THE PUSH GUIDE TO
WHICH UNIVERSITY 2007-8

D1328913

SERIES EDITOR Johnny Rich
EDITOR Anthony Leyton
WRITTEN BY Alice Tarleton
ADDITIONAL MATERIAL Ruth Bushi, Anthony Leyton, Johnny Rich
SUB-EDITORS Paul Crowney, David Whisson

12TH EDITION
ASSISTANT EDITOR Polly Calvert
EDITORIAL ASSISTANT Terrie Chilvers
RESEARCHERS Mairead Aitken, Robert Alderson, Yad Barzinji, Chloe Bennett, Donna-Louise Bishop,
Andrew Bogie, Laura Brown, Sophie Bull, Rachel Burley, Nicola Casey, Simon Cooper, John
Ellingsworth, Laura Fanthorpe, Rory Gallivan, Hannah de Haan, Emma Durgan, Greg Easter, Amy
Glendinning. Jo Gudgeon, Kat Kennedy, Rachel Levy, Anna Lomax, Reshma Madhi, Andrew Novak,
Martin Philip, Nicholas Piachaud, Shaina Riley, Julia Round, Katie Spong, Samuel Stow, Mary Sweeney,
Kenn Taylor, Amy Tyndall, Nkeiruka Uhgaonu, Peter Walsh, Emma Woolerton, Vivienne Yong

THANKS TO Mairead Aitken, Laura Brown, Evelyn Cole, Simon Cooper, Sarah Mackness
SPECIAL THANKS TO Caroline Jelves, Nicole Linhardt-Rich, Jacqueline Palmer, Paul Pensom, Katie Spong,
Sam Stow, Vivienne Yong

PUSH ONLINE www.push.co.uk

In association with THE INDEPENDENT

ORDERS Please contact Bookpoint Ltd,
130 Milton Park, Abingdon, Oxon OX14 4SB.
TELEPHONE (44) 01235 827720,
FAX (44) 01235 400454.
Lines are open from 9.00am to 5.00pm, Monday to
Saturday, with a 24-hour message answering
service. You can also order through our website
www.hoddereducation.co.uk

BRITISH LIBRARY CATALOGUING IN PUBLICATION DATA
A catalogue record for this title is available from
the British Library.

First published in 1992 as *PUSH 93* (The
Polytechnic and University Students' Handbook)
A catalogue record for this book is available from
the British Library

ISBN-10: 0 3409 2958 8
ISBN-13: 9 780340 929582

Impression number 6 5 4 3 2 1
Year 2006

PICTURES Getty Images
PRINTED IN Malta for Hodder Education, a division
of Hodder Headline, 338 Euston Road, London
NW1 3BH.

Hodder Headline's policy is to use papers that are natural, renewable and recyclable products and
made from wood grown in sustainable forests. The logging and manufacturing processes are
expected to conform to the environmental regulations of the country of origin.

Flunk rates are calculated by Push from data published by the Higher Education Statistics Agency,
who produce Performance Indicators in Higher Education on behalf of the four UK funding bodies.
Source of data: HESA Performance Indicators in Higher Education in the UK 2002/03, Table T5. Data
used by permission of the Higher Education Statistics Agency. HESA cannot accept responsibility for
any inferences or conclusions derived from the data by third parties.

NOTE FROM PUSH The Push Guides have just about the best research methods you could hope for. We
visit every university and produce more pages of research than is healthy for the world's rainforests.
Yet, even the best make mistakes occasionally. We do everything in our power to avoid it (including
checking everything at least three times), but if we've got something wrong or it's changed since we
went to press, then we're really sorry, but, basically, bite me – it's not our fault. Go stew. But do let us
know first, okay? Not only will we put it right, we'll give you a credit for it, too.
Text in the university profiles in italics is Push's opinion – take it or leave it.

CONTENTS

PUSH POWER

Push is an independent organisation that collects the largest ever resource of information about student life in the UK.

Push distributes that information through a variety of services:

THE PUSH GUIDE TO WHICH UNIVERSITY The best-selling guidebook (tip: you're reading it) with essential facts, figures and opinions on every university in the UK.

THE PUSH GUIDE TO CHOOSING A UNIVERSITY Top advice about choosing the right university.

THE PUSH GUIDE TO MONEY: STUDENT SURVIVAL The lowdown on what you'll have to spend, what you'll have to spend it on and how the cost varies at each of the UK's universities.

PUSH ONLINE (WWW.PUSH.CO.UK) Regularly updated information, advice and links about student life and choosing a university with a uniquely powerful University Chooser feature for site members.

PUSH VISITS The personal touch: in association with Lloyds TSB, Push experts visit schools and colleges to give specialist advice.

THE INDEPENDENT Through Push's ongoing relationship with the Independent, Push supplies facts, figures and grassroots knowledge, especially during the newspaper's exclusive coverage of UCAS's official clearing listings.

DID YOU KNOW?

Push has employed more than 500 researchers, photographers and writers over the past 14 years.

Push researchers visit every university in the UK in person.

Push's research probes the universities themselves, students' unions, public and Government bodies and thousands of students.

Each year Push generates over 15,000 pages of exclusive research.

Push's entire database of information is fully updated every year.

Push information has all been checked at least three times.

The Push team is made up of high-flying students, recent graduates and education experts.

Push is the UK's most widely used resource about student life, used by students, teachers, careers advisors, parents, universities, Government bodies, political parties, media organisations and many others.

Push always strives to provide the most up-to-date information in the most accessible style and at an affordable cost.

Everything we do is by students for students.

We love hearing glowing praise. Harsh criticism leaves us weeping into our cocoa. If you have the former, or, if you must, the latter or just want to be involved with life in the Push lane and think you cut the mustard, drop us a line at:

The Push Guides
Independent News & Media
191 Marsh Wall
London E14 9RS
Tel: (+44/0)20-7005 3654

Or by e-mail to editor@push.co.uk

PUSH START

Foreword by Gemma Tumelty, President of the National Union of Students

Choosing the right university and course for the next three years of your life can feel like a daunting process, however Push is a comprehensive resource to help you make the right choices for you.

University is a fantastic experience with innumerable opportunities. As well as the obvious benefits that a degree provides, you'll have the chance to get involved in countless projects for often the first, and sometimes only, time in your life. And university communities can be an eclectic mix of personalities, with people from all sorts of different backgrounds working, living and socialising together.

The factors that will influence your decision are varied. Distance, welfare provision, nightlife, entertainment, halls of residence, extra-curricular activities, graduate employment and beer prices may be reasons for and against choosing a particular course, location and university. This year, the decision is made much harder for prospective students as a result of top-up fees. Universities should offer a range of bursaries to their prospective students so it is vital that you speak to institutions and find out what support is on offer and about the level of fees you will be expected to pay. Make a shortlist of your favourite places and take advantage of the open days on offer. This will give you a great opportunity to meet real students and find out if you really want to go there. You may have older siblings, parents or friends who have already been to university and can give you advice on what university and course to choose, but remember it's your future and your choice.

As soon as you arrive on campus, make a beeline to the students' union and check out all the activities on offer. You may want to join a club or society, sit on your Union Council or be a student representative, try out for the sports teams, join a voluntary project in your local community, write for the union newspaper or find a part-time job. The SU will be able to advise you on all these opportunities. Visit www.nusonline.co.uk for information on everything to do with student life, including advice, updates on NUS campaigns, events, details of benefits available to you through our student card and fun stuff like music downloads and competitions.

As well as being the best days of your life, university will help you develop skills that will be invaluable once you go out into the world of full-time work. Whatever your interests and experience you can be sure student life will be as diverse and cosmopolitan as you make it. Don't forget that NUS represents over five million students in the UK and your SU will be able to support you on campus during your studies.

Good luck in making your choices and I wish you all the best for your time at university.

Gemma Tumelty
NUS president
www.nusonline.co.uk

PUSHOVER

Using The Push Guide is a pushover. A five-year-old child could understand it, but before you rush out to find a five year-old child because you can't make head nor tail of it, here's the idiot's guide to The Push Guide – also invaluable for gifted five year-olds, vastly over-qualified academics and you...

The Push Guide has been designed and devised to make it as easy to use as possible, whatever you want to do with it.

Well, maybe if you want to use it as a pet, you're probably better off with a shitzu, but as a guide to real life at the UK's universities and colleges, it's the best there is.

The Push Guide isn't trying to replace UCAS or the colleges' own prospectuses. We're just lending a hand in what is frankly the sort of decision that has most people reaching for the pin cushion. The Push Guide provides the sort of information you really want to know in order to decide, not all that stuff about course codes and quotas which appears everywhere else.

And don't let anyone tell you your decision doesn't matter. Manchester Metropolitan, Warwick and Cambridge Universities may each do a Maths course, but students are letting themselves in for more than algebra and calculus. Differentiation and integration mean something quite different when your chosen university becomes your home for the next few years.

Push tells you the real story and tells it straight. But there's no point just telling you that one university is the best and that everyone should go there. Everyone wants something different and every university offers something unique. What The Push Guide does is match you with the university of your dreams... or near enough.

The Push Guide backs up nearly everything with facts, figures and statistics and when nothing tells it better than an honest opinion, we're not ashamed to admit that it's a personal view – even if it is the best-informed opinion available any-

where. In fact, we slap it in italics just so you know. Although our judgements are scrupulously researched and representative, we still advise a pretty hefty accompanying dose of salt. After all, even Push's opinion is still only an opinion.

With The Push Guide you can make comparisons and pin-point the features that you're looking for. The symbols, charts and maps give a quick and easy reference to the sort of factors that might really sway your decision, not just courses. The profiles for each university make it possible to check out whether they make the grade in the important parts other unis cannot reach.
For help getting to grips with Push's icons, ratings and other features, read on.

WHEN TO USE THE PUSH GUIDE

Choosing a course is obviously one of the first things to do and The Push Guide provides a table of all courses on offer (see 'Push, of course', page 705). Since you don't want to see essentially the same course listed under 93 different names in 203 different places, Push has standardised the names and listed them alphabetically by subject areas.

This means that you don't have to wade through pages of different institutions to find the few that offer the course you're looking for. A word of warning: the standardisation of nearly 10,000 degree courses means that some get grouped together in a way which would perhaps be objectionable to those who appreciate the finer differences between Phonic Linguistics and Linguistic Phonemics. For exact details of any course, its contents and with which other courses it may be combined, check availability with the institutions themselves, their prospectuses or UCAS's listings.

If you know more or less what course you want to study and that course is not unusual – like Maths or English Literature, but not Cartesian Astrophysics with a side order of Sewage Management – then, no problem, you can choose entirely on the strength of other factors as outlined in each college's Push profile. However, if the course is only offered at a few universities, you should make a shortlist from the 'Push, of course' lists (page 705) and then turn to the profiles for the clinching factors: Where is it? Is there any social life beyond a non-alcoholic cocktail bar and regular bus-spotting conventions? Is there a croquet club? Will it be possible to buy cigarettes at 3 in the morning?

Even for quite unusual courses, there are so many institutions to choose from that you should take the opportunity to get pushy – to demand exactly what you want or as near as damn it.

But maybe you don't know what course you want to study, don't care or just haven't quite finalised it yet (it's still a toss up between Fine Art or Chemical Engineering, for example). Well, then there are no constraints – you can choose entirely on the basis of where you'd like to study and in what environment, rather than what you'd like to study. Either way, The Push Guide is the best key to all the vital factors students have to put up with on a day-to-day basis.

To make life a bit easier, we've used icons (explained a bit further on) to give you an at-a-glance feel for accommodation and booze prices, facilities for welfare and sports provisions, and for academic rankings. Mostly, the icons are based on official statistics – which can't possibly tell the whole story. Push knows that only a fool would decide where to spend three years of their life based on a thumb – so do yourself a favour and read the text in each profile for the bigger picture.

NAMES AND CROSS-REFERENCING

When all the old polytechnics became universities way back at the start of the 90s, we suddenly found ourselves with lorry-loads of universities with wacky names like De Montfort University (formerly Leicester Poly) and Liverpool John Moores University (formerly Liverpool Poly) which is named after the bloke who founded the Littlewoods Pools. However, since old habits die hard, if you look up a college under the old name you will find it cross-referenced to its new name anyway.

All the profiles are arranged alphabetically (ignoring the words 'University' or 'University of'), but some places like UEA (University of East Anglia) are sent simply to try the brains behind Push. Should it be U for 'UEA'? E for 'East'? Or A for 'Ah, we're in Norwich'? Well, if you can't beat 'em... put it under all three. However

you try to look up even the most awkward of names you should find it cross-referenced.

THE PUSH SYMBOLS

On the last page you'll find the key to the Push symbols – handy and at hand.

GLOSSARY & ABBREVIATIONS

It's a jargon jungle out there. Everything in higher education would be so easy to understand if the colleges didn't insist on using acrid acronyms and tedious terminology all the time. In fact, it's a plot to stop the unemployed from becoming professors, but that's another (paranoid) story. Push unleashes the lingo in its 'Short, sharp Push' (Abbreviations, page 625) and 'When Push comes to shove' (Glossary, page 618).

OTHER OPTIONS

Even though all the old polytechnics are now universities, you should still remember that higher education doesn't begin and end there. The choice for prospective students is bigger than Victoria Beckham's wardrobe allowance. There's thousands more universities abroad. And how about vocational training, rather than a degree? Free your mind and your pants will follow.

    The Push Guide can't include all the options – it would be thousands of pages long, years out of date, cost the earth and be impossible to pick up, let alone read. Apart from that, we like the idea.

GETTING IN TOUCH

We crave feedback. We love it. We would crawl naked over splintered glass to hear what you have to say about Push. Unless, that is, you just want to slag us off or sue us for libel. Assuming you have some worthwhile and constructive response, not necessarily positive, please feel free to write to The Push Guides, Independent House, 191 Marsh Wall, London E14 9RS or e-mail us at editor@push.co.uk.

    For next year's edition, we will again need researchers with an unassailable sense of duty and a streak of masochism – if you think we might not slam the door in your face while doubling up in fits of giggles, please drop us a line with reasons why you meet Push's exacting standards.

MAKING THE MOST OF THE UNIVERSITY PROFILES

NAMES

As a headline, The Push Guide uses the name most students use or the most convenient title. So, for example, LSE is LSE, not the London School of Economics & Political Science. The institution's exact name is used in the address, in case you really need to know.

ADDRESSES

For each university, The Push Guide lists the address and telephone number of the administration and of the students' unions, as well as any e-mail or web addresses there might be. We've given the address of the main site, or if there is more than one main site, we say, what the hey, and give them all.

GENERAL ⓊⓊⓊⓊⓊⓊⓊⓊⓊⓊⓊⓊⓊ

STATISTICS

All statistics were right up to the minute of going to press and Push is really, really cut up if they're wrong later, but, hell, that's the way it goes. To keep that to a minimum though, where possible we've used official, nationally comparative figures from HESA (the Higher Education Statistics Agency). Some institutions, for various reasons, don't release certain statistics. Although we are not known for willingly taking 'no' for an answer, Push follows the old journalistic maxim: 'If in doubt, leave it out'. We suggest readers should follow the cynics' maxim: 'What are they trying to hide?' We've used 'n/a' where figures weren't relevant to an institution, or we just couldn't get hold of them.

FOUNDED Many institutions have hazy histories either too deep in the clouds of time or involving too many complicated mergers and changes of name to have just one founding year. Some newer institutions, desperate to appear venerable and ivy-covered, prefer to give the founding date of an obscure technical college on the other side of town that eventually morphed into the current institution after 14 name changes and multiple mergers. Push, however, has used the latest techniques (a step beyond the 'Eeny-Meeny-Miny-Mo Principle') to select just one year and, if further clarification is worthwhile, it's explained elsewhere in the profile.

FULL-TIME U'GRADS This includes students on sandwich courses, which are nothing to do with learning what to put between slices of bread, but courses where some time is spent not actually studying but on a work placement.

PART-TIME Those on undergraduate courses only. Official figures from HESA include students writing theses or career folk doing short, full-time courses. Push has used this figure too because it can give you a feel of what being on campus – the atmosphere, facilities and student make-up – is like. But statistics being the pesky buggers that they are can complicate things. For instance, while HESA's part-time figure at, say Oxford University, is rather high, you can't actually apply to do a part-time undergrad degree there. Don't blame Push, we don't make this stuff up you know.

POSTGRADS Full-time postgraduate students (who've already taken a degree).

NON-DEGREE Often HND (Higher National Diploma) students but all sorts of vocational, access and pre-degree courses might be offered, especially at newer universities. Again, figures are for full-time students.

AVE COURSE Strictly speaking, for the pedantic statisticians out there, this is the modal length of courses. Or, in English, the most common course length.

ETHNIC Some institutions prefer not to ask their students to classify themselves into one racial box or another; others are concerned to keep tabs on the ethnic origins of students, in order to ensure no bias or discrimination is occurring. Criteria for definition will vary but this figure should give a pretty good idea of the cultural mix at a particular institution. Oxbridge colleges in particular can be a bit cagey about giving this figure; we leave it up to you to decide what to make of that.

STATE:PRIVATE SCHOOL The ratio of undergraduates educated at state schools to those from privately-funded secondary schools. Nationally (across the UK) the proportion of students from private schools is about 13%.

FLUNK RATE This is an indication of the percentage of full-time undergraduates who, for one reason or another, don't successfully complete their course by being awarded a degree. The national average is 14% (around one in seven) with figures for individual institutions ranging from 1% to 37% – which means that well over a third of students come away with nothing. Nada. Zilch. Not even a cuddly toy.

Our flunk rates use data supplied by HESA. These figures project how many students who started in the academic year 2002–03 will neither gain a degree nor transfer to another university or course.

MATURE STUDENTS Those aged 21 or over at the time of starting their courses. Postgrads aren't included in this figure.

INTERNATIONAL STUDENTS Includes EU students from outside the UK.

DISABLED STUDENTS Colleges, if they keep records at all, often define 'disabled' differently. Some include only registered disabled students, others extend the definition to students with dyslexia, asthma or any students who, for whatever reason, choose to define themselves as disabled. So, for a bit of consistency, Push's figures come from HESA, and refer to the number of full and part-time students in receipt of the Disabled Students' Allowance. Not all disabled students have to tell the university they're receiving this, or even classify themselves as disabled. However, it can be a useful guide to how well your needs may be catered for and whether there may be others in the same dinghy as you.

LOCAL Students who were resident within 30 miles of the institution when they applied. A higher percentage of local students can affect the atmosphere, from giving it a more independent spirit to meaning that the campus is a ghost town at weekends.

ACADEMIC RANKING (Oxbridge colleges) Based on the Norrington (Oxford) and Tompkins (Cambridge) tables, which rank colleges according to students' end-of-year or final exam results. Rankings are relative to other colleges in the same university, and were correct at the time of going to press.

ATMOSPHERE
This section in the profiles, more than any other, gives the real feel of the place.

TOWN DETAIL
As well as describing what the nearest city or town is like, we've given a breakdown of population, distance from the city centre to the university and weather details. Do you need to pack a sun hat or a shower cap? This is the place to look. High and low temperatures are given in centigrade. Rainfall is given in millimetres.

TRAVEL
TRAINS AND BUSES Fares given are the best we've been able to find at the time of writing (though it can be beyond even Push to get a straight answer out of National Rail Enquiries at times). That means the cheapest possible return journey with a student discount card or apex ticket. Some of these don't apply at certain times of the day and apex tickets have to be bought at least two weeks in advance.
HITCHING Push would like to warn readers that if they don't know that hitching can be dangerous, then there is something wrong with them. Push accepts no responsibility for students who have bad experiences when thumbing it, such as waiting six hours in the rain for a lift, being picked up by Micra-driving Cheese String obsessives or being made to listen to Chico on the car stereo.
UNIVERSITY Transport listed here is that which the institution lays on, sometimes free, sometimes not.

CAREER PROSPECTS
What kind of careers facilities there are, including how many full- and part-time staff there are. You'll also find the graduate unemployment rate listed here – that's the number of students who don't go on to employment or further study within six months of graduating.

FAMOUS ALUMNI
A bit of celebrity gossip – who went where. Just

so students can boast that they're going to the same college as that famous 1920s Swiss serial killer or whoever.

FURTHER INFORMATION

Prospectuses are absolutely essential if you're seriously considering applying to an institution and invaluable for seeing what the college would like you to think of them. However, they are sales documents and while almost every word will be true, it will not be the truth, the whole truth and nothing but the truth. They are available from the address at the top of each profile. On the other hand, some students' unions publish 'alternative' prospectuses, which present the point of view of students at the college. Also worth getting, although the views contained are almost exclusively biased and, since the writers have rarely visited a representative number of colleges, not very comparative.

We've also listed any videos, CD-Roms, websites or other sources of information. Some are just prospectuses dumped on the net – others are more revealing. Where possible we give the address for the SU website, as well as the official university one. If you've got the time and the facilities, check them out.

ACADEMIC 〇〇〇〇〇〇〇〇〇〇〇〇〇〇

The teaching standard is:

 Barely hovering

 Flying

 Soaring high

ACADEMIC STATS

RANGE OF POINTS REQUIRED FOR ENTRANCE You'll need to know whether you're likely to be able to get in and so here's the top and bottom benchmarks that the college uses based on the UCAS points tariff (see Entrance requirements', page 606). Not every course requires the same points though. You may need 300 points to get into a university's law degree, for instance, but be able to get into the same place to do catering and tourism with just 80. But it's not as cut and dried as some people make out. It depends how you gather your points – what qualifications and in what subjects. You can have 360 points in English, French and History A Levels, but it won't get you in to study Physics even if they claim to only want 200 points. In the end, you'll have to double check with the university anyway about what points they'd want from you for an individual course but, for what it's worth, we've also given the average points students have on entry.

APPLICANTS PER PLACE The average number of students battling it out for a place in Toenail Biology or whatever.

CLEARING The percentage of students who entered through the UCAS clearing system. Some institutions have (sometimes undeserved) reputations as UCAS dumping grounds. This figure should give an idea of the number of students whose presence isn't entirely by choice. UCAS don't release figures for individual institutions and, understandably, some universities are a little coy about revealing this figure.

NUMBER/LENGTH OF TERMS Different colleges split up the year differently. Some have three short terms, others have two long ones (semesters). It may not seem all that important, but, apart from anything else, if the vacations are shorter, odds are you won't be earning as much money during them.

STAFF/STUDENT RATIOS This isn't as straightforward as it may appear. Part-time staff and students can muddy the statistical waters. But it gives you a rough idea of whether tutorials are going to be cosy little sherry sessions a deux, or rugby scrums with the tutor as the ball.

STUDY ADDICTS The percentage of students who stay on for further helpings after a first degree.

TEACHING Based on students' own assessments made in the 2005 National Student Survey (NSS). The star rating is based upon each university's students' overall satisfaction with the teaching on their course, taking into account the whole learning caboodle of resources and support available, course organisation and the general brilliance of their lecturers. The more stars, the higher the average survey score, relative to other universities. Where NSS results were not available, (for example, at Scottish universities), we've used data from the Quality Assurance Agency for Higher Education's (QAA) most recent assessment.

RESEARCH The average figure for the college based on the last Government-funded Research

Assessment Exercise (RAE). For undergrads, the level of research isn't as directly important as colleges would like you to think, but it is a good general indicator of a top-notch department. Push represents the teaching and research figures by 1–5 stars, where more stars means higher scores relative to the other institutions. Bear in mind though that these are average scores. Those particularly interested in how a particular department or subject rates would do well to investigate further.

ADMISSIONS
Whether applications should be made through UCAS, GTTR etc., or whether the institutions can be approached directly, for example, for part-time or mature study.

SUBJECTS
We've given an indication of the main subjects studied. Where courses scored more than 4.0 in the NSS, we've named them in this section (which means that students thought provisions and teaching for those courses were particularly snazzy).

LIBRARIES
Unless otherwise stated, we give the total number of books and study places in all the college libraries, not just the main library. The spend per student is shown as a five-level rating where more pound signs means a higher spend.

COMPUTERS
We give the number of computer workstations available for general use and don't include places or terminals set aside exclusively for students on a particular course. Spend per student is again shown as a five-level rating, where more pound signs means a higher spend.

ENTERTAINMENT

Drinks are:

 pricey

 average

 bargainous

BEER, WINE AND SOFT DRINKS
Prices of beer, wine and soft drinks are given as the average at student bars and in towns.

SOCIAL

The SU's activities are:

 frozen stiff

 lukewarm

 hot, hot, hot

CLUBS AND SOCS
Clubs and societies have been split into sporting and non-sporting, which isn't always easy. Push puts them under whichever heading the college uses and you'd be well advised to check under both headings if the existence of a certain club is really important to you. Since it would get a bit repetitive otherwise, we've missed out the ones which crop up just about everywhere in the college profiles, but to be sure that the club you want is at the college you're looking at, turn to the 'clubs' tables at the back (page 736). The only ones usually missed out are the course-related societies (for sucking up to tutors).

Of course, if you've decided that somewhere is perfect apart from the fact that it doesn't have a 'South Park' Fan Club, you shouldn't dismiss it out of hand. At most colleges it's fairly easy to start a society – you only need to find between 20 and 50 others to say they want to join and the SU may well give you a packet to spend on parkas, overpriced merchandising and that vital sight-seeing trip to Colorado.

SPORTS

Student sport is:

 slobbish

 average

 active and triumphant

ACCOMMODATION

The average rent is:

🏠 ⊞ 👎 expensive

🏠 ⊞ ✊ average

🏠 ⊞ 👍 cheap

Push's icons tell you how expensive accommodation is, both living out (on the left) and in college (on the right).

ACCOMMODATION

Universities tend to transform mysteriously into conference centres the moment vacations start, so if you're in halls you may well get turfed out with all your belongings to allow some panty-hose salesman to attend a corporate beerfest. The Push Guide gives a weekly cost and how many weeks you're going to be paying. Also given are the percentages of full-time undergraduates living in catered and self-catered accommodation. Bear in mind that 'catered' can mean anything from the full-board of three square meals a day and a Harrods hamper for your picnics, to a single 'pay-as-you-eat' canteen which you have to catch a bus to get to and which serves cockroaches in the soup.

As well as costs, The Push Guide also gives you details of the availability and standard of college accommodation and the kinds of security arrangements you can expect. As if that weren't enough there's even information on local housing. We even give you a rough idea of what contents insurance might set you back (the quotes we got were based on £2,500-worth of possessions, including a computer). More £ signs means more expensive.

WELFARE

The welfare provision is:

❤️ 👎 poor

❤️ 🤚 passable

❤️ 👍 pampering

CRIME RATE The crime rate comes from figures published by the Home Office. They're not based on incidents on campus or university property, but are a general idea of what goes on in the town or city. The rating ranges from one (low) to five (high) exclamation marks.

FINANCIAL

ACCESS FUNDS When student loans were introduced in 1990, the Government made some money available to colleges to help avoid the problems that were likely to arise for students who were less able to pay. The figures given are the total amount each college is currently allocated. Students who want a slice of the cake should apply annually to their university, but not until they get there. Other sources of available income are listed below this figure.

SUCCESSFUL APPLICATIONS The number of students who get a slice of the cake gives an indication of how large a slice they each got. Some colleges were only willing or able to provide figures as a percentage. Others couldn't give us any figures at all, or wouldn't because they're 'orrible.

PUSH LINKS: OTHER SERVICES FROM PUSH

Push is an independent organisation that does more annual research into UK student life than anyone else.

The Push Guide to Which University is just one of the services we provide to university applicants. Since all of our services are designed to work together to help you make the best decision and to support you once you've made it, we might as well take this opportunity to plug the others.

THE PUSH GUIDE TO CHOOSING A UNIVERSITY

What's the point of half the information contained in The Push Guide to Which University? Stuff like the price of beer – that's obviously important, but why, for instance, should anyone care how many staff the careers service has or whether the accommodation is catered or self-catering?

These are the very things that really affect student life and mean that no two universities are the same. They differ radically, with strengths and weaknesses, quirks and habits.

The Push Guide to Choosing a University explains all those differences, why they matter and how they affect life as a student. It's also jam-packed with tips about choosing and it dissects the application process, student funding and, perhaps best of all, has Push's unique University Chooser Questionnaire to help design your ideal institution and match which comes closest.

PUSH ONLINE (www.push.co.uk)

The ultimate online guide to UK universities.

For members, our interactive tools take the guesswork out of finding the perfect university, including the interractive University Chooser function. Want to be close enough to home to take your washing home but don't want the folks turning up unnanounced? No problem – punch in your preferences and let Push do the searching for you.

Once you've got your shortlist, go check out your top choices to compare entertainment, accommodation, sport, travel and every other aspect of student life with Push's in-depth university profiles.

There's plenty of free stuff too, from short, sharp university profiles to articles about everything student-related, plus extra goodies for members.

THE PUSH GUIDE TO STUDENT MONEY 2007/8

Perhaps the biggest issue for students today is the cost of it all. In Push's unique tell-it-like-it-is style, we explain what you'll have to spend, what you'll have to spend it on and how to get by.

The Push Guide to Student Money also gives unique details of how important costs differ at every university in the UK.

THE PUSH SCHOOLS TOUR

Push has teamed up with Lloyds TSB to visit schools and colleges all over the UK, giving advice about choosing a university and student life. If you or your school fancies a slot on our itinerary, contact us at editor@push.co.uk.

MORE COMING SOON...

Push's ongoing commitment to applicants means we'll not rest until we've provided every goddamn thing we can think of to help you pick the right university.

Already our experts give talks in schools and colleges throughout the country and we'll be launching yet more new books and services soon. Watch this space.

PUSHING IN: GETTING INTO UNIVERSITY

So. How do you get into university? Some say you need a degree to understand how to apply for a degree. Push cuts through the jargon and tells you how it really works.

The first acronym to learn is UCAS (pron 'you-cass'), the Universities and Colleges Admissions Service. They manage the application process for most universities and colleges in the UK for first degrees, foundation degrees and some diplomas, though they don't have anything to do with deciding who actually goes where.

UCAS applications used to involve a forest of paper forms and therefore a lot of worry about whether your handwriting might make you look like a psycho. Nowadays, like pop music, poker and Push, UCAS uses the internet.

From May, applicants can register and complete their application forms online (it doesn't have to be done in one sitting) by feverishly clicking their way through the process at www.ucas.com/apply.

There are spaces on the application form to apply to up to six courses, but you don't have to use them all. You can apply to the same course at up to six different universities, six different courses at the same university or, indeed, six different courses at six different universities. If you're applying for some medicine-related or Art & Design courses, you may not get the full six bites of the cherry – you may only have three or four choices.

Next you need to answer all sorts of questions about your past grades, what exams you're taking in the future and how you justify your existence to date. It's the main chance to convince the universities how committed you are to the course you've chosen, how brilliant you'll be at it and what a generally happening person you'd be to have around. You can get useful tips about filling in your personal statement and about the application process in general from Push Online (www.push.co.uk).

There's also a section on the form for your school or college to fill in either singing your praises or dissing you like a wrong 'un. They'll also say what they think you're likely to get in your A Levels, Highers or other exams. Unfortunately, you don't get to see what they've said about you because they only add their comments once you've submitted your bits to UCAS. (However, under the Data Protection Act, you can ask to be shown your reference, which is handy if you think you've been given a tabloid smear job.)

If you apply as an individual – ie. not through a school – you'll be responsible for pasting your reference in yourself. You should give your referee the UCAS how-to guidelines on what they should be bigging up and ask them to send it back to you electronically so that you don't have to type it all out again yourself. Needless to say, don't be tempted to add a few literary flourishes of your own – it'll stick out like George Bush at a peace rally and the universities you're applying to won't be impressed.

UCAS starts accepting applications from the end of September. If you're applying for Oxbridge or to do medicine, dentistry or veterinary science it'll need to be in by 15th October, otherwise you've got till 15th January to get your act together. And for Route B Art & Design courses, it's 24th March.

It's best not to leave it later than mid-November because there may be hundreds of other applicants after the same course as you and the universities aren't holding their breath before getting the bums booked onto the seats. It's a whole early-bird-doomed-worm scenario.

Meanwhile, if your application arrives after the deadline dates, UCAS will still process your application, but they'll mark it as 'late' and universities will only consider it if they've got places left. And if you don't get your application in until after 30th June (12th June for those Route B Art & Design courses), you'll be in Clearing (see below), which is a bit like being at the back of the queue on a club night.

Whenever they get it, you should get an acknowledgement fairly quickly that UCAS have received the form and they'll give you an application number and a record of what they think you've applied for – which you should check.

Meanwhile, the universities and colleges get copies of your application and they write to you direct with their decisions. There are basically four things they might do.

They could make you a conditional offer. In effect this says if you get certain grades in your A Levels or other forthcoming exams, then they'll take you.

Or they might make an unconditional offer, saying they'll take you whatever your grades, but this isn't likely unless you've already done some A Levels, Highers or equivalent.

Or they might turn you down outright. Or they might ask you for interview. In which case it's a good opportunity to check out the place. If you get an interview, be prepared. Be keen. Be enthusiastic. Above all, be yourself. (As if being anyone else was an option.) If you're worried about it, grab your careers advisor or nearest friendly teacher and insist they help you. Remind them that they chose their atrociously paid profession for love rather than money.

After the interview, the university or college will either make you a conditional or unconditional offer or they'll reject you. If you don't get in, console yourself with the fact that thousands of other hopeful students also got turned down and, besides, you didn't want to go to that stinky dump anyway.

UCAS will send you a note of the universities' decisions as they make them. Whatever they say, you don't have to respond until you've got a full set of replies from all the universities you applied to. You should hear from them all, one way or another by, at the latest, the end of April. You can follow the whole process online using the Track system at UCAS's website (www.UCAS.com) or you can just phone them.
If you've got any unconditional offers, you can reject them right away or accept one, go away, relax and prepare to start that course at the beginning of the next year.

If you've got more than two conditional offers, then you've got to dump some. You've also got to say which is your favourite and firmly accept it. That means that if you manage to meet whatever conditions they've made, then that's where you're off to. You're allowed to keep a back up (or 'insurance') offer by provisionally accepting another offer with easier conditions. That means if you don't make the grades for your first choice, you've still got somewhere to go.

It is possible that none of your choices will make you an offer or maybe that you'll decide after an interview, open day or visit that you don't like the place. On the other hand, maybe you just won't make the grade for either of the two offers you've kept. In this case, you've got two choices. Either take a year out and go through the whole process again. Or try to go through Clearing.

Clearing is the mad scramble that takes place between the day the exam results come out and the first day of the universities' new terms. During these few weeks, students without a university place try to get matched up with university courses that don't have enough students. Although it's all masterminded by UCAS in theory, in practice its the universities themselves that deal with the nitty gritty and this time you get to approach them directly.

Be careful, though, if you do end up in Clearing, not just to jump at the first place you get offered. Clearing gets even the coolest cats hot and bothered and it's easy to end up on a course you don't like at a university you hate.

It's important to pick a course and a university that suit you as an individual – if you don't, you may live to regret it. Nearly one in seven students doesn't successfully complete the course they start and the proportion is highest among those who get in through Clearing.

If you're not at school or college in the UK, you can still apply online at www.ucas.com or phone +44 (0)870 1122211.

HARD PUSHED: STUDENT FINANCE

Nowadays, being a student is almost the same as being in debt, but there are ways of stashing the cash and diverting the debts.

If you're thinking about embarking on a course of study at a UK university or college, you should be thinking about debt at the same time. The two go together like cream cheese and bagels (only less tastily). Debt has become such a fact of life for most students that some fall into a state of paralysis about the whole thing and never really deal with the problem. Push can't wave a magic cliché and make debts disappear, but we can come up with a few ideas to help students make the best out of a situation roughly equivalent to swimming the Atlantic with John Prescott strapped to your knees.

At the brink of a promising career, starting with being accepted to university or college, most students don't want to think of the poverty they're going to have to put up with until they land that cushy job in merchant banking, marketing or medicine. Still less, if they are looking forward to a career where the greatest reward will be the warm glow of job satisfaction, such as teaching, social work or even acting.

However, there's little point starting a course you're not going to be able to afford to finish. Students have to ask themselves how they're going to make ends meet.

If the answer is that your parents are so phenomenally wealthy and indulgent that they'll give you all the cash you need, then your problems are over. But, for those on this side of the rainbow, there are a number of issues to consider.

In fact, there are so many that we've produced a book all about it – The Push Guide to Student Money. It covers everything to do with student finance – what you'll have to spend, what you'll have to spend it on and how to put the fun back into funding. Rush out and steal a copy now (it's only £9.99, but you might as well start saving now).

If you didn't take that advice and you're still reading, the following brief guide may help till you realise you need that truly excellent publication.

ECONOMISE

Whatever other options you take, economy is always the one that puts shoes on your feet. Decide what's important and pay for that. Then see how much money you have left and decide what else you'd like if possible. Plan expenditure – on a weekly basis, if your income's tight – and stick to your plan.

Be pessimistic. Optimistic students don't check their balance when they shove their cards in the cash machine and sooner or later their card gets swallowed. Realists check their balance and then get out half the amount they wanted. Pessimists don't bother going to the cashpoint because they know it was only ever created in order to swallow cards. That way, they preserve enough readies to live a miserly, but not miserable existence.

As with many things, sensible moderation is the key. Students who are so desperate to economise that they never set foot in the SU bar and don't buy anything not directly related to food, shelter or academic survival may come out the other end with a first-class degree and a bank balance not too far out of the black. Chances are, though, they'll also have missed out on much of the stuff that makes a degree course worthwhile. Students may have to accept that Maserati and Armani aren't going to be on the shopping list for the next few years, but the odd pint of beer or the next Arctic Monkeys CD aren't going to cast you into the fiery furnace of debt hell.

GOVERNMENT FUNDING

Few things in life get quite so confusing as the student funding situation over the last few years. Push, as ever, is here to help you tell the wood from the deforestation trucks and find out how you'll be affected.

First off, although top-up fees (see below) are moving the balance towards students, the

Government still pays most of the tuition fees for most first-degree students. What students themselves have to pay is a portion of the wad that's needed to pay for all those libraries, loos and lecturers. Unfortunately, however, that money's paid direct to the university by the Local Education Authorities (LEAs) and the like. Students don't even get so much as a sniff of it, but they shouldn't forget to apply for it – or they could end up paying out themselves.

GRANTS

The LEAs also make a decision about grants. These aren't the grants of ancient history that paid for everything, but a hand-out of up to £2,700 a year. How much you get depends on how much your folks earn, but something from the full whack to a crisp £50 note should be available to about half of students – those from the poorest families. If your parents earn less than £17,500 a year, you'll get the maximum. If they earn between £17,500 and £37,425, you'll get a partial grant. Better than a swift kick in the guts, but only a really hard one. Apart from that and the loans and bursaries (see below), students are on their own to find the readies for their living costs (or maintenance as they call it).

TUITION FEES

Right, pay attention, because this is the big banana. This year, the whole system of university fees became about as easy to grasp as a final-year astrophysics exam. It varies according to where you live, where you want go to university, and quite possibly whether or not you can stand on your head and juggle jam-jars.

As Push was going to press, all but eight UK universities have decided to whack students with the full £3,000 a year in tuition fees from September 2006. Of the institutions that aren't going with the flow, four are covered in this book. They are: Thames Valley University; Northampton University; Greenwich University and Leeds Metropolitan University.

If you're considering any of these universities, have a scoot over to the fees section of their profiles to see how much moolah you're going to save on the three grand. Granted you may not be saving enough to buy a secondhand Robin

Reliant, but it's (marginally) better than a smack in the privates.

Now, about actually paying the damned fees. You don't. Or not straight away. The Student Loans Company will pay them while you're studying and will only start sending the heavies round once you're earning over £15,000. Then they'll take 9% of whatever you earn over £15,000 – so, on a salary of £15,001, you'll pay back 9p a year. Or, more realistically, on an £18,000 salary, you'll be paying £5.19 a week, or around £270 a year.

And just to show they have a heart, the SLC will wipe out any remaining debt 25 years after you walk out the university gates for the final time. Roll on 2035, eh?

In case that's not quite bewildering enough, the whole system varies for students studying outside the country they live in:

• Scottish students on courses at Scottish universities and colleges don't have to pay fees. Instead they pay an 'endowment' of about £2,200 when they graduate. However, students from the rest of the UK who study at Scottish institutions will have to pay fees – expected to be £1,700 – for the whole of their course (including the extra year that most degrees last in Scotland).

• Scottish students on courses at English universities will have to pay top-up fees, and they'll get a loan to cover them, just like English students do.

• All Welsh and non-UK EU students on courses at universities in Wales – in 2006 at least – will pay a fixed fee of around £1,200 and they'll be able to get a loan to cover it. From 2007, all Welsh unis will hit the £3,000 mark, but Welsh students should get an extra grant to make up for the price-hike.

• Students on a year abroad or industrial placement year will usually pay a third of their normal tuition fee for that year.

• International students have to pay full fees, except students from the EU. In England they'll pay top-up fees and can get a loan to pay for the fees (just like the English). In Wales they'll

· ·

pay the fixed fee of around £1,200 (until 2007) and in Scotland they'll pay the same as Scottish students.

Whatever the case and whatever your parents' income, you should still apply to your LEA for tuition fees awards or you'll end up paying rather more than the full £3,000 a year.

BURSARIES

What with a degree now costing more than a small house somewhere up north, universities are being encouraged to set up extensive bursary systems to keep their students from, well, starving in gutters. Any of the universities who want to charge the full £3,000 of top-up fees (ie. most of them) will have to make sure that students on the full £2,700 maintenance grant get at least another £300 from the university – which should mean they can cover the whole three grand, and often more. Essentially, if they want to charge top whack, they have to top it up. Hard to explain when you're drunk.

Of course, many universities already have (often quite generous) bursary systems in place. Almost all universities and colleges also have cash to hand out. It's called the Access to Learning Fund ('access fund', to its mates). The idea is to help students who need it most – which usually means having nowhere else to turn for basic funds (not simply wanting free moolah for a bit of bling).

Some universities and colleges are a bit more splash-happy with the cash than others. They have their own sponsorships, scholarships and bursaries, many of which are only open to students studying a certain subject or who were born in a particular county on a Thursday when Aquarius was in the ascendant. We might be talking pennies, but occasionally it's big bucks, so it's always worth checking out the possibilities. In many cases, these hand-outs are being adapted to take account of the strange new world of student funding.

Students with special needs can also get special bursaries and awards – usually if they're a parent or have a disability. If you qualify, you should be able to get your hands on this cash no matter which university you're studying at.

LOANS

A loan is money borrowed and don't you forget it.

There are two fundamental problems with borrowing money: (i) sooner or later, whoever lent it will want it back, and (ii) they will want more than they lent in the first place. This applies whether it is borrowed from a bank, the Student Loans Company, a building society, whoever.

There are two possible exceptions. If they can afford it, students' parents often give them interest-free loans and many recognise that the likelihood of seeing it again is somewhat smaller than meeting June Whitfield at a death metal concert. Sometimes, friends can be persuaded to lend each other a few quid to get by, but this is usually the quickest way to lose friends – especially if they're students too, because the chances are they'll have financial problems of their own.

Student bank accounts often offer free overdraft facilities of £1,000 and even more. After the limit though, interest rates can be gob-stoppingly high, especially if the overdraft is unagreed. Students who intend to exceed their agreed limit, should tell the bank about it first. It's frightening as hell, but they're much nicer when they know what's going on and they send fewer rude letters and charge lower interest. They might, of course, say no, but they rarely cut students off without a penny so long as they've shown a responsible attitude.

Each year, almost all students can also apply for a Government-funded Student Loan from the inspiringly titled Student Loans Company. These used just to be doled out for living expenses. Now they include money to meet the top-up fees, so you could well be saddled with almost £9,000 of debt before you've even really got started.

It's not, as rumour sometimes has it, interest-free. Interest is fixed at the rate of inflation; it's a cheaper loan than most, but it's not just a grant which has to be paid back. Repayments will start when a student has graduated and is earning £15,000 a year and it's usually just taken out of their pay by their employer. However, the amount they have to pay back each month is linked to how much they earn, rather than how much they've borrowed.

To get a Student Loan, you need to apply to your LEA or, in some cases, the SLC (check with your

LEA) as part of the process of applying for them to pay a share of your tuition fees. There's a small section at the end of the form where you can indicate whether you want to take a loan and, if so, how much you want to borrow. This means that you can get everything sorted before you start your course, which should be handy for paying your first rent cheque.

With the new maintenance grant, how much cash you can borrow will vary. Some will get the full £2,700 grant hand-out, with the option to borrow more on top. Others will get a smaller grant and, maybe, larger loans. Others – that's around 50% of students – will get loans only and have to pay back every penny.

Postgrads and international students can't get student loans (or at least, not these ones), but if you don't believe us or you're not sure, it's best to check your eligibility.

The amount students are allowed to borrow depends on how much cash their parents have. As The Push Guide went to press, students were entitled to the maximum following amounts for each full year and for the final year (which doesn't include the summer). It'll go up in 2007, but the bean-counters at the SLC aren't yet saying by how much:

	Full year	Final year
Students living away from parents:		
In London	£6,170	£5,620
Elsewhere	£4,405	£4,080
Students living with parents:	£3,415	£3,085

Not everyone can borrow that much, however – those who are eligible for the maintenance grant get their loan entitlement reduced accordingly. And those with the richest parents are only allowed to take up to 75% of the total loan, as their parents are expected to cough up a bit more to make up the difference.

There are other operations students can borrow from, such as credit card companies and loan sharks, but if you do go down this path, check out the interest rates first and see what advance Satan will give on your soul. (It may be a better offer.)

JOBS, SPONSORSHIP AND MORE

Earning a bob or two helps maximise income and, since working time can't be spent spending, it can even help minimise outgoings. The problem is finding a good job. For those who can find work from the employment agencies which don't have 'No Students' signs in the windows, too often it's a toss-up between valuable work experience for less than a condom machine earns in a convent, or dreadful drudgery for only reasonable readies.

There's also the problem of a job interfering with study. Students rarely find time to do more than a little bar work during term and just because some people call that five week period between terms 'the holidays', it doesn't mean students don't have dissertations, essays, field trips, projects and so on. Some unions and colleges run their own employment agencies (aka jobshops) or offer work to their own students – obviously they're much more likely to be sympathetic about the need to juggle paid work with academic commitments.

Earning extras is all very well, but except for those with a specially marketable talent (such as being bilingual, able to type at 80wpm or having insider knowledge about the 2:30 at Chepstow), students should never rely on what they might make. Therefore, pessimism intact, it's best to leave it out of the equation when calculating budgets.

Some employers offer schemes whereby students are subsidised for the duration of their courses, usually in exchange for work during the vacation or after graduation. The armed forces and science/technology based organisations are usually the best bet for this – if you're one of those admirably and unfeasibly sussed people who mapped out what they wanted to do with their lives at the age of 12, it could be worthwhile contacting employers in your chosen field and seeing what they have to offer.

For some students, financial salvation comes in the form of a sandwich course. These involve doing a work placement at some point in the course for periods of anything from a few months up to a whole year. Apart from getting work experience, sandwich students usually get paid while they're working. It may not clear all their debts, but it can certainly fill a pretty big hole at the bank.

TOP TIPS
Finally a couple of cunning ploys to employ...

1. Do your homework. If you haven't guessed already, the funding system is horrendously complicated, and varies from country to country, university to university, course to course, person to person, and sub-atomic particle to sub-atomic particle.

What we've said here is just an overview and you need to know how it applies to you. Make sure you know what to expect. Did we mention The Push Guide to Student Money? Did we mention it's only £9.99?

2. Make a budget. Work out how much you're going to get from your loan, your parents and any other sources of income and then subtract your rent, allowances for food, bills, travel, clothes, books and other stuff you need for your course, insurance and even a bit for beer money. This will probably be a scary and educational process, striking such fear into you that you take a sensible attitude to money throughout your student career. If it isn't scary, either you're very rich, very brave or you've got your sums wrong.

3. Whether you think you need it or not, you should take up as big a student loan as they'll let you have. You'll almost certainly need it and it's better to have the money in the bank waiting than realise you're stony broke and only then start the application process which, if you're desperate for cash, seems to take forever. It's certainly better than making futile attempts to stay in the black. They won't work and won't last.

4. Even if you definitely don't need one, take out a student loan anyway and invest it elsewhere. The interest charged on a student loan is pegged to the rate of inflation, currently 3.1% pa. Bunging it in an ISA or a long-term savings account will earn you at least 4% interest and will usually give you instant access to your money. You're quids in, whatever.

5. Students who can apply for state benefits, should do. Unfortunately, students are the only members of society not entitled to normal benefits because of their occupation. Students are not allowed to collect unemployment benefit during their vacations if they cannot find work and are not allowed to claim housing benefit. However, students with disabilities or with dependants will still find they can claim some benefits.

6. Stay friends with your bank. Never go beyond your overdraft limit without getting permission. If you do, they'll send you really helpful letters but – to add insult to injury – they'll charge you for them. They'll also fine you for breaking the rules and whack a big interest rate on your borrowings.

PUSHING OUT THE BOAT: A YEAR OUT

A look at the pros and cons of taking a year out before going on to higher education.

Why do students consider taking a year off? They're only young once, so why waste time not getting on with life? Why don't they just get a degree, get a job and get an income? Why don't they choose life, choose a pension plan, choose 2.4 kids, a Tesco loyalty card and a 34-inch telly with surround sound and a boob-job thrown in? Why don't they take the short cut and just coat themselves in compost and rot?

Why? Because it's more fun to spend a year getting up to the kind of thing they can only do when they've got the youth and the opportunity, when they haven't got kids and when slumming it round the Amazon basin doesn't leave bits of mosquito in their dentures.

But it's not all fun and opportunity-seizing, there are real practical advantages too. Far from the old view that time out is worthless bumming around, a constructive year off is now an immense asset in the competitive job market.

An extended CV is better than a brown envelope stuffed with used fifties when it comes to sending out job applications. Students who've taken a year out or spent their long vacations broadening their horizons, have got more to offer to a potential employer. They stand out from the crowd at every opportunity and not just because they smell funny. It won't get them a position for which they're not qualified, but all things being equal, it helps.

With little or no real work experience, employers will have to make judgements based on qualifications and nobody's fooled for a moment into thinking that a degree in politics or an A Level in physics is a perfect preparation for a career in marketing, management or merchant banking. If they can find something to pick a student out from the rest of the pack, they'll home in like missiles over Baghdad. Many employers even discriminate against students who spent long summer vacations living with their parents, staying in bed and watching Neighbours.

Another reason for taking a year out is simply to work and store up a nest egg to see them through university. The average student is now expected to graduate with £15,000- worth of debt. There are very few ways to avoid being in debt after graduation, but one of them is to stash some cash before you start.

But during a year out, time can be even more valuable than money. Even if money's tight, with time, you can always find a way to get away or get up to something worthwhile. Time is necessary – money isn't. Even a bout of globe-trotting doesn't have to cost the earth. It's all too easy to think cash is needed for a good time and so students sit around waiting for a job that doesn't turn up. They'd be better off using that waiting time to get out of the rut and out of the country.

Of course, some ventures do require money – for example, for a six-month expedition across Africa, a least a grand up front would be needed. But there are also ways of getting overseas for less than £100, such as crewing on a yacht to the Caribbean or being a youth leader at an American summer camp. One thing leads to another and other opportunities open up. Travel breeds confidence, which breeds success.

If you plan to work and travel overseas, it's worth pausing to consider aims and objectives. To promote the environment? To conserve wildlife? To make some money? Or simply have a unique experience, filled with self-discovery? These things are all very well, but never forget the fun factor.

You shouldn't worry about what you think you should do – you should do what you really want to. Time out doesn't have to be politically correct – a year spent skiing and mountain biking in Switzerland is not inferior to one spent helping orphans in India or saving a rainforest in South East Asia.

Whatever you end up doing – even if you eventually decide to stay at home and get work experience (or re-sit exams) – you shouldn't expect non-stop action. You're unlikely to complete a trans-Africa expedition without getting stomach problems, very unlikely to sail across the Atlantic without getting sea-sick and there's no chance of going to Australia without getting hungover. But new friends, knowledge, self-confidence and experience will make the sacrifices worthwhile.

When, after a year out, a student becomes a fresher, you can always tell they're not straight from school. They're the ones for whom new challenges are not quite such a fresh experience. Or maybe just the insufferably smug ones.

PUSHING ON A BIT: MATURE STUDENTS

A few wise words for mature students and those returning to higher education.

First off, a mature student isn't necessarily someone who wears cardigans and shakes their greying head in a responsible way saying, 'It's not like it was in my day'. Nor necessarily are they pushing on a bit.

Students can be classified as mature from as young as 21. If you were alive when Bros were getting crew cuts and wondering when they'd be famous, you're probably old enough to be a mature student. The only generally accepted definition is that mature students are not the same age as conventional students and they are (with a few exceptions) not coming to higher education straight from school.

If you are returning to education, there are special considerations which vary enormously from one college to another. There's no need to accept sloppy seconds and just make do when it comes to higher education – there's enough choice to put your foot down and set an agenda according to your own specific needs.

Most students' unions (SUs) provide some facilities for mature students such as common rooms, mature student groups and specialised welfare advice. Make a checklist of needs from housing through to entertainment which will make a difference to which college you choose.

Although mature students often have roots and ties which may be an incentive to look no further than the most local college, many will find that special provisions for mature students may make a broader search worthwhile.

Some colleges provide specialised packages which are centred on people who have not just left the parental home. For example, many offer off-campus self-catering accommodation, others have specific flats for mature students with their partner (usually only if married) and even their children, though it's rare to find places that can accommodate more than one child per couple. The college will probably also provide house hunting info for those who'd rather go it alone. The Accommodation Officer will be most handy for this – SUs' accommodation help is generally geared mainly to 'conventional' students.

As for social life, most entertainments centre around the SU rather than the college. The Push Guide gives the low-down on the goings-on. Bear in mind that bars may be full of students who, for the first time, don't have to prove their age to buy a pint. Discos will be aimed at groovy young things who think Depeche Mode is a setting on their hi-fi (though you can always wow them with your intimate knowledge of 80s pop lyrics on retro night). From gigs to grub, what do you want to do? And does the college you're looking at provide it?

If appropriate, check about childcare facilities as many universities are only beginning to develop services in this area. The Push Guide tells you whether there's a crèche, but under that description can be anything from well-staffed care at subsidised cost for children from 6 months to 5 years old to some nobody who fancied a spot of babysitting, surrounded by squealing brats and tipped-up paint pots. In most colleges, the SU is either the main provider of childcare facilities on campus or knows best what provisions are available and will give an honest opinion of how good they are. Either get in touch with the person – talk to the Welfare Officer – or ask for a copy of the SU handbook or alternative prospectus.

Although many students are aged over 21, many facilities still cater for the 18+ age range. Mature students can feel isolated and so it's useful if there are others in the same boat and a forum for them to meet. Some SUs provide better support than others and many mature student groups organise their own functions. Under the Welfare section, The Push Guide says whether there's a mature students' association.

Also in the vital statistics panel in the general section of each college profile, we provide figures for the percentage of mature students. That can vary from the single digits to a few universities where 18-year-olds are the freaks. Naturally enough, this is one of the best indicators of how well geared up the university may be for mature students. After all, there's safety in numbers. Or failing that, other people to moan with.

POORLY PUSH: WELFARE

Student life has its ups and downs and welfare – the support system provided by universities and colleges to help students with their health and happiness – is the safety net for the down times. Push seeks out a friendly ear.

Universities do worry about students beyond whether they get their essays in and pay their tuition fees on time. They worry about their welfare. After all, if students aren't healthy, wealthy (or solvent) and happy, they're hardly likely to get their essays in or pay their tuition fees on time. Some care more than others. However, most do provide services to look after students including some, if not all the following:

HEALTH doctors, nurses and, sometimes, physiotherapists, chiropractors, psychiatrists and so on.

WELL-BEING AND HAPPINESS counsellors and advisors trained to deal with all the problems likely to be faced by students, including exam stress, depression and sexual problems. There may also be access to groups and advisors with specific concerns, such as for lesbian, gay, bisexual and transgender students; those with disabilities; women and so on.

FINANCE debt counsellors, hardship funds, emergency loans, bursaries and some scholarships.

OTHERS help finding housing and dealing with accommodation problems, legal advice, chaplains, help landing a job (part-time, temporary or a career), crèches and nurseries and so on.

Often some or even all of these services are provided by the students' union or they provide complementary services, such as academic appeals representation, financial help and Nightline – a Samaritans-style free and confidential phone service, staffed by trained students. As well as the provisions from the universities and unions (found in the Welfare section of each college profile), here are some other helpful contacts:

THE NATIONAL BISEXUAL HELPLINE (0845) 450 1264 (Tues and Wed 7.30–9.30pm; Sat 10.30am–12.30am).

EATING DISORDERS ASSOCIATION (EDA) Offers support and mutual care to those suffering from Anorexia or Bulimia Nervosa, binge eating, and other eating-related problems. (0845) 634 7650 (callers 18 and under Mon–Fri 4–6.30pm and Sat 1–4.30pm) or e-mail talkback@edauk.com. See also www.edauk.com

GET CONNECTED A free confidential helpline for young people that will put them in touch with the right help they need. (0808) 808 4994 (every day from 1pm–11pm), or e-mail help@getconnected.org.uk

LONDON LESBIAN AND GAY SWITCHBOARD A national service for lesbians, gays and anyone needing support regarding their sexuality. Information, advice, listening and referral. (020) 7837 7324 (24 hours) or www.llgs.org.uk

NATIONAL AIDS HELPLINE For anyone concerned about HIV/AIDS. Offers information and advice, can make referrals: (0800) 567 123 (24 hours). See also www.playingsafely.co.uk for general links on matters sexual.

TALK TO FRANK Resources for anyone concerned about drug misuse, including users, families, friends and carers – (0800) 77 66 00 (24 hours). See www.talktofrank.com

THE SAMARITANS Providing confidential, emotional support to anyone in need: (08457) 90 90 90 (UK) or (1850) 60 90 90 (ROI). E-mail: jo@samaritans.org

SEXWISE Information, advice and guidance for young people on sexual health and sexuality. See the website (www.ruthinking.co.uk) or call (0800) 28 29 30 (7am–midnight every day).

NATIONAL DEBTLINE Exactly what it says on the tin. (0800) 808 4000 or see www.nationaldebtline.co.uk

PUSHING BACK THE FRONTIERS: STUDENTS WITH DISABILITIES

Having a disability doesn't mean your needs can't be met at University. Skill (the National Bureau for Students with Disabilities) points the way...

Being disabled doesn't mean going to higher education will be different for you – the other information in The Push Guide is as relevant to you as anyone else – but if you do have a disability, medical condition or specific learning difficulty, you may have a few more things to think about before you apply.

The Disability Discrimination Act is in force to ensure disabled students aren't treated any less favourably than non-disabled students. Universities have to make reasonable adjustments to make sure you're not at a disadvantage because of a disability. While you'll need to know if your disability-related needs can be met by the college or university, don't be tempted to make disability the only criteria you use when making choices – remember that the subject you're going to study, the social life, where provisions are geographically located and so on are all just as important to you as to a non-disabled student.

Skill produces a guide, Into Higher Education, which gives advice about applying. It includes contact details of all institutions offering higher education courses, with details of some of the facilities they offer disabled students. You can also find out information from prospectuses, the SU, internet, league tables and by talking to other disabled students. Don't be afraid to contact institutions before applying. If you're not sure what's available, never be afraid to ask.

It's also a good idea to visit before applying. Open days are a good way for you to check out the university's facilities and attitude. Consider all areas of student life – it may be just as important for you socially to get into the bar and meet other students as it is for you academically to get into the library and find books.

As long as you meet eligibility criteria there's a Disabled Students' Allowance to help with disability-related costs in studying. Skill produces a lot of information about these allowances and how to apply for them.

Skill's Information Service is available for telephone enquiries (Tuesday 11.30am–1.30pm and Thursday 1.30pm–3.30pm) on (0800) 328 5050, textphone (0800) 068 2422 or e-mail at info@skill.org.uk. You can also post messages for other students and access a range of information booklets at Skill's website, www.skill.org.uk.

There's no need for you to do everything on your own. Most colleges have disability advisors/co-ordinators and union welfare officers to help make sure your experience at university is of great benefit to you both academically and socially, and there may be disabled students' groups. Skill also has a membership scheme and a newsletter for students called 'Notes and Quotes'. So if you have any questions, hit any problems or if you would like to be involved in Skill's work, why not get in touch?

PUSHGRADS: POSTGRADUATES

Some students become addicted to student life and think, what the hell, I'll do another degree. But life as a postgrad is very different from the lazy, hazy daze of undergrad life and it can be just as troubled financially. Here are some of the pitfalls for postgrads.

There are a whopping half a million postgrad students in UK universities at the moment, including those who stayed on after graduating or returned to take postgraduate courses. The reasons vary greatly, from putting off the 9–5 grind, worries about getting employment at all, sheer love of particle physics (it happens) or pure love of student life.

But those simply expecting an extension of

undergrad life are sorely misled. Postgrads study all year round with no long holidays to recharge batteries or bank accounts.

Funding, too, is harder to come by – very few postgrads are guaranteed financial support for any course (trainee teachers are one notable exception). This applies not just to maintenance costs (postgrads aren't allowed to apply for student loans), but also to tuition costs, all of which postgrads have to meet themselves, regardless of income. What grants are available are awarded on a competitive basis and so it's a good idea to have a pretty damn impressive first degree (even a good 2.i may be cutting it fine for humanities and arts subjects because there's less funding about). It also helps if you're able to apply to a funding council who are more generous with grants.

There are also Government-subsidised Career Development Loans mostly for courses which can claim some kind of vocational element (translating obscure Abyssinian limericks probably doesn't count) and which pay out between £300 and £8,000. See www.lifelonglearning.co.uk/cdl for the fine print.

At the end of the day, a postgrad qualification may solve the financial problems it creates. Postgrads stand out from the crowd to potential employers and can expect to earn more. However, some employers prefer to train recent undergraduates and postgrads can find themselves overqualified. Some postgrads become professional academics, but the financial rewards alone are not likely to be a temptation.

Postgraduate courses split into two broad types – those that centre on research and those that are mainly taught.

Researchers study for one or two years to get a Masters degree or MPhil, or three years for a Doctorate (PhD). However, these are minimum periods – many students take a bit longer, sometimes up to twice as long. That extra time, including the costs of living, eating and socialising, also racks up the final bill.

Funding for research is available from Research Councils, charities or on research contracts from the institutions themselves – see www.rcuk.ac.uk Commercially valuable research can often attract industrial sponsorship so delving into new types of plastic is likely to be less financially fraught than examining the philology of Philo.

Although there's no teaching in a research degree, postgrads' work is supervised and it's important the supervisor is appropriately clued up. Postgrads should interview whoever will be supervising them before accepting a place – it's important not only that supervisors are able to appreciate the subtleties of their postgrads' work, but also that they get on well.

As for taught courses, they are usually part of an extended career ladder or a stepping stone to a research degree. They are either for students who want to specialise in a particular field or want to convert their qualifications to a different area. Conversion courses in particular vary greatly in what they offer, so students should be sure not just that it's suitable, but also why it is. Awards for these courses are available from the same sources as for research degrees.

UNITED WE PUSH: STUDENTS' UNIONS

Call them talking shops, bop shops, shopping centres or advice centres, what are students' unions? Who are they? Over to the NUS...

Inescapable, unavoidable and absolutely essential. Within minutes of arriving at university you'll find yourself in your students' union (SU).

SUs form the collective voice of the student body. Each student is automatically a member of the SU and each will be involved in running the union through general meetings and electing executive officers. It costs you zero and you can't get much cheaper than that. The union represents you and your interests and whatever you want to do, you can, because you own and run your union and you can make it happen.

SUs work in different ways. If you want to know where to find accommodation, contraception, more money, even how to get a job, they have trained staff and student officers to help. If you want to disco till dawn, eat, drink and be merry, this is the place to be. But it's more than top bands, cheap drink, decent food and good advice. If you want to join any one of the thousands of different student sporting, social, political, cultural or special interest clubs and societies, from the flat cap society to Alan Partridge appreciation, then get down to the union.

If you've a particular gripe – if there aren't enough books in the library, minibuses for the hockey teams or you've got problems in your halls of residence – union officers will take on the university administration and sort it out by representing your views at meetings and making sure that the student voice is heard.

Your union will also probably be a member of the National Union of Students. NUS is a confederation of unions representing over 5 million students in the UK and gives you national representation, letting Parliament and the press know exactly what you think and lobbying for change. NUS also provides back-up and training for all your individual elected union officers.

PUSHING THE PENNIES: CHARITY RAGS

Today's Rag is all things to all people. Whatever you want out of student life, Rag can provide it. The Rag network is an instant and no-hassle social life. At the same time Rag exists to raise thousands of pounds for needy causes. UKRag explains the ins and outs of being a good Samaritan.

So, what exactly do Rags do? Each one's different, but overall they exist to raise funds for charity through student activity. It might mean organising Rag balls, concerts, pantos, clubnights, sponsored runs, bungee jumps...

pretty much anything. They also offer the chance to travel the UK, for free, so you could find yourself spending a Saturday collecting for charity in some far flung city. One of the most fun parts of Rag is the chance to go to Megaraids, where loads of Rags collect in one place, and have a massive party afterwards.

While beer and parties are good, when it comes after a long day when you've achieved something for other people, when you've had a laugh with some of the best mates you will ever meet – then it's absolutely priceless.

Not only that, but it'll give you those extra-curricular skills employers always seem to harp on about. If you want a good job you need more than just your degree: interpersonal skills; team experience; ICT; project-management. By joining Rag, and putting in as much or as little time as you want, you'll get back much more than you could possibly want out of your time at Uni.

If you want to get involved get in touch with your Rag, as soon as you get to campus, if not before. Of course, some universities/colleges won't have a Rag group set up yet but there are plenty of resources and help out there if you have the nouse to start one yourself. www.UKRag.net has the gen on the best way to go about it.

Everyone brings something unique to the mix – business skills, leadership, a love of money, computer skills – so don't assume that 'warm and fuzzy' is all that's required. Last year Rags all over the UK raised several million pounds for charity, beating cancer, feeding the starving, housing the homeless, fighting AIDS, helping kids, as well as caring for the sick, desperate and deserving. It's a serious mission, but in return for your time and effort you'll be part of the biggest, most fun and most useful student network the UK's ever seen.

Rag is a tradition that spans centuries as an essential part of UK university life. It was even the inspiration behind Comic Relief and Red Nose Day. There's a massive community of us out here, and plenty of help and support is always available, especially on www.UKRag.net, a community of Raggies, Rags, and charity reps and we'd love to see you there.

"JUST TELL ME. WHICH IS THE BEST UNIVERSITY?"

Wouldn't it be great if you could just say what you want from a university and someone told you how and where to get it?

That's just what Push Online does.

The most powerful, most detailed, downright most bestest way to find the right university for you, to help you get a place and to prepare you for student life

Visit Push Online
at www.push.co.uk

Join up for access to
the really flashy extra
bits at just £14.99 a year

A

UNIVERSITY OF ABERDEEN

UNIVERSITY OF ABERTAY DUNDEE

ABERYSTWYTH, UNIVERSITY OF WALES

➤ **APU**
see Anglia Ruskin University

➤ **ANGLIA POLYTECHNIC**
see Anglia Ruskin University

ANGLIA RUSKIN UNIVERSITY

UNIVERSITY OF THE ARTS, LONDON

ASTON UNIVERSITY

A UNIVERSITY OF ABERDEEN

O THE UNIVERSITY OF ABERDEEN University Office, King's College, Aberdeen, AB24 3FX **TEL** (01224) 272 090
E-MAIL sras@abdn.ac.uk **WEBSITE** www.abdn.ac.uk/sras **O UNIVERSITY STUDENTS' ASSOCIATION** Luthuli House,
50/52 College Bounds, Old Aberdeen, AB24 3DS **TEL** (01224) 272 965 **E-MAIL** ausa@abdn.ac.uk **WEBSITE** www.ausa.org.uk

GENERAL ◑◑◑◑◑◑◑◑◑◑◑◑◑

The first university the alphabet has to offer is way, way up north in the *affectionately* named Granite City. Aberdeen lies on the east coast of Scotland, suitably placed to be the oil capital of Europe and *spanned all round by spectacular castles, coastline, beaches and lochs and the majesty of the Grampian Highlands – even Push gets poetic at the thought.* The city itself's a pretty place too with flowers, parks and great architecture. The University is based on three sites which once made up two separate universities. In fact, Aberdeen had two universities back when that was the total number in the whole of England. The larger, main site is King's College in Old Aberdeen, *a satisfying eyeful* of 15th-century buildings, modern blocks, green space and cobbled streets, 1,200m north of the city centre. The Medical School at Foresterhill is a mile and a half from the main campus. The concretey Hilton campus houses the School of Education, a theatre, a library and various accommodation blocks.

SEX RATIO: ♂46 ♀54	**FOUNDED:** 1495
FULL-TIME U'GRADS: 10,300	**PART-TIME:** 1,060
POSTGRADS: 3,159	**NON-DEGREE:** 915
AVE COURSE: 4YRS	**ETHNIC:** 6%
STATE:PRIVATE SCHOOL: 84:16	**FLUNK RATE:** 17%
MATURE: 19%	**INTERNATIONAL:** 13%
DISABLED: 165	**LOCAL:** 36%

ATMOSPHERE
Most Aberdonian students enjoy the beautiful and relaxed environment for their four years of study. A strong sporting ethos and an exciting nightlife complement the academic end of the tunnel and town/gown relations couldn't be cosier.

ABERDEEN
O POPULATION 211,250 **O CITY CENTRE** 1 MILE
O LONDON 410 MILES **O DUNDEE** 67 MILES
O EDINBURGH 126 MILES
O HIGH TEMP 17 **O LOW TEMP** 0 **O RAINFALL** 61
Aberdeen is a very old city made prosperous over the past century thanks to its strong associations with the North Sea oil industry. *The flammable black ooze from the dawn of time has brought the city a varied cultural cocktail from all over the UK, a predictable industrial presence and a lot of tankers. The fishing trade that once dominated is headed to Davy Jones's locker as a result,* but the salty scent of sea-life still swirls the streets. The city centre's *gorgeous* architecture and *ample*

amenities *are contrasted by the outskirts, which contain some of the grimmer aspects of 70s civil engineering.* Just outside the city, swathes of countryside continue on and on and on and on before arriving at anywhere vaguely urban. *It's a self-contained town and it has to be – it's bloody miles from anywhere.*

TRAVEL
TRAINS *Despite being so far north* (the same latitude as St Petersburg), rail connections are *quite good, if expensive.* Among others, services are offered to London (from £71.20 return), Glasgow (£34.50) and Birmingham (£68.05).
BUSES National Express coach services to London (£42), Glasgow (£21.80), Birmingham (£39.50) and others. For coach journeys within Scotland there's Scottish Citylink. Stagecoach also run services. Megabus deals are cheapest, running to Glasgow and Edinburgh for £6 rtn.
CAR A92, A93, A94 and A96. Two miles to the nearest junction.
AIR Inland flights around the UK and to some European cities.
FERRIES There's a ferry service to Lerwick in the Shetlands.
HITCHING *The A92 is fairly major and once hitchers have got to the M90, it's plain sailing. But the hitch of hitching is that it's a long, long road and going west inland is nigh on impossible.*
LOCAL Good bus services run anywhere in the city from 35p, *useful for getting into the centre from King's.*
TAXIS *Useful late at night, but expensive* – £6 from the station to King's, £10-12 from the airport.
BICYCLES *Despite the heavy traffic and the cold winds,* many students take to cycling. Some halls are only 1,200m from the campuses so pedal power can be just the ticket. Bike theft is as rare as any other crime in Aberdeen.

CAREER PROSPECTS
O CAREERS SERVICE O NO. OF STAFF 9 FULL
O UNEMPLOYED AFTER 6 MTHS 3%
The Careers & Appointments Service organises seminars and workshops, weekly job update e-mails and performs that fave corporate fad – psychometric testing. Also newsletters, bulletin boards, interview training and job fairs *ago-go.*

FAMOUS ALUMNI
Nicky Campbell (DJ); Iain Crichton-Smith (poet); Iain Cuthbertson (actor); Alistair Darling MP (Lab, Secretary of State); Sandy Gall (veteran journalist); Denys Henderson (Chair of ICI); Tessa Jowell MP (Culture Secretary); Kenneth McKellar (singer); David McLean MP (Con); James Naughtie (BBC Radio 4 'Today' presenter).

FURTHER INFO

○ PROSPECTUSES UNDERGRAD; POSTGRAD; SOME DEPARTMENTAL; INTERNATIONAL.

○ OPEN DAYS
Applicants receive a guidance pack containing advice, accommodation info and a pamphlet for parents to pore over. The admissions website is www.abdn.ac.uk/sras.

ACADEMIC ⊕⊕⊕⊕⊕⊕⊕⊕⊕⊕⊕⊕

Since many academic staff are involved in national and international level research staff/student relations are fairly cosy – *a sort of 'we're all in this learning malarky together' vibe.* Teaching comprises lectures and compulsory tutorials, with the odd one-to-one session thrown in here and there. Fourth year brings with it the *perils* of dissertation.

ENTRY POINTS: 216-348	AVE POINTS: N/A
APPLICATIONS PER PLACE: 7	CLEARING: 6%
NO. OF TERMS: 3	LENGTH OF TERMS: 12WKS
STAFF TO STUDENT RATIO: N/A	STUDY ADDICTS: 29%
TEACHING: ★★★	RESEARCH: ★★★
YEAR ABROAD: 2%	SANDWICH STUDENTS: <1%
1STS: 7%	2.2s: 19%
2.1s: 37%	3RDS: 2%

ADMISSIONS

○ APPLY VIA UCAS

SUBJECTS

UNUSUAL Belgian Law; Gender Studies; Marine & Coastal Resource Management.

LIBRARIES

○ 1,050,000 BOOKS ○ 1,548 STUDY PLACES
○ 24-HR ACCESS
There's *oodles* of shelf space spread over four large libraries and some smaller departmental libraries and archives. The main Queen Margaret library has self-service issue and return facilities and (along with the Taylor and Medical libraries) has wireless facilities – *so students can play online poker while they work.* It gets chock-a-block – a *much-needed* new library is in the pipeline to cope with the University's history of expanding *like a belly at a buffet.* Bookworms can study until 10pm most nights a week. Members of the public are allowed into all libraries on a 'look but don't touch' basis.

COMPUTERS

○ 1,000 WORKSTATIONS ○ 24-HR ACCESS
PCs in the libraries, halls and the main IT centre in the Edward Wright Building. All PCs have CD readers and writers and all students have a page on the University's network, which contains exam results, library loans, tuition and hall fees and *other useful but Big Brotherish info.*

OTHER LEARNING FACILITIES

Aberdeen houses the European Documentation Centre as well as language labs, drama studio, rehearsal rooms, CAD lab, media centre and practice courtroom.

ENTERTAINMENT ⊕⊕⊕⊕⊕⊕⊕⊕⊕

THE CITY
○ PRICE OF A PINT OF BEER £2
○ GLASS OF WINE £2.30
○ CAN OF RED BULL £2.20
CINEMAS Vue and the UGC are there for *brainless popcorn-guzzling.* The Belmont Picturehouse provides artier flicks.
THEATRES His Majesty's Theatre attracts big-time ballet and opera on tour as well as less elite delights like pantos. Its biggest seller is the Student Charities Campaign show. The Aberdeen Arts Centre is smaller and hosts more fringe theatre, am dram and some student productions.
PUBS *A mixture of old men's pubs and pretentious glittery bars with little dance floors, made up for with a healthy supply of student-friendly venues.* Pushplugs: the Illicit Still; the Bobbin; St Machar Bar.
CLUBBING *Aberdeen has enough clubs to keep hip hips moving.* Liquid, Espionage, Priory and Ministry *around Belmont Street are good for movers and shakers.*
MUSIC VENUES Folk music *infests* most pubs at some point, *but the indie scene is on the rise with venues like the Tunnels, Moshulu and Drummonds keeping alt bands in business.* The Music Hall does a mixture of classical, rock, pop, jazz and more folk. The Lemon Tree is a 'concept' venue, *meaning it's quite small, has a stage and that Radiohead once played here.*
OTHER Bundles of museums and galleries. *Worthy of note* are the Zoology Museum, Aberdeen Art Gallery and Stratosphere – *where you can play with the exhibits like some kind of crazy child.*
EATING OUT *A bit pricey.* Pushplugs: Café 52 and The Olive Tree *for French;* Buffet King *for Oriental nibbling;* Blue Elephant Tandoori *for the best Aberdeen has to offer in Indian;* Estaminet *for tapas and* Lamba *for boozed-up Mexican dishes and dancing on chairs.*

UNIVERSITY
○ PRICE OF A PINT OF BEER £1.75
○ GLASS OF WINE £1.90
○ CAN OF RED BULL £2.10
The financially flailing Union has had to slash and burn its once-mighty bar scene, leaving the only the glowing embers to warm student cockles. Luckily, they appear to have found £8m down the back of the sofa and are building a central Union 'Hub' that will act as bar-cum-food-court-cum-services-centre-cum-pelican-sanctuary. (Push has just learned the pelican bit's been cancelled. Shame).

Words in italics are Push's point of view — take it or leave it...

BARS A once-healthy bar scene was culled to leave just two (capacity 440) to prop up of an evening in Littlejohn Street. The Union, (as one bar is called), hosts karaoke, quizzes and other pubby pursuits.

THEATRES The theatre at the Hilton campus gets an airing now and then, as do some of the town venues (see above). *Despite the Centre Stage Society's attempts to thesp up their fellow students, it's sport not soliloquising that appeals to most.*

MUSIC VENUES Thursdays in the Union alternate between live bands and open mic efforts.

FOOD *Zeste Café is a relaxing 70s style joint that does everything to be found in motorway services plus takeaways. A big café/bar and a food court should be cooking on gas come September 2006.*

OTHER Quiz nights and bingo *aren't just for grannies.* There are Departmental balls throughout the year as well.

SOCIAL ⭕⭕⭕⭕⭕⭕⭕⭕⭕⭕⭕⭕⭕

ABERDEEN UNIVERSITY STUDENTS' ASSOCIATION
o **6** SABBATICALS   o TURNOUT AT LAST BALLOT 57%   o NUS MEMBER

The student body are by and large political animals and AUSA regularly herds them into protests and strikes against hiked up tuition fees and is showing no sign of giving up any time soon.

SA FACILITIES
Two bars in the Union on Littlejohn Street. The daytime building will have an internet café, café/bar, food court, shops, food court, careers office, accommodation offices and drop-in centres.

CLUBS (NON-SPORTING)
Anime & Manga; Bahai; Balanese; Gamelan; Capoeira (Brazilian Dancing); Celtic (not the football club); Chinese; Concert Band; Creative Writing; European; Expedition; Jazz; First Aid; Forestry; German; Gilbert & Sullivan; Hispanic; Hong Kong & Cantonese; Humanitarian Long-term Projects; International; Italian; Live Acts; Leaf & Loam; Marrow UK (Leukaemia charity); Natural History; Niteline; Pagan; Pan-African Students; Poker; Pool; Reiki; Role-playing; Russian; Scandinavian; Scottish Nationalist; Scottish Dance; SCROLL; Shared Planet; Singapore Students; Wilderness Medical. **See also Clubs tables.**

OTHER ORGANISATIONS
DEBATER As well as AUSA students become members (free and automatically) of Debater, one of the country's oldest mooting societies that does nothing but host discussions on topics of every breed and flavour and come to conclusions (or not) about them. *It's popular, fun and not as pompous and Toryfied as the Oxbridge debating unions.*

OTHERS Weekly paper 'Gaudie' is a *geriatric* 70 years old and, *unusually for a student newspaper, actually contains news.* As part of the Charities Campaign, the annual Torcher Parade – *not as medieval or painful as it sounds* – is the largest torchlit parade in Europe and Jailbreak – *not as criminal as it sounds* – sends penniless students as far away from the city as they can in 36 hours. Thespies congregate in Centre Stage and Treading the Boards (for musicals), but whinge that they don't have enough space to rehearse or perform. *Luvvies, eh?* SCA (Student Community Action) is the *energetic* local help organisation run by student volunteers.

RELIGIOUS
o **11** CHAPLAINS (COFE, RC, METHODIST, QUAKER, RC GREEK ORTHODOX, MORMON), IMAM, RABBI

Two chapels and a small mosque in the University. Locally, apart from St Mary's Cathedral (Catholic), St Andrew's Cathedral (Episcopal) and St Machar's Cathedral (Presbyterian), there are places of worship for most faiths.

PAID WORK
o JOB BUREAU

Union-run JobLink helps find part-time, vacation and temp work (see www.ausa.org.uk/joblink for job ads). Students can sometimes find work in the oil industry, particularly those with studies in a relevant field. *If not, it's time to get out the rod and go fish.*

SPORTS ⭕⭕⭕⭕⭕⭕⭕⭕⭕⭕⭕⭕⭕

o RECENT SUCCESS SKIING   o BUSA RANKING 29

AUSA runs and sails a tight sporting ship. Sporting success is highly regarded and consequently highly frequent. Instructional classes are available in various things, including yoga, boxercise, Pilates, dance and sports conditioning. Fitness consultations and therapy services are also available to tone those flagging muscles.

SPORTS FACILITIES
Most facilities available on both sites. The Butchart Recreation Centre (King's) has been refurbished and contains a sports hall, gym, cardiovascular equipment, fitness and testing room, weights room, four squash courts and a climbing wall. Also two more squash courts, playing fields, three all-weather tennis courts (or sometimes an all-weather pitch instead) and a swimming pool. The main sports fields are at Balgownie, two miles north, where there are more playing fields for football, rugby, hockey and cricket (bringing the total to just under 20 acres), a running track, golf course and dry ski slope. Elsewhere, the University has a boathouse on the River Dee, a glider at Aboyne and a mountain hut at Lochnagar. All facilities and

fitness classes cost a *nice, round* £1 per session. The University has got into the Citcy Council's pocket in order to develop an Olympic-standard regional sports centre.

SPORTING CLUBS
Aikido; Boat; Boxing; Curling; Field Sports; Gaelic Football; Gliding; Hurling; Ju-Jitsu; Lacrosse; Lifesaving; Mountain-biking; Potholing & Caving; Rifle; Rollerhockey; Shinty; Skydiving; Surf; Table Tennis; Tai Chi; Triathlon; Ultimate Frisbee; Underwater Hockey; Waterpolo. **See also Clubs tables.**

ATTRACTIONS
The local football team, a kick away from campus, is one-time Scottish giants Aberdeen FC – alias 'the Dons'.

ACCOMMODATION ◍◍◍◍◍◍◍◍◍

IN UNIVERSITY
◎ **CATERED** 10% ◎ **COST** £87-105 (38WKS)
◎ **SELF-CATERING** 17% ◎ **COST** £54-75 (38/48WKS)
◎ **1ST YRS LIVING IN** 15% ◎ **INSURANCE PREMIUM** £
AVAILABILITY All first years can be housed, then most students find themselves living out for at least two years. The *bog standard 70s and 80s style* halls are spread over the city. The Hillhead Halls are the largest, about 1,200m north of King's, a mixture of halls (*with tiny rooms*) and flats. *Popular Hillhead is the most spirited hangout, as well as the cheapest.* Crombie-Johnston Halls are closer and dearer. Corridors and floors tend to be single-sex. There are 24-hr reception desks and student welfare staff. Most halls have launderettes, study spaces, TV rooms and gaming facilities, some have an on-site bar. The self-catering accommodation is split between blocks of flats, shared between three to seven students, and local flats and houses either owned or leased by the University, a few of which are available for married couples. Elphinstone Road flats are usually reserved for older students and postgrads. The University has a deal with Aberdeen Student Village, which manages four halls of residence in the city centre.
CAR PARKING: Parking *isn't too much of a problem* with a permit, but the city's green policy means the authorities are attempting to discourage students from bringing cars.

EXTERNALLY
◎ **AVE RENT** £65 ◎ **LIVING AT HOME** 5 PER CENT
AVAILABILITY: 61% of Aberdeen's students have gone off to seek their domestic fortunes alone, which can be a tricky affair given that most local landlords are trying to pipe into the oil industry for tenants. *Sandilands is cheap (and rough), house-hunters are better off trying their luck in Ferryhill, Seaton, King Street, George Street,* Urquhart Road and Rosemount, *for example.*
HOUSING HELP The Union accommodation service advertises widely and offers advice on living out. The University sticks to advising on its owned or managed flats.

WELFARE ◍◍◍◍◍◍◍◍◍◍◍

SERVICES
◎ **LGBT SOCIETY** ◎ **ETHNIC MINORITIES OFFICERS & SOCIETY** ◎ **WOMEN'S OFFICER & SOCIETY** ◎ **MATURE STUDENTS' SOCIETY** ◎ **INTERNATIONAL STUDENTS' OFFICER & SOCIETY** ◎ **POSTGRAD OFFICER & SOCIETY** ◎ **DISABILITIES OFFICER & SOCIETY** ◎ **SELF-DEFENCE CLASSES** ◎ **NIGHTLINE** ◎ **TAXI FUND** ◎ **COLLEGE COUNSELLORS** 4 FULL ◎ **CRIME RATING** !!!
Aberdeen's welfare safety net has few holes. The SA has a welfare sabbatical officer as well as a finance advisor.
HEALTH Four GPs and two nurses staff the University's *comprehensive* medical practice which has a full range of NHS services. King's campus has a dental health unit.
CRECHES/NURSERY 47 places are available for munchkins up to 5yrs.
DISABILITIES It's a very old city with a very old university built in times when disabilities were symptoms of witchcraft, so *wheelchair access is none too hot.* Improvements are being made and the SA's *pretty determined* they should be. Ramps have been added, doors widened and induction loops fitted. The University's prepared to re-schedule lectures and all departments have a disabilities co-ordinator. Accommodation is adapted as needed.

FINANCE
◎ **AVE DEBT PER YEAR** £1,509 ◎ **HOME STUDENT FEES** £1,700
FEES Postgrads pay £3,085/ International fees start at £8,316. *Lucky* Scottish students don't need to fork out at all.
◎ **ACCESS FUND** £250,000 ◎ **SUCCESSFUL APPLICATIONS/YR** 1,031 ◎ **AVE PAYMENT** £200
SUPPORT There are about 150 endowments, bursaries, external grants and trusts available for school leavers coming to Aberdeen University. *Some are very obscure:* for one, applicants must be from Cabrach (a *tiny* village 40 miles away) and promise not to drink or smoke throughout their degree. *As if.*

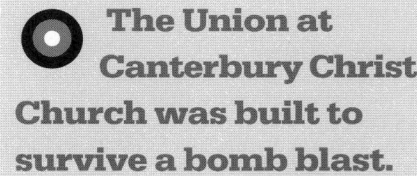

The Union at Canterbury Christ Church was built to survive a bomb blast.

UNIVERSITY OF ABERTAY DUNDEE

FORMERLY DUNDEE INSTITUTE OF TECHNOLOGY

○ **THE UNIVERSITY OF ABERTAY DUNDEE** Bell Street, Dundee, DD1 1HG **TEL** (01382) 308 000
E−MAIL sro@abertay.ac.uk **WEBSITE** www.abertay.ac.uk ○ **UNIVERSITY OF ABERTAY STUDENTS' ASSOCIATION** Bell Street,
Dundee, DD1 1HG **TEL** (01382) 308 950 **E−MAIL** j.weir@abertay.ac.uk **WEBSITE** www.abertayunion.com

GENERAL ◑◑◑◑◑◑◑◑◑◑◑◑◑

A bertay, Dundee's newest university, divides itself among five main blocks ranging from a 16th century castle to the *brand spanking new* student centre. The main site, set around a *green and pleasant* quad, *is like a warren inside*. All the buildings are a couple of minutes walk from the middle of town. The University has undergone a facelift over the past few years, which means that *while parts of it look like Joan Collins in the morning, others resemble a radiant and freshly botoxed Catherine Zeta-Jones.*

SEX RATIO: ♂51 ♀49	**FOUNDED:** 1888
FULL−TIME U'GRADS: 4,009	**PART−TIME:** 506
POSTGRADS: 450	**NON−DEGREE:** 200
AVE COURSE: 4YRS	**ETHNIC:** 14%
STATE:PRIVATE SCHOOL: 97:3	**FLUNK RATE:** 15%
MATURE: 32%	**INTERNATIONAL:** 19%
DISABLED: 90	**LOCAL:** 62%

ATMOSPHERE
There's a *fondness* for Abertay that stems largely from the high proportion of local students. *That can spell homesickness for Sassenachs and international students*, but overall it's a *friendly, techie* kind of place with *more of a chip on the shoulder* about Dundee University than the local residents, *most of whom put up with students without too much fuss.*

DUNDEE see Dundee University
○ **CITY CENTRE** 0 MILES

TRAVEL see Dundee University
Dundee station is 10 mins walk from the University. There's an *extensive* local bus service, which ferries between halls and campus for 80p.

CAREER PROSPECTS
○ **CAREERS SERVICE** ○ **NO. OF STAFF** 2 FULL/3 PART
○ **UNEMPLOYED AFTER 6** MTHS 5%
Newsletters, bulletin boards and job fairs. The new student centre has online careers resources.

FAMOUS ALUMNI
David Jones (inventor of Grand Theft Auto); Maurice Malpass (Dundee Utd); Andy Nicoll, Craig Redpath, Tom Smith (rugby internationals); George Simpson (former Chief Executive, GEC); Brian Souter (Stagecoach Chairman).

FURTHER INFO
○ **PROSPECTUSES** UNDERGRAD; POSTGRAD; VIDEO
○ **OPEN DAYS**

ACADEMIC ◑◑◑◑◑◑◑◑◑◑◑◑◑

Abertay's a techie university split into four schools: contemporary science, the Business School, computing and advanced technology and social/health sciences. *Not a layabout English Lit student in sight.*

ENTRY POINTS: 168−264	**AVE POINTS:** N/A
APPLICATIONS PER PLACE: 5	**CLEARING:** 10%
NO. OF TERMS: 2	**LENGTH OF TERMS:** 15WKS
STAFF TO STUDENT RATIO: 1:17	**STUDY ADDICTS:** 17%
TEACHING: ★★	**RESEARCH:** ★★★
YEAR ABROAD: <1%	**SANDWICH STUDENTS:** 3%
FIRSTS: 7%	**2.2s:** 35%
2.1s: 36%	**3RDS:** 11%

ADMISSIONS
○ **APPLY VIA UCAS**
A Wider Access University, so there's active recruitment of varying ages, abilities and nationalities. Postgrads and part-timers can apply direct.

SUBJECTS
BUSINESS SCHOOL 24%   **CONTEMPORARY SCIENCES** 15%
COMPUTING 26%   **SOCIAL & HEALTH SCIENCES** 35%

LIBRARIES
○ **120,000** BOOKS ○ **700** STUDY PLACES

COMPUTERS
○ **1,500** WORKSTATIONS ○ **24−HR** ACCESS

OTHER LEARNING FACILITIES
The new crime scene for the Forensic sciences department was opened by Inspector Rebus creator Ian Rankin. There's also a fully-equipped language learning centre.

ENTERTAINMENT

THE CITY see <u>Dundee University</u>

UNIVERSITY
- **PRICE OF A PINT OF BEER** £1.50
- **GLASS OF WINE** £1.70
- **CAN OF RED BULL** £1.40

BARS The main bar opens six days a week, with occasional happy hours, karaoke, quiz nights, pool comps, PS2 tournaments, and food. Decked out in royal blue velour, it *looks a bit like an airport lounge*. The sports bar has, *unsurprisingly*, a big screen for daily Sky sports viewing.
FILM There's a cinema in the new student centre.
CLUBBING Wednesday club night themes include Las Vegas, 70s and Playboy Mansion (*tasteful eh?*), but overall ents are pretty flaccid. Colin and Edith from Radio One have popped up to DJ.
FOOD The two bar/cafés in the new student centre are the best place for grub. *Nothing special but it's cheap and does the job.*

SOCIAL

UNIVERSITY OF ABERTAY DUNDEE STUDENTS' ASSOCIATION
- **3 SABBATICALS** **TURNOUT AT LAST BALLOT** 20%
- **NUS MEMBER**

Relations between the SU, *the college suits and the students are pretty snug, and in a wee place like Abertay, they have to be.*

SA FACILITIES
The Student Centre includes: bars and nightclub facilities; study spaces and meeting rooms; gym; family areas and children's play areas; advice and support services; open plan office space for students and support staff; online careers support; cinema; theatre; exhibition space; food court; debating chamber. The SA also has: pool tables; minibus hire; photocopying/fax/printing services; TV lounge; juke boxes; stationery shop; vending machines; bookshop; launderette.

CLUBS (NON-SPORTING)
Computer Games; Film; Football Manager 2006; Indian Students; International Students; Japanese Film & Animation; Organic Gardening; Piping & Traditional Music; Poker; Rock; Role-play. **See also Clubs tables.**

OTHER ORGANISATIONS
Student publication the Abertay Times comes out every few months. There are occasional charity bashes (Halloween, etc.).

RELIGIOUS
- **5 CHAPLAINS (RC, COFS, EPISCOPALIAN)**

A chaplaincy centre is available for those of 'all faiths and none'. There's a Muslim Prayer Room.

PAID WORK see <u>Dundee University</u>
- **JOB BUREAU**

Work is easiest to find outside term. The careers service can help find work during.

SPORTS

- **RECENT SUCCESS** GAELIC WOMEN'S/MEN'S FOOTBALL
- **BUSA RANKING** 73

Abertay are plucky overachievers, given the size of the place. Facilities *aren't anything to write home about*, but students *bound for sporting immortality* can make use of the Elite Athletics programme (golf, athletics, swimming etc.), which gives advice on diet and coaching.

SPORTS FACILITIES
Football, hockey and all-weather pitches; tennis, squash, basketball and netball courts; sports hall; swimming pool; running track; athletics field; multigym; aerobics studio; golf course. Dundee has a leisure centre, athletics field, squash and tennis courts, ice rink and another golf course. Special deals for students at local facilities. Then there's the *rugged* Scottish countryside, with mountains and rivers *to climb, jump off and plunge into.*

SPORTING CLUBS
Airsoft; Gaelic Football; Hurling; Rowing; Shinty; Skydiving; Ultimate Frisbee. **See also Clubs tables.**

ATTRACTIONS see <u>Dundee University</u>

ACCOMMODATION

IN COLLEGE
- **SELF-CATERING** 19% **COST** £44-69 (36WKS)
- **INSURANCE PREMIUM** £

AVAILABILITY Livers-in forage for themselves but halls are *reasonably kitted out*. Some even have dishwashers. All first years are offered rooms, but some may have to share. One in five rooms have en suite facilites. Corso Street and Meadowside Hill halls are *in vogue* with mature and European students. Alloway and Hillside *are the halls of choice for gregarious first years*. There's wheelchair access at Hillbank Hall.
CAR PARKING *Ridiculously easy.*

EXTERNALLY see <u>Dundee University</u>
- **AVE RENT** £50

AVAILABILITY Many local students save rent by staying at home. Those who live out can expect

Words in italics are Push's point of view — take it or leave it...

A

to have *a fairly easy time* finding semi-furnished flats close to university. Perth Road is *popular, but getting quite expensive.* Most try to avoid *slumming* it on the city's east side.

HOUSING HELP *Not much to set students on their way, only an approved landlord list.*

WELFARE ☺☺☺☺☺☺☺☺☺☺☺☺☺

SERVICES
⊙ INTERNATIONAL STUDENTS' OFFICER ⊙ DISABILITIES OFFICER ⊙ UNIVERSITY COUNSELLORS 2 FULL/4 PART **⊙ CRIME RATING** !!

CRECHES/NURSERY Links with local nurseries and University crèche in the new Student Centre.

DISABILITIES Access depends on subject studied – some departments *are nearly impossible,* although the Disabilities Officer can make arrangements including relocating classes.

FINANCE
⊙ AVE DEBT PER YEAR £2,440

FEES No top-up fees in Scotland. Fees of £1,175 for students from England, Northern Ireland and Wales. International (non-EU) undergrads have to cough up £7,250 for the privilege. Postgrad fees are £3,085 (home) or £7,750 for (international).

SUPPORT There's a cool £100,000 sloshing around in the hardship fund, plus a mature students' bursary for Scottish students, sporting excellence fund, a £1,000 centenary scholarship and a couple of other funds paying out the odd £500.

ABERYSTWYTH UNIVERSITY

THE COLLEGE IS PART OF THE UNIVERSITY OF WALES

⊙ **UNIVERSITY OF WALES** Aberystwyth, Old College, King Street, Aberystwyth, SY23 3AX **TEL** (01970) 622 021
E–MAIL ug-admissions@aber.ac.uk **WEBSITE** www.aber.ac.uk ⊙ **URDD MYFYRWYR/ABERYSTWYTH GUILD OF STUDENTS**
Penglais, Aberystwyth, Ceredigion, SY23 2DX **TEL** (01970) 621 700 **E–MAIL** undeb.llywydd@aber.ac.uk/union.president@aber.ac.uk

GENERAL ☺☺☺☺☺☺☺☺☺☺☺☺☺

Aberystwyth – *or 'Aber' as it's known to those in the know* – is sitting pretty on the mid-Wales coast. It's a quiet, seafront market town, miles away from...*well everywhere, really,* except the main Penglais campus (1–2 mile from the town centre). The not-quite-mountains, the bay and the river Rheidol trickling through the town make for an *inspiring* backdrop to one of the University of Wales's oldest colleges. The campus is a *hotchpotch* of classic Victorian constructions and *blocky 60s beasties.* The Llanbadarn campus is a mile from Penglais campus in a village of the same name a*nd is a pleasant, secluded spot, even by Aber's standards.*

SEX RATIO: ♂51 ♀49	**FOUNDED:** 1872
FULL-TIME U'GRADS: 6,163	**PART-TIME:** 1,493
POSTGRADS: 757	**NON-DEGREE:** 137
AVE COURSE: 3YRS	**ETHNIC:** 3%
STATE:PRIVATE SCHOOL: 94:6	**FLUNK RATE:** 11%
MATURE: 12%	**INTERNATIONAL:** 8%
DISABLED: 290	**LOCAL:** 4%

ATMOSPHERE
In a town relatively dominated by students it's hard to get around without running into friends and arch-nemeses. Having said that, friendliness and fellow-feeling fills the air (when it's not raining at least – then it's usually water) and many love the cosy community atmosphere so much they have to be unglued from the campus after graduation. At such distance from the rest of the world there are few who make the effort to go home regularly, so the campus is just as humming at weekends and vacations as term time. Relations with the locals are better than reputed, though it's probably best to leave sheep-shagger gags well alone.

ABERYSTWYTH
⊙ **POPULATION** 25,300 ⊙ **CITY CENTRE** 1 MILE
⊙ **LONDON** 235 MILES ⊙ **MACHYNLLETH** 18 MILES
⊙ **ABERAERON** 20 MILES ⊙ **HIGH TEMP** 18 ⊙ **LOW TEMP** 2
⊙ **RAINFALL** 88

Aberystwyth is one of the major towns in the Welsh region of Ceredigion *and as such, has more than to offer than might be expected for a place of its size.* The town was chartered by Edward I in 1277 and has a lot of museums *to prove it,* as well as castle ruins and ancient Celtic archives. *The stones of the past are all tossed with a salad of the modern* – banks, supermarkets, bookshops and markets. *It's not a shopper's paradise* but coachloads of tourists breeze through in the summer to wander the castle gardens or the *luscious beaches.* Outside the town, there's the Ynyshir Nature Reserve for *budding plant-botherers* and animal sanctuaries for spotting kites, dolphins and seals.

TRAVEL

Remoteness is one of Aber's advantages. Getting away from it all is easy; getting back the other way ain't so dandy. Delays, engineering works and the like mean getting around the wilds of Wales usually ends up taking longer than expected.

TRAINS Aberystwyth station is about 800m from the main campus, with direct main-line connections to London (from £35.20 return), Birmingham (£24.30) and Manchester (£27.05).
COACHES Trans Cambria and National Express services – London (£25), Birmingham (£21.50).
CAR A487 and A44 – *not exactly Spaghetti Junction.*
HITCHING *Without any major roads to Aber, it's mainly thumbs down, although the Welsh do take pity on hitchers.*
LOCAL *Reliable* local buses run until 11pm. Services run from the station to the main campus and to Llanbadarn every 20 mins, 50p. Students can buy a discounted annual pass. Britain's longest electric cliff railway, which leads to a camera obscura on the headland cliff, is *strictly for tourists.*
UNIVERSITY A free bus service runs to and from town throughout the day.
TAXIS £2 from the station to the main campus.
BICYCLES *Students need legs like girders to pedal up the hills – worth it for those who are into pain and hyperventilation.*

CAREER PROSPECTS

○ **CAREERS SERVICE** ○ **NO. OF STAFF** 3 FULL
○ **UNEMPLOYED AFTER 6 MTHS** 7%
An advisory service with careers library, bulletin boards, job fairs and interview training.

FAMOUS ALUMNI

Neil Hamilton (*ex-MP, TV personality and panto star*); Mel Jones (actor and writer); Ahmad Kabbah (President of Sierra Leone); Dr Jeremy Leggat (Greenpeace); Sharon McGuire (Bridget Jones director); John Morris QC (Attorney General); David Prosser (CE of Legal & General plc); Tom Singh (founder of New Look); Simon Thorpe (editor, Viz). Prince Charles studied Welsh here for three months before his investiture.

SPECIAL FEATURES

The on-site National Library of Wales is a copyright library so it has at least one of everything published in Britain and Ireland. *This gives the town one of the highest books to people ratios in the world, which is handy for aspiring academics.*

FURTHER INFO

○ **PROSPECTUSES** UNDERGRAD; POSTGRAD; DEPARTMENTAL; ALTERNATIVE.
○ **OPEN DAYS**

ACADEMIC ◖◖◖◖◖◖◖◖◖◖◖◖◖

Highly rated teaching in most subjects. International Politics, History and Welsh History among others are particularly strong. Courses are credit-based and modular, with students taking 120 credits per year. Modularisation varies: some courses have relatively few optional modules, others are less rigid.

ENTRY POINTS: 180-340	**AVE POINTS: N/A**
APPLICATIONS PER PLACE: 5	**CLEARING: 7%**
NO. OF TERMS: 2	**LENGTH OF TERMS: 15WKS**
STAFF TO STUDENT RATIO: 1:20	**STUDY ADDICTS: N/A**
TEACHING:	**RESEARCH: ★★★**
YEAR ABROAD: 2%	**SANDWICH STUDENTS: 2%**
FIRSTS: 9%	**2.2s: 32%**
2.1s: 51%	**3RDS: 5%**

ADMISSIONS

○ **APPLY VIA UCAS**
Aber caters for applicants from non-traditional academic backgrounds and has a relaxed attitude to mature students without formal qualifications.

SUBJECTS

ART/HUMANITIES 21%   **ART & DESIGN** 17%   **BUSINESS** 9%   **EDUCATION** 15%   **ENGINEERING** 1%   **MATHS, IT & COMPUTING** 7%   **SCIENCES** 22%   **SOCIAL SCIENCES** 23%
BEST Agriculture; Biology; Communications & Information Studies; Computer Science; Economics; English; Finance & Accounting; History; Human & Social Geography; Performing Arts; Law; Physical Geography & Environmental Science; Physical Sciences; Politics.
UNUSUAL Aber's International Politics course was the first of its kind in the galaxy. Horsey types can bring their own filly to campus for Equine Studies and Space Science and Robotics *keeps the Robot Wars contingent busy.*

LIBRARIES

○ **730,436 BOOKS** ○ **1,143 STUDY PLACES**
○ **SPEND PER STUDENT** ££
The Hugh Owen library and its three baby brothers are backed up by the *humungous* National Library of Wales, free to Aber students.

COMPUTERS

○ **677 WORKSTATIONS** ○ **24-HR ACCESS**
The number of computers ain't such a drag as most student rooms can jack into the net. There's also an in-house PC shop and maintenance department, and an on-going project to provide wireless networking on campus for laptop-toting students.

OTHER LEARNING FACILITIES

Language labs; rehearsal rooms; CAD lab; media centre and an astonishing five drama studios. A science visualisation centre (*where experiments can be done without, um, actually being done*) is in the pipeline. Aber provides web-posting space to all who want it so hundreds of student web pages are accessible from the main site, ranging from extensive drunken photo galleries to detailed analyses of different types of peat. *Whatever clicks your button, eh?*

ENTERTAINMENT ○○○○○○○○○

THE CITY
- **PRICE OF A PINT OF BEER** £1.80
- **GLASS OF WINE** £2
- **CAN OF RED BULL** £1.80

CINEMAS The Commodore is *crumbly but cosy* and gets *new(ish) releases* right in the town centre.
THEATRES A small theatre by the harbour hosts touring productions (everything from cabaret to Brecht). Performances by professional groups also appear at the University's Arts Centre.
PUBS *Warm, cosy and somewhat pricey.* Pushplugs: Rummers (old-school); Glengower; Varsity; Lord Beechings; The Cambrian; Harleys (good for sport); Academy (converted church); Orangery (classy coffee bar atmosphere with Wi-Fi access). *There's a Wetherspoons – Starbucks of the pub world – for cut-price liquids. Students tend to avoid the Nag's Head and Black Lion.*
CLUBBING *Not exactly cutting edge. The Pier and the Footie are all pretty run-of-the mill. The Bay has occasional indie/grunge aspirations.*
MUSIC VENUES Local bands play at a few of the pubs (local legend has it that Robert Plant and Jimmy Page - of Led Zeppelin fame - once turned up to jam in the back room of the Angel). In the true Welsh spirit, Aber has its own male voice choir. There's also annual jazz and world music festivals.
COMEDY/CABARET Karaoke can be found at the Inn on the Pier, *if you really want to look.*
EATING OUT *An excellent variety of local restaurants, especially for fresh fish. Harry's is top choice when parents visit – it's too expensive for more regular visits. Sherlock's (Portugese) and Little Italy (guess) offer cheaper special occasion fare. Rumbletums promises an affordable Sunday lunch and Shilaam does all-you-can-eat Indian for a fiver during the day. There's no shortage of cafés and pubs for cheap scoffage during the day, or greasy kebab shops to ease the midnight munchies. Serendipity and Gannets are both popular bistros.* Other Pushplugs: Agra and The Light of Asia (curry), Little Italy *(guess)*, Le Café Noir *(guess again)*, Mandarin *(no, not oranges)* and the *publicious* Varsity, Bar Essential and the Brasserie on the Pier.

UNIVERSITY
- **PRICE OF A PINT OF BEER** £1.80
- **GLASS OF WINE** £2
- **CAN OF RED BULL** £1.50

BARS The Joint The Union has a bar (Bar 9) and a club keeps the beer flowing till 1 or 2am (not Sundays) *and is rush-hour busy most nights. Mondays are the time for film screenings or a poker night, and there's a friendly café-atmosphere during the day. Hall bars are a popular place to start the party:* Cwrt Mawr Bar by one of the halls juggles Pound-a-Pint nights, TV sports events and, oh Lord, karaoke. Rosser has fewer organised events *but still draws in quite a crowd.* The wee Outback in Llanbadarn is open till 1am on Thursdays.
THEATRES The Arts Centre is *proper swish* and hosts productions by both students and *real people.* The Theatre, Film & TV Studies department is *particularly mighty* and spawns its drama-babies in several studios, including the *nearly-new* Parry Williams building.
FILM *Two films a day ensure distraction is always available. Varied cocktail of mainstream, arthouse and world cinema. There's a small, cosy screening room at the National Library of Wales used mainly for classics and Welsh celluloid.*
MUSIC VENUES The Union's main venue pumps out warbles from ickle indie and rock bands nearly every week. The Arts Centre has a *cluttered calendar of all kinds of musical events throughout the year.*
CLUBBING The *poptastic* Reload (Wed) and the *dancier* Wired (Fri) are the Union's biggest nights. Visiting DJs have included Judge Jules and Bethan and Huw off Radio One. Weekend theme nights and fancy dress fun *cater for those who like their nightlife with a dollop of extra cheese.*
COMEDY/CABARET Fortnightly Tuesday Comedy Network nights at the Union. The Arts Centre has *laughable musings from the likes of Jack Dee, Ben Elton and Jeremy Hardy every so often too.*
FOOD Aber's 'food loyalty card' functions a bit like a phone top-up card and can be spent in any of the many catering outlets. *The system has saved more than a few from budget-related starvation.* Dining rooms in halls of residence operate on a pay-as-you-eat basis. Food's up for grabs till 1am.
OTHER The Union-hosted May Ball is the biggest black-tie bonanza of the year. Jools Holland and Goldie Lookin' Chain strutted their stuff last year. Two galleries at the Arts Centre display photos and artworks to *gawp* at.

SOCIAL ○○○○○○○○○○○○

ABERYSTWYTH GUILD OF STUDENTS
- **5 SABBATICALS** **TURNOUT AT LAST BALLOT** 30%
- **NUS MEMBER**

The Guild is subdivided into the UMCA (Welsh Speakers Students Union – *the acronym works in Welsh*), which has its own sabbatical officer and looks after the Welsh contingent. The Guild recently scrapped its Campaigns Officer post, but still finds time to kick up a right old fuss over the likes of tuition fees and recent problems with University-overseen private accommodation. *Relations between the Guild and University bigwigs are smooth and co-operative. Politics comes in a fairly left-wing form, although round these parts PC means Plaid Cymru rather than Political Correctness.*

SU FACILITIES
Four bars (two union-run); three cafeterias; snack bar; fast food joint; pool tables; meeting rooms; Endsleigh Insurance Office; Abbey National and HSBC ATMs; general store; stationery shop; post office; new and secondhand bookshops; gaming and vending machines; travel agency; launderette; fax and printing services; photocopier; photo booth; payphones; advice centre; TV lounge.

CLUBS (NON-SPORTING)
Anime; Aber Paras; Bell Ringing; Chinese; Clandestine Insurgent Rebel Clown Army; Comics; Juggling; Methodist Punk; Retro; Warp (War Games and Role Play). **See also Clubs tables.**

OTHER ORGANISATIONS
The Courier is Aber's award-nominated student mag, its editor sits on the Guild Exec. There's also Yr Utgorn for Welsh-speakers. Bay Radio broadcasts four programmes a day in the Union building, and recently got an online licence *in order to extend its tentacles further.* Aber Rag is one of Europe's biggest and regularly raises five-figure sums, but then, they do have four minibuses which shoot off round the country every weekend to hassle strangers for cash. The excellent Community Action group is called 'Dim Prob' *(which is not a reflection on the Aberystwyth intellect of the participants,* but Welsh for 'No Problem'), spends its selfless time gardening for the elderly, giving parties for disabled kids *and generally being nice to everyone.* Budding thesps in The Nomadic Players put on a range of shows.

RELIGIOUS
The University has its own chapel and several chaplains. Town has churches for most Christian denominations as well as a mosque.

PAID WORK
⊙ **JOB BUREAU** ⊙ **PAID WORK** TERM-TIME 40%; HOLS 60%
Bar, cleaning and supermarket work are all available, especially in the summer when the tourists are in town. Aber's Job Link service *does its best* to find work for those who need it – bar and cleaning gigs are common.

SPORTS ⓊⓊⓊⓊⓊⓊⓊⓊⓊⓊⓊⓊ

⊙ **RECENT SUCCESS** FENCING; BASKETBALL
⊙ **BUSA RANKING** 62
Despite the *ultra-competitive* annual Rugby 7s competition, *the Aber attitude to sport is friendly and open to even the most wimpish athlete. There are a good many water-based sports and*

Aber is nearly top of the list when it comes to getting wet and sweaty. About half the students are members of the Athletics Union, which is run by a sabbatical officer.

A

SPORTS FACILITIES
A *mighty selection:* 12 football, four rugby, four hockey, an all-weather and two cricket pitches; 13 squash, eight tennis, two basketball and four netball courts; two sports halls; swimming pool; athletics field; gym; multigym; aerobics studio; climbing wall; golf course; lake and river (Rheidol) access and a boathouse *for larking about on the Irish Sea or watching bronzed bikinied beauties or speedoed studs splashing around – you sick puppy.* Costs £25 a year for full access, *which is better value than any luxury 'gym'.* Locally: golf course; swimming pool; bowling green.

SPORTING CLUBS
American Football; Cheerleaders; Caving; Dodgeball; Expeditions; Lacrosse; Mountaineering; Surfing; Ultimate Frisbee; Walking. **See also Clubs tables.**

ACCOMMODATION ⓊⓊⓊⓊⓊⓊⓊⓊⓊ

IN COLLEGE
⊙ **CATERED** 18% ⊙ **COST** £79 (29WKS)
⊙ **SELF-CATERING** 40% ⊙ **COST** £70 (36WKS)
⊙ **1ST YRS LIVING IN** 100% ⊙ **2ND YRS LIVING IN** 10%
⊙ **3RD YRS LIVING IN** 50%
⊙ **INSURANCE PREMIUM** £
AVAILABILITY All 1st years can live in (less than 3% sharing) and the majority of finalists return to halls in their 3rd year. Most 2nd years live out. There's a wide selection of accommodation from larger halls on campus to the *enormous* Pentre Jane Morgan Student Village and *adorable little places on the seafront. All rooms are good quality and well looked-after and secure* – CCTV, hall wardens and blokes tend to be put on the ground floor *so murderers can get them first.* Student rooms come complete with insurance cover, *which is handy.* Neuadd Pantycelyn hall houses a treasury of old Welsh stuff (paintings and musical instruments). There's a bring-your-own bedding policy but bedding-packs are available *for a reasonable price – just don't expect satin sheets.* Alexandria Halls, a new private development on the seafront overseen by the uni, *got off to a shaky start in 2004 with building work still in progress when the first students moved in. The rooms – now completed – are luxurious and priced accordingly.*
CAR PARKING Easy at Penglais campus (permits required, £20/yr), less so in the town. The seafront pads have no facilities for cars.

A

EXTERNALLY

☉ AVE RENT £55 **☉ LIVING AT HOME** 3%

AVAILABILITY Aber's too small to fit all its eggs in one basket so some have to go elsewhere to seek their bed. *It's not too tricky and accommodation in the area is on the cheap side and far from scummy. The influx of tourists in the summer keeps prices down for students year-round, although there's usually a summer retainer to pay. Unsurprisingly, the seafront is popular.*

HOUSING HELP *The proactive Accommodation Service is dedicated to domestic well being – no one gets left out in the cold.* They approve and blacklist landlords, publish vacancy lists and bulletin boards, offer legal/contract advice, hold safety seminars and will intervene in domestic disputes – *that's wrangles with landlords, not The Great I'm Not Making The Tea War of 2007.*

WELFARE ⊍⊍⊍⊍⊍⊍⊍⊍⊍⊍⊍⊍⊍⊍

SERVICES

☉ LGBT OFFICER & SOCIETY ☉ ETHNIC MINORITIES OFFICER & SOCIETY ☉ WOMEN'S OFFICER & SOCIETY ☉ MATURE STUDENTS' OFFICER & SOCIETY ☉ INTERNATIONAL STUDENTS' OFFICER & SOCIETY ☉ POSTGRAD OFFICER & SOCIETY ☉ DISABILITIES OFFICER & SUPPORT GROUP ☉ NIGHTLINE ☉ TAXI FUND ☉ COLLEGE COUNSELLORS 4 FULL **☉ CRIME RATING** !

There's a Welsh language group. Town provides a rape crisis line. All students have personal tutors they are required to see three times a term.

HEALTH Students Health Centre with doctors and nurse, but students are also asked to register with a local GP and dentist. There are plenty of willing surgeries, *though waiting times can be a problem.*

WOMEN Attack alarms available for £2.50.

CRECHES/NURSERY The University runs a crèche facility with 63 places, 6mths–4yrs.

DISABILITIES *Though improving, wheelchair access is problematic for geographical reasons. The University has a welcoming attitude, but short of flattening the whole town, there's not much they can do.* Disabled applicants are encouraged to get in touch for an individual assessment. *Facilities for sight-impaired students are good and dyslexia is well supported with assessment, academic assistance and weekly group meetings.*

CRIME *'Lowest crime rate in Britain' echoes through the valleys.*

FINANCE

☉ AVE DEBT PER YEAR £2,860 **☉ HOME STUDENT FEES** £3,000

FEES International students pay between £7,890 and £10,025 depending on whether it's an arts or science degree, part-timers pay £98 per 10 credit module. The Welsh Government has introduced a fee remission grant of £1,800 for those students who already call Wales home.

☉ ACCESS FUND £450,000 **☉ SUCCESSFUL APPLICATIONS/YR** 800 **☉ AVE PAYMENT** £600

SUPPORT The Student Financial Support Office provides help and advice for all matters fiscal. There are a good many scholarships available: exam-based Entrance Scholarships are worth up to £3,600, some courses award Excellence Bursaries of up to £2,000 for good A level performance, and other chances to shine include Merit Awards - a one-off payment of £450. There are also hardship funds and bursaries for students from low-income families.

ANGLIA RUSKIN UNIVERSITY

FORMERLY ANGLIA POLYTECHNIC UNIVERSITY (APU)

☉ ANGLIA RUSKIN UNIVERSITY East Road, Cambridge, CB1 1PT **TEL** 0845 271 3333 **E–MAIL** answers@anglia.ac.uk **WEBSITE** www.anglia.ac.uk **☉ ANGLIA RUSKIN STUDENTS' UNION** Room Hel 125, 1st Floor, Helmore Building, East Road, Cambridge CB1 1PT **TEL** (01223) 460 008 **E–MAIL** info@apusu.com.

GENERAL ⊍⊍⊍⊍⊍⊍⊍⊍⊍⊍⊍⊍⊍⊍

Along with Ulster and De Montfort, *this is as close as a university's different sites get to being separate colleges.* In fact, Anglia Ruskin University's two main campuses were once separate colleges – Cambridge College of Art & Technology (CCAT) and the Essex Institute of Higher Education in Chelmsford – until they merged in 1989, became a poly in 1991 and a university in 1992. *All in the time it takes to get a degree. They're merged in the loosest sense,*

because they're still geographically and socially quite distinct. In 2005 it became the last institution in the UK to purge itself of the dreaded 'P' word, finally swapping 'Polytechnic' for the surname of Victorian intellectual John Ruskin, who opened the School of Art in 1858 . **See below for details of each site.**

SEX RATIO: ♂34 ♀66	FOUNDED: 1989
FULL-TIME U'GRADS: 11,406	PART-TIME: 11,307
POSTGRADS: 4,310	NON-DEGREE: 1,117
AVE COURSE: 3YRS	ETHNIC: 22%
STATE:PRIVATE SCHOOL: 97:3	FLUNK RATE: 17%
MATURE: 71%	INTERNATIONAL: 20%
DISABLED: 180	LOCAL: 60%

ENTRY POINTS: 140–280	AVE POINTS: 207
APPLICATIONS PER PLACE: N/A	CLEARING: 15%
NO. OF TERMS: 2	LENGTH OF TERMS: 18WKS
STAFF TO STUDENT RATIO: 1:30	STUDY ADDICTS: 24%
TEACHING: ✲✲	RESEARCH: ✲
YEAR ABROAD: <1%	SANDWICH STUDENTS: 2%
1STS: 10%	2.2s: 34%
2.1s: 48%	3RDS: 3%

ATMOSPHERE
The spirit at each site varies as much as the place names on the train tickets and there's no common overtone. The Cambridge site's about as far removed from its illustrious neighbour as it's possible to get, both in distance from the historic town centre and in attitude: there's a definite defiance at being part of Anglia Ruskin rather than <u>Cambridge</u>. *Chelmsford (see below for fuller description) has more mature students and part-timers, so it's not as self-consciously studenty as the Fens-based campus.*

CAMBRIDGE see <u>University of Cambridge</u>
◉ CITY CENTRE 800M
See below for details of the Chelmsford site.

TRAVEL see <u>University of Cambridge</u>

CAREER PROSPECTS
◉ CAREERS SERVICE ◉ NO. OF STAFF 4FULL/1PART
◉ UNEMPLOYED AFTER 6 MTHS 5%
Chelmsford has six full time advisors. A mentoring scheme matches second years up with local employers.

FAMOUS ALUMNI
Adam Ant (80s pop icon); Lord Ashcroft (Business); Fluck and Law (creators of Spitting Image); Kim Howells MP (Lab); Baroness Patricia Scotland QC (first black female judge); Ronald Searle (cartoonist); Tom Sharpe (writer); Mike Smith (broadcaster).

FURTHER INFO
◉ PROSPECTUSES UNDERGRAD; POSTGRAD; SOME DEPARTMENTAL
◉ OPEN DAYS

ACADEMIC ()()()()()()()()()()()()

While Anglia Ruskin may not have all that much in common with its Cambridge neighbour it does have a *respected* widening participation programme, which means a lot of first-generation students and others who might not otherwise have been able to experience the university thing. It's hottest on vocational courses and the Audio & Music Technology courses have a *decent* rep. With a few exceptions (Accounting; Business & Management; Computing; Law; Marketing; Social Work), most courses are offered only at one of the two sites. Anglia Ruskin accredits degrees from over 30 regional colleges.

ADMISSIONS
◉ APPLY VIA UCAS

SUBJECTS
ANGLIA INTERNATIONAL BUSINESS SCHOOL 20%
ARTS, LAW & SOCIAL SCIENCES 21%   **EDUCATION:** 9%
HEALTH & SOCIAL CARE 26%   **SCIENCE & TECHNOLOGY** 24%
BEST Art & Design; Law; Management.
UNUSUAL Animal Behaviour; Complementary Medicine; Computer Gaming & Animation; Music Therapy; Time-based Art; Real Estate Management.

LIBRARIES
◉ 352,000 BOOKS ◉ 1,024 STUDY PLACES
◉ SPEND PER STUDENT: £££
Books are held and shared between the two sites. Non-print materials are increasing, with the full text of 25,000 books online. Students should be able to wangle a card for Cambridge University's library if that's still not enough.

COMPUTERS
◉ 2,500 WORKSTATIONS ◉ 24-HR ACCESS
Training is available on both campuses for the IT illiterate.

ENTERTAINMENT ()()()()()()()()()()

THE CITY see <u>University of Cambridge</u>
See below for information about other sites.

CAMBRIDGE CAMPUS
◉ PRICE OF A PINT OF BEER £2
◉ GLASS OF WINE £3.50
◉ CAN OF RED BULL £1.60
BARS Kudos (cap 200) gets busy at lunchtimes and evenings. Weekly quiz nights, *popular* paninis and late opening from Wed-Sat. The Academy (cap 400) is directly downstairs for club nights *and, despite the stage's strange acoustic set-up, gigs.*
THEATRES *Strong* drama scene with the Mumford Theatre (cap 250) to showcase the output of a *small but keen thespy crew.*
MUSIC VENUES Regular tunesters ranging from Arab Strap and Hard-Fi to Jo O'Meara and Ladytron. Fortnightly open mic nights too. The Mumford feeds classical music needs.
CLUBBING Wednesdays start at Kudos and wind up at Twenty Two (in town). Fewer club nights at the Academy since the Alternative Music Society

imploded, but there's still a decent dancy selection, including Fridays' Touch (pop, cheese, retro) and Saturdays' U Know What's Up (R'n'B). Dave Pearce and Tim Westwood have captained the decks.

COMEDY/CABARET Fortnightly *jest-fests* from circuit names.

FOOD *Good cheap* grub at the refectory and the SU bar. The Café does snacks and the hot brown caffeinated stuff.

SOCIAL ()()()()()()()()()()()()

ANGLIA STUDENTS' UNION
○ **6 SABBATICALS** ○ **TURNOUT AT LAST BALLOT** 10%
○ **NUS MEMBER**

The Union and University cuddle up quite comfortably. Split between two sites, the Union struggles to get students into a lather about much and therefore spends a lot more time running welfare-related campaigns than climbing up tall buildings in a Batman suit. Just don't refer to them as ARSU, okay?

SU FACILITIES
Bar; canteen, coffee shop, fast food joint; pool table; meeting room; minibuses and cars to hire; ATMs; photocopying/fax services; payphones; photo booth; advice centre; juke box; video games; general store and stationery shop; vending machines.

CLUBS (NON-SPORTING)
Afro-Caribbean; Art; Anglia Theatre; Buddhist; DJ; European Law Students; Film & Communications; Hindu; Make Poverty History; Optic; Roots and Shoots (environmental); Student Radio; Sikh; Social Policy; Wildlife. **See also Clubs tables.**

OTHER ORGANISATIONS
SU-run 'Apex' newspaper hits monthly. The community liaison team is a University-led scheme to get students volunteering in the local area. The drama society is *mighty*. RAG *hoovers in the cash* with the likes of a naked calendar. *Ooh er, missus.*

RELIGIOUS
○ **2 CHAPLAINS (COFE, RC)**
For religion in Cambridge see University of Cambridge

PAID WORK see University of Cambridge
○ **JOB BUREAU** ○ **PAID WORK** TERM-TIME 50%; HOLS 95%
As the University of Cambridge forbids its students from working, Anglia Ruskin students have a *distinct advantage* in bagging part-time and summer jobs.

SPORTS ()()()()()()()()()()()()

○ **RECENT SUCCESS** CRICKET ○ **BUSA RANKING** 109
Anglia Ruskin's part of the Cricketing School of Excellence. Sports bursaries are worth £500-£1,000 and students can train as sports coaches for free.

SPORTS FACILITIES
Football, rugby, hockey and cricket pitches; tennis courts; gym. For sports facilities in town see University of Cambridge.

SPORTING CLUBS
Cheerleading; Ju-Jitsu; Rowing; Skydiving; Snowsports; Wing Tsun. **See also Clubs tables.**

ATTRACTIONS see University of Cambridge

ACCOMMODATION ()()()()()()()()()

IN UNIVERSITY
○ **SELF-CATERING** 11% ○ **COST** £78 (40WKS)
○ **1ST YRS LIVING IN** 58%
○ **INSURANCE PREMIUM** £

AVAILABILITY There's a place for any first year who hails from more than 25 miles from Cambridge, and some older students are also squeezed in. Halls in Cambridge *are rather good*, and are bolstered by local flats and houses (head tenancy). Shared launderette and kitchen facilities in all halls and phone and data points in most rooms. Wheelchair access at Swinhoe and Peter Taylor Halls. Sedley Court is a new privately run hall *popular with Ruskinites*.

CAR PARKING Cambridge is *a nightmare of a place to keep a car* and there's no parking at Anglia Ruskin.

EXTERNALLY see University of Cambridge
○ **AVE RENT** £73 ○ **LIVING AT HOME** LOTS

WELFARE ()()()()()()()()()()()()

SERVICES
○ **LGBT SOCIETY** ○ **ETHNIC MINORITIES SOCIETY**
○ **INTERNATIONAL STUDENTS' OFFICER & SOCIETY**
○ **WOMEN'S OFFICER** ○ **SELF-DEFENCE CLASSES**
○ **UNIVERSITY COUNSELLORS** 1 FULL ○ **CRIME RATING** !

The Union runs an advice centre and student volunteers man Linkline.

HEALTH Campus nurses available all day to help with basic problems. GPs are available by appointment on weekday mornings and Monday afternoons.

WOMEN Free attack alarms available.
CRECHES/NURSERY 50 places for kids aged 12wks-5yrs.
DISABILITIES Most of the campus is *accessible*.

FINANCE
- **AVE DEBT PER YEAR** £4,097 ○ **HOME STUDENT FEES** £3,000
- **SUCCESSFUL APPLICATIONS/YR** 1,500

○ **AVE PAYMENT** £200-500
SUPPORT Financial advisors on both campuses. The *tempting* Anglia Ruskin Award gives students cash for completing each year and there are scholarships *for sporting godliness* and study abroad.

CHELMSFORD CAMPUS

○ **CHELMSFORD CAMPUS** Bishop Hall Lane, Chelmsford, CM1 1SQ **TEL** 0845 271 3333 **E-MAIL** answers@anglia.ac.uk
WEBSITE www.anglia.ac.uk ○ **CHELMSFORD SU OFFICE** 1st Floor, Tindal Building, Rivermead Campus, Bishop Hall Lane, Chelmsford CM1 1SQ **TEL** (01245) 258 178

Chelmsford's about 80 mins drive from Cambridge. It's a commuter town 37 miles outside London with decent amenities, *but not much of a studenty feel.* There are *plenty* of mature and part-time students kicking around.

CHELMSFORD CAMPUS
- **POPULATION** 157,200 ○ **CITY CENTRE** 800M
- **LONDON** 37 MILES ○ **COST OF LIVING** £
Chelmsford isn't exactly Thrill City but nor is it Dullsville. It's a run-of-the-mill commuter town (which means that London's accessible enough) with an adequate selection of clubs and pubs. It isn't a student city in the sense of Cambridge and, unless the students are able to integrate with the local community, they might as well stay on campus for three years. Currently in a bit of an in-between stage, the campus is being gradually relocated and swankier student facilities should eventually bloom.

TRAVEL
Most things in the town are within walking distance, which is handy. Chelmsford Station is two mins from campus, with direct trains into London Liverpool Street (£9.55) and it's *easy enough* to change for Manchester (£41.80) and others. National Express coaches and cars are a regular feature of student travels. Stansted's just down the road for inland and domestic flights. Parking is tricky, particularly at the Rivermead campus, but there are affordable multistoreys not too far away.

ACADEMIC
There's a new academic campus in Rivermead, *which has taken some of the pressure off the teaching space* and is still expanding – it should absorb the *shabby* Central Campus completely in the next few years. Schools based in Chelmsford include those for Law, Education and the Ashcroft International Business School. The new library at the Ashcroft International Business School is spacious and computer facilities *aren't bad*.

ENTERTAINMENT
CHELMSFORD: Cinema; three theatres; V festival at Hylands Park every year. The town's been spruced up a bit and now has chain (Edward's, J D Wetherspoon) and non-chain bars, as well as some *quaint* country pubs out of town. Varied *if predictable* restaurants (Pizza Hut, Café Rouge) but also a *smattering* of Thai, Chinese and Indian *scoff-stops*.
SITE: The new Kudos bar in the Tindal building, *which is strangely similar to its namesake at the Cambridge campus, has been gratefully received.* The Placcy is a *friendly* sort of bar which runs club nights three times a week. *Decent* food at Tindal building, but the refectory in Ashcroft is *more popular*.

SOCIAL
Student reps divide their time between Chelmsford and Cambridge. A few societies: Christian Union; Environmental Planning; Rock; Mission Croatia (charity). Facilities include: Bar; photocopying; minibus hire; general shop; games room; common room; vending machines; advice centre. The *ambitious* new student centre will give the current facility a *much-deserved* retirement. Given the demographics of the student body, paid work is common – 50% pull in the pennies during term and 95% top up the coffers during vacations.

SPORTS
Gym; two hockey pitches; badminton and basketball courts; sports hall; playing fields. The new sports centre has added badminton courts and a cutting-edge fitness room.

ACCOMMODATION
ON SITE
○ **SELF-CATERING** 4% ○ **COST** £54-79 (40WKS)
Housing at Chelmsford is *good quality but overpriced*. The *plush* new student village at Rivermead has *proved popular despite the costly rooms*.

EXTERNALLY

☉ AVE RENT £40-65

Chelmsford's adapting to its expanded student population though some landlords are still a bit wary. Most places are safe but the Broomfield estate is best avoided.

WELFARE

No doctor at the Rivermead site but a local surgery is close to the halls. The University-run counselling unit employs three full-time counsellors, four part-timers and a registered doctor. There's a chaplaincy in the student village with a Muslim prayer area. Study skills are taught on all sites.

▶ **ANGLIA POLYTECHNIC**
see Anglia Ruskin University

UNIVERSITY OF THE ARTS LONDON

FORMERLY THE LONDON INSTITUTE

1. **☉ UNIVERSITY OF THE ARTS LONDON** 65 Davies Street, London, W1K 5DA **TEL** (020) 7514 6000 **E-MAIL** info@arts.ac.uk **WEBSITE** www.arts.ac.uk **☉ UNIVERSITY OF THE ARTS STUDENTS' UNION** 2-6 Catton Street, Holborn, London, WC1R 4AA **TEL** (020) 7514 6270 **E-MAIL** info@su.arts.ac.uk; **WEBSITE** www.suarts.org
2. **☉ CENTRAL ST MARTIN'S COLLEGE OF ART AND DESIGN** Southampton Row, London, WC1B 4AP **TEL** (020) 7514 7022 **E-MAIL** info@csm.arts.ac.uk **WEBSITE** www.csm.arts.ac.uk
3. **☉ LONDON COLLEGE OF COMMUNICATION** Elephant & Castle, London, SE1 6SB **TEL** (020) 7514 6569 **E-MAIL** info@lcc.arts.ac.uk **WEBSITE** www.lcc.arts.ac.uk
4. **☉ CHELSEA COLLEGE OF ART AND DESIGN** Millbank, London, SW1P 4RJ **TEL** (020) 7514 7751 **E-MAIL** enquiries@chelsea.arts.ac.uk **WEBSITE** www.chelsea.arts.ac.uk
5. **☉ LONDON COLLEGE OF FASHION** 20 John Princes Street, London, W1G 0BJ **TEL** (020) 7514 7344 **E-MAIL** enquiries@fashion.arts.ac.uk **WEBSITE** www.fashion.arts.ac.uk
6. **☉ CAMBERWELL COLLEGE OF ARTS** Peckham Road, London, SE5 8UF **TEL** (020) 7514 6302 **E-MAIL** enquiries@camberwell.arts.ac.uk **WEBSITE** www.camberwell.arts.ac.uk

GENERAL ◖◗◖◗◖◗◖◗◖◗◖◗◖◗

The University of the Arts was called the London Institute until recently, but they decided that the largest art school in Europe should have a name *that sounds less like a prison for the clinically insane*. Students study at one of five separate institutions, all of which are *dripping arty street cred in their own right*. Although the University as a whole signs the degree certificates, students apply to the individual colleges. For general information about London see University of London

SEX RATIO: ♂40 ♀60	**FOUNDED: 1989**
FULL-TIME U'GRADS: 9,022	**PART-TIME: 600**
POSTGRADS: 1,607	**NON-DEGREE: 7,304**
AVE COURSE: N/A	**ETHNIC: N/A**
STATE:PRIVATE SCHOOL: 97:3	**FLUNK RATE: 13%**
MATURE: 30%	**INTERNATIONAL: 30%**
DISABLED: 415	**LOCAL: N/A**

ATMOSPHERE

Not only is the University the sum of five separate colleges, but these are in turn fragmented into 16 different sites all over London – so the opportunities for bonding sessions across the whole University are pretty slim. Even so, the students tend to be similar in many ways: *trendy in the extreme and committed to their courses. The days of self-conscious artists wallowing in an existential mire of absinthe and syphilis may have passed, but the image lives on and the students try to live up to it.*

COLLEGES

CENTRAL ST MARTIN'S COLLEGE OF ART AND DESIGN: (Art & Design, Performance) *Made famous by Jarvis Cocker cadging rum and coke off a sculptress in* Common People, the College in Holborn crawls with *worryingly hip artsters*. Like a Russian doll, Saint Martins also consists of further sites at Charing Cross, Clerkenwell and Byam Shaw. Most students here do foundation courses and can stay on for the follow-up degree. The SU has a representative on site.

LONDON COLLEGE OF COMMUNICATION (FORMERLY LONDON COLLEGE OF PRINTING (9,000 students – Media, Printing, Marketing, Graphic Design). Based at *unappealing* Elephant & Castle (which has neither an elephant nor a castle – see South Bank University) in Southwark. The site's had a *sleek* transformation and includes a state-of-the-art Media School, as well as an IT centre. LCC has an SU rep on hand, *should anyone need representing*. An Enterprise Centre supports keenos wishing to start their own businesses.

CHELSEA COLLEGE OF ART AND DESIGN (Art & Design) Next door to Tate Britain on the riverbank. SU rep.

LONDON COLLEGE OF FASHION (Fashion) Three sites around the *posher* stretch of Oxford Street and East London. *Stuffed with designer goodies like* a catwalk venue, media suites, salons and studios. The Union has a bar and a rep here.

CAMBERWELL COLLEGE OF ARTS (Art & Design). Set in a *mutant hybrid* of Victorian and modern architecture with two annexes 15 mins walk away. *This part of South London is shabby, but chic and relatively cheap.*

LONDON see University of London

TRAVEL see University of London
ST MARTIN'S Holborn (Central, Piccadilly lines) for Southampton Row. Farringdon (Circle, Hammersmith & City) for Clerkenwell. Covent Garden (Piccadilly) for Long Acre. Tottenham Court Road (Central, Northern) for Charing Cross Road.
LCC Elephant & Castle (Bakerloo and Northern, also overground and Thameslink).
CHELSEA (MILLBANK) Pimlico (Victoria line).
LCF Oxford Circus (Central, Bakerloo and Victoria) or Bond Street (Central and Jubilee) for Oxford Street sites. Barbican (Circle and Hammersmith & City) or Old Street (Northern) for City sites.
CAMBERWELL No Tube but Peckham Rye station has frequent trains to London Bridge, Victoria and Blackfriars and lots of buses all over.

CAREER PROSPECTS
❂ **CAREERS SERVICE** ❂ **NO. OF STAFF** 3 FULL/2 PART
❂ **UNEMPLOYED AFTER 6 MTHS:** 9%
The Careers Service publishes a monthly job list. Some of the courses are more vocational than others (for instance at LCC), but those who hope to hit the starry heights of fame are no doubt bolstered by the alumni list.

FAMOUS ALUMNI
Lionel Bart (composer); Quentin Blake (illustrator); Dirk Bogarde (actor, writer); Neville Brody (graphic designer); Pierce Brosnan (James Bond); A S Byatt (writer); Jarvis Cocker (Pulp); Terence Conran (entrepreneur); Tara Fitzgerald (actress); Colin Firth (actor); Nicole Farhi, John Galliano, Katherine Hamnett, Stella McCartney, Alexander McQueen, Bruce Oldfield, Rifat Ozbek, Zandra Rhodes (fashion designers); Gilbert & George (artists); PJ Harvey (*moody songstress*); Mike Leigh (film director); Henry Moore (sculptor); Chris Ofili (Turner Prize-winning painter); Alexei Sayle (comedian); Vivian Stanshall (*eccentric musician*); Joe Strummer (The Clash singer); Mark Wallenger (sculptor).

FURTHER INFO
❂ **PROSPECTUSES** FROM INDIVIDUAL COLLEGES

ACADEMIC ❁❁❁❁❁❁❁❁❁❁❁❁❁

Anything and everything to do with art, fashion, , communication, design or performance is found at one College or another *and they all have decent enough reps to brag about at parties. St Martin's, for instance, is widely celebrated/ gently mocked for its record in Fine Art. Courses tend to be vocational only in the religious sense of the word – these cats are following their dreams, man.*

APPLICATIONS PER PLACE: N/A	CLEARING: 4%
NO. OF TERMS: 3	LENGTH OF TERMS: 11WKS
STAFF TO STUDENT RATIO: 1:17	STUDY ADDICTS: N/A
TEACHING: ★★★★	RESEARCH: ★★★★★
YEAR ABROAD: 0%	SANDWICH STUDENTS: 10%
1STS: 10%	2.2s: 36%
2.1s: 44%	3RDS: 10%

ADMISSIONS
❂ **APPLY VIA UCAS**
Arts courses care more about portfolios and interview performance than A Level points.

SUBJECTS
ART & DESIGN 85%   **SOCIAL SCIENCES** 2%
ARTS/HUMANITIES 6%   **BUSINESS/MANAGEMENT** 7%
BEST LCC: Graphic Design; Marketing & Management; Printing & Publishing; Retail Studies. Camberwell: Art & Design.

LIBRARIES
❂ **350,625 BOOKS** ❂ **1,014 STUDY PLACES**
Each site has at least one library – St Martin's has two, Chelsea, three. The intra-library computer network means students can see the catalogues of all eight. LCC has just got hold of late filmmaker Stanley Kubrick's archive, one of the biggest collections of film production-related material in the world.

COMPUTERS
❂ **2,426 WORKSTATIONS**
Each college has its own computer-stash, with specialised software for various IT-heavy courses.

OTHER LEARNING FACILITIES
The University owns several galleries and the Camberwell Press. Other than that language labs, drama studio, rehearsal rooms, theatre, several famous archive collections, CAD labs and a media centre.

The Sex Pistols played their first proper gig at St Martin's (part of University of the Arts).

A

ENTERTAINMENT ◑◑◑◑◑◑◑◑◑

THE CITY see <u>University of London</u>

UNIVERSITY
- **PRICE OF A PINT OF BEER** £1.80
- **GLASS OF WINE** £1.10
- **CAN OF RED BULL** £1.50

The ents side of things suffers greatly from the lack of a main venue and the Union's inaction when it comes to University-wide events. Many students schlep off to <u>Goldsmiths</u>' bar instead.
BARS: *The biggest and best of the University bars is the Boiler Room at LCC, where most events take place.* There are also bars at Chelsea, Back Hill, Camberwell (jazz nights, digital TV, karaoke, DJs, table football), LCF (ditto) and Red Lion Square (ditto plus cocktails).
THEATRES: The Cochrane is a *professional standard theatre – frequently overrun by drama students.*
MUSIC VENUES: Open mic nights at Chelsea bar; live music of a Thursday at LCC.
FOOD: The LCC and Camberwell bars serve jacket potatoes and other such nosh. Catering on all sites is handled by an outside contractor *to less than universal approval.*
OTHER: Plenty of opportunities for the arty types to exhibit the fruits of their labours – the annual Xhibit is open to Joe Public and Unfinished at LCC shows work that's just that.

SOCIAL ◑◑◑◑◑◑◑◑◑◑◑

UNIVERSITY OF THE ARTS STUDENTS' UNION
- **2 SABBATICALS** ● **TURNOUT AT LAST BALLOT** 10%
- **NUS MEMBER**

Because of the fragmented nature of the University (and even of some of its component bodies) and the lack of a SU venue, there's less social cohesion than at a Liverpool/Everton mix & mingle.

SU FACILITIES
Across the sites, collectively, there's a lot to be desired. Individually, it varies enormously.

CLUBS (NON-SPORTING)
Art of Living; B.E.A.N.S.;Charity; Comic Arts; Digital Arts; DJ; Kashka; Kunst; Latin American; Life Drawing; Painting; RESPECT. **See also Clubs tables.**

OTHER ORGANISATIONS
The award-winning Union newsletter, 'Less Common More Sense', circulates monthly. There's a radio station on the horizon, broadcasting out to the bars and the interwebbynet.

RELIGIOUS
- **3 CHAPLAINS**

For religion in London see <u>University of London</u>

PAID WORK see <u>University of London</u>
- **JOB BUREAU** ● **PAID WORK** TERM-TIME 60%; HOLS 80%

Vacancy lists are plastered around the Union and the net.

SPORTS ◑◑◑◑◑◑◑◑◑◑◑◑

Art and sport don't exactly play nicely together and the University has no facilities of its own as a result. For those who'd actually be prepared to wear a rugby shirt in public, there are more than enough facilities scattered across the city. See <u>University of London</u>.

SPORTING CLUBS
Ballet; Breakdance; Jiu Jitsu; Ski/Snowboard; Street Dance; Skate; Surf. **See also Clubs tables.**

ATTRACTIONS see <u>University of London</u>

ACCOMMODATION ◑◑◑◑◑◑◑◑◑

IN UNIVERSITY
- **SELF-CATERING:** 19% ● **COST:** £116 (39-52WKS)
- **1ST YRS LIVING IN:** 90%
- **INSURANCE PREMIUM:** £

AVAILABILITY: Most, though not all, first years can be squeezed in. Priority is given to under-18s, those from outside London and students with special requirements. Just over half the rooms have en suite facilities. Accommodation is in five blocks of mostly 60s design, split between Battersea and Tooting. The new Ewen Henderson Court has free fast internet and a *pricey but posh* hall will open in Camberwell in September 2006. All halls have TV rooms and launderettes; only some have computer access.
CAR PARKING: *The Millennium Dome was a better idea than trying to park anywhere near most of the sites.*

EXTERNALLY see <u>University of London</u>
- **AVE RENT:** £93 ● **LIVING AT HOME:** 5%

HOUSING HELP: There's an accommodation service with housing lists, a find-a-flatmate service and an online forum.

WELCOME ⊙⊙⊙⊙⊙⊙⊙⊙⊙⊙⊙⊙⊙

♥ ✊

SERVICES
⊙ **LGBT SOCIETY** ⊙ **POSTGRAD SOCIETY** ⊙ **INTERNA-TIONAL STUDENTS' OFFICER & SOCIETY** ⊙ **NIGHTLINE** ⊙ **UNIVERSITY COUNSELLORS** 7 PART ⊙ **CRIME RATING:** !!!!!

During term there's a student services office at the colleges, doling out advice. There's also a year-round advisor at the Central Student Services office and the Union has an Education & Welfare Officer.
HEALTH: Health centres at accommodation sites.

CRECHES/NURSERY: 34 places for 6mths-5yrs at LCC.
DISABILITIES: *Long distances between sites can make access cumbersome for wheelchair users.* Dyslexia co-ordinators at colleges and a deaf students' forum.

FINANCE
⊙ **AVE DEBT PER YEAR** £3,586 ⊙ **HOME STUDENT FEES** £3,000
FEES FE courses cost £6,400. International students pay £9,800.
SUPPORT Bursaries of up to £1,000 for home students. Scholarships can be bagged from the likes of the British Board of Film Classification and British Printing Industries Federation and there's help for students from the Americas.

ASTON UNIVERSITY

⊙ **ASTON UNIVERSITY** Aston Triangle, Birmingham, B4 7ET **TEL** (0121) 204 3000 **E-MAIL** ugenquiries@aston.ac.uk **WEBSITE** www.aston.ac.uk ⊙ **ASTON STUDENTS' GUILD** Aston University, Aston Triangle, Gosta Green, Birmingham, B4 7ES **TEL** (0121) 359 6531 **E-MAIL** guild.liaison@aston.ac.uk **WEBSITE** www.astonguild.org.uk

GENERAL ⊙⊙⊙⊙⊙⊙⊙⊙⊙⊙⊙⊙⊙

Just five mins leg action from the centre of Birmingham is the *not-quite-triangular* Aston Triangle – *a modern, green, landscaped campus of brown, brick buildings.* Within them lie over three miles of corridors and the oldest public swimming pool in the country (1860). And a University. A pair of *intimidating* sky lifts slide up and down the main building, *which although 'futuristic' in appearance, is beginning to look a bit dated, paradoxically enough. It's what the 60s thought the future would look like – watching '2001: A Space Odyssey' has the same effect. Despite the campus's compact size there's also the Vice-Chancellor's Lake – work, play and hangovers all mix on the lakeside lawns when the sunshine hits.* For general info about Birmingham see University of Birmingham

courses is central to this and many students spend time on additional summer placements, tutoring and voluntary work. The small campus setting means everyone knows everyone else – the law of the Aston Loop means that everyone can be linked, like Kevin Bacon, to everyone else by six people. It's cosy enough but the bright lights of Brum are all around if things get stifling.

BIRMINGHAM see University of Birmingham

TRAVEL see University of Birmingham
TRAINS New Street Station is 15 mins walk away.
COACHES Digbeth is a National Express station, five mins taxi-ride from the campus.
CAR There's no parking on campus and the nearby streets are limited. There are several pay & displays in walking distance – *but not many students bother with cars.*
COLLEGE The Residents' Association (ACRA) runs a minibus service to local supermarkets *so there's no excuse to go hungry.* Coaches and minibuses also go to the recreation site.
BICYCLES: Bikes are more and more common thanks to Birmingham's improved cycle network. *Locked shelters on campus help deter wandering hacksaws.*

CAREER PROSPECTS
⊙ **CAREERS SERVICE** ⊙ **NO. OF STAFF** 9 FULL/1 PART
⊙ **UNEMPLOYED AFTER 6 MTHS** 6%
Aston is top of the job pops when it comes to graduate employment. The Careers Service is a part of student life from the word 'matriculate'. It offers the usual careers shebang (library, newsletters etc.) plus e-mail updates, visiting employers, mock interviews, Microsoft courses, placement support and tutorials.

👤👤👤👤👤👤👤👤👤👤👤👤👤👤👤👤👤👤👤

SEX RATIO: ♂49 ♀51	**FOUNDED:** 1895
FULL-TIME U'GRADS: 6,300	**PART-TIME:** 259
POSTGRADS: 1,200	**NON-DEGREE:** 0
AVE COURSE: 4YRS	**ETHNIC:** 24%
STATE:PRIVATE SCHOOL: 90:10	**FLUNK RATE:** 8%
MATURE: 8%	**INTERNATIONAL:** 15%
DISABLED: 75	**LOCAL:** 25%

ATMOSPHERE
Aston's an unusual kettle of squid in that it's never been a polytechnic yet places a hefty emphasis on vocational degrees and career-angled learning. Students are more than keen for the complete fun-fuelled, drink-drenched package, but make sure they gather a few precious CV points on the way. The placement year of most

FAMOUS ALUMNI
Gregor Townsend (Rugby); Laura Jones (BBC reporter); Lord Rooker (Labour peer); Jasper Carrott has an honorary degree. *It's unclear why.*

FURTHER INFO
○ **PROSPECTUSES** UNDERGRAD; POSTGRAD; DEPARTMENTAL; INTERNATIONAL; DVD
○ **OPEN DAYS**

ACADEMIC ○○○○○○○○○○○○○

While not a 'vocational' university as such, teaching could be considered more career-training than knowledge-gathering. The University pioneered the sandwich course and the year-long work placements are common. Overall grades are a combination of second year results, placement year performance, dissertations and mainly *the dreaded* final year exams. Lectures take up a *middling* 8-15hrs a week and there's an emphasis on team projects and presentations – *how CV-friendly*. The *swankily-housed* Business school is *highly esteemed* and Aston's *strong in languages, health sciences and engineering*, too.

ENTRY POINTS: 240-340	**AVE POINTS: 342**
APPLICATIONS PER PLACE: 8	**CLEARING: 6%**
NO. OF TERMS: 3	**LENGTH OF TERMS: 10WKS**
STAFF TO STUDENT RATIO: 1:15	**STUDY ADDICTS: 10%**
TEACHING: ✶✶✶✶	**RESEARCH: ✶✶✶✶**
YEAR ABROAD: 11%	**SANDWICH STUDENTS: 70%**
1STS: 10%	**2.2s: 27%**
2.1s: 59%	**3RDS: 4%**

ADMISSIONS
○ **APPLY VIA UCAS**

SUBJECTS
ART & DESIGN 4%   **ART/HUMANITIES** 2%
BUSINESS/MANAGEMENT 30%   **ENGINEERING** 13%
MEDICAL SCIENCES 20%   **MODERN LANGUAGES** 8%
SCIENCES 13%   **SOCIAL SCIENCES** 10%
BEST Business; Languages; Medicine; Pharmacy; Politics.
UNUSUAL Audiology; Logistics; Optometry; Translation Studies.

LIBRARIES
○ **320,000 BOOKS** ○ **700 STUDY PLACES**
Aston's main library is open seven days and *although it's not quite a literary powerhouse*, intranet facilities are extensive, with searchable online catalogues and reservations.

COMPUTERS
○ **800 WORKSTATIONS** ○ **24-HR ACCESS**
Wireless internet access across campus, including in all student bedrooms for £10 a month.

OTHER LEARNING FACILITIES
A maths drop-in centre is available *to all those who forget how to count.* Rehearsal rooms, CAD lab, media centre, and *top-notch* labs for neurosciences and optometry. Tons of language labs and not restricted to those on language courses. There are also some *sketchy* online resources.

ENTERTAINMENT ○○○○○○○○○○

THE CITY see University of Birmingham
Aston students *favour* city-centre bars like Hidden, Mackenzies and Bar Risa. Other areas for a *good night out in Brum* are Moseley, Harborne and Digbeth (lots of Irish pubs). For gigging there's the National Indoor Arena and Birmingham Academy (five mins saunter from campus) – Goldfrapp, Black Eyed Peas and Super Furry Animals played recently.
CLUBS Air, Gas Street and the Works – big student nights.
EATING OUT *Loads* of eats across the city, and not just limited to balti. Plenty near campus – try Michelles (French), Johns Fish Bar and Big Wok (*stuff-ya-face Chinese*).
OTHER The new Bull Ring shopping Centre is massive and has a fair few diversions (and is also a good source of part-time work).

UNIVERSITY
○ **PRICE OF A PINT OF BEER:** £1.65
○ **GLASS OF WINE:** £1.80
○ **CAN OF RED BULL:** £1.75
A *respectable roster of revelry, but the SU struggles to lure students from the cheaper pubs and bars nearby.*
BARS Einstein's is a *pubby, popular* affair that keeps the liquor swilling till 2am on ent nights. The Loft is the *sportsman's choice*, while the Blue Room is a coffee bar by day which gets boozy in the evenings with the adjoining Guild Hall till 2am. Café Astons has a more *mature* air – it's postgrads and staff only. Thursday night is Larryoke, named in honour of Larry the Eternal Barman, *supposedly a student who never got round to leaving.* This is honoured by karaoke and play-your-cards-right. *Naturally.*
THEATRES The Great Hall draws in student and professional thesps.
FILM One free indiscriminate blockbuster shown every week.
CLUBBING/MUSIC VENUES The Guild Hall (940) crams dancers in four nights a week: School Days – *uniform fetishes and Rick Astley – is the biggest heel-clicker.* Rag organises Freakers, *which has a sexual fantasies theme – nurses, bored house-wives, llama farmers, etc.* Not a big gig venue, but Jamelia and Trevor Nelson have appeared recently.

COMEDY/CABARET The Blue Room hosts comedy nights where 80s *relics* Timmy Mallett, the cast of Rainbow, Keith Harris & Orville and the like up the comedy kitsch factor.

FOOD Café Lago offers refectory-style dining and made-to-order pizzas three times a day. La Serre does *cheap* takeaway sarnies, and there's a Costa Coffee and a Subway on campus. Grub can be had from bars and the Guild Hall till 11pm most nights.

OTHER Lavish May Ball and Graduation Ball, *a mean* Fresher's Week and the summer term 'Astonbury' music festival..

SOCIAL ◯◯◯◯◯◯◯◯◯◯◯◯◯

ASTON STUDENTS' GUILD
◉ **5 SABBATICALS** ◉ **NUS MEMBER**
The Union is a massive part of student life – socially and sportingly at least. They're not the most political banana in the bowl but it's all hands on deck come student election time.

SU FACILITIES
Purpose-built nightclub and music venue; five bars; two cafeterias; pool/snooker tables; loads of meeting rooms; three minibuses for hire; NatWest, HSBC and Lloyds TSB banks with ATMs; photocopiers; photo booth; fax and printing service; payphones; advice centre; games room; hairdresser; vending machines; general store; stationery shop; bookshop; ticket agency; launderette.

CLUBS (NON-SPORTING)
Extreme BBQ; Extreme Ironing; Formula Student Car Racing; Greek; Hiking; Queueing; Urban & Salsa Dancing. **See also Clubs tables.**

OTHER ORGANISATIONS
There's a student mag five times a term. *Rag is a busy little beaver*, raising hefty sums through a *crammed calendar* of pub crawls, slave auctions, *colossal piss-ups and the usual tomfoolery.* There's *gazillions of different community groups* who do a mixture of conservation work, coaching in local schools and community stuff.

RELIGIOUS
◉ **3 CHAPLAINS (FC, COFE, RC)**
The multi-faith chaplaincy and variety of prayer rooms cater for Christian, Sikh, Hindu, Jewish and Islamic faiths. Birmingham city centre has many more.

PAID WORK see University of Birmingham
◉ **JOB BUREAU** ◉ **PAID WORK** TERM-TIME 60%; HOLS 85%
The Guild's job shop advertises local jobs (bars, pubs, clubs, shops and restaurants) and the Union also employs a few itself. There's also a vacation work placement scheme which helps find course-related positions with decent wages.

SPORTS ◯◯◯◯◯◯◯◯◯◯◯◯◯

◉ **RECENT SUCCESS** N/A ◉ **BUSA RANKING** 97
Sport is popular across the student body, reflected in a healthy BUSA performance. The University takes it seriously too, having spent 200 thou on a new fitness suite, redeveloping the gym (including personal trainers) and spewing £300K on new all-weather pitches. They may be followed by a new sports centre within the next few years.

SPORTS FACILITIES
No shirking on the facilities front: nine football/rugby pitches; one cricket, four hockey and two all-weather pitches. Five squash, four tennis and two basketball courts; two sports halls; swimming pool; multigym; gym; aerobics studio; climbing wall; snooker and table tennis tables; solarium; large pavilion with three bars. Fitness centre membership costs £40 for three months, sports hall hire £12 an hour. Locally, the Tamworth Snow Dome is a few chugs down the train line.

SPORTING CLUBS
Lacrosse; Mountaineering; Table Tennis. **See also Clubs tables.**

ATTRACTIONS see University of Birmingham

ACCOMMODATION ◯◯◯◯◯◯◯◯◯

IN UNIVERSITY
◉ **SELF-CATERING** 38% ◉ **COST** £67 (39WKS)
◉ **1ST YRS LIVING IN** 80%
◉ **INSURANCE PREMIUM** £££
AVAILABILITY Aston accommodation comes in en suite (£89) or standard (£58). All halls and flats are on campus and *consequently over-subscribed* but first years are guaranteed a place. A third of those living in have a toilet to call their throne and the en suite rooms are in *sexy, modern* lakeside low-rises. *The standard variety is older and smaller, built when comfort wasn't a priority and plumbing was just a few steps ahead of some straw in the corner. It's not all that grim though – there are postcard views across Birmingham from the high-rises.* There's the options of single-sexed/mixed and smoking/non-smoking. Students can buy a meal deal pass for £250 a term that gives them ten refectory meals a week, *but many then struggle to get there on time for their grub.* Halls are swipe card entry and porters are on duty day and night. There's CCTV and bobbies on the beat drop by.
CAR PARKING: *Don't even go there.*

EXTERNALLY see University of Birmingham
○ **AVE RENT** £55 ○ **LIVING AT HOME** 20%
AVAILABILITY The second year campus exodus *usually winds up* in Erdington or Aston Brook Green, which are relatively cheap and campus-accessible. New developments by people like UNITE are springing up in the city and are *proving popular as well as encouraging private landlords to keep standards high.*
HOUSING HELP Vacancies, approved landlord lists, contract and legal assistance from the Housing Office.

WELFARE ◖◗◖◗◖◗◖◗◖◗◖◗◖◗◖◗◖◗◖◗◖◗

SERVICES
○ **LGBT SOCIETY** ○ **ETHNIC MINORITIES SOCIETY**
○ **MATURE STUDENTS' OFFICER** ○ **INTERNATIONAL STUDENTS' OFFICER** ○ **POSTGRAD OFFICER**
○ **DISABILITIES SOCIETY** ○ **SELF−DEFENCE CLASSES**
○ **NIGHTLINE** ○ **COLLEGE COUNSELLORS** 5 FULL/3 PART
○ **CRIME RATING:** !!!!
HEALTH The campus health service has three doctors, four nurses, a dentist and an optometrist.
WOMEN Some single-sex flats for women as well as women-only pool and gym sessions.
CRECHES/NURSERY 50 places on campus for kids 6wks–5yrs.
DISABILITIES Campus is *compact, flat and self-contained* and there are ramps and lifts in most buildings for wheelchair users. There's a small number of adapted bedrooms and parking permits are free to disabled students. Hearing loops and dyslexia support tutor.
CRIME: Two rozzers patrol the campus. There are the usual town crime concerns but *they don't encroach on campus.*
DRUGS: There's an annual safe drinking campaign and a zero tolerance policy on drug users.

FINANCE
○ **AVE DEBT PER YEAR:** £3,747 ○ **HOME STUDENT FEES:** £3,000
FEES: Foundation years cost £1,200. Postgrad fees are a *whopping* £10,000. International students pay £8,000-10,000.
○ **ACCESS FUND:** £500,000
○ **SUCCESSFUL APPLICATIONS/YR:** 700
SUPPORT: Hardship funds, travel bursaries and an assortment of other prizes, including the Aston bursary (£1,500), are available to those who need them.

○   **Rupert Murdoch had to buy the copyright for The Sun from Aston University – it was the name of their first Students' Union newspaper.**

BANGOR, UNIVERSITY OF WALES

▶ BARTS
see *Queen Mary, University of London*

UNIVERSITY OF BATH

BATH SPA UNIVERSITY

▶ BATH SPA UNIVERSITY COLLEGE
see *Bath Spa University*

▶ BCUC
see *Buckinghamshire Chilterns University*

▶ BEDFORD
see *University of Luton*

▶ BEDFORD COLLEGE OF HIGHER EDUCATION
see *De Montfort University*

▶ BELFAST, QUEEN'S UNIVERSITY
see *Queen's University of Belfast*

BIRKBECK, UNIVERSITY OF LONDON

UNIVERSITY OF BIRMINGHAM

▶ BIRMINGHAM CONSERVATOIRE
see *UCE Birmingham*

▶ BOLTON INSTITUTE FOR HIGHER EDUCATION
see *University of Bolton*

UNIVERSITY OF BOLTON

BOURNEMOUTH UNIVERSITY

▶ BOURNEMOUTH POLYTECHNIC, DORSET INSTITUTE
see *Bournemouth University*

UNIVERSITY OF BRADFORD

BRIGHTON UNIVERSITY

UNIVERSITY OF BRISTOL

▶ BRISTOL, UNIVERSITY OF THE WEST OF ENGLAND
see *UWE Bristol*

▶ BROOKES UNIVERSITY
see *Oxford Brookes University*

BRUNEL UNIVERSITY

UNIVERSITY OF BUCKINGHAM

BUCKINGHAMSHIRE CHILTERNS UNIVERSITY

▶ BUCKINGHAMSHIRE CHILTERNS UNIVERSITY COLLEGE
see *Buckinghamshire Chilterns University*

B

BANGOR, UNIVERSITY OF WALES

B

1) ● **UNIVERSITY OF WALES** Bangor, Gwynedd, LL57 2DG **TEL** (01248) 351 151 **E-MAIL** admissions@bangor.ac.uk
WEBSITE www.bangor.ac.uk ● **UNIVERSITY STUDENTS' UNION NAME** Undeb Myfyrwyr Bangor Student's Union, Deiniol Road,
Bangor, Gwynedd, LL57 2TH **TEL** (01248) 388 000 **E-MAIL** undeb@undeb.bangor.ac.uk **WEBSITE** www.undeb.bangor.ac.uk
2) ● **SCHOOL OF EDUCATION** University of Wales, Bangor, Gwynedd, LL57 2PX **TEL** (01248) 383082
3) ● **FACULTY OF HEALTH STUDIES** Wrexham Technology Park, Wrexham, LL13 7YP **TEL** (01978) 316 316

GENERAL ◖◖◖◖◖◖◖◖◖◖◖◖◖

Didn't we have a lovely time the day we went
to Bangor?' Probably not if it was pouring
with rain and we were after a big night out.
Bangor is a small city to be found between the
rugged beauty of Snowdonia and the Menai
Strait, which divides Anglesey from the rest of
Britain. That's Wales, for the geographically
hazy, and deepest rural Wales at that. The city
is unmistakably pretty with gorgeous scenic
views, and a modest crop of high street chains.
It's surrounded by quaint little towns with their
own castles – places like Beaumaris, Conwy
and Caernarfon. The main University building
is a cathedral-esque creation, though some others
on the College Road resemble old country hotels.

🚶🚶🚶🚶🚶🚶🚶🚶🚶🚶🚶🚶🚶🚶🚶🚶🚶🚶🚶🚶🚶🚶🚶

SEX RATIO: ♂37 ♀63	**FOUNDED:** 1884
FULL-TIME U'GRADS: 6,221	**PART-TIME:** 2,210
POSTGRADS: 1,933	**NON-DEGREE:** 2,500
AVE COURSE: 3-4YRS	**ETHNIC:** 6%
STATE:PRIVATE SCHOOL: 94:6	**FLUNK RATE:** 17%
MATURE: 29%	**INTERNATIONAL:** 9%
DISABLED: 295	**LOCAL:** 20%

ATMOSPHERE
This is cagoule and sensible footwear country
rather than planet party, but if it's the peaceful life
that appeals, there are probably few better places.
Bangor is laid-back, comfortingly small with a tight
and huggy student community. Students almost
double the city population during term-time and
relations with the locals are largely easy. The
University is a hit with native Welsh speakers and
there's a sizeable Irish population, attracted by the
close quarters of Holyhead.

SITES
SCHOOL OF EDUCATION (1,528 students – Education,
Sport Science) Welcome to north Walian suburbia.
The community is extraordinarily close, with plenty
of curtain twitching and gossip mongering. The
central college buildings are about a mile away and
buses stop outside the department.
WREXHAM (Radiography, Nursing & Midwifery) 60
miles from Bangor, the Wrexham site is actually on
a science park on the edge of town. Chester, 12
miles further, is the focus of student attention. It's a
tourist trap, with plenty of worthy historic sites to
yawn around, as well as a far more exciting set of
bars, pubs, clubs and theatres. Most students at
this site are from the local area anyway.

BANGOR
● **POPULATION** 111,173 ● **LONDON** 236 MILES
● **CARDIFF** 180 MILES ● **MANCHESTER** 85 MILES
● **HIGH TEMP** 19 ● **LOW TEMP** 3 ● **RAINFALL** 70
The sea breeze blows squalls of tourists into the
city, to marvel at the admittedly marvellous
views. There are lots of shops – though not much
in the way of variety – as well as a tolerably
funky night scene.

TRAVEL
TRAINS The station is 800m from the main
University buildings. Trains take about four
hours direct to London (from £42.20 return). Just
about everywhere else involves a change at
Crewe (£12.85).
COACHES National Express to London (£31.50)
takes between 9-12 hours. Birmingham
(£21.50), Cardiff (£42.50) and other destinations
are also available.
CAR More for escaping than getting around.
LOCAL Buses run around town and all across
Gwynedd, though Bangor is dinky enough get
around fine on foot. Day trips on the ferry to
Ireland cost £9, and there's an incredible single
carriage steam train ride up Snowdon.
TAXIS Not too costly (average £1.80) as there's
nowhere far to go in the city. CHUBBS has
female drivers and is student-friendly.
BICYCLES Bangor is hillsville, and pedalling
demands thighs of steel. Still, sporty Bangorites
seem to get a kick out it and cycling's
surprisingly popular.

CAREER PROSPECTS
● **CAREERS SERVICE** ● **NO. OF STAFF** 13 FULL/8 PART
● **UNEMPLOYED AFTER 6 MTHS** 6%
The careers service is involved in the GO
Wales/Cymru Prosper Wales work experience
project, promoting employment for students who
live in Wales.

FAMOUS ALUMNI
Danny Boyle (film director); Tim Haines
(Producer, BBC's Walking with Dinosaurs); Mark
Hughes (former Wales football team manager).
Richard Attenborough and Carol Vorderman are
honorary fellows.

FURTHER INFO
● **PROSPECTUSES** UNDERGRAD; POSTGRAD; DEPARTMENTAL;
VIDEO; CD-ROM.
● **OPEN DAYS**
Bilingual prospectuses. SU also does an info pack
– see the web.

Words in italics are Push's point of view — take it or leave it...

B

ACADEMIC

A *magnet* for sport and exercise science students, *Bangor has an increasingly bitchin' psychology department*. Also runs a *respected* Welsh degree, which lures a lot of local students.

ENTRY POINTS: 200-300	AVE POINTS: 288
APPLICATIONS PER PLACE: 5	CLEARING: 2%
NO. OF TERMS: 2	LENGTH OF TERMS: 15wks
STAFF TO STUDENT RATIO: 1:17	STUDY ADDICTS: 21%
TEACHING: ★★★★	RESEARCH: ★★★
YEAR ABROAD: <1%	SANDWICH STUDENTS: <1%
1STS: 12%	2.2s: 40%
2.1s: 38%	3RDS: 10%

ADMISSIONS
○ APPLY VIA UCAS

SUBJECTS
ARTS & SOCIAL SCIENCES 34% **EDUCATION** 21%
HEALTH STUDIES 15% **SCIENCE & ENGINEERING** 30%
BEST Biological Sciences; Chemistry; Forestry; Music; Ocean Sciences; Psychology; Theology & Religious Studies; Welsh.
UNUSUAL Environmental Forensics; Law with Modern European Languages; Marine Chemistry; Oceanography & Computing; Three-Language Honours.

LIBRARIES
○ **850,500** BOOKS ○ **1,173** STUDY PLACES
○ SPEND PER STUDENT £
Two main faculty and five smaller departmental libraries.

COMPUTERS
○ **800** WORKSTATIONS ○ **24**-HR ACCESS
○ SPEND PER STUDENT £

OTHER LEARNING FACILITIES
The Ocean Sciences department has a multi-million pound research ship to *probe the depths of the high seas*.

ENTERTAINMENT

THE CITY
○ PRICE OF A PINT OF BEER £2
○ GLASS OF WINE £3 ○ CAN OF RED BULL £3
CINEMAS The Apollo has a couple of screens. Those with wheels make the trip to the Cineworld multiplex in Llandudno Junction (20 mins drive) or the Creative Enterprise Centre (Galeri) in Caernarfon (ten mins).
THEATRES Theatr Gwynedd has its own production company and also hosts touring shows.
PUBS *The quayside pubs are small and personable.* Pushplugs: Patricks (aka Paddy's, *small, stupidly cheap, very student-friendly*); Joott

(late licence, *obligatory* dancefloor); O'Shea's (*chirpy, chirpy, cheap, cheap*); Belle Vue (*luvvie hang-out*).
CLUBBING The University *bears the clubbing brunt*, but Octagon draws a *horde* on student night (Wednesday) and Saturday (*cheese-a-rama*).
EATING OUT *Pub grub ago-go.* Wetherspoons and Costa are *predictably popular*. Pushplugs: Star Kebab; The Pizza House; Mike's Bites (*cheap grease*); Late Stop.

THE UNIVERSITY

○ PRICE OF A PINT OF BEER £2
○ GLASS OF WINE £2.50 ○ CAN OF RED BULL £2
BARS NUS only, unlike the University club. The main bar, Academi, has lounge seating area, plasma screen TV, sound system and a dancefloor, plus a smaller cocktail and bottle bar. Things keep going til 2am. The smaller Jock's bar has pool tables, games machines and *a jukebox to remove the need for conversation*.
THEATRES There's a *small but committed* thesp set made up of three societies: Rostra (am dram); BEDS (English drama); Soda (musicals). All use the Theatr Gwynedd next door to the SU.
FILM Theatr Gwynedd doubles up as a screen for arty films, and Academi hosts a film night a couple of times a month.
MUSIC VENUES Recent visitors have included El Presidente, Towers of London and *local(ish) nutters* Goldie Lookin Chain.
CLUBBING *In a strange reversal of normal affairs* the town looks to the University for thrills. Time/Amser is a *ferry-shaped yet curiously barn-like sort of place* open to all until 3am and consequently rammed. A 60s-90s night on Mondays *gets everyone jiggy*, and after that there's everything from R'n'B to house nights. Fancy dress is also *inexplicably popular*.
COMEDY/CABARET Monthly gigs at the Academi from up-and-coming gag merchants.
FOOD Freddy's, the SU fast-food place, *provides the grease*. Y Glan Newydd does more *wholesome* lunches and the University runs self-service joint Bistro 1. There's also Dylans; Mrs P's (deli); Ceri's Diner.
OTHER A summer ball *extravaganza* and plenty of halls' balls to boot.

Students from Bangor Rag once 'closed' the island of Anglesey by erecting an 'Anglesey Full' sign.

Words in italics are Push's point of view – take it or leave it...

SOCIAL ○○○○○○○○○○○○○

BANGOR STUDENTS' UNION/ UNDEB MYFYRWYR BANGOR
○ **7** SABBATICALS ○ TURNOUT AT LAST BALLOT 12%
○ NUS MEMBER
The SU gets along well with the University suits. *They tend to concentrate on welfare and services over party politicking.* There's also a Welsh language officer and society for keepin' it Cymru.

SU FACILITIES
Union building: two bars; one club; café; snack bar; shop; Natwest bank; STA travel shop; meeting room; games room; photo booth; laundrette; parking space; minibus hire.

CLUBS (NON SPORTING)
Archaeology; Chinese; Duke of Edinburgh; Earth Religions (paganism, witchcraft, Druidism and the like); Geography; Guides & Scouts; Hellenic (Greek); Indian; Japanese; Latino; Law; Speculative Analysis (budding stockbrokers); Stage Crew; United Nations; War Gaming and Role-playing. **See also Clubs tables.**

OTHER ORGANISATIONS
Monthly student newspapers in English ('Seren') and Welsh ('Y Ddraenen') and a student radio station ('Storm'). Thesps find their niche at either ROSTRA (the Uni's oldest drama soc), SODA (musical theatre) or BEDS (English drama). The Student Volunteering group *does its bit* for the local community. RAG *shakes its buckets.*

RELIGIOUS
○ TEAM OF CHAPLAINS (COFE, RC)
The CofE chaplaincy centre also has 28 self-catered rooms *for the really keen* and an ecumenical centre where followers of all faiths can drop in. Locally, there's a Cathedral as well as Catholic, Methodist, Church of Wales and Baptist churches, a Quaker house and a mosque.

PAID WORK
○ JOB BUREAU ○ PAID WORK TERM-TIME 55%; HOLS 76%
Jobs can be *hard to come by*, although Welsh speakers are at an advantage for office/admin work. GoWales provides 97 paid placements in north-west Wales during vacations and after graduation. The Portfolio Worker Project helps develop freelancing abilities.

SPORTS ○○○○○○○○○○○○○

○ RECENT SUCCESSES RUGBY, KAYAKING
○ BUSA RANKING 107
Poor pitches are holding back otherwise-successful outdoor sports teams.

SPORTS FACILITIES
Six football pitches; hockey pitch; two rugby pitches; all-weather pitch; cricket ground; four squash courts; two tennis courts; four basketball courts; three netball courts; three sports halls; running track; athletics field; gym; aerobics studio; multigym; climbing wall. In town, the JJB Fitness Centre does student discounts. The Uni uses Bangor's swimming pool.

SPORTING CLUBS
Canoe Polo; Cheerleaders; Christians in sports; Dance; Gaelic football; Gymnastics; Ki-Aikido; Octopush (underwater hockey); Rowing; Surfing; Ultimate Frisbee; Windsurfing. **See also Clubs tables.**

ATTRACTIONS
Bangor FC *barely raise a cheer* but local facilities are *pretty good.* There's a leisure centre, swimming pool, athletics field, squash and tennis courts, a *sporty* sort of river, pot-holing caves, and mile upon mile of *glorious hikeable* mountainside (snowdonia's not far away). Llandudno has a dry ski slope. The national centres for watersports and mountaineering are accessible from Bangor.

ACCOMMODATION ○○○○○○○○○○

IN COLLEGE
○ SELF-CATERING 19% ○ COST £56 (37WKS)
○ 1ST YRS LIVING IN 67% ○ 2ND YRS LIVING IN 18%
○ 3RD YRS LIVING IN 10% ○ FINALISTS LIVING IN 10%
○ INSURANCE PREMIUM £
AVAILABILITY Accommodation is guaranteed for all first years – even those who come through Clearing get a bed *sooner or later.* Halls are scattered, so students are usually allocated to the one nearest their department. Some share, but it's *filthily* cheap at £49 a week.. Quality varies wildly: The Ffriddoedd site is Bangor's *finest*, with *pricier* en suite rooms, net connections, on-site launderette, halls office, coffee shop, bar and newsagent. *Things are less pretty at the older style halls of the Ffrid site and Rathbone where some shoddy facilities have been reported*, though inmates are usually too busy making their own entertainment to care much. There's one hall for Welsh-speaking students, which *proves popular for the close-spun community.*
CAR PARKING A year's parking permit costs £9.00, *though spaces can be limited.*

EXTERNALLY
○ AVE RENT £45 ○ LIVING AT HOME 5%
AVAILABILITY *Digs costing from £45 are scattered all over Bangor.*
HOUSING HELP The Accommodation Office advertises vacancies and provides a code of standards for landlords to sign up to.

WELFARE 🅞🅞🅞🅞🅞🅞🅞🅞🅞🅞🅞🅞🅞🅞

SERVICES
🅞 **LGBT OFFICER & SOCIETY** 🅞 **INTERNATIONAL STUDENTS' SOCIETY** 🅞 **DISABILITIES SUPPORT GROUP** 🅞 **SELF-DEFENCE CLASSES** 🅞 **NIGHTLINE** 🅞 **UNIVERSITY COUNSELLORS** 13 PART 🅞 **CRIME RATING** !
There's a welfare advisor in the Student Services Centre and a student counselling service Halls of residence also have support.
HEALTH Student nurse on campus. A nearby surgery has five GPs on the books.
CRIME: *Rarer than a Frenchman's steak. Neverthless Bangor's introduced self-defence classes and cheap attack alarms in case any supervillains come to town.*
DISABILITIES Accommodation for wheelchair users, but some of the older buildings have *very poor* access. The Dyslexia Student Service provides *internationally-renowned* support.

FINANCE
🅞 **AVE DEBT PER YEAR** £4,004
🅞 **HOME STUDENT FEES** £3,000
FEES £1,200 for home students in 2006; up to £3,000 from 2007 but Welsh residents should then get an annual £1,800 fee grant. £7,600-£8,000 for international students. Part-time undergrads: £80-90 per 10 credit module. Postgrads courses: £4,685 for MA Banking Finance; £8,560 for an MBA; £1,175 for a PGCE; others £3,085. Part-time postgrads: £1,543.
🅞 **ACCESS FUND** £470,000 🅞 **SUCCESSFUL APPLICATIONS/YR** 550 🅞 **AVE PAYMENT** £800-2,000
SUPPORT *Dosh-happy* academic scholarships, access bursaries for single parents, post-graduate access bursaries, start-up bursaries for mature students relocating to the Bangor area, and a SU £500 emergency fund for those in dire dosh straits. The Money Support Unit doles out advice and deals with paperwork.

B

⯈ BARTS
see *Queen Mary, University of London*

UNIVERSITY OF BATH

🅞 **THE UNIVERSITY OF BATH** Claverton Down, Bath, BA2 7AY **TEL** (01225) 388 388 **E-MAIL** admissions@bath.ac.uk
WEBSITE www.bath.ac.uk 🅞 **UNIVERSITY OF BATH STUDENTS' UNION** Claverton Down, Bath, BA2 7AY **TEL** (01225) 386 612

GENERAL 🅞🅞🅞🅞🅞🅞🅞🅞🅞🅞🅞🅞🅞

At the foot of the Cotswolds, an energetic stone's throw south-east of Bristol, is Bath – one of England's *most beautiful and unspoilt cities*. The Celts sniffed around the springs and the Romans built the first settlement here, but it was in Georgian times that it became the *pretty place* we know today – *although, as all tight-trouser fans will be aware, Jane Austen called it 'a monstrosity of epic proportion', but then set half her novels there, so what did she know?*
The many tourists don't come just to see the Roman Baths and the golden stones of the historic city but also the local countryside, the Mendip Hills and the Severn Estuary. *Unfortunately*, the University, being on a small 60s campus nine miles from the city centre, *shares very little of this elegance. It's a disorienting place at first, with no immediately apparent focus or entry point. The buildings, with all the concrete charm of a shopping precinct, are definitely not the best feature. Still, there's loads of grassy and leafy bits to frolic in as well as the itsy bitsy University lake – perfect*

for those Mr Darcy moments – compensating a bit for the windy location.

SEX RATIO: ♂54 ♀46	FOUNDED: 1966
FULL-TIME U'GRADS: 8,285	PART-TIME: 1,222
POSTGRADS: 2,977	NON-DEGREE: N/A
AVE COURSE: 3-4YRS	ETHNIC: 12%
STATE:PRIVATE SCHOOL: 38:14	FLUNK RATE: 4%
MATURE: 21%	INTERNATIONAL: 17%
DISABLED: 215	LOCAL: N/A

ATMOSPHERE
Bath babies may be a touch isolated from the city (which isn't exactly Shangri-La to begin with) but they don't mind too much. Although serious about studies, both the library and the bars bustle merrily away throughout the day and students find plenty of time for sports, other activities, and then some more sports. Many are rather well-off – they'd have to be to live in Bath – but there's no real snobbery or pretentiousness, more a generous helping of community spirit, topped with lashings of charity work and garnished with a volunteering side salad. Delicious.

BATH
⊙ **POPULATION** 169,040 ⊙ **CITY CENTRE** 1.5 MILES
⊙ **LONDON** 100 MILES ⊙ **BRISTOL** 11 MILES
⊙ **HIGH TEMP** 21 ⊙ **LOW TEMP** 2 ⊙ **RAINFALL** 72

Bath's a *strikingly beautiful* city and one of only three on the planet to win a place on UNESCO's World Heritage list. Its most distinguishing feature is the hot water spring that produces a quarter of a million gallons of hot liquid a day, giving the city its name. The Roman Baths are a *necessary touristy* stop off. So too will be the Bath Spa public baths – *when and if they ever open* – which will draw on the same thermal water source and allow visitors to see what the Romans were on about. The spa resort heritage and *gorgeous* surroundings flood the city with tourists and their associated cash, but the *flipside is the wealth of amenities and cultural attractions can leave the humble student significantly out of pocket.* The two institutions (see also <u>Bath Spa University</u>) bring some *much-needed* youth to the city and the atmosphere *can get lively and interesting for those who know where to go.* Outside the city there's Bristol *for urban thrills*, Stonehenge, Salisbury Plain and Glastonbury *if you like your culture served quasi-mystical* and Claverton Cats & Dogs Home (close to the University) – *always appreciative of volunteer dog-walkers and cat-cuddlers.*

TRAVEL
TRAINS Bath Spa Station roughly two miles away has services to London Paddington (from £25.10 return), Bristol (£3.55), Birmingham (£25.70) and beyond.
COACHES Bath Coach Station has several National Express and First Group services, including London (£20.40) and Bristol (£3.80).
CAR Bath's nine miles off the M4 down the A46 and on the A4. The city centre's bus gate makes it *pretty much unnavigable.* The Council is planning to introduce a parking scheme to stop students and staff clogging residential streets with cars. Students living on campus or living privately in BA1 or BA2 postcodes are not eligible for annual permits. For others, they cost between £103 and £155 depending on location.
AIR Bristol Airport 18 miles away has flights inland and to main European destinations.
HITCHING *Many students cadge lifts up the hill to the University and the M4's good for thumbing down to London.*
LOCAL The SU has negotiated with First Bus to bring about the 'Bright Orange' bus service (No. 18) which operates between the city and Bath University every six mins during term. A ride on the city bus costs £1.40; cheaper tickets can be bought in bulk.
TAXIS Well stocked for cabs. A ride from the station to campus is around a fiver.
BICYCLES Some of the more energetic students and staff do cycle to campus *but the distance is prohibitive to, well, normal people. Bathwick and Widcombe Hills are definitely not for the*

faint-hearted or unfit. There's a cycle shed at the bottom of Bathwick for those who prefer the bus up the hill, plus sheds on campus.

CAREER PROSPECTS
⊙ **CAREERS SERVICE** ⊙ **NO. OF STAFF** 8 FULL/2 PART
⊙ **UNEMPLOYED AFTER 6** MTHS 6%

The *ass-kicking* careers service runs a variety of aids for all students including personal skills workshops, aptitude testing, computer-aided guidance systems (*nothing to do with controlling missiles*), job fairs and employer presentations. A lot of Bath students do vacation placements while studying, arranged by the careers folk.

FAMOUS ALUMNI
Don Foster (local Lib Dem MP); 'Dr' Neil Fox (Radio DJ, Pop Idol judge and *pillock*); Charles Lewington (ex-Tory Director of Communications); Jon Sleightholme (rugby player); Russell Senior (formerly of Pulp).

FURTHER INFO
⊙ **PROSPECTUSES** UNDERGRAD; POSTGRAD; INTERNATIONAL.
⊙ **OPEN DAYS**
The International Office produces an International Students' Handbook – see www.bath.ac.uk/international-office. Other prospectuses can be ordered online (www.bath.ac.uk/admissions) or by phone. Open days in June and September.

ACADEMIC ⊙⊙⊙⊙⊙⊙⊙⊙⊙⊙⊙⊙⊙

⊙ **1994 GROUP**
Apart from having one of the most meaningless Latin mottos – 'Generatim discite cultus' ('Learn each field of study according to its kind') – Bath has a strong record of providing professional courses, particularly in sciences and engineering. It's a *firm believer* in the powers of the placement year and study years abroad. Three in five students pack their bags for industrial placements in the public or private sector, or for a year studying abroad during their degree courses. There's no institutional assessment scheme as many courses are accredited by external, professional bodies. *On the one hand students can be sure of learning up-to-date professional skills, on the other some may feel a tad uneasy spending several years being moulded into cogs for the industrial machine.* Students can opt to take a learning unit outside their main course – *most opt for career-bolsterers like languages or management.* the semester system means students come back after Christmas for a couple of weeks classes, before being plunged into exams.

ENTRY POINTS: 280-360	AVE POINTS: 324
APPLICATIONS PER PLACE: 7	CLEARING: 2%
NO. OF TERMS: 2	LENGTH OF TERMS: 15wks
STAFF TO STUDENT RATIO: 1:14	STUDY ADDICTS: 15%
TEACHING: ****	RESEARCH: *****
YEAR ABROAD: 1%	SANDWICH STUDENTS: 48%
1STS: 19%	2.2S: 19%
2.1S: 57%	3RDS: 3%

ADMISSIONS

⊙ APPLY VIA UCAS

Bath operates a student-centred admissions policy, meaning that, *in theory at least,* they judge applications by whether the student will benefit intellectually rather than how much money they can make out of them. *Quite sweet really.*

SUBJECTS

CROSS −FACULTY PROGRAMMES: 6% **HEALTH** 4% **HUMANITIES & SOCIAL SCIENCES** 28% **LIFELONG LEARMNING:** 11% **MANAGEMENT** 7% **ENGINEERING AND DESIGN** 20% **SCIENCE** 29% **BEST** Biology & related; Business; Civil, Chemical, & Other Engineering; Economics; Electronic & Electrical Engineering; European Languages & Area Studies; Mathematical Sciences; Mechanically-based Engineering; Medical Science and Pharmacy; Physical Science; Politics; Social Policy & Anthropology; Sports Science; Sociology.

LIBRARIES

⊙ 545,000 BOOKS ⊙ 1,100 STUDY PLACES
⊙ 24-HR ACCESS ⊙ SPEND PER STUDENT £££

Two main faculty and five smaller departmental libraries.

COMPUTERS

⊙ 2,000 WORKSTATIONS ⊙ 24-HR ACCESS
⊙ SPEND PER STUDENT: £££££

There are several computer rooms and a PC suite. *Despite recent improvements, there are still often queues to get onto one.* A new wireless environment around the Central Parade is in the process of being created. All bedrooms have intranet access.

OTHER LEARNING FACILITIES

There's a self-access language centre on level 5 of the library with audio-visual resources. The Arts Theatre has rehearsal space for dance and drama, and there are music rehearsal rooms, a design lab and a tv centre.

ENTERTAINMENT ◑◑◑◑◑◑◑◑◑◑

THE CITY

⊙ PRICE OF A PINT OF BEER £2.40
⊙ GLASS OF WINE £2.60
⊙ CAN OF RED BULL £1.80

CINEMAS The ABC's an *old school town-centre cinema with character,* showing major releases one by one. *The locally cherished Little Theatre*

Cinema has two screens for mainstream/arthouse *flicks* and there's an Odeon – both do student discounts. There's also a film festival.

THEATRES The *popular* Georgian Theatre Royal shows musicals and West End stuff with the occasional B-list celebrity appearance. The smaller Ustinov Studio attached to it is a *good* place to catch quirky fare like puppet shows, local am dram and one-man events. Rondo Theatre's an *intimate* studio spot with a *diverse* line-up. All offer student deals. The *dinky* Kingswood and Mission Theatres host local and visiting shows.

PUBS *Quaint and plentiful with many a potent pint, but expensive. Many are designed purely to part the tourist trade from their money, but most are welcoming enough.* Pushplugs (or *maybe Bathplugs*): The Boater; the Bell; the Chequers Inn (as yet undiscovered by tourists – *shh*); Flan O'Briens (rugby shown); Saracen's Head (Bath's oldest); the Huntsman; the Pulteney Arms; the Porter; the Pig & Fiddle.

CLUBBING *Not a huge deal going on, but things are more lively than the staid, touristy image might suggest.* Pushplugs: Cadillacs (*very pink*, Monday is student night); Po Na Na; Moles (live music and DJs); Ts; Babylon; Qube.

MUSIC VENUES *Up-coming indie rockers congregate in Moles on a Saturday night. Porter Butt is also good for guitar-based rockeries. Bath Pavilion puts on the odd big name gig. The Bell and Doolally's get all types of weird and wonderful tuneage.*

EATING OUT The dozens of chintzy tea rooms aimed at tourists have been replaced by various chain coffee outlets, *but they go down just as well with visiting parents (and their wallets).* Other, more student-friendly Pushplugs: Café Retro (*lively and cheap*); Porter Bar (homemade veggie); Eastern Eye and Pria do *good* curries; Schwartz Bros (*non-plastic* fast food); Café Cadbury (food made from chocolate); Green Park Brasserie (live jazz; three-course nosh for under a tenner on week nights). Try Sally Lunn's – *totally touristy,* but everything comes with a traditional Bath bun.

OTHER *Brilliant for museums and art galleries: the Holbourne Museum, Victoria Art Gallery, Royal Photographic Centre and the museums of Costume, Native Art and East Asian Art are all worth spending pennies in (actual pennies, not weeing).*

THE UNIVERSITY

⊙ PRICE OF A PINT OF BEER £1.85
⊙ GLASS OF WINE £2
⊙ CAN OF RED BULL £1.80

BARS The Plug Bar attached to the Venue club is the *classic student boozer,* stuffed with arcade machines (including giant Jenga and Connect 4) and puts on sports and film nights, karaoke and *ultra-popular* theme parties. The Parade bar *is pricier and a bit more pretentious* with wooden floors and *an older crowd. Opening hours are erratic, although it does have a late licence. Warning to quiet-lovers: the* volume gets turned up big style around 9pm. The Sports café is also licensed.

THEATRES The Arts Theatre is the home of BUST (Bath University Student Theatre), which puts on 3-5 shows a year. Professional companies also visit.

FILM Membership of the film society gets varied regular filmic fare, screened in a stereoequipped lecture theatre.

CLUBBING The Venue *does its bit for the disco dollies* and sets the stage for karaoke, dance, cheese etc. *Horny is the popular Friday night meat market.* Sports clubs take over on Wednesdays. There's a cocktail bar – *but it's not Tom Cruise-quality.* The Union hosts a club night in Po Na Na (in the city) on Mondays.

COMEDY Plug Bar gets a local *chuckle-monster* in once a month.

FOOD The *dull-looking but cheap* Choices food court has a *shopping-mall style* selection of oriental, pizza, market and traditional foodstuffs and is backed up by fast food Pitstop (pre-order online for a 5% discount), Munchies (free pizza delivery around campus), the bars, and several delis, cafés and snack-stops.

OTHER At least two balls a year (Rag and Graduation).

SOCIAL ⊍⊍⊍⊍⊍⊍⊍⊍⊍⊍⊍⊍⊍⊍

UNIVERSITY OF BATH STUDENTS' UNION
○ **6 SABBATICALS** ○ **TURNOUT AT LAST BALLOT** 23%
○ **NUS MEMBER**

They may not be the most powerful political force in the galaxy but BUSU is quietly confident when it comes to matters like welfare support, commercial enterprise, ents, societies and community-polishing volunteer projects. Most importantly, the University actually makes a point of listening to them and representatives' views go straight to the highest echelons of command. 98% of Bath students are involved in some form of club or soc.

> ◉ **'Always plan for practice fire alarms at three in the morning: extra bodies in a hall of residence are difficult to explain.' – Michael Fish, weatherman.**

SU FACILITIES
BUSU's based at Norwood House, where it offers: two bars; nightclub; cafeterias; snack bars; the Pitstop; pool tables; Barclays, NatWest and HSBC banks and ATMs; general shop; convenience store; travel agency; new and secondhand bookshops; hairdressers; vending and gaming machines; photocopiers; payphones; fax and printing service; advice centre; launderette.

CLUBS (NON-SPORTING)
Airsoft Society; Bath Anglican; Bath Area Malaysian & Singaporean Association; Bath Computer Science; Bath Orthodox Student; Bath Real Ale; Bath Uni Football; Bath University Curry Appreciation; Bath University Guides and Scouts; Bath University Motorcycle Club; Bath University Music Production; Bath University Soap; Bath University Student Musicals; Bath University Student Theatre; BodySoc (dance); Breakdancing; Buddhist Meditation; Campus Television; Chamber Choir; Cheerleaders; Chess and Board Games; Chinese Students; Chocolate; Choral and Orchestra; Cocktail; Eggplant (vegetarian); French Connection; German; Gospel; Acapella; Soul and Pop; Gravity Vomit (juggling & circus skills); Greek Dancing; Hellenic; Impact (newspaper); Investment; Islamic; Jewish; Korean; Mandarin; MusicSoc; One World (human rights, justice, environment); Rocksoc; Russian; Salsa; Saudade – Brazilian & Portuguese; Scandinavian; Spanish & Italian; Students For a Free Tibet; SU Food Co-operative; Thai Association; Visual Arts; Welsh; Wine. **See also Clubs tables.**

OTHER ORGANISATIONS
The Union publishes the *advert-heavy* 'Impact' every fortnight. University Radio Bath can be heard all over campus and there's a student TV station. *Never-resting* Rag has a sabbatical coordinator and sucked £85,000 out of the public last year, through a series of ridiculous stunts and events, including the annual duck race – where several thousand rubber ducks are deposited into the river Avon from a crane-suspended 15ft egg. *And, Push promises, they've done much crazier things than that.* BUSCA – Bath University Students' Community Action – *is very active* in arranging volunteer initiatives and events on local and international levels.

RELIGIOUS
○ **9 CHAPLAINS (COFE, RC, URC, ORTHODOX, QUAKER, METHODIST, BAPTIST)**
The Chaplaincy Centre provides a non-denominational meeting place for the faithful. There's a Muslim prayer room with washing facilities on campus. Bath has plenty of churches, a mosque and Buddhist groups. The nearest synagogues and Sikh Gurdwaras are in Bristol..

PAID WORK
○ **JOB BUREAU** ○ **PAID WORK** TERM-TIME 20%; HOLS 35%
Bath's ever-flowing stream of tourists provides plenty of seasonal work. SU-run JobLink *is a far cry from the typical tatty Union notice board* and operates similarly to a council job centre, advertising casual part-time work and keeping

B

to a strict Code of Practice. On-campus there's work available in shops, bars and admin.

SPORTS

O **RECENT SUCCESSES** BADMINTON, TENNIS, NETBALL, SWIMMING O **BUSA RANKING** 2

Sport takes a high priority at Bath – *none of this wimpy crap about it only being a game.* Facilities are world class, tuition is expert and there's also a sports training village. The Uni battles *arch-rival* Loughborough to top the student sports table. In 2002 the elite Team Bath became the first student team to reach the first round of the FA cup in 100 years. Bath Uni's been declared a Regional Centre for Sporting Excellence and facilities are being extended and improved all the time. *Everybody's favourite loser Tim Henman got very excited by the new tennis courts a while back.*

SPORTS FACILITIES

The excellent amenities are all on campus: two sports halls; 95 acres of playing fields; 50m pool; four squash courts; two all-weather pitches; eight indoor/ten outdoor tennis courts; two Astroturf hockey pitches; three netball courts; two basketball courts; athletics field; 132m indoor running straight; climbing wall; weights room; multigym; sauna; bobsleigh push-start track; fencing salle; judo dojo; indoor shooting range. *The best thing is it's all as free as sunshine to students,* except the members-only fitness suite. Next door there's a golf course and in town further facilities like a bowling green, river and so on.

SPORTING CLUBS

American Football; Ballroom Dancing; Floorball; Gliding; Gymnastics; Hot Air Ballooning; Ju-Jitsu; Kite; Kung Fu & Kickboxing; Lacrosse; Life Saving; Motor Club (cart racing); Parachuting; Paragliding; Rifle Club; Sky-diving; Surfing; Table Tennis; T'ai Chi Chuan; Triathlon; Ultimate Frisbee; Wakeboard & Waterski; Waterpolo; Windsurfing. **See also Clubs tables.**

ATTRACTIONS

Bath Rugby Club for the cauliflower-eared. Bath City FC is in the Nationwide Conference League.

ACCOMMODATION

IN UNIVERSITY

O **SELF-CATERING** 31% O **COST:** £73 (35-38WKS)
O **1ST YRS LIVING IN** 98% C**2ND YRS LIVING IN:** 1%
O **3RD YRS LIVING IN:** 1% C**FINALISTS LIVING IN:** 5%
O **POSTGRADS LIVING IN:** 10% O **INSURANCE PREMIUM:** £

AVAILABILITY All first years and international students are offered a place in the University housing, mostly on campus. Bath has some complexes in town, but they're generally used by locals, matures and late-comers. More than half of the rooms are en suite and all take the form of 5-13 bedrooms clustered around a shared kitchen. Launderettes are plentiful. *Some of Eastwood's a bit basic and a shade shabby but the low rents make it ideal for scrimpers and savers* and parts were recently refurbished. *Malborough and Solsbury Court are at the glamorous and expensive end.* Some off-site family flats for those with children and single-sex accommodation available upon request. There are no curfews, *but heavy metal gigs or atom bomb testing after 11.30pm are frowned upon.* CCTV, entry phones and 24-hour security office *fight the forces of evil. No tuck-in service though.*

EXTERNALLY

O **AVE RENT** £64 (INC BILLS) O **LIVING AT HOME** 2%
AVAILABILITY *Bath's a wealthy town and house prices reflect it* but it's still possible to find the odd *habitable hovel.* Provided students put any thought of the gracious Regency terraces out of their minds and concentrate on the less central areas, living out is manageable. *Oldfield Park and Coombe Down are good bets, but avoid smeggy Twerton and Fairfield Park.*
HOUSING HELP The five accommodation office staff maintain a private lettings database and a notice board. It works in conjunction with the Union's AWARE housing office to provide contractual advice. No property vetting, but Bath Council has an accreditation scheme.

WELFARE

SERVICES

O **LGBT SOCIETY** O **ETHNIC MINORITIES SOCIETY**
O **WOMEN'S SOCIETY** O **MATURE STUDENTS' SOCIETY**
O **INTERNATIONAL STUDENTS' SOCIETY** O **POSTGRAD SOCIETY** O **DISABILITIES OFFICER & SOCIETY**
O **NIGHTLINE** O **CRIME RATING** !

The SU AWARE centre is the focal point of student support and holds a weekly solicitor's surgery.
HEALTH On-campus Medical Centre with three medical officers and three nurses, as well as a Dental Centre with real live dentist.
CRECHES/NURSERY The award-winning Westwood Nursery *is one of the best in the country* and has 48 places for kids 6mths to school age.
DISABILITIES Access around the compact campus is *generally good:* all major buildings have ramps and lifts, but some areas *can be limiting.* There's an extensive range of support services for students with dyslexia, including weekly workshops, specialist library equipment and software, plus laptop/tape-recorder loans. The Bath Assessment Centre gives students the choice of 'high tech', 'low tech' or 'no tech' levels of support – *good for students who resent special treatment.*
CRIME *A notoriously crime-free city.*

B

FINANCE
◗ AVE DEBT PER YEAR £2,683 **◗ HOME STUDENT FEES** £3,000
FEES The common or garden postgrad fee is £3,660 but it varies. International postgrads pay £9,300 for arts and £11,900 for sciences. International undergrads pay £8,600 for Arts courses; £11,000 for sciences. Fees halve for part-timers. The top-up fees sting will be softened by Bath bursaries of up to £1,500 for those on all or part of the maintenance grant.

◗ ACCESS FUND £299,136 **◗ SUCCESSFUL APPLICATIONS/YR** 326
SUPPORT Students who have to do vacation and field study can apply for special awards. There's a sports scholarship scheme where exceptional students can take an extra year for their degrees combined with intensive training. There are some subject-specific bursaries up for grabs. Hardship fund (£45,000) also available for those who can't ask for Access to Learning funds – primarily international students.

BATH SPA UNIVERSITY

FORMERLY BATH SPA UNIVERSITY COLLEGE, BATH COLLEGE OF HIGHER EDUCATION

1) **◗ BATH SPA UNIVERSITY** Newton St Loe, Bath, BA2 9BN **TEL** (01225) 875 875 **E-MAIL** enquiries@bathspa.ac.uk **WEBSITE** www.bathspa.ac.uk **◗ BATH SPA UNIVERSITY STUDENTS' UNION**, Newton Park Campus, Newton St Loe, Bath, BA2 9BN **TEL** (01225) 875 588 **E-MAIL** bathspasu@bathspa.ac.uk **WEBSITE** www.bathspasu.co.uk
2) **◗ BATH SPA UNIVERSITY**, Sion Hill, Lansdown, BA1 5SF **TEL** (01225) 875 875 **◗ BATH SPA STUDENTS' UNION**, Somerset Place, Lansdown, BA1 5SF **TEL** (01225) 875 684)

GENERAL ○○○○○○○○○○○○○

Like the University of Bath, the main site of Bath Spa isn't actually in Bath, nor even in the town of Keynsham nearby, but around five miles away, with *the main Newton Park site amidst hilly countryside more National Trust than NUS. The buildings themselves are, for the most part, built with golden-coloured Bath stone in the classic Regency style that can make every day feel like an episode of 'Pride and Prejudice'. The unwritten rule obeyed by all the students, that no one drops litter, preserves the beauty of the place (unless you're into post-modern garbage collages, that is).* The buildings of the Newton Park campus are *caked in history* – the chandeliered administrative centre is a former manor house, complete with trapdoor in what was the master bedroom for the maid to do some after-hours 'room service'.

👫👫👫👫👫👫👫👫👫👫👫👫👫👫👫👫👫

SEX RATIO: ♂30 ♀70	**FOUNDED:** 1983
FULL-TIME U'GRADS: 3,360	**PART-TIME:** 117
POSTGRADS: 1,302	**NON-DEGREE:** 676
AVE COURSE: 3YRS	**ETHNIC:** 6%
STATE:PRIVATE SCHOOL: 80:20	**FLUNK RATE:** 6%
MATURE: 40%	**INTERNATIONAL:** 7%
DISABLED: 190	**LOCAL:** 26%

ATMOSPHERE
The high number of female and mature students has a significant effect, shifting the focus from traditional alcoholic boisterousness towards a quieter and more friendly little university, where everyone knows everyone else and staff seem to genuinely care about their charges. It's the sort of place that you wouldn't mind having in your own backyard, if you had a backyard big enough. The students are generally quietly wealthy and content with their lot. The main party nights are on weekdays, and the campus has a tendency to empty faster than bowels after a vindaloo come the weekend, meaning that those who live there can feel isolated. Contact with Bath locals is at a minimum, thanks to the remoteness of the location.

OTHER SITES
SION HILL (Bath School of Art & Design) Exclusively for Arts students to frolic in, the *peaceful and pretty* Sion Hill Campus is sat atop a *sizeable* hill in a *quiet* residential area within walking distance of Bath town centre. It has computing facilities, refectory, bar, purpose-built sculpture studio and accommodation. Somerset Place, the main bit of the campus, is the longest stretch of Georgian Crescent with a single owner in the galaxy. *Or something.*

BATH see University of Bath

TRAVEL see University of Bath
CAR *A motor is very handy given the remoteness of the place,* although first years living in halls aren't allowed them on campus. Others require free permits *but parking isn't a worry.*
LOCAL Buses are far and away best for the Newton Park-Bath journey, two an hour, *quite reliably,* until around 3am. The Bright Orange (418) runs between town, Bath Spa and Bath University and does season tickets.

Words in italics are Push's point of view – take it or leave it...

B

TAXIS The University has a deal with a local firm – it's a flat £7.50 into town.
BICYCLES *Strictly for recreational use since it's just too darned far to pedal anywhere useful.*

CAREER PROSPECTS
○ **CAREERS SERVICE** ○ **NO. OF STAFF** 1 FULL/4 PART
○ **UNEMPLOYED AFTER 6 MTHS** 5%
Bulletin board, careers library, workshops, and a host of online resources, including computer guidance software and a job database that the careers staff have just blasted into cyberspace.

FAMOUS ALUMNI
Andy Bradshaw (novelist); Howard Hodgkin (Turner Prize painter); Anita Roddick (Body Shop); Jason Gardner (athlete); Clive Deamer (musician, Portishead); Andy Davis (musician, Goldfrapp). William Harbutt, the inventor of plasticine, lectured here.

SPECIAL FEATURES
The Newton Park campus is built on Duchy of Cornwall land (meaning Prince Charles is the landlord), so although there's plenty of space, *getting planning permission for new buildings is nearly impossible.* The grounds were originally designed by 17th-century landscaping revolutionary, Capability Brown.

FURTHER INFO
○ **PROSPECTUSES** UNDERGRAD; POSTGRAD; CD-ROM.
○ **OPEN DAYS**
Ring the University to get hold of any prospectus or check out the detailed one that lives on the web. In addition to open days, there are visit afternoons generally on the last Wednesday of every month.

ACADEMIC ○○○○○○○○○○○○○○

Courses *err on the side of the vocational and Bath Spa's focus is on its highly-rated teaching rather than research.* Degree programmes are spread between seven academic schools and are *thoroughly modular.*
 Students take six modules a year and flexibility of course options increases in the second and third years. More than 200 Bath Spa students take their first year at associated FE colleges around Wessex. Media and performing arts are *swelling*, with a new dance and drama centre set to open in October 2006, and there's a healthy contingent of science and education students along with the creative types – *quite a mixed bag for such a pint-sized place.*

ENTRY POINTS: 200–260	AVE POINTS: N/A
APPLICATIONS PER PLACE: 5	CLEARING: 5%
NO. OF TERMS: 2	LENGTH OF TERMS: 15WKS
STAFF TO STUDENT RATIO: 1:22	STUDY ADDICTS: 5%
TEACHING: ★★★★	RESEARCH: ★★
YEAR ABROAD: N/A	SANDWICH STUDENTS: 1%
1STS: 7%	2.2S: 26%
2.1S: 53%	3RDS: 2%

ADMISSIONS
○ **APPLY VIA UCAS/DIRECT FOR PART-TIME**
The University *laps up* applications from mature students and from those with non-traditional backgrounds.

SUBJECTS
ART & DESIGN 14%   **COMBINED AWARDS** 29%
EDUCATION 25%   **ENGLISH & CREATIVE STUDIES** 4%
HISTORICAL & CULTURAL STUDIES 3%
MUSIC & PERFORMING ARTS 14%   **SCIENCES** 11%
BEST Business; Communications; Education; English; History; Psychology; Sociology.
UNUSUAL The Remote Sensing course (studying satellite/aircraft surveillance of Earth) is part of the Geographic Information Systems qualification and is unique to Bath Spa; Writing for Young People (MA).

LIBRARIES
○ **172,000 BOOKS** ○ **291 STUDY PLACES**
Libraries at Newton Park and Sion Hill stock course-relevant material, DVDs and other handy audio-visual paraphernalia. Despite welcome expansions, book and computer facilities *could do with being bigger and better – if only Bonnie Prince Charlie would allow it.*

COMPUTERS
○ **650 WORKSTATIONS**
Both libraries have workstations and there are several other open-access computer rooms, available till about 10pm. Course documents, announcements from tutors and online discussion groups are available on the Virtual Learning Environment – *ideal for those that that prefer not to talk to real people.* All campus accommodation has wi-fi access.

OTHER LEARNING FACILITIES
A drama studio and music rehearsal rooms. Sion Hill has some specialised art, design and sculpture rooms.

ENTERTAINMENT ○○○○○○○○○

THE TOWN see University of Bath
Spa-ites hang out at the same places as their Bath counterparts, but mingling betwixt the two is as rare as a tequila slammer at a church tea party.

B

THE UNIVERSITY
- **PRICE OF A PINT OF BEER** £1.60
- **GLASS OF WINE** £1.50
- **CAN OF RED BULL** £1.20

BARS The Newton Park bar (700 capacity) is the biggest and most popular, with two late (til 2am) nights a week and quizzes, salsa and karaoke. The Sion Hill Bar *is less of a favourite, although some enjoy the low-key 'local' feel of the place.*

THEATRES Student productions have to find a stage in the city, though the forthcoming drama centre should change all that.

FILM Contemporary and classic flicks are shown at Sion Hill.

MUSIC VENUES The bar at Newton Park has weekly live, generally student, bands. The Michael Tippett Centre catches bigger birds.

CLUBBING *A brace of big ones* (cheese and dance, respectively) in the Newton Park Bar.

FOOD Eat@Moreton and Deli@Moreton serve sandwiches, soups and similar lunch goodies. Small snackages sold by the SU shop.

OTHER Three balls a year, visiting hypnotists and other *nearly entertaining shenanigans.*

SOCIAL ●●●●●●●●●●●●●

BATH SPA UNIVERSITY STUDENTS' UNION
- **3 SABBATICALS** ○ **TURNOUT AT LAST BALLOT** 12%
- **NUS MEMBER**

The SU has facilities on both sites, with the Newton Park branch recently rehoused in a modern building. *Political opinions are treated as thought-crime at Bath Spa, with the focus firmly on welfare and ents rather than rabble-rousing and the University and Union happily embroiled in a mutual love-in over their clean, civilised campus.*

SU FACILITIES
Spread between the sites: two bars; shop; two cafeterias; canteen; three pool tables; juke box; two meeting rooms; minibus for hire; NatWest ATMs; photocopier; fax and printing service; payphones; photo booth; advice centre; post office; new and secondhand bookshops; vending and gaming machines; launderette.

CLUBS (NON-SPORTING)
Beat Poetry; Chess; Mature students; OTC (Officers Training Corps); Pool; Salsa; Sweets From Strangers (alternative music); Video Games; Writers. **See also Clubs tables.**

OTHER ORGANISATIONS
The SU produces the *eminently readable* 'H20' fortnightly. Rag is finding its fundraising feet. A Student Community Action group organises environmental and art projects, and goes into local schools doing nice things to children.

RELIGIOUS
- **5 CHAPLAINS (COFE, RC, URC, ORTHODOX, METHODIST)**
A small chaplaincy runs a drop-in centre on campus.
Religion in Bath see <u>University of Bath</u>

PAID WORK see <u>University of Bath</u>
- **JOB BUREAU** ○ **PAID WORK: TERM-TIME** 50%: **HOLS** 80%
The job shop provides part-time work for students – quite literally, since it employs three students itself – and maintains an online job database.

SPORTS ●●●●●●●●●●●●●●

- **BUSA RANKING:** 122
Sport remains a forgettable diversion to the majority, with the sports hall so under-used it was turned into a new house for the SU. The University has been putting money into local sports facilities instead, as there's so little space on campus.

SPORTS FACILITIES
Football pitch; cricket pitch; two tennis courts; netball court, rugby pitch.

SPORTING CLUBS
Aikido; Boardsports; Cheerleading; Equestrian; Five-a-side Football; Kickboxing; Mini Golf. **See also Clubs tables.**

ATTRACTIONS see <u>University of Bath</u>

ACCOMMODATION ●●●●●●●●●●

IN UNIVERSITY
- **SELF-CATERING** 42% ○ **COST** £70 (40WKS)
- **1ST YRS LIVING IN** 90-95%
- **INSURANCE PREMIUM** £

AVAILABILITY Priority goes to firtst years coming from over 30 miles away but 5-10% still end up without a room. *No one else has a hope in hell.* 4% share. The accommodation is split into a village right on the campus doorstep and the *box-fresh* Waterside Court, about three miles away between the campus and town. At Sion Hill, the *beautiful* converted Georgian Crescent has room for 100. No catered accommodation. 24-hour security.

CAR PARKING No livers-in can park, but commuters can register for a free permit.

EXTERNALLY see <u>University of Bath</u>
- **AVE RENT** £70

AVAILABILITY *Oldfield Park is a popular option. Whiteway and Twerton are on the rougher side of inhabitable but some students end up landing*

there regardless. *Locals can get sick of sharing streets with pesky students, but tend to air any gripes in a curtain-twitching, letter-writing fashion rather than with their fists. The city is small enough for livers-out to walk everywhere – except, that is, to campus.*
HOUSING HELP: The University and SU Accommodation Offices employ two full-time staff that can help with finding vacancies, emergency housing and warn of blacklisted landlords & properties.

WELFARE ⓤⓤⓤⓤⓤⓤⓤⓤⓤⓤⓤⓤⓤⓤ

SERVICES
○ **LESBIAN/GAY/BISEXUAL OFFICER & SOCIETY**
○ **WOMEN'S OFFICER** ○ **INTERNATIONAL STUDENTS' OFFICER** ○ **NIGHTLINE** ○ **UNIVERSITY COUNSELLORS** 3 PART ○ **CRIME RATING** !
As well as the specialist counsellors, there are two full-time welfare staff to advise on finances and *generally mop up the tears.*
HEALTH A doctors' surgery visits the campus twice a week *so injuries have to be carefully scheduled.*
WOMEN £1 attack alarms from the SU.
CRECHES/NURSERY Nursery service with 30 places for crawlers to toddlers.
DISABILITIES *Listed buildings don't help matters,* but BSUC has undertaken a major works programme to improve access on both campuses. *The 1.5-mile spread of teaching rooms will still cause problems.* Both campuses have ramps, hearing loops, stair lifts, automatic doors and adapted accommodation. There's a full-time Disability Officer who assesses individual needs.

FINANCE
○ **AVE DEBT PER YEAR** £3,173
○ **HOME STUDENT FEES** £3,000
FEES International students pay £6,680-£8,440 or £8,320 for postgrad courses. UK postgrads cough up £3,200.
○ **ACCESS FUND** £434,873
○ **SUCCESSFUL APPLICATIONS/YR** 326
○ **AVE PAYMENT** £500-£2,500
SUPPORT Bursaries of up to £1,150 and scholarships of £1,000 a pop for various subjects.

▶ **BATH SPA UNIVERSITY COLLEGE**
see *Bath Spa University*

▶ **BCUC**
see *Buckinghamshire Chilterns University*

▶ **BEDFORD**
see *University of Luton*

▶ **BEDFORD COLLEGE OF HIGHER EDUCATION**
see *De Montfort University*

▶ **BELFAST, QUEEN'S UNIVERSITY**
see *Queen's University, Belfast*

BIRKBECK, UNIVERSITY OF LONDON

THE COLLEGE IS PART OF THE UNIVERSITY OF LONDON AND STUDENTS ARE ENTITLED TO USE ITS FACILITIES.

○ **BIRKBECK, UNIVERSITY OF LONDON** Malet Street, Bloomsbury, London, WC1E 7HX **TEL** (020) 7631 6000 **E-MAIL** admissions@bbk.ac.uk **WEBSITE** www.bbk.ac.uk ○ **BIRKBECK STUDENT'S UNION**, Malet St, Bloomsbury, London, WC1E 7HX **TEL** (020) 7631 6335 **E-MAIL** president@bcsu.bbk.ac.uk **WEBSITE** www.bbk.ac.uk/su

GENERAL ⓤⓤⓤⓤⓤⓤⓤⓤⓤⓤⓤⓤⓤ

The College was originally founded as the London Mechanics' Institution in a pub on the Strand. It's changed a bit since then – *no more lectures over a pint or ten, Push supposes.* Specialising in courses for mature students with jobs, people otherwise occupied during the day or the unemployed, most Birkbeck teaching occurs in the twilight hours between six and nine. Almost all Birkbeck students are part-time and courses have an excellent reputation. The main building is a *stark redbrick* construction close to Trafalgar Square and handy for ULU. For general information about London see *University of London*

Words in italics are Push's point of view – take it or leave it...

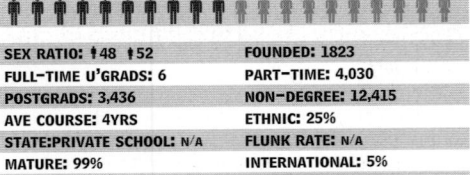

SEX RATIO: ♀48 ♂52	**FOUNDED:** 1823
FULL-TIME U'GRADS: 6	**PART-TIME:** 4,030
POSTGRADS: 3,436	**NON-DEGREE:** 12,415
AVE COURSE: 4YRS	**ETHNIC:** 25%
STATE:PRIVATE SCHOOL: N/A	**FLUNK RATE:** N/A
MATURE: 99%	**INTERNATIONAL:** 5%
DISABLED: 41	**LOCAL:** 85%

ATMOSPHERE

What with *heavy* commitments, it's not the average student scenario. *There's an industrious vibe and while people are friendly, they're busy and are often mid-rush, so laid back chat is rare.* The majority are adults hoping to change careers or improve themselves professionally and *there's a great deal of respect for the college and the life-changing opportunities it affords.*

LONDON see University of London

TRAVEL see University of London
TRAINS Euston Station and Kings Cross (for national and local travel) are within walking distance.
COACHES Kings Cross has services from National Express and most major companies.
LOCAL Buses *aplenty* serve the site (10, 24 29, 73 and 134 from Gower Street; 7 and 188 from Russell Square; 10, 24, 29, 73, 13 from Tottenham Court Road). Euston and Goodge Street stations are both close by for Victoria line tube travel (Northern and Central lines).
BICYCLES *No problems cycling with parking spaces provided.*

CAREER PROSPECTS
❍ CAREERS SERVICE
Birkbeck uses the University of London careers service (ULCS). It offers facilities from drop-in services to longer advisory interviews. The Graduate Career Resource Centre, the largest in London, is also accessible to students and graduates.

FAMOUS ALUMNI
Dido (singer); Ed Davey MP (Lib Dem Shadow Secretary); Phillipa Forester (TV presenter); Ramsay Mcdonald (former PM); Laurie Taylor (media sociologist); Tracy Thorn (Everything but the Girl); Helen Sharman (first British astronaut); Sandy Shaw (barefooted 60s babe); Jah Wobble (80s punk rocker).

FURTHER INFO
❍ PROSPECTUSES UNDERGRAD; POSTGRAD
❍ OPEN EVENINGS
See website for dates of open evenings.

ACADEMIC ◖◗◖◗◖◗◖◗◖◗◖◗◖◗◖◗◖◗◖◗◖◗

❍ 1994 GROUP
Study's what Birkbeck's all about, *everything else is just icing.* It's one of a handful of universities specialising in part-time evening study, mostly taught by formal lecture. Some courses are vocational. It gets top marks for teaching. Birkbeck has four faculties (Arts, Science, Social Science and Continuing Education) with 16 schools teaching a number of different courses.

NO. OF TERMS: 3	**LENGTH OF TERMS:** 12WKS
STAFF TO STUDENT RATIO: 1:18	**STUDY ADDICTS:** N/A
TEACHING: ★★★★	**RESEARCH:** N/A
1STS: 15%	**2,2S:** 27%
2.1S: 56%	**3RDS:** 3%

ADMISSIONS
❍ APPLY DIRECT
Those over 21 (most students) can apply without formal qualifications.

SUBJECTS
ARTS & HUMANITIES 31%   **CONTINUING EDUCATION** 39%
SOCIAL SCIENCES 12%   **OTHER** 18%
BEST Archeology; Biology; Computer Science; Creative Arts; Economics; English-based Studies; European Languages; Geography; Law; Mathematics; Management; Other Languages; Politics; Psychology; Social Geography.

LIBRARIES
❍ 350,000 BOOKS ❍ 335 STUDY PLACES
❍ SPEND PER STUDENT: £££££
The main library is open seven days a week and there are several others locally. The college runs UK Libraries Plus, which lets borrowers access 120 higher education libraries in the UK.

COMPUTERS
❍ 650 WORKSTATIONS ❍ 24-HR ACCESS
❍ SPEND PER STUDENT: ££££
Got the essentials (printers, PCs), helpdesk and some special needs provision.

ENTERTAINMENT ◖◗◖◗◖◗◖◗◖◗◖◗◖◗◖◗◖◗

THE CITY see University of London

THE UNIVERSITY
❍ PRICE OF A PINT OF BEER £1.70
❍ GLASS OF WINE £2..25
❍ CAN OF RED BULL £1.50
When half the busy students have to leg it home to feed the plant, water the cat and put the kids out for the night (or whatever), demand is low.

Bigger things come from the shared University of London facilities.

BARS *The reasonably busy SU bar is more of a convenience than a social hangout, but students can at least enjoy a sneaky tipple after lectures. The ents net is widening with salsa and beach party nights and occasional stand-up, poetry, live music and DJs on Fridays.*

FOOD Malet Street and Gordon Square have small refuelling stops.

SOCIAL

BIRKBECK STUDENTS' UNION
○ 1 SABBATICAL ○ NUS MEMBER
Politically dud, sportingly non-existent, socially lacklustre, the SU is there for essentials alone.

SU FACILITIES
Common room; TV lounge; pool table; photocopier; shop; 'Lamp & Owl' magazine. The University also has a crèche, payphone, advice centre and post office. There's an independent stationers, printing service and general store.

PAID WORK
○ JOB BUREAU ○ PAID WORK: TERM−TIME 99%: HOLS 99%
Since students generally have work already, there's only ULU's (*admittedly massive*) jobshop and careers service.

SPORTS

Sport's purely recreational. The footy team did okay, but the Birks have to use ULU's facilities.

ACCOMMODATION

IN COLLEGE
○ 1ST YRS LIVING IN 0%
○ INSURANCE PREMIUM: £££££
If required places are available in London's inter-collegiate accommodation. The University of London accommodation office is there for students to use and abuse.

EXTERNALLY see University of London.

WELFARE

SERVICES
○ POSTGRAD OFFICER & SOCIETY ○ NIGHTLINE
○ CRIME RATING !!!!!
Advice available through the SU, but the age range of the students means a lot of help comes via academic tutors. While there's a crèche, everything else comes from the University of London.
DISABLED The Disabilities Office supports students with special needs, a disabled students allowance is available for special equipment, software, orthopaedic chairs, induction loops for the hard-of-hearing and so on. Ramps and rails have been installed in the old buildings.

FINANCE
○ AVE DEBT PER YEAR £776 ○ HOME STUDENT FEES £1,122
FEES £3,180 for international undergrads and £9,804-£14,796 for international postgrads. UK postgrads: £3,168 for full-time; £2,124 for part-time; £1,500 for research.
○ ACCESS FUND N/A ○ SUCCESSFUL APPLICATIONS/YR 151
○ AVE PAYMENT £100-£2,625 (PART-TIME) OR £3,500 (FULL-TIME)
SUPPORT Hardship funds, college research funds (which can cover fees and/or maintenance).

UNIVERSITY OF BIRMINGHAM

○ **UNIVERSITY OF BIRMINGHAM** Edgbaston, Birmingham, B15 2TT **TEL** (0121) 414 6727 **E−MAIL** admissions@bham.ac.uk **WEBSITE** www.bham.ac.uk ○ **BIRMINGHAM UNIVERSITY GUILD OF STUDENTS (BUGS)** The University of Birmingham, Edgbaston Park Road, B15 2TU **TEL** (0121) 251 2300 **E−MAIL** enquiries@bugs.bham.ac.uk **WEBSITE** www.bugs.bham.ac.uk

GENERAL

Forget everything you think you know about Birmingham. Well, not quite everything: this is still the UK's second-biggest city, an old *industrial* splurge of a conurbation in the *dead-eye centre of* England. And yes, that Black Country accent *still has acres of comic potential for plummy southern types. But that's as far as it goes:* Birmingham's had a fuller facelift than Wacko Jacko. Built around the Bull Ring centre, the city has *just*

Words in italics are Push's point of view — take it or leave it...

everything a student could hanker after: a *swanky* Selfridges and a smaller Harvey Nicks for *Sloanes and trendies*, every high street chain *imaginable* and a jewellery quarter. Then there's the entertainment: IMAX cinema, NEC for big gigs, a 60m big wheel imported from Paris, *loads* of bars and restaurants, an *infamous* clubbing scene and several miles of Balti houses, selling Brum's very own Indian invention.

The University, 2.5 miles from the town centre and *an island of greenery* amid the bustle of Edgbaston, is *self-consciously* redbrick, although the central area of the campus is *grandly traditional*. Many students are pretty *focused on their degrees, although a lot of them aren't (sport is the main distraction)*.

SEX RATIO: ♀43 ♂57	**FOUNDED:** 1900
FULL-TIME U'GRADS: 19,548	**PART-TIME:** 4,180
POSTGRADS: 7,500	**NON-DEGREE:** 1,690
AVE COURSE: 3YRS	**ETHNIC:** 7%
STATE:PRIVATE SCHOOL: 80:20	**FLUNK RATE:** 7%
MATURE: 12%	**INTERNATIONAL:** 25%
DISABLED: 375	**LOCAL:** 26%

ATMOSPHERE

Cheery, chummy, varied and accommodating. Birmingham is a *welcoming* place to study, although relations with the locals *can be fraught, particularly in student-heavy areas of town, where traffic cone battles at 3am can fray tempers.* Students are *proud* of the University's top-flight status for study and sport. As with many of the redbrick places, it's *pretty middle class,* with big smiles and brownie points for achievement in the sports hall and the exam hall. The student concentration at Selly Oak means that it's *hard to go anywhere without bumping into a familiar face,* but the city's size means that it's *easy to disappear into the shadows if necessary.*

BIRMINGHAM

- **POPULATION** 977,087 ⊙ **CITY CENTRE** 2.5 MILES
- **LONDON** 105 MILES ⊙ **MANCHESTER** 75 MILES
- **COVENTRY** 20 MILES
- **HIGH TEMP** 20 ⊙ **LOW TEMP** 2 ⊙ **RAINFALL** 64

Shopping trollies have been hooked out of canals, concrete has been cobbled or paved, some of the worst architectural monsters have been slain and the whole place is revamped, spruced up and ready to entertain.

TRAVEL

TRAINS Uniquely, there's a station on campus, connecting to Birmingham New Street for mainline links to London (from £9.90 return), Manchester (£18.40), Edinburgh (£58.55) and *just about every other city in the country.*

COACHES £17.60 rtn to London on National Express. Also Manchester (£9.20), Edinburgh (£40.50) and all over. West Midlands Travel and London Liner are on hand too.

CAR A38, M5, M6, M42 are the best roads to get to the University. *Avoid rush-hour unless staring at motionless bumpers sounds like a fun day out.*

AIR My Travel Lite, Duo, Ryanair, FlyBe and other budget airlines jet out of Birmingham International Airport, nine miles east from the campus, with flights to the USA, Europe, Ireland and domestic routes.

HITCHING *Birmingham is the motorway Mecca of England. Pick a junction and get thumbing.*

LOCAL Bus services are late-night-running and *abundant but busy.* It's also easy to get into town, but hard to get around the edge. Overground trains run around the city – *they're faster than buses, but more expensive and unreliable. Possibly useful for those in Selly Oak.*

COLLEGE The University lays on a free bus between Edgbaston and Selly Oak (pass needed), and another from halls to various places around campus with uni ID.

TAXIS About £6 from town to college. *As usual,* minicabs undercut the black cabs.

BICYCLES Bikes are *commonplace* on campus and there are cycle lanes and *plenty* of places to lock them up.

CAREER PROSPECTS

- ⊙ **CAREERS SERVICE** ⊙ **NO. OF STAFF:** 12 FULL/5 PART
- ⊙ **UNEMPLOYED AFTER 6 MTHS:** 4%

Accessible and helpful service with bulletin boards, vacancy lists, employer contacts, website, skills training and other events.

FAMOUS ALUMNI

Hilary Armstrong MP (Chief Whip); Tim Curry (Rocky Horror star); Philippa Forrester (TV presenter); Jeff Green (writer, comedian); Simon Le Bon (Duran Duran); Desmond Morris (zoologist); Sir Paul Nurse (Cancer Research, Nobel winner); Chris Tarrant (TV and radio presenter); Victor Ubogu (rugby player); Ann Widdecombe MP (Con); Victoria Wood (comedian).

FURTHER INFO

- ⊙ **PROSPECTUSES** UNDERGRAD; POSTGRAD; SOME DEPARTMENTS.
- ⊙ **OPEN DAYS**

See www.marketing.bham.ac.uk/admissions/ for more info.

ACADEMIC ⓤⓤⓤⓤⓤⓤⓤⓤⓤⓤⓤⓤ

⊙ **RUSSELL GROUP**

Good library and academic staff and a strong reputation in subjects including medicine, European languages, psychology, sport science, engineering, history and social sciences. Workload is *fairly high* – students have to put in about 40 hours a week during the 15-week semesters. Assessment is a mixture of essays, multiple choice questions, presentations, class tests, practical/laboratory work and formal written exams with some group work involved too.

B

ENTRY POINTS: 260–360	AVE POINTS: 320
APPLICATIONS PER PLACE: 9	CLEARING: 4%
NO. OF TERMS: 2	LENGTH OF TERMS: 15wks
STAFF TO STUDENT RATIO: 1:14	STUDY ADDICTS: 26%
TEACHING: ****	RESEARCH: *****
YEAR ABROAD: 5%	SANDWICH STUDENTS: 2%
1STS: 12%	2.2s: 28%
2.1s: 56%	3RDS: 4%

ADMISSIONS
○ APPLY VIA UCAS/GTTR/DIRECT FOR POSTGRAD

SUBJECTS
ARTS & SOCIAL SCIENCES 28%   **ENGINEERING & PHYSICAL SCIENCES** 26%   **LIFE & HEALTH SCIENCES** 28%
BEST Biology & Related Sciences; Business; Civil, Chemical & Other Engineering; Computer Science; Electronic Engineering; English-based Studies; European Languages & Area Studies; Finance & Accounting; Management; Human & Social Geography; Law; Mechanical Engineering; Medicine & Dentistry; Other Languages & Area Studies; Physical Geography & Environmental Science; Physical Science; Technology.

LIBRARIES
○ **2,500,000** BOOKS ○ **2,280** STUDY PLACES
Even with a gigantic library and nine smaller ones, there's still pressure on spaces. 60,000 of the books are rare tomes in a special collection.

COMPUTERS
○ **2,402** WORKSTATIONS
Students are *chuffed* with the *techie wizardry* on offer. There's free broadband in 80% of rooms and wireless facilities for laptops, video editing suites and assistive technology booths for special needs students around campus. All catered University rooms have internet connections.

ENTERTAINMENT ○○○○○○○○○○

THE CITY
○ PRICE OF A PINT OF BEER £2.30
○ GLASS OF WINE £2.80
○ CAN OF RED BULL £2.50
The town is *jam-packed* with temptations and opportunities. The shopping is *superior*, there's booze and Balti galore and the cinemas, theatres, clubs and music venues *would make a Londoner jealous*. If boredom sets in, Alton Towers, Cadbury's World and Stratford-upon-Avon are all on tap nearby.
CINEMAS The blockbusting UGC multiplex does student discounts and there are three others if that doesn't appeal. Push counted 38 screens in the big cinemas alone and there are various smaller cinemas, including specialist Indian ones and the arty Electric.
THEATRES The Birmingham Rep is *one of the best* in the country. There's also the Alexandra Theatre and the Hippodrome for ballet as well as loads of smaller operations.

PUBS Brum pubs come in handfuls, but not all are student-friendly. Pushplugs: Three Horseshoes; Gun Barrels. *The Station, the Goose and Soak are best avoided.*
CLUBBING An *awesome* club scene has developed recently. Pushplugs: Renaissance; God's Kitchen (Fridays); Miss Moneypenny's; Babooshka; Sundissential.
MUSIC VENUES Stadium stars rock the NEC and NIA, but the *best* venue is Birmingham Academy, whose recent guests have included Primal Scream, Starsailor, The Coral, Athlete, Kings of Leon, Basement Jaxx, Ocean Colour Scene, The Flaming Lips and Black Rebel Motorcycle Club. There's also Ronnie Scott's (jazz) and the Symphony Hall (classical).
OTHER There's the Silver Blades Ice Rink and Merry Hill, which is one of the largest shopping centres in Europe and houses a multiplex cinema and bowling alley. There's also the *eye-catching* Bull Ring shopping centre, home to Selfridges and Harvey Nicks.
EATING OUT Whatever tickles the tastebuds is somewhere in Birmingham. Pushplugs: Polaris; Kushi; Livingroom; Magic Bean (cheap veggie); the Mud Café (*good value* Italian); Selly Sausage (*huge* portions); House of Phoenix (Persian). Otherwise it's local curry houses in Selly Oak.

THE UNIVERSITY
○ PRICE OF A PINT OF BEER £1.90
○ GLASS OF WINE £2.40
○ CAN OF RED BULL £1.65
BARS Joe's (cap 700) is the main hangout and gets *pretty raucous*. There's also the Underground, a recently refurbished club-cum-pub that fits 400. For *pubbier traditionalists*, the Beorma bar does real ale and sofas. There are also bars in all the halls.
THEATRES Brum is *thesp central* – a *serious number* of theatre groups all put on three plays a year. The Allardyce Nicholl Theatre within the guild raises the curtain on many of them.
FILM Various film groups hold screenings around campus.
CLUBBING Fab and Fresh (£3) takes over Joes and The Underground every Saturday night for garage, house, cheese and disco classics. Stomp is the Friday night indie/cheese session and, just to warm up, Villy Vodkas Vodka Factory takes over Joes every Thursday.
FOOD The University has a *clutch* of culinary options: Café Connections (pasta, paninis, coffee) is *pleasant*; Food Court (kebabs, jackets, fry-ups and pasta) is cheap but busy; Avanti (baguettes, pasta, spuds, curries etc.) also *gets hectic*; Go (sandwich bar); Cafégo (deli bar); Go2 and Cybergo (variations on the theme); and loads of other sandwich bars.
OTHER Balls *ago-go* provide *OTT celebrations* for freshers, graduates, departments and others.

Words in italics are Push's point of view — take it or leave it...

B

SOCIAL ()()()()()()()()()()()()

BIRMINGHAM UNIVERSITY GUILD OF STUDENTS (BUGS)
○ **7** SABBATICALS   ○ TURNOUT AT LAST BALLOT 11%
○ NUS MEMBER
Birmingham isn't much of a political hotspot.
Instead, the 14-strong SU executive look after
welfare and ents and *cosy up nicely* to the
University suits.

SU FACILITIES
The Guild building provides: three bars; nightclub;
two canteens; four snack bars; a fast-food outlet;
pool tables; meeting rooms; minibus/car/van hire;
Endsleigh Insurance; HSBC banks and ATMs;
photocopiers; fax; printing; photo booth;
payphones; advice centre; crèche; TV/video games;
jukeboxes; general store; stationery shop; post
office; vending machines; bookshop; STA travel;
ticket agency; launderette; CD shop.

CLUBS (NON-SPORTING)
AngSoc; Animal Campaigner; Alternative
Performing Arts; Astronomical; Ballroom Dancing;
Bridge; BALD (Before and After Lecture
Drinking); BUST the war; Carnival; Cheerleading;
Chess; Circus; Debating; Duke of Edinburgh;
Fetish; Gliding; Goth; International Volunteers;
Iranian Students; Korean; Malaysian; LINKS
(St Johns Ambulance) Mauritian; Medieval
Excursions & Drinking; Mexican; Motor Club;
Nordic; Pagan; Paintball; Photo; Pool & Snooker;
Palestinian; Portuguese; Real Ale; Sikh;
Singaporean; Sri Lankan; Stop AIDS; Students
with Disabilities; Taiwanese; Talking Heads;
Turkish Students; Wilderness Medicine; Women's
Association. **See also Clubs tables.**

OTHER ORGANISATIONS
Free student paper 'Redbrick' is published
regularly by Bugs. 'Burn FM' broadcasts on the
airwaves and the web. There's a TV station and a
very active Rag group, Carnival. A couple of
community action groups help out around Brum.

RELIGIOUS
○ UNIVERSITY CHAPLAINCY (MULTI-FAITH)
The University's St Francis Hall is a
multi-denominational centre, catering for all
Jewish and Christian hues. There's also a Muslim
prayer room. Birmingham itself is a multicultural
city and has cathedrals and churches of all types,
as well as mosques, temples and synagogues.

PAID WORK
○ JOB BUREAU   ○ PAID WORK TERM-TIME 30%; HOLS 30%
The Job Zone arranges jobs and placements with the
help of the careers centre's services. Loads of
opportunities around campus in the kitchens, libraries,
bars, alumni office, careers service and so on.

SPORTS ()()()()()()()()()()()()()

○ RECENT SUCCESSES FOOTBALL, HOCKEY, RUGBY
○ BUSA RANKING 3
Birmingham think of Loughborough in roughly
the same way that Oxford think about
Cambridge: horrid little upstarts who need to be
taught a lesson (but who usually win). The rivalry
is intense and Brum are deservedly proud of their
sporting record.

SPORTS FACILITIES
Five multi-purpose pitches for football, rugby and
hockey; cricket pitch; squash court; tennis court;
basketball court; netball court; sports hall;
swimming pool; running track; athletics field;
gym; aerobics studio; sauna/steam room; lake at
Edgbaston; river at Worcester; gymnastics centre;
climbing wall; martial arts centre; sports shop.
Courses are £11 for a term of ten classes; gym
membership is £95 a year (off peak), £131 peak.
Club membership £60 a year.
IN THE CITY a sports centre; running track; tennis
and squash courts; swimming pool; ice rink;
croquet/bowling green; golf course; and a dry
ski slope.

SPORTING CLUBS
10-pin bowling; American football; Cricket;
Gymnastics & Trampolining; Ice Hockey; Ju-Jitsu;

> ◉ **'It was a time when the number of times one
> could get laid was exceeded only by the
> number of job opportunities – a state of affairs
> which applies only in the House of Commons. And
> to think we did it on local authority grants'** – the
> late Tony Banks MP, on his student days.

Words in italics are Push's point of view – take it or leave it...

Korfball; Kung Fu; Lacrosse; Lifesaving; Mountaineering; Ninpo-Budo; Orienteering; Rowing; Sailing; Ski-Snowboard; Squash; Street Sports; Surf; Table Tennis; Tae Kwon Do; Tennis; Triathlon; Ultimate Frisbee; Volleyball; Water Polo; Windsurfing; Wing Chun. **See also Clubs tables.**

ATTRACTIONS
The national golf centre has hosted the Davis Cup, the NEC held the 2003 world indoor athletics championships. Edgbaston is a Test cricket ground and home to Warwickshire CCC. Local football teams are Aston Villa and Birmingham (*decent*), Wolves (*less decent*), West Brom (*middling*) and Walsall (*dire*).

ACCOMMODATION

IN UNIVERSITY
○ **CATERED** 9% ○ **COST** £100 (31/42WKS)
○ **SELF-CATERING** 22% ○ **COST** £78 (35/42/50WKS)
○ **1ST YRS LIVING IN** 90%
○ **INSURANCE PREMIUM** £££
AVAILABILITY Most first years are guaranteed accommodation, although those who make it to Brum through clearing or live locally aren't always lucky. Accommodation is *fiercely expensive*, although much has been refurbished and caters for disabled students. Most halls are in one of three student villages, the Vale village is the latest to get a facelift. 80% of accommodation is within 25 mins hot-foot from college. *None are heinously awful.* Shackleton Hall, in the Vale, *is the address of choice.* Cleaners only look after communal areas, although in the summer vacation rooms are cleaned and *cleared of any students buried by their own overflowing ash-trays.* Some of the self-catering *inmates* can buy a 'MEAL plan', which lets them *gorge themselves silly* in University canteens.
CAR PARKING Available but *strictly rationed.* A (free) permit is needed.

EXTERNALLY
○ **AVE RENT** £50
AVAILABILITY *It's tough to find a decent pad at a pretty price.* But as just about everyone descends on the same neighbourhood – Selly Oak – *they're all in the same boat.*
HOUSING HELP Housing services runs a property registration scheme, checking out houses before they're advertised. There's also advice for those *plagued by dodgy private landlords.* The Guild's advice and representation centre offers advice on housing issues. The University has a hand in www.birminghamstudentpad.co.uk for online hunting.

WELFARE

SERVICES
○ **LGBT OFFICER & SOCIETY** ○ **WOMEN'S OFFICER & SOCIETY** ○ **MATURE STUDENTS' OFFICER & SOCIETY** ○ **INTERNATIONAL STUDENTS' OFFICER & SOCIETY** ○ **ETHNIC MINORITIES OFFICER & SOCIETY** ○ **POSTGRAD OFFICER & SOCIETY** ○ **DISABILITIES OFFICER & SOCIETY** ○ **NIGHTLINE** ○ **UNIVERSITY COUNSELLORS** 3 FULL/7 PART ○ **CRIME RATING** !!!!
Brum *knows how to look after students.* There are University welfare and Guild services and students have welfare tutors.
HEALTH On-campus NHS practice with eight GPs, five nurses, an osteopath, a part-time health visitor and a part-time midwife. On-campus dental practice with three dentists and dental nurses.
WOMEN Women's association runs welfare drop-ins and has a women's room with advice leaflets, books and chill out space. There are harassment advisers at the University for all students.
CRECHES/NURSERY Two nurseries with 124 places (3mths-5yrs).
DISABILITIES Campus is *large and hilly* with several listed buildings that can't be properly adapted, although the newer buildings are a *bit better.* Sports facilities are adapted for access. There's also dyslexia tuition, note-taking, assisted technology (kurzweil, jaws, texthelp, inspiration) and extended loans in the libraries.
CRIME Burglary can be a bit of a problem *in PlayStation-heavy student areas.* The police *do their bit* with a 'safer students' programme.
DRUGS *Guild membership is whisked away if they find your stash.*

FINANCE
○ **AVE DEBT PER YEAR** £3,546
○ **HOME STUDENT FEES** £3,000
FEES International student fees: £9,000 (non-lab), £11,700 (lab), £21,300 (clinical). UK postgrads pay a *high* £4,000.
○ **ACCESS FUND** £902,155 ○ **SUCCESSFUL APPLICATIONS/YR** 1,413 ○ **AVE PAYMENT** £100-3,500
SUPPORT A range of bursaries is offered by both University and Guild, for academic success and financial hardship. Amounts vary from £1,000 to full payment of fees and maintenance payments at ESRC rate.

▶ BIRMINGHAM CONSERVATOIRE
see *UCE Birmingham*

▶ BOLTON INSTITUTE FOR HIGHER EDUCATION
see *University of Bolton*

Words in italics are Push's point of view – take it or leave it...

B

UNIVERSITY OF BOLTON

FORMERLY BOLTON INSTITUTE OF HIGHER EDUCATION

○ **THE UNIVERSITY OF BOLTON** Deane Road, Bolton, Lancashire, BL3 5AB **TEL** (01204) 900 600 **E-MAIL** enquiries@bolton.ac.uk **WEBSITE** www.bolton.ac.uk ○ **UNIVERSITY OF BOLTON STUDENTS' UNION** Deane Road, Bolton, Lancashire, BL3 5AB **TEL** (01204) 900 850 **E-MAIL** bisu@bolton.ac.uk **WEBSITE** www.ubsu.org.uk

GENERAL ◖◗◖◗◖◗◖◗◖◗◖◗◖◗◖◗◖◗◖◗◖◗◖◗

Growing up amongst the likes of Liverpool, Manchester and Preston wouldn't do much for a smaller industrial town's confidence, but Bolton is big and hard enough to stand its ground as a major Northern civic centre. Of eight universities in the North West, Bolton is the newest (it changed its name to reflect its university status in 2005), although its origins as a centre for vocational and educational training date back to the early 19th century. Just outside the town centre the main Deane campus is a child of the 60s, dominated by the new £6m glass-fronted Design Studio. *This isn't the place to get back to nature – the only green bits are hungover students –* but there's the Lake District, moors and dales not too far away *for communing with Mother Earth.*

SEX RATIO: ♂51 ♀49	**FOUNDED:** 1982
FULL-TIME U'GRADS: 2,641	**PART-TIME:** 1,588
POSTGRADS: 1,388	**NON-DEGREE:** 2,269
AVE COURSE: 3YRS	**ETHNIC:** 28%
STATE:PRIVATE SCHOOL: 97:3	**FLUNK RATE:** 32%
MATURE: 86%	**INTERNATIONAL:** 25%
DISABLED: 35	**LOCAL:** 80%

ATMOSPHERE

Studying at Bolton can be a quiet experience – except for the noise of traffic from the surrounding roads. Large numbers of mature students and locals means that the University is more of a drop-in lecture centre than a cosy student bubble, although that's not to say there's nothing in the way of ribaldry and frolicking – just on a smaller scale than at other places.

SITES

DEANE CAMPUS The largest campus with most of the students and facilities, including the SU, sports hall, the Design Studio and a range of cafés. Prone to fits of redevelopment, (i.e. holes and scaffolding), until the new student centre is up and humming.
CHADWICK CAMPUS (Arts, Education and Cultural & Creative Studies) 800m from the Deane Campus, Chadwick holds a theatre, refectory and shop as well as teaching facilities. *Students are a little more laid back and there's more evidence of pleasant greenery.*

BOLTON

○ **POPULATION** 261,037 ○ **CITY CENTRE** 800M
○ **LONDON** 182 MILES ○ **MANCHESTER** 10 MILES
○ **BLACKPOOL** 35 MILES
○ **HIGH TEMP** 20 ○ **LOW TEMP** 1 ○ **RAINFALL** 68

Bolton is a busy industrial town – *think Phoenix Nights –* and the area around the University is *something of a strip mall –* thick with roads, supermarkets and drive-thru burger joints. *The upside of the setting is the number of modern amenities (malls). The downside is it looks a bit grim.* Relics of the cloth industry include the Tonge Moor Textile Museum. The Last Drop Village is *Bolton's answer to the theme park,* an 18th-century converted farmhouse extended to create a *picturesque* village with cottages, pub, restaurant, hotel, craft shops and other *would-be tourist traps (if there were any tourists). The world is waiting for Bolton Council to formally apologise for Sara Cox.*

TRAVEL

TRAINS Bolton mainline station is 800m from the University and offers connections to Manchester (£3.20) every 15 mins.
COACHES The coach station (next to the railway) has National Express services to most major cities. Return to London from £18.50.
CAR The devilish A666, M61, M62 and A679 all serve Bolton. *Parking is as easy as a drunken hooker* with plenty of free space on campus for student cars. The town is *cheapish* for parking too.
AIR Manchester Airport (EasyJet) is 30 mins by car.
HITCHING *The network of main roads means hitching isn't a crazy option.*
LOCAL Buses are *refreshingly regular,* with many using the *inexpensive* services to get to and from halls until 11.30pm. A nightbus from Manchester chugs in at 1am, 2.30am at weekends.
TAXIS *More than enough.* Town to halls costs about two or three quid.
BICYCLES Even with cycle lanes, busy roads mean *cycling in Bolton can seem like running a gauntlet of death. That doesn't stop people nicking bikes though. They probably use them for car parts.*

CAREER PROSPECTS

○ **CAREERS SERVICE** ○ **NO. OF STAFF** 1 FULL/3 PART
○ **UNEMPLOYED AFTER 6 MTHS** 7%

The Student Centre *looks weedy but punches well above its weight:* newsletters, bulletin boards, careers library, interview training and CV surgery sessions.

FAMOUS ALUMNI

Stephen Blyth (Gregory award poet); Josie Cichockyi (paralympic champion and first female in a wheelchair to break the three hour barrier in the London marathon); Peter White (former Coates Viyella).

B

SPECIAL FEATURES
Bolton has two student intakes a year, accepting applications for February and September entry.

FURTHER INFO
⊙ **PROSPECTUSES** UNDERGRAD; POSTGRAD; SOME DEPARTMENTAL
⊙ **OPEN DAYS**
There are nine open days a year – see website for all admission details.

ACADEMIC ⓊⓊⓊⓊⓊⓊⓊⓊⓊⓊⓊ

Bolton the town is big on industry. Bolton the University is big on industrial courses. *Business and materials-based courses are big boomers and the textiles department gets brownie points for designing the material for Man U football shirts.* Psychology, Health Studies, Education and Community Nursing *are other strong points* and the Uni also does a lot of design work for the Ministry of Defence (*all a bit hush hush*). Courses are modular, *meaning if a student bails before three years are up they'll still take home a certificate in something.* Teaching is spread throughout the day (9am-9pm) so there's a good deal of flexibility in learning (*or drinking*) schedules. Most notes and study aids are on the web *for those who didn't pay attention first time around.*

ENTRY POINTS: 140-280	AVE POINTS: 174
APPLICATIONS PER PLACE: 3	CLEARING: 25%
NO. OF TERMS: 2	LENGTH OF TERMS: 18wks
STAFF TO STUDENT RATIO: N/A	STUDY ADDICTS: 26%
TEACHING: **	RESEARCH: *
YEAR ABROAD: 8%	SANDWICH STUDENTS: 15%
1STS: 7%	2.2S: 42%
2.1S: 32%	3RDS: 11%

ADMISSIONS
⊙ **APPLY VIA UCAS**
The admissions policy is geared towards roping in what they call 'non-traditional students', *although that's a bit of a meaningless umbrella.*

SUBJECTS
ART & DESIGN 14%   **BUILT ENVIRONMENT** 4%
BUSINESS STUDIES 14%   **CULTURAL & CREATIVE STUDIES** 7%   **EDUCATION** 2%   **ENGINEERING & DESIGN** 7%   **HEALTH & SOCIAL SCIENCE** 14%
PSYCHOLOGY & LIFE SCIENCE 13%
BEST Nursing.
UNUSUAL Animation and Illustration; Community Health and Wellbeing; Computer Games Design; Criminological & Forensic Psychology; Media, Writing & Production; Sport & Exercise Psychology; Special Effect Development.

LIBRARIES
⊙ **175,000** BOOKS   ⊙ **941** STUDY PLACES
⊙ **SPEND PER STUDENT** £££
Libraries at Deane Street and Eagle Mall. *Okay, but not really enough books.*

COMPUTERS
⊙ **522** WORKSTATIONS   ⊙ **24**-HR ACCESS
⊙ **SPEND PER STUDENT** £££££
There's a 24-hour PC lab with more computers stashed in various departments.

OTHER LEARNING FACILITIES
Chadwick has a drama studio and a CAD lab for budding e-designers. A £17m redevelopment of Deane campus completed in summer 2004 includes a new design centre and a face-lift for the textile labs. There's an incubator unit for business start-ups (*not baby chickens*).

ENTERTAINMENT ⓊⓊⓊⓊⓊⓊⓊⓊⓊ

BOLTON
⊙ **PRICE OF A PINT OF BEER** £1.80
⊙ **GLASS OF WINE** £2.30   ⊙ **CAN OF RED BULL** £2.30
PUBS *Plenty of liver-curdling possibilities.* 'The drunken mile' is a row of about 20 bars – *the bar-boom has hit Bolton hard and new ones are opening all the time. Some town centre pubs can get a bit grumpy at students but many are amiable enough. Malloney's is popular during cocktail hour for those at the posher end.* Pushplugs: J2 (four floors of mainstream music); BL1 (cheap); Cattle Market (near halls); Varsity; Swan; Macaulays; Reflex; Hawthorns (*where you might bump in to Danny from McFly if you're, um, lucky*).
CINEMAS Three miles away, the ten-screen UGC *is a bit of a hike.* The Vue (13 screens) charges students £3.50 and 'The Valley' (14 screens) is a snip at £2.50.
THEATRES The Octagon hands out free student tickets for a mix of modern plays, Shakespeare and panto at Xmas. Book three days in advance to get a student discount.
CLUBBING *J2 has the variety to keep punters keen.* Refles, Swan, Baracuda and Macaulays do student nights and Hawthorn's is an indie hang-out. *Atlantis & IKON are worth notice too.*
MUSIC VENUES Various venues with anything from rock to Ravel. Pushplugs: Oscar's Café (jazz, blues, rock); Gypsy's Tent (alternative); Albert Hall Complex (classical, blues); Mosegate (tribute bands); Bar No. 15 (local bands).

⊙ **The vice-chancellors of 33 universities are paid more than the Prime Minister.**

EATING OUT *Kentucky fried creatures and various McNibbles can be caught and eaten over the road but there's not much doing for the dedicated epicure.* Pushplugs: Olive Press; Tiggi's (pizza) is cheap; Cook in the Books is veggie.

THE UNIVERSITY

- **PRICE OF A PINT OF BEER** £1.60
- **GLASS OF WINE** £2.30 **CAN OF RED BULL** N/A

The SU makes a token effort but generally all is quiet on the entertainment front.

BARS The Venue bar in the *freakin' ugly* Union building opens 11am-11pm and shows *loads of sport on the permanently playing big screen TV. The cool kids pop down for a few drinks then make tracks for town.*

THEATRES *Minimal provision* since the drama department shut.

FILM The film society puts on a few screenings a year.

CLUBBING/MUSIC VENUES Lesser known visiting bands and guest DJs use the Venue as a venue (*so that's why...*). Several club nights go on but most clubland fun is based around the SU's Macauley's sponsorship deal.

COMEDY/CABARET *Occasionally found at the Venue, but don't hold your breath.*

FOOD *There are several slop-stops and café clusters around the campuses.* The Venue dishes up from breakfast till 6pm with pizza and a pint deals *seemingly every other day.*

OTHER Black-tie balls for Christmas, Spring, Graduation and various sports.

SOCIAL ◑◑◑◑◑◑◑◑◑◑◑◑◑

UNIVERSITY OF BOLTON STUDENTS' UNION

- **2** SABBATICALS **TURNOUT AT LAST BALLOT** 14%
- **NUS MEMBER**

SU FACILITIES

Not one for the politicos, the SU concentrates on running its various drinking societies (sorry, 'sporting clubs') and keeping its ents afloat. Relations with the University have been positively glowing since the new Vice Chancellor started. The Union has bagged extra funding and is due a new (and hopefully less architecturally offensive) building by 2008.

SU FACILITIES

One bar; one café; pool room; three meeting rooms; juke box; gaming machines; general store; stationery shop; photocopier, printing and fax services; photo booth; advice centre.

CLUBS (NON-SPORTING)

Alternative Therapy; Christian Union; Co-operative Forum; Disabled Students Action Group; Film; Friends of Palestine; Mature Students; Motor Sports. **See also Clubs tables.**

OTHER ORGANISATIONS

Bolton has eight proud pages in Student Direct – the *ad-laden* free weekly mag run jointly with Salford and Manchester. No Rag, but there is a volunteering group to keep *do-gooding types occupied.* A group on Chadwick campus does work on sexing-up the local area.

RELIGIOUS

- **1** CHAPLAIN (COFE)

The University also has four volunteer chaplains for Muslim, Hindu and other Christian faiths. There's a multi-faith prayer room on campus and facilities in town for Muslims, Hindu, RC, CofE, Baptist, URC, Methodist, Quaker and Scientology practitioners.

PAID WORK

- **JOB BUREAU**

The job shop at the Student Centre posts part-time vacancies. Bar, restaurant and supermarket work is fairly common.

SPORTS ◑◑◑◑◑◑◑◑◑◑◑◑◑

- **BUSA RANKING** 96

The SU runs all sports clubs and arrangements and keeps costs to a minimum to preserve sports for all levels of involvement. Sports Hall and gym induction costs £4, and then a *bargainous* £15 will buy membership for a whole year. *Team competitions occur more in the pub than in the field. Boat races at Bolton are more likely to entail beer and bar stools than boats.*

SPORTS FACILITIES

Two football pitches; rugby, hockey and all-weather pitches; cricket wicket; basketball, squash and netball courts; sports hall, gym, multigym; running track; croquet lawn/bowling green; climbing hall; health and fitness centre and sporting lake available.

SPORTING CLUBS

Circuit Training, Gaelic Football; Hung Kuen (Shaolin Kung Fu); Snowboarding; Tai Chi; Women's Hockey. **See also Clubs tables.**

ATTRACTIONS

Bolton Wanderers FC are kicking around nearby.

ACCOMMODATION ◑◑◑◑◑◑◑◑◑

IN UNIVERSITY

- **SELF-CATERING** 21% **COST** £55 (40WKS)
- **1ST YRS LIVING IN** 15%
- **INSURANCE PREMIUM** ££££

AVAILABILITY *First years have guaranteed accommodation on campus to look forward to and, bearing in mind that most mature students* look after themselves and many others are local, few are left in the lurch. Halls are good quality, with shared kitchens and bathrooms. Orlando village houses 380 in a collection of flats ten mins walk from the Deane campus. Hollins Halls attract a fair few (perhaps it's the red-light area location...). Both have net access. Beefy security guards fend off intruders and throw out guests come midnight – pyjama parties not allowed. **CAR PARKING** Car parks at both halls, but finding a space can be a pain in the axle.

EXTERNALLY
○ **AVE RENT** £40
AVAILABILITY Accommodation is reasonably easy to find and of decent quality to boot. In the Great Home Quest, the first task is to look for a shared house preferably in Chorley Old Road, Chorley New Road, Heaton Park Road, Queen's Park Road or just Park Road. Rough Darcy Leaver and the crime-ridden Mencroft Avenue area are best avoided – otherwise speak softly and carry a large dog.
HOUSING HELP The Student Centre helps vet contracts, gives legal advice and publishes vacancy lists.

WELFARE ○○○○○○○○○○○○○

SERVICES
○ **WOMEN'S OFFICER** ○ **MATURE STUDENTS' SOCIETY** ○ **INTERNATIONAL STUDENTS' SOCIETY** ○ **SELF-DEFENCE CLASSES** ○ **NIGHTLINE** ○ **UNIVERSITY COUNSELLORS** 1 PART ○ **CRIME RATING** !!!
The Advice Unit gives out financial and immigration help.
DISABILITIES A University Disabilities Officer provides support on all campuses. Wheelchair access is generally very good, especially in the SU. Braille, ramps, adapted accommodation and large print signs for the visually impaired (medically or alcoholically).

FINANCE
○ **AVE DEBT PER YEAR** £3,356 ○ **HOME STUDENT FEES** £3,000 **FEES** Non-UK students pay around £7,500. A PGCE costs £2,000; other postgrad courses vary.
○ **ACCESS FUND** £600,000 ○ **SUCCESSFUL APPLICATIONS/YR** 344
SUPPORT Budget advice, hardship funds, emergency loans and some bursaries available. The Bolton Bursary is worth up to £300 to poorer students; the Bolton Scholarship (non means-tested) offers £700 to those who came to the University after studying at a partner college.

▶ **BOLTON INSTITUTE FOR HIGHER EDUCATION**
see University of Bolton

BOURNEMOUTH UNIVERSITY

FORMERLY BOURNEMOUTH POLYTECHNIC AND DORSET INSTITUTE

1) ○ **BOURNEMOUTH UNIVERSITY** Talbot Campus, Fern Barrow, Bournemouth, BH12 5BB **TEL** (01202) 524 111 **E-MAIL** enquiries@bournemouth.ac.uk **WEBSITE** www.bournemouth.ac.uk ○ **THE STUDENTS' UNION AT BOURNEMOUTH UNIVERSITY**, Talbot Campus, Fern Barrow, Bournemouth, BH12 5BB **TEL** (01202) 965 765 **E-MAIL** subu@bournemouth.ac.uk **WEBSITE** www.subu.org.uk
2) ○ **BOURNEMOUTH UNIVERSITY** Lansdowne Campus, Christchurch Road and Holdenhurst Road, Bournemouth, BH1 3LT

GENERAL ○○○○○○○○○○○○○

Bournemouth is the largest of three towns rolled into one, with Poole to the west and Christchurch to the east and 350,000 people shared out between them. Following the coast east, the New Forest stretches inland. The main Talbot Campus of the University is technically in Poole, 2.5 miles north of Bournemouth town centre. It's a modern campus, resembling beige Lego linked by brick pathways. This is reflected in its single-minded, career-oriented philosophy.

SEX RATIO: ♂45 ♀55	FOUNDED: 1976
FULL-TIME U'GRADS: 10,106	PART-TIME: 3,569
POSTGRADS: 1,526	NON-DEGREE: 2,058
AVE COURSE: 4YRS	ETHNIC: 9%
STATE:PRIVATE SCHOOL: 93:7	FLUNK RATE: 13%
MATURE: 21%	INTERNATIONAL: 8%
DISABLED: 410	LOCAL: 17%

ATMOSPHERE
The student body tends to be middle-class, clean-cut and car-owning. It's a high spec world with teeth gritted for the free market, a more economic, plastic substitute for the original

B

ivory tower. *The focus is getting a return on the investment of time and money, rather than a four year holiday. Having said that, in the last few years, the expansion of the University has made Bournemouth less of an undertaker's waiting room and more of a happening funville, full of eager students.*

SITES

LANSDOWNE CAMPUS (4,500 students – Health, Community Studies, Design, Engineering, postgrad Business School) Lansdowne is *less of a campus and more a collection of buildings* in Bournemouth's town centre, near the bus and train stations and less than a mile from the sea. SUBU's nightspot, the Old Fire Station, is based here.

BOURNEMOUTH/POOLE

- **POPULATION** 138,400 - **CITY CENTRE** 2.5 MILES
- **LONDON** 100 MILES - **SOUTHAMPTON** 26 MILES
- **BRISTOL** 60 MILES
- **HIGH TEMP** 22 - **LOW TEMP** 2 - **RAINFALL** 67

In summer, Bournemouth's a bristling, bustling town full of tourists, little hotels, sandy beaches, sea and ice-cream melting down your wrist. It doesn't totally close in winter, but there's a little less fun to be had. It does have 2,000 acres of parks in town though and *has enough shops to keep students kitted out, although true shopaholics may start to feel faint and shaky after a while.* The urban village of Winton, less than a mile from the campus, has shops for *mundane necessities.* Not far away, just to the west of Poole/Bournemouth, is the World Heritage Site – the Jurassic Coast – which is now a *major* tourist attraction and area of interest to naturalists *and Alan Titchmarsh fans.*

TRAVEL

TRAINS From Bournemouth station, two miles from the campus, to London (£27.00), Brighton (£19.95) and all over.
COACHES Megabus run twice daily to and from London (from £1 each way) – *third world transport at third world prices.* National Express also run (as low as £3 if you pre-book).
AIR Bournemouth International Airport is about five miles away. Ryanair fly from there to Dublin, Glasgow and Barcelona. Rockhopper fly to the Channel Islands. Budget flights include various European destinations from Thomsonfly and Belfast (Jet2).
CAR The A38, A31 and A35. *Many Bournemouth students have cars, despite parking shortages, particularly at Lansdowne Campus.*
FERRIES From Poole's busy port to the Channel Islands and France.
UNIVERSITY The University subsidises the Unilinx bus service (35p a go), which nips between the campuses and town.
TAXIS Taxis are *frequent and easy to pick up* from the town centre and other locations. Average cost varies but between £2.50 and £7 will take you most places around town. Some firms offer discounts or frequent user deals. It's often cheaper to book ahead.
BICYCLES *Top notch* cycle routes lead to and from the University's Talbot Campus. The local area is

fairly bike-friendly (some hills, but also paths that follow former railway lines into the towns and out into the countryside). Bike lock-ups/sheds on both campuses. *The aptly named Cemetery Junction roundabout is deadly.*

CAREER PROSPECTS
- **CAREERS SERVICE** - **NO. OF STAFF** 6 FULL-TIME
- **UNEMPLOYED AFTER 6 MTHS** 21%

Workshops in CV writing, interview skills, assistance with finding placements, links with local business. *Bar sitting the interviews for them, the University does just about everything in its power to hoist students up onto the career ladder.* Personal Development Planning is taken seriously and learners are encouraged to make themselves employable from day one.

FAMOUS ALUMNI
Toby Farrow (playwright); Michael Jackson (*not that one*, the former *big cheese* at C4); Rachel Jones (Radio One breakfast show producer *and target of Chris Moyles' jibes*); Paul Kavanagh (computer animator, The Phantom Menace); Tom Lawton (inventor); Rachel McTavish (ITV newsreader); Tommy Sandhu (TV presenter).

SPECIAL FEATURES
The first bunch of *budding Hiltons* should take up their places at the world's first fully commercial teaching hotel, in which the University has a hand, in 2008.

FURTHER INFO
- **PROSPECTUSES** UNDERGRAD; POSTGRAD.
- **OPEN DAYS**

Also a CD-Rom for international students, an accommodation DVD and a handy 'Money Matters' leaflet..

ACADEMIC ⓤⓤⓤⓤⓤⓤⓤⓤⓤⓤⓤⓤ

Bournemouth's *best known* for its media school (which fittingly enough has just been made the UK's only Centre of Excellence in Media Practice) with courses in journalism, PR, computer animation and scriptwriting – *just take a look at the alumni.* Most are sandwich courses involving work placements for a year. *The record of getting into these cut-throat industries at the end is impressive.* There's also a burgeoning Peer Assisted Learning Scheme, where second years enourage freshers to *get their noses to the grindstone.*

ENTRY POINTS: 180-300	**AVE POINTS: 259**
APPLICATIONS PER PLACE: 5	**CLEARING: 7%**
NO. OF TERMS: 3	**LENGTH OF TERMS: 11 WKS**
STAFF TO STUDENT RATIO: 1:12	**STUDY ADDICTS: 5%**
TEACHING: ★★	**RESEARCH: ★★★**
YEAR ABROAD: 2%	**SANDWICH STUDENTS: 62%**
1STS: 10%	**2.2S: 34%**
2.1S: 53%	**3RDS: 3%**

Words in italics are Push's point of view — take it or leave it...

ADMISSIONS
○ **APPLY VIA UCAS/DIRECT FOR PART-TIME COURSES/NMAS FOR NURSING**
Summer schools ease returnees to study back in gently.

SUBJECTS
BUSINESS & LAW 25%   **CONSERVATION SCIENCES** 6%
DESIGN/ENGINEERING/COMPUTERS 24%   **MEDIA** 22%
HEALTH/COMMUNITY STUDIES 6%   **SERVICES** 17%
BEST Communications/Information Studies; Finance/Accounting; Psychology; Technology.
UNUSUAL Food Marketing; Forensic Archaeology; Sports Management (golf).

LIBRARIES
○ **400,000 BOOKS** ○ **1,000 STUDY PLACES**
The library has a network of tutor librarians specialising in each of the University's academic areas.

COMPUTERS
○ **1,700 WORKSTATIONS** ○ **24-HR ACCESS**
Many lecturers put lecture notes online and there've been experiments into the *wonderful world* of podcasts and setting up a Virtual Learning Environment– *good news for slackers*. Some of the IT equipment is *flashy stuff*, such as the UK's National Centre for Computer Animation and a CAD lab modelling facility (*that's computer modelling, not the other kind*). Not everyone gets to play with them though.

OTHER LEARNING FACILITIES
Music rehearsal studio; audio and TV editing suites including fully working TV studio.

ENTERTAINMENT ○○○○○○○○○○

BOURNEMOUTH/POOLE
○ **PRICE OF A PINT OF BEER** £1.90
○ **GLASS OF WINE** £2.50
○ **CAN OF RED BULL** £2
CINEMAS Bournemouth has an IMAX, ABC and Odeon and Poole, a UCI and the Lighthouse Arts Centre.
THEATRES The Pavilion for 'shows', *in the spangly-costumed sense of the word*. The Lighthouse is for *serious* plays and musicals (with student discounts).
PUBS Around Old Christchurch Road there's a popular strip of pubs. *Try Walkabout, Bliss and Consortium (alternative feel).*
CLUBBING *A great long string* of clubs down Holdenhurst Road, Christchurch Road and down by the pier. Alcatraz is a *home-from-home* for many international students with Latin sounds and Eurohits. *Most prefer Union-run theme nights at the Old Fire Station.* Berlins offers cheap nights and a foam party. The *hugely popular but slightly townie* Opera House offers 'Slinky' at weekends and 'Hot And Horny' on Thursdays. The Great Escape provides R'n'B,

house and breakbeats. Lots of table dancing clubs too, *if that's your cuppa coffee.*
MUSIC VENUES Bournemouth's *muscling its way* on to the gigging scene and attracts the likes of Girls Aloud, Stereophonics and Scissor Sisters. The Lighthouse is the home of the Bournemouth Symphony Orchestra – one of the UK's major orchestras. BIC has big rock names. The Villa is a step down in size from that. The Consortium in Bournemouth Square hosts alternative music. Mr Smiths *is a scuzzy, fun little place if you like rock, punk and metal ska.* The Gander and O'Neills host local bands.
COMEDY/CABARET Peter Kay, Jo Brand and Eddie Izzard have all garnered the giggles at BIC.
EATING OUT *Plenty to hasten a slide into obesity,* from Dominoes to Café Rouge and El Gringoes (Mexican) to beachside seafood joints. Charminster Road is good for curry at Coriander and *appetising* Middle Eastern bites at the Baraca Café and Restaurant. The Caribbean Café Bar on Old Christchurch Road has a student night Mondays with special promos, plus Salsa and Reggae nights and an all-day eat-as-much-as-you-like buffet for £5 on Sundays.

THE UNIVERSITY
○ **PRICE OF A PINT OF BEER** £2.10
○ **GLASS OF WINE** £3.20
○ **CAN OF RED BULL** £1.50
BARS SU-run Dylan's is a non-smoking pub-style bar with the odd live band playing, quiz nights and *good value* food during the day. D2 is a café bar with *more pretensions (less grease, table service).*
THEATRES Drama isn't strong but the Allsebrook Lecture Theatre is there for the annnual SU thesp-athon.
FILM There's the Good Film Club.
MUSIC VENUES Bands like Hard-Fi and, er, Karl Kennedy off 'Neighbours' have stormed through the Old Fire Station (cap 1,200).
CLUBBING The *hugely popular listed-building-cum-bopspot* Old Fire Station tries to cover all bases and *mostly succeeds* with Fancy Dress Mondays – from chavs to Playboy bunnies. Wednesday nights alternate between the Comedy factory and Rock City. Friday is Lollipop (pop anthems), Also: Loveshack (Sat, retro and contemporary) and other parties.
COMEDY/CABARET Every two weeks at the Old Fire Station and at Talbot.
FOOD All the bars do food. Dylan's and D2 do *great* pizzas for £2.50 and *the best wedges in the world*. The Student Refectory (8.30am-3.30pm) is *very busy at lunchtimes but quiet earlier, when they do a fab brekkie.* Jumbucks is an 'Australian Pie Bar' franchised into the University (£2.75 a meal, *possibly kangaroo meat or possum kidneys*). Studio Café Bar is a cyber café with muffins, danish etc.
OTHER The largest SU summer ball in the country (6,000 students) as well as Freshers' and Graduation Balls.

Words in italics are Push's point of view – take it or leave it...

B

SOCIAL

STUDENTS' UNION AT BOURNEMOUTH UNIVERSITY (SUBU)
- **3 SABBATICALS** **TURNOUT AT LAST BALLOT** 10%
- **NUS MEMBER**

Bournemouth never used to be a hotbed of radicalism, Trotskyism or any kind of -ism. Except maybe careerism.

SU FACILITIES
Endsleigh Insurance; cafeteria; hall; bar; advice centre; video games; photocopier and fax service; four pool tables; three minibuses; a general store; stationery shop; new and secondhand bookshops; launderette; Barclays Bank with ATM; volunteering office the Old Fire Station Bar in town.

CLUBS (NON-SPORTING)
Archaeology; Bournemouth African Caribbean; BU Riders; Chinese Students & Scholars Association (CSSA); Climbing Club; Drama; Duke of Edinburgh; E Sports; Forensic; Indonesian; International Students'; Islamic; Jewish; Law; Motorsports; Performing Arts (PARTS); Photography; Real Ale; Scandinavian; See Live Centre; SHOUT! (Gay & Lesbian); St John Ambulance Links; Terra Firma at Kingston Maurward.**See also Clubs tables.**

OTHER ORGANISATIONS
The Nerve Media Network is *Bournemouth students' answer to Rupert Murdoch.* It consists of a website, a radio station, a TV station, an events department and the *professional-looking* 'Nerve' Magazine. Newspaper Student Press isn't part of the Union but has a high student readership and *a leftwing slant only slightly at odds*

> **Plans are afoot to build the world's first fully commercial teaching hotel at Bournemouth University where hospitality students will practise their craft in the four-star 200-bedroom building.**

with their 'student page-3 girls' (not topless, Push should point out). There's RAG and a community action group for those that prefer to *get down with the people rather than just write about them.* PARTS is the drama society.

RELIGIOUS:
- **2 CHAPLAINS (COFE, RC)**

The inter-faith chaplaincy has a central meeting area on the Talbot Campus which includes a quiet room and a Muslim prayer room. Two rabbis (Reform, Orthodox) and an imam are available. The chaplains run a 'Global Café' every Wednesday in Jumbucks.

PAID WORK
- **JOB BUREAU** **PAID WORK** TERM-TIME 54%; HOLS 87%

There's a steady demand for students in local hotels, bars, clubs etc. B&Q and Asda also *lick their lips hungrily* at the start of every academic year. The SU has an 'Investors in People' award for its staff development programmes and employs about 220 students.

SPORTS

- **RECENT SUCCESSES** GOLF, ARCHERY, HURDLING
- **BUSA RANKING** 42

Bournemouth's *clawing its way up* the BUSA rankings, putting in a *storming* gold performance. The University's insistence on scheduling lectures on Wednesday afternoons *hampers activity. What do they think this is, an educational institution?*

SPORTS FACILITIES
Bournemouth's *particularly chuffed* about being able to use Dean Park, a county standard cricket ground. Also: two football/rugby pitches; fitness suite; climbing wall; sports hall; squash courts; golf simulator. For a joining fee of £10 students can use all these facilities and get discounts at the swimming pool and other facilities in town.

SPORTING CLUBS
Motorsports; Rowing; Surfing; Wakeboarding & Waterski. **See also Clubs tables.**

ATTRACTIONS
Bournemouth FC have found a *comfortable niche* at the upper end of the Coca-Cola league.

ACCOMMODATION

IN UNIVERSITY
- **SELF-CATERING** 15% **COST** £68 (40WKS)
- **1ST YRS LIVING IN** 68% **INSURANCE PREMIUM** £

AVAILABILITY Availability: International students get priority but there's enough accommodation for most first years that want it (one in 20 has to make other arrangements). Most first years end up at Purbeck

House at Landsdowne. Living in Talbot means being close to the University action, living in Lansdowne means being close to the Old Fire Station and the town. *What a dilemma.* The non-smoking student village on the Talbot campus only has places for 250 first years (*ie. not a lot*), with one in four sharing rooms. The houses *look like the set of Brookside and are shared between four, five or seven students. They're not cheap and a bit far from shops – a bit far from anything except the campus for that matter,* but they've got en suite showers and internet sockets in each room. The *extremely lively* Cranborne (499 students) and Hurn House (152 students) are based near the Lansdowne Campus and are *more popular* than the student site. There's £50 a year in extras (admin and insurance) and a £365 returnable deposit.

CAR PARKING: All students based in University housing can get a parking permit (£50/yr), but *space is limited everywhere.*

EXTERNALLY
O **AVE RENT** £90 O **LIVING AT HOME** 20%
AVAILABILITY After the summer, there's plenty of housing in the Winton and Charminster areas near all the studenty pubs and clubs. The University manages 250 private houses through the Unilet scheme (£61-70) and also makes arrangements with hotels and guest houses from £70/wk (sharing) to £92 (single) including breakfast and evening meal.
HOUSING HELP The Accommodation Service manages and lets the local housing mentioned above. They can also help find other options if needed.

WELFARE ()()()()()()()()()()()()()()

SERVICES
O **LGBT OFFICER** O **MATURE STUDENTS' OFFICER**
O **INTERNATIONAL STUDENTS' OFFICER AND SOCIETY**
O **DISABILITIES OFFICER** O **UNIVERSITY COUNSELLORS** 4 FULL, 1 PART O **CRIME RATING** !!!
Counselling and advice services are contracted out to the local authority. Drop-in service for international students. The SU runs an advice centre with four full-time staff who offer advice on legal woes, accommodation wrangles, academic worries and other sleep-deprivers. Ever at the cutting edge of new media, welfare advice podcasts are on the way.
HEALTH/CRECHES/NURSERY The medical centre in Talbot House has a doctor and nurses and is also home to the Talbot Woods Day Nursery for babies 3-30mths and nursery school rugrats 2-5. Also a half-term play scheme for 5-12 yrs. The SU offer £10 childcare vouchers to students with sprogs.
DISABILITIES All buildings have ramps and automatic doors, lifts are fitted with voice instructions and Braille keypads. There are dedicated parking bays for disabled drivers. The learning support unit assists students with dyslexia and other special needs.

FINANCE
O **AVE DEBT PER YEAR** £3,162 O **HOME STUDENT FEES** £3,000
FEES International students pay £6,900-£8,400. UK postgrads are charged £3,800-£5,300.
O **ACCESS FUND AVE PAYMENT** £850
SUPPORT Means-tested bursaries (non means-tested for students at partner colleges) of up to £3,000.

▶ **BOURNEMOUTH POLYTECHNIC, DORSET INSTITUTE**
see *Bournemouth University*

UNIVERSITY OF BRADFORD

1) O **UNIVERSITY OF BRADFORD** Richmond Road, Bradford, West Yorkshire, BD7 1DP **TEL** (0800) 073 1225
E-MAIL course-enquiries@bradford.ac.uk **WEBSITE** www.bradford.ac.uk
O **UNIVERSITY OF BRADFORD UNION**, Longside Lane, Bradford, West Yorkshire, BD7 1DP **TEL** (01274) 233 300
E-MAIL ubu-communications@bradford.ac.uk **WEBSITE** www.ubuonline.co.uk
2) O The School of Management, Emm Lane, Bradford, BD9 4JL **TEL** (01274) 234 393 **E-MAIL** management@bradford.ac.uk

GENERAL ()()()()()()()()()()()()()()

Bradford was built on woolly sheep, *which is better than being built by woolly sheep,* but means it's historically a dense, industry-driven town. Despite being one of the ten largest cities in the UK, Bradford *gets a fair bit of schtick for its grim, gritty northern image but amidst the 60s concrete architecture and traffic 'mares, there are pretty bits*

of architecture dotted around and a passable pedestrian centre. The £200m being pumped into the city regeneration fund should give it a bit more edge. The Brontë sisters painted their pictures of passionate and idyllic English country life from Haworth (eight miles outside town). The campus is close to the city centre, and is *compact, modern and high-rise,* with plenty of room to park cars – assuming students can get them through Bradford's *linguine-like* web of roads and roundabouts.

Words in italics are Push's point of view — take it or leave it...

B

SEX RATIO: ♂49 ♀51	FOUNDED: 1966
FULL-TIME U'GRADS: 7,245	PART-TIME: 1,025
POSTGRADS: 1,200	NON-DEGREE: 655
AVE COURSE: 3YRS	ETHNIC: 51%
STATE:PRIVATE SCHOOL: 94:6	FLUNK RATE: 19%
MATURE: 32%	INTERNATIONAL: 22%
DISABLED: 140	LOCAL: 59%

ATMOSPHERE

The campus springs to life on a Monday morning, although by the weekend it's drained of it – probably because of the large number of local and mature students. It's a laid back ethnic melting pot with a decent social scene that leans heavy on Manchester and Leeds for fireworks. There's a strong sporting scene and a pumped-up political atmosphere railing against racism, the BNP and various big businesses.

SITES

THE SCHOOL OF MANAGEMENT (1,300 students) The 14-acre parkland site is about three miles from the main campus, which is connected via a shuttle bus. *And given the level of excitement on offer out in Bradford's 'burbs, students will need it.*
SCHOOL OF HEALTH STUDIES Situated in the Unity Building on Trinity Road, 5 mins walk from the main campus.

BRADFORD

⊙ **POPULATION** 467,665 ⊙ **CITY CENTRE** 800M
⊙ **LONDON** 180 MILES ⊙ **LEEDS** 9 MILES
⊙ **MANCHESTER** 30 MILES
⊙ **HIGH TEMP** 19 ⊙ **LOW TEMP** 1 ⊙ **RAINFALL** 73
Bradford's a scrimping student's paradise – it's rumoured to be the cheapest place to study in the whole of these fair isles. In fact, it has been rated as one of the few places where the cost of living is actually less than the maximum student loan. *And there are enough ways to blow cash, too*, with plenty of bars, cinemas, theatres and curry houses. There's even a *cursory nod towards culture* with the *fabulous* National Museum of Photography and the Alhambra Theatre. *The cash-splash civic sex-up going on is* improving the shopping side of things, and also restoring the famous 'Brown Muff' building. *Push's mind boggles too.*

TRAVEL

TRAINS National Rail trains to Edinburgh (from £46.05 return), Leeds (£2.20), London King's Cross (£47.50), Manchester (£8.65), York (£8.30) and Sheffield (£7.00).
COACHES National Express from Bradford Interchange to Leeds (£2.50), London Victoria (£24.50), Manchester (£8.20), York (£5.40) and Sheffield (£6.50).
CAR Just a few minutes off the M62 down the M606, on the A58, A658 and A650. Be warned: *the one-way system around town is bad enough, but Bradford also has some of the worst drivers in the country.*
AIR Leeds & Bradford Airport (6.5 miles away)

operates flights inland and to Europe, Ireland and North America.
UNIVERSITY A *nippy* shuttlebus runs between the main campus and the School of Management. The SU's free weeknightly safety bus drops students at home (within two miles of campus).
LOCAL Buses are *cheap and convenient* for campus, town and the Emm Lane site. West Yorkshire DayRover: a one-day leisure ticket for unlimited travel in West Yorkshire. £3.80 bus only, £4.50 bus and train. £6 family DayRover (covers bus and train).
TAXIS *Not too expensive*, costing £4 from the campus to the station. Bradford's compact and local journeys are cheap.
BICYCLES *Bradford and the campus are a bit hilly so students need to be riding something with as many gears as spokes.*

CAREER PROSPECTS

⊙ **CAREERS SERVICE** ⊙ **NO. OF STAFF** 14 FULL/7 PART
⊙ **UNEMPLOYED AFTER 6 MTHS** 6%
Lots of vocational courses, much-touted collaboration with industry employers, a *well-stocked* careers service with online vacancies and an e-mail advice service to make job-hunting *a little less stressful*. Someone or other voted them number two in the country for grad employment.

FAMOUS ALUMNI

David Bailey (photographer); The Rt Hon Betty Boothroyd (former Speaker of the House of Commons, H DLitt); Lord Melvyn Bragg (Member of the House of Lords and TV presenter); David Hinchliffe, Steve McCabe (Lab MPs), Baroness Taylor (Lab peer); John Hegley (poet); David Hockney (artist); Tom Ingall (BBC Look North presenter); Al Kelly (radio presenter); Jon McGregor (writer); Sir Tony O'Reilly (Irish millionaire tycoon). Lord David Puttnam has an honorary scroll. Duncan Preston (actor) is an honorary graduate and Imran Khan the current Chancellor.

FURTHER INFO

⊙ **PROSPECTUSES** UNDERGRAD; POSTGRAD; DEPARTMENTAL
⊙ **OPEN DAYS**
For open day info: www.bradford.ac.uk/openday or give them a bell. A Mature Students' Guide can be had from course-enquiries@bradford.ac.uk or call the University.

ACADEMIC ʘʘʘʘʘʘʘʘʘʘʘʘ

Bradford's always been big on vocationally driven courses and has recently been beefing up its academic arsenal with meaty development plans. Placements and sandwich courses are commonplace, particularly in Health Studies (*its poster-child faculty*), commerce and industry. There's a lot of investment in the pharmaceutical department, funding *brainy types in white coats to work on potentially mind-altering drugs.*

Words in italics are Push's point of view — take it or leave it...

ENTRY POINTS: 200-320	AVE POINTS: 265
APPLICATIONS PER PLACE: 7	CLEARING: 18%
NO. OF TERMS: 3	LENGTH OF TERMS: 11wks
STAFF TO STUDENT RATIO: 1:19	STUDY ADDICTS: 8%
TEACHING: ★★★	RESEARCH: ★★★★
YEAR ABROAD: 0%	SANDWICH STUDENTS: 19%
1STS: 12%	2.2s: 42%
2.1s: 41%	3RDS: 5%

ADMISSIONS

○ APPLY VIA UCAS/NMAS FOR NURSING/
DIRECT FOR PART-TIME

*They're keener than mustard on mature
students and big believers in recruiting from the
local area.*

SUBJECTS

ARCHAEOLOGICAL, GEOGRAPHICAL &
ENVIRONMENTAL SCIENCES 4%   ENGINEERING,
DESIGN & TECHNOLOGY 11%   HEALTH STUDIES 15%
INFORMATICS 15%   LIFE SCIENCES 26%
LIFELONG EDUCATION AND DEVELOPMENT 1%
MANAGEMENT 11%   SOCIAL AND INTERNATIONAL
STUDIES 17%

BEST Accounting; Anatomy, Physiology &
Pathology; Civil Engineering; Forensic &
Archaeological Science; French Studies;
Iberian Studies; Law; Management Studies;
Marketing; Microbiology; Opthalmics;
Pharmacology; Toxicology & Pharmacy;
Physical Geography & Environmental Science;
Psychology; Sociology.
UNUSUAL Cancer Biology; Creative Writing &
Identity; Design for Computer Games; Economics
& Development Studies; Forensic & Archaeological
Sciences; French with Crime Studies; Peace
Studies; Robotics with Artificial Intelligence.

LIBRARIES

○ 592,433 BOOKS ○ 1,085 STUDY PLACES
○ 24-HR ACCESS

One big bookstack at JB Priestley library and a
couple of smaller ones at the Management and
Health Studies sites.

COMPUTERS

○ 1,000+ WORKSTATIONS ○ 24-HR ACCESS
Commendable cyber-credentials all round –
halls are 100% jacked in to (free) broadband
and a wireless network has been set up on
campus and all halls of residence have free
broadband for all. Discounted laptops are
available to students to rent or buy.

OTHER LEARNING FACILITIES

A recent £130m's worth of 'corporate initiative' is
intended to *sex up the campus no end*, with new
lecture theatres, a digital arts studio and an
Institute of Cancer Therapeutics on the horizon.
There's a 'languages for all' programme for those
who fancy speaking in tongues and a 'virtual
learning environment', i.e. *lecturers have learned
to use the internet.*

ENTERTAINMENT ○○○○○○○○○

THE CITY

○ PRICE OF A PINT OF BEER £1.90
○ GLASS OF WINE £2 ○ CAN OF RED BULL £1.50
*Pulling itself up by the bootstraps, but still put in
the shade by the bright lights of Leeds.*
CINEMAS A 16-screen Cineworld shows *everything*
from Hollywood to Bollywood. Also an IMAX
with a *behemoth* of a screen and the Cubby
Broccoli Cinema in the National Museum of Film
and Photography *for anything with subtitles or
sex.* The Bradford Film Festival runs for 16 days
every Spring.
THEATRES Alhambra is Bradford's answer to the
West End and shows *suitably showy shows* –
musicals, opera, ballet and pantos with
washed-up soap stars. The Studio Theatre
next door does smaller-scale touring pieces
and new writing.
PUBS The 'West End' area has several enormous
chain pubs (Wetherspoons, Flares, Varsity) with
cheap drinks offers. *Any cheaper and they'd be
giving away tenners as beer mats. There are
some quality alehouses and whisky dens if you're
prepared to explore.* Pushplugs: Dr Livingstones
(cheesy pub/club).
CLUBBING *Loads of cheesy clubs with student
nights, but nothing for the more discerning
clubber – try Leeds.*
MUSIC VENUES St George's Hall for *biggish* bands
(Franz Ferdinand, Stereophonic-style *dirge*;
Morrissey, Jools Holland), comedy (The Mighty
Boosh and, *god help us,* the Chuckle Brothers)
and spoken tours. Bradford Cathedral puts on
regular orchestral fare.
EATING OUT *Curry houses and kebab shops to die
for (rather than after).* Pushplugs: Lahore, Royal
Balti and Sanam (*spice heaven*), Fusia (noodles),
the Fair trade (organic veggie).
OTHER The SDC Colour museum is Britain's only
one dedicated *to, er, colour.*

THE UNIVERSITY

○ PRICE OF A PINT OF BEER £1.50
○ GLASS OF WINE £1,90
*The Union is trying to boost its dance credentials
but the nightlife still looks a little tame in
comparison to other city universities. Plenty of
plays and films to veg out in front of, mind.*
BARS The *picks of the pack* are the Courtyard Bar
(quiz nights and Sky Sports footie) and the
cavernous Basement, which runs some of the
biggest club nights in town.
THEATRES *Thesp-ville. Drama-minded* students put
plays on all the time at the Theatre in the Mill on
Shearbridge Road.
FILM The 9m-wide biggest student cinema screen
in the world (*...ever?*) shows the latest blockbusters and old classics every fortnight and all for
free. *Bonus.*

Words in italics are Push's point of view – take it or leave it...

B

CLUBBING *There's plenty going on most week-nights, but the big, stonking cheese-fest has to be the evergreen Friday Night Disco.* GO DJ brings together pro and amateur disc-spinners and Transmission is a weekly indie night in Escape.

MUSIC VENUES The Tamsin Little Music Centre deals with the *respectable, classical side of things* and even has practice rooms to entice *true musos*, while the Basement hosts *popular stuff*.

FOOD *Plenty of options*: The Mondiale Refectory on the main campus does three hot meals a day. Posher fodder on offer at Coffee With Principles. Jazzman's serves sandwiches and snacks until the early evening. Halal sarnies on offer in the Union shop.

OTHER On-campus art gallery.

SOCIAL ◑◑◑◑◑◑◑◑◑◑◑◑◑

UNIVERSITY OF BRADFORD UNION
◉ **6 SABBATICALS** ◉ **TURNOUT AT LAST BALLOT** 13%
◉ **NUS MEMBER**
Way more political than most places, UBU campaigns *on all sorts of leftie platforms*, from boycotting Nestlé, Bacardi and Esso to protests against BNP local election candidates. UBU also runs the Commie (shorthand for the Communal Building), and is *heavily involved* with the University's decision-making.

SU FACILITIES
The Commie – *not particularly pretty* three-storey building with five bars; two canteens; coffee bar; eight pool tables; meeting rooms; minibus hire; Endsleigh Insurance; Natwest bank & ATMs; photocopying/ printing/fax services; photo booth; payphones; advice centre; crèche; juke boxes; video games; general store and post office; new and secondhand bookshops; travel agency; launderette.

CLUBS (NON-SPORTING)
Afro-Carribean; Bugs (computer games); Duke of Edinburgh; Indian; Indie; Irish; Jazz band; Magic; Nigerian; Omani; Operas & Musicals; Pakistani; People & Planet; Pirate; Real ale; Respect; Role playing; St John's Ambulance; Saudi; Sikh; Student Action for Refugees; Twirl (dance, not chocolate). **See also Clubs tables.**

OTHER ORGANISATIONS
'Kinetic' is the Union mag. 'What's On' is the fortnightly newsletter. Ramair (www.ramairfm.co.uk), the longest-running student radio in the country, broadcasts on AM across the campus. Bradford University Theatre Group (BUTG) *shows off its wares* at the Mill (see entertainment section). There's also the UCAN volunteering project which gets students helping out in *needy* parts of the city, particularly on projects related to their degree subjects or future career plans.

RELIGIOUS
◉ **TEAM OF CHAPLAINS (RC, COFE, LUTHERAN, METHODIST) AND MUSLIM ADVISORS**
The University has a quiet room and an interfaith prayer room. The city has an Anglican cathedral and other places of worship for Christians, Jews, Muslims, Sikhs and Hindus plus a plethora of Islamic bookshops and food stores.

PAID WORK
◉ **JOB BUREAU** ◉ **PAID WORK** TERM-TIME 75%; HOLS 80%
The JobShop helps students find part-time work, which many do in cinemas, theatres, SU bars and shops plus pubs, restaurants and offices in town.

SPORTS ◑◑◑◑◑◑◑◑◑◑◑◑◑

◉ **RECENT SUCCESSES** RUGBY, WEIGHTLIFTING
◉ **BUSA RANKING** 122
Students are *generally sporty and active* and facilities are *decent enough.* But there's a *hefty* fee for student membership: £100-250 a year depending on which bits users want unlimited access to. Otherwise it's a one-off fee of £45, then £1.50 a visit. Along with Leeds, the University is part of a centre of cricketing excellence and Elton sailing lake holds an annual event for University boatsmen from across the country.

SPORTS FACILITIES
Over 23 acres of sports grounds including: four footie, three rugby, hockey, astroturf and cricket pitches; squash, tennis, basketball and netball courts; sports hall for ball-type sports; swimming pool; gym/multigym; weights room; sauna and spanking new solarium; aerobics studio; river. In Bradford there's a leisure centre; squash and tennis courts; swimming pool; ice rink; golf course; hills for walking/climbing/hang-gliding; artificial snow ski slope; and pot-holing caves.

SPORTING CLUBS
Aerobics; Ice Hockey; Ju-Jitsu; Pilates; Rowing; Tai Chi; Ultimate Frisbee; Water Polo; Weights; Yoga. **See also Clubs tables.**

ATTRACTIONS
The Bradford Bulls play with an oval ball, Bradford FC with a round one.

ACCOMMODATION ◑◑◑◑◑◑◑◑◑

IN UNIVERSITY
◉ **SELF-CATERING** 23% ◉ **COST** £68 (39/51WKS)
◉ **1ST YRS LIVING IN** 40%
◉ **POSTGRADS LIVING IN** 40%
◉ **INSURANCE PREMIUM** ££££
AVAILABILITY All first years can be accommodated and the University tries to give them the halls they ask for. No one has to share. Most

accommodation is on campus, and the rest is only five mins walk away. University halls and Bradford halls are dead in the centre of campus, *but they've seen some hard times and they're starting to creak.* International House, All Saints Hall and Venon Barnaby Hall are aimed at international students and returners and are *the nicest but costliest* (£78/wk for en-suite). Wardley House is privately run by Unipol Housing.
CAR PARKING Parking's available everywhere except for Wardley House, although it's *limited* at all halls. There's some free parking around campus and in nearby residential bits of town. A campus permit costs undergrads £19, £25 for grads.

EXTERNALLY
◒ AVE RENT £35
AVAILABILITY Rent is *rock-bottom* and there's *tons of choice – although some students share rather grotty hovels with mice.* Housing a short walk from campus can cost as little as £25 a week. Great Horton is *popular with bed-addicts* as it's near campus. *Not everyone likes Manningham* (former red light district).
HOUSING HELP Unipol on campus helps students find a room of their own in the local area.

WELFARE ◒◒◒◒◒◒◒◒◒◒◒◒

SERVICES
◒ **LESBIAN/GAY/BISEXUAL OFFICER & SOCIETY**
◒ **ETHNIC MINORITIES OFFICER** ◒ **WOMEN'S OFFICER & SOCIETY** ◒ **MATURE STUDENTS' OFFICER**
◒ **INTERNATIONAL STUDENTS' OFFICER & SOCIETY**
◒ **DISABILITIES OFFICER** ◒ **LATE-NIGHT MINIBUS**
◒ **UNIVERSITY COUNSELLORS** 1 FULL/3 PART
◒ **SU COUNSELLORS** 2 ◒ **CRIME RATING** !!!
HEALTH Health service and eye clinic. Good medical centre with four GPs and a few nurses.
CRIME Halls and campus buildings are close enough for comfort, with plenty of CCTV spies.
WOMEN: Attack alarms free from the SU.
CRECHES/NURSERY 45 places for under 3 1/2yrs and 26 places for 3 1/2 to 5 yrs.
DISABILITIES *Access is reasonable* although the campus is *rather hilly.*
DRUGS 'No drugs' policy on campus, according to the SU.

FINANCE
◒ **AVE DEBT PER YEAR** £3,001
◒ **HOME STUDENT FEES** £3,000
FEES Sandwich years cost £600. International undergrads pay £7,790 (social sciences/management) or £10,060 (science/engineering). Domestic postgrads are looking at £3,168.
◒ **ACCESS FUND** £457,046 ◒ **SUCCESSFUL APPLICATIONS/YR** 931 ◒ **AVE PAYMENT** £452
SUPPORT Ten scholarships of half the fees for international students. Hardship loans (£500); income-assessed bursaries; 20 postgrad bursaries (£1,000); travel awards.

BRIGHTON UNIVERSITY

FORMERLY BRIGHTON POLYTECHNIC

1) ◒ **UNIVERSITY OF BRIGHTON** Mithras House, Lewes Road, Brighton, BN2 4AT **TEL** (01273) 644644 **E-MAIL** admissions@brighton.ac.uk **WEBSITE** www.brighton.ac.uk ◒ **UNIVERSITY OF BRIGHTON STUDENTS' UNION** Cockcroft Building, Lewes Road, Brighton, BN2 4GJ **TEL** (01273) 642 870 **E-MAIL** ubsu@brighton.ac.uk **WEBSITE** www.ubsu.net
2) ◒ **GRAND PARADE CAMPUS** Grand Parade, Brighton, BN2 0JY ◒ **UNIVERSITY OF BRIGHTON STUDENTS' UNION** Main Building, 58-67 Grand Parade, Brighton, BN2 0JY **TEL** (01273) 643 190
3) ◒ **FALMER CAMPUS** Falmer, Brighton, BN1 9PH ◒ **UNIVERSITY OF BRIGHTON STUDENTS' UNION** Village Way, Brighton, BN1 9PH **TEL** (01273) 643 328
4) ◒ **EASTBOURNE CAMPUS** Trevin Towers, Gaudick Road, Eastbourne, BN20 7SP ◒ **UNIVERSITY OF BRIGHTON STUDENTS' UNION** Bishopsbourne, 32 Carlisle Road, Eastbourne, BN20 7SP **TEL** (01273) 643 816
5) ◒ **UNIVERSITY CENTRE HASTINGS** Havelock Road, Hastings, TN34 1DQ **TEL** (08456) 020 607

GENERAL ◒◒◒◒◒◒◒◒◒◒◒◒◒

Brighton enjoyed its heyday in the late 90s, when the sun was always out and it was okay to like Tony Blair. A few things have changed, but the city (including its more staid Siamese sibling, Hove) is still a south-coast hotspot driven by drinking, dancing and lounging around on the beach. The University is spread over four campuses, one of which isn't in Brighton – in fact it's some way east along the south coast in Eastbourne. Each of the sites is noticeably different and only a fool would apply without making sure exactly which campus they were heading for.

Words in italics are Push's point of view – take it or leave it...

B

SEX RATIO: ♂37 ♀63	**FOUNDED:** 1853
FULL-TIME U'GRADS: 15,937	**PART-TIME:** 5,737
POSTGRADS: 4,080	**NON-DEGREE:** 1,423
AVE COURSE: 3YRS	**ETHNIC:** 20%
STATE:PRIVATE SCHOOL: 92:8	**FLUNK RATE:** 15%
MATURE: 51%	**INTERNATIONAL:** 13%
DISABLED: 365	**LOCAL:** 44%

ATMOSPHERE

Brighton is a youthful, fast-paced city – a bit like the better bits of London, set by the sea. There's top shopping, with loads of cool boutiques and psychedelic bazaars scattered around a healthy dose of high-street names. Plus of course enough clubbing action to scare seals witless. A couple of festivals come to town in the summer, including a mammoth arts fest (mammoth as in big, not hairy, tusky and extinct) in May, as do droves of sun-seekers on bank holiday weekends. There's plenty of greenery in the centre of town, which adds to the chilled-out feel. The atmosphere varies at each site, but it's generally creative and cosmopolitan.

SITES

MOULSECOOMB The main admin hub. Two miles from the seafront, it even has its own train station.
GRAND PARADE CAMPUS (1,852 students – Art & Design, Fashion, Humanities) *Slap in the middle of town, easy enough on the eyes and chock-full of arts students doing their best to be radical.*
FALMER CAMPUS (6,014 students – Education, Social Sciences, Languages) Three miles out of town and *feels a bit isolated* even though there's an *easy* rail link with the city centre. The medical school – a joint venture with Sussex University – lives here too.
EASTBOURNE CAMPUS (2,250 students – Sport & Leisure, Nursing, Leisure Management & Marketing) Dotted across the centre of Eastbourne, a town *with a reputation for being full of things on sticks – that's lollipops and geriatrics, not cocktail sausages.*
UNIVERSITY CENTRE HASTINGS (500 students – Education, Business, Tourism, Computing, Health) Not just a Brightonian baby but managed by the University and run in partnership with other institutions in the region to give access to higher education for all.

BRIGHTON

◉ **POPULATION** 247,817 ◉ **CITY CENTRE** 0-3 MILES
◉ **LONDON** 55 MILES ◉ **SOUTHAMPTON** 56 MILES
◉ **EASTBOURNE** 26 MILES
◉ **HIGH TEMP** 20 ◉ **LOW TEMP** 2 ◉ **RAINFALL** 61
Brighton's eclectic population rubs shoulders without too many problems. It's posher than the average kiss-me-quick coastal town with craft shops rather than candy floss and fashion boutiques in place of bawdy-postcard hawkers. North Laines is dreadlocked hipsterville, and South Laines is rammed to the hilt with trendy clothes, jewellery and antique shops. The lavish excesses don't mask a serious problem with homelessness, though.

Eastbourne, long the butt of oldie jokes, really is dominated by Mr Burns types. But that leaves the nightlife to the students, which is no bad thing. It's not nearly as eye-catching as Brighton and the shopping isn't really up to scratch – it's possible to buy more than hair nets and dog food, but not a lot more.

TRAVEL

TRAINS Connections to London (from £15 rtn), Bristol (£29.35), Sheffield (£46.95) and beyond.
COACHES National Express routes to London (£8.40), Bristol (£33.20), Sheffield (£32.80). Megabuses run to London – prices are microscopic if you book far enough in advance.
CAR A23 connects to London (M25) via the M23. *Parking is a nightmare*, and complicated by a pre-pay voucher system.
AIR 23 miles from Gatwick on the A23.
LOCAL Trains every 15 mins from Brighton for Moulsecoomb and Falmer. *The south coast is better travelled by train than the timely but sluggish bus services.*
COLLEGE Free minibus between Varley Halls of Residence and Falmer campus.
TAXIS Lots of taxi firms, all charging *extortionate* prices (£10 for three miles).
BICYCLES Campuses have bike racks and sheds and cycle lanes are on the increase, but traffic is chaotic and the hills *thigh-busting. Good* cycle lanes between Moulsecoomb and Falmer.

CAREER PROSPECTS

◉ **CAREERS SERVICE** ◉ **NO. OF STAFF** 7 FULL/8 PART
◉ **UNEMPLOYED AFTER 6 MTHS** 7%

FAMOUS ALUMNI

Kate Allenby (Olympic bronze – Modern Pentathlon); Helen Chadwick (late artist); Norman Cook aka Fatboy Slim (DJ); Harvey Goldsmith (promoter); Emily Gravett (children's author); Alison Lapper (artist, her statue's in Trafalgar Square); Julien McDonald (designer); Helen Rollason (late BBC sports reporter); Tanya Streeter (world champion freediver); Keith Tyson (Turner Prize winner); Jo Whiley (Radio 1 DJ); Rachel Whiteread (plaster-mad artist).

FURTHER INFO

◉ **PROSPECTUSES** UNDERGRAD; POSTGRAD; ALTERNATIVE
◉ **OPEN DAYS**
The SU's alternative prospectus is available online.

ACADEMIC ◖◖◖◖◖◖◖◖◖◖◖◖

Subjects are divided into five faculties. Brighton runs some *fairly outlandish-sounding* courses, such as Editorial Photography and Horse Studies. Arts students typically have around ten hours a week in university. There's a new Culinary Arts studio and a Centre of Excellence in Design and Creativity (the latter is shared with Sussex University).

Words in italics are Push's point of view — take it or leave it...

ENTRY POINTS: 180–320	AVE POINTS: 240
APPLICATIONS PER PLACE: 6	CLEARING: 10%
NO. OF TERMS: 2	LENGTH OF TERMS: 16wks
STAFF TO STUDENT RATIO: 1:22	STUDY ADDICTS: 70%
TEACHING: **	RESEARCH: *
YEAR ABROAD: 1%	SANDWICH STUDENTS: 20%
1STS: 10%	2.2S: 34%
2.1S: 47%	3RDS: 8%

ADMISSIONS
○ APPLY VIA UCAS/NMAS FOR NURSING/GTTR FOR PGCE

SUBJECTS
ART & ARCHITECTURE 12%   EDUCATION & SPORT 21%
HEALTH 24%   MANAGEMENT & INFORMATION
SERVICES 22%   PARTNER COLLEGES 6%   SCIENCE &
ENGINEERING 13%
BEST Business; Finance & Accounting.; History;
Management; Physical Geography &
Environmental Science; Sports Science.
UNUSUAL Oenology & Viticulture (wine studies);
Oriental Medicine; Sports Journalism (BA).
Foundation courses in Wine Business and Wine
Production. are also available.

LIBRARIES
○ 500,000+ BOOKS ○ 1,400 STUDY PLACES
○ SPEND PER STUDENT ££
A large main library is bolstered by smaller
departmental ones on each campus. A learning
resource centre at University Centre Hastings
includes a library and IT facilities.

COMPUTERS
○ 3,300 WORKSTATIONS ○ 1,429 INTERNET ACCESS
POINTS ○ SPEND PER STUDENT: ££
Every room in halls has internet access. The
Computer Pool rooms have PCs, Macs, printing
and scanning. The student cultural website is
the place for e-mail, course materials and
library services.

ENTERTAINMENT ◡◡◡◡◡◡◡◡◡◡

THE CITY
○ PRICE OF A PINT OF BEER £2.75
○ GLASS OF WINE £2.75
○ CAN OF RED BULL £2
*Brighton's not cheap. In fact it's positively
pocket-sorry so students tend to stick to the
cheaper chain pubs. Luckily, the beach is free.
It's a friendly and liberal-minded place, so there
are few no-go areas. It's also one of the UK's
most prominent (not to mention flamboyant)
gay scenes.*
CINEMAS Three cinemas including the *arty* Duke
of York Picturehouse, UGC (week-long student
discount) and Odeon multiplexes.
THEATRES Theatre Royal caters for mainstream
West End-style tastes. The out-of-town Gardner
Arts centre is *lower-key and lefter-field.*

PUBS *Expensive.* Pushplugs: Roundhill (local); Font
(cheap); Mash Tun (*classier*) AliCats (shows free
films every night).
CLUBBING Brighton's clubs are *legendary*, led by
The Beach (home to Big Beat Boutique).
Pushplugs: Ocean Rooms; Audio (*less cheese
than a vegan restaurant*); Beach/Honeyclub
/Event 2 (*more cheese than a deli counter*).
MUSIC VENUES/COMEDY A *varied* music scene with
summer showpiece festivals. The Brighton Dome,
the Event and the Brighton Centre host big
names. Concorde 2 showcases *big fishes and
unsigned minnows alike.* Komedia has a weekly
student night and attracts the likes of Electric
Soft Parade.
EATING OUT *Anything and everything edible
abounds.* Push can plug a few: Donatellos (3
course deal); Big Momma Cherris (soul food); La
Tasca (Spanish).

THE UNIVERSITY
○ PRICE OF A PINT OF BEER £1.80
○ GLASS OF WINE £2
○ CAN OF RED BULL £1.75
BARS *There are small bars on the campuses, but
they can't hold a flickering candle to the bright
lights of the city.*
THEATRES The drama society organises trips, but
the thesp scene *isn't exactly thriving* – students
look to town to tread the boards, *and we don't
mean the pier.*
FILM The Falmer bar shows free films on a
Sunday night.
MUSIC VENUES The Sallis Benney theatre for
occasional world music and jazz.
CLUBBING *SU facilities verge on the non-existent,
but the town more than makes up for it.*
COMEDY/CABARET Brighton's a stop on the circuit
travelled by comedy folk such as Adam Bloom
and Sean Collins.
FOOD *Loads* of snack bars, coffee bars and
refectories at all sites.
OTHER Regular balls in Eastbourne and Brighton.
Tickets *can be hard to lay hands on.*

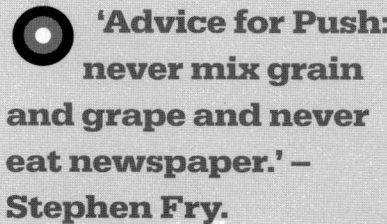

**'Advice for Push:
never mix grain
and grape and never
eat newspaper.' –
Stephen Fry.**

B

SOCIAL

UNIVERSITY OF BRIGHTON STUDENTS UNION
○ **5 SABBATICALS** ○ **TURNOUT AT LAST BALLOT** 5% ○ **NUS MEMBER**
So-so facilities are spread across the sites. *UBSU is as political as a brained squid.*

CLUBS (NON-SPORTING)
See Clubs tables.

OTHER ORGANISATIONS
A new glossy mag is just being launched, and there's also the UBSU newsletter. The University runs @ctive Student, which is both an initiative to get students involved in community work and *an example of gratuitous typographical brand-imaging*.

RELIGIOUS
Prayer rooms for all denominations. Town has places of worship for all the major faiths.

PAID WORK
○ **JOB BUREAU** ○ **PAID WORK** TERM-TIME 12-15%; HOLS 12%
There are plenty of jobs going in bars, shops and restaurants around town, *although most of them are during the summer vacation.*

SPORTS

○ **BUSA RANKING** 25
Facilities at Eastbourne are *good*, thanks to sports degrees.

SPORTS FACILITIES
Three sports halls; playing fields; athletics track; swimming pool (at Eastbourne) – for something bigger try the sea, 50+miles to France; floodlit tennis courts, 5-a-side football pitch and netball court; climbing wall; gyms; multigym; putting green; sauna; cardiovascular gym (Moulsecoomb); Sport & Racquet club (£10 membership for students at Falmer).

SPORTING CLUBS
American Football; Boxing; Circuit Training; Gaelic Football; Ju-Jitsu; Kendo; Kickboxing; Korean Martial Arts; Lacrosse; Motor Sports; Mountaineering; Table Tennis; Tae Kwon Do; Triathalon; Wakeboard; Windsurfing. **See also Clubs tables.**

ATTRACTIONS
Portsmouth and Southampton are the south coast's footballing *heavyweights*. Brighton and Hove Albion are *less impressive.*

ACCOMMODATION

IN UNIVERSITY
○ **SELF-CATERING** 28% ○ **COST** £74 (39/50 WKS)
○ **1ST YRS LIVING IN** 58% ○ **POSTGRADS LIVING IN** 60%
○ **INSURANCE PREMIUM** ££
AVAILABILITY *Basic but functional halls. There's some new and super-modern accommodation at Eastbourne, but it comes at a price* (£70-75 a week). Those who defer places or accept unconditional offers before the end of June are guaranteed places, as are most international students. There's a limited number of couples' flats. Most halls have disabled facilities. Insurance is included in the rent.
CAR PARKING Falmer and Moulsecoomb have a few parking spaces, but *traffic in Brighton is horrendous. Adding to the congestion is not a great idea.*

EXTERNALLY
○ **AVE RENT** £70 ○ **LIVING AT HOME** 12%
AVAILABILITY Most choose to live in Moulsecoomb or the London Road area. *Central Brighton and Hove are out of most students' leagues and nowhere is especially cheap. Digs in Eastbourne cost a bit less and Hastings is the cheapest of the lot.*
HOUSING HELP The University has a list of registered properties and manages some private sector accommodation.

WELFARE

SERVICES
○ **DISABILITIES SOCIETY** ○ **LATE NIGHT MINIBUS**
○ **NIGHTLINE** ○ **UNIVERSITY COUNSELLORS** 2 FULL/5 PART
○ **CRIME RATING** !!!
Brighton's Student Services department is the proud owners of a 'Matrix Standard', *meaning that it's quite good at patching up dodgy karma and looking after its brood.*
HEALTH Each site has a medical centre, but students tend to register with local practices *to take the pressure off.*
CRECHES/NURSERY Crèches at Moulsecoomb, Grand Parade and Eastbourne. 70 places for children aged 2-5yrs.
DISABILITIES Ramps and hearing loops. Special accommodation is provided on all sites. The University's welfare office has a dedicated dyslexia support department.

FINANCE
○ **AVE DEBT PER YEAR** £1,895 ○ **HOME STUDENT FEES** £3,000
FEES International students pay £7,800/yr
○ **ACCESS FUND** £750,000 ○ **SUCCESSFUL APPLICATIONS/YR** 1,500 ○ **AVE PAYMENT** £100-3,500
SUPPORT Bursaries of £500-£1,000 for students from poorer backgrounds.

UNIVERSITY OF BRISTOL

○ **UNIVERSITY OF BRISTOL** Senate House, Tyndall Avenue, BS8 1TH **TEL** (0117) 928 9000 **E-MAIL** admissions@bristol.ac.uk
WEBSITE www.bristol.ac.uk ○ **UNIVERSITY OF BRISTOL STUDENTS' UNION** Queens Road, Clifton, BS8 1LN **TEL** (0117) 954 5800
E-MAIL communications-ubu@bris.ac.uk **WEBSITE** www.ubu.org.uk

B

GENERAL ◑◑◑◑◑◑◑◑◑◑◑◑◑

Bristol sits on the river Avon, by the mouth of the Severn, in the armpit of Wales and south-west England. *That's about as close to an armpit as it gets, though, as Bristol is actually quite scenic and pleasant. The countryside that surrounds the town is lush and lovely.* There's an attractive hotchpotch of old and new buildings, the best of the lot being in Clifton, the *posh and quite exclusive* home to the main University.

University Precinct is *imposing* – the *splendid* Gothic tower of the Wills Memorial Building *dominates the cityscape.* Converted Victorian houses form the Arts departments, and the 18th-century mansion Royal Fort House adds *a little decadent splendour. Unfortunately, there's a large and unlovely maggot in the apple* – the Union building is an *ugly concrete block that's out for demolition.*

👤👤👤👤👤👤👤👤👤👤👤👤👤👤👤👤👤👤👤👤

SEX RATIO: ♂47 ♀53	FOUNDED: 1876
FULL-TIME U'GRADS: 10,600	PART-TIME: 3,900
POSTGRADS: 2,663	NON-DEGREE: N/A
AVE COURSE: 3/4YRS	ETHNIC: 12%
STATE:PRIVATE SCHOOL: 61:39	FLUNK RATE: 4%
MATURE: 10%	INTERNATIONAL: 20%
DISABLED: 180	LOCAL: 7%

ATMOSPHERE
They're not exactly happy about it, but Bristol students have a reputation as sloaney Oxbridge rejects. The Trustafarian, faux boho image is one the University would sooner kick loose, and the SU's doing its best to play up a state school slant in admissions. Whatever, Bristol's a serious academic university in a buzzing city, still enjoying the cachet of its late-90s trip-hop cool. The SU comes to life at night, with loads of facilities and enough to occupy the most committed of work-shirkers.

BRISTOL
○ **POPULATION** 393,900 ○ **CITY CENTRE** 0 MILES
○ **LONDON** 111 MILES ○ **BIRMINGHAM** 77 MILES
○ **CARDIFF** 29 MILES
○ **HIGH TEMP** 21 ○ **LOW TEMP** 2 ○ **RAINFALL** 72
Bristol's *effectively* the capital of the south-west. It was, until the 19th century, as important as London, Brum or Manchester, but the old maritime industry has gone now and the docks have been redeveloped with offices for *yuppies and bars and clubs to keep them off the streets.*
Bristol's *highlights* include: the Cabot Tower (which, from below, can be seen from almost anywhere and, from the top of which,

almost anything can be seen) and the *outrageous* Clifton Suspension Bridge, designed by Brunel. Also designed by Brunel in 1843 is the SS Great Britain, now in dry dock at the Maritime Heritage Museum. For science *with knobs on*, try @bristol on the waterfront, for art and nature, the City Museum & Art Gallery and for caged animals slowly losing their minds, Bristol Zoo. In some ways, Bristol is the British San Francisco: *beautiful, quirky, culturally thriving, but with a few too many hippies and hills.*

TRAVEL
TRAINS Bristol Temple Meads is one of the country's centres for mainline routes: London (from £39 return), Birmingham (£36.50) and elsewhere. Bristol Parkway for Wales.
COACHES Similarly well served by coach services, including National Express buses to, among other places, London (£20), Birmingham (£17.40) and Cardiff (£8.10). Arrow and Bakers Dolphin also offer cheap return trips to London. Megabus can get you to London for £1 each way *and it's only a bit manky.*
CAR On the way to the Severn Bridge, the M4 bypasses Bristol with the M32 going into the city. The M5 comes down from the Midlands, and the A38, A4 and A37 also all visit Bristol. *The city itself is a parking nightmare, however.*
AIR Bristol Airport, seven miles outside the city centre, has flights inland, to Europe and beyond.
LOCAL There are several British Rail stops in and around the city providing a reliable, frequent and comprehensive service without staggering cost. Local buses fill in where trains can't go, costing £1 from Temple Meads Station to the Union.
UNIVERSITY The UBU Bus services run in the evening between Stoke Bishop, via Clifton and the Union, down to the city centre, and back. It's £1 a trip and several services visit halls of residence. Buses run till 11.30pm.
TAXIS *Useful for students who go home when the kebab vans close. But it's about a fiver a trip – about a large doner and chips.*
BICYCLES Cycle lanes are appearing around the city. *They'll keep the nuttier drivers at bay, but not the thigh-busting hills.*

CAREER PROSPECTS
○ **CAREERS SERVICE** ○ **NO. OF STAFF** 12 FULL/15 PART
○ **UNEMPLOYED AFTER 6MTHS** 6%

FAMOUS ALUMNI
Paloma Baeza (actress); David Bamber (actor); Paul Boateng (MP); Josh Lewsey (England rugby player); Derren Brown (magician/mindreader/*charlatan*); Alex Cox (film director); Dominik Diamond (one-time Gamesmaster presenter); Judy Finnegan (daytime TV's *greatest old soak*); Caroline Goodall (actress);

Words in italics are Push's point of view – take it or leave it...

B

Sahar Hashemi (founder of Coffee Republic); Will Hutton (TV journalist/producer); Sue Lawley; Sarah Montague (ex- and current Radio 4 Today presenters); Matt Lucas, David Walliams (comedians, Little Britain); Caron Keating (late TV presenter), Dick King Smith (writer of *The Sheep Pig*, on which the film Babe was based); Chris Langham (writer/actor/director); Sheena McDonald (TV presenter/newsreader); Chris Morris (Brass Eye); Lembit Opik, MP (Lib Dem); Simon Pegg (actor); Iain Percy (Olympic gold medallist, sailing, 2000); Timothy Pigott-Smith (actor); Colin Sell (pianist in Radio 4's I'm Sorry I Haven't A Clue); Alastair Stewart (news presenter).

FURTHER INFO
◉ PROSPECTUSES UNDERGRAD; POSTGRAD **◉ OPEN DAYS** **◉ VIDEO**
UBU's alternative prospectus available online.

ACADEMIC ◡◡◡◡◡◡◡◡◡◡◡◡◡

◉ RUSSELL GROUP
Strong reputation and pretty successful across the board. Especially good for engineering.

ENTRY POINTS: 240-360	AVE POINTS: N/A
APPLICATIONS PER PLACE: 11	CLEARING: 0%
NO. OF TERMS: 3	LENGTH OF TERMS: 10wks
STAFF TO STUDENT RATIO: 1:10	STUDY ADDICTS: 17%
TEACHING: ★★★★	RESEARCH: ★★★★★
YEAR ABROAD: 3%	SANDWICH STUDENTS: 6%
1STS: 16%	2.2S: 14%
2.1S: 55%	3RDS: 15%

ADMISSIONS
◉ APPLY VIA UCAS/GTTR FOR TEACHING

SUBJECTS
ARTS 21%   **DENTISTRY & MEDICINE** 12%
ENGINEERING 14%   **MEDICAL & VETERINARY SCIENCES** 11%
SCIENCE 22%   **SOCIAL SCIENCES & LAW** 20%
BEST Agriculture; Biology; Civil/Chemical/Other Engineering; Computer Science; Electric & Electrical Engineering; English-based Language Studies; European languages; Finance & Accounting; Law; Management; Mathematics; Medical Sciences & Pharmacy; Medicine & Dentistry; Philosophy/Theology/Religious Studies; Physical Geology & Environmental Science; Physical Science; Technology; Veterinary Science.
UNUSUAL Deaf Studies; Engineering Design.

LIBRARIES
◉ 1,400,000 BOOKS ◉ 2,100 STUDY PLACES
◉ SPEND PER STUDENT £££
Bit of a pot-luck library situation: one large *but inadequate* Arts & Social Sciences library and lots of smaller departmental ones, *some of which (eg. Geography and Medical) are top-notch.* There are plans to expand and tidy things up over the next couple of years.

COMPUTERS
◉ 1,200 WORKSTATIONS ◉ 24-HR ACCESS
Computer rooms and internet points in all halls.

ENTERTAINMENT ◡◡◡◡◡◡◡◡◡◡

THE CITY
◉ PRICE OF A PINT OF BEER £2.60
◉ GLASS OF WINE £2.75 **◉ CAN OF RED BULL** £2
CINEMAS A *wide* range of flicks in all kinds of picture palaces. Try the Arts Centre Cinema, the Watershed and the Arthouse Cinema at the city's *superlative* dockside arts complex, the Arnolfini. The *shabby but bargainous* (£2.50) Orpheus is ten minutes from the halls at Stoke Bishop. The *trendy* Cube puts on *cutting edge alt fare*, and at the other end of the scale there's a multi-screen Vue at the Cribbs Causeway shopping complex.
THEATRES The Old Vic is England's oldest working theatre and hosts *high-brow, high-minded* shows – its 'pay what you can' nights are *cheapskate heaven*. Newer kids on the block: The Tobacco Factory (good for Shakespeare); the Arnolfini (experimental *weirdy stuff*); The Hippodrome (West End re-runs).
PUBS Whiteladies Road has a *ridiculous number* of pubs lining it. Pushplugs: Babushka (retro); Jersey Lilly; Penny Farthing and Vittoria (in Bohemia); the Baroque, the Hatchet; the Bell (near the University); Clifton Wine Bar is in, er, Clifton, as is the Coronation Tap; Revolution (*vodka heaven*) and the Bar Room Bar in the city.
CLUBBING *A few to tickle the fancy*. Pushplugs: Carling Academy (big-name DJs); Warehouse (student-only cheese and RnB); Dojo (hip-hop); Reflex (big bars and small queues); The Works (foam parties – *says it all really*); Thekla (underground); Blue Mountain (breakbeat and hip-hop).
MUSIC VENUES Bristol built a *cutting-edge* reputation by *churning out* artists like Roni Size, Portishead, Tricky and Massive Attack. *That golden age has passed, but there are lots of good venues in town.* Pushplugs: Colston Hall (eclectic, rock to orchestra); Victoria Rooms (classical); Anson Rooms (rock, alternative); Bierkeller (unsigned bands of a Tuesday). The Carling Academy and the Fleece and Firkin are *rated* for gig line-ups.
COMEDY/CABARET Quirky shows happen at the Hatchet pub near campus, and there's cabaret at gay bar The Pineapple of a Saturday. There are Jesters and Jongleurs clubs *if you like your laughter tinged with corporate moneybags*.
EATING OUT *Lots of nice places close to campus including:* Chandos Deli (sarnies); Boston Tea Party (late breakfasts and caffeinated *treats*); Saha (Moroccan); Rocatillos (*greasy* diner).

B

THE UNIVERSITY
◉ **PRICE OF A PINT OF BEER** £1.30
◉ **GLASS OF WINE** £1.50
◉ **CAN OF RED BULL** £1

BARS The newly-refurbished Epicurean ('The Epi', cap 650) on the third floor of the Union Building is the *gravitational* centre of student social life. The Avon Gorge Bar is on the fifth floor with roof garden and events, and the *noisy* Ar2 (or Mandela Bar) on the first floor hosts the odd bit of live music. The University runs a number of other bars in the halls.

THEATRES *Luvvie-heaven*. Bristol's *one of the strongest* for student drama with more than 30 productions last year and nearly a dozen student societies for those of a performing bent. Winston Theatre and Lady Windsor Studio are both run by the Union. The drama department uses the Glynn Wickham Studio and the Victoria Rooms (700) are used for *large-scale* productions. Bristol usually sends something to the Edinburgh Fringe.

FILM The Fine Film society shows the best of modern and classic flicks and the Film-making society *lets budding Tarantinos have a go*.

MUSIC VENUES Epi showcases student bands *and their heroes*. Recent visitors include Franz Ferdinand, Coldplay and the White Stripes.

CLUBBING Occasional club nights at the Union, Anson Room and the Epi. The regular repairs for clubbers are student nights in the city's clubs.

FOOD Café Zuma has a *famous* all-day breakfast at a *famously friendly price* (£2).

SOCIAL ◗◗◗◗◗◗◗◗◗◗◗◗◗◗◗

UNIVERSITY OF BRISTOL UNION
◉ **7 SABBATICALS** ◉ **TURNOUT AT LAST BALLOT** 20% ◉ **NUS MEMBER**

UBU's building is *one of the largest and best equipped in the country*. The Union has a significant say in the University but *still doesn't attract much interest from students*. Campaigns include trying to get the Union moved, *which would require a very big crane*.

SU FACILITIES
At the Union building: three bars; restaurant; snack bar; vending machines; travel agent; huge new general shop; secondhand bookshop; NatWest cash machines; video arcade; market stalls; swimming pool; two dark-rooms; music rooms; pottery workshop; art studio; pool; two theatres; launderette; hairdresser and barber; study rooms; photo booth.

CLUBS (NON-SPORTING)
About 170 including: Algerian; All You Can Eat; Anime & Manga; Artofficial; Asian Cultural; Association for British & Chinese University Students (ABACUS); BREATHE (Bristol Breaks; Techno; House & Electro); Bridge; Bristol Indie; Bristol Information Technology (BITS); Bristol Real Ale (BRA); BUMS (Bristol University Music Society); Bristol Volunteers For Development Abroad (BVDA); Caledonian; Chinese; Chinese Chess & Calligraphy; Chinese Lion Dance Troupe; Chinese Students & Scholars Association (CSSA); Chocolate; Church Choir; Coalition For Tibet; Colombian Solidarity Campaign; Comedy; Computer Gaming (COGS); Conservation; Debating; DramSoc (Drama); Equine; Fair Trade; Fine Film; Film-making (UBFS); Flat Caps & Ferrets (Northerners); Folk; Football Supporters; Friends of Falun Dafa; Hellenic (Greek); Hispanic Society; Hong Kong; Hot Air Ballooning; International Affairs; Japanese; Jazz Funk Soul Connection; Justice for Palestine; Jungle; Korean; Live; Madrigal Ensemble; Make a Wish; Marrow; Malay Cultural; Malaysian-Singaporean Students Association (MSSA); Massage; Model United Nations (MUN); Music Theatre Bristol; Organ Donation (UBODS); PantoSoc; People & Planet; PhotoSoc; Polish; Portuguese; Pottery; Red Cross; Reggae; RESPECT; Revelation (Gospel); Russian; Save The Children; Scandinavian; Socialist Students Save Free Education; Students Supporting Street Kids (SSSK); Stage Technicians Association (STA); St John Ambulance (Volunteer); Stop Aids; Student Action for Refugees (STAR); Student Security; Soul; Symphonia; Tea; Thai; Vegetarian & Vegan; Welsh; Wilderness Medical; Wine Circle. **See also Clubs tables.**

OTHER ORGANISATIONS
UBU's regular 'Epigram' is the *excellent* fortnightly newspaper. 'Burst FM' is the student radio station. Do-gooders do good through the Bristol-wide charity Rag and the active Students Community Action, involved in over 29 local projects.

RELIGIOUS
◉ **12 CHAPLAINS (ANGLICAN; CATHOLIC; CHARISMATIC FREE; FREE CHURCH; JEWISH ORTHODOX; JEWISH PROGRESSIVE; LUTHERAN; METHODIST; MUSLIM; ORTHODOX; QUAKER; URC)**

The Ecumenical Chaplaincy Centre houses meetings and services. Also a quiet room for prayer and reflection. In town, worshippers of every species have everything from Sikh temples and the Salvation Army to the Vedanta Movement and synagogues.

PAID WORK
◉ **JOB BUREAU** ◉ **PAID WORK** TERM-TIME 18%; HOLS 20%

There's always go-go dancing, but otherwise just the normal limited selection of bar work and restaurants. The SU runs a student employment office.

Words in italics are Push's point of view — take it or leave it...

SPORTS

○ **BUSA RANKING** 11

Pull on your boots, flex those pecs – this is one of those places where students are *as likely to be carrying Deep Heat as they are dope.* Bristol are clawing their way back up the BUSA league and the emphasis is *firmly* on sports for the sporty, and *even slobby couchers can turn into Mr Motivator in this environment.* There's also a high performance squad for top international players, fancy that.

SPORTS FACILITIES

If a sport's worth playing, facilities are probably slotted in for it somewhere around the University. The sports centre by the main University buildings houses a gym and facilities for many indoor sports. Under the Union building is a swimming pool and further out, by the halls of residence at Stoke Bishop and at Coombe Dingle, there are 38 acres of playing fields, a floodlit artificial pitch and 16 grass tennis courts. Hockey's played on an Astroturf pitch and there's an indoor tennis centre (also to be used by the LTA). There are further sports provisions at the halls including squash and tennis courts. Sailors swing their booms down at Chew Valley sailing club and rowers use the boathouses on the Avon. A Sportspass costs £185 (two years) or £260 (for three). In Bristol there's a sports hall, running track, squash and tennis courts, croquet/bowling green, golf course, lake and river and mountains and caves for potholing.

SPORTING CLUBS

Aikido; American Football; Boating; Clay Pigeon Shooting; Exploring; Gliding; Jiu Jitsu; Korfball; Kuro Hebi; Lacrosse; Lifesaving; Polo; Roller Hockey; Shorinji Kemo; Skydiving; Snooker; Snowboarding; Surfing; Table Tennis; Triathlon; Ultimate Frisbee; Underwater Sports; Wakeboarding; Waterski; Windsurfing. **See also Clubs tables.**

ATTRACTIONS

Bristol Rugby Club, Bristol Packers, local American Football team and, with round balls, Bristol Rovers and Bristol City FCs. Gloucestershire County and Cricket Club. Yellow balls fly at the Redland Lawn Tennis Championship.

ACCOMMODATION

IN UNIVERSITY

○ **CATERED** 17% ○ **COST** £91 (38WKS)
○ **SELF-CATERING** 19% ○ **COST** £66 (38WKS)
○ **1ST YRS LIVING IN** 91% ○ **POSTGRADS LIVING IN** 18%
○ **INSURANCE PREMIUM** £££

AVAILABILITY Most first years live in halls, but they're out on their ears after that. Halls are based in three areas: six large halls at Stoke Bishop (just under two miles north of the University Precinct); three halls near the *gorgeous gorge* in Clifton (less than a mile west); and student houses in and around the Precinct itself, which are all self-catering and scarce. There are five catered halls (*with food to die from, rather than for*), four self-catering halls (two of which are blocks of shared flats) and 19 houses for 9-25 students. *Stoke Bishop may be cut off, but the camaraderie's a real seller.*

CAR PARKING Cars only allowed with a permit and there's *more chance of selling a salad to Jo Brand than getting hold of one.*

EXTERNALLY

○ **AVE RENT** £72 ○ **LIVING AT HOME** 4%

AVAILABILITY *Finding a pad should be easy, although prices are ever on the up.* Although local relations are *quite good,* some areas of Bristol are *as rough as it comes.* St Paul's and Knowle *have crackheads and dealers on the corners but some students live there for the gutter cred.* Most bite the rent bullet and opt for Clifton and Redland in order to be within walking distance of campus. Bishopston and Cotham are also okay and areas 'south of the river' like Windmill and Southville are growing in popularity, even though they're a bit mingy around the edges. Wherever students lay their hat, they find it hard to park their car.

HOUSING HELP: The University accommodation office keeps a vacancies register and database and provide general help, landlord blacklist and advice.

WELFARE

SERVICES

○ **LESBIAN/GAY/BISEXUAL OFFICER & SOCIETY**
○ **ETHNIC MINORITIES OFFICER & SOCIETY**
○ **WOMEN'S OFFICER** ○ **MATURE STUDENTS' OFFICER**
○ **INTERNATIONAL STUDENTS' OFFICER** ○ **POSTGRAD OFFICER & SOCIETY** ○ **DISABILITIES OFFICER & SOCIETY**
○ **MINIBUS** ○ **NIGHTLINE** ○ **UNIVERSITY COUNSELLORS**
4 FULL ○ **SU COUNSELLORS** 1 PART ○ **CRIME RATING** !!!!!

> ◉ **A first year student at the University of Bristol sold her virginity online for £18,000 to try to avoid student debt.**

Words in italics are Push's point of view — take it or leave it...

HEALTH Sickly students can drag themselves to the health service at University Precinct. Up to nine doctors and medical officers and ten nurses dole out the drugs, bandages and bedside sympathy.

CRIME *Little cause for concern on campus, but things get edgier further afield and around some of the halls of residence.*

CRECHES/NURSERY Two nurseries. University Day nursery has 34 places for kids aged 2-5yrs & 22 places for babies from 3mths. Langford Nursery at the School of Clinical Veterinary Science has 15 places for children aged 2-5yrs and five places for babies from 3mths.

DISABILITIES Old buildings and hilly terrain make access *tricky* despite the University's efforts.

DRUGS *Bristol's something of a herbal harbour, but hey, at least it's not slaves anymore.*

FINANCE
- **AVE DEBT PER YEAR** £2,224 ⊙ **HOME STUDENT FEES** £3,000
FEES Postgrads pay £3,500 for arts and £3,700 for sciences. Non-EU students pay £9,600 for arts courses, £12,400 for sciences and 23,100 for clinical years.
- **ACCESS FUND** £365,000 ⊙ **SUCCESSFUL APPLICATIONS/YR** 484 ⊙ **AVE PAYMENT** £800-1,800
SUPPORT Convocation bursaries (£1,000) to low-income students from schools in Avon. Sports scholarships for the talented, plus the usual compulsory top-up-related bursaries for those receiving the maintenance grant.

▶ **BRISTOL, UNIVERSITY OF THE WEST OF ENGLAND**
see *UWE Bristol*

▶ **BROOKES UNIVERSITY**
see *Oxford Brookes University*

BRUNEL UNIVERSITY

⊙ **BRUNEL UNIVERSITY** Uxbridge, Middlesex, UB8 3PH; **TEL** (01895) 274 000 **E-MAIL** courses@brunel.ac.uk **WEBSITE** www.brunel.ac.uk ⊙ **UNION OF BRUNEL STUDENTS** Cleveland Road, Uxbridge, Middlesex, UB8 2PH **TEL** (01895) 462 200 **E-MAIL** su.president@brunel.ac.uk; **WEBSITE** www.brunelstudents.com

GENERAL ()()()()()()()()()()()()()()

Uxbridge is a *metallic satellite-town* on the western end of the Metropolitan and Piccadilly Lines *with space-age offices, a slick, spick'n'span shopping mall and a few quaint streets.* A mile south of Uxbridge proper are the redbrick and grey concrete buildings of Brunel University, which is in the final throes of a £250m redevelopment programme that should leave it academically, sportily, socially and foodily enhanced. Dystopian nightmare 'A Clockwork Orange' was filmed here and, *although the newer buildings are slightly less conducive to ultra-violence than the 60s monstrosities, the campus is drably practical rather than sexy.* Grassy patches and a stream (*the optimistically titled 'River' Pinn*) help create a feeling of space. *Thankfully.*

ATMOSPHERE
Brunel used to be overrun with geeks who told maths jokes that could make hyenas look glum. This image is no longer accurate as in recent years more students are studying humanities (though they can tell pretty dodgy jokes too). However, students still tend to be focused on careers rather than careering through student scrapes, and though it is a fun place to study, the work ethic is strong and the research ethic stronger.

LONDON see University of London

UXBRIDGE
Uxbridge is a modern town with all the required boxes ticked – supermarkets, banks and so on. It's been gradually face-lifted and tummy-tucked over the past few years and now has a look of a modern town about it, including a new cinema, bars and malls to loiter menacingly in. It's still quite a trek from the centre of London though (40 mins by tube) and the Uxbridge site is 20 mins walk from the town centre, but this does mean that the site has a leafy, rural feel to it. Thankfully, London is just about accessible for special occasions – necessary for any serious stimulation.

SEX RATIO: ♂55 ♀45		**FOUNDED:** 1966	
FULL-TIME U'GRADS: 8,933		**PART-TIME:** 848	
POSTGRADS: 2,515		**NON-DEGREE:** 202	
AVE COURSE: 3/4YRS		**ETHNIC:** 53%	
STATE:PRIVATE SCHOOL: 79:8		**FLUNK RATE:** 12%	
MATURE: 25%		**INTERNATIONAL:** 18%	
DISABLED: 215		**LOCAL:** 48%	

Words in italics are Push's point of view — take it or leave it...

TRAVEL see University of London

TRAINS West Drayton and Hayes are the stations nearest to the Uxbridge site both a short bus ride away (Uxbridge tube station is closer). There are trains to Bristol, Cardiff, Slough and other cities in the south-west served by trains out of London Paddington (at least 45 mins away, £6.30 return from West Drayton). For other services, the *quickest route is usually* via London mainline stations.

BUSES National Express and London Country coach services bypass Uxbridge. The nearest stop is Heathrow Airport (25 mins by bus).

CAR Brunel is on the London escape route to the west, near the M25 (two miles), and on the M4, M40, A4, A40 and A30.

AIR Heathrow is four miles from the Uxbridge campus.

HITCHING *No shortage of main roads (although hitchers have to get on to them to start with), but drivers aren't too enthusiastic.*

LOCAL Uxbridge is still within London's local transport network, *which is convenient but expensive.* It's served by buses 207, 222, U1, U3, U4, U7, Express Coach 607 and Night Bus N89 (which goes right into London's West End, though it can take a while).

UNDERGROUND Uxbridge station (a mile from campus) is the last stop on the Metropolitan and Piccadilly Lines and *offers an arduous and expensive service* into London (£5.40 off-peak one day travel card).

TAXIS Cabs charge London and Heathrow prices. Town centre to campus is £5.

BICYCLES *Bikes are useful for local trips although the busy roads can make it hell.* Increased security and installation of bike sheds has made the bikes safer, *if not their owners.*

CAREER PROSPECTS
O **CAREERS SERVICE** O **NO. OF STAFF:** 9 FULL/4 PART
O **UNEMPLOYED AFTER 6MTHS:** 11%

FAMOUS ALUMNI
Tony Adams (ex-Arsenal and England); Jo Brand (comedienne); Linford Crawford (first black barrister on the Bar Council); James Cracknell (Olympic gold coxless 4s); Audley Harrison (boxing Olympic gold medallist); Richard Hill (member of England's Rugby World Cup-winning team); Patricia Hodge (actress); Lee Mack (comedian); Alan Pascoe, Marcia Richardson, Kathy Smallwood (athletes); Iwan Thomas (British 400m record-holder).

FURTHER INFO
O **PROSPECTUSES** UNDERGRAD; POSTGRAD; DEPARTMENTAL
O **OPEN DAYS**

ACADEMIC ○○○○○○○○○○○○○○

Brunel has traditionally taught sciences, social sciences and engineering, but in more recent years has been dabbling in arts and humanities.

Half the students study 'thin sandwich' courses, comprising a chunk of industrial placement for two terms in the first three years of study and a lumpy spread of academic study for the rest of the time. Performance in work placements is taken into account by the examiners, *bless 'em.*

ENTRY POINTS: 240-340	**AVE POINTS:** 276
APPLICATIONS PER PLACE: 7	**CLEARING:** 23%
NO. OF TERMS: 3	**LENGTH OF TERMS:** 12WKS
STAFF TO STUDENT RATIO: 1:19	**STUDY ADDICTS:** 14%
TEACHING: ★	**RESEARCH:** ★★★★
YEAR ABROAD: 6%	**SANDWICH STUDENTS:** 27%
1STS: 13%	**2.2S:** 29%
2.1S: 51%	**3RDS:** 4%

ADMISSIONS
O **APPLY VIA UCAS**

SUBJECTS
ART & DESIGN 8%   **BUSINESS/MANAGEMENT** 22%
ENGINEERING 17%   **SCIENCES** 15%
SOCIAL SCIENCES 12%   **SPORT & EDUCATION** 13%
INFORMATION SYSTEMS COMPUTING & MATHS 9%
BEST Anthropology; Drama; Economics; Education; General Engineering; Health Studies; Mathematics; Politics; Psychology; Sociology; Sports Sciences.
UNUSUAL Aviation Engineering; Design for Sport.

LIBRARIES
O **428,393 BOOKS** O **1,049 STUDY PLACES**
O **SPEND PER STUDENT £££**
The library has doubled in size in the past few years and is now the proud owner of an Assistive Technology Centre.

COMPUTERS
O **520 WORKSTATIONS** O **24-HR ACCESS**

OTHER LEARNING FACILITIES
Free classes in photography, ceramics, painting, drawing and drama. Free weekly rehearsals for choirs, orchestra and chamber groups.

ENTERTAINMENT ○○○○○○○○○

THE CITY see University of London

UXBRIDGE
O **PRICE OF A PINT OF BEER** £2.40
O **GLASS OF WINE** £2.70
CINEMAS The nine-screen Odeon does a 10% student discount.
THEATRES The Beck Theatre in Hayes can't compete with the West End but it has regular plays, musicals, jazz and classical music.
PUBS *Lots of traditional pubs, which get packed out by business lunchers – try Load of Hay (beer garden); the Malt Shovel; the Swan & Bottle. Wetherspoons and the Hogshead are student-friendly.*
MUSIC VENUES *Royale's is a cheap and tacky*

pick-up joint. *Most students prefer to hit London's expensive and tacky pick-up joints. Oceana in Kingston is a cab-ride away.*
EATING OUT *Pub grub is usually a good deal.* Pushplugs: the Three Tuns; the Metropolitan; Auberge (pricey, but big portions of, er, mussels and chips).

THE UNIVERSITY
○ **PRICE OF A PINT OF BEER** £1.70
○ **GLASS OF WINE** £2 ○ **CAN OF RED BULL** £2
BARS The bars stay *busy* throughout the day. The main Union bar, Loco (cap 400) is *perky enough* with weekly quizzes and occasional music nights; the Hubs *looks like an airport lounge*; Sports Bar *is more relaxed. It's hard to avoid big-screen sports at the weekend.*
THEATRES Several productions every year at the Howell Theatre in conjunction with the University's arts centre.
MUSIC VENUES The Academy (600) is the University's largest site for sounds.
CLUBBING The Academy sees *cool, underground* names like Pendulum, Scratch Perverts and, *er,* Chesney Hawkes. *There's an excuse to avoid beauty sleep every night of the week,* with cheese and chart on Wednesdays, commercial dance on Fridays, and the themed nights (think Doctors & Nurses or Skool Disco) to fill in the gaps.
CABARET Fortnightly acts from the alternative comedy circuit, with recent mirthsters including Will Smith, Rufus Hound and Sean Collins.
FOOD The *airy* Union-run Refractory for *good, cheap* scoff; Café Direct for a coffee hit, Locos Kitchen for table service and *proper* meals; Chicken Joes for fast food. The University canteen, the Stephenson Room, does *affordable* meals.

SOCIAL ○○○○○○○○○○○○○

UNION OF BRUNEL STUDENTS
○ **4 SABBATICALS** ○ **TURNOUT AT LAST BALLOT** 12%
○ **NUS MEMBER**
Emphasis and energy is devoted to clubs and societies, which maintain a broad involvement in the Union's gamut of goings on. Politically speaking, Brunel students are notoriously uninterested.

SU FACILITIES
Two bars; two catering outlets; the Academy nightclub; information and advice centre; Endsleigh Insurance office; four minibuses; photo booth; vending and games machines; juke box; pool tables; conference and function rooms; mini supermarket; HSBC bank/ATM.

CLUBS (NON-SPORTING)
Alternative Music; Arab; Arian; B-Pak (Pakistani); Brunel Motor Club; Brunel Television; Brunel Turkish; B.U.G.S (Gaming); Chinese Great Wall; Current Affairs; Dope On Plastic Events; Eastern

European; Every Nation; Hacky Sack; Hellenic; Hindu; Indian; International Students; Korean; Krishna Consciousness; Latin; Persian; Respect (political party); Sikh; Sinhalese; Student Community Action; Thai; Tamil; The Rock Foundation; UNYSA Brunel (UN youth roleplay sessions). **See also Clubs tables.**

OTHER ORGANISATIONS
'Le Nurb' (*geddit?*) is the *rickety but well-meaning* monthly mag. There's also 'B1000 Radio'. Rag do the fundraising thing with a Rag Week and heaps of sponsored events organised through the other clubs and societies. The community action group is funded by the SU, and concentrates on helping the very old or the very young.

RELIGIOUS
○ **6 CHAPLAINS**
The Meeting House chaplaincy welcomes believers of all faiths and there's also a small mosque. There are local churches for most flavours of Christianity.

PAID WORK see University of London
○ **JOB BUREAU**

SPORTS ○○○○○○○○○○○○○

○ **RECENT SUCCESSES** SUPER HEAVYWEIGHT BOXING, JITSU, KARATE, RUGBY, WOMEN'S HOCKEY, FOOTBALL
○ **BUSA RANKING** 26
For a small university, Brunel has some big-time facilities – including a £6.5m outdoor complex and a £7m athletics and netball centre – and has bagged a small quarryload of silverware in recent years.

SPORTS FACILITIES
Two large and one small multi-purpose sports hall; facilities and support for elite athletes; all-weather facilities (including a floodlit 6-lane track); pavilion; five football, one all-weather hockey, and two rugby pitches; two synthetic playing fields; four squash courts; *highly-rated* climbing wall, fitness suite; weights room; sports bar; boathouse on the Thames; sailors make use of the Queen Mother Reservoir. Scholarships are available to students who aren't taking sports academically, but who are particularly nifty at them.

SPORTING CLUBS
BOMB (Mountain Biking); Boxing; Capoeira; Chinese Boxing; Dance; Handball; Jitsu; Rowing; Ten Pin; Thai Boxing; Ultimate Frisbee; Skydiving. **See also Clubs tables.**

ATTRACTIONS see University of London
The MCC's second cricket ground is in Uxbridge and Queen's Park Rangers are the local football team. For a flutter on the nags, there's nearby Kempton and Sandown.

Words in italics are Push's point of view — take it or leave it...

B

ACCOMMODATION ○○○○○○○○○

IN UNIVERSITY

- **SELF-CATERING** 36% ○ **COST** £78 (36/51WKS)
- **1ST YRS LIVING IN** 74%
- **INSURANCE PREMIUM** £££

AVAILABILITY Only first years and postgrads have *the luxury* of living in; everyone else has to try their luck elsewhere. Meal tickets can be bought cheaply in bulk from the *scrummy food court*, meaning *there's no excuse for living on Pot Noodles*. Faraday and Fleming Hall are the *most sought after*, with big en suite rooms. The newest halls have full-time wardens. Isambard Hall is *reportedly prone to break-ins*. 400 *unpretty* rooms are off-campus in a building let out by RAF Uxbridge. Lots of new but *costlier* accommodation is being built as part of the University's 40th anniversary *celebratory blowout*.

CAR PARKING Permit parking (£36-130pa). Clamping in operation.

EXTERNALLY see University of London
- **AVE RENT** £70 ○ **LIVING AT HOME** 15%

AVAILABILITY Hayes is close but has a *rough reputation*. Cowley, Hillingdon, Uxbridge and West Drayton are *popular nesting spots*. The area *has its fair share of unsalubrious landlords and cheap rents can end up bad value in the long-run*.

There are, however, *enough vacancies for students to have some choice in the matter*. **HOUSING HELP** The Union-run accommodation office takes its duties seriously, giving out advice and recovering £8,000 worth of stolen bonds through the small claims court last year.

WELFARE ○○○○○○○○○○○

SERVICES
- **EQUALITY & DIVERSITY OFFICER** ○ **LGBT OFFICER & SOCIETY** ○ **MATURE STUDENTS' OFFICER & SOCIETY** ○ **INTERNATIONAL STUDENTS' OFFICER & SOCIETY** ○ **POSTGRAD SOCIETY** ○ **ETHNIC MINORITIES OFFICER** ○ **DISABILITIES OFFICER** ○ **LATE-NIGHT/WOMEN'S MINIBUS** ○ **UNIVERSITY COUNSELLORS** 3 FULL/2 PART ○ **CRIME RATING** !!!

HEALTH NHS practice on campus.
DISABILITIES Disability and dyslexia service provide *good* support and Brunel tells us all buildings are now adapted for wheelchairs.

FINANCE
- **AVE DEBT PER YEAR** £3,403 ○ **HOME STUDENT FEES** £3,000

FEES International students stump up £8,000-£10,200 a year. Postgrad courses cost from £3,085 up to a *whopping* £51,250.
○ **ACCESS FUND** £517,000 ○ **SUCCESSFUL APPLICATIONS/YR** 785 ○ **AVE PAYMENT** £400
SUPPORT Hardship loans, and some new bursaries available.

UNIVERSITY OF BUCKINGHAM

○ **UNIVERSITY OF BUCKINGHAM** Hunter Street, Buckingham, MK18 1EG **TEL** (01280) 814 080 **E-MAIL** info@buckingham.ac.uk **WEBSITE** www.buckingham.ac.uk ○ **UNIVERSITY OF BUCKINGHAM STUDENTS' UNION** Tanlaw Mill, University of Buckingham, MK18 1EG **TEL** (01280) 822 522 **E-MAIL** student.union@buckingham.ac.uk

GENERAL ○○○○○○○○○○○○

Naming Buckinghamshire after Buckingham *is every bit as daft as calling Greater London Tootingshire, but at least it's got a nice ring to it*. Stretching from the north-west of London, the *jewel* of the Home Counties contains many bigger towns – the *great urban experiment* Milton Keynes, for one. For over 1,000 years Buckingham *has been a quiet market town and shows no signs of stopping*. Just on the edge of town are the University's two eight-acre sites: Hunter Street (Business & Humanities) and Verney Park (Law & Sciences). *The buildings are mostly modern and attractive* – although a converted mill, milk factory and chapel date back a century or so and the River Ouse wanders through

the Hunter Street site. *The surrounding fields, trees and old stone buildings make it seem completely cut off from the outside world – and in one sense, it is*. Buckingham is a unique university; the only private institution of its kind in Britain. This means no government funding and almost £7,500 a year in fees alone. *Ouch*.

SEX RATIO: ♂45 ♀55	FOUNDED: 1974
FULL-TIME U'GRADS: 486	PART-TIME: 40
POSTGRADS: 137	NON-DEGREE: 91
AVE COURSE: 2YRS	ETHNIC: 68%
STATE:PRIVATE SCHOOL: N/A	FLUNK RATE: N/A
MATURE: 61%	INTERNATIONAL: 75%
DISABLED: N/A	LOCAL: 4%

ATMOSPHERE

Bucking the general HE trend and dumping the Government has worked so far, although the full fee whammy has given Buckingham an elitist image which it's eager to shed – ditching Maggie Thatcher as Chancellor was a start. Those who can afford to come here for two-year fast track degrees fall into three broad categories: *international students (they'd probably pay more in the long run doing a three-year course elsewhere); rich students; and mature students who see it as the quickest, easiest way of acquiring employable qualifications.* Aware that many take a gamble in coming here, the University is very customer-driven and strives to provide good service and value for money. *Naturally, the condensed degree course means the workload is heavy and there's very little time for extra-curricular activities or drunken shenanigans. Life here isn't just like riding the assembly line of a degree factory – the small size and campus ethos make for a strong sense of community: everyone's in the same canoe.* Couple that with the huge number of international students – harking from over 80 different countries – and you have what *may be the most self-contained and multicultural village on the planet, with all the positive (open-minded and cosmopolitan) and negative (nationalist cliquiness) aspects that entails.*

BUCKINGHAM
- **POPULATION** 13,000 **CITY CENTRE** 400M
- **LONDON** 50 MILES **OXFORD** 21 MILES
- **MILTON KEYNES** 14 MILES
- **HIGH TEMP** 20 **LOW TEMP** 0 **RAINFALL** 54

Buckingham's a pretty town, but as Meatloaf might say, it sure has a helluva lot to learn about rock and roll. It's got everything necessary to keep its inhabitants alive – banks, bookshops, beauticians and boutiques – but not a lot to keep them lively. The closest thing to an all-night party is the fish counter at the 24-hour Tesco's. Milton Keynes is fun-o-rama by comparison, but even its giant multiplex pales in comparison to the entertainment available in every other major city in the world. And in most large boxes, come to mention it.

TRAVEL

TRAINS The nearest stations are at Bicester and Milton Keynes (London to MK from £14.20 return).
BUSES/COACHES Buses take 20 mins to get to MK and National Express services go from there all over the country. The X5 half-hourly Stagecoach Express goes between Oxford and Cambridge, taking in Buckingham, Bedford and MK en route. Also coaches to Northampton (£8.50), Leicester (£14.20) and Nottingham (£18).
CAR *Students who can afford Buckingham's fees can often afford a car as well – there's a thriving used-car sale scene in the Union – more free enterprise.* Parking presents few problems and permits are free if students ask nicely. Routes include the M1, which bypasses MK, the A5, going straight through it, or the A43. Direct roads include A413, A421

and A422.
AIR London Luton is the closest international airport (36 miles), with *hangars stuffed with easyjet planes.*
HITCHING *Hitching in the Home Counties is like carving a roast with chopsticks – it's just about possible, but it takes a long time, you end up covered in meat, and there are easier ways.*
LOCAL The No. 40 bus meanders around Buckingham and calls at Tesco.
UNIVERSITY The University runs a shuttle service weekdays between the main Hunter Street site and the law school at Verney Park *for those who find a ten-min walk too demanding.*
TAXIS Some firms offer student discounts but *since the town is so small and long-distance travel too expensive, taxi rides are largely pointless luxuries.*
BICYCLES *What with the quality and quantity of fresh air, the rural rarity of traffic and the 800m between the sites a bike is a handy asset indeed – if hills aren't too off-putting.*

CAREER PROSPECTS
- **CAREERS SERVICE** **NO. OF STAFF** 3 FULL
- **UNEMPLOYED AFTER 6MTHS** 11%

The careers service has a library, publishes a newsletter, arranges job fairs and practice interviews. It's also open to the public, for a small charge of course (*all in the best free market tradition*).

FAMOUS ALUMNI

Marc Gene (Formula 1 driver); Alex Jovy (film director); Bob Taverner (CEO Twinings/Ovaltine) Chris de Lapuente (President, Global Hair Care, Proctor and Gamble).

SPECIAL FEATURES

No enforced autumn starts for Buckingham students (*it's that free market again*): there's a chance of beginning in January, July, September and October. Many courses start in the beginning of the calendar year, leaving what would be an autumn term free for travel . This gives international students opportunity to take a top-up course in English before their courses start. It also means that students can graduate six months before students at other universities, giving them a head start in the race for employment. *Sly.*

FURTHER INFO
- **PROSPECTUSES** UNDERGRAD; POSTGRAD; SOME DEPARTMENTAL; INTERNATIONAL
- **OPEN DAYS**

ACADEMIC ⊙⊙⊙⊙⊙⊙⊙⊙⊙⊙⊙⊙

Cramming three years of study into two years is a bit like trying to swallow a beach ball. The four intense ten-week terms give students less vacation time, but when they're paying so much

B

to be there, *too much holiday seems like poor value for money.* Contact teaching hours fill about 24 hours a week, and a good many more are taken up with private study. It's only the last 18 months of study that influence the final grade, so students have six months *to get in the swing before the panic sets in.* Being a private university, Buckingham is largely left to its own devices when it comes to *pesky* Government interference. Exams, however, are externally graded, so a degree from here is just as valid as one from any other university – *the Law School in particular has a good rep.* Plans are afoot to offer fast-track medical degrees from 2008, *thus luring in more potential high earners.*

ENTRY POINTS: 160–240	**AVE POINTS:** 220
APPLICATIONS PER PLACE: 1	**CLEARING:** 0%
NO. OF TERMS: 4	**LENGTH OF TERMS:** 10wks
STAFF TO STUDENT RATIO: 1:9	**STUDY ADDICTS:** 32%
YEAR ABROAD: 0%	**SANDWICH STUDENTS:** 1%
1STS: 10%	**2.2S:** 39%
2.1S: 36%	**3RDS:** 7%

ADMISSIONS
○ **APPLY VIA UCAS/DIRECT**

SUBJECTS
ARTS/HUMANITIES 4%   **BUSINESS/MANAGEMENT** 22%
INTERNATIONAL STUDIES 14%   **EDUCATION** 5%
FOUNDATION ENGLISH 3%   **LAW** 41%
INFORMATION SYSTEMS 3%   **SOCIAL SCIENCES** 2%
UNUSUAL Business Enterprise, Marketing with Psychology, PGCE (postgrad teaching course) designed specifically for private school teachers.

LIBRARIES
○ **93,461** BOOKS ○ **215** STUDY PLACES
○ **SPEND PER STUDENT** ££££
The Hunter Street Library spans three floors of Business and Humanities books and was once the barracks of the Royal Bucks Hussars – some 19th-century bits remain. The Franciscan Library at Verney Park houses Law and Science volumes. Student computers are available in both. 24-hour access during exams.

COMPUTERS
○ **130** WORKSTATIONS ○ **24-HR ACCESS**
○ **SPEND PER STUDENT** ££££
Computer rooms are spread around both sites. All student rooms have internet access points. Wireless hotspots have sprung up in the libraries, refectory and group study areas.

OTHER LEARNING FACILITIES
Language lab with Audio/Video and computer-based learning facilities; CAD lab and Satellite TV room with channels from all over the globe.

ENTERTAINMENT ○○○○○○○○○

THE TOWN
○ **PRICE OF A PINT OF BEER** £2.20
○ **GLASS OF WINE** £2.50
○ **CAN OF RED BULL** £1,80
For a fix of fun or culture, Buckingham is as happening as a pork chop in a synagogue. Students either have to tone down their entertainment requirements or leg it to Oxford, MK or London.
CINEMAS/THEATRES There is a local am dram group, but MK *is the only option* for sit-down entertainment.
PUBS *There are several traditional-style pubs within walking distance of the campus but many are fairly expensive.* Pushplugs: the Mitre (pool tables and snuggly log fire); the New Inn (Sri Lankan food, live music); the Woolpack (riverside beer garden); the King's Head (cocktails) and the White Hart (regular karaoke and themed nights).
MUSIC VENUES A few pubs host local bands (eg. the New Inn, the Woolpack). The White Hart and Grand Junction have DJ nights and late licences at weekends.
EATING OUT *Not a great deal to tempt the discerning budget diner but 'budget' isn't always a relevant concept here.* There are quite a few Indians offering discounts, like Buckingham Fort and Dipalee Tandooris. *Beijing, the China Cottage and Cheng Du are the places to go for Chinese; Prego is popular for Italian.* Most of these also do student discounts.

THE UNIVERSITY
○ **PRICE OF A PINT OF BEER** £2
○ **GLASS OF WINE** £1.70
○ **CAN OF RED BULL** £1.75
BARS George's Bar opens lunchtimes and evenings – *all-day benders don't seem to be the done thing. George is a busy man when he's open though.* The bar shows big screen sport and MTV and has special events/quizzes towards the weekend.
THEATRES The Radcliffe Centre for student productions, some of which come from the pulsing pens of the Buckingham Arts & Theatre Society (BATS).
FILM Buckingham's premier lecture theatre is comandeered for new and old film screenings on Friday and Saturday nights.
CLUBBING/MUSIC VENUES The Refectory occasionally clears out the crockery to host student and local bands. Clubbers have to head further afield to strap on their dancing shoes.
FOOD The Refectory's big enough to feed all Buckingham students, which it does from around £2.50 a meal until 4.30pm. BBQs and themed days crop up every so often. The Verney Park Coffee Bar dishes out hot meals, snacks and cakes – bar snacks are available til late.
OTHER The Graduation Swan Ball every February.

SOCIAL ()()()()()()()()()()()()()()

UNIVERSITY OF BUCKINGHAM STUDENTS' UNION

○ 1 SABBATICAL ○ TURNOUT AT LAST BALLOT 28%

A dead gerbil in a tutu makes more of a political statement than Buckingham SU ever have – but since many students are only spending a short time in the UK, politics isn't a priority. With the restricted amount of leisure time and the exec being changed twice a year rather than annually, *there's not a lot the SU can do.* It provides services, co-ordinates clubs and runs the annual Rag week and Ball, *but beyond that, students aren't aware of its existence except when they need embassy details, train times or party booking.*

SU FACILITIES

The SU's based on the Hunter Street site in the converted Tanlaw Mill, which also houses the refectory and some indoor sports amenities. The SU runs: bar; cafeteria; Sky TV; games machines; three pool tables; snack bar; fax service and juke box. Other facilities: photocopiers; post office; new and secondhand bookshops; TV lounge; launderette; stationery shop; vending machines; Wellness centre (complimentary therapies).

CLUBS (NON-SPORTING)

See Clubs tables.

RELIGIOUS

A Muslim prayer room is available. There are CofE, RC and Methodist churches in town.

PAID WORK

○ PAID WORK TERM-TIME 14%; HOLS 19%

There are few opportunities, needs or time for moonlight occupations. *There are a couple of restaurants, pubs or shops in the town that recruit students, and the Union bar and library night shifts are student-staffed.* The University's careers department lends a hand finding temporary jobs and things like the Grand Prix or mayoral elections crop up and need workers from time to time.

SPORTS ()()()()()()()()()()()()()()

○ RECENT SUCCESSES NONE **○ BUSA RANKING** 122

Many don't find time to hit the pitch, but this means that those who play sports can do so for fun without suffering any serious competitive urges (racket rage etc.). Or any major successes, for that matter.

SPORTS FACILITIES

In the Tanlaw Mill: fitness centre (£40/year); aerobics and martial arts room; a snooker room. There are also table tennis tables, basketball, netball and tennis courts, an all-weather five-a-side pitch, a floodlit training area and 32 acres of playing fields for football, rugby and cricket. Local sports centres cost cash, but provide a broader choice of provisions including a swimming pool and sports classes.

SPORTING CLUBS

Aerobics; Belly Dancing; Pilates; Power Yoga; Snooker; Table Tennis; Salsa; Kickboxing; Squash; Football; Running; Tennis; Basketball. **See also Clubs tables.**

ACCOMMODATION ()()()()()()()()()()

IN UNIVERSITY

○ SELF-CATERING 72% **○ COST** £75 (40WKS)
○ 1ST YRS LIVING IN 75%
○ 2ND YRS/FINALISTS LIVING IN 50%
○ POSTGRADS LIVING IN 25%
○ INSURANCE PREMIUM £

AVAILABILITY All first years and a fair few second years are given rooms in the various halls on campus: a fair few of the rooms stay empty. No one has to share but most accommodation divides kitchen/bathroom facilities between two to eight people. Most rooms have their own washbasin and a baby fridgelet, phone/internet connections and TV aerial sockets. The smaller rooms are in corridor-style halls; others take the form of shared flats. Hunter Street has the refectory and bar on its doorstep and Mitre Court and Hunter Street halls are *popular* for larger rooms and en suite

'Have you seen how many people have gone back to school now? It just keeps the unemployment figures down and produces millions of half-educated old coots.' – Mark E Smith (the Fall) holds forth on mature students.

Words in italics are Push's point of view – take it or leave it...

facilities, but *there's no truly shameful housing.* Mature and postgrad students have their own block. Blokes get plonked on ground floors and there are some women-only corridors.

EXTERNALLY
O AVE RENT £90

AVAILABILITY Buckingham itself offers *limited and expensive* housing, which can be a problem given that the University requires all students live within ten miles. Parental purchasing power is a plus point for many students, however, and prices *aren't prohibitive to the majority*, who find themselves living all over Buckingham and local villages.

HOUSING HELP The Accommodation Officer keeps a list of agencies in the area.

WELFARE ꙮꙮꙮꙮꙮꙮꙮꙮꙮꙮꙮ

SERVICES
O POSTGRAD OFFICER O UNIVERSITY COUNSELLORS 1 FULL/1 PART **O CRIME RATING** !
The small student body and good staff relations means most students have good contact with personal tutors.

HEALTH The town's North End Surgery has five GPs available Mon-Fri.

CRIME *Buckingham's crime rate is similar to that of a nunnery, though several cars have been broken into on campus. Those pesky nuns...*
DISABILITIES: *The converted buildings are lacking on the access front but things are improving.* The Disability Support Department offers support for most physical and mental disabilities including ramps, hearing loops, note-takers and special academic arrangements for dyslexics.

FINANCE
O AVE DEBT PER YEAR £6,311
O HOME STUDENT FEES £7,500

FEES According to the laws of physics, every action has an equal and opposite reaction. and sure enough, while top-up fees are making most universities costly from 2006, tuition will actually get cheaper at Buckingham. Home counties-dwellers already get a fee discount of £4,040, which will be extended to all UK/EU students in 2006. International student fees: £12,500. Postgrads: £8,600.

SUPPORT With no government support there's also no access fund, although there are some hardship funds (loans only) and sponsorship deals available for certain subjects and from some local organisations. The Rotary Club, for example, has sponsored students in the past. Graduates get discounts on further study based on academic results. For more on scholarships (including for local, mature and marketing/media/journalism students) see the website. Accommodation and tuition fees can be paid in installments.

BUCKINGHAMSHIRE CHILTERNS UNIVERSITY

1) **O BUCKINGHAMSHIRE CHILTERNS UNIVERSITY** Queen Alexandra Road, High Wycombe, HP11 2JZ **TEL** (01494) 522 141 **WEBSITE** www.bcuc.ac.uk **O BUCKINGHAMSHIRE CHILTERNS STUDENTS' UNION** Queen Alexandra Road, High Wycombe, HP11 2JZ **TEL** (01494) 446 330 **E-MAIL** president@bcuc.ac.uk Website: www.bcsu.net
2) **O WELLESBOURNE CAMPUS** Kingshill Road, High Wycombe, HP13 5BB
3) **O CHALFONT CAMPUS** Gorelands Lane, Chalfont St Giles, HP8 4AD

GENERAL ꙮꙮꙮꙮꙮꙮꙮꙮꙮꙮꙮ

Halfway down Buckinghamshire, *within whistling distance* of the M40, is a *densely populated* commuter belt, home to people *rich enough to live this close to London and still see trees.* It's called High Wycombe, *not because of the house prices*, but because it's set amidst the rolling Chiltern Hills. *But what's in a name? Well, Buckinghamshire Chilterns shouldn't be confused with the University of Buckingham,* which is in, er, Buckingham. And it's not a university *in the strictest sense*, although it's been dealing in degrees since 1996. One of

the sites is in Chalfont St Giles, *which is great rhyming slang, but no bustling metropolis. But then again, maybe long country walks and lungfuls of unpolluted air are more your bag.*

SEX RATIO: ♀43 ♂57	FOUNDED: 1893
FULL-TIME U'GRADS: 6,020	PART-TIME: 3,140
POSTGRADS: 140	NON-DEGREE: 844
AVE COURSE: 3YRS	ETHNIC: 10%
STATE:PRIVATE SCHOOL: N/A	FLUNK RATE: 12%
MATURE: 30%	INTERNATIONAL: 13%
DISABLED: 185	LOCAL: 24%

Words in italics are Push's point of view — take it or leave it...

ATMOSPHERE

Abandon hope of thumping party action all ye who enter Wycombe. It's a pleasant but drowsy market town whose main tourist attraction is a chair museum. True, the concrete labyrinth of the University site isn't going to be bringing home architectural awards, but it's not going to frighten babies either. Stumbling into the bar is light relief – funky Ministry of Sound décor and chill-out gas in the air add to the all-round feeling of warm, unassuming community.

SITES

WELLESBOURNE CAMPUS (Leisure & Tourism) Wellesbourne is a collection of nondescript 60s buildings a couple of miles from the main campus. *Very green and very quiet,* it's connected by a regular bus service (£1).
CHALFONT CAMPUS (1,900 students – Business School, Health Studies) The Chalfont campus is a *self-contained* 18th-century mansion in Chalfont St Giles – about nine miles from Wycombe. Minibuses take students to and from the main campus, although the *only call* to go there is for SU events.

HIGH WYCOMBE

- **POPULATION** 162,000 **CITY CENTRE** 0 MILES
- **LONDON** 40 MILES **OXFORD** 35 MILES
- **BIRMINGHAM** 122 MILES
- **HIGH TEMP** 22 **LOW TEMP** 1 **RAINFALL** 48

Wycombe is your average, everyday, friendly neighbourhood market town – identikit shops, Daily Mail readers, and a handful of diverting amenities. There's a cinema, *a scattering of student-friendly pubs and a club, but that's about the lot. Unless it's chairs that tickle your fancy.*

TRAVEL

TRAINS The station is 400m from the main campus; services go direct to London Marylebone (from £10.05 return, 40 mins) and Birmingham (£16.10). From Chalfont, Chalfont and Latimer is on the Metropolitan tube line (Zone 5) and overground trains stop at the station also.
COACHES National Express coaches go to London (£18.80), Oxford (£8.40), Reading (£14.60) and all over.
CAR Wycombe is right next to the M40 and Chalfont is close to the M25. No student parking at college though.
AIR Heathrow is 40 miles away.
LOCAL Buses have the surrounding countryside covered *but there's not much to travel for.*
TAXIS Station to campus costs three quid.
BICYCLES *The town's not huge, but it's hilly. Not exactly bikers' paradise.*

CAREER PROSPECTS

- **CAREERS SERVICE** **NO. OF STAFF** 2 FULL/1 PART
- **UNEMPLOYED AFTER 6MTHS** 10%

FAMOUS ALUMNI

Howard Jones (80s teen idol); Zandra Rhodes (fashion designer).

FURTHER INFO

- **PROSPECTUSES** UNDERGRAD; POSTGRAD; DEPARTMENTAL
- **OPEN DAYS**

E-mail marketing@bucuc.ac.uk for more info.

ACADEMIC ()()()()()()()()()()()()

Business, health and design are the major degrees, taught by the usual combination of lectures, seminars and tutorials. *Less run-of-the-mill* is the choice of courses, ranging from equine management to jewellery studies. The music department is a *mini-Motown* with its very own record label. All courses are modular.

ENTRY POINTS: 140–180	AVE POINTS: 140
NO. OF TERMS: 3	LENGTH OF TERMS: 12WKS
STAFF TO STUDENT RATIO: 1:10	CLEARING: 9%
TEACHING: *	RESEARCH: *
SANDWICH STUDENTS: 1%	

ADMISSIONS

- **APPLY VIA UCAS/NMAS**

SUBJECTS

APPLIED SOCIAL SCIENCES & HUMANITIES 10%
BUSINESS 19% **DESIGN** 24% **HEALTH STUDIES** 20%
LEISURE & TOURISM 10% **TECHNOLOGY** 17%
UNUSUAL Equine Industry Management; Equine Sports Performance; Furniture Design & Craftsmanship; Furniture Restoration & Conservation; International Music Management; Jewellery (BA).

LIBRARIES

- **1,770,000 BOOKS**

The main library opens late most days to *accommodate the dreaded essay crises.*

COMPUTERS

- **150 WORKSTATIONS**

Computers in all libraries and some of the halls of residence. Lecture notes are slapped up on the e-learning Blackboard for online access.

ENTERTAINMENT ()()()()()()()()()

THE TOWN

- **PRICE OF A PINT OF BEER** £2
- **GLASS OF WINE** £3.60
- **CAN OF RED BULL** £1,90

CINEMAS A six-screen UCI in town does student discounts. There's another one at Gerrard's Cross, just a *quick hop* on the train.
THEATRES The Wycombe Swan is the thespy outlet, *but it's not exactly highbrow fare.*
PUBS *Mainly traditional towny pubs,* but a couple are *student-savvy.* Pushplugs: Firkin, Hobgoblin. *Avoid the Saracen's Head and White Horse or risk a healthy portion of shoe supper.*

B

B

CLUBBING *Chances to dance at Club Eden (student night on Wednesdays), the Attic and Time, though they can be a bit rough.*

MUSIC VENUES *There's a stunted sort of indie scene in the Nag's Head but London's a better bet and not too far.*

EATING OUT *Hardly Cordon Bleu territory.* Pushplugs: L'artista; Fusions (restaurant/bar).

THE UNIVERSITY
- **PRICE OF A PINT OF BEER** £1.80
- **GLASS OF WINE** £2 ○ **CAN OF RED BULL** £1.90

BARS The White Room (cap 800) in the Union has regular nights including a *cheesefest* at Club Tropicana. Bar Two in Chalfont (cap 600) also does regular nights *to try and shake the cabin fever.* A watering hole at Westbourne with sofas, computers, a TV and, *to remind drinkers they're not just sitting in their living room,* a DJ booth.

FILM Occasional offerings from the SU and Film Soc.

FOOD Every site has a refectory. The White Room in Wycombe does sandwiches and snacks. Bar Two serves *pubbier* grub.

OTHER The May Ball summons a few big names. Mr Blobby, Goldrush and DJ Dazzler have appeared at the University recently.

BUCKINGHAMSHIRE CHILTERNS STUDENTS' UNION
- **3 SABBATICALS** ○ **TURNOUT AT LAST BALLOT:** 7%
- **NUS MEMBER**

The SU concentrates on ents rather than political foment.

SU FACILITIES
Bars; nightclub; shop; photocopier; payphone; video games; fax; juke box; sandwich bar; late-night minibus; vending machines; photo booth; pool tables.

CLUBS (NON-SPORTING)
DJ; Gospel Choir; Performers. **See Clubs tables.**

OTHER ORGANISATIONS
Magazine 'the Noise' comes out five times a year. A radio station is *clogged up in the pipeline somewhere.* Student Volunteering and the V Team are active in the local community, helping out at schools, running talent shows etc. RAG gets *cheesy for charidee.*

RELIGIOUS
- **1 CHAPLAIN (COFE)**

Places of worship for Christians, Muslims and Sikhs.

PAID WORK
- **JOB BUREAU**

SU bars employ students, as do bars, restaurants, call centres and temping agencies in town.

SPORTS ○○○○○○○○○○○○○

- **RECENT SUCCESSES** GOLF, RUGBY ○ **BUSA RANKING** 94

Sport's more for fun than shiny cups and trophies, but the University attracts the occasional athletic wunderkind.

SPORTS FACILITIES
Wycombe campus: fitness, aerobics and weights room; gym; tennis courts; football pitches. Wycombe town: Leisure centre; golf course; sauna and solarium; dry ski slope. Chalfont campus: sports hall; swimming pool; multigym; tennis courts; athletics field; all-weather pitch; gym. There are outdoor facilities at Wellesbourne. An annual membership card (£35) gives access to everything and a discount at the swimming pool.

SPORTING CLUBS
Cheerleading; Outdoor Pursuits. **See also Clubs tables.**

ATTRACTIONS
Wycombe Wanderers is the local football club. They're a *good deal less entertaining* than Wasps, the rugby union side. *And a good deal less entertaining than the stinging insects too, come to think of it.* The University has partnerships with both.

ACCOMMODATION ○○○○○○○○○

IN UNIVERSITY
- **SELF-CATERING** 19% ○ **COST:** £60 (32WKS)
- **1ST YRS LIVING IN** 90%
- **INSURANCE PREMIUM** £

AVAILABILITY Pressure on space at halls is *pretty intense.* Newland Park is the largest hall, with 700 places. Another 500 are divvied between Brook Street Hall and John North Hall, both in the centre of Wycombe. St Peter and St Giles Halls are both on Chalfont campus.

CAR PARKING *Ludicrous* on campus in Wycombe, although *it's not too silly* in halls and an *entirely rational* prospect at Chalfont.

EXTERNALLY
- **AVE RENT** £60

AVAILABILITY *There for the taking, though prices reflect the outer London location rather than the quality.* Most students set up camp around Chalfont or High Wycombe. The best bits are Wycombe town, Desborough, Green Street and Upper Street. Gerrards Cross is nice but with *prices to match while West Wycombe is cheaper.*

HOUSING HELP The accommodation office does its best to help students set up shop nearby.

WELFARE ◑◑◑◑◑◑◑◑◑◑◑◑◑

SERVICES
- ○ LGBT SOCIETY ○ INTERNATIONAL STUDENTS' SOCIETY
- ○ MATURE STUDENTS' SOCIETY ○ POSTGRAD SOCIETY
- ○ DISABILITIES SOCIETY ○ ETHNIC MINORITIES SOCIETY
- ○ LATE–NIGHT MINIBUS ○ SELF–DEFENCE CLASSES
- ○ NIGHTLINE ○ UNIVERSITY COUNSELLORS 4 FULL
- ○ SU COUNSELLORS 2 FULL ○ CRIME RATING !!

The SU's Advice & Representation Centre *does its bit to help with life's woes.*

HEALTH Three GPs at Wycombe, three at Chalfont.
DISABILITIES Wheelchair access on campus is *passable.*
CRIME *Pretty safe, though waving a fancy phone around is never a good idea.*

FINANCE
- ○ AVE DEBT PER YEAR £2,983
- ○ HOME STUDENT FEES £3,000

FEES International students pay a *pretty low* £4,600-£7,100.
- ○ ACCESS FUND AVE PAYMENT £300

SUPPORT Bursaries of £1,000, University and faculty scholarships of £300.

▶ BUCKINGHAMSHIRE CHILTERNS UNIVERSITY COLLEGE
see *Buckinghamshire Chilterns University*

CAMBERWELL COLLEGE OF ARTS
see *University of the Arts, London*

▶ **UNIVERSITY OF CAMBRIDGE**
Christ's College, Cambridge
Churchill College, Cambridge
Clare College, Cambridge
Corpus Christi College, Cambridge
Downing College, Cambridge
Emmanuel College, Cambridge
Fitzwilliam College, Cambridge
Girton College, Cambridge
Gonville & Caius College, Cambridge
Homerton College, Cambridge
Hughes Hall, Cambridge
Jesus College, Cambridge
King's College, Cambridge
Lucy Cavendish College, Cambridge
Magdalene College, Cambridge
New Hall College, Cambridge
Newnham College, Cambridge
Pembroke College, Cambridge
Peterhouse, Cambridge
Queens' College, Cambridge
Robinson College, Cambridge
Selwyn College, Cambridge
Sidney Sussex College, Cambridge
St Catharine's College, Cambridge
St Edmund's College, Cambridge
St John's College, Cambridge
Trinity College, Cambridge
Trinity Hall, Cambridge
Wolfson College, Cambridge

▶ **CANTERBURY**
see *The University of Kent*

CANTERBURY CHRIST CHURCH UNIVERSITY

CARDIFF UNIVERSITY

▶ **CARDIFF INSTITUTE**
see *UWIC*

▶ **CARLISLE**
see *University of Central Lancashire*

▶ **CARTREFLE TEACHER TRAINING COLLEGE**
see *North East Wales Institute*

▶ **CAYTHORPE**
see *University of Lincoln*

▶ **UNIVERSITY OF CENTRAL ENGLAND**
see *UCE Birmingham*

UNIVERSITY OF CENTRAL LANCASHIRE

▶ **CENTRAL LONDON POLY**
see *University of Westminster*

▶ **CENTRAL ST MARTINS COLLEGE OF ART & DESIGN**
see *University of the Arts, London*

▶ **CHARING CROSS & WESTMINSTER HOSPITAL**
see *Imperial College, London*

▶ **CHARLOTTE MASON**
see *Lancaster University*

▶ **CHARLES FREARS COLLEGE OF NURSING AND MIDWIFERY**
see *De Montfort University*

▶ **CHELSEA COLLEGE OF ART & DESIGN**
see *University of the Arts, London*

▶ **CHELTENHAM & GLOUCESTER COLLEGE OF HIGHER EDUCATION**
see *University of Gloucestershire*

CHESTER UNIVERSITY

▶ **UNIVERSITY COLLEGE CHESTER**
see *University of Chester*

▶ **CHESTER COLLEGE OF HIGHER EDUCATION**
see *University of Chester*

UNIVERSITY OF CHICHESTER

▶ **UNIVERSITY COLLEGE CHICHESTER**
see *University of Chichester*

▶ **CHICHESTER COLLEGE**
see *University of Chichester*

▶ **CIRENCESTER**
see *Royal Agricultural College*

CITY UNIVERSITY

▶ **CITY OF LONDON POLY**
see *London Metropolitan University*

▶ **COLERAINE**
see *University of Ulster*

COURTAULD INSTITUTE OF ART, LONDON

COVENTRY UNIVERSITY

CREATIVE ARTS UNIVERSITY COLLEGE

▶ **CREWE & ALSAGER COLLEGE OF HIGHER EDUCATION**
see *Manchester Metropolitan University*

C

CAMBRIDGE UNIVERSITY

○ UNIVERSITY OF CAMBRIDGE Admissions Office, Fitzwilliam House, 32 Trumpington Street, Cambridge, CB2 1QY
TEL (01223) 333 308 **E-MAIL** admissions@cam.ac.uk **WEBSITE** www.cam.ac.uk **○ CAMBRIDGE UNIVERSITY STUDENTS' UNION**
11/12 Trumpington Street, Cambridge, CB2 1QA **TEL** (01223) 356 454 **E-MAIL** info@cusu.cam.ac.uk **WEBSITE** www.cusu.cam.ac.uk

GENERAL ○○○○○○○○○○○○○○

Surrounded by the flat and marshy Fenlands, the ancient city of Cambridge sits smugly on the edge of East Anglia, bulging arse-end of England – *geographically speaking, no offence to East Anglians*. The reason for the city's smugness lies in the sprawl of colleges, faculties and departments that make up the University. About a century after the trend started in Oxford, higher education sprouted in Cambridge and now, nearly 800 years later, these are among the *most famous, most highly revered and possibly the most extraordinary universities in the world*. The University remains (much more than at Oxford) the focal point of the *stunning city, which is largely composed of attractive buildings* in light golden stone. The University buildings are its colleges – 31 in all – and they are as attractive examples of English architecture spanning eight centuries as are likely to be found anywhere. *The area they cover is remarkably compact and to the outsider has a slightly surreal feeling hanging in the air, aided and abetted by the bizarre language students use – 'backs', 'cuppers', 'bedders', 'bumps'.*

These words are part of the world inhabited by the elite – a controversial word to which the University objects. They can pretend all they want that they're firmly grounded in the real world – and, don't get us wrong, there are plenty of 'normal' people here – but the truth is that, from the moment you sign in at the Porter's Lodge to the day you graduate at Senate House, you're really not in Kansas any more.

SEX RATIO: ♂52 ♀48	FOUNDED: 1284
FULL-TIME U'GRADS: 11,982	PART-TIME: 0
POSTGRADS: 5,499	NON-DEGREE: 0
AVE COURSE: 3YRS	ETHNIC: 19%
STATE:PRIVATE SCHOOL: 57:43	FLUNK RATE: 1%
MATURE: 7%	INTERNATIONAL: 13%
DISABLED: 50	LOCAL: N/A

ATMOSPHERE

Okay, so Cambridge and Oxford are more similar than Kylie's arse and a ripe melon and only their prospectuses would claim they're completely different. Like Oxford, most of the students' social concerns and the intense academic life revolve around the colleges, which run themselves, arrange their own admissions and are fiercely competitive with each other. However, unlike Oxford, there are plenty of opportunities to switch courses and an even stronger sense that this is a student city.

Cambridge's picturesque façade hides a rigorous work ethic – three years' studying here is one of the most intense educational experiences anyone can hope to have with their clothes on. In this compact and University-dominated city, there is virtually no escape. It can be challenging, it can be claustrophobic and it can be compared to being locked in a prison cell with 50 double-glazing salesmen. That's just the work side of things though – those who know all work and no play makes Jack reach for the Kalashnikov try to cram every waking hour with extra-curricular activity: sport; drama; journalism; music; politics; archaic drinking clubs; whatever. Cambridge students do a lot of whatever. They need to have good time management skills or learn them pretty quick.

Life in the colleges is even more cosseted, closeted and all-consuming and they range in size from Lucy Cavendish (120 undergrads) to Trinity College (more than 700). Most colleges have around 400 undergraduates and many students experience a little shock when they emerge into the big, bad real world ('What do you mean "make my own bed?"'). The colleges themselves do vary more than Kylie's arse and a ripe melon, however, and it's a foolhardy fool who uses the pinprick picking method. Odd ceremonies and traditions persist, and it remains the case that students from 'non-Cambridge' backgrounds (state schools, women, ethnic minorities) may take longer to adjust than others, whatever the prospectuses may say.

The following Push entries expose the naked truth and the neatly garbed falsehoods about the undergrad colleges. Push doesn't cover Darwin or Clare Hall, which are postgrad colleges. *We suggest you write to the above address or the colleges themselves if this upsets you (letters of complaint to Push will be duly noted and used as coffee filters).*

CAMBRIDGE

○ POPULATION 108,863 **○ LONDON** 58 MILES
○ OXFORD 77 MILES **○ NORWICH** 57 MILES
○ HIGH TEMP 22 **○ LOW TEMP** 1 **○ RAINFALL** 46
The Romans didn't know what they were letting the world in for when they first settled here. If the University hadn't come to town at the end of the Middle Ages, the city would most likely have remained as the legionaries left it – a small, insignificant fenland village of eel fishers. Now, of course the city bustles all year round with snap-happy tourists, students and a number of bemused locals who don't see what all the fuss is about. All the basic ingredients are here – although a single city-centre Sainsbury's can't feed everybody, and the club scene is lame if not legless. There's tons of traditional real ale pubs,

bookstores ago-go, a fabulous daily market, *Kettles Yard Art Gallery and a mass of museums. The wheels of commercialism are grinding on though, and some central streets are in danger of being swamped by chain stores and restaurants – although several quirky and trendy one-offs are fighting the flood. The River Cam is the summertime highlight, littered with ducks and drunken punters at every lazy meander. Locals don't have much problem with the students – the primary civic moneyspinners – but they do have their quibbles with the University and its colleges which own most of the land in the city and plague planning permission applications. Everyone, however, hates the tourists. More or less, the centre point of Cambridge (for the purpose of measuring distances to the colleges in Push entries, at any rate) is the breath-stoppingly beautiful King's Parade.*

TRAVEL
TRAINS Cambridge's *smallish* station connects to London King's Cross (three an hour, £16.95 rtn), Liverpool Street (£19.15), Liverpool Lime Street, Birmingham (£26.05), Bristol (£40.95) and more. Incidentally, the station is some way beyond the city centre because the *University authorities didn't want rough common London folk coming too close to the sensitive young undergraduates – they might catch cockney diseases.*
COACHES The *shabby* outdoor bus station on Drummond Street runs plenty of competitive services. Greenline, Premier Travel and National Express run to London (£12.80 rtn), Bristol £52.50), Oxford and elsewhere.
CAR Circled by the A14 and just a few minutes off the M11 from London. Also the A428 and A10. *The city centre's practically devoid of cars and the limited multi-storey parking costs more than a night with Julia Roberts.* There is, however, a park & ride service on the edge of the city. Students aren't allowed to keep cars without good reason.
AIR Cambridge Airport for private jets. London Stansted, 23 miles down the M11, is on a direct train link and has loads of budget flights.
HITCHING Variable – *aim towards M11 junctions, or A10/Trumpington Road for London.*
LOCAL Stagecoach runs bus services as *regular as prunes* to the surrounding villages, Ely, Huntingdon, the station and the outer colleges.
TAXIS *The short distances between places means cab companies are comfortable hiking up prices – similar length journeys would be cheaper in larger cities – but there are always plenty of black cabs around.* Some colleges have free taxi arrangements at night. See separate entries.
BICYCLES *Bikes are virtually a prerequisite for living in Cambridge – and it's not just the student stereotype of books in a basket, scarf flapping in the breeze – many locals push pedals too.* There are ample racks around town and in the colleges, *though there's also a lucrative trade in bike-napping and cycle skeletons are to be seen on railings across the city.*

CAREER PROSPECTS
⊙ **CAREERS SERVICE** ⊙ **NO. OF STAFF** 10 FULL/20 PART
⊙ **UNEMPLOYED AFTER 6 MTHS** 3%
Although '(Cantab)' after your name might not be the sure-fire guarantee of a top job it once was, a Cambridge education rarely does harm on a CV and, supposedly, employers find Cambridge students more down-to-earth than those from Oxford (who must surely then be abject space cadets). The careers people operate a load of facilities, including a *substantial library,* one-on-one CV/interview/advice sessions, job fairs, weekly e-mail bulletins *from the moment a student signs up till the day they die,* employer presentations and a GradLink service – which puts *starry-eyed hopefuls* in touch with graduates in their chosen professions.

FAMOUS ALUMNI see individual colleges
Cambridge seems particularly strong on spies, Tory MPs and comedians. Draw your own conclusions.

SPECIAL FEATURES
Undergrads have to 'keep term', which means that they may not live more than three miles from the church of St Mary's in the centre of the city and they must get permission before going away during term time.

FURTHER INFO
⊙ **PROSPECTUSES** UNDERGRAD; POSTGRAD; DEPARTMENTALS; ALTERNATIVE
⊙ **OPEN DAYS**
Get online or contact the Cambridge Admissions office for prospectuses. Postgrads should contact the Board of Graduate Studies (01223) 766 606. The Colleges have their own prospectuses and open days.

ACADEMIC ◡◡◡◡◡◡◡◡◡◡◡◡◡

⊙ **RUSSELL GROUP**
Eight-week terms may sound cushy, but Cambridge students have anything but an easy academic ride – the constant pressure and unrelenting deadlines ruin all hopes of long vacations watching 'Deal Or No Deal'. The actual cushy part is that, three years after graduating, students get handed an MA on a plate, simply for still being alive (the University wanted to give MAs immediately upon graduation simply because they figured the gruelling study merited them, but, understandably, other universities argued them down).

ENTRY POINTS: 340–360		AVE POINTS: N/A	
APPLICATIONS PER PLACE: 4		CLEARING: 0%	
NO. OF TERMS: 3		LENGTH OF TERMS: 8WKS	
STAFF TO STUDENT RATIO: 1:12		STUDY ADDICTS: 42%	
TEACHING: *****		RESEARCH: *****	
YEAR ABROAD: 6%		SANDWICH STUDENTS: 1%	
1STS: 20%		2.2S: 20%	
2.1S: 50%		3RDS: 5%	

Words in italics are Push's point of view — take it or leave it...

ADMISSIONS
⊙ APPLY VIA UCAS
Some courses require tests in addition to interviews, namely: the National Admission Test for Law; Sixth Term Examination Papers in Maths (STEP); the Bio-Medical Admissions Test (BMAT); and the Thinking Skills Assessment Test (TSA). Several colleges and courses require a portfolio of essays to be submitted in addition to UCAS forms and the Cambridge Application Form (CAF). At the end of the day, it's down to the colleges to say who's in or out and there's also the 'pooling' system – *sort of like a baby version of clearing. Naturally, all the pitfalls of clearing apply to pooling too. Cambridge has never been free from accusations of snobbery when it comes to admissions although it has a programme of widening participation in state schools.*

SUBJECTS
ARCHITECTURE 2%   **ART & DESIGN** 2%   **EDUCATION** 3%
ENGINEERING 11%   **HUMANITIES** 23%
MATHEMATICS & COMPUTING 10%
MEDICINE/VETERINARY MEDICINE 14%   **SCIENCES:** 17%
SOCIAL, ECONOMIC, POLITICAL & LEGAL STUDIES 18%
SUBJECTS ALLIED TO MEDICINE 2%
BEST All. Can't really argue with that.

LIBRARIES
⊙ **7,000,000** BOOKS ⊙ **988** STUDY PLACES
⊙ **24**-HR ACCESS
The *great 60s phallus* that is the University Library (www.lib.cam.ac.uk) is one of six copyright libraries in the country and as such has the right to claim a copy of every new book published in the UK. Every year, the number of new additions, if laid end to end, would extend the collection by a mile. The library attracts loads of top academics and intellectual celebrities like Germaine Greer can regularly be spotted perusing its endless shelves. *As if the UL weren't enough,* every college has its own library and there are more than 30 libraries devoted to individual subjects – *quite a few books, then.*

COMPUTERS
⊙ **2,800** WORKSTATIONS
Most colleges have their own variable computing facilities but the central computing service has a number of cutting-edge IT suites for student use.

OTHER LEARNING FACILITIES
There are more specialised facilities and labs than most students will ever realise exist, including astronomy observatory, open-access language labs, music rehearsal rooms and the ADC theatre.

ENTERTAINMENT ◑◑◑◑◑◑◑◑◑

THE CITY
⊙ **PRICE OF A PINT OF BEER** £2.80-3
⊙ **GLASS OF WINE** £3
⊙ **CAN OF RED BULL** £2.50
CINEMAS The *massive mall-style multiplex* at the Grafton Centre gets all the big movies, but the Arts Picturehouse on St Andrews Street does a range of new releases, art house, world cinema, cult classics, *good beer and really great crêpes.* Homerton students like the new cinema near the station, *others haven't really noticed it.*
THEATRES The Arts Theatre shows popular mainstream drama and the *annual Christopher Biggins panto.* The Junction shows more eclectic material.
PUBS *Cambridge has many a quality alehouse, although the prices seem attached to London's. Riverside pubs are popular student haunts. In particular: The Mill, which spills onto 'Beer Island' – a summertime barbecue oasis circled by the Cam; The Anchor (watch fat American tourists fall off their punts). The King's Street Run is a legendary alternative hangout, whilst quieter, quainter pubs like the Pickerel and the Eagle (where Watson & Crick discovered DNA) provide pleasant inebriation. The Maypole gets packed, especially as it is one of the few pubs to embrace the new licensing laws with glee, serving pints until 2am at weekends. Other Pushplugs: The Cow (ultratrendy, cocktail deals); the Vaults; the St Radegund (smallest pub in town). Students would do better staying at home and sticking pins in their faces than going into Wetherspoons or the Rat & Parrot on weekends.*
CLUBBING *It is possible to have a good night out with the aid of large amounts of malted hops, but college ents are by far the most popular nights. Nonetheless Pushplugs: Soul Tree; Club 22; Ballare (still known by its ten years out-of-date title 'Cindy's'); the Junction (Dot Cotton gay night once a month, Boogie Wonderland on Fridays); Mondays at The Fez.*
MUSIC VENUES The Corn Exchange has big name bands, *seemingly alternating weekly with The Levellers,* while pub venues like the Man on the Moon and the Portland Arms have *respectable* local giggers.
OTHER Mainstream comedy comes to the Corn Exchange. CAMRA (Campaign for Real Ale) hits town in summer and winter for beer festivals and the annual Strawberry Fair on Midsummer Common is a *fun hippy festival of moozic and booze. Let's not forget punting on the Cam, the archetypal Cambridge pastime* – there are punt stations at Quayside and by the Anchor, the requisite strawberries and champagne are available in Sainsbury's.
EATING OUT *It's customary to take out one's parents or at least their credit cards. Many cafés are just pricey tourist traps and chains are increasing their stranglehold on the city centre,*

but there are a few pubs and restaurants that do good value, good quality food. Pushplugs: Eraina Taverna (Greekish); the Bun Shop (tapas); Teriyaki (Japanese); Dojo's (Oriental). The burgers at the Alma are possibly divine in origin.

UNIVERSITY

BARS The University has no central bar of its own but the individual colleges have at least one, varying like airport lounges like Trinity to opium dens like King's and cutesy pubbettes like Pembroke. Some are for college members and their guests only, but it's never too hard to crash.

THEATRES The newly refurbished, fully equipped and student-run ADC theatre shows two productions four nights a week, year-round, ranging from the inspired to the despised. There's also the tiny Playroom for more intimate performances and many colleges have their own performance spaces, notably Queens' Fitzpatrick Hall. In May Week, almost every college offers some kind of drama in its gardens, usually Shakespeare. Cantabrian thespians hit Edinburgh by the dozen every year.

FILM Most colleges have their own film club, which usually amounts to rented videos in the JCR, although some are more professional (especially at St John's, Queens', Peterhouse and the Cambridge Union Society). Being run by students, these, of course, show just about anything students might want to see and often just what the projectionist wants to.

MUSIC VENUES The University Concert Hall hosts mainly classical concerts including the University's many orchestras, choirs and chapel music groups. The college JCRs are prepared to use almost any room available for more contemporary noises.

CLUBBING In-college ents are the biggest nights going – no one minds how loud, dingy and sweaty they can be. CUSU borrows local clubs for a quartet of events: the LGBT's popular Unique at Club 22 (cheese); Top Banana at Ballare (cheese/chart); Melamondo at Fez and Urbanite at Soul Tree.

COMEDY/CABARET The Cambridge Footlights Revue has given birth to some of the world's best chuckle-mongers including half the Monty Python Team, Peter Cook & Dudley Moore, Smith & Jones, Fry & Laurie, Clive Anderson, Clive James, Emma Thompson, Tony Slattery and so on ad ridiculum, although the talent scouts haven't been so ready with their chequebooks in recent years. Cambridge Comedy is unkillable, though,

and the Footlights show goes on (and on and...). Occasional comedy nights in the Colleges often surpass them in the hilarity stakes.

FOOD Livers-in (ie. the vast majority) eat in college dining halls, but there are also cafeterias and sandwich bars in some departments and the University Library. Meals are cheap but that's because they're subsidised by the Kitchen Fixed Charge that all students pay at the beginning of term. So even if you go out for the other kind of KFC, you've paid for your meal already. All colleges hold 'formal halls' at least once a week – some of the larger ones daily – which are generally formal table-service affairs with better than average food. For many students they're a good excuse to get trashed on cheap wine and the traditional practice of 'pennying' (putting a penny in someone's glass, obliging them to down the contents in order to stop the queen from drowning, or something equally archaic and ridiculous). Big, candle-lit, roast-pig-with-fruit-rammed-up-every-orifice dinners still go on, just not every day.

BALLS Wild parties in penguin suits and ball frocks which usually end up covered in strawberries and vomit. Most colleges have one (or share one with another college) and some are huge (such as Trinity's). The one thing they almost all have in common is a discussion with the bank manager – a double ticket can cost in excess of £180 (plus the dry-cleaning bill) for 11 hours of all-inclusive extravagance and big-name bands. Some colleges have cheaper versions with fewer thrills and frills. The odd thing is the balls are almost all in June and yet are called May Balls. May Week also includes 'Suicide Sunday' – nothing to do with exam pressure but a day to begin alcoholic consumption at 9am and carry on until oblivion.

OTHER Terribly civilised entertainments flourish, especially in the last few weeks of the summer term when exams are over and all students have to do is hang around sipping Pimms during the annual college/society/faculty garden party crawl.

SOCIAL ◖◗◖◗◖◗◖◗◖◗◖◗◖◗◖◗◖◗◖◗◖◗◖◗

CAMBRIDGE UNIVERSITY STUDENTS' UNION

○ **6 SABBATICALS** ○ **TURNOUT AT LAST BALLOT** 22%
○ **NUS MEMBER**

The colleges' JCRs and MCRs have really plugged the gap that students' unions usually fill and CUSU (which, to be fair, is good at what it

---

● **Legend has it that Cambridge University was actually founded by Oxford scholars fleeing town-gown violence back in the 13th Century.**

does) doesn't have much of a profile – in part due to the continuing non-existence of a central SU building, for which it's been fighting for years. CUSU co-ordinates many campaigns (Target Schools, Green and so on) and concentrates on keeping the wheels of student admin turning. *Amazingly*, it's one of the poorest student unions in the country and its sabbaticals are amongst the poorest paid – *its facilities are also a poor reflection of Cambridge's stature.* CUSU publishes various (*largely unread*) handbooks (Societies Guide, Diary, Alternative Prospectus, termly paper, Sex Guide – '*wear gloves, use lube*' – and Green Guide) and *lashings of political hackery. However, the politics is limited, because most students get all the (non-party) politics they need through their own JCR. On the quiet, CUSU does all sorts of valiant representation and welfare work in the University,* trains and advises JCR officers and co-ordinates more societies than there are days in the academic year.

SU FACILITIES
CUSU's services HQ has moved from Trumpington Street to the New Museum Site – *could this be the start of a unified building?* In the meantime, facilities at the CUSU Offices include: *cheap* photocopier, shop, fax, stationery, condoms; minibus hire. Practically speaking, it aims at providing for JCRs who then provide amenities for individual students.

CLUBS (NON-SPORTING)
This list doesn't include college-based societies. What do you want, the moon on a stick? Abacus; Action Aid; Air Squadron; Anglo-Japanese; Anti-Bloodsports; Archimideans; Art; Assassin's Guild; Baby Milk Action; Backgammon; Baha'i; Ballet; Bangladesh; Birders; Black & Asian Caucus; Bone Marrow; Brass Band; Bridge (community); Buddhist; Campus Children's Holidays; Canadian; Canal; Cannabis Legalisation; Ceilidh; Chamber Choir; Chocolate; Christian Music; Christian Science; Cobblers; Cognitive Science; Comic (the paper variety not stand-up); Community Church; Computer; Contact (helping the elderly); Cuba; Cycle Safety; Dance; Detective Fiction; Diamond Way; Diplomacy (game); Disabilities; Dr Who; Duke of Edinburgh Award; Early Music; Eating Disorders; Enterprise (Star Trek); Environment Action; Esperanto; Essex; European; European Theatre Group (international touring company); Excitium; Explorers & Travellers; Field Sports; Film & TV; First Aid; Fisher Society (Catholic); Footlights; Freaky Comics; Free (libertarian); Freemasonry; French; Friends of the Earth; Gamelan (gongs); German; Go (game); Greenlink; Grimsoc (professional Northerners); Hellenic; Heraldic; Hillwalking; Hindu; Hispanic; Holistic Medicine; Hong Kong & China; Hungarian; Imfundo (South African Educational Trust); India; International; Iran; Israel; Italian; Jews & Christians; Jomborg the New (fantasy); Jugglers; Kettle's Yard (visual arts); Light Entertainment; Link Africa; Linkline;

Literary; Madhouse Theatre; Mah-Jong; Malaysia & Singapore; Marlowe Dramatic; Massage; Medical Action; Methodist; Middle East; Mummers; Mystical; Officers' Training Corps; Opera; Orthodox; Overlanders (rough travel); Oxfam; Pakistan; Poetry; Pottery; Progressive Jewish; Punjabi; Quorum; Radio; Railway; Raleigh; Revolver & Pistol; Roleplaying; RN; Science Fiction; Scientists for the Earth; Scottish & Irish; Scouts & Guides; Seres (Chinese magazine); Sheila & Her Dog (relapse into childhood); Slavonic & East European; Sri Lanka; Strathsprey & Reel (Scottish dancing); Student Christian Movement; Support for the Homeless; Survival (tribal rights); Tibet Support; Tolkien; Transcendence; Troubadours; Ugandan Children; Underwater Exploration; Union Society; Union Society Boycott; United Nations; Up Shit Creek Without a Paddle (ignore exams); Visual Arts; Welsh; West End; Wine; Young Friends (Quakers). **See also Clubs tables.**

OTHER ORGANISATIONS
MEDIA *Proper papers* 'Varsity' and 'the Cambridge Student' (TCS) vie for the attention of both students and locals on a weekly basis. Varsity is the elder – the first student paper to go full colour – *but has become more tabloidy in recent years.* Other publications come and go. 'Cambridge University Radio' (CUR) broadcasts from Churchill to nowhere in particular. A few *unfortunate* local cable-owners unintentionally pick up the programmes produced by 'Cambridge University Television' (CUTE).
RAG Colleges compete in raising money for the University's charity Rag. With competition spurring them on, they raise vast sums every year. The biggest event of the year is the Rag Blind Date where students are assigned dates based on how fit the Rag reps think they are, *then spend an entire evening failing to sleep with a stranger.*
STUDENT COMMUNITY ACTION As shown by the list above, there are a number of Cambridge clubs with a conscience. Some of these and other organisations – in all about 50 – do voluntary work in all sectors of the community.
MUSIC Cambridge offers *the perfect opportunity to get together and make sweet music,* mostly of the classical variety with the Chamber Orchestra (CUCO), the Music Society (CUMS), the *dangerously acronymed* Cambridge University Musical Theatre Society or in any of the many college orchestras, choirs, etc. Contemporary musicians either form bands the usual way or use the Musician's Directory to find each other. Basically, whatever toots your flute, there'll be a society, club or association devoted to it.

RELIGIOUS
Every denomination of Christianity is here and virtually no religion is unrepresented (including a few religious orders started by students wanting to avoid poll tax in the 90s). Most colleges have a CofE or multi-faith chapel/chaplain, Corpus Christi has a mosque. Try the following for some *communal God-squadding:* the Christian Union

(Anglican); the Fisher Society (Catholic); the Methodists; the Islamic Society (linked to local mosque); not one, but two Jewish societies, Progressive and Orthodox (with a synagogue, rabbi and kosher restaurant of their own) and so on. There are local places of worship for Hindus, Sikhs and Buddhists.

PAID WORK

○ PAID WORK: TERM TIME 10%; HOLS 50%

Cambridge University authorities officially debar their students from working more than six hours a week. As a result, many students ignore them and get bar or baby-sitting jobs around town, and most take on temporary holiday work. Life-modelling opportunities for local artists are common and can provide some quick cash for those who don't mind getting their kit off.

SPORTS

○ BUSA RANKING 6

Face it, Cambridge breeds many more than its fair share of sporting deities. Many of the rulers of rugby, captains of cricket and angels of athletics have come running from Cambridge's sporting fields. However even the weediest wimps are encouraged to exert themselves in anything from tiddlywinks to boxing, but most often, rowing. Intercollegiate rivalries perk up the sporting calendar no end, as do Varsity fixtures with the University of Oxford – the annual boat race is still a huge national event and rugby prompts much chest-thumping. Whatever the game, it's probably played in a college society or team and, if not there, in the University as a whole.

SPORTS FACILITIES

Each College has its own facilities to a varying degree, but the University as a whole doesn't have all that much to call its own, except for *endless* playing fields, a squash centre, three new indoor cricket lanes, a gym and one of the country's few real tennis clubs – *a cross between tennis and extreme violence.* There's funding galore for redressing deficiencies, however, and the city itself offers several important amenities. Kelsey Kerridge Sports Centre has a swimming pool, climbing wall and sports courts, and the River Cam offers the rowing teams, canoeists and inadvertent swimmers plenty of moist recreation.

SPORTING CLUBS

See individual college entries for the bigger picture. American Football; Boxing; Caving; Clay Pigeon Shooting; Croquet; Drag Hunt; Eton Fives; Field Sports; Gymnastics; Hang Gliding; Hill Walking; Korfball; Lacrosse; Life Saving; Parachuting; Pétanque; Polo; Power Lifting; Rambling; Real Tennis; Revolvers & Pistols; Rifles; Rugby League; Surf Squad; Trampoline; Ultimate Frisbee; Windsurfing. **See also Clubs tables.**

ATTRACTIONS

As if the University's own sports didn't satisfy every possible desire to spectate, there's always Cambridge United & City Football and Rugby Clubs. *The more Sloaney set can don their toff hats and pop off to Newmarket for the races and lose all daddy's money.*

ACCOMMODATION

IN COLLEGE

○ CATERED 95% **○ 1ST YRS LIVING IN** 100% **○ INSURANCE PREMIUM** £

AVAILABILITY *One of Cambridge's best features is being able to live in college accommodation.* Most colleges have room for all first years and finalists, and second years who can't be squeezed into the college itself will usually be offered some kind of college-owned housing nearby. *The rooms vary from palatial suites to pokey cupboards without central heating, although most are fairly impressive.* Older rooms around the college courts can look *spectacular* from the outside, but the *more modern tend to offer better living conditions.* Sharing a room is rare, but sets (two linked rooms with lounge/study area) are fairly common. *On the flipside, there can be a reality-shock when students graduate after having been shielded for three years from the unpleasantness of cooking, cleaning and domestic budgeting.* There's limited availability for couples and even less for students with children. At many colleges, the best rooms are reserved for Scholars – those who get firsts in exams. Each college makes its own arrangements so check the college entries.

CAR PARKING *Students aren't technically allowed to bring cars to their colleges, but some outer colleges (where parking is less impossible) aren't as staunch sticklers for policy.*

EXTERNALLY

○ AVE RENT £80-120

AVAILABILITY Pretty much everyone lives in college, but for those few that don't (postgrads and some others) accommodation can be tough to source. *The hand-me-down housing method has kept the severest problems at bay but students do have to keep an eye open for a few landlords who're willing to make a fast buck from a student's bad luck.* Usually livers-out share houses. *Relations with the local community are generally pretty good and there are no student ghettos, although quirky, cosmopolitan Mill Road and, although rarely from choice, Milton Road are popular. The only place students should rule out is the north of the city, because it's easy enough to find something closer.* Students who choose to live out have to find somewhere within three miles of the city centre.

HOUSING HELP For fast relief students can refer to the Accommodation Syndicate (Kellet Lodge)

C

who keep a list of suitable accommodation, *often a little pricier than those on the open market but always up to scratch.*

WELFARE ⓤⓤⓤⓤⓤⓤⓤⓤⓤⓤⓤⓤⓤ

SERVICES

- **LGBT OFFICER & SOCIETY** ○ **WOMEN'S OFFICER & SOCIETY** ○ **MATURE STUDENTS' OFFICER**
- **INTERNATIONAL STUDENTS' OFFICER & SOCIETY**
- **DISABILITIES OFFICER & SOCIETY** ○ **ETHNIC MINORITIES OFFICER & SOCIETY** ○ **NIGHTLINE**
- **UNIVERSITY COUNSELLORS** 7 FULL/7 PART
- **CRIME RATING** !!

CUSU has no full-time welfare staff – that's another job for the colleges – but there is the University Counselling Service, which a number of students turn to at some point during their time here: academic pressure is high. There are support groups of every flavour, including HIV/AIDS, and most colleges have a society of some description for postgrads.

HEALTH Most colleges have their own nurses or doctors and the University operates a dental service for students' teething troubles.

WOMEN Several colleges have only started to allow women students over the last two decades and *some are still reeling from the shock. As female numbers grow the situation and the facilities improve, but the academic staff of some departments and colleges are still ominously predominantly male. The prevailing chauvinism is that of a previous generation and some women end up pedalling on a lower gear just to show they can. The most blatant m-c-piggery rears its head in some college bars where the tone can border on the oppressive.* But, in the face of aggression, women have taken steps. There's a Women's Council, Women's Executive, Women's Handbook, free rape alarms and so on.

CRECHES/NURSERY Queens' has run a University-wide staff & student crèche for some years and Gonville & Caius is now following suit. The University nursery has 88 places for staff and students' kids.

LESBIAN/GAY/BISEXUAL Cambridge has the largest LGBT Society in the UK and *there's a long tradition of relative sexual tolerance in the University. Gay icons such as E M Forster, Sir Ian McKellen and Stephen Fry have passed through its portals.*

DISABILITIES Cambridge was not originally built with wheelchairs in mind, although it is blessed with a lack of hills. However, a fair amount of building has been going on over the last 20 years and there has been a *genuine attempt* to make these new buildings accessible at least. Individual colleges have provisions for disabled students. The Disability Resource Centre (DRC) has a number of advisors and resources. For sight-impaired students, large print or Braille exam papers are available. Access in the colleges varies, *but students with motor disabilities should look at Robinson, Fitzwilliam and New Hall first.*

CRIME Not a huge problem in the city, *but trouble lurks on open spaces like Jesus Green, and Parker's Piece should be avoided at night.*

DRUGS The colleges officially have a zero tolerance policy, *but cannabis possession isn't a hanging offence (walk on the roof however, and you're out). Harder drugs, particularly cocaine, aren't uncommon among male sloanes – but then, they can get away with anything, really.*

FINANCE

○ **AVE DEBT PER YEAR** £3,308 ○ **HOME STUDENT FEES** £3,000

FEES Cambridge is charging the whole three grand for tuition fees, but bursaries dependent on parental income will help with living costs. There'll be up to £5,000 a year for mature students. Other costs: postgrads pay £5,098, which includes a college fee of £2,013. International students cough up from £10,845 (Arts) to £13,584 *for the pleasure of being able to say they studied in quaint olde England.*

SUPPORT Most financial assistance comes from the colleges and takes the form of hardship funds, academic prizes or *archaic* bursaries (cash for Catholic girls whose parents converted from Judaism, for instance).

> ◎ **'When I started at Cambridge, I was anxious to be Prime Minister but uncertain through which political party this might best be arranged. I therefore joined the Liberals, the Labour Party and the Conservative Party as it seemed wise not to put all my eggs in one basket.' – Matthew Parris, journalist and ex-MP**

Words in italics are Push's point of view — take it or leave it...

CHRIST'S COLLEGE, CAMBRIDGE

THIS COLLEGE IS PART OF THE UNIVERSITY OF CAMBRIDGE AND STUDENTS ARE ENTITLED TO USE ITS FACILITIES

CHRIST'S COLLEGE Cambridge, CB2 3BU **TEL** (01223) 334 900 **E-MAIL** admissions@christs.cam.ac.uk
WEBSITE www.christs.cam.ac.uk **CHRIST'S COLLEGE STUDENTS' UNION** Cambridge, CB2 3BU **TEL** (01223) 465 545
E-MAIL christs-jcr@lists.cam.ac.uk **WEBSITE** www.christsjcr.com

GENERAL

Christ's is only 300 metres from King's Parade and is *slap bang in the middle of the city*, right by the shops and the bus station (and Burger King). It is one of the older and *most beautiful* colleges, built around four courts (with some parts dating back to the 15th-century), except for 'the Typewriter', the 70s accommodation block, which, *visually, is a poke in the eye, but, socially, a pat on the back. Academic standards are very high which can up the pressure (there are showers in the library for students working a little too energetically). There's a cheerful, supportive, sociable atmosphere that helps let off some academic steam.*

SEX RATIO: ♂62 ♀38	**FOUNDED:** 1448
FULL-TIME U'GRADS: 440	**PART-TIME:** 0
POSTGRADS: 114	**MATURE:** N/A
STATE:PRIVATE SCHOOL: 54:46	**DISABLED:** N/A
ACADEMIC RANKING: 4	**INTERNATIONAL:** 15%

Smallish Buttery Bar; two bops/term, biennial balls; theatre/venue (200); film soc; Plumb auditorium for recitals; music rehearsal rooms; *mighty lung-ed* chapel choir; *strong* drama at the purpose built New Court Theatre; media centre. 'Christ's Pieces' termly newspaper (£1); Milton Society for dining/debating. Three libraries (120,000 books); 40 computers, 24-hr; internet access points in all rooms. Video hire service. *Strong* Christian Union; CofE chapel. JCR taxi reimbursement scheme with College; vending machines. Successes in men's football, rugby and hockey; squash courts on site, but most sports facilities (four football, one cricket and two rugby pitches, two squash courts) a mile away; new boats in the boat club; *active* societies for table tennis, squash or in Jesus Lane hostels; *decent rooms but the kitchens don't have ovens.* Canteen and formal meals. CCTV; college sick bay; nurse; late-night taxi service; free rape alarms; LGBT, International Students' and Women's Officer (and Men's Officer if welfare officer isn't a bloke). Means-tested bursaries and academic scholarships.

FAMOUS ALUMNI

Sacha Baron-Cohen (aka Borat/Ali G, *booyakasha*); Charles Darwin (revolutionary evolutionary); John Milton (poet); Lord Mountbatten of Burma; ; C P Snow (writer); Richard Whiteley (*late Countdown love-god*).

CHURCHILL COLLEGE, CAMBRIDGE

THIS COLLEGE IS PART OF THE UNIVERSITY OF CAMBRIDGE AND STUDENTS ARE ENTITLED TO USE ITS FACILITIES

CHURCHILL COLLEGE Cambridge, CB3 0DS **TEL** (01223) 336000 **E-MAIL** admissions@chu.cam.ac.uk
WEBSITE www.chu.cam.ac.uk **CHURCHILL JCR** Storey's Way, Cambridge, CB3 0DS **E-MAIL** jcr-president@chu.cam.ac.uk
WEBSITE http://jcr.chu.cam.ac.uk

GENERAL

A mile from King's Parade and looking rather *prison-ish, Churchill isn't the most attractive or best located of colleges. It is however one of the more modern, progressive and larger, and home of the University radio. Its newness offers other advantages over more traditional Cambridge colleges in terms of facilities and space (being well-endowed in the grounds department helps). More students come from state schools and there are more scientists (and a few arty sorts, though), so pretensions and stereotypes get funny looks rather than approval.*

SEX RATIO: ♂69 ♀31	**FOUNDED:** 1960
FULL-TIME U'GRADS: 484	**PART-TIME:** 0
POSTGRADS: 306	**MATURE:** 1%
STATE:PRIVATE SCHOOL: 60:40	**DISABLED:** 48
ACADEMIC RANKING: 18	**INTERNATIONAL:** 19%

Spacious bar; 'the pav' every Friday (free weekly ent with themes – *great if you've got a nappy to showcase*); spring ball; film theatre (cap 300); GODS theatre group; jazz; music recitals; orchestra; *Active* JCR with reading, TV, games and party rooms. 'Winston' mag for goss; University radio station. Four libraries (45,000 books); 37 computers, 24-hr; free language

Words in italics are Push's point of view – take it or leave it...

courses for all students. Chapel. Sports pitches on-site (tennis, football, cricket, hockey); squash courts; multigym. All except most fourth years live in; all accommodation on site; biggest dining hall in Cambridge, (non-formal); phone and internet in all rooms; cafeteria, access to self-catering; veggie options; *decent kitchens*. CCTV; swipe cards. Nurse; some disabled facilities; free late night taxi service and attack alarms; scholarship, travel grants, 'Winston Bursary' and hardship funds.

FAMOUS ALUMNI
Geoff Travis (founder of Rough Trade record label)

CLARE COLLEGE, CAMBRIDGE

THIS COLLEGE IS PART OF THE UNIVERSITY OF CAMBRIDGE AND STUDENTS ARE ENTITLED TO USE ITS FACILITIES

◉ CLARE COLLEGE Trinity Lane, Cambridge, CB2 1TL **TEL** (01223) 333 200 **E–MAIL** admissions@clare.cam.ac.uk **WEBSITE** www.clare.cam.ac.uk **◉ UNION OF CLARE STUDENTS** Memorial Court, Queens Road, Cambridge, CB2 1TL **TEL** (01223) 333 200 **E–MAIL** ucs@clare.cam.ac.uk **WEBSITE** http://ucs.clare.cam.ac.uk

GENERAL
Clare's *proud* of its history – it's the second oldest college in Cambridge, with the oldest bridge, linking parts of the college that sit *elegantly* on either bank of the Cam. It's a *gorgeous and gleaming* riverside college with *an unpretentious attitude and a healthy social mix*. The *renowned* Clare Cellars hosts bands and DJs a couple of times a week. *Students from other colleges (Push will let them remain anonymous) have been heard to say that, if they had their application over again, they'd put Clare at the top of their list.*

SEX RATIO: ♂51 ♀49	FOUNDED: 1326
FULL-TIME U'GRADS: 469	PART-TIME: 0
POSTGRADS: 198	MATURE: 1%
STATE:PRIVATE SCHOOL: 56:44	DISABLED: 9
ACADEMIC RANKING: 9	INTERNATIONAL: 10%

Atmospheric cellars (bar cap 200) have a University-wide ents reputation; two venues – bar and a chill-out room; pool table, juke box; weekly theme nights, DJs, jazz; comedy; extensive gardens used for annual May Ball attended by 950 students (*most romantic in Cambridge*). College paper, 'Clareification'. Two libraries (33,000 books); DVD loan service, 24-hr law reading room f*or reading law, natch*; 40 computers; all rooms have internet access. CofE chapel used for classical recitals; semi-professional choir. Sports fields (four acres) 1.5 miles away; football and rowing strong; table football *for the less athletic*. Almost all are guaranteed rooms. Secure bike compound. Most students eat in the dining hall (*Italian bias* with veggie option). CCTV; SU welfare officers, nurse; counselling; hardship fund, travel and book grants.

FAMOUS ALUMNI
Sir David Attenborough (TV naturalist); Peter Lilley MP (Con); Paul Mellon (philanthropist); Matthew Parris (ex-MP, Times sketch writer); Siegfried Sassoon (poet); Cecil Sharp (folk music historian); Richard Stilgoe (entertainer/lyricist); James Watson (discovered DNA); Andrew Wiles (proved Fermat's Last Theorem).

CORPUS CHRISTI COLLEGE, CAMBRIDGE

THIS COLLEGE IS PART OF THE UNIVERSITY OF CAMBRIDGE AND STUDENTS ARE ENTITLED TO USE ITS FACILITIES

◉ CORPUS CHRISTI COLLEGE Cambridge, CB2 1RH **TEL** (01223) 338 000 **E–MAIL** admissions@corpus.cam.ac.uk **WEBSITE** www.corpus.cam.ac.uk **◉ CORPUS CHRISTI JCR** Corpus Christi College, Cambridge, CB2 1RH **WEBSITE** www.corpus.cam.ac.uk/jcr

GENERAL
Corpus Christi, founded by the townsfolk to train priests, is downtown (on King's Parade), more or less opposite St Catharine's. *The dark stone of many of its buildings at first seems spooky and austere but after a while the shadowy gatehouse becomes warm and welcoming – like the students inside.* The Old Court is mid-14th century; its modern equivalent New Court was

completed in 1827 by the designer of the National Gallery. As members of one of the smallest colleges, *Corpus folk like to see themselves as one big, huggy family. It's a tight community with a strong sense of identity.*

SEX RATIO: ♂58 ♀42	FOUNDED: 1352
FULL-TIME U'GRADS: 270	PART-TIME: 0
POSTGRADS: 190	MATURE: N/A
STATE:PRIVATE SCHOOL: 41:59	DISABLED: 3
ACADEMIC RANKING: 16	INTERNATIONAL: 21%

Bar with regular 'slacks' – live music – and bops; *enthusiastic* drama, owns the experimental Playroom theatre in town; two or three concerts in the Master's Lodge each term; May Ball every year. Two libraries – a hi-tech and *cyber-savvy* third is being built that will more than double the book stock (over 100,000 books including the largest medieval manuscript stash in the UK); 15 PCs/Macs; Ethernet in all rooms. Weekly newsletter (Corporeal); CofE chapel; *involved* JCR. *Good rowers and ruggers;* three acres of sports fields 10 mins away; squash courts, bowling green, snooker room. Annual sports tournament with Corpus Christi, Oxford – *frequently unsuccessful.* Everyone lives in; gates closed at 11pm – students have keys; thrice weekly candlelit dinner with waiter service; cafeteria. Three rooms for mobility-impaired students; *access not brilliant.* Finance tutor to help with money worries; bursaries, scholarships and hardship fund.

FAMOUS ALUMNI
Christopher Isherwood (writer); Christopher Marlowe (playwright); Lord Sieff (M&S); E P Thompson (historian).

DOWNING COLLEGE, CAMBRIDGE

THIS COLLEGE IS PART OF THE UNIVERSITY OF CAMBRIDGE AND STUDENTS ARE ENTITLED TO USE ITS FACILITIES

◉ **DOWNING COLLEGE** Cambridge, CB2 1DQ **TEL** (01223) 334 800 **E-MAIL** admissions@dow.cam.ac.uk **WEBSITE** www.dow.cam.ac.uk ◉ **JUNIOR COMMON ROOM** Downing College, Cambridge, CB2 1DQ **TEL** (01223) 334 825 **E-MAIL** president@downingjcr.co.uk **WEBSITE** www.downingjcr.co.uk

GENERAL
A little over 500 metres from King's Parade is the *elegant* Downing College, a *welcoming* expanse of *spacious* lawns and neoclassical architecture from the last 200 years. *It's sat roughly where town meets gown geographically speaking, a tad further out than the other city centre colleges – perhaps this is why its students are more down-to-earth. The College is noted for sporting achievements, but if your idea of exertion is feeding the vast squirrel population then fear not, there's plenty more on offer, including a thriving music society. Social indulgence can take precedence over banner-waving, but Downing students are active on the University-wide hack scene as well.*

SEX RATIO: ♂56 ♀44	FOUNDED: 1800
FULL-TIME U'GRADS: 448	PART-TIME: 0
POSTGRADS: 230	MATURE: 1%
STATE:PRIVATE SCHOOL: 58:42	DISABLED: 180
ACADEMIC RANKING: 15	INTERNATIONAL: 10%

Large, *plush* student-run bar, longest hours in the University; *popular* baguette bar; student bands, cabaret, films and drama in Howard Building (cap 120), *luvvied-up* drama soc shows in the Dining Hall; weekly bops in Party Room, cheesy/jazz/theme discos and karaoke; music practice rooms; annual ball. Bi-termly college mag, 'Griffin'. Library (47,000 books); 40 computers, 24-hr access; intranet sockets in most bedrooms (£25 per term); CofE chapel; Student community action group. *Sportilicious – strong on rowing, football, rugby and hockey;* swanky boathouse plus nine acres of playing fields a mile away, gym on-site. Everyone lives in; *quality* rooms; CCTV, entry phones; two flats for couples; pay-as-you-eat meals; three candlelit formals a week; LGBT, Women's, Men's, Mature, International, Postgrad and Ethnic Minorities Officers; nurse, physio and nearby medical practice; free pregnancy tests and attack alarms; fortnightly women's council meeting; *good* access, adapted rooms; hardship fund, travel grants.

FAMOUS ALUMNI
Michael Apted (director, James Bond); Mike Atherton (former England cricket captain); Quentin Blake (illustrator); John Cleese (comedian); Andy Hamilton (comedian & script writer); Thandie Newton (actress); Trevor Nunn (theatre director); Michael Winner (*bad* film director/restaurant critic).

Words in italics are Push's point of view — take it or leave it...

EMMANUEL COLLEGE, CAMBRIDGE

THIS COLLEGE IS PART OF THE UNIVERSITY OF CAMBRIDGE AND STUDENTS ARE ENTITLED TO USE ITS FACILITIES

⊙ **EMMANUEL COLLEGE** Cambridge, CB2 3AP **TEL** (01223) 334 290 **E-MAIL** admissions@emma.cam.ac.uk
WEBSITE www.emma.cam.ac.uk ⊙ **JUNIOR COMMON ROOM** Emmanuel College, Cambridge, CB2 3AP
E-MAIL online@ecsu.org.uk **WEBSITE** www.ecsu.org.uk

GENERAL

Emma (as Emmanuel's *affectionately* known),
500 metres from King's Parade, is a collection of
dignified 16th-century buildings, 60s
accommodation blocks, *elegant* landscaped
gardens and a duck pond, replete with resident
ducks. *Emmanuel's perceived by other students
as unpretentious, approachable, party-lovers,
who are well represented in University activities.*

SEX RATIO: ♂47 ♀53	FOUNDED: 1584
FULL-TIME U'GRADS: 460	PART-TIME: 0
POSTGRADS: 207	MATURE: 5%
STATE:PRIVATE SCHOOL: 61:39	DISABLED: 32
ACADEMIC RANKING: 5	INTERNATIONAL: 7%

Split-level bar (cap 200); ball/event every year;
theatre in new Queen's building; films, DJ
nights, quizzes, live funk, indie and jazz nights;
college music and drama societies. Weekly 'Roar'
mag. Library (51,500 books); 30 computers in two
rooms, 24-hr; all rooms networked on-site, help
provided for off-site net set up. Chapel designed
by Christopher Wren. Sports fields (2.5 acres)
and *impressive* pavilion 20 mins away; squash
courts; outdoor swimming pool in the grounds;
boats. *Rowers by tradition.* All undergrads live in
(£68/wk); internet connections in all rooms.
Optional formals; veggie and vegan options.
CCTV; part-time nurse; part-time counsellor; free
condoms and pregnancy tests; exam-time
stressbusters (yoga, study skills workshops);
Women's group & Officer; Disabilities and
Access officers.

FAMOUS ALUMNI

Graham Chapman (Monty Python's Brian);
Michael Frayn (playwright); Eddie George
(ex-Gov, Bank of England); F R Leavis (lit crit);
Rory McGrath (TV *personality*); Lord Cecil
Parkinson (Tory); Griff Rhys Jones (comic).

FITZWILLIAM COLLEGE, CAMBRIDGE

THIS COLLEGE IS PART OF THE UNIVERSITY OF CAMBRIDGE AND STUDENTS ARE ENTITLED TO USE ITS FACILITIES

⊙ **FITZWILLIAM COLLEGE** Storey's Way, Cambridge, CB3 0DG **TEL** (01223) 332 000 **E-MAIL** admissions@fitz.cam.ac.uk
WEBSITE www.fitz.cam.ac.uk ⊙ **JUNIOR MEMBERS' ASSOCIATION** Fitzwilliam College, Storey's Way, Cambridge, CB3 0DG
WEBSITE www.srfc.ucam.org/fitzjcr

GENERAL

Fitz isn't a typical Cambridge college. For a start, its
main buildings are modern and red-brick. It admits
more state school students than most. *It prides
itself on being friendly, down to earth and not
claustrophobic or overwhelming.* It's set apart from
the other colleges, a mile from King's Parade at the
top of Cambridge's only hill (*well, a shallow slope*)
next to New Hall in the city's *business* area. *The
location may contribute to its sociable atmosphere –
students have to make more of an effort than most
to meet people outside the college walls.*

SEX RATIO: ♂61 ♀39	FOUNDED: 1869
FULL-TIME U'GRADS: 491	PART-TIME: 0
POSTGRADS: 191	MATURE: 1%
STATE:PRIVATE SCHOOL: 65:35	DISABLED: 15
ACADEMIC RANKING: 13	INTERNATIONAL: 12%

Large *departure-loungey* bar hosts quizzes and
karaoke; Fitz Entz twice a term, *big and very
popular*; concerts in chapel; Fitz Barbershop
singers; swing band; regular theatre; *state-of-the-
art* 250-cap venue, cinema, concerts and sports;
termly Events (mini-balls); annual
(*maxi-*)ball. Good JCR facilities; Weekly 'Billy
Bulletin' newsletter. Library (38,000 books); 40
computers, 24-hr; cybercafé. Chapel. *Good* sports
fields (seven acres) including a boathouse 600m
away plus facilities on site; tennis and squash
courts, multigym; *successful football.* All years
can live in College or College-owned houses;
internet points in rooms. CCTV, swipe cards;
shared nurse, welfare officers; free taxis and
attack alarms; Linkline listening service. Two
en suite disabled rooms; chairlift access; ramps.

FAMOUS ALUMNI

Nick Clarke (broadcaster); Charlotte Hudson
(Watchdog presenter); Derek Pringle (cricketer);
Sir David Starkey (TV historian); Sarah
Winckless (Olympic rower).

Words in italics are Push's point of view – take it or leave it...

GIRTON COLLEGE, CAMBRIDGE

THIS COLLEGE IS PART OF THE UNIVERSITY OF CAMBRIDGE AND STUDENTS ARE ENTITLED TO USE ITS FACILITIES

◉ **GIRTON COLLEGE** Huntingdon Road, Cambridge, CB3 0JG **TEL** (01223) 338 972 **E–MAIL** admissions@girton.cam.ac.uk **WEBSITE** www.girton.cam.ac.uk ◉ **JUNIOR MEMBERS' ASSOCIATION** Girton College, Huntingdon Road, Cambridge, CB3 0JG **TEL** (01223) 338 898 **WEBSITE** www.girtonjcr.com

GENERAL

Founded in 1869 as a women-only college Girton was built two and a half miles from the city centre *to protect the city's hapless male undergrads from marauding Girtonian wenches.* Mixed since 1979, this *liberal and relaxed* college now has an even balance of chaps and chapesses. Being out of town gives it the benefit of over 50 acres of grounds surrounding the *imposing* Gothic redbrick buildings. *The distance means integration with the rest of the University can prove difficult – wags at other colleges often quip that more of them have been to India than to Girton – although fun-loving Girtonians seem quite proud of their distinctive lifestyle.*

SEX RATIO: ♂49 ♀51	
FULL-TIME U'GRADS: 528	PART-TIME: 0
POSTGRADS: 195	MATURE: 2%
STATE:PRIVATE SCHOOL: 55:45	DISABLED: 4
ACADEMIC RANKING: 24	INTERNATIONAL: 14%

Bar; regular ents; film nights, annual garden party; annual revue; *successful and comparatively cheap* spring ball; Dramatic society; the prestigious choir tours and records choral CDs. JCR newsletters: termly 'Angle' and *anarchic* fortnightly 'Bogsheet'; *Environmentally-minded* JCR. Library (100,000 books, open till 11pm); 44 computers, 24-hrs. Chapel. *Sports facilities on site (the only college with an indoor heated swimming pool – nice) and the necessary bike ride into town keeps Girtonians fit.* All students live in, some second years in 'Wolfie' (Wolfson Court) closer to town; weekly formal meals; reciprocal dining rights with Pembroke and Downing. Nursery with 80- places. Free taxis on Thurs and Sat evenings; self-defence classes; night porter. International students', Ethnic Minorities', Green, Women's, Men's & LGBT Officers. Assorted cashflow help available.

FAMOUS ALUMNI

Lady Brenda Hale (first woman lawlord); Queen Margarethe of Denmark; Joan Robinson (economist); Arianna Stassinopoulos (writer); Angela Tilby (writer and TV producer); Sandi Toksvig (*dinky* comedian).

GONVILLE & CAIUS COLLEGE, CAMBRIDGE

THIS COLLEGE IS PART OF THE UNIVERSITY OF CAMBRIDGE AND STUDENTS ARE ENTITLED TO USE ITS FACILITIES

◉ **GONVILLE & CAIUS COLLEGE** Cambridge, CB2 1TA **TEL** (01223) 332 447 **E–MAIL** admissions@cai.cam.ac.uk **WEBSITE** www.cai.cam.ac.uk ◉ **GONVILLE & CAIUS STUDENTS' UNION** Gonville & Caius College, Cambridge, CB2 1TA **TEL** (01223) 332 447 **WEBSITE** http://gcsu.cai.ucam.org

GENERAL

The most important thing about Gonville & Caius is to pronounce its name correctly. Gonville's okay, apart from sounding like a Muppet character and most people drop that bit anyway, but Caius is pronounced 'keys'. Caius is based on two sites, eight mins walk apart. The main building's at one end of King's Parade and is centred on the *fine* old Renaissance Caius Court, next to *French-Chateau-style* Tree Court, the only college court in Cambridge with, er, trees. Sitting on the Backs (meadow banks) across the river is '60s building Harvey Court, the first year accommodation, *which bears more than a passing resemblance to a multi-storey car park. (Although pretty views provide some compensation). There's a friendly enough atmosphere and a good social mix.*

SEX RATIO: ♂57 ♀43	FOUNDED: 1348
FULL-TIME U'GRADS: 543	PART-TIME: 0
POSTGRADS: 221	MATURE: 1%
STATE:PRIVATE SCHOOL: 42:58	DISABLED: 0
ACADEMIC RANKING: 2	INTERNATIONAL: 12%

Bar hosts karaoke, quizzes and cross-dressing extravaganza, 'Miss Caius' competition; Bateman concert room; annual ball. Caiustone newsletter; many drinking/dining clubs; *active* music soc. Working library and old library (90,000 books); 52 PCs, some 24-hr. Chapel; CofE chaplain. *Good* sports facilities in College and 400m away (three acres and a bar); *successful* rowers. All first and third years live in hall, second years in *crummier* College hostels; almost all rooms have internet points; work in progress on a new accommodation block next to Harvey Court. *Was*

C

worst food in Cambridge, getting better; occasional formal meals; some accommodation for married students. Swipe cards; nurse, pregnancy tests, free condoms; Ethnic minorities, Women's and Access Officers; bursaries; scholarships; grants and book grants. Ground floor accommodation and ramps for disabled students; lift access to Cockerell Library.

FAMOUS ALUMNI
Harold Abrahams (Olympic runner, featured in Chariots of Fire); Alistair Campbell (former Labour *Spin-King*); Kenneth Clark MP (*cigar-sucking* Tory); David Frost (broadcaster); William Harvey (discovered circulation of blood); Titus Oates (of Popish plot fame); Dr Venn (as in Venn diagram).

HOMERTON COLLEGE, CAMBRIDGE

THIS COLLEGE IS PART OF THE UNIVERSITY OF CAMBRIDGE AND STUDENTS ARE ENTITLED TO USE ITS FACILITIES

○ **HOMERTON COLLEGE** Cambridge, CB2 2PH **TEL** (01223) 507 252 **E-MAIL** admissions@homerton.cam.ac.uk
WEBSITE www.homerton.cam.ac.uk ○ **HOMERTON UNION OF STUDENTS** Homerton College, Cambridge, CB2 2PH
TEL (01223) 507 236 **WEBSITE** www.husonline.co.uk.uk

GENERAL
Homerton's probably the least Cambridgey Cambridge college, because of its location (a mile and a half out of town) and its academic set-up (formerly teaching education, though, since it became a bona fide Cambridge college in 2001, most subjects are now available). *It's less wealthy than some other colleges so has to court the conference trade. Being a relatively new arrival on the Cam collegiate scene, it's keen to get itself established but it's an outgoing, enterprising place filled with 'can-do' types who make the most of what's on offer. Students tend to socialise in College, but Homerton folk have made their University-level mark in sport, journalism and more.*

SEX RATIO: ♂30 ♀70	FOUNDED: 1695
FULL-TIME U'GRADS: 557	PART-TIME: N/A
POSTGRADS: 631	MATURE: 5%
STATE:PRIVATE SCHOOL: 70:30	DISABLED: 4
ACADEMIC RANKING: 26	INTERNATIONAL: 7%

Big bar; live bands in the Main Hall (300); dance/drama studio; steel band; choirs; chamber orchestra; wind band; annual ball; art room; *politically active* JCR with sabbatical president (only one in Cambridge). 'Hush' College mag. Library (60,000 books, 24-hr opening); 70 computers, 24-hr. Sports fields (25 acres) which, *unusually for Cambridge, are* on site; squash and tennis courts; shared boathouse. All-day buttery; dining hall; *food on the up.* Accommodation for all first years and finalists; *expensive but modern, good quality and largely en suite* internet access in rooms. Nurse; half-term crèche. Mature, International, LGBT, Women's, Ethnic Minorities' and Skills Training Officers; *large* LGBT soc; 24/7 welfare phone line. Travel and choral scholarships; hardship fund; mature student bursaries. All accommodation has disabled access.

FAMOUS ALUMNI
Julie Covington (actress/singer); Dawn French (*rotund Dibley vicar*)Nick Hancock (former presenter of They Think It's All Over – *he is now*); Nick Hornby (*pricklit* author) Cherie Lunghi (actress); Ben Oakley (British windsurfing coach); Kieran West (Olympian).

HUGHES HALL, CAMBRIDGE

THIS COLLEGE IS PART OF THE UNIVERSITY OF CAMBRIDGE AND STUDENTS ARE ENTITLED TO USE ITS FACILITIES

○ **HUGHES HALL** Mortimer Road, Cambridge, CB1 2EW **TEL** (01223) 331 897 **E-MAIL** ugadmissions@hughes.cam.ac.uk
WEBSITE www.hughes.cam.ac.uk ○ **HUGHES HALL MCR** Wollaston College, Cambridge, CB1 2EW
WEBSITE http://mcr.hughes.cam.ac.uk

GENERAL
Ten minutes stroll through the centre of Cambridge, over the wide, green grounds of Parker's Piece and far from the tourist bustle, is Hughes Hall, the oldest grad college in town. It's a small place alright, but a lot bigger than it

looks at first sight. Modern buildings give way to *attractive,* concealed gardens and 1900s red-brick architecture, *creating a tardis effect that's easy to get lost in. It may not be a vital stop on the tourist trail, but it's focused and friendly. Students are pretty proud of their college and, whereas the porters and staff at other colleges occasionally have to restrain themselves from punching snap-happy*

Americans, the good-natured chaps at Hughes are more likely to invite passers-by in for coffee and cake. Bless. Although it's traditionally for graduates, they've recently started taking in a handful of undergrads (whose numbers are increasing annually), although everyone – in both age and outlook – is mature.

SEX RATIO: ♂76 ♀24	FOUNDED: 1885
FULL-TIME U'GRADS: 95	PART-TIME: 0
POSTGRADS: 425	MATURE: 100%
STATE:PRIVATE SCHOOL: 50:50	DISABLED: 27
ACADEMIC RANKING: 29	INTERNATIONAL: 26%

Small but friendly bar, bedecked with oars; fortnightly themed bops, karaoke, quizzes, pool, big screen sport/politics. Active music and drama societies; several recitals per term; newly reinvented May Ball. Titchy library (3,540 books, 46 study spaces), but in the process of being enlarged; 298 computers, also set to increase;

network access in rooms (£25 termly connection fee), computer in every student room on the main site. Apolitical but strongly representational MCR; coffee room with newspapers and cinema screen (for weekend showings); cosy, hotel-style lounge with balcony and excellent view of cricket on Parker's Piece; yearbook. Strong rowers, footballers and cricketers. All first years and finalists can live in (£70-£84 p/w); some flats for couples; high-standard rooms (especially in new Fenners Building) with well-kitted kitchens; swipe cards; entry phones; guidebook for those living out. Students eat in functional dining hall; great food; Saturday brunches; weekly formal meals. Limited car parking for those who need it (medics and PGCEs); oversubscribed bike racks. Welfare, Ethics and Complaints Officers; nearby doctor's surgery; cheap rape alarms; CCTV.

FAMOUS ALUMNI
Alison Uttley (kids' writer).

JESUS COLLEGE, CAMBRIDGE

THIS COLLEGE IS PART OF THE UNIVERSITY OF CAMBRIDGE AND STUDENTS ARE ENTITLED TO USE ITS FACILITIES

○ **JESUS COLLEGE** Jesus Lane, Cambridge, CB2 8BL **TEL** (01223) 339 339 **E-MAIL** undergraduate-admissions@jesus.cam.ac.uk **WEBSITE** www.jesus.cam.ac.uk ○ **JESUS COLLEGE STUDENT UNION** Jesus College, Cambridge, CB2 8BL **E-MAIL** jcsu_president@jesus.cam.ac.uk **WEBSITE** www-jcsu.jesus.cam.ac.uk

GENERAL
Jesus College, built around an old convent with buildings dating from the 12th century, is five mins walk from King's Parade. Its chapel (built 1140) is the oldest building in Cambridge. It's seen as a posh, trendy college and combines sporting enthusiasm with a liberal, if not radical, ethos. It makes a genuine effort to recruit more women and students from state schools. The bar is the social suction point and is usually full by nightfall.

SEX RATIO: ♂56 ♀44	FOUNDED: 1496
FULL-TIME U'GRADS: 542	PART-TIME: 0
POSTGRADS: 228	MATURE: 1%
STATE:PRIVATE SCHOOL: 55:45	DISABLED: 3
ACADEMIC RANKING: 7	INTERNATIONAL: 8%

Bar, cliquey but well-equipped with TV screen, pool table, games machines; classical concerts in the Chapel (250); active choir; annual May Ball; music practice room. College mags: 'Red & Blackmail' and 'Peripheral Vision'. Two libraries (25,000 books); 26 computers, 24-hr; Ethernet in all rooms. CofE chapel. Excellent sports; squash and tennis courts, sports fields (four acres) and pavilion on site; boathopuse. Football, hockey and cricket especially strong. All students can live in (£73-£138/wk, 24wks); second and third years in desirable converted houses on College perimeter; eat in dining hall; formal meals five times weekly; self-catering facilities. Night porter; CCTV, entry-phones; nurse; physiotherapist; subsidised rape alarms; Women's and Welfare officers; bursaries, hardship fund and travel grants.

FAMOUS ALUMNI
S T Coleridge (poet); Alistair Cooke (late broadcaster); Thomas Cranmer (former Archbishop of Canterbury); Ted Dexter (cricketer); Prince Edward; Wilfred Hadfield (invented double yellow lines); Nick Hornby (writer); Richard Lacey (food safety guru); Thomas Malthus (economist).

 Sacha Baron Cohen, aka Ali G, set up the "All stars" College 3rds Football Team at Christ's.

KING'S COLLEGE, CAMBRIDGE

THIS COLLEGE IS PART OF THE UNIVERSITY OF CAMBRIDGE AND STUDENTS ARE ENTITLED TO USE ITS FACILITIES

◉ KING'S COLLEGE King's Parade, Cambridge, CB2 1ST **TEL** (01223) 331 100 **E-MAIL** undergraduate.admissions@kings.cam.ac.uk **WEBSITE** www.kings.cam.ac.uk **◉ JCR** King's College, King's Parade, Cambridge, CB2 1ST **TEL** (01223) 331 454 **WEBSITE** www-kcsu.org.uk

GENERAL

King's College, on King's Parade, *has many a dreaming spire and the famous* King's chapel (started in 1446). *There's a good mix of all Cambridge's different types and awe-inspiringly ancient surroundings. King's has a somewhat leftist tradition, relaxed and down to earth with an unusually high proportion of state school students (by Cambridge standards). Its porters are reputed to be the nicest in Cambridge.*

College bar open lunchtimes and seven evenings a week. Every term there's a Mingle (mini ball), June Event is a deluxe version. 'Red Dragon Pie' student mag; *breath-stopping* Ecumenical chapel. Main library (130,000 books) with *extensive* document archives; Rowe music library; 33 computers, 24-hr. Sports fields; multigym; shared boathouse, boats and canoes. All students can live in either on site or in a College-owned hostel nearby and eat in the dining hall; *cheap rents* (£58-£92); weekly formal meals during Michaelmas and Lent terms. Entry-phones; nurse; LGBT, Ethnic Minorities and Access Officers; a few rooms for wheelchair users.

SEX RATIO: ♂56 ♀44	FOUNDED: 1441
FULL-TIME U'GRADS: 407	PART-TIME: 0
POSTGRADS: 181	MATURE: <1%
STATE:PRIVATE SCHOOL: 72:28	DISABLED: 4
ACADEMIC RANKING: 10	INTERNATIONAL: 12%

FAMOUS ALUMNI

David Baddiel (comedian); Martin Bell MP (Ind); Rupert Brooke (poet); Zadie Smith (novelist); Alan Turing (computers); Johns Bird & Fortune (comedians); E M Forster (writer); John Maynard Keynes (economist); Michael Mates MP (Con); Salman Rushdie (writer).

LUCY CAVENDISH COLLEGE, CAMBRIDGE

THIS COLLEGE IS PART OF THE UNIVERSITY OF CAMBRIDGE AND STUDENTS ARE ENTITLED TO USE ITS FACILITIES

◉ LUCY CAVENDISH COLLEGE Lady Margaret Road, Cambridge, CB3 0BU **TEL** (01223) 332 190 **E-MAIL** lcc-admissions@list.cam.ac.uk **WEBSITE** www.lucy-cav.cam.ac.uk **◉ THE STUDENTS' UNION** Lucy Cavendish College, Cambridge, CB3 0BU **WEBSITE** www-kcsu.org.uk

GENERAL

Four of the buildings of Lucy Cavendish College (600 metres from King's Parade) date from the end of the 19th century, the rest are modern, including the library. The site's full of trees, *tranquil and quite beautiful,* complete with a tiny Anglo-Saxon herb garden – *perfect for peaceful study.* Only women over 21 years old are admitted and the average age is 30. *There's no bitchy boarding school atmosphere – it's a refreshingly diverse and progressive college where dedication, creativity and flexibility are rated higher than early educational success. There's a healthy dose of partying along with the intellectual exertions though and students are increasingly making their mark on the wider University stage.*

SEX RATIO: ♂0 ♀100	FOUNDED: 1965
FULL-TIME U'GRADS: 128	PART-TIME: 10
POSTGRADS: 113	MATURE: 100%
STATE:PRIVATE SCHOOL: 100:0	DISABLED: 3
ACADEMIC RANKING: 27	INTERNATIONAL: 23%

Café-style bar with jazz nights; music pavilion for practice and recitals; k*eeno choir. Modern, attractive* library (20,000 books, 24-hr); special collection of Victorian kids' books; 18 computers; network points in all bedrooms (£25 a term). Gym on site; rowing team. *College not known for athletic miracles, but, hey, they're only small. Quality* rooms are split between on site (£53-£68) or flats and houses spattered around town (£80.50-£202.50); provision for students with spouses or sprogs. Students and staff eat together (*a refreshing change*); formal dinners every Thursday; *admirable* self-catering facilities.

MAGDALENE COLLEGE, CAMBRIDGE

THIS COLLEGE IS PART OF THE UNIVERSITY OF CAMBRIDGE AND STUDENTS ARE ENTITLED TO USE ITS FACILITIES

○ **MAGDALENE COLLEGE** Cambridge, CB3 0AG **TEL** (01223) 332 100 **E–MAIL** admissions@magd.cam.ac.uk
WEBSITE www.magd.cam.ac.uk ○ **MAGDALENE JCR** Magdalene College, Cambridge, CB3 0AG
E–MAIL jcr.president@magd.cam.ac.uk **WEBSITE** http://jcr.magd.cam.ac.uk

C

GENERAL

If you want to cause a sudden embarrassed hush at parties say 'Maggdalleen'. To flow with wit and wisdom pronounce it correctly as 'Maudlin' – to be in the in-crowd, call it 'The Village'. The atmosphere at this college – 700 metres from King's Parade and with more river frontage than any other – *is far from maudlin and the lively social scene revolves around the bar.* Magdalene's one of the smaller colleges and *tradition and camaraderie pervade. An international flavour lends an air of culture to the atmosphere and the location gives students barely rivalled ease-of-access to pubs and eateries.* The College features medieval and 15th- and 16th-century courts as well as Pepys' Library, but *unfortunately, it hasn't escaped clumsy postwar architecture at some residential blocks.*

SEX RATIO: ♂51 ♀49	FOUNDED: 1542
FULL–TIME U'GRADS: 359	PART–TIME: 0
POSTGRADS: 183	MATURE: 1%
STATE:PRIVATE SCHOOL: 43:57	DISABLED: 3
ACADEMIC RANKING: 20	INTERNATIONAL: 15%

Bland bar; common room with widescreen Sky TV, pool table, ents; termly karaoke and quizzes; classical and jazz concerts in Benson Hall (cap 100); annual musical and freshers' play; annual garden party; biennial ball (*one of the best, very posh*). 'Ars Magna' termly College mag and biweekly 'Magd In' and 'Magd Out' e-mail newsletters. Three libraries (30,000 books in main one); 23 computers, 24-hr. CofE chapel. *Good* sports fields (eight acres) 500 metres away, shared with St John's; boathouse shared with Queens'. All students live in; *accommodation varies,* all rooms networked; canteen and self-catering facilities; *nightly formal meals, among Cambridge's finest.* CCTV; nurse; free rape alarms, condoms and pregnancy tests. International, Environmental and Ethics and LGBT officers; Equal Opps Rep. Scholarships.

FAMOUS ALUMNI

Katie Derham (ITN newsreader); Bamber Gascoigne (quizmaster, writer); Gavin Hastings (former Scottish rugby captain); Charles Kingsley (author); Charles Stewart Parnell (19th-C Irish nationalist); Samuel Pepys (diarist); Alan Rusbridger (editor, the Guardian); John Simpson (*danger-loving* BBC reporter).

NEW HALL, CAMBRIDGE

THIS COLLEGE IS PART OF THE UNIVERSITY OF CAMBRIDGE AND STUDENTS ARE ENTITLED TO USE ITS FACILITIES

○ **NEW HALL** Cambridge, CB3 0DF **TEL** (01223) 762 100 **E–MAIL** admissions@newhall.cam.ac.uk
WEBSITE www.newhall.cam.ac.uk ○ **NEW HALL UNION** New Hall College, Cambridge, CB3 0DF
E–MAIL jcr-president@newhall.cam.ac.uk **WEBSITE** www.newhall.cam.ac.uk/students/jcr

GENERAL

Founded in 1954 to up Cambridge's female population, New Hall's situated 1,200 metres from King's Parade and is capped with a *striking* dome roof – the only college dome in Oxbridge. *Free from excess history, tradition or accumulated wealth,* New Hall concentrates on supporting its students in their academic pursuits. *It can take itself too seriously sometimes, but the youth of the college means it's evolving and can be an exciting place to study.* New Hall has remained resolutely single-sex and *while students are perky enough about this, they tend to socialise elsewhere.*

SEX RATIO: ♂0 ♀100	FOUNDED: 1954
FULL–TIME U'GRADS: 387	PART–TIME: 4%
POSTGRADS: 69	MATURE: 0.6%
STATE:PRIVATE SCHOOL: 60:40	DISABLED: 21
ACADEMIC RANKING: 25	INTERNATIONAL: 19%

Bar (cap 100, open four times a week), *giant* TV, film, jazz nights; pool table, ice cream vending machine; concerts, drama soc, student bands and *popular club-style* events at the Dome (cap 300) three times a year; Vivien Stewart Room (60), Fellows' Drawing Room (45 and a Steinway) or the Long Room (200). Library (60,000 books); 24 computers, 24-hrs; art room

Words in italics are Push's point of view – take it or leave it...

C

(largest collection of contemporary women's art in Europe); darkroom. JCR newsletter, 'New-S Worthy'. *Successful* boat club; multigym; squash and tennis courts. 96% of undergrads live in; *good-quality* rooms, wide price range, most with internet connections; pay-as-you-eat canteen (*could be better but good for veggies*); formals once a week; permit parking; some CCTV; swipe cards; nurse; LBGT, International,

Target and Women's Officers; various support funds, including interesting expeditions *but New Hall's far from rolling in it.*

FAMOUS ALUMNI
Jocelyn Bell Burnell (discovered Pulsars); Frances Edmonds (writer); Joanna MacGregor (pianist); Sue Perkins (of Mel & Sue); Tilda Swinton (actress).

NEWNHAM COLLEGE, CAMBRIDGE

THIS COLLEGE IS PART OF THE UNIVERSITY OF CAMBRIDGE AND STUDENTS ARE ENTITLED TO USE ITS FACILITIES

◉ **NEWNHAM COLLEGE** Sidgwick Avenue, Cambridge, CB3 9DF **TEL** (01223) 335 700 **E-MAIL** lcc-admissions@newn.cam.ac.uk **WEBSITE** www.newn.cam.ac.uk ◉ **NEWNHAM COLLEGE JCR** Sidgwick Avenue, Cambridge, CB3 9DF **WEBSITE** http://newnhamjcr.com

GENERAL
In 1870 university education for ladies was a new and dangerous idea. In 1871 Newnham college *gave the establishment the finger* and started life as a house for young women who had to travel to learn. Only 1,200 metres from King's Parade, *Newnham is a distinctive Victorian building set in huge gardens. Gone are the days when righteous young Newnhamites had to fight for equal status within the university – until 1948 the ladies of Cambridge had the dubious honour of receiving only a title of degree, or 'BA tit' – but Newnhamites still make their voices heard on the issues of the day. The College buzzes with enthusiasm and, ahem, love of learning. Students have some of the most diverse backgrounds of the colleges and a determination to get everything out of the Cambridge experience.*

SEX RATIO: ♂0 ♀100	FOUNDED: 1871
FULL-TIME U'GRADS: 400	PART-TIME: 0
POSTGRADS: 149	MATURE: 1%
STATE:PRIVATE SCHOOL: 51:49	DISABLED: 4
ACADEMIC RANKING: 21	INTERNATIONAL: 15%

Boilerhouse bar open Tuesday and Saturday evenings (*nice and cheap*), regular live bands, comedy nights, quizzes and pool/table football tournaments; classical concerts and clubbing in the College Hall (cap 250); performing arts

studio; *pretty* Old Labs performance space; choir; orchestra; biennial ball; garden parties; plays performed in theatre studio, hall or garden; *posh* pianos. JCR provides TV, video and DVD, vending machines, photocopier. Observatory; *improved* library (90,000 books, 50 study places with net access points); 35 computers, 24-hr access; JCR women's library; art room. 'N-Vie' college paper; 'Newbiles' (Newnham-Bisexual-Lesbian) e-mail list; *active* JCR; fair trade stall twice-weekly;. Footie; rugby; lacrosse; sports field on site; multigym; tennis and netball courts. Most students live in; *assortment of room standards,* some with antiques, all rooms have network points. *Food is non-fatal,* self-catering facilities are *good;* six student parking spaces. Nurse; chaplain; rooms for wheelchair users; free condoms and pregnancy tests; special finance tutor. Women's, LGBT, Green, International and Ethnic Minorities Officers. Scholarships and hardship funds; grants for books, sport and travel.

FAMOUS ALUMNI
Diane Abbott (Britain's first black female MP, Lab); Joan Bakewell (broadcaster); Eleanor Bron, A S Byatt, Margaret Drabble, Katherine Whitehorn (writers); Germaine Greer (*female eunuch,* academic and *unlikely* Celebrity BB contestant); Patricia Hewitt MP (Lab); Dorothy Hodgkin (Chemistry Nobel laureate); Ann Mallalieu (Labour peer); Miriam Margolyes (actress); Julia Neuberger (female rabbi); Sylvia Plath (poet); Emma Thompson, Olivia Williams (actresses).

The Junior Common Room at Peterhouse, Cambridge, is called the Sex Club.
Former members include former Conservative leader Michael Howard.

Words in italics are Push's point of view – take it or leave it...

PEMBROKE COLLEGE, CAMBRIDGE

THIS COLLEGE IS PART OF THE UNIVERSITY OF CAMBRIDGE AND STUDENTS ARE ENTITLED TO USE ITS FACILITIES

PEMBROKE COLLEGE Cambridge, CB2 1RF **TEL** (01223) 338 100 **E-MAIL** admissions@pem.cam.ac.uk **WEBSITE** www.pem.cam.ac.uk **JUNIOR PARLOUR** Pembroke College, Cambridge, CB2 1RF **E-MAIL** jp-president@pem.cam.ac.uk **WEBSITE** www.pem.cam.ac.uk/jp

GENERAL

14th-century architecture and *lush* gardens mingle with redbrick buildings and '90s constructions. Just off King's Parade but away from most of the tourists, Pembroke College is *a pant-ruiningly attractive place to study.* The place has a *reputation for academic excellence and a wealth of extracurricular activities.* Plays are put on in the grounds and *the whole place is oozing with studyish enthusiasm. Students are well integrated with university existence, but things can get a bit insular. Sport and partying blow off steam.*

SEX RATIO: ♂52 ♀48	FOUNDED: 1347
FULL-TIME U'GRADS: 450	PART-TIME: 0
POSTGRADS: 202	MATURE: 2%
STATE:PRIVATE SCHOOL: 55:45	DISABLED: 12
ACADEMIC RANKING: 6	INTERNATIONAL: 12%

Bar; Old Cellars theatre (cap 50); concerts in Old Library; student bands in Junior Parlour and New Cellars; bops twice a term; library (60,000 books); music room; 26 computers; 24-hr lab; all rooms have internet connection. CofE chapel. 'Pembroke St' newsletter; 'Pem' arts mag. Pembroke runs a community centre in South London (where students can also stay). Winnie the Pooh Society, plus *sackloads* of other socs. *Especially good for the sporty;* rowing; sports fields and courts; 24-hr gym; aerobics; athletics; multigym; oldest bowling green in Europe. All students live in college or college houses; the newest block, Foundress Court, has a Japanese garden *for meditative types;* students eat in canteen; optional formal every night; *good food and veggie options; great* deli-made sarnies; *limited* self-catering in college; night porters; nurse; grants and scholarships; attack alarms and self-defence classes for women; Equal Opportunities, Anti-racism, Green, LGBT and Women's Officers.

FAMOUS ALUMNI

Peter Cook (comedy *god*); Raymond Dolby (audio inventor); Thomas Gray, Edmund Spenser (poets); Ted Hughes (late poet laureate); Eric Idle (Monty Python *funnyman*); Clive James (writer, presenter); Jonathan Lynn (writer, director); Bill Oddie (*comic and bird-fancier*); Pitt the Younger (PM); Tom Sharpe (writer); Chris Smith MP (former Lab); Sir John Sulston (Genome project).

PETERHOUSE, CAMBRIDGE

THIS COLLEGE IS PART OF THE UNIVERSITY OF CAMBRIDGE AND STUDENTS ARE ENTITLED TO USE ITS FACILITIES

PETERHOUSE Cambridge, CB2 1RD **TEL** (01223) 338 223 **E-MAIL** admissions@pet.cam.ac.uk **WEBSITE** www.pet.cam.ac.uk **PETERHOUSE JCR** Cambridge, CB2 1RD **E-MAIL** jcr@pet.ca.ac.uk **WEBSITE** www.srcf.ucam.org/pet-jcr

GENERAL

The smallest, oldest and *most traditional* of the Cambridge colleges, with *beautiful and well-kept* gardens. With high standards and fierce competition for places, even for Cambridge, Peterhouse *sucks in the academic elite and spits them out into top jobs.* It's rich and *well-respected, and although they're less true these days, the 'old boys' club' jibes from fellow colleges still get hurled around. Being so small, energetic movers and shakers play on the wider University stage.* Alcohol, sport, drama and alcohol are the *more popular pastimes.*

SEX RATIO: ♂63 ♀37	FOUNDED: 1284
FULL-TIME U'GRADS: 282	PART-TIME: 0
POSTGRADS: 122	MATURE: 3%
STATE:PRIVATE SCHOOL: 57:43	DISABLED: 19
ACADEMIC RANKING: 22	INTERNATIONAL: 13%

Bar; Music Room (cap 100) for clubbing and student bands, *but college tutors disapprove if it gets too boisterous;* theatre (180) for drama and classical concerts; biennial ball; drinking and debating societies; *irreverent and borderline tasteless* termly mag, 'the Sex'. Library (40,000 books, network points and five reading rooms), 16 computers; *net access all over the shop.* CofE chapel. *Fairly athletic types;* sports facilities

C

(eight acres shared with Clare College a mile away); squash court and gym on site; boathouse. All students live in College-maintained or arranged housing (£48-131 a week); most eat in the *gorgeous* dining hall; *limited self-catering (best at Parkside, off-site housing)*. Nurse; women's advisors; hardship fund; prizes and scholarships. Alternative prospectus online (www.srcf.ucam/ pet-jcr/prospectus/main.php).

FAMOUS ALUMNI

Charles Babbage (computing pioneer); Thomas Campion (poet); Stephanie Cook (Olympic gold medallist); Richard Crashaw (poet); Sir Christopher Cockerell (invented the hovercraft); Colin Greenwood (Radiohead); Michael Howard MP (Con ex-leader); James Mason (actor); Sam Mendes (director); Max Perutz (Nobel Prize winner); Michael Portillo MP (Con); Frank Whittle (invented the jet engine).

QUEENS' COLLEGE, CAMBRIDGE

THIS COLLEGE IS PART OF THE UNIVERSITY OF CAMBRIDGE AND STUDENTS ARE ENTITLED TO USE ITS FACILITIES

QUEENS' COLLEGE Cambridge, CB3 9ET **TEL** (01223) 335 511 **E-MAIL** admissions@quns.cam.ac.uk **WEBSITE** www.queens.cam.ac.uk **QUEENS' COLLEGE JCR** Cambridge, CB3 9ET **E-MAIL** jcr_president@quns.cam.ac.uk **WEBSITE** http://jcrwww.quns.cam.ac.uk

GENERAL

Queens' is halfway along Silver Street, a *major* student pipeline to the main arts faculties. *It's a mixture of beautiful Elizabethan courts, a passable redbrick thing and one of Cambridge's many iffy Cripps Court concrete uglies*. It's right opposite the Anchor pub, a *favourite* riverside student and tourist hang-out. *It has an amiable, laid-back charm – a sort of bastion of innocent fun – and a healthier state/private mix than some colleges. It's notoriously thespy and holds a high-profile drama competition every year.*

SEX RATIO: ♂58 ♀42	FOUNDED: 1448
FULL-TIME U'GRADS: 535	PART-TIME: 0
POSTGRADS: 323	MATURE: 0
STATE:PRIVATE SCHOOL: 54:46	DISABLED: 0
ACADEMIC RANKING: 8	INTERNATIONAL: 8%

Spacious, conservatory-endowed bar Fitzpatrick Hall (380) for 'Bats' drama soc performances,

student bands and *among the best* college club nights in Cambridge as well as Jingles (*cheese*); films; biennial ball; three music rooms; annual outdoor performance in Cloister Court. 'The Drain' student mag. *Successful* Rag. Two libraries (70,000 books); 12 PCs, three Macs, 24-hr. CofE chapel. Multigym and squash courts onsite; *big* sports fields (15 acres shared with Robinson) 800m away; *very modern* boathouse; *success* in male and female footie. All undergraduates can live in, except a few fourth years; Ethernet points in all rooms; *good* food in dining hall; nightly formals; *practically zilch* self-catering. *Limited* disabled access; Equal Opps/Welfare, Target, Women's, Environmental, LGBT Officers. Nurse; crèche; free pregnancy tests. Hardship fund (usually pays crèche fees); scholarships.

FAMOUS ALUMNI

Erasmus (Renaissance humanist); Mike Foale (first Brit in space); Stephen Fry (the *inimitable* writer, actor, comedian and *luvvie*); Michael Gibson, John Spencer (rugby players); Tom Holland (Bond's Q 1986-89); Graham Swift, T H White (writers).

ROBINSON COLLEGE, CAMBRIDGE

THIS COLLEGE IS PART OF THE UNIVERSITY OF CAMBRIDGE AND STUDENTS ARE ENTITLED TO USE ITS FACILITIES

ROBINSON COLLEGE Grange Road, Cambridge, CB3 9AN **TEL** (01223) 339 100 **E-MAIL** undergraduate-admissions@robinson.cam.ac.uk **WEBSITE** www.robinson.cam.ac.uk **ROBINSON COLLEGE STUDENTS' ASSOCIATION** Grange Road, Cambridge, CB3 9AN **WEBSITE** www-stud.robinson.cam.ac.uk/rcsa

GENERAL

Looks aren't everything, which in Robinson's case is just as well. It's a bit of a car park. As so often in life though, the College makes up for *pug-ugly features with a nice personality. It's modern, the only historically mixed-sex place in Cambridge and it's handy for the University library. Anywhere more than five mins walk from King's Parade is a world away in Cambridge, so Robinson, at about 15 mins brisk stroll, is considered far out, although it does sit helpfully* on the University Library's doorstep and the arts faculties are *handily* close. *There's a friendly community between the years, who mingle along the bedroom corridors. Most unusually of all, they don't mind people walking on the grass.*

SEX RATIO: ♂61 ♀39	**FOUNDED:** 1979
FULL-TIME U'GRADS: 425	**PART-TIME:** 0
POSTGRADS: 86	**MATURE:** 3%
STATE:PRIVATE SCHOOL: 64:36	**DISABLED:** 4
ACADEMIC RANKING: 11	**INTERNATIONAL:** 10%

Two bars (Sunday night meal deal: plate and a pint for £3.40); bands, concerts and plays in the Auditorium (cap 250); *humming drama society (Brickhouse Theatre); mixed choir; oodles of* other socs. Frequent club nights. Fortnightly newsletter, termly mag. Two libraries (50,000 books); 30 computers, 24-hr. Chapel with *famous* organ. Sports fields (15 acres shared with Queens') 1,200m away; shared boatclub; some facilities on site. All students live in, either on site or 20 mins bike ride away; most rooms en suite with phone and net connections, *spiffing* self-catering. Doctor and nurse; *cuddly* JCR welfare; free rape alarms and taxis for the stranded; financial tutor; various funds and scholarships; *excellent* disabled access. *Stodgily thorough* alternative prospectus online.

FAMOUS ALUMNI
Morwenna Banks (comedian); Adrian Davies (Welsh rugby); Charles Hart (lyricist); Gary Sinyor (film director).

SELWYN COLLEGE, CAMBRIDGE

THIS COLLEGE IS PART OF THE UNIVERSITY OF CAMBRIDGE AND STUDENTS ARE ENTITLED TO USE ITS FACILITIES

● **SELWYN COLLEGE** Grange Road, Cambridge, CB3 9DQ **TEL** (01223) 335 896 **E-MAIL** admissions@sel.cam.ac.uk **WEBSITE** www.sel.cam.ac.uk ● **SELWYN JCR** Grange Road, Cambridge, CB3 9DQ **E-MAIL** jcrpresident@sel.cam.ac.uk **WEBSITE** www-jcr.sel.cam.ac.uk

GENERAL
Set in lovely, tranquil gardens, Selwyn's been called Cambridge's best-kept secret. *It's a bit of an exaggeration, but the cluster of pretty neo-Gothic buildings behind the arts faculties and across the road from Newnham College is certainly low-profile compared with the more raucous river colleges. Like most of Cambridge, it's scarred with a Cripps building. Nevertheless, it's one of the more friendly colleges (rather like Pembroke, Robinson or Queens'), with a lively bar scene and not much in the way of any sort of attitude.*

SEX RATIO: ♂58 ♀42	**FOUNDED:** 1882
FULL-TIME U'GRADS: 384	**PART-TIME:** 0
POSTGRADS: 152	**MATURE:** 1%
STATE:PRIVATE SCHOOL: 63:37	**DISABLED:** 7
ACADEMIC RANKING: 19	**INTERNATIONAL:** 8%

Fun-stuffed bar hosts popular 'Selwyn Sessions'; theatre and weekly bops in Selwyn Diamond (cap 600), live music in Main Hall and JCR; themed events; famous Snowball at Xmas. College mag, 'Kiwi'. Library (48,000 books); 23 computers. CofE chapel. Two drama societies, *strong* music scene, *competent* Chapel choir; sports fields 600m away shared with King's; rowing's *especially strong*. All can live in; varied accomodation including 44 *brand-spanking-new* en-suite rooms in *tasteful* Ann's Court; Ethernet points in all rooms; *limited* self-catering; two *renowned* formals a week. *Decent* college food. Nurse; sickbay; bursaries, scholarships, prizes; free attack alarms; some disabled facilities.

FAMOUS ALUMNI
Clive Anderson (TV host, lawyer); John Gummer MP (Con); Simon Hughes MP (Lib Dem); Hugh Laurie (comedian, actor); Malcolm Muggeridge (journalist); Rob Newman (comedian, novelist).

> ● **The race around Trinity College Great Court in Chariots of Fire was actually filmed at Eton because Cambridge dons weren't impressed with the script and didn't want to co-operate.**

Words in italics are Push's point of view — take it or leave it...

SIDNEY SUSSEX COLLEGE, CAMBRIDGE

THIS COLLEGE IS PART OF THE UNIVERSITY OF CAMBRIDGE AND STUDENTS ARE ENTITLED TO USE ITS FACILITIES

◉ **SIDNEY SUSSEX COLLEGE** Sidney Street, Cambridge, CB2 3HU **TEL** (01223) 338 800 **E-MAIL** admissions@sid.cam.ac.uk **WEBSITE** www.sid.cam.ac.uk ◉ **SIDNEY SUSSEX COLLEGE JCR** Sidney Street, Cambridge, CB2 3HU **TEL** (01223) 338 800 **E-MAIL** sscsu.president@sid.cam.ac.uk **WEBSITE** www.jcr.sid.ucam.org/site

GENERAL

Sidney's *one of the prettier* colleges, with red-brick *just about complementing the grander* late 16th-century stuff. *It's small enough to be undaunting, but big enough to avoid being stifling. And best of all*, Sainsbury's is about 20 metres away. There's an *active* JCR, some of the *best* accommodation in Cambridge and students have a *high profile* in University drama and Rag. It's also one of the least *stuffy* places in town – around 65% of students are from sate schools, it was one of the first colleges to let girls in and the Master is a mistress.

SEX RATIO: ♂55 ♀45	**FOUNDED:** 1596
FULL-TIME U'GRADS: 370	**PART-TIME:** 0
POSTGRADS: 178	**MATURE:** 2%
STATE:PRIVATE SCHOOL: 44:56	**DISABLED:** 4
ACADEMIC RANKING: 14	**INTERNATIONAL:** 10%

Only student-run bar in Cambridge (cap 175) used for fortnightly bops; William Mary Hall, (80 seated); biennial ball. 'Sid News' newsletter and *rowdy* 'El Sid' mag, Yearbook. Library (40,000 books); 36 computers, 24-hr; net access in all rooms. Chapel. Sports fields (22 acres) 1.5 miles away; boathouse; squash court, croquet lawn and gym on site. All live in (£58-80/week), some en suite rooms, most within five mins of College; eat in dining hall (food *improving*, veggie option); *adequate* self-catering. CCTV; chaplain; nurse; hardship fund; bursaries; book grants; prizes. Rooms for disabled students, some lifts. Alternative Prospectus.

FAMOUS ALUMNI

Asa Briggs (historian); Oliver Cromwell (Lord Protector); Lord Owen (ex-SDP leader); Andrew Rawnsley (journo); Carol Vorderman (*fawning daytime telly mathmo*).

ST CATHARINE'S COLLEGE, CAMBRIDGE

THIS COLLEGE IS PART OF THE UNIVERSITY OF CAMBRIDGE AND STUDENTS ARE ENTITLED TO USE ITS FACILITIES

◉ **ST CATHARINE'S COLLEGE** Cambridge, CB2 1RL **TEL** (01223) 338 300 **E-MAIL** undergraduate.admissions@caths.cam.ac.uk **WEBSITE** www.caths.cam.ac.uk ◉ **ST CATHARINE'S COLLEGE JCR** Cambridge, CB2 1RL **WEBSITE** http://hadriel.caths.cam.ac.uk/jcr

GENERAL

Catz, as *St Catharine's is known by the hipsters*, is set back from the beginning of King's Parade opposite Corpus Christi and bears witness to more than five centuries of building – much of it *pretty impressive. It's big enough to be diverse but small enough to be intimate. The kidz at Catz compliment their strong academic record with lots of sporty and musical pursuits. Although they enjoy one another's company, their love of uni-wide competitions and ents means that they don't ignore the rest of the University altogether. Like so much of Cambridge, Catz is mobbed by tourists in the summer, although most are more interested in King's next door and the porters do their best to fight off the hordes.*

SEX RATIO: ♂51 ♀49	**FOUNDED:** 1473
FULL-TIME U'GRADS: 467	**PART-TIME:** 0
POSTGRADS: 168	**MATURE:** <1%
STATE:PRIVATE SCHOOL: 52:48	**DISABLED:** 2
ACADEMIC RANKING: 1	**INTERNATIONAL:** 8%

Bar (*beating social heart* for most of the college); bops a few times a term; Sky TV in JCR; Octagon theatre (cap 150) and chapel (100) used for concerts; biennial ball. 'Catzeyes' magazine. Two libraries (70,000 books), 24hr; 38 computers, scanning, printing; internet access in all rooms; record library and classical CD collection. CofE chapel. Sports fields (three acres, new pavilion) 1,200m away; only Astroturf pitch in a Cambridge college; *success in rowing*. All students can live in (second years in the octagonal St Chad's building), £50-£87p/w; eat in cafeteria; self-catering *limited*; CCTV. Green, Target and Equal Opps Officers. Nurse; sick bay; five rooms for wheelchair users; *good* access. Some financial support; academic scholarships and prizes.

FAMOUS ALUMNI
Peter Boizot (founded Pizza Express); Kevin Greening (XFM); Sir Peter Hall (theatre director and RSC founder); Malcolm Lowry (*booze-hound* writer); Sir Ian McKellen (actor); Jeremy Paxman (BBC *bulldog*).

ST EDMUND'S COLLEGE, CAMBRIDGE

THIS COLLEGE IS PART OF THE UNIVERSITY OF CAMBRIDGE AND STUDENTS ARE ENTITLED TO USE ITS FACILITIES

◉ **ST EDMUND'S COLLEGE** Cambridge, CB3 0BN **TEL** (01223) 336 250 **E–MAIL** admissions@st-edmunds.cam.ac.uk **WEBSITE** www.st-edmunds.cam.ac.uk ◉ **ST EDMUND'S COLLEGE COMBINATION ROOM** Cambridge, CB3 0BN **WEBSITE** www.st-edmunds.cam.ac.uk/student

GENERAL
Plonked ten minutes schlep from the city centre, students at St Edmund's (*'Eddies' to those in the know*) are either mature (*in age, not necessarily attitude*) or affiliated, so *work takes precedence over binge drinking. It's friendly, with a close community and a bop that attracts Cambridge's more discerning ents socialites.* While it's been around since the end of the 19th- century, it's only been a full card-carrying college of the University since 1965. It's one of the University's six graduate colleges but slips in around 100 mature undergrads too.

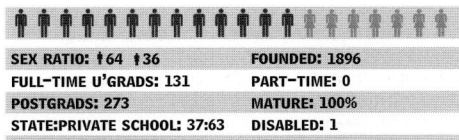

SEX RATIO: ♂64 ♀36	FOUNDED: 1896
FULL-TIME U'GRADS: 131	PART-TIME: 0
POSTGRADS: 273	MATURE: 100%
STATE:PRIVATE SCHOOL: 37:63	DISABLED: 1
ACADEMIC RANKING: 28	INTERNATIONAL: 48%

Bar; *buzzy music society; new library; May Ball; success at Bumps (intercollegiate rowing competition); shared boatclub with Trinity Hall; fitness suite, gym, tennis, table tennis and croquet facilities. Rooms for 200 students (£61-78 a week); some family maisonettes for two adults, two children (£130 a week); ethernet in all rooms; *limited* cooking facilities – most accommodation is catered. Daily worship, RC chapel. Academic prizes and scholarships; hardship fund.

ST JOHN'S COLLEGE, CAMBRIDGE

THIS COLLEGE IS PART OF THE UNIVERSITY OF CAMBRIDGE AND STUDENTS ARE ENTITLED TO USE ITS FACILITIES

◉ **ST JOHN'S COLLEGE** Cambridge, CB2 1TP **TEL** (01223) 338 700 **E–MAIL** admissions@joh.cam.ac.uk **WEBSITE** www.joh.cam.ac.uk ◉ **JCR** St John's College, Cambridge, CB2 1TP **TEL** (01223) 338 685 **E–MAIL** spresident@sjcjcr.com **WEBSITE** http://jcr.joh.cam.ac.uk

GENERAL
This is as good as life in an Oxbridge College gets – think 'Brideshead Revisited'. John's is a posh, sporty, wealthy riverside college large enough to cater for most (stereo)types although so big that some students can feel lost. Tourists flock to see the Gothic splendour of New Court and the beautiful Bridge of Sighs, and tickets for the luxuriant May Ball (*rivalled only by Trinity's extravaganza*) are like chocolate-coated gold dust.

SEX RATIO: ♂59 ♀41	FOUNDED: 1511
FULL-TIME U'GRADS: 597	PART-TIME: 0
POSTGRADS: 299	MATURE: 2%
STATE:PRIVATE SCHOOL: 54:46	DISABLED: 14
ACADEMIC RANKING: 12	INTERNATIONAL: 11%

Bar; Pythagoras Building (theatre); art and music rooms; Palmerston Room (cap 350) for bands; Old Music Room (100) for concerts; Boiler Room (100) for fortnightly bops; *legendary* annual ball. Lady Margaret Players (*major* drama society); *loads* of societies; regular JCR newsletter and twice termly 'Cripptic mag'; cable TV. Two libraries (120,000 books); 45 computers, 24-hr. Large *cathedral-ish* CofE chapel. Large on-site sports hall, renowned Lady Margaret Boat Club, *superb* sports teams and extensive sports fields 200m away; cardiovascular and free weights gyms. Everyone lives in or in hostels; *good* self-catering. CCTV, swipe cards. Two nurses; chaplain. *Very good* disabled access and provisions. LGBT Society; Equal Opps, Welfare and Access Officers. *Excellent* financial support: book grants and help for students suffering unexpected hardship.

FAMOUS ALUMNI
Douglas Adams (author); Rob Andrew (former England rugby player); William Wilberforce (anti-slavery campaigners); Derek Jacobi (*luvvie*); Lord Palmerston (PM); William Wordsworth (poet).

Words in italics are Push's point of view – take it or leave it...

TRINITY COLLEGE, CAMBRIDGE

THIS COLLEGE IS PART OF THE UNIVERSITY OF CAMBRIDGE AND STUDENTS ARE ENTITLED TO USE ITS FACILITIES

○ **TRINITY COLLEGE** Cambridge, CB2 1TQ **TEL** (01223) 338 400 **E–MAIL** admissions@trin.cam.ac.uk **WEBSITE** www.trin.cam.ac.uk
○ **TRINITY COLLEGE STUDENTS' UNION** Trinity College, Cambridge, CB2 1TQ **TEL** (01223) 367 424
E–MAIL tcsu-president@trin.cam.ac.uk **WEBSITE** www.tcsu.net

GENERAL

Trinity, which *sprawls* between the backs and the centre of town, is Cambridge's largest and *arguably grandest* college. The main buildings are *breath-stopping* medieval affairs and pictures of the portly founder Henry VIII bedeck the walls. *Its students jostle with tourists to get across Great Court, home of the largest covered fountain in Europe, for whatever that's worth. Insanely wealthy, Trinity is the third largest landowner in the country, after the Crown and the Church – there's some very pissed-off tenant villages in Suffolk. Almost bottomless pockets are generously dipped into to help less well-off students, and the College is slowly redressing its white public-schoolboy image – freaks, geeks, sloanes, jocks, hacks and downright normal folk now co-exist in relative harmony. Emphasis on the 'relative'.*

SEX RATIO: ♂59 ♀41	FOUNDED: 1546
FULL–TIME U'GRADS: 745	PART–TIME: 0
POSTGRADS: 361	MATURE: 2%
STATE:PRIVATE SCHOOL: 44:56	DISABLED: 13
ACADEMIC RANKING: 3	INTERNATIONAL: 21%

Airport-lounge bar with juke box, pool, quiz machine and table football; Chapel (200) and Combination Room (100) for live music (*prestigious* choir) and fortnightly *sweaty* bops in Wolfson Party Room (150); biggest annual ball (2,000 tickets); regular jazz, fortnightly Magpie &

Stump comedy debating and theatre in gardens or Great Hall. JCR with widescreen TV, DVD player. *Countless ever-changing societies. Widespread political disinterest, with pockets of arch-conservatism.* Two libraries, one for law, *imposing* (Christopher) Wren Library (300,000 books); 70 24-hr computers in three computer rooms; internet access in most rooms. CofE chapel; three chaplains; charity fund-raising. Extensive sports fields 800m from College; *success* in rowing and rugby. Everyone lives in; rooms vary (attics with oak beams, grand rooms with high ceilings, modern with en suite facilities; mixed sex couples can choose to share; eat in *dark and moody* Great Hall; *popular and riotous* formal hall every night; *varied kitchen facilities*; booze-dispensing buttery, *vast* wine cellar. CCTV, swipe cards; nurse; Women's and Access Officers, LGBT rep; *wheelchair access dreadful*, some adapted rooms. *Generous* financial support, usually in the form of *bizarre* prizes; choral and organ scholarships.

FAMOUS ALUMNI

Francis Bacon (artist); Lord Byron (*mad, bad* poet); Prince Charles; Earl Grey (one of six ex-PMs who went to Trinity); Lord Hurd (Con, former Foreign Secretary); Lord Macaulay (historian); Vladimir Nabokov (writer, Lolita); Isaac Newton (scientist); Enoch Powell ("rivers of blood" MP); Bertrand Russell, Ludwig Wittgenstein (philosophers); Alfred, Lord Tennyson (*less mad* poet); Lord Whitelaw (ex-Tory minister).

TRINITY HALL, CAMBRIDGE

THIS COLLEGE IS PART OF THE UNIVERSITY OF CAMBRIDGE AND STUDENTS ARE ENTITLED TO USE ITS FACILITIES

○ **TRINITY HALL** Cambridge, CB2 1TJ **TEL** (01223) 332 500 **E–MAIL** admissions@trinhall.cam.ac.uk
WEBSITE www.trinhall.cam.ac.uk ○ **TRINITY HALL JCR** Cambridge, CB2 1TJ **TEL** (01223) 332 500 **E–MAIL** jcr@trinhall.cam.ac.uk
WEBSITE http://hall.trinhall.cam.ac.uk/jcr

GENERAL

Tit Hall (the nickname's only amiably abusive) is a river college that *peeps out from* behind Clare, Caius and Trinity colleges, tucked away just off King's Parade. It's the fourth smallest in Cambridge, *which means it's friendly and intimate, or stifling and incestuous, depending* on who you ask. It has a rather pretty Georgian courtyard and lovely gardens although the new academic spirit might mean you won't spend all your time dossing in them.

SEX RATIO: ♂51 ♀49	FOUNDED: 1350
FULL-TIME U'GRADS: 383	PART-TIME: 0
POSTGRADS: 231	MATURE: 1%
STATE:PRIVATE SCHOOL: 55:45	DISABLED: 3
ACADEMIC RANKING: 17	INTERNATIONAL: 9%

Small, pubbish bar; indie and dance bands; open mic nights; fortnightly themed 'Viva!' bops; June Event (baby ball); 'Suicide Sunday' garden party; lecture theatre for drama and music (cap 270). 'Hallmark' weekly newsletter; *enthusiastic* Rag. *Eclectic* range of socs including Air Squadron *(for wannabe Mavericks)*, Cheerleading, Martial Arts and Fair Trade. Two libraries (85,000 books) *but can get more cramped than a sardine moshpit*; 20 computers, 24-hrs; Ethernet in all rooms. CofE chapel. Sports fields (3 acres) a mile away; gym, two squash courts, boathouse shared with St Edmund's, *'boaty' rep*. Most live in: accommodation split between college, Bishop Bateman Court & St Clement's (five mins walk) and the Wychfield site (15 mins). *Rooms on the titchy side; few* self-catering facilities. Green, Women's, LGBT and Welfare Officers; nurse; hardship fund (£50,000), book loans, scholarships. *Miniature* Alternative Prospectus online.

FAMOUS ALUMNI
Lord Howe (Con, former Cabinet Minister); Nicholas Hytner (National Theatre director); Donald Maclean (spy for the USSR); Andrew Marr *(gesticulating* journalist with *marr-velous ears)* J B Priestley (writer); Tony Slattery (comedian); Terry Waite (former church envoy held hostage in Beirut); Rachel Weisz (actress).

WOLFSON COLLEGE, CAMBRIDGE

THIS COLLEGE IS PART OF THE UNIVERSITY OF CAMBRIDGE AND STUDENTS ARE ENTITLED TO USE ITS FACILITIES

- **WOLFSON COLLEGE** Barton Road, Cambridge, CB3 9BB **TEL** (01223) 335 900 **WEBSITE** www.wolfson.cam.ac.uk
- **WOLFSON COLLEGE STUDENT ASSOCIATION** Cambridge, CB3 9BB **WEBSITE** www.wolfson.cam.ac.uk/wcsa

GENERAL
Originally and *uninspiringly* known as 'University College', Wolfson's a graduate and mature affair, which takes affiliated medical students as well as undergrads for the whole gamut of Cam degrees. *It's less champagne and hierarchy-driven than most of the other colleges,* with no JCR/SCR division and a *hardcore approach to work. They like to think of themselves as modern, cosmopolitan and lively, and even though they're not exactly party animals, they ain't poopers either.*

SEX RATIO: ♂56 ♀44	FOUNDED: 1965
FULL-TIME U'GRADS: 138	PART-TIME: 0
POSTGRADS: 500	MATURE: 100%
STATE: PRIVATE SCHOOL: 75:25	DISABLED: 3
ACADEMIC RANKING: 23	INTERNATIONAL: 46%

Bar; meeting and music rooms. Art society. Library, 24-hrs; 18 PCs, some for student rental; all rooms networked (net use £15 a term). 'Wolf Sun' college paper. Shared boatclub, footie, rugby, squash, badminton, and basket ball facilities; snooker tables, multigym, tennis courts and aerobics club. All first years guaranteed a bed (£61-79 a week); some college-owned flats (£102 -177); choice of termly or annual tenancy agreements; canteen grub in dining hall – staff and students eat together; formal dinners twice a week. *Some* disabled facilities. 12 international student scholarships; hardship fund.

▶ CANTERBURY
see *University of Kent at Canterbury*

> ◉ **'If I was called upon to mention the prettiest corner of the world, I should ... point the way to the gardens of Trinity Hall.' – Henry James**

CANTERBURY CHRIST CHURCH UNIVERSITY

FORMERLY CANTERBURY CHRIST CHURCH UNIVERSITY COLLEGE

1. ○ **CANTERBURY CHRIST CHURCH UNIVERSITY** North Holmes Road, Canterbury, Kent, CT1 1QU **TEL** (01227) 782 900 **E−MAIL** admissions@canterbury.ac.uk **WEBSITE** www.canterbury.ac.uk ○ **CHRIST CHURCH STUDENTS' UNION** North Holmes Road, Canterbury, Kent, CT1 1QU **TEL** (01227) 782 416 **E−MAIL** su.president@canterbury.ac.uk **WEBSITE** www.c4online.net
2. ○ **BROADSTAIRS CAMPUS** Canterbury Christchurch University, Northwood Road, Broadstairs, Kent, CT10 2WA **TEL** (01843) 280 600 **WEBSITE** www.canterbury.ac.uk/broadstairs ○ **CANTERBURY'S STUDENTS' UNION** Room CG13, Northwood Road, Broadstairs, Kent, CT10 2WA **TEL** (01843) 609 182 **E−MAIL** su.broadstairs@canterbury.ac.uk

GENERAL ○○○○○○○○○○○○○

CCCU, *as absolutely no one but lazy typists call it*, is mostly found in Canterbury, but three other little pieces of it are scattered around Kent – namely: Broadstairs, Chatham and Tunbridge Wells. It's been handing out degrees ever since the Church of England set it up as a teacher training college in 1962 and it finally became a university proper in 2005. With the main site in the centre of one of England's most visited cities (see University of Kent), it's *pretty popular*. The main campus at Canterbury *blends in nicely with its leafy, Kodak-moment surroundings, but once inside it's also modern and well-equipped.*

SEX RATIO: ♂28 ♀72	**FOUNDED:** 1962
FULL−TIME U'GRADS: 6,438	**PART−TIME:** 5,097
POSTGRADS: 3,089	**NON−DEGREE:** 2,680
AVE COURSE: 3YRS	**ETHNIC:** 11%
STATE:PRIVATE SCHOOL: 97:3	**FLUNK RATE:** 16%
MATURE: 50%	**INTERNATIONAL:** 7%
DISABLED: 170	**LOCAL:** 82%

ATMOSPHERE
The main campus is surprisingly self-contained, considering eight out of ten students come from the local area. There's a warm, friendly atmosphere that's only slightly soured by occasional disputes about noise with the local residents and some alleged hassle from the lager-fuelled townie youths who aren't actually studying here.

SITES
BROADSTAIRS CAMPUS (1,000 students – Business, Education, Nursing, Media, Music, Policing) Thanet's 18 miles from Canterbury, not far from the Kent coast and Margate and Ramsgate. It's *not as pretty* as the main site but *those into aesthetics can always head over to the beaches and watersports, or pop into Horizons bar and the refectory.* Most students are local and/or mature.
CHATHAM, MEDWAY (Health, Education, Policing) CCCU recently shipped its first batch of students over to the *fancy new* Medway site, which is part of the Universities at Medway partnership (jointly with University of Kent and Greenwich University).

SALOMONS CAMPUS, TUNBRIDGE WELLS CCCU's associate campus 40 miles from Canterbury is a training centre for public sector professionals, so *most students will never even know it exists.*

CANTERBURY see University of Kent

TRAVEL see University of Kent
LOCAL A minibus shuttles between sites.

CAREER PROSPECTS
○ **CAREERS SERVICE** ○ **NO. OF STAFF** 4 FULL/3 PART
○ **UNEMPLOYED AFTER 6** MTHS 4%
Second year BA/BSc students undergo a Career Development Programme during the last three weeks of the academic year which involves advice and work placements or short courses. Career seminars cover a variety of *useful* subjects.

FAMOUS ALUMNI
Kate Blewett (award-laden documentarian); Jane Carter (Classical honcho, BBC Music); Jonathan Holmes (writer and presenter); Geraldine McCaughrean (author).

FURTHER INFO
○ **PROSPECTUSES** UNDERGRAD; POSTGRAD; INTERNATIONAL; ALTERNATIVE; DVD
○ **OPEN DAYS**

ACADEMIC ○○○○○○○○○○○○○

The University's one of the top three providers of teacher training in the country and specialises in churning out graduates for useful jobs in the public services: nurses, social care, policing and the like. The media and sports science programmes are *fairly rammed*, too. *Facilities are new and shiny as a freshly-minted coin.*

ENTRY POINTS: 160−240	**POINTS:** 160
APPLICATIONS PER PLACE: 10	**CLEARING:** 21%
NO. OF TERMS: 3	**LENGTH OF TERMS:** 12WKS
STAFF TO STUDENT RATIO: N/A	**STUDY ADDICTS:** 19%
TEACHING: ★★★	**RESEARCH:** ★
YEAR ABROAD: 0%	**SANDWICH STUDENTS:** <1%
1STS: 9%	**2.2s:** 43%
2.1s: 37%	**3RDS:** 10%

ADMISSIONS
❍ APPLY VIA UCAS
Widening participation *is the name of the game* at the admissions office (*Monopoly got boring after a while*), and they encourage applications from international, mature and part-time students with or without formal qualifications, so long as they can show they're up to the job. Cranially well-endowed candidates can occasionally leapfrog the first year and go straight into the second.

SUBJECTS
ARTS/HUMANITIES 17%   **BUSINESS & SCIENCE** 25%
EDUCATION 32%   **HEALTH** 26%
BEST American Studies; Art; Applied Social Sciences; Business & Management; Hospitality Management; Nursing & Midwifery; Programmes Allied to Medicine; Radio, Film & Television Studies; Religious STudies; Science; Sport Science; Tourism.

LIBRARIES
❍ 276,066 BOOKS ❍ 655 STUDY PLACES
❍ SPEND PER STUDENT £
There are libraries at all sites, although the one at Broadstairs is the *dwarf of the fellowship*.

COMPUTERS
❍ 740 WORKSTATIONS ❍ 24-HOUR ACCESS
Although students have their quibbles every now and then, the IT people at Canterbury are doing their best to improve matters. Most halls at Canterbury have net access and all do at Broadstairs. There are internet cafés at Canterbury and Chatham.

OTHER LEARNING FACILITIES
Language labs; open-access drama studio; CAD lab; media centre; courtroom; sports science lab; nursing lab.

ENTERTAINMENT ◖◗◖◗◖◗◖◗◖◗◖◗

THE CITY see University of Kent

UNIVERSITY
❍ PRICE OF A PINT OF BEER £1.50
❍ GLASS OF WINE £2.50
❍ CAN OF RED BULL £1.75
BARS Unusually, the bar in the Union building at Canterbury is actually run by the University. It offers *all the usual bar essentials and a bit more* (quizzes, three lounges, two TV rooms, a coffee shop, two club nights a week and, obviously, booze). Broadstairs students also have the *intimate* Horizons bar. Chathamites quaff at the Drunken Sailor.
THEATRES *With all the media students around you'd expect a bit of thesping.* Student productions are *quite well known* in the area.

FILM/COMEDY Newish releases are shown by the Union once a month. Monthly comedy attracts laugh-inducers like Rob Deering and Tony Law.
MUSIC VENUES The SU runs an unplugged evening every Thursday. The University-run main hall (cap 400) has seen acts ranging from Girls Aloud to Electric 6 and Liberty X.
CLUBBING Funky Fridays runs on, yes, a Friday and provides a mountain of *cheesy pop* for fans to slalom down. On Wednesday nights the University's sports teams run their own party.
FOOD The canteen-style Food Court is the *prime* munchery and keeps a-ladlin' till 7pm. The South Room café and the Union Bar also do snacks and there are other outlets on all sites.
OTHER CCCU *is ball heaven (or ball hell)* with six of the things throughout the year including the *legendary* summer ball, known in these parts as The Big One. Usually 4,000 students attend with big *(but not necessarily good)* acts like Blue in the main hall and tribute bands like the Bandit Beatles and Coolplay nearby. There are also beer tents and games across the whole campus till 6am.

SOCIAL ◖◗◖◗◖◗◖◗◖◗◖◗◖◗◖◗◖◗

CHRIST CHURCH STUDENTS' UNION
❍ 4 SABBATICALS ❍ TURNOUT AT LAST BALLOT 10%
❍ NUS MEMBER
What it lacks in size, it makes up for in bustle. The Union's *refreshingly active* considering its location in the *smugly affluent* end of Kent. *They don't shirk on the ents front either, arranging distractions every night of the week.*

SU FACILITIES
Most facilities are run by the University (bars, cafés etc.) but the Union also has two pool tables, a minibus, a TV lounge, an advice centre, gaming machines, and a new and secondhand bookshop. *Facilities are still relatively limited.*

CLUBS (NON-SPORTING)
Pagan; World (international events). **See also Clubs tables.**

OTHER ORGANISATIONS
The free fortnightly student newspaper has the *uncharacteristically bloodthirsty* title of 'Bluebeard'. 'Canterbury Student Radio', a joint venture between Christ Church and Kent, will entertain cyberspace and beyond from September 2006. C4TV (nothing to do with Channel 4) pulls off televisual stunts like locking ten students in a room for a week, 'Big Brother'-style. A charity Rag *helps the helpless*.

RELIGIOUS
❍ 2 CHAPLAINS (COFE)

PAID WORK see University of Kent

⊙ JOB BUREAU ⊙ PAID WORK TERM TIME 70%; HOLS 75%
The Jobshop's vacancy board and e-bulletins can help find part-time work during studies, including the possibility of doing up to 15 hours a week for the SU, as well as relevant vacation opportunities. Hospitality, retailing and clerical support are the *front runners* in the local area.

SPORTS ⟨⟩⟨⟩⟨⟩⟨⟩⟨⟩⟨⟩⟨⟩⟨⟩⟨⟩⟨⟩⟨⟩⟨⟩

⊙ BUSA RANKING 88
The University spends a fair few notes on sport and *they get good value for money with plenty of participation in sports teams. It's not all about the sweet smell of stonking triumph and the humiliating agony of defeat, however – students can be involved to whatever level they wish (as long as they're prepared to schlep off-campus to the facilities).*

SPORTS FACILITIES
Very little on site, but students can use: four football pitches; rugby pitch; three tennis courts; two sports halls with one netball and four basketball courts; gym. For £29 a year (plus user fee) students can go for the burn at the St George's Fitness Centre, five mins away from the University, where there are weights and *everything else you need to become as ripped as a Metallica track.* The Kent Coast is a *top spot* for watersports.

SPORTING CLUBS
American Football; Cheerleading; Horseriding; Pool. **See also Clubs tables.**

ATTRACTIONS
Kent County Cricket Club and Gillingham FC are the local teams. See University of Kent.

ACCOMMODATION ⟨⟩⟨⟩⟨⟩⟨⟩⟨⟩⟨⟩⟨⟩⟨⟩⟨⟩

IN UNIVERSITY
⊙ CATERED 2% **⊙ COST** £64 (36WKS)
⊙ SELF-CATERING 34% **⊙ COST** £76 (39/44WKS)
⊙ 1ST YRS LIVING IN 28%
⊙ INSURANCE PREMIUM £
AVAILABILITY All first years who want to can live in. Priority goes to students younger than 24 who live further away, but all younger international and all disabled students are guaranteed a bed. *For the majority who make it into the ivory tower, standards are pretty high.* The catered halls operate on a 'pay as you eat' system, so food costs extra. The halls vary from blocks of 20 rooms to a 300-room student village (Parnham Road) and are at most a 25-min walk from the University. About a third are en suite. Quibble-wise, *it can sometimes take the powers that be a while to deal with problems.* The village at Parham Road is furthest away from campus, located in a *less well turned-out area of*

Canterbury, and there have been reports of theft. Christ Church campus is right in the middle of town, *which is great,* but it means locals use it as a short cut, *inevitably* leading to some vandalism and bike theft. Porter patrols try to prevent this and security has been *beefed up.* There's nothing available for couples and all accommodation is single-sex where possible. There's also some housing at Broadstairs.
CAR PARKING *Difficult. Scarce parking facilities on campus and not much around it.* Parnham Road has a few spaces, as does Pin Hill, but at a charge of £1 a day. *Otherwise, bring a bike.*

EXTERNALLY see University of Kent
⊙ AVE RENT £76
HOUSING HELP The Accommodation Office lists private sector landlords and operates a house-mate matching scheme. The SU holds accommodation fairs and *blacklists baddies.*

WELFARE ⟨⟩⟨⟩⟨⟩⟨⟩⟨⟩⟨⟩⟨⟩⟨⟩⟨⟩⟨⟩⟨⟩

SERVICES
⊙ LGBT OFFICER & SOCIETY ⊙ ETHNIC MINORITIES OFFICER ⊙ MATURE STUDENTS' OFFICER ⊙ INTERNATIONAL STUDENTS' OFFICER ⊙ DISABILITIES OFFICER ⊙ NIGHTLINE ⊙ UNIVERSITY COUNSELLORS 2 PART **⊙ CRIME RATING** !
There's an *okay* spread of support services but the Union is pressing for extra funds for the likes of a late-night minibus.
HEALTH Contracted GP services, providing a range of NHS specialists.
WOMEN Student Union provides attack alarms for £2.
CRECHES/NURSERY 20 places at the nursery on Havelock Street by the main campus for kids aged 3mths-4yrs.
DISABILITIES Recent work has meant most campus buildings are now accessible, *although there are still obstacles here and there.* Induction loops, ramps, lifts, Braille facilities, note-takers, adapted rooms and dyslexia support are all on-hand.
CRIME *Most students have crime-free lives, although tensions with the contingent at the local barracks cause trouble occasionally.* North Holmes Road down the side of the University is one of five local roads that've been identified as problem areas by local police. A few foreign students have come in for harassment from an *inbred* minority in the town.

FINANCE
⊙ AVE DEBT PER YEAR £3,611 **⊙ HOME STUDENT FEES** £3,000
FEES £3,200 for postgrads (approx). International students pay £6,990 (undergrad) or £7,640 (postgrad).
SUPPORT A hundred £300 Young Student Bursaries for those under 21 when starting their course. Mature students can grab up to £500.

CARDIFF UNIVERSITY

INCLUDES THE FORMER WALES COLLEGE OF MEDICINE

○ **CARDIFF UNIVERSITY** Cardiff, CF10 3XQ **TEL** (029) 2087 4839 **E-MAIL** prospectus@cardiff.ac.uk
WEBSITE www.cardiff.ac.uk ○ **CARDIFF UNIVERSITY STUDENTS' UNION** Park Place, Cardiff, CF10 3QN **TEL** (029) 2078 1400
E-MAIL studentsunion@cf.ac.uk **WEBSITE** www.cardiffstudents.com

GENERAL ○○○○○○○○○○○○○

Cardiff's been *spruced up* in the last few years and is now a *giant, sparkly gem in the country's crown*. It's the *biggest, brightest* city in Wales and has been the capital city since 1955. It's *green and pleasant* by day, *bright and raucous* by night. The University is *dead in the middle* of town, five mins from the main shopping centre. It's spread along a single street, so it *feels like a little town of its own*. The buildings are *pretty fancy* and even the newer ones have lots of green space *to lounge about in (although Push wouldn't in mid-January when things get nippy)*. Wales College of Medicine has been part of the package since 2004, adding an extra campus at Heath Park and making Cardiff the biggest university in Wales as a consequence.

SEX RATIO: ♠44 ♀56	**FOUNDED:** 1883
FULL-TIME U'GRADS: 15,548	**PART-TIME:** 292
POSTGRADS: 3,882	**NON-DEGREE:** 54
AVE COURSE: 3YRS	**ETHNIC:** 10%
STATE:PRIVATE SCHOOL: 85:15	**FLUNK RATE:** 5%
MATURE: 15%	**INTERNATIONAL:** 17%
DISABLED: 250	**LOCAL:** 22%

ATMOSPHERE
Perhaps owing in part to the tabloid-friendly antics of Wales' favourite fallen angel Charlotte Church, Cardiff has something of a reputation as a 24-hr party city, which isn't too far from the truth. Cash keeps rolling into the city and it feels like a young, fast-paced kind of place. Partying is on a par with hitting the books and the sports pitch.

OTHER SITES
HEATH PARK CAMPUS (3,200 students – Schools of Medicine, Dentistry, Healthcare Studies, Nursing & Midwifery Studies) A *short* bus ride (or 20 mins *beating the streets*) from the main University buildings. It's *quietish* with *a few cafés, bars and libraries to call its own. But it's very much in the orbit of the main deal*, especially since the College of Medicine became officially hitched.

CARDIFF
○ **POPULATION** 305,200 ○ **CITY CENTRE** 0 MILES
○ **LONDON** 143 MILES ○ **BRISTOL** 30 MILES
○ **SWANSEA** 40 MILES
○ **HIGH TEMP** 21 ○ **LOW TEMP** 2 ○ **RAINFALL** 87
Massive redevelopment has made Cardiff a proper 21st-century city. The *most obvious bit* is the Millennium Stadium, which is *mighty impressive outside and breathtaking inside*. The Millennium Centre is the next part of it, and will house lots of Wales's *arty stuff*. Cardiff's sorted for *lower-brow* culture, too, with *lots* of bars in the mix. *With a largely pedestrianised centre, it can often feel more like a large – albeit very well-equipped – town than a big scary capital city, which is no bad thing. Like most cities, though, it can get a bit hairy on Saturday night.*

TRAVEL
TRAINS Direct trains from Cardiff Central: London (£35.65 rtn); Birmingham (£25.20); Manchester (£35.50).
COACHES National Express to most places including London (£26 rtn) and Birmingham (£21).
CAR To get to Cardiff there's the M4, A470 and A48. There's not much call for a car in the city and parts of the city centre are pedestrianised but they can be handy for exploring the South Wales countryside, just five miles away.
AIR Cardiff International Airport has flights to the Channel Islands, Ireland and even the USA, as well as inland trips.
HITCHING The A48's a bonus – only five mins walk from the campus – and the Welsh are willing.
LOCAL Local bus services run every 20–30 mins all round town: reliable with an average trip costing 50p.
TAXIS Lots of firms will happily rip off anyone that can't, or can't be bothered, to walk home.
BICYCLES Everything's within pedalling distance and there are sheds at all the halls. Bike-rustling is a bit of problem, though.

CAREER PROSPECTS
○ **CAREERS SERVICE** ○ **NO. OF STAFF** 7 FULL
○ **UNEMPLOYED AFTER 6 MTHS** 5 %
A *huge* range of services, including help for *budding* Bransons and *media-wannabes*. There's also participation in Cymru Prosper Wales, which includes paid summer placements for graduates with Welsh businesses.

FAMOUS ALUMNI
Huw Edwards (BBC TV newsreader); Arwel Hughes (conductor); Karl Hyde, Rick Smith (Underworld); Neil and Glenys Kinnock; Professor Bernard Knight (ret'd Home Office Pathologist, crime writer); Sian Lloyd (weatherwoman); Philip Madoc (actor); Sian Philips (actress); Tim Sebastian (BBC reporter).

Words in italics are Push's point of view — take it or leave it...

C

FURTHER INFO
- **PROSPECTUSES** UNDERGRAD; POSTGRAD; SOME DEPARTMENTAL
- **OPEN DAYS**

ACADEMIC ◐◐◐◐◐◐◐◐◐◐◐◐◐

- **RUSSELL GROUP**

Like black pepper, Cardiff's a *good all-rounder and pretty hot on lots of courses*. The science departments have had *lots of money chucked at them*, including from the merger with the College of Medicine, and *posh* new schools of chemistry, optometry and life sciences. It's a traditional academic university, but courses take a fairly flexible format and there are some opportunities to learn languages or do industrial placements as well.

ENTRY POINTS: 240–360	AVE POINTS: 375
APPLICATIONS PER PLACE: 7	CLEARING: 3%
NO. OF TERMS: 2	LENGTH OF TERMS: 15WKS
STAFF TO STUDENT RATIO: 1:6	STUDY ADDICTS: 9%
TEACHING: ★★★★	RESEARCH: ★★★★★
YEAR ABROAD: 4%	SANDWICH STUDENTS: 9%
1STS: 14%	2.2S: 26%
2.1S: 56%	3RDS: 3%

ADMISSIONS
- **APPLY VIA UCAS**

There are a *brain-boggling* 28 academic schools – everything from the School of Architechture to the School of Welsh.

SUBJECTS
BUSINESS & LAW 16% **HEALTH/LIFE SCIENCE** 14%; **ENGINEERING/PLANNING** 10% **HUMANITIES** 27% **HEALTHCARE** 22%   **PHYSICAL SCIENCES** 11%
BEST Architecture; Biology/Bio-Sciences; Business; Chemistry; Earth Sciences; Education; Engineering; English, Communication & Philosophy; Finance & Accounting; History & Archaeology; Journalism; Languages; Law; Maths; Music; Optometry; Pharmacy; Physics; Politics; Psychology; Religious Studies; Social Sciences; Town Planning.
OTHER *Japanese*. Also the joint Cardiff-Bordeaux scheme offers a Cardiff degree in Politics and a diploma from the institute of Political science in Bordeaux. Students study for two years in each country.

LIBRARIES
- **1,286,874** BOOKS **3,408** STUDY PLACES
- **SPEND PER STUDENT** £££

Technically an *alarming-sounding* eleven libraries, but they are really all one inter-connected *whopper*. Main ones are Arts & Social Studies, the Aberconway and Science.

COMPUTERS
- **5,500** WORKSTATIONS **24-HOUR ACCESS**
- **SPEND PER STUDENT** £

The University is *kitting out* student rooms with internet points.

ENTERTAINMENT ◐◐◐◐◐◐◐◐◐

THE CITY
- **PRICE OF A PINT OF BEER** £1.90
- **GLASS OF WINE** £1.40

Cardiff students like the finer drinks in life (champers and cocktails) as well as slumming at pound-a-pint nights. Plenty of both on offer.
CINEMAS The Chapter Arts Centre's arthouse screen adds more *refined/pretentious* culture to the several mainstream multiplexes in the city.
THEATRES Five theatres, including the Chapter Arts Centre (which also has a dance studio and exhibition centres), the New Theatre (home of the Welsh National Opera), the Sherman Theatre and the new Wales Millennium Centre, which houses art exhibitions as well as stage productions.
PUBS *Some excellent boozers, the usual chain suspects and some very average theme pubs that aren't worth the effort. Pushplugs: The Woodville Arms (aka the Woody – a student haven); Macintosh (skittles in the summer); Cantaloupe (cocktails and offers with neighbouring club Creation). The redeveloped docks are full of pubs and clubs, which are generally student-supporting.*
CLUBBING *Tons of clubs to choose from, some with stickier carpets than others. Pushplugs: Liquid (Mondays); Creation; Sunday Service at Jumpin Jaks; Dewis.*
MUSIC VENUES *Megastars call at International Arena and the Millennium Stadium when on tours. Mere musical mortals make do with St David's Hall or the Jazz bar.*
COMEDY/CABARET *Jongleurs at the Plaza and various acts at the theatres.*
OTHER For *culture-hounds*, there's the Museum of Welsh Life and Techniquest, a *big* hands-on science exhibition.
EATING OUT *Cardiff boasts an entire street (Caroline Street) of kebab shops, which gets literally hidden under a carpet of polystyrene wrappers and semi-masticated donkey/doner meat on a Friday night. Pushplugs: Ethnic Deli (£10 for five dishes); Las Iguanas and Old Orleans (Tex-Mex); Ramone's (greasy spoon); Bistro 116; The Pear Tree (Cathays community centre); Taurus (steakhouse).*

UNIVERSITY
- **PRICE OF A PINT OF BEER:** £1.60
- **GLASS OF WINE:** £1.75
- **CAN OF RED BULL:** £1.50

The Union has facilities to match any in the country and students know how to make the most of them.

BARS A *huge* choice of bars. The Taf has a *large and loyal* following and has been extended to keep up with *boozers'* demands.

THEATRES Nothing belonging to the University, but the drama group can hire the Sherman Theatre (in town).

MUSIC VENUES The Great Hall is a stop on *regular high-profile* tours. Recent visitors include Hard-Fi, KT Tunstall, Supergrass and Arctic Monkeys. Student music is *relegated* to a small room behind Solus.

CLUBBING Solus is the second-biggest nightclub in south Wales, cramming in 1,900 *sweaty revellers* to the sounds of indie, hip hop, cheese, dance anthems and *drunken shouting*. During the day it's a refectory.

COMEDY/CABARET Comedy circuit shows roll into the Great Hall every month.

Food: CF10 has check tablecloths and hot food until 3.30pm. University refectories serve food all day and Solus *keeps clubbers' spirits high with late-night pizzas*.

OTHER 5,000 went to the Summer Ball last year at Cardiff Castle, as did Tony Christie, Chappers & Dave and, *er*, 911. Sports and media balls too.

SOCIAL ()()()()()()()()()()()()()()()()

CARDIFF UNIVERSITY STUDENTS' UNION
- **6 SABBATICALS** - **TURNOUT AT LAST BALLOT** 29%
- **NUS MEMBER**

The Union does a *grand job* of running its facilities and *keeping the political furnace stoked*. There's an *active* student rep system and *keen* interest in Union elections, with the president last year even setting up a special hotline in case any of the *wannabe* leaders started to crack under the pressure of the campaign trail. There's a new working area for students running societies. 2,000 have enrolled with the *hugely popular* student development unit for training in skills ranging from meditation and public speaking to management and Welsh lessons. The Union has a Welsh language policy and all signs and many publications are bilingual. Fair trade is *the new hot ethically-produced potato* and Cardiff is angling for official fair trade status.

SU FACILITIES
Nine bars; five cafeterias/sandwich bars; minibus hire; printing and photocopying; two shops (general, food, stationery, new and secondhand books); Thresher's off-licence; travel centre; payphones; phone messaging service; photo booth; mobile phone store; video games and vending machines; radio lounge; juke box; eight pool tables; four snooker tables; media suite; volunteer suite; IT suite; TV lounges (*or should that be suites?*); study rooms; job shop; function rooms; conference hall; nightclub; Endsleigh Insurance.

CLUBS (NON-SPORTING)
Take a deep breath: A Cappella; Act One; Afro-Caribbean; AIESEC; Amnesty International; Art; BACCUP; Baha'i; Bell Ringing; BioMedical; Broadway Dance; Business; Canadian; Cardiff Castle Appreciation; Cardiff Marrow; Catholic; ChemSoc; Chess; Chinese; Christian Union; Civil Engineering; Cocktail; Conservative; Debating; Duke of Edinburgh; Dynamic Yoga; Earthsoc; EWB; English; Erasmus; Film; French; Funky Arse Dance; Gatecrash; German; Greek; GRIMSoc; Gym Gym; Harry Potter; History; Hoffi Coffi; Hong Kong; Iranian; IRIS; Islamic; Japanese; Jazz; Jewish; Journalism; Labour Students; Law; LGBT; Lib Dems; Links; Live Music; Loafers; MMM; Malaysian; Mature Students; Mechanical Engineering; Medical; MedSoc; MICE; MicroSoc; Mind the Gap; MOMED; Music; Neighbours; Navigators; NeuroScience; Nigerian Students; Nightline; Oddsoc; Omani; One Mission; Optometry; Pagan; People & Places; Photographic; Plaid Cymru; Politics; Pool; Postgrad; Psychology; Puddle Jumping; RAG; Real Ale & Cider; Roleplaying; Save The Children; SAWSA; Scandinavian; Scientific Dive; Sci-Fi; SCM; Scout & Guide SHAG; SPEAK; Speleological; Sri Lankan; STAR; Table Football; Table Tennis; UNA Exchange; Welsh History; Wind Band; Wine Appreciation; WPSA; Xpress Radio; Yuva. **See also Clubs tables.**

OTHER ORGANISATIONS
There's a *small drama puddle* and Rag raises money with *sporadic spates of silliness, but Cardiff students prefer world domination* – media and politics are the well-established student scenes. Free and *much-garlanded* student paper 'Gair Rhydd' ('Free World') is run by the SU. 'Xpress Radio' broadcasts all day in the Union and has a couple of stints on FM every year.

RELIGIOUS
Cardiff has two cathedrals (RC, CofE) and churches of most sorts, including Church of Scotland, Orthodox, Methodist, Quaker. United Reform has an ecumenical chaplaincy on campus. There are also places of worship for Muslims, Jews, Hindus, Sikhs and Buddhists.

PAID WORK
- **JOB BUREAU** - **PAID WORK** TERM-TIME 80%; HOLS 73%

The University Job Shop employs 700 students a year for up to 15 hours a week in various clerical, administrative, cleaning and catering jobs around the campus. Some students get work in the admissions team (eg. PR, recruitment, campaigns) and end up staying there after graduation. *Handy, eh?*

SPORTS

⊙ BUSA RANKING 22

Between the city and the University, *Cardiff is kitted out for just about everything. Rugby pulses through its veins as though nothing else matters, and far be it from Push to disagree.*

SPORTS FACILITIES

Four sports centres; 33 acres of playing fields for all the usual field games; small athletics track; floodlit artificial pitch; Astroturf pitch; tennis and squash courts. Expert advice and fitness assessments also available. Indoor facilities at Talybont (residential complex a mile from the main campus) include two sports halls, a fitness studio, free weights room and five-a-side soccer pitch, martial arts dojo. The Union has facilities for table tennis, squash, fencing, darts, snooker and pool. Other facilities (swimming pool, shooting range, sailing centre and boathouse) are hired locally by the University. Water sports on the Taff and climbing, walking, jumping, grunting on the nearby mountains. Locally: swimming pool, dry ski slope. The brand new International Sports Village – a £700m development scheme on the waterfront – includes a snow dome.

SPORTING CLUBS

Aikido, American Football; Cave; Cheerleading; Dance; Extreme Sport; Ju-Jitsu; Kickboxing; Kite Surf; Korfball; Kung Fu; Lacrosse; Motorsports' Mountaineering; Mountain Bike; Rambling; Rifle; Rowing; Snooker; Surf; Ultimate Frisbee; Waterpolo; Windsurf; Yoga. **See also Clubs tables.**

ATTRACTIONS

The *jaw-droppingly impressive* Millennium Stadium hosts English domestic cup finals as well as Welsh international football. *The real passion is still rugby, though.* There's also Ninian Park for Cardiff FC, Glamorgan Cricket Club at Sophia Gardens and the Cardiff Devils ice hockey team.

ACCOMMODATION

IN COLLEGE

⊙ CATERED 2% **⊙ COST** £70 (39WKS)
⊙ SELF-CATERING 32% **⊙ COST** £70 (39/41WKS)
⊙ 1ST YRS LIVING IN 97%
⊙ INSURANCE PREMIUM ££

AVAILABILITY All non-clearing first years are guaranteed their own room in halls. Catered accommodation is gradually being phased out. There are 13 halls, *all within walking distance* of University. The biggest are the Talybonts north and south and University Hall. Aberdare Hall is girls-only.

CAR PARKING Limited but available at several halls. A yearly pass is *pricey* at £90 though.

EXTERNALLY

⊙ AVE RENT: £51

AVAILABILITY *Students can bunk up within staggering distance of the University at prices that leave plenty of loan over for drinks and sweeties.* The north of the city is *most popular* for living out. There's a *student ghetto* at Cathays and Roath (for its pubs and chippies) in shared houses and flats. *Push would steer clear of Grange Town and nearby Riverside.*

HOUSING HELP The Residence office does vacancy and landlord lists and legal advice. Cardiff's in the process of setting up its own letting agency *in an attempt to keep students well-housed.*

WELFARE

SERVICES

⊙ LGBT SOCIETY ⊙ ETHNIC MINORITIES SOCIETY
⊙ MATURE STUDENTS' OFFICER
⊙ INTERNATIONAL STUDENTS' SOCIETY
⊙ POSTGRAD SOCIETY
⊙ DISABILITIES OFFICER & SOCIETY
⊙ LATE-NIGHT/WOMEN'S MINIBUS ⊙ NIGHTLINE
⊙ UNIVERSITY COUNSELLORS 5 FULL/2 PART
⊙ CRIME RATING !!!!

The Student Support Centre is capable of dealing with most likely crises, and both it and the University *devote a good deal of time and effort into keeping everybody smiling (or at least grimacing non-committally).*

HEALTH Three each of doctors and nurses at the University health centre.

WOMEN Student Union provides attack alarms for £2.

CRECHES/NURSERY 20 places at the nursery on Havelock Street by the main campus for kids aged 3mths-4yrs.

DISABILITIES Access is pretty good all round but possible problems in the SU and some halls. Also a Dyslexia Resource Centre with four full-time specialists.

FINANCE

⊙ AVE DEBT PER YEAR £3,457 **⊙ HOME STUDENT FEES** £1,200

FEES Top up fees come in from 2007, but Welsh students and non-UK EU students get an £1,800 fee grant to ease the pain - other UK students pay a *full-fat* £3K. Part-timers are charged £588. International undergrads pay £8,250 for arts and £10,620 for sciences. Postgrad courses cost a *fairly standard* £3,085.

⊙ ACCESS FUND £800,000
⊙ SUCCESSFUL APPLICATIONS 1,136

SUPPORT Hardship fund available *if things are really tough.* The Oldfield Davies Trust can help women with health problems and there's also a range of course/background specific trusts and bursaries plus short-term loans and small grants for finalists.

Words in italics are Push's point of view — take it or leave it...

C

➤ CARDIFF INSTITUTE
see *UWIC*

➤ CARLISLE
see *University of Central Lancashire*

➤ CARTREFLE TEACHER TRAINING COLLEGE
see *North East Wales Institute*

➤ CAYTHORPE
see *De Montfort University*

➤ UNIVERSITY OF CENTRAL ENGLAND
see *UCE Birmingham*

UNIVERSITY OF CENTRAL LANCASHIRE

FORMERLY PRESTON POLYTECHNIC, LANCASHIRE POLYTECHNIC

1. ⊙ **UNIVERSITY OF CENTRAL LANCASHIRE** Preston Campus, Foster Building, Preston, Lancashire, PR1 2HE **TEL** (01772) 201 201
E‑MAIL cenquiries@uclan.ac.uk **WEBSITE** www.uclan.ac.uk ⊙ **UCLAN STUDENTS' UNION** Fylde Road, Preston, Lancashire, PR1 2TQ
TEL (01772) 893 000 **E‑MAIL** suinformation@uclan.ac.uk **WEBSITE** www.yourunion.co.uk
2. **PENRITH CAMPUS** Newton Rigg, Penrith, Cumbria, CA11 0AH **WEBSITE:** www.uclan.ac.uk/cumbria
3. **CARLISLE CAMPUS** University of Central Lancashire, Paternoster Row, Carlisle, CA3 8TB **TWEBSITE** www.uclan.ac.uk/penrith

GENERAL ⓾⓾⓾⓾⓾⓾⓾⓾⓾⓾⓾⓾⓾

Preston, which sits on the River Ribble, *rules the Lancashire roost*. It was officially made England's 50th city to mark Her Madge's 50th Jubilee (*that's Elizabeth II, not Mrs Ritchie*). It's the second largest city in Lancashire and the county's administrative capital. *That means it's big(ish) and bright(ish), but outshone by Blackpool (in more ways than one)*. The University was established as the Preston Institution for the Diffusion of Knowledge and *though it doesn't quite pulsate with academic radioactivity, it just about looks the part*. It's cementing its position as the fifth biggest University in the whole, wide country with a *heap of new bricks and mortar*, most notably the *swanky* SU building. A 38-acre campus *near* the city centre carries two main blocks and a *mishmash of styles, most notably redbrick, concrete and glass*. There's a converted church to house the Arts Centre. 70 miles away in the *moist but attractive* Lake District is the remote, land-based outdoors-y course campus of Penrith. 30 miles from that is the Carlisle campus for business-types, bang in the centre of – *can you guess what it is yet?* – Carlisle.

SEX RATIO: ↑42 ↓58	**FOUNDED:** 1828
FULL-TIME U'GRADS: 15,066	**PART-TIME:** 9,312
POSTGRADS: 2,808	**NON-DEGREE:** 13,450
AVE COURSE: 3YRS	**ETHNIC:** 11%
STATE:PRIVATE SCHOOL: 96:4	**FLUNK RATE:** 19%
MATURE: 62%	**INTERNATIONAL:** 15%
DISABLED: 360	**LOCAL:** 66%

ATMOSPHERE
There are two types of students in Preston – level-headed bookish types with a thirst for learning but not much more beyond; and their racier colleagues, with a taste for life's thrills, who tack the learning bit on as an inconvenient extra. The latter are in the majority – or at least that's how it feels. They don't mix much, though.

OTHER SITES
PENRITH (Land Studies, Equine Studies, Computing, Business, Forensic Science, Tourism & Outdoor Pursuits) The *tiny and isolated* community town of Penrith sweeps the Cumbrian contingent into similar courses to Preston, *with a sligtly more rural educational sprinkling*. The Cumbria Academy for Animal Studies is based here, along with an SU rep and welfare, activities and ents committees. 300 students live in halls (catered or otherwise).
CARLISLE (Business, Management) Also for Cumbria-tied students, the small city campus enjoys the benefits of city life that Penrith lacks

and is within (energetic) spitting distance of Hadrian's Wall. The SU is represented here *so though they may be out of the way, they ain't out of the loop.* 200 students live in shared flats on site.

PRESTON
○ **POPULATION** 129,600 ○ **CITY CENTRE** 500M
○ **LONDON** 202 MILES ○ **MANCHESTER** 25 MILES
○ **HIGH TEMP** 19 ○ **LOW TEMP** 0 ○ **RAINFALL** 71
Preston gets a *double thumbs-up*: one for cost and one for quality of life. *It's not really a student city, but there are enough cheap drinks promos to keep the pub-bound in pocket.* The Lancashire countryside is *beautiful, as are some of the north-west's seaside towns (Southport, Morecambe etc.).*

TRAVEL
TRAINS Preston Station, 400m from campus, runs direct trains to London (£39.80 rtn), Manchester (£7.95) and beyond.
COACHES National Express services to, among other places, London (£26.50) and Manchester (£5.90).
CAR Preston is on the A6, A49, A59 and A677, and just off the M6, M55 and M61. The town centre can get congested, although there's a new park and ride in the 'burbs.
AIR Manchester International is the closest for cheap international and domestic flights.
LOCAL Local buses keep to a *pernickety* fare system (no change given). Discounted Rambler tickets (anywhere in town, £5.20/week) are available.
UNIVERSITY The Union runs a bus between Penrith, Carlisle and Preston, *but it's really quite a voyage.*
TAXIS *Cheap and plentiful – like a chav's jewellery.*
BICYCLES Bikes are *popular* for getting around the campus *sprawl, but it's not much fun humping them around the hills.*

CAREER PROSPECTS
○ **CAREERS SERVICE** ○ **NO. OF STAFF** 2 FULL/4 PART
○ **UNEMPLOYED AFTER 6 MTHS** 6%
Bulletin boards, jobs fairs, careers library and interview training to help repay those *mountainous* overdrafts.

FAMOUS ALUMNI
Mark Beaumont (NME hack); Victoria Derbyshire, Ian Payne (BBC Radio 5 Live); Simon Kelner (Editor, the Independent); Joe Lydon (rugby league); Phil MacIntyre (pop promoter); Alastair Mann (Match of the Day); Vicky Marsden (Radio 1 DJ); Tjinder Singh, Ben Ayres (Cornershop).

FURTHER INFO
○ **PROSPECTUSES** UNDERGRAD; POSTGRAD; SOME DEPARTMENTAL
○ **OPEN DAYS**
For open day and campus tour information call (01772) 201 201.

ACADEMIC ○○○○○○○○○○○○○

Lots of vocational and practical subjects *boosted by cosy links with local industries.* The NCTJ journalism course is *pretty well respected* and oversubscribed as a result. Some courses offer a year out or sandwich placements.

ENTRY POINTS: 120-300	**AVE POINTS: 238**
APPLICATIONS PER PLACE: 5	**CLEARING: 22%**
NO. OF TERMS: 2	**LENGTH OF TERMS: 15WKS**
STAFF TO STUDENT RATIO: 1:18	**STUDY ADDICTS: 9%**
TEACHING: ★★	**RESEARCH: ★★★**
YEAR ABROAD: N/A	**SANDWICH STUDENTS: 9%**
1STS: 8%	**2.2S: 41%**
2.1S: 42%	**3RDS: 6%**

ADMISSIONS
○ **APPLY VIA UCAS/NMAS FOR NURSING**

SUBJECTS
BUSINESS SCHOOL 16%
CULTURAL LEGAL & SOCIAL STUDIES 27%
DESIGN & TECHNOLOGY 21%   **HEALTH** 22%
SCIENCE 14%
BEST Education; English; History & Archaeology; Journalism; Law; Nursing; Physical Geography & Environmental Science; Physical Science; Psychology; Sociology, Social Policy & Anthropology; Social Work; Subjects allied to Medicine.
UNUSUAL Deaf Studies & British Sign Language; Motor Sports (students actually get to race).

LIBRARIES
○ **607,858 BOOKS** ○ **1,582 STUDY PLACES**
○ **24-HOUR ACCESS** ○ **SPEND PER STUDENT** ££££
The main library's housed in one of the campus's *more modern* buildings. In addition to the folding paper variety, there are 10,000 e-books to scroll through. The library's open till 2am on school nights, for *post-pub essay crises.* The other two sites both have libraries and IT centres.

COMPUTERS
○ **1,000+ WORKSTATIONS** ○ **24-HOUR ACCESS**
○ **SPEND PER STUDENT** ££
Wireless hotspots are springing up around the campus.

OTHER LEARNING FACILITIES
Language labs; music rooms; CAD lab; media centre; 3D visualisation lab; practice courtroom; TV/radio studios; crime scene house; clinical skills lab.

ENTERTAINMENT ◖◗◖◗◖◗◖◗◖◗◖◗◖◗◖◗

THE CITY
○ **PRICE OF A PINT OF BEER** £1.80
○ **GLASS OF WINE** £2.10 ○ **CAN OF RED BULL** £2.26
The University scene makes up for the town's shortcomings.
CINEMAS Two, with 17 screens between them. Penrith has a cinema; Carlisle too.
Theatres: The Charter Theatre, 15 mins walk from campus, serves up a diet of amateur and touring plays.
PUBS *Generally student-hardened. Perfect skivespot the Ship is in the middle of campus and gets painted a different colour each year (maybe watching the stuff dry isn't actually that boring). The Assembly is a good bet in town.* Both Penrith and Carlisle keep the students in drink.
CLUBBING/MUSIC VENUES *Precious little – 53 Degrees (see below) has captured students' hearts (and even some of the locals'). Not a mighty club scene in Carlisle, but, amazingly, Penrith has one or two clubby spots.*
EATING OUT *Varied, cheap and open well after McDonald's has turfed out. Pushplugs: Isis Café bar; ultimate student friendly Chill-Out Zone; Tiggi's (50% student discount); Bella Pasta (half-price on Wednesdays).*

UNIVERSITY
○ **PRICE OF A PINT OF BEER** £1.80
○ **GLASS OF WINE** £2.70
○ **CAN OF RED BULL** £1.80
The new SU building's already bagged one big ents award – not bad at all, especially for a University with a fair amount of local students.
BARS *A drinktastic trio with matching black and red decor.* Main boozer Source has big TVs and pool tables and stays open till 3am at weekends. For club nights it joins forces with 53 Degrees, which has a smaller club bar and a music venue. The Gin Case bar at Penrith *provides the social centre, but Carlisle kids have to make do with the city's offerings.*
THEATRES Semi-official alt drama scene uses St Peter's Arts Centre for all sorts of productions.
FILM: A new arthouse cinema will screen 7-10 shows a week.
CLUBBING Saturdays are cheesy and charty in the Source and 53 Degrees puts on some popular midweek fare. Trevor Nelson has stopped by recently, as have Jon Carter and Fergie.
Music venues: 1,200 pairs of ears can fit into 53 Degrees, making it one of the biggest live venues in the local area. Supergrass, Hard-Fi and Fun Lovin Criminals have graced the stage and there's an indie night on Thursdays.
COMEDY/CABARET Fortnightly comedy in 53 Degrees gets the likes of Adam Bloom.
FOOD *Top of the lunchboxes* is The Green Olive, a coffee shop and tapas bar, *which makes a change from the usual grease or sarnies.* Source does *decent* bar food until 9pm and Fresh 2 Go sells sandwiches and similar snackage. *Cheap but boring canteen fare* at the Foster Restaurant. The Brambles restaurant at Penrith offers weekday meals. Carlisle has a canteen.

SOCIAL ◖◗◖◗◖◗◖◗◖◗◖◗◖◗◖◗◖◗

UCLAN STUDENTS' UNION
○ **7 SABBATICALS** ○ **TURNOUT AT LAST BALLOT** 5%
○ **NUS MEMBER**
The SU are pretty close to the University authorities and there's not a lot of politicking to be done in Preston.

SU FACILITIES
53 Degrees – the new SU building – is *so new the paint's still wet.* Three bars including clubbing and live music space; coffee shop/tapas bar (University-owned); shop; Advice Centre; Print Shop.

CLUBS (NON-SPORTING)
Anime & Manga; Bahai; Chinese; Green Medicine; Hellenic; International Sudents; Invention; Journalism; Links (St John's Ambulance); Mature Students; Malaysian; Musical Theatre; Pagan; Paintball; Poker; PR. Penrith: Conservation Volunteers; Forestry Club; Hawk Club; Re-enactment; Shooting; Scout & Guide; Working Ferret. **See also Clubs tables.**

OTHER ORGANISATIONS
The weekly paper, 'Pluto', isn't a Disney comic, but a *strong* student newspaper staffed by *keenos* from the journo department. Their companions on the airwaves are Frequency 1350AM. *At long last, Rag has gots its wheels in motion* and volunteering takes place through a *highly regarded* University scheme.

RELIGIOUS
○ **2 CHAPLAINS (RC, MULTI-FAITH)**
Multi-faith centre for prayer worship and quiet reflection. The city has a cathedral, churches and places of worship for Muslims, Hindus, Sikhs, Buddhists and Jews.

PAID WORK
○ **JOB BUREAU** ○ **PAID WORK** TERM-TIME 34%; HOLS 75%
Jobshop ('the Bridge'). *Loads* of vacancies round college and in Preston for part-timers.

SPORTS ◖◗◖◗◖◗◖◗◖◗◖◗◖◗◖◗◖◗

○ **RECENT SUCCESSES** FOOTBALL, GOLF, HOCKEY
○ **BUSA RANKING** 66
Sports facilities are *pretty extensive* and students *take advantage of everything they can*

find in the city. There's an annual Lancashire Cup competition against Lancaster University.

SPORTS FACILITIES

65 acres of sports fields including: 12 football, four hockey, six rugby and four cricket pitches; squash, tennis, netball and basketball courts; sports halls; running track and athletics field; gym/multigym; aerobics studio; climbing wall. The Foster Sports Centre has studios for health and fitness, martial arts and fencing, as well as a weights room and courts for a variety of ball sports. The local area has athletics and running space; squash and tennis courts; swimming pool, ice rink; bowling green; golf course; dry and artificial snow ski slopes; pot-holing caves, lakes and rivers for splashing about in. Joint membership of Preston Sports Arena and University facilities costs £28/term or £45/yr.
PENRITH Sports hall with climbing wall and tree; indoor equine area; shooting range.
CARLISLE No university facilities, but students can get discounts locally.

SPORTING CLUBS

Aikido; Dance; Womens' Football; Gaelic Football; Jitsu; Shaolin Kung Fu; Mountaineering; Rugby League; Womens' Rugby Union; Skydiving; Snowboarding; Surf; Windsurf. Penrith: Clay Pigeon Shooting; Fell Running; Paddling; Mountain Activities; Ski/Snowboarding. **See also Clubs tables.**

ATTRACTIONS

Preston's home to the National Football Museum. Preston North End are the *less glamorous* local team.

ACCOMMODATION ◑◑◑◑◑◑◑◑◑

IN UNIVERSITY

○ **SELF–CATERING** 10% ○ **COST** £56 (37WKS)
○ **1ST YRS LIVING IN** 50%
○ **INSURANCE PREMIUM** £
AVAILABILITY Accommodation's reserved for first years, annd most students land either in halls or uni-arranged private accommodation. The halls are *bog-standard* student digs, mainly with shared kitchens and bathrooms and 400 rooms at the top of the price bracket with en suite facilities. All rents include bills. A few rooms are adapted for disabled students and almost all are on campus. 24-hour security's *tight* and there's a free internal phone system in all college rooms.
CAR PARKING *Easy enough* with a permit.

EXTERNALLY

○ **AVE RENT** £58 ○ **LIVING AT HOME** 45%
AVAILABILITY *Hardly a hassle* to find a house in Preston, the standard's *decent*, too. Students *prefer* to live in Plungington and Broadgate rather than Deepdale or Ashton. Lots of private halls have sprung up in the last few years. It's a *small city*, so students *don't tend to worry about long and tedious* commutes into college.
HOUSING HELP Eight staff in the accommodation office *spread their net all over town.*

WELFARE ◑◑◑◑◑◑◑◑◑◑◑◑

SERVICES

○ **LGBT OFFICER & SOCIETY** ○ **RACE RELATIONS GROUP**
○ **WOMEN'S OFFICER & SOCIETY**
○ **INTERNATIONAL STUDENTS' OFFICER & SOCIETY**
○ **POSTGRAD OFFICER & SOCIETY**
○ **DISABILITIES OFFICER & SOCIETY** ○ **TAXI FUND**
○ **ALL–NIGHT MINIBUS** ○ **SELF–DEFENCE CLASSES**
○ **UNIVERSITY COUNSELLORS** 1 FULL/7 PART
○ **CRIME RATING** !!!!
The University's 'i' Student Advice Centre takes care of academic, financial and general welfare gubbins and the Union's advice centre is the place for money advice and general welfare needs.
HEALTH A health centre on campus has five GPs and two nurses.
CRECHES/NURSERY 70 places for ages 1-5yrs.
DISABILITIES *Good* access all across campus with wheelchair access, hearing loops and special accommodation.
CRIME muggings on campus have been reported recently.

FINANCE

○ **AVE DEBT PER YEAR** £3,937 ○ **HOME STUDENT FEES** £3,000
FEES International students pay £7,950 (undergrad) or £8,650 (postgrad). Most UK postgrads pay £3,130. Part-time students pay by the module.
○ **ACCESS FUND** £1,500,000
○ **SUCCESSFUL APPLICATIONS/YR** 3,800
○ **AVERAGE PAYMENT** £100-3,500
SUPPORT A small hardship fund is available to international and some part-time students and emergency loans of up to £250 *can keep the more desperate in baked beans and Wotsits for as long as necessary.* 'Ones to Watch' scholarships offer a grand to full-time undergrads who come from mid-income families.

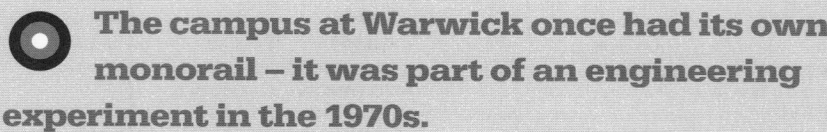

The campus at Warwick once had its own monorail – it was part of an engineering experiment in the 1970s.

▶ **CENTRAL LONDON POLY**
see *University of Westminster*

▶ **CENTRAL ST MARTINS COLLEGE OF ART**
see *University of the Arts, London*

▶ **CHARING CROSS & WESTMINSTER HOSPITAL**
see *Imperial College, London*

▶ **CHARLOTTE MASON**
see *Lancaster University*

▶ **CHELSEA COLLEGE OF ART**
see *University of the Arts, London*

▶ **CHELTENHAM & GLOUCESTER COLLEGE OF HIGHER EDUCATION**
see *University of Gloucestershire*

CHESTER UNIVERSITY

FORMERLY UNIVERSITY COLLEGE CHESTER; CHESTER COLLEGE OF HIGHER EDUCATION

1. ◑ **UNIVERSITY OF CHESTER** Parkgate Road, Chester, CH1 4BJ **TEL** (01244) 511 000 **E−MAIL** enquiries@chester.ac.uk
WEBSITE www.chester.ac.uk
2. **WARRINGTON CAMPUS** Crab Lane, Warrington, WA2 0DB **TEL** (01925) 534 206 **WARRINGTON SU TEL** (01925) 534 375
E−MAIL csuw.vp@chester.ac.uk

GENERAL ◑◑◑◑◑◑◑◑◑◑◑◑◑

Soap fans, take note. The antics of the disproportionately blonde and unfeasibly attractive students of the Chester-set (though not necessarily Chester-filmed) 'Hollyoaks' are fiction. In reality, the newly-crowned University of Chester is a far more sedate place than its TV counterpart, without an obvious serial killer or convoluted family tragedy in sight (although far be it from Push to cast aspersions on the attractiveness of its student body). Located in the north-west of England to the south of Liverpool and Manchester, Chester University was founded as the country's first teacher training college (its other claim to fame) in 1839. It gained offical university status in 2005. The main site is in the pretty, historic city of Chester and there's a smaller campus at Warrington.

SEX RATIO: ♂38 ♀62	FOUNDED: 1839
FULL−TIME U'GRADS: 5,321	PART−TIME: 510
POSTGRADS: 1,579	NON−DEGREE: 3,110
AVE COURSE: 3YRS	ETHNIC: 4%
STATE:PRIVATE SCHOOL: 97:3	FLUNK RATE: 13%
MATURE: 19%	INTERNATIONAL: 3%
DISABLED: 75	LOCAL: 32%

ATMOSPHERE
More cosiness than cliffhanger. A small

University with a community feel, everyone seems to know everyone else and students have a good relationship with the staff. A reasonably high proportion (nearly a third) of students from the local area. While most lap up the niceness like contented felines, those with a revolutionary bent might find it stifling. If it does all get a bit much, the grittier bustle of Liverpool isn't far away.

OTHER SITES
WARRINGTON (1,287 students – Business; Computer Science; Media; Sport & Exercise Sciences) 0 miles from the main site, on the outskirts of Warrington, *a reasonably pleasant but fairly unremarkable town. The site's got its own well-equipped library, nosh outlets, sports facilities and some accommodation plus an SU Vice-President and manager to keep students in the loop.*
WIRRAL EDUCATION CENTRE, LEIGHTON EDUCATION CENTRE (440 students, 360 students) Satellite nursing sites at hospitals near Birkenhead and Crewe.

CHESTER
◑ **POPULATION** 118,207 ◑ **CITY CENTRE** 10 MINS
◑ **LIVERPOOL** 28 MILES
◑ **HIGH TEMP** 17 ◑ **LOW TEMP** 5 ◑ **RAINFALL** 42
Unmistakably historical, Chester wears its postcard-friendly heritage on its sleeve. Encased by the remainder of a Roman Wall, its olde streets are rich with beautiful architecture – tudor buildings house high street chains.

TRAVEL

TRAINS Direct trains from Chester station, ten mins walk from campus, to Cardiff (£9.05 rtn) and London (£23.70); book at least a week early to avoid the price doubling.

COACHES Services from Chester coach station: London (£26.40); Liverpool (£6.50); Birmingham (£11.60).

CAR A55, M56/M6, M53 are all nearby, or try the A5268, A5116, A548, A540, A51, and A41. More than a third of full-time students have a motor (*the rest just have a car, presumably*). Parking on campus is free to those that can get a permit, but the University has reduced the number in an attempt *to stop the planet overheating* (applicants must live at least three miles away to be in with a chance). Parking locally costs about £3 a day.

LOCAL A free University minibus between the Chester and Warrington campuses, or the train between costs £6.25.

TAXIS Fares start from £2.20 in Chester (free phone in the Union bar). Those at Warrington rarely need a chauffer.

BICYCLES The car is the *vehicle of choice*, but new cycle parks and better shower/locker areas might make peddling easier. The campus is close to a main cycle path to the city centre, but otherwise roads are busy.

CAREER PROSPECTS

○ **CAREERS SERVICE** ○ **NO. OF STAFF** 7 FULL/5 PART
○ **UNEMPLOYED AFTER 6MTHS** 3%

Interview training, jobs fairs, CV feedback, careers library, newsletters, workshops, bulletin boards and a jobshop to boot.

FAMOUS ALUMNI

Jim Bowen ('Bullseye'); John Carelton, Jon Sleightholme (former England Rugby Union players), Peter Williams (ditto plus Rugby League for Wales); 'Comedy' Dave Vitty (Chris Moyles' *sidekick*); Rob Wotton (Sky Sports). *Honorary bits of paper* have been given to Sir Bernard Lovell (Astronomer); Gerald Scarfe (satirical cartoonist); Pete Waterman (*poptastic* music producer) and the Duke of Westminster.

FURTHER INFO

○ **PROSPECTUSES** UNDERGRAD; POSTGRAD; ALL DEPARTMENTS; INTERNATIONAL; VIDEO; ALTERNATIVE
○ **OPEN DAYS**

ACADEMIC ⦿⦿⦿⦿⦿⦿⦿⦿⦿⦿⦿⦿⦿

Learners take eight modules a year, one of which (in the second year) can be abroad. Students are *pretty happy* with the teaching, of which they get an average of 12 hrs a week. The Performing Arts & Drama department is *particularly strong*.

ENTRY POINTS: 220-300	**AVE POINTS:** N/A
APPLICATIONS PER PLACE: 3	**CLEARING:** 0%
NO. OF TERMS: 4	**LENGTH OF TERMS:** 8WKS
STAFF TO STUDENT RATIO: 1:12	**STUDY ADDICTS:** 42%
TEACHING: ★★★★★	**RESEARCH:** ★★★★★
YEAR ABROAD: 6%	**SANDWICH STUDENTS:** 1%
1STS: 20%	**2.2S:** 20%
2.1S: 50%	**3RDS:** 5%

ADMISSIONS

○ **APPLY VIA** UCAS/GTTR/NMAS/DIRECT FOR PROFESSIONAL COURSES

SUBJECTS

ART & DESIGN 9% **ARTS/HUMANITIES** 10%
BUSINESS/MANAGEMENT 13% **EDUCATION** 5%
ENGINEERING 1% **MEDIA** 8% **MEDICAL SCIENCES** 24%
(MODERN) LANGUAGES 4% **SCIENCES** 14%
SOCIAL SCIENCES 12%

BEST Art & Design; Business; English; History & Archaeology; Performing Arts; Sociology; Theology & Religious Studies.

UNUSUAL Advertising & Marketing; Cardio-vascular Rehabilitation (MSc); Psychology & Counselling

LIBRARIES

○ **271,655** BOOKS ○ **738** STUDY PLACES
○ **SPEND PER STUDENT** £££

24-hr access is planned for the main library on the Chester campus from 2006-07. Specialist libraries on the other sites.

COMPUTERS

○ **980** WORKSTATIONS ○ **SPEND PER STUDENT** £££

All halls have computers and are the only place where geeks can type 24hrs a day.

OTHER LEARNING FACILITIES

Language lab; drama studio; media centre; practice courtroom. TV studio, AV edit suites and photography suite in the main library.

ENTERTAINMENT ⦿⦿⦿⦿⦿⦿⦿⦿⦿

THE CITY

○ **PRICE OF A PINT OF BEER** £2.30
○ **GLASS OF WINE:** £2.50 ○ **CAN OF RED BULL** £1.55

CINEMAS The pair of seven-screen multiplexes (Odeon and UGC) do student discount, the latter has a bar.

THEATRES The Gateway tries to entice students with a 2-4-1 ticket deal.

PUBS *Posh* wine bars (Living Room) and cocktail joints (Fiesta Havanas) *jostle for space* with traditional boozers like the Bouverie Arms and Irish pubs eg. Number 15. Pushpugs: the Red Lion, Loaf and the Coach & Horses (penny-pinchingly cheap).

CLUBBING An *unholy clubbing trinity* – Reflex (80s student night on Mondays), RB's (commercial dance and R'n'B) and Brannigan's (student night on Wednesdays). *That's yer lot.*

MUSIC VENUES Dozens of pubs are hosts to live music, especially in the Uplands area.
EATING OUT *Everything from kebaberies to posh cuisine, assuming, of course, that the loan will stretch to more than a packet of Cup-a-Soup.*

UNIVERSITY
- **PRICE OF A PINT OF BEER** £1.45
- **GLASS OF WINE** £2

Student drama is made-up head and costumed shoulders above the rest of the Chester's ents, not that that's saying much, really.
BARS Drinks and *other distractions* (Sky Sports, pool tables, karaoke, quizzes *and the like*) at Max 250/Overdraft (cap 480), which is open from 9am-11pm every day.
THEATRES *A super-keen show-off contingent* puts on about ten productions a year. The North-West Media Centre is on the Warrington campus, Molloy Hall has 500 seats and there's a drama studio at the Chester campus.
MUSIC VENUES Overdraft can hold 240 pairs of ears, but rarely gets live acts in to entertain them.
FOOD Chritchley Café does the *cheapest* main meals and sarnies. There are also four *canteen-style* dining halls and eight snack bars, but everything stops serving by 6.30pm.
OTHER A summer ball in June and a sports presentation evening in March.

SOCIAL ()()()()()()()()()()()()

CHESTER STUDENTS' UNION
- **3** SABBATICALS   **TURNOUT AT LAST BALLOT** 10%
- **NUS MEMBER**

The Union building's a friendly place with the feel of a youth club – a smattering of events and facilities keep students happy but there's little to set the world on fire. Politics is about as popular as a thermal vest in the desert. The Union and University enjoy a mutual love-in – the SU president is also a University governor.

SU FACILITIES
Two bars; music venue; five canteen/cafés; nine pool tables; minibus hire; Endsleigh Insurance; ATM (Alliance & Leicester); photocopier; photobooth; payphones; advice centre; crèche; juke box; video/gaming machines; general store; stationery shop; vending machines; new bookshop; second hand bookshop; launderette.

CLUBS (NON-SPORTING)
Centre Stage Warrington; Chester Cheer; Chester Dance; Chester Pride (LGBT); Chester SUDS; Christian; Christian Union Warrington; Criminology; Debating; DJ; Juggling & Circus Skills; Live Music; Martial Arts Warrington; Mature Students; Poker; Rock; Roleplay; Self-defence; Student Scout & Guide Organisation; Vision. **See also Clubs tables.**

OTHER ORGANISATIONS
'The JIP' is the free monthly rag, while 'Student News' is the *tediously on-message* staff and student newspaper. 'CAT' (radio) broadcasts daily over the internet and 'UCTV' is the fledgling online telly station. RAG raised a *reasonable* £2,000 last year through various sponsored shenanigans.

RELIGIOUS
Good new for Christy-types – the Christian Union is active on campus and there's a *plethora* of churches in Chester itself.

PAID WORK
- **JOB BUREAU**   **PAID WORK** TERM-TIME 18%; HOLS 78%

Chester has all the usual job suspects near campus – students earn crusts in retail, call centres and hospitality. *Pocket money opportunities* around the Warrington campus *are harder to come by.*

SPORTS ()()()()()()()()()()()()()

- **RECENT SUCCESSES** RUGBY LEAGUE   **BUSA RANKING** 80

Rugby league has competed nationally, but the emphasis at Chester is on having fun rather than bringing home the silverware. Free access to all the facilities (apart from squash and the fitness suite) means everyone can get a bit of the sporting action.

SPORTS FACILITIES
Facilities are spread out over two sites. Seven football pitches; two rugby pitches; two all-weather pitches; cricket pitch; two tennis courts/netball court; 25m swimming pool; sauna/steam room; athletics field and running track; *prehistoric* climbing wall; gym; multi-gym; aerobics studio; boathouse; two sports halls with ten badminton courts, two volleyball courts, two cricket nets, two basketball courts; two netball courts. Locally there's also a golf course, swimming pool and leisure centre.

SPORTING CLUBS
See also Clubs tables.

ACCOMMODATION ()()()()()()()()()

IN UNIVERSITY
- **CATERED** 7%   **COST** £90 (34/40WKS)
- **SELF-CATERING** 14%   **COST** £62 (40WKS)
- **1ST YRS LIVING IN** 80%   **INSURANCE PREMIUM** £

AVAILABILITY Chester's student numbers have been expanding faster than its accommodation. There are plans to get more *home sweet homes*, but last year 15% of first years had to make other living arrangements. Priority goes to those from more than 35 miles away, international students and

those with special needs . The lucky ones get a choice between catered (all meals), semi-catered (ten meals a week) and self-catering halls. All are less than two miles from the campus, but facilities are *functional but spartan*. There's accommodation for disabled students and some single-sex accommodation. Nearly a third of rooms have en suite facilities. A handful of rooms are shared. A head tenancy scheme gives 110 (mainly older) students a place to live. There are 371 places in halls and houses at Warrington.
CAR PARKING No student parking on campus.

EXTERNALLY
◉ AVE RENT £63 **◉ LIVING AT HOME** 24%
AVAILABILITY *The stampede in student numbers (see above) has increased competition for rented bricks and mortar, but most house-hunters can find a nest (usually a five bed house with a living room) near the Union.*
HOUSING HELP Accommodation Office offers an approved landlord list and vacancy list, legal help and advice, bulletin board and fire/gas certificate checks.

WELFARE ◉◉◉◉◉◉◉◉◉◉◉◉

SERVICES
◉ LGBT OFFICER & SOCIETY ◉ ETHNIC MINORITIES OFFICER ◉ WOMEN'S OFFICER ◉ INTERNATIONAL STUDENTS' SOCIETY ◉ MATURE STUDENTS' SOCIETY ◉ POSTGRAD SOCIETY ◉ DISABILITIES OFFICER ◉ EQUAL OPPORTUNITIES OFFICER ◉ SELF-DEFENCE CLASSES ◉ UNIVERSITY COUNSELLORS 3 PART **◉ CRIME RATING** !
The Union and University both offer welfare help. Voluntary and *presumably insomniac* tutors give full-time pastoral cover from 6pm to 9am.
HEALTH NHS practices near both campuses and an on-site nurse-led pratice on the Warrington site.
DISABILITIES *Good* access to all new buildings, but things are *trickier* in some of the older Grade II listed buildings such as the Blue Coat School. The University *is on the ball* and will arrange timetables around access issues. Also dyslexia screening, support tutorials and 'Read and Write' word prediction software.

FINANCE
◉ AVE DEBT PER YEAR £3,137 **◉ HOME STUDENT FEES** £3,000
FEES International students pay £6,720-£7,484 (undergrad) and £7,848-£9,120 (postgrad). UK postgrads pay £2,760-£5,580 or, for part-timers, £230-£465 per module.
◉ ACCESS FUND £412,547
◉ SUCCESSFUL APPLICATIONS/YR 1,160
◉ AVERAGE PAYMENT £510
SUPPORT: Means-tested bursaries of £450-£1,350.

▶ UNIVERSITY COLLEGE CHESTER
see *University of Chester*

▶ CHESTER COLLEGE
see *University of Chester*

UNIVERSITY OF CHICHESTER

◉ UNIVERSITY OF CHICHESTER Bishop Otter Campus, College Lane, Chichester, West Wsussex, PO19 6PE **TEL** (01243) 816 000 **E-MAIL** admissions@chi.ac.uk **WEBSITE:** www.chiuni.ac.uk **◉ UNIVERSITY OF CHICHESTER STUDENTS' UNION** Bishop Otter Campus, College Lane, Chichester, West Sussex, PO19 6PE **TEL** (01243) 816 390 **E-MAIL** su@chi.ac.uk **WEBSITE** See below for details of other sites.

GENERAL ◉◉◉◉◉◉◉◉◉◉◉◉

Chichester upgraded from university college to fully-fledged university status in 2005. Despite the name, only one of its main sites is in Chichester itself. The Bishop Otter Campus, named after the 19th-century religious leader *and aquatic mammal*, is a 38-acre site just outside the centre of this *pretty* cathedral city, 20 miles from Portsmouth. It was founded in 1839 as Bishop Otter College. They merged in 1977 and both sites (see below for details of the Bognor Regis site) have several modern additions. A high proportion of students are on teaching-related or sports courses. The University used to offer degrees in association with the Isle of Wight College, but recently stopped in order to focus on degrees on the mainland.

SEX RATIO: ♂32 ♀68	**FOUNDED:** 1839
FULL-TIME U'GRADS: 2,260	**PART-TIME:** 315
POSTGRADS: 1,133	**NON-DEGREE:** 235
AVE COURSE: 3YRS	**ETHNIC:** 4%
STATE:PRIVATE SCHOOL: 96:4	**FLUNK RATE:** 13%
MATURE: 32%	**INTERNATIONAL:** 4%
DISABLED: 75	**LOCAL:** 67%

ATMOSPHERE

Given the size of the campuses, it's not surprising that there's a close-knit, amicable atmosphere. It feels as though everyone knows everyone else, but luckily, the students are laid back and lively enough to keep things from getting too claustrophobic. Half sports students, half everyone else can sometimes lead to a bit of a culture clash, but nothing bad tempered. This isn't party central, or even party outskirts – most places shut by midnight and students rub shoulders with the blue rinse brigade in town. The two campuses are six miles apart and free buses run between them.

OTHER SITES

HORSHAM (Education & English) This small, friendly satellite campus in Horsham was originally set up for mature students. Most Horsham students also spend a day a week at one of the main campuses. See below for details of the Bognor Regis site.

CHICHESTER

● **POPULATION** 106,450 ● **CITY CENTRE** 800M
● **LONDON** 75 MILES ● **PORTSMOUTH** 20 MILES
● **BRIGHTON** 32 MILES
● **HIGH TEMP** 21 ● **LOW TEMP** 2 ● **RAINFALL** 75
The Bishop Otter campus is set in parkland on the outskirts of Chichester, a historic cathedral city known to the locals as 'Chi' (pronounced to rhyme with 'eye'). It's a cream tea and antiques kind of place. Although four Georgian shopping streets add a bit of bustle to the centre, quaintness is never far away. See below for details of Bognor Regis.

TRAVEL

TRAINS Chichester Station (15 mins walk from campus) has direct services to London Victoria (90 mins, £15.70 rtn); Portsmouth (45 mins, £6.35 sgl); Brighton (55 mins, £11.20 rtn); Southampton (50 mins, £12.95).
COACHES The coach station (15 mins walk from campus) has services to London Victoria (£13.80, 5 hrs); Portsmouth and Brighton (2.5hrs, £6.40); Southampton (2.5 hrs, £6.50).
CAR Decent road links to London including M25 London orbital (1.25 hr via A27/A3); Bristol (3 hrs via A27/M27/A36); Birmingham (3.5 hrs via A27(M)/A34/M40). Parking isn't a nightmare, and should be even sweeter when the promised park & ride scheme gets off the ground.
AIR Flights from Southampton (34 miles), Gatwick (43 miles) and Heathrow.
LOCAL Buses and trains from/to campuses cost £5 and £3.40 return respectively.

UNIVERSITY Free coaches nip between sites, though they're not suitable for wheelchairs or those with mobility problems. They run weekdays, hourly during the day, latest service 11.20pm.
BICYCLES Pedal pushers can get between campuses in 30-40 mins. And why not, with plenty of bike spaces and no major theft problem?

CAREER PROSPECTS

● **CAREERS SERVICE** ● **NO. OF STAFF** 2 FULL/1 PART
● **UNEMPLOYED AFTER** 6 MTHS 9%
Bulletin boards, library, teaching fair, job fairs, one-to-one guidance and interview training.

FAMOUS ALUMNI

Jason Merrills (actor, Casualty/Cutting It/Waterloo Road).

FURTHER INFO

● **PROSPECTUSES** UNDERGRAD; POSTGRAD; INTERNATIONAL
● **OPEN DAYS**
Mature student evenings and taster days in some depts where applicants can sample lectures or workshops. Four open days a year.

ACADEMIC ❂❂❂❂❂❂❂❂❂❂❂❂❂

Modular undergrad courses, with a cosy touch to them. Teaching is based on seminars, workshops, syndicates and small group learning rather than lectures, with the oodles of contact time often making it feel more like a school than a uni. Most courses involve about 12 hrs a week, 20 for teaching, visual and performing arts courses. Assessment methods range from seminar presentations to exams, dissertations in the final year. Teaching and Sports Science are the traditional high flyers.

ENTRY POINTS: 160-300	**AVE POINTS:** 236
APPLICATIONS PER PLACE: 5	**CLEARING:** 5%
NO. OF TERMS: 2	**LENGTH OF TERMS:** 15WKS
STAFF TO STUDENT RATIO: 1:17	**STUDY ADDICTS:** 1%
TEACHING: ✱✱✱	**RESEARCH:** ✱
YEAR ABROAD: 4%	**SANDWICH STUDENTS:** 4%
1STS: 6%	**2.2S:** 48%
2.1S: 40%	**3RDS:** 6%

ADMISSIONS

● **APPLY VIA UCAS**
The University considers applicants from non-traditional backgrounds (so good for mature students without formal qualifications). Some courses involve auditions. International students need equivalent qualifications.

SUBJECTS

CULTURAL STUDIES 17%   **PHYSICAL EDUCATION** 14%
SOCIAL STUDIES 20%   **SPORT SCIENCES** 16%
TEACHER EDUCATION 13%   **VISUAL/PERFORMING ARTS** 20%
BEST Dance.
UNUSUAL Adventure Education; Business with Dance.

Words in italics are Push's point of view – take it or leave it...

C

LIBRARIES
- **258,820** BOOKS - **504** STUDY PLACES
- **SPEND PER STUDENT** £££

Library on each campus (Bishop Otter's is the bigger, with 160,000 books and 410 study spaces). An integrated system means students can borrow, request and return books from either library. CDs, DVDs and videos can be also used in either library. *With headphones, natch.*

COMPUTERS
- **260** WORKSTATIONS - **SPEND PER STUDENT** £££££

IT provisions at Bishop Otter are housed in the library, where there are also three laptop points. Computer rooms *don't open late enough to suit nocturnal candle-burners.*

OTHER LEARNING FACILITIES
Drama facilities; media centre; music rooms; art gallery. The dance studios are *impressive.*

ENTERTAINMENT ⓞⓞⓞⓞⓞⓞⓞⓞⓞⓞ

THE CITY
- **PRICE OF A PINT OF BEER** £2
- **GLASS OF WINE** £2.50 - **CAN OF RED BULL** £2

See below for details of other sites.

CINEMAS The New Park Centre (within walking distance of campus) has a bar and shows up to five arthouse films and new releases a day (one screen), as well as hosting an annual 18-day film festival. Student discounts here and at the nearby ten-screen Cineworld.

THEATRES Next door to campus the *famous* Chichester Festival Theatre and its extension, the Minerva Theatre, put on a wide variety of shows.

PUBS *With the notable exception of Wetherspoons, most pubs cater for the needs of the wealthier, non-student residents.* Pushplugs: Wetherspoons (cheap); the Havana; the Vestry; West (cocktails and good value grub).

CLUBBING Thursdays is the place to go on Tuesdays (*naturally*). Drayton has an 80s-style student night on Tuesdays and 90s, Garage and R'n'B occasions the rest of the week. Chicago Rock Café is at Chichester Gate Leisure Park.

MUSIC VENUES Local bands across the musical spectrum play at pubs like the Four Chestnuts, the Fountain, the Swan and the Chichester Inn.

EATING OUT *Wetherspoons is typically popular* and there's KFC and McDonald's in the new Southgate complex. There are *truckloads of* sandwich shops and tea rooms around the town, but *some can be expensive. Picnic on the green spaces around the Cathedral when the sun shines.* For evening eating, the Charcoal Grill *offers drunken punters salvation in the form of their kebabs,* and Perfect Pizza *is also open till midnight.*

OTHER Aside from the *rolling serenity of the* South Downs and the Sussex coast, culture and calm can be found in Chichester Cathedral, Arundel Castle, the Pallant House Gallery and Goodwood Sculpture Park.

UNIVERSITY
- **PRICE OF A PINT OF BEER** £1.70
- **GLASS OF WINE** £1.70-£2
- **CAN OF RED BULL** £1.70

BARS The Zeebar building has space for 600 *boozy* girls and boys and is packed most nights. Themed nights – karaoke, pool tournaments, live music, sports night or 'club land' – get the party started, *but things tend to fizzle out, pumpkin-like, by midnight.*

THEATRES The Showroom Theatre hosts professional and student performances. *Strange as it may sound,* the Chapel is also used for music and dance nights.

CLUBBING/MUSIC VENUES Local and unsigned bands make a beeline for the Zeebar. Open mic nights are *supremely popular with the show-off contingent. There's fun to be had on the Zeebar's dancefloor, though describing it as a club is about as accurate as calling Bognor a surf beach – only an amateur would be fooled.* Jo from S Club and Tim Westwood have popped down lately.

COMEDY Once a month in – *where else?* – the Zeebar.

FOOD The College-run canteen can hold 150 *munchers and keeps sporty students fuelled with healthy nosh.* Holts Café is *popular* with mature students and there's also a *tiddly* grub shop.

OTHER Students finally get the chance to stay up past midnight at four *impressive* balls a year, which include the likes of fun fairs and ice sculptures but only set revellers back £10-£20.

SOCIAL ⓞⓞⓞⓞⓞⓞⓞⓞⓞⓞⓞⓞ

UNIVERSITY OF CHICHESTER'S STUDENTS' UNION
- **2** SABBATICALS - **TURNOUT AT LAST BALLOT** 15%
- **NUS MEMBER**

Politics isn't the name of the SU's game, but it does organise ents, sports clubs/teams and socs and *sticks up for its members whenever necessary.* The SU building, Zeebar, is £1.6m *well spent* – it's a multi-purpose bar/meeting area that's open all day and usually *buzzing.* Relations with the University are *warm and toasty.*

SU FACILITIES
Two bars; two canteens; chapel; pool tables; two minibuses for hire; cashpoint; photocopier; fax; photo booth; phone; games machine; vending machine; shop; launderette.

CLUBS (NON-SPORTING)
Mutual Appreciation; Queueing; Vampire. **See also Clubs tables.**

Words in italics are Push's point of view — take it or leave it...

OTHER ORGANISATIONS

'The Clash' is the SU paper (free, twice termly, but *unfortunately for budding journos* produced mainly by union officials rather than students). Rag *did well* in raising three grand last year for good causes.

RELIGIOUS

○ 1 CHAPLAIN (COFE)

The on-site chapel is also used for non-religious events. There are CofE, RC and Baptist churches in and around Chichester. Other faiths *might have to look a little harder.*

PAID WORK

○ JOB BUREAU ○ PAID WORK term time 42% hols 45%
Jobshop for internal and external jobs and vacancies board. The careers service does what it can to help students find vocational/vacation work. The University employs a number of students in catering, marketing, accommodation etc., and the town itself has a few retail opportunities.

SPORTS ○○○○○○○○○○○○○○

○ RECENT SUCCESSES BASKETBALL, CRICKET, HOCKEY, NETBALL, RUGBY
○ BUSA RANKING 45

A healthy contingent of sports students and decent facilities keep sporting success high on the agenda. The SU organises recreational sporting shenanigans and the PE Department looks after the academic side of things. *A bit of internal wrangling goes on over whether the University provides competitive sport or sport for all – it tries its best to do both.* The University sports staff were heavily involved with some of the 2004 Olympics' athletes.

SPORTS FACILITIES

Nine acres of sports fields; lacrosse pitch. The sports centre at Bishop Otter includes a sports hall, indoor and outdoor climbing walls, fitness suite, Astro pitch, tennis/netball courts and two gyms. It's possible – *and popular* – to take a coaching qualification. Sports clubs train free; other students get membership at a maximum of £90 a year. The *large* Westgate Leisure Centre in town has courts, swimming, gym, classes, sauna and jacuzzi. The Chichester Lawn Tennis & Squash Club offers a yearly subscription. The beach and Chichester lake are handy for watery sports.

SPORTING CLUBS

Rock Climbing; Surfing **See also Clubs tables.**

ATTRACTIONS

Goodwood race course puts on horse and motor racing and shows, and employs plenty of students to serve nibbles in the summer.

ACCOMMODATION ○○○○○○○○○○

IN UNIVERSITY

○ CATERED 8% **○ COST** £117 (30WKS)
○ SELF-CATERING 5% **○ COST** £95 (30WKS)
○ 1ST YRS LIVING IN 47% **○ INSURANCE PREMIUM** £
AVAILABILITY Accommodation is allocated on a first-come, first-served basis, and with such a high proportion of local students there's usually a bed for those that want it, though not necessarily at the same site at which they're studying. Halls are a stone's throw from the union, and take the form of *clusters of cosy cottage affairs rather than gaping tower blocks.* Nearly half the rooms are en suite and there's a launderette. All rooms have internet access. Two rooms are adapted for disabled students. Insurance is included in the rent. There's a 24-hr security guard and a student warden system, where *old hands keep an eye out for the new recruits.* A new self-catering block should open for business in Autumn 2006.
CAR PARKING By £10 permit. *Plenty of space to stash a bike; less for a car.* First years living on campus aren't allowed parking. About 70% of students have wheels. *Some have cars too.*

EXTERNALLY (CHICHESTER)

○ AVE RENT £60 **○ LIVING AT HOME** 47%
AVAILABILITY The influx of summer visitors means 9-month contracts are pretty common – these are a *handy way of keeping costs low over the long vacation.* Most students live in privately rented houses, flats or homestays (ie. with a landlord or family, perhaps including meals). *Gownies rub shoulders with townies, rather than holing up in student ghettos. Lodgings are cheaper further away from campus.*
HOUSING HELP The accommodation office provides advice and an approved landlord list.

WELFARE ○○○○○○○○○○○○

SERVICES

○ MATURE STUDENTS' OFFICER
○ INTERNATIONAL STUDENTS' OFFICER
○ EQUAL OPPORTUNITIES OFFICER
○ DISABILITIES OFFICER
○ UNIVERSITY COUNSELLORS 1 FULL/2 PART
○ SU COUNSELLORS 3 FULL/9 PART
○ CRIME RATING !
HEALTH Full-time nurse; GP surgeries twice a week.
CRIME Not a problem. Halls are handily close to the union for late night (*well, midnight, this is Chichester after all*) returners.
WOMEN Cheap attack alarms supplied by the SU. There's a *bizarre* taxi scheme where, in emergencies, a student card is ransomed to the cabbie until the penniless person scrapes

C

together the cash for the fare.
DISABILITIES *Access isn't comprehensive, but the campus is flat and most central buildings and two teaching buildings are accessible.* The disability support team helps with technical stuff like note-taking, readers, communicators and non-medical helpers. There are taping, Braille and large screen computer facilities and plans for a guide dog pen.

FINANCE
⊙ **AVE DEBT PER YEAR** £3,115 ⊙ **HOME STUDENT FEES** £3,000
FEES Part-time students pay £150 a module. Postgrad fees are £2,425-£3,190, or £6,900-£7,650

for international (non-EU) students. International students cough up £6,900 for classroom-based courses, £7,650 for research-based ones.
⊙ **ACCESS FUND** £250,000 ⊙ **SUCCESSFUL APPLICATIONS/YR** 346
⊙ **AVERAGE PAYMENT** £800
SUPPORT Various scholarships are available from various departments. Bursaries of £250-£1,000 are available to students eligible for the government's maintenance grant.

⮞ **UNIVERSITY COLLEGE CHICHESTER**
see *University of Chichester*

⮞ **CHICHESTER COLLEGE**
see *University of Chichester*

⮞ **CIRENCESTER**
see *Royal Agricultural College*

BOGNOR REGIS

⊙ **UNIVERSITY OF CHICHESTER** Bognor Regis Campus, Upper Bognor Road, Bognor Regis, West Sussex, PO21 1HR
TEL (01243) 816 000

GENERAL
The site dates from 1947 and is centred on a Georgian mansion terrace in the seaside resort of Bognor Regis. Its 1,200-odd students create a *buzzing atmosphere similar to that found seven miles away at the Chichester site. Students studying at the other site often live in Bognor anyway, as the accommodation's cheaper.*

BOGNOR REGIS
A traditional, laid-back seaside resort with plenty of easily-accessible coastline to pull in watersports lovers. It's popular with tourists, particularly in the summer.
TRAVEL Bognor has its own mainline railway station within walking distance of the site (1.75 hrs direct to London Victoria) and good road links to the rest of the country. Driving times to the Bognor Regis Campus are 15 mins longer than those given above for Chichester. Disabled parking spaces are available. The University lays on hourly coaches between the two sites.

ACADEMIC
Teacher Education, Business Studies IT and Tourism Management are all based at Bognor. A Learning Resource Centre provides 70 study spaces, 100,000 books and 70 computers, all with internet access.

ENTERTAINMENT
THE TOWN *All the fun of the seaside.* Pushplugs:

Hatters/Wetherspoons (*cheap, heaving and unhampered by anything unpleasant like atmosphere*); The Beach House (*mad atmosphere*, DJs like the Minestrone of Sound or the Chemistry Brothers); the Waiting Room (more DJs, *very student-friendly*); Esplanade (pool and music till 1am); The Mud Club (student friendly, music); The Prom/Bottle bar (weekend DJs, late-opening); William Hardwick (*pricey but quiet and comfy*). As well as *the usual range* of fast food outlets and fish and chip shops there are *a few reasonable restaurants.* The Alexandra Theatre has plays and films, and the old-fashioned Picturedrome shows recent releases. Clubwise, there's Vision (student nights on Tuesdays and Thursdays) and Oceans 11 (alternative music on Wednesdays).
SITE The Mack has a main bar with sports shown on a big screen upstairs and a cocktail affair below. Entertainment of the open mic or karaoke variety is laid on nearly every night. Pool tournaments happen on Mondays. Tuesdays are *'club'* nights. There's also free Playstation 2 as well as pool tables and arcade machines *to while the hours away.* The refectory is run by the same company as the main site, *so don't expect Bognor delicacies.*

SOCIAL
ON SITE Shop; refectory; common room; prayer room. One of the Union's sabbs is based in Bognor.

Words in italics are Push's point of view — take it or leave it...

SPORT

There are tennis courts on site, but the bulk of sporty shenanigans are found at Chichester. The Arun Leisure Centre (swimming pool, gym, courts, classes) is *within strolling distance* of the campus. The waveside setting means *watersports freaks* can get wet sailing, windsurfing, surfing, waterskiing, kitesurfing or kayaking.

ACCOMMODATION

ON SITE 260 rooms and flats of various sizes on-campus, 160 with en suite facilities and there's a *handful* with twin beds. 20 women-only rooms at the Dome. Two rooms are suitable for disabled students.

BOGNOR REGIS
⊙ **AVE RENT** £58 ⊙ **LIVING OUT** 80%
As in Chichester, homestay plans and 9-month contracts are available.

WELFARE

There's an on-site nurse and visiting doctors.

CITY UNIVERSITY

1. ⊙ **CITY UNIVERSITY** Northampton Square, London, EC1V 0HB **TEL** (020) 7040 5060 **WEBSITE** www.city.ac.uk city
   ⊙ **UNIVERSITY STUDENTS' UNION** Northampton Square, London, EC1V 0HB **TEL** (020) 7040 5606 **E−MAIL** cusu@city.ac.uk
   WEBSITE www.cusuonline.org
2. ⊙ **CASS BUSINESS SCHOOL** 106 Bunhill Row, London, EC1Y 8TZ
3. ⊙ **ST BARTHOLOMEW SCHOOL OF NURSING & MIDWIFERY** 24 Chiswell Street, London EC1A 7QN

GENERAL ⓤⓤⓤⓤⓤⓤⓤⓤⓤⓤⓤⓤⓤ

City University sits at the point *where Islington hip hits City slick, with achingly edgy Hoxton and Shoreditch to the east. If picking a university is like buying a house – location, location, location – then City has it all.* Of course, like anywhere in London, *wealth and splendour butt up against poverty and crime and the rich/poor divide is abundant in Islington. But this is a student-dominated hotspot, which provides something of a buffer to the rougher side of London life.* £20m has recently been spent on the impressive Social Sciences building and the glass-fronted Cass Business School near Finsbury Square *seems rather swanky.*

👤👤👤👤👤👤👤👤👤👤👤👤👤👤👤👤👤👤👤	
SEX RATIO: ♀43 ♂57	**FOUNDED:** 1894
FULL−TIME U'GRADS: 6,506	**PART−TIME:** 1,730
POSTGRADS: 4,568	**NON−DEGREE:** 9,088
AVE COURSE: 3YRS	**ETHNIC:** 46%
STATE:PRIVATE SCHOOL: 70:30	**FLUNK RATE:** 15%
MATURE: 42%	**INTERNATIONAL:** 29%
DISABLED: 5	**LOCAL:** 15%

ATMOSPHERE

The syllabus is dominated by business and technology and an *appropriate work ethic has been instilled in students. Fun comes second to getting a good degree and student politics take a sorry third.* A popular group study space was opened last year although *it probably would have been more popular had one of the Union's two bars not been closed to house it.* The University is divvied up across three main sites *and can feel fragmented,* especially with the *high proportion* of postgrads and the *rival attraction of city life over City life. The diversity* of the local area is reflected in a *rich mixture* of social and ethnic backgrounds and City draws almost three-quarters of students from state schools. *There's a bustling, friendly atmosphere to halls of residence and college corridors, although things on the main site calm down as soon as the working day is done.*

OTHER SITES

CASS BUSINESS SCHOOL (1,166 students – Finance, Management & Statistics, Actuarial Science) The Business School is ten mins walk from the main campus. *Its only real role is as a swish new teaching building and the centre of gravity remains Northampton Square.*
ST BARTHOLOMEW SCHOOL OF NURSING & MIDWIFERY (Adult Nursing, Applied Biological Sciences, Applied Psychosocial Sciences, Child Health, Child Health Research & Policy Unit, Department of Mental Health & Learning Disability, Midwifery & Public Health and Primary Care Unit) Like the business centre, St Bart's is really an extension of Northampton Square, *where the extra-curricular action is based.*

LONDON see University of London

Like a lot of London, Islington *can blow a crater in your pocket.*

TRAVEL see University of London

TRAINS Liverpool Street and King's Cross (soon to be Regent Quarter) mainline stations are within ten mins walk. Underground stations: Angel (Northern Line), Farringdon or Barbican (both Circle, Hammersmith and City, Metropolitan, Thameslink).
COACHES Victoria coach station is the closest – about 15 mins on the tube from Angel or 25 mins on the number 73 bus.

Words in italics are Push's point of view – take it or leave it...

BUSES 4, 19, 30, 38, 43, 55, 56, 73, 171, 196, 214, 243, 279, 341, 505; N19, N21, N73, N92, N96.
CAR Islington council has an *unquenchable thirst* for emptying the pockets of traffic infringers. That means clamps, hefty fines and *mind-boggling* parking fees where you do find a space. City's inside the congestion charge zone.
UNIVERSITY Transport from lectures to accommodation is laid on for nursing students in Hackney.
TAXIS Black cabs, minicabs, but all at a cost – *that's London.*
BICYCLES Bikes are popular with students, and there are bike racks in Northampton Square (40 spaces, one-off £10 fee). But be warned – there's a *huge problem* with cycle and scooter theft in Islington. *Buy the best bike-lock you can afford and get the bike security stamped.*

CAREER PROSPECTS
✪ CAREERS SERVICE ✪ NO. OF STAFF 6 FULL
✪ UNEMPLOYED AFTER 6 MTHS 5%
The vocational nature of many courses (even arts courses have a professional slant) means most students are highly employable on graduation.

FAMOUS ALUMNI
Brendan Barber (TUC president); Michael Fish (*veteran* ex-weatherman); Stelios Haji-Ionnau (Easy group); Ruby Hammer (Ruby & Millie make-up); Dermot Murnaghan (newsreader); Sophie Raworth (BBC newsreader); Jack Warner (Dixon of Dock Green – *ask your gran*).

FURTHER INFO
✪ PROSPECTUSES UNDERGRAD; POSTGRAD; DEPARTMENTAL
✪ OPEN DAYS
Open days can be arranged by schools. Frequent campus tours let potential recruits have a *good sniff around.*

ACADEMIC ◖◖◖◖◖◖◖◖◖◖◖◖◖

City has made vocational business and technology courses its niche and has an *impressive* reputation, notably in the journalism department, whose postgraduate diploma is *world-renowned.* Music also has a good reputation (City's associated with Guildhall School of Music & Drama) and free French, German and Spanish classes are available to linguistically-inclined students.

ENTRY POINTS: 220-360	AVE POINTS: N/A
APPLICATIONS PER PLACE: N/A	CLEARING: 21%
NO. OF TERMS: 3	LENGTH OF TERMS: 10WKS
STAFF TO STUDENT RATIO: 1:14	STUDY ADDICTS: 15%
TEACHING: ★★★	RESEARCH: ★★
YEAR ABROAD: 2%	SANDWICH STUDENTS: 6%

ADMISSIONS
✪ APPLY VIA UCAS/NMAS

SUBJECTS
ALLIED HEALTH SERVICES 12% **ARTS/HUMANITIES** 12%
CASS BUSINESS SCHOOL 23%
ENGINEERING & MATHEMATICAL SCIENCE 10%
INFORMATICS 3% **SOCIAL SCIENCES** 9% **LAW** 9%
NURSING & MIDWIFERY 22% **SOCIAL SCIENCES** 9%
BEST Art & Design; Business & Management; Economics; Electrical & Electronic Engineering; Librarianship & Information Management; Mathematical Sciences; Nursing; Other studies allied to Medicine; Psychology.

LIBRARIES
✪ 363,683 BOOKS ✪ 1,222 STUDY PLACES
✪ SPEND PER STUDENT ££
Two main libraries are supplemented by several departmental ones and 100,000 volumes of periodicals *bolster* the bookshelves. The Cass Business library is *ultra-modern and sorted* for everything students need.

COMPUTERS
✪ 600 WORKSTATIONS ✪ 24-HOUR ACCESS
✪ SPEND PER STUDENT ££
Despite a *reasonable* spread of computers across the site there can be a *lot of pressure* on places. Some wireless access at Northampton Square and internet access of the plug-in variety in all student rooms.

OTHER LEARNING FACILITIES
Broadcast suite.

ENTERTAINMENT ◖◖◖◖◖◖◖◖◖

THE CITY see University of London
✪ PRICE OF A PINT OF BEER: £2.50
✪ GLASS OF WINE £3 **✪ CAN OF RED BULL** £2
Islington, Shoreditch and the City have their share of *diverse* entertainments including pubs, clubs, bars, a welter of restaurants and snack bars, galleries, theatres, cinemas and more.
CINEMAS The Screen on the Green and a Vue next to the Islington Academy cater for cult and mainstream tastes respectively. The *comfy* alternative cinema at the Barbican is a bus ride away.
THEATRES Sadler's Wells is just across the road, and shows ballet, contemporary dance and international theatre. Also the Anna Scher Theatre and the Old Red Lion (*hip new and newish* playwrights).
PUBS A trip from lectures to the Bull *is like staggering out of the back door and finding a raucous party in the shed. The Peasant's rather upmarket and has a reputation as a hip gastropub. Neither could be described as cheap, even though the Bull feels as though it should be (fish finger sarnies are a popular speciality – go figure). Nevertheless, they're popular with students, despite rivalry from Islington and Clerkenwell's other boozers.*
CLUBBING Fabric and Turnmills (Clerkenwell/

Farringdon) are within easy stomping distance. Alternative clubnights (eg. XFM night) at the Islington Academy and Slimelight is a legendary Saturday night goth club for *those that know how (and dare) to get in.*

MUSIC VENUES The Islington Academy (in the N1 centre) hosts a lot of hot young indie bands. Daniel Powter, PKGO and the Wonder Stuff were recent visitors. The Garage (Highbury) and the Scala also get tunesters and the Hope and Anchor is the place for local acts.

COMEDY/CABARET *Mirthsters* can be found at the Purple Turtle bar (Essex Road), Red Rose Club (Seven Sisters Road) and the Courtyard Theatre.

EATING OUT Kebab houses and chip shops are *ten a penny* almost anywhere in London, but in Islington so are bistros, gastropubs, sandwich/coffee shops and *credit-card-busting* posher places.

UNIVERSITY
- **PRICE OF A PINT OF BEER** £1.50
- **GLASS OF WINE** £2
- **CAN OF RED BULL** £1.50

There are regular *cheap and cheerful* nights in the University bar, with weekly pool comps and quiz nights *providing a break* from the drinks and dancing. The *regulation cheese-fests* play second fiddle to a *more bling* brand of ents which attract *big names* from the UK urban scene.

BARS Saddlers bar *gets packed and sweaty* during the week, but isn't always open at weekends *owing to lack of interest.*

CLUBBING Bhangra, hiphop and R'n'B get regular outings in the bar, plus plenty of *Parmesan-infused* fun – Quids In on Wednesdays in Saddlers Bar, Candyfloss (Mondays) and a weekly Bar FTSE night, where drinks prices change to meet demand.

FOOD The University runs two refectories – *convenient canteen fare.* Saddlers bar serves snacks and sandwiches. There's a Café Ritazza, a City Trader shop and a Taste sandwich bar, plus several fair trade outlets. *As university fodder goes, nowhere's particularly cheap, but readjust to London prices, and it's not criminally costly.*

OTHER The Freshers Ball is *a chance to pull on the penguin suit.*

SOCIAL ◑◑◑◑◑◑◑◑◑◑◑◑◑

CITY UNIVERSITY STUDENTS' UNION
- **7 SABBATICALS** ◉ **TURNOUT AT LAST BALLOT** 4%
- **NUS MEMBER**

CUSU did a *canny* bit of business in turning the social scene management over to university hands, but it has left the student rep body *without a great amount to do.* Facilities are *lightweight* in comparison to ULU, which City

students are not entitled to use (*although many do*).

SU FACILITIES
Bar; committee room; general shop; games area; minibus hire; snooker and pool tables; vending machines and video games; travel shops; secondhand book stall.

CLUBS (NON-SPORTING)
Ahlul Bayt (Islamic); AIESEC (work abroad scheme co-ordinators); Art of Living; Chinese; Cypriot; Economics; Finance & Investment; Hellenic; Hindu; Korean; Law; Malaysian; Mauritian; Nordic; Optometry; Student CND; Vulture magazine. **See also Clubs tables.**

OTHER ORGANISATIONS
The glossy CUSU-run student magazine, 'Massive', is published two or three times a term and 'Vulture' is its new rival. 'Divercity radio' can be caught on the net and in the SU foyer but *goes largely unnoticed.* City has a *long tradition* of charity rag, and has held events ranging from the *sexy* (World's largest Ann Summers Party, erotic dance nights) to the *stupid* (life sized carrot costumes).

RELIGIOUS
- **5 CHAPLAINS (METHODIST/FC; COFE; RC; GREEK ORTHODOX), RABBI**

There's a Muslim prayer room on site, but London provides well for all faiths. The Islamic Society is *particularly active* on campus.

PAID WORK
- **JOB BUREAU** ◉ **PAID WORK** TERM-TIME 18%; HOLS 30%

There are *plenty* of opportunities for students to find work and the university job bureau helps students on their way after graduation. There's some low-paid work on offer in the Union's bar and shop and unpaid placements and internships in the likes of media, marketing, management and training and research.

SPORTS ◑◑◑◑◑◑◑◑◑◑◑◑◑

- **BUSA RANKING** 116

City is *decidedly sluggish, with study and partying higher on most agendas.*

SPORTS FACILITIES
City owns a *modest* sports centre, providing: aerobics; basketball courts; gym; martial arts; netball courts; squash courts; sports hall; sauna and steam room. Membership costs £20 per month. Shared rugby, hockey, football, tennis and cricket grounds are dotted around north London and the rowing club has a boathouse at Chiswick. Surfers can use the Queen Mary Sailing Club.

SPORTING CLUBS

Aikido; Bridge; Dance; Hiking; Shorinji Kempo; Snowboarding; Wrestling. **See also Clubs tables.**

ATTRACTIONS

Arsenal are the local football team, although chances of getting tickets are *slim*. *Otherwise there's the pick of London's plethora of teams across just about every possible sport.*

ACCOMMODATION ○○○○○○○○○

IN UNIVERSITY

○ **SELF-CATERING** 11% ○ **COST** £98 (35-51WKS)
○ **INSURANCE PREMIUM** £

AVAILABILITY Accommodation is *generally good, secure and close to university*. The prices may seem *steep* but a quick look at the private rental market in the area says students are getting *a bit of a steal*. Francis Rowley Court is *the address of choice*. Walter Sickert Hall is *less desirable*. Most accommodation has shared kitchens and laundrette facilities; cleaners are also on hand in some locations. There are 599 first year rooms to go around, which the University reckons is enough to house everyone from outside the Greater London area, *but it's still as well to apply early.*
CAR PARKING *No way, no how.*

EXTERNALLY

○ **AVE RENT** £88 ○ **LIVING AT HOME** 20%

AVAILABILITY Finding *affordable digs* anywhere this near the centre of London is a *nightmare,* particularly if you can't pay more than £80 a week. *Hackney, Camden and Stoke Newington are all good bets with easy bus routes into Islington. Clapton is harder to get to, but (perhaps as a result) is cheaper.*
HOUSING HELP The University-run accommodation service has an approved landlord list, vacancy list and property vetting.

WELFARE ○○○○○○○○○○○○○

SERVICES

○ **LGBT OFFICER & SOCIETY** ○ **ETHNIC MINORITIES OFFICER** ○ **WOMEN'S OFFICER**
○ **MATURE STUDENTS' OFFICER** ○ **POSTGRAD OFFICER**
○ **INTERNATIONAL STUDENTS' OFFICER & SOCIETY**
○ **DISABILITIES OFFICER & SOCIETY**
○ **SELF-DEFENCE CLASSES** ○ **NIGHTLINE**
○ **UNIVERSITY COUNSELLORS** 1 FULL/9 PART
○ **CRIME RATING** !!!!!

The Student Advice Centre doles out wise words on finance, housing, academic issues and the like. Every student has a personal tutor.
HEALTH There's close contact with a GP service, as well as a nurse advisory service and University optometry clinics. Under-24s can have a free Meningitis C jab.
WOMEN The Women's Officer is the *main port of call.*
CRECHES/NURSERY No crèche on site, but the University has an established relationship with a local nursery for 2-5-year-olds.
DISABILITIES Not all of Northampton Square is accessible to disabled students, but the University will *jiggle* classroom timetables around as necessary. T-loops, some special accommodation, lifts and note-takers.

FINANCE

○ **AVE DEBT PER YEAR** £2,825 ○ **HOME STUDENT FEES** £3,000
FEES Fees vary for international, postgraduate and EU students.
SUPPORT The Sir John Cass Foundation offers 14 scholarships a year to undergraduates from London studying Computing, Engineering, Mathematics and Actuarial Science or Nursing and Midwifery. Awarded to second and third year students, they're worth £1,000 per year for up to three years. The Reeves Foundation and Finsbury Educational Trust offer scholarships to Greater London students. NHS bursaries of £6,859 to nursing students and up to £2,837 for other courses are available.

▶ **CITY OF LONDON POLY**
see *London Metropolitan University*

▶ **COLERAINE**
see *University of Ulster*

◉ **'I think that's the problem with a university education. You just end up thinking too much.' – Ed O'Brien (Radiohead)**

Words in italics are Push's point of view — take it or leave it...

COURTAULD INSTITUTE OF ART

THE COLLEGE IS PART OF UNIVERSITY OF LONDON AND STUDENTS ARE ENTITLED TO USE ITS FACILITIES

⊙ **THE COURTAULD INSTITUTE OF ART** Somerset House, Strand, London, WC2R 0RN **TEL** (020) 7848 2645
E–MAIL ugadmissions@courtauld.ac.uk **WEBSITE** www.courtauld.ac.uk
⊙ **COURTAULD STUDENT'S UNION** Somerset House, Strand, London, WC2R 0RN **TEL** (020) 7848 2717

C

GENERAL ()()()()()()()()()()()()()

The Courtauld is *appropriately* housed in one of Europe's *most elegant* 18th-century public buildings, Somerset House, located on a huge site between the north bank of the Thames and the Strand. Formerly the public record office, the building's been opened up to the public and is now chocka with cafés, restaurants and art, including the Courtauld Collection. The Institute's the UK's only college specialising solely in the history of art. Somerset House is plastered with paintings, sculptures, architectural features and the Institute's own *remarkable collection*. Only 500m from Trafalgar Square and the rest of central London, it's *extremely well served for entertainments, culture and other disturbingly expensive activities.* For general information about London see University of London.

SEX RATIO: ♀40 ♂60	**FOUNDED: 1932**
FULL–TIME U'GRADS: 150	**PART–TIME: 0**
POSTGRADS: 200	**NON–DEGREE: 0**
AVE COURSE: 3YRS	**ETHNIC: 20%**
STATE:PRIVATE SCHOOL: 40:60	**FLUNK RATE: 1%**
MATURE: 10%	**INTERNATIONAL: 15%**
DISABLED: 5	**LOCAL: 20%**

ATMOSPHERE

A high proportion of students come from public schools. Quite a few are relatively well-off and happy to have London licking their wallets clean every weekend. The Institute is making a concerted effort to encourage applicants without a silver spoon in any part of their anatomies, but in the meantime there are still an unsettling number of pashminas in evidence. There's a community atmosphere, with undergrads and postgrads mixing more happily than in many larger institutions (although with so few people they have little choice). Many students also form strong ties with their counterparts at other London colleges, especially if they start off by living in intercollegiate halls. As the Institute has no sports or entertainments facilities of its own, the focus is on work.

LONDON see University of London

TRAVEL see University of London
TRAINS Waterloo, Charing Cross and Blackfriars are a ten minute stomp away.
BUSES Students are spoilt for choice: 1, 4, 25, 59, 68, X68, 76, 168, 171, 176, 188, 341, 501, 505, 521,

N1, N175, N176 stop nearby.
UNDERGROUND Covent Garden, Temple, Holborn and Charing Cross are all close.
BICYCLES A *popular way* of getting around with bike facilities on campus.

CAREER PROSPECTS
⊙ **CAREERS SERVICE** ⊙ **UNEMPLOYED AFTER 6 MTHS** 5%
See University of London.

FAMOUS ALUMNI
Anthony Blunt (former director of the Institute and Russian spy, *the rotter*); Anita Brookner (writer); Andrew Graham-Dixon (art historian); Neil MacGregor (National Gallery); Vincent Price (*creepy actor*); Nicholas Serota (Tate); Brian Sewell (*sickeningly posh* art critic).

FURTHER INFO
⊙ **PROSPECTUSES** UNDERGRAD; POSTGRAD
⊙ **OPEN DAYS**
Find the prospectuses online (www.courtauld.ac.uk/prospectivestudents/courses2006/ug/index.htm) *rather than on trees.*

ACADEMIC ()()()()()()()()()()()()()()

The Institute has the distinct advantage of having many of the subjects of their subjects in the Gallery. Focus is on seminar-based small-group teaching, though there are also lectures. Assessment's based on course work and end of year exams.

ENTRY POINTS: 300-360	**AVE POINTS: N/A**
APPLICATIONS PER PLACE: 5	**CLEARING: 0%**
NO. OF TERMS: 3	**LENGTH OF TERMS: 10WKS**
STAFF TO STUDENT RATIO: 1:8	**STUDY ADDICTS: 20%**
TEACHING: ✭✭✭✭✭	**RESEARCH: ✭✭✭✭✭**
1STS: 17%	**2.2S: 15%**
2.1S: 78%	**3RDS: 0%**

ADMISSIONS
⊙ **APPLY VIA UCAS**
Candidates with no qualifications but who actually know something about the history of art are encouraged to give it a go.

SUBJECTS
ARTS 100%
BEST History of Art.

C

LIBRARIES
○ **180,000 BOOKS** ○ **65 STUDY PLACES**
The libraries are among the country's best sources for art history with 1,600,000 reproductions. 800,000 photographs, but they're only open till 9pm and *students aren't known for keeping sensible hours*. All their paintings, drawings and sculptures are online, plus there's a *big* (200,000) slide library and a *ridiculously big* photo library (1.8 million).

COMPUTERS
○ **32 WORKSTATIONS** ○ **SPEND PER STUDENT** £
All 'puters have web access, but inaccessible after 9pm. Students can also use facilities at King's College, next door.

OTHER LEARNING FACILITIES
Good links with public lectures at places like the National Gallery, which the Institute encourages students to attend.

ENTERTAINMENT ◖◗◖◗◖◗◖◗◖◗◖◗

THE CITY see University of London

UNIVERSITY
Your average art historian could probably outdrink an entire rugby tour, yet there are no bars at the Institute. Still, students have access to King's College and University of London bars and the rest of ULU's stuff. There are also *well-attended* union-organised events eg. quiz and game nights at local boozers or the café.
FILM The film society puts on free showings of uber-cool movies or students' own creations.
MUSIC Occasional music nights with student bands and DJs.
FOOD There's a refectory (cap 100). *It's quite nice, though the metallic furniture and bricks all over the shop make it feel like a museum.* Food is *tasty* but the price (£3.40) makes it worth popping next door to King's.
OTHER A bit of a mass knees-up in a *trendy* outside location twice a term and a *massive* summer ball.

SOCIAL ◖◗◖◗◖◗◖◗◖◗◖◗◖

COURTAULD STUDENTS' UNION
○ **1 SABBATICAL** ○ **NUS MEMBER**
The SU (no sabbs, *but they're working on it*) is, *in theory*, an ents-based organisation, but is yet to really pull its finger out. There are 15 part-time officials, which is a *fair whack* of the student population. *How communist.*

SU FACILITIES
A lounge and *very popular* pool table (*with a long queue*). An internet café is in the offing.

CLUBS (NON-SPORTING)
Business of Art; Life Drawing; Yoga. **See also Clubs tables.**

OTHER ORGANISATIONS
There's a sporadic newspaper and 'Dualogue', a joint magazine project with Chelsea Institute of Art.

RELIGIOUS
○ **1 CHAPLAIN (COFE), RABBI**
See University of London

PAID WORK see University of London
○ **JOB BUREAU** ○ **PAID WORK** TERM-TIME 25%; HOLS 70%
Normal London chances of getting a job, slightly improved with the help of University of London's *epic* job shop.

SPORTS ◖◗◖◗◖◗◖◗◖◗◖◗◖◗

SPORTS FACILITIES
No sports facilities of their own, but *also no real inclination to do anything sportier than running to the loo. There've been sporadic attempts to set up mixed-sex football teams that might one day come to fruition.* University of London's facilities are, as ever, available.

SPORTING CLUBS
See Clubs tables.

ATTRACTIONS see University of London

ACCOMMODATION ◖◗◖◗◖◗◖◗◖◗

IN COLLEGE
○ **CATERED** 27% ○ **COST** £118 (38WKS)
○ **1ST YRS LIVING IN** 90% ○ **INSURANCE PREMIUM** £
AVAILABILITY Courtauld has 40 places in the University of London's inter-collegiate housing, and 26 students *hole up* in a converted old hotel 100m down the road. *The Uni would dearly love to improve accommodation, but don't hold your breath – this is London after all.*
CAR PARKING *No way, no how.*

EXTERNALLY see University of London
○ **AVE RENT** £80 ○ **LIVING AT HOME** 2%
AVAILABILITY *London has many a cheap and quality student house, but, as they're hidden behind the masses of expensive or seriously dodgy ones, a note of caution is advised. Hackney and Bethnal Green are popular*

stomping grounds, unless Daddy is footing the bill for a *West End pad.*

WELFARE ◔◔◔◔◔◔◔◔◔◔◔◔◔

SERVICES
- **COLLEGE COUNSELLORS** 1
- **CRIME RATING:** !!!!!

All of the University of London's vast services are available, and there's an NHS practice in Gower Street.

DISABILITIES Ramps/lifts, *good* wheelchair access. The Institute tries to make adjustments and provide necessary facilities for any disabled students to attend courses.

FINANCE
- **AVE DEBT PER YEAR** £1,575 ● **HOME STUDENT FEES** £3,000

FEES Postgrads fork out £3,085 a year, while part-timers shell £1,543 for the privilege. International undergrads have £9,700-£11,500 *to worry about.*
- **ACCESS FUND** £8,500 ● **SUCCESSFUL APPLICATION/YR** 20
- **AVE PAYMENT** £300

SUPPORT Postgrad scholarships and disability support through the hardship fund. There are four bursaries of £4,000 each, loads of £300 yearly grants and bursaries to help pay the rent.

COVENTRY UNIVERSITY

FORMERLY COVENTRY POLYTECHNIC

● **COVENTRY UNIVERSITY** Priory Street,CV1 5FB **TEL** (02476) 790 790 **E−MAIL** info.rao@coventry.ac.uk **WEBSITE** www.coventry.ac.uk ● **COVENTRY UNIVERSITY STUDENTS' UNION** Priory Street, Coventry, CV1 5FJ tel: (024) 7679 5200. **E−MAIL** suexec@coventry.ac.uk **WEBSITE** www.coventry.ac.uk/cusu

GENERAL ◔◔◔◔◔◔◔◔◔◔◔◔◔

Old Coventry, one of the Midland's *most historical cities*, was completely destroyed during a single night's bombing in WWII. The locals disapproved and rebuilt it again almost as quickly – *and it kind of shows. The inner city resembles a huge futuristic machine with giant chimneys and intestinal roads wind between buildings.* In the middle there's a *sprawling* shopping centre and, *handily*, the University. Near *grander* civic buildings (the sports centre, art gallery, museum and *famous* glass cathedral) the redbrick campus has been *tarted up* with sculptures, flowerbeds, paved squares and, *bizarrely*, gravestones. A recent *shopping spree* has endowed the University with an eclectic collection of additions: a performing arts & media centre; a design and modelling facility; and an aerospace lab, complete with Harrier Jump Jet and Scout helicopter.

to having a fair amount of students knocking around the place and consequently town/gown relations are good.

COVENTRY
- **POPULATION** 300,700 ● **LONDON** 88 MILES
- **BIRMINGHAM** 16 MILES
- **HIGH TEMP** 20 ● **LOW TEMP** 2 ● **RAINFALL** 55

Coventry's past is flaunted, like Lady Godiva's buttocks, in a number of museums, galleries and tourist attractions. Some outer areas look like they were inspired by a breezeblock, but most have been built with consideration, often for practicality. A mile-long pedestrianised shopping centre has enough shops to *suck at the most carefully guarded loan.* The city is constantly being renovated for the future under such ongoing plans as the Millennium Initiative. *A growing number of festivals also liven things up a bit.*

TRAVEL
TRAINS The main station's about a mile from campus and on the main line to London (£22.20 rtn) and Birmingham (£3.95).
COACHES National Express, Bharat and Harry Shaw run loads of services, including London (£17.20 rtn), Birmingham (£4.30) and Manchester (£14.40).
CAR *Being slap-bang in the middle of the country*, it's easy to get to (via the M6, M69, M45 and A45) and it's close to the M1, M40, M42 and A5), *but once there the one-way streets are bad for the blood pressure.*
AIR Birmingham Airport is less than ten miles away.
LOCAL Buses 17 and 27 leave the station every ten minutes for the University and then on to the city centre, Leamington Spa and beyond.

SEX RATIO: ♂53 ♀47		**FOUNDED:** 1843	
FULL−TIME U'GRADS: 9,635		**PART−TIME:** 1,508	
POSTGRADS: 2,384		**NON−DEGREE:** 4,545	
AVE COURSE: 3YRS		**ETHNIC:** 38%	
STATE:PRIVATE SCHOOL: 96:4		**FLUNK RATE:** 18%	
MATURE: 30%		**INTERNATIONAL:** 15%	
DISABLED: 290		**LOCAL:** 48%	

ATMOSPHERE
Coventry students like a giggle. Priority-wise, politics comes behind sport, which comes far behind having a good time. Students are friendly and largely from state schools. Locals are used

TAXIS *The town's snug so for £2 you can go far.*
BICYCLES *A nice, flat landscape but roads are busy and bikes go walkies.*

CAREER PROSPECTS
⊙ **CAREERS SERVICE** ⊙ **NO. OF STAFF** 3 FULL/2 PART
⊙ **UNEMPLOYED AFTER** **6** MTHS 8%

FAMOUS ALUMNI
John Kettley (weatherman); Steve Mattin (Mercedes designer); Andrea Mclean (TV presenter); Michael Rodber (designed Eurostar); Alison Snowden (Oscar-winning animator); Chris Stevenson & Piere Webster (Ford Ka designers); David Yelland (Talk Radio owner).

FURTHER INFO
⊙ **PROSPECTUSES** UNDERGRAD; POSTGRAD; PART-TIME
⊙ **OPEN DAYS**
Five open days a year, between July and October.

ACADEMIC ⦿⦿⦿⦿⦿⦿⦿⦿⦿⦿⦿⦿

31 academic departments grouped into five faculties/schools. Strong in Engineering, Automotive Design, Health and Disaster Management. They're pretty proud of their online learning tool, Web CT, too. The University has a hand in three new Centres of Excellence in Teaching in Learning (Design, Maths Support and Health & Social Care), *which means extra kudos and extra cash. Students moan about having to go to different departments to hand in assignments (due to a merger into faculties).*

ENTRY POINTS: 160–300	AVE POINTS: 230
APPLICATIONS PER PLACE: 6	CLEARING: 14%
NO. OF TERMS: 3	LENGTH OF TERMS: 8–12WKS
STAFF TO STUDENT RATIO: 1:15	STUDY ADDICTS: 20%
TEACHING: ***	RESEARCH: **
YEAR ABROAD: <1%	SANDWICH STUDENTS: 24%
1STS: 13%	2.2S: 31%
2.1s: 40%	3RDS: 4%

ADMISSIONS
⊙ **APPLY VIA UCAS**

SUBJECTS
ART & DESIGN 14%   **HEALTH & LIFE SCIENCES** 31%
BUSINESS, ENVIRONMENT & SOCIETY 29%
ENGINEERING & COMPUTING 26%

BEST Agriculture & Related Subjects; Architecture; Biology & related Sciences; Building & Planning; Business; Economics; English-based Studies; European Languages & Area Studies; History & Archaeology; Human & Social Geography; Management; Mathematical Sciences; Nursing & Other Subjects Allied to Medicine; Other Languages & Area Studies; Performing Arts; Physical Geography & Environmental Science; Physical Science; Politics; Psychology; Social Policy & Anthropology; Social Work; Sports

Science; Sociology; Tourism, Transport, Travel & Others in Business & Administrative Studies.
UNUSUAL Clothing Design & Marketinng; Creative Industries Management; Digital Entertainment Technology; Forensic & Investigation Studies; Games Technology; Global Security & Disaster Management; Intelligent Product Design; Lifestyle Management.

LIBRARIES
⊙ **350,000** BOOKS ⊙ **1,200** STUDY PLACES
⊙ **SPEND PER STUDENT** ££
The library has a café. A well-placed bookshop takes up the slack for those with the dough.

COMPUTERS
⊙ **2,000** WORKSTATIONS ⊙ **24**–HOUR ACCESS

ENTERTAINMENT ⦿⦿⦿⦿⦿⦿⦿⦿⦿

THE CITY
⊙ **PRICE OF A PINT OF BEER** £2.60
⊙ **GLASS OF WINE** £3 ⊙ **CAN OF RED BULL** £2.75
For what Coventry lacks, proximity to Birmingham, Wolverhampton and other cities means alternatives can be hunted down.
CINEMAS Three ten-screeners, two on the edge of town and the Skydome complex in the centre.
THEATRES *Belgrade Theatre for run-of-the-mill dramatic fayre with early bird discounts.*
PUBS *Some local pubs (eg. Courtyard and Graduates) aren't all that student-friendly,* but Push plugs: Prague, Dogma, the Lounge.
CLUBBING The main student nights are at Colosseum (Mondays), where drinks prices *plumb the depths* of 50p a shot and Lava Ignite (Wednesdays).
MUSIC VENUES Most go to Birmingham and Wolverhampton.
EATING OUT *Something cheap and cheerful for everyone, except possibly those blokes who eat lightbulbs:* Scream bars (Yellow Card discount); Browns (home cooking); Pizza Express; TGI Friday's; Varsity's; Yates's.
BALLS Coventry students hold their balls annually.

UNIVERSITY
⊙ **PRICE OF A PINT OF BEER** £1.80
⊙ **GLASS OF WINE** £2.35
⊙ **CAN OF RED BULL** £1.40
The club and music venues are pint-sized and Coventry doesn't attract big names, but the cheap and cheerful watering holes are well-attended and there are plenty of events and days out laid on. Just don't expect cutting edge sophistication, okay?
BARS FiftyFour has three rooms, each with a bar, and *bears the brunt of the ents mission with super-popular* drinks promotions, karaoke, quiz, pool comp, band and club nights. It's open every day and until 2am three nights a week. Coffee

Revolution is a *relaxed* licensed coffee bar and *popular daytime skivespot*.

THEATRE Regular student productions in the Ellen Terry building.

FILM Free flicks every Friday in Coffee Revolution.

MUSIC VENUES Student and local bands *are let out* to play on Sundays.

CLUBBING Weekly club nights include Flirt (Fridays) and Trollied (*for all your Edam requirements*) plus *less frequent* themed nights. Judge Jules, Westwood and N-Trance have all played.

COMEDY/CABARET *Giggle merchants* and hypnotists once a term in FiftyFour.

FOOD Subway in FiftyFour is the priciest place on campus but serves until late. Reunion does *standard* eats. Also hidden round campus are Chapters; Brakes; the Pavilion Bar.

SOCIAL ◖◗◖◗◖◗◖◗◖◗◖◗◖◗

COVENTRY UNIVERSITY STUDENTS' UNION
◉ **5 SABBATICALS** ◉ **TURNOUT AT LAST BALLOT** 9%
◉ **NUS MEMBER**

CUSU has been making a real effort to stir the student body from its cryogenically frozen attitude to politics. Now they're just apathetic and uninformed, which is an improvement. It has two separate buildings, one on Priory Street opposite the Cathedral and the ents shrine FiftyFour on Cox Street.

SU FACILITIES
The SU building provides: general shop; bars; four minibuses for hire; photo booth; video games; hairdresser; vending machines; pool tables; three meeting rooms, IT and printing and fax facilities. The Junction has a music rehearsal room, meeting rooms, prayer rooms and the Source radio staion.

CLUBS (NON-SPORTING)
Enterprise; Gospel; Hellenic; Hong Kong; Links (St John's Ambulance); Source FM. **See also Clubs tables.**

OTHER ORGANISATIONS
There's monthly magazine 'Source' as well as 'Source Radio'. A new RAG team has started to rake in the pennies with RAG raids, talent competitions, *insomnia marathons* and pub crawls. The community action group raises money for and participates in local voluntary work.

RELIGIOUS
◉ **3 CHAPLAINS (COFE; RC; FC)**
There's a Muslim prayer room on campus. Locally there are pious palaces of prayer for many faiths, *most notably*, the Anglican Cathedral.

PAID WORK
◉ **JOB BUREAU**
Futureworks is the SU jobshop and some work is available at the Union itself.

SPORTS ◖◗◖◗◖◗◖◗◖◗◖◗◖◗◖◗

◉ **BUSA RANKING** 59
Students are more interested in sports than politics – but what does that say? Facilities are good, though.

SPORTS FACILITIES
An *ultra-modern* facility on campus has: a four-court sports hall and a two-court minor hall; dance/martial arts studio; large fitness suite; sports injury clinic. Otherwise, Westwood Heath has: three football pitches; three rugby pitches; cricket pitch; floodlit hockey pitch; nine-hole golf course; four tennis courts. *Generous* bursaries and scholarships for elite athletes. The local sports centre has an Olympic sized swimming pool, squash courts and student discounts. Warwick has two council-owned golf courses. The 2005 Millennium development added a new arena and leisure complex.

SPORTING CLUBS
Boxing; Break dancing; Cheerleading; Football (Womens); Gliding; Karting; Mountain Bike; Mountaineering; Paint ball; Rugby League (Mens); Rugby League (Womens); Samurai Jiu Jitsu; Scuba diving; Surf/Snow/Skate; Tetsudo; Thai boxing; Womens Basketball; World Federation Ju-Jitsu; Wutan. **See also Clubs tables.**

ATTRACTIONS
Coventry FC's the local side, based at the Ricoh Arena, which also attracts some biggie events. Warwick has horse racing. See also University of Warwick.

ACCOMMODATION ◖◗◖◗◖◗◖◗◖◗◖◗◖◗

IN UNIVERSITY
◉ **CATERED** 6% ◉ **COST** £85 (40WKS)
◉ **SELF-CATERING** 17% ◉ **COST** £62 (40/50WKS)
◉ **1ST YRS LIVING IN** 22% ◉ **INSURANCE PREMIUM** £££££
AVAILABILITY Four halls of residence (*ranging from the excellent to the execrable*) and 1,000 places in head tenancy schemes. First years get priority and lots of mature and local students are already sorted. A minority have to share and most accommodation is single sex. The rent for most rooms is inclusive of internet access and membership at the University's sports centre. Most places are in Priory Hall (*old but big rooms*) on campus *but Singer Hall is the nicest* (600). Caradoc Hall (64 single bedsits and 62 twin flats) is the cheapest but three miles away in the

middle of a council estate and there are also 350 places in University-owned houses in town, though *some get grumpy about living so far out.* A security service is shared between the halls. The University allocates rooms in the privately-owned and *super swanky* Trinity Point and students also live in three other halls.
CAR PARKING Rare but some availability at Singer Hall (priority to residents there) at an extra cost.

EXTERNALLY
○ AVE RENT £55 **○ LIVING AT HOME** 26%
AVAILABILITY Previously students have been snagging cheap gaffs, but *landlords are starting to catch on. Stoke is the best student area, followed by the nicer and pricier Counden and Earlsdon. Hill Fields is Coventry's Bronx. Parking is so rare and costly, it's not worth trying.*
HOUSING HELP The Accommodation Office checks out every place on its books, offers a handbook and contract advice.

WELFARE ○○○○○○○○○○○○○

SERVICES
○ LGBT SOCIETY ○ UNIVERSITY COUNSELLORS 2 FULL/5 PART
○ SU COUNSELLORS 2 FULL
○ CRIME RATING !!!
A new drop-in advice centre should be in place by September 2006, when the SU will have four full-time welfare advisors. The campus's medical centre has eight doctors, both male and female, and nurses.
CRECHES/NURSERY There's a crèche *but demand is high and places not guaranteed.*
DISABILITIES Disabled Students' Forum. The Disabilities Office has staff and facilities for students with various forms of disability, especially sight impairments. The University will try to adapt courses, assignments or venues as needed.
CRIME/DRUGS *The city has had a bit of a rep for drugs but things are improving and, anyway, the University seems unaffected.*

FINANCE
○ AVE DEBT PER YEAR £3,831 **○ HOME STUDENT FEES** £3,000
○ ACCESS FUND £648,000 **○ SUCCESSFUL APPLICATIONS YR:** 1,226 **○ AVE PAYMENT** £100-£3,500
SUPPORT Scholarships are available for some sexy new vocational 'STAR' courses, which include the likes of Clothing Design & Marketing and Games Technology. There's also a small welfare fund for the desperate, short-term loans and arts and sports bursaries, the latter worth up to £750 a piece.

CREATIVE ARTS UNIVERSITY COLLEGE

FORMERLY THE SURREY INSTITUTE OF ART & DESIGN UNIVERSITY COLLEGE, KENT INSTITUTE OF ART & DESIGN

○ **UNIVERSITY COLLEGE FOR THE CREATIVE ARTS** at Farnham, Falkner Road, Farnham, Surrey, GU9 7DS **TEL** (01252) 722 441 **E-MAIL** info@ucreative.ac.uk **WEBSITE** www.ucreative.ac.uk **STUDENTS' UNION** University College for the Creative Arts at Farnham, Falkner Road, Farnham, Surrey, GU9 7DS **TEL** (01252) 710 263 **E-MAIL** chaslam@ucreative.ac.uk **WEBSITE** www.uccasu.com

GENERAL ○○○○○○○○○○○○○

Still in the first throes of newlywed passion, the Surrey Institute of Art & Design (SIAD) and the Kent Institute of Art & Design teamed up in 2005 to *spawn a five-campused beast going under the lengthy new married name of* University College for the Creative Arts at Canterbury, Epsom, Farnham, Maidstone and Rochester. *Phew.* About 6,500 students are spread out across the sites, two of which (Epsom and Farnham) are based in Surrey while the others are in Kent. *No prizes for guessing which Institute each used to belong to.* The biggest campus is at Farnham, which houses about a third of the University College's 6,500 students. The University College hopes to get the full University title by 2007 – watch this space.

SEX RATIO: N/A		**FOUNDED:** 2005	
FULL-TIME U'GRADS: 4,000		**PART-TIME:** N/A	
POSTGRADS: N/A		**NON-DEGREE:** N/A	
AVE COURSE: 3YRS		**ETHNIC:** N/A	
STATE:PRIVATE SCHOOL: N/A		**FLUNK RATE:** 8%	
MATURE: N/A		**INTERNATIONAL:** N/A	
DISABLED: 310		**LOCAL:** N/A	

Words in italics are Push's point of view – take it or leave it...

C

ATMOSPHERE

Although the University College is keen to stress its unity with all the fervour of a blissful bride, there's a definite distinction between the three Kent and two Surrey campuses – not really that surprising given the physical distances (up to 100 miles) between them. Mind you, a bit of space led to many a happy marriage and it's not clear whether more integration will be desirable or even practical. All campuses are far from equal in terms of facilities – the Surreyites tend to think they have the edge over the Kent 'newcomers'. Set in the quaint, sedate, most homiest of home counties, the sites are, incongruously, stuffed with trendoid creative types.

SURREY

On the home counties trail from London to Southampton, Farnham is an old rural market town *full of quaint shops and beige jackets. However, many residents are commuters, so the town has more of a suburban than a village feel. Both the Farnham and Epsom campuses provide peaceful environments where students can work and rabidly pursue fashion trends. Despite purple hair, piercings and carefully outrageous dress-sense, students are down-to-earth, work-minded and cheerful. Reactions amongst the local rugged, rich folk (whose idea of crazy is orange wellies) are mixed, but don't really stray past grumbling disapproval. Being a bit out-of-the-way, some students could feel cut off from ents. Not that there are that many, moreover public transport can wind down from 6pm.*

FARNHAM

- **POPULATION** 115,600 **TOWN CENTRE** 450M
- **LONDON** 42 MILES **READING** 19 MILES
- **SOUTHAMPTON** 31 MILES
- **HIGH TEMP** 22 **LOW TEMP** 1 **RAINFALL** 54

Farnham's small, Georgian leafy townlet with quaint shops and boutiques lining narrow streets and cobbled lanes. It's dominated more by upper class locals than pub-crawling students and is home to the Maltings Centre, with music, arts, theatrical and entertainment events. It also has a castle dating back to the 12th-century. They should get a new one. See below for details of the other sites.

TRAVEL

TRAINS Farnham station is less than a mile from the College, on the line to London (£6.65) and Guildford.
COACHES Services to London (£8.50), Birmingham (£20.75) and Manchester (£27.50), among others.
CAR Farnham's *bedevilled by one-way systems* and best approached from the A325, the M25 to the A3 past Guildford or the A31 from the south-west. *A motor's a handy accessory as Farnham's hardly a seething metropolis. As a result, the free car park on campus is becoming crowded.*
AIR Heathrow and Gatwick both less than 30 miles.
HITCHING *No one's going anywhere useful even if they do pick up.*

LOCAL

LOCAL *Buses in Farnham are fairly regular. Taxis are reliable and easy to find.*
BICYCLES *No hills, lots of places to leave bikes and little theft. Narrow streets put a lot of students off, though.*

CAREER PROSPECTS

- **CAREERS SERVICE** **NO. OF STAFF** 2 FULL/2 PART
- **UNEMPLOYED AFTER 6 MTHS** N/A

Help until graduation and beyond. Services include: newsletters, bulletin boards, job fairs, interview training and a careers library.

FAMOUS ALUMNI

Linda Barker (interior designer/*gurning Curry's gimpette*); Michael Dudok de Wit, Daniel Greaves (Oscar-winning animators); Tracey Emin (*bonkers* artist) Karen Millen, Owen Gaster, Gharani Strok (fashion designers); Suzie Templeton (BAFTA winner).

FURTHER INFO

- **PROSPECTUSES** UNDERGRAD; POSTGRAD; DEPARTMENTAL
- **OPEN DAYS**

Info available online.

ACADEMIC ()()()()()()()()()()()()

As well as the five colleges, there's a school of Architecture at Canterbury. All courses offer direct professional training. Work's done in groups and independent projects. *The emphasis is more on workshops, which means fewer lectures to sleep through.*

ENTRY POINTS: 180–240	AVE POINTS: N/A
APPLICATIONS PER PLACE: 3	CLEARING: 0%
NO. OF TERMS: 2	LENGTH OF TERMS: 15wks
STAFF TO STUDENT RATIO: 1:15	STUDY ADDICTS: 2%
TEACHING: N/A	RESEARCH: ✱✱✱
YEAR ABROAD: <1%	SANDWICH STUDENTS: 7%
1STS: 16%	2.2S: 47%
2.1S: 32%	3RDS: 5%

ADMISSIONS

- **APPLY VIA UCAS**

SUBJECTS

UNUSUAL Animation; Design Management; Digital Screen Arts; Product Design Sustainable Futures.

LIBRARIES

- **44,000 BOOKS** **250 STUDY PLACES**

The library at Farnham's in the award-winning Library & Learning Centre (LLC) and is open all week *but not very late.*

COMPUTERS

- **423 WORKSTATIONS** (BETWEEN EPSOM AND FARNHAM)

Extensive IT resources are in the IT Centre. Open access computers for independent study are based in the LLC and can be booked.

C

ENTERTAINMENT ◗◗◗◗◗◗◗◗◗◗

THE CITY
- **PRICE OF A PINT OF BEER** £1.60
- **GLASS OF WINE** £1.75 ● **CAN OF RED BULL** £1.20

Farnham's as dead as disco. Plenty of pubs, but not much else. Guildford, 11 miles away, has a bunch of clubs, a smattering of pubs, a dollop of cinema and a leisure centre (see University of Surrey*). London's not too far.*

CINEMAS/THEATRE A cinema in Farnham shows weekly new releases. The Odeon in Guildford, on the banks of the River Wey, is within easy walking distance of the main station. The Maltings Centre in Farnham has film events and theatre.

PUBS *Most, though not all, of the pubs welcome students.* Pushplugs: the Hogs Head (cheap).

CLUBBING/MUSIC The Maltings fields local musical talent. *For clubbing, Guildford is the only real local option. Elsewhere clubbing only happens to students if they stray on to the wrong farmer's land. Oh, and there's* London.

EATING OUT Farnham has many locations for a *dignified scoff and a host of good takeaways for all your cholestrol needs.* Pushplugs: Pizza Express; Zizzi's; Hogs Head (cheap).

UNIVERSITY
- **PRICE OF A PINT OF BEER** £1.55
- **GLASS OF WINE** £1.20
- **CAN OF RED BULL** £1.60

BARS The Union (cap 600) is the centre of social activity, with many theme nights and cheap drinks promotions plus food during the day.

FILM Irregular screenings for £2 *an ogle.*

MUSIC/CLUBBING The Union is open until 2am three times a week – Monday is School Disco, Thurday is the mainstream Sublime of Flirt and Saturdays' MINT spins alternative rock/indie records. Elextric, DJ Boco and Mint have appeared recently. Buses are laid on between the Surrey sites when events kick off.

COMEDY/CABARET Fortnightly comedy club (£3) gets *chucklemonsters* from the local circuit.

FOOD *Foodies are hardly spoilt for choice –* Scolarest sells pizza, pasta, sarnies and soup until 4pm and Upper Crust does drinks and baguettes at lunchtime.

OTHER All the sites get involved in a freshers' ball and there's a graduation ball too.

SOCIAL ◗◗◗◗◗◗◗◗◗◗◗◗

UNIVERSITY COLLEGE FOR THE CREATIVE ARTS STUDENTS' UNION
- **3 SABBATICALS** ● **TURNOUT AT LAST BALLOT** 10%
- **NUS MEMBER**

The 'global' president (*that's in the context of UCCA, not the world*) is elected by all the students and based at the Farnham campus. The other sites each have a vice-president to take care of their own affairs. The SU a*voids big politics unless it can't help it and concentrates on student services.* When campaigning kicks off though it gets involved and students are *enthusiastic*, most recently about banning smoking from the Union building before 4.30pm. The SU doesn't actually own its own facilities and therefore *has had some trouble running activities.*

SU FACILITIES
(Including facilities at Epsom) Two bars; canteen; three snack shops; pool tables; meeting rooms; minibus hire; photocopier; vending machines; fax; payphone; late night minibus; juke boxes; advice; games machines; launderette.

CLUBS (NON-SPORTING)
See Clubs tables.

OTHER ORGANISATIONS
'Tab', the student newspaper, comes out three times a year. Rag's enthusiastic, *but doesn't raise vast sums.* They've promised to improve.

RELIGIOUS
- **2 CHAPLAINS**

Local CofE and Baptist churches.

PAID WORK
- **JOB BUREAU**

The jobshop has a regularly updated notice board. Supermarket, pub and bar work are the best bets. The College also employs students as cleaners and security staff and at the SU for bar work.

SPORTS ◗◗◗◗◗◗◗◗◗◗◗◗

- **RECENT SUCCESSES** FOOTBALL

It's a fearsome thing to behold when art students start getting sporty, but it's happening here. The College's football team is the holder of the Surrey Midweek County Cup. It's even more worrying to know the College has no real facilities of its own and has to rent local ones. We're scared too.

SPORTS FACILITIES
Local facilities are: sports centre; pitches; swimming pool, croquet lawn and bowling green, golf courses; squash courts tennis courts.

SPORTING CLUBS
See Clubs tables.

ATTRACTIONS
Local rugby team.

ACCOMMODATION ◖◗◖◗◖◗◖◗◖◗◖◗

IN COLLEGE
○ **SELF-CATERING COST: £63** ○ **1ST YRS LIVING IN** 70%
○ **INSURANCE PREMIUM** £
AVAILABILITY 381 students can be housed at
Farnham. First years are not guaranteed a place;
accommodation is provided according to distance
and mobility. The Student Village has won
awards, *(of the housing standards variety, not
Oscars or poetry contests).*
CAR PARKING Parking is by free permit,
but *difficult.*

EXTERNALLY
○ **AVE RENT** £75
AVAILABILITY *Suitable, cheap accommodation may
prove hard to find. Wrecclesham, Upper Hale,
Dollis Drive and Tilford Road are all convenient.
Some move out as far as Aldershot where
accommodation is in more abundant supply and
cheaper, but comes with a dodgy reputation.*
HOUSING HELP Housing help runs vacancy lists
and a bulletin board.

WELFARE ◖◗◖◗◖◗◖◗◖◗◖◗◖◗◖◗◖◗◖◗◖◗

SERVICES
○ LGBT OFFICER & SOCIETY ○ WOMEN'S OFFICER
○ INTERNATIONAL STUDENTS' OFFICER & SOCIETY
○ DISABILITIES OFFICER
○ LATE-NIGHT/WOMEN'S MINIBUS
○ SELF-DEFENCE CLASSES
○ UNIVERSITY COUNSELLORS 3 FULL/2 PART
○ CRIME RATING !
HEALTH The College doctors and nursing staff are
available on campus at specific times, or at their
own practices nearby. On-site surgeries are
offered three times a week through a local
medical practice; a nurse is available once
a week.
DISABILITIES Wheelchair access is *generally
adequate at best, although all Student Services
are accessible to wheelchair users.* Hearing loops
are installed in key areas and the learning and
teaching co-ordinator manages a team of ten
dyslexia support tutors.

FINANCE
○ **AVE DEBT PER YEAR** £4,713 ○ **HOME STUDENT FEES** £3,000
SUPPORT 80 £2,000 bursaries a year available to
those who meet the criteria, but all UK students with a full grant are entitled to a £300
handout.Hardship Loans of up to £500 for
students in trouble and part-timers under 55. The
College offers a small number of bursaries and
research studentships for postgrads, to be used
as a contribution to fees.

EPSOM

○ **UNIVERSITY COLLEGE FOR THE CREATIVE ARTS** at Epsom, Ashley Road, Epsom, Surrey, KT18 5BE **TEL** (01372) 728 811
○ **STUDENTS' UNION** University College for the Creative Arts, Ashley Road, Epsom, Surrey, KT18 5BE **TEL** (01372) 702 443

GENERAL
Home to 1,100 students and *eerily similar,* at
first glance to the Farnham campus (32 miles
away). It makes sense, therefore, to see also the
Farnham section above.

EPSOM
Home of the famous racecourse, Epsom's *a little
more suburban* than Farnham. There are *oodles*
of pubs, bars and restaurants, as well as a
theatre and leisure centre with a *top* swimming
pool (student rates). It's only 17 miles from
London's entertainment scene.

TRAVEL
Nearer to London than Farnham, trains to
Central London cost £3.10 (return) and the
station's just five mins walk from campus. The
A24 is the closest *big road.* Parking on campus
is *tricky* – permits are given to those that live
furthest away. Local buses *aren't bad.*

ACADEMIC
(Fashion, Fashion Journalism, Fashion
Promotion and Illustration, Graphic Design and
Graphic Design: New Media). The library has
42,000 books and 150 study spaces plus other
resources including an *impressive* 150,000 slides.
There are *extensive* IT resources including open
access computers for independent study are
based in the LLC and can be booked.

ENTERTAINMENT
THE TOWN The main attractions in town come in
the form of the Boogie Lounge (popular on a
Monday), Chicago rock café and the Salt House.
The Playhouse does comedy, film, concerts and
decidedly low brow plays. The Rising Sun is a
student-friendly pub doing food and Pierre
Victoire also *dishes up dinner.*
SITE The Retreat is the bar on campus. The
refectory does *canteen grub* during the day and
there's a coffee shop.

SOCIAL
ON SITE LGBT and Ethnic Minorities Officers. TV lounge, pool table and a break dancing society.

ACCOMMODATION
ON SITE Halls of residence completed in 2003 house 54 students. All are en suite with a communal kitchen/dining area. The University also runs eight flats a mile from Epsom

(34 beds) – shared kitchen, lounge and shower rooms in each.

EPSOM
⊙ AVE RENT £79-84
Rents reflect Epsom's proximity to London, unfortunately.
HOUSING HELP Vacancy lists and a bulletin board.

CANTERBURY

⊙ UNIVERSITY COLLEGE FOR THE CREATIVE ARTS at Canterbury, New Dover Road, Canterbury, Kent, CT1 3AN **TEL** (01227) 817302
UCCA STUDENTS' UNION New Dover Road, Canterbury, Kent, CT1 3AN **TEL** (01227) 817337

GENERAL
Formerly part of the Kent Institute of Art and Design, the Canterbury site is 100 miles from Farnham and is *studyville* for 1,000 students.

CANTERBURY see University of Kent

TRAVEL
There's no transport provided between the Kent sites. Training it to Maidstone takes 55mins (£10.30 rtn), and Rochester 45mins, (£8.70).

ACADEMIC
Fine Art, School of Architecture, School of Departments of Further Education and Architecture are all based here. The library has 30,000 books, DVDs and videos.

ENTERTAINMENT
The SU is represented through the 'global' system, but doesn't run to organising ents at Canterbury. The college runs a small canteen and there's a small bar. The film club screens fortnightly arthouse and cult films in the Craig Lecture Theatre. 'SOUP' is the student mag and there are plans to join the other local

universities in a radio station. The Global society organises trips to places of interest.

SPORTS
No University sports facilities, but students can join a local sports centre for £130 a year. The Men's Football and Basketball teams have made it as far as the Kent College League (*well, it's a start*). Other clubs on site: Mixed Hockey; Netball; Kung-Fu; Jive Dancing; plus an annual ski trip to Europe and termly visits to the Milton Keynes Snowdome.

ACCOMMODATION
ON SITE Space for 100 sleepers. One self-catering hall on site with 57 beds, plus two halls off site, many with ensuite facilites. All cost more than £3,000 a year.

CANTERBURY
⊙ AVE RENT £67
See University of Kent

WELFARE
A trained counsellor is available on site.

MAIDSTONE

⊙ UNIVERSITY COLLEGE FOR THE CREATIVE ARTS at Maidstone, Oakwood Park, Maidstone, Kent, ME16 8AG **TEL** (01622) 620 000
UCCA STUDENTS' UNION Oakwood Park, Maidstone, Kent, ME16 8AG **TEL** (01622) 621 108

GENERAL
Between 800-900 arty types study on the site. *And study is about all they can do, with the bar and café having recently closed.*

TRAVEL
London is 50mins on the train (£12.50 rtn), Canterbury is an hour (£12.50 rtn) and Rochester 30mins (£4.50 rtn).

ACADEMIC
Media, Arts & Communication Design and Further Education are based here. There are about 25,000 books and bits in the library.

SOCIAL
ON SITE A Union sabb is based here. No ents facilities, but there's an Animation Club, Film Club, Football Team, Breakdance Classes and Christian Union to keep students *entertained, healthy and spiritually fulfilled.* 'INK' magazine is being set up at Maidstone.

ACCOMMODATION
ON SITE 134 accommodation places.

WELFARE
There's a counsellor on site, and the advice centre is open all week, 10am-2pm.

Words in italics are Push's point of view – take it or leave it...

ROCHESTER

● UNIVERSITY COLLEGE FOR THE CREATIVE ARTS at Rochester, Fort Pitt, Rochester, Kent, ME1 1DZ **TEL** (01634) 888 702
UCCA STUDENTS' UNION Fort Pitt, Rochester, Kent, ME1 1DZ **TEL** (01634) 888 754

GENERAL
The site houses 1,400 students.

TRAVEL
Chatham and Rochester stations are both five mins walk from the site. London is 40 mins down the train tracks (£9.50 rtn). Gillingham and Maidstone aren't far away.

ACADEMIC
Fine Art, the School of Architecture and Further Education are based here. The library has around 30,000 books.

ENTERTAINMENT
UNIVERSITY The K-Bar holds 200 drinkers and doubles up as a café during the day. The SU organises *old school* events on Tuesdays and Thursdays along the lines of Tarts & Vicars and Doctors & Nurses. *You can't beat a classic.* There's also a refectory for *canteen-style cuisine.*

THE TOWN Student nights every Sunday at the Old Post Office.

SOCIAL
One of the Union's sabbs is based in Rochester.

SPORTS
There are no University sports facilities, *but students have found it in themselves to set up a belly dancing club.* There's a local sports centre (discounted membership for students) and Rochester has a football team and netball team.

ACCOMMODATION
ON SITE First years get priority. 241 places in the hall of residence.

ROCHESTER
● AVE RENT £60-75

WELFARE
There's a trained counsellor on site.

CREWE & ALSAGER COLLEGE OF HIGHER EDUCATION
see *Manchester Metropolitan University*

'I bleed for these Students' Unions that have been hijacked by a bunch of lefties. We're sick of them wasting our money on their pathetic marches, demos and women's things. We should tell students to go stuff themselves.' – Peter Hitchens, former assistant editor of the Daily Express and profound educational philosopher.

Words in italics are Push's point of view – take it or leave it...

DE MONTFORT UNIVERSITY

▶ UNIVERSITY OF DERBY

▶ DERBYSHIRE COLLEGE OF HIGHER EDUCATION
see *University of Derby*

▶ DISTRIBUTIVE TRADES
see *University of the Arts, London*

DUNDEE UNIVERSITY

DURHAM UNIVERSITY

D

DE MONTFORT UNIVERSITY

FORMERLY LEICESTER POLYTECHNIC

⊙ **DE MONTFORT UNIVERSITY LEICESTER** The Gateway, Leicester, LE1 9BH **TEL** (08459) 454 647 **E-MAIL** enquiries@dmu.ac.uk **WEBSITE** www.dmu.ac.uk ⊙ **DE MONTFORT UNIVERSITY STUDENTS' UNION**, 1st Floor, Campus Centre Building, Mill Lane, Leicester, LE2 7DR **TEL** (0116) 255 5576 **WEBSITE** www.mydsu.com See below for details about other sites

GENERAL ◖◗◖◗◖◗◖◗◖◗◖◗◖◗

De Montfort University *is a curious beast*. When Leicester Polytechnic stopped being Leicester Polytechnic in 1992, *the powers-that-be began a colonisation project almost imperialist in scope*, setting up academic outposts in Bedford, Lincoln and Milton Keynes. *Ten or so years later, the empire began to crumble and DMU is withdrawing its troops and consolidating power at home.* The Milton Keynes site was closed in 2003 and the Scraptoft site in Leicester has also been, *er, scrapped.* Bedford's twin campuses are in the process of combining and in August 2006 *are expected to defect to a different empire altogether*, merging with Luton to become what will probably be called the University of Bedfordshire. DMU's 'distributed' status has been *a bit of a double-edged sword: on the one hand, it can offer one of the widest ranges of courses in the UK; on the other, there's no sense of a central university identity except in name. Hopefully, the forthcoming changes will alter that.* The main Leicester City campus *in the groovy bit of town has recently realised the error of its 60s architectural ways, demolished all the brutalist blocks, flung up some more appealing modern buildings and created an intriguing (and much less depressing) gathering of architectural styles, including the medieval Trinity building.*

👤👤👤👤👤👤👤👤👤👤👤👤👤👤👤👤👤👤👤👤

SEX RATIO: ♂41 ♀59	**FOUNDED:** 1969
FULL-TIME U'GRADS: 12,570	**PART-TIME:** 1,519
POSTGRADS: 3,751	**NON-DEGREE:** 5,007
AVE COURSE: 3YRS	**ETHNIC:** 37%
STATE:PRIVATE SCHOOL: 96:4	**FLUNK RATE:** 16%
MATURE: 26%	**INTERNATIONAL:** 5%
DISABLED: 365	**LOCAL:** 5%

ATMOSPHERE
Students tend to be committed to having a good time, getting a good degree then going on to a good job. The University is simply too spread out to make generalisations about atmosphere, however – it'd be like comparing Australia to Canada – so see details for the Bedford campus, town and travel at the end.

LEICESTER SITES
CHARLES FREARS CAMPUS (Nursing & Midwifery) Just outside the city centre, *briskly walkable and even more briskly busable* from the main City site, Charlie Frears has his own medical library and teaching facilities in a *pleasant enough* setting.

LEICESTER
See Leicester University
⊙ **CITY CENTRE** 0 MILES

TRAVEL
See Leicester University
UNIVERSITY A shuttlebus service connects both Leicester sites with the city centre and the train station. It's used by the public too, but DMU students get *hefty* discounts.
CARS There's no student parking at the main campus, but a *limited* number of spaces at Charles Frears.

CAREER PROSPECTS
⊙ **CAREERS SERVICE** ⊙ **NO. OF STAFF** 8 FULL
⊙ **UNEMPLOYED AFTER 6 MTHS** 9%
Careers DMU is *highly focused on shifting graduates into business.* It has a contract with the local adult guidance network and provides newsletters, bulletin boards, e-mail updates and job fairs in addition to interview training, workshops, presentations, career-selection software, workshops, CV writing guidance, psychometric testing and assessment preparation.

FAMOUS ALUMNI
Charles Dance (actor); Eddie 'the Eagle' Edwards; Engelbert Humperdinck (60s singer); Prolapse (indie band); Janet Reger (*nice knickers*); Kendra Slawinski, OBE (netball); Liz Tilberis (late editor, Vogue); Simon Wells (director); Debra Veal (Atlantic rower). Jimmy Choo (the shoe man) holds an honorary doctorate in Design.

SPECIAL FEATURES
De Montfort takes its name from Simon De Montfort, the 13th-century Earl of Leicester. The earl banned Jews from the city, tried to over-throw the king, led the baronial revolt, kidnapped Henry III and his son, all before he finally got his head chopped off and put on a spike. His father, also called Simon, fought in the Fourth Crusade. His son, *er*, also called Simon, *may or may not have fornicated his way through Kent. None of them, however, had any firm policies on lifelong education, the rights of all to get academic and professional qualifications or indeed the merits of charity shop clothing.*

FURTHER INFO
⊙ **PROSPECTUSES** UNDERGRAD; POSTGRAD; SOME DEPARTMENTS
⊙ **OPEN DAYS**
Prospectuses can be ordered online or by calling (08457) 443 311. A guide for international students is published annually. Faculty open days held throughout the year.

Words in italics are Push's point of view – take it or leave it...

ACADEMIC ◑◑◑◑◑◑◑◑◑◑◑◑

DMU offers *a jaw-dropping variety* of courses, most with an intensely vocational bent – *let's face it, no one is going to take a BA in Adventure Recreation out of idle curiosity* – and teaching methods/hours *vary widely* from course to course. All undergrad degree courses are modular, with students taking four to six modules over the course of each year. Degree grades are based on performance in the second and third years, with the final year doubly weighted.

ENTRY POINTS: 160–300	AVE POINTS: **229**
APPLICATIONS PER PLACE: **5**	CLEARING: 16%
NO. OF TERMS: 3	LENGTH OF TERMS: 12 WKS
STAFF TO STUDENT RATIO: 1:19	STUDY ADDICTS: 11%
TEACHING: ★★	RESEARCH: ★★★
FIRSTS: 7%	2.2s: 38%
2.1s: 42%	OTHERS: 8%

ADMISSIONS
◔ **APPLY VIA UCAS**
DMU is especially friendly towards local and mature applicants, under-represented groups and those with alternative experience and non-traditional backgrounds. Research-wise, DMU has been praised for being the best post-1992 research institute in the UK, *which sceptics might call a 'Very Good, Considering...' type accolade.*

SUBJECTS
ART & DESIGN 19%   **BUSINESS & LAW** 19%
COMPUTING SCIENCES & ENGINEERING 13%
EDUCATION & CONTEMPORARY STUDIES (BEDFORD) 14%
HEALTH & LIFE SCIENCES 22%   **HUMANITIES** 13%
BEST Business; English Studies; Finance & Accounting; History & Archaeology; Law; Pharmacy; Politics.
UNUSUAL Adventure Recreation; Audiology (all course fees paid by NHS); Broadcast Technology; Contour Fashion; Creative Writing; Electronics Games Technology; Footwear Design; Forensic Computing; Game Art Design; International Business/International Relations & Globalisation; Music, Technology & Innovation; Public & Community Health; Radio Production.

LIBRARIES
◔ **586,218 BOOKS** ◔ **1,770 STUDY PLACES**
◔ **SPEND PER STUDENT** ££
The Leicester site has a library on each of its two campuses. The Kimberlin library (city campus) is the largest and is open till 10pm. The Charles Frears Library is a tenth of the size and stocks books on nursing and midwifery. *Which is handy for nurses and midwives.*

COMPUTERS
◔ **2,000 WORKSTATIONS** ◔ **SPEND PER STUDENT:** ££

OTHER LEARNING FACILITIES
Since there are a lot of specialist courses, there's also a lot of specialist facilities: language labs; drama studios; music technology studio; pharmacy practice suite; working newsroom.

ENTERTAINMENT ◑◑◑◑◑◑◑◑◑

LEICESTER
See Leicester University

UNIVERSITY
◔ **PRICE OF A PINT OF BEER** £1.70
◔ **GLASS OF WINE** £1.70
◔ **CAN OF RED BULL** £1.70
The SU has waned in size and *students are disappointed with its lean ents programme.*
BARS *Level 1 is relaxed during the day and hots up at night.* There's also the Graduate Bar.
THEATRES The drama society puts on an annual production in the Phoenix Arts Centre (in town).
CLUBBING/MUSIC VENUES Level 1 *flashes its lasers* at weekly regulars ranging from Thursday's Kinky (70s, 80s, & 90s cheese) to Wednesday's UniVibe (bhangra) music to Friday's 2oothpaste (rock). Tickets sold from SU reception throughout the week. El Presidente, Steve Lamacq and Huw Stephens are among those who've appeared.
COMEDY/CABARET Level 1 (*where else?*) hosts a comedy/magic night, Random, on Sundays.
FOOD Level 1 does sandwiches, toasties and – *after an embittered battle with the authorities* – cheesy chips. *Oh glory.* There are also a couple of cafés, one of which sells fairtrade food and drink *for a warm toasty glow.* Everywhere stops serving by 4pm.
OTHER Festive Snow Ball at Christmas time. A summer ball is stuck somewhere in the pipeline.

SOCIAL ◑◑◑◑◑◑◑◑◑◑◑◑

DE MONTFORT UNIVERSITY STUDENTS' UNION
◔ **7 SABBATICALS** ◔ **NUS MEMBER**
◔ **TURNOUT AT LAST BALLOT** 3-4%
The Global Union (*which sounds more like something created to fight the Dark Side*) represents all sites but is based in Leicester, but there are also site-specific officers responsible for Bedford's SU branch. They're *fairly* political and ethically minded, boycotting Nestlé and so on.

SU FACILITIES
Two bars; purpose-built nightclub/venue; cafeteria; fast food outlet; two pool tables; meeting room; minibus hire; HSBC ATM; photocopier; fax service; photo booth; payphones; general store with dry cleaning, alterations and photo-developing service; stationery shop; vending and gaming machines; new bookshop.

D

Words in italics are Push's point of view — take it or leave it...

CLUBS (NON SPORTING)
Disabled Students. **See also Clubs tables**.

OTHER ORGANISATIONS
Student paper 'the Demon' speaks out fortnightly while radio station 'Demon FM' broadcasts online and twice a year through the Leicester airwaves. There's also a TV station, 'DMU TV'. A *shame-faced Rag is struggling to maintain students' flagging interest*. The independent theatre group rises to an annual panto but not much more.

RELIGIOUS
⊙ **TEAM OF CHAPLAINS (COFE, RC)**
Muslim prayer room at City campus. See Leicester University for details of provisions in the city.

PAID WORK
⊙ **JOB BUREAU** ⊙ **PAID WORK** TERM-TIME 40-50%; HOLS 65%
Work Bank is a privately run company that caters for all DMU sites and matches local jobs with student needs. Jobs Live is an online vacancy database that allows CV posting so potential employers can check out the talent. The SU employs students in bars and shops.

⊙ **BUSA RANKING** 86
DMU are regulars in the BUSA leagues, and students at the Leicester site *enjoy a kickabout as much as the next man and his dog. Leicester used to feel like the couch potato in comparison to the Bedford site's swankier facilities.*

SPORTS FACILITIES
Swing hammer, swing. At Leicester City Campus the John Sandford Sports Centre is about to be knocked down, then rebuilt. For now it has: fitness studio; weight training suite; courts for badminton, tennis, four-a-side football, squash and basketball; solarium; sauna; table tennis tables . Access to the centre is either by day pass or yearly Leisure Card (£36). There's also: football, rugby, cricket, hockey and all-weather pitches; swimming pool; climbing wall; athletics field; aerobics studio. The lake and the River Soar near the campus are *handy* for a paddle. See Leicester University for local facilities.

SPORTING CLUBS
Capoeira; Cheerleading; Rowing. **See also Clubs tables**.

ATTRACTIONS
See Leicester University
The John Sandford Sports Centre is also home to British Basketball league team, the Leicester Riders.

IN COLLEGE
⊙ **SELF-CATERING** 22%   ⊙ **COST:** £70 (38-43WKS)
⊙ **1ST YRS LIVING IN** 73%
⊙ **INSURANCE PREMIUM** ££
AVAILABILITY More than half of all first years are accommodated at Leicester, and none have to share. Students are given five preferences when it comes to choosing halls, most of which are private. No one has more than a ten min walk and five *sexy* new(ish) halls all have en suite facilities and network points. Buildings are fitted with secure entry systems, CCTV and night porters. Lockable cycle pods in all halls. Single sex flats available.
CAR PARKING Permits at halls are only for the disabled.

EXTERNALLY
See Leicester University
⊙ **AVE RENT** £53 ⊙ **LIVING AT HOME** 25%
AVAILABILITY The majority of second and third years live out, generally sharing houses around Leicester, which are pretty cheap on the whole. Standards vary depending on the rent. Finding a place is quite a hassle-free process as long as it's started early. Narborough Road is a popular area near Campus Centre.
HOUSING HELP The University Accommodation Office (has a presence at all sites) has a bulletin board and newsletter plus online database. It works with Leicester City Council and the Leicester Landlords Association on an accredited housing scheme.

SERVICES
⊙ **LGBT OFFICER & SOCIETY** ⊙ **WOMEN'S OFFICER**
⊙ **MATURE STUDENTS' OFFICER & SOCIETY**
⊙ **INTERNATIONAL STUDENTS' OFFICER & SOCIETY**
⊙ **DISABILITIES OFFICER & SOCIETY**
⊙ **LATE NIGHT MINIBUS** ⊙ **SELF DEFENCE CLASSES**
⊙ **UNIVERSITY COUNSELLORS** 4 FULL/2 PART
⊙ **CRIME RATING** !!!!
There are University and Union welfare services on all sites. A mental health co-ordinator is on hand to support students with histories of mental illness, raise awareness and reduce social stigma.
HEALTH The City campus health centre houses five GPs, four nurses, physio, health visitor and a midwife.
DISABILITIES There's an ongoing programme of access improvement – all buildings now have ramps and/or lift access and pushpad/automatic doors. There are a few adapted study bedrooms and there's a dyslexia support worker.

D

D

FINANCE
- **AVE DEBT PER YEAR** £2,495
- **HOME STUDENT FEE** £3,000

FEES International students are charged from £7,990 to £8,955. UK postgrads cough up £3,162.

- **ACCESS FUND** £1,200,000 ○ **SUCCESSFUL APPLICATIONS PER YR** 1,000 ○ **AVE PAYMENT** £1,200

SUPPORT The University reckons two-thirds of students will qualify for some of their largesse, although students are only allowed to grab one bursary a year. Bursaries of £300 for those that get full maintenance grants and £500 for those that just get a partial one. Academic awards of up to £1,000 *dangle invitingly* for those with more than 280 UCAS points and sports scholarships give the same *to bionic people* representing Britain or England. Hardship funds are available to cover childcare, travel, accommodation etc.

DE MONTFORT UNIVERSITY, BEDFORD

AT TIME OF WRITING, THE SITE WAS DUE TO MERGE WITH LUTON UNIVERSITY. PUSH STRONGLY ADVISES CHECKING WITH THE UNIVERSITIES AND UCAS FOR UP-TO-DATE INFORMATION ON APPLICATIONS.

1. ○ **DE MONTFORT UNIVERSITY BEFORD** 37 Lansdowne Road, Bedford, MK40 2BZ **TEL** (01234) 793 484 **FAX** (01234) 350 833
2. ○ **DE MONTFORT UNIVERSITY BEFORD** Polhill Avenue, Bedford, MK41 9EA **TEL** (01234) 793 012
E-MAIL bed-admissions@dmu.ac.uk **WEBSITE** www.dmu.ac.uk./ecs ○ **DE MONTFORT UNIVERSITY STUDENTS'**
UNION (BEDFORD) 37 Lansdowne Road, Bedford, MK40 2BZ **TEL** (01234) 793 012 **E-MAIL** suenqquiries@dmu.ac.uk

Forty miles from the much larger Leicester site, De Montfort's baby brother Bedford is home to 2,378 students (Humanities, Performing Arts, Education, Sports Science, Business and Social & Cultural Studies). There are two sites: the Lansdowne (sporty) and Polhill (arty) campuses, two miles apart on the outskirts of the town. The *relaxed atmosphere is not unlike that of a sixth form college and students have little or no contact with their counterparts at Leicester, so it can feel like an entirely separate institution.* Soon it will be – the site is expected to merge with Luton in August 2006. DMU's extensive redevelopment programme is running full steam ahead and by July 2007 all Lansdowne operations should be transferred to a new and improved Polhill. Plans include: swathes more land, 500 new student rooms, teaching facility extensions, and a new campus central building with bar and catering facilities, and a 350-seat theatre.

BEDFORD
- **POPULATION** 147,911 ○ **LONDON** 50 MILES
- **LEICESTER** 40 MILES ○ **CAMBRIDGE** 30 MILES

Bedford is a quiet county town – founded by Beda, an 8th-century Saxon chief *for those who aren't yet boring enough in the pub* – impaled by a pretty stretch of the River Ouse and surrounded by *what people insist on calling 'unspoilt countryside', diddy villages and signposts with delusions of grandeur: 'Bedford – A Progressive County'. Quite what a regressive county would involve, Push can't say. It's got the usual gamut of shops, pubs and the odd club (that's 'odd' in both senses of the word) but its more vivacious inhabitants thank their lucky stars that London is less than an hour away.*

TRAVEL
London 40 mins away by train from Bedford station, ditto Leicester. Luton Airport a mere 17 mins, for quick getaways. The A1, M1 and M25 are easily accessible. DMU runs a shuttlebus between campuses, the town and station. Some on-site student parking.

ACADEMIC
The Bedford library facilities are smaller than Leicester's with 128,868 books, 361 study places and 137 web-enabled workstations for student use. The £6m Polhill Library and Information Centre boasts a state-of-the-art IT suite. There are also biochemistry and physiology labs, dance studios and sports science labs.

ENTERTAINMENT
LOCAL Bedford is less of a studenty, cosmopolitan city than Leicester but it has a fair few ye olde ale houses and a couple of *passable* night spots. *Student pubby, clubby, grubby faves include the New York, New York; Oxygen; Bankers Draft; The Rose; Enigma; Foresters; Chicago's clubs; Gulshan's Tandoori.* Also: Aspects Complex near Polhill with a six-screen cinema and 10-pin bowling; an annual regatta; and the *notoriously dangerous* beer festival. Dedicated party animals make the trek to Kettering, Northampton or London.

UNIVERSITY The Bowen West Theatre *is a little more dynamic than its Leicester counterpart* – probably because the performing arts courses are based here. Many contemporary dance and drama shows are put on throughout the year.

> **Researchers at De Montfort University have perfected a technique for turning pig manure into energy.**

Other than that, *the site's in a bit of a relocation limbo* – the bar recently shut its doors and scoffwise there's a refectory at each site and a small coffee shop. The new Campus Centre (due January 2007) will take responsibility for stomach-filling.

SOCIAL & POLITICAL
Two sabbatical SU officers liaise with the larger Union body in Leicester and offer social and welfare support to Bedford-bound students. There's a performing arts society to add to the socs list and the campus has its own chaplain.

SPORTS
○ **BUSA RANKING** 58
Alexander Sports Hall is huge and has: courts for basketball, volleyball, tennis and badminton; a climbing wall; sauna and solarium; and a health and fitness suite. The Lansdowne campus has a swimming pool, dance studios and a gym. Astroturf, cricket, football and rugby pitches are there for the tramping. Polhill has not one but two new gyms. Charges are the same as at the Leicester campus. Sports coaching is available as are sports scholarships. Locally there's a large leisure complex with pool, athletics stadium and a hockey centre. The site has its own men's and women's rugby union, hockey, netball and football teams – *Leicester students need not apply.*

ACCOMMODATION
ON SITE
○ **CATERED COST** £71 (38WKS)
○ **SELF-CATERED COST** £64 (38WKS)
Bedford's three halls offer 300 rooms – meaning that 13% of students based here can be accommodated, usually first years. The halls are a combination of converted Victorian houses and purpose-built blocks. Most places at Bedford are catered (ten meals a week) and usually only people with special dietary requirements will get into a self-catered hall. *Not liking the canteen food probably doesn't count.* 24/7 security patrols and lockable cycle pods. Parking is disabled only. Limited head tenancy schemes. Things are about to change, however, and soon all accommodation will be self-catered with 558 ensuite bedrooms on offer by September 2007.
EXTERNALLY
○ **AVE RENT** £53 ○ **LIVING OUT** 66%
Living costs and rents in Bedford are cheaper than Leicester and below the national average. *Bonus.*

WELFARE
HEALTH Polhill has a medical centre. Physiotherapy's also available.
CRECHES/NURSERY: There's a crèche on the Polhill campus providing day care for 2-5-yr-olds.
DISABILITIES: The new Polhill library and info centre is riddled with lifts, and has adapted desks on each of its four floors.
CRIME: Pretty low. Sleep easily.

UNIVERSITY OF DERBY
FORMERLY DERBYSHIRE COLLEGE OF HIGHER EDUCATION
○ **UNIVERSITY OF DERBY** Kedleston Road, Derby, DE22 1GB **TEL** (08701) 202 330 **E-MAIL** enquiries-admissions@derby.ac.uk **WEBSITE** www.derby.ac.uk ○ **UNIVERSITY OF DERBY STUDENTS' UNION**, Kedleston Road, Derby, DE22 1GB **TEL** (01332) 591 507 **E-MAIL** info@udsu.co.uk **WEBSITE** www.udsu.co.uk

GENERAL ◖◖◖◖◖◖◖◖◖◖◖◖◖

At the southern tip of the *beautiful Derbyshire Peak District is the not-quite-so-stunning city of Derby,* in the north of the Midlands. The University is based at eight sites around the city *and can be something of a labyrinth to navigate,* though work is underway to condense most of it on to two campuses, with Arts students getting a new base on the Markeaton campus. The main site is (and will remain as) the Kedleston Road campus just outside town to the north-west, amidst *rather pleasant* open countryside. Modern, brightly coloured and *welcoming – the authorities haven't ignored the feng shui effects of a good water feature.* Having taken the leap from a College of Higher Education to University in 1992, Derby now offers a wide range of subjects, many of which are vocational. The University of Derby College, Buxton, attached to Derby University, has recently moved to the town centre and offers a variety of

Degree-level/FE courses: A Levels, HNDs, NVQs *and several alphabets' worth of other acronyms.*

SEX RATIO: ♂59 ♀41	**FOUNDED:** 1851
FULL-TIME U'GRADS: 8,592	**PART-TIME:** 2,951
POSTGRADS: 2,476	**NON-DEGREE:** 601
AVE COURSE: 3YRS	**ETHNIC:** 20%
STATE:PRIVATE SCHOOL: 95:5	**FLUNK RATE:** 27%
MATURE: 33%	**INTERNATIONAL:** 3%
DISABLED: 170	**LOCAL:** 52%

ATMOSPHERE
The Kedleston campus is a friendly, buzzing environment and its inhabitants are largely a casual, down-to-earth crew, many of them from the local area. The big fashion department polarises students into those who think they look cool and those who think there are better things to care about, but all share a good vibe.

Words in italics are Push's point of view – take it or leave it...

SITES

An intersite bus service makes getting around easy.
KEDLESTON ROAD The largest site, containing most of the students and University admin blocks.
MICKLEOVER (1,000 students – Health & Community Studies, Education, Social Science). Mainly concrete site, two miles from the city centre, with some halls of residence.
GREEN LANE (100 – Film & TV) Bang in the city centre, three miles from Kedleston, is this listed Victorian building – a purpose-built art college.
BRITANNIA MILL (800 – Art & Design) Arty atmosphere in a converted mill, also in the city centre.
CEDARS (400 – Occupational Therapy) An Edwardian building juxtaposed with modernist chunks three miles from the main site.
JACKSON'S MILL (200 – Art & Design) Close to the halls of residence at Bridge Street but 20 mins walk to the main campus for books, food and beer.
DERBY ROYAL INFIRMARY (DRI) 300 students – Radiography.
MARKEATON CAMPUS (50 students – Motorsports) Ten mins from Kedlestone Road, this site is being developed in anticipation of Derby becoming a two-hub campus with Kedlestone Road.

DERBY

○ **POPULATION** 221,700 ○ **CITY CENTRE** 2 MILES
○ **LONDON** 128 MILES ○ **NOTTINGHAM** 15 MILES
○ **BIRMINGHAM** 41 MILES
○ **HIGH TEMP** 20 ○ **LOW TEMP** 1 ○ **RAINFALL** 59
Those who dismiss Derby as being as ugly as a warthog with eczema are missing the historical significance of the place (if not the general appearance). After all, Derby played an important role in the Jacobite Rebellion and a crucial part in the Industrial Revolution. *So there.* Like many small cities it's growing rapidly, and as new shops appear, the old ones get more upmarket. It has 600 listed buildings, a good number of parks, lots of useful shops and amenities and three museums: the Derby Museum, Industrial Museum and Pickford House, as well as attractions like the Arboretum Park and, outside town, Elvaston Castle, Shipley Country Park and Chatsworth House – most of which are essentially large old houses with gardens.

TRAVEL

TRAINS Derby station is 2.5 miles from Kedleston Road: London (from £30.15 return), Sheffield (£9.40) and beyond.
COACHES National Express and other services operate to London (£22.00) and Sheffield (£7.30), among other places.
CAR Derby is eight miles from the M1 and on the A6, A38, A50, A52.
AIR East Midlands is the closest airport, 8 miles south-east of town, with flights inland and to Europe.
HITCHING *Kindly motorists on long hauls on the main roads. Some lard-guzzling truckers too, but that's the way it goes in this game.*
LOCAL Reliable buses run every 10 mins to the town centre from the main campus. Multi-ride passes offer a 50% discount. Regular buses between sites.
TAXIS £2-3 between sites and city centre – several

companies offer 10% student discounts.
BICYCLES Plans for a bike link between city and sites are still plans: *roads are too busy for all but the most stubborn or suicidal cyclist.*

CAREER PROSPECTS

○ **CAREERS SERVICE** ○ **NO. OF STAFF:** 5 FULL/4 PART
○ **UNEMPLOYED AFTER** 6 MTHS 6%
The Career Development Centre emails fortnightly vacancy and careers information bulletins, offers free online psychometric testing, arranges seminars, workshops and job fairs and keeps a physical and online library of careers resources. See www.derby.ac.uk/careers for resources for staff, students and graduates, prospective students and employers.

FAMOUS ALUMNI

Cedric Brown (former British Gas fat-cat); Jyoti Mishra (White Town).

FURTHER INFO

○ **PROSPECTUSES** UNDERGRAD; POSTGRAD; ALTERNATIVE; VIDEO
○ **OPEN DAYS** Around four open days a year, info hotline: 08701 202 330. Successful applicants are invited to attend course-specific visit days to view the campus and facilities. Prospectuses can be ordered at www.derby.ac.uk/prospectus

ACADEMIC ○○○○○○○○○○○○○

Derby's five sites have a wealth of courses stashed in them *ranging from the mundane to the implausible,* at degree, HND and Further Education levels. *There are a mind-boggling number of part-time options* – hence a sizeable part-time student body – and a wide-ranging Combined Subject and Joint Honours degree programme, *meaning that subjects as different as chalk and chinchillas can often be studied together.* Traditional subjects are thin on the ground and lag behind Derby's acknowledged strong points – business, design and technology-related courses.

ENTRY POINTS: 160–280		**AVE POINTS:** N/A	
NO. OF TERMS: 3		**LENGTH OF TERMS:** 12 WKS	
STAFF TO STUDENT RATIO: 1:22		**STUDY ADDICTS:** 9%	
TEACHING: ★		**RESEARCH:** ★	
YEAR ABROAD: <1%		**SANDWICH STUDENTS:** 1%	
1STS: 7%		**2.2s:** 36%	
2.1s: 43%		**OTHERS:** 9%	

ADMISSIONS

○ **APPLY VIA UCAS**

SUBJECTS

BEST Business; English-based Studies; Law; Physical Science; Psychology; Subjects Allied to Medicine.
UNUSUAL 3D Design; Aseptic Services; Beauty & Spa Services; Complementary Therapies; Early Childhood Studies; Events Management; Forensic

Science; Global Hazards; Illustration for Animation; International Spa Management; Sex, Sexuality & Gender; Third World Development.

LIBRARIES

⊙ **323,000** BOOKS ⊙ **1,680** STUDY PLACES

Five libraries – *obtusely* known as 'Learning Centres' – one at each site, all course-specific. Study space *is pretty cramped* but the Learning Centre at Kedleston has added more space. Buxton and Cedars Libraries are closed at weekends.

COMPUTERS

⊙ **850** WORKSTATIONS ⊙ **1,680** STUDY PLACES

There are IT rooms at all sites except Cedars. All halls of residence are networked to the University.

OTHER LEARNING FACILITIES

Language labs (for undergrads and the wider community); drama studio; rehearsal rooms; CAD lab; audio/TV centre; a practice courtroom for budding Perry Masons. A Virtual Campus is up and humming, so students can access online modules, assessments and subject message boards.

ENTERTAINMENT ◑◑◑◑◑◑◑◑◑

THE CITY

⊙ PRICE OF A PINT OF BEER £1.80
⊙ GLASS OF WINE £2.50

CINEMAS There are two multiplexes with 22 screens between them. QUAD, the new arts centre, has an arthouse cinema.

THEATRES The Derby Playhouse has its own repertory company and offers 10% discounts

PUBS Nearby Burton is the brewing capital of England. Walkabout, Coyote Wild and Walkabout are the main *jam-packed* student hangouts. The Ashbourne Mile is *a renowned bar crawl.*

CLUBBING Derby is picking up speed on the club front. *Pushplugs: Blue Note; Gatehouse; McCluskys.*

> ⊙ **Students at the University of Chicago have created a porn magazine which features an erotic photo story shot inside the University's library.**

MUSIC VENUES No massive venues, but several large enough to attract more than local strummers and drummers. Victoria Inn and the Flower Pot and the Loft host live *muzak.* The Assembly Rooms has major bands *but they charge the earth.*

EATING OUT The pizza chains do student discounts. The Ram near halls does a *tasty* burger for a couple of quid. Curzon Street and Normanton Road embody the curry nexus. *Pushplugs: Friargate (Cantonese); Excelsior (Chinese); Moghul (Indian); Plug Tonic (posh); Antibo's (Italian); Cactus Café (Mexican). New Normanton, ten mins from city centre, is good for all sorts of restaurants.*

UNIVERSITY

⊙ PRICE OF A PINT OF BEER £1.65 ⊙ GLASS OF WINE £2
⊙ CAN OF RED BULL: £1.50

BARS Blends on Kedleston Road is a *relaxed* booze-plying café-style affair that shuts at 6pm. *Lonsdale bar has the most life in it, stretching to proper pub hours and featuring aspiring record-riders.* A new plasma screen-laden bar with a linked grandstand overlooking the rugby pitch is set to open in 2006.

FILM Cinema facilities at Green Lane campus.

CLUBBING/MUSIC VENUES Plans are afoot to host bands and hold club nights on campus when the new bar opens. For the meantime, Spank at Zanzibar in town is an NUS *cheese-fest indieshrine.* Lonsdale bar has open mic nights and acoustic evenings.

FOOD The Atrium in the large entrance hangar at Kedleston does inexpensive snacks and meals, and there are other outlets at most sites.

OTHER The Graduation Ball and the May Ball *are a truly massive pair that have attracted Girls Aloud, Happy Mondays and Goldie Lookin Chain (to play, that is, not to pretend they're students for the night).*

SOCIAL ◑◑◑◑◑◑◑◑◑◑◑

UNIVERSITY OF DERBY STUDENTS' UNION

⊙ **4** SABBATICALS ⊙ TURNOUT AT LAST BALLOT 10 %
⊙ NUS MEMBER

Links between the SU and the University are *much better* than previously. The *good vibes* are also showing in imported sports facilities, the new radio station, and a bigger and better bar.

SU FACILITIES

Three bars; cafeteria; snack bar; six pool tables; meeting room; minibus for hire; Endsleigh Insurance branch; Natwest bank and Lloyds TSB ATM; fax and printing service; photocopier; photo booth; advice centre; payphones; hair salon; Waterstone's; general and stationery stores at Kedleston, Britannia Mill and Buxton; juke boxes; gaming machines.

Words in italics are Push's point of view — take it or leave it...

CLUBS (NON SPORTING)

Anime/Manga; Computing; Events (organise everything from club nights to forays into the Peak district); Greek; Kids Team (volunteer work with local children); Motor Sport; Poker; Radio; Sikh. **See also Clubs tables.**

OTHER ORGANISATIONS

'Dusted' is the *impressive* monthly mag and 'D1' is the campus radio station. There's now a permanent member of staff in charge of Rag so the figures are growing. The Community Development Area also *gets up to a lot of good*.

RELIGIOUS

⦿ 5 CHAPLAINS (COFE, RC , RUSSIAN ORTHODOX,FC)
Hindu, Muslim, Sikh, Jewish, Baha'i and Buddhist faith advisors are also available. The Religious Resource & Research Centre has prayer facilities at both Kedleston and Mickleover and there's a Muslim prayer room at Kedleston. In Derby, there's an Anglican cathedral and provisions for Christians of every hue, Hindus, Muslims, Sikhs and Jews.

PAID WORK

⦿ JOB BUREAU   ⦿ PAID WORK TERM-TIME 25%; HOLS 50%
The active Career Development Centre doubles as a part-time *piggy bank filler*, maintaining the online jobs@hand database as well as running the Student Employment Agency. UDSU has a number of ongoing positions available in bars, shops, admin, gyms etc. All are minimum wage.

⦿ RECENT SUCCESSES WOMEN'S HOCKEY/BADMINTON, RUGBY UNION **⦿ BUSA RANKING** 114
There isn't exactly a sporty slant, especially in comparison with the nearby *bionic triangle* of Loughborough, Nottingham and Leicester, but *occasional smudges of athletic achievement and not inconsiderable facilities* mean bats and balls do collide regularly.

SPORTS FACILITIES

Facilities are based at Mickleover. Fizeek Fitness Studio; five football and two rugby pitches; swimming pool; all-weather pitch; climbing wall; multigym; running track; badminton court; American football pitch. Derbyshire adds various other goodies like golf courses, cricket facilities, the river and, of course, the Peak District.

SPORTING CLUBS

American Football; Cheerleading; Rowing; Yoga; Snow Sports; Judo; Tae Quon Doe; Kickboxing. **See also Clubs tables.**

ATTRACTIONS

Derby County FC and Derbyshire Cricket Club. As for the Derby horse race – that's in Epsom. *We know, it's confusing.*

IN UNIVERSITY

⦿ SELF-CATERING 24%   **⦿ COST** £48 (42WKS)
⦿ 1ST YRS LIVING IN 75%   **⦿ INSURANCE PREMIUM** £
AVAILABILITY First years are pretty much guaranteed hall accommodation and provisions aren't overly stretched thanks to the number of local students living at home. Residences are all *shiny, modern, purpose-built jobs in gazeworthy grounds* but there's a *hefty walk* (15 mins or more) to get to campus. Top of the building blocks is Peak Court, which has en suite rooms and is nearish the main site, closely followed in popularity by Sir Peter Hilton Court. Nunnery Court is built around Derby's oldest building and *trendy* Lonsdale Hall (*less pretty but with a pumping bar*) offers the option of renting a room for only five days a week if so desired. Princess Alice Court is full of freshers while St Christopher's Court is reserved for returning students. Laverstoke Court is the oldest and *least plush*. CCTV, entry phones, and a 24-hour watch scheme *stop most things going bump in the night*. Less than 5% have to share and rooms for disabled students are spread out among the halls. Apply online at www.dsrl.co.uk.
CAR PARKING Most halls have car parks, although places are limited. A permit costs £60-100.

EXTERNALLY

⦿ AVE RENT £45   **⦿ LIVING AT HOME** 25%
AVAILABILITY Heaps of *fairly bog-standard* rental accommodation, often old railway worker's houses. The surplus means standards are improving, *although if a student has specific needs for a grime-infested rathole, they'll have no trouble finding one.* Most of studentville is on direct bus routes to the University, to the south-east of the main campus – Kedlestone Road, Ashbourne Road, Uttoxeter New Road and the city centre are the most popular pockets of habitation. Normanton and Peartree are the red-light districts – *if that's of any interest one way or the other.* An accredited landlord scheme means four out of five students are living some-where *with all the walls in the right place*. There's a database on the University website.
HOUSING HELP The six staff in Derby Student Residences post vacancies and offer advice and assistance, as can the SU.

SERVICES

⦿ LGBT OFFICER   ⦿ MATURE STUDENTS' OFFICER ⦿ INTERNATIONAL STUDENTS' OFFICER   ⦿ DISABILITIES OFFICER   ⦿ WOMEN'S OFFICER   ⦿ 24-HR ADVICE LINE

D

● UNIVERSITY COUNSELLORS 4 FULL/10 PART **● UNION COUNSELLORS** 1 FULL/1 PART **● CRIME RATING** !!!
HEALTH GP practice and nurse surgeries on campus.
CRECHES/NURSERY The private Discovery Day Nursery can take in students' kids 3mths-14yrs.
DISABILITIES Wheelchair access is variable according to site – all new developments are *excellent*. The University is rightly proud of its Deafness Studies Unit – there are BSL signers available, as well as enlarged texts, Braille signs and tape recordings available for the visually impaired. Also help for dyslexic students.
CRIME Security guards and CCTV on campus.

FINANCE
● AVE DEBT PER YEAR £2,960
● HOME STUDENT FEES £3,000
● FEES Foundation course fees slosh around the £1,250 mark. International students pay £7,200. Postgrad course costs are a steep £7,800 for a taught masters, £8,700 for an MBA, £15,600 for a MPhil and £23,400 for a PhD.
● ACCESS FUND £800,000 **● SUCCESSFUL APPLICATIONS/YR** 1,200-1,400 **● AVE PAYMENT** £100-£3,500
SUPPORT Means-tested bursaries to ease the new fees, including help for local (Derby) students.

▶ DERBYSHIRE COLLEGE OF HIGHER EDUCATION
see *University of Derby*

▶ DISTRIBUTIVE TRADES
see *University of the Arts, London*

DUNDEE UNIVERSITY

1. **● UNIVERSITY OF DUNDEE** Dundee, DD1 4HN **TEL** (01382) 344 000 **E-MAIL** srs@dundee.ac.uk
WEBSITE www.dundee.ac.uk **● DUNDEE UNIVERSITY STUDENTS' ASSOCIATION**, Airlie Place, Dundee, DD1 4HE
E-MAIL dusa@dusa.co.uk **WEBSITE** www.dusa.co.uk
2. **● UNIVERSITY OF DUNDEE** Kirkcaldy Campus, Forth Avenue, Kirkcaldy, KY2 5YS **TEL** (01592) 268 888

GENERAL ○○○○○○○○○○○○○

Tucked onto the northern side of the Firth of Tay and a trundle down the east coast of Scotland from Aberdeen, is Dundee. The Tay estuary, the surrounding expanse of sandy shore and the highlands rising inland are *very picturesque – although, the same can't really be said for the city*. A mile west of the city centre, in an area of town scenically overlooking the river, is the self-contained main campus of Dundee University. It's gone *redevelopment crazy* in the last few years and whole chunks of the campus are being dug up, added to, taken from and *generally diddled with* in a major revamp scheduled to finish in 2007. So, while there may be workers drilling through walls for a while, the facilities should be vastly improved soon, if not sooner. This is in keeping with the University's history of buildings *sprouting in spurts throughout the last century or so, which explains its jumbled architecture. Despite the campus's spaciousness, greenery is, literally, thin on the ground.* Following a cluster of mergers over the past decade, the University has spread over various other campuses around the city, notably the medical departments at Ninewells Hospital and Gardyne Campus (social work and education). There's also the Kirkcaldy Campus in the scenic (and touristy) town of Kirkcaldy, Fife, 30 miles away.

SEX RATIO: ♂37 ♀63	**FOUNDED:** 1967
FULL-TIME U'GRADS: 9,454	**PART-TIME:** 1,417
POSTGRADS: 4,993	**NON-DEGREE:** 732
AVE COURSE: 4YRS	**ETHNIC:** 8%
STATE:PRIVATE SCHOOL: 93:7	**FLUNK RATE:** 16%
MATURE: 29%	**INTERNATIONAL:** 9%
DISABLED: 140	**LOCAL:** 50%

ATMOSPHERE
The main campus is compact and the University untraditional. The mix of students on campus is broad – more than two-thirds from Scotland, one in five from elsewhere in the UK (especially Northern Ireland). *It's full of normal, unpretentious people and, although there's fun to be had, the joint is hardly rocking.*

SITES
KIRKCALDY CAMPUS: (Nursing & Midwifery) Based about 30 miles away in a *dinky* Fife town (pop: 47,000), about 15 miles from Edinburgh.

DUNDEE
● POPULATION 142,700 **● CITY CENTRE** <1 MILE
● LONDON 384 MILES **● EDINBURGH** 50 MILES
● ABERDEEN 60 MILES
● HIGH TEMP: 19 **● LOW TEMP** 0 **● RAINFALL** 55
Nowhere near as ugly as it used to be, Dundee has

---

settled comfortable into modern townhood (ie. it's got a big shopping complex). The Tay, Riverside and the port area have certain attractions and there are 1,300 acres of parkland including golf courses, a zoo and nature trail. Two bridges span the Tay, both of which are more successful than the first bridge which collapsed in 1879 shortly after it was built, killing 75 people (as described in the world's worst poem by William McGonagall). The people are friendly enough too. The city has the requisite bunch of museums, galleries and historic buildings to keep residents from boredom-inspired killing sprees, including Bonar Hall (a University-owned exhibition centre). Worth an ogle are the Observatory on Balgay Hill and Captain Scott's ship 'Discovery'.

TRAVEL
TRAINS Dundee station has services to London (from £65.15 rtn), Glasgow (£21.60) and routes to most parts of Scotland and England.
COACHES National Express, Stagecoach and Citylink services including London (£41) and Glasgow (£12).
CAR From the south, the M90 goes up to Perth (19 miles west) from where there's the A90, or the A914 which crosses the Tay. From the north, there's the A92, A929 and A923. The University is strict about parking the four-wheeled monsters – an annual permit costs £150 or it's a fiver upfront then about 40p an hour.
AIR Dundee (Riverside Park) Airport serves UK destinations and the odd international.
HITCHING Not easy. Too many roundabouts around Dundee where hitchers can get stuck all day. The best bet is to get a lift on the A92 along the coast and try to swing by Edinburgh.
LOCAL The good bus service is fairly cheap (80p across town, exact fare only), but the last is at around 11.15pm.
UNIVERSITY A free minibus nips from the main campus to the Medical School and Education and Social Work Schools. The Students' Association provides a night bus that takes, erm, tired and emotional students back to halls after a night at the Union.
TAXIS Cheapest in Scotland.
BICYCLES Not too hilly and theft isn't a major problem, but bikes aren't really that necessary.

CAREER PROSPECTS
◉ CAREERS SERVICE ◉ NO. OF STAFF 3 FULL
◉ UNEMPLOYED AFTER 6 MTHS 4%
The usual gamut of interview prep, bulletin boards and career fairs.

FAMOUS ALUMNI
Kate Atkinson (novelist); Sir James Black (Nobel laureate, medicine; current Chancellor); Stewart Campbell (rugby); Lynda Clark (Scottish Advocate General); Brian Cox (actor); Fred MacAulay (comedian); Lord Robertson of Port Ellen (Secretary General, NATO); Albert Watson (photographer).

FURTHER INFO
◉ PROSPECTUSES UNDERGRAD; POSTGRAD; ALL DEPARTMENTS: ALTERNATIVE; INTERNATIONAL; VIDEO
◉ OPEN DAYS
The website is one of the most applicant-friendly

going and the SA provides a dirt-dishing guide for freshers and prospective students.

ACADEMIC ◖◖◖◖◖◖◖◖◖◖◖◖◖

Medicine, Life Sciences and Art & Design all raise studious eyebrows and Dundee maintains strong links with industry, especially pharmaceuticals. Courses are modular, meaning students pick'n'mix subjects and many of the courses run continual assessment. 20 lucky students each year get to take part in the Transatlantic Student Exchange programme and jet off to the States to go to toga parties – we mean study – in America or Canada for a year. 20% of the students are distance learners.

ENTRY POINTS: 180–360	AVE POINTS: 240
APPLICATIONS PER PLACE: 6	CLEARING: 7%
NO. OF TERMS: 2	LENGTH OF TERMS: 15WKS
STAFF TO STUDENT RATIO: 1:10	STUDY ADDICTS: 21%
TEACHING: ★★★★	RESEARCH: ★★★★
1STS: 9%	2.2s: 22%
2.1s: 36%	OTHERS: N/A

ADMISSIONS
◉ APPLY VIA UCAS/CATCH FOR NURSING & MIDWIFERY

SUBJECTS
ART & DESIGN 14%   **ARTS & SOCIAL SCIENCES** 18%
LAW & ACCOUNTANCY 10%
EDUCATION & SOCIAL WORK 6%
ENGINEERING & PHYSICAL SCIENCE 9%
LIFE SCIENCES 9%
MEDICINE, DENTISTRY & NURSING 38%

LIBRARIES
◉ 762,000 BOOKS ◉ 1,609 STUDY PLACES
◉ SPEND PER STUDENT ££££
More than half the books are in the Main Library, but there are eight other various book stashes across the campuses and departments, reflecting their subjects.

COMPUTERS
◉ 2,626 WORKSTATIONS
16 separate IT suites and various other PC places.

ENTERTAINMENT ◖◖◖◖◖◖◖◖◖

THE CITY
◉ PRICE OF A PINT OF BEER £1.95
◉ GLASS OF WINE £3 **◉ CAN OF RED BULL** £1.50
CINEMAS The UGC and Odeon multiplexes (ten screens each) see to students' cravings for bangs, gags and fluffy endings. Or the arty, two-screen DCA for subtitled films and soul-destroying endings plus a bar in which to drink away the high intellect.
THEATRES The Dundee Rep for more hardcore theatre. Caird Hall for ballet, opera and pantos.

PUBS Being Scotland, pubs are open *virtually all the time. Pushplugs: Bar Rio; Amsterdam; Nether Inn. Avoid the Speedwell and the Taybridge – old men alert.*

CLUBBING *Dundee's clubs may not be world-renowned, nor indeed cheap, but that doesn't scare off desperate students.* There's certainly no shortage. Fat Sam's and The Social are the main alternative *for students bored with DUSA.*

MUSIC VENUES Gigs at Fat Sam's. Caird Hall hosts classical and pop while the West Port pub swings to Cajun and Mexican rhythms.

EATING OUT Pubs are usually a good starting point – most of the student favourites do food beyond pork scratchings in cider sauce. *Pushplugs: Braes; Visocchi's; Anatolia (Turkish).*

OTHER For fun before nightfall, there are the zoo and wildlife sanctuary and the beaches.

UNIVERSITY

⊙ **PRICE OF A PINT OF BEER** £1.70 ⊙ **GLASS OF WINE** £3
⊙ **CAN OF RED BULL** £1.50

BARS £4.8m has been spent refurbishing the Union. The Liar Bar draws the DJs for big club nights. *The balcony attached to Mono Bar is a vomit-related accident waiting to happen.* There is also the Air Bar.

THEATRES LIP Theatre Company pulls on the hose and doublets at the Dundee Rep Theatre.

FILM The film society shows one movie a week, normally mainstream. Also weekly viewings at the local cinema.

MUSIC VENUES Mylo, Editors, and the Thrills have played. Floor 5 has band nights for student strummers.

CLUBBING Mono holds the *funkiest* club nights. Tim Westwood, Queens of Noize, and Colin & Edith from Radio 1 have all swabbed the decks.

FOOD Yum Yum is the main eatery in the Union and does everything from deep-fried to rabbit food at a reasonable price. Otherwise there's the Union shop for sarnies.

OTHER Graduation ball, sports ball and diddier faculty bashes.

SOCIAL ◖◖◖◖◖◖◖◖◖◖◖◖◖

DUNDEE UNIVERSITY STUDENTS' ASSOCIATION

⊙ **3 SABBATICALS** ⊙ **TURNOUT AT LAST BALLOT** 8%
New students could be forgiven for blinking at the sight of the *modernist mirrored glass visual assault of a building* where DUSA is based. *The students can also be a bit whingy about the services they get out of the SA, but to be fair, they do a good job of keeping the ents boat afloat. Politically though, most students don't care if they're right, left or hanging from the ceiling by their ankles (DUSA's not affiliated to NUS), so long as the beer doesn't run out.*

SA FACILITIES

The SA provides: five bars; canteen; coffee bar; fast food place; two meeting rooms; three minibuses and a van; RBS bank with ATM; Clydesdale ATMs; photo booth; crèche; general store; stationery shop; vending machines; new & secondhand bookshops; advice centre; TV lounge; post office; swimming pool; 'I-walls' for web-surfing.

CLUBS (NON SPORTING)

Bands; Chocolate Eaters; Development & Research Expeditions; Finnish; Hellenic; Hispanic; International Students; Lip Theatre; Mooting; Music; Natural History; Nigerian; Operatic; People & Planet; Poker; Self-defence; Role-playing; Young Entrepreneurs. **See also Clubs tables.**

OTHER ORGANISATIONS

'The Student Times' is the monthly SA-centric rag. Radio station, 'Vertigo', broadcasts across the city and on the internet. DUMS does Raggish charity stuff.

RELIGIOUS

⊙ **9 CHAPLAINS (RC, METHODIST, BAPTIST, EPISCOPALIAN, CONGREGATIONAL, ORTHODOX, FCOFS)**
Only one chaplain is full-time, but the others are found often enough at the chaplaincy, which also caters for other flavours of faith (*quite literally, actually – they've got a coffee bar*). Also a Muslim prayer room.

PAID WORK

Most people who want work can get it – there's no end of part-time *McJobs* in the city centre. Apart from listing these on its website, DUSA hires quite a few people itself and holds recruitment fairs to entice the next generation of ent, security and bar staff into its clutches.

SPORTS ◖◖◖◖◖◖◖◖◖◖◖◖◖

⊙ **RECENT SUCCESSES** SKIING ⊙ **BUSA RANKING** 53
Interest's not as hot as the facilities.

SPORTS FACILITIES

Six football pitches; four rugby pitches; three hockey pitches; three all-weather fields; cricket pitch; four tennis courts; four netball courts; swimming pool; gym; climbing wall; running track; aerobics studio; four squash courts; four basketball courts; sports hall; sauna... *you work up a sweat just listing them.* Annual membership costs £65.

SPORTING CLUBS

Boat; Boxing; Gaelic Football; Hurling; Ju-Jitsu; Kickboxing; Rollerhockey. **See also Clubs tables.**

ATTRACTIONS

Dundee United and Dundee FC *bicker on and off the pitch.*

ACCOMMODATION ()()()()()()()()()()

IN UNIVERSITY
◉ **SELF-CATERING** 14% ◉ **COST** £71 (37WKS)
◉ **1ST YRS LIVING IN** 43% ◉ **INSURANCE PREMIUM** £
AVAILABILITY In theory, first years are guaranteed a place in halls if they want one, although this will be easier in practice when the building work is finished. Self-caterers try to get elbow-room at the cooker with five other students on average (*not a bad sharing rate*). Peterson Hall is non-smoking. There's a launderette in each hall. The University is in cahoots with the police which, coupled with CCTV and night porters, *ensures beauty sleep is normally undisturbed.*
CAR PARKING £60 gets a parking permit and there's usually room to stash bikes in the entrances to halls.

EXTERNALLY
◉ **AVE RENT** £67 ◉ **LIVING AT HOME** 23%
AVAILABILITY More than 80% live out, many in their parents' or their own homes. *So they're alright, Jack.* There's enough choice around for students to be able to pick somewhere near where they study. Choice pitches include Perth Road, but even this is getting to be quite expensive and students are moving further and further out. The east side and city centre are *a bit too rough for more sensitive souls.*
HOUSING HELP The University Residences Office, apart from allocating University places, offers bulletin boards, advice and booklets, provided by eight staff. DUSA runs an online service.

WELFARE ()()()()()()()()()()()()

SERVICES
◉ **LGBT SOCIETY** ◉ **POSTGRAD SOCIETY**
◉ **INTERNATIONAL STUDENTS' OFFICER & SOCIETY**
◉ **DISABILITIES OFFICER** ◉ **LATE-NIGHT MINIBUS**
◉ **UNIVERSITY COUNSELLORS** 4 FULL ◉ **CRIME RATING** !!
DUSA's Information & Support Service offers drop-in lunchtime sessions and arranges police and solicitor's clinics. A student support worker helps with anything from landlords to loneliness and co-ordinates 'Peer Connections', a mentoring scheme for students to look after each other.
HEALTH The Student Health Service has a part-time doctor and two nurses.
CRECHES/NURSERY 40 places for kids over 2yrs.
DISABILITIES Disability Support Officers in each department are there to see students get what they need. There's also a special IT suite and dyslexia service.

FINANCE
◉ **AVE DEBT PER YEAR** £1,461
◉ **HOME STUDENT FEES** £1,700
◉ **FEES** Non-Scottish students will have to *kiss bye-bye* to £3,000 in fees. Part-timers cough up £196 per 20 credit module. Postgrads pay £3,085 and international students are charged £8,000.
◉ **ACCESS FUND** £500,000
◉ **SUCCESSFUL APPLICATIONS/YR** 900
SUPPORT: Through the Student Money Advisor and assistant, the SAS (*that's the Student Advisory Service, not the balaclava-headed crack assassins*) provides financial advice and there are bursaries for mature students.

D

◉ **Dundee University staff and students rehearsed and produced 'Seven Brides for Seven Brothers' in 23 hours and 30 mins and now hold the world record for the fastest ever staging of a musical.**

Words in italics are Push's point of view — take it or leave it...

DURHAM UNIVERSITY

1) ❂ **DURHAM UNIVERSITY** University Office, Durham, DH1 3HP **TEL** (0191) 334 2000 **E-MAIL** admissions@durham.ac.uk **WEBSITE** www.durham.ac.uk ❂ **DURHAM STUDENTS' UNION**, Dunelm House, New Elvet, Durham, DH1 3AN **TEL** (0191) 334 1777 **E-MAIL** enquiries@dsu.org.uk **WEBSITE** www.dsu.org.uk
2) ❂ **DURHAM UNIVERSITY** Queen's Campus, University Boulevard, Thornaby, Stockton-on-Tees, TS17 6BH **TEL** (0191) 334 2000

D

GENERAL ◍◍◍◍◍◍◍◍◍◍◍◍

Durham City, laced by the River Wear, lies in the heart of the Geordie-speaking North-East, near the Northumbrian Moors, ten miles from the North Sea and 52 miles south of the Scottish border. The University is planted in the middle of the ancient, small city and on weekdays during term students dominate it socially as much as the cathedral and castle do physically. The castle is actually one of the University's 16 colleges, which spread out in three main groups across the city giving the advantages of a collegiate, civic and campus university as well as a handy defence against invading Vikings. The University has two branches outside Durham itself: a small Catholic college four miles outside the city, and the Queen's Campus, an entirely modern and separate site in Stockton, 21 miles away, and a mini university in itself, that could hardly be more different from Durham's quiet and old-world charm if it tried.

👤👤👤👤👤👤👤👤👤👤👤👤👤👤👤👤👤👤👤👤👤

SEX RATIO: ♂47 ♀53	**FOUNDED:** 1832
FULL-TIME U'GRADS: 11,410	**PART-TIME:** 97
POSTGRADS: 1,047	**NON-DEGREE:** 3,531
AVE COURSE: 3YRS	**ETHNIC:** 7%
STATE:PRIVATE SCHOOL: 40:34	**FLUNK RATE:** 4%
MATURE: 7%	**INTERNATIONAL:** 15%
DISABLED: 80	**LOCAL:** 16%

ATMOSPHERE

As England's third oldest university, there's something of the Oxbridge about Durham with its traditions, its formal dinners and balls (*of the black-tie variety*). *One major difference though is the strength of its central SU. Although the weather's chilly, the hearts are warm.* The college system and the size of the city create a communal, almost school-like atmosphere, that some find claustrophobic. *The city's becoming more student-friendly, though locals can resent the hordes of students getting their town dirty.*

THE COLLEGES

Much of a student's social life is centred on the college where they eat, sleep and drink. Students remain members of their college even if they don't live there. However, unlike Oxbridge, teaching is not college-based. The main colleges are grouped into three areas and each group has a flavour of its own. So it's important to pick the right college – *each one tastes different.*

The oldest colleges are on 'the Peninsula', along 'the Bailey', *and they appeal particularly to those who* admire their architecture and tradition (*if not their facilities*) *and to raging Sloanes.* These colleges are:
UNIVERSITY COLLEGE OR 'CASTLE' (217) The first college and one of the most over-subscribed (16 applications per place). *Students sacrifice a few creature comforts to live in a castle in their third year (if they're lucky).* Founded in 1072, the castle is the oldest building used for student accommodation in the country.
HATFIELD (234) *Rugby and beer. Not the place for shy, retiring, sensitive types.*
ST CHAD'S (101) *Croquet and Pimms. Very small but with character.*
ST JOHN'S (116) *Small, quaint and in cahoots with the Church.* Predominantly Christian. First years get to live next to the cathedral, *the jammy beggars.*
ST CUTHBERT'S SOCIETY (705) 80% live out of college. Many mature students, but this is balancing out. *It's sporty, and the bar actually feels like a pub rather than a youth club.*

The Hill Colleges, near the science departments, were mostly built in the 60s *and tend to be more progressive.* These colleges are:
ST AIDAN'S (267) *Motivated and progressive students. They have to be to climb that hill and still party.*
VAN MILDERT (318) *Like Aidan's but less motivated and not on a hill.* The most cosmopolitan college, *with a reputation for fundraising.*
TREVELYAN (196) *'Trevs' has honeycomb maze architecture and, for no special reason, rather arty students.*
ST MARY'S (213) After many years as an all-female bastion, Mary's is now mixed. *The atmosphere (a strange mix of the knitting and nighties brigade and sporty party monsters) is likely to change for good. Possibly the most attractive buildings of the hill colleges.*
GREY (274) *Slightly more character than its name suggests.*
COLLINGWOOD (347) The youngest hill college is *media hacksville but unpretentious.*

The third area isn't really a group. It's the hilly north bank of the Wear where the largest college,
ST HILD & ST BEDE (368), stands alone on a 16-acre site. Its students are a mixture of all sorts, *variously accused of being too insular or too dominant.*

USTINOV (1,900) is for postgrads only.
USHAW is a Catholic seminary four miles out of the city.
JOSEPHINE BUTLER, a new self-catering 400-bed college, is due to open in Autumn 2006 next to Ustinov, about a mile from Durham centre. *First years will be able to whip up their own easycook pasta as though they're in a 'normal' modern*

university, *rather than getting caught up in the whole formal meal and college tradition thing.* **JOHN SNOW** (388) and **GEORGE STEPHENSON** (453), are based at the Queen's Campus at Stockton, *which is completely unlike Durham in terms of atmosphere, history, geography and absence of pomp. It feels like a completely separate university,* with its own union and ents, but maintains the same infrastructure.

DURHAM

- **POPULATION** 87,709 ○ **CITY CENTRE** 0 MILES
- **LONDON** 240 MILES ○ **NEWCASTLE** 15 MILES
- **HIGH TEMP:** 19 ○ **LOW TEMP** 0 ○ **RAINFALL** 54

Durham used to be the epicentre of the North-East's mining tradition. Nowadays there's not much in Durham not connected to the University or the cathedral. It does have a shopping mall, an open-air and a covered market, lots of quaint shoppes, army and arts museums and certainly carries an air of its own history but, well, *there's no buzz. Things are picking up but thrill-seekers and hardened shoppers sneak into Newcastle when Durham's not looking.*

Stockton, 21 miles south of Durham, but only 3 miles out of Middlesbrough, is the birthplace of the steam engine and the Industrial Revolution, *but don't expect it still to be so cutting edge.* Manufacturing industries went out with Maggie Thatcher and left Stockton in need of the kind of rejuvenation that Durham's Queen's Campus was intended to bring. See University of Teesside for local details.

TRAVEL

TRAINS Mainline connections from Durham to London King's Cross (£60.35) and handy trains to Newcastle (£6.10). Stockton is near Darlington train station, on the London-Edinburgh line.
COACHES National Express and Blue Line services to many destinations including London (£34) and Newcastle (£3.50).
CAR Five mins off the A1, but the city operates a congestion charge in the centre and around town, walking is easy enough (and the riverside paths are *blissful*). Stockton connects to the A1 via the A66.
AIR Newcastle and Teesside Airports are close to both campuses – flights to London, Northern Ireland and Europe.
HITCHING *Not bad* from the A1.
LOCAL Good bus services *that lazy students use to get up the hills in Durham.* Fares from 30p. A frequent-but-slow service runs between Durham and Queen's Campus.
TAXIS Some of Britain's cheapest taxis (min fare £1, £15 Durham-Newcastle) make it a worthwhile share.
BICYCLES A *bit hilly* for bikes.

CAREER PROSPECTS

- **CAREERS SERVICE** ○ **NO. OF STAFF** 20
- **UNEMPLOYED AFTER 6** MTHS 16%

SPECIAL FEATURES

Teikyo University, a Japanese college, has set up an outpost at Durham University, where its students can come for a year, get a taste of English students and go home all the wiser. It includes two small halls of residence, but some students also stay at the neighbouring St Mary's College.

FAMOUS ALUMNI

George Alagiah, Hazel Irvine, Jeremy Vine (BBC presenters); Will Carling, Phil de Glanville (England rugby captains); Jack Cunningham MP (Lab); Hunter Davies (journalist); Jonathan Edwards (triple jumper); Harold Evans (ex-Sunday Times ed); Will Greenwood (England rugby centre); Nasser Hussain (ex-England cricket captain); Cmdr Tim Lawrence (Princess Anne's hubby); Edward Leigh MP (Con); Andrew Strauss (cricketer and Ashes winner) James Wilby (actor).

FURTHER INFO

○ **PROSPECTUSES** UNDERGRAD; POSTGRAD; ALTERNATIVE; MATURE; INTERNATIONAL.

ACADEMIC ○○○○○○○○○○○○○○

○ **1994** GROUP

ENTRY POINTS: 280–360	AVE POINTS: 360
APPLNS PER PLACE: 8	CLEARING: 3%
NO. OF TERMS: 3	LENGTH OF TERMS: 9WKS
STAFF TO STUDENT RATIO: 1:19	STUDY ADDICTS: 36%
TEACHING: *****	RESEARCH: *****
YEAR ABROAD: 3%	SANDWICH STUDENTS: 1%
1STS: 16%	2.2S: 21%
2.1S: 58%	OTHERS: 3%

ADMISSIONS

○ **APPLY VIA UCAS**
Students normally choose a college on their application form – worth getting it in early as each college only has a certain number of places up for grabs.

SUBJECTS

ARTS/HUMANITIES 26%   **SCIENCES** 35%
SOCIAL SCIENCES & HEALTH 39%
BEST Archaeology; English; European Language & Area Studies; History; Human & Social Geography; Law; Medicine; Philosophy; Physical Science; Theology & Religious Studies.
WORST Spanish.

LIBRARIES

○ **1,500,000** BOOKS ○ **1,667** STUDY PLACES
○ **SPEND PER STUDENT** £££
As well as the main library, there are four other libraries (including education, ecclesiastical and special collections). Each college and many departments also have their own libraries.

COMPUTERS

○ **1,200** WORKSTATIONS ○ **24**-HR ACCESS
Despite six classrooms, several computer rooms, 24-hr access and all colleges having net capabilities, getting at a computer *can still*

occasionally prove tricky. 1,250 study places in the library have networked PCs or wireless capacity. Around 5,000 student rooms have high-speed net access. Introductory courses in web design, spreadsheets and general techno guff are available.

ENTERTAINMENT ◖◖◖◖◖◖◖◖◖◖

THE CITY
- **PRICE OF A PINT OF BEER** £1.60
- **GLASS OF WINE** £2
- **CAN OF RED BULL** £2.50

Durham's a bit dinky and still can't fully quench the student thirst. Most find it safest to leave the city to the locals at weekends and many sidle off to Newcastle in search of good times – see Newcastle University *for further info.*

CINEMAS The Gala Cinema in Durham has one screen but boasts an IMAX and occasional theatre too.

THEATRES The Gala, *er,* Theatre (cap 510). One stage, but boasts a cinema and, *oh never mind...*

PUBS *A few, not all are student-friendly* but some serve real ale *if that's your cup of tea. Pushplugs: Bar Arabia (parties and shisha tobacco); the Fish Tank (live bands, DJs and poetry readings, free food); Duncow Inn (here be ale); Jimmy Allen's (student discounts, drum & bass sets); Vennels (café/wine bar with live music). Probably best avoided are Yates' and the Fighting Cocks.*

CLUBBING *Klute is a Durham institution, in that it's rubbish, but like a much beloved but lame dog, you can't bring yourself to shoot it through the head, despite it being named 'n' shamed as the second Worst Club in Europe.* There's also DH1, Café Rock and Studio, *but Newcastle has better options.*

MUSIC VENUES Classical, blues and jazz at the Gala. Otherwise it's pub music only. The Jug has regular bands. *The Fishtank is tiny, but hosts decent alternative music and comedy.*

EATING OUT *Little choice really, but one or two to help students recover from beans on toast and Pot Noodle overdoses. Hides is a 'Ra' hangout, even though it serves coffee and traditional English rather than diamond-encrusted cocktails. Pushplugs:* Ricardos (Chinese, *only kidding,* Italian); Brown Sugar (*pricey but popular,* especially the cakes).

UNIVERSITY
- **PRICE OF A PINT OF BEER** £1.40
- **GLASS OF WINE** £1.60

BARS Kingsgate is the SU's main bar, complete with a pool table and sports TV. It's open from lunchtime until 12.30am most nights, 1.30am on Fridays and Saturdays. Each college has its own bar too, where most of the serious drinking gets done and around which a lot of college life revolves (*that's what happens when you drink too much*). The Queen's campus has the Rocket Union.

THEATRES Student drama is well represented, with regular shows at The Assembly Room theatre and some going on to the Fringe plus an annual drama festival in shivery February. *Beware though, levels of theatre-ness can change dramatically from year to year.*

FILM No cinema, but there are film societies and Hild/Bede students are liberal with the use of DVDs on their OHP.

CLUBBING/MUSIC VENUES The Ballroom (cap 750), Riverside Café (150) in Dunelm House are used along with a smaller room and Stockton's Rocket Union. The colleges have smaller facilities that they don't bother using much. Friday night's Planet of Sound *cums on and feels the noize* (hiphop and dance) all over campus and an indie night is planned for Saturdays. *Most big-name acts think Durham is what you do with drumsticks* but Stiff Little Fingers, the Damned, the Buzzcocks, DJ Luck & MC Neat and Goldie have all found their way up the motorway.

COMEDY/CABARET The comedy society *haven't yet laughed their way up to organising a regular night.*

FOOD Kingsgate (pizza) and Riverside (*comfy seats, sandwiches and snacks*) and Rocket do *pretty standard stuff.*

BALLS Each college puts on at least one a year, costing from a few quid to £130+ for a double ticket at Castle's *elitist* June Bash. There's also the Freshers' Ball *where Durham's posh kids (easily spotted, they're the ones whose over-bite appears to have swallowed their chin) get a bit squiffy and embarrass the family name.*

> ◎ **Durham University shelled out £100,000 on software which would generate the undergraduate timetable but when it wouldn't work properly staff tried to finish the job by hand. They eventually decided to leave the previous year's timetable unchanged.**

Words in italics are Push's point of view — take it or leave it...

SOCIAL ◗◗◗◗◗◗◗◗◗◗◗◗◗

DURHAM STUDENTS' UNION
◗ 4 SABBATICALS ◗ TURNOUT AT LAST BALLOT 21%
◗ NUS MEMBER
DSU doesn't just keep the students quiet with booze. It's a politically shrewd union with a representative voice in the University and a tendency to grab headlines, appear on television and launch political careers. Less political students sometimes complain that this is at the expense of other aspects of the Union's responsibilities. Regardless, the students rally together for one of the country's largest (and silliest) collections of clubs and societies at any university. Rather than the central SU, colleges are the first and foremost point of contact of most students and its college reps that keep the SU in touch with the word on the (cobbled) street.

SU FACILITIES
The large Union building, Dunelm House, is placed right in the middle of Durham where it offers: three bars; a ballroom; Riverside Room Cafeteria; small hall; shop; travel agency; launderette; stationery shop; secondhand bookshop; advice centre; ticket agency; pool tables; minibus; car and van hire; fax, print and photocopier services; meeting room; games and vending machines; juke box; public phone; photo booth.

CLUBS (NON SPORTING)
Aegis (genocide prevention); Alt-music; Amnesty International; Anglo-Japanese; Anti-Sweatshop Campaign; Arts; Assassins; Astronomical; BALADS (waltz, jive, tango, quickstep & cha cha cha for beginners); Belly Dancing, Big Band, Caledonian (dance Scottish reels); Hill Walking, Hill Orchestra; Hong Kong; Improvised Comedy; Instep Dance; Intercollegiate Darts; Italian; Jazz & Grove; Kendo-Japanese sword techniques; Labour; Latin American; Light Opera; LINKS-first aid; Meditation; Methodist; Mixed Martial; Model United Nations; Motor Sports; Music; Natural Science; Neighbours *('everybody needs good...')*; Nigerian Students; Orchestral; Philosophical; Photography; Pimm's; Pink (LGBT); Poker; British Red Cross; Revelation Rock & Gospel Choir; Sc-Fi; Shorinji-Kempo (Japanese martial arts); Scout & Guide Group; Seagal appreciation; SGIA News (International Students); Singapore; Spanish; SPEAK (religious volunteering society); Students Supporting Street Kids; Student Theatre; Team (society which aims to aid students who want to socialise outside their college 'family'); Treasure Trap (live-action, role-playing game society); Welsh; Whisky Appreciation; Wing Chun Kung Fu; Yoga; Young Federal Union. **See also Clubs tables.**

OTHER ORGANISATIONS
'Palatinate', the student newspaper, has won awards recently. 'LIP' (Level Information Project) is a national mag aimed at a pro-multicultural student readership. 'Purple' is the fledgling online radio station. www.durham21.co.uk (three times NUS website of the year) is a not-for-profit online newspaper, with all proceeds going to Durham University Charity Week (aka DUCK). DUCK, incidentally, is what they call their *phenomenally active* charity Rag (following the ban of Rag after, *reputedly, students broke in to Durham Top Security Prison*). Student Community Action acts as an umbrella for projects including SPARK, which promotes work with local youngsters. The Durham Union Society (DUS) is the long-standing debating society, which offers more than just debating – *often seen as a right-wing alternative to DSU or as a refuge for the sophisticated Sloane* – either way it costs £35 to get in, runs a bar, TV room, café and a range of events.

RELIGIOUS
There's a 1,500 year-old Christian heritage, so finding a church is easy. As well as the cathedral, there are Anglican, Catholic, Methodist, Quaker and United Reformed churches. Most colleges have their own chapel. For Muslims a prayer-room is provided and St Mary's does halal nosh, but the nearest mosque is in Sunderland. Everyone else has to go to Newcastle to find a *worship shop*.

PAID WORK
◗ JOB BUREAU
Work can be found in the University bars, libraries or locally and there's a comprehensive jobshop to find folk work, *but jobs are still hard to come by*.

SPORTS ◗◗◗◗◗◗◗◗◗◗◗◗◗◗

◗ RECENT SUCCESSES ROWING, CANOEING, CRICKET, MEN'S HOCKEY **◗ BUSA RANKING** 5
Durham tends to wow when it comes to sports, possibly because they pump so much money into it or, in the case of rowing, hire ex-Olympian alumni to coach the team. Or maybe it's the fresh air. Whatever, they take it seriously.

SPORTS FACILITIES
Sports hall; 64 acres of playing fields; all-weather pitch; multigym; athletics and running track; gym; fitness suite; croquet lawn and bowling green; tennis and squash courts; the River Wear. Outdoor pitches are floodlit. Most colleges have their own gym. Durham City also has a public baths. Stockton will have all-weather floodlit pitches and there's a public sports centre nearby with watersports facilities.

SPORTING CLUBS
Boardriders; Boat; Boxing; Bridge; Clay Pigeon; Fives; Freefall; Gliding; Hang Gliding & Paragliding; Lacrosse; Mountaineering; Polo; Table Tennis; Ultimate Frisbee; Water polo. *See also Clubs tables*.

ATTRACTIONS

The Durham Regatta is one of the top annual university rowing events. Durham University doesn't actually run it though, but does do well in it. Durham city has a strong cricket team. Newcastle, Sunderland and Middlesbrough FCs are nearby.

ACCOMMODATION ((((((((((

IN COLLEGE

○ **CATERED** 39% ○ **COST** £117 (30/33WKS)
○ **SELF-CATERING** 17% ○ **COST** £85 (38WKS)
○ **1ST YRS LIVING IN** 98% ○ **INSURANCE PREMIUM** £
AVAILABILITY Almost all first years live in and some colleges can provide accommodation for a further year. Housing is mixed and disabled facilities are available. With so many different colleges, what students call home *varies big time*, from *cold but atmospheric chambers* in the Castle with limited facilities to en suite modern rooms at most of the hill colleges. *University College's housing is the worst, Collingwood's the best.* Sharing is pretty common, *though students seem to think it's all part of the Durham fun. Most shared kitchens, being pants, make it hard to create anything more substantial than toast and a cuppa, especially in the catered rooms.* Security's *good*, with night porters on patrol. Students *are stung* with an extra charge per night if they stay during the Christmas and Easter holidays, even though their stuff's still in their room. Stockton's two colleges are self-catering (shared kitchens).
CAR PARKING A permit is required to get at the few spaces available. What with the congestion charge too *there's little point having a car if living in.* Stockton has a bit more space for cars, though.

EXTERNALLY

○ **AVE RENT** £58 ○ **LIVING AT HOME** 1%
AVAILABILITY Most second years and some third years live out. Costs can vary from £45 to £120, depending on location. The best houses, near the city centre, go *quicker than cocaine at a celebrity party.* Housing is expensive and rare in the local area, so many students resort to the surrounding villages, which aren't too far away. In the city there are Victorian terraced houses that tend to share between three and five. The Viaduct (£60/wk) is a sought-after spot, closely followed by Bowburn and Langley Moor. Gilesgate and Crossgate are near the University, but pricier. *The pit villages should be avoided. Cars are unnecessary and the cause of much local tension,* but people still bring them.
HOUSING HELP There's a web-based house search for all students and the University keeps a list of approved landlords. St Cuthbert's Society helps its own guys.

WELFARE ((((((((((((

SERVICES

○ **LGBT OFFICER** & **SOCIETY** ○ **MATURE STUDENTS'**
OFFICER & **SOCIETY** ○ **INTERNATIONAL STUDENTS'**
SOCIETY ○ **POSTGRAD OFFICER** & **SOCIETY**
○ **DISABILITIES OFFICER** & **SOCIETY** ○ **WOMEN'S OFFICER**
○ **SELF-DEFENCE CLASSES** ○ **LATE-NIGHT MINIBUS**
○ **NIGHTLINE** ○ **UNIVERSITY COUNSELLORS** 3 FULL/10 PART
○ **CRIME RATING** !
Welfare provision is *very good*: union reps cover most areas as well as professionally-trained staff, so-called 'moral tutors' in the colleges and a student health centre (colleges also allocate their students to local NHS practices). There's even free legal advice and an 85-capacity crèche.
DISABILITIES Durham University Service for Students with Disabilities (DUSSD) offers help to get around the fact that, being old, Durham wasn't designed with any kind of disability in mind. Modern, purpose-built Stockton is much more accessible.
CRIME It's a small, safe city with little to fear bar the occasional college break-in.
DRUGS Are bad, in the University's eyes, and it has no time for those caught taking them.

FINANCE

○ **AVE DEBT PER YEAR** £1,975
○ **HOME STUDENT FEES** £3,000
FEES Foundation courses cost £1,200 and part-time undergrads pay £1,500. International students pay about £9,120-£11,895.
○ **ACCESS FUND** £512,236 ○ **SUCCESSFUL**
APPLICATIONS/**YR** 594 ○ **AVE PAYMENT** £776
The top-up fight has been fought and lost, but Durham's one of the Holy Trinity of universities (along with Oxford and Cambridge, *natch*) offering the full three grand of support to students from families with less than £16,000 yearly income. The hardship fund also gives out £50,000 a year. Although it's not unheard of, to get more than £2,000 from the hardship or access fund requires exceptional circumstances (*being 'thirsty' doesn't count*). The Union tells students how to get money out of the University, but doesn't offer any itself. Academic prizes are up for grabs, as are awards for students who want to do some worthy extra-curricular stuff but can't afford it.

Words in italics are Push's point of view — take it or leave it...

EALING COLLEGE OF HIGHER EDUCATION
see *Thames Valley University*

EAST 15 ACTING SCHOOL
see *University of Essex*

UNIVERSITY OF EAST ANGLIA

UNIVERSITY OF EAST LONDON

ECONOMICS
see *LSE*

UNIVERSITY OF EDINBURGH

EDINBURGH BUSINESS SCHOOL
see *Heriot-Watt University*

EPSOM
see *Creative Arts University College*

UNIVERSITY OF ESSEX

EXETER UNIVERSITY

E

▶ **EALING COLLEGE OF HIGHER EDUCATION**
see _Thames Valley University_

▶ **EAST 15 ACTING SCHOOL**
see _University of Essex_

UNIVERSITY OF EAST ANGLIA

○ **UNIVERSITY OF EAST ANGLIA** Norwich, NR4 7TJ **TEL** (01603) 591 515 **E-MAIL** admissions@uea.ac.uk **WEBSITE** www.uea.ac.uk
○ **UNION OF UEA STUDENTS**, Union House, University of East Anglia, Norwich, NR4 7TJ **TEL** (01603) 593 272
E-MAIL su.comms@uea.ac.uk **WEBSITE** www.ueastudent.com

GENERAL ○○○○○○○○○○○○○

Things that are flat: _car parks, still water and East Anglia._ East Anglia's northern bit is also soggy because of the Broads – miles of lakes, waterways and fenlands _which also means tourists._ When Norwich was Britain's second biggest city, the Broads were full of traders instead of Americans, but times change. During the Industrial Revolution other cities cottoned on to cotton or cashed in on coal, Norwich made it with mustard and still has a thriving industry. Nowadays Norwich, _a rather hilly market town considering its surrounding topography,_ is a tourist attraction, administrative centre for Norfolk and home to 270 acres of premium university known as the 'University Plain' (_seeing herds of students moving across it at sunset can be quite emotional_). 2.5 miles out of town, between a 40s council estate and a conservation area, UEA is a concrete complex surrounded by greenery and its very own lake. Its recent shopping budget _would put even Sharon Osbourne to shame,_ with £250m _splashed out_ on new accommodation, a library extension and SU facilities.

SEX RATIO: ♂39 ♀61	**FOUNDED:** 1963
FULL-TIME U'GRADS: 8,508	**PART-TIME:** 2,461
POSTGRADS: 2,127	**NON-DEGREE:** 0
AVE COURSE: 3YRS	**ETHNIC:** 15%
STATE:PRIVATE SCHOOL: 88:12	**FLUNK RATE:** 13%
MATURE: 53%	**INTERNATIONAL:** 15%
DISABLED: 125	**LOCAL:** 44%

ATMOSPHERE

An easy-going, informal but sometimes cliquey atmosphere in a largely white, middle-class environment. Many first years rarely leave the campus. Those who can cope with this, lousy weather and the tumbleweed at the weekends (despite good ents) will enjoy themselves. When the claustrophobia's too much to bear, the town's only a short bus or bike trip away. UEA's a true greenfield site, so don't expect cutting-edge style or busting rhymes on street corners.

NORWICH

○ **POPULATION** 121,700 ○ **CITY CENTRE** 2 MILES
○ **LONDON** 103 MILES ○ **BIRMINGHAM** 139 MILES
○ **CAMBRIDGE** 62 MILES
○ **HIGH TEMP** 20 ○ **LOW TEMP** 1 ○ **RAINFALL** 55

Locals like to remind students that Norwich is a city, not a town. It does, after all, have not one but two cathedrals and contains all the amenities including a _whole bunch_ of supermarkets, late-night shops, bookshops, banks and _cunningly-located_ cashpoints. Apart from the cathedral glut, tourists _quite like_ the Norman castle, which has been converted into two museums and an art gallery. The area between the University and the town is known as 'the Golden Triangle', with lots of students and amenities and a _community feel. For UEA students, Norwich is like a favourite grandparent, warm and friendly, but unlikely to offer much in the way of high-octane excitement._ A fair proportion of graduates like it so much, they stay on and make it their home.

TRAVEL

TRAINS Nearest station is Norwich, three miles from campus. Direct services to London (£24.05), change there for other destinations or via Peterborough for the North.
COACHES Various services include London (£20.50) and Birmingham (£28.50).
CAR The A11, A47, A140 and A146 go via Norwich.
AIR Flights inland and to about 200 cities worldwide from Norwich Airport.
LOCAL Buses 25, 26, 27 and 502 regularly run from nearby St Stephen's Meadow and St Stephen's Street in town to the main campus. Taxis can work out cheaper than taking a bus if in a group and most firms give a special rate to/from UEA. If heading into the city, make sure you ask for 'the city' and not 'the town'; _locals are particular._
BICYCLES _Some cycle lanes near UEA, but it's advisable to wear a gas mask on the ring road. Otherwise it's good territory for two wheelers._

CAREER PROSPECTS

○ **CAREERS SERVICE** ○ **NO. OF STAFF** 5 FULL
○ **UNEMPLOYED AFTER 6 MTHS** 7%
Interview training, jobs fairs, careers library and Matrix, an online training service.

Words in italics are Push's point of view – take it or leave it...

FAMOUS ALUMNI

Jenny Abramsky (Radio 5 Live); Trezzo Azopardi, Martyn Bedford, Tracy Chevalier, Kazuo Ishiguro, Toby Litt, Ian McEwan, Clive Sinclair, Rose Tremain (writers); Jack Davenport (actor); Charlie Higson, Arthur Smith, Paul Whitehouse (comedians); Paul Nurse (Nobel Prize-winning scientist); Dr Rihab Taha (*notorious* Iraqi biological weapons boss).

FURTHER INFO

- **PROSPECTUSES** UNDERGRAD; POSTGRAD; ALTERNATIVE
- **OPEN DAYS**

ACADEMIC ())))))))))))))

- **1994** GROUP

UEA is particularly renowned in two areas. The first is English and American Studies, including the *world-famous* MA in writing (check out the alumni). The other is Environmental Studies, which although it contains meteorology and the like, *isn't quite as green as it sounds.* Development Studies, Law, History and Social Work prop up the table of academic strengths. A fair amount of genetic *meddling* goes on at the John Innes Centre. Degrees are modular, meaning assessment is ongoing (*no slacking*). Students are allowed to take a module in something unrelated to their course – most opt for Creative Writing or a language. Learning support tutors are on hand to advise on time management and study skills.

ENTRY POINTS: 240-360	AVE POINTS: 276
APPLICATIONS PER PLACE: 6	CLEARING: 7%
NO. OF TERMS: 3	LENGTH OF TERMS: 12wks
STAFF TO STUDENT RATIO: 1:17	STUDY ADDICTS: 20%
TEACHING: ****	RESEARCH: ****
YEAR ABROAD: 3%	SANDWICH STUDENTS: 0%
1STS: 9%	2.2S: 28%
2.1S: 56%	3RDS: 6%

ADMISSIONS

- **APPLY VIA UCAS**

SUBJECTS

ARTS & HUMANITIES 25%   **INSTITUTE OF HEALTH** 32%
SCIENCES 18%   **SOCIAL SCIENCES** 25%
BEST American Studies; Art History; Biological Sciences; Drama; Economics; Film Studies; Management; Maths; Philosophy; Physiotherapy; politics; Subjects allied to Medicine.

LIBRARIES

- **750,000** BOOKS ○ **1200** STUDY PLACES

Adequate opening hours and a *good range* of different materials.

COMPUTERS

- **2000** WORKSTATIONS ○ **24-HR ACCESS**

Lots of computers. All students are cleared out of the IT centre when the library closes and let back in with their swipe cards. *Which is odd.*

OTHER LEARNING FACILITIES

Most students can take part in an exchange year which counts towards their final degree.

ENTERTAINMENT ()))))))))))

THE CITY

- **PRICE OF A PINT OF BEER** £2.70
- **GLASS OF WINE** £3
- **CAN OF RED BULL** £2

Discounting holidays, a student could get drunk in a different pub every night of the year (and die of acute alcohol poisoning but that's by the by). Food and music aside, there's a pretty decent representation of fun in Norwich that should keep all but the most picky occupied.

CINEMAS Cinema City (currently being spruced up) is the place for independent flicks. There's also the arty Playhouse, as well as Vue, Hollywood and UCI multiplexes.

THEATRES The Theatre Royal is the largest (cap 2,000), providing mainstream fare, opera and Shakespeare. *The Norwich Playhouse is a bit more radical and Norwich Arts Centre yet more so.* Norwich Puppet Theatre is one of only three in the country dedicated to puppetry, *if that's your thing.*

PUBS Norwich has a massive amount of pubs, over 300 in all. The best are clustered in the Golden Triangle. Pushplugs: Garden House; Café Da (vodka bar); Mad Moose (rugger buggers). Best to avoid pubs on certain estates like West Earlham and Larkham.

CLUBBING A varied selection which has nurtured Norwich's hitherto lame nightlife. *Pushplugs: Mercy (cap 2,000); Liquid (Tuesday student night, free entry); Zoom (indie/garage); Marvel (hip hop/acid jazz) and Gas Station (soul/funk) at The Loft; Ikon (student nights); Mojo's Club (trip hop/drum 'n' bass); Optic; Time.*

MUSIC/COMEDY The Arts Centre (cap 350) offers an eclectic selection of music and even comedy, though the University is still *probably the best* venue in East Anglia. There's also a monthly Comedy Store night at the Forum.

EATING OUT The *worryingly titled 'Tombland' is a restaurant-heavy part of town that boasts a variety of eaterie ethnicities, often with student discounts. Pushplugs: Tree House (wholefood); Pedro's (Mexican); Unthank Kitchen (greasy spoon).*

UNIVERSITY

- **PRICE OF A PINT OF BEER** £1.70
- **GLASS OF WINE** £2.10
- **CAN OF RED BULL** £1.50

As the town is for pubs, UEA is for music. While most of its entertainments are decent, its music borders on the legendary. The arts centre is pretty stonking too.

BARS The Union Pub is the main watering hole,

offering pool tables and assorted drinky bargains. It's half non-smoking. The *pubby* Grad bar is aimed at the over-21 crowd.

THEATRES The UEA Drama Studio is the site of some fine work by dram and non-dram students alike, who've also taken shows to the Fringe. Touring companies like to stop by too.

FILM Two films a week in the 300 capacity cinema, ranging from blockbuster to arthouse and back again.

MUSIC VENUES Two Union venues, LCR (on campus) and Waterfront (in the city centre), are among East Anglia's biggest music venues and see a *huge variety* of top acts including, among many others: Supergrass, KT Tunstall, Blondie, Mylo. For more classical tastes the site for sound is the small concert hall (150).

CLUBBING LCR hosts plenty of student nights, with Tues and Sat leaving the least elbow room. Zane Lowe and Scott Mills have DJ'd.

COMEDY/CABARET Fortnightly in the Hive. Lee Mack, Richard Herring and Adam Bloom *have braved the giggle-hungry mobs.*

FOOD Campus has eight *face-stufferies*, from canteen fare in Zest to the *scrummy* Sportspark refectory. The Hive Coffee Bar in the Union is an *essential* daytime snack stop and Mango coffee shop *does good baguettes.*

OTHER The *incredible* Sainsbury Centre for Visual Arts on campus has a *very impressive* array of tribal, modern and other art. It was built for a collection owned by *the supermarket bloke* and has pieces by Francis Bacon, Henry Moore and Alberto Giacometti. There are also Latin parties, and balls every summer, Christmas and graduation.

SOCIAL ⊙⊙⊙⊙⊙⊙⊙⊙⊙⊙⊙⊙⊙

UNION OF UEA STUDENTS
⊙ **4 SABBATICALS** ⊙ **TURNOUT AT LAST BALLOT** 20%
⊙ **NUS MEMBER**

UEA is working on restoring its rep as a left-wing hotbed. Relations with the administration tend towards the Alaskan side. A portion of the student body are uninterested in politics, another part wave banners like they were surgically attached. Campaigns have included a boycott of Nestle, a huge Environment Week, and the ongoing gripe about the lack of a freshers' week. The Union has reps on every University committee and there's a course rep system to give student voices a bit of amplification.

SU FACILITIES
In Union House and elsewhere on campus: five bars; shop; newsagent; post office; travel shop; secondhand bookshop; Waterstones; games room; common room; print room; photocopying; advice; women's room; snack bar; vending machines; minibus hire; snooker tables; launderette; ticket agency; Barclays, HSBC and NatWest banks and ATMs.

CLUBS (NON SPORTING)
African students; Anarchist; Anime; Art Of Living (new age stuff); Art; Ballroom & Latin American Dancing; Buddhist; Capoeira; Cocktail; Cooking; Creative Writing; Deviant (rock); Duke of Edinburgh; East Asian; Folked; Football Supporters; French; Games (board games, roleplay, LARP); Hellenic; LINKS (St John's Ambulance); Japan; Juggling; Latin Dancing; Malaysian; Medsin; Mexican; Middle Eastern; Music; Nordic; Nightline; Politics; Pub Crawl; RAG; Revelation Rock Gospel Choir; Speak (social justice); STAR(Student action for refugees); Streetjazz; UEA Canaries (Norwich City FC supporters). **See also Clubs tables.**

OTHER ORGANISATIONS
Weekly newsletter ('the Rabbit'), and an independent fortnightly newspaper ('Concrete', winner of national awards) let the student body know what's going on. Livewire radio broadcasts upstairs in the Union pub, while Nexus TV screens downstairs. A volunteer co-ordinator helps students find work with voluntary organisations and *Rag throws together* theme nights.

RELIGIOUS
Non-denominational chaplaincy on campus and a worship room for Muslims. In the city there's a *splendid* Anglican cathedral and another for Catholics, as well as prayer areas for Jews, Muslims and Buddhists.

PAID WORK
⊙ **JOB BUREAU** ⊙ **PAID WORK** HOLS 80%

The jobshop is jointly run by the SU and the University. There's less unemployment in East Anglia than most of the country and apart from the usual bar work, students can get better paid jobs in local government and other areas.

SPORTS ⊙⊙⊙⊙⊙⊙⊙⊙⊙⊙⊙⊙⊙

⊙ **BUSA RANKING** 56

Stellar sports facilities of a size that stretches eyes as well as limbs. Athletic activity is a mass participation thing and the SU has a 'sports-for-all' policy, but some people are put off by the cliqueiness of the sports clubs.

SPORTS FACILITIES
Push gets tired just listing them all. Most facilities are on campus, including: sports hall; gym; badminton courts; multigym/gym; indoor football pitches; 50m swimming pool with moveable floor; baseball diamond; squash courts (charged); tennis courts; cricket nets; two artificial pitches; county athletic track; climbing wall; aerobics studio; martial arts room; rugby pitch; hockey pitches; sports injury clinic; coaching centre. On the edge of University Plain are 40 acres of playing fields; locally there are the Norfolk Broads for water sports and the city for swimming pool and golf course.

SPORTING CLUBS

10-Pin Bowling; American Football; Ballroom Dancing; Cheerleading; Frisbee; Kayak; Korfball; Lacrosse; Mountaineering; Rock Climbing; Rowing; Snooker; Table Tennis; Windsurfing; Yoga. **See also Clubs tables.**

ATTRACTIONS

A few miles from the University is the massive Norwich Sports Village – a multi-million squid sports centre. There's a dry ski slope at Trowse (4 miles away), an indoor kart club, snooker hall, 10-pin bowling and Quasar laser skirmishes to be had in the city. Norwich FC has Delia Smith on the board.

ACCOMMODATION ◑◑◑◑◑◑◑◑◑◑

IN UNIVERSITY
- **SELF-CATERING** 40% ◉ **COST:** £66 (38WKS)
- **1ST YRS LIVING IN** 80%
- **2ND YRS LIVING IN** 33%
- **FINALISTS LIVING IN** 21%
- **POSTGRADS LIVING IN** 10%
- **INSURANCE PREMIUM** £

AVAILABILITY *Plenty to go around* – first years who come from 12 miles or more away are guaranteed a place, disabled students get priority and non-EU students are guaranteed accommodation throughout their course. There's been *hefty* spending on accommodation, with lots of new blocks *up-and-renting* and more to come. Most rooms on campus are in mixed halls and are on the *small side, but facilities are box-fresh and kitchens are spacious.* Norfolk and Suffolk Terraces are Grade 2-listed buildings *but that doesn't mean their ziggurat design is aesthetically pleasing.* 24-hr security, emergency phones and CCTV on all campuses. All halls are self-catering.
CAR PARKING: For first years who have to travel and the disabled only.

EXTERNALLY
- **AVE RENT** £50

AVAILABILITY *It's not too hard to find rooms in Norwich.* The Golden Triangle is full of them – try Unthank, Earlham and Dereham Roads. *It's a bit of a yuppie ghetto but that's where the good pubs and the 24-hr shops are so, funnily enough, it's where the students go too. Avoid Larkham and West Earlham like they were really dodgy estates.*
HOUSING HELP Homerun's the SU's online housing bureau, which vets properties and offers advice. There's also the standard housing bureau, who do the same thing face-to-face.

WELFARE ◑◑◑◑◑◑◑◑◑◑◑

SERVICES
- **INTERNATIONAL STUDENTS' OFFICER & SOCIETY**
- **DISABILITIES SOCIETY** ◉ **WOMEN'S OFFICER & SOCIETY** ◉ **LGBT SOCIETY** ◉ **MATURE STUDENTS' SOCIETY**
- **POSTGRAD SOCIETY** ◉ **ETHNIC MINORITIES SOCIETY**
- **NIGHTLINE** ◉ **UNIVERSITY COUNSELLORS** 5 FULL/5 PART/3 TRAINING ◉ **SU COUNSELLORS** 5 FULL
- **CRIME RATING** !!!!

UEA's health and welfare services *are comprehensive*, there are *reasonable* considerations made for *pretty much anything happening short of alien experimentation* and the health centre even has a midwife.
HEALTH 24-hr health centre on campus with nurses, GP service, dentist and psychiatrist.
WOMEN Personal alarms and a women's group, and a delayed fare system in late-night taxis.
CRECHE Nursery on campus for 6wks to school-age kids.
DISABILITIES *Wheelchair access is pretty good, mainly because the campus is so flat, but there are also plenty of lifts, ramps and all that good stuff, as well as a special needs awareness society.* There's a dyslexia support society and HEFCE funding for students with dyslexia and hearing problems.

FINANCE
- **AVE DEBT PER YEAR** £2,601
- **HOME STUDENT FEES** £3,000

FEES Postgrads pay £3,085. International student fees: £8,700 (Arts & Social Sciences); £11,300 (Sciences); £17,100 (Medicine).
ACCESS FUND £306,755
SUCCESSFUL APPLICATIONS/YR 400
SUPPORT A veritable buffet of grants, bursaries and scholarships. Guidance also available from the advice centre in the SU.

Words in italics are Push's point of view – take it or leave it...

UNIVERSITY OF EAST LONDON

FORMERLY POLYTECHNIC OF EAST LONDON, NORTH EAST LONDON POLYTECHNIC.

1. ◉ **UNIVERSITY OF EAST LONDON** University Way, London, E16 2RD **TEL** (020) 8223 3000 **E-MAIL** admiss@uel.ac.uk **WEBSITE** www.uel.ac.uk ◉ **UNIVERSITY OF LONDON STUDENT'S UNION** University Way, London, E16 2RD, RM8 2AS **TEL** (020) 8223 2420 **WEBSITE** www.uelsu.net
2. ◉ **UNIVERSITY OF EAST LONDON, STRATFORD CAMPUS** Romford Road, London, E15 4LZ **UEL STUDENTS' UNION**, Romford Road, London, Stratford, E15 4LZ **TEL** (020) 8223 4209

E

GENERAL ◖◗◖◗◖◗◖◗◖◗◖◗◖◗◖◗

The University of East London (UEL) divides its time, its students and itself between two East London sites, four miles from each other, *sprawling from the reclaimed wasteland* that is the Docklands to the Stratford Campus to the north. Stratford (nothing to do with Shakespeare), five miles north-east of Trafalgar Square, has the main building, *a grand chunk of listed Victorian architecture that doesn't exactly fit the surroundings (imagine it in Albert Square).*The Docklands Campus *is made of strangely shaped, brightly coloured, not-quite-award-winning waterside buildings, which is all very modern, but a bit like the set of a TV programme for three year-olds.* For general information about London see University of London.

👫👫👫👫👫👫👫👫👫👫👫👫👫👫👫👫👫👫👫👫

SEX RATIO: ♂45 ♀55	**FOUNDED:** 1970
FULL-TIME U'GRADS: 8,980	**PART-TIME:** 3,052
POSTGRADS: 5,186	**NON-DEGREE:** 3,354
AVE COURSE: 3YRS	**ETHNIC:** 64%
STATE:PRIVATE SCHOOL: 96:4	**FLUNK RATE:** 26%
MATURE: 78%	**INTERNATIONAL:** 25%
DISABLED: 475	**LOCAL:** 80%

ATMOSPHERE
Go to UEL to quietly get on with the studious part of being a student. Despite being on the edge of London between its notorious East End and the more recently notorious Essex, crazy student antics (like gangster-baiting and drink-your-loan-dry days) just don't happen. This is gutting for some, but great for the high proportion of study-minded mature students. While facilities may be wanting, the interesting cultural cocktail – many students are local and/or from ethnic minority backgrounds – makes for a tolerant and friendly atmosphere in which to study (more than a platform for politics).

LONDON see University of London

THE EAST END, DOCKLANDS AND DAGENHAM
Stratford and the rest of London's East End are traditionally the home of London's dispossessed: first, Jews; nowadays Asians, yuppies and the occasional unfortunate but accurate stereotype (wearing a shellsuit, calling some bird a 'shlaaag'). The lively community atmosphere though is hard to find elsewhere. Petticoat Lane market may be a bit more gimmicky than it used to be, but Brick Lane *is an overdose for the shopaholic, even late at night.* The 2012 Olympic juggernaut *is thundering towards Stratford with a cargo of cash* for better transport links and regeneration of the area.

Docklands is a strangely soulless mix of warehouses converted into loft apartments for rich city brokers, Barratt homes, business parks, out-of-town shopping centres, dual carriageways and the Thames Barrier. Floating above are the small trains of the Docklands Light Railway monorail and the small planes landing at London City Airport.

TRAVEL see University of London
BUSES There are a few buses running between sites, but it requires lots of changing and waiting. Plenty of services run into central London (particularly the City) and back.
TRAINS For Stratford the nearest rail stations are Startford and Maryland (ten mins from London Liverpool Street). The Docklands Light Railway Cyprus Station is right at the entrance of the Docklands Campus.
CAR *It's London, so expect traffic trickiness. Parking can cause friction with the locals.*
AIR London City Airport is so near the Docklands Campus, *students almost have to duck and although it's mostly business flyers, there are occasional budget deals.*
HITCHING *Usually impossible inside London, hitchers have to get to the outskirts and, as a rule of thumb, Essex is a no-go. However, some of the dual carriageways around the Docklands campus (such as the A13) might be worth a try.*
UNDERGROUND Stratford is on the Central Line; Barking (District and Hammersmith & City during peak times) and Plaistow are good for some buildings.
UNIVERSITY Regular minibuses pottle between campuses.
BICYCLES *If black nostrils cause no concern, biking is the cheap option for students, until their bike gets nicked. Some decent bike lanes and green routes around the area.*

CAREER PROSPECTS:
◉ **CAREERS SERVICE** ◉ **NO. OF STAFF** 3 FULL/4 PART
◉ **UNEMPLOYED AFTER 6MTHS** 6%
Lots of potentially useful vocational courses and a standard job shop for part-time term-time work.

Words in italics are Push's point of view – take it or leave it...

FAMOUS ALUMNI
Jake Chapman (Young British Artist™ and Chapman Brother); Daljit Dhaliwal (TV presenter); Ian MacAlister (Chair of Network Rail); Terence Stamp (actor); Lord Trotman (Chair of ICI); Sam Taylor-Wood (artist). Honorary degrees for Trevor Brooking, Billy Bragg and Terence Stamp.

FURTHER INFO
○ **PROSPECTUSES** UNDERGRAD; POSTGRAD
○ **OPEN DAYS**

ACADEMIC ⓊⓊⓊⓊⓊⓊⓊⓊⓊⓊⓊⓊⓊ

Heavy emphasis on vocational studies, particularly when it comes to psychology, teaching and law. New academic buildings, labs and lecture theatres are *popping up* as part of the expansion programme. The PGCE course has been highly rated by the education watchdog, OFSTED. A choice of start dates (February or the traditional September) is becoming more common.

ENTRY POINTS: 120-300		**AVE POINTS: 210**	
APPLICATIONS PER PLACE: 4		**CLEARING: 46%**	
NO. OF TERMS: 2		**LENGTH OF TERMS: 15wks**	
STAFF TO STUDENT RATIO: 1:29		**STUDY ADDICTS: N/A**	
TEACHING: ✱		**RESEARCH:** ✱	
YEAR ABROAD: 0%		**SANDWICH STUDENTS: 5%**	
1STS: 6%		**2.2S: 45%**	
2.1S: 36%		**3RDS: 13%**	

ADMISSIONS
○ **APPLY VIA UCAS**
Mature students who don't have typical entry requirements are encouraged to apply and normally get an interview. They're told about short courses to help them qualify and the mature student advisors can give further advice.

SUBJECTS
ARCHITECTURE 7%   **ART & DESIGN** 10%
ARTS/HUMANITIES 15%   **BUSINESS MANAGEMENT** 15%
COMPUTING AND TECHNOLOGY 12%   **EDUCATION** 8%
LAW 8%   **PSYCHOLOGY** 7%   **SCIENCES** 12%
SOCIAL SCIENCES 8%
BEST Architecture; Art & Design; Civil Engineering; Politics; Psychology.
UNUSUAL Complimentary Therapy; Computer Games & Interactive Entertainment; Digital Journalism; Forensic Science.

LIBRARIES
○ **297,056 BOOKS** ○ **24-HR ACCESS**
Three libraries, all with 24-hr access Mon–Thurs in term.

COMPUTERS
○ **1000 WORKSTATIONS**
Computers are spread across the campuses, *but with terminals shared between thousands of students who work instead of getting sozzled, expect difficulties.*

ENTERTAINMENT ⓊⓊⓊⓊⓊⓊⓊⓊⓊ

THE CITY see University of London

EAST LONDON
○ **PRICE OF A PINT OF BEER** £1.90
○ **GLASS OF WINE** £2 ○ **CAN OF RED BULL** £1.80
Apart from the occasional Spearmint Rhino strip joint, The Docklands are a bit of an entertainments abyss. Stratford's a lot more lively.
CINEMAS Multiplexes at Romford and Gant's Hill, Ilford (ten screens in all), a four-screener at Stratford and Warner Bros in Dagenham who sponsor the student mag and do freebies.
THEATRES The Theatre Royal Stratford East do shows that transfer to the West End where they're more expensive, so *use your noggin.* Stratford Circus Arts Centre *has a bit of everything, from theatre to music to poetry to club nights.*
PUBS *Many a cheerful boozer keeps the East Enders warm at night and TV/film clichés are made up from little bits of all of them. Common sense suggests avoiding the dodgy gaffs (people flying through windows: bad. Happy, unbloodied clientele: good). Most places are cheaper but less varied than central London. Pushplugs: The Spotted Dog; The Golden Grove; King Edward; Princess Alice; The Pigeons.*
CLUBBING *East End clubs; nature's way of culling the student population. Go to London, Benjies on Mile End Road (indie nights); The Rex; The Pigeons Club (complements SU events) and Fabric (trendy, has beds).*
EATING OUT The diversity of food stops matches the diversity of people and *the best stuff is on the ethnic end of the foodometer. Try: Sombrero Steak House (Ilford); Raj (Barking); Galleria (Barking good veggie option).*

UNIVERSITY
○ **PRICE OF A PINT OF BEER** £1.80
○ **GLASS OF WINE** £1.80
○ **CAN OF RED BULL** £1.60
BARS Each campus has its own bars (Duel 1, 2 and 3), *with Docklands being the most studenty, Barking the most ents-based and Stratford the most popular. The student bars are an alternative to the not-always pukka local options.* Happy hours are from 5-7pm every weekday.
CLUBBING/MUSIC Regular nights at Stratford and Barking, including 'Back to the Old School', 'Fusion' and the *more worrying* 'Abomination'. Bands are rare but do happen.
COMEDY/CABARET A regular comedy night called 'Mirth Control'.
FOOD Eight *budget-friendly* cafeterias exist across the three campuses, *varying from swish to friendly to bog standard at best. No shortage, but not much excitement. The £1.75 fry-ups are about as good as it greasily gets.*

E

Words in italics are Push's point of view — take it or leave it...

OTHER Two main balls a year, for freshers and in summer.

SOCIAL

UNIVERSITY OF EAST LONDON STUDENTS' UNION
○ **6 SABBATICALS** ○ **NUS MEMBER**
Unlike many other unis these days, UEL still has a fiery streak reminiscent of the golden age of student radicalism and the Union has overtly political ambitions. Even the graffiti is political ('Did Blair pay tuition fees? No! Do you pay tuition fees? Yes!'). Hot on race and welfare issues.

SU FACILITIES
Collectively, the sites offer: two bars; two cafeterias; four coffee bars; four pool tables; meeting rooms; a minibus; insurance; Barclays and Natwest banks and ATMs; photocopier/fax/printing; photo booth; payphones; advice; a crèche; women's room; juke box; bookshops; launderette; games machines; vending machines; stationers; internet café.

CLUBS (NON SPORTING)
Advertising; African Law; Architecture Rocks; Anthropological Film; Barking Bateria (samba); Computer Games; Capoeira; Dandelion n Burdock; Entrepreneurship; Fashion; Fine Art; Fairy Tales; Gnarly Grinders (skateboarding); Graphic Design; High Sensation (organises hip hop & dance nights); Hindu; Hip-hop; Historical/Cultural; Intercultural; International Development; Kegites (Nigerian culture); Live Innovative Performance (LIPS); Megalithic Art Appreciation (MAAS); Malaysian; Neo-Radical Anthropological Forum (NRAF); PD2006 (social group based around a passion for product design); Pub Crawl; Pattern Cutting; RESPECT; Samba; Sikh & Punjabi; Snow White n Unit 7; Sub Zero (music); Unicef on campus; Urban Sweetz (music & dance); Verbal Warnin (MCs); World Issues; World Music. **See also Clubs tables.**

OTHER ORGANISATIONS
'Refuel', the student paper, focuses on local and global issues. The student radio station (Cr:uel) broadcasts over the net only.

RELIGIOUS
○ **1 CHAPLAINS (COFE)**
Muslim prayer room availible in the T Block at Barking, Catholic church literally next door and most religions are catered for in the area.

PAID WORK see University of London
○ **JOB BUREAU**
Limited work to be had in the various bars and cafés, but the Job Shop helps students to scour locally. Workbank helps students find work, the Enterprise Zone helps 'em develop skills and *CV-bigging-up prowess.*

SPORTS

○ **RECENT SUCCESSES** RUGBY
The sporting spirit is decidedly diluted and facilities are limited, although the latter could get a kick up the ass of Olympic proportions. UEL is a partner of the London Olympic Institute and it's possible a new aquatic centre will become a University facility – watch this space.

SPORTS FACILITIES
Four tennis courts; fitness suite; squash courts; sports hall; swimming pool; two gyms; sauna/steam room; sunbeds.

ATTRACTIONS see University of London
Newham Sports Centre is well-stocked. Nearby is a dry ski slope, athletics track and amenities for most sports. With London set to host the 2012 Olympics, *the best is yet to come. An Olympic stadium will turn up on UEL's doorstep as part of a flurry of regeneration.* West Ham (say 'Wess Tam' to blend in) is the local footie side. Leyton Orient and Charlton Athletic are close by too.

ACCOMMODATION

IN UNIVERSITY
○ **SELF-CATERED** 10% ○ **COST** £81 (30WKS)
○ **INSURANCE PREMIUM** £
AVAILABILITY 900 self-catering single rooms spread across the Barking and Docklands campuses. Plans to build halls at Stratford have been delayed until 2010. Even *with so many local and mature students, demand for places is high* and priority is given to first years, disabled students and those from abroad. Four halls (currently under construction) will shoot the number of beds at Docklands up to 1,250 (from 380).
CAR PARKING: *Quite a distance from London's parking purgatory, so not too bad,* but a permit is needed.

EXTERNALLY see University of London
○ **AVERAGE RENT** £80
AVAILABILITY Most mature students have their homes already sorted. *East London is cheaper than many other parts of the capital. It's possible to live quite far out and still be on the doorstep. Students don't even try to live in the Canary Wharf area unless they're rich enough to clean their teeth with caviar.* Stratford is a likely local as are Leyton, Beckton, Goodmayes, Ilford, Dagenham, Forest Gate and East Ham. Also Leytonstone and Walthamstow, *but they're a bit of a trek.* It depends which campus students are based at.

HOUSING HELP The three accommodation offices employ six full- and three part-time staff.

WELFARE

SERVICES
- **LGBT SOCIETY** ○ **ETHNIC MINORITIES OFFICER**
- **WOMEN'S OFFICER** ○ **MATURE STUDENTS' OFFICER**
- **INTERNATIONAL STUDENTS' OFFICER**
- **DISABILITIES OFFICER** ○ **SELF-DEFENCE CLASSES**
- **NIGHTLINE** ○ **UNIVERSITY COUNSELLORS** 5 FULL
- **CRIME RATING** !!!!

Advice on a variety of issues comes from the Union's Advice and Info Service and the sabbatical officers are *keen* to help with personal and academic problems. Immigration advice is available for international students.

HEALTH Medical centres on two sites are staffed by nurses.

WOMEN & ETHNIC MINORITIES UEL has a *crusading* equal opportunities policy, reflected in the high proportion of students from ethnic minorities, *which is particularly important given local social and racial tensions.* The Black Mentor Scheme pairs up black students with successful black mentors in their chosen field.

CRECHES/NURSERY Barking Campus has a daytime nursery for children *that don't poo everywhere when the staff's backs are turned.*

DISABILITIES Newer buildings, like Docklands, are designed with disabled access in mind. Meanwhile, there are also a disabilities advisor, Arkenstone readers for the sight-impaired in the main library, a Minicom for the hearing-impaired, specialist tutors and workshops for dyslexia sufferers on all campuses.

FINANCE
- **AVE DEBT PER YEAR** £2,313
- **HOME STUDENT FEES** £3000
- **ACCESS FUND** £300,000
- **SUCCESSFUL APPLICATIONS/YR** 1,000

SUPPORT Loans of up to £500 and payments of £700 to £1,500 are available in cases of hardship, as are 200 £1,000 scholarships for achievements in one of four fields: Academic, Citizenship, Cultural and Sport. Students who progress from their first semester into their second get £500 just for staying around, and those who get the full maintenance grant get another £300.

 ECONOMICS
see LSE

UNIVERSITY OF EDINBURGH

○ **UNIVERSITY OF EDINBURGH**, Old College, South Bridge, Edinburgh, EH8 9YL **TEL** (0131) 650 1000
E-MAIL communications.office@ed.ac.uk **WEBSITE** www.ed.ac.uk
○ **EDINBURGH UNIVERSITY STUDENTS' ASSOCIATION**, EUSA, The Potterrrow, 5/2 Bristo Square, Edinburgh, EH8 9AL
TEL (0131) 650 2656 **E-MAIL** enquiry@eusa.ed.ac.uk **WEBSITE** www.eusa.ed.ac.uk

GENERAL

Scotland's capital, Edinburgh, sits on the Firth of Forth on the east coast. *Anyone who's read any Irvine Welsh might think they've a fairly good idea what to expect: scag, hoorin', fitba and so on. Then there's the festival clichés: a lot of arty types descend for a month and block the streets with performance art and mime shows.* The reality is *somewhere between the two, although Push reckons there's more chance of bumping into a juggling unicyclist on the Royal Mile than Franco Begbie down Easter Road.* Like most cities there are some *darker* streets, but student life mainly revolves around *gorgeous, historic buildings and beautifully planned gardens.* There are four universities in town: Napier, Heriot-Watt, Queen Margaret College and the University of Edinburgh itself, which is the sixth oldest in Britain. The three main sites are at George Square/Old College (city centre), King's Buildings (science and engineering campus, two miles south) and the residential Pollock Halls site (east, near Holyrood Park). Even the more modern buildings are *attractive,* built in local stone *with concern for the city's beauty.*

> ◎ **Edinburgh's Teviot Row House is the oldest custom-built Student's Union in the world.**

Words in italics are Push's point of view — take it or leave it...

SEX RATIO: ♀44 ♂56	FOUNDED: 1582
FULL-TIME U'GRADS: 15, 095	PART-TIME: 1,055
POSTGRADS: 3,275	NON-DEGREE: N/A
AVE COURSE: 4YRS	ETHNIC: N/A
STATE:PRIVATE SCHOOL: N/A	FLUNK RATE: 6%
MATURE: 13%	INTERNATIONAL: 18%
DISABLED: 420	LOCAL: 50%

ATMOSPHERE

With 50,000 students at the four universities *there's a large and visible presence in the city and just as the buildings are integrated throughout the city, so are the students.* Edinburgh's *arguably more anglicised* than Glasgow (there's a 40% Sassenach population). *Relations with the locals are good, bars and books are hit with equal vigour and the city has a lively feel about it. The University attracts a sizeable contingent of 'Yahs' – plummy-voiced public school types who have slightly more time for their non-yah counterparts than the old feudal barons had for the peasant classes, but only just.*

EDINBURGH

- **POPULATION** 435,430 ⊙ **CITY CENTRE** 1.5 MILES
- **LONDON** 391 MILES ⊙ **GLASGOW** 44 MILES
- **NEWCASTLE** 93 MILES
- **HIGH TEMP** 18 ⊙ **LOW TEMP** 1 ⊙ **RAINFALL** 53

Edinburgh's built on seven hills, with mini-mountain (and recently active volcano) Arthur's Seat topped by the castle in the middle. The architecture *reflects some rich history*, with a medieval city centre and the New Town to the north. There are three main streets running parallel: Queen Street, George Street and Princes Street. The Royal Mile, a series of small interlinked streets, runs through the centre of town. It's a *major* stop on the tourist track: Holyrood Palace, the Museum of Scotland, the National Gallery, the castle and much more. The nightlife is *famous, particularly for late licensing.* Of course there are rougher areas, *but staying safe isn't a huge problem.*

TRAVEL

TRAINS Edinburgh Waverley Station is the most central with a direct line to Glasgow (from £7.70 return) and London (£62.10). Connections to Birmingham and Bristol.
COACHES National Express, Stagecoach and Citylink services to London (£36), Glasgow (£8.90) and others.
CAR The M8 and M9 connect with the A8 to the west. There are also the A1, A7, A68, A70, A71, A702, A703 and A90. Coming into Edinburgh through Biggar can be *a bit of a slow process, but at least the scenery is spectacular.*
AIR Edinburgh (Turnhouse) Airport, 5.5 miles west of the city centre, has a range of international and internal flights (from £69 return to London).
HITCHING *The A1 is good for getting into the city, but not so hot for getting out. The M8 and M9 are good for Glasgow and Perth.*
LOCAL Bus services are good all round the city and

quite cheap (from 50p). A frequent night bus runs all over the town.
TAXIS £3 across town. *A happy luxury.*
BICYCLES *Useful, but remember those hills. And bikes that aren't chained down get ghosted off.*

CAREER PROSPECTS

- **CAREERS SERVICE** ⊙ **NO. OF STAFF** 23 FULL/9 PART
- **UNEMPLOYED AFTER 6MTHS** 8%

A pretty comprehensive service: careers consultations; information centres; skills development workshops; online vacancies. See www.careers.ed.ac.uk.

FAMOUS ALUMNI

James Barrie, Arthur Conan Doyle, Walter Scott, Robert Louis Stevenson (authors); Dr Barry (world's first qualified woman doctor – she impersonated a man to study and practise); David Brewster (invented the kaleidoscope); Gordon Brown MP, the late Robin Cook MP (Lab); Thomas Carlyle (historian/philosopher); Charles Darwin (revolutionary evolutionary); David Hume (philosopher); Eric Liddell (Chariots of Fire runner) and Ian Charleson, who played him; Lord Mackay of Clashfern; Julius Nyerere (ex-President, Tanzania); Malcolm Rifkind (Con, ex-minister, ex-MP); Peter Roget (of Thesaurus fame); Kirsty Wark (TV presenter, Newsnight); James Watt (engineer/inventor).

SPECIAL FEATURES

Rectors are elected every three years by students. Previous post holders have included Magnus Magnusson, Winston Churchill, Muriel Gray, Donnie Munro (of Runrig), Sir David Steel and James Robertson Justice.

FURTHER INFO

- **PROSPECTUSES** UNDERGRAD; POSTGRAD; ALTERNATIVE
- **OPEN DAYS**

EUSA produces an alternative prospectus and an essential guide to househunting etc. See the websites for more info.

ACADEMIC ○○○○○○○○○○○○○

⊙ **RUSSELL GROUP**
Scotland's leading research university, with a *top-flight reputation* across a wide range of subjects. Some four-year degrees have the option to pursue several different options during the course and arts courses are *elastically flexible*, with no need to hone it down to just one subject until the final year. *Heavy emphasis* is placed on personal study and self-motivation.

ENTRY POINTS: 120–290	AVE POINTS: 240
APPLICATIONS PER PLACE: N A	CLEARING: 5%
NO. OF TERMS: 2	LENGTH OF TERMS: 11wks
STAFF TO STUDENT RATIO: 1:17	STUDY ADDICTS: 21%
TEACHING: ✶✶✶	RESEARCH: ✶✶✶✶✶
YEAR ABROAD: <1%	SANDWICH STUDENTS: 1%

Words in italics are Push's point of view – take it or leave it...

ADMISSIONS
- **APPLY VIA UCAS**

SUBJECTS
BEST Accounting; Cellular & Molecular Biology; Chemistry; Computer Studies; Electrical & Electronic Engineering; European Languages; Finance; Geology; History; Maths; Organismal Biology; Physics; Social Policy; Social Work; Sociology; Statistics; Veterinary Medicine; Body fullout para style. Body fullout para style.

LIBRARIES
- **2,700,000 BOOKS** **3,500 STUDY PLACES**

There's an enormous Main Library and six other more specialised ones (Divinity; Law; the Europa Institute; Medicine; Music; Science & Veterinary Medicine).

COMPUTERS
- **1,500 WORKSTATIONS**

ENTERTAINMENT ❍❍❍❍❍❍❍❍❍

THE CITY
- **PRICE OF A PINT OF BEER** £2.50
- **GLASS OF WINE** £2.30
- **CAN OF RED BULL** £2

Edinburgh is a *party city* all year round, but it *really kicks off* in August when the festivals come to town. The Edinburgh Festival is the world's biggest arts bash, and the fringe (hundreds of student and low-budget shows) turns *almost any space imaginable* into a theatre. At the same time there are film, dance, jazz, TV and book festivals *and a lot of drinking and shagging goes on, too.* Of course, this is outside term time, *but it would be bordering on the criminal not to make the most of the time at Edinburgh to get involved.*
CINEMAS Eight cinemas with more than 40 screens between them.
THEATRES 13 theatres, but of course the festivals bump this up to the hundreds. *Things are arty all year round.* The *grandest* theatres are the Festival Theatre (*what else?*), The Royal Lyceum, King's Theatre and the *cutting-edge* Traverse.
PUBS Most don't chuck out till 1am *and it's a good idea to get a taste for Scotch.* Try the Grassmarket area for the best boozers. *Why Not? is the 'yah' bar (which probably answers the question) while the Junction is cheap but gritty.* Pushplugs: Bar Salsa (cheap); Brass Monkey (loungey backroom with cushions on the floor); the Auld Hoose (food and darts).
CLUBBING *A decent, if not quite legendary clubbing scene.* Pushplugs: Liquid Room (pricey drinks but plenty of students); Ego, Establishment or Subway *for chemically-enhanced dancemoves; I Fly Spitfires at Cabaret Voltaire for indie.*
MUSIC VENUES Pubs and clubs are hot for live music, but there is a *glut* of other venues *all scraping by.* Pushplugs: Usher Hall (classical, including the Scottish National Opera); Queen's Hall (indie and more); Playhouse (AOR); The Venue (indie); Rocking Horse (metal mayhem).
EATING OUT *Edinburgh eateries are among the best in Scotland. As such, they're among the most fearsomely expensive too. Them's the breaks.* Pushplugs the Mosque (dirt cheap curry); Monster Mash (spoilt for bangers and mash choice); Palmera Pizza.
OTHER *Lots for tourists, who come to see kilts, bagpipes and funny hats.* There's cabaret *everywhere* and the Tattoo, a military parade at the castle. The City Art Centre has six exhibition spaces and free admission.

UNIVERSITY
- **PRICE OF A PINT OF BEER** £1.50
- **GLASS OF WINE** £1.95

With the University so spread out, there are *plenty of options for the footloose reveller.*
BARS Dotted across the main sites. The main ones are the Teviot Row House, with five bars, and a 400 capacity club, the Potterow union bars and the Pleasance bar, *which is rather pubby.*
THEATRES The drama scene is, *unsurprisingly, very strong.* The Bedlam Theatre Company runs its very own theatre.
FILM The Film Society has scooped the Best Student Film Society award recently. *Not quite an Oscar, but good going nonetheless.* Films are screened throughout the week. Members can buy a £15 pass to see more than 60 films a year.
MUSIC VENUES The Union at Potterow features *popular* acts like Mylo, Har Mar Superstar and Belle & Sebastian. It also features *godawful abominations* of the airwaves like the Cheeky Girls and Natasha Hamilton. *Shame.*
CLUBBING Pleasuredome (dance) is the *big night*, but indie, funk, soul and cheese are all catered for. The Big Cheese lures the masses to the Potterow for a *huge* Saturday night bash.
COMEDY/CABARET The Pleasance is a *major stop* on the comedy circuit, featuring names like Dave Gorman, Miles Jupp and Andy Zaltzman.
FOOD 13 EUSA outlets *feed the famished* until 10pm.
OTHER Balls throughout the year. The *glittering night* of the social calendar is the Societies Oscars in February.

SOCIAL ❍❍❍❍❍❍❍❍❍❍❍❍

EDINBURGH UNIVERSITY STUDENTS' UNION ASSOCIATION
- **4 SABBATICALS** **TURNOUT AT LAST BALLOT** 13%

Edinburgh has just boarded the decks of the big ship NUS after 30 years rowing along in their own dinghy of independence. Nevertheless, student representation at the University is *brain-achingly complicated* – EUSA is an umbrella for the SRC (Student Representative Council) which does political and representative work, and The Union which provides student services. There's also an Advice Place for welfare needs. There's a strong sense of community and plenty of student societies to get het up about the issues of the day.

SU FACILITIES

TEVIOT ROW five bars; jukeboxes; snack bar; two cafeterias; restaurant; games room; music room; satellite TV..

KING'S BUILDINGS HOUSE sports facilities; mature, international and postgrad students' lounge; welfare advice; shop; bar; the University's largest catering outlet.

POTTERROW 1,200-capacity nightclub and music venue; games room; eateries. A popular lunchtime meeting place and has the biggest and busiest EUSA shop.

THE PLEASANCE bar; Societies Centre; catering; technical equipment hire; theatre (cap 270); meeting/function rooms.

ALSO print service; five shops; crèche; NatWest, Halifax and Royal Bank of Scotland cashpoints; library; photo booths; pool tables; games and vending machines; travel agency; TV lounges; meeting rooms; launderettes.

CLUBS (NON SPORTING)

Aberdeen FC Supporters; Action (social work); African & Arabic Dance Society; Agricultural; AIESEC; Air Squadron; All Tomorrow's Parties (Save the Children); Anime & Animation; Art; Asian Dharma (Buddhist); Baha'i; BBQ; Beatles Appreciation; Benelux; Boycott Coca-Cola; Bridge Club; Capoeira; Celtic Supporters; Chamber Choir; Chess; Children's Holiday Venture; Chill-out; Chinese (x3); ChocSoc; Christian Action & Thought; Contact Improvisation Dance; Creative Writing; Cuddle Club (charity); Diagnostic (debate); Ditch the Duke (want Prince Philip to resign as Chancellor); Drumming; Duke of Edinburgh; Edinburgh Alpha for Students; Edinburgh Global Partnerships; Edinburgh Television Production; Electronic Music Society; Escogriffes; Ethical Economics; Exposure Magazine; Fair Trade Café; Flamenco; Folk Song Society; Football Supporters; Frequently Asked Questions (collectible and non-collectible card and board games); GEAS (roleplay); Guild of Changeringers; Harry Potter; Hellenic; Highland; iCUE (buisness consultancy); Intercourse; Japanese; Juggling; Korean; Lutheran; Macintosh

Users; Malaysian; Marchmont Street Party; Marrow; Mediterranean Gastronomic; Mexicanos En Edimburgo; Model United Nations; Mooting (legal debate); Neighbours Appreciation; Nightline; Oddsoc (Scandinavian); Offbeat 25 (arranging arts events); Omani; Pagan; Paintball; Palestine Solidarity; Para Los Ninos (charity); PC Gamers; Perfidious Albian (medieval re-enactment); Persian; Poker; Pollock Chinese Christian Fellowship; Portuguese & Brazilian; Pub; Red Cross; Reeling (Scottish dancing); Renaissance Singers; Revelation Rock Gospel Choir; Rhubarb [satire newspaper]; Savoy Opera Group; Scottish Romanian Language Link (SCROLL); Sign ; Singapore; Singers (EU); SIS: Skills; Standing Ovation (theatre trips); Stop Aids; Student Action for Refugees (STAR); Students Against NUS at Edinburgh; Studio Opera; Swahili; Swing Dance; Tai Chi Chuan; Taiwanese Society; Tandem (pairs British and International students); Tango; Tennet's Lager Appreciation; Tenteleni (charity); Teviot Library Appreciation; The Inside Line; Tibet; Trading & Investment; United World Colleges; Untapped Talent (music performance); Wargames; Water of Life (whisky); Wine; Women of the World; Yoga; Young Federal Union. **See also** Clubs tables.

OTHER ORGANISATIONS

'Student' is a weekly independent paper, 'Hype' is the fortnightly EUSA rag. Other publications include 'Nomad' (travel) and 'Piffle' magazine. 'Fresh Air' broadcasts over the net and in the Union. ESCA's the Rag organisation and SCAG helps out in the community, as does Settlement. The Debates Committee *is more like the Unions of Oxford and Cambridge than a run-of-the-mill debating club.*

RELIGIOUS

◐ 1 CHAPLAIN (ANGLICAN)
Local places of worship include all sorts of churches as well as places for Sikhs and Jews.

PAID WORK

◐ JOB BUREAU ◐ PAID WORK TERM-TIME 40%; HOLS 80%
Loads of opportunities to work in the thriving city centre, especially showing tourists round in the summer. The University/Union-run Student Employment Service helps out with adverts for part-time and vacation work.

◉ **When elected at the tender age of 21, Gordon Brown became the youngest ever rector of Edinburgh University (and Chairman of the University Court), a post that he held from 1972-1975.**

Words in italics are Push's point of view — take it or leave it...

SPORTS () () () () () () () () () () () () () ()

◎ BUSA RANKING 9
Students *are far from duffers* on the field (the attractions of the city *help prise back the blinkers a little*) *but there isn't the same sporting fever as at some other universities* (think Birmingham, Loughborough). Students get automatic membership of the sports Union (free) and annual membership of the Pleasance sports centre costs £72.

SPORTS FACILITIES
Outdoor facilities at Peffermill Sports Ground (including 25 acres of playing fields and three clay tennis courts); playing fields with a floodlit synthetic grass pitch; tennis courts; golfing facilities. At the Uni Sports Centre (ten mins from Pollock Halls) there's a sports hall, a small hall, fitness room, ten squash courts, table tennis studios, a combat salle, a rifle and archery range. At the Firbush Point Field Centre 80 miles from Edinburgh: sailing, canoeing, skiing and hills to walk. The city has many golf courses, a large swimming pool, ice rink and the Meadowbank Stadium. Half the city is made of parks and open spaces (including Queen's Park and Arthur's Seat).

SPORTING CLUBS
Athletics; Badminton; Basketball; Boat; Boxing; Curling; Exmoor Pony Trekking; Gliding; Hare & Hounds; Hillwalking; Hot Air Balloon; Ice Hockey; Judo; Ju-Jitsu; Kendo; Korfball; Lacrosse; Motorsport; Mountaineering; Netball; Orienteering; Riding; Rifle; Roller Hockey; Shinty; Skydiving; Table Tennis; Triathlon; Ultimate Frisbee; Weightlifting; Windsurfing & Surfing. **See also Clubs tables.**

ATTRACTIONS
Hibs and Hearts divide the city across similar partisan lines as Celtic and Rangers in Glasgow. But the teams are *nowhere near as wealthy, entertaining or high profile and there's a lot less of the sectarian sentiment about their supporters.* Murrayfield is the home of the *currently woeful* Scottish rugby team. Edinburgh, the club rugby side, are a *bit more* successful. There's also athletics at Meadowbank.

ACCOMMODATION () () () () () () () () () ()

IN UNIVERSITY
◎ CATERED 13% **◎ COST** £116 (33WKS)
◎ SELF-CATERED 18% **◎ COST** £69 (38/52WKS)
◎ 1ST YRS LIVING IN 100%
◎ POSTGRADS LIVING IN 15%
◎ INSURANCE PREMIUM £
AVAILABILITY All first years who want to live in can,

although a *minority* have to share. There are mixed and single-sex flats, some fitted out for wheelchair access. The standard is *pretty good* and all halls are within ten mins *trot* of the main campus. About a quarter of rooms have en suite facilities. Kitchens are basic (microwave, kettle, toaster, fridge) and they, along with other communal areas, *are kept from festering* by University cleaners. Pollock Halls are the *yah lair – pashminas and pearls abound.*
CAR PARKING Okay in halls, although a pass is needed (free for disabled students, then £50-80 depending on location). But it's a *horrorshow* trying to park on campus.

EXTERNALLY
◎ AVERAGE RENT £65 **◎ LIVING AT HOME** 16%
AVAILABILITY Accommodation is easy to find, as long as you avoid August (festivals) and September (last-minute panics). *Enterprising students with an eye for a quick buck rent a flat at the beginning of the summer and sub-let it at an extortionate price to visiting thesps with a budget to blow; less lucky students are turfed out unceremoniously so their landlord can do the same. The best areas are Marchmont, Bruntsfield and Newington: studenty, quite central and homely. Avoid Niddrie, Pilton and Wester Hailes.*
HOUSING HELP The Accommodation Service helps out with registered landlords, property vetting, a bulletin board, contract approval and legal advice. The University acts as a lettings agency, *so many livers-out are really living in. Sort of.*

WELFARE () () () () () () () () () () () ()

SERVICES
◎ LESBIAN/GAY/BISEXUAL SOCIETY
◎ EQUAL OPPORTUNITIES OFFICER ◎ WOMEN'S SOCIETY ◎ INTERNATIONAL STUDENTS' SOCIETY
◎ POSTGRAD OFFICER ◎ DISABILITIES OFFICER & SOCIETY ◎ NIGHTLINE (6PM-8AM) ◎ UNIVERSITY COUNSELLORS 1FULL/15 PART **◎ CRIME RATING** !!
EUSA's Advice Place is responsible for welfare and acts as a drop-in centre for all sorts of problems.
HEALTH The Student Health Centre has six doctors as well as nurses, a psychologist, physiotherapist, pharmacist and family planning unit.
CRECHES/NURSERY 39 places for kids 5wks-6yrs.
DISABILITIES *Access isn't great,* thanks to the University's age and locations. But the disability office and Special Needs Committee *do their best* to be accommodating, even up to making building improvements, if given early notice. There's also a dyslexia advisor available to help.

E

FINANCE
- **AVE DEBT PER YEAR** £2,884
- **HOME STUDENT FEES** £1,700
FEES: Non-Scottish students are looking at the full £3K *wallop.*
- **ACCESS FUND** £742,308

- **SUCCESSFUL APPLICATIONS/YR:** 750
- **AVE PAYMENT** £300-2,000
SUPPORT 100 bursaries for undergrads in financial trouble. Also postgrad scholarships available to Chinese, Canadian, Indian and American students.

▶ EDINBURGH BUSINESS SCHOOL
see Heriot-Watt University

▶ EPSOM
see *Creative Arts University College*

UNIVERSITY OF ESSEX

1. ● **UNIVERSITY OF ESSEX** Wivenhoe Park, Colchester, Essex, CO4 3SQ **TEL** (01206) 873333 **E-MAIL** admit@essex.ac.uk **WEBSITE** www.essex.ac.uk ● **UNIVERSITY OF ESSEX STUDENTS' UNION** Wivenhoe Park, Colchester, Essex, CO4 3SQ **TEL** (01206) 863211 **E-MAIL** su@essex.ac.uk website: www.essexstudent.com
2. ● **EAST 15 ACTING SCHOOL** Hatfields, Rectory Lane, Loughton, Essex, IG10 3RY **TEL** (020) 8508 5983 **WEBSITE** www.east15.ac.uk
3. ● **UNIVERSITY OF ESSEX SOUTHEND** Princess Caroline House, 1 High Street, Southend-on-Sea, Essex, SS1 1JE **TEL** (01702) 339 888 **WEBSITE** www.essex.ac.uk/southend

GENERAL ◗◗◗◗◗◗◗◗◗◗◗◗◗

Forget the Essex Girl jokes – the University isn't in the famously maligned part of Essex *that's full of parked Ford Capris and peroxide blondes.* It's 2.5 miles from Colchester, a thoroughly modern Roman town located a bit further from London. It's one of the *dinkiest* fully-fledged universities according to student numbers, but it's set amid three large lakes in 200 acres of *scenic parkland*, designed to hold a much larger institution – the University slowed its ambitious expansion a few years after it was founded (*although it's now catching up for lost time*). It has remnants of the big plans, though: the campus contains shops, eating places and facilities *which betray the grander designs*. They're all arranged in a *confusing* series of interlinked courtyards and modern concrete buildings, flanked by towering multi-storey residential blocks. The Uni, along with the University of East Anglia, is also opening a new campus in Suffolk, mainly to attract local students *to get qualified*.

SEX RATIO: ♂51 ♀49	**FOUNDED:** 1964
FULL-TIME U'GRADS: 5,610	**PART-TIME:** 234
POSTGRADS: 2,211	**NON-DEGREE:** N/A
AVE COURSE: 3YRS	**ETHNIC:** 10%
STATE:PRIVATE SCHOOL: 96:4	**FLUNK RATE:** 14%
MATURE: 17%	**INTERNATIONAL:** 38%
DISABLED: 475	**LOCAL:** 22%

ATMOSPHERE
Being such a small University, based in a big campus (if you include the parkland), there's quite a sense of community. This can either be seen as friendly solidarity or as busy-body nosiness, close-knit groups or cliques. Whatever, most of the atmosphere is tightly focused on the bars and things are particularly, er, vibrant at weekends. Less gregarious students can have a hard time and relations with the locals aren't particularly warm. Run-ins with pissed-up squaddies are rare, possibly because most students have the sense to steer clear of enemy territory (the Hippodrome on a Saturday night – which should be treated as No Man's Land in any case.)

SITES
EAST 15 ACTING SCHOOL (253 students – acting) The drama department's based on the Hatfields campus on the outskirts of London, 50 miles from the main University campus. It's set in the residential area of Loughton near Epping Forest. Specialist facilities include 14 rehearsal rooms, music room, dance and radio studio, purpose-built theatre and screening room, with £1.3m new facility with a costume department and rehearsal rooms. The University tries to help students find accommodation locally.
SOUTHEND (Health, Entrepreneurship & Business, Education, Creative Industries).Specialising in education for local folk, the Southend campus is set to get newer and shinier with the arrival of £23m worth of bricks in 20077.

COLCHESTER

⊙ POPULATION 155,796 **⊙ CITY CENTRE** 2 MILES
⊙ LONDON 40 MILES **⊙ IPSWICH** 17 MILES
⊙ HIGH TEMP 20 **⊙ LOW TEMP** 0 **⊙ RAINFALL** 67

The Romans started Colchester, although they went home some time ago. It's the oldest recorded town in the country – *and the town plan hasn't been greatly changed since.* But, as when all the bits of a car have been replaced so many times you have a new car (*in these parts, usually with wooden spoilers and neon under-lighting*), Colchester has established many modern pockets: shopping centres and light industry, busy roads and modern architecture and *Leisureworld (possibly the bastard relation of skate rink Rollerworld) – an alternative universe of slidy, splashy fun with fitness facilities to boot*. There are still many *pretty* parts, old houses and ancient buildings, not least the original Roman Wall and the castle (built by William the Conquerer) which houses a museum. *The area's most recent claims to fame, ex-Mods/reborn slackers Blur, have left less of an impression on the town, as has strip-happy PR-whore Jodie Marsh, who started her 'career' in this neck of the woods.*

TRAVEL

TRAINS The nearest mainline station to the campus is Colchester North, three miles away. Colchester Town station is nearest the town centre, but with fewer services. Direct services run into London Liverpool Street (from £14.85 return). Connections via London are possible all over the country including Birmingham (£34.25), Bristol (£62) and Edinburgh (£49). Some trains also stop at Hythe (between Colchester and Wivenhoe).
COACHES National Express services to London (£13.40), Birmingham (£28.50) and more.
CAR Colchester is visited by the A120, A12, A133 and the A604.
FERRIES To the Hook of Holland from Harwich and Felixstowe, 22 and 27 miles away, respectively.
AIR Stansted is 32 miles west on the A120. Regular buses run between the airport and the town centre.
HITCHING *The slip roads of the A12 are the best bet, but trying to get a lift in Essex is basically the same as simply waving a thumb at passing cars.*
LOCAL *Buses are expensive, but they're reliable* and tour the local villages which is *useful* for those living there. A new line serves University Quays, the new accommodation development.
UNIVERSITY *Night owls can hop on the late-night minibus.*
TAXIS Some firms are less expensive than others, *but Push wouldn't use the word 'cheap' for any of them.* Luckily, the SU has done a wheeler deal with a local company that means the SU will stump up the fare if a student can't foot the bill. *To be repaid, obviously.*
BICYCLES There's a cycle network around Colchester and *Essex is quite flat.*

CAREER PROSPECTS

⊙ CAREERS SERVICE ⊙ NO. OF STAFF 8 FULL/6 PART
⊙ UNEMPLOYED AFTER 6MTHS 9%

Services include: newsletters; bulletin boards; careers library; job fairs; interview training.

FAMOUS ALUMNI

Oscar Arias (President of Costa Rica & Nobel Prize winner); John Bercow (Tory MP); Virginia Bottomley MP (Con); Brian Hanrahan (BBC reporter); Rodolfo Neri Vela (Mexico's first astronaut); Ben Okri (writer); Chandra Sonic (Asian Dub Foundation); Mike Todd (Chief Constable of Greater Manchester Police).

SPECIAL FEATURES

There are a lot of ducks on the three lakes, and around the campus there are more rabbits than students. Each year, much to the distress of the students, the University carries out a bunny cull (*to weed out myxomatosis not for the sheer hell of it*).
The University has a collection of Sigmund Freud's letters and Europe's only public collection dedicated exclusively to modern and contemporary Latin American art.

FURTHER INFO

⊙ PROSPECTUSES UNDERGRAD; POSTGRAD; ALL DEPARTMENTS; ALTERNATIVE; INTERNATIONAL
⊙ OPEN DAYS

The alternative prospectus can be found at www.essexfirst.co.uk and postgrads can e-mail pgadmit@essex.ac.uk

ACADEMIC ⦿⦿⦿⦿⦿⦿⦿⦿⦿⦿⦿⦿⦿

⊙ 1994 GROUP

Essex hits above its size in terms of academic reputation. Courses are flexible and it's possible to switch courses at the end of the first year, circumstances permitting.

ENTRY POINTS: 240-340	AVE POINTS: 311
APPLICATIONS PER PLACE: 13	CLEARING: 11%
NO. OF TERMS: 3	LENGTH OF TERMS: 10WKS
STAFF TO STUDENT RATIO: 1:14	STUDY ADDICTS: 25%
TEACHING: ★★★	RESEARCH: ★★★★
YEAR ABROAD: 2%	SANDWICH STUDENTS: N/A
1STS: 10%	2.2S: 33%
2.1S: 46%	3RDS: 9%

ADMISSIONS

⊙ APPLY VIA UCAS

SUBJECTS

⊙ HUMANITIES AND COMPARATIVE STUDIES 22%
⊙ LAW 10% **⊙ SCIENCE AND ENGINEERING** 27%
⊙ SOCIAL SCIENCES 36%
BEST Biological Sciences; Economics; Film and Theatre Studies; Government; History; Language and Linguistics; Law; Literature; Management; Sociology; Sports Science.
UNUSUAL English & French Law LLB (taught jointly at Essex and the University of Paris); Human Rights; Marine & Freshwater Biology (which includes field trips to the Honduras and remote islands of Indonesia).

Words in italics are Push's point of view — take it or leave it...

LIBRARIES
⦿ **953,000 BOOKS** ⦿ **1,156 STUDY PLACES** ⦿ **SPEND PER STUDENT** £££££

As well as your average bookshelf, the Library has pamphlets, microfilms and special collections of international importance. A large reading room is open 24-hrs during term.

COMPUTERS
⦿ **540 WORKSTATIONS**

Networked computers whirr in open-access labs on campus. There's an IT helpdesk and in halls, internet points in bedrooms. Essex also run IT courses *for repentant Luddites*.

OTHER LEARNING FACILITIES
Language lab; drama studio; music rehearsal rooms; media centre; multimedia lab.

ENTERTAINMENT ⦿⦿⦿⦿⦿⦿⦿⦿⦿

THE TOWN
⦿ **PRICE OF A PINT OF BEER** £1.65
⦿ **GLASS OF WINE** £2 ⦿ **CAN OF RED BULL** £1.55

CINEMAS Students can grab a discount at the ten-screen Odeon multiplex.

THEATRES The excellent Mercury Theatre hosts a rep company.

PUBS *Students more usually stick to their own bars or the pubs close by, since the local pubs are full of soldiers. A few Pushplugs: The Lamb (noisy); Hole in the Wall (goth/indie); Wig & Pen; Horse & Groom (aka the Doom & Gloom); the King's Arms and the Lamb's Arms for real ale; Wetherspoons (bargain basement beer prices) is quiet enough from Monday to Wednesday, but otherwise avoid the larger town centre chains unless you appreciate velour tracksuits and brainless violence.*

CLUBBING *The real stiletto-heeled, mini-skirted cattle markets are in Southend (40 miles away) and Chelmsford (24 miles). Colchester's clubs are slower lane, more down-to-earth, but still tacky. Students don't often bother. Terrace (student DJs, but no student groovers, sadly); Hippodrome (large, sweaty, crowded). Avoid Chicago's. Route is popular.*

MUSIC VENUES *The Hippodrome has naff PAs. Better stick to The Twist (blues, rock and teeniemetal), The Arts Centre (indie, reggae) and the Charterhall (various). Better still, go up to London.*

EATING OUT Colchester has restaurants of every description – *worth checking out those with student discounts* – and junkyards of fast food. *Pushplugs: The Red Lion (historic hotel with an expensive but reliable menu); Food on the Hill (veggie); Jade Garden (cheap Chinese); Granata's; The Lemon Tree (pricey); Thai Dragon; Rose & Crown for parental purchasing; Playhouse; Wig & Pen (cheap pub grub); Sloppy Joe's (Tex-Mex); The Noodle Bar; Valentino's (romantic atmosphere, garlicky food - what a combo). The famous Talbooth in Dedham is a good choice for those with rich parents and cars; ditto The Barn Brasserie. Some kebab shops and the like are open till 4am.*

UNIVERSITY
⦿ **PRICE OF A PINT OF BEER** £1.65
⦿ **GLASS OF WINE** £2.40
⦿ **CAN OF RED BULL** £1.70

BARS The SU's Main Bar is, *unsurprisingly, the chief quaffing spot*, holding 1,000 thirsty people when it's chocka. This and the Level 2 bar, which hosts society, quiz and karaoke nights, were recently refurbished. The Underground is open late for club-style events. A facelift is planned to make it bigger and comfier by Autumn 2006. *The newest and smallest kid on the block is Café Mondo, a swish affair famed for its salsa nights.* The SU also runs Top Bar, which holds 300.

THEATRES The University is *well-equipped* and the Lakeside Theatre has many visits from national companies. Student shows are also *enthusiastically produced* – some make it to the Edinburgh Fringe.

FILM Several film societies organise regular showings in lecture theatres.

MUSIC VENUES The Underground (cap 1,000) gets the headline acts. Local and up-and coming bands appear at Level 2.

CLUBBING Regular clubnights and specialist dance acts at The Underground. Tim Westwood, Trevor Nelson and Judge Jules all did the honours last year.

COMEDY/CABARET Weekly comedy nights at Level 2.

FOOD The snacks in the Blues Café, SX Express and the Top Bar *are beyond the pockets of many students, who tend to stock up on eats in the main SU bar.* Mondo also *dishes up grub in swisher surroundings. Other snackage can be had at Café Vert, Take 3 and Food on 3.*

OTHER The Law Soc, Christmas and Summer Balls are big events. The University has a purpose-built exhibition gallery and a sculpture trail for *art-finding fun.*

SOCIAL ⦿⦿⦿⦿⦿⦿⦿⦿⦿⦿⦿

UNIVERSITY OF ESSEX STUDENTS' UNION
⦿ **5 SABBATICALS** ⦿ **TURNOUT AT LAST BALLOT** 20-25%
⦿ **NUS MEMBER**

Essex had a radical reputation as a red-hot hot-bed, then became known for a few blue-eyed Thatcherites, but the students are somewhat more apathetic nowadays. However, UESU was a major player in the campaign against tuition fees, so maybe politics isn't dead.

SU FACILITIES
In SU building: four bars; two nosh places (the uni has another six); minibus hire; printing services; general shop; pool tables; Barclays and Lloyds TSB banks; NatWest ATM; Endsleigh Insurance office; function room (cap 100); TV room; three meeting rooms; secondhand bookshop.

Words in italics are Push's point of view — take it or leave it...

CLUBS (NON-SPORTING)

Loads, including: American Society; American Studies Society; AFM Society; Art Film; Art; Biological Sciences; Buddhist Society; Bollywood Film; Chinese Christian Fellowship; Choir; Classical Music Society; Clubbing Society; Comedy Society; CSSA; Cypriot Society; Discordian; DJ Society; Drum and Bass; European Society; Explore UK; French Connection; Goth Society; German Society; Gregorian Society; Game Design; Green Alternative Society; Hong Kong Chinese; Human Rights Fairtrade Society; Indian Cultural Society; Italian Society; Japanese International; Jazz Society; Jesus Alive Fellowship; Korean; Latin American; Latin American Women's Society; Law; Lazy Exercise Society; Malaysian; Mature Students' Society; Media; Metal Soc; Mexican; Model UN; Multiplayer Gaming; Musical Performance Society; MUSOC; New Music; New Noise Music Society; Nordic; Persian Friends; Pakistani Cultural Society; Peace Campaign; Philosophy; Polish; Poker; Politics; Psychology; RnB; Punk; RESPECT Society; Rocky Horror; Russian; Roleplaying; Sikh; Sisters Society; Socrates; Spanish Fiesta; St Johns LINKS; Student Action for Refugees; Sociology; SWD; Syrian (pending ratification); Taiwanese; Thai; Theatre Arts; Turkish. **See also Clubs tables.**

OTHER ORGANISATIONS

The student media includes the fortnightly newspaper 'the Rabbit' and Red AM 1404, which broadcasts 24 hours. V-Team, the Community Action group, gets students stuck into projects such as sports coaching, mentoring young offenders and conservation work and has been awarded cash by the Home Office for group volunteer work. Rag raised £2,000 last year for local charities.

RELIGIOUS

○ **CHAPLAINS (COFE, RC, URC, UNITARIAN, QUAKER, BAPTIST, CONGREGATIONAL, ORTHODOX, JEWISH, METHODIST, ISLAMIC, BUDDHIST)**

There's a worship area in the University Chaplaincy centre for use by all religions. During term, there are Anglican services each Sunday and Mass three times a week. There are religious provisions *for all colours of the spiritual rainbow*, including Jewish, Muslim, Buddhist and Chinese Christian Fellowship. *There aren't really enough prayer spaces for the increasing numbers of Islamic students.* The Islamic Society organises a prayer schedule and has a deep freeze with Halal meat. A kosher kitchen supplies the general shop.

PAID WORK

○ **JOB BUREAU**

The University and SU give students paid shop, bar and office work. The Jobshop helps students find work on- or off-campus. It has vacancy boards, a regularly-updated website and it advises on CVs and employment-related issues such as tax and National Insurance.

SPORTS ○○○○○○○○○○○○○○

○ **RECENT SUCCESSES** WOMEN'S FOOTBALL, VOLLEYBALL, CRICKET
○ **BUSA RANKING** 78

As with many other things, the University has sports facilities that were intended for somewhere much larger. *But who's complaining?* Sports bursaries *attract the odd bionic wonderkid*, including students who have cycled and hurdled at an international level – the latter making it to the Athens Olympics, *no less.* There's a *good level of participation* among the *mere mortals* as well.

SPORTS FACILITIES

A purpose-built sports science laboratory currently takes *pride of place* while 40 acres of the parkland are used for sports including: playing fields; a grass athletics track; a floodlit synthetic sports pitch; three all-weather tennis courts; an exercise circuit ('the Squirrel Run') and the only 18-hole frisbee golf course in the country. Also a gym and sports hall including six badminton courts, another tennis court, a climbing wall (largest in the south-east), six squash courts (four elsewhere on campus); fitness room; archery range; weights and other indoor sports facilities. Students get special rates on University sport facilities, eg. £1.10 for the fitness room, £3.30 for netball courts, £1.70 for aerobics. Colchester also provides swimming pools and a roller rink.

SPORTING CLUBS

10-Pin Bowling; American Football; Women's

In 1981, an 18-hole disc golf course - the first in Britain - was installed on Essex University campus. The course has since hosted the Essex Open Frisbee Championships and the UK Championships.

Basketball; Boxing; Brazilian Jiu-Jitsu; Capoeira (a combination of martial arts and acrobatics); Cheerleading; Disc Sports; Essex Dance; Women's Football; Gliding; Jitsu; Kickboxing; Kung Fu; Motorsports; Pool; Rowing; Women's Rugby Union; Rugby League; Skydiving; Snowsports; Table Tennis; Triathlon. **See also Clubs tables.**

ATTRACTIONS
Colchester United is the local football team; *Ipswich Town attract a lot of local support from those in denial about residing in Essex.* There's also Essex County Cricket Club.

ACCOMMODATION ◖◖◖◖◖◖◖◖◖◖

IN UNIVERSITY
- **SELF-CATERED** 53% ● **COST** £66 (39/50WKS)
- **1ST YRS LIVING IN** 71%
- **2ND YRS LIVING IN** 22%
- **3RD YRS LIVING IN** 35%
- **POSTGRADS LIVING IN** 58%
- **INSURANCE PREMIUM** £

AVAILABILITY There are six tower blocks on campus which *are reckoned to provide a good social life for the undergrads who inhabit them.* Apparently, the architect was a bit eccentric and based the campus design on an Italian hill town. A *newish* development, University Quays, has given 760 more students a place to rest their heads. *Not a bad selection,* meaning that the University is able to guarantee accommodation (usually on the campus) to all first years who apply in time, and house *an impressive* 53% of all undergrads. All international students are housed by the university unless they don't want to be. Rooms are all single, mostly in shared flats for between four and six students. Many are *quite spacious and well-equipped. Students' main gripe is the lack of common or TV rooms.* Most flats are mixed, although some single-sex flats are available. Security is *excellent,* particularly in the newer, *Fort Knox-like* accommodation blocks.
CAR PARKING Automotive students living on or near campus have to pay and display.

EXTERNALLY
- **AVERAGE RENT** £55 ● **LIVING AT HOME** 11%

AVAILABILITY Finding suitable accommodation in Colchester, Wivenhoe (*peaceful*), Greenstead (*cheap but mild ASBO-territory*) or other surrounding villages *presents few problems. Students should avoid Lexden (too expensive) and Tollgate is just too far.* If living out, *a car is handy, but the cost of parking should be brought into the reckoning.*
HOUSING HELP The University Accommodation Office provides general help, approves some houses and flats and can fix students up in lodgings (with live-in landlord/lady).

WELFARE ◖◖◖◖◖◖◖◖◖◖◖◖

SERVICES
- **LGBT SOCIETY** ● **MATURE STUDENTS' OFFICER & SOCIETY** ● **INTERNATIONAL STUDENTS' OFFICER & SOCIETY** ● **POSTGRAD OFFICER & SOCIETY**
- **WOMEN'S OFFICER** ● **DISABILITIES OFFICER**
- **LATE-NIGHT MINIBUS** ● **NIGHTLINE** ● **UNIVERSITY COUNSELLORS** 8 FULL/ 6 PART ● **CRIME RATING** !

The SU Advice Centre provides help and referral for students with all manner of difficulties. It's staffed by student volunteers, trained and supported by professional staff. The University has a welfare advisor in the Student Support Office. In general, *the welfare provision is extensive and well-structured at every level.*
HEALTH The campus health centre provides one full- and two part-time counsellors, three nurses, five doctors, two physios and an administrator. Nurse appointments are *swift,* but those needing the doc face a 7-10 day wait.
WOMEN There's a late night minibus and women's officer. Attack alarms available from Nightline.
CRECHES/NURSERY 100 places for littl'uns (aged 0-5).
DISABILITIES There's a disability support team and departmental liaison officers. Special provisions and representative channels for students with all forms of special needs, including a Braille map of the campus, induction loops in lecture theatres and adapted housing for wheelchair users in the houses on campus. Accessibility and provisions are *among the best in the country.*

FINANCE
- **AVE Debt PER YEAR** £2,683
- **HOME STUDENT FEES** £3,000

FEES Postgrads pay around £3,168, less for part-timers. Non-EU students: £8,700 (classroom-based); £11,175 (lab-based).
- **ACCESS FUND** £336,000 ● **SUCCESSFUL APPLICATIONS/YR** 770 ● **AVE PAYMENT** £53-3,500

SUPPORT Fees are being topped up to the max, but there are a few things in place *to ease financial pain.* Those from poorer backgrounds will get cash maintenance bursaries, and students on four year degrees with a foundation year will get an initial fee reduction (£1,200 rather than £3,000 in the first year of study). The Sports Bursary scheme is open to athletes who compete at national and international level. It includes financial support, free access to University and local sports facilities (and a bunch of other non-financial perks). The J P Morgan Fleming Bursary is meant for mature students from the local area. Up to £500 is awarded to clever maths applicants. NHS support (up to full tuition fees) is available for Biomedical sandwich students and Clinical Physiology (Cardiology) students. The Vera Carmen Lord Fund is, *bizarrely,* available for students connected with the Worthing area or Jamaica. There are also bursaries for refugees or the children of refugees, disabled students, those with children and the Marie Helen Luen Charitable Trust Fund helps UK undergrads who've fallen on hard times.

Words in italics are Push's point of view — take it or leave it...

EXETER UNIVERSITY

1. ◔ **UNIVERSITY OF EXETER** Northcote House, The Queen's Drive, Exeter, EX4 4QJ **TEL** (01392) 661 000
E-MAIL admissions@exeter.ac.uk **WEBSITE** www.exeter.ac.uk ◔ **EXETER STUDENTS' GUILD** Devonshire House, Stocker Road, EX4
4PZ **TEL** (01392) 263 528 **E-MAIL** ask@guild.exeter.ac.uk **WEBSITE** www.guild.exeter.ac.uk or www.fxu.org.uk for Cornwall Campus
2. ◔ **UNIVERSITY OF EXETER IN CORNWALL** Cornwall Campus, Penryn, Cornwall, TR10 9EZ **TEL** (01326) 371 801
E-MAIL cornwall@exeter.ac.uk

GENERAL ◔◔◔◔◔◔◔◔◔◔◔◔◔

Down in *deepest, darkest Devon*, the River Exe
flows out into the English Channel in a wide
estuary with the golden, sandy beaches of south
Devon all around. Where the river starts to
widen, nine miles from the coast, there's Exeter,
not a big city, but a *pretty* one. Although the
place was almost wiped out by a single night's
bombing in World War II, the Luftwaffe didn't
manage to destroy any major landmarks, such as
the ancient cathedral (built in 1050), the city walls
(built by the Romans) or the Guild Hall. Among
the other things not destroyed by bombing was
the University – mainly because it wasn't built
until 1955. Some of its buildings date from the
last century though, but most were built in the
50s and 60s and are *low-rise* blocks in light stone.
The University is about a mile from the recently
redeveloped city centre in a *particularly hilly and
green area*. The setting is *stunning, perfect for
both town and country*, with two streams and
ponds dotted about the campus.

SEX RATIO: ♂48 ♀52	**FOUNDED:** 1955
FULL-TIME U'GRADS: 8,460	**PART-TIME:** 1.509
POSTGRADS: 3.589	**NON-DEGREE:** 0
AVE COURSE: 3YRS	**ETHNIC:** 5%
STATE:PRIVATE SCHOOL: 76:24	**FLUNK RATE:** 6%
MATURE: 10%	**INTERNATIONAL:** 13%
DISABLED: 345	**LOCAL:** 40%

ATMOSPHERE

*Exeter once had a reputation for attracting rich
kids who couldn't make it to Oxbridge though
things are a bit more mixed these days. It's a very
friendly place and the gorgeous setting is more
than enough compensation for the odd bit of
social friction. Lots of student houses are spread
across the city and relations with locals are pretty
good generally.*

SITES

ST LUKE'S CAMPUS (1,500 students – Education,
Sports Science) Although it's only a mile and a
half from the main campus this site *feels a bit like
a separate institution* and there's a concerted
effort to include the 'Lukies' in Guild activities,
*though it does have a community spirit all of its
own.* St Luke's Hall has housing for 209 students.
CORNWALL CAMPUS (Earth & Environment Science,
Conservation Biology, Geography, English,
History, Law, Politics, Renewable Energy,

Geology, Mining Engineering) 100 million
smackers worth of *hot* new campus action,
Tremough may be *billions of miles* from Exeter
(*that's right, billions*), and shared with *the far
more geographically-qualified* University College
Falmouth, but *the University is particularly
pleased* with its new outpost by the surf-lashed
Cornish shores. It's the proud centrepiece of the
Combined Universities in Cornwall Initiative and
the home of Exeter's *favourite toy* – its mineral
analysis machine used in forensic investigation.
Push prefers its Tracy Island. 500 en suite
self-catering bedrooms are available in Glasney
Parc, the student village, together with bars,
restaurant and sports centre.

EXETER
◔ **POPULATION** 111,200 ◔ **CITY CENTRE** 1 MILE
◔ **LONDON** 170 MILES ◔ **BRISTOL** 69 MILES
◔ **PLYMOUTH** 46 MILES
◔ **HIGH TEMP** 21 ◔ **LOW TEMP** 2 ◔ **RAINFALL** 64
While it's never going to be a party in a tin,
according to the EU, the *cute and cuddleable* city
of Exeter has the highest quality of life of any
English city and is *far from devoid of zesty perks*.
In part, this must be due to the *ample* selection of
high street shops, supermarkets and banks, and
to *numerous, wholesome* cafés. *There's even a
half-decent club or three lying around.* Tourist
attractions include the ancient cathedral, the
historic Guild Hall and various museums,
including the Royal Albert Museum and Art
Gallery, with its *amusing* giraffe. *Devon at large
has its own appeal* – *spooky* Dartmoor, for one
thing, as well as a *staggering number* of
breweries, cider presses and Buckfast Abbey,
where generations of monks have made what
they call 'tonic wine' and *Push calls 'liquid tar'*. A
few miles away there's the Jurassic Coast with
various fossilised mini-dinosaurs and, of course,
the sea.

TRAVEL
TRAINS Exeter St David's Station is half a mile
from the University. There are direct lines to
London (from £33.65), Bristol (£16.50),
Birmingham (£20) and connections all over.
BUSES National Express services all over the
country. The new Megabus (www.megabus.com)
takes five hours to get to London and there's
nowhere to put your stuff, *but at £1.50 each way,
that's forgivable*.
CAR Exeter is at the southern end of the M5, or
there's the A30, A377 and A38.
AIR Exeter Airport (six miles) offers inland and
European flights with FlyBe.

Words in italics are Push's point of view – take it or leave it...

LOCAL *Local buses are reliable and quite comprehensive, but not cheap. The same can be said of local trains* – there are four stations around the city, *but they're not very usefully placed.*
TAXIS: £2.50-3 from Streatham campus to city centre; Hackney cabs can be hailed in the street.
BICYCLES Bikes are *frequently* used by students, despite the hills. The campus has numerous places to lock up bikes and there are cycle paths around the city.

CAREER PROSPECTS
⊙ **CAREERS SERVICE** ⊙ **NO. OF STAFF** 15 FULL/5 PART
⊙ **UNEMPLOYED AFTER 6MTHS** 5%
There's a databank of 500 alumni willing to offer careers advice to current students (*but probably none of those listed below*). It's possible to do work experience modules as part of a degree. There's also plenty of careers *gumpf* like business placements, personal development plans, Earn & Learn jobshop, guidance interviews and so on.

SPECIAL FEATURES
There's an e-learning facility with 4,000 students doing 120 courses online.

FAMOUS ALUMNI
Toby Amies (MTV); Emma B (Radio 1 presenter); Felix Buxton (Basement Jaxx); Anastasia Cooke (TV presenter); Paul Downton, Richard Ellison (England cricketers); Richard Hill (former England rugby captain); Paul Jackson (TV producer); John O'Farrell (comic author/columnist); Stewart Purvis (former ITN chief exec); J K Rowling (writer, Harry Potter); Sam Smith (tennis player); David Sole (former Scotland rugby captain); Matthew Wright (TV presenter); Will Young (*lantern-jawed* Pop Idol); Thom Yorke (Radiohead).

FURTHER INFO
⊙ **PROSPECTUSES** UNDERGRAD; POSTGRAD; DEPARTMENTAL; CD ROM; VIDEO
⊙ **OPEN DAYS**
Virtual tours are available online.

ACADEMIC ⊙⊙⊙⊙⊙⊙⊙⊙⊙⊙⊙⊙⊙

⊙ **1994 GROUP**
There are 26 academic departments spread across 12 Schools, including the Peninsula Medical School, run with the University of Plymouth.

ENTRY POINTS: 240-400	**AVE POINTS:** 360
APPLICATIONS PER PLACE: 9	**CLEARING:** 5%
NO. OF TERMS: 3	**LENGTH OF TERMS:** 12WKS
STAFF TO STUDENT RATIO: 1:14	**STUDY ADDICTS:** 22%
TEACHING: ★★★★	**RESEARCH:** ★★★★★
YEAR ABROAD: 10%	**SANDWICH STUDENTS:** 2%
1STS: 12%	**2.2S:** 28%
2.1S: 58%	**3RDS:** 2%

ADMISSIONS
⊙ **APPLY VIA UCAS OR DIRECT FOR PART-TIME**

SUBJECTS
⊙ **ARAB & ISLAMIC STUDIES** <1%   ⊙ **BIOSCIENCES** 6%
⊙ **BUSINESS**/**MANAGEMENT** 11%   ⊙ **CLASSICS, ANCIENT HISTORY & THEOLOGY** 4%   ⊙ **EDUCATION & LIFELONG LEARNING** 2%   ⊙ **ENGINEERING, COMPUTER SCIENCE & MATHS** 12%   ⊙ **ENGLISH** 8%   ⊙ **GEOGRAPHY, ARCHAEOLOGY & EARTH RESOURCES** 8%   ⊙ **HISTORICAL, POLITICAL & SOCIAL SCIENCES** 12%   ⊙ **LANGUAGES** 11 %   ⊙ **LAW** 6%   ⊙ **MEDICAL SCIENCES** 3%   ⊙ **PERFORMANCE ARTS** 4%   ⊙ **PHYSICS** 3 %   ⊙ **PSYCHOLOGY** 4%   ⊙ **SPORTS SCIENCES** 4%
BEST Biosciences; Business; Conservation Biology & Ecology; Economics; English; European Languages & Area Studies; Finance & Accounting; Geography; History & Archeology; Human & Social; Management; Mathematical Sciences; Mathematically based Engineering; Performing Arts; Philosophy; Physical Geography & Environmental Science; Physical Science; Politics; Psychology; Sociology; Social Policy & Anthropology; Sport Sciences; Theology & Religious Studies; .
UNUSUAL Arab & Islamic Studies; Conservation Biology & Ecology (both at Cornwall campus); Renewable Energy (Cornwall again); European Law (four-year dual qualification combining both UK & French/German law degree); Modern languages with teaching English as a second language.

LIBRARIES
⊙ **1,200,000 BOOKS** ⊙ **1,733 STUDY PLACES**
⊙ **SPEND PER STUDENT** ££££
The library includes an Arab World Documentation Unit and 40,000 cinema history-related artefacts in the Bill Douglas centre. Their Special Collections include an *impressive* amount of works by, and material relating to, Agatha Christie, Daphne du Maurier and John Betjeman. The main library opens til 10pm on weekdays.

COMPUTERS
⊙ **1,000 WORKSTATIONS** ⊙ **24-HR ACCESS**
The majority of rooms in halls have internet access (annual fee £60 but no usage charge). Wireless access to the university network in the main campus library.

OTHER LEARNING FACILITIES
Specialist financial and stockmarket software (Bloomberg, Micropal, Datastream).

E

ENTERTAINMENT ()()()()()()()()()

THE TOWN
- **PRICE OF A PINT OF BEER** £2.35
- **GLASS OF WINE** £2.70
- **CAN OF RED BULL** £2

CINEMAS There's a three-screen Odeon; one-screen Phoenix Arts Centre (students £1 off) and the *friendly, sophisticated* Exeter Picture House (two-screen) for arthouse stuff.

THEATRES The Northcott on campus is the main regional theatre, but the Barnfield and the Arts Centre *encourage less commercial fare.*

PUBS *Plenty in town. Pushplugs: the huge Wetherspoons near campus, Mount Radford (for Lukies); Double Locks (a bit far, but worth it in summer).*

CLUBBING Most clubs, such as Warehouse, Arena, Club Rococo's and Volts, are mainstream; *Pushplugs: Rococco's; The Cavern; Timepiece (eclectic indie).*

MUSIC VENUES The Cavern provides a *more intimate, less mainstream alternative* to the University. Phoenix Arts Centre also puts on bands. Westpoint gets big arena tours.

FOOD *Not a huge selection of cheap eats but you won't starve either. Late night food can be hard to come by unless you're near a 24-hr garage. Pushplugs: Chadni for Indian; Mad Meg's (supposedly haunted by a medieval cook); Harry's (pizza, Mexican, steaks); the Blue Fish; Double Locks (pub lunches by the river).*

UNIVERSITY
- **PRICE OF A PINT OF BEER** £0.85
- **GLASS OF WINE:** £2 ● **CAN OF RED BULL** £1.60

BARS The Ram's *hugely popular* throughout the day, maybe because it looks like a proper pub, *albeit one that does fantastic hot white chocolate and toffish coffees.* There are two Union bars and four non-Union ones. The Lemon Grove (Lemmy) has a varied programme of events including big screen sport and games evenings. The halls have their own bars, only open to residents of that hall and their guests. Cross Keys at St Luke's (cap 700) turns into a club at weekends and shows sports in the week. Clydes House at the postgraduate centre does food and theme nights. Cornwall campus has a bar too.

THEATRES Northcott Theatre (cap 433) is based on campus and student companies put on occasional productions there, as well as jaunts up to Edinburgh and other parts of the country.

FILM *Sporadic screenings.*

MUSIC VENUES The Lemon Grove (cap 1,300) hosts varied club nights twice a week. Live sounds *pound* there and in the Great Hall (cap 1,700), which doesn't actually belong to the Guild, but is regularly borrowed from the University and is one of the biggest venues in the South West with top indie and rock acts – Joss Stone, Mr Scruff, Franz Ferdinand, Motorhead and the Zutons played last year. Cornwall campus has the Stannary (cap. 1,000), where Jack Johnson, Dizee Rascal and DJ Yoda *have got down and dirty.*

CLUBBING The Lemmy has a live DJ on Fridays and a student-only night on Saturdays.

FOOD The Refectory opens for lunch and dinner and the *good-value* Coffee Bar is popular all day. The Ram bar does *good, freshly-cooked* food and snacks in the evenings. The Coffee Bar serves *awesome* breakfasts – £2 for ten items all day long.

OTHER Many big balls, the highlight being summer's. The monthly Café Scientifique at the Phoenix gets guest speakers *to discuss all things geeky.*

SOCIAL ()()()()()()()()()()()()

EXETER STUDENTS' GUILD
- **6 SABBATICALS** ● **TURNOUT AT LAST BALLOT** 25%
- **NUS MEMBER**

The Guild's facilities are based in Devonshire House and are shared with various University activities. Both St Luke's and Cornwall campuses have Guild representatives (called the FXU at Cornwall, see University College Falmouth) *who communicate with the mothership and keep everybody nicely represented.* The Guild is politically neutral and *gets on well* with the University.

SU FACILITIES
Advice centre; two bar/clubs; shop; crèche; coffee shop; fast food; meeting rooms; minibus; Natwest Bank; launderette; post office; new and secondhand bookshop; travel agency; ticket agency; fax and printing service.

CLUBS (NON-SPORTING)
Arts; Beats & Bass; Brass Ensemble; Breakdance; Buddhists; Campus Bands; Chinese; Chocolate; Circus; Cocktail; Duke of Edinburgh; Folk Dance; Friends of Palestine; Games; Ghandi; Gilbert & Sullivan; Japanese; Malaysian; Motosoc; Tolkien; Turkish; Wine; X-rated. **See also Clubs tables.**

OTHER ORGANISATIONS
Impressive newspaper, 'Exeposé'; Xpression FM; Xnet (interactive website); XTV which pumps award-winning drama plus comedy, news and music into bars. There is also a charity OutRAGeous (*see what they did there?*), which raises *loads* and organises the Safer Sex Ball, the largest World AIDS Day event in the country. The major league volunteering organisation has four paid staff plus a student council overseeing 22 projects including work with kids' camps.

RELIGIOUS
- **7 CHAPLAINS**

Worship shops for the major faiths in town.

PAID WORK
⊙ JOB BUREAU ⊙ PAID WORK TERM-TIME 35%; HOLS 40%
A few local jobs for students in the tourist trade and some bar and clerical work in the Guild. The Works, the online jobshop, finds part-time and vacation work, and students can sign up to be campus tour guides, outreach ambassadors and *general PR monkeys* to bring in some pennies.

SPORTS ⊙⊙⊙⊙⊙⊙⊙⊙⊙⊙⊙⊙

⊙ RECENT SUCCESSES CLIMBING, SNOOKER, HOCKEY, KARATE, SAILING, WIND-SURFING **⊙ BUSA RANKING** 12
Big spending on sport over the past few years seems to have paid off, with the University sitting near the top of the BUSA tree.

SPORTS FACILITIES
Four indoor & four outdoor tennis courts; climbing wall; four squash courts; fitness suite; two exercise studios; four sports pitches; outdoor swimming pool; training suite; physiotherapy suite. St Luke's campus: sports hall; gymnasium hall; fitness studio; indoor pool.
OFF-CAMPUS ACCESS TO two football pitches, two cricket squares; lacrosse facilities; 60 acre playing field; 13 outdoor tennis parks; fleet of dinghies. Annual membership for £25 plus participation fee or £165 for annual Gold membership (unlimited gym use) and £190 for Platinum (unlimited everything). The sea, the River Dart and the moors are also assets.

SPORTING CLUBS
American Football; Expedition; Lafrowda; Methang; Pub Sports; Skydiving. **See also Clubs tables.**

ATTRACTIONS
Exeter FC is the local footy team and there are rugby and hockey outfits as well. The races are also popular round here – horses at Newton Abbot, speedway, dogs and people in town.

> ◎ **Because of an architect's error, the Psychology building at Exeter University was built back-to-front.**

ACCOMMODATION ⊙⊙⊙⊙⊙⊙⊙⊙⊙⊙

IN UNIVERSITY
⊙ CATERED 47% **⊙ COST** £110 (30WKS)
⊙ SELF-CATERED 26% **⊙ COST** £73 (34/39/50 WKS)
⊙ 1ST YRS LIVING IN 92%
⊙ POSTGRADS LIVING IN 20%
⊙ INSURANCE PREMIUM £
AVAILABILITY All first years can be housed and there's still space for many from other years. One in ten have to share a room. The majority of first years choose to live in the catered halls, which, with the exception of St Luke's Hall, are right next to the campus and vary in style from 19th-century buildings to *new very plush halls*. Most students who live in after their first year are housed in the self-catering flats. *Prices are steep but standards, especially in the newer accommodation, are very high.* There are also 142 places in a head tenancy system and 16 flats for families. The Cornwall campus has a new student village with 500 self-catering en suite rooms and surfboard lockers.
CAR PARKING Permit parking available for students living more than 1.5 miles from campus *or with a convincingly forged doctor's note.*

EXTERNALLY
⊙ AVERAGE RENT £60 **⊙ LIVING AT HOME** 5%
AVAILABILITY *Finding private accommodation in Exeter is easy peasy.* Some car-owners travel quite a way into the countryside (*but find beautiful country homes there). The best places are St James and Pennsylvania near the campus and Newtown nearer the St Luke's site.*
HOUSING HELP The accommodation office keeps a list of possible lodgings.

WELFARE ⊙⊙⊙⊙⊙⊙⊙⊙⊙⊙⊙

SERVICES
⊙ ETHNIC MINORITIES OFFICER & SOCIETY ⊙ POSTGRAD OFFICER & SOCIETY ⊙ WOMEN'S OFFICER & SOCIETY ⊙ MATURE STUDENTS' OFFICER & SOCIETY ⊙ INTERNATIONAL STUDENTS' OFFICER & SOCIETY ⊙ DISABILITIES OFFICER & SOCIETY ⊙ SELF-DEFENCE CLASSES ⊙ NIGHTLINE ⊙ UNIVERSITY COUNSELLORS 2 FULL/4 PART **⊙ CRIME RATING** !!
HEALTH Two GPs, six nurses. A trained mental health specialist works with students with anorexia, depression and *similar nasties.*
CRECHES/NURSERY 53 place nursery for 6wks-5yr-olds. Half-term playschemes for 5-14-yr-olds.
DISABILITIES The campus is *hilly and difficult to get around by wheelchair* but all buildings offer disabled access. Disability Resource Centre helps students with study problems or other difficulties. The library has a special equipment including a voice recognition synthesiser.

FINANCE

- **AVE DEBT PER YEAR** £3,199
- **HOME STUDENT FEES** £3,000
FEES £8,760-£10,860 for international students. UK postgrads pay £3,540.
- **ACCESS FUND** £435,777 ● **SUCCESSFUL APPLICATIONS**/**YR** 946 ● **AVE PAYMENT** £300

SUPPORT Sports bursaries (free accommodation and £1,000 a year) are available, as well as the Vice Chancellor's Excellence Scholarship for £5,000 a year and the Jubilee Science Scholarships for £3,000. There's a variety of Access bursaries (up to £2,000 for locals or students from poorer backgrounds).

E

▶ FALMOUTH COLLEGE OF ARTS
see *University College Falmouth*

UNIVERSITY COLLEGE FALMOUTH

▶ FARNHAM
see *Creative Arts University College*

▶ FASHION
see *University of the Arts, London*

F

▶ **FALMOUTH COLLEGE OF ARTS**
see *University College Falmouth*

UNIVERSITY COLLEGE FALMOUTH

FORMERLY FALMOUTH COLLEGE OF ARTS

○ **UNIVERSITY COLLEGE FALMOUTH** Woodlane, Falmouth, TR11 4RH **TEL** (01326) 211 077 **E−MAIL** admissions@falmouth.ac.uk **WEBSITE** www.falmouth.ac.uk ○ **FALMOUTH & EXETER STUDENT UNION** The Annex, Tremough Campus, Treliever Road, Penryn, Cornwall, TR10 9EZ **TEL** (01326) 251 447 **E−MAIL** office@fxu.org.uk website www.fxu.org.uk

GENERAL ○○○○○○○○○○○○○○

Way, way way down on England's big toe is Falmouth, port, tourist town and *haven for floaty creative types*. In it is Cornwall's only university — or University College, to be more precise. It's been spooning out Arts Ed since 1902 but only won its degree-doling rights in 2004. Falmouth's a *small but perkily formed seaside town and the main Woodlane campus is entirely in proportion, diddiness-wise. It's shockingly warm (for England, at least)* round these parts and leafy palms and subtropical plants flourish, *so the whole area can feel more like a holiday resort than a place of intense bookworming.* There's another academic outpost just down the road at Tremough.

SEX RATIO: ♂42 ♀58	**FOUNDED:** 1902
FULL-TIME U'GRADS: 1,706	**PART-TIME:** 58
POSTGRADS: 193	**NON-DEGREE:** 150
AVE COURSE: 3YRS	**ETHNIC:** 3%
STATE:PRIVATE SCHOOL: 93:7	**FLUNK RATE:** 17%
MATURE: 30%	**INTERNATIONAL:** 9%
DISABLED: 225	**LOCAL:** 22%

ATMOSPHERE
The winning combo of arts subjects and decent surfing makes for a campus so mellow it could pass out at any moment. There's a real commune feel floating in the air and the fact that everyone says 'hello' as they pass by can be a bit like living on the set of Heartbeat. Only with palm trees.

OTHER SITES
TREMOUGH (Design; English; Journalism) The *lush* 70-acre campus is centred on an old manor house and is shared with Exeter as part of the Combined Universities in Cornwall initiative. Falmouth students are separate academically from Exeter's, but the top drawer facilities and social lives are *cosily communal. It's a sexy, modern place,* ten mins stroll from the *dinky town* of Penryn and ten mins on the bus from Woodlane.

FALMOUTH
○ **POPULATION** 87,861 ○ **CITY CENTRE:** <1 MILE
○ **LONDON** 265 MILES ○ **TRURO** 15 MILES
○ **EXETER** 95 MILES
○ **HIGH TEMP** 16 ○ **LOW TEMP** 7 ○ **RAINFALL** 43

The *cutesy* seaside town of Falmouth first popped up on the map in the 17th Century, established as a port and centre for all things ocean-going, including a healthy smuggling trade. *It's still that way today, although smuggling's less fashionable* and alongside the boat-building, shipping and poncing around on yachts, there's a massive tourist injection come the summer. *It's a quaint and quirky little town, yet to be despoiled by big high street chains.* It does, however, boast the *enviable* title of '3rd largest deep-water harbour in the world', for what that's worth. Nearby, the Eden Project, Pendennis Castle, the Lost Gardens of Heligan (a *stunning* subtropical landscape) and Falmouth's own *gorgeous* beaches *keep the tourists, students and locals smiling.*

TRAVEL
TRAINS Falmouth Town Station is about a mile from campus. Connect to Truro (15 miles away) for the longer haul. From here you can get to London (from £44.20 return) and lots of other places.
COACHES Falmouth coach station (1 mile) has National Express services that scoot all the way to Glasgow (£60) and other destinations.
CAR The M5, A30 and A39 are all handy bits of tarmac. *Parking in Falmouth isn't much of a headache but at the College itself, it's a different (and more painful) story.*
AIR Newquay airport's just shy of 30 miles away and runs Ryanair and FlyBe budget flights.
LOCAL 50p gets you into Penryn and back on the College-subsidised bus service, £2.40 gets you a day trip into Truro. There's also the local overland train (£2.50 sgl to Truro)
TAXIS *Not a popular form of student transport and not really a necessary one either.*
BICYCLES *Cycling's even easier than pie around here* and theft barely registers on the radar.

CAREER PROSPECTS
- ○ **CAREERS SERVICE** ○ **NO. OF STAFF** 2 FULL
- ○ **UNEMPLOYED AFTER** 6MTHS 4%

The Careers Advisory Service runs drop-in advice sessions and appointments, as well as the usual gamut of job fairs, vacancy bulletins and interview training.

FAMOUS ALUMNI
Sophie Benzig (Radio 5 Live); Tacita Dean (artist and Turner Prize loser); Lorna Dunkley (Sky News presenter); Angus Walker (ITN).

FURTHER INFO
- ○ **PROSPECTUSES:** UNDERGRAD; POSTGRAD; ALL DEPTS
- ○ **OPEN DAYS** E-mail opendays@falmouth.ac.uk to plan a visit.

ACADEMIC ○○○○○○○○○○○○

Falmouth dabbles exclusively in the arts and all its students are either artists, designers, media-types *or lost*. Courses have a strongly vocational slant and a hefty practical element. As a result, a lot of work is workshop/studio-based. Students can expect to do around seven work experience placements and get a wide variety of lectures from visiting industry professionals. Most courses don't have exams (*woohoo*) but are assesed on final year studio work and dissertations.

ENTRY POINTS: N/A	AVE POINTS: 220
APPLICATIONS PER PLACE: 4	CLEARING: 3%
NO. OF TERMS: 3	LENGTH OF TERMS: 10WKS
STAFF TO STUDENT RATIO: 1:3	STUDY ADDICTS: 4%
TEACHING: ***	RESEARCH: N/A
YEAR ABROAD: 0%	SANDWICH STUDENTS: 0%
1STSS: 9%	2.2S: 33%
2.2S: 49%	3RDS: 4%

ADMISSIONS
- ○ **APPLY VIA UCAS**

All part-time, postgrad or foundation course applications are handled by Falmouth's Admissions department.

SUBJECTS
ART 33%   **DESIGN** 33%   **MEDIA** 33%
BEST Art; Design.

LIBRARIES
- ○ 100,000 BOOKS ○ 304 STUDY PLACES
- ○ SPEND PER STUDENT ££

The large library at Tremough and the smaller one at Woodlane aren't intended for night-owls – everything's closed by 9pm.

COMPUTERS
- ○ 240 WORKSTATIONS

As with libraries, so with computers. *No midnight Belgian porn fests.* There is a campus-wide wireless network though.

OTHER LEARNING FACILITIES
Specialised geography and biology labs; music and TV production studios; media centre; CAD lab.

ENTERTAINMENT ○○○○○○○○○

THE TOWN
- ○ **PRICE OF A PINT OF BEER** £2.20
- ○ **GLASS OF WINE** £2.20 ○ **CAN OF RED BULL** £2

While the students may not exactly be able to go largin' it for a fat one on a night out, there's enough going on around town to keep most entertained.

CINEMAS *Indie, arty fare* at the Falmouth Arts Centre. The Plaza in Truro for all your multiplex needs.

THEATRES The Falmouth Arts Centre for local board-treaders and small scale professional shows. The Hall at Cornwall has the big touring productions.

PUBS *Warm and welcoming local hostelries*, including the Boathouse, Bunters Bar, the Waterfront and the Star & Garter. Wetherspoons is cheap. *Go figure.*

CLUBBING Three, (*count them, three*) clubs in Falmouth. The Quayside is the fave.

MUSIC Major players head for the Eden Project. Smaller scale strummers at the Star & Girder or the Waterfront.

EATING OUT *Generally good grub around town.* Highlights include: 5 Degrees West, Blue South and the Shed.

UNIVERSITY
- ○ **PRICE OF A PINT OF BEER** £1.50
- ○ **GLASS OF WINE** £1.60
- ○ **CAN OF RED BULL** £1.75

BARS The enormous Stannary bar/venue is the centrepoint of campus social life and has a *hectic* weekly events schedule. And a late licence.

THEATRES Absolutely zilch, except involvement in local am dram.

FILM One or more student-made flicks per week are shown for free in the media centre.

MUSIC VENUES The Stannary plays host to some live music. Lemon Jelly stopped by last year.

CLUBBING Again, the big nights are in the Stannary. Friday's Hex clubnight (£2 before 10pm, £4 after) gets the beats (*and the sweat*) a-pumpin. Mr Scruff's been by recently.

COMEDY/CABARET Circuit comics in the Stannary every Thursday.

FOOD All students self-cater so there's not a vast selection of edibles. The Stannary does *good* pizza and other mains. The refectory dishes out cafeteria fare. *The nearby Asda wins out every time, though.*

OTHER: Three black tie balls a year — Freshers', Christmas and Graduation.

F

SOCIAL

FALMOUTH & EXETER STUDENT UNION (FXU)
○ **3** SABBATICALS ○ TURNOUT AT LAST BALLOT 10%
○ NUS MEMBER

Falmouth doesn't have a union of its own but has joined forces with Exeter's Guild of Students to form the *mighty* FXU. *It's not in fact a new mobile phone model,* but rather the ents and welfare student *powerhouse* based on the Tremough campus. *Politics is a dirty word in these parts.*

SU FACILITIES
Nightclub; two bars; cafeteria; pool tables; meeting rooms; minibus hire; ATM; photocopier; payphones; creche; general store; stationery shop; post office; vending machines; launderette. Termly visits from booksellers and second hand sales.

CLUBS (NON-SPORTING)
Filmmaking; Human Rights. **See also Clubs tables.**

OTHER ORGANISATIONS
'Exepose' — Exeter's paper gets flicked through by Falmouthites, as does 'Substance', Falmouth's own SU mag (more will be hitting the press this year). 'Radiowave' broadcasts over the intranet and a newly-established RAG is gearing up for *charity mugging tomfoolery.*

RELIGIOUS
○ CHAPLAIN

The chaplain is based at the Tremough campus and most Christian stylings are addressed by the local churchs. Other faiths — Muslims in particular — *might do better in another county.*

PAID WORK
○ JOB SHOP ○ PAID WORK TERM-TIME 80%; HOLS 80%

FXU has some input into the running of the Careers Advisory Service. Falmouth has a ton of possibilities for the cash-seeker, as long as they're after bar or retail slog.

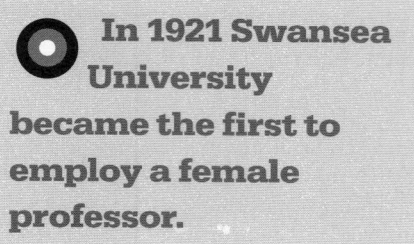
In 1921 Swansea University became the first to employ a female professor.

SPORTS

The University has a *big fat bloody stake* in the Sports Centre, which is also open to the public, leaving FXU to organise the teams and post-match revelry. Being coastal Cornwall, *there's a hefty bias for the wet stuff* and sailing and diving are favourites.

SPORTS FACILITIES
There's nowt in the way of sports fields, but the Sports Centre has a multigym, aerobics studio and a hall for bouncing balls about. Costs vary but students are subsidised. Some other sporty frolics are catered for locally, with an athletics field, squash and tennis courts, a pool, ice rink, bowling green and golf course. The hills, caves, river and the sea itself, *provide nature's own gym.*

SPORTING CLUBS
Capoeira; Circus; Kung Fu; Sea Swimming; Snowboarding; Ultimate Frisbee. **See also Clubs tables.**

ACCOMMODATION

IN COLLEGE
○ SELF-CATERING 18% ○ COST £75 (39/50WKS)
○ INSURANCE PREMIUM £

AVAILABILITY Falmouth has no accommodation of its own but has done a deal with the Sanctuary Housing Association that lands most roof-needing first years in one of 11 blocks (some shared with Exeter). Flats consist of five en-suite bedrooms and a communal kitchen/*dossing room.* Rooms have TVs — *so no one has to miss Richard & Judy* — and phone and network sockets. Kitchens are fully kitted out, communal areas are cleaned 4 days a week and laundry rooms *get whites whiter than brown.* Insurance is included in the rent. International students get priority. Some ground floor flats for disabled students.
CAR PARKING *Pretty tight.* Students with special needs are in with a chance.

EXTERNALLY
○ AVE RENT £70 ○ LIVING AT HOME 5%

AVAILABILITY As long as it's not tourist season (*that's visiting, not hunting them*), *finding a house is as easy as finding a needle in a sewing box* and it's mostly within 15 mins bus ride from campus.
HOUSING HELP The Accommodation Office keeps lists of approved landlords and vacancies, *but there's still a few fingers it could lift.*

WELFARE ◡◡◡◡◡◡◡◡◡◡◡◡◡◡

SERVICES

◉ WELFARE LIAISON OFFICER ◉ LGBT SUPPORT GROUP
◉ WOMEN'S OFFICER ◉ NIGHTLINE ◉ COLLEGE
COUNSELLORS 4 FULL ◉ CRIME RATING !
HEALTH Twice weekly nurse's clinic at Tremough.
Several local GPs.
NURSERY/CRECHE Day nursery for one-year-olds and
above. After school and holiday clubs for
younglings up to eight.

DISABILITIES *Lumpy* geography doesn't help
wheelchair access, nor do some old buildings at
Woodlane. Ramps, lifts and ground floor housing
make getting around a little easier. Diagnosis and
tuition for dyslexic students is available.
DRUGS Zero tolerance — searches are carried out
occasionally.

FINANCE

◉ AVE DEBT PER YEAR £3,617 ◉ HOME STUDENT FEES £3,000
SUPPORT Annual bursaries based on household
income available (£250-£675).

⯈ FARNHAM
see *Creative Arts University College*

⯈ FASHION
see *University of the Arts, London*

F

➡ **GEORGE'S HOSPITAL**
see *St George's, University of London*

GLAMORGAN UNIVERSITY

UNIVERSITY OF GLASGOW

GLASGOW CALEDONIAN UNIVERSITY

➡ **GLASGOW POLYTECHNIC**
see *Glasgow Caledonian University*

UNIVERSITY OF GLOUCESTERSHIRE

GOLDSMITHS, LONDON

➡ **GORDON UNIVERSITY**
see *Robert Gordon University*

GREENWICH UNIVERSITY

➡ **GUY'S HOSPITAL**
see *King's College London*

G

GLAMORGAN UNIVERSITY

FORMERLY POLYTECHNIC OF WALES

1. ◉ **UNIVERSITY OF GLAMORGAN** Treforest, Pontypridd, Wales, CF37 1DL **TEL** 0800 716 925 **E-MAIL** enquiries@glam.ac.uk **WEBSITE** www.glam.ac.uk ◉ **UNIVERSITY OF GLAMORGAN UNION** University of Glamorgan Union, Forest Grove, Treforest, Mid Glamorgan, Wales, CF37 1UF
2. ◉ **UNIVERSITY OF GLAMORGAN** Glyntaff Campus, University of Glamorgan, Cemetery Road, Glyntaff, Pontypridd, Wales, CF37 4BL

GENERAL ◑◑◑◑◑◑◑◑◑◑◑◑

In South Wales, up the Taff Valley from Cardiff, is the market town of Pontypridd. A mile away is the terraced, ex-mining village of Treforest and overlooking it on a steep hillside are the 70 acres of the University of Glamorgan. It's a mix of different buildings, old Welsh stone, demountables and redbrick with a *squat, white and controversially expensive block* in the middle. When the sun comes out students get dazzled by the *extraordinary views over the valleys and remember why they went there in the first place. Then the sun goes in again and they go to the pub.* Cardiff's a mere 12 miles away – *handy for those craving a bit of Big City Action.* Adventurous types are *happy to make-do with stunning* local countryside, which is *perfect* for everthing from walking to rock-climbing and from swimming to surfing.

SEX RATIO: ♂49 ♀51	**FOUNDED:** 1913
FULL-TIME U'GRADS: 9,833	**PART-TIME:** 8,521
POSTGRADS: 2,972	**NON-DEGREE:** 1,792
AVE COURSE: 3YRS	**ETHNIC:** N/A
STATE:PRIVATE SCHOOL: 97:3	**FLUNK RATE:** N/A
MATURE: 40%	**INTERNATIONAL:** 13%
DISABLED: 180	**LOCAL:** 60%

ATMOSPHERE

Small and weather-dependent, Glamorgan can feel *nigh on perfect in the summer when the students are scattered over the grass with their books and pints, drinking in the view. On other days it's clear that a valley is essentially just a big hole in the ground and in this case a soggy one.* 'Glam' *students have gained a bit of a rep as drinkers, but they know how to work when it counts.* Most people are friendly and robustly cheerful and everyone who frequents the small Union knows each other, *often biblically.*

OTHER SITES

GLYNTAFF CAMPUS (Law, Care Sciences, Welsh Institute of Health & Social Care) 15 mins walk from the main campus. *It's not so much a campus as a bunch of lecture rooms and a lounge, but they had to call it something.* Care sciences lives in a *swanky* new building with computer labs and clinical practice suites. The University also has associations with a number of local colleges. Creative courses (eg. Animation; Design; Drama; Culture & Society) are set to move to a 'Cardiff

School of Creative and Cultural Industries', a new campus in Cardiff city centre due to open in 2007. *Watch this space.*

PONTYPRIDD

◉ **POPULATION** 33,500 ◉ **CITY CENTRE** 1 MILE
◉ **LONDON** 145 MILES ◉ **CARDIFF** 12 MILES
◉ **BIRMINGHAM** 90 MILES
◉ **HIGH TEMP** 21 ◉ **LOW TEMP** 2 ◉ **RAINFALL** 87

Pontypridd, or Ponty, *is rather cramped. It's mostly a single road with shops on it.* There's an indoor market and an outdoor one once a week, and a large park *that takes people by surprise (not by jumping out and demanding their valuables, but because it's hidden down a side street).* Ponty and Treforest together have all the basic amenities and Cardiff is a short train journey away. It's Cardiff most students will go to for a big night out, see <u>Cardiff University</u>.

TRAVEL

TRAINS From Treforest station, right outside campus, trains go to Cardiff every 20 mins (£3.70 return). Change there for London (from £36.30 return), Swansea (£11.40) and Manchester (£34.30). Buy tickets in advance or the price can double. The last train back from Cardiff is at 11.27pm.
COACHES National Express run a host of services departing from nearby Cardiff.
CAR Treforest is on the A470 and about 8 miles off the M4.
AIR Cardiff International, 11 miles from the city centre, is the nearest airport.
HITCHING *The Welsh take pity on hitchers and once on the M4 prospects are good, but remember it's pronounced 'Pontypreeth'.*
LOCAL Walking is *no hardship,* with Ponty and the Glyntaff site ten mins from *compact* Treforest. Bus services go every 20 mins to Ponty and every 25 to Cardiff. A free student shuttle within a ten mile radius of campus runs after 10.30pm.
TAXIS About £1.50 into Ponty and £20 back from Cardiff.
BICYCLES *The hills put people off and bikes can disappear. Positively though, the Taff Trail is a straight and exceptionally scenic cycle route straight into Cardiff.*

CAREER PROSPECTS

◉ **CAREERS SERVICE** ◉ **NO. OF STAFF** 12 FULL/1PART
◉ **UNEMPLOYED AFTER 6MTHS** 6%

There's a job shop and Cymru Prosper Wales are active in the area. They find relevant work experience for students and also help graduates

G

SPECIAL FEATURES
The University claims to be Britain's greenest, with recycling facilities and a car share scheme among the *tree-hugging initiatives*.

FAMOUS ALUMNI
Max Boyce (entertainer); Gareth Davies (Funeral for a Friend); Ian Hamer (Olympic athlete); Jonathan Humphreys (rugby player); Rupert Moon (rugby player and broadcaster); Michael Owen (the rugby player, not the footballer). Patrick Moore is an honorary fellow, as is Lord Richard Attenborough.

FURTHER INFO
○ **PROSPECTUSES** UNDERGRAD; POSTGRAD; DEPARTMENTAL
○ **OPEN DAYS**

ACADEMIC ○○○○○○○○○○○○○

Many courses are vocational. A big emphasis on links with 'real' work and getting hands-on experience.

ENTRY POINTS: 80–300		**AVE POINTS:** 210	
APPLICATIONS PER PLACE: 4		**CLEARING:** 20%	
NO. OF TERMS: 3		**LENGTH OF TERMS:** 12–15WKS	
STAFF TO STUDENT RATIO: 1:17		**STUDY ADDICTS:** 15%	
TEACHING: ★★★		**RESEARCH:** ★	
YEAR ABROAD: N/A		**SANDWICH STUDENTS:** 19%	
1STS: 14%		**2.2S:** 34%	
2.1S: 38%		**3RDS:** 14%	

ADMISSIONS
○ **APPLY VIA UCAS**
Local students from partner schools may get lower offers than those from afar.

SUBJECTS
ART & DESIGN & PERFORMING ARTS 14%
ARTS/HUMANITIES 13%   **BUILT ENVIRONMENT** 3%
BUSINESS/MANAGEMENT 23%
ENGINEERING & TECHNOLOGY 15%
MATHS, SCIENCE, IT AND COMPUTING 13% **SCIENCES** 19%
SOCIAL SCIENCES 14%
BEST Care Sciences; Creative Arts; English; Law; Management; Sociology; Social Policy & Anthropology; subjects allied to medicine.
UNUSUAL Astrobiology; Chiropractic; Computer System Security; Police Sciences; Outdoor Learning & the Science of Adventure, Science Fiction.

LIBRARIES
○ **236,955 BOOKS** ○ **785 STUDY PLACES**
The Learning Resource Centre (LRC) offers all the usual library stuff plus 24-hr book return. *It's not that big though and students sometimes go to Cardiff to get the books they need.*

COMPUTERS
○ **1,450 WORKSTATIONS** ○ **24–HR ACCESS**
Computer access can be irksome at deadline time as the rooms are often clogged by students and lectures. The LRC loans laptops overnight.

OTHER LEARNING FACILITIES
The LRC doubles as the media centre, with TV and audio studios and equipment hire.

ENTERTAINMENT ○○○○○○○○○

PONTYPRIDD For Cardiff, see <u>Cardiff University</u>
○ **PRICE OF A PINT OF BEER** £2.30 ○ **GLASS OF WINE** £2
○ **CAN OF RED BULL** £1.50
Ponty, being small and imperfectly-formed for nightlife, sends students to Cardiff in droves. Apart from pubs, students learn to do a lot of socialising at home.
CINEMAS *Costly but convenient* Showcase Natgarwr has 12 screens. Ponty's Muni (one screen) shows *arty and popular* films. *Locals go there to shout advice at the characters and have sex.*
PUBS Treforest has eight pubs *within a stagger:* the Otley (*drama student den*); the Forest (*cheap*).
CLUBBING Ponty has a club or two with *entertaining fights* at the weekend. *Best go to Cardiff.*
EATING OUT *All of the pubs do serviceable nosh. Also numerous take-aways and grease-joints –* JJ's and Uni Takeaway are the favourites.

UNIVERSITY
○ **PRICE OF A PINT OF BEER** £1.75
○ **GLASS OF WINE** £2 ○ **CAN OF RED BULL** £1.90
The Union's facilities may be small and cute but it manages to get an impressive amount of things to happen. It's at the top of a hill – difficult going up, painful rolling down.
BARS The Union venues are right next to each other and open every evening. The Baa Bar (cap. 300) and Smiths (500) downstairs have food, pool tables and Sky TV.
THEATRES Visiting companies and an *enthusiastic* drama contingent use the theatre.
CLUBBING/MUSIC VENUES Shafts (500 capacity) is the mainstay nightclub and the doors open into the Baa Bar to *create Glamorgan's answer to a superclub*. Cheese, dance, house, guest DJs and live rock bands *all grace the place on various nights. The novelty wears off though* and buses ship students to Creation in Cardiff on a Monday.
COMEDY/CABARET The Union's on the Paramount Comedy circuit. Fortnightly *mirthsters pack the punters* into Shafts.
FOOD The bars serve pub food that's *cheap, hot and often nice*. Three sandwich shops and a couple of canteens *ease the rest of the tummy rumbles*.

G

SOCIAL ○○○○○○○○○○○○

UNIVERSITY OF GLAMORGAN UNION
○ **6 SABBATICALS** ○ **TURNOUT AT LAST BALLOT** 10-15%
○ **NUS MEMBER**
The Union campaigns a lot for local charities and issues close to home, like keeping Wednesday afternoons free. *Tending not to be too political, it keep its head down on improving its own students' lot and gets on well with the University as a result*

UNION FACILITIES
The building is small but crammed with goodness. The Union is responsible for three bars, one of which becomes the nightclub; cafeteria; media training centre; restaurant; minibuses; travel agency; general shop; cashpoints; insurance office; photocopier; photo/phone booths; gaming and vending machines; pool tables; juke box; launderette; fax machine; printing service; advice centre.

CLUBS (NON-SPORTING)
Cheerleading; Chiropractic; Christian Encounter; Hellenic; Live Music; Pagan; Scientific Diving; Socialist Students; War Games & Role Playing. **See also Clubs tables.**

OTHER ORGANISATIONS
GTFM, the award-winning FM/net radio, has teamed up with the local community to be Wales' first 'Access Radio' and broadcasts 24/7. Glam Rag raised an *admirable* £10,000 last year and *drags 200 boffins a week out with a popular* quiz night in the Union. Leek, the student newspaper, is published 2-3 times a year. GlamTV is the new TV station.

RELIGIOUS
○ **3 CHAPLAINS (COFE, FC, RC)**
The Mosque on campus has facilities for ablutions and male and female prayer rooms.

PAID WORK
○ **JOB BUREAU** ○ **PAID WORK** TERM-TIME 60%; HOLS 85%
A handful of jobs available on campus and locally, more for those willing to go to Cardiff or sell their body to medical science. Jobshop, open days and Cymru Prosper Wales (see above).

SPORTS ○○○○○○○○○○○○

○ **RECENT SUCCESSES** ATHLETICS, KARATE
○ **BUSA RANKING** 68
Everyone from the All Blacks to Cardiff City FC have used the University's facilities for training, *which sounds like high praise to Push*. There are plenty of individual sporting stars and in many team sports – rugby league and union, football,

Women's hockey, squash, cricket, and netball – Glamorgan sits near the top of the leagues. More than 50 muscle-straining activities, from belly dancing to circuit training, are laid on once a week.

SPORTS FACILITIES
30 acres of playing fields (some flood-lit); all-weather pitch; cricket pitch; nine other pitches; flood-lit trim trail; sports hall; four squash courts; climbing wall; fitness room; multigym; sauna/steam room; two gyms; golf practice area; archery range; boules, bowls and croquet lawns; flood-lit tennis court and a sports injury clinic. Membership ranges from £29-40 a year.

SPORTING CLUBS
Gaelic Football; Ju-Jitsu; Rugby League & Union; Snowboard & Waterpolo. **See also Clubs tables.**

ATTRACTIONS
Rugby Union in Ponty and mountains, lakes, caves, the River Taff, a golf course and a swimming pool locally.

ACCOMMODATION ○○○○○○○○○

IN UNIVERSITY
○ **SELF-CATERING** 11% ○ **COST** £63 (37WKS)
○ **INSURANCE** £
AVAILABILITY Preference is given to first years, but *not many get places in halls – a lot* of students live locally anyway. The University tries to *cram* in most of those who accept an unconditional UCAS offer by March and sort the rest out with approved private accommodation. The halls are a *decent* standard and 70% of rooms are en suite. Philip Evans and Squire are the older halls. Halls are self-catered, but £25 a week buys a voucher book for any of the grub on campus.
CAR PARKING *Parking's really tough*. Students have missed lectures because they can't find spaces. £100 a year gets a residents' permit.

EXTERNALLY
○ **AVE RENT** £45 ○ **LIVING AT HOME** 70%
AVAILABILITY Most available houses in the immediate area are taken by students. *Houses aren't hard to find. However, nice houses and honest landlords can be particularly dodgy and students are warned off housing agencies in Treforest. Every house should be thoroughly scrutinised before signing anything.*
HOUSING HELP The University runs an accommodation service and a *vital* list of reputable landlords.

Words in italics are Push's point of view – take it or leave it...

G

WELFARE ()()()()()()()()()()()()()

SERVICES
○ **LGBT** ○ **OFFICER & SOCIETY** ○ **ETHNIC MINORITIES OFFICER & SOCIETY** ○ **WOMEN'S OFFICER & SOCIETY**
○ **MATURE STUDENTS' OFFICER**
○ **INTERNATIONAL STUDENTS' OFFICER & SOCIETY**
○ **DISABILITIES OFFICER & SOCIETY**
○ **LATE-NIGHT/WOMEN'S MINIBUS**
○ **SELF-DEFENCE CLASSES**
○ **UNIVERSITY COUNSELLORS** 3 FULL/5 PART ○ **CRIME RATING** !
The Student Support centre helps with careers, legal advice, counselling and advice, health, student finance, disability and dyslexia. It also has resident personal tutors and an international support unit.
HEALTH *Sickly* students can walk-in to a nurse-led health centre on campus.
CRECHES/NURSERY Full and part-time care for kiddies aged 3 mths-5yrs, plus a holiday playscheme and an after-school club.
DISABLED *Effort has been made for disabled students. The newer buildings have been purpose-designed but it's on a hill – not easy for wheelchair users, who also have to go outside to go downstairs at the Union. Otherwise Glamorgan has tactile maps, guide dog pens, Braille facilities, dyslexia considerations and support workers. Accommodation can be adapted to suit needs.*
CRIME There've been recent attacks on students, allegedly by a group of local youths, but for the most part this or any other kind of crime is *rare as underdone steak.*

FINANCE
○ **AVE DEBT PER YEAR** £2,170 ○ **HOME STUDENT FEES** £1,200
FEES Welsh students don't have to pay the full £3K fee hike. Others are not so lucky.
○ **ACCESS FUND** £920,284 ○ **SUCCESSFUL APPLICATIONS/YR** 1,192 ○ **AVE PAYMENT** £720
SUPPORT A *bulging* sack of scholarships and bursaries available, getting more than 240 UCAS points, completing each academic year, and living more than 45 miles from campus, among others.

UNIVERSITY OF GLASGOW

1. ○ **THE UNIVERSITY OF GLASGOW** University Avenue, Glasgow, G12 8QQ **TEL** (0141) 330 2000 **EMAIL** prospectus@gla.ac.uk **WEBSITE** www.gla.ac.uk ○ **STUDENT REPRESENTATIVE COUNCIL** University Avenue, Glasgow, G12 8QQ
2. ○ **THE UNIVERSITY OF GLASGOW** Crichton Campus, University of Glasgow, Rutherford Mccowan Buildings, Dumfries, DG1 4ZL **TEL** (01387) 702 001 **EMAIL** information@crichton.gla.ac.uk **WEBSITE** www.cc.gla.ac.uk

GENERAL ()()()()()()()()()()()()()

G lasgwegians have endured enough jokes about Irn Bru, deep-fried Mars Bars and incomprehensible men in kilts head-butting one another to last anyone a lifetime. These days they're desperate to convince anyone who'll listen that Glasgae is the Scottish Florence, which is just about true, although it says more about Scotland than Italy. The old industrial town now has an upmarket shopping centre, some pretty impressive parks, cinemas, museums, galleries and a pleasantly laid-back West End café district. One thing they're not going to change, though, is the weather. Cold, wet, wet, cold and wet. And cold. The University's the UK's fourth oldest, founded by Papal Bull (that's an ordinance, not an energy drink) in 1451. It's been on Gilmorehill, in the West End, since 1870, although many of the buildings date from the 50s and 60s. There's a splendid chapel, some peaceful secluded quads, the academic centre in the Landmark Gilbert Scott Building and the Hunterian Museum.

SEX RATIO: ♀42 ♂58		**FOUNDED:** 1451
FULL-TIME U'GRADS: 15,890		**PART-TIME:** 4,565
POSTGRADS: 3,780		**NON-DEGREE:** 4,536
AVE COURSE: 4YRS		**ETHNIC:** 14%
STATE:PRIVATE SCHOOL: 86:14		**FLUNK RATE:** 14%
MATURE: 15%		**INTERNATIONAL:** 13%
DISABLED: 215		**LOCAL:** 42%

ATMOSPHERE
Some Glasgow students definitely consider themselves a cut above the rabble, which isn't necessarily a good thing. Within the University there's a liberal, cosmopolitan feel, but it stems from a high-trendy middle-class insecure sort of safety in numbers. Most of the insecurity focuses on the townies, known as neds, who (unwittingly) receive a regular slagging in the stuck-up University newspaper. Still, students are well in with the locals, partly because many of them are locals.

OTHER SITES
CRICHTON CAMPUS (275 students – Faculty of Arts & Engineering) In Dumfries, about 80 miles from Glasgow and with its own accommodation block, swimming pool, gym and nine hole golf course. Video links to the main campus supplement on-site teaching.

Words in italics are Push's point of view — take it or leave it...

GLASGOW
- **POPULATION** 609,370 ● **CITY CENTRE** 1 MILE
- **LONDON** 367 MILES ● **EDINBURGH** 52 MILES
- **HIGH TEMP** 21 ● **LOW TEMP** 0 ● **RAINFALL** 79

The city sits on the banks of the Clyde, which flows out towards the Isle of Arran to the west. The Strathclyde hills *yaw* off to the east and the *skeletons of the once-mighty* steel and shipping industries *rattle their chains* all around. Glasgow's been *dragging itself out of recession and is now a modern, cultured European city*. There are 35 museums and galleries, an IMAX cinema, some *big* music venues and the *best upmarket shopping this side of Knightsbridge*. But the underbelly is *dark, dangerous and druggy*. Some areas have *serious* drug problems with crime figures to match.

TRAVEL
TRAINS Queen's Street and Central Stations are the main ones, with regular services to London (from £62.10 return), Birmingham (£58.55), Inverness (£23.10), Aberdeen (£23.10), Dundee (£15.30) and more. Partick Station's closest to the University, though the main stations are *only* a five min subway ride away.

COACHES Eurolines coaches go to Paris, Amsterdam and Brussels. National Express goes to London (£36), Birmingham (£40.50), Cardiff (£49.50) and others. Buchanan Bus station is the main terminus, again five mins by subway.

CAR *Good* connections all over the country including the M74, A8/M8, A80/M80, A82, A77 and A736. Parking's fairly restricted; students need permits on University property.

AIR Glasgow International Airport (£5 by bus) is the main airport. Glasgow Prestwick (£5 train ride) offers Ryanair flights to Paris Beauvais, Brussels and Belfast.

LOCAL Buses around the city centre (55p/£1) are *frequent and cheap*. Local rail services are *pretty good too*, stopping all over the city. A termly (10-week) pass is £339. The subway, known locally as the Clockwork Orange, is 90p a trip. Strathclyde Public Transport issues a travelcard. (£12.10/week) for unlimited weekly travel.

COLLEGE Free Campus-to-Halls Minibus Service until 10.30pm. The bus is driven by student drivers and stops at residences including Murano Street, Queen Margaret Residence, Winton Drive, Wolfson Hall, Cairncross House, Kelvinhaugh Street and Maclay Hall/Park Circus. *Not wheelchair friendly, though.*

TAXIS Black hackneys and privates *charge like the Light Brigade. Worth it for the very rich/very drunk.*

BICYCLES Hills, *snarly* traffic and *decent* public transport mean bikers are in a minority, but cycle routes between campus and residences ensure those that choose pedal power are provided for.

CAREER PROSPECTS
- **CAREERS SERVICE** ● **NO. OF STAFF** 17
- **UNEMPLOYED AFTER 6**MTHS 4%

The service participates in the Club 21 scheme, which places students with big graduate employers like AMEC and Deutsche Bank.

FAMOUS ALUMNI
John Boyd Orr (nutritionist); William Boyd, A J Cronin (writers); Gerard Butler (actor); Menzies Campbell MP (Lib Dem leader); Donald Dewar (Scotland's late First Minister); the Delgados; James Herriot (vet, writer); Pat Kane (Hue & Cry); Lord Kelvin (of the temperature scale); Charles Kennedy (ex-Lib Dem leader); Dr Kamal Ketuly (Deputy Minister for Human Rights in Iraq); Joseph Lister (pioneer of antiseptics); John Logie Baird (invented TV); Anne Louise McIlroy (pioneering woman in medicine); Professor Macquorn Rankine (wrote first engineering textbook); Shereen Nanjiani (TV presenter); Andrew Neil (TV politico); Emma Richards (yachtswoman); Adam Smith (economist); John Smith (late Labour leader); Frederick Soddy (scientist); James Watt (inventor).

FURTHER INFO
- **PROSPECTUSES** UNDERGRAD; POSTGRAD; SOME DEPTS
- **OPEN DAYS**

ACADEMIC ○○○○○○○○○○○○○○

- **RUSSELL GROUP**

The University's got a *proud* reputation and has churned out *lots of eminent* inventors, politicians and so on. Degrees are *quite* flexible, and some students can mix and match bits from other courses and faculties. Arts, Science and Social Science students choose three subjects to study in their first year.

ENTRY POINTS: 180-340	AVE POINTS: N/A
APPLICATIONS PER PLACE: 7	CLEARING: 2%
NO. OF TERMS: 2	LENGTH OF TERMS: 12WKS
STAFF TO STUDENT RATIO: 1:12	STUDY ADDICTS: 16%
TEACHING: ★★★	RESEARCH: ★★★★★
YEAR ABROAD: 1%	SANDWICH STUDENTS: 7%
1STS: 8%	2.2s: 20%
2.1s: 42%	3RDS: 4%

ADMISSIONS
- **APPLY VIA UCAS**

SUBJECTS
ART 26%   **CRICHTON CAMPUS** 2%   **EDUCATION** 5%
ENGINEERING 8%   **LAW & FINANCIAL STUDIES** 8%
MEDICINE 12%   **SCIENCE** 25%   **SOCIAL SCIENCES** 12%
VETERINARY MEDICINE 3%
BEST Classics; Economics; Geography; History; Law; Theology & Religious Studies.
UNUSUAL: Astronomy; Avionics; Battlefield Archaeology (MLitt); Countryside Management; Neuroinformatics; Parasitology; Virology.

LIBRARIES
- **2,000,000+** BOOKS ● **3,200** STUDY PLACES
- **SPEND PER STUDENT** ££££

The University Library also stocks electronic journals, periodicals and manuscripts, *as well as lots of dusty rooms full of specialist books and* scholars gathering cobwebs. Politics and history are particularly well endowed. Slack-jawed window-gazing over the city is best done on the 11th floor.

COMPUTERS
◉ 683 WORKSTATIONS
There are computers all over the University Library and faculties and wi-fi is *extending its tendrils*. The facilities *aren't brilliant* and the lack of 24-hr access is *a sore point*. All students are required to pass a Basic IT Competence test *to ensure they don't pour coffee in the keyboards or chew floppy disks*. All rooms are networked.

OTHER LEARNING FACILITIES
Media Centre; theatre; language labs; CAD studio; rehearsal rooms; practice courtroom; animal hospital.

ENTERTAINMENT ◍◍◍◍◍◍◍◍◍

THE CITY
◉ **PRICE OF A PINT OF BEER** £2.20 ◉ **GLASS OF WINE** £2.50 ◉ **CAN OF RED BULL** £1.50

There's *loads* to do in Glasgow, but thanks to council *killjoys*, happy-hour bingeing's no longer one of them. Bars can only serve cheap booze if they agree that the cheap prices will be permanent. *So it can be pricey*.

CINEMAS 35 screens in the city, including a *colossal* Cineworld multiplex, an IMAX 3D screen, the arty Glasgow Film Theatre and *uber-arty* Centre for Contemporary Arts (CCA) and the *plush* independent Grosvenor (serves *cheap* beer all day).

THEATRES *A few to choose from*, including the King's Theatre (*mainstream* family musicals), the Theatre Royal (*posh* ballet and opera), Tron (contemporary plays and performance art) and the Arches (Shakespeare and much more).

PUBS *Pubbers paradise*. Sauchiehall Street in the city centre is a *major* pub crawl with Firewater, the Hall, Driftwood and Nice 'n' Sleazy playing commercial pop and indie. The Brunswick Cellars, Babooshka, Buddha and the Local cater to *more expensive tastes – mostly not those of students*. The Merchant City area has Bargo (*perfect in summer but pricey*) and Blackfriars (live music, *popular* on Sundays). Princes Square's October (*cheap* vodka/Red Bull) is *popular pre-club*. Off the little side lanes from Buchanan Street there are cosy bars with DJs: Bar 10; Bar Soba; or the Lab. *Keep well away from the Rangers and Celtic pubs in Paisley Road West and Gallowgate.*

CLUBBING *A fast-moving and fast-changing scene is beloved by Glasgow students*. Pushplugs: Chinawhite (£8 but worth it); Polo Lounge (gay *baroque*). Student prices and cheese are at Destiny, Jumpin Jack's and the Shed. There's also the Cathouse (goth) and Blanket (cheese/R&B). The Tunnel (once legendary) and the Garage (cheese hell) are best avoided.

EATING OUT *All of the pubs do serviceable nosh. Also numerous take-aways and grease-joints – JJ's and Uni Takeaway are the favourites.*

MUSIC VENUES *Lots of variety*, including the Barrowlands and Carling Academy for international acts and club nights; the CCA for *almost everything*; ABC for indie club nights and big indie bands; the award-laden King Tut's Wah Wah Hut for up-and-coming indie acts; and the *gargantuan* SECC.

COMEDY/CABARET *Giggles* every night at the Stand (*cheap and cosy*), which entices the likes of Adam Bloom, Nick Revell and Alan Carr to *stand-up and be laughed at*. Glasgow International Comedy Festival *brings out the big guns* for two and a half weeks each year.

EATING OUT Chainy and cheap. Kebabish does fancy-kebab-cum-curry scoff with lunches costing around £3. The West End, untainted by Starbucks, has cut-above cafés open until 11pm or midnight – try Offshore (bright and shiny with free wi-fi); Bibliocafé (second-hand books); Beanscene (candlelit cosiness).

UNIVERSITY
◉ **PRICE OF A PINT OF BEER** £1.25 ◉ **GLASS OF WINE** £1.25 ◉ **CAN OF RED BULL** £2

BARS Twelve bars are split between two Glasgow SUs (see below for more details on Unions). At Glasgow University Union (GUU) late licences and cheap drinkies abound – there's the Beer Bar (*pubby refuge*); Deep 6 (sports and bands); the Playing Fields (sports); Altitude (chilled out with pool tables); the Cocktail Bar (cocktails, *duh*); and the Billiard Hall (snooker). At Queen Margaret Union (QMU) there's Jim's Bar (*great* acoustic open mic night); Qudos (*legendary* club nights) and the Coffee Bar (*relaxed, eco-conscious hippy chill-out*).

THEATRES The Gilmorehill Centre has a theatre space for student groups' public performances.

FILM Sproadic screenings, veering from arthouse to mainstream.

MUSIC VENUES QMU *takes music seriously*. It *prides itself* on the acts it attracts and has its own record label. Nirvana and Red Hot Chili Peppers have both appeared and nowadays it attracts *cool big names* like Magic Numbers, Gary Numan and KT Tunstall. The debating hall (1,500 cap) at GUU gets *soon-to-be-greatness* along the lines of Arcade Fire.

CLUBBING Qudos is *the place to be seen*. Cheesy Pop's *an old fave*, Revolution (nu-metal/alternative) *a young pretender*. GUU's Hive club is *regarded as the best in town*.

FOOD QMU has the Food Factory (sarnies and soup) and a fairtrade coffee bar, as well as a Delice de France café (toasties and bagels). The GUU Servery does hot and cold food all day and is *easy on the pocket*.

OTHER The QMU Christmas extravaganza is the 12-hr Cheesy – *the name sums it up*. For *more civilised* sporting types, the GUSA Annual Awards celebrates those who've *run, jumped and sweated the best* during the year. GUU's annual Daft Friday is a *ginormous* black tie ball.

G

Words in italics are Push's point of view — take it or leave it...

SOCIAL ()()()()()()()()()()()()()()

STUDENT REPRESENTATIVE COUNCIL/GLASGOW UNIVERSITY UNION/QUEEN MARGARET UNION

O 4 SABBATICALS O TURNOUT AT LAST BALLOT 6%

Take a deep breath – this is complicated. There are five SUs in Glasgow, with two in competition. First, there's the Student Representative Council (all students get automatic membership), which organises student representation, welfare, clubs and societies. *It's gently left-wing and not very high profile.* Next come the two services unions. A student can be a member of only one of these and they must choose in their first few weeks. The rivalries mean a *ferociously busy* freshers week and students can use the facilities at both most of the time, but can only vote in their own union. Not joining either means no use of facilities at either. *So there.* Glasgow University Union, originally a men-only affair, has a large centre in a listed building near the centre of the campus. It organises debates, as well as services, and *rates with the Oxbridge Unions* for the speakers it attracts. Fans of QMU (formerly the Women's union) would argue that theirs *is where the cool people who don't like rugby hang out and ents are given priority over public school-esque drinking games.* GUU used to be the bigger, but QMU has overtaken it in recent years. The fourth union is the Sports Association (GUSA). Finally, there's the Postgraduate Research Club, PRC. None of the unions is a member of NUS, but they're members of Northern Services, a 'buying consortium', *ie. cheap beer.*

SU FACILITIES

SRC Printing; secondhand bookshop; vending machines.
GUU Seven bars; cafeteria; restaurant; minibus; travel agency; six pool tables; ten snooker tables; canteen shop; 24-hr student facilities; print shop; photocopying; games machines; pool; juke box; vending machines; two libraries; meeting and conference rooms; launderette; Bank of Scotland ATMs.
QMU Three bars; cafeteria; restaurant; sandwich bar; print shop; photocopying; shop; games and vending machines; two pool tables; study rooms; juke box; snooker room (members only); TV lounge; meeting rooms; customised nightclub; launderette; Bank of Scotland ATM.

CLUBS (NON-SPORTING)

AEGEE - The European; Caribou House Canadian; Cecilian (Musical & Operatic Club); Chamber Choir; Chess; Chinese; Student Christian Movement; Cuckoo's Nest (live role-playing); University Dialectic (debating); Dirty Weekenders Conservation; East Timor & Indonesia Group; Exploration; Gaming (role-playing); table-top battles; collectible card games); GUARDS World of Darkness Roleplaying; Hellenic; Hindu; Hong Kong; Humanist; Indian Cultural; International; IO (science fiction & fantasy); Italian; Japanese; Korean; Linux; Literary; Living Marxism; Malaysia; Medical Ethics Debating; Network Gaming; Ossianic; Science Journalism; Scottish Country Dance; Glasgow University Scottish Nationalist Association; (GUSNA); Singapore; Slavonic; STAR: student action for refugees; Student Volunteers Abroad (SVA); Student Travellers Association (holidays); Turkish; Turnbull Catholic; Visual Art Club; Glasgow University Young European Movement. **See also Clubs tables.**

OTHER ORGANISATIONS

'The Guardian' (not that one) is an award-winning yet scurrilous newspaper. QMU's fortnightly 'Qmunicate' has listings and highbrow culture stuff. The *artsy* 'Glasgow University Magazine' is the oldest student publication in Scotland and mixes lighthearted and serious content *pretty effectively.* 'SubCity' broadcasts on FM for a month of every year across the West End; 'GUST' TV wins regular awards for its occasional broadcasts, which are repeated *endlessly* in the bars. Rag raises cash for causes all year, and there are *countless* opportunities for *conscience-led* volunteers.

RELIGIOUS

CofE, Methodist, Free Church, Baptist, RC and CofS chaplaincies on campus. In town there's Glasgow (CofS) and St Andrew's (RC) Cathedrals. Also places of worship locally for Muslims, Jews, Buddhists, Hindus and Sikhs.

PAID WORK

O JOB BUREAU

Loads of information and training, student advisors try to lend a hand. The GU Templine places candidates in temporary jobs, and the Jobcentre in Partick's also *geared towards* students. The SRC posts vacancies too. *Glasgow's a busy, bustly place and there are plenty of pubs, clubs and shops that actively seek out students to do the gruntwork.*

SPORTS ()()()()()()()()()()()()()

O RECENT SUCCESSES FOOTBALL, HOCKEY, LACROSSE, NETBALL, RUGBY, SQUASH, SWIMMING **O BUSA RANKING** 18

There's a *well-organised* sporting scene with *okay – and getting okayer by the year* – facilities.

SPORTS FACILITIES

92 acres of sports fields; two rugby pitches; grass shinty/lacrosse pitch; squash and tennis courts; sports halls; two basketball courts; swimming pool; gym/multigym; aerobics studio; sauna. In and around Glasgow: leisure centre; running track; squash and tennis courts; swimming pool; ice rink; croquet lawn/bowling green; golf course. Use of the

facilities costs £30 a year. A new development at the Garscube outdoor site will house another swimming pool, eight badminton courts, a gym and a health suite. The river, mountains and dry and artificial snow ski slopes *give further amusement.*

SPORTING CLUBS

Aikido; American Football; Boats (rowing); Boxing; Cheerleading; Curling; Gaelic Football; Hares & Hounds (outdoor running/street orienteering); Lacrosse; Glasgow University Motor Sports Club (GUMSC); Mountaineering; Muay Thai; Parachuting; Potholing; Rifle & Sporting Gun; Shinty; Ski & Snowboarding; Shorinji-Kempo (martial art); Snooker; Surfing & Kitesurfing; Swimming & Waterpolo; Ultimate Frisbee; Windsurfing. **See also Clubs tables.**

ATTRACTIONS

Celtic and Rangers are the *bitterest* of rivals, as well as the *only teams in Scotland worth watching.*

ACCOMMODATION ◖◖◖◖◖◖◖◖◖◖

IN UNIVERSITY

◉ **CATERED** 1% ◉ **COST** £100 (40WKS)
◉ **SELF-CATERING** 21% ◉ **COST** £74 (40WKS) ◉ **1ST YRS LIVING IN** N/A ◉ **INSURANCE PREMIUM** ££££
AVAILABILITY Priority in halls goes to non-Weedgies though the University usually finds space for everyone who needs it – around 15% have to share (they do try to avoid sticking chalk with cheese though). Most first years who want to can live in, and 25% of rooms are reserved each year for returning students. Standards and facilities vary from *passable to plush, and unsavoury to en suite.* Queen Mag's halls are popular. Murano St halls *border a dodgy area – beware.* All are within 25 mins walk of campus. Wardens *ward off evildoers* 24/7 but break-ins are *all too common* (113 last year). Disabled and family accommodation also available.
CAR PARKING *Not too hard* at most halls (apart from the student apartment complex) with a permit (£15).

EXTERNALLY

◉ **AVE RENT** £60 ◉ **LIVING AT HOME** 27%
AVAILABILITY Rent in the West End is *rising but reasonable* and standards *pleasantly high.* There are *cheaper* bits of Glasgow, but *none so convenient.*
HOUSING HELP Vacancy database, annual housing help day, and access to the Private Accommodation Database (Pad) which covers all five Glasgow institutions and accredits *decent* private housing.

WELFARE ◖◖◖◖◖◖◖◖◖◖◖◖◖

SERVICES

◉ **LGBT OFFICER & SOCIETY** ◉ **WOMEN'S OFFICER**
◉ **MATURE STUDENTS' SOCIETY**
◉ **INTERNATIONAL STUDENTS' OFFICER** ◉ **POSTGRAD SOCIETY** ◉ **DISABILITIES OFFICER** ◉ **LATE-NIGHT MINIBUS**
◉ **NIGHTLINE** ◉ **UNIVERSITY COUNSELLORS** 6 FULL/2 PART ◉ **CRIME RATING** !!!
HEALTH Free University health service with GPs, psychiatrist, clinical psychologist.
CRECHES/NURSERY 74 places for newborns up to 5yrs.
DISABLED Facilities in newer halls of residence are *okay* and there's a specially adapted learning centre in the library, but *even the best intentions can't stop the main building being old and inaccessible.*
DRUGS *An ugly druggy scene in the city. Proceed with caution.*
CRIME Car theft's a *problem* around campus and the lighting is *poor, but there's little else to cry about so long as students keep their wits about them –* those that don't (or are just plain unlucky) can fall victim to occasional attacks.

FINANCE

◉ **AVE DEBT PER YEAR** £2,419 ◉ **HOME STUDENT FEES** £1,700
FEES Scottish universities don't charge top-up fees – to Scottish students, at least. £3,000 for other UK and EU students and £8,300-£19,000 for internationals.
◉ **ACCESS FUND** £774,550
SUPPORT The Carnegie Trust pays tuition fees, the mature students' bursary helps with childcare costs. The University has a scholarship programme for *talented* athletes, which pays bursaries of £300-1,500 and the Beaton Scholarship has £1,500 up for grabs for the best sob story.

The Archbishop of Canterbury is the only person in the country who can award degrees personally, and legally speaking, he is a university.

GLASGOW CALEDONIAN UNIVERSITY

FORMERLY GLASGOW POLYTECHNIC

○ **GLASGOW CALEDONIAN UNIVERSITY** Cowcaddens Road, Glasgow, G4 0BA **TEL** (0141) 331 3000 **E-MAIL** rhu@gcal.ac.uk **WEBSITE** www.caledonian.ac.uk ○ **GLASGOW CALEDONIAN UNIVERSITY STUDENTS' ASSOCIATION**, 70 Cowcaddens Road, Glasgow, G4 0BA **TEL** (0141) 332 0681 **EMAIL** student.president@caledonian.ac.uk **WEBSITE** www.caledonianstudent.com

GENERAL ○○○○○○○○○○○○○○

For general information on Glasgow: see University of Glasgow. Glasgow Caledonian's a modern-faced institution with a historical background. It began in 1875 as a small college with a *mere* 100 students. These days it's a *much bigger, heartier* University with a load more students and is moored in the heart of Glasgow's city centre. Recent cash-splashing means that facilities are *good*, especially for healthcare students.

SEX RATIO: ♂39 ♀61	**FOUNDED:** 1875
FULL-TIME U'GRADS: 10,662	**PART-TIME:** 2,836
POSTGRADS: 2,362	**NON-DEGREE:** N/A
AVE COURSE: 4YRS	**ETHNIC:** 4%
STATE:PRIVATE SCHOOL: 97:3	**FLUNK RATE:** 18%
MATURE: 44%	**INTERNATIONAL:** 3%
DISABLED: 145	**LOCAL:** 90%

ATMOSPHERE

The student population is *overwhelmingly* local and/or mature. It's a *functional sort of place* that teaches degrees and *not a lot more, something most of the students appreciate. They're happy to get on with studying and leave the student capers to the trendies at the s/wankier University of Glasgow.*

GLASGOW see University of Glasgow
○ **CITY CENTRE** 0 MILES

TRAVEL

See University of Glasgow
The tube and a big bus depot are just next door to the City campus and Queen Street station is 10 mins walk away. *Handy, eh?*

CAREER PROSPECTS
○ **CAREERS SERVICE** ○ **NO. OF STAFF** 7 FULL
○ **UNEMPLOYED AFTER 6**MTHS 7%

FAMOUS ALUMNI

Cathy Jamieson (Scottish Executive Justice Minister); Andy Kerr (Scottish Executive Health & Community Care Minister); Rhona Martin MBE (Olympic gold medal winning curler).

FURTHER INFO
○ **PROSPECTUSES** UNDERGRAD; POSTGRAD ○ **OPEN DAYS**

ACADEMIC ○○○○○○○○○○○○○○

The business school's the *glittery trinket in Caledonian's tiara*. It's the biggest one in Scotland and was opened by Michelle Mone, business-woman and creator of the gel-filled bra (*madam, Push salutes you*). There's a *healthy medical rep*, with one in five of Scotland's nurses and healthcare professionals training here. Teaching-wise, lectures and tutorials are the norm. Engineering, Science and Computing students have their own labs with specialist equipment. There's also a clinical simulation lab (mock hospital) for *Florence Nightingale types* and Microsoft had a hand in the new games technology lab.

ENTRY POINTS: 160-320	**AVE POINTS:** 285
APPLICATIONS PER PLACE: 6	**CLEARING:** 3%
NO. OF TERMS: 2	**LENGTH OF TERMS:** 15WKS
STAFF TO STUDENT RATIO: 1:10	**STUDY ADDICTS:** 92%
TEACHING: ✶	**RESEARCH:** ✶✶
YEAR ABROAD: 1%	**SANDWICH STUDENTS:** 8%
1STS: 11%	**2.2S:** 36%
2.1S: 50%	**3RDS:** 3%

ADMISSIONS
○ **APPLY VIA UCAS/CATCH FOR NURSING & MIDWIFERY**
Access is *wider than a sumo wrestler's bottom*, with 27% of students coming from non-traditional backgrounds.

SUBJECTS
ART & HOSPITALITY 8%   **BUILT ENVIRONMENT** 6%
BUSINESS & LANGUAGES 25%   **COMPUTING** 8%
ENGINEERING 10%   **GENERAL STUDENTS** 1%
HEALTH 19%   **MATHS** 1%   **SOCIAL SCIENCES** 11%
SCIENCE 11%
BEST Biomedical Sciences; Computing; Engineering; Nursing; Optometry.

LIBRARIES
○ **350,000 BOOKS** ○ **1,800 STUDY PLACES**
The new Saltire Centre is a *seriously snazzed-up study space* – as well as books, desks and the usual library gubbins, there are plastic-palm tree lights, inflatable bubbles in which to sit and piped-in birdsong. *It might sound like a step too far towards the poncy side of zen, but with its huge, airy atrium, sofas, beanbags and balconies, the well-equipped building is deservedly popular as a daytime hang-out. Full futuristic geek points.*

G

COMPUTERS
◉ **1,550 WORKSTATIONS**
The Saltire centre has 500 machines and 150 laptops to loan. All first year rooms have internet points.

OTHER LEARNING FACILITIES
Games technology lab.

ENTERTAINMENT ◗◗◗◗◗◗◗◗◗

THE CITY see University of Glasgow

UNIVERSITY
◉ **PRICE OF A PINT OF BEER** £1.75 ◉ **GLASS OF WINE** £1.30
A new SA building's pencilled in for a grand opening (*perhaps by another lingerie designer*) sometime soon. It should have two bars, an internet café, games room and more. *As things stand, though, the SA pales in comparison to the modern University buildings and ents are at a sorry ebb. Students look to the city for kicks.*
BARS The Bedsit contains two bars: the Main Bar and the Back Bar. *They're nothing spectacular. The entertainment only goes as far as the occasional quiz and karaoke session.*
CLUBBING *Weekend frolics were cancelled because of lack of interest.* Funky Fridays has drinks offers and chilled-out choons from 3pm-3am. Radio Onesters Trevor Nelson, Vernon Kay and Colin & Edith have DJ'd.
FOOD *Legendary* baguette shop upstairs in Bedsit. The City campus refectory is *pretty expensive*, although the coffee shop *isn't too bad*.
OTHER Two graduation balls and a sports ball *fill the frill quota* every year.

SOCIAL ◖◗◗◗◗◗◗◗◗◗◗◗◗◗

GLASGOW CALEDONIAN UNIVERSITY STUDENTS' ASSOCIATION
◉ **4 SABBATICALS** ◉ **TURNOUT AT LAST BALLOT** 13%
◉ **NUS MEMBER**
The SA have *vague* ambitions to political agitation, *especially* if it involves the Scottish end of the Free Education Movement.

SA FACILITIES
SA building (the Bedsit): three bars; canteen and pizza café; pool tables; meeting room; Bank of Scotland ATM; photocopying/printing services; photo booth; payphones; advice centre; crèche; video games; stationery shop; new book shop and book-trading service.

CLUBS (NON-SPORTING)
Alpha Course (Christian conversion); Chinese; Go Team Events (first aid, teambuilding etc.); Hellenic; Music. *See also Clubs tables.*

OTHER ORGANISATIONS
Re:Union's the *light-hearted* glossy mag (six times a year), run and paid for by the SA. Rag week bundles most of the University's charity work into seven *frenzied* days once a year.

RELIGIOUS
◉ **1 CHAPLAIN**
Chaplaincy room and Muslim prayer room. Religion in Glasgow: see University of Glasgow

PAID WORK
◉ **JOB BUREAU**

SPORTS ◖◗◗◗◗◗◗◗◗◗◗◗◗◗

◉ **RECENT SUCCESSES** MEN'S VOLLEYBALL, MEN'S HOCKEY
◉ **BUSA RANKING** 75

SPORTS FACILITIES
With no outdoor facilities to call its own, the University makes do with its sports complex the Arc which has: gym; massage service; various yoga/pilates/aerobic classes; trampolining; netball; karate; judo; basketball; table tennis; Muay Thai boxing; handball; volleyball. *Not bad, and cheap to boot* at £35 a year. The University has links with the local Cartha Queens Park Rugby club for training and facilities.

SPORTING CLUBS
Adventure; Muay Thai Boxing; Mountaineering; Paintball & Airsoft; Rowing; Sailplane & Gliding; SkyDiving; Snowboarding; Table Tennis. **See also Clubs tables.**

ATTRACTIONS see University of Glasgow

ACCOMMODATION

IN UNIVERSITY
◉ **SELF-CATERING** 6% ◉ **COST** £75 (37WKS)
◉ **INSURANCE PREMIUM** ££££
AVAILABILITY Facilities in Caledonian Court are *far from ideal*. There's not room for *anything like* the whole fresher intake, and anyone outside the first year can *dream on*. The accommodation that's there is *okay – modern and close to town* – about half of all rooms are en suite and there are flats adapted for disabled students.
CAR PARKING *Limited* in halls. Most student drivers leave cars in local car parks (about £7 a day).

EXTERNALLY see University of Glasgow
◉ **AVE RENT** £65
AVAILABILITY Two private halls near campus – one UNITE, one the *plush but pricey* Victoria Halls –

G

mop up the fresher excess and are popular with second years too. Beware of straying into nearby rough areas, though. The West End is popular, although it's a way away from Cally. Woodlands is also popular and the Gorbals and Clydeside are cheaper but less salubrious.

HOUSING HELP The University accommodation office vets landlords and posts vacancies.

WELFARE ()()()()()()()()()()()()()()()()

SERVICES
- **LGBT OFFICER & SOCIETY**
- **WOMEN'S OFFICER** ○ **MATURE STUDENTS' SOCIETY**
- **INTERNATIONAL STUDENTS' OFFICER** ○ **DISABILITIES OFFICER** ○ **LATE-NIGHT MINIBUS** ○ **NIGHTLINE**
- **UNIVERSITY COUNSELLORS** 5 FULL
- **SA COUNSELLORS** 1 ○ **CRIME RATING** !!!

The Base, in the Saltire Centre, gives academic advice.

NURSERY The Beechwood Nursery looks after kids while mum/dad hits the books.

DISABILITIES Good facilities in the modern buildings, with all the necessary ramps, lifts, loops and so on.

FINANCE
- **AVE DEBT PER YEAR** £3,496
- **HOME STUDENT FEES** £1,700

FEES Scots just have to pay the graduate endowment. Other UK undergraduates are stung for up to £1,700 and internationals pay £7,000-8,000.

- **ACCESS FUND** £240,000

SUPPORT Emergency loans (£20-50) are available and the hardship fund will shell out £400-500 at a throw. Scholarships are available for undergrads and grads studying travel and tourism. The University helps with some students' childcare costs. £2,000 sport scholarships are available for those with talent on the track, field, rink etc.

▶ **GLASGOW POLYTECHNIC**

see *Glasgow Caledonian University*

UNIVERSITY OF GLOUCESTERSHIRE

FORMERLY CHELTENHAM AND GLOUCESTER COLLEGE OF HIGHER EDUCATION

1. ○ **UNIVERSITY OF GLOUCESTERSHIRE** Park Campus, The Park, Cheltenham, GL50 2RH **TEL** (08707) 210210 **EMAIL** admissions@glos.ac.uk **WEBSITE** www.glos.ac.uk
○ **UNIVERSITY OF GLOUCESTERSHIRE STUDENTS' UNION (PARK CAMPUS)** The Park, Cheltenham, GL50 2RH **TEL** (01242) 714 360 **EMAIL** pksu@glos.ac.uk **WEBSITE** www.ugsu.org
2. ○ **FRANCIS CLOSE HALL CAMPUS** Swindon Road, Cheltenham, GL50 4AZ **TEL** (01242) 532 900
○ **UNIVERSITY OF GLOUCESTERSHIRE STUDENTS' UNION (FCH CAMPUS)** Swindon Road, Cheltenham, GL50 4AZ **TEL** (01242) 543 439 **EMAIL** fchsu@glos.ac.uk
3. ○ **PITTVILLE CAMPUS** Albert road, Cheltenham, GL52 3JG **TEL** (01242) 532 210
○ **UNIVERSITY OF GLOUCESTERSHIRE STUDENTS' UNION (PITVILLE CAMPUS)** Albert Road, Cheltenham, GL52 3JG **TEL** (01242) 532 219 **EMAIL** pvsu@glos.ac.uk
4. ○ **OXSTALLS CAMPUS** Oxstalls Lane, Longlevens, Gloucester, GL2 9HW **TEL** (01242) 532 210
○ **UNIVERSITY OF GLOUCESTERSHIRE STUDENTS' UNION (PITVILLE CAMPUS)** Albert Road, Cheltenham, GL52 3JG **TEL** (01452) 876 659 **EMAIL** oxsu@glos.ac.uk

---

GENERAL ()()()()()()()()()()()()()

The two towns of Cheltenham and Gloucester are less than seven miles apart amidst the *genteel* hills of Gloucestershire, beyond the end of the Bristol Channel, where it gives up being the Severn Estuary and becomes the River Severn. The main site at Park Campus (originally a botanic and zoological garden, note the Africa-shaped lake) is a *leafy retreat* 1.5 miles from Cheltenham town centre, with *elderly* buildings, *elegant* grounds and an *extraordinary* garden. Among the tennis courts and the large pond where the ducks occasionally allow students to

row, it's one of the few places in England where Wellingtonia trees can be found. They have very soft bark, *which can be punched or head-butted without fear of pain – it's not good for the trees but handy for students wandering home drunk.* Gloucestershire University has *reinvented itself more times than Madonna* – beginning life as the Mechanics' Institutes in Cheltenham and Gloucester in the early 1800s, then dabbling in the waters of teacher training for just under a century before various separations and mergers morphed it into an Arts and Technology College and finally, in 2001, a university. A new site opened in Gloucester in 2002, which meant that the University's previous name was briefly accurate, before they immediately changed it. Nowadays, the University spreads its talents over four sites. There's also the Urban Learning Foundation, an affiliated centre in London catering for postgrad education students, *about which most students neither know nor care.*

SEX RATIO: ♦45 ♦55	**FOUNDED:** 1834
FULL-TIME U'GRADS: 6,446	**PART-TIME:** 3,204
POSTGRADS: 1,573	**NON-DEGREE:** N/A
AVE COURSE: 3–4YRS	**ETHNIC:** 6%
STATE:PRIVATE SCHOOL: 94:6	**FLUNK RATE:** 14%
MATURE: 30%	**INTERNATIONAL:** 7%
DISABLED: 185	**LOCAL:** 30%

ATMOSPHERE
With its spotlessly clean white walls and soothing ambience, the Park Campus in Cheltenham would make a great rehab centre for drug-pickled celebs. Like the town, the friendly student body is mostly middle-England and middle-class, with just a pinch of eccentricity and vague aspirations towards something a bit cooler. With nearly a third of students coming from the local area, *the place tends towards the cosy rather than the crazy.*

OTHER SITES
FRANCIS CLOSE HALL Teachers have been trained at the Francis Close Hall Campus for over 150 years. Social Sciences, Theology, Religious Studies, Environmental Programmes and Humanities are more recent additions. FCH is *picturesque and classically academic-looking with an Oxbridge-style gothic* quadrangle and clock tower. Notable facilities include the Gloucester Suite training restaurant for Hospitality students and a studio and lab for environmentalists.

PITTVILLE CAMPUS (2,500 students – Art & Design, Media) Just outside Cheltenham town centre, near the racecourse, overlooking the *beautiful* Cotswolds, *is peaceful and laid-back* – a home to sculpture, painting and print-making studios, a graphics editing suite, multi-media suites, a broadcast journalism studio and an art gallery.

OXSTALLS CAMPUS (Sport & Leisure) Five mins from the centre of Gloucester (nine miles from Cheltenham) is a *newish* £19m campus with two halls of residence housing 308 students. Gloucester itself is *riddled with history* and chunks of Roman paraphernalia are scattered around. The city possesses a *stunning* medieval cathedral (which was used for corridor scenes in the Harry Potter films).

CHELTENHAM
- ● **POPULATION** 110,000 ● **CITY CENTRE** 1 MILE
- ● **LONDON** 95 MILES ● **BRISTOL** 40 MILES
- ● **BIRMINGHAM** 43 MILES
- ● **HIGH TEMP** 22 ● **LOW TEMP** 1 ● **RAINFALL** 60

Cheltenham became a fashionable resort in the 18th century when the famously demented George III decided that its spring water would be good for him. The result can still be seen in the elegant Regency architecture that sprang up at the time. However, the spa ran dry in 2003 and these days it's probably horses and spies which are the town's main claims to fame. GCHQ, *the top-secret-in-a-very-British-way (ie. everybody knows about it but officially it doesn't exist) snoop centre is just up the road. Despite its staid appearance, the town does manage to attract well-respected jazz and literary festivals every year.*

TRAVEL
CHELTENHAM
TRAINS Cheltenham Spa station is a mile from Park Campus, offering direct links to London (from £29.70 return), Birmingham (£11.10), Manchester (£23.10) and elsewhere.
COACHES National Express, Marchants and Swanbrook operate coach services from Cheltenham's Royal Well bus station; a return trip to London costs around £20, but advance fares on National Express start much lower.
CAR Main road links to the A40, M5 (junction 11) and M40. Cheltenham has a tricky one-way system to master.
UNIVERSITY The free Unimotion bus service shuttles between campuses twice an hour hops from Cheltenham station to the Park Campus in five mins.
AIR Heathrow's less than two hours away but Birmingham International, Staverton and Bristol airports are closer by for *less ambitious* flights.
BICYCLES The University offers a subsidy to students who want to buy bikes.

GLOUCESTER
TRAINS Gloucester to London Paddington for around £24 return, Bristol Parkway for £10.10.
COACHES The National Express service runs between Gloucester and London Victoria (prices as Cheltenham), and elsewhere.
CARS The M5 runs close by.

CAREER PROSPECTS
- ● **CAREERS SERVICE** ● **NO. OF STAFF** 1 FULL/6 PART
- ● **UNEMPLOYED AFTER 6MTHS** 8%

Impressive integration with the academic side of things – several of the careers advisors are also lecturers and rather than just being an add-on, careers advice is also doled out during classes.

FAMOUS ALUMNI
Chris Beardshaw (TV gardener); Chris Broad, Sarah Potter (cricketers); David Bryant (bowls champion); Adam Buxton (the Adam & Joe show); Jonathan Callard (rugby international); Peter Edwards (artist); Beverley Knight (R&B diva); Roger Lovegrove (wildlife broadcaster); P H Newby (writer).

FURTHER INFO
- ● **PROSPECTUSES** UNDERGRAD; POSTGRAD; SOME DEPARTMENTS; DVD; INTERNATIONAL; NEWSLETTER
- ● **OPEN DAYS**

The *snazzy* DVD 'brochure' was made by former students and follows seven finalists at the end of

G

summer term. International students should contact the international office – intoffice@glos.ac.uk

ACADEMIC ⊙⊙⊙⊙⊙⊙⊙⊙⊙⊙⊙⊙

129 fields – *that's courses to you and Push* – in nine subject areas are grouped into four faculties. The University's long tradition of teacher training has made it something of a *hotspot* for education courses. Assessment is flexible – final marks are calculated either from final grades or average results over the previous two years, whichever's better, *helping students breathe more easily.* Courses lean towards the vocational and are modular, allowing joint and major/minor subject combinations. First years face compulsory modules in study skills and personal development (leadership, teamwork etc.).

ENTRY POINTS: 100-280	AVE POINTS: 200
APPLICATIONS PER PLACE: 5	CLEARING: 6%
NO. OF TERMS: 2	LENGTH OF TERMS: 15wks
STAFF TO STUDENT RATIO: 1:20	STUDY ADDICTS: 13%
TEACHING: **	RESEARCH: ***
YEAR ABROAD: 3%	SANDWICH STUDENTS: 20%
1STS: 6%	2.2s: 36%
2.1s: 35%	3RDS: 21%

ADMISSIONS
⊙ **APPLY VIA UCAS OR DIRECT FOR PART-TIME**
The University welcomes applications from mature students on Access courses and works in partnership with local education colleges and the Gloucestershire Open College Network to help plan and approve Access programmes. International students can get help with obtaining and completing application forms from their local British Council office.

SUBJECTS
ART, MEDIA & DESIGN 15% **BUSINESS** 31%
EDUCATION 5% **ENVIRONMENT** 7% **HUMANITIES** 12%
SPORT & LEISURE 19%

BEST Agriculture, Building & Planning; Creative Arts; English; History/Archaeology; Human & Social Geography; Languages; Management; Philosophy; Physical Geography & Environmental Science; Physical Science; Politics; Psychology; Social Work; Sociology; Social Policy & Anthropology; Teacher Training; Theology & Religious Studies.
UNUSUAL Adventure Leisure Management; Events Management; Heritage Management; Interactive Games Design; Media and Music Management; Photojournalism; Playwork; Popular Music; Water Resource Management.

LIBRARIES
⊙ **243,000 BOOKS** ⊙ **821 STUDY PLACES**
There are subject-specific libraries on each site. Park Campus is the largest, with nearly half the University's book provision.

COMPUTERS
⊙ **470 WORKSTATIONS**
Each campus has an IT-equipped Learning Centre, open 70 hours a week during term but also has some 24-hr provision. Some student rooms have internet access.

OTHER LEARNING FACILITIES
Language labs; CAD labs; media centre and specialised facilities on each campus.

ENTERTAINMENT ⊙⊙⊙⊙⊙⊙⊙⊙⊙⊙

THE CITY
THE TOWNS
⊙ **PRICE OF A PINT OF BEER** £2.20
⊙ **GLASS OF WINE** £2.50 ⊙ **CAN OF RED BULL** £2
CINEMAS A seven-screen Odeon in Cheltenham and a UGC in Gloucester, but *the more discerning* hit the Blue Room at Gloucester's Guildhall *for cult films.*
THEATRES The *high-brow* Everyman (touring productions) is half price for students. The Bacon offers 10% off its many musicals and concerts. The Playhouse stages over 20 amateur productions a year and the Guildhall has *real live dramas as well as its screens.*
PUBS *A fairly typical mix of pubs and wine bars, most of which at least tolerate students. Pushplugs: Fray & Fiddle; Pulpit; Wetherspoon and Scream (Cheltenham); Dick Wittington's (Gloucester). Try the Montpellier Run – a string of good pubs close-ish by.*
CLUBBING *Drinkers are better served than dancers, but there are a few clubs worth mentioning in Cheltenham – try Blush, Fez and the Hub (indie). Gloucester has Liquid and Interaction.*
MUSIC VENUES Cheltenham Town Hall hosts symphony orchestras, opera, folk festivals and the Cheltenham International Jazz Festival every spring, as well as the Fringe Music Festival. In Gloucester, the Guildhall is *a haven for the artily weird*, with African drum classes, belly dance lessons, cult movies and gigs.
COMEDY/CABARET Slacks in Cheltenham is the *top laughspot* and most theatres lay on weekly chucklemonsters.
EATING OUT Plenty of pubs do *better than average* grub and Cheltenham's café culture is *on the up. Cheltenham Pushplugs: Zizzi's (chain Italian); Jim Thompson's (Oriental); the Conservatory (café bar). Gloucester Pushplugs: Haus (bit of everything); the Comfy Pew (café/pub with church furnishings).*
OTHER *Festival heaven.* The annual Cheltenham Literary Festival draws oodles of bookish types down to talk, workshop and *bitch about each other.* There are also jazz, folk and music festivals to get excited about.

UNIVERSITY
- **PRICE OF A PINT OF BEER** £1.70
- **GLASS OF WINE** £2 ● **CAN OF RED BULL** £1.05

BARS One per campus. Most of the Union's main events (karaoke, pool comps, quizzes, bands, cocktail parties and so on) kick off at the *colossal* Park Bar in Cheltenham which is *nicely laid-back* during the day, *loud and vibrant* by night. Pittville and the Francis Close (big screen sports) both have *more mellow* hang-outs. Gloucester's got the newer Oxtalls bar *where all the sports posse pose after a hard day learning how to break people like match-sticks.*

THEATRE The Chapel hosts music and drama *once every month of blue moons.*

FILM The Film Society puts on *culty arty weirdness* in lecture theatres.

MUSIC VENUES Monthly nights in the bars. The Park campus bar attracts local and not-so-local bands, mostly hopefuls.

COMEDY/CABARET *One-off specials for charidee.*

CLUBBING Pre-parties for a couple of clubs in town.

FOOD Refectory on each campus, open til 6-8pm Mon-Fri. Francis Close students can have their peers cook for them in the Gloucester Suite training restaurant – *go in summer, they know what they're doing by then.*

OTHER Five balls a year. The Summer Ball's held at Cheltenham Racecourse and keeps going till a *comparatively wussy* 2am. *Big (but not necessarily clever) names* are persuaded to drop by, including the likes of Goldie Lookin' Chain, Judge Jules, Orson and Sara Cox.

SOCIAL ()()()()()()()()()()()()()()()

UNIVERSITY OF GLOUCESTERSHIRE STUDENTS' UNION
- **4 SABBATICALS** ● **TURNOUT AT LAST BALLOT** 10%
- **NUS MEMBER**

The bright and welcoming SU is on a mission to entertain – politics would just be a hindrance – and jealously protects its members from the lures of town entertainments by keeping the ents calendar stuffed to bust.

SU FACILITIES
Club; four bars; four canteens; four snack bars; 12 pool/snooker tables; a whole load of meeting rooms; Alliance & Leicester ATM; photocopier, fax and printing service; photo booth; payphones; advice centre; juke box; games machines; general store; stationery shop; vending machines; laun-derette.

CLUBS (NON-SPORTING)
United Nations (debating). *See also Clubs tables.*

OTHER ORGANISATIONS
The free SU paper is called Space and there's a new radio station which puts out podcasts. Rag is *pretty eager*, arranging frequent (*and frequently ridiculous*) events in the name of charity. Volunteering Now is about the only student group that really mixes with the local population and gathers a fair few CV points as it does. The volunteering and training department does courses like first aid and football training.

RELIGIOUS
- **2 CHAPLAINS (COFE)**

The 1908 Chapel at Francis Close is the University's god spot. *Other faiths aren't so lucky* although a prayer room for all faiths is being developed at Park. There are also world faith advisors.

G

PAID WORK
- **JOB BUREAU** ● **PAID WORK** TERM-TIME >50%; HOLS >90%

The SU hires over 100 students and has its own employment agency for part-time work and links with BUNAC. UCAS is based in Cheltenham and often employs students, as do other local head offices for Kraft Foods, Bird's Eye Walls, British Energy and many others. Festivals can bring in serious temporary money, especially the Gold Cup. Organisers recruit temps at the twice yearly Jobs Fayre, where an assortment of local companies put in appearances.

SPORTS ()()()()()()()()()()()()()()

- **RECENT SUCCESSES** CYCLING, WOMEN'S RUGBY
- **BUSA RANKING** 37

They may never crack the Olympics, but Gloucestershire jocks are launching a determined attack on the BUSA leagues.

SPORTS FACILITIES
Small but sportily-formed. Football, hockey, cricket, rugby and all-weather pitches; squash, netball, basketball and three tennis courts; sports hall; pavilion; multigym; swimming pool; gym; aerobics studio; boathouse. Free gym membership. Cheltenham town's facilities include: the Balcarras Sports Centre, Chapel Rock Gymnasium, Cloud 9 Ladies' Health Club; squash courts; running track; pool; lake and river. Gloucester offers a couple of leisure centres.

SPORTING CLUBS
Board-riders (surf, skate, snow, ski); Capoeira; Cheerleading; Go-Karting; Lacrosse; Gymnastics; Kendo; Kick/Thai-boxing; Paintball; Pool; Rowing; Street & Break-dancing. **See also Clubs tables.**

ATTRACTIONS
Cheltenham Town FC are the local team. There's Beaufort Sports & Polo Centre for horsey types and the racecourse, natch.

Words in italics are Push's point of view – take it or leave it...

ACCOMMODATION ◔◔◔◔◔◔◔◔◔

IN UNIVERSITY
- **SELF-CATERING** 20% ⊙ **COST** £75 (41WKS)
- **1ST YRS LIVING IN** 80% (41WKS)
- **INSURANCE PREMIUM** £

AVAILABILITY About 80% of first years can be housed but there's no guarantee – *get that form in sharpish*. Accommodation standards are high – it's mainly en suite rooms with shared kitchens, which *bizarrely* have microwaves and grills but no cookers – *learn to love those ready meals*. Students can normally be housed near where they study, *which is handy*. Park Campus has an award-winning student village with its own refectory, bar and shop. The *most popular* halls are Eldon and Merrowdown as they're *attractive* Regency buildings near the campus and the town centre (the annexes are the most modern). Regency Halls are also *slap-bang* in the centre of Cheltenham. Shaftesbury Hall at Francis Close is the latest addition and is *pretty special*. In Gloucester, Oxstalls Hall on campus is the *best option for lazybones*, Upper Quay and Ermin Hall *are prettier and slightly cheaper while Pittville has the most green space*. All campus-based halls have 24-hr security. Others have a *patchier* system.

CAR PARKING Parking on the streets round campus is free but *spaces are scarce* during term. Campus parking's reserved for students living outside halls (with a £30 permit).

EXTERNALLY
- **AVE RENT** £58 ⊙ **LIVING AT HOME** 25%

AVAILABILITY Standards *vary wildly* but there's plenty of accommodation in both Cheltenham and Gloucester. *The pricey properties around the Park campus are in much demand. The living is easier around Francis Close Hall.*

HOUSING HELP The accommodation offices at Francis Close and Oxstalls *offer wise words* and maintain a database of registered flats and houses, available online.

WELFARE ◔◔◔◔◔◔◔◔◔◔◔◔◔

SERVICES
- **LGBT SOCIETY** ⊙ **MATURE STUDENTS' OFFICER & SOCIETY** ⊙ **ETHNIC MINORITIES SOCIETY**
- **INTERNATIONAL STUDENTS' OFFICER**
- **DISABILITIES OFFICER & SOCIETY**
- **WOMEN'S OFFICER**
- **UNIVERSITY COUNSELLORS** 1 FULL/2 PART
- **CRIME RATING** !!

The UniMotion shuttle bus runs until 11pm, or 2am on event nights.

HEALTH Park Campus has a medical centre with GP surgeries, information and advice. Physiotherapy sessions are available for those sporting sporting injuries.

CRIME Campuses are secure and well-lit.

CRECHES/NURSERY 50 places for 6mths-5yrs, 8am-6pm. Also a Pre-School Centre for those too young to ship off to school (*quite a waiting list*) and an after-school club for 4-11-year-olds.

DISABILITIES *Good* access on all campuses. Ramps everywhere and plenty of power-assisted doors. *Competent* Student Disability Advisors will help with access or study problems. Note-takers and sign interpreters are available.

DRUGS Testing for *naughty things (that's chemicals, not whoopee cushions)* on the door of SU nights.

FINANCE
- **AVE DEBT PER YEAR** £2,861
- **HOME STUDENT FEES** £3,000 ⊙ **ACCESS FUND** £536,272
- **SUCCESSFUL APPLICATIONS/YR** 650

FEES Scots just have to pay the graduate endowment. Other UK undergraduates are stung for £3,000 and internationals pay £7,000-8,000.

- **ACCESS FUND** £240,000

SUPPORT There's a Student Finance Officer offering guidance on money matters and hardship assistance– *all the fun of a bank manager with none of the guilt*. Help for those from poorer households – see www.glos.ac.uk/fees for more. In addition to subject-specific bursaries, a disabled students' allowance provides help buying specialist equipment and with other costs.

> ◎   **Basil Spence designed the campus and some of the buildings are supposed to look like interesting objects from the air. There's the Gardner Arts centre (a roll of film), Falmer House (a camera), Lecture halls A1 & A2 (a butterfly) and the library (an open book).**

Words in italics are Push's point of view – take it or leave it...

GOLDSMITHS, UNIVERSITY OF LONDON

THE COLLEGE IS PART OF THE UNIVERSITY OF LONDON AND STUDENTS ARE ENTITLED TO USE ITS FACILITIES.

○ **GOLDSMITHS, UNIVERSITY OF LONDON** New Cross, London, SE14 6NW **TEL** (020) 7919 7171 **E-MAIL** admissions@gold.ac.uk **WEBSITE** www.goldsmiths.ac.uk ○ **GOLDSMITHS STUDENTS' UNION**, Dixon Road, New Cross, London, SE14 6NW **TEL** (020) 8692 1406 **E-MAIL** gcsu@gold.ac.uk **WEBSITE** www.gcsu.org.uk

GENERAL ◖◖◖◖◖◖◖◖◖◖◖◖◖◖

The main sight that greets anyone arriving in New Cross Gate by train is a giant scrapyard, and it's a pretty good symbol of this chunk of south-east London – rather tatty, careworn and in need of a good seeing to. But that's inner-city life and the good news is that Goldsmiths is a bit of a beacon in the gloom. The surroundings have inspired some seriously big names in the arts, from Lucien Freud to Damien Hirst, Malcolm McLaren and half of Blur. The main college building is a (relatively) clean, attractive three-storey affair with a patch of green space at the back. Most of the university buildings don't exactly leap out of the landscape, but they're modern and house a lively, diverse, creative bunch of students. If there's one landmark addition, it's the Ben Pimlott Building, which features a sculptural 'scribble' – so it's a bit more 'urban scrawl' than 'urban sprawl'. New Cross is docklands territory, and the Dome is just visible from the library – whether that's an inspiring sight is a matter of opinion.

SEX RATIO: ♂33 ♀67	FOUNDED: 1891
FULL-TIME U'GRADS: 3,406	PART-TIME: 1,255
POSTGRADS: 2,612	NON-DEGREE: 91
AVE COURSE: 3YRS	ETHNIC: 35%
STATE:PRIVATE SCHOOL: 91:9	FLUNK RATE: 18%
MATURE: 34%	INTERNATIONAL: 15%
DISABLED: 75	LOCAL: 38%

ATMOSPHERE

If the London colleges are like Friends, then Goldsmiths is Phoebe – artsy, conscience-bound and decked out with big earrings and plastic jewellery. That's not to say the place doesn't have a lot of less kooky attributes, with a streetwise vibe and non-arty students also well provided for. The emphasis on the creative arts adds to a laid-back attitude and students get on well with the locals, helped hugely by close community links. It's absolutely not City-slick suit-and-boot-land – breadheads beware. The Brand Council have, er, branded Goldsmiths 'cool' several times in recent years, which is a source of much pride for the college authorities and of faint embarrassment for the students – a bit like mum developing an interest in hip-hop.

LONDON see University of London
○ **CITY CENTRE** 5 MILES
New Cross and Lewisham are pretty dingy and at a 15 minute train journey away are removed from the frantic bustle of central London. But the Docklands redevelopment has rubbed off in spots, particularly in Greenwich, where the famous Observatory and Maritime museum lend culture. It's cheap, too, for London.

TRAVEL see University of London
TRAINS New Cross and New Cross Gate have direct services into London Bridge.
BUSES Loads including numbers: 21, 36, 53, 136, 171 (to the West End) and night-buses too.
CAR Just off the south circular and outside the congestion zone, both of which help. But finding a parking spot isn't much fun. Road-rage sufferers be warned.
UNDERGROUND New Cross and New Cross Gate are on the East London line. DLR and Jubilee lines pass through the area, but the quickest route into town is by train.
BICYCLES Two wheels are better than four, and students know it. Bike facilities in college help.

CAREER PROSPECTS
○ **CAREERS SERVICE** ○ **NO. OF STAFF** 2 FULL/2 PART
○ **UNEMPLOYED AFTER 6 MTHS** 3%
The careers service provides an e-mail service with vacancies, workshops, employment fairs, discussion forums and careers advice.

FAMOUS ALUMNI
Alex James and Graham Coxon (of Blur fame); Martin Brabbins (conductor); John Cale (Velvet Underground); Vic Charles (karate champ); Julian Clary (comedian); Wendy Cope (poet); Lucien Freud, Damien Hirst, Tom Keating, Bridget Riley (artists); Tessa Jowell MP (Lab); Linton Kwesi Johnson (dub poet); Malcolm McLaren (Sex Pistols creator); Brian Molko (Placebo); Molly Parkin (writer); Mary Quant (designer); Lord Melvyn-Rees (former Home Secretary); Gillian Wearing (Turner prize-winning artist); Colin Welland (playwright/actor); Vivienne Westwood (fashion designer).

FURTHER INFO
○ **PROSPECTUSES** UNDERGRAD; POSTGRAD; ALTERNATIVE
○ **OPEN DAYS** ○ **VIDEO**
Prospectuses also available for study-abroad, PGCE and part-time students. Alternative prospectus at http://mcserver.gold.ac.uk/journalism/ba/2006/alt.gold/index.htm

G

ACADEMIC ⭕⭕⭕⭕⭕⭕⭕⭕⭕⭕⭕⭕

⊙ 1994 GROUP

A big name in the artistic field, Goldsmiths's end of term exhibitions and degree shows generally excite a lot of interest. It's not all just paints and brushes, mind – they boast academic clout in several other areas, particularly Sociology and Media & Communications. They may or may not have invented the word 'interdisciplinarity' but, either way, it describes the ideas frequently exchanged between their departments and, if well positioned, scores highly in Scrabble. Work is assessed by a mix of exams, dissertations, shows, exhibitions, coursework, performances and, of course, more exams.

ENTRY POINTS: 240-340	AVE POINTS: 285
APPLICATIONS PER PLACE: 8	CLEARING: 19%
NO. OF TERMS: 3	LENGTH OF TERMS: 10WKS
STAFF TO STUDENT RATIO: 1:10	STUDY ADDICTS: 13%
TEACHING: ****	RESEARCH: ***
YEAR ABROAD: <1%	SANDWICH STUDENTS: <1%
1STS: 10%	2.2S: 35%
2.1S: 49%	3RDS: 6%

ADMISSIONS
⊙ APPLY VIA UCAS

SUBJECTS
ANTHROPOLOGY 3%   **COMPUTING** 8%   **DESIGN** 6%
EDUCATIONAL STUDIES 7%   **ENGLISH** 11%   **HISTORY** 4%
MEDIA & COMMUNICATIONS 11%   **MUSIC** 4%   **POLITICS** 5%
PROFESSIONAL & COMMUNITY EDUCATION 3%
SOCIOLOGY 8%   **VISUAL ARTS** 9%   **VISUAL CULTURES** 5%
BEST English and Comparative Literature; History; Media & Communications; Psychology; Sociology.

LIBRARIES
⊙ 221,000 BOOKS   ⊙ 470 STUDY PLACES
⊙ 24-HR ACCESS
The Rutherford Information Services Building houses a *modern* library.

COMPUTERS
⊙ 582 WORKSTATIONS
Online learning is in place for some subjects *so students can go to college without getting out of bed.*

OTHER LEARNING FACILITIES
The glossy new Ben Pimlott building opened in 2005 with *up-to-date* studios and facilities for *budding Damien Hirsts – dead sheep and formaldehyde not included.*

ENTERTAINMENT ⭕⭕⭕⭕⭕⭕⭕⭕⭕⭕

THE CITY see University of London
⊙ PRICE OF A PINT OF BEER £1.80
⊙ GLASS OF WINE £1.90 **⊙ CAN OF RED BULL** £1.40
CINEMAS Multiplexes at Greenwich, Peckham and Surrey Quays are *cheaper, plusher and newer than some in the West End.*
THEATRES Try the Albany in Deptford and the Jack in Brockley, *but again the West End is the best bet.*
PUBS *Pushplugs:* Montague Arms (*indie trash with a nautical motif*); Amersham Arms; New Cross Inn; Marquis of Granby; Rosemary Branch; Paradise Bar; Goldsmiths Tavern.
MUSIC VENUES The *ever-popular* Brixton Academy is nearby.
CLUBBING *Pushplugs:* Bubblegum in Deptford.
EATING OUT *Lots of good, easy-on-the-pocket ethnic restaurants. Pushplugs:* The Thailand (*one of the best in London*); Café Creme; Moonbow Jakes; Marie's Café; Gem's; Mr Cheung; Raj Bhujan.

UNIVERSITY
⊙ PRICE OF A PINT OF BEER £1.80
⊙ GLASS OF WINE £1.90 **⊙ CAN OF RED BULL** £1.40
BARS The Green Room is the *main bar, with all the usual trimmings:* bar snacks, karaoke, cheap booze, cheesy music and a pub quiz.
THEATRES *With all these arty types, there's a strong thesp scene,* which is boosted by a huge stage and active drama group.
FILM The film society has a screen of its own and shows *appropriately leftfield films, with the occasional blockbuster thrown in for good measure.* The Stretch Bar has a weekly film night.
MUSIC VENUES Old boys Blur popped back for a tenth anniversary gig, and other *biggish* indie/alternative acts (eg. Athlete, Lady Sovereign) also turn up *from time to time.*
CLUBBING Club Sandwich is a *popular weekly cheese-fest,* rivalled by Friday's SE14 (hip-hop and drum and bass) *for those who prefer to keep their music credible.* Pendulum, DJ Yoda and Scratch Perverts have popped by recently.
FOOD *Decent but pricey fare* at Loafer's coffee shop and the Refectory, and *pleasant enough* dining at the newly revamped Stretch. *Good* bar snacks at the Green Room and at Revolution.
OTHER Four balls a year and regular hall and society events, like a one-off Burlesque strip for Breast Cancer Awareness. *No one can accuse these folks of lacking imagination.*

There's more to student life than poverty and fun... See the clubs & socs tables

Words in italics are Push's point of view – take it or leave it...

SOCIAL ◗◗◗◗◗◗◗◗◗◗◗◗◗

GOLDSMITHS STUDENTS' UNION
◗ **5 SABBATICALS** ◗ **TURNOUT AT LAST BALLOT** 15%
◗ **NUS MEMBER**
The Union has a reputation as a *vocal, lefty* kind of student body, and uses links with the College's *more celebrated* old boys to good effect. Campaigning issues are *many and various* with a *wider world-view* than just top-up fees and student access.

SU FACILITIES
Advice centre; two bars; bank and ATM (NatWest); canteen; three snack/coffee bars; general store; juke-box; laundrette; minibus hire; photo booth; three pool tables; vending machines; video games.

CLUBS (NON SPORTING)
Alternative Culture; Chess; Chinese; Hindu; Korean; Made in Goldsmiths (craft); Meditation; Music; Musical Theatre; Persian; Poi (dance); Respect Party (yep, that's MP and Big Brother loser George Galloway's mob); Sikh; Swing. **See also Clubs tables.**

OTHER ORGANISATIONS
Guardian award-winning monthly student mag Smiths, student radio station Wired. Community outreach eg. a sports ambassador scheme encourages *altruistic types to integrate into the local area, and are probably a darn sight more sensible in the mean streets of New Cross than traditional student fundraisers like jumping around in fancy dress shaking a collection tin.*

RELIGIOUS
◗ **4 CHAPLAINS (COFE, RC , METHODIST, URC), IMAM**
Religion in London: see University of London

PAID WORK
◗ **JOB BUREAU** ◗ **PAID WORK** TERM-TIME 35%; HOLS 80%
Part-time jobs are easily had in London, and there are plenty on campus.

SPORTS ◗◗◗◗◗◗◗◗◗◗◗◗◗

◗ **RECENT SUCCESSES** FOOTBALL ◗ **BUSA RANKING** 122
Students are *generally a bit more Brecht than Beckenbauer*, but the SU has an increasing sports agenda and offers classes in yoga, circuit training, etc.

SPORTS FACILITIES
21 acres of playing fields eight miles away in Sidcup. Students are entitled to use ULU facilities, *which are a bit better.* A £10 Student Activities Card allows students to dip into clubs and societies without paying full membership fees.

An on-campus fitness centre should be up and running by autumn 2006 with a subsidised student rate of £15-£20 a month.

SPORTING CLUBS
Capoeira; Ju Jitsu; Kickboxing; Ski and Snowboarding. **See also Clubs tables.**

ATTRACTIONS see University of London
Local football team Millwall have *cleaned up their act since the bad old days, while Crystal Palace loiter around the top end of the Championship after a brief visit to the Premiership big boys. Charlton Athletic are currently having a whale of a time,* and have a *high-flying* ladies football side.

ACCOMMODATION ◗◗◗◗◗◗◗◗◗◗

IN COLLEGE
◗ **SELF-CATERING** 28% ◗ **COST** £87 (39/50WKS)
◗ **1ST YRS LIVING IN** 58% ◗ **2ND YRS LIVING IN** 6%
◗ **FINALISTS LIVING IN** 4% ◗ **INSURANCE PREMIUM** £££
AVAILABILITY All accommodation is *within five minutes walk of campus – handy that –* and around 3/4 of rooms have en suite facilities. Quality is *top-notch* and nobody needs to share. *Loring Hall has a reputation as the party palace.* Swipe card entry and night-time security patrols *let residents sleep easy.*
CAR PARKING Two halls have parking (registration with Goldsmiths required); disabled students have priority.

EXTERNALLY see University of London
◗ **AVE RENT** £70
AVAILABILITY House-hunting is easier and cheaper south of the river, which just about makes up for relatively poor transport links. New Cross is a student haven, with plenty of wallet-friendly big houses to rent. Brockley and Deptford prove popular despite being a bit shabby. Brixton's still tarred with the 'cool' brush and has more than its fair share of trustafarians getting all ghetto-fabulous as a result.
HOUSING HELP The college and GSU provide a *hands-on* service and help students through every stage of finding a new place.

WELFARE ◗◗◗◗◗◗◗◗◗◗◗◗◗

SERVICES
◗ **LGBT OFFICER AND SOCIETY** ◗ **ETHNIC MINORITIES OFFICER** ◗ **WOMEN'S OFFICER AND SUPPORT GROUP** ◗ **MATURE STUDENTS' OFFICER** ◗ **INTERNATIONAL STUDENTS' OFFICER** ◗ **POSTGRAD OFFICER**
◗ **DISABILITIES OFFICER AND SUPPORT GROUP**
◗ **SELF-DEFENCE CLASSES** ◗ **NIGHTLINE** ◗ **COLLEGE COUNSELLORS** 1 FULL/3 PART ◗ **CRIME RATING:** !!!!
The college looks out for its students, has *good*

G

facilities and welfare provisions *by the bucket. Some of the older college buildings are tricky for disabled students, though.*

HEALTH Medical centre on campus with two full-time GPs and two practice nurses.

CRIME *New Cross has a bad rep for street crime, but with a bit of common sense most students get by unscathed.* There's CCTV coverage from the uni right down to the station.

CRECHES/NURSERY Crèche with 20 places for 3mths-5yrs.

DISABILITIES Newer buildings have *decent* access and facilities (ramps, lifts, hearing loops, Braille signs) but sharp corners and stairs make older parts *difficult.* There's also a full-time dyslexia tutor on hand.

FINANCE

○ **AVE DEBT PER YEAR** £1,923 ○ **HOME STUDENT FEES** £3,000 **FEES** A postgrad course costs £3,085 for home students; £8,745 for internationals. International student fees: £8,745-£11,875.

○ **ACCESS FUND** £365,000 ○ **SUCCESSFUL APPLICATIONS/YR** 600 ○ **AVE PAYMENT** £100-£3,500 **SUPPORT** A postgrad scholarship scheme makes payments of up to £1,000. The alumni discounts scheme grants £500 at a time and there's accommodation bursaries of £285-£995 with a deadline that lets the clearing contingent get in on the cash too.

G

▶ **GORDON UNIVERSITY**
see *Robert Gordon University*

GREENWICH UNIVERSITY

FORMERLY WOOLWICH POLYTECHNIC, THAMES POLYTECHNIC

(1. ○ **THE UNIVERSITY OF GREENWICH** Old Royal Naval College, Park Row, Greenwich, London, SE10 9LS **TEL** (020) 8331 8000 **EMAIL** courseinfo@gre.ac.uk **WEBSITE** www.gre.ac.uk ○ **UNIVERSITY OF GREENWICH STUDENTS' UNION** Cooper Building, King William Walk, Greenwich, London, SE10 9JH **TEL** (020) 8331 7629 **WEBSITE** www.suug.co.uk
(2. ○ **THE UNIVERSITY OF GREENWICH** Old Royal Naval College, Park Row, Greenwich, London, SE10 9LS **TEL** (020) 8331 8000 **EMAIL** courseinfo@gre.ac.uk **WEBSITE** www.gre.ac.uk ○ **UNIVERSITY OF GREENWICH STUDENTS' UNION** Cooper Building, King William Walk, Greenwich, London, SE10 9JH **TEL** (020) 8331 7629 **WEBSITE** www.suug.co.uk
(3. ○ **THE UNIVERSITY OF GREENWICH** Old Royal Naval College, Park Row, Greenwich, London, SE10 9LS **TEL** (020) 8331 8000 **EMAIL** courseinfo@gre.ac.uk **WEBSITE** www.gre.ac.uk ○ **UNIVERSITY OF GREENWICH STUDENTS' UNION** Cooper Building, King William Walk, Greenwich, London, SE10 9JH **TEL** (020) 8331 7629 **WEBSITE** www.suug.co.uk

GENERAL ○○○○○○○○○○○○○○

Greenwich University comprises a *stately* threesome of campuses, two of which live up to their name by being in the borough of Greenwich – *where the time comes from.* The main site, Maritime Greenwich, revolves around the *stunning,* partly Wren-designed Old Royal Naval College, birthplace of kings and a *firm filmic favourite.* Avery Hill, a few miles away, is a combination of Victorian mansion and more modern buildings, swathed in parkland and *generally very pleasant all over.* Then there's Chatham in Kent, a former naval barracks on the historic dockyard, *and the feeling here is much more rural.* The different sites offer different courses and students considering applying should check where they'd be based, *since, despite strong transport links, they're largely self-contained and as different as chalk and chutney.*

SEX RATIO: ♂47 ♀53	**FOUNDED:** 1890
FULL-TIME U'GRADS: 9,121	**PART-TIME:** 1,781
POSTGRADS: 5,203	**NON-DEGREE:** 2,898
AVE COURSE: 3YRS	**ETHNIC:** 53%
STATE:PRIVATE SCHOOL: 95:5	**FLUNK RATE:** 25%
MATURE: 46%	**INTERNATIONAL:** 19%
DISABLED: 190	**LOCAL:** 54%

ATMOSPHERE

The University's far enough away from the city centre to feel relaxed, but plenty of student activity means life is far from dull. The two major SU venues, particularly Bar Latitude in Greenwich and the Dome at Avery Hill, provide a social focus which would otherwise be lost in the distances between sites. This and the social melting pot of many ethnic groups help to provide a sense of fun and an extra-curricular buzz that's missing at some of the other 'new' universities. There's a livelier social scene at Avery Hill, while students at the Maritime site display a stronger devotion to the great god of work.

OTHER SITES

AVERY HILL (6,000 students – Education & Training, Health & Social Care, Architecture & Construction) An attractive site, three miles south of Woolwich, set in an 86-acre park with a listed mansion as the main building and gorgeous Winter Gardens. New buildings worth £14m are on the way, including a sports and teaching centre and, *how eco-friendly*, 100 trees. The nearest major shopping area is Eltham, a mile away.

MEDWAY (2,000 students – Engineering, Natural Resources Institute, Science, Pharmacy) Based at Chatham and in association with the Natural Resources Institute. It has a robotics centre, computer-aided design studio and satellite technology base. *Wowsers*. It's also currently being developed as an integrated campus with the University of Kent and Canterbury Christ Church University College.

LONDON see University of London
The London borough of Greenwich, which hugs the south bank of the river at the eastern end of the Thames, is firmly a tourist top-spot, thanks in part to features like the Cutty Sark and the Royal Observatory. Meanwhile, residents and students are kept happy with enough shops, bars and clubs to shake several sticks at. The *ever-ailing* Dome is no longer open, but current plans are to transform it into a waterfront sports, leisure and entertainment complex. *Woo hoo*. It's *easy enough* to get into central London on the DLR railway – *the absence of the tube proper means Greenwich is a bit of a respite from the maddening crowds, and outside of tourist-hunting season has a chilled, laid-back air.*

TRAVEL see University of London
TRAINS Avery Hill, Falconwood or New Eltham stations (both 15 mins walk). Chatham station for Medway. There's a DLR station (Cutty Sark) at Greenwich. London Bridge is the nearest tube and mainline train station, 15 mins from Greenwich, 20 mins from Avery Hill and just over an hour from Medway.
BUSES All sites are served by a wide range of regular London bus services.
UNDERGROUND London Bridge (Northern, Jubilee) is the nearest tube.
UNIVERSITY Free inter-site shuttlebuses run four times a day plus three times in the evening – timetables available from the SU.
CAR Local parking permits are needed. There are student spaces at Avery Hill and Medway, but not Greenwich.
BICYCLES *Your life in the hands of juggernaut drivers.*

CAREER PROSPECTS

CAREERS SERVICE **NO. OF STAFF** 2 FULL/2 PART
UNEMPLOYED AFTER 6 MTHS 14%
The University's service has a *poorly advertised but pretty comprehensive package* to students and recent graduates. Services include: online key skills training; mentoring for ethnic minority students; job shop; job fairs; interview training; careers library; bulletin boards.

FAMOUS ALUMNI

Natasha Bedingfield (songstress); Hale & Pace (*unamusing* double act); Rachel Heyhoe Flint (cricketer); Graham Ingham (BBC TV reporter); Brian Jacks (former judo champ); Prof Charles Kao (inventor of fibre optics); William G Stewart (Fifteen to One).

FURTHER INFO (BODY SUBHEAD)

PROSPECTUSES UNDERGRAD; POSTGRAD; SOME DEPARTMENTS; INTERNATIONAL STUDENTS **OPEN DAYS** Visit the admissions website for open day details, course introductions, student testimonials and virtual tours.

ACADEMIC ○○○○○○○○○○○○○

Research, scientific and technical-based studies are *what Greenwich does best, academically speaking*. Teaching is getting in on the technology act with innovations like the online campus. Some distance learning options are offered. Final grades are *the bastard children of* second and final year exams and coursework.

ENTRY POINTS: 100–300	AVE POINTS: 200
APPLICATIONS PER PLACE: N/A	CLEARING: 21%
NO. OF TERMS: 2	LENGTH OF TERMS: 15wks
STAFF TO STUDENT RATIO: 1:20	STUDY ADDICTS: 12%
TEACHING: ✱✱	RESEARCH: ✱✱
YEAR ABROAD: 1%	SANDWICH STUDENTS: N/A
1STS: 9%	2.2s: 41%
2.1s: 32%	3RDS: 14%

ADMISSIONS

APPLY VIA UCAS

SUBJECTS

ARCHITECTURE & CONSTRUCTION 7%
BUSINESS/MANAGEMENT 28%
COMPUTER SCIENCE & MATHS 14%   **EDUCATION** 11%
ENGINEERING 6%   **HEALTH & SOCIAL CARE** 8%
HUMANITIES 20%   **SCIENCES** 6%
BEST Biosciences; Building, Land & Property Management; Business & Management; Civil Engineering; Economics; Education; Hospitality, Leisure, Recreation, Sport & Tourism; Nursing; Pharmacology & Pharmacy; Philosophy; Psychology; Politics; Sports Science; Theology & Religious Studies; Town & Country Planning.

LIBRARIES

456.500 BOOKS **1,821 STUDY PLACES**
SPEND PER STUDENT £
Not bad at all, apart from the fact that they're closed on Sundays. The good news though is that each site has at least one library open until 9pm.

COMPUTERS

1,086 WORKSTATIONS **SPEND PER STUDENT** ££££
Computers are based in the libraries at all three sites, *so all the same opening hour quibbles apply*. The Queen Anne building was recently given *an extra shot* of hardware.

Words in italics are Push's point of view — take it or leave it...

OTHER LEARNING FACILITIES

Language laboratory; media centre; TV studio.

ENTERTAINMENT ◖◗◖◗◖◗◖◗◖◗◖◗◖◗

THE CITY see University of London
- **PRICE OF A PINT OF BEER** £1.75
- **GLASS OF WINE** £2.85 ○ **CAN OF RED BULL** £2.10

Except Greenwich itself, there is little to do outside college as the sites aren't exactly in London's most jumping joints.

CINEMAS Students get discounted tickets at Greenwich Film Works (UCI, 14 screens) and the *heaving* Bluewater.

THEATRES The Greenwich Playhouse and the Greenwich Theatre (a former Victorian music hall) have both had students tread their boards.

PUBS *Pushplugs: the Ordnance; the Trafalgar in Greenwich.* There's a *newish* Wetherspoons next to Greenwich DLR Station *which proves popular when desperate.*

CLUBBING/MUSIC VENUES Various late night bars offer live tunes. *Try Up the Creek (also good for comedy) or the late-opening St Christophers or Live Bar. Clubs tend towards the stagger-in-drunk rather than the plan-a-visit-when-sober, but there's fun to be had at the Meantime club (dance) and a couple of cheese emporiums.*

EATING OUT *Budget-conscious students grab a cheap bite at Goddard's Pie House, Tae Won Mein and Noodle Time. Pubs along the river are a pricier alternative.*

OTHER The *vibrant and thrilling* Greenwich and Docklands International Festival invades the borough each June.

UNIVERSITY

- **PRICE OF A PINT OF BEER** £1.70 ○ **GLASS OF WINE** £1.30

BARS The main ones are happy-hour-fuelled Bar Latitude at Greenwich, the Dome at Avery Hill (made up of Jester's and Mazey's bars and open til 2am twice a week), the more traditional Drunken Sailor, and the Sparrows Farm Sports Bar, *where drunken football nuts go karaoke crazy.* Bar Latitude shuts at 7pm on Fridays – *Push wasn't joking when we said there's a strong study vibe on the Maritime campus.*

THEATRES Nothing on campus – student thesps get involved in productions at local theatres.

FILM There's a film society, though no screenings at present.

MUSIC VENUES The Dome at Avery Hill can hold 1,000 punters. Recent offerings include Jamelia and Big Brovaz. There's also a jazz night at Bar Latitude.

CLUBBING Three or four club nights a week, *usually serving up commercial, cheese or R'n'B grooves.* The likes of Trevor Nelson and Tim Westwood have appeared. *Pushplugs: Dizzy at the Dome, a Friday night delight for many.*

COMEDY/CABARET The Dome hosts a regular comedy night, which features laughtersmiths

from the Up the Creek comedy circuit.

FOOD A range of eateries, notably Greengages and Pembroke canteen-style restaurants and the *smaller, nibblier* Queen Anne coffee shop. Halal food available. Excellent *waist-expanding* scoff at Bar Latitude. Some club nights are catered.

OTHER Summer ball and sports and societies award dinner.

SOCIAL ◖◗◖◗◖◗◖◗◖◗◖◗◖◗◖◗

UNIVERSITY OF GREENWICH STUDENTS' UNION

- **5 SABBATICALS** ○ **TURNOUT AT LAST BALLOT** 4%
- **NUS MEMBER**

The concentration of SU facilities at Greenwich and Avery Hill tends to leave the further-flung members somewhat out of the equation, although representation at Medway has improved in recent years. The entertainment facilities are well used, but politics is a cold potato. Instead, the SU plays it safe and stays politically neutral, which could be why its relationship with the University is warm and back-slappy.

SU FACILITIES

Four main and three smaller bars; three minibuses; three shops; post office; vending and games machines; pool tables; juke box; photocopying; fax; printing; photo booth; payphone; advice centre; STA travel; Endsleigh Insurance; launderette; TV lounge; three meeting rooms.

CLUBS (NON-SPORTING)

Arabic; Explore UK; Hindu; Nigerian; Sikh; Cypriot; Turkish; Iranian. **See also Clubs tables.**

OTHER ORGANISATIONS

The student magazine, 'Sarky Cutt', is published every six weeks. There's an *active* Rag and Community Projects bursaries for voluntary groups. 'Longitude' radio started broadcasting in 2005. BITE offers skills sessions and workshops *intended to make students more employable.*

RELIGIOUS

- **5 CHAPLAINS (COFE, RC, CHINESE, ASSOCIATE CHAPLAINS FOR OTHER FAITHS)**

The Maritime campus chapel is open to the public every day. Muslim prayer rooms available at each site. All faiths are represented in London at large, but around Greenwich it can vary.

PAID WORK

- **JOB BUREAU**

SPORTS ○○○○○○○○○○○○○○○

○ RECENT SUCCESSES MEN'S FOOTBALL, RUGBY, HOCKEY, BOAT CLUB, ATHLETICS, TAE KWON DO **○ BUSA RANKING** 81
For a University mostly inside the M25, Greenwich has some pretty good sports facilities, but only a certain proportion of the students get into the spirit. Successes tend to be individual rather than team efforts. Sports facilities are concentrated at the Avery Hill site.

SPORTS FACILITIES
AVERY HILL Sports centre with multigym, squash courts, snooker tables; gym; football, rugby and hockey pitches; tennis courts; running track. **MEDWAY** Sports hall.

SPORTING CLUBS
American Football; Cheerleading; Rowing; Snowsports. **See also Clubs tables.**

ATTRACTIONS see University of London
Charlton Athletic, Millwall and Gillingham are the respective local football teams.

ACCOMMODATION ○○○○○○○○○

IN UNIVERSITY
○ SELF–CATERING 11% **○ COST** £101 (40WKS)
○ 1ST YRS LIVING IN 12% **○ INSURANCE PREMIUM** ££
AVAILABILITY The University guarantees to house all first years who request it, although this might mean private accommodation (head tenancy or housing association schemes). There's something at each site but the majority of University-owned housing is in *friendly* halls at Avery Hill. All sites have disabled facilities, CCTV, entry-phones and 24-hr security. There's one hall just for postgrads. 75% of rooms are en suite. There are also 50 places in *pricier* studio flats (£120-150), *a few of which* are suitable for couples.
CAR PARKING Parking is by permit sticker only. *Plenty of room for motors at Avery Hill and Medway, less so at Greenwich.*

EXTERNALLY see University of London
○ AVE RENT £95 **○ LIVING AT HOME** 55%
AVAILABILITY East and South-East London, especially Woolwich and Plumstead, are cheaper than north of the river, but you get what you pay for. Some parts, such as Thamesmead, are a bit deficient on the safety front.

HOUSING HELP The University runs a housing office on each site. Bulletin boards, vacancy lists and approved landlord lists keep students in the know. Advisors can check contracts and help with legal stuff.

WELFARE ○○○○○○○○○○○○○

SERVICES
○ LGBT OFFICER AND SOCIETY ○ WOMEN'S OFFICER
○ MATURE STUDENTS' OFFICER
○ INTERNATIONAL STUDENTS' OFFICER
○ POSTGRAD OFFICER
○ DISABILITIES OFFICER AND SOCIETY
○ SELF–DEFENCE CLASSES ○ NIGHTLINE
○ UNIVERSITY COUNSELLORS 3 FULL **○ CRIME RATING** !!!!
Something on every site. The SU runs a welfare and advice department and the University runs a counselling service, *easily accessible on the larger sites only.* They organise workshops for coping with stress, anxiety and so on. *Sadly*, the minibus doesn't run late.
HEALTH Greenwich: two off-campus NHS practices with four GPs and three nurses. Avery Hill: practice with five GPs and three nurses. Medway: practice with three GPs and one nurse.
WOMEN There's a women's officer (non-sabbatical).
CRECHES/NURSERY 30 places are available for children aged 6mths-5yrs (term-time only).
DISABILITIES Disabled parking and wheelchair access to the campuses are *pretty good, although the 18th-century buildings at Maritime Greenwich can be tiring to navigate.* Facilities for taping lectures, portable word processors, portable loops and conversers and disabled parking are all in place. The Disability and Dyslexia Service *does oodles* to help people with learning difficulties, offering software advice, study skills workshops and more. Disabled students get priority when it comes to allocating accommodation and the University have *a bit of cash* set aside to make any individual adaptations that might be needed. Incidentally, Greenwich topped the league table in employing disabled professors.

FINANCE
○ AVE DEBT PER YEAR £3,343
○ HOME STUDENT FEES £2,500
FEES With the exception of its pharmacy courses, Greenwich is one of the handful of places not going the whole top-up fees hog. International students, however, usually pay £8,000 for classroom-based courses and £8,650 for lab-based.
SUPPORT Bursaries are doled out to mature students and high-achievers (300+ A Level points).

➡ **GUY'S HOSPITAL**
see *King's College London*

⬛ HALLAM
see *Sheffield Hallam University*

HARPER ADAMS UNIVERSITY COLLEGE

⬛ HARROGATE COLLEGE
see *Leeds Metropolitan University*

⬛ HATFIELD POLYTECHNIC
see *University of Hertfordshire*

HERIOT-WATT UNIVERSITY

UNIVERSITY OF HERTFORDSHIRE

HEYTHROP COLLEGE, UNIVERSITY OF LONDON

⬛ HOLLOWAY
see *Royal Holloway, University of London*

⬛ HOPE, LIVERPOOL
see *Liverpool Hope University*

UNIVERSITY OF HUDDERSFIELD

⬛ HUDDERSFIELD POLYTECHNIC
see *University of Huddersfield*

UNIVERSITY OF HULL

⬛ UNIVERSITY OF HUMBERSIDE
see *University of Lincoln*

H

▶ **HALLAM**
see *Sheffield Hallam University*

HARPER ADAMS UNIVERSITY COLLEGE

○ **HARPER ADAMS UNIVERSITY COLLEGE**, Newport, Shropshire, TF10 8NB **TEL** (01952) 815 000
E−MAIL admissions@harper-adams.ac.uk **WEBSITE** www.harper-adams.ac.uk ○ **HARPER ADAMS STUDENTS' UNION**
TEL (01952) 815 313 **E−MAIL** su@harper-adams.ac.uk **WEBSITE**: www.harper-adams.ac.uk/su

GENERAL ○○○○○○○○○○○○○

Welcome to the countryside. Harper Adams isn't just a rural campus – it lives, breathes and exists for the sticks. The small, self-contained college is set in 700 acres of *rustic-est* Shropshire, specialises in agricultural topics and has its own 343 hectare working farm. It's cut off from urban civilisation by *distance, limited* transport links and the smell of cows, *but that's part of the charm.*

SEX RATIO: ♂62 ♀38	
FULL−TIME U'GRADS: 929	**PART−TIME:** 11
POSTGRADS: 83	**NON−DEGREE:** 360
AVE COURSE: 4RS	**ETHNIC:** 1%
STATE:PRIVATE SCHOOL: 78:22	**FLUNK RATE:** 13%
MATURE: 16%	**INTERNATIONAL:** 4%
DISABLED: 75	**LOCAL:** 27%

ATMOSPHERE
Friendly and intense, not unlike an Enid Blyton-style boarding school, but with rosy cheeks and wellies instead of gymslips and hockey sticks. Everyone knows everyone else and there's not much getting away from the intimate social scene. Of course that's not for everybody – cabin fever sufferers might be best to steer clear – for others it's a welcome safety net. The specialised nature of the syllabus means that everyone knows why they're there and most of them are pretty happy about it. About 10% of students come from Ireland *and all are keen to disassociate themselves from their rivals at Royal Agricultural College. The revolution starts here.*

NEWPORT
○ **POPULATION** 10,814 ○ **TOWN CENTRE** 3 MILES
○ **LONDON** 146 MILES ○ **TELFORD** 10 MILES
○ **BIRMINGHAM**: 36 MILES
○ **HIGH TEMP** 20 ○ **LOW TEMP** 0 ○**RAINFALL** 58
Newport is a one-horse town, so it's lucky there's a lot more livestock to hand at college. The beautiful Shropshire countryside can only be stared at admiringly for so long so it's fortunate that Telford and Shrewsbury *are nearby, though neither could be called mindblowing. Luckily it takes less than an hour to get to* Birmingham, *so urban fun is not out of the question.*

TRAVEL
TRAINS The nearest stations are in Telford (10 miles) and Stafford (16 miles). Trains will take you to destinations including London (from £25.80 return) and Birmingham (£7.55).
COACHES National Express services run from Telford to London (£19.60), Birmingham (£4.30) and all over.
CAR M6, M54, A41. Parking on campus is *free and easy which is just as well as cars are quite heavily relied upon.*
AIR Birmingham International (45 miles) for low-cost internal and international flights (Ryanair, FlyBe, Mytravel).
LOCAL Buses are *infrequent and unreliable. Cars, bikes or – oh horrors – walking are better options.*
TAXIS *They're very popular and easy to get, but there's more chance of hitching a lift on a Friesian than hailing one in the street.* Some companies do £2.50 to Newport or £10 to Stafford deals.
BICYCLES A cycle lane connects town and campus. There are also pods and racks at college.

CAREER PROSPECTS
○ **CAREERS SERVICE** ○ **NO. OF STAFF** 2
○ **UNEMPLOYED AFTER 6 MTHS** 3%
Bulletin boards, newsletters, vacancy lists, job fairs etc.

FURTHER INFO
○ **PROSPECTUSES** UNDERGRAD; POSTGRAD; DEPARTMENTAL; SHORT COURSE BROCHURES
○ **OPEN DAYS**

ACADEMIC ○○○○○○○○○○○○○

The College runs a *highly specialised* set of subjects concentrating on land and agricultural studies. There are five main subject groups: Animals, Business & Agri-food, Rural Affairs & Environment, Engineering and Crops. *Teaching Quality is a College buzzphrase and the obligatory placement year is a significant boon when it comes to graduate employability. Agriculture and Forestry merit a special mention. There are plenty of staff to go around, so students get to know their tutors well.*

ENTRY POINTS: 160–300	AVE POINTS: 220
APPLICATIONS PER PLACE: 3	CLEARING: 3%
NO. OF TERMS: 3	LENGTH OF TERMS: 13/11 WKS
STAFF TO STUDENT RATIO: 1:7	STUDY ADDICTS: 2%
TEACHING: ★★★★★	RESEARCH: ★
1STS: 8 %	2.2s: 38 %
2.1s: 47%	3RDS: 2 %

ADMISSIONS
○ **APPLY VIA UCAS.**

SUBJECTS
AGRICULTURE 29% **ANIMALS & VETERINARY NURSING** 11%
BUSINESS & AGRI-FOODS 11% **COUNTRYSIDE,**
ENVIRONMENT, LEISURE & TOURISM 12%
ENGINEERING 15% **RURAL ENTERPRISE & LAND**
MANAGEMENT (REALM) 19%
BEST Agriculture; REALM.
UNUSUAL Dairy Herd Management; Off-road
Vehicle Design.

LIBRARIES
○ **50,000 BOOKS** ○ **143 STUDY PLACES**
○ **SPEND PER STUDENT** ££££
The Bamford Library is a recent addition,
comprising a two-storey library, a JCB
Engineering Design Centre, an exhibition hall and
the Kaldi Café. Its *impressive* eco-credentials
include a rainwater harvesting system unit and a
natural ventilation system – *which is not another
phrase for 'draughty' apparently.*

COMPUTERS
○ **268 WORKSTATIONS** ○ **SPEND PER STUDENT** ££££
Halls and the library have wireless access.

OTHER LEARNING FACILITIES
Language labs; drama studio; CAD lab; rehearsal
rooms; Engineering Design Centre; indoor field
(to test vehicles).

ENTERTAINMENT ○○○○○○○○○○

THE TOWN
○ **PRICE OF A PINT OF BEER** £2
○ **GLASS OF WINE** £1.80
CINEMAS UCI multiplex in Telford.
THEATRES Telford's Oakengates has hosted Paul
McKenna and Al Murray. Wolverhampton or
Birmingham for proper drama.
PUBS 17 waterholes in town, and *students
sometimes venture into local territory. Pushplugs:
the Bridge; the Barley; Ozzey's Wine Bar
(promotions a-plenty); the Phez.*
CLUBBING *Cheesier than a sweaty foot in a Wotsits
factory.* Zanzibar, Athena and Barley all provide
some groove action. Shrewsbury has Flares and
Liquid; Birmingham and Liverpool have the
bright lights of the big city.
MUSIC VENUES Weston Park, 15 mins from campus,
is the host site for the annual V festival.
EATING OUT *Homely pub grub* at the Fox and the
Bridge in Newport. A handful of Indians and takeaways and bigger chains in Telford, Shrewsbury
and Stafford keep hunger pangs at bay, *just don't
expect anything terribly exciting.*

THE UNIVERSITY
○ **PRICE OF A PINT OF BEER** £2
○ **GLASS OF WINE** £1
With the town *bottoming* out on entertainment,
the *bulk* of the fun has to come from the Uni.
Thankfully, the SU do a *sterling* job.
BARS The main bar's busiest on Wednesday
(sporty types' *big night out*) and it opens till late
on weekends. The daily haunt is the Lounge.
THEATRE The QMH drama society *thesps about the
place a bit.*
FILM There's a film on once a week in the
Lounge bar.
MUSIC VENUES Live bands in the main bar every
week, *but this isn't TOTP territory.*
CLUBBING Fancy dress nights in the main bar on
Wednesdays – *think PVC, Fur & Feathers,
Hookers & Haymakers and other similarly kerazy
themes.* Sara Cox, Chappers & Dave and Scott
Mills have all taken time out from Radio One
to DJ.
COMEDY Fortnightly drop-ins from the likes of John
Oliver and Andy Zaltzman.
FOOD The dining hall is a *school-dinnery* kind
of canteen, while the Cafeteria *(aka the Kak)*
and LRC do café snacks. *Hardy fare, but
hardly tantalising.*
OTHERS Big Summer all-night ball, plus
Christmas Ball and Paddies Ball, organised for
St Patrick's Day by the, *you guessed it,* Irish
society, Harper Ireland.

SOCIAL ○○○○○○○○○○○○

HARPER ADAMS STUDENTS' UNION
○ **1 SABBATICAL** ○ **TURNOUT AT LAST BALLOT** 36%
The 10-strong executive *gets on pretty well* with
the University powers that be. Its *main* role is to
look after welfare and provide ents to *distract
from the rural plod.*

SU FACILITIES
Bar/club/music venue; lounge bar; three
canteens; two pool tables; meeting room;
photocopier/fax/printing service; payphones;
late-night minibus; TV lounge; general store;
stationery shop; vending machines; bookshop;
launderette.

CLUBS (NON SPORTING)
Flamenco; Harper Cymru (Welsh); International;
Ploughing; Remote-control Cars. **See Clubs tables.**

OTHER ORGANISATIONS
Rag raised an *impressive* £5,000 for charidee last
year, through the likes of quizzes, days out to
Stafford and its annual magazine.

Words in italics are Push's point of view – take it or leave it...

RELIGIOUS
⊙ 4 CHAPLAINS (COFE, RC , METHODIST)
Prayer room on campus. *Most Christian denominations have godstops in the local area. Everyone else will have a job on their hands.*

PAID WORK
⊙ JOB BUREAU ⊙ VACANCIES BOARD
⊙ PAID WORK TERM-TIME 38%; HOLS 90%
Careers Service, intranet job postings and summer jobs bulletin board.

SPORTS ()()()()()()()()()()()()()

⊙ BUSA RANKING 86 **⊙ RECENT SUCCESSES** RUGBY, HOCKEY
A strong reputation, especially at rugby, where the college punches way above its weight. Everyone's encouraged to get involved in sport of some kind.

SPORTS FACILITIES
Two football pitches; three rugby pitches; hockey pitch; cricket pitch; tennis courts; netball court; sports hall; swimming pool; croquet lawn; gym; new multigym; climbing wall; shooting ground. There's a golf course and driving range in the vicinity and ice rink, bowling and dry ski slope in Telford. The nearby mountains are great for climbing, hang gliding, *falling off* and so on. Gym membership costs £50 per year.

SPORTING CLUBS
4x4ing; Air Rifle; Clay-pigeon Shooting; Circuit training; Fishing; Gaelic Football; Lacrosse; Parachuting; Polo; Pool; Rowing; Skydiving; Ultimate Frisbee; Windsurfing. **See Clubs tables.**

ACCOMMODATION ()()()()()()()()()

IN COLLEGE
⊙ CATERED 41% **⊙ COST** £100 (32WKS)
⊙ SELF-CATERING 19% **⊙ COST** £66 (32WKS)
⊙ INSURANCE PREMIUM £
AVAILABILITY Almost all the livers-in are first years, who are guaranteed accommodation. *Some of them live like lords and ladies of the manor* – en suite facilities, cleaners and a laundry service (returning cleaned and ironed clothes to the door), and three meals a day. All halls are on campus and security is tight. Kitchens are shared between 6-8 students in self-catering flats. One hall is all male and what was intended to be an all-female hall is currently a collection of single-sex floors.
CAR PARKING *This deep into the countryside, cars are useful.* There's parking for all students but a (free) permit is required.

EXTERNALLY
⊙ AVE RENT £55 **⊙ LIVING AT HOME** <5%
AVAILABILITY Accommodation in Newport is *easy enough to find* and it caters for the *essentials* – close to campus, clean and pretty civilised.
HOUSING HELP A student advisor helps find housing. The office keeps a vacancy list and blacklist of villainous landlords, helps out with safety checks etc.

WELFARE ()()()()()()()()()()()()

SERVICES
⊙ POSTGRAD OFFICER & SOCIETY ⊙ INTERNATIONAL STUDENTS' OFFICER & SOCIETY ⊙ LATE-NIGHT MINIBUS ⊙ COLLEGE COUNSELLORS 1 PART **⊙ CRIME RATING** !!
Student wardens are available to help with personal problems, as are the part-time counsellor, personal tutors and student services staff.
HEALTH An on-campus NHS practice runs five days a week with a nurse available on Wednesdays. There's also a surgery in town.
DISABILITIES The old building has *poor* access, although some of the accommodation is *a bit better* and more alterations are under way. *Dedicated dyslexia support.*

FINANCE
⊙ AVE DEBT PER YEAR £2,459 **⊙ HOME STUDENT FEES** £3,000
FEES International students pay £7,200. Postgrad fees are £3,200 for a diploma or £3,950 for an MSc.
⊙ ACCESS FUND: £50,000 **⊙ SUCCESSFUL APPLICATIONS/YR:** 75 **⊙ AVE PAYMENT** £667
SUPPORT An *extensive* range of scholarships and bursaries for new students each year. £1,000 bursaries for those with household incomes of less than £17,500 and £500 or £750 for other incomes up to £37,500. Prizes are awarded by key employers to outstanding students.

➤ **HARROGATE COLLEGE**
see *Leeds Metropolitan University*

➤ **HATFIELD POLYTECHNIC**
see *University of Hertfordshire*

Words in italics are Push's point of view — take it or leave it...

HERIOT-WATT UNIVERSITY

○ **HERIOT-WATT UNIVERSITY**, Edinburgh, EH14 4AS **TEL** (0131) 449 5111 **E-MAIL** enquiries@hw.ac.uk **WEBSITE** www.hw.ac.uk
○ **HERIOT-WATT UNIVERSITY STUDENTS' ASSOCIATION**, Riccarton, Edinburgh, EH14 4AS **TEL** (0131) 451 5333 **E-MAIL** hwusa@hw.ac.uk **WEBSITE** www.hwusa.org

GENERAL ◖◖◖◖◖◖◖◖◖◖◖◖

6 5 miles from the ancient stones of Edinburgh University sit *the much less geriatric bricks* of Heriot-Watt University's Edinburgh Campus. 380 acres of parkland provide an *almost soporific* natural backdrop to what was once the site of an old mansion house and is now the wooded home of HWU, which has been indulging a neo-Napoleonic scheme of expansion and acquisition for the past 50 years. *It's not the most exciting place in the world, but the woodland and the artificial lake make for a pleasant afternoon's wandering.* In 2005 they threw their net further afield and opened a new campus way out in Dubai to teach Dubai- type subjects (management, IT, Science and Commerce, etc.) to Dubai-type people. For general information about Edinburgh, see University of Edinburgh.

SEX RATIO: ♂60 ♀40	FOUNDED: 1821
FULL-TIME U'GRADS: 5,100	PART-TIME: 250
POSTGRADS: 1,600	NON-DEGREE: 40
AVE COURSE: 4YRS	ETHNIC: 20%
STATE:PRIVATE SCHOOL: 92:8	FLUNK RATE: 17%
MATURE: 39%	INTERNATIONAL: 28%
DISABLED: 100	LOCAL: 40%

ATMOSPHERE
The self-contained Edinburgh campus is a serene, relaxed, 9-to-5 kind of place. Most students who live off campus don't hang around come teatime, leaving the place a bit bleak, except for the lesser-spotted fresher who can be observed, flitting nervously through his (and the male is the dominant gender here) brick habitat. There's little contact with other local species except in Edinburgh, where students are such a common breed that trouble is rare.

SITES
SCOTTISH BORDERS CAMPUS (600 students – Textiles, Design and some Management) SBC (as it's abbreviated) is the campus formerly known as the Scottish College of Textiles. It's in the *small but attractive* town of Galashiels, 37 miles from the main campus at Edinburgh (a shuttle-bus runs between the two). *There's not a lot to do around here – especially since the outpost of the SA closes throughout the weekend but students can bus it to the Edinburgh campus to catch some top gigs.* Many students spend some of their time studying on both campuses.
ORKNEY CAMPUS (Marine and Environment-related courses) Situated in Stromness (the second largest town in the Orkney islands – *not that that says much*), the campus consists of The International

Centre for Island Technology *where they concentrate on marine energy and the environment.*

EDINBURGH see University of Edinburgh
○ **CITY CENTRE** 6.5 MILES

TRAVEL see University of Edinburgh
CAR The Edinburgh campus is about a mile outside the A720 Edinburgh ring road, just off the A71 on its way out of the city. There are parking spaces on the campus.
LOCAL Buses run in and out of Edinburgh town centre from 5.30am till 4am. The N25 night service runs every hour from 12.15am to 4.15am and costs £2. Daytime service to the town costs £1.
UNIVERSITY There's a shuttle bus running to the Scottish Borders Campus and back again. It's free but places must be pre-booked.
TAXIS 20-min rides to Waverley Station are convenient, but prices climb to £13 at night.
BICYCLES *A bit far to the city centre, but the union canal and other cycle paths improve access to the town. Cycling is popular despite the lumpy surroundings.*

CAREER PROSPECTS
○ **CAREERS SERVICE** ○ **NO. OF STAFF** 7 FULL
○ **UNEMPLOYED AFTER 6 MTHS** 10%
The Careers Advisory Service's calendar is *chock-full* of job fairs, recruitment programmes, CV clinics and talks. Short and long-term vacancies are posted in online and printed newsletters. There's also a *helpful* Alumni Mentoring Programme whereby graduates offer phone and e-mail advice to current students – *particularly useful for international students.*

○ **The grounds of Heriot-Watt University contain a disused ticket office – all that remains of Edinburgh's proposed underground train system.**

Words in italics are Push's point of view — take it or leave it...

FAMOUS ALUMNI

Nigel Brockton (World Championship Speed Skier); Adam Crozier (CE, Royal Mail); Craig Joiner (rugby player); Archy Kirkwood (Lib Dem peer); Henry McLeish (former First Minister of Scotland); Martin O'Neill (Labour peer); Jim Telfer (Director, Rugby, Scottish Rugby Union plc); Irvine Welsh ('Trainspotting' author).

SPECIAL FEATURES

The name Heriot-Watt has nothing to do with cow-invading TV vet James Heriott. James Watt (1736-1819) was one of the innovators of the Industrial Revolution with his work on steam engines. George Heriot (1563-1623), known as 'Jinglin' Geordie', was a jeweller and financier to James VI of Scotland (James I of England).

FURTHER INFO

○ **PROSPECTUSES** UNDERGRAD; POSTGRAD; ALTERNATIVE
○ **OPEN DAYS**

'Fresh', the alternative prospectus, is a collaboration between students and staff. A brief prospectus is also available in Braille. A Scholar Programme that goes into high schools is intended to ease the transition between school and university. See www.hw.ac.uk/recruitment for more info.

ACADEMIC ○○○○○○○○○○○○○○

The courses on offer at Heriot-Watt broadly cover the interests of its two namesakes: science, industry, engineering and textiles. It has strong links with modern industry and has one of the UK's two specialised centres in actuarial maths and statistics. Logistics, Photonics and Petroleum Engineering are among its poster-subjects. Students are assigned a course tutor as a mentor to consult about academic stuff.

ENTRY POINTS: 180–280	AVE POINTS: N/A
APPLICATIONS PER PLACE: 5	CLEARING: 7%
NO. OF TERMS: 3	LENGTH OF TERMS: 10 WKS
STAFF TO STUDENT RATIO: 1:14	STUDY ADDICTS: 16%
TEACHING: ★★★★★	RESEARCH: ★★★★
YEAR ABROAD: 3 %	SANDWICH STUDENTS: <1%
1STS: 12%	2.2S: 33%
2.1S: 43%	3RDS: 7%

ADMISSIONS

○ **APPLY VIA UCAS**

HWU has a policy of pulling in under-represented groups and broadening participation – especially when it comes to mature, local and disabled students.

SUBJECTS

BUILT ENVIRONMENT: 14% **ENGINEERING & PHYSICAL SCIENCES**: 25% **LIFE SCIENCES**: 9% **MANAGEMENT & LANGUAGES** 24% **MATHS & COMPUTER SCIENCES**: 18%
TEXTILES & DESIGN: 8%
BEST: Engineering & Computing; European Languages.
UNUSUAL: Brewing & Distilling.

LIBRARIES

○ **156,500 BOOKS** ○ **780 STUDY PLACES**

There's a main library at the Edinburgh campus, where Irvine Welsh allegedly wrote most of 'Trainspotting'. *Which can only be worrying.* There are also collections in some departments and at least one library at each of the other sites.

COMPUTERS

○ **460 WORKSTATIONS** ○ **24-HR ACCESS**

Most University residences have networked workstations with 24-hour access. Some buildings now have wireless laptop connection points. The Scott Russell Building has 48 PCs available all night; other computer centres on both campuses close comfortably before midnight.

OTHER LEARNING FACILITIES

Language labs, a design lab and a media centre.

ENTERTAINMENT ○○○○○○○○○○

THE CITY see University of Edinburgh

THE UNIVERSITY

○ **PRICE OF A PINT OF BEER** £1.75
○ **GLASS OF WINE** £1.60
○ **CAN OF RED BULL** £1.80

BARS Three in the Union: Liberty's (a daytime snack-café that gets more alcoholic at night), Zero° (more of a nightclub/event venue) and Jinglin' Geordies (*pubby* with a gaming area – pool, video games and juke box). An external company runs the bar in the conference centre.
FILM £5 a year gets the pleasure of viewing one *mainstream or cultish* film per week in Zero°.
CLUBBING/MUSIC VENUES/COMEDY Zero° has a club night, Jam, on Fridays and bands every Thursday. Underbelly, Amplifico and El Presidente have all played. There's a comedy club every other Tuesday and open-mic/karaoke on Sundays.
FOOD The University Refectory dishes out three meals a day. All the bars provide food of some description. Jinglin' Geordies Tea Time Special has full meals from £1.50 and keeps the platters coming till midnight.
OTHER Weekly pub quizzes and the odd ball.

SOCIAL ○○○○○○○○○○○○○

HERIOT-WATT UNIVERSITY STUDENTS' ASSOCIATION

○ **4 SABBATICALS** ○ **TURNOUT AT LAST BALLOT** 6%
○ **NUS MEMBER**

Politics is generally a bigger turn-off for Heriot-Watt students than Chris Moyles in a tutu smeared in Marmite, although this was one of the first unions to campaign against top-up fees and the like. As far as most are concerned, however, the Student Association is first and foremost a services organisation and it's recently started bussing students between the Edinburgh and Borders campus for special events. *The University tolerates the Union but worries that it encourages students to party too much, which seems a bit like worrying that 'Blue Peter' encourages under-age sex and violence, but nevermind.*

SA FACILITIES
The Association's building, named The Union, contains: three bars; disco; cafeteria; shop; travel agency; PA hire; welfare library; meeting rooms. The Scottish Borders Campus has a union building designed by SBC students.

CLUBS (NON SPORTING)
Brewing; Duke of Edinburgh; Enterprise; Fiction Library; Flunky (Christian events); HW 4 Peace; Jazz; Libyan Students; Life Aquatic; Mag-Net (mature & graduate network); MASSUE (Malaysian & Singaporean); Parthenon Hellenic; Poker; Radio Station; Table Football; Watt Gamers. **See Clubs tables.**

OTHER ORGANISATIONS
Watts On' is the free paper three times a term. Lots of volunteering goes on and TiTs is the *innovative* Theatre Society.

RELIGIOUS
◉ 1 CHAPLAIN (COFS)
The multi-faith chaplaincy has several honorary chaplains (CofE, RC, Methodist, Greek, Orthodox, Free Church of Scotland) and there's a Muslim prayer room.

PAID WORK see University of Edinburgh
◉ JOB BUREAU ◉ PAID WORK TERM-TIME 75% HOLS 85%
Jobs on campus are posted by the University jobshop (an offshoot of the Careers Advisory Service).

SPORTS ◉◉◉◉◉◉◉◉◉◉◉◉

◉ BUSA RANKING 55 **◉ RECENT SUCCESSES** RUGBY, TENNIS, HOCKEY
With such large grounds, the University has provided some *excellent* sporting facilities *that have attracted a fair number of muscle-bound Olympians.* The Sports Union co-ordinates all sports activities and remains entirely independent of the SA. Scholarships are available for badminton, golf and squash.

SPORTS FACILITIES
The Edinburgh campus boasts the *impressive* National Squash Centre and a pro-quality Sports Academy (in conjunction with Hearts football club, who also train there). There are: five grass pitches; three astro pitches; indoor astrodome; two rugby pitches; two outdoor cross country tracks; two sports halls with four badminton

courts; three volleyball courts; basketball court; netball court; climbing wall; martial arts space; fitness suite; two free weights rooms. Sports Union Membership costs £10 (one-off payment) of £3 (single year). See also University of Edinburgh.

SPORTING CLUBS
Aikido; Boat; Curling; Gaelic Football; Rifle; Table Tennis. **See Clubs tables.**

ATTRACTIONS see University of Edinburgh.

ACCOMMODATION ◉◉◉◉◉◉◉◉◉◉

IN UNIVERSITY
◉ CATERED 6% **◉ COST** £85 (33WKS)
◉ SELF-CATERING 26% **◉ COST** £66 (39WKS)
◉ 1ST YRS LIVING IN 60%
◉ INSURANCE PREMIUM £
AVAILABILITY
All first years get a room *(that's not a euphemism for getting frisky),* if they want one. Any that pass up the chance can live in the following year, if they really want. All halls are on campus (1,800 beds) and consist of single study bedrooms with small shared kitchen in catered and bathroom (although many self-catered halls have en suites). The University houses 240 students in a head tenancy scheme based in town centre flats. There's not much to choose between halls. *However, the catered halls are older, do more unpleasant things with concrete and are beginning to look run-down. Security patrols hunt down bogeymen at night.*
CAR PARKING Free permits.

EXTERNALLY see University of Edinburgh
◉ AVE RENT £65
AVAILABILITY Students tend to remain close to campus in areas like West Side, Slateford, Grogie and Morningside.
HOUSING HELP The Accommodation Office has three staff providing a bulletin board and advice. *Many homeless students find the Student Pad website run by* University of Edinburgh *helpful.*

WELFARE ◉◉◉◉◉◉◉◉◉◉◉

SERVICES
◉ LGBT OFFICER ◉ INTERNATIONAL STUDENTS' OFFICER
◉ WOMEN'S OFFICER ◉ DISABILITIES OFFICER
◉ SELF-DEFENCE CLASSES ◉ TAXI FUND
◉ UNIVERSITY COUNSELLORS 1 FULL
◉ SU COUNSELLORS 2 FULL/1 PART **◉ CRIME RATING** !!
The SA Vice-President is responsible for student welfare on the Scottish Borders Campus.
HEALTH The main campus has a medical centre with four GPs, three nurses, a dentist and a physio.
CRECHES/NURSERY The University nursery on the

Edinburgh campus has full-day or part-day places (birth upwards).

DISABILITIES *Access to some departments and buildings is just great and awareness is good, but considering how modern a campus this is, there have been some omissions.* The Union has been refurbished to improve access. There are 22 specially adapted rooms and there's a Special Needs Advisor.

FINANCE

○ **AVE DEBT PER YEAR** £1,655 ○ **HOME STUDENT FEES** £1,700 **FEES** Non-Scottish Brits are still fleeced for £3,000 in tuition fees. International undergrads pay

£7,350–9,600, postgrads £3,200 (home) or up to £9,700 (int'l). Distance learning modules are available – costs vary.
○ **ACCESS FUND** £360,000 ○ **SUCCESSFUL APPLICATIONS/YR** 569 ○ **AVE PAYMENT** £400
SUPPORT In addition to the access fund, several bursaries and scholarships can be plundered, including a fee waiver for part-timers, living support for students under 25 from low-income families, hardship loans, a hardship fund, sports scholarships and mature students bursary scheme (for married students over 25 who have been self-supporting for three years).

UNIVERSITY OF HERTFORDSHIRE

FORMERLY HATFIELD POLYTECHNIC

H

1. ○ **UNIVERSITY OF HERTFORDSHIRE**, College Lane, Hatfield, Hertfordshire, AL10 9AB **TEL** (01707) 284 800 **E-MAIL** admissions@herts.ac.uk **WEBSITE**: www.herts.ac.uk ○ **UNIVERSITY OF HERTFORDSHIRE STUDENTS' UNION**, College Lane, Hatfield, Hertfordshire, AL10 9AB **TEL** (01707) 285 004 **E-MAIL** ushu@herts.ac.uk **WEBSITE** www.ushu.herts.ac.uk
2. ○ **FACULTY OF LAW**, St Albans Campus, University of Hertfordshire, 7 Hatfield Road, St Albans, Hertfordshire, AL1 3RS

GENERAL ○○○○○○○○○○○○○○

Barely eight miles from the outskirts of London, Hatfield is the University of Hertfordshire's centre of operations. *Being a commuter town, it's a sleeping satellite and a fairly uninteresting one at that, although it's aware of its failings and has been attempting a makeover for some time now.* Hertfordshire is one of the *less trite* Home Counties with *sprinklings of pretty* rural villages and the *attractive* St Albans. *The main campus seems divorced from everything but the A1, which runs right along one edge. It's a couple of miles away from the train station in Hatfield – and in Hatfield, the station is the most appealing feature, at least until the town's revamp kicks in. The 30-year architectural history of uninspiring blocks that made up most of the campus is thankfully being phased out, with the brighter and more modern buildings of the new de Havilland campus leading the way into the future.*

🚹🚹🚹🚹🚹🚹🚹🚹🚹🚹🚹🚹🚹🚹🚹🚹🚹🚹🚹🚹

SEX RATIO: ♂45 ♀55	**FOUNDED:** 1952
FULL-TIME U'GRADS: 2,300	**PART-TIME:** 3,800
POSTGRADS: 3,330	**NON-DEGREE:** 760
AVE COURSE: 3YRS	**ETHNIC:** 11%
STATE:PRIVATE SCHOOL: 98:2	**FLUNK RATE:** 18%
MATURE: 23%	**INTERNATIONAL:** 11%
DISABLED: 250	**LOCAL:** 29%

ATMOSPHERE

The fact that the immediate vicinity isn't the most socially happening slab of commuter-land hasn't dampened students' spirits. In fact, it galvanises them to build fun factories of their own. This doesn't, however, distract them from their main

purpose in coming to Herts – the old 'choose university, choose degree, choose career' mantra. Town/gown relations aren't exactly hugs and bunnies, particularly when it comes to parking. There are, however, plans for a new car park at Angerland Common, so there's another 800 reasons to be cheerful on the way. Insularity is an issue on campus – locals and internationals tend to stick to their own kind rather than integrate and the significant part-time contingent coming and going scuppers any continuous sense of community. The SU are working on it and a number of community initiatives and Rag projects are oiling the joints somewhat.

SITES

COLLEGE LANE CAMPUS (All subjects not based at other sites) This 93-acre site is the main campus, but *the least attractive – it's the sort of place that will take over the world when the Orwellian nightmare begins. Sadly, a few colourful drainpipes don't do enough to redeem the overall aesthetic.*

FACULTY OF LAW, ST ALBANS (1,100 students – Law) About 6 miles from Hatfield in the *pretty* Roman town of St Albans is the heart of the local legal community and the University's law faculty lives right in the middle of it. *It's a much more exciting eye-candy town than Hatfield, which is why it's a bit of a drag there's no student accommodation on or near this site.*

DE HAVILLAND CAMPUS (Humanities & Education) Just a mile across Hatfield from College Lane perches the £120m phoenix that rose from the ashes of Watford and Hertford campuses. It's an *ultra-modern, glassy arrangement* of giant auditorium, giant learning resource centre (LRC), giant blocks of student accommodation and *not-so-giant refectory that somehow manages to* *look a bit flimsy*. There's no SU bar, so the University Bus Service *is a must* to get to College Lane for a beer, but there is the Sports and Social club for *a quieter night close to home*.

HATFIELD
- **POPULATION** 97,600 ● **TOWN CENTRE** 1 MILE
- **LONDON** 8 MILES ● **ST ALBANS** 5 MILES
- **HIGH TEMP** 21 ● **LOW TEMP** 1 ● **RAINFALL** 49

Hatfield is essentially a springboard into London and has thus never really bothered to acquire much personality of its own. Having said that, there are some historical gems – Old Hatfield *is the nice bit*, home to Hatfield House, *a charming Jacobean mansion where Queen Bessie I used to hang out. The newer bit of town is nondescript, bordering on drab. Architectural magnificence or fun stuff have never been of much interest to the pharmaceutical and computing industries that Hatfield is at the centre of – useful for sandwich placements though. The massive Galleria shopping centre on the outskirts has distracted a few, but St Albans is far and away friendlier, prettier and more popular with students.*

TRAVEL
TRAINS Hatfield station is 1.5 miles from the main campus, useful for the direct service to London King's Cross to the south (from £9 return) and Stevenage to the north (£6.10). From these stations there are also direct services all the way to York, Newcastle and Edinburgh and connections to the rest of the country. Hertford station is about half an hour from London (£9.50).

COACHES No National Express service to Hatfield. The nearest stops are London's Victoria Coach Station and Luton (12 miles away). London Country and Greenline buses run services to and from London.

CAR The A1(M) runs right by the campus. The A1000 passes through Hatfield, as does the A414 which also goes to Hertford. All sites are within five miles of the M25. The Galleria shopping centre has free parking, and there are pay & displays around College Lane (50p/day) – but there's no parking at all on the de Havilland site. The University has established a car-sharing policy.

AIR Luton Airport, offering international and inland flights, is 11 miles north-east.

HITCHING *The Home Counties as a rule aren't good for picking up lifts but the A1 is just about the best road to be on. Try the junction with the M25, six miles down the road.*

LOCAL *Buses aren't the cheapest in the country, and can be irritatingly slow.* Routes to Hatfield, St Albans, Stevenage, Watford and Welwyn Garden City.

UNIVERSITY The Universities Uno bus service does subsidised student fares.

TAXIS Numerous firms, *but prices rocket beyond any of the town boundaries.*

BICYCLES *A bike's a useful way of rolling around the campuses.*

CAREER PROSPECTS
- **CAREERS SERVICE** ● **NO. OF STAFF** 1 FULL/4 PART
- **UNEMPLOYED AFTER 6MTHS** 12%

The Careers Advisory Service provides vacancy newsletters, bulletin boards, a programme of talks, workshops, mock interviews and aptitude testing.

FAMOUS ALUMNI
Sanjeev Bhaskar (Goodness Gracious Me, The Kumars); Ian Dowie (footballer); Helen Lederer (comedian); Lady Parkinson (wife of Cecil); Jayne Zito (mental health campaigner).

FURTHER INFO
● **PROSPECTUSES** UNDERGRAD; POSTGRAD; DEPARTMENTAL; ALTERNATIVE; VIDEO ● **OPEN DAYS**

There are three general open days annually, although mid-week campus tours occur throughout the year. There are specific open days for Art & Design and Nursing & Midwifery. See website for prospectuses and details.

ACADEMIC ◍◍◍◍◍◍◍◍◍◍◍◍◍

Hertfordshire's six faculties have undergone rapid expansion in recent years, with the School of Pharmacy being the latest new toy, *and the academic balloon ain't gonna stop inflating any time soon.* The University's also responsible for a number of students in the local college consortium: Hertford Regional, Oaklands, North Hertfordshire and West Herts colleges. Management and other vocational courses are big business – the University was one of the first to offer a sandwich degree and links with industry are superglue strong. The *wound-licking* Physiotherapy and Nursing departments are also good. Weekly lectures are backed up by weekly tutorials. *Forget any notion of cosy fireside chats over cherry brandy, however* – most tutorials contain 20-25 students. The majority of courses divide into four modules each term, assessment for some is 100% coursework-based. The *techno-savvy* StudyNet system allows online access to module materials, lecture notes, message boards and LRC resources.

ENTRY POINTS: 80-240	AVE POINTS: 230
APPLICATIONS PER PLACE: 4	CLEARING: 15%
NO. OF TERMS: 2	LENGTH OF TERMS: 15 WKS
STAFF TO STUDENT RATIO: 1:30	STUDY ADDICTS: 15%
TEACHING: **	RESEARCH: **
1STS: 10 %	2.2s: 41 %
2.1s: 37%	3RDS: 3%

ADMISSIONS
● **APPLY VIA UCAS/NMAS FOR NURSING/GTTR FOR PGCE**

Herts is beefing up its Equal Opps policy to encourage minority groups, including those with no formal qualifications. Mature Students and those working while studying can use the Credit & Accumulation Transfer Service (CATS), which allows students to choose their own pace of study. Application packs for Counselling courses available from (01707) 284 800.

SUBJECTS

ART & DESIGN 7%   **ARTS, HUMANITIES & EDUCATION** 16%
BUSINESS/MANAGEMENT 16%   **CONSORTIUM COLLEGES** 5%
ENGINEERING 14%   **HEALTH & HUMAN SCIENCES** 30%
INTERDISCIPLINARY STUDIES 7%   **LAW** 6%
UNUSUAL Paramedic Science.

LIBRARIES

◉ **500,000 BOOKS** ◉ **2,940 STUDY PLACES**
◉ **SPEND PER STUDENT** £££££ ◉ **24-HR ACCESS**
The de Havilland and College Lane LRCs keep
going through the night and cover all subjects
except Law – the smaller library at St Albans is
stuffed with weighty legal tomes.

COMPUTERS

◉ **2,900 WORKSTATIONS** ◉ **24-HR ACCESS**
Staffed computer rooms on all sites and magic
laptop sockets for web access in the libraries. The
1,600-room halls of residence at de Havilland
come complete with broadband access included
in their rent. Technophobes beware.

OTHER LEARNING FACILITIES

Language labs are annexed to the LRCs. There's
also a CAD lab, music rehearsal rooms, mock
pharmacy and a media centre.
The practice courtroom at St Albans was donated
to the University by Hatfield Magistrates Court.
Presumably they'd finished with it.

ENTERTAINMENT ◑◑◑◑◑◑◑◑◑◑

THE TOWN

◉ **PRICE OF A PINT OF BEER** £1.80
◉ **GLASS OF WINE** £2.20
◉ **CAN OF RED BULL** £1.80
*The sheer nocturnal dullness of Hatfield has obliged
many students to throw themselves wholeheartedly
into the Union ents scene. Or in front of a train. Or
onto a train bound for London.* The pubs scene
doesn't exactly embrace students open-armed so
much as stare at them open-mouthed. *Luckier
lawyers enjoy St Albans, which is bigger, more
cosmopolitan, and densely stuffed with pubs.*
CINEMAS The nine-screen UCI in the Galleria
complex has reduced student tickets (£4.50-
5.50). Watford and Stevenage have similar
celluloid centres.
THEATRES Plenty of performances hit St Alban's
Theatre on their way to London.
PUBS *Mai Tai's (which changes its name with
alarming frequency) in the Galleria is really the
only place students bother with – probably
because of the boozy deals on offer.* Cross Keys
and the Bell are popular with the lawyers.
Hatfield's The Cavendish and the aptly-named
Harrier aren't exactly student-friendly.
CLUBBING Batchwoods (chart, cheese, urban, dance),
based in a converted manor in St Albans, is gaining
momentum thanks to the Pub2Club Thursday night
deal with the Union. £3 gets entry, a drink, and
return bus travel to and from funkytown.

MUSIC VENUES Live tunesters grace several of the
bars in St Albans, most notably the Factory,
which has hosted KT Tunstall and the Cooper
Temple Clause. For bigger fish, Knebworth and
Wembley are a 30-min drive.
COMEDY/CABARET In St Albans, O'Neils, the
Maltings Arts Centre and the Alban Arena.
EATING OUT The Galleria's many eateries include
MacDonald's and other *plastic food* in plastic
packs. Hatfield has a few restaurants (Indian,
Italian, Greek and Chinese) and snack shops,
such as burger bars, chippies and spud places.
Celeb chef Jean-Christophe Novelli's lakeside
restaurant Auberge du Lac is one for gourmets
and those with bulging wallets. *St Albans,
Hertford and Watford also have tasty but
somewhat expensive eateries.*

THE UNIVERSITY

◉ **PRICE OF A PINT OF BEER** £1.90
◉ **GLASS OF WINE** £2.50
◉ **CAN OF RED BULL** £1.75
BARS The biggest, *loudest, busiest* bar is the Font
Bar on the main campus, with lively daytimes,
different entertainments and open doors till 1am
every night. Hutton Hall bar's got live music
events and the Elephant House bar is blessed
with karaoke, film and sports nights.
THEATRES The new Auditorium at de Havilland
seats 450 and shows both student and touring shows.
The dedicated University Arts Programme is
responsible for over 60 productions a year, including
drama, dance, music and other cultural events.
FILM The Ele House shows a weekly mainstream
film, £2.
CLUBBING/MUSIC VENUES Bonk and Flirt are the big
nights in the Font Bar. Paul Eden, Tim Westwood
and Trevor Nelson have all hit the decks. Guest
crooners have included Lemar, Phantom Planet
and Goldie Lookin' Chain.
COMEDY/CABARET Fortnightly comedy at the Ele
House.
FOOD The Font Bar spoons out a mixture of *lovely
junk* and Oriental goodies till midnight. Elephant
House has all manner of speedy snacks on offer,
which are usually cheaper than refectory food.
The Union shop does halal fare.
OTHER The June Ball is held jointly with Luton
University – *that's the official line anyway. Luton
can't afford their own so have hijacked
Hertfordshire's – it's a grand affair,* with live
bands, casino, fairground rides, food court and
gallons and gallons of fermented goodness.

SOCIAL ◑◑◑◑◑◑◑◑◑◑◑◑◑

UNIVERSITY OF HERTFORDSHIRE STUDENTS' UNION

◉ **5 SABBATICALS** ◉ **TURNOUT AT LAST BALLOT** 7%
◉ **NUS MEMBER**
The Elephant House at the Hatfield site is the SU's

own building, but it also has offices in the University's Hutton Block. *It's strictly a leave-your-politics-at-the-door affair*, and political societies are banned out of policy – *not that that's a bone of contention, many students are more interested in playing massive message board games of Mallett's Mallet than in following a cause.* The focus is on immediate issues (namely rent and parking), and *the exec do a pretty good job of representing student views to the powers above.*

SU FACILITIES
Bars; nightclub; two snack bars; canteen; two fast food outlets; two pool tables; meeting room; minibus hire; car for hire; Endsleigh Insurance office; Lloyds TSB and NatWest ATMs; general store; stationary shop; bookshop; travel agency; vending & gaming machines; fax & printing services; photocopiers; payphones; photo booth; advice centre; launderette.

CLUBS (NON SPORTING)
Curry; Students United Against Discrimination. **See Clubs tables.**

OTHER ORGANISATIONS
'Newsletter University' comes out five times a year, also online. 'Horizon', the University paper, is monthly. There's also 'Solar', a weekly e-mail newsletter mainly containing events listings. Radio station Crush claims to be the oldest student radion station in the galaxy (or at least the country) and broadcasts online and around campus and bars till 1am. The Hertfordshire Rag has been *raking it in* (in the region of £10,000 a year) and is introducing a year-round calendar of charity stunts instead of its previous one-off Rag Week. There's a volunteer centre to get students involved in the local community, which is nice.

RELIGIOUS
◉ 1 CHAPLAIN (MULTI-FAITH)
On campus facilities for Muslim and Christian worship, including an ecumenical chaplaincy and a Muslim prayer room. Also Anglican, Catholic and Evangelical churches in Hatfield.

PAID WORK
◉ JOB BUREAU ◉ PAID WORK TERM-TIME 80%; HOLS 55%
Vacancy boards are posted and updated by the recruitment office. There are plenty of term-time and vacation pocket-lining opportunities at the Galleria complex and in local supermarkets. The Union has casual work available in bars and shops and an online vacancy notice board. The University Student Ambassador Scheme helps find casual local jobs.

SPORTS

◉ RECENT SUCCESSES AMERICAN FOOTBALL, FENCING, FOOTBALL AND WOMEN'S FOOTBALL **◉ BUSA RANKING** 59
Hertfordshire Sports Village has become one of the University's top selling points – *the standard of sporting success has lagged behind the variety and quality of the facilities, but things are improving.* There are links with Saracens rugby, Watford football and Arsenal ladies football team.

SPORTS FACILITIES
Hertfordshire Sports Village at de Havilland has an indoor cricket hall, eight-lane swimming pool, climbing and bouldering wall, 100-station fitness suite, 12 badminton courts, two floodlit Astroturf pitches and extra outdoor sports fields. Students get massive discounts on season passes or per session. Locally there's Hatfield leisure centre and swimming pool, plus a huge gym and a golf course.

SPORTING CLUBS
Aikido Yoshinko; Lacrosse; Skydiving; Yoga. **See Clubs tables.**

ATTRACTION
Hatfield Town FC is nearby. Milton Keynes now has Wimbledon FC and the Snowdome.

ACCOMMODATION ◖◖◖◖◖◖◖◖◖

IN UNIVERSITY
◉ CATERED 6% **◉ COST** £85 (33WKS)
◉ SELF-CATERING 26% **◉ COST** £68 (39WKS)
◉ 1ST YRS LIVING IN 60% **◉ INSURANCE PREMIUM** £
AVAILABILITY First years are guaranteed accommodation if application deadlines are met but few others get a look-in. The de Havilland campus has 1,600 *luxury* rooms – with en suite and broadband – and is *popular as a result*, despite being in the most expensive price band. Accommodation takes the form of clustered flats, *so there's a sense of community. The halls on the far edge of College Lane are a bit on the dreary side but affordability makes them popular regardless.* Mixed sex couples are easily housed, single sex accommodation is also available. There's no catered accommodation, *and the kitchens can have up to 11 students trying to microwave lasagne simultaneously.* Security has been improved and there are plans to add another 1,400 high quality rooms at some point in the future.
CAR PARKING De Havilland is strictly car-free.

EXTERNALLY
◉ AVE RENT £65
AVAILABILITY St Albans *is the plum position, but pricey.* Hatfield and Welwyn Garden City are also popular, but have fewer bars and shops *in which to run up debts.* Since the closure of the Watford and Hertford campuses, the number of students trying to find external housing in Hatfield at the same time has caused problems. The January house-hunt is *competitive*, with losers forced out of the town centre and into suburbs or nearby villages. The University's head tenancy scheme

and 'digs' arrangements with local families help, *but not enough to keep everyone happy.* Hazel Grove is close to College Lane *and is therefore the most convenient place to be for many students. Fat chance of finding a place to live there, though.*
HOUSING HELP The Accommodation Office run the head tenancy scheme and offer advice. The Union-run advice service posts vacancies *and is handy for finding hassle-free accommodation that is actually habitable. By humans.*

WELFARE ⟲⟲⟲⟲⟲⟲⟲⟲⟲⟲⟲⟲⟲

SERVICES
⊙ LGBT OFFICER & SOCIETY ⊙ MATURE STUDENTS' OFFICER & SOCIETY ⊙ INTERNATIONAL STUDENTS' OFFICER & SOCIETY ⊙ POSTGRAD OFFICER & SOCIETY ⊙ DISABILITIES OFFICER & SOCIETY ⊙ WOMEN'S OFFICER & SOCIETY ⊙ ETHNIC MINORITIES OFFICER & SOCIETY ⊙ LATE-NIGHT MINIBUS ⊙ NIGHTLINE ⊙ UNIVERSITY COUNSELLORS 4 ⊙ SU COUNSELLORS 2 ⊙ CRIME RATING !! The Advice Support Centre doles out advice on everything from accommodation to money. *Oh, and free condoms.*
HEALTH On-campus NHS practice with GPs and nurses.
CRECHES/NURSERY The campus nursery has places for children up to 5yrs. Demand is high.
WOMEN A minibus nips around three late nights a week.

DISABILITIES Despite some steep slopes between buildings the Hatfield campus has *comparatively excellent access* and special accommodation provisions including rooms for carers. Also various amenities for hearing- and sight-impaired students. Many lecture theatres have hearing loops, all main switchboards are equipped with minicoms and there's *good support for dyslexics* in conjunction with the local Access Centres.
CRIME Campus crime is low – partly thanks to a University Watch scheme run jointly with the police and Unisecure. Off-campus there've been spates of burglary (made more painful by a lack of contents insurance in some cases). A few idiotic local youths have caused problems for students in the past, with racially motivated crime *not unheard of.* There are two community police officers on site to ease matters.
DRUGS The Union operates a zero tolerance policy and there's often random sniffer dog testing at venue entrances. *Needless to say, drug abuse is not common as a consequence.*

FINANCE
⊙ **AVE DEBT PER YEAR** £2,869
⊙ **HOME STUDENT FEES** £3,000
FEES Postgrads pay £3,100. Internationals shell out £8,700-£9,500.
⊙ **ACCESS FUND** £841,000
SUPPORT Some departmental awards – Engineering and Science students with more than 360 UCAS points can bag £3,000 scholarships.

HEYTHROP COLLEGE, UNIVERSITY OF LONDON

THE COLLEGE IS PART OF THE UNIVERSITY OF LONDON AND STUDENTS ARE ENTITLED TO USE ITS FACILITIES

⊙ **HEYTHROP COLLEGE, UNIVERSITY OF LONDON**, Kensington Square, London, W8 5HQ **TEL** (020) 7795 6600 **E-MAIL** enquiries@heythrop.ac.uk **WEBSITE** www.heythrop.ac.uk ⊙ **HEYTHROP COLLEGE STUDENTS UNION**, Kensington Square, London, W8 5HQ **TEL** (020) 7795 4255 **E-MAIL** hsupresident@heythrop.ac.uk

⊙ **If you have any comments about Push, or fancy being involved in the next edition, drop us a line: editor@push.co.uk**

GENERAL ⟲⟲⟲⟲⟲⟲⟲⟲⟲⟲⟲⟲

Right next door to Kensington Tube is one of London's smallest and oldest institutions. Over the centuries Heythrop has been on an international pilgrimage, starting off in Louvain, Belgium, in 1614, pausing for breath at Liège, and moving on through Stonyhurst, North Wales and Oxford before landing in this *appealing* little Victorian campus in the *poshest part* of London. Originally a breeding-ground for Jesuit priests *(if they're allowed to breed, that is)* it offers courses in philosophy and theology. It's still a Catholic institution though – *this is not the place to look for Shaolin kung fu monks, devil worshippers or Ian Paisley.* The *charmingly eccentric* campus shares its space with a number of other

Words in italics are Push's point of view — take it or leave it...

institutions, including an American college and an assortment of religious groups, *all of which add different flavours to the social stew pot.* For general information on London see University of London.

SEX RATIO: ♂44 ♀56	FOUNDED: 1614
FULL-TIME U'GRADS: 277	PART-TIME: 4
POSTGRADS: 359	NON-DEGREE: 86
AVE COURSE: 3YRS	ETHNIC: 19%
STATE:PRIVATE SCHOOL: 80:20	FLUNK RATE: 17%
MATURE: 26%	INTERNATIONAL: 8%
DISABLED: N/A	LOCAL: 15%

ATMOSPHERE
Kensington High Street may be frighteningly busy and jammed with braying trustafarians, bemused tourists looking for Harrods and largely ignored Big Issue sellers, but the air surrounding Heythrop College couldn't be more tranquil if you filled it with cannabis fumes. Many students and staff are members of religious orders or wannabes, which gives it a very close-knit, cosy feel with no 'them & us' divide between the two (lots of matures help). Many students fall in love with the Escher-esque curio of a campus and the atmosphere of quiet reflection at first sight. Others find the aura of reverence and deathly hush of the common room suffocating. There are a fair few more lively attractions in the locale though, including a number of snug old pubs, achingly trendy bars and the Royal Court Theatre. Kensington Palace, Britain's loveliest council flat, is nearby too.

LONDON see University of London.

TRAVEL see University of London.
TRAINS Kensington Olympia is the nearest mainline station.
BUSES 9, 10, 27, 28, 31, 49, 52 *are the lucky numbers for this bus route lottery.*
UNDERGROUND High Street Kensington tube is next-door.
BICYCLES *Kensington's generally quite flat and bike-able, and many Heythropians find it the best way to get around.*

CAREER PROSPECTS
⊙ **CAREERS SERVICE** ⊙ **UNEMPLOYED AFTER 6MTHS** N/A
See University of London

FAMOUS ALUMNI
Frederick Copleston (philosopher); Gerard Manley Hopkins (poet); Nick Stuart (TV presenter).

FURTHER INFO
⊙ **PROSPECTUSES** UNDERGRAD, POSTGRAD, DEPARTMENTAL; VIDEO ⊙ **OPEN DAYS**

ACADEMIC ⊍⊍⊍⊍⊍⊍⊍⊍⊍⊍⊍⊍

The sheer diddiness means small class sizes, with one-to-one tutorials for undergrads, but a fair share of more conventional lectures and seminars are thrown in. There are two schools, one for each discipline. Theology students have exams and assessed coursework each year; philosophy students store up all their assessment until the third year.

ENTRY POINTS: 120-260	AVE POINTS: 189
APPLICATIONS PER PLACE: 5	CLEARING: 13%
NO. OF TERMS: 3	LENGTH OF TERMS: 12 WKS
STAFF TO STUDENT RATIO: 1:8	STUDY ADDICTS: 25%
TEACHING: ★★★	RESEARCH: ★★
1STS: 8%	2.2s: 41%
2.1s: 34%	3RDS: 8 %

ADMISSIONS
⊙ **APPLY VIA UCAS**

SUBJECTS
ARTS/HUMANITIES 100%
BEST Philosophy, Theology.
UNUSUAL Philosophy, Religion & Ethics.

LIBRARIES
⊙ **200,000** BOOKS ⊙ **60** STUDY PLACES
Heythrop keeps one of the largest specialist philosophy libraries *in the known universe. No Danielle Steele, then?*

COMPUTERS
⊙ **NO. OF WORKSTATIONS** 20
The main library has networked 'puters – an odd juxtaposition with 500-year-old manuscripts. There's also campus-wide wireless.

ENTERTAINMENT ⊍⊍⊍⊍⊍⊍⊍⊍⊍

THE CITY see University of London.

THE COLLEGE
With very few entertainment facilities on campus, most venture into Kensington to find the fun.
THEATRES *There's a fully teched-up stage space that doesn't get much use.*
FILM *Free sporadic screenings of arty, foreign fare.*
FOOD The Maria Assumpta Canteen doles out *divine* nosh till 7pm.
OTHER Two black-tie balls a year, including the Summer Ball at the *uber-posh* Institute of Directors on Pall Mall.

H

SOCIAL

HEYTHROP STUDENTS UNION
○ **TURNOUT AT LAST BALLOT** 35% ○ **NUS MEMBER**

There's very little to argue about in Heythrop, so the SU isn't the most political pea in the pod, mainly focusing on the events calendar. Positions are available on the College governing body and various committees for some subjects.

SU FACILITIES
Pool table; meeting room; photocopier; stationery shop; new and secondhand bookshops; table football; DVD player; widescreen TV and personal lockers (£5/yr). College-run TV lounge; snack bar; cafeteria; payphones; advice centre; vending machines also available.

CLUBS (NON SPORTING)
Real Ale. See Clubs tables.

RELIGIOUS
○ **2 CHAPLAINS (RC, BAPTIST)**
Heythrop's *Jesuit past doesn't have the stranglehold on faith that it once did. The college makes provisions for a variety of religious beliefs (or non-beliefs), although Christianity is still big daddy.* Mass is celebrated daily in the chapel and there's a college-wide mass *(or extended lunch break)* on Thursdays. A Muslim prayer room is available.

PAID WORK see University of London.
○ **PAID WORK** TERM-TIME 50%; HOLS 80%
Kensington High Street has plenty of shops, bars and restaurants for *gruntwork*.

SPORTS

○ **RECENT SUCCESSES** NONE.

SPORTS FACILITIES
One all-weather, all-purpose pitch – *though finding anything resembling a ball might be tricky*. The football team kicks around the London intercollegiate league *but students' minds are generally on more spiritual goals*.

SPORTING CLUBS
See Clubs tables.

ATTRACTIONS see University of London
Chelsea, Fulham and QPR football grounds are close by.

ACCOMMODATION

IN COLLEGE
○ **CATERED** 5% ○ **COST** £66
○ **SELF-CATERED** 7% ○ **COST** £65
○ **1ST YRS LIVING IN** 90% ○ **INSURANCE PREMIUM** £££
AVAILABILITY Also access to the UoL Intercollegiate halls as required. *Kitchens in the catered halls are utility-laden.* The Maria Assumpta Halls are women-only.
CAR PARKING Few spaces on campus (by arrangement with the College) *but cars aren't popular anyway*.

EXTERNALLY see University of London
○ **AVE RENT** £110
AVAILABILITY *Living conditions are rarely anything but plush in Kensington. House-rents are rarely anything but satanic.*
HOUSING HELP see University of London

WELFARE

SERVICES
○ **NIGHTLINE** ○ **UNIVERSITY COUNSELLORS** 1 FULL-TIME
○ **CRIME RATING** !!!
One of the chaplains is a trained counsellor.
HEALTH UoL's health service is on Gower Street.
DISABILITIES Chair-lifts, stair-lifts and ramps have been fitted where possible, *but the stair-crazy college buildings make access damned difficult.* Signings in lectures have been arranged in the past and UoL offers dyslexia support.
CRIME *Not generally a Christian pastime. Kensington is about as safe as large, expensive, security-conscious houses.*

FINANCE
○ **AVE DEBT PER YEAR** £2,738 ○ **HOME STUDENT FEES** £3,320
FEES Home student fees for undergrads are slightly above average, *probably because the college is more excited about postgraduate study*, for which students pay a relatively gentle £3,160. International undergrads pay £4,880.
SUPPORT Limited access fund and a few small bursaries.

⇨ **HOLLOWAY**
see *Royal Holloway, University of London*

⇨ **HOPE, LIVERPOOL**
see *Liverpool Hope University*

UNIVERSITY OF HUDDERSFIELD

FORMERLY HUDDERSFIELD POLYTECHNIC

1. ○ **UNIVERSITY OF HUDDERSFIELD**, Queensgate, Huddersfield, HD1 3DH **TEL** (01484) 422 288 **E-MAIL** prospectus@hud.ac.uk **WEBSITE** www.hud.ac.uk ○ **HUDDERSFIELD UNIVERSITY UNION**, University of Huddersfield, Queensgate, Huddersfield, HD1 3DH **TEL** (01484) 538 156 **E-MAIL** student.union@hud.ac.uk **WEBSITE** www.huddersfieldstudent.com
2. ○ **UNIVERSITY CENTRE OLDHAM**, Cromwell Street, Oldham, OL1 1BB **TEL** (0800) 0850 374 **E-MAIL** oldham@hud.ac.uk
3. ○ **UNIVERSITY CENTRE BARNSLEY** Church Street, Barnelsey S70 2AN **TEL** (01226 602 262) **E-MAIL** barnsley@hud.ac.uk

GENERAL ○○○○○○○○○○○○○

First-time visitors are forgiven a double take. If the green and fieldy area around Huddersfield looks strangely familiar it's because it provided the setting for crusty comedy Last of the Summer Wine and more recently The League of Gentlemen. Huddersfield's just east of the Pennines in the middle of northern England, not too far from Leeds and Manchester. Millions of quids of recent development into campus buildings have been like much-needed botox shots.

SEX RATIO: ♂44 ♀56	**FOUNDED: 1992**
FULL-TIME U'GRADS: 8,242	**PART-TIME: 1,219**
POSTGRADS: 3,404	**NON-DEGREE: 5,011**
AVE COURSE: 3-4YRS	**ETHNIC: 18%**
STATE:PRIVATE SCHOOL: 97:3	**FLUNK RATE: 20%**
MATURE: 55%	**INTERNATIONAL: 8%**
DISABLED: 235	**LOCAL: 45%**

ATMOSPHERE

There's a bluff heartiness to both town and gown – welcoming and friendly without any nancying around. It's a multicultural society with a 'work hard, play hard' attitude. The University powers that be are still gloating about having enticed new Chancellor and local luvvie Patrick 'Make it so' Stewart to the helm.

MINOR SITES

BARNSLEY AND OLDHAM *The Uni recently launched a bid for world – or at least Yorkshire – domination,* with two small satellite campuses opening in Barnsley and Oldham aimed at attracting students from the local area. Tuition fees are *cheaper* than at the Huddersfield site.

HUDDERSFIELD

○ **POPULATION** 388,900 ○ **CITY CENTRE** 0 MILES
○ **LONDON** 174 MILES ○ **LEEDS** 14 MILES
○ **MANCHESTER** 23 MILES
○ **HIGH TEMP** 19 ○ **LOW TEMP** 1 ○ **RAINFALL** 73
Recent years have brought *much-needed regeneration* to the town, which was *badly hit* by recession and the swift demise of native manufacturing. Now there's a *whopping great* shopping centre, a *glut* of trendy bars and a *few* more jobs to go around. *Someone forgot to turn on the bright lights though, so fun-seekers tend to hop on the train to Leeds or Manchester.*

TRAVEL

TRAINS The station is ten mins walk from campus. Services go direct to Leeds (from £4.60 return) and Manchester (£6.60) several times an hour. London trains (£31) are via Wakefield.
COACHES National Express to London (£24), Birmingham (£18.80) and elsewhere.
CAR A few minutes from the M62 via the A62, A642, A629 and A616.
AIR Leeds Bradford or Manchester airport for low-cost national airlines.
HITCHING *A62 or a short hop on a bus to Junction 24 of the M62.*
LOCAL *Not bad at all.* Various buses and trains locally.
UNIVERSITY There's a free shuttle bus service to Storthes Hall Park student village.
TAXIS *Taxis are plentiful and plenty cheap.*
BICYCLES *Only a true glutton for punishment would take on Huddersfield's hills.*

CAREER PROSPECTS

○ **CAREERS SERVICE** ○ **NO. OF STAFF** 9 FULL/3 PART ○ **UNEMPLOYED AFTER 6MTHS** 5%

FAMOUS ALUMNI

George Buckley (CEO of the Brunswick corporation); Gordon Kaye (Rene in 'Allo 'Allo); Wilf Lunn (eccentric inventor).

FURTHER INFO

○ **PROSPECTUSES** UNDERGRAD; POSTGRAD; SOME DEPARTMENTS; CD-ROM ○ **OPEN DAYS** Open days in June, September and October.

ACADEMIC ○○○○○○○○○○○○○

Sandwich courses are Huddersfield's thing, and the vocational edge they give to the courses *helps keep the grad employment rate up*. There's also a *relatively high* number of arts courses on offer for a former poly. The University's *worked hard at getting tight* with local industry and health service providers. The business incubator programme hatches a *hefty* number of young entrepreneurs every year.

ENTRY POINTS: 180–340	**AVE POINTS:** 189
APPLICATIONS PER PLACE: 4	**CLEARING:** 13%
NO. OF TERMS: 2	**LENGTH OF TERMS:** 15 WKS
TEACHING: *****	**RESEARCH:** ****
STAFF/STUDENT RATIO: 1:15	**STUDY ADDICTS:** 25%
YEAR ABROAD: 0%	**SANDWICH STUDENTS:** 20%
1STS: 8%	**2.2S:** 41%
2.1S: 34%	**3RDS:** 8%

ADMISSIONS

APPLY VIA UCAS/NMAS FOR NURSING
Students with non-traditional backgrounds (eg. work experience) are *warmly welcomed*. Foundation degrees and HNDs are common routes on to degree courses.

SUBJECTS

ART & DESIGN 17%   **ARTS/HUMANITIES** 17%
BUSINESS 18%   **COMPUTING & ENGINEERING** 15%
EDUCATION & PROFESSIONAL DEVELOPMENT 6%
HUMAN & HEALTH SCIENCES 17%   **SCIENCES** 10%
BEST FOR History; Performing Arts; Physical Sciences; Politics; Psychology; Subjects Allied to Medicine.
UNUSUAL Air Transport & Logistics Management; Events Management; Podiatry; Popular Music Production; Sports Journalism; Sports Promotion & Marketing.

LIBRARIES

400,000 BOOKS   **1,100 STUDY PLACES**
24–HR ACCESS   **SPEND PER STUDENT** £
The library runs a delivery system for part-timers.

COMPUTERS

2,300 WORKSTATIONS   **24–HR ACCESS**
SPEND PER STUDENT £££
Resources include electronic journals and audio-visual study aids. Broadband connections in all halls.

OTHER LEARNING FACILITIES

Part of the old SU facility has been *magically transformed* into drama studios, where Chancellor Patrick Stewart plies his trade leading theatrical workshops. There are also media studios at the town centre Queensgate campus.

ENTERTAINMENT ⓤⓤⓤⓤⓤⓤⓤⓤⓤⓤ

THE TOWN

PRICE OF A PINT OF BEER £2
GLASS OF WINE £2
CAN OF RED BULL £1.50
Huddersfield is racing with (and lagging behind) neighbouring Leeds when it comes to trendying up. The social culture is more pubby than clubby, but sexy new independent shops, bars and cafés are adding to the urban hum.
CINEMAS A nine-screen Odeon at Galpharm Stadium, ten mins walk from campus.
THEATRES The Lawrence Batley Theatre for mainstream productions and musicals.

PUBS *Real ale country*, though traditional pubs now rub shoulders with *ubiquitous* chain bars. Late licences abound around Zetland Street, near campus. Most pubs are student-friendly. *Pushplugs: Tokyo; Cotton Factory; College Arms; Zephyr.*
CLUBBING *Howlingly awful club scene requires swallowing pride along with a few stiff drinks. Heavy-hearted Pushplugs: Visage (cheesy Tuesdays are fun for freshers, passe for elders); Tokyo (a stagger away from the Students' Union); Camel Club (two student nights a week); Session.*
MUSIC VENUES Bar 1 twenty holds *decent* accoustic nights. Up-and-coming bands up and come to the Corner House. Brass bands are *popular* locally.
COMEDY/CABARET The Cellar Theatre hosts a fortnightly Comedy Cellar night.
EATING OUT *Varied and cheap.* Yates, Scream and Lloyds are handy for budget scoff. *Pushplugs: Mensahib (Indian); Shamus O'Donnell's (pub-grub); Blue Rooms (veggie).*

THE UNIVERSITY

PRICE OF A PINT OF BEER £1.50
GLASS OF WINE £1.90
CAN OF RED BULL £1.60
BARS The Venue hosts a regular quiz night and indie/rock night but *struggles to lure* students in from the nearby town centre drinking holes.
THEATRES There's a drama society and the purpose-built Milton Theatre. *Getting into character has gone up in the popularity stakes since Patrick Stewart got involved with the Uni.*
MUSIC VENUES *Zilch for gig lovers* as, despite having concert facilities, the Union only has a licence to run one room at a time. The music department puts on weekly recitals of the classical variety at St Paul's Hall.
CLUBBING A free student night at the Venue every Friday.
COMEDY/CABARET There's a monthly comedy night at – *you've guessed it* –The Venue. Ben Foley and Marlon Davies have appeared.
FOOD *Loads of places to graze, mainly cheap and cheerful coffee shops and canteens.*

SOCIAL ⓤⓤⓤⓤⓤⓤⓤⓤⓤⓤⓤⓤⓤ

UNIVERSITY OF HUDDERSFIELD STUDENTS' UNION

5 SABBATICALS   **TURNOUT AT LAST BALLOT** 17%
NUS MEMBER
UHSU aren't the most active of student bodies and though they put the effort into welfare, the emphasis is firmly on local issues rather than national political campaigns. Relations with the Uni are positively glowing. 2005 saw the new clean, colourful and modern Union facility enter the world.

SU FACILITIES

Bars and coffee bars; social areas; cafeteria; music/comedy venue; printing service; general shop; photocopying; pool room; games and vending machines; juke box; function rooms.

CLUBS (NON SPORTING)

Cocktail Critics (book group); Friends of Falun Gong; Boardriding; Role Playing; Juggling; Marketing; Medieval Re-enactment; Motorcycle; Real Ale; SLAGS (Spirit & Liquor Awareness & Guidance Society). **See Clubs tables.**

OTHER ORGANISATIONS

Budding hacks at the Huddersfield Student have previously scooped 'Best on a Small Budget' Guardian award. Ultra FM broadcasts for one month a term within five miles of Milton Hall. The SU has a dedicated sabbatical officer to raise money for good causes, and Hands On Volunteering organises good works. RAG raised £12,000 last year.

RELIGIOUS

○ 3 CHAPLAINS (RC, COFE, FC)
The interdenominational chaplaincy and Muslim prayer room are bonuses in a town *well-provided for most faiths.* The chaplaincy also holds a weekly Quaker meeting and Buddhist meditation.

PAID WORK

○ JOB BUREAU ○ PAID WORK TERM-TIME 53%; HOLS 71%
The job shop helps local businesses find student employees. The SU employs 70 students part-time a year and the university takes on 400 students during vacations. *Three supermarkets near campus provide oodles of opportunity for shelf-stacking shenanigans.*

SPORTS ()()()()()()()()()()()()()

○ RECENT SUCCESSES RUGBY LEAGUE **○ BUSA RANKING** 120
The town is better kitted out than the University for sporting satisfaction and success. A Kirklees Passport (£6/year) gives discounted rates at local facilities. The Students' Union has been *attempting to lure more students into the world of jogging and jockstraps. Not in a fetish way.*

SPORTS FACILITIES

15 acres of playing fields two miles from campus; sports hall; athletics field; Astroturf pitch; squash courts; multigym; fitness gym. The town doubles up on all of these and also has a croquet lawn, bowling green, running track, swimming pool, golf courses, tennis courts, saunas and an all-weather pitch. There's a lake, river and hills nearby.

SPORTING CLUBS

Boxing; Caving; Gaelic Football; Jiu Jtisu; Wing Chun. *See Clubs tables.*

ATTRACTIONS

Galpharm Stadium is home to Huddersfield FC and their *more successful* Rugby League counterparts, the Huddersfield Giants (who are sponsored by the University, doncha know). The Uni Rugby Union team also has close links with the local side and many students play for Huddersfield Heat, the nationally-ranked local basketball team.

ACCOMMODATION ()()()()()()()()()()

IN UNIVERSITY

○ SELF-CATERING 21% **○ COST** £70 (32WKS)
○ 1ST YEARS LIVING IN 90%
○ INSURANCE PREMIUM ££££
AVAILABILITY The University has deals with various private halls (run by Digs – see www.campusdigs .com) including the plush Storthes Hall (four miles from campus, with shuttle bus, minimarket, café, DVD library, TV lounge, launderette, gym and bars) and Ashenhurst (less than a mile away but at the top of a *near-vertical* hill; unsuitable for disabled residents). Storthes and Ashenhurst are mainly for first years and international students; *ages are a more mixed bag in the others. Security is good with CCTV cameras aplenty.* Four other halls (Firth Point, The Bridge, Aspley Hall and Snow Island) within 400m of campus are run by other companies – see www.accommodationfor students.com for more info. Applicants with Huddersfield as their first choice are guaranteed accommodation (dependent on deadlines and deposits, *yadi yada yada*).
CAR PARKING Free parking at Ashenhurst.

EXTERNALLY

○ AVE RENT £50 **○ LIVING AT HOME** 20%
AVAILABILITY *There's no shortage of digs and the quality increases further out. Springrove, Newsome are top spots; Bradford Road, Birkby and Lockwood are also good. Sheepridge, Deighton and Fartown (the red light district, allegedly) are a bit rough and probably worth avoiding.*
HOUSING HELP The Uni allocates places in its preferred suppliers halls (the Students' Union is the place for independent advice), and helps liver-outers find a roof to go over their heads.

Words in italics are Push's point of view — take it or leave it...

WELFARE ⓄⓄⓄⓄⓄⓄⓄⓄⓄⓄⓄ

SERVICES
- Ⓞ **MATURE STUDENTS' OFFICER** Ⓞ **LGBT OFFICER**
- Ⓞ **DISABILITIES OFFICER** Ⓞ **INTERNATIONAL STUDENTS' SOCIETY** Ⓞ **POSTGRAD SOCIETY** Ⓞ **LATE−NIGHT MINIBUS**
- Ⓞ **NIGHTLINE** Ⓞ **TAXI FUND** Ⓞ **UNIVERSITY COUNSELLORS** 2 FULL/1 PART
- Ⓞ **SU COUNSELLORS** 1 FULL/1 PART Ⓞ **CRIME RATING** !!

The University Advice centre is *well-run, efficient and helpful*. The chaplaincy *doles out* free tinned food to hard-up students – there goes the harvest festival collection.

HEALTH A *top-notch* on-campus NHS practice has 20 staff including three GPs.

CRECHES/NURSERY 24 places for children aged 6wks-5yrs.

DISABILITIES All buildings on the main campus have wheelchair access, *though hills can be tricky*. Hearing loops, note-takers and specialist help for dyslexics are available. There are adapted rooms in Storthes Hall.

DRUGS The University has a zero tolerance approach to drugs.

FINANCE
- Ⓞ **AVE DEBT PER YEAR** £3,815
- Ⓞ **HOME STUDENT FEES** £3,000

FEES Students at the Barnsley and Oldham centres pay £2,000 rather than £3,000 and there are no fees for anyone on a sandwich year. International students pay £6,870-£7,740. UK postgrads pay £3,316 or £5,530 for an MBA; international postgrads pay £7,895 and £8,630 respectively.
- Ⓞ **ACCESS FUND** £799,000 Ⓞ **SUCCESSFUL APPLICATIONS/YR** 505 Ⓞ **AVE PAYMENT** £1,582

SUPPORT Local student bursaries for West Yorkshire students who are the first in their family to go to university. Some individual course bursaries.

▶ **HUDDERSFIELD POLYTECHNIC**
see *University of Huddersfield*

UNIVERSITY OF HULL

- Ⓞ **UNIVERSITY OF HULL**, Hull, HU6 7RX **TEL** (0870) 126 2000 **E−MAIL** admissions@hull.ac.uk **WEBSITE** www.hull.ac.uk
- Ⓞ **HULL UNIVERSITY UNION**, University House, Cottingham Road, Hull, HU6 7RX **TEL** (01484) 466 000
E−MAIL H=hullstudent@union.hull.ac.uk **WEBSITE** www.hullstudent.com Ⓞ **SCARBOROUGH CAMPUS**, Filey Road, Scarborough, YO11 3AZ **TEL** (01723) 362 397 Ⓞ **HULL UNIVERSITY UNION − SCARBOROUGH CAMPUS**, Filey Road, Scarborough, YO11 3AZ **TEL** (01723) 367 258 **E−MAIL** scarborough@union.hull.ac.uk

GENERAL ⓄⓄⓄⓄⓄⓄⓄⓄⓄⓄⓄⓄ

Hull (full title Kingston upon Hull) has long been the butt of rather unkind jokes, largely because it had a few brushes with the ugly tree on the way to the civil engineer's. In reality, however, the less industrialised bits of this north-eastern city are rather pretty and the nearby coastline is stunning. The campus is large, leafy, low-lying and modern-ish (mostly built within the last 80 years). It's spoiled only by some ugly 60s architecture. It's a couple of miles from the town centre and since 2001 has incorporated University College Scarborough, *though beware – this is 40 miles from the main site.*

SEX RATIO: ♂47 ♀53	**FOUNDED:** 1927
FULL-TIME U'GRADS: 9,769	**PART-TIME:** 7,575
POSTGRADS: 2,387	**NON-DEGREE:** 4.700
AVE COURSE: 3YRS	**ETHNIC:** 13%
STATE:PRIVATE SCHOOL: 93:7	**FLUNK RATE:** 12%
MATURE: 30%	**INTERNATIONAL:** 10%
DISABLED: 380	**LOCAL:** 56%

ATMOSPHERE
Hull is a classic civic campus: integrated with the town, but far enough removed to provide a haven of dirt-cheap beer, student accommodation and even learning. The town, by turn, provides a bustling escape should campus life begin to stifle. It punches above its weight in the nightlife stakes, although cynics might suggest that's no great achievement. Students tend to be no-nonsense, northern types with a good sense of humour (which is handy as they're spending three years in

---

a blustery fish port). Overall, Hull lacks a certain je ne sais quoi. Perhaps it's joie de vivre.

SITES

SCARBOROUGH CAMPUS (1,400 students – Creative Music, Business, Education, Technology, Drama & Dance, Coastal/ Marine Sciences) Scarborough campus is, perhaps not surprisingly, in Scarborough, 40 miles from Hull. The town is seasonally quiet in the winter and has the *bare essentials* – a few shops and pubs, but the nearest *shiny lights* can be found in York. *It has a great reputation for its creative technology subjects* and Scarborough students are *fiercely protective of their own campus*, although it doesn't offer *anything like the souped-up student microcosm* to be found in Hull.

HULL

⊙**POPULATION** 243,400 ⊙**CITY CENTRE** 2 MILES
⊙**LONDON** 165 MILES ⊙**YORK** 34 MILES ⊙**LEEDS** 50 MILES
⊙**HIGH TEMP** 21 ⊙**LOW TEMP** 1 ⊙**RAINFALL** 54

Hull was built on fish and is now driven by large-scale industries, particularly chemical manufacture. *Neither are particularly fancy-dan trades* and the town's boasts of having its own telephone system, suspension bridge and record-sized submarium *are unlikely to set student hearts a-flutter. The glamourless* reputation puts off the tourists and there's been none of the trendification that's hit the likes of Leeds and Manchester, but Hull is *perfectly adequate* for the essentials of daily life. Shops, banks, bookshops, art galleries and so forth are all present *and correct* and, for the town's size, there's a *decent* range of drinking dens. Hull employs a *large* number of students and this eases relations between town and gown, *although Saturday night boozing often stirs things up again*.

TRAVEL

TRAINS Trains travel from Hull to Newcastle (from £17.80 return), London (£27), Birmingham (£35.25) and beyond.
COACHES Clipper and National Express services all over the country including London (£22.50), Birmingham (£17.75) and Newcastle (£16.75).
CAR From the south the M18 connects the M1 with the local Hull motorway, the M62. From the north, take the M1 then M62 which leads into the A63, then look out for the A1079.
AIR/FERRY Humberside Airport, 12 miles south across the Humber is mainly for inland flights, although it has some to Europe. Boats pop over to Amsterdam (from £60).
HITCHING *There's a semi-official hitch pitch on the A63 that all traffic has to pass*.
LOCAL: There are two *fiercely competitive* bus companies running until midnight-ish.
TAXIS *Sharing taxis is often cheaper than catching a bus or train*.
BICYCLES Hull is very flat with straight wide roads and cycle lanes between the residential and functional parts of the University. *Buy a bike lock – theft is rife*.

CAREER PROSPECTS
⊙ **CAREERS SERVICE** ⊙**NO. OF STAFF** 2 FULL/4 PART
⊙**UNEMPLOYED AFTER 6MTHS** N/A

FAMOUS ALUMNI

Lord Dearing (of Dearing Report fame); John Godber, Jonathan Harvey (playwrights); Lord Hattersley; Philip Larkin (poet); Sally Lindsay ('Coronation Street'); John McCarthy (former hostage) & Jill Morrell (his campaigning ex-partner); Roger McGough (poet); Anthony Minghella ('English Patient' director); Sarah Greene, Juliet Morris, Jenni Murray (broadcasters); Tom Paulin (Oxford don and TV arts critic); John Prescott MP (Lab); Michael Stock (S****, Aitken & Waterman); Ben Watt & Tracey Thorn (Everything But The Girl).

FURTHER INFO
⊙ **PROSPECTUSES** UNDERGRAD; POSTGRAD; ALL DEPTS; DVD/CD-ROM ⊙ **OPEN DAYS**

ACADEMIC ⊍⊍⊍⊍⊍⊍⊍⊍⊍⊍⊍⊍⊍

The University has a *good reputation* for the sciences, particularly chemistry and things involving the wider world – American Studies, Geography, Politics and International Studies. Both sites are good for drama and the digital arts. Teaching centres around seminars (compulsory) and lectures (optional, but *useful*) and the workload on most courses is *about average*. The University is doing *its best to embrace the new millennium* and invests in modern learning methods, while the medical school pools resources with York.

ENTRY POINTS: 180-340	AVE POINTS: 253
APPLICATIONS PER PLACE: 4	CLEARING: 10%
NO. OF TERMS: 2	LENGTH OF TERMS: 15 WKS
STAFF TO STUDENT RATIO: 1:15	STUDY ADDICTS: N/A
TEACHING: ✶✶✶✶✶	RESEARCH: ✶✶✶✶
1STS: 7%	2.2s: 35 %
2.1s: 48%	3RDS: 3 %

ADMISSIONS
⊙ **APPLY VIA UCAS**

Local students can apply for University bursaries *but with only 40 to go around it's pretty competitive*.

SUBJECTS

ARTS/HUMANITIES 9.6% **ARTS & SOCIALSCIENCE** 41.8%
BUSINESS/MANAGEMENT 15.2% **COMPUTER SCIENCE** 4.7%
DRAMA & MUSIC 4% **LAW** 6%
(MODERN) LANGUAGES 10% **NURSING** 13.1%
PSYCHOLOGY 5.3% **SCIENCES** 29.8%
UNUSUAL Citizenship & Social Justice; Medical Product Design; War & Security Studies.

LIBRARIES
⊙ **1,000,000 BOOKS** ⊙ **1,600 STUDY PLACES**
A large collection of books *is all well and good,*

but Hull really trumps its rivals in the staring out-of-the-window department. The view from the Brynmor Jones library over the Humber estuary is awesome. This is where Philip Larkin was a librarian (and, supposedly, masturbated in his office). It's pretty up-to-speed in terms of technology and opens till 10pm on weekdays. It also offers a free bus service to the British Library. The Keith Donaldson library at Scarborough has 80,000 books and gets twice-weekly deliveries of other tomes from Hull.

COMPUTERS
○ 1,100 WORKSTATIONS ○ 24-HR ACCESS
Brynmor Jones is well kitted out with 24-hr access, Bluetooth wireless access and computers on every floor. There's network access in all University accommodation too.

OTHER LEARNING FACILITIES
A 21st-century playground with CAD-labs, language labs, music rehearsal rooms and a drama studio.

ENTERTAINMENT ◖◗◖◗◖◗◖◗◖◗

THE CITY
○ PRICE OF A PINT OF BEER £1.80
○ GLASS OF WINE £2 **○ CAN OF RED BULL** £1.50
Hull conforms precisely to the stereotype of a port town: awash with pubs, many with dubious nautical themes, if not genuine 17th-century salty seadogs. There's a good range and most are student-friendly, though sticking to the Union at weekends could prove less painful.

CINEMAS All multi-screen, two offering student discounts.

THEATRES The more highbrow is the New Theatre for posh plays, opera and ballet. Spring Street Theatre is a rep base, the home of the excellent Hull Truck Theatre company and also hosts cabaret nights.

PUBS Watch out for those with stuffed fish on the walls and glass balls in nets and you won't go far wrong. Pushplugs: Gardener's Arms (definitely a student haven); Haworth Arms (sponsors sports teams); Mission. The Bev Road Run, a 12-pub crawl, is a good bet for the hollow-legged. Probably best to avoid the city centre on football match days, especially if Leeds United are your team of choice.

CLUBBING Currently in vogue are Pozition on Thursdays and Waterfront on Mondays. There's little to satisfy the diehard clubber though. Stay away from Heaven and Hell on pain of... well, pain.

MUSIC VENUES A decent indie scene and Hull City FC's shiny new KC stadium hosts the occasional megastar, although that may mean Elton John. Pushplugs: the Piper (up-and-coming/indie) and City Hall (Sugababes, Chris Rea and Hull Philharmonic Orchestra plus 'comedy' from the likes of Roy Chubby Brown and Ben Elton).

EATING OUT Enough delis and cafés around campus to keep the hunger pangs at bay, but nothing worth putting on weight for. Pushplugs: Mensahib (spiceadelic Indian).

THE UNIVERSITY
○ PRICE OF A PINT OF BEER £1.50
○ GLASS OF WINE £1.80
○ CAN OF RED BULL £1.80
Students are spoilt with a large and varied range of bars and even a purpose-built and pretty successful club.

BARS Sanctuary bar is the biggie, with real ale, big screens, outside seating, snackage plus a fistful of quizzes, pool tournaments and, lord help us, karaoke. Scarborough has Calvino's bar, which lays on a couple of annual balls.

THEATRES The chest-pounding, board-treadingly popular student drama scene displays its wares in the on-campus theatre.

FILM The film society regularly shows cult films.

MUSIC VENUES Asylum features mainstream acts like Arctic Monkeys, Franz Ferdinand and Fun Lovin' Criminals.

CLUBBING Asylum is a well-named, tailor-made social hub of a superclub, which can cram in 1,100 sweaty revellers, occasionally to the beats of names as big as DJ Yoda and Trevor Nelson. It's cheap, cheerful and hugely popular.

COMEDY/CABARET Weekly gags at the union from established circuit funnymen, such as Dan Atkinson.

FOOD Campus food ranges from the cultured to the congealing, all at reasonable prices.

OTHER Posh-frocks donned for the end of year mega-bash ball and throughout the year for individual department knees-ups.

SOCIAL ◖◗◖◗◖◗◖◗◖◗◖◗

HULL UNIVERSITY UNION
○ 8 SABBATICALS ○ TURNOUT AT LAST BALLOT 11%
○ NUS MEMBER
Besides the ubiquitous Nestlé boycott and a move towards fair trade, there's a notable absence of firebrand student politics. But the Union does an ok job of maintaining its facilities, and generally keeps University authorities sweet, too.

SU FACILITIES
Union facilities are top drawer. Pride of place goes to Asylum (see above), but facilities include: ATMs (HSBC and Natwest); four bars; canteen; crèche; insurance sales; general store; eight meeting rooms; four minibuses for hire; payphones; photo booth; eight pool tables; snooker room; printing service; new/secondhand bookshop; two snack bars; sports and fitness centre; stationery shop; ticket agency; travel agency; TV lounge; video games; women's room; launderette; hair salon; Humberside police office.

CLUBS (NON SPORTING)
Big band; Conservative Future; Drum & Bass; Real Ale; Student Action for Refugees. **See Clubs tables.**

OTHER ORGANISATIONS
'Hullfire' is the self-financing student paper, run by the students themselves and published monthly. The student radio station 'JAM1575' broadcasts daily on an AM frequency. HUSSO (Hull University Social Services Organisation) is a Union-run charity which does community projects like refugee aid, mental health-care and prison education. RAG tries to raise a not-at-all-bad £25,000 a year. *All very worthwhile and great CV brownie points.*

RELIGIOUS
⊙ 9 CHAPLAINS (COFE, RC, ORTHODOX, METHODIST, BAPTIST, URC, FRIENDS), RABBI
The University is close to a number of Christian churches and a mosque. University facilities are *limited*, but a Muslim prayer room is available.

PAID WORK
⊙ JOB BUREAU ⊙ PAID WORK TERM-TIME 50%; HOLS 80%
The town employs *tons* of students and the Union has a job exchange with facilities for helping students find work: e-mail bulletins; links with local businesses; jobs fairs; NASE membership; vacancy board.

SPORTS ⊙⊙⊙⊙⊙⊙⊙⊙⊙⊙⊙⊙⊙

⊙ RECENT SUCCESSES CLAY SHOOTING, CRICKET, FENCING
⊙ BUSA RANKING 71
Despite a *full roster* of sports facilities – the university is a *premier* coaching centre – Hull students remain *duffers on the pitch*, with 11 teams slipping down to lower BUSA leagues last year. *Keen but unconvincing.*

SPORTS FACILITIES
At the Sports & Fitness Centre: indoor sports; fitness and weight training; two multigyms; sauna and solarium; jacuzzi. At the Sports Centre (close to the Union): gym; two sports halls; badminton and six squash courts; outdoor pitches; posh astroturf pitch; climbing wall. 11 playing fields on the campus and near the Lawns Halls, an athletics and running track, 11 tennis courts and a boathouse at Beresford Avenue. Netball/5-a-side courts. The city also has a swimming pool and an ice rink.

SPORTING CLUBS
American football; Clay pigeon shooting; dodgeball. **See Clubs tables.**

ATTRACTION
Hull City FC have a new ground and have started pulling in *whopping crowds*, given their size. Also two *major* rugby league clubs.

ACCOMMODATION ⊙⊙⊙⊙⊙⊙⊙⊙⊙

IN UNIVERSITY
⊙ CATERED 14% **⊙ COST** £91 (31WKS)
⊙ SELF-CATERING 12% **⊙ COST** £67 (31-50WKS)
⊙ 1ST YRS LIVING IN 56% **⊙ INSURANCE PREMIUM** ££££
AVAILABILITY All first years can live in University accommodation – *the des res is the Lawns*, three miles from campus and the *hub of fresher life*. There's more expensive accommodation at Taylor Court, *better suited to mature students and postgrads*. Single and mixed-sex digs are available and the overall standard is *basic but decent*. Grassy areas and balconies *would be perfect if Hull had a Mediterranean climate*. Halls are kitted out with laundrettes, TV common rooms and network internet access. Accommodation is *secure* and university cleaners keep it *habitable*. There's some provision for disabilities and hearing problems, but apply early. Scarborough has 220 catered rooms and the University manages another 200 private places.
CAR PARKING *Plentiful*. By permit only – free in halls, £75 per year at Taylor Court.

EXTERNALLY
⊙ AVE RENT £45 **⊙ LIVING AT HOME** 10%
AVAILABILITY *Housing is easy to come by and among the cheapest in the country* – £45 per week keeps students *living in comfort*. Beverley Road is the *top* student spot, *although things can get less friendly further out*. The Trees are privately-owned student flats five minutes from campus.
HOUSING HELP Information on private housing is available from the SU's Advice Centre. The University has close links with private landlords. Confusingly, the University and the council each run separate accreditation schemes.

> ⊙ **The registrar and finance directors at Hull University once agreed to live on £10 each for a week to see what life was like for hard-pressed students.**

WELFARE ◖◖◖◖◖◖◖◖◖◖◖◖◖

SERVICES
⊙ LGBT OFFICER & SOCIETY ⊙ WOMEN'S SOCIETY ⊙ MATURE STUDENTS' SOCIETY ⊙ INTERNATIONAL STUDENTS' OFFICER & SOCIETY ⊙ POSTGRAD OFFICER & SOCIETY ⊙ ETHNIC MINORITIES SOCIETY ⊙ LATE–NIGHT/WOMEN'S MINIBUS ⊙ SELF–DEFENCE CLASSES ⊙ NIGHTLINE ⊙ TAXI FUND ⊙ UNIVERSITY COUNSELLORS 5 FULL ⊙ CRIME RATING !!!!!
Welfare support comes with the housing: residential pastoral staff in halls and non-resident staff for houses and flats. Also advice centres for personal and legal problems.
HEALTH *Not brilliant*. No health facilities on campus although local GPs tout for work in Freshers' Week.
WOMEN Attack alarms are available, as are appointments with the equal opportunities officer.

CRECHES/NURSERY ,A crèche has *limited* places for children from 3mths-5yrs.
DISABILITIES T-loops, ramps and note-takers are in place and the area around campus is flat as a pancake. The Union building is well-designed but access in the central ,administration building is *pretty shabby*.
CRIME A part-time police officer plods around campus.

FINANCE
⊙ AVE DEBT PER YEAR £4,113
⊙ HOME STUDENT FEES £3,000
FEES Years abroad or in industry and foundation years cost £1,500. Part-time fees are £550.
⊙ ACCESS FUND N/A ⊙ AVE PAYMENT N/A
SUPPORT Financial assistance is available in the form of hardship funds, emergency funds, bursaries (£1,000), scholarships (£1,500) and a postgrad teaching support scheme.

➤ UNIVERSITY OF HUMBERSIDE
see *University of Lincoln*

IMPERIAL COLLEGE LONDON

I

IMPERIAL COLLEGE LONDON

THE COLLEGE IS PART OF THE UNIVERSITY OF LONDON AND STUDENTS ARE ENTITLED TO USE ITS FACILITIES.

⊙ **IMPERIAL COLLEGE LONDON** South Kensington Campus, London, SW7 2AZ **TEL** (020) 7589 5111 **E-MAIL** info@imperial.ac.uk
WEBSITE www.imperial.ac.uk ⊙ **IMPERIAL COLLEGE UNION** Prince Consort Road, London, SW7 2BB **TEL** (020) 7594 8060
E-MAIL president@imperial.ac.uk **WEBSITE** www.union.imperial.ac.uk

GENERAL ◖◗◖◗◖◗◖◗◖◗◖◗◖◗

J am sandwiched between the Natural History Museum and the Royal Albert Hall in South Kensington, 1.5 miles from Trafalgar Square, is Imperial College. It was formed in 1907, when the Royal School of Mines, City & Guilds College and the Royal College of Science merged. The Medical School *joined the party* in the late 80s and Wye College (which specialised in farming and environmental courses) in 2000. *The main building is what Prince Chas would call a 'carbuncle' – a towering, oversized portakabin of aluminium, smoked glass and concrete.* The two new buildings, the Sir Alexander Fleming and the Tanaka Business School (which will provide a new entrance to the campus), were designed by top architects Foster & Partners. *Inside, it's well ordered – echoing walkways with glass displays and cabinets full of scientific paraphernalia, all adding to the sense of awesome thinkology.* Overshadowing all this is the Queen's Tower, which has now been locked off. *Allegedly, too many frustrated finalists were flinging themselves from the parapet, knowing at least enough physics to realise it was a surefire way of getting out of exams.* Apart from the campus at South Kensington and the various hospital campuses, Imperial has the agricultural research centre at Wye in Kent and a 260-acre site at Silwood Park, near Ascot, mainly for scientific fieldwork. The whole shebang comes under the University of London umbrella, *but the College is currently in the process of striking out, Braveheart-style, as a university in its own right – watch this space.*

SEX RATIO: ♂ 63 ♀ 37	**FOUNDED:** 1907
FULL-TIME U'GRADS: 8,050	**PART-TIME:** 0
POSTGRADS: 4,247	**NON-DEGREE:** N/A
AVE COURSE: 4YRS	**ETHNIC:** 30%
STATE:PRIVATE SCHOOL: 59:41	**FLUNK RATE:** 4%
MATURE: 5%	**INTERNATIONAL:** 38%
DISABLED: 25	**LOCAL:** 24%

ATMOSPHERE

Just because Imperial's students are overwhelmingly male and all studying science, technology or medicine, doesn't mean they're all geeks. There are a few nerds, spods, boffins and dweebs as well. No, that's not really fair, but they do work very hard, on a 9-to-5 basis mostly and academic standards are world-renowned. Outside hours, they know how to chug a pint and there's a substantial sporty set as well. Relations with the immediate locals (posh Kensingtonians) are next to non-existent. With the sex ratio at two-to-one, the main problem for Imperial's (straight) males is, of course, intense sexual frustration.

SITES

Medical students spend most of their first two years at the main South Kensington site, after which they study at one of the other four sites in West London:
ST MARY'S (190 students) Two miles from Imperial, in Paddington, and part of the faculty of Medicine. *If you thought the scientists worked hard, the doctors-to-be do even more.* Despite this, they have time to use the recreation centre on site, as well as the swimming pool and bar.
ROYAL BROMPTON (140 students) What used to be known as the National Heart and Lung Institute is now the Royal Brompton site in Chelsea, a mile from the main site. Apart from academic facilities, *fun-time is restricted to a sarnie shop.*
CHARING CROSS (225 students) Not, despite its name, anywhere near Charing Cross, this site is three miles from the main site, in Hammersmith. There's a bar and a café.
HAMMERSMITH (347 students) Formerly the Royal Postgraduate Medical School, this site is mostly for postgraduates.
SILWOOD PARK 100 postgrad students.
WYE CAMPUS This rural outpost is the base for students taking degrees in Applied Business Management taught by the University of Kent.

LONDON see University of London
The area immediately surrounding the College is a *prim quad with privet hedges in the relative peace* of South Kensington ('South Ken', to his friends). Kensington itself is a well-to-do area with Harrod's just round the corner in Knightsbridge (*although we don't recommend students use it for their weekly shop).* The area's full of expensive boutiques and delicatessens. *Even the kebab joints have French names round here.* It's also an erudite part of London, brimming with museums and libraries and educational institutions. It's way too pricey to live in South Ken itself. Shepherd's Bush or Earl's Court are a likelier bet. However, it's well connected for the West End and ULU only takes 20 mins by tube or slightly longer by bus.

TRAVEL see University of London
TRAINS The nearest mainline BR stations are Paddington and Victoria, each about 1.5 miles away, but on direct bus routes.
BUSES 9, 10, 14, 51, 74 and C1. Night buses: N14 and N97.

Words in italics are Push's point of view — take it or leave it...

CAR Parking at the college is limited to those with disabilities. The congestion charging zone is not far away and it might swallow South Ken in the future.
UNDERGROUND Gloucester Road and South Kensington (both on the District, Circle and Piccadilly Lines).

CAREER PROSPECTS
◉ **CAREERS SERVICE** ◉ **NO. OF STAFF** 6 full/1 part
◉ **UNEMPLOYED AFTER 6 MTHS** 9%
The careers service offers just about everything you could want (*bar a foot massage*): psychometric testing, internship and market trends info, careers events, employer presentations and drop-in sessions, and interview training. Potential employers, particularly in scientific and technical areas, regard Imperial as a *goldmine of bright bods.*

FAMOUS ALUMNI
Mary Archer (*bigwig scientist, no really, she is, even though her husband Lord Jeff says so too*); Sir Roger Bannister (four minute miler); Sir Alexander Fleming (discovered penicillin); Rajiv Gandhi (late Indian Prime Minister); W G Grace (cricketer); David Irving (revisionist 'historian'); David Livingstone (explorer); Brian May (*large-haired Queen guitar hero*); Trevor Phillips (Chair of the Commission for Racial Equality); Joan Ruddock MP (Lab); Simon Singh (author, Fermat's Last Theorem); H G Wells (writer); J P R Williams (rugby player); Francis Wilson (weatherman).

SPECIAL FEATURES
Imperial's mascot is a 185lb micrometer, which avoids the trend among London colleges of stealing each other's mascots.

FURTHER INFO
◉ **PROSPECTUSES** UNDERGRAD; POSTGRAD; SOME DEPARTMENTS
◉ **OPEN DAYS** International students get a special guide once they receive an offer.

ACADEMIC ◗◗◗◗◗◗◗◗◗◗◗◗◗

◉ **RUSSELL GROUP**
Imperial's academic standards are renowned worldwide and over 20% of students get first-class degrees. Although it's famous for its science and technology work, a few arts and language courses are also on offer. Most courses offer a year abroad or in industry. Some graduates end up with unusual letters after their names (such as ARCS, ARSM and ACGI) showing they're now associates of Imperial's constituent colleges. 99% of the teaching staff have PhDs and students can get their hands dirty with real research too through the Undergraduate Research Opportunities Programme (UROP) where they can help out postgrads and staff with their work and maybe get their names on scientific publications

even before graduating (*impressive for sure*). Things don't quieten down too much outside term either. In the summer vacation, some students get a bursary based on the level of those paid to postgrads for helping out (particularly popular with international students who don't need work permits for UROP projects).

ENTRY POINTS: 274-353	AVE POINTS: 341
APPLICATIONS PER PLACE: 6	CLEARING: 1%
STAFF TO STUDENT RATIO: 1:10	STUDY ADDICTS: 31%
TEACHING: ***	RESEARCH: *****
YEAR ABROAD: 6%	SANDWICH STUDENTS: 3%
1STS: 21%	2.2s: 17%
2.1s: 42%	3RDS: 2%

ADMISSIONS
◉ **APPLY VIA UCAS**

SUBJECTS
ENGINEERING 39%   **LIFE SCIENCES** 12%
MEDICAL SCIENCES 26%   **PHYSICAL SCIENCES** 23%
BEST Biology; Business; Management; Computer Science; Civil, Chemical, and Other Engineering; Electronic & Electrical Engineering; Technology; Mathematical Sciences; Other subjects allied to Medicine.
UNUSUAL Biomedical Engineering; Physics with Studies in Musical Performance (joint with the Royal College of Music).

LIBRARIES
◉ **950,000 BOOKS** ◉ **2,400 STUDY PLACES**
There are 17 libraries in all, including the Central Library, the Science Museum Library, six medical libraries and eight departmental libraries. These house 13,000 full text electronic journals as well as nearly a million books. *Not bad, eh?*

COMPUTERS
◉ **2,000 WORKSTATIONS**
There are workstations in every department and 450 general access workstations in the Central Library. The College has a high speed, wireless network so students can access onsite and off-site resources.

OTHER LEARNING FACILITIES
Language lab; drama studio; music rooms; CAD lab; media centre. The Silwood Park powerhouse has an arboretum; greenhouse facilities; wind tunnel; reactor and a rain simulator – for scientific purposes, not just Gene Kelly-inspired dancing outbursts. If so inclined, most students can take a language, humanities or management course.

ENTERTAINMENT ◗◗◗◗◗◗◗◗◗◗

THE CITY see <u>University of London</u>
South Ken has a fair level of entertainments of its own, but it's mainly wine bars and posh clubs, although the Queen's Arms is *popular*. The West End is within an *energetic stroll's distance* and

many of the areas around Kensington *offer some thrills and spills* (Notting Hill, Earl's Court, Hammersmith, Chelsea, Fulham, Putney). Other locals worthy of a Pushplug: Rat & Parrot and Finnegan's Wake.

UNIVERSITY
- **PRICE OF A PINT OF CIDER** £1.40
- **GLASS OF WINE** £1.45
- **CAN OF RED BULL** £1.90

The South Ken campus has the biggest of everything, but there are also ents facilities of some description on all the smaller sites.

BARS The five bars at the main site include Da Vinci's (*still looks like a Butlin's leisure lounge despite having been done up*), Southside (*pipe 'n' slippers pub*), Union Bar (*also pubby, popular with rugby gorillas*) and dBs (*womb-like venue bar*).

THEATRES Imperial has two halls, which are both eminently suitable as theatres for the *strangely strong dramatic contingent*, including medical opera and drama societies (*for medics, not medical operas and dramas*). Not only do they take shows to the Edinburgh Fringe, they rent a whole theatre there and sub-let it to other groups.

FILM Imperial has the largest student cinema screen in the country and shows two mainstream films a week. It's one of the cheapest flick factories in the West End, *though that's not saying much.*

MUSIC VENUES The Great Hall has a capacity of 600 and there's also the Concert Hall (cap 450) and dBs (450).

CLUBBING Several club nights every week: the mainstream Pop Tarts; Common People (indie); Hedonizm (dub); Shaft (70s) and more.

COMEDY/CABARET Once a fortnight, in the Union building, there's a comic on the bill.

FOOD The JCR does a self-service all-day breakfast bar, which gets chocka at lunchtimes. QT in the Sherfield Building sells snacks in the daytime as well as the Main Dining Hall which serves *slightly more substantial* scoff. dBs does baguettes. There are also cafés in several department buildings, including the Sir Alexander Fleming building (*watch out for the penicillin experiments – it's a type of mould, y'know*).

OTHER Two big balls a year, occasionally in *posh* London hotels. Also Christmas and departmental binges and three carnivals a year.

SOCIAL ◖◗◖◗◖◗◖◗◖◗◖◗◖◗

IMPERIAL COLLEGE STUDENTS' UNION
- **7 SABBATICALS** **TURNOUT AT LAST BALLOT** 15%

The Union is politically independent, even of the NUS. It exists to provide services to its members, *who lap them up when they can tear themselves away from work. Urging the students into any*

political activity is harder than learning Gujurati from a Martian. Also ULU: see University of London

SU FACILITIES
The Union has facilities at the main site, St Mary's, Wye and Charing Cross. At South Ken, the Union building, called Beit Quad, is on the other side of the road. In all, the Union offers bars, a cafeteria, sandwich bar, travel agency, resources centre, two shops, minibus hire, photo booth, video and games machines, juke boxes, cinema and fax service. There's a new centre housing advice, welfare, chaplaincy services, a media centre, store and library.

CLUBS (NON SPORTING)
Arabic; Alternative Music; Anime; Bangladeshi; Bridge; Buddhist; Bruneian; Chamber Music; Cheese; Choir; Cypriot; Contemporary Music; Croatian; Disco; Exploration; Fashion; Film Appreciation; Finance; French; German; Hellenic; Hindu; Home Brewing; Indonesian; Indian; Iranian; Italian; International Tamil; International; Japanese; Jazz & Rock; Jazz Big Bad; Juggling; Ju-Jitsu; Karting; Kenyan; Korean; Latin-American; Lebanese; Linux Users; Malaysian; Mauritian; Methodist; Model UN; Musical Theatre; Natural History; Orthodox Christian; Outdoor; Pakistan; Palestinian Society; Poker; Polish; Political Philosophy; Postgraduate; Portuguese; Radio; Robot Wars; Scandinavian; Singapore; Singaporean Medical; Spanish; Sri Lankan; St. John Ambulance; String Ensemble; Sufi; Taiwan; Transportation; Turkish; UNICEF; War Games; Welsh; West Indian; Wine Tasting. **See also Clubs tables.**

OTHER ORGANISATIONS
Felix is the Union's weekly newspaper and there's also a radio station (Imperial College Radio) and a TV station (STOIC – Student Television of Imperial College). Imperial College's Rag *is very energetic, although as much energy goes into oh-so-wacky stunts as into actual fund-raising.* There's the annual tiddlywink race down Oxford Street and *legends abound of the naked parachute leap which ended in nude students being bundled out of a van at Harrod's. Felix claims to have photos.* The Science Fiction Society has more than 7,500 books and is thought to be the biggest student-run library in Europe. *Wowsers.*

RELIGIOUS
- **2 FULL-TIME CHAPLAINS (COFE, RC);**
- **2 PART-TIME (COFE)**

The College has links with Methodist, Free Church and Lutheran chaplains. There's an Islamic Prayer room and the Regent's Park Mosque (one of the country's largest) is nearby. The Chaplaincy Centre can point other believers in the right direction and has a prayer room for use by individual Christians and Buddhists. Religion in London: see University of London.

PAID WORK see University of London
Imperial students can appeal to the firms constantly vying for their talents for vacation work or there's Imperial's UROP scheme (see above) where they help lecturers with their research work and can expect to earn cash and many brownie points. The Careers Service advertises any part-time job opportunities that come its way.

SPORTS

● BUSA RANKING 47
Bearing in mind that Imperial students are entitled to use ULU and the University's facilities as well as their own *excellent* amenities, they've got the world at their feet like a football. Imperial is top of the London colleges in the student sports league.

SPORTS FACILITIES
Imperial has 60 acres of playing fields at Harlington (15 miles from Kensington), and 12.5 acres at Teddington with four tennis courts. The College lays on buses two days a week to get to Harlington so that students can use the pavilion and pitches (including an all-weather pitch). Meanwhile, over the road at the South Ken ranch, there's a swimming pool; spa; gym; sauna; aerobics studio; squash courts; sports hall and climbing wall. St Mary's campus has a swimming pool; sports hall; gym; basketball & volleyball courts; badminton courts; martial arts & aerobics studio. A boathouse in Putney satisfies the dedicated rowing contingent and there's a mountain hut in Snowdonia *for hardy types*.

SPORTING CLUBS
Aikido; Aerobics; American Football; Bowling; Boxing; Billiards & Snooker; Caving; Croquet; Curling; Fitness; Gymnastics; Ice Hockey; Kickboxing; Kung Fu; Kendo; Lacrosse; Lifesaving; Mountaineering; Parachuting; Polo; Rifle; Softball; Table Football; Table Tennis; Ultimate Frisbee; Windsurfing; Water polo; Waterski; Wrestling; Yachting; Yoga. **See also Clubs tables.**

ATTRACTIONS see University of London

ACCOMMODATION

IN COLLEGE
● CATERED 5% **● COST** £102 (38WKS)
● SELF-CATERING 34% **● COST** £94 (34/38/51WKS)
● 1ST YRS LIVING IN 94%
● INSURANCE PREMIUM £
AVAILABILITY Imperial accommodates all its first years either in their own halls or intercollegiate halls, but College housing is limited for other

students. There are 11 halls in all and four *so-called* student houses. A *whopping* 50% of students in College accommodation have to share rooms, sometimes even in triple rooms, but they are charged less. The halls are mostly around South Ken, but also spread throughout west London, the furthest being a 40-minute *tube grind away*. There's some cheaper, mainly catered, accommodation on the Wye campus and space for 125 postgrads in five halls at Silwood Park. All the London's accommodation's get-your-own-grub apart from Linstead Hall which provides a *piddly* one meal a weekday. Swipe card entry and security guards in all halls and there's a choice of smoking or non-smoking. There are 60 flats available to couples, 16 of which are suitable for families. Women have to apply to the University for intercollegiate rooms if they want all-female housing.
CAR PARKING *Very tricky* in South Kensington (permit required); easier at Wye and Silwood Park.

EXTERNALLY
● AVE RENT £125
AVAILABILITY Hammersmith is the closest location *for those who haven't struck lucky on the scratch cards*.
HOUSING HELP The Union has a housing advice scheme and the University Private Housing Office provides housing lists, legal advice and a bulletin board.

WELFARE

SERVICES
● LGBT SOCIETY ● MATURE STUDENTS' OFFICER & SOCIETY
● INTERNATIONAL STUDENTS' OFFICER & SOCIETY
● POSTGRAD OFFICER & SOCIETY
● DISABILITIES OFFICER ● SELF-DEFENCE CLASSES
● NIGHTLINE ● TAXI FUND
● COLLEGE COUNSELLORS 1 FULL/3 PART
● CRIME RATING !!!
HEALTH The Health Centre is home to five doctors, two nurses, NHS dentists, psychotherapists, physiotherapists and one full-time and three part-time counsellors. There's also a visiting psychiatrist, weekly sports medicine physician and private alternative therapists.
WOMEN With less than one woman to every two men, *the most severe problem is solitude*, although the increasing number of medical students is levelling the figures out.
CRECHES/NURSERY Space for 54 tots aged 6mths-5yrs at South Ken and 15 more at Hammersmith, but there's a 1-2yr waiting list for babies.
DISABILITIES The South Kensington campus is fairly compact, *but access could still be improved in places*. To this end, the College is refurbishing older buildings and newer ones have *good* facilities. There's specially designed accommodation for wheelchair users and

hearing- and sight-impaired students. The College employs a Disabilities Officer, and anyone thinking of studying is encouraged to get in touch. There are hearing loops in some lecture theatres and lifts around the main building.

FINANCE

○ **AVE DEBT PER YEAR** £4,542 ○ **HOME STUDENT FEES** £3,000 **FEES** International undergrads have to cough up five figures – £12,700 for life sciences to £17,500 for Engineering. Standard postgrad fees are £3,168 for UK students and £14,650 for international students, but some courses charge *premium flog-your-granny rates*.

○ **ACCESS FUND** £365,737 ○ **SUCCESSFUL APPLICATIONS**/**YR** 325 ○ **AVERAGE PAYMENT** £1,060 **SUPPORT** Many, many scholarships and sponsorships are available. As for tuition fees, help will be particularly good for those studying science, engineering and medicine. Those on the full maintenance grant who meet the UCAS deadline for accepting an offer AND get top grades in at least three A-levels are up for an *astonishing* four grand's worth of bursary booty.

 **Imperial College, London has its own nuclear reactor.**

KCL
see *King's College London*

KEELE UNIVERSITY

KENNEDY INSTITUTE OF RHEUMATOLOGY
see *Imperial College, London*

UNIVERSITY OF KENT

KENT INSTITUTE OF ART & DESIGN
see *Creative Arts University College*

KING'S COLLEGE LONDON

KINGSTON UNIVERSITY

KINGSTON POLYTECHNIC
see *Kingston University*

KCL
see *King's College London*

K

KEELE UNIVERSITY

○ **KEELE UNIVERSITY** Keele, Staffordshire, ST5 5BG **TEL** (01782) 621 111 **E-MAIL** undergraduate@keele.ac.uk
WEBSITE www.keele.ac.uk ○ **KEELE UNIVERSITY STUDENTS' UNION (KUSU)**, Keele, Staffs, ST5 5BJ **TEL** (01782) 583 700
E-MAIL sta15@kusu.keele.ac.uk **WEBSITE** www.kusu.net

GENERAL ()()()()()()()()()()()()()

Keele University is situated near the 'Potteries' towns of Stoke-on-Trent and Newcastle under Lyme in the north Midlands, *but at the same time manages to feel a million miles from anywhere. It's an army camp-like arrangement of geometric blocks in a square mile of parkland, mostly modern but including the bootylicious Keele Hall, the oldest building (19th-century) on the estate* which these days hosts conferences rather than students. Keele gained a bit of a rep in the post-war higher education expansion for its flexibility of study, *which many institutions have since stolen – sorry, emulated –* and its communal atmosphere.

SEX RATIO: ♂40 ♀60	**FOUNDED:** 1962
FULL-TIME U'GRADS: 5,500	**PART-TIME:** 12
POSTGRADS: 3,000	**NON-DEGREE:** 2,500
AVE COURSE: 3YRS	**ETHNIC:** 11%
STATE:PRIVATE SCHOOL: 83:9	**FLUNK RATE:** 10%
MATURE: 15%	**INTERNATIONAL:** 8%
DISABLED: 70%	**LOCAL:** 26%

ATMOSPHERE
Keele is a small, busy but friendly university, with 70% of students and many of the staff and their families living on campus. Newcastle under Lyme and Stoke offer some respite if the atmosphere starts to cloy, but even they don't have much to offer the discerning thrill-seeker. Whether the familiar community feel is relished or resented is a matter of taste, but the bustling campus could never be called 'humdrum', and Push won't even try.

KEELE for Stoke, see <u>Staffordshire University</u>

○ **POPULATION** 122,000 ○ **CITY CENTRE** 3.5 MILES
○ **LONDON** 147 MILES ○ **MANCHESTER** 34 MILES
○ **BIRMINGHAM** 43 MILES
○ **HIGH TEMP** 20 ○ **LOW TEMP** 0 ○ **RAINFALL** 56
Keele, with as few pubs as its name has syllables, only just makes it to village status. The surrounding area was built on the 19th-century pottery industry, hence the name The Potteries. Wedgwood, Spode and Royal Doulton pottery all came from round here. *Habitat and Tupperware didn't.* Local facilities in the old market town of Newcastle are *a tad limited, however, there's more than enough to get by* – all the major banks and a *fair few* shops. For more commercial trappings, Hanley (one of the six towns that make up the city of Stoke-on-Trent) *is better equipped and The Potteries Shopping Centre could just about support a spending spree.* Local attractions include all the various Pottery Museums, the once industrial, but now leisure canals, Festival Park (shops, cinema, dry ski slope), the Stoke City Museum & Art Gallery and Alton Towers, *the theme park-cum-vomit factory,* half an hour down the road.

TRAVEL
TRAINS The nearest train station is five miles away at Stoke – London (from £31 return), Manchester (£7.80).
COACHES London to Stoke by National Express takes five hours (£21).
CAR From the south, leave the M6 at Junction 15 and follow the signs for Newcastle under Lyme. From the north, leave the M6 at Junction 16 and take the A500 for Crewe and Nantwich. Finding the University is infinitely easier than finding a parking space on campus.
LOCAL From Stoke-on-Trent station the No. 29 bus heads for campus every 15 mins.
COLLEGE Safety bus runs between campus, halls and the area.
TAXIS An essential after clubbing. Costs £5-6 to campus from Newcastle and nearly double that from Stoke (Hanley).
BICYCLES *Handy on campus but everything else is too far away and too darn hilly.*

CAREER PROSPECTS
○ **CAREERS SERVICE** ○ **NO. OF STAFF** 3 FULL/2 PART
○ **UNEMPLOYED AFTER 6MTHS** 4%
The careers service website has vacancies and news plus the Windmills Programme, a virtual career coach.

FAMOUS ALUMNI
Don Foster MP (LibDem); Michael Mansfield QC (Barrister); Lord Melchett (of Greenpeace, not Blackadder); Alun Michael MP (Trade & Industry minister); Nick Partridge (AIDS campaigner); Clare Short MP (Lab); Phil Soar (author); Jack Straw MP (Foreign Secretary); Adelaide Tambo (MP, African National Congress).

FURTHER INFO
○ **PROSPECTUSES** UNDERGRAD; POSTGRAD; DEPARTMENTS; CD-ROM FOR INTERNATIONAL STUDENTS
○ **OPEN DAYS**

ACADEMIC ()()()()()()()()()()()()()

Flexibility's the name of the game – 90% of students do joint honours degrees, so arts students find themselves dabbling in science and vice versa. The upside is students get an insight into matters they might have otherwise ignored, but some might find

Words in italics are Push's point of view — take it or leave it...

it a travesty of the natural order. Timetabling is, therefore, a work of art, although students have griped about schedules in the School of Politics, International Relations & Philosophy (SPIRE) apparently because learner numbers have swelled without a corresponding increase in staff. Keele has stuck the European Quality Label for Mobility on its correspondence, owing to the fact that almost every student has the chance to spend a semester at a sister institution in America, Australia, South Africa or Europe. Non-language students have the chance to gain a lingo certificate, too. The Keele University School of Medicine recently opened at the City General Hospital. Would-be doctors and won't-be patients rejoiced.

ENTRY POINTS: 160–340	**AVE POINTS: 240**
APPLICATIONS PER PLACE: 7	**CLEARING: 6%**
NO. OF TERMS: 2	**LENGTH OF TERMS: 15WKS**
STAFF TO STUDENT RATIO: 1:11	**STUDY ADDICTS: 13%**
TEACHING: ★★★	**RESEARCH: ★★★**
YEAR ABROAD: 3%	**SANDWICH STUDENTS: <1%**
1STS: 9%	**2.2S: 40%**
2.1S: 47%	**3RDS: 2%**

ADMISSIONS
○ APPLY VIA UCAS/NMAS FOR NURSING

SUBJECTS
HEALTH 11% **HUMANITIES** 20%
NATURAL SCIENCES 22% **SOCIAL SCIENCES** 47%
BEST Biology; Biochemistry; Business; Human Resource Management; Music; History; Philosophy; American Studies; English Studies; Modern Languages; Law; Mathematics & Statistics; Medicine; Physical Geography & Environmental Science; Geology; Pharmacy; Physics & Astronomy; Economics; Politics; Social Work; Sociology; Social Policy.

LIBRARIES
○ **598,700** BOOKS ○ **607** STUDY PLACES
○ SPEND PER STUDENT ££££
A big push on the electronic journal front has made essay research maybe not a breeze, but at least a light gust. 24-hr access would be nice, but in a place this size, it ain't likely.

COMPUTERS
○ **445** WORKSTATIONS ○ SPEND PER STUDENT £
Most systems now have Windows XP *and all the trimmings. Wi-fi is on the way.* All bedrooms on campus have fast network access.

OTHER LEARNING FACILITIES
Language lab, music rehearsal rooms.

ENTERTAINMENT ○○○○○○○○○

NEWCASTLE UNDER LYME/HANLEY
for Stoke, see <u>Staffordshire University</u>
○ PRICE OF A PINT OF BEER £2.10
○ GLASS OF WINE £1.75
○ CAN OF RED BULL £2
CINEMAS Eight-screen Vue in Newcastle under Lyme and ten-screen Odeon in nearby Festival Park.
THEATRES The New Vic in Newcastle and the Regent in Hanley both offer NUS discounts.
PUBS *Students don't bother with Keele's sole offering, the Sneyd Arms (good for food but expensive), but thankfully there's no shortage of pubs in Newcastle under Lyme.* Even the old town hall has been converted into one. *Wetherspoons is popular (because it's cheap).* The Old Brown Jug does *great* cider and live music.
CLUBBING Flares, Walkabout and Chicago Rock *do their same old, same old chain thing.* The Void, Creation and Fluid in Hanley all offer student nights. In Newcastle there's the Sutherland Arms for rockers and Longton's for all kinds of dancefloor tunes.
MUSIC VENUES Two rock pubs in Newcastle, Full Moon and the Black Friar, support live bands.
EATING OUT George Street in Newcastle *has something for everyone in possession of a mouth, teeth and digestive tract* with four kebab houses, a French restaurant, an Italian, three Chinese, a couple of Indians, a Thai, a chippy. Pushplugs: *Art of Siam (Thai)* in Hanley; *Pablo Frankies (Mexican/Latin/tapas).*

UNIVERSITY
○ PRICE OF A PINT OF BEER £1.60
○ GLASS OF WINE £1.90
○ CAN OF RED BULL £1.60
When it was built, the Students' Union was the largest purpose-built entertainment venue in Staffordshire, *which may not be as impressive as it sounds when you think about what the rest of Staffordshire is like, but it's still something to say to those who think of Keele as a sleepy backwater.*
BARS Nine different bars, from the *sofatastic* Lounge Bar and the *poky* BJs to the *Cheers*-style decor of the University-owned Union Square. Hall bars *of note* include the Lindsey Bar and Hawthorns.
THEATRES Most summers there's outdoor Shakespeare from the Drama Society in the Clockhouse Courtyard, indoors boards are trodden *exuberantly* throughout the year.
FILM Free films are shown every fortnight in the Union (usually alternative).
MUSIC VENUES *Not bad for the back of beyond –* acts from Rachel Stevens and the Coral to Funeral for a Friend and the Subways hit the *extremely impressive* 1,100-capacity Ballroom, which has a *nifty* sprung dancefloor and a bottle bar. K2 has *smaller, but no less perfectly formed* gigs now and then.

K

Words in italics are Push's point of view – take it or leave it...

CLUBBING The usual DJ suspects Trevor Nelson and Dave Pearce have taken a spin on the decks at The Ballroom. Four regular nights a week pick from the pop/cheese/retro/alternative/dance record boxes. Punk, metal and thrash get their occasional days in the dark as well. K2 does its share of club-hosting for the *smaller* nights.
COMEDY/CABARET Paramount Comedy Club acts every fortnight. Alan Carr appeared recently.
FOOD Harvey's Sandwich bar is *good for the healthy option, swiftly nullified by* a trip to the Diner for a fry-up, or Wednesday's kebab and curry night *(surely that should be kebab OR curry night?)*. The University offers Comus Restaurant for *fancy fare*, Le Café, Vite & Eat, the Italian Job for *dining in style*, Union Square for *bargainous* pizzas, burgers etc. and Hawthorn's Restaurant for Sunday roasts.
OTHER Six balls a year, including Grad, Christmas and Athletics. Six months after the Freshers Fair, the Refreshers Fair *doesn't distribute fizzy sweets* but rather reminds students of clubs and societies they might have missed.

SOCIAL ◖◗◖◗◖◗◖◗◖◗◖◗◖◗◖◗◖◗◖◗◖◗◖◗

KEELE UNIVERSITY STUDENTS' UNION (KUSU)
◉ **4 SABBATICALS** ◉ **TURNOUTAT LAST BALLOT** 26%
◉ **NUS MEMBER**
This is almost an old-fashioned banner-waving, barricade-building political Union, but not quite. Politically, it's full of wide-eyed interest and growing out of a non-party political past to become increasingly factionalised. A UKIP society formed recently, *much to the disgruntlement of some international students. Welfare is the SU's forte* – it recently joined forces with the University to lobby the bus company for more services to campus.

SU FACILITIES
The Union Building in the middle of campus has: eight bars; three cafés; two snack bars; fast food outlet; ten pool/snooker tables; meeting rooms; four minibuses; Endsleigh Insurance office; Natwest Bank; two cashpoints (Lloyds TSB, Co-op); photocopier; fax & printing service; photo booth; payphone; advice centre; TV lounge; and a secondhand book exchange.

CLUBS (NON SPORTING)
Cheese & Port; Chinese Students & Scholars Association; Christian Drama; Circus; Computer; Concert Band; Dance Music Kollective; Dancesport; Desi; East Asian Community; Eco Group; Harry Potter; International Student; Keele Airsoft (paintballing); Keele Ale & Cider; Keele Association of Guides & Scouts; Sri-Lankan; Links (St John Ambulance); Multicultural Urban (street dance); Musicians; Nightline; Philosopher's Guild; Revelation Rock Gospel Choir; STAR (Student Action For Refugees) Taekwon-do; Tai-Chi; UKIP. **See also Clubs tables.**

OTHER ORGANISATIONS
Free Union newspaper 'Concourse' comes out fortnightly. *Super-keen* 'KUBE FM' radio station broadcasts on the net and across campus during term. A voluntary group, Active, *lives up to its name.*

RELIGIOUS
◉ **4 CHAPLAINS (RC, CATHOLIC LAY, COFE, FC)**
The big inter-denominational Christian chapel is a *bizarre* grey, brick structure, rectangular with two cylindrical turrets at one end. Muslim prayer room provided on campus. In Newcastle and Stoke, apart from various churches, there are places of worship for Muslims, Sikhs and Buddhists.

PAID WORK
◉ **JOB BUREAU**
The SU pretty much has a monopoly on employment; *everything else is too far away.* Luckily, it employs about 300 students.

SPORTS ◖◗◖◗◖◗◖◗◖◗◖◗◖◗◖◗◖◗◖◗◖◗◖◗

◉ **RECENT SUCCESSES** MEN'S RUGBY LEAGUE AND UNION, TENNIS ◉ **BUSA RANKING** 109
A fairly good level of facilities and involvement, both competitive and recreational. £46 a semester lets students go wild on the gym facilities.

SPORTS FACILITIES
Close to the principal parts of the University (halls of residence, the SU and the main teaching areas), the sports facilities spread over 50 acres including eight football pitches, a hockey pitch, two cricket pitches, three rugby pitches, all-weather pitch, six squash courts, two basketball courts, three sports halls, 12 tennis courts, four netball courts, running track, gym, climbing wall, running track, aerobics studio, sunbeds and five-a-side football in the Leisure Centre.

SPORTING CLUBS
Ju-Jitsu; Korfball; Lacrosse; Mountain Biking; Roller Hockey; Table Tennis; Ultimate Frisbee. See also Clubs tables.

ATTRACTIONS
Locally, there's Stoke City and Port Vale Football Clubs, Uttoxeter Race Course, the Potteries Marathon and, most years, the Lombard Rally. Keele also hosts the National Karate Championships.

Words in italics are Push's point of view — take it or leave it...

ACCOMMODATION ◡◡◡◡◡◡◡◡◡

IN UNIVERSITY
- **SELF-CATERING** 58% ○ **COST** £69 (33/37/42/52WKS)
- **1ST YRS LIVING IN** 85%
- **2ND YRS LIVING IN** 30%
- **FINALISTS LIVING IN** 95%
- **POSTGRADS LIVING IN** 30%
- **INSURANCE PREMIUM** £

AVAILABILITY Living in is the norm. *It's one of the big pluses about Keele as far as Keele is concerned.* First years actually have to apply to live out rather than to live in. As a result, almost all are housed in the University's five halls on campus. *Conditions vary depending on how much you pay – in some halls shared kitchens are fought over by 30 people.* All halls are self-catering (some have pay-as-you-eat refectories and snack bars), vary in size from 400 to 800 places and some offer single-sex blocks. Two halls are blocks of flats for four students sharing a kitchen and bathroom, although these are mainly for finalists. Some space is available on campus for mature students and single parents. All the halls have bars and Lindsey is popular. Hawthorns is the furthest away (about 15 mins walk).

CAR PARKING Not enough to go around. Permits, which keep clampers at bay rather than guaranteeing a space, cost *a painful* £50.

EXTERNALLY
- **AVE RENT** £50 ○ **LIVING AT HOME** 5%

AVAILABILITY *It's pretty easy to find cheap rooms a bus ride away from campus, but there's nothing close. Newcastle or Silverdale are the preferred options, being on a handy bus route, although Hanley and parts of Stoke are also on the house-hunter's checklist. A privately-run hall is also popular. Knutton and Cobridge are a bit rough and Parkside is getting worse. If living out, a car wouldn't go unused.*

HOUSING HELP The University's Accommodation Office has three full-time officers, a vacancies newsletter and a housing approval scheme.

WELFARE ◡◡◡◡◡◡◡◡◡◡◡

SERVICES
- **LGBT OFFICER & SOCIETY** ○ **ETHNIC MINORITIES OFFICER** ○ **WOMEN'S OFFICER** ○ **MATURE STUDENTS' OFFICER** ○ **INTERNATIONAL STUDENTS' OFFICER**
- **POSTGRAD OFFICER** ○ **DISABILITIES OFFICER**
- **LATE-NIGHT/WOMEN'S MINIBUS** ○ **NIGHTLINE**
- **UNIVERSITY COUNSELLORS** 2 FULL/2 PART
- **SU COUNSELLORS** 5 FULL/1 PART ○ **CRIME RATING** !!

The University's Counselling Service, assisted by the chaplains, *keeps emotions on an even keel (geddit?).* The Union runs an independent Advice Unit which offers a free and confidential listening service, financial and legal advice, help for international students, drugs info and support for lesbian and gay students. Freshers are assigned a resident tutor.

HEALTH The Keele General Practice is based on campus and employs a male and a female doctor, two nurses and a dentist. As well as normal health care, it offers a psychiatry clinic.

CRÈCHES/NURSERY 124 places for 12wks-5yrs. Links with local schools provide three after-school clubs for 5-11-yr-olds.

DISABILITIES *The sprawling campus is difficult to get around by wheelchair* but support for deaf, blind and dyslexic students is *commendable.*

CRIME *Students used to think Keele was an old-skool village and leave their doors unlocked. Students got burgled, big-style. CCTV on campus and smarter students mean things are now okay.*

FINANCE
- **AVE DEBT PER YEAR** £2,335
- **HOME STUDENT FEES** £3,000

FEES Postgrads pay £3,400-£9,950 and international students are charged £7,500-£9,900.
- **ACCESS FUND** £296,850 ○ **SUCCESSFUL APPLICATIONS/YR** 450 ○ **AVERAGE PAYMENT** £100-£3,500

SUPPORT Hardship loans and opportunity bursaries (for students from low-income families) and mature student bursaries are available, as well as other help for students with children. The SU and chaplaincy have further arrangements for small emergency loans and grants.

➡️ **KENNEDY INSTITUTE OF RHEUMATOLOGY**
see *Imperial College, London*

K

Keele University once charged a student £45 for damage to a soap dish.

UNIVERSITY OF KENT

● **UNIVERSITY OF KENT** The Registry, Canterbury, Kent, CT2 7NZ **TEL** (01227) 764 000 **E-MAIL** recruitment@kent.ac.uk **WEBSITE** www.kent.ac.uk ● **UNIVERSITY OF KENT STUDENTS' UNION** Mandela Building, University of Kent, Canterbury, Kent, CT2 7NW **TEL** (01227) 824 200 **E-MAIL** union-president@kent.ac.uk **WEBSITE** www.kentunion.co.uk

GENERAL ○○○○○○○○○○○○○

The county of Kent *may be the Garden of England or its compost heap depending on how you look at it* – or how you react to the smell of the hops that it grows and brews. Canterbury, despite its idyllic old England countryside setting and wealth of medieval stonework, *is more than a slice of ye olde heritage industrie – it's a modern city with a six-century history.* The University it's home to doesn't share its ornate architecture, being largely 60s redbrick, *but with nothing like as much concrete as could be expected.* The 300 acres of campus land are 1.5 miles from the city centre and are set in *a lovely patch of green space and landscaped garden. The University overlooks the city and cathedral, making the view beautiful but the air blustery.* It's split into four distinct colleges and also lays claim to the University of Kent at Medway in Chatham.

SEX RATIO: ♀49 ♂51	**FOUNDED:** 1965
FULL-TIME U'GRADS: 9,442	**PART-TIME:** 2,970
POSTGRADS: 1,504	**NON-DEGREE:** 364
AVE COURSE: 3YRS	**ETHNIC:** 13%
STATE:PRIVATE SCHOOL: 88:12	**FLUNK RATE:** 12%
MATURE: 18%	**INTERNATIONAL:** 10%
DISABLED: 185	**LOCAL:** 51%

ATMOSPHERE

Kent's collegiate system is a double-edged sword. On the one blade, it's created a real sense of loyalty and competition within the colleges. On the other, cliques form and there's little reason to mix between colleges that well, especially as each has its own mini Union and ents, and there's no real unifying community across sites. There's little difference in life at the colleges (about 1,500 undergrads in each) and students rarely express a preference when applying (nor is it necessarily a good idea to do so). Since a fair few students are from the Home Counties, weekends bring a small but noticeable exodus from campus. *Those that stay pile into the Venue and have fun behind their backs. Canterbury and campus have meshed well over the years. Local businesses appreciate the cash students bring in, and the only real complaints levelled at them revolve around noise.*

SITES

THE UNIVERSITY OF KENT AT MEDWAY (1,500 students – IT, Sports Science, Health & Social Sciences, Law, Creative Events, Music Technology, Tourism Management, Pharmacy) Together with the University of Greenwich and Canterbury Christ Church University, Kent has moved some of its departments and students 30 miles away to Medway. *The SU on site is working harder to get more on-campus solidarity in place but the whole experiment has yet to hit its stride.* In particular, there's no on-campus housing, though there is University-managed housing locally. *Rents are cheap in the surrounding town – but travel costs balance this out* (no intersite services laid on by the University). Chatham, a *compact dockland community, is industrial, residential and not exactly beautiful.* New shopping and entertainment centres will be *welcome* additions once they're completed. The Dickens connections (Charlie boy lived here as a child) keeps tourists occupied. Once that's out of the way students head to Rochester *for kicks.*

CANTERBURY

● **POPULATION** 135,278 ● **CITY CENTRE** 1 MILE
● **LONDON** 60 MILES ● **DOVER** 30 MILES
● **RAMSGATE** 30 MILES
● **HIGH TEMP** 22 ● **LOW TEMP** 1 ● **RAINFALL** 63
Canterbury has most of the amenities of a large city with the added treasures that come with being a small town in a beautiful place. Most people head straight for the grand and imposing cathedral – effectively the centre of the Anglican universe. The medieval city walls are still standing firm and historical buildings litter the city. Old lanes intertwine with newer streets, making *simply wandering around a leisure activity in itself. More modern developments and giant chain stores are encroaching from the outskirts, and it does have a slightly shoddy underbelly, but who'd hold that against a place that has managed to stay so pretty for so long? It's not most people's idea of a student town, let alone a party animal's paradise, but there's fun to be had – just not the crazy, pulsing 24-hour kind.*

TRAVEL

TRAINS Canterbury East is the station for London Victoria (from £13.75 rtn), and connections to Edinburgh (£73.35), Birmingham (£35.20) and Bristol (£38.30). Canterbury East is closer, for Charing Cross and Waterloo East. International travel is typically faster than getting around Blighty. Paris is 2hrs 20mins away (Canterbury West, change at Ashford for Eurostar) whereas it takes around that just to get to Heathrow, Stansted, Luton or Gatwick airports (change in central London).
COACHES Canterbury Bus Station in the town centre has National Express services running all over the country, including London Victoria (£13.80).
CAR The A2 and M2 connect London with Canterbury while the A28 runs to the south

K

coast. *The M20 can be handy.* Although the centre of town is pedestrianised, there are plenty of car parks around the University, and a few around town. The student car park costs £2 a day for those who don't have a £20 permit – available to students who live over a mile away.

HITCHING *Enough busy roads to make it seem a possibility – especially the A2 and the A28 – but Kentish drivers are surprisingly keen on travelling alone.*

LOCAL Useful Stagecoach buses 4a and 4u run through the campus every 15 mins during the day (every 30 mins evenings and weekends) until around midnight. Students can splash out on an annual bus pass (£170-290) or supersaver ticket if they're keen on public transport.

UNIVERSITY A Unibus trundles to and from the town centre in term seven days a week (though sporadically on Sundays). Two free late-night services leave Rutherford car park nightly. The 11.30 does Blean, Whitstable and Herne Bay; the 11.40 does Canterbury, Wincheap and Sturry (plus request stops). Women get priority.

TAXIS Two ranks on campus. Cabs are private hire only and can cost anything from £4-7 from campus to town, depending on time of day.

BICYCLES *Common sights around University even though campus is on a big hill.* There are loads of cycle lanes in the city and around the campus, along with parking racks.

MEDWAY London Victoria's a 55-min choo-choo from Chatham and there are direct services from Ramsgate and Dover Priory (for ferry services). The M2 & M20 are *useful for drivers*, along with a host of A roads. Parking's free in the Historic Dockyard. Buses tootle between the railway station and Dock Road (for campus) every ten mins at peak times: the 100, 101, 140, 141, 151 and the 196 all make the journey

CAREER PROSPECTS
⊙ CAREERS SERVICE ⊙ UNEMPLOYED AFTER 6 MTHS 3%
The Careers Advisory Service caters for Kent students as well as a variety of smaller local colleges. It offers a full library, application advice and Carousel, a skills analysis programme. Medway campus also has an advisory service.

FAMOUS ALUMNI
Paul Ackford (rugby player and journalist); Alan Davies (frizzy-haired comedian); Gavin Esler (journalist); Anna Hill (broadcaster); Kazuo Ishiguro (writer); Wayne Otto (karate champ); Paul Ross (TV presenter); David Walsh (historian); Charles Wigoder (mobile phone entrepreneur); Tom Wilkinson (actor).

FURTHER INFO
⊙ PROSPECTUSES UNDERGRAD; POSTGRAD; INTERNATIONAL; ALTERNATIVE
⊙ OPEN DAYS
Prospectuses can be ordered online or from (01227) 827 272. Open days are held twice a year though visitors are welcome any time – contact the Admission & Recruitment Office for more information.

ACADEMIC ⊙⊙⊙⊙⊙⊙⊙⊙⊙⊙⊙⊙⊙

Three faculties comprising 28 departments with courses in humanities, science, technology and medical studies, social sciences and other bits 'n' bobs. Drama's particularly rated. There's also a law clinic that handles real cases and enables law students to gain some practical experience of casework. Humanities and social sciences courses often incorporate learning a foreign language and the opportunity for a year abroad. Eight modules are studied per course; those in Sciences and Computer Studies are continuously assessed, rather than by a final piece of work. Kent's adopted the European Credit Transfer System, which is internationally recognised. Around half the credits gained on each module are ECTs. Sandwich years in industry are common choices. Kent students have rated the University the best in the South East for teaching.

ENTRY POINTS: 260-320	**AVE POINTS: 288**
APPLICATIONS PER PLACE: 5	**CLEARING: 2%**
NO. OF TERMS: 3	**LENGTH OF TERMS: 15 WKS**
STAFF TO STUDENT RATIO: 1:16	**STUDY ADDICTS: 21%**
TEACHING: ★★★	**RESEARCH: ★★★★**
YEAR ABROAD: 1%	**SANDWICH STUDENTS: 13%**

ADMISSIONS
⊙ APPLY VIA UCAS/DIRECT
'Widening Access' is a University committee buzz-phrase, especially as far as the Medway campus is concerned. Diploma students can apply direct. Mature students can squeeze in without traditional qualifications. A foundation year is open to those who need to brush-up language and study skills before undertaking a degree.

SUBJECTS
ARTS/HUMANITIES: 27%   **SCIENCE, TECHNOLOGY & MEDICAL STUDIES:** 22%   **SOCIAL SCIENCES** 51%
BEST Architecture; Art & Design; Biological Sciences; Business; Computer Science; Creative Arts; Economics, Politics & Sociology; Electronic & Electrical Engineering; English-Based Studies; European Languages & Area Studies; History & Archaeology; Law; Management; Performing Arts; Philosophy; Physical Science; Psychology; Social Policy & Anthropology; Sports Science; Theology & Religious Studies.
UNUSUAL Biodiversity; Health & Fitness; Internet & Multimedia Communications; Sports Therapy; War Studies; Wildlife Conservation.

LIBRARIES
⊙ 1,000,000 BOOKS ⊙ 1,286 STUDY PLACES
⊙ SPEND PER STUDENT ££
The main Templeman library has a bundle of special collections. The Centre for the Study of Cartoons & Caricature has 90,000 cartoons, *of the satirical/political type, not the South Park box set.* There's a learning resource centre at the Medway campus *but not many need to use it.* Students can

K

access full text newspaper articles and e-books online. The colleges have their own baby collections and the cathedral library has shelf upon shelf of dusty tomes – not for the likes of plebby undergrads, mind. The University buys 16,000 new books a year.

COMPUTERS
⊙ 630 WORKSTATIONS ⊙ 24-HR ACCESS
95% of student rooms have free internet/network access – but there's a *crafty* annual hook-up charge of £68 for those who want to plug their own 'puter into it. Others can reach a couple of 24-hr PCs. The Drill Hall library at Medway (home of the LRC) has 370 workstations.

OTHER LEARNING FACILITIES
There's a design lab and language labs for students doing languages as part of their course. Greenwich and Kent Universities have between them *coughed up to the tune of* £5m for new labs at Medway.

ENTERTAINMENT ◖◖◖◖◖◖◖◖◖◖

CANTERBURY
⊙ PRICE OF A PINT OF BEER £1.60
⊙ GLASS OF WINE £2.50
⊙ GLASS OF WINE £1.50
CINEMAS The Odeon has two screens.
THEATRES The Marlowe Theatre is the city's main venue for touring drama and sex-soap pretty boy panto. *Literary types might like to know* T S Eliot's play Murder in the Cathedral was written for and performed in Canterbury Cathedral. *Skint types might be more interested to know there's a student discount.*
PUBS The city has *firkinfuls of* traditional ale pubs, largely thanks to the hop-soaked beer factories that populate the county. *Students don't just drink 'Manky Brian's Famous Whippleweasel' though: trendy joints like Alberry's Wine Bar pull in a fair few, the Scream pub is popular for its cheap prices and the Cherry Tree's range of flavoured vodkas has titillated a taste bud or two in its time.* Casey's (Irish), the Cricketers and Hobgoblin *are also faves.*
CLUBBING *Canterbury isn't Club City but it's occasionally worth ignoring that the Works is a dirt-cheap cheesy dive and that the Chicago Rock Café's horrendously overpriced during the week. The Rock's still nicer than Baa-Baa's three floors though, which is saying something.*
MUSIC VENUES Classical concerts are held in the cathedral, the Marlowe Theatre has a few big names *(and mouths)* warbling now and then (Van Morrison, Vonda Shepherd). Local Heroes Records is a record shop: the club on the first floor does a *nice line in eclectic* sounds (World, Jazz, Folk). Several pubs provide local bands with excuses to perform.
COMEDY/CABARET The Marlowe attracts the likes of Ricky Tomlinson.

EATING OUT Local scoff shops are geared to the student and tourist trade and there are *plentiful* Indian, Italian, Mexican, Chinese, French and vegetarian restaurants, as well as various fish'n'chip shops and other takeaways. *Pushplugs: Café Naz (Indian with discounts); Café des Amis (Mexican, natch); Ask (pizza).*

MEDWAY
Students at Medway get outta town to party, with SU buses to Maidstone's Ikon, Amadeus and other nightclubs. The Riverside Tavern is a *popular* gay pub with a dance floor. The Ship & Trades has *good* dockside views from the patio. The Central Theatre is *retro tribute band hell, or heaven, if that's your groove.* Rochester, a ten min taxi ride away, furnishes *more variety,* including a UGC multiplex complete with loyalty discounts.

UNIVERSITY
⊙ PRICE OF A PINT OF BEER £1.70
⊙ GLASS OF WINE £1.50
⊙ GLASS OF WINE £2
Despite a mixed bag of campus ents, students in Canterbury tend to head for the bright(ish) lights of the city. Students in Medway have a bar, nightclub and pubby ents (pool tables, TV, games).
BARS In addition to the four college bars, the Union has three *larger* boozeries. The Lighthouse does tons of food and opens its second room for club nights. Woody's serves the main halls of residence and has *a buzzing atmosphere,* different ents every night of the week, and food. The Venue is *the biggest and the busiest* (on campus and in Canterbury), juggling promotions every night. The University's four other bars *tend to be cosy but more low key.*
THEATRES The Gulbenkian Theatre on campus is *very well kitted out* but is shared with the wider community. It hosts touring productions, concerts and the annual Canterbury festival, as well as a good many plays put on by the student drama society. Kent has one of the largest drama departments in the country.
FILM Cinema 3 is another shared venue that shows several *mainstream-ish* films a week for £3.50. Kent Student Cinema stock their own DVD library and produce a termly magazine.
MUSIC VENUES The Gulbenkian Theatre runs a number of live performances, usually world music, classical and jazz-orientated.
CLUBBING The Venue *is well-named given it's pretty much the only club option going in Canterbury.* Past *greats* have included DJ Spoony, Judge Jules and Trevor Nelson but the youth of today *slate it for it's lack of atmosphere/space, and an overabundance of cheese. Hard-core clubbers remain true to the faith,* while the Ministry of Sound tour always pulls in the masses.
COMEDY/CABARET Jimmy Carr, Dave *'sideburns'* Gorman and The Great Suprendo have all *piff-paff-poofed into the Gulbenkian in the name of*

entertainment. The drama department runs one comedy show weekly and the Union brings in the professionals *when that falls flat*.

FOOD Catering is mainly centred in individual college refectories *but the bars dish out till late evening*. Eliot and Rutherford Colleges have *traditional* dining halls, Eliot also has Mungo's bistro. The Lighthouse has a Costa Coffee franchise that dishes out paninis. The Gulbenkian Café does *gourmet nibbling though the prices aren't as bad as names of dishes suggest (not so much McChicken as 'chicken liver parfait' – ooh, get them)*. Arriving students are given a 'cashless card' a top-up debit card which can be used in some of the shops and cafes on campus. Points and discounts can also be earned which knocks a few pennies off the cost of chow. There are catering outlets/Union shop at Medway too.

OTHER Apart from college and society dos, there's at least one major event a term, including balls for Freshers, Rag, Jocks and everyone else.

SOCIAL ⚫⚫⚫⚫⚫⚫⚫⚫⚫⚫⚫⚫⚫⚫

UNIVERSITY OF KENT STUDENTS' UNION
⚫ **5 SABBATICALS** ⚫ **TURNOUT AT LAST BALLOT** 20%
⚫ **NUS MEMBER**

The Union's come-over all Why Don't You at the moment, having launched three new strategies. Shout Out! sounds like it was inspired by 70s kiddies' TV, but is actually about raising student awareness of the SU and its superhero-like powers of democracy. There's also a 'fair accommodation for students' campaign and a drive to get independence for Medway Union's ents. *It's not exactly Free Nelson Mandela, but you get the pic.* They also nudged the University towards its new Fair Trade status. *As if all that didn't warrant a lie-down,* there'll also be developments in student media and new standards for academic regulation, *which demonstrates the hand-and-blister relationship they have with the Uni bigwigs. Students, on the other hand, feel their input and ideas aren't always acknowledged.*

SU FACILITIES
The SU owns three buildings: Mandela Building, the Virginia Woolf Building and the Venue, er, venue. There are seven bars in total and a nightclub to boot. Also: a travel agency; fax and printing service; minibus hire; Endsleigh Insurance office; payphones; general shop; secondhand bookshop; five pool tables; juke box; vending machines; TV lounge; two meeting rooms; launderette; stationery shop; photocopier; photo booth; van hire. Also HSBC, NatWest and Lloyds TSB banks with ATMs on campus.

CLUBS (NON SPORTING)
Adventure Gaming; Anime Arabic; Art; Ballroom & Latin Dancing; Believers Love World; Belly Dance; Buddhist Meditation; Capoeira; Chinese; CPAS (Christian Performing Arts); Creative writing; Critical lawyers; Current Affairs; Drum

& Bass; East African; Erasmus; European Affairs; Film; Finance; French; German; Good Food; Hellenic; Hip hop; Hong Kong; In.Visible; Japanese; Kent Dance; Kent Cinema; Kinksoc; Latin American; Malasyian & Bruneian; Mauritian; MUN; Music; National Union of Journalists; Open UP1; Pagan; Paintball; Persian Armenian; Pirate; P.O.P; Pro-Life; Respect; Salsa; Shiatsu & Earth Healing; Sri Lankan; SWSS; Space; Spanish; Stage Spiders; Subtext; Tai Chi; Talk Russian; Temple; UKCD; United East; Vox Humana.

AT MEDWAY Christian Faith Academy; Christian Union; Future Aspirations; Medway Law Group; LGBT; Talk Thoughts. **See also Clubs tables.**

OTHER ORGANISATIONS
The Union produces 'Kred' every month, the *cringingly-named* student paper. The film society churns out the termlly film-making mag, 'Big Lens'. 'UKCR', the 24-hr campus radio station, has finally snagged its community radio licence (the first to be granted to an SU), and is now called 'CSR'. Rag raises a *fair amount* of cash through its annual Snow Ball, auctions and other *deranged* events, for local and national charities – they're aiming for £25,000 this year. 'YOUTHACTION' mag (from the Jobshop) has volunteering ops and contacts in the back.

RELIGIOUS
⚫ **2 CHAPLAINS (COFE, RC)**
Ten part-time chaplains cover most Christian denominations and Jewish, Islamic, Buddhist and Baha'i faiths. The Eliot Chapel is the campus prayer place although there are various makeshift worship shops in colleges as well as a Muslim prayer room. In town, there's the cathedral, of course, *but Christians who fancy something a little less lofty don't have to worry about any kind of theological drought. Non-Christians may get a bit more spiritually thirsty.* Prayer room in the Blake Building at Medway, plus access to Chaplains on campus.

PAID WORK
⚫ **JOB BUREAU** ⚫ **PAID WORK** TERM-TIME 20%; HOLS 75%
The Union jobshop has vacancy boards, newsletters, advice *and a good rep with local employers.* In the summertime, the Garden of England needs harvesting, and there are hop and fruit picking jobs going. *A foreign language can be helpful for getting a job dog-walking some of the millions of tourists.* There's bar and admin work in the Union and similar stuff in the city. Students at Medway also won't go short of pocket money.

K

SPORTS ◖◗◖◗◖◗◖◗◖◗◖◗◖◗

○ RECENT SUCCESSES HOCKEY **○ BUSA RANKING** 44
Intercollegiate rivalry gets pretty heated on the pitch, if a little lukewarm on the national level. £53/yr buys time on most facilities, £60 also gets peak access to the Cardio Theatre. There's been some sprucing up of existing kit, with planned pitches and pavilion extension. Outstanding athletes can receive awards of up to £1,500.

SPORTS FACILITIES
The Sports Centre on the Canterbury campus is also open to locals: two multi-purpose halls (the main hall fitted with a sprung Taraflex floor) for badminton, netball, basketball, five-a-side football & volleyball; four refurbed squash courts; cricket nets; climbing wall; over 40 fitness/dance classes per week; sun beds & sauna; fitness suite; free weights; cardio theatre; individual fitness assessments & programmes; 12 outdoor tennis courts; beach volleyball court; playing fields with floodlit all-weather pitch for hockey & soccer; sports pavilion; grass pitches & cricket squares. Medway students have, er, a gymnasium and a sports centre. Canterbury's also got: leisure centre; pool; bowling green; dry ski slope; golf course; more racket sport courts and caves; the river and a lake are available for those who like to take it outside. Medway has the gear for snow sports, crazy, crazy golf, tennis and outdoor swimming.

SPORTING CLUBS
10-Pin Bowling; Aikido; Caving; Falconettes (Cheerleading); Falcons (American Football); Go-Carting; Kendo; Kickboxing; Korfball; Kung Fu; Mountaineering; Paintball; Sailing & Windsurfing; Skydiving; Snow Sports. **See also Clubs tables.**

ATTRACTIONS
Gillingham FC *(who?)* and Kent County Cricket Club practise their art nearby. Dog racing and windsurfing at Whitstable.

ACCOMMODATION ◖◗◖◗◖◗◖◗◖◗

IN COLLEGE
○ CATERED 14% **○ COST** £96 (31WKS)
○ SELF-CATERING 28% **○ COST** £83 (38/52WKS)
○ 1ST YRS LIVING IN 100%
○ INSURANCE PREMIUM £
AVAILABILITY There are a total of 4,000 undergrad rooms available so in theory just under half of them can be accommodated – first years are guaranteed if they apply by August. Whether or not they live in, students remain members of their colleges throughout their courses. Living on campus is undoubtedly convenient, *but those in college halls can*

finish the year more out of pocket than they'd expected. Only brekkie's included in rents, and no cooking facilities means eating in the college refectories or dining on micro-filth, *which quickly adds up.* Rents are London-like, which can cause injury to the wallet given loans and grants don't come with London weighting in these here parts. Come the witching hour, hall access is only for keycard-equipped residents. Most halls have a JCR *(basically a communal chill-out zone).* Self-catering University houses like Beckett Court *are popular with second and third years, as is Park Wood,* a little village of student houses with its own bar and shop set in *charming* woodland. Launderettes are available to all. The University's *not too keen on re-engineering the Black Death* so cleaners are called in – at students' cost – if rooms and communal areas *start showing signs of non-human life.* There's enough accommodation that no-one need share, and the majority of twin rooms are occupied by just one person. Five halls, including Park Wood, are set aside for postgrads – all of whom live in.
CAR PARKING *Not too much of a problem* for those living at Park Wood (£30 permit though). Permits for those living more than a mile away start at £20 *but good luck finding a spot around residences.*

EXTERNALLY
○ AVE RENT £65 **○ LIVING AT HOME** 2%
AVAILABILITY Finding somewhere to live in *Canterbury is like rooting for truffles (easy enough if you keep your nose to the ground) and the January house-hunt isn't as frenetic as it might be.* An increasing number are moving out to Herne Bay, Hales Place and, *under protest,* Whitstable (five or six miles north), *where rents are cheaper, places more plentiful and life more dull. For those who are bed-wettingly keen for something closer to the action, Wincheap and Downs Road are the places to aim for. The council's trying to disguise the dodgy Sturry Road with posh new housing, but not many students are falling for it.*
HOUSING HELP The four guys in the Accommodation Office place first years on campus, manage an off-campus vacancy list and help with legal wrangles. *The SU is much more hands-on in its advice-giving.*

WELFARE ◖◗◖◗◖◗◖◗◖◗◖◗◖◗

SERVICES
○ LGBT OFFICER & SOCIETY ○ WOMEN'S OFFICER & SOCIETY ○ MATURE STUDENTS' OFFICER & SOCIETY ○ ETHNIC MINORITIES OFFICER & SOCIETY ○ INTERNATIONAL STUDENTS' OFFICER & SOCIETY ○ POSTGRAD OFFICER & SOCIETY ○ DISABILITIES OFFICER & SOCIETY ○ LATE-NIGHT MINIBUS ○ SELF-DEFENCE CLASSES ○ COLLEGE COUNSELLORS 4 FULL **○ CRIME RATING** !
The *unfeasibly caring* Union also appoints a Men's Officer and a Students with Dependants'

K

Officer. The taxi fund is for SU staff only.

HEALTH The University Medical Centre comes complete with six doctors, six nurses (including one psychiatric liaison) and a residential sick bay. Medway students are advised to register with surgeries in town.

WOMEN Security measures – not just for women – include free personal alarms. The 'campopo' – *campus copper to you* – will walk students to their doors.

CRÈCHES/NURSERY The University crèche looks after up to 50 children between 6wks-4yrs. SU subsidises costs for students and demand is high. Medway has the Jigsaw Nursery for 65 tots.

DISABILITIES Priority parking, lifts and ramps for all buildings. The Disability Support Unit provides support and information for all disabled students, including screening and exam arrangements for dyslexics.

FINANCE

- **AVE DEBT PER YEAR** £3,446
- **HOME STUDENT FEES** £3,000/YR

FEES International students pay £8,580/yr for non-lab courses or £11,130/yr otherwise. Applications to Kent have risen by 3% this year, so not everyone's in a huff over top-up fees.

- **ACCESS FUND** £160,000

SUPPORT Some academic, music, art and sport bursaries available to those with talent (rugby and cricket in particular), plus a range of bursaries to help top-up afflicted students. The Master of each college has £200 or so kicking around for anyone who really needs it and emergency loans are available. High-achieving International students can get two grand off first year fees or a 10% loyalty discount if another family member has attended.

▶ KENT INSTITUTE OF ART AND DESIGN

see *Creative Arts University College*

KING'S COLLEGE LONDON

1. **◉ KING'S COLLEGE LONDON** University of London, The Strand, London, WC2R 2LS **TEL** (020) 7836 5454 **E-MAIL** ceu@kcl.ac.uk **WEBSITE** www.kcl.ac.uk ◉ **KING'S COLLEGE STUDENTS' UNION** Macadam Building, Surrey Street, London, WC2R 2NS **TEL** (020) 7848 1588 **E-MAIL** student.life.support@kclsu.org **WEBSITE** www.kclsu.org
2. **◉ GUY'S CAMPUS: KING'S COLLEGE LONDON** School of Medicine, Dental Institute, School of Biomedical & Health Sciences, London, SE1 1UL ◉ **KING'S COLLEGE STUDENTS' UNION** Boland House, London, SE1 1UL **TEL** (020) 7848 1588
3. **◉ KING'S COLLEGE LONDON, DENMARK HILL CAMPUS** Weston Education Centre, Bessemer Rd, London, SE5 8AF

GENERAL ◍◍◍◍◍◍◍◍◍◍◍◍

In 1829 King George IV and the Duke of Wellington got together and came up with King's College as their gift to Higher Education (*'Duke's College' somehow isn't as punchy*). It's the second oldest college of the University of London and its *genteel rivalry with the top-spot holder, UCL, remains intense*. Its biggest site is situated at one end of the Strand, *which places it roughly where 'Chance' is on the Monopoly board*. The Thames is a boulder's throw away, as are Fleet Street, the Courtauld Institute of Art, LSE and Aldwych (a five-lane crescent curving round Bush House, the HQ of the BBC World Service). *King's also edges on to the West End so it's a prime entry point into London's social and cultural hub. The 70s front of the King's College main building is in stark contrast to the more traditional buildings that surround it. It's made of* various shades of grey, concrete, glass and even has a giant internet screen in reception. *Hidden away at the back of the building, overlooking the Thames, is much finer Georgian architecture, but that far into the building it's hard to find your way out again.* The Waterloo, Guy's and St Thomas's campus sites are just across the river; there's also Denmark Hill campus in Camberwell. For general information about London: see University of London.

SEX RATIO: ♂40 ♀60	FOUNDED: 1829
FULL-TIME U'GRADS: 12,101	PART-TIME: 1,743
POSTGRADS: 4,693	NON-DEGREE: 1,218
AVE COURSE: 3YRS	ETHNIC: 43%
STATE:PRIVATE SCHOOL: 55:27	FLUNK RATE: 7%
MATURE: 29%	INTERNATIONAL: 15%
DISABLED: 115	LOCAL: 46%

Words in italics are Push's point of view — take it or leave it...

K

ATMOSPHERE
Like London at large, KCL is a heady, cosmopolitan jumble. The College pulses with life and academic rigour and, far from being a lofty spire, is firmly embedded in the city around it. Strand, Guy's and Waterloo are the focus of studying and social life although there's also the University of London central Union and the legion of local venues. The Strand in particular is at the heart of it all, so some of the more distant sites can end up feeling more like the kidneys. The college's medical departments are renowned, and the hospital campuses have an air of professionalism about them – but there are very few students in any department who don't take their course seriously. No time-wasters, please.

SITES
THE STRAND (6,250 students – Humanities, Law, Physical Sciences, Engineering, Social Sciences) This is the eastern end of the West End. *There are a million ways to spend money but nowhere to live and not many places to do the weekly shopping without your daily bread costing more than your dough.* The SU's based at this site and the nearest college halls are just ten mins walk away. Inside *currently resembles a building site,* but the £40 million worth of *improved academic and social facilities should be worth it.*
GUY'S CAMPUS (6,000 students – Medicine, Dentistry, Biomedical & Health Sciences) A collection of *Georgian style* buildings close to London Bridge. From the top of Guy's Tower there's an *incredible view across the city.* It's two miles from the Strand site on the Thames's South Bank. There's also a *fairly new* teaching base and facilities to match at Guy's campus as well as an SU and welfare provisions.
WATERLOO CAMPUS (3,000 students – Biomedical & Life Sciences, Nursing & Midwifery, Social Sciences) Half a mile from the Strand, *dead centre of the cultural strip that is the South Bank,* the site has a *more subdued atmosphere,* probably because it's the centre of college administration.
ST THOMAS'S HOSPITAL (aka *Tommy's* – medical) 1,200m from Trafalgar Square, opposite the Houses of Parliament on the south side of the Thames, is Tommy's modern 70s open-plan development with *bright, clean,* inter-connected buildings and a bar but no canteen.
DENMARK HILL CAMPUS (1,000 students – Psychiatry, Medicine, Dentistry). King's College Hospital in Camberwell. *A different kettle of cod altogether,* Camberwell's in South London and, *almost necessarily, shabbier as a result. It's not London's safest area (or its worst – London gets much worse), but it's cheap, residential and good for shopping. Camberwell's getting better for entertainment though still a bit old-men's-pubville but it's very well connected for the West End. The campus has its own social life anyway.*

LONDON see University of London

TRAVEL see University of London
TRAINS Charing Cross is the most accessible mainline station for the Strand site. Waterloo station for (ahem) Waterloo, Denmark Hill for King's Hospital and London Bridge for Guy's.
BUSES Strand: 1, 4, 6, 9, 11, 13, 15, 23, 26, 59, 68, 76, 77a, 91, 168, 171 (*mathematicians may want to calculate the sequence there).* Denmark Hill: 12, 35, 40, 45 and others. 108, 501 and 133 go near Guy's and Waterloo; 77 and 507 go to Tommy's. The Riverside bus RV1 connects the Strand, Guy's and Waterloo. *Plenty* of night-buses cover all bases.
UNDERGROUND Temple (District & Circle) or Holborn (Piccadilly & Central) for the Strand site. Northern and Bakerloo lines for Waterloo; London Bridge (Northern) for Guy's; Lambeth North (Bakerloo) for Tommy's. The Jubilee line serves students based at both Guy's and Waterloo.
COLLEGE A bus is provided for medical students travelling between Guy's and Tommy's.
BICYCLES *Chances of being mown down by cars are slim since most vehicles in the area tend to be stationary, although choking to death on exhaust fumes is no one's idea of a giggle. Still the fastest way of getting around though.*

CAREER PROSPECTS
◉ **CAREERS SERVICE** ◉ **NO. OF STAFF** 11 FULL/1 PART
◉ **UNEMPLOYED AFTER 6 MTHS** 4%
The Grad Club, as they call it, provides the Full Monty: newsletters, bulletin boards, vacancy lists, interview training, job fairs, seminar programmes and career consultations on each campus.

FAMOUS ALUMNI
Rory Bremner (impressionist); Anita Brookner, Susan Hill, Hanif Kureishi (novelists); George Carey (Archbishop of Canterbury); Arthur C Clarke (sci-fi writer); John Eliot Gardner (composer/conductor); W S Gilbert (Sullivan's other half); Thomas Hardy (*depressing novelist, miserable poet*); Njongonkulu Winston Ndungane (Archbishop of Cape Town); Chapman Pincher (writer/journalist); Ian Shaw (jazz singer); Desmond Tutu (Archbishop *and source of student rhyming slang*); Maurice Wilkins (Nobel Laureate DNA Scientist).

SPECIAL FEATURES
With a £400m refurb under its belt, *KCL is pretty smug.* It's also one-quarter of SIMFONEC (with the RVC, City University and St Mary's), a *ginormous* scientific business enterprise specialising in teaching entrepreneurship and encouraging business innovation in the London universities.

FURTHER INFO
◉ **PROSPECTUSES** UNDERGRAD; POSTGRAD; SOME DEPARTMENTAL
◉ **OPEN DAYS**
All info from admissions. KCL website has an online prospectus, virtual tour and allows cyberchat with current students. E-mail for international applicants: international@kcl.ac.uk. There's a widening participation office – *full marks for good intentions.*

Words in italics are Push's point of view – take it or leave it...

ACADEMIC 〇〇〇〇〇〇〇〇〇〇〇〇〇

〇 RUSSELL GROUP
More than 200 courses available, ranging from traditional core subjects to *ludicrously innovative fields*. The College is split not quite down the middle into medical sciences on one side and everything else on the other. *Biomedical Sciences on Guy's campus are particularly cutting-edge.* From 2007, the College is getting into line with most other institutions, bringing in a modular system where students have to complete 360 credits during a typical three-year degree – each credit should involve about ten hours work (including researching, private study and assessment), *so now you know.*

ENTRY POINTS: 120–170	**AVE POINTS:** 389
APPLICATIONS PER PLACE: 6	**CLEARING:** 7%
NO. OF TERMS: 2	**LENGTH OF TERMS:** 14wks
STAFF TO STUDENT RATIO: 1:9	**STUDY ADDICTS:** 20%
TEACHING: ****	**RESEARCH:** ****
YEAR ABROAD: <1%	**SANDWICH STUDENTS:** N/A
1STS: 16%	**2.2s:** 25%
2.1s: 55%	**3RDS:** 4%

ADMISSIONS
〇 APPLY VIA UCAS
Not a stickler for A levels, KCL also considers Access courses, BTEC or other vocational courses. Relevant work experience can be counted rather than quals for courses like nursing.

SUBJECTS
BIOMEDICAL & HEALTH SCIENCES 18%
DENTAL INSTITUTE 7%   **HUMANITIES** 16%
INSTITUTE OF PSYCHIATRY N/A   **LAW** 8%
MEDICINE 17%   **NURSING & MIDWIFERY** 15%
PHYSICAL SCIENCE & ENGINEERING 11%
SOCIAL SCIENCES & PUBLIC POLICY 9%
BEST Dentistry; European Languages; Geography; History; Medicine; Law; Pharmacy; Philosophy; Theology & Religious Studies.
UNUSUAL Portuguese & Brazilian Studies; Turkish & Greek.

LIBRARIES
〇 900,000+ BOOKS 〇 2,800 STUDY PLACES
〇 SPEND PER STUDENT £££
As well as the vast University of London library at Senate House, KCL students have several libraries at their disposal and every campus has some kind of book and computer shed. The main Maughan Library used to be the Public Record Office and is now the largest new university library in Britain since WWII. It's also got the only remaining Victorian zinc ceilings, *which is apparently more exciting than it sounds.* Open till 10pm weekdays.

COMPUTERS
〇 1,400 WORKSTATIONS 〇 24–HR ACCESS 〇 SPEND PER STUDENT £££££
PAWs (Public Access Workstations – *otherwise*

known as 'computers') are sprinkled across campus, including in the libraries. Assorted opening times, but there's also wireless access, for *essential e-mail checking on the go*, as well as college-network access in a number of buildings. The virtual learning environment is WebCT Vista, *of which the college is pretty proud.*

OTHER LEARNING FACILITIES
Language labs offer seven levels of teaching in various foreign languages. Music rehearsal rooms are available; there's also access to teaching at the Royal Academy of Music. The 'Virtual Campus' allows some online learning.

ENTERTAINMENT 〇〇〇〇〇〇〇〇〇

THE CITY see University of London
〇 PRICE OF A PINT OF BEER £2.80
〇 GLASS OF WINE £2.80
〇 CAN OF RED BULL £2.50

COLLEGE see University of London
〇 PRICE OF A PINT OF BEER £1.80
〇 GLASS OF WINE £2
〇 CAN OF RED BULL £1.90
KCL's ents are dwarfed by the larger social scene at the University of London Union. The proximity of London's West End is also an issue, drawing King's students out of the campus and into the glittering nightlife of the city.
BARS Three bars at the Strand, including the Waterfront *which can get packed*, and Tutu's (the flagship venue), *offers a great view of the Thames and a reasonable cocktail menu.* Denmark Hill, Guy's, Tommy's and Waterloo have bars too.
THEATRES The Greenwood Theatre has Question Time, Jackanory, Countdown and Jo Brand on its CV and it's been tarted up even more since its TV glory days. 20+ productions each year with regular jaunts to Edinburgh. *King's Players rule the dramatic roost but other societies and departments get a look-in too.*
CLUBBING/MUSIC VENUES *The truth is, ULU's far better at doing this sort of thing.* Still, Tutu's (cap 620) holds regular cheesy club nights of which Phase is *the most popular*, as does the Penthouse Bar at Denmark Hill. Inverse (cap 500) pulses underground at Guy's campus. Tutu's is the main gig venue – Alanis Morissette, Richard Ashcroft, El Presidente and We Are Scientists have strummed and warbled recently.
FOOD King's restaurant in the Strand site flogs *cheap* pie 'n' chips concoctions. Tutu's and its sibling bars sell food late into the night, the hospitals have canteens and there are *cheap, chirpy* cafés on most sites.
OTHER Yearly bevy of black-tie balls. The Summer Ball is the *biggest* and ULU schedules some *top* formal nights as well.

K

Words in italics are Push's point of view — take it or leave it...

SOCIAL ◖◖◖◖◖◖◖◖◖◖◖◖

KING'S COLLEGE LONDON STUDENTS' UNION
- **5 SABBATICALS** ○ **TURNOUT AT LAST BALLOT** 15%
- **NUS MEMBER**

KCLSU is the oldest union in London *but it certainly ain't the most political, casting itself instead as a charitable force taking students under its wing. The overall feel is businesslike rather than Bolshevik and the focus is on events and facilities rather than revolution. Not unlike the Tories under a newly-elected Dave Cameron, KCLSU believes in co-operating with the University rather than scoring points against it and consequently the pair enjoy a mature and respectfully chummy relationship.*

SU FACILITIES
Five bars; four cafeterias; nightclub; four coffee/snack bars; two fast food outlets; eight pool tables; Endsleigh Insurance branch; at least two ATMs on each site; payphones; crèche; two bookshops (one Blackwells); STA travel branch; general store; vending machines; stationery shop; juke boxes; TV lounge; meeting rooms; photocopier; fax service; printing service; photo booth; advice centre. There's a new student centre at Waterloo.

CLUBS (NON SPORTING)
ABACUS (Chinese culture and language); Afro-Caribbean; Ahlul Bayt (a branch of Islam); Anaesthetics; Arabic; Asian; Ballroom; Bangladesh; Bikers; Breakin' KCL (hiphop and breakdancing); Chinese; Clio (history); Dance; Dead Parrot; Entrpreneurial & Investment; European; French; G&S (Gilbert & Sullivan); General Practice; German; Mature Students; Hellenic; Hindu; Hip-Hop; India; Iranian Persian; Islamic; Jain; Jewish; Kenyan; King's Players (drama); Krishna Consciousness; LINKS (first aid); Make Up; Malaysian Singaporean; Mauritian; Maxwell (physics); Médecins Sans Frontières; Medical Ethics; MedACT (charity); MUN (Model United Nations); Musical Theatre; Paediatrics; Pakistan; People & Planet; Physio; Quality Stuff (from wargaming and roleplaying to anime, manga and contemporary Japanse film); Resturant; Rock; Sai; Sikh; Snooker&Pool; Sri Lankan; Surgical; Thai; Turkish; War Studies; Windband; Women's Health; Yoga. **See also Clubs tables.**

OTHER ORGANISATIONS
'Roar' is the SU mag (including listings). KCLSU Community Action gets students away from the beer and the books and out to help needy souls. *The Rag's beer races with UCL go down well and London colleges have a penchant for pinching each other's mascots. King's mascot was Reggie, a quarter-ton red copper lion, until he was stolen by City & Guilds who castrated him. The new mascot was filled with concrete and was quickly stolen with the aid of trucks and winches. Now they've got a copper lion again, which is just asking for it.*

RELIGIOUS
- **4 CHAPLAINS (COFE, RC, ORTHODOX, FC)**

Chapels at the Strand and Guy's, Muslim prayer rooms are located on various sites.

PAID WORK see University of London
- **PAID WORK** TERM-TIME 45%; HOLS 65%

Some paid work is available with the SU, mainly bar work.

SPORTS ◖◖◖◖◖◖◖◖◖◖◖◖◖◖

- **BUSA RANKING** 60

Things are surprisingly sporty considering the outdoor facilities are divided around Cobham, New Malden, Dulwich and Honour Oak Park – all more than a light jog away. In the past, 40% of University of London team members have been King's students.

SPORTS FACILITIES
13 football pitches; six rugby pitches; hockey pitch; six cricket wickets; two squash courts; 19 tennis courts; two basketball courts; eight netball courts; sports hall; two swimming pools; running track; athletics field; K4 fitness gym; multigym; aerobics studio; four rounders pitches. *Most of which are bloody miles away, but at least they're free to use.* There's a testosterone-heavy shooting range at Strand, while Guy's has a swimming pool and a gym. Locally there are public facilities and the courtyard of the Courtauld Institute becomes an ice rink at Xmas time.

SPORTING CLUBS
Boat (rowing); Cheerleading; Fencing; FITE (a female-only environment for exercise, currently focusing on the martial art form of Muay); Kickboxing; Kung Fu; Lacrosse; Rifle; Waterpolo; Table Tennis; Ultimate Frisbee; Windsurfing. **See also Clubs tables.**

ATTRACTIONS see University of London

ACCOMMODATION ◖◖◖◖◖◖◖◖◖

IN UNIVERSITY
- **CATERED** 9% ○ **COST** £104 (40/51WKS)
- **SELF-CATERING** 18% ○ **COST** £79 (40WKS)
- **1ST YRS LIVING IN** 75%
- **INSURANCE PREMIUM** £

AVAILABILITY Eight halls of residences dotted around London, most within a four-mile radius of the Strand. The Hampstead Halls are *in demand for their posh, leafy looks, even though they're at the other end of town,* while Stamford Street is *the most luxurious, with swish en suites* and basement fitness centre. There are

K

single-sex halls as well as some provision for couples. All halls have launderette facilities, and most have common rooms and TV lounges. Self-catered kitchens have *plenty of appliance goodies*. A handful (66) have to share but pay less *for the privilege*. King's also has 595 spaces in London University inter-collegiate halls. All accommodation-hopeful first years can be squeezed in somewhere within the first few weeks of term.
CAR PARKING Almost *impossible* at almost all halls. Permits are *trickier to get hold of than epileptic eels*, but the Residence Office has a few for special cases.

EXTERNALLY see University of London
⊙ **AVE RENT** £75
HOUSING HELP The accommodation office works in conjunction with the University of London to help those living out. Bulletin boards and legal advice are available from KCL, otherwise see the University of London's facilities.

WELFARE ◖◖◖◖◖◖◖◖◖◖◖◖◖

SERVICES
⊙ **POSTGRAD OFFICER** ⊙ **SELF−DEFENCE CLASSES**
⊙ **COLLEGE COUNSELLORS** 1 FULL/12 PART
⊙ **CRIME RATING** !!!!!
Student welfare advisors take care of *the tea and*

sympathy side of things with advice on finance, benefits, housing, legal stuff and immigration.
HEALTH The College runs a Counselling and Medical Centre with four doctors, three nurses, consultant psychiatrist, a counsellor and a psychotherapist. Full dental service available in the College Hospitals.
CRECHES/NURSERY King's offers subsidised places with a private local nursery.
DISABILITIES *Good intentions, but old buildings don't lend themselves easily to wheelchair use. There are a number of Disability Advisers and a guide for disabled students, but accommodation is limited to a handful of adapted rooms.*
CRIME/DRUGS Denmark Hill is *a bit rougher around the edges than the others and drug-related crime is a concern.*

FINANCE
⊙ **AVE DEBT PER YEAR** £3,099
⊙ **HOME STUDENT FEES** £3,000
FEES International students can pay up to £25,726 for clinically based degrees and a slightly less fearsome £13,844 for classroom-based courses.

⊙ **ACCESS FUND** £634,683 ⊙ **SUCCESSFUL APPLICATIONS/YR** 930 ⊙ **AVERAGE PAYMENT** £100-3,500
SUPPORT New bursaries and scholarships (*unambiguously* titled myBursary and myScholarship) from 2006 for full-time students, in addition to other scholarships, bursaries and hardship funds for internationals.

K

KINGSTON UNIVERSITY

FORMERLY KINGSTON POLYTECHNIC

⊙ **KINGSTON UNIVERSITY** River House, 53-57 High Street, Kingston upon Thames, Surrey, KT1 1LQ **TEL** (020) 8547 2000 **E−MAIL** admissions-info@kingston.ac.uk **WEBSITE** www.kingston.ac.uk ⊙ **KINGSTON UNIVERSITY STUDENTS' UNION**, Penrhyn Road, Kingston upon Thames, Surrey, KT1 2EE **TEL** (020) 8547 8868 **E−MAIL** studentsunion@kingston.ac.uk **WEBSITE** www.kingstonsu.com

GENERAL ◖◖◖◖◖◖◖◖◖◖◖◖◖◖

Kingston didn't used to be in London, but the city's swell means that King Henry VIII's one-time country retreat is now a part of the big smoke, *even if there's a lot less smoke and a lot more greenery than the rest of the capital*. It's south-west London, some ten miles from Trafalgar Square and *retains some of the character of its historical glory*. Hampton Court Palace is the obvious highlight, surrounded by acres of deer-parks. Across the *handsome* Kingston Bridge sit the four sites of the university, *all of which lack palatial splendour, to say the least*. The buildings are within four miles of one another and vary from *whitewashed charm to new-fangled mangle*. A £30 million spending spree's currently underway, meaning buildings should be *shinier and bigger* by 2007.

SEX RATIO: ♂48 ♀52	**FOUNDED:** 1971
FULL−TIME U'GRADS: 14,410	**PART−TIME:** 1,691
POSTGRADS: 2,552	**NON−DEGREE:** 2,426
AVE COURSE: 3YRS	**ETHNIC:** 47%
STATE:PRIVATE SCHOOL: 92:8	**FLUNK RATE:** 17%
MATURE: 32%	**INTERNATIONAL:** 14%
DISABLED: 240	**LOCAL:** N/A

ATMOSPHERE
Students have a strong affinity for their college, which isn't diluted by the multiple sites or the occasionally depressing architecture. The main site at Penrhyn Road (7,500 students) is an intimate hive of activity, with campaigning, drinking, dressing up and general riotousness in full show. Knight's Park (2,000) has more of a thoughtful, arty feel to it, whereas Roehampton Vale (800) is a bit nerdier – lots of engineers either engineering or keeping things low-key. The halls

site at Kingston Hill (6,000) has a strong sense of community.

LONDON see University of London
- **POPULATION** 147,600 ⊙ **TOWN CENTRE** 0.5 MILES
- **LONDON** 10 MILES ⊙ **BIRMINGHAM** 106 MILES
- **EDINBURGH** 423 MILES
- **HIGH TEMP** 22 ⊙ **LOW TEMP** 4 ⊙ **RAINFALL** 49

KINGSTON

A *lively* town centre focuses on the 700-year-old marketplace. There's a *village-like character which stops just short of buxom milkmaids with a glint in their eye.* The re-developed Charter Quay has courtyards, walkways, bars and shops. There's also a high-profile bluechip industry presence, where *serious men in suits and geeks in labcoats* make *stacks of cash* for companies like Nikon, Sitel and Unichem.

TRAVEL see University of London
TRAINS A standard single from Waterloo to Kingston (30 mins) costs £3.60.
CAR *Acres* of car parking space but unfortunately also thousands upon thousands of cars too, *so balancing the two isn't always easy.*
AIR Kingston's *quite convenient* for Gatwick and Heathrow.
UNIVERSITY Free buses cover the different sites and run every 15 mins, 9am-6pm Mon-Fri.
TAXIS £8 from station to student residence. There's a *lot of competition*, which *can only be a good thing* for students who can be bothered to haggle.
BICYCLES Students make full use of a good cycle lane network.

CAREER PROSPECTS
- **CAREERS SERVICE** ⊙ **NO. OF STAFF:** 5 FULL/4 PART
- **UNEMPLOYED AFTER 6 MTHS** 4%
Offices at Penrhyn Road, Roehampton Vale and Kingston Hill.

FAMOUS ALUMNI

Richard Archer (lead singer, Hard-Fi); Glenda Bailey (editor, US Harper's Bazaar); Angie Bowie (Dave's first wife); Lawrence Dallaglio (former England rugby captain); Trevor Eve (actor); Patrick Forge (DJ); Caryn Franklin (TV presenter); Richard James (the Aphex Twin); Graeme Le Saux (football pundit); John Richmond, Helen Storey (fashion designers); Stella Tennant (posh model). Sir Gulam Noon (*one-man chicken tikka masala empire*) has an honorary doctorate.

FURTHER INFO
- **PROSPECTUSES** UNDERGRAD; POSTGRAD
- **OPEN DAYS**

ACADEMIC ○○○○○○○○○○○○

A broad range of subjects on offer and decent module-based teaching. Kingston's at the forefront of the online learning revolution – the vast majority of course modules are now online.

ENTRY POINTS: 40-320	**AVE POINTS: 288**
APPLICATIONS PER PLACE: 3	**LENGTH OF TERMS: 12**WKS
STAFF TO STUDENT RATION: 1:11	**STUDY ADDICTS: 19%**
TEACHING: ★★	**RESEARCH:★★**
YEAR ABROAD: 3%	**SANDWICH STUDENTS: 3%**
1STS: 9%	**2.2S: 36%**
2.1S: 39%	**3RDS: 3%**

ADMISSIONS
- **APPLY VIA UCAS**
Kingston is a massive academic arachnid with a web of partner colleges.

SUBJECTS
ART, DESIGN & ARCHITECTURE 13%   **ARTS & SOCIAL SCIENCES** 24%   **BUSINESS & LAW** 22%   **COMPUTING, INFORMATION SYSTEMS & MATHEMATICS** 9%   **ENGINEERING** 10%   **HEALTH & SOCIAL CARE SCIENCES** 9%   **SCIENCE** 13%
BEST Biology & Related Sciences; Civil, Chemical & Other Engineering; English-based studies; Finance & Accounting; History & Archaeology; Medical Science & Pharmacy; Social Work; Subjects Allied to Medicine.
UNUSUAL The only Aircraft Engineering Foundation course in the country.

LIBRARIES
- **431,293 BOOKS** ⊙ **1,359 STUDY PLACES**
Four main libraries, one on each site, devoted to the faculties based there. Doors are open from 10am-5pm at weekends, apart from those at Roehampton Vale, *which stay firmly shut.* A few special collections, including Knights Park Slide Library (250,000 slides) and Penrhyn Road's Mineralogical library. A £3 million extension should be done and dusted by 2007, unleashing another 430 study places and 300 computers.

COMPUTERS
- **1,800 WORKSTATIONS**
Blackboard's the Virtual Learning Environment of choice. Penrhyn's computers are available until midnight during term-time and most halls have internet access for a one-off fee.

OTHER LEARNING FACILITIES
Students on the Aircraft Engineering foundation degree get a *real life* Learjet to play with.

Words in italics are Push's point of view – take it or leave it...

ENTERTAINMENT ()()()()()()()()()

LONDON see University of London

KINGSTON UPON THAMES
- **PRICE OF A PINT OF BEER** £2.20
- **GLASS OF WINE** £2.40
- **CAN OF RED BULL** £2

CINEMAS A 14-screen Odeon in the *fatly-named* Rotunda centre does a neat 20% student discount.
THEATRES The Rose of Kingston is in the *swish* Quays development.
PUBS About 20 to choose from *so ideal for pub golf*. They include the *very nice, very classy and very expensive. Pushplugs: Bar Casa, Ha Ha's, Kingston Mill (It's a Scream chain)*.
CLUBBING Oceania is a *whopping* eight-room club on the site of the old bus station. Monday and Wednesday are student nights. Otherwise, The Works (seven bars and two clubs, *renowned* R'n'B nights). Bacchus somehow *makes a dingy cellar seem like a decent venue* and Bar Eivissa plays all sorts.
MUSIC VENUES The Grey Horse has live music most nights, tickling the indie, rock, accoustic, R'n'B and alternative earbones, among others. *Useless trivia*: the Lost Prophets played one of their first gigs in Kingston.
COMEDY/CABARET The Crack Comedy club at the Grey Horse gets well-known names and unheard-of newbies on Sundays.
EATING OUT *Lots of chains. Pushplugs: Wagamama; Nando's; Blue Hawaii; Little Italy; Pizza Express; Frango*.

UNIVERSITY
- **PRICE OF A PINT OF BEER** £1.80
- **GLASS OF WINE** £2.25

BARS Bar Zen is the biggest and holds theme nights in its neon-lit, grungy interior. The *slightly more leftfield* Knight's Park bar has DJ nights, indie rock evening, events and live bands. It *somehow manages to achieve a laid-back ambience while being packed tighter than Linford Christie's shorts*. Hannafords (inside a World War Two military cinema, no less), on the Kingston Hill campus, is a community boozer and the Tolworth Court sports bar is *jocksville*, especially on a Wednesday.
THEATRES The drama course has *vamped up the thesp levels*. Kingston now sends productions to the Edinburgh Fringe and has its own studio theatre.
FILM The society *sticks up a screen whenever it finds a room spare* and shows cult classics. Hannafords relives its past with a screening every Saturday – *gas masks and ration books optional*.
MUSIC VENUES Bar Zen and Knight's Park both host live bands.

CLUBBING KUSU has sorted out a deal with Oceania and The Works for *cheap* student nights – Mondays and Wednesdays are the big boogies. Students can hop the queues and get discounted tickets.
COMEDY/CABARET Paramount Comedy network visitors crack gags twice a mont, plus Hannafords hosts a monthly Avalon laugh sesh.
FOOD Two eateries at Penrhyn Road – the *bustling* Food Store and the *cosier* Picton Room, both doing hot food and snacks. Bar Zen and Hannafords both do grub,there's a Subway sandwich bar and, if all else fails, there's the University shop.
OTHER A *glitzy* summer ball and sports ball, plus a summer fete which turns into a masquerade in the evening.

SOCIAL ()()()()()()()()()()()()()()

KINGSTON UNIVERSITY STUDENTS UNION
- **4 SABBATICALS** ● **TURNOUT AT LAST BALLOT** 6%
- **NUS MEMBER**

The left-leaning Union has recently cast aside its rebellious teenage past to get on better with the University. KUSU still want longer library opening hours, and better social and prayer space, mind. Some sabbs hot-footed it down to Westminster recently to sign a motion against top-up fees being raised further.

SU FACILITIES
The *portacabinesque* Union Building is based at Penrhyn Road and offers bars with TVs, pool tables and games machines, a travel office, bookshop, photocopying and printing. Each site has its own Union office and bar (except Roehampton Vale).

CLUBS (NON SPORTING)
Aegis; Alternative Music; Ahmadiyya Muslim; AMISOC; Bar; Believers Loveworld; Big Degrees Motorcycle; Circus & Juggling; Colours; FACT (film & cult TV); Faith Debate; Fore Crime; Hindu; International; Korean; KUALA; KUSEDS; Liberal Democrats; Living Word; Music and Design; Oriental; Oriental Sport; Register; Research; RESPECT; SKA (architecture); Sikh; Sports; Tamil; Training. **See also Clubs tables.**

OTHER ORGANISATIONS
The weekly Union-run broadsheet 'SUblime' (not bad at all) is filled with student contributions. 'STONE Radio' is *battling with bureacracy* to get itself set up. Students and staff do a *fair deal* of community work painting schools, working with kids and so on and Rag raises cash through abseils and other *(not quite so) high jinks*.

RELIGIOUS
There are a number of churches, mosques, temples and synagogues in the local area and an interdenominational prayer room provided by the

Words in italics are Push's point of view – take it or leave it...

University. For religion in London see University of London

PAID WORK see University of London
⊙ **PAID WORK** TERM-TIME 60%; HOLS 90%

There's *no need* to go job-hunting in central London when there are *plenty of opportunities* on the doorstep. Shopping centres, Union bars, Uni admin, tutoring, office temping, bar work are *all there for the taking* – the Careers Service has a list on their website, *handily*.

SPORTS

⊙ **RECENT SUCCESSES** HOCKEY, BADMINTON, ROWING, SWIMMING, TAE KWON DO, CRICKET, FENCING, BADMINTON, KARTING, TRAMPOLINING
⊙ **BUSA RANKING** 77

Excellent sporting facilities as the University runs a Talented Athlete Scheme to help top sportsmen and women compete nationally and internationally. Talented athletes get bursaries, free use of the Uni's fitness centre, free sports massage, professional office backup and 'flexible' workload – ie. *not too much of it*.

SPORTS FACILITIES
The University owns a whole lot of pitches at Tolworth Court, including ten football pitches, two hockey pitches, tennis courts, a gym at Kingston Hill; and a fitness centre with gym and aerobics studio at Penrhyn Road. Off-peak membership costs £28.25 for four months or £51.50 for a year, while the full monty is priced at £45 or £90. Also a local public leisure centre and swimming pool.

SPORTING CLUBS
American Football; Caving; Jitsu (of the Jiu variety); Karate Goju Rhu; Karate Shotokan; Motorcycle; Mountaineering. **See also Clubs tables.**

ATTRACTIONS see University of London
World class rugby at Twickenham is close by and there's racing at Sandown Park. Wimbledon for the tennis – and strawberries at a pound each – after summer exams.

ACCOMMODATION

IN UNIVERSITY
⊙ **SELF-CATERING** 20%   ⊙ **COST** £91 (40/48/50WKS)
⊙ **1ST YRS LIVING IN** 20%
⊙ **INSURANCE PREMIUM** £

AVAILABILITY Halls are *generally of a pretty decent standard*, although some are a *bit of a trek* from campus. The cost *ain't bad by London standards, but that doesn't mean it's cheap*. Clayhill Hall has had a major refurb and is no longer referred to by students as *'Clayhell'*. Middlemill Halls, near the campus, are the *most popular*. Some rooms are modified for wheelchair access. Most (70%) are en suite. A head tenancy scheme mops up any excess.
CAR PARKING *Fine* in halls, *forbidden* in Uni.

EXTERNALLY see University of London
⊙ **AVE RENT** £85   ⊙ **LIVING AT HOME** 30%

AVAILABILITY Most accommodation is to be found two miles from campus in Surbiton (*of The Good Life fame*) but many letting agents *run a mile* at the sniff of a student. Plenty of housing on the market, but *it's not cheap, either*.
HOUSING HELP The University accommodation office does *its best* to help out, with a daily vacancy list and an online student-to-student messageboard.

WELFARE

SERVICES
⊙ **LGBT OFFICER & SOCIETY** ⊙ **INTERNATIONAL STUDENTS' OFFICER** ⊙ **UNITY (ETHNIC MINORITIES) OFFICER** ⊙ **WOMEN'S OFFICER** ⊙ **DISABILITIES OFFICER** ⊙ **POSTGRAD OFFICER** ⊙ **MATURE STUDENTS' OFFICER** ⊙ **UNIVERSITY COUNSELLORS** 3 FULL/2 PART
⊙ **CRIME RATING** !!

There's a Citizens' Advice Bureau on campus that deals with all sorts of welfare issues.
HEALTH There are four GPs, a nurse and counsellors at the on-campus NHS practice, plus

K

> 'I met a girl who was going to Oxford. I said to her, "Why can't you read bloody Pride and Prejudice in the f***ing kitchen? Why do you have to go to Oxford?" No Answer.' – Jeffrey Barnard, writer and bon viveur.

Words in italics are Push's point of view — take it or leave it...

access to specialist clinics and even complementary stuff.

WOMEN Attack alarms are available for cautious types of both genders.

CRECHES/NURSERY 24 places in the nursery for kids from 2-5yrs.

DISABILITIES Disabled parking, a technical support centre and decent access in the main bulidings. There's also a dyslexia support officer.

CRIME Kingston is the first SU in the country to be designated a Third Party Reporting Site, (a place where local hate crimes can be reported). *Which doesn't mean the University is especially danger-ous, just on the ball.*

FINANCE

- **AVE DEBT PER YEAR** £3,092
- **HOME STUDENT FEES** £3,000

FEES The full £3k for all undergraduate degrees bar Nursing, Midwifery, Radiography and Physio. Foundation years cost £1,200. International under-grads are charged £8,250-£9,350 and international postgrads £1,100 to £7,475. UK postgrads cough up £4,320-£7,200. *Not literally, of course. That would be a medical miracle.*

SUPPORT Students eligible for a government maintenance grant also qualify for a bursary of at least £300. Hardship loans are available and there's an access fund.

▶ KINGSTON POLYTECHNIC

see *Kingston University*

LA SAINTE UNION
see *University of Southampton*

LAMPETER UNIVERSITY OF WALES

LANCASHIRE POLYTECHNIC
see *University of Central Lancashire*

LANCASTER UNIVERSITY

LEEDS UNIVERSITY

LEEDS METROPOLITAN UNIVERSITY

LEEDS POLYTECHNIC
see *Leeds Metropolitan University*

LEICESTER UNIVERSITY

UNIVERSITY OF LINCOLN

LINCOLN SCHOOL OF ART AND DESIGN
see *University of Lincoln*

LINCOLNSHIRE SCHOOL OF AGRICULTURE
see *University of Lincoln*

UNIVERSITY OF LIVERPOOL

LIVERPOOL HOPE UNIVERSITY

LIVERPOOL HOPE UNIVERSITY COLLEGE
see *Liverpool Hope University*

LIVERPOOL INSTITUTE OF HIGHER EDUCATION (LIHE)
see *Liverpool Hope University*

LIVERPOOL JOHN MOORES UNIVERSITY

LIVERPOOL POLYTECHNIC
see *Liverpool John Moores University*

LONDON HOSPITAL MEDICAL COLLEGE
see *Queen Mary, University of London*

UNIVERSITY OF LONDON

LONDON METROPOLITAN UNIVERSITY

LONDON SOUTH BANK UNIVERSITY

LONDON COLLEGE OF COMMUNICATION
see *University of the Arts, London*

LONDON COLLEGE OF FASHION
see *University of the Arts, London*

LONDON COLLEGE OF PRINTING
see *University of the Arts, London*

LONDON GUILDHALL UNIVERSITY
see *London Metropolitan University*

LONDON SCHOOL OF ECONOMICS
see *LSE*

LONDON SCHOOL OF MEDICINE AND DENTISTRY
see *Queen Mary, University of London*

LOUGHBOROUGH UNIVERSITY

LSE

UNIVERSITY OF LUTON

LUTON COLLEGE OF HIGHER EDUCATION
see *University of Luton*

L

▶ **LA SAINTE UNION**
see *University of Southampton*

LAMPETER, UNIVERSITY OF WALES

FORMERLY ST DAVID'S COLLEGE
PART OF THE UNIVERSITY OF WALES

◉ **UNIVERSITY OF WALES, LAMPETER** Lampeter, Ceredigion, SA48 7ED **TEL** (01570) 422 351 **E−MAIL** recruit@lamp.ac.uk
WEBSITE www.lamp.ac.uk ◉ **UNIVERSITY OF WALES, LAMPETER, STUDENTS' UNION** Lampeter, Ceredigion, SA48 7ED **TEL**
(01570) 422 619 **E−MAIL** ents@lamp.ac.uk **WEBSITE** www.lamp.ac.uk/su
www.lamp.ac.uk/su

GENERAL 🌙🌙🌙🌙🌙🌙🌙🌙🌙🌙🌙

Deep in the hills of south-west Wales, where valleys and leylines meet, is the *tiny* market town of Lampeter. In this virtual village, *around the corner from nowhere, is the correspondingly* small University – the oldest degree-awarding institution in Wales and the third oldest in Britain. Modelled on an Oxbridge college, *its elegant stone buildings, which engulf the town, are quietly impressive, with none of the pomp and grandeur of their Oxbridge counterparts. For the wiccans of the world, the whole area is a channelling point for mystical energy. Beyond the borders of the town are the beautiful, rugged hills from which Stonehenge was cut – then lugged 300-odd miles for some twisted, druidic reason. The red kite soars above the valleys and, around the coast, dolphins frolic. Aw.*

👤👤👤👤👤👤👤👤👤👤👤👤👤👤👤👤👤👤

SEX RATIO: ♀39 ♂61	FOUNDED: 1822
FULL−TIME U'GRADS: 829	PART−TIME: 118
POSTGRADS: 503	NON−DEGREE: 27
AVE COURSE: 3YRS	ETHNIC: 13%
STATE:PRIVATE SCHOOL: 60:40	FLUNK RATE: 23%
MATURE: 37%	INTERNATIONAL: 11%
DISABLED: 105	LOCAL: 8%

◎ **Lampeter University's Archaeology and Anthropology Department offers an MA in Death Studies.**

ATMOSPHERE
Lampeter has one of the smallest campuses in Britain and can be a very quiet place when students are buried in the bar/library. The student body is a mixture of sensible country folk and happy hippies who manage to perk things up in a laid back sort of way. Staff/student closeness is one of the plus points and social and academic life combine in a strong sense of community where it's well-nigh impossible not to know everyone else. Because of the size of the town and the age of the University, locals are more of a clique than the dominant community and relations are friendly as a result.

Some, particularly those who've woken up here after clearing, can find the remoteness tricky to adjust to, but doing a degree here is not entirely unlike spending three years in the chillout tent at Glastonbury – with all the ancient spookiness both places share. Hauntings and possessions have been reported, but then there are lots of mushrooms growing on them there hills.

LAMPETER
◉ **POPULATION** 3,000 ◉ **TOWN CENTRE** 0 MILES
◉ **LONDON** 220 MILES ◉ **CARMARTHEN** 23 MILES
◉ **ABERYSTWYTH** 27 MILES
◉ **HIGH TEMP** 18 ◉ **LOW TEMP** 2 ◉ **RAINFALL** 71
To call Lampeter a town would be *stretching things* – it's got about 20 shops, a pub for each night of the week *and that's it. Lampeter has a remote and forgotten feel to it, as though it's been hidden away from the world.* There's no station – the nearest is in Carmarthen which is about three times the size, relatively good for shopping but still a far cry from a buzzing metropolis. Students head to Aberystwyth for the *comparatively* big noise. *The local area is dripping with history, natural beauty, award-winning organic food and sheep.* There's a Roman goldmine; plenty of ruins; Talley Abbey; Pembrokeshire National Park; the National Botanical Garden of Wales, Aberglasney; and the famous Devil's Bridge. For those into literary research, Lampeter town and campus got a significant (and somewhat satirical) mention in Malcolm Pryce's novel 'Last Tango in Aberystwyth'.

Words in italics are Push's point of view — take it or leave it...

TRAVEL

TRAINS From Carmarthen you can get mainline trains to London (from £35.65 return), Cardiff (£11.55) and Birmingham (£27.60). Aberystwyth station is better for northbound journeys.

COACHES Traws Cambria buses make the three-hour chug to Cardiff (£11) twice daily. Connections also to Camarthen and Aberystwyth.

CAR *A car – or failing that, a rocket pack – makes a big difference to the quality of life. Daytrips and shopping become feasible for a start.* 18 miles off the A40.

AIR Cardiff International or Birmingham are the closest – *which is to say they're both several inconvenient hours away.*

HITCHING *Without any major roads, it ain't easy. Allow a day to get anywhere and take a sleeping bag just in case. To make things a little easier – bring a car with you too.*

LOCAL The buses stick to the timetables, hourly till about 5.30pm. It's £2.65 return to Carmarthen with a similar service to Aberystwyth (£3.40).

UNIVERSITY Occasionally organises trips to Swansea, Cardiff and Aberystwyth.

TAXIS *Sure, there are taxis, but frankly, students can't afford them – about £20 to Carmarthen. Maybe worth it to have a night out in town if sharing the ride back.*

BICYCLES There are sheds, not too many hills and virtually no theft, *but without motorised legs, most places are out of cycle reach.*

CAREER PROSPECTS

◉ **CAREERS SERVICE** ◉ **NO. OF STAFF** 4 FULL
◉ **UNEMPLOYED AFTER 6**MTHS 9%

The Employability Unit is a job centre and career guidance facility, sending newsletters, sorting out job fairs, distributing all sorts of useful booklets and giving interview practice.

FAMOUS ALUMNI

Juliet Foster (Sky News); Jack Higgins (thriller writer); Adrian Mourby (Head of Drama, BBC Wales); Sulak Sivaraksa (Thai human rights campaigner); Rebecca Wheatley (Casualty actress).

SPECIAL FEATURES

Single honours degrees may be started in January as well as the more usual late September. Super keen beans can also complete modules during the summer, meaning a degree could be whizzed through in less than three years.

FURTHER INFO

◉ **PROSPECTUSES** UNDERGRAD; POSTGRAD; SOME DEPARTMENTS; ALTERNATIVE
◉ **OPEN DAYS**

There's an online overseas guide offering practical information for international students, as well as a mature students' guide, both via the main website. Lampeter attracts a large number of long distance learners – *understandable since it's such an effort to actually get there.* E-mail the SU for alternative info.

ACADEMIC ◉◉◉◉◉◉◉◉◉◉◉

Lampeter specialises in Arts, Humanities and Social Sciences. *Its small size means that seminars and tutorials can be intimate affairs and students have a clearer vision of the academic staff as actual people rather than talking books.* With no science subjects to complicate the schedules, all students can expect between 10-20 contact hours per week, less in the third year. The modular credit-based system is flexible, so units from other department can also be studied.

ENTRY POINTS: 160–260	**AVE POINTS:** 200
APPLICATIONS PER PLACE: 4	**CLEARING:** 2%
NO. OF TERMS: 3	**LENGTH OF TERMS:** 11/8WKS
STAFF TO STUDENT RATIO: 1:8	**STUDY ADDICTS:** 27%
TEACHING: ✭✭✭✭	**RESEARCH:** ✭✭✭
YEAR ABROAD: 3%	**SANDWICH STUDENTS:** 0
1STS: 7%	**2.2S:** 34%
2.1S: 52%	**3RDS:** 7%

ADMISSIONS

◉ **APPLY VIA UCAS**

Lampeter has a good record for widening access and considers applications on individual merits.

SUBJECTS

ARTS/HUMANITIES 91% **BUSINESS** 9%
UNUSUAL Australian Studies; Chinese Studies; English with Creative Writing; Islamic Studies.

LIBRARIES

◉ **230,000 BOOKS** ◉ **200 STUDY PLACES**

Two libraries: the Founder's (22,000 historical books, documents and manuscripts) and the Main Library. *Both adhere to slightly archaic hours, closing early at weekends and blink-and- you'll-miss-it opening on Sundays.*

COMPUTERS

◉ **200 WORKSTATIONS** ◉ **24-HR ACCESS**

Five labs, including one in the Main Library. There's a Mac lab for Apple lovers, and every room on campus is wired up to the interweb.

OTHER LEARNING FACILITIES

The *ultra-sexy* Media Centre is open 9-5 and has a range of facilities, including a film and TV studio, video editing/conferencing suite, digital printing and scanning, subtitling, digital camera and web streaming equipment – all for free.

ENTERTAINMENT ◉◉◉◉◉◉◉◉◉◉

LAMPETER

◉ **PRICE OF A PINT OF BEER** £2.20
◉ **GLASS OF WINE** £2 ◉ **CAN OF RED BULL** £1.80

It's a tiny place, but it's got all the basics and one or two unexpected luxuries. Boredom isn't much of a problem – there's enough to do to keep all but the most fundamentalist clubthumper amused. With no need for taxis, nights out come in cheap.

THEATRES Theatr Felinfach: theatr fach fywiog yn werth ymweld a hi. *If you don't understand that, don't bother.*

CINEMAS *Um, there's a huge DVD and video shop. Does that count?*

PUBS 14 pubs within a 1.5 mile radius, *of which the most popular are the Black Lion (attractive and fun) and the Cwmanne Tavern (cheaper, friendly and sociable) There are no 'locals-only' haunts, but best leave your sheep jokes at home.*

MUSIC VENUES Local and student bands play at some pubs, such as the Cwmanne Tavern.

CLUBBING The Quarry stays open late and holds student night on Thursdays.

EATING OUT There are a few eateries and plenty of cosy cafés. *The Ram Inn's food is tasty, cheap and big. Pushplugs: Shapla Tandori (Indian); Nehar (Indian takeaway); Mama Mia(kebab house; good pizza); Lloyds Fish & Chips.*

UNIVERSITY

○ **PRICE OF A PINT OF BEER** £1.80
○ **GLASS OF WINE** £1.80
○ **CAN OF RED BULL** £1.50

BARS *Students and staff mix in the Old Bar, which has a late licence when it needs one and holds regular karaoke, music and talent events. The Extension acts as bar-cum-club.* There's also a small but cosy Refectory Bar in the Uni.

THEATRES The Arts Hall's a multimedia performance venue, *which means it's essentially a large room with no specialist equipment.* The drama society puts two or three plays on a year.

FILM The Arts Hall or a lecture theatre becomes a cinema for five or six films a week. There are three different film societies so the schedule is wildly varied from Disney to Polanski to George A Romero. Screenings are free during the week, and cheap as chips at the weekend.

MUSIC VENUES The Extension reaches places the Arts Hall can't, with regular open mic nights *and the odd appearance by local or little-known artists.* There are also classical music events.

CLUBBING Regular nights at The Extension keep students up past their bedtime. DJ Yoda, Cantalop, Annie Mac and Fabio & Grooverider have performed.

FOOD The Refectory offers basic school dinnery stuff, but the portions are generous. Pooh's Corner and the Pizza Bar in the SU are more likely to tempt jaded palates. The shop offers *the three nutritional staples*: the pasty, the sandwich and the packet of crisps.

OTHER The President's Ball has been *a typical marquee job (big name + bar + dance tent x alcohol = wasted)*, but is set to include a bit more family-friendly fun as lots of parents and siblings come along for the ride.

LAMPETER, UNIVERSITY OF WALES, STUDENTS' UNION

○ **3 SABBATICALS** ○ **TURNOUT AT LAST BALLOT** 35%
○ **NUS MEMBER**

The small size of the University makes it hard to escape SU involvement and societies flourish. *Party politics doesn't often go beyond discussions on the ethical status of Twiglets: the Union Exec prides itself on being completely unbiased and there's an overall feeling of tolerance and liberalism. The Vice Chancellor has a pro-student stance, so relations with the authorities are harmonious.*

SU FACILITIES

The Union building has a bar; cafeteria; restaurant; advice centre; printing and photocopying; payphones; general shop; pool tables; juke box; TV room; function room; bookshop; gaming and vending machines and minibus hire. The Union Extension provides a dance floor, bar, nightclub facilities and a conference suite.

CLUBS (NON-SPORTING)

Anime; Archaeology; Arts & Crafts; Battle; Board Games; Buddhist; Chinese; Circus; Geek; Lampeter Organic Garden; Masquerade; NurfSoc (Neighbours and surfing); Pagan; Patrick McGoohan Appreciation; Pudding; Rock; Role Play; Punk; Underground Music; Video Games; Warhammer. **See also Clubs tables.**

OTHER ORGANISATIONS

'1822' is the University's satirical magazine, four times a term. Rag organises the *customary three-legged pub-crawl.*

RELIGIOUS

○ **1 CHAPLAIN (COFE)**

There's a *dinky little* chapel, a mosque and a Buddhist prayer room. *The pagan society's adventures take them off into the woods. Other faiths will have further to travel.*

PAID WORK

○ **JOB BUREAU**

The Employability Unit helps find local vacancies. Some jobs are up for grabs in the Union and the bar. Local pub and shop work isn't out of the question but besides that and the organic food packing centre, there's not a lot about.

L

SPORTS 🌙🌙🌙🌙🌙🌙🌙🌙🌙🌙🌙🌙🌙

◉ RECENT SUCCESSES RUGBY **◉ BUSA RANKING** 122
Lampeter's the oldest rugby-playing institution in Wales. Considering it's such a weeny place, sporting success is surprisingly frequent but the emphasis is on fun and the attitude is encouraging to all.

SPORTS FACILITIES
There's a *stark* modern sports hall, five acres of playing fields, squash and tennis courts, basketball/netball court; swimming pool, multigym (£13/term). *The river (Afon Teifi) is useful for some sports but not large enough for any aquatic Olympics.* Around town, there's a golf course and pony trekking and the mountains are excellent for rambling, climbing, hang-gliding *and getting cold.* Students can use the town swimming pool gratis at certain times.

SPORTING CLUBS
Extreme Frisbee; Hiking; Jitsu; Kung Fu & Tai Chi; Rock Climbing. **See also Clubs tables.**

ACCOMMODATION 🌙🌙🌙🌙🌙🌙🌙🌙🌙

IN COLLEGE
◉ SELF-CATERING 61% **◉ COST** £50 (37WKS)
◉ 1ST YRS LIVING IN 85% **◉ 2ND YRS LIVING IN** 65%
◉ FINALISTS YEARS LIVING IN 75%
◉ POSTGRADS LIVING IN 35% **◉ INSURANCE PREMIUM** £
AVAILABILITY The majority of undergrads live in, first years are guaranteed accommodation and about half who live in have en suite facilities. All accommodation is on campus and *no one gets turfed out when it comes to vacation – which is popular with finalists.* Those who live in for three years get a 10% rent discount in the second and third year. Kitchens are shared with 4-7 others and every room has a network connection.*There are a few dodgy digs and damp is a problem but most students swallow their pride and are content with the basics.* Mixed-sex couples are accommodated as are those sharing, with twin beds, larger rooms and a reduction (a tenner per person per week). There are all-night porters *but that's more of a token gesture than a security measure as crime in halls is uncommon to say the least.*
CAR PARKING Not a problem.

EXTERNALLY
• AVE RENT £45 **• LIVING AT HOME** 6%
AVAILABILITY There's plenty of accommodation within walking distance of campus and, given the miniature size of the place, live-outers can almost feel as though they're still in halls.

WELFARE 🌙🌙🌙🌙🌙🌙🌙🌙🌙🌙🌙

SERVICES
◉ LGBT OFFICER & SOCIETY ◉ WOMEN'S OFFICER & SOCIETY ◉ INTERNATIONAL STUDENTS' OFFICER & SOCIETY ◉ DISABILITIES OFFICER & SOCIETY ◉ NIGHTLINE ◉ COLLEGE COUNSELLORS 1 FULL/4 PART **◉ CRIME RATING:** !
HEALTH The University shares the town GP service which has four doctors and a nurse.
WOMEN Free attack alarms and a walk-home service from chivalrous security staff.
CRECHES/NURSERY 30 places for kids between newborn (ish) and 5yrs. There's a playscheme during vacations.
DISABILITIES *The age of the buildings can present some access problems but the campus itself is compact and largely doable.* Plans are in place to make things better. Ramps, hearing loops and adapted accommodation all feature.
CRIME *Lowest in the UK, so the police say.*
DRUGS *Arts & Humanities students, mushrooms growing locally – go figure.* The University has a zero tolerance policy *and a few blind spots.*

FINANCE
◉ AVE DEBT PER YEAR £2,448 **◉ HOME STUDENT FEES** £3,000
FEES International undergrads are looking at £8,040, postgrads at £3,200. It'll be 2007 before top-up fees hit, *but the Union is steadily mounting a strong defence.*
◉ ACCESS FUND £175,000 **◉ SUCCESSFUL APPLICATIONS/YR** 400 **◉ AVE PAYMENT** £500
SUPPORT University scholarships are worth £500 and departmental ones £1,000, plus a *flurry* of other awards and buraries.

L

▸ LANCASHIRE POLYTECHNIC
see *University of Central Lancashire*

LANCASTER UNIVERSITY

○ **LANCASTER UNIVERSITY** Bailrigg, Lancaster, LA1 4YW **TEL** (01524) 65201 **E-MAIL** ugadmissions@lancs.ac.uk
WEBSITE www.lancs.ac.uk ○ **LANCASTER UNIVERSITY STUDENTS' UNION** Bailrigg, Lancaster, LA1 4YW **TEL** (01524) 593 765
WEBSITE www.lusu.co.uk

GENERAL ○○○○○○○○○○○○

A few miles south of the *lovely Lake District*, the county town of Lancaster dates from Roman days *and still has plenty of honey-coloured Georgian buildings left to show off at parties*. Flanked by countryside in most directions, with *lumpy Cumbria beckoning to the north*, it reaches out to Morecambe and Heysham four miles away on the north-west coast, as well as to the treeless Forest of Bowland – *starter for ten: 'forest' means crown property for hunting, trees are an added feature*. Two miles from the city centre and perched on a hill, the University of Lancaster is comprised of nine colleges that form the large Greenfield campus. Many of the 60s buildings are *beginning to look uglier than Pete Burns without his makeup* but the University has forked out *squillions* on a number of redevelopments and extensions. The campus centre is Alexandra Square, a large paved area surrounded by light brick buildings and filled with students walking, chatting, working, sleeping and putting up posters. Circling the campus 250 acres of landscaped woods, parklands and fields provide a *serene* rural backdrop to the college buildings and the *bustling* University atmosphere.

SEX RATIO: ♂47 ♀53	**FOUNDED:** 1964
FULL-TIME U'GRADS: 8,216	**PART-TIME:** 42
POSTGRADS: 2,834	**NON-DEGREE:** 1,447
AVE COURSE: 3YRS	**ETHNIC:** 16%
STATE:PRIVATE SCHOOL: 91:9	**FLUNK RATE:** 5%
MATURE: 8%	**INTERNATIONAL:** 24%
DISABLED: 185	**LOCAL:** 12%

ATMOSPHERE

The most pronounced influence on the University's atmosphere is the collegiate system (although nowhere near the extent of Oxbridge) which gives a 'community within a community' air. Although the colleges are little more than glorified halls of residence, most teaching is college-orientated and the social life tends to hang itself around college bars. The colleges themselves don't conduct admissions, although students can express a preference when applying – not that there's that much to prefer since the only obvious difference is in size, varying between 750 and 1,350-odd students. There's a varied crowd, with all sorts of different backgrounds mingling nicely and an ethnically-mixed bag including Chinese and Asian communities. Despite the lack of a major ents venue on site, students are happy to keep the fun on campus, with the occasional jaunt into town for big nights out. Having said that, the work ethic's keener than Anne Diamond in a sweetshop, and you'll find few slackers. The town-gown relationship is good, but it's less rosy the further past the train station that you get.

LANCASTER

○ **POPULATION** 133,914 ○ **CITY CENTRE** 2.5 MILES
○ **LONDON** 250 MILES ○ **PRESTON** 26 MILES
○ **MANCHESTER** 48 MILES
○ **HIGH TEMP** 19 ○ **LOW TEMP** 1 ○ **RAINFALL** 71

Lancaster's a rather sweet and quaint city, with tourist-fuls of history oozing down its winding little streets. The Ashton memorial dominates the skyline on one hill while the castle and the priory gaze down from another. The castle's dual function as tourist attraction and prison neatly mirrors the atmosphere of the city and its people: ancient architecture and English-rose beauty compete with a whiff of small-town bigotry and a fashion sense reliant on baseball caps and excessive gold jewellery. Lancaster has the usual deck of amenities: supermarkets, late-opening shops, bookstores and libraries, as well as the Maritime Museum. The new student complex *is good for frittering away student loans.* Manchester's nearby *for city hi-jinks*, as is the Lake District *for wandering lonely as a cloud. And everyone goes to Morecambe, a miniature version of the fabulously tacky, coin-slot heaven that is Blackpool (also relatively close).*

TRAVEL

TRAINS Lancaster station, three miles from the campus (around 45mins walk away), has direct connections to London (from £20.50 return), Manchester (£9.40), Birmingham (£30.70) and other places, *some nice, some nasty. So it goes.*
COACHES *The considerate people at* National Express have plonked a coach stop on the campus with passing routes to a number of major cities – *dangerously tempting after a tankard or eight.*
CAR The M6 bypasses Lancaster from north to south, slicing past the edge of the campus. The A6 and A683 go right into the centre. *Parking's okay, though the University isn't keen on students having cars and buses are very accessible.*
AIR Manchester Airport 50 miles away has most major budget airlines.
HITCHING *There's a special shelter on campus and an established point in town for pick-ups for trips to and from the University although most students don't use it since the University and the Union have been telling hitching horror stories. For longer journeys the M6 is a good option. There are also offers of lifts and car-pooling on notice boards.*
LOCAL There's a big bus stop right in the middle of the campus. Trips into town are £1.10 (sgl) and

£1.75 (rtn), although students can fork out £120 for a yearly pass. *Check online first, though: there are discounts aplenty lurking in cyberspace.*

TAXIS *Taxis tend towards the wallet-emptying*: £6 between town and the campus. *Pre-booking with one of the local firms is advisable – flagging them down is a bad idea.*

BICYCLES There's a cycle path running from the campus to the city centre and Morecambe. *Hills are good for you, apparently, so the students are in luck there.*

CAREER PROSPECTS

○ CAREERS SERVICE ○ NO. OF STAFF 8 FULL/7 PART
○ UNEMPLOYED AFTER 6MTHS 6%

Five careers advisors (one part-time) can advise how to score a job as Wayne Rooney's personal massage therapist and the like. Vacancy newsletters, a library, interview training and job fairs. The online resources at http://careers.lancs.ac.uk are *pretty damn comprehensive.*

FAMOUS ALUMNI

Richard Allinson (DJ); Anna Lawson (actor); Oly Marsden (skier); Alan Milburn MP (Lab); Jason Queally (Olympic cycling gold medallist); Andy Serkis (the face and voice behind Gollum, and the 'man behind the monkey' behind King Kong); Simon Smith (rugby player); Gary Waller MP (Tory); Peter Whalley and Marvin Close (Coronation Street writers).

SPECIAL FEATURES

Infolab 21 – not a secret Government alien-probing pod but a £15m communication and IT centre. It looks like *a gigantic lego brick*, but it's packed to the gills with research expertise, training and skills-learning facilities and, er, 'business incubation'.

The new Lancaster Environment Centre will house the largest group of environmental scientists in Europe. *The Guinness Book of Records has yet to show interest.*

FURTHER INFO

○ PROSPECTUSES UNDERGRAD; POSTGRAD; ALTERNATIVE; VIDEO
○ OPEN DAYS

Two open days a year, plus conducted campus visits on the 1st and 3rd Wednesday of every month. Places can be booked by phoning up or completing the form in the prospectus. The relevant dates for your diary can be found at www.lancs.ac.uk/depts/schools/visit.htm

ACADEMIC ○○○○○○○○○○○○○

○ 1994 GROUP

Undergraduate teaching at Lancaster has reaped an award or two and its sociology, statistics and management departments *have a few feathers stuffed* in their research caps. The first year

doesn't usually count in final marks (but you have to pass it to continue) and uses a 'tripos' system, meaning you read a major and two minor subjects. So second year students can *transfer to a completely different course than the one they applied for, if they so desire.* Workloads vary – *around 14 contact hours a week for your common-or-garden scientist, far fewer for the lesser-spotted postgrad.* The Management School's £9.5m extension has bestowed a *lucrative* Leadership Centre, an entrepreneurial institute working with regional businesses.

ENTRY POINTS: 260-360	AVE POINTS: 293
APPLICATIONS PER PLACE: 6	CLEARING: 9%
NO. OF TERMS: 3	LENGTH OF TERMS: 10WKS
STAFF TO STUDENT RATIO: 1:15	STUDY ADDICTS: 25%
TEACHING: ✶✶✶✶✶	RESEARCH: ✶✶✶✶✶
YEAR ABROAD: 9%	SANDWICH STUDENTS: 7%
1STS: 12%	2.2S: 29%
2.1S: 53%	3RDS: 5%

ADMISSIONS

○ APPLY VIA UCAS

Lancaster *likes* mature students, who need a minimum of two A levels or equivalent to apply.

SUBJECTS

ARTS & SOCIAL SCIENCES 51%   **COMBINED STUDIES** 5%
MANAGEMENT SCHOOL 23%
SCIENCE & TECHNOLOGY 27%   **SOCIAL SCIENCES** 24%
BEST Applied Social Science; Art; Biology; Computer Science; Economics; Educational Research; General Engineering; English Language & Literature; Environmental Studies; European Languages & Culture; French; Geography; History; Italian; Law; Linguistics; Management School; Music; Philosophy; Physics; Politics & International Relations; Psychology; Pure Mathematics; Religious Studies; Statistics & Applied Statistics; Sociology (incorporating Women's Studies); Spanish; Theatre Studies.
UNUSUAL Operations, Work & Technology *(the psychological and philosophical side of marketing. In other words, advanced studies in parting a fool and his cash).*

LIBRARIES

○ 1,000,000 BOOKS **○ 900** STUDY PLACES
○ SPEND PER STUDENT ££

The University Library (open 8am-midnight) at the centre of the campus contains audio and visual playback equipment, 140 PC workstations, microfilm reading and a rare books room. And books of course. The Ruskin Library has an *extensive* collection of books, letters and manuscripts centred around Pre-Raphaelite art critic *and priggish paedophile,* John Ruskin.

COMPUTERS

○ 1,500 WORKSTATIONS **○ 24-**HR ACCESS

24 computer labs around campus, the largest being in the main library. Students get their mitts on some *respectable kit,* including a *wide variety* of course-specific software.

OTHER LEARNING FACILITIES

Lancaster has rehearsal rooms, drama studio, language labs, practice courtroom, design lab and a TV centre with digital video editing suite.

ENTERTAINMENT ◗◖◗◖◗◖◗◖◗◖◗◖

THE CITY

- ◉ **PRICE OF A PINT OF BEER** £1.80
- ◉ **GLASS OF WINE** £2 ◉ **CAN OF RED BULL** £2.30

CINEMAS The two-screen Regal oozes character from its old bones and does student discounts (£3 tix). The Dukes is home to arty-farty flicks and theatre, while Morecambe's ten-screen is a 20-min bus ride away for blockbuster action.

THEATRES The Dukes covers the touring circuit as well as open-air 'Promenade plays' (there's no stage – the audience follows the action around the grounds) at the stunning Williamson Park every summer.

PUBS *Chain bars are springing up like chicken pox in Lancaster, as in most cities,* but there are still loads of traditional real ale pubs in the city. *Pushplugs: Wetherspoons; Red; Walkabout; Scream; Varsity and Keystone's (sport).*

CLUBBING The Sugarhouse is the main venue – owned and run by the SU but situated in the city centre – and it draws in the bigger gigs. Liquid has 'Monday Madness' – £2.50 entry *for your fill of Dairylea 'n' dance.* The Carleton *out-cheeses them all, though,* and does disco (Wed) and rock (Fri).

MUSIC VENUES Loads of pubs stage live music, so cheap tunes are easy to come by.

EATING OUT *Not a vast selection, but all bar the pickiest palates will be satisfied. Pushplugs: Nawaab Tandoori (excellent value balti); Sultan's (Indian, in a converted church); Paulo Gianni's (Italian, student discounts); Whaletale Café (veggie); Marco's; Icky's; Bodrums.*

UNIVERSITY

- ◉ **PRICE OF A PINT OF BEER** £1.75
- ◉ **GLASS OF WINE** £1.70
- ◉ **CAN OF RED BULL** £1.80

BARS Each college has a bar, *popular* with its own students. Cross-fertilisation only usually happens when there's an event on somewhere or students play 'Bar Golf' (a pint in each college bar in turn, doubling back for an 18-hole course). Lonsdale's new bar is *chic and minimalist,* while County's is *sociable and popular.* Grad bar is *most* like a traditional pub, with real-ale and live bands.

THEATRES There's the purpose-built Nuffield, *but drama's not to die for here.* A couple of plays are performed each term.

FILM Recent blockbusters and more are shown five times a week by *one of the biggest and best-equipped student film clubs in the country* (admission £2, free to society members).

MUSIC VENUES *The Sugarhouse rules:* The Coral and The Music have been lured in for Union ents. *Trying to prove postgrads still know how to swing their pants,* Graduate Bar hosts 'Gradstock' (geddit?). The uni's Great Hall stages concerts, discos, balls etc.

CLUBBING The Sugarhouse again: Wednesdays (9pm-2am) and Saturdays (9pm-3am). *For those opposed to leaving home to get their groove on* there are two clubs on-campus. Hussle is half retro club, half pub while Lounge always has the *obligatory* dance floor and the occasional *very welcome* free entry.

COMEDY/CABARET *Laugh-a-minute* every fortnight in the Sugarhouse, thanks on a Thursday to the Comedy Network. Rob Deering, Al Pitcher and Russell Howard have all done a stint behind the mike.

FOOD Most colleges provide snackage in some form. Fylde's coffee bar is *popular with study groups* but County's is *said to be the best place to grab a bite on campus.* The Venue coffee shop is *nicey but pricey.* There's also Baker House Farm (food court), Café 21, Wibbly Wobbly Burger (*er,* burgers), Wong's Kitchen (Chinese), Spice Hut (Indian). Diggles, Mamma Mia and Pizzeria satisfy the craving for melted cheese and hot bread. 'Cause cheese on toast don't do, apparently.

OTHER Two or three balls a year, including Graduation.

SOCIAL ◗◖◗◖◗◖◗◖◗◖◗◖◗◖

LANCASTER UNIVERSITY STUDENTS' UNION

- ◉ **6 SABBATICALS** ◉ **TURNOUT AT LAST BALLOT** 27%
- ◉ **NUS MEMBER**

LUSU *runs its empire* from Edward Roberts Court *and is pretty encompassing in its outlook.* Representation, ents and services are also provided on a college level through Junior Common Rooms (JCRs). *Students here are more politically aware than some we could mention with JCRs getting involved in Uni decisions.* Recent actions include pressing for more space for sports and societies.

SU FACILITIES

Nine college bars; Sugarhouse venue; cafeteria; snack bars; pool tables; meeting rooms; Barclays and HSBC ATMs; photocopiers; printing service; payphones; advice centre; travel agent; new bookshop. Also around the campus there are banks, a post office, petrol station, bookshops (new and secondhand), hairdresser, chemist, newsagent, supermarket, bakery, ticket agency and a few smaller shops.

CLUBS (NON-SPORTING)

Buddhist; Chinese; Finnish; Jugglers; Motoring; Poetry; United Nations Association. *See also Clubs tables.*

OTHER ORGANISATIONS

'SCAN' (Student Comment & News) is the free fortnightly *Union-issue toilet roll*. 'Bailrigg FM' keeps going 24-hrs a day, broadcasting on 87.7FM and online. *Rag pimps its ass for charity, and does it well* - they raised over £10,000 last year, and even have their own mag. LUVU is a voluntary group that works in the local community.

RELIGIOUS

◉ 3 CHAPLAINS (COFE, RC, METHODIST)
Two chapels (Anglican and Roman Catholic) as well as rooms for the Jewish community with a Kosher kitchen. There's a non-denominational Chaplaincy Centre on campus, which hosts visits from ministers of most religions, and a Muslim prayer room. There are various places of worship in town, including a number of different churches and a mosque.

PAID WORK

◉ JOB BUREAU ◉ PAID WORK: TERM-TIME: 25%; HOLS: 70%
The job bureau helps find extra cash *for penny-chews and Panini stickers*, and local shops and bars have openings during the tourist seasons, *but generally speaking, there's not much on offer.*

SPORTS ◖◗◖◗◖◗◖◗◖◗◖◗◖◗◖◗

◉ BUSA RANKING 69
Friendly but fierce college rivalries emerge in tussles for the Carter Shield. When they gang up to take on other universities... well, they lose. They do have a good record of snatching the annual Roses Cup from the hands of <u>York University</u> *however, so all is not lost.*

SPORTS FACILITIES

18 acres of playing fields *(which allegedly provide a fine harvest of magic mushrooms in season)*; all-weather pitches (including two astro-turf); sports hall; eight tennis and eight squash courts; croquet lawn; bowling green; 25m swimming pool; climbing wall; multigym; sauna and solarium; gym; weights rooms (male and female); dance studio; athletics area; golf practice area; archery range; floodlit hard playing area; and the University's Lake Carter. Locally, a golf course and the River Lune (where the University has a boat house). The Sailing Club uses the Glasson Dock marina.

SPORTING CLUBS

American Football; Korfball; Lacrosse; Riding; Rowing.; Snowboarding; Table Tennis. **See also Clubs tables.**

ACCOMMODATION ◖◗◖◗◖◗◖◗◖◗◖◗◖◗◖◗◖◗

IN UNIVERSITY

◉ SELF-CATERING 57% **◉ COST** £71 (33/40WKS)
◉ 1ST YRS LIVING IN 95% **◉ INSURANCE PREMIUM** £
AVAILABILITY All first years get rooms if Lancaster's their first choice. Students returning from sandwich placements or years abroad get accommodation guaranteed as well, but second years are largely out on their own. Lancaster's colleges use self-catering halls (single rooms, some en suite, with shared kitchen) and a number of furnished houses as part of their head tenancy scheme. *Porters keep a close eye on things overnight.* Some colleges have single-sex floors and flats whilst couples can *get down to it* in some of the flatlets and twin rooms available. 'Cos of the college thang, students in halls have access to bars, study areas, games rooms and TV lounges. *Heaps of* recent re-development means *scores of* new places to lay one's head – Cartmel and Lonsdale are newly buffed and polished, while Fylde and Furness are currently being spruced. Rents are reasonable and include bills. They don't include vacations though.
CAR PARKING *Limited* free parking 5-10 mins from the colleges. *Even more limited permit parking nearer*, but first years aren't allowed to bring cars. Bike parking's *easy* all over campus, though.

EXTERNALLY

◉ AVE RENT £48 **◉ LIVING AT HOME** 3%
AVAILABILITY Living costs in Lancaster are at the lower end, so students can afford to shop around for a decent pad. *Places are fairly easy to find – Bowerham is the most convenient, but Galgate, Dale Street and Blade Street are worth considering. Skerton is to be avoided, no questions asked.*
HOUSING HELP The Union runs a house-finding service, backed up by the University Accommodation Office. They post vacancies, keep a list of accredited landlords *and make sure that money-grabbing opportunists with outhouses for rent don't get a look in.*

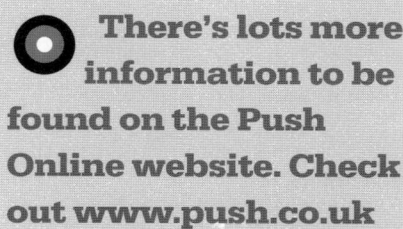

There's lots more information to be found on the Push Online website. Check out www.push.co.uk

---

Words in italics are Push's point of view — take it or leave it...

WELFARE ⓤⓤⓤⓤⓤⓤⓤⓤⓤⓤⓤⓤ

SERVICES

◉ LGBT SOCIETY ◉ WOMEN'S OFFICER ◉ MATURE STUDENTS' ASSOCIATION ◉ INTERNATIONAL STUDENTS' SOCIETY ◉ LATE–NIGHT WOMEN'S MINIBUS ◉ NIGHTLINE ◉ COLLEGE COUNSELLORS 7 FULL/2 PART ◉ SU COUNSELLORS 1 FULL ◉ CRIME RATING !!

LUSU's Welfare Officer works in close cahoots with the University Welfare staff advising and supporting all types of tear-jerking trauma. The student support service helps with budgeting, emergency loans etc. The Uni's said to be particularly pro-gay & lesbian (hey, welcome to the 21st century).

CRIME Crime is low on-campus, but – as with any university town – there's occasional student-baiting off it.

HEALTH The Bailrigg Medical Centre contains a practice staffed with male and female GPs. There's a 24-nurse unit, a dentist and an alternative therapies centre.

WOMEN Attack alarms are available and there are minibus runs home from the Sugarhouse on club nights for women only, 7pm-2am.

CRECHES/NURSERY The paying pre-school centre has 30 places for under-twos and 82 for older children.

DISABILITIES *Lancaster gets kudos for making almost the whole of its compact campus accessible.* Several adapted bedrooms are available and the library has a Kurzweil text-reading machine and Braille embosser. Hearing loops in lecture theatres. Dyslexic students get extra support. Most importantly, all college bars have ramp access.

FINANCE

◉ AVE DEBT PER YEAR £2.803
◉ HOME STUDENT FEES £3,000
FEES EU students pay £8,250, other internationals will pay more like 10k. Part-timers pay £392 per part 1 subject or £294 per part 2 unit.
◉ ACCESS FUND £450,000 ◉ SUCCESSFUL APPLICATIONS/YR 550-600 ◉ AVE PAYMENT £100-3,500
SUPPORT *Terrific* financial support for disabled students, including an equipment allowance and a non-medical helper's allowance. Postgrads can apply for up to £5,640 a year.

LEEDS UNIVERSITY

◉ THE UNIVERSITY OF LEEDS Leeds, LS2 9JT TEL (0113) 243 1751 E-MAIL ask@leeds.ac.uk WEBSITE www.leeds.ac.uk
◉ LEEDS UNIVERSITY UNION PO Box 157, Leeds, LS1 1UH TEL (0113) 231 4254 E-MAIL comms@union.leeds.ac.uk
WEBSITE www.luuonline.com

GENERAL ⓤⓤⓤⓤⓤⓤⓤⓤⓤⓤⓤⓤⓤ

Leeds University celebrated its centenary in 2004 but in the last hundred years it's gone from being the cloistered academic institution represented by the *virginally white* clock tower of Parkinson House to an institution which sprawls across the city. About 13% of Leeds residents are students and together with neighbouring Leeds Metropolitan University they occupy a massive *studentland* conurbation of lecture theatres, halls and *Victorian terraced houses decorated with badly blu-tacked posters.*

SEX RATIO: ♂45 ♀55	FOUNDED: 1904
FULL–TIME U'GRADS: 22,175	PART–TIME: 1,519
POSTGRADS: 6,210	NON–DEGREE: 3,713
AVE COURSE: 3YRS	ETHNIC: 10%
STATE:PRIVATE SCHOOL: 74:26	FLUNK RATE: 8%
MATURE: 10%	INTERNATIONAL: 9%
DISABLED: 525	LOCAL: 21%

ATMOSPHERE

The sheer number of students and the variety of entertainment available might mean frantic hedonism and furious activity – but scepticism and apathy have a pretty palpable presence too. *An observer crueller than Push would say few consider anything more deeply than the bottom of their glass – the Union Bar's always busy, of course. In a city this size with a social scene rivalling Manchester, there's fun to be had for those that want it – and many that don't. The main site's in the heart of the city, and the University's one of the bigger kids on the block. Town/gown relations are on the whole very good, with the rare exception of student monopolies like Headingley: the penchant for traffic cones, a sea of to-let signs and hiked-up prices don't sit too well with locals who live there year-round. Whether it turns into a full-on backlash remains to be seen, but the Batman & Robin like partnership of the two universities is a force for good and douses upsets with community initiatives.*

SITES

As Push writes, The School of Performance and Cultural Industries at Bretton Hall, 17 miles south of Leeds, is packing its bags for the trip back to the main campus in 2007, when everything will be located on one, central site. A regular bus service links the sites in the meantime.

LEEDS
- **POPULATION** 715,500 ● **CITY CENTRE** 0 MILES
- **LONDON** 189 MILES ● **MANCHESTER** 40 MILES
- **HIGH TEMP** 19 ● **LOW TEMP** 1 ● **RAINFALL** 58

Although the bombs of WWII missed Leeds, the 60s developers and town planners didn't. At the top of Parkinson House there's amusement to be had watching hapless drivers trying to navigate the spaghetti-tangle of bypasses and one-way systems. Of course it's not quite so much fun for the people doing the driving but at least they might see the glorious Victorian buildings of the Town Hall, City Museum, Henry Moore Gallery and Opera North's home at the Grand Theatre. If you believe the hype/awards, Leeds is the best city in the galaxy to live, study, work, shop and part-ay. Millions have already been pumped into regenerating the city, with another coupla hundred grand aimed at cramming in even more excuses for retail therapy. *The semi-pedestrianised main street, Briggate, has every local amenity a student could possibly want and many they couldn't, including a branch of Ab-Fab favourite Harvey Nicks.*

TRAVEL
TRAINS Leeds station is the centre of the *very efficient* West Yorkshire metro train network serving all the local Yorkshire towns (Bradford, Wakefield, Sheffield and York). There are also direct services to London (from £47.25 return), Manchester (£10.05), Edinburgh (£46.05) and elsewhere.
COACHES National Express to London (£24), Manchester (£8.40), Edinburgh (£35) and other destinations. Also served by Blueline.
CAR Ten mins off the M1 and on the M62 to Manchester. *Cars aren't necessary for local travel – public transport's pretty good and most places you'd want to be in staggering distance of are.*
AIR Leeds/Bradford Airport for inland and European flights. Manchester Airport's around an hour away for international trips.
HITCHING *Chances of a lift are good on the M1 or M62, but obviously there are safer ways of getting around.*
LOCAL *Very reliable and frequent* trains and buses (maximum off-peak fare is 80p). A monthly student Metrocard (bus and train) is £39.50, the Student First travel card (£34 a month) is valid on bus routes from the University to the city centre.
TAXIS Local taxi firms will accept student cards in place of a fare for those caught short. They then claim the money off the University who return the card on repayment. *Handy, huh?*
BICYCLES There are plenty of cycle paths (and hills) but also a need for state-of-the-art security *to protect your bike from certain light-fingered locals.*

CAREER PROSPECTS
- **CAREERS SERVICE** ● **NO. OF STAFF** 27 FULL/19 PART
- **UNEMPLOYED AFTER 6MTHS** 10%

The careers service is *highly efficient – but it'd have to be with the legions of staff.* Performing Arts students get an in-house casting service and those interested in becoming self-employed have a dedicated service, Spark. The work placement centre helps find internships and work experience.

FAMOUS ALUMNI
Steve Bell (cartoonist); Mark Byford (ex-BBC boss); Barry Cryer (writer/comedian); Paul Dacre (editor, Daily Mail); Jeremy Dyson (League of Gentlemen); David Gedge (singer, Wedding Present); Alastair McGowan (funnyman impressionist); Mark Knopfler (Dire Straits); Claire Short MP; Jack Straw (Foreign Secretary and ex-SU president); Wole Soyinka (poet & playright); Nicholas Witchell (BBC newsreader, ex-editor of 'Leeds Student'); Alan Yentob (BBC *big cheese*).

FURTHER INFO
- **PROSPECTUSES** UNDERGRAD; POSTGRAD; SOME DEPARTMENTS; ALTERNATIVE ● **OPEN DAYS**

A guide for mature students is also available. Open days in June and September.

ACADEMIC ○○○○○○○○○○○○○

- **RUSSELL GROUP**

Leeds is strong on research and traditional subject areas like Law, English, Medicine, the Sciences and Engineering. Performance arts are getting a boost through a spurt of initiatives including a £1.5m theatre, performance design studio and the relocation of the Bretton facilities. They've also raided the piggy bank for refurbishments across lots of departments including Linguistics, Genetics, Medical & Biological Sciences and the Cancer Research facility. Links with 20 international universities *make the world an oyster for those who fancy a year studying abroad, but most students aren't keen on seafood.*

ENTRY POINTS: 260–360	**AVE POINTS:** 387
APPLICATIONS PER PLACE: 7	**CLEARING:** 4%
NO. OF TERMS: 3	**LENGTH OF TERMS:** 10WKS
STAFF TO STUDENT RATIO: 1:15	**STUDY ADDICTS:** 24%
TEACHING: ★★★	**RESEARCH:** ★★★★★
YEAR ABROAD: 10%	**SANDWICH STUDENTS:** 2%
1STS: 12%	**2.2S:** 26%
2.1S: 59%	**3RDS:** 3%

ADMISSIONS
- **APPLY VIA UCAS**

SUBJECTS
ARTS/HUMANITIES 12% **BIOLOGICAL SCIENCES** 8%
BUSINESS/MANAGEMENT 4% **EARTH & ENVIRONMENT** 5%
ENGINEERING 9% **MATHS/PHYSICAL SCIENCES** 5%
MEDICAL SCIENCES 16% **PERFORMANCE, VISUAL ARTS & COMMUNICATIONS** 16% **SOCIAL SCIENCES** 16%
BEST Biological Sciences; Computer Science; Education; English-based Studies; Electronic & Electrical Engineering; European Languages & Area Studies; History; Human & Social Geography; Mathematical Sciences; Medical Science & Pharmacy; Medicine & Dentistry; Other languages & area studies; Philosophy; Physical Geography & Environmental Science; Physical Science;Theology; & Religious Studies; Psychology; Social Work.
UNUSUAL Nanotechnology, Product Design.

LIBRARIES

⊙ **2,782,000** BOOKS ⊙ **4,000** STUDY PLACES
⊙ SPEND PER STUDENT ££££

'Third largest library facilities in the country', *read headlines across the land. Well, in Leeds anyway. Okay, only at the library. Probably.* Two main libraries and seven departmental, with collections on everyone from Will Shakespeare to Barbara Taylor Bradford. Librarians are subject specialists, *not just droning 'Sssh'-machines.*

COMPUTERS

⊙ **1,700** WORKSTATIONS ⊙ **24**-HR ACCESS

Despite the stonking general provision, only some halls enjoy the pleasures of networking.

OTHER LEARNING FACILITIES

Language labs; drama studio; rehearsal rooms; media centre. Each department has a floor of the Nathan Bodington Building to provide subject-specific resources. The Bodington Common website offers other interactive learning tools.

ENTERTAINMENT ◑◑◑◑◑◑◑◑◑◑

THE CITY

⊙ PRICE OF A PINT OF BEER £2.50
⊙ GLASS OF WINE £2 ⊙ CAN OF RED BULL £1.90

Leeds' rapidly developing nightlife has more than cottoned on to the possibilities of the student market. Headingley in particular has morphed from scraggy city centre satellite to sparkly student boozing heaven.

CINEMAS Two independent single-screen fleapits, three multiplex. The Hyde Park Picture House is an old-fashioned fave *(arty, Bollywood, Hollywood, student-made).*

THEATRES *Everything* from opera at the Grand to Alan Ayckbourn and am dram. The West Yorkshire Playhouse is a world-renowned modern repertory theatre complex. The City Varieties may be the oldest surviving music hall in the country, *but that's no excuse for bankrolling Ken Dodd.*

PUBS This is the home of Yorkshire bitter *and there are few local pubs that don't serve a decent pint. Serious imbibers should contemplate the Otley Run, a 14-pub crawl of mythical proportions, including the Eldon, the Skyrack, the Original Oak and the Dry Dock (on a boat). Pushplugs (Headingley): Woodies ('local' but good range of beers); the Three Horseshoes (sporting); the New Inn (beer garden); Headingley Taps; the Arc (attached to the Lounge Cinema, has cocktail bar, balcony, DJs - popular enough to queue). City centre waterholes worth draining a firkin in: North Bar (European beers); Fab Café (built by cult TV geeks for cult TV geeks); Velvet (gay-friendly); Arts Café.*

CLUBBING Leeds is an all-night city thanks to a tolerant council licensing policy. It's also home to some *great* clubs, if you can squeeze past the queues. *The Push posse would want to be on the*

guest-list for: Gatecrasher (dance/trance), Oceana, Hi Fi Club, Mint Club, Space, Halo.

MUSIC VENUES *Leeds is a compulsory stop for touring bands from big names to the biggest and there's a thriving live scene. Pushplugs: the Cockpit; Joseph's Well; the Irish Centre (all indie).*

COMEDY/CABARET Comedy at the Hi-Fi Club. The Music Hall has hosted Patrick Kielty, Dylan Moran and Chumbawamba, *but we forgive them.*

EATING OUT *Grubstops to satisfy all palates and pockets. Pushplugs: Citrus and Dare in Headingley; Wokmania (all-u-can-eat); Salvos (Italian – may require a parent with a credit card); Baraka (Moroccan); Original Oak (pub lunches); Clock Café; Grove Café; Manuela's; Dino's; Fujihiro and Little Tokyo (cheap Japanese food).*

OTHER For those who don't drink, eat, dance or watch stuff, Leeds has a fair few afternoon-fillers – the Royal Armouries, Tropical World and Kirkstall Abbey being three of them.

UNIVERSITY

⊙ PRICE OF A PINT OF BEER £2
⊙ GLASS OF WINE £2
⊙ CAN OF RED BULL £1.70

BARS Mine is far from the pits when it comes to ents: open daily for food and then re-opening at 9pm with a varied cocktail of comedy, live music, DJs, film, concerts and clubbing. Everyone back to Mine, then? The Old Bar is open until 12am for karaoke and quiz nights and there's a bar at Bretton too.

THEATRES *Lively board-walkers get as far as Edinburgh every year.* Riley Smith Hall and the Workshop Theatre host them on campus.

FILM Two mainstream films a week in Mine.

MUSIC VENUES The Refectory is Leeds' largest live music venue with recent acts like The Kaiser Chiefs, *which is a bit disloyal given most of them graduated from the uni next door.*

CLUBBING Stylus and Bar Coda *are the Union's premier party nights.* Stylus has won its share of awards and, with Mine and Coda tacked on, has the potential for being a *gigantical* venue (1,600 cap). Brighton Beach pulls up on a Friday, Valve SoundSystem passes through twice a year, and Public Enemy and the likes have also gestured their through.

COMEDY/CABARET Mine, again.

FOOD *The refectory's best for fuelling-up before lectures. MJ's coffee bar deals with snacks and the bars all serve up a good range of eats.* The Union's supermarket is good for food on the move. There are sarnie and snack shops dotted about campus, some of which stock Fair Trade munchies.

OTHER One of the biggest graduation balls in the country with 5,000 people. A freshers' do in October and a summer black-tie event. Some halls have formal dinners.

SOCIAL ⦿⦿⦿⦿⦿⦿⦿⦿⦿⦿⦿⦿⦿

LEEDS UNIVERSITY UNION
⦿ 13 SABBATICALS ⦿ TURNOUT AT LAST BALLOT 12%

Most other student bodies would be delighted to have an operation on the scale of LUU to represent them but size brings its own problems. When the executive tried to remove the sabbatical posts at the Nightline and Student Radio, they were overwhelmingly voted down. So they don't rule the roost. Most of the time as long as the beer's cheap and the ents are up to scratch most people are happy. There's a fair bit of politicking going down, too.

SU FACILITIES
Bars; travel agency; book shop; ATMs; opticians; Endsleigh Insurance; hair salon; photo booth; games machines; newsagent; insurance broker; off licence; Waterstone's.

CLUBS (NON-SPORTING)
Acapella singers; AIESEC; Anime; Art; Backstage; Ballet; Band; Bangladeshi Students; Belly Dancing; Boxercise; Break Dance; Bretton Hall Music; Bridge; British Born Chinese; Buddhist Meditation; Café Babel; Celebrating Him in Print; Change Ringers; Cheese; Chess; Chinese; Comedy; Commercial & Investment Banking; Compassion for Animals; Creative Writing; Dance Band; Dance Expose; Disabled Students; Duke of Edinburgh; Egyptian; English Heritage Workshop; Forum of Composers & Musicians; Fresh Funk; Game Development; Hellenic; Hindu Students Forum; Hong Kong; House Music (DJ); Indian Students Association; Indonesian; Iranian; Irish Dancing; ISKCON; Japanese; Juggling & Circus Skills; Kabal; Kite; Korean; Latin American & Portuguese; Leeds Review; Leeds Student Television; Lippy Magazine; Live Action Roleplay; Live Music Appreciation; Luso-Brazillian; LUST; Malaysian; Malaysian & Singaporean; Medsin; Mexican; Modern Dance; Music; Musical Theatre; Omani Students; Orthodox Christian; Palestinian Solidarity Group; Parkour; Political & Campaigning; Pool; Punk; Real Ale; Respect; Revelation Rock-Gospel Choir; Revolution; Roleplay; Scottish Country Dancing; Scout & Guide; Sign Language; Singaporean; SIS; Skateboarding; Soulciety; Spanish; Speak; Speleological St Johns Ambulance; Sri Lankan; Stage Musical; Student Action for Refugees; Student Stop AIDS; Sudanese; Swing Dance; Tea; Thai Students; Theatre Group; Tibet; Turkish; Union Music Library; United Nations Association; Vietnamese; Wine; World Music. **See also Clubs tables.**

OTHER ORGANISATIONS
'Leeds Student' is the award-winning weekly paper. The radio station ('LSR FM') is a joint venture with Leeds Met. 'LS:TV' shows an hour a day throughout the Union. Rag raises several grand for worthwhile causes each year. CALM (another joint operation) runs 60 *effective* local help projects.

RELIGIOUS
⦿ 9 CHAPLAINS (COFE, BAPTIST, RC, LUTHERAN, METHODIST, ORTHODOX, QUAKER, SALVATION ARMY, URC), IMAM AND RABBI

Ecumenical Chaplaincy Centre with the above Christian churches working together. Prayer rooms and other facilities for Jews, Hindus, Muslims and Sikhs. The Islamic Society says daily prayers on campus. The city offers places of worship for all strains of god-fearer; Hindus, Muslims and Sikhs are *particularly well-catered for*. Leeds has the largest Jewish student population outside Manchester.

PAID WORK
⦿ JOB BUREAU

The *usual* bar work and stewarding at Union ents and joblink run by the SU with the emphasis on safe employment practices. Leeds as a city is *teeming* with bar and retail opportunities.

SPORTS ⦿⦿⦿⦿⦿⦿⦿⦿⦿⦿⦿⦿⦿

⦿ BUSA RANKING 15

Facilities and precedents are there for sporting success and there's no end of hopefuls. SportsLeeds organises intramural comps and tournaments: they're now sponsored by *big league Deloitte so there may be more cash to spend on shell suits and sweat bands*. Recent upgrading of the Sports Centre has meant a few more bits of kit.

SPORTS FACILITIES
£45/yr buys time at all facilities. The Sports Centre has: fitness room; weight training room; sports halls; six squash courts; table tennis facilities;an aerobics centre; cardiovascular room; climbing wall. Weetwood, close to the halls, has 100 acres to kick/throw balls in, tennis courts and a floodlit, synthetic pitch. The University also has outdoor centres in the Yorkshire Dales and the Lake District.

SPORTING CLUBS
10-pin bowling; Aikido; American Football; Boat; Boxing; Capeoira Heranca; Cheerleading; Dancesport; Gliding; Gymnastics; Hiking; Kickboxing; Korfball; Lacrosse; Motor Sport; Mountaineering; Rifle; Rugby League; Rugby Union; Samurai Jui Jistu; Skydiving; Surfing; Table Tennis; Tai Chi; Thai Boxing; Ultimate Frisbee; Windsurfing. **See also Clubs tables.**

ATTRACTIONS
This is *the heartland* of rugby league and with Leeds United at Elland Road, international cricket at Headingley and Olympic swimming facilities only a paddle away, there's something to see all year round.

L

ACCOMMODATION ○○○○○○○○○○

IN UNIVERSITY
- **CATERED** 7% **COST** £97 (31/39WKS)
- **SELF-CATERING** 24% **COST** £80 (40WKS)
- **1ST YRS LIVING IN** 60%
- **INSURANCE PREMIUM** £££££

AVAILABILITY All first years who want to can live in a variety of *highly comfortsome* halls. The older ones, such as Bodington and Devonshire (both catered), require 10% of students to share but that does keep the rent down. The self-catering flats hold anything from four to 14 students. Catered halls come with *snack-enabled* kitchens and 14-19 meals a week (veggie and porkless options too). Internet and laundry facilities plus access to common rooms, sports facilities and bars. *There are complaints about restrictions (on sticking posters up, for example) and about cleaners arriving at what they coyly describe as 'inopportune' moments.*

CAR PARKING *Expensive, unnecessary and in short supply.*

EXTERNALLY
- **AVE RENT** £58

AVAILABILITY *Most students stick to the large quantity of late 19th-century back-to-back terraced housing. Conditions vary but the UniPol code of practice has sorted out a few problems with unscrupulous landlords. Favourite student destinations are Headingley (a massive student enclave), Woodhouse and Hyde Park, but the local goodwill is rubbing a bit thin as a result. Most choose not to live in somewhat rough and druggy Chapeltown.*

HOUSING HELP UniPol, the joint University and Leeds Metropolitan University SUs' housing service provides lots of help and advice with a code of standards and an *excellent* internet search service. It also keeps tabs on the worst landlords. *Watch out for local letting agents (of the devil) announcing a housing shortage and pressuring students into renting before the Unipol list goes up.*

WELFARE ○○○○○○○○○○○○

SERVICES
- **LGBT SOCIETY** **ETHNIC MINORITIES OFFICER & SOCIETY** **MATURE STUDENTS' OFFICER & SOCIETY** **INTERNATIONAL STUDENTS' OFFICER & SOCIETY** **POSTGRAD OFFICER & SOCIETY** **DISABILITIES OFFICER & SOCIETY** **WOMEN'S OFFICER & SOCIETY** **LATE-NIGHT MINIBUS** **NIGHTLINE** **TAXI FUND** **UNIVERSITY COUNSELLORS** 7 FULL/9 PART **CRIME RATING** !!!!!

Nightline is one of only two in the country with a sabbatical officer at the helm. Self-defence classes cost £1 per session. Free safety alarms. The free late bus between Union and front doors is available to men and women travelling alone.

HEALTH The student health service has its very own mini-hospital with doctors, a seven-bed sickbay and even a minor operation suite. In total there are 13 GPs, eight nurses and eight sickbay attendants. There's a website dedicated to mental health.

CRECHES/NURSERY The SU's Bright Beginnings has 60 places for kids 6mths-5yrs.

DISABILITIES The University and the Union are making efforts to improve access and have adapted the entire Union building. Campus has *middling* wheelchair access, but key buildings have been fitted with automatic doors and card entry – a map's available that shows wheelchair-friendly routes. Also 35 designated disabled parking bays. Solid dyslexia support.

FINANCE
- **AVE DEBT PER YEAR** £2,883
- **HOME STUDENT FEES** £3,000

FEES Part-time students pay £1,500. Postgrads pay £3,085. International undergrads pay between £8,600 for Arts, Law and Education courses and and £11,400 for Science and Engineering.
- **ACCESS FUND** £1,027,536
- **SUCCESSFUL APPLICATIONS** 1,055 **AVE PAYMENT** £974

SUPPORT Scholarships are available for students from less affluent Leeds suburbs. There's the usual bursaries/welfare funds and a range of budgeting advice, debt counselling and even – *a sign of the times* – help with bankruptcy. The Union offers emergency loans of up to £100.

There's more to student life than poverty and fun.... See the clubs & socs tables.

LEEDS METROPOLITAN UNIVERSITY

FORMERLY LEEDS POLYTECHNIC

LEEDS METROPOLITAN UNIVERSITY Course Enquiries, Freepost LS6440, Leeds, LS1 3HE **TEL** (0113) 283 3113 **E-MAIL** course enquiries@leedsmet.ac.uk **WEBSITE** www.leedsmet.ac.uk **LEEDS METROPOLITAN UNIVERSITY STUDENTS UNION** B Building, Calverley Street, Leeds, LS1 3HE **TEL** (0113) 209 8400 **E-MAIL** enquiries@leedsmetsu.ac.uk **WEBSITE** www.leedsmetsu.org.uk

GENERAL

R ight in the middle of Leeds there's a university. Right next-door is another one. *Somewhere one ends and the next begins, but it's not easy to tell where.* Like its more elderly neighbour, the Met's buildings are a jumble of old and new, but it centres on seven *brooding* concrete tower blocks, *from which the Metropolitan proudly reminds us that Leeds hasn't gone entirely soft since the arrival of Harvey Nicks and the rest. It's a sobbing shame that* the site cannot be shifted en masse to the Headingly Campus, three miles out in a *chocolate box* wooded site arranged *tastefully* around a cricket square. The University's making amends with planned developments, *although with the Rose Bowl lecture theatre and a new building for Business students, it's not earth-shatteringly exciting. The Met's slightly overwhelmed by the bigger boy next door, but although there are still lots of joint endeavours (which tend to be run 'jointly' by Leeds University) there are signs that this baby's almost ready to fly solo.*

SEX RATIO: ♂49 ♀51	**FOUNDED:** 1970
FULL-TIME U'GRADS: 14,151	**PART-TIME:** 1,871
POSTGRADS: 3,241	**NON-DEGREE:** 11,469
AVE COURSE: 3YRS	**ETHNIC:** 19%
STATE:PRIVATE SCHOOL: 97:3	**FLUNK RATE:** 15%
MATURE: 21%	**INTERNATIONAL:** 10%
DISABLED: 320	**LOCAL:** 46%

ATMOSPHERE

Leeds Met has a hefty helping of part-time stu-dents but this hasn't affected the atmosphere. In fact, grumbly locals would probably suggest that all the students seem to be part-time, judging by the numbers of them out and about every night. That's a bit unfair, though. In such a friendly, sociable town there are bound to be temptations. Leeds fully deserves its reputation as Party Central and Leeds Met students are more than happy to play their central part in keeping it so. The Civic Quarter campus is next to, and dwarfed by, big bro Leeds University, but the high number of scholars milling around makes for a compact, studenty pleasure zone.

SITES

HEADINGLY CAMPUS Three miles from the city campus, Headingly is in 100 acres of woods and parkland, affording *panoramic* views across Leeds and based round a main building dating back to 1913. It's home to various departments (including Business, Education, IT, Law, Sports Sciences and Languages) and the main sports facilities. There could be more mixing between sites, especially as locals aren't as loved-up with students as in the town centre.

HARROGATE CAMPUS Titchy site that contains FE provisions (ie, Harrogate College) so not much use to the University's other students, except that there's potential to blag cheap haircuts at the trainee beauty salon on site.

LEEDS see Leeds University

TRAVEL see Leeds University

COLLEGE A bus service runs between the sites every six to ten mins.

LOCAL First Bus serves Headingley Campus, Kirkstall Brewery Residences and the city centre via the civic quarter campus. There's a free bus that shuttles between the bus station, Civic Quarter and the train station.

TAXIS Students finding themselves short at the end of the night, can give the taxi driver their student card instead of paying. The University then pays and students get their card back when they pay the University. *Cunning, eh?*

CAREER PROSPECTS

 CAREERS SERVICE **NO. OF STAFF** 5 FULL/4 PART **UNEMPLOYED AFTER 6MTHS** 4%

The Careers Service runs development work-shops and lends a hand with job applications and laying hands on work experience.

FAMOUS ALUMNI

Marc Almond (singer); Glen Baxter (cartoonist); Betty Boothroyd (former Speaker of the Commons); Peter Cattaneo (film director); Jeremy Dyson (League of Gentlemen writer); Brendan Foster (Olympian & Current chancellor); Austin Healy (Rugby Union); Sir Henry Moore (sculptor); Ron Pickering (late sports commentator); Eric Pickles MP (Con); Keith Waterhouse (writer); Ricky Wilson (Kaiser Chief).

FURTHER INFO

 PROSPECTUSES UNDERGRAD; POSTGRAD

Words in italics are Push's point of view — take it or leave it...

ACADEMIC ◐◐◐◐◐◐◐◐◐◐◐◐

Leeds Met is strong on vocational degrees, particularly those that involve fun: Hospitality, Sport, Leisure and Tourism. The Business School, Events Management and PR courses also have a good reputation. Students need to achieve a minimum number of credit points and standard of work each year to progress to the next.

ENTRY POINTS: 120–320	**AVE POINTS:** 236
APPLICATIONS PER PLACE: 6	**CLEARING:** 10%
NO. OF TERMS: 2	**LENGTH OF TERMS:** 14/6wks
STAFF TO STUDENT RATIO: 1:18	**STUDY ADDICTS:** 21%
TEACHING: ★★	**RESEARCH:** ★★
YEAR ABROAD: <1%	**SANDWICH STUDENTS:** 29%
1STS: 8%	**2.2S:** 41%
2.1S: 42%	**3RDS:** 9%

ADMISSIONS
○ **APPLY VIA UCAS/GTTR FOR PGCE**
They're *flexible* in their recruitment policy and will take experience into account as much as bits of paper.

SUBJECTS
ARTS & SOCIETY 24% **BUSINESS & LAW** 24%
HEALTH 11% **INFORMATION & TECHNOLOGY** 16%
INTERNATIONAL FACULTY 8% **SPORT & EDUCATION** 17%
BEST Biology; Civil Engineering; Computer Science; Economics; English Studies; History; Information Services; Landscape Design; Marketing; Social Sciences; Subjects Allied to Medicine; Social Policy; Social Work; Sports Science.
UNUSUAL Loads, due to the University's vocational stance: Animation Techniques & Special Effects; Club & Casino Management; Cybercrime & Society; Enterprise, Event Fundraising & Sponsorship; Exercise Science & Obesity Management; Fire Safety; Garden Art & Design; Human Centred Design; Information & Library Systems; Lifestyle Management; Managing Cultural & Major Events; Playwork; Resort Management; Sport & Media Broadcasting; Visualisation & Simulation.

LIBRARIES
○ **365,002 BOOKS** ○ **2,082 STUDY PLACES**
○ **24-HR ACCESS**
24/365 opening suits book worms and study addicts.

COMPUTERS
○ **1,578 WORKSTATIONS** ○ **24-HR ACCESS**
○ **SPEND PER STUDENT** ££££
There are facilities in the libraries as well as wireless internet access in residences. Laptops can be loaned. Web CT lets users tap into course information, lecture notes and the library catalogue.

OTHER LEARNING FACILITIES
Some students get to hang their *masterpieces* in the University's *groovy* gallery. Helpzones across campus answer queries *about pretty much anything (related to student life; we're not sure how they fare on pub quiz conundrums).* Some courses are available with distance-learning options.

ENTERTAINMENT ◐◐◐◐◐◐◐◐◐

THE CITY see Leeds University

UNIVERSITY
○ **PRICE OF A PINT OF BEER** £1.80
○ **GLASS OF WINE** £2 ○ **CAN OF RED BULL** £1.70
BARS The Met Bar is heaving throughout term thanks to the cheap food during the day and solid sounds three nights a week. It's got the biggest TV screen in the town, *so Leeds Utd's triumphs and travesties can be scrutinised in magnified detail.* Becketts Sports Bar at Headingly has big and plasma screens for the football, games machines, five pool tables and an internet café. *It's a particular fave with the sporting crowd,* but is generally packed. Sugarwell Court Bar is a new addition to the SU stable and does a similar thing to Headingly's. Kirkstall residences have a two-floor bar (pub grub served downstairs) with cyber café, quiz nights and a cheese-based club night once a week.
THEATRE The Gallery and Studio Theatre hosts regional tours *but student thesping's rarer than roast beef.*
CLUBBING The SU plays host to Star (Indie) & Electrichead every Friday. Occasional club nights at Met Bar.
MUSIC VENUES Leeds Met has a become a *major venue on national tours, completely overshadowing its more staid neighbour.* The Lost Prophets, the Darkness, Damien Rice, Athlete, New Found Glory, Coldplay, Doves, Oasis and the Thrills have all popped into the Met Bar recently. Local bands play free gigs at Headingly.
CABARET Lyrically Justified (open mic night) in Headingly's Bar once a month.
FOOD Metceno is a food court which includes Horizons (world meals), Ceno's (pizza, pasta) and Ainsley's (pastries). The Met Bar comes with a Diner (9am-7pm). The main refectory, the Depot, *offers good value for limited dosh.* The Grapevine is *a posher affair where the lecturers hang out.* The refectory at Headingly is *confusingly also called the Depot and Costa Coffee has somehow infiltrated the main University building.* The Terrace Café Bar offers sandwiches alongside its pool tables.

Words in italics are Push's point of view — take it or leave it...

SOCIAL ◡◡◡◡◡◡◡◡◡◡◡◡

LEEDS METROPOLITAN UNIVERSITY STUDENTS' UNION (LMUSU)
◉ 5 SABBATICALS ◉ TURNOUT AT LAST BALLOT 5%
◉ NUS MEMBER
Politics isn't exactly cut-throat. Students aren't really bothered who's running things. They're more concerned about who scored the winning try, what's gone wrong this week at Leeds Utd and whose round it is. The SU are trying to rattle students' cages by appointing a few more sabbs. We'd hate to see them when they get really narked.

SU FACILITIES
The main facilities are at the City Campus where there are: two bars; five coffee bars; two print rooms; Endsleigh Insurance; games & vending machines; a health and fitness suite; general and stationery shops; bookstore. At Headingly, there's not only another bar, but also a café, bank, photo booth, games machines, pool tables, TV lounge, a disco and a juke-box.

CLUBS (NON-SPORTING)
Friends of India; Hindu; Malaysian; Musician's Network; Sikh; Skateboarding; Sri Lankan; St John's Ambulance (LINKS); The Social (politics); Walking. **See also Clubs tables.**

OTHER ORGANISATIONS
'LiME' is the student mag; 'The Met' is the free newssheet, no longer run in collaboration with Leeds Uni *after a lovers' tiff*. 'Leeds Student Radio' (www.lsrfm.com), still run jointly, broadcasts locally 24-hrs a day from September 2005. There are Rag events, *but a co-ordinating committee is a wistful extra at the mo'. In the meantime,* CALM (Community Action at Leeds Met) makes a few headlines with *wide-ranging* campaigns such as safety, mental health and sexual health.

RELIGIOUS
Six chaplains are shared with Leeds University. Meanwhile, there's an advisor and not one, but two prayer rooms for Muslims. Jews make do with just an advisor and, Push presumes, pray wherever the mood takes them.

PAID WORK see Leeds University
◉ JOB BUREAU ◉ PAID WORK: TERM-TIME: 42%; HOLS: 53%
The *excellent* job shop has filled well over 2,000 vacancies and is available online. Students on the Retailing BA can gather academic credits from working for a range of retail chains (Asda, IKEA, Debenhams etc.).

SPORTS ◡◡◡◡◡◡◡◡◡◡◡◡◡

◉ RECENT SUCCESSES RUGBY, CRICKET **◉ BUSA RANKING** 23
Sports for all policy, and partnerships with national organisation such as the Lawn Tennis Association and British Gymnastics, which mean students can make use of professional coaching and contacts. *While BUSA points don't come easy, the Mets take their frustrations out by kicking Leeds University's ass at the yearly varsity match.* The University's trying to raise sport in the student consciousness: sponsoring Headingly stadium and offering sports scholarships are some of the weapons in their arsenal.

SPORTS FACILITIES
The facilities at Headingly include: 14 acres for sport; the new Centre of Excellence for Tennis; the Carnegie Regional Gymnastics Centre; dance studio; swimming pool; squash courts; athletics and playing fields (including 12 football pitches, four rugby, one lacrosse, two synthetic floodlit and one five-a-side pitch); climbing wall; multigym; weights room; running track; tennis courts and regular aerobics classes. These facilities were acquired through lottery funding, which means that the public also get to use them, but students can buy an annual pass for £35, *which works out as cheap as low-fat chips.* The city has its own leisure centre, pool, sauna, ski slope, a lake and river, a bowling green and golf course. See Leeds University for local facilities.

SPORTING CLUBS
Boxing; Club Captains 05; Dance; Dodgeball; Gaelic Football; Gymnastics; Handball Club; Ju Jitsu; Kayaking; Lacrosse; Shaolin Kung Fu; Snowboarding; Table Tennis; Tai Jitsu; Triathlon; Waterpolo; Weightlifting. **See also Clubs tables.**

ATTRACTIONS see Leeds University

ACCOMMODATION ◡◡◡◡◡◡◡◡◡

IN UNIVERSITY
◉ SELF CATERING 22% **◉ COST** £70 (41/43WKS)
◉ 1ST YRS LIVING IN 51% **◉ INSURANCE PREMIUM** £££££
AVAILABILITY Just over half of first years live in (non-locals have priority), either at the *popular and evocatively named* Kirkstall Brewery complex in the centre of town or the *less popular* Sugarwell Court a mile or so further out. The rest are handled by UniPol, *not an international crime-fighting agency, but the Leeds universities' first-rate joint student property management scheme.* The Met's halls are placed at *quite a distance* from each other, although most are close to the University. 20% of rooms are en suite and about six students jostle for use of each kitchen. CCTV and keycard entry systems help *them sleep soundly.* See also Leeds University.

L

CAR PARKING *Free parking + first-come, first-served + not many spaces = well, you work out the maths.*

EXTERNALLY see Leeds University
○ **AVE RENT** £55
HOUSING HELP *UniPol to the rescue once again. Certain unscrupulous local letting agents try to tell newbies there's a housing shortage to get them to sign contracts before the UniPol list is up.* Leeds Met also has its own Accommodation Office and, so far, nobody's ended up sleeping on the gym floor. First years who don't get into halls are invited to meet and get to know each other with a view to house-sharing *with people who won't end up killing each other over the washing-up.*

WELFARE ○○○○○○○○○○○○○○

SERVICES
○ **LGBT OFFICER & SOCIETY** ○ **MATURE STUDENTS' OFFICER & SOCIETY** ○ **WOMEN'S OFFICER & SOCIETY** ○ **INTERNATIONAL STUDENTS' OFFICER & SOCIETY** ○ **ETHNIC MINORITIES' OFFICER & SOCIETY** ○ **DISABILITIES OFFICER & SOCIETY** ○ **SELF-DEFENCE CLASSES** ○ **NIGHTLINE** ○ **TAXI FUND** ○ **UNIVERSITY COUNSELLORS** 2 FULL/2 PART

○ **SU COUNSELLORS** 4 FULL-TIME ○ **CRIME RATING** !!!!!
The SU student advice service counsels on issues such as discrimination, immigration, housing, money, debt and so on.
HEALTH Health centres on each campus treat minor illnesses and accidents, plus offer sexual health advice, condoms, etc. There's access to Leeds University's Nightline.
CRECHES/NURSERY A crèche takes care of students' mini-mes.
DISABILITIES Some buildings can't be adapted for wheelchair users. UniPol (see above) makes an extra effort to accommodate students with disabilities. There's a full-time dyslexia support officer and induction loops at Headingly.

FINANCE
○ **AVE DEBT PER YEAR** £3,458 ○ **HOME STUDENT FEES** £2,000
FEES International students pay fees in three bands ranging between £8-£10k. Leeds Met's one of the rare places not charging the full whack three grand top-up.
○ **ACCESS FUND** £1M ○ **SUCCESSFUL APPLICATIONS/YR** 1,266 ○ **AVE PAYMENT** £800
SUPPORT Debt counselling is available from the Budget Advisor and two part-timers. There's an emergency fund for international students and top musclers can apply for a sports scholarship. Bursaries for applicants from low-income families.

▶ **LEEDS POLYTECHNIC**
see *Leeds Metropolitan University*

UNIVERSITY OF LEICESTER

○ **UNIVERSITY OF LEICESTER** University Road, Leicester, LE1 7RH **TEL** 0116 252 2522 **E-MAIL** postmaster@le.ac.uk or admissions@le.ac.uk ○ **UNIVERSITY OF LEICESTER STUDENTS' UNION** Percy Gee Building, University Road, Leicester, LE1 7RH **TEL** (0116) 223 1111 **E-MAIL** lusu@le.ac.uk **WEBSITE** www.leicesterstudent.org

GENERAL ○○○○○○○○○○○○○

Leicester (along with Nottingham to the north and Northampton to the south) is one of the principal cities of the East Midlands. *But it doesn't really feel all that big. It's something about the attitude of the people, which is generally full of small-town small-talk friendliness. The suburbs are attractive, but the centre, tarred and feathered with history, has a few dodgy areas.* Parts have been pedestrianised, mainly the shopping areas. A mile from the centre, opposite a large cemetery and the *rather pretty* Victoria Park, is the city's older University – bigger sibling of De Montfort. It's a mixture of pleasant old architecture, such as the original Georgian and Edwardian buildings, and *new-fangled* post-war bits 'n' bobs. Three of these are particularly prominent on the skyline: the Attenborough Building, 18 storeys high, which won a design award (but then, France won the 1998 World Cup); the ten-storey Charles Wilson Building; and the Engineering block, which is Grade II listed, having won an award in the 1960s for its use of aluminium – *although, today, it's about as sexy as a non-stick frying pan.*

SEX RATIO: ♂47 ♀53	FOUNDED: 1921
FULL-TIME U'GRADS: 7,708	PART-TIME: 1,799
POSTGRADS: 8,170	NON-DEGREE: N/A
AVE COURSE: 3-4YRS	ETHNIC: 9%
STATE:PRIVATE SCHOOL: 88:12	FLUNK RATE: 4%
MATURE: 10%	INTERNATIONAL: 8%
DISABLED: 175	LOCAL: N/A

ATMOSPHERE

Leicester's scholarly types are into having a good time, whether on the playing fields or in the bars. They're a very friendly and welcoming crowd and the substantial international contingent offers a multicultural mix that the more staid student can find somewhat intimidating. The huge amount of greenery surrounding the campus promises plenty of frolicking, but heightens the impression that the University is slightly divorced from the rest of town, physically as well as socially.

LEICESTER

- **POPULATION** 279,921 - **CITY CENTRE** 1 MILE
- **LONDON** 98 MILES - **BIRMINGHAM** 33 MILES
- **NOTTINGHAM** 28 MILES
- **HIGH TEMP** 21 - **LOW TEMP** 0 - **RAINFALL** 49

The city of Leicester is a *fairly* thriving commercial centre with the odd throwback to Roman times dotted about – as any visitor to the Jewry Wall and its attached museum will no doubt be told. The Guildhall in the centre of the city is medieval and, nearby, the discerning tourist finds the 700-year-old covered market – still one of the largest in Europe. *The castle and cathedral are worth a look-in, but let's stop dwelling in the past and enjoy the place as it is now – a heady cosmopolitan* mixture of people with a *huge* Asian population and a *full deck* of modern amenities like restaurants, curry houses, shops, pubs, curry houses, galleries, more curry houses and Gary Lineker's dad's fruit stall. For those not satisfied with what's on offer in town, Bradgate Park – former home of Lady Jane Grey (who was queen for nine days) – has *lovely, rolling greenery* and lots of deer, while Rutland Water – the biggest man-made reservoir this side of the Orient Express – *offers everything worth getting wet for.*

TRAVEL

TRAINS Leicester Station operates many services direct all over the Midlands and the rest of the country, including London (from £26.40 return), Sheffield (£12.15), Edinburgh (£61.05), Leeds (£20.05) and beyond.

COACHES National Express and other services to London (£20.50), Sheffield (£10.40), Edinburgh (£46) and elsewhere.

CAR The M1 skirts the edge of Leicester and the M69 connects with the A5 from the city's outskirts. Also the A6, A46, A47, A50 and A607.

AIR Flights from East Midlands Airport (16 miles away) inland and to Europe. Birmingham International – a 45-min drive – offers more exotic destinations.

HITCHING *Excellent for London or Birmingham. Catch a bus out to near the M1 or M69 motorway junctions.*

LOCAL *Buses are reliable, cheap (60p from campus to town),* well used and run until 11pm.

TAXIS £3 for an average journey from halls to town.

BICYCLES Leicester, 'Britain's First Environmental City', has introduced cycle ways and there are racks on campus.

CAREER PROSPECTS

- **CAREERS SERVICE** - **NO. OF STAFF** 13 FULL
- **UNEMPLOYED AFTER 6MTHS** 5%

The *thorough* careers service gives careers a good servicing, which means sending out regular newsletters and e-mail vacancy updates, throwing job fairs and employer presentations, giving CV, application, interview and assessment assistance and offering advice on starting a business – *anything from double-glazing to porn empires.*

FAMOUS ALUMNI

Sir Malcolm Bradbury (writer); Sue Cook (TV presenter); Sue Campbell (sportswoman); Heather Couper (TV astronomer); Carol Galley (City whizz kid); Michael Jack MP (Con); Bob Mortimer (comedian, Vic's other half); Pete McCarthy (late comedian, TV presenter); Michael Nicholson (ITN newscaster); Adele Parks (chicklit scribbler); Andrew Taylor (chief exec McDonald's); Tony Underwood (rugby player); Sir Alan Walters (economist); Sir John Stevens (Comissioner of the Met Police).

FURTHER INFO

- **PROSPECTUSES** UNDERGRAD; POSTGRAD - **OPEN DAYS**

Prospective undergrads get the choice of three open days and two info days a year.

ACADEMIC ⓤⓤⓤⓤⓤⓤⓤⓤⓤⓤⓤⓤⓤ

A range of *traditional, but forward-thinking* courses with tons of combined honours and joint degree options. Every subject is modular, with students taking 120 credits a year. *Physics and Space Science have always had a bit of a reputation – which contributed in part to the arrival of the National Space Science Centre in Leicester.* The University is keen to teach key skills along with the subject in question, so even a student of Medieval Baking should come out of it with basic numerical and IT ability. (NB. *Sad to say, Medieval Baking is not actually on offer.*)

ENTRY POINTS: 240–400	AVE POINTS: 370
APPLICATIONS PER PLACE: 8	CLEARING: 5%
NO. OF TERMS: 2	LENGTH OF TERMS: 16WKS
STAFF TO STUDENT RATIO: 1:13	STUDY ADDICTS: 35%
TEACHING: *****	RESEARCH: ***
YEAR ABROAD: 17%	SANDWICH STUDENTS: 1%
1STS: 12%	2.2s: 30%
2.1s: 53%	3RDS: 5%

ADMISSIONS

- **APPLY VIA UCAS**

Leicester relishes applications from mature and international students as well as those from schools with little record of sending students on to university. Applicants with 'suitable advanced qualifications' can fast-track straight into the second year.

Words in italics are Push's point of view – take it or leave it...

L

SUBJECTS

ARTS/HUMANITIES 22%   **BUSINESS/MANAGEMENT** 3%
MEDICAL SCIENCES 27%   **EDUCATION** 3%   **(MODERN)**
LANGUAGES 3%   **LAW** 12%   **SCIENCES** 18%   **SOCIAL
SCIENCES** 21%
BEST Biological Sciences; Communications;
Economics; English; Geography; History &
Archaeology; Law; Medicine; Modern Languages;
Physical Science; Politics; Psychology.
UNUSUAL Genetics (DNA fingerprinting was
invented here, doncha know?).

LIBRARIES

◍ 1,100,000 BOOKS ◍ 1,200 STUDY PLACES
Currently in the middle of a £12million redevelopment, which should be done and dusted by 2007.
In addition to the *fatly stocked* main library, there
are smaller, specialised libraries for Education,
Clinical Sciences and Law. The main library
opens till midnight on weekdays and has
squirrelled away some *impressive* special stuff,
including a collection of early kids' books and the
letters and manuscripts of *barmy* farce
playwright, Joe Orton.

COMPUTERS

◍ 728 WORKSTATIONS
Computer clusters are, er, clustered around the
campus including in the libraries. Some rooms are
open till 2am and most have printer access. There
are NTL network points in all bedrooms.

OTHER LEARNING FACILITIES

Leicester students have access to language labs
(open to all, not just linguists), rehearsal rooms, a
theatre for drama, a media centre and a room to
practise mooting (*that's debating to you and me*).

ENTERTAINMENT ◡◡◡◡◡◡◡◡◡◡◡

LEICESTER

◍ PRICE OF A PINT OF BEER £2
◍ GLASS OF WINE £2.80
◍ CAN OF RED BULL £1.90
CINEMAS The 12-screen Odeon (Freeman's Park) is
nearby and puts on the odd premiere in
conjunction with the Uni. There's also the
Cannon (for mainstream movies and the
occasional Indian film), a Warner multiplex, the
Phoenix Arts centre (for arthouse flicks) and
Capital Cinema (for Asian epics).
THEATRES The Haymarket hosts populist productions
and touring companies and, again, the Phoenix for
fringe and cult dramatic fodder. Touring London
hits wash up at the De Montfort Hall.
PUBS *Gazillions. Pushplugs: Varsity, the Dry Dock
and the Loaded Dog stay open late and dole out
student discount cards; Time, Terrace and Show
Rooms (for cocktails); Wetherspoons (wallets will
be thankful); Pause (classy); Revolution (vodka
heaven); Nomads (good service). Don't bother with
the Braunstone (anti-student) or the Angel (unless
you support Leicester City).*

CLUBBING *Leicester has enough clubs to suit all but
the most pernickety of tail-feather shakers,
although some aren't up to much. Pushplugs:
Planet (trance/acid, big queues); SHAG at
Zanzibar (which the SU has a hand in); Attik
(ambient/drum'n'bass); the Fan Club and Mosh
(indie); Streetlife (gay); Junction 21 (hip hop, dub);
Mosquito Coast (NUS night indie/retro). Po Na
Na's is good for guest DJs but slow for service.*
MUSIC VENUES De Montfort Hall, *an important indie
venue,* shouldn't be confused with De Montfort
University, which is also *not too bad for gigs.* The
Charlotte, Half Time Orange and the Shed have
smaller indie bands.
COMEDY *The comedy scene here is funtastic –
check out Club Jongleurs and the Leicester
Comedy Festival which is the biggest in Britain,
attracting over 40,000 people a year.*
EATING OUT *Leicester's curry scene almost, but not
quite, rivals Bradford's, especially outside the
centre. Among the dozens of options, Akash,
Shireen and Manzel's stand out, but there are
plenty more. Other Pushplugs: Que Pasa
(Mexican); the Good Earth (veggie); Lynn's Café
(greasy spoon); Café Brussels; Bread & Roses
(veggie); Dino's (Italian); Fat Cat Café; San Carlo
(Italian); The Curry House (Britain's oldest).*
OTHER Leicester's numerous ethnic communities
add to the party calendar with annual Caribbean
and Mela (Asian) carnivals and Diwali (Hindu)
celebrations. Glastonbury's spawn, The Summer
Sundae, took place in the grounds of De Montfort
Hall.

UNIVERSITY

◍ PRICE OF A PINT OF BEER £1.40
◍ GLASS OF WINE £1.50
◍ CAN OF RED BULL £1.50
The Union scooped the Club Mirror award – *a
prestigious ents prize* – for Best Student Union in
2005, *which bodes well for those who like to come
out and play.*
BARS *The Redfearn's mix of regular events, pub
food and amber nectar make it the most popular
bar,* but there's back-up boozery at Elements and
the Global Café which does international nights.
THEATRES Leicester's assorted drama groups share
the thesping in Queen's Hall several times a year.
FILM The Attenborough film theatre is
purpose-built. Haphazard schedule of themed
seasons organised by various departments.
Nothing revolutionary.
MUSIC VENUES The Venue draws some class acts,
who've included The Subways, The Wedding
Present, the Go! Team and Graham Coxon. Sound
Asylum in Elements hosts local unsigned bands
and student gigs. Classical recitals take place in
the Charles Wilson Building.
CLUBBING Wednesday's aptly named cheesefest,
Red Leicester, always packs The Venue. Friday's
'Mad Fer-It' brings in the likes of Karl Kennedy
from Neighbours and *perma-tanned* Bargain
Hunter David Dickinson. *Unfortunately. Brighton
Beach is a must for mods and those whose ears*

L

got stuck in the 60s. Trevor Nelson and Dizzee Rascal have DJ'd.

COMEDY/CABARET Comedy happens fortnightly (in conjunction with Paramount) in Elements every Monday. The Charles Wilson building gets in on the act with the odd special event.

FOOD The University offers a discount card for food bought on campus. Scoff stops include: Snappers Diner; Loafer's for cafeteria fare and scrummy sarnies; Costa Coffee; the Venue Food Court does *cheap and chompable fare* while the Café Piazza has a *pricey continental style*. The Union shop stocks *a stellar array of* sandwiches.

OTHER There's a Summer Ball in The Venue – Jools Holland played last year. The Union lays on other events as and when it feels like it.

SOCIAL ◗◗◗◗◗◗◗◗◗◗◗◗◗

UNIVERSITY OF LEICESTER STUDENT'S UNION

○ **5 SABBATICALS** ○ **TURNOUT AT LAST BALLOT** 15%
○ **NUS MEMBER**

The SU enjoys a good relationship with the University administration and with the students. Housed in the labyrinthine Percy Gee building, it concentrates on organising successful ents and advisory services and on keeping the money machine in motion (not that they print their own or anything). Issues revolve around awareness and information and, rarely get overly political – that's the societies' business.

SU FACILITIES

Three bars; nightclub; cafeteria; snack bar; fast food outlet; three pool tables; meeting room; three minibuses for hire; NatWest and HSBC banks with ATMs; photocopier; fax service; payphones; advice centre; TV lounge; vending and gaming machines; general store; print shop; travel agency; secondhand bookshop.

CLUBS (NON-SPORTING)

Academia; Arab; Archaeology; AstroSoc; Ballroom & Latin American Dance; Band; Big Band; British Culture; CAMRA; Changeringers; Chemistry; Chess; Chinese; Choral; Classical; Cyprus; Duke of Edinburgh; Economics; Engineering; English; Football Supporters; Free Tibet; Friends of Falun Gong; Games; Geography; Geology; Hindu; History; Ideological; Italian; Investors; Japanese Animation; Jedi; Law; LeSEDS (space science); Let Us Play; Malaysian; Mass Communications; Maths & Computing; MedBioGen; MedSIN; Modern Dance; Modern Languages; Museum Studies; PC; Poetry; Politics; Pro Evolution Soccer; Psychology; PsyNeuro; Saudi; Scandinavian; Sikh; Singapore; SLUGS (Scout & Guides); Sociology; Street Jazz; Student Action for Refugees; Style Council (design); Taiwanese; Turkish; Travel; Umoja Gospel Choir; Viking; Welsh. *See also Clubs tables.*

OTHER ORGANISATIONS

As well as 'Ripple', the independent student newspaper (fortnightly), there's also Leicester University Student Television or 'LUST' for short and 'LUSH FM' – which recently got back on air and can be heard at www.lushfm.org. The charity Rag has a full-time sabbatical organiser and sets its sights on breaking its fund-raising record each year through parachute jumps, beer festivals and the ilk. 'Contact' is the student community group, which helps keep town-gown relations ticking over by running local help projects with more than 500 student volunteers. Luvvie soc the LUT organises an *annual Oscars night* to give pats-on-the-back to thesps and non-thesps alike.

RELIGIOUS

○ **7 CHAPLAINS** (**COFE, RC, METHODIST, URC, QUAKER, SALVATION ARMY, INTERNATIONAL STUDENTS**)

The Gatehouse Chaplaincy Centre welcomes students of all denominations and maintains links with Jewish, Hindu, Buddhist, Muslim and Sikh faith representatives. It has a TV lounge and offers cheap lunches – *so it's not all about God.* There's a Muslim prayer room on campus. Locally, there are churches and places of worship for every brand of god-fearer including a Jain Centre, unique outside the Indian subcontinent.

PAID WORK

○ **JOB BUREAU** ○ **PAID WORK** TERM-TIME 50%: HOLS 60%

The Union-run jobshop matches students with casual jobs and, failing that, there's always the Walkers Crisps factory. The University runs a student employment centre allowing local companies to recruit directly from the student body.

SPORTS ◗◗◗◗◗◗◗◗◗◗◗◗◗◗

○ **RECENT SUCCESSES** FOOTBALL, HOCKEY
○ **BUSA RANKING** 92

The Athletics Union is one of the best-funded around and *although they're no champs (Loughborough University takes most of the*

> ◎ **Six of the MPs elected in Labour's 1997 landslide were former presidents of the National Union of Students.**

L

trophies in this neck of the Midlands), the Leicester lot haven't thrown in any towels just yet. Competitive egos are soothed slightly by regular redbrick victories against local ex-poly rivals De Montfort. Rugby Union (men's and women's) and women's football are also starting to make waves.

SPORTS FACILITIES

The swanky Manor Road Sports Hall plays host to five-a-side, volleyball, netball, four badminton courts, two cricket nets, tennis, table tennis and runs fitness programmes. The Charles Wilson Sports Hall is the main onsite facility, offering all of the above plus frisbee, judo, fencing, karate and a sports shop. Three squash courts are sited near the School of Education. Leicester has 25 acres of playing fields, including an all-weather pitch, athletics track and nine tennis courts, plus Greenhouse 1 & 2, its well-equipped health and fitness suites. Facilities are free with a Sports Card for £45 a year. Leicester itself adds a croquet lawn/bowling green, seven swimming pools, four squash courts, hockey pitch, sports injury clinic, snooker and pool facilities, roller-blading rink, health and fitness club, golf course, basketball centre, dry ski slope, sauna and solarium, and the River Soar.

SPORTING CLUBS

American Football; Canoeing; Fell Walking; Ju Jitsu; Lacrosse; Mountaineers; Rifle; Rugby League; Rugby Union; Snowboarding; Table Tennis; Ultimate Frisbee. **See also Clubs tables.**

ATTRACTIONS

Apart from Leicester City FC, there are the Tigers (rugby), the Riders (basketball), the Panthers (American Football), Leicestershire Cricket Club, Cannons sports complex (very expensive though) and the Cycling Stadium.

ACCOMMODATION ⓤⓤⓤⓤⓤⓤⓤⓤⓤ

IN UNIVERSITY

◉ **CATERED** 18% ◉ **COST** £105 (30WKS)
◉ **SELF-CATERING** 34% ◉ **COST** £69 (39/42WKS)
◉ **1ST YRS LIVING IN** 90% ◉ **2ND YRS LIVING IN** 45%
◉ **FINALISTS LIVING IN** 45%
◉ **INSURANCE PREMIUM** ££

AVAILABILITY First years are guaranteed a place in university accommodation if they want it, and international students and returning finalists have priority too. The choice is between the five catered halls at Oadby, 2.5 miles from the campus (60s blocks and Edwardian houses beautifully set in the University's Botanical Gardens), the hall at Knighton (halfway to Oadby) or the five self-catering student houses and blocks, some at Knighton, but most nearer the campus. Freshers tend to make a beeline for the catered halls, which have an excellent pastoral care with prefect-type sub-wardens to keep students on the rails. Gilbert Murray Hall is non-smoking only. Plush Opal Court apartment complex appeared in 2003 and offers 669

self-catered places very near campus – mainly sought after by returning postgrads – the University is a bit precious about its new baby, however, and demands a £200 damage deposit in case students burn it down or poo on the walls. Less than 10% of hall residents have to share (cheaper) rooms and all halls are mixed, although sexes are split into corridors. The rooms themselves are a decent size – some are very new and have en suite facilities (Beaumont and Stamford for example) and the halls are well kitted-out with most having bars that buzz almost every night of the week, JCRs and, about half, computing facilities. The houses have single rooms and each is single sex but groups of houses are mixed. Some halls have night porters, wardens or postgrads that live on site.

CAR PARKING Plenty of spaces at most halls – with a £35 permit required for two of them.

EXTERNALLY

◉ **AVE RENT** £50 ◉ **LIVING AT HOME** <5%
AVAILABILITY A decent standard at pretty reasonable prices for those prepared to look. Trendy Evington and Clarendon Park are the most popular spots, so get hunting early. Other good bets include the Tudor Road and Narborough Road areas, Knighton and the city centre. Highfields is the cheap but dodgy district, so only those who enjoy being stalked at night should try it. Parking is about as difficult as getting a needle through the eye of a camel without the RSPCA complaining.

HOUSING HELP The University has the obligatory accommodation service that gives legal help and contract approval while the Union-run Accommodation Office advertises streetloads of vacancies and provides help and advice in the great home-hunt.

WELFARE ⓤⓤⓤⓤⓤⓤⓤⓤⓤⓤⓤⓤⓤ

SERVICES

◉ **LGBT OFFICER & SOCIETY** ◉ **ETHNIC MINORITIES OFFICER & SOCIETY** ◉ **WOMEN'S OFFICER & SOCIETY**
◉ **MATURE STUDENTS' OFFICER & SOCIETY**
◉ **INTERNATIONAL STUDENTS' OFFICER & SOCIETY**
◉ **DISABILITIES OFFICER & SOCIETY** ◉ **POSTGRAD OFFICER & SOCIETY** ◉ **LATE-NIGHT MINIBUS** ◉ **SELF-DEFENCE CLASSES** ◉ **NIGHTLINE** ◉ **UNIVERSITY COUNSELLORS** 15 FULL/2 PART ◉ **UNION COUNSELLORS** 4 FULL
◉ **CRIME RATING** !!!!

The comprehensive welfare service covers everything from dyslexia difficulties to counselling care. The Union runs a minibus back to halls on Wednesdays and Fridays after club nights at 1.40am and 2.15am (£1).

HEALTH The Freemen's Common Health centre offers six doctors and three nurses. The Hugh Binnie sick bay can give up to ten poorly peeps 24-hour care during term time.

CRIME Shouldn't be a problem, with the usual

caveat of exercising a bit of common sense – stick to well-lit areas and don't pootle around alone in Victoria park late at night. Those insistent on braving the *mean streets* of Highfields also do well to walk in groups. **DISABILITIES** There's the Richard Attenborough Centre for Disability and the Arts, a disability co-ordinator and an Accessibility Centre for students with specific difficulties. *The campus is easily accessible to wheelchair users.*

FINANCE
- **AVE DEBT PER YEAR** £3,556
- **HOME STUDENT FEES** £3,000

FEES International students' fees start at £8,200 and soar up to £10,950 (undergrad) or £19,500 (postgrad). UK postgrads pay from £3,085.
- **ACCESS FUND** £438,757 **SUCCESSFUL APPLICATIONS** 808 **AVERAGE PAYMENT** £500

SUPPORT Numerous hardship funds exist, some for specific groups (mature students, overseas students etc.), scholarships for physics, engineering and sports bursaries. The SU giv es hardship loans up to £100 and special needs students are given priority.

UNIVERSITY OF LINCOLN

FORMERLY UNIVERSITY OF LINCOLNSHIRE AND HUMBERSIDE

- **UNIVERSITY OF LINCOLN** Brayford Pool, Lincoln, LN6 7TS **TEL** (01522) 882 000 **E-MAIL** enquiries@lincoln.ac.uk **WEBSITE** www.lincoln.ac.uk **SU OFFICE (LINCOLN)** ULSU Co-operative, Brayford Pool, Lincoln, LN6 7TS **TEL** (01522) 886006 **E-MAIL** sureceptionlinc@lincoln.ac.uk **WEBSITE** www.lincolnsu.com

GENERAL ◑◑◑◑◑◑◑◑◑◑◑◑◑

Lincoln's a young University that's *traditionally* had strong links with Humberside. The town's *pretty, although when the most notable feature is a cathedral, the party-free alarm bells should start clanging.* Since emerging from the University of Lincolnshire and Humberside, Lincoln's *flexing its muscles and trying to prove it can stand on its own two feet* and has recently opened an *impressive* £5.4m science facility. *The place has got quite a taste for expansion: a veritable feast of new buildings is in the pipeline,* new courses are being laid on the Uni hopes to have 10,000 students by 2009.

SEX RATIO: ♀45 ♂55	**FOUNDED:** 1861
FULL-TIME U'GRADS: 8,292	**PART-TIME:** 662
POSTGRADS: 692	**NON-DEGREE:** 1,200
AVE COURSE: 3YRS	**ETHNIC:** 1%
STATE:PRIVATE SCHOOL: 97:3	**FLUNK RATE:** 18%
MATURE: 49%	**INTERNATIONAL:** 3%
DISABLED: 365	**LOCAL:** N/A

ATMOSPHERE
This modern (but not gruesomely so) £70m development on the edge of an ancient harbour in the historic city of Lincoln is primed for continued expansion. Recent additions include the £10m school of Architecture. Lincoln has lots of eager types, keen to better themselves in a development that looks more like a conference centre than an academic facility. There are several sites in Lincoln itself, the main one being the marina-side Brayford campus. *Students at Hull, an hour away, might feel like they're at a different university. University of Hull, possibly.*

SITES
BRAYFORD CAMPUS (6,985 students) Home to the main teaching building, library sports centre, Architecture and Media Communications. There's also the main library and *most importantly*, the SU bar. The campus is in the city centre, so there's no need for a car. The newish science building houses all the science courses and has all the usual technical mcgubbins.

RISEHOLME CAMPUS (327 students) Five miles from Lincoln's city centre and in a rural setting – *which is just as well, really*, as it's home to the countryside and animal-related courses. There are over 1,000 acres of farmed land and nearby there's woodland, deer parks, swimming pool, indoor riding arena and golfing. *Campus or holiday park, Push wonders.* The student bar recently had a revamp and there's one catered hall.

CATHEDRAL CAMPUS (327 students – Arts, Design, Conservation & Crafts)

HULL CAMPUS (800 students – Health & Social Care; Management Development) An hour from Lincoln, 45 mins from Leeds or Scarborough. The University's invested £4m into the City Centre Campus, as it's known, which means a new Learning Resource Centre and lecture theatres.

HULL see University of Hull

LINCOLN
- **POPULATION** 85,600 **CITY CENTRE** 0 MILES
- **LONDON** 132 MILES **HULL** 44 MILES
- **HIGH TEMP** 20 **LOW TEMP** 1 **RAINFALL** 58

Lincoln's a *beautiful* cathedral city surrounded by *peaceful, boring* countryside. A host of student-friendly bars, restaurants and clubs have been springing up since local amenity providers *recently woke up to the (allegedly lucrative)* student market.

Words in italics are Push's point of view — take it or leave it...

TRAVEL

HULL see University of Hull

LINCOLN

TRAINS The station, a few mins walk from the campus, has services to London (from £33.40 return), Birmingham (£17.95), Edinburgh (£54.65) and more.
COACHES National Express run services to London (£25), Birmingham (13.80) and other destinations.
CAR The A1 runs nearby, intersecting with the A46 at Newark and the A57 near Retford. Lincolnshire has no motorways.
BICYCLES *A hill from hell – use gears wisely.*

CAREER PROSPECTS

- **CAREERS SERVICE** ○ **NO. OF STAFF:** 4 FULL
- **UNEMPLOYED AFTER 6**MTHS 10%

FAMOUS ALUMNI

Antonio Berardi (fashion designer); Elliott Morley MP (Lab); Mary Parkinson (TV presenter).

FURTHER INFO

- **PROSPECTUSES** UNDERGRAD; POSTGRAD; VIDEO
- **OPEN DAYS**

Magazine and newsletter also available on request.

L

ACADEMIC ()()()()()()()()()()()()()()

There are now five faculties: Art, Architecture & Design; Technology; Business & Law; Media & Humanities; Health, Life & Social Sciences. There are also other departments of Health Leadership, Educational Leadership, Theology, Professional & Continuing Education. The Lincolnshire School of Agriculture is *one of the country's best*, for, er, learning about agriculture.

ENTRY POINTS: 240–400	**AVE POINTS: 370**
APPLICATIONS PER PLACE: 8	**CLEARING: 5%**
NO. OF TERMS: 2	**LENGTH OF TERMS: 16**WKS
STAFF TO STUDENT RATIO: 1:13	**STUDY ADDICTS: 35%**
TEACHING: ***	**RESEARCH: ***
YEAR ABROAD: 17%	**SANDWICH STUDENTS: 1%**
1STS**: 12%**	**2.2**S**: 30%**
2.1S**: 53%**	**3**RDS**: 5%**

ADMISSIONS

- **APPLY VIA UCAS**

SUBJECTS

ART & DESIGN 23%   **ARTS/MEDIA** 18%   **BUSINESS/LAW** 25%   **SOCIAL SCIENCES/HEALTH** 27%
UNUSUAL Advertising Art Direction; Animation; Conservation & Restoration; Golf Studies; Herbal Medicine; Interactive Screen-based Graphics; Museum & Exhibition Design.

LIBRARIES

- ○ **250,000 BOOKS** ○ **1,541 STUDY PLACES**

Opening hours are 8.30am till a red-eyed midnight. Provisions have improved following the recent expansions. The new £6m library opened last year and has already bagged several awards.

COMPUTERS

- ○ **1,200 WORKSTATIONS**

ENTERTAINMENT ()()()()()()()()()()

HULL see University of Hull

LINCOLN

- ○ **PRICE OF A PINT OF BEER** £2.60
- ○ **GLASS OF WINE** £2.95 ○ **CAN OF RED BULL** £2

CINEMAS There's a new multiplex cinema *almost within popcorn-throwing distance* of the campus.
THEATRES Board-treading *in abundance* at the Theatre Royal and Bishop's Palace. New venue Drill Hall puts on touring shows and community theatre.
PUBS/CLUBS The high street and Marina area have seen an explosion in student haunts, among them Revolution, Yate's, Edward's, Walkabout, the Annexe, Orgasmic and Dogma. *Pushplugs: Dogma; Bar Ln2; Kind. Pulse, Ritzy, Jumpin Jaks and Po Na Na are the most popular clubs.*
MUSIC VENUES *Lincoln's hardly on the big name circuit, but* Grafton House and O'Rourke's host local indie wannabes and O'Rourke's also has jazz nights. Drill Hall puts on *a decent musical smorgasbord*, ranging from classical and ballet to jazz and rock and roll.
EATING OUT Thai, Mexican and general scrumminess in Bailgate; Indian and many others dotted around the city.

UNIVERSITY

- ○ **PRICE OF A PINT OF BEER** £1.25 ○ **GLASS OF WINE** £2

No great shakes at present, but with the new student building (due summer 2006) set to include new club facilities, bars, and a music venue with 1,500 capacity, ents should breed like a rabbit on speed.
BARS Delph, the bar at Lincoln (cap 360) has DJ nights and live bands.
MUSIC VENUES Various bars in the new student centre will showcase Lincoln's *finest stage-strutters.*
CLUBBING Fuse is the indie/rock night at Delph; You're 'avin' a Giraffe brings out the crazy funsters.
FOOD The main Refectory is *usually packed* and everyday nosh is *pretty good*, but service stops at *a tummy-rumblingly early* 3.30pm.
OTHER Occasional balls and a drama society.

SOCIAL ⓊⓊⓊⓊⓊⓊⓊⓊⓊⓊⓊ

LINCOLN STUDENTS' UNION
◉ **6 SABBATICALS** ◉ **TURNOUT AT LAST BALLOT** 30%
◉ **NUS MEMBER**
The SU has suffered over the years from a bad case of spreading themselves too thin over different sites. Things are looking up, with the £6 million Student Centre (operated by the Uni in partnership with the Union) on the way. As well as bars, eats, shops and a music venue, the monster will house the various clubs and societies.

CLUBS (NON-SPORTING)
Breakdancing; Cheerleading; Chinese; Conservation; Fine Arts; History; Illustration; International Relations & Politics; Law; Outdoor Activities; Poker; Radio; Sci-fi; UNICEF; Video Gaming. **See also Clubs tables.**

OTHER ORGANISATIONS
SU mag is 'Bullet' and there's an indie Student paper, 'the Defender'. 'Siren FM' will have a full-time licence from 2007. Annual Rag week in April.

RELIGIOUS
◉ **CHAPLAIN**

PAID WORK
◉ **JOB BUREAU**

SPORTS ⓊⓊⓊⓊⓊⓊⓊⓊⓊⓊⓊⓊⓊ

◉ **RECENT SUCCESSES** BOXING ◉ **BUSA RANKING** 84
A recently added £5m sports facility should make its mark soon. *Ish.* The football team plays in BUSA's top division.

SPORTS FACILITIES
Football, all-weather and hockey pitches; squash, basketball and netball courts; sports hall; gym, multigym, sauna; aerobics studio; climbing wall; golf course; lake. There's also a *popular* canoeing club and two public pools in Lincoln.

SPORTING CLUBS
American Football; Boxing; Equine; Dodgeball; Gliding; Kickboxing; Motor Racing; Paintballing & Airsoft; Polo; Rowing; Snowsports. **See also Clubs tables.**

ACCOMMODATION ⓊⓊⓊⓊⓊⓊⓊⓊⓊ

IN UNIVERSITY
◉ **CATERED** 2% ◉ **COST** £102(33WKS)
◉ **SELF CATERING** 14% ◉ **COST** £102 (33WKS)
◉ **1ST YRS LIVING IN** 30% ◉ **INSURANCE PREMIUM** £

AVAILABILITY Rooms on a first come, first served basis, though the University tries to house as many non-local first years as possible. There are 1,134 self-catering study bedrooms arranged in courts of 8-14 on campus at Lincoln. Most are en suite and there are facilities for disabled students too. There are also accommodation staff on site to give support where needed.
CAR PARKING The Brayford Pool campus has *limited spaces* and parkers must get a £600 permit. But as it's slapbang in the city centre, *the Uni reckon a car should be an unnecessary, cash-consuming, enviromentally-unfriendly luxury anyway.*

EXTERNALLY

HULL see University of Hull

LINCOLN
◉ **AVE RENT** £80 ◉ **LIVING AT HOME** 5%
AVAILABILITY *Because Lincoln isn't yet swamped with house-hungry students there's enough private accommodation going, especially the relatively cheap Victorian houses around Monks Road and West Parade. The areas near the football ground are somewhat grimmer.*
HOUSING HELP Information on private housing is available from the SU. The University has close links with private landlords and there's a code of practice.

WELFARE ⓊⓊⓊⓊⓊⓊⓊⓊⓊⓊⓊⓊ

SERVICES
◉ **LGBT OFFICER & SOCIETY** ◉ **INTERNATIONAL STUDENTS' OFFICER** ◉ **ETHNIC MINORITIES' OFFICER** ◉ **WOMEN'S OFFICER** ◉ **DISABILITIES OFFICER & SOCIETY**
◉ **NIGHTLINE** ◉ **UNIVERSITY COUNSELLORS** 2 FULL/2PART
◉ **CRIME RATING** !!!!
The University advice office, with 15 staff, *does a top-notch job* of dealing with life's *little and not so little* troubles. There are also welfare drop-in sessions on both campuses.
HEALTH The student health service is staffed by three nurses.
DISABILITIES The University's Disability Access, Resources & Technology service (DART) gives info on allowance payments, arranges dyslexia assessments and equipment or facilities (notetakers, readers and so on). Facilities are available at both campuses.

FINANCE
◉ **AVE DEBT PER YEAR** £3,112
◉ **HOME STUDENT FEES** £3,000
◉ **ACCESS FUND** £500,000
◉ **SUCCESSFUL APPLICATIONS/YR** 1,500
SUPPORT The University waives fees for part-time undergraduates on income support.

Words in italics are Push's point of view — take it or leave it...

▶ **LINCOLN SCHOOL OF ART AND DESIGN**
see *University of Lincoln*

▶ **LINCOLNSHIRE SCHOOL OF AGRICULTURE**
see *University of Lincoln*

UNIVERSITY OF LIVERPOOL

◉ **UNIVERSITY OF LIVERPOOL** 150 Mount Pleasant, Liverpool, L69 3GD **TEL** (0151) 794 2000 **E–MAIL** ugrecriutment@liv.ac.uk
Website: www.liv.ac.uk ◉ **THE UNIVERSITY OF LIVERPOOL GUILD OF STUDENTS** 160 Mount Pleasant, Liverpool, L69 7BR **TEL**
(0151) 794 4128 **E–MAIL** gensec@liv.ac.uk **WEBSITE** www.liverpoolguild.org.uk

GENERAL ◖◗◖◗◖◗◖◗◖◗◖◗◖◗

From Gerry and his Pacemakers to the dearly departed Brookside and the legends that were the Beatles to new noisemakers like The Zutons and The Coral, Liverpool has always dipped its toes in the waters of youth culture. Merseyside's sliced in two by the River Mersey, dividing Liverpool from the Wirral. The city began as the primary seaway of the North-West and is still a bustling port. *Lucky Northerners get two major cities for the price of one as* Manchester is only 28 miles away. A major programme of redevelopment has been underway for some years now, and investors are still pouring their cash in, so attractive modern buildings are springing up amongst the art deco and post-industrialist architecture.

Liverpool's first university (joined by Liverpool John Moores University in 1992) battles Manchester for the title of the original 'redbrick' institution. The word was coined to describe the University's Victoria Building on Brownlow Hill. Many of the other buildings are redbrick too but others are more modern – *well, 60s and 70s –* based on a 100-acre site (*big for an inner city campus*) in the Mount Pleasant area of town, gazing out on the city from the brow of a hill.

SEX RATIO: ♂50 ♀50	FOUNDED: 1881
FULL–TIME U'GRADS: 13,623	PART–TIME: 622
POSTGRADS: 927	NON–DEGREE: 1,906
AVE COURSE: 3YRS	ETHNIC: 15%
STATE:PRIVATE SCHOOL: 85:15	FLUNK RATE: 6%
MATURE: 21%	INTERNATIONAL: 11%
DISABLED: 215	LOCAL: 38%

ATMOSPHERE

Liverpool students tend to be enveloped by the atmosphere of the city: down-to-earth, unpretentious and with a deeply ingrained sense of fun. Like the locals, the students have a strong sense of loyalty to their town that extends beyond a passing appreciation of its musical and footballing history through to its cultural, social and academic possibilities. They know they're here to work and they enjoy some excellent academic facilities, but with one of the best-equipped Unions in the country and some of the most stomping club venues, partying and studying mix together as smoothly as a double vodka and Red Bull.

OTHER SITES

The Vet school is at Leahurst in the Wirral. There's a free coach, *which is nice.*

LIVERPOOL

◉ **POPULATION** 439,473 ◉ **CITY CENTRE** 800M
◉ **LONDON** 201 MILES ◉ **CHESTER** 26 MILES
◉ **MANCHESTER** 28 MILES
◉ **HIGH TEMP** 21 ◉ **LOW TEMP** 2 ◉ **RAINFALL** 63
Having snatched the prestigious title of European Capital of Culture 2008 from under Newcastle's nose, Liverpool's come a long way from its roots as a prosperous mercantile port and is now recognised for its *thriving social scene and city-wide cultural infusion.* The sense of history still pervades, however – grand Victorian houses are still dotted around and ancient streets built for carriages still wind their way throughout the town. *It's not all glitzy olde worlde glamour though – there are still some areas that put the 'void' in 'avoidable'.* But away from the rough edges there's oodles of fun to be had – *Liverpool's bar scene and nightlife are buzzing* and the musical heritage – largely thanks to Lennon and Co. – is still a source of intense civic pride, as testified by the mind-boggling quantity of Beatles tours and paraphernalia available to the discerning musical tourist. The city centre is handily compact and The Albert Dock drags in droves of sightseers eager to check out the unmistakable Liverpudlian waterfront, with its vast array of shops, swanky bars, restaurants, museums and galleries.

TRAVEL

TRAINS Liverpool Lime Street is about ten mins walk down the road, offering mainline services to London (from £37.75 return), Manchester (£6.95), Leeds (£15.70), Birmingham (£17.55) and loads of other cities, big and small.
COACHES The National Express station on Norton

Street is 800m from campus and runs regular coaches to Leeds (£12.80), Birmingham (£11.60), London (£27) and hourly to Manchester (£6.80). **CAR** M53, M56, M57, M58 and M62 (good for North-West and Wales). There's a multi-storey car park sat beside the campus, £3 a day. *Parking on University premises is not an encouraging prospect.* **AIR** Liverpool Airport is eight miles from the city. It covers national and international destinations and runs cheap flights through easyjet and Keen. **FERRY** Liverpool's the main port for Belfast and there are other regular ferries to Ireland. *And, of course, there's the famous ferry 'cross the Mersey.* **HITCHING** *Good connections are a boon when it comes to lift-scrounging. Edge Lane is a top spot to pick up lifts just before it hits the motorway and the M57's not a bad option either. The University's dead against hitching.* **LOCAL** Arriva buses 86 and 26 are *useful, reliable* services to get to and from the University. Student fares cost £1 or so, but yearly or termly passes are *cheaper and less faffy* – check the Arriva website for discount deals. The *handy* Merseyrail trains trundle from the train station in the city centre to the suburbs and coastal towns like Southport (£2 rtn). **UNIVERSITY** Passes are available for the University bus service which runs between the Guild and halls of residence. **TAXIS** Plenty of black cabs crawl the kerbs – *complete with proud-to-be-Scouse, seen-it-all cabbies* – but pre-booking with local companies Delta or Botanics often works out cheaper. **BICYCLES** *It's not a hilly city, but Liverpool's a bit large and car-orientated for cycling to be the best transport choice.*

CAREER PROSPECTS
◉ **CAREERS SERVICE** ◉ **NO. OF STAFF** 25 FULL
◉ **UNEMPLOYED AFTER 6MTHS** 4%
The *excellent* Careers Service is a subdivision of the Centre for Lifelong Learning and offers students job alert e-mails, a fortnightly job bulletin, career fairs, employer presentations, work seminars and *a wealth of* application, CV and interview guidance.

FAMOUS ALUMNI
Steve Coppell (footballer and manager); Barry Horne (footballer, Everton and Wales); Maurice Colclough, Oliver Lodge (wireless radio pioneer); Tony Neary (rugby union); Hugh Jones (marathon runner); Chris Lowe (Pet Shop Boy); Alison Mowbray (Olympic rower); Phil Redmond (TV mogul and the brains behind Brookside, Grange Hill and Hollyoaks); Prof. Joseph Rotblat CBE (Nobel prize winning physicist); Patricia Routledge (actress). Jon Snow (TV news supremo) was thrown out for student protest-type activities before he graduated.

FURTHER INFO
◉ **PROSPECTUSES** UNDERGRAD; POSTGRAD; INTERNATIONAL; ALTERNATIVE ◉ **OPEN DAYS**
In addition to the annual open days independent visits can be arranged by contacting lstewart@liverpool.ac.uk. Prospectuses can be ordered via the main website which also offers a *comprehensive but plug-heavy* virtual tour of the campus.

ACADEMIC ◉◉◉◉◉◉◉◉◉◉◉◉

◉ **RUSSELL GROUP**
Liverpool's hot stuff academically, with a wide range of professionally directed, forward thinking courses up for the taking. It was the first place in the UK to open up departments in Architecture, Biochemistry, Civic Design and Oceanography and its English department was one of the first to admit that Science Fiction might be worth a second academic glance. As well as being an early pioneer in the academic study of Veterinary Science, the Uni has one of only two centres for tropical medicine in the country. Eight Nobel Prize winners have come and gone – it was here the link was made between mosquitoes and malaria – so there must be something good going on. Thirty-two departments are grouped into eight faculties – students are allocated a personal tutor from their faculty's staff, with whom they check-in twice a term. Teaching is a mix of seminars, compulsory lectures and practicals (as necessary). Courses are accessed through coursework, exams, presentations and projects; final grades are totted up as a combo of exam results over the course.

ENTRY POINTS: 280-390	AVE POINTS: N/A
APPLICATIONS PER PLACE: 7	CLEARING: 5%
NO. OF TERMS: 2	LENGTH OF TERMS: 19WKS
STAFF TO STUDENT RATIO: 1:13	STUDY ADDICTS: N/A
TEACHING: ★★★	RESEARCH: ★★★
YEAR ABROAD: 4%	SANDWICH STUDENTS: 1%
1STS: 12%	2.2S: 28%
2.1S: 48%	3RDS: 3%

ADMISSIONS
◉ **APPLY VIA UCAS**
Liverpool has an open door policy when it comes to providing Higher Education for people of all ages and backgrounds. Those with non-traditional qualifications or experience *need not be scared to apply.*

SUBJECTS
ARTS 20% **DENTISTRY** 3% **ENGINEERING** 8% **HEALTH SCIENCE** 4% **MEDICINE** 11% **SCIENCE** 21% **SES** 27% **VETERINARY MEDICINE** 4%
BEST Agriculture; Architecture; Biology;

L

◉ **Sheffield Rag once tried to paint a zebra crossing on the M1.**

Communications & Information Studies; English; European Languages & Area Studies; History & Archaeology; Human & Social Geography; Maths; Mechanically-based Engineering; Medical Science & Pharmacy; Physical Geography & Environmental Sciences; Physical Sciences; Psychology; Performing Arts; Veterinary Science. **UNUSUAL** Irish Studies (only course in the world).

LIBRARIES
◉ 1,800,000 BOOKS ◉ 1,678 STUDY PLACES
◉ SPEND PER STUDENT £££££
Of the four biggest libraries, the Sydney Jones Library is the daddy, but the Harold Coen Library alone would be big enough for most universities. The Law and Education Libraries are fairly chunky too, and there a large number of smaller, departmental book stashes.

COMPUTERS
◉ 1,388 WORKSTATIONS ◉ 24-HR ACCESS
◉ SPEND PER STUDENT ££
Brownlow Hill computer lab is 24-hr access – as long as students cough up £10 a year for the privilege. Workstations are available in the libraries and departmental labs. Study bedrooms now all have broadband facilities.

OTHER LEARNING FACILITIES
Drama studio to prance in; rehearsal rooms to *dance in.*

ENTERTAINMENT ◗◗◗◗◗◗◗◗◗◗

THE CITY
◉ PRICE OF A PINT OF BEER £2
◉ GLASS OF WINE £2 **◉ CAN OF RED BULL** £2
CINEMAS Two in the city centre, a bog-standard Odeon and Fact – the first purpose-built arts project in Liverpool for 60 years. The £10m complex houses three cinema screens (old, new and arty films) – one of which has comfy sofas – two galleries, a media lounge and *the trendiest of trendy bars.* Multiplexes and one-screen shacks are dotted around the suburbs.
THEATRES The Empire is a pre-West End stopover for touring shows. The smaller and more *daring* Everyman Theatre has an *innovative and unconventional slant.* The Liverpool Playhouse in the centre hosts some major productions and there's also the *small but perfectly formed Unity Theatre for an appealing array of comedy, dance and drama.*
PUBS *The boom in swish trend-setting bars and national chain pubs has hit Liverpool with all the force of the tenth tequila slammer. There are now lots of new places worthy of student attention,* including the *very sophisticated* Tea Factory, *the funky but cheesy Baa Bar – which does loads of £1 shooters –* and The Pilgrim, which is *popular with the arty student set.* Brookhouse is a *popular* pub in the middle of a student housing area and has the added bonus of drawing in the *unfeasibly*

attractive stars of Hollyoaks. Students jostle along with locals in *traditional boozers (and onetime Beatle haunts)* Ye Cracke and Jacaranda. *There are too many other places to mention, but Cava (cosy tequila bar), Magnet, Korova (indie chic), Roadkill (nu rock/metal), Blue Bar, Revolution, Walkabout and Tru Bar & Grill are all good places to start.*
CLUBBING *More choice than any dedicated dance-fiend could ever deserve. Medication at Nation (Wed) piles the punters into its three rooms – a mix of urban, dance and cheese. Vodka Nation at Garlands (Thurs) is student night but's better at the weekends for those not into dance and Scouse House. Vod Bull at The Office is a popular Tuesday pastime. Top pulling spot The Krazy House is a bit more alternative but lures in all sorts with its cheap drinkage. The Blue Angel (aka The Razz) could be cleaner but there's something so seductive about its relentless onslaught of cheesy pop every night of the week.*
COMEDY/CABARET The Rawhide Royal Court hosts variety and comedy shows.
MUSIC VENUES *The new Carling Academy is one of the few places in the world where it's still acceptable to shout 'Let's Rock!' without being ironic.* Barfly gets up-and-comers plus lots of local live acts. The Philharmonic Hall holds the city's orchestra plus serious muso acts such as Sigur Ros and Morrissey. *There's heaps of other smaller venues, including Zanzibar and the intimate Magnet.*
EATING OUT *It's entirely possibly to live without a kitchen in Liverpool – although only the supremely minted would consider dining out all the time. There are some good value eateries though: Shere Khan is close to being the finest curry house in the world – or at least Liverpool – with funky décor and extensive menu. Cheap and cheerful Kimos has a half-hearted Mediterranean theme but does divine kebabs. St Petersburg is a rare thing - a Russian restaurant. Caesar's Palace is the venue for posh dates without posh prices and Tabac, Magnet, The Quarter (Italian) and Ask are also popular. China Town has eateries aplenty, or May Sum in the town centre does an eat-till-you-puke buffet with a student discount.*

UNIVERSITY
◉ PRICE OF A PINT OF BEER £1.20
◉ GLASS OF WINE £1.40
◉ CAN OF RED BULL £1.40
BARS There are ten bars in and around the Guild and University. *Most popular is the Liver Bar, an art deco-style haven of purple, pink and pound-a-pint* offers all day every day. The Gilmour Bar is *highly ornate,* with a listed ceiling. The Ken Saro Wiwa bar (named after the executed Nigerian political prisoner) is *a modern place that's a good spot for a cheap lunch.* The other lounge, basement and balcony bars get an airing on club nights.
THEATRES The Stanley Theatre in the Guild was recently refurbished and there's a drama studio to boot. The two active drama societies put quite a few shows on each year, usually one up in Edinburgh too.

Words in italics are Push's point of view — take it or leave it...

FILM A *large screen* in the Guild puts on free film nights from time to time.

MUSIC VENUES The Liverpool Academy 1, 2, 3 and 4 are major venues both for the University and the rest of the city. Venue sizes range from a stonking 2,000 to an intimate 150. The year-round programme of gigs has featured Editors, KT Tunstall and Goldfrapp.

CLUBBING Monday's Double Vision at the Guild is now *one of the largest nights going in the UK* featuring indie, dance, hip hop, R&B – *everything really* – in three rooms, including the Live Lounge where upcoming talent is showcased. The bar is often reputed to run dry by the end of the night. Time Tunnel, the Saturday retro night, is now over ten years old *and hasn't yet lost its sense of kitsch*. Mr Scruff has DJ'd.

COMEDY/CABARET Regular comedy in Academy 1 brings in some big names.

FOOD The bars all serve some kind of food or other, with pizza in the Liver Bar and bargain breakfasts at Reilly getting a big digestive thumbs up. The 700-seat Courtyard *makes the Guild the culinary and social centre of the campus and completely eliminates the need for a main University refectory*. Several departments have *itty bitty* snack bars.

OTHER All major departments arrange balls *which pale in comparison to the enormous Graduation Ball in July.*

SOCIAL ◖◖◖◖◖◖◖◖◖◖◖◖◖

THE UNIVERSITY OF LIVERPOOL GUILD OF STUDENTS
◉ 4 SABBATICALS ◉ TURNOUT AT LAST BALLOT 13%
◉ NUS MEMBER

With the second-largest Union building in Europe (Paris holds the top spot), *Liverpool students are a lucky bunch, especially when it comes to entertainment* – which the ents officer lays on *thick and fast. The exec is a slick, professional organisation with a number of commercial interests that help to stock its ample piggybank.* Relations with the University are co-operative – both the Guild and Uni authorities are prepared to *listen to each other and the SU is represented on most University committees. Although not overly political, students have launched a few volleys against 'Top-Up' Tony's tuition fee proposals.*

SU FACILITIES
Ten bars; five cafeterias; print shop; general shop; photographers; optician; Little Cohen library with study area; travel agency; ticket agency; advice centre; Royal Bank of Scotland with ATMs; prayer room; international lounge; launderette; hairdresser; table tennis; snooker/pool tables; Mountford Hall; theatre; new bookshop; dark room; band practice room; function rooms; photo booth; post office; games and vending machines; film-making facilities; minibus hire; photocopying.

CLUBS (NON-SPORTING)
AIESEC; Anime; Band (rock/pop); Break dancing; Chinese; CND; Cocktail; Dance Music; Drum & Bass; Friends of Palestine; Fusion (Christian); Hindu; Hip-hop; Indian; Jazz; Funk & Soul; JAM (Joint Anglican Methodist); Juggling; LINKS (St John Ambulance); Malaysian; MatSoc; Meditation; Mexican; Mountaineering; Music; Neighbours; Open Air; Paintballing; PopSoc; Potholing; Ras-Malaii (Asian women's culture); Real Ale; Roleplay gaming. Sikh; Singapore; SLAGS (Scouts & Guides); STAR (refugee action); Sri-Lankan; plus many departmental societies. **See also Clubs tables.**

OTHER ORGANISATIONS
'Liverpool Student'' is a city-wide publication that John Moores and Liverpool Hope also have hands in. It and its hacks have been noticed several times by the Student Media Awards. 'Icon' radio broadcasts daily on the net. Liverpool Rag is *lively* and bagged £8,500 for charity last year, while Liverpool Student Community Action goes forth and does good works. The drama society is *popular and well-run*, and the 'Give It A Go' scheme lets students try out new activites. LUSTI (Liverpool University Student Trainers Initiative) organises free skills training.

RELIGIOUS
◉ 2 CHAPLAINS (COFE, RC) RABBI

There's a Muslim prayer room in the Union and an Anglican chaplaincy on campus. Two cathedrals in town, Catholic and Anglican, in *strongly contrasting* architectural styles, and both within praying distance of the Union. There are plenty of churches (including Swedish and Greek Orthodox), more synagogues than in any other English town this size and a few mosques, as well as temples for Hindus, Buddhists and Hare Krishnas.

PAID WORK
◉ JOB BUREAU
◉ PAID WORK TERM-TIME 55-70%; HOLS 70-90%

PULSE is run through the Careers Service and sources part-time and temporary vacancies which it advertises through e-mail and text alerts. The Business Bridge scheme can help with finding placements in local companies. Liverpool itself has a high unemployment rate, but the tenacious job-seeker should be able to find bar, shop call-centre or restaurant work.

SPORTS ◖◖◖◖◖◖◖◖◖◖◖◖◖◖

◉ RECENT SUCCESSES WOMEN'S BASKETBALL, TRIATHLON
◉ BUSA RANKING 40

Only three years younger than the University itself the Athletics Union lures around a third of the student body into *its oiled and muscular grip. Facilities are among the best of any university in the country*, and include a four-court sports hall, changing facilities, *state-of-the art* dance and fitness centre and disabled facilities in the pool. *Sporting successes of the past couple of years have lifted competitive spirits.*

SPORTS FACILITIES

Strewth: over 70 acres of playing fields for athletics, football, rugby, hockey, lacrosse and cricket spread over the area around halls of residence. There are more playing fields at Maryton Grange and Widnes (served by University minibuses). Two sports centres on campus include: swimming pool; climbing wall; dance studio; multigym; basketball/netball courts. Thrown into the bundle are the boathouse at Knowsley Park and the outdoor activity centre all the way over in Snowdonia. Membership of the AU costs £24/year. Liverpool itself adds extra facilities into the mix, including the River Mersey, a dry ski slope, a golf course and a number of *high quality* leisure centres (Toxteth, Everton and Kirby, for example).

SPORTING CLUBS

10-Pin Bowling; Dance; Diving & Waterpolo; Lacrosse; Multi-sports; Rifle; Table-Tennis. **See also Clubs tables.**

ATTRACTIONS

Liverpool FC are still legendary in the world of football and have kept one of the most impressive records in English club history. That's not to say that their neighbours Everton haven't done pretty damn well for themselves though – ditto their *less famous but still feisty friends* the Tranmere Rovers. The Grand National venue Aintree Race Course is around and about, as well as some other *diamond* spectator-spots. Golfwise, Merseyside has some of the best links courses in the UK.

ACCOMMODATION ◗◗◗◗◗◗◗◗◗◗◗

IN UNIVERSITY

- ◉ **CATERED** 15% ◉ **COST** £97 (32WKS)
- ◉ **SELF CATERING** 9% ◉ **COST** £69 (38/40/42WKS)
- ◉ **1ST YRS LIVING IN** 81% ◉ **INSURANCE PREMIUM** £
AVAILABILITY Liverpool's halls are almost exclusively stocked with first years, although there aren't quite enough rooms for all of those that want them. Rent prices include cleaning of communal areas and, in catered accommodation, two entirely edible meals a day. Mulberry Court and Philharmonic Court Halls *are popular by virtue of their closeness to campus*, but Greenbank and Carnatic – both on *pleasant green sites* three miles away – have strong social atmospheres and are served by a University bus service morning and evening. Most halls have laundry facilities, TV lounge, sports facilities on hand, computers and a bar. Security is pretty tight.
CAR PARKING Limited permit-only parking.

EXTERNALLY

◉ **AVE RENT** £55
AVAILABILITY *Generally no problem* finding somewhere to live, but the crème de la caramel is always gone by mid-February so – *as when showering in prisons* – it pays to be vigilant. The biggest problem students face is finding somewhere close to their place of study, but few end up miles away. *Smithdown Road is popular for its easy bus routes. Some areas have developed as decidedly studenty, such as Wavertree (a veritable student ghetto), Sefton Park (more expensive, but arty, converted flats), Allerton, Mossley Hill, Aigburth, Old Swan and the famous Penny Lane. Some areas are less appealing, such as Toxteth and Walton, but students do live there quite happily. Kensington and Toxteth are also worth a mention – many choose to live there for the cheapness despite bad press. Plenty of central but soulless private halls have sprung up over the past few years.*
HOUSING HELP Liverpool University and John Moores joined forces to create Liverpool Student Homes – an accommodation-finding service that has branches on campus, at Mount Pleasant and on Edge Lane. Contract approval, safety checks and vacancy posting are all within its remit.

WELFARE ◗◗◗◗◗◗◗◗◗◗◗◗◗

SERVICES

◉ **LGBT OFFICER & SOCIETY** ◉ **ETHNIC MINORITIES SOCIETY** ◉ **WOMEN'S OFFICER & SOCIETY** ◉ **MATURE STUDENTS' OFFICER & SOCIETY** ◉ **INTERNATIONAL STUDENTS' OFFICER & SOCIETY** ◉ **POSTGRAD OFFICER & SOCIETY** ◉ **DISABILITIES SOCIETY** ◉ **LATE-NIGHT/ WOMEN'S MINIBUS** ◉ **NIGHTLINE** ◉ **UNIVERSITY COUNSELLORS** 2 FULL/2 PART ◉ **CRIME RATING** !!!!!
The Student Advice Centre and the sabbatical Welfare Officer act as first points of contact for troubled students – they either dole out advice or refer to one of the University's specialist support services. As well as the above there are nine associate volunteer counsellors (professionally trained). Student Health Services and the Medial Faculty have a part-time clinical psychologist each.
HEALTH The Brownlow Group Practice based at the Student Services Centre offers full-time surgeries all year round, as well as emergency treatment and medical services at halls.
WOMEN: Women-only swimming lessons, self-defence classes and priority on the University bus service. Not all at the same time, mind.
CRECHES/NURSERY 68 places for kiddies younger than 5.
DISABILITIES *Access isn't entirely peachy*, but there's been serious investment towards ramps and lifts in some campus buildings. There's a Disabled Students' Working Party as well as particular provisions for hearing-impaired and students with dyslexia.

CRIME *Not much of a problem*, but minor thefts are common enough to warrant caution.
DRUGS There's a help service on campus for students with drug problems, but these are few and far between. There are the usual drug issues in the city.

FINANCE
○ **AVE DEBT PER YEAR** £4,730
○ **HOME STUDENT FEES** £3,000
FEES Foundation year fees are £1,200 and a year abroad/sandwich year costs £600. Part-timers pay £375 per 15 credit module. Postgrads pay £3,085. International student fees: arts £8,350; sciences £10,750; clinical £16,650; foundation year £8,350. Overseas postgrad students pay between £8,350 (arts) and £13,500 (MBAs).
○ **ACCESS FUND** £650,000 ○ **SUCCESSFUL APPLICATIONS/YR** 1,200 ○ **AVE PAYMENT** £650
SUPPORT The University offers financial advice and assistance to students with holes in their piggy banks. As well as the standard government help, the Uni's Liverpool Bursary offers up to £1,300 a year to those in need.

LIVERPOOL HOPE UNIVERSITY

FORMERLY LIVERPOOL INSTITUTE OF HIGHER EDUCATION, LIVERPOOL HOPE UNIVERSITY COLLEGE

1. ○ **LIVERPOOL HOPE UNIVERSITY** Hope Park, Liverpool, L16 9JD **TEL** (0151) 291 3000 **E-MAIL** admission@hope.ac.uk
WEBSITE www.hope.ac.uk ○ **LIVERPOOL HOPE STUDENTS' UNION WEBSITE** www.hopesu.ac.uk
2. ○ **HOPE AT EVERTON** Haigh street, Liverpool, L3 8QB

GENERAL ○○○○○○○○○○○○○

Five miles from the centre of Liverpool sits the *calm and collected* world of Liverpool Hope. It began its life by linking St Katherine's and Notre Dame Colleges of Teacher Education for Women, annexed their male equivalent, Christ Church, spent a brief spell as the Liverpool Institute for Higher Education in 1980, pupated into a university college in 1995 before gaining *full-on, hardcore* university status in 2005. Phew. It's always had *strong godly leanings* and maintains a *firmly* religious outlook – although it's by no means as Jesus-centric as it once was. The campus itself is a compact collection of *drab* bricks and glass, which conceal some of the *much more exciting* architecture of the original buildings and chapels at the campus's centre. For general info about Liverpool: see University of Liverpool.

SEX RATIO: ♂34 ♀66	**FOUNDED:** 1844
FULL-TIME U'GRADS: 4,176	**PART-TIME:** 991
POSTGRADS: 1,180	**NON-DEGREE:** 1,080
AVE COURSE: 3YRS	**ETHNIC:** 7%
STATE:PRIVATE SCHOOL: N/A	**FLUNK RATE:** 24%
MATURE: 30%	**INTERNATIONAL:** 6%
DISABLED: 200	**LOCAL:** N/A

ATMOSPHERE
The Hope community is cosy almost to the point of stifling – even woollen airlocks couldn't be this close-knit. Most students treat their workload with relaxed determination, intent on getting the job done then getting a job, without too much excitement en route. In fact, 'University life' is a bit of an oxymoron here. Students drain from the campus at weekends – even the cafés close – but the SU musters enough enthusiasm for an ent or two midweek. The bulk of the party action, however, is orientated around Smithdown Road, where many students live out. Relations with locals have moments of tension due to noise and parking.

SITES
EVERTON (1,000 students – Creative Arts) Four miles from Hope Park and closer to the city centre, this site is situated in a newly-developed residential area and provides accommodation blocks and some of the *artier* facilities, plus the Great Hall theatre venue, a bar and a café.

○ **Hollyoaks often films at Liverpool Hope. The halls and gym are often used, while the library doubles as a court room.**

LIVERPOOL see University of Liverpool

TRAVEL see University of Liverpool
TRAINS Mossley Hill, about three miles away, is the nearest station, but Liverpool Lime Street, 5.5 miles away, is *a better bet* for national journey-making.
COACHES National Express Coaches trundle out of Edge Lane Drive, 1.5 miles from campus.
CAR *Like a whalebone corset, parking regulations on campus are both morally controversial and restrictive* – there are very few spaces and visitors have to book in advance. The neighbourhood is residential, so on-street parking is a possibility, *but this isn't going down too well with the residents themselves.*
LOCAL Buses 75 and 78 make the half-hour journey into the city centre every 10 mins for £1.
UNIVERSITY A free hourly shuttlebus runs between both main sites. Students living in Aigburth or Everton halls get a discounted bus pass in deference to their distance.
BICYCLES *Barely any bike theft on or around campus, largely because there's barely any bikes to thieve.*

CAREER PROSPECTS
 ⊙ **CAREERS SERVICE** ⊙ **NO. OF STAFF** 8 FULL/1 PART
 ⊙ **UNEMPLOYED AFTER 6**MTHS 6%
The Career Development Service provides guidance, e-guidance *(we don't mean drugs advice)*, a library, interview training, vacancy lists and arranges job fairs. Someone is always available out of hours to *deal with career emergencies – of the 'Help! My professional development is swerving dangerously off course' type.*

FAMOUS ALUMNI
Willy Russell (playwright, Shirley Valentine).

FURTHER INFO
 ⊙ **PROSPECTUSES** UNDERGRAD; POSTGRAD; DEPARTMENTAL; INTERNATIONAL; PGCE; VIDEO ⊙ **OPEN DAYS**

ACADEMIC ⊙⊙⊙⊙⊙⊙⊙⊙⊙⊙⊙⊙

The University's strong ecumenical background means that even the academic side of life has a strong religious aftertaste – instead of faculties or departments, students study in one of five 'deaneries'. Courses are modular and very flexible, particularly in the second and third years, when students can find themselves studying several diverse subjects as part of the same course. There's no scheduled one-to-one lecturer contact as such, *but since everyone's so darned friendly and accessible*, individual help is always available. Course-wise, teacher training is probably its *biggest hitter.*

ENTRY POINTS: 220	AVE POINTS: 220
NO. OF TERMS: 3	LENGTH OF TERMS: 10WKS
STAFF TO STUDENT RATIO: 1:23	STUDY ADDICTS: 14%
TEACHING: ***	RESEARCH: **
YEAR ABROAD: N/A	SANDWICH STUDENTS: N/A
1STS: 5%	2.2s: 46%
2.1s: 42%	3RDS: 7%

ADMISSIONS
 ⊙ **APPLY VIA UCAS/DIRECT FOR PART-TIME COURSES**
LHU is predisposed to applicants with some sort of religious conviction and also looks positively on hopefuls who are mature, disabled, international or who need to remain in the North West for any reason *(except maybe house arrest).*

SUBJECTS
ARTS & COMMUNITY 16%   **BUSINESS & IT** 14%
EDUCATION 36%   **HUMANITIES** 12%
SCIENCES/SOCIAL SCIENCES 22%
BEST Art & Design; Biology; Business; Computer Science; Education; English; Geography; Health; History; Management; Performing Arts.
UNUSUAL Computer Gaming; Psychology students can take a parapsychology option. *Wooh, spooooky!*

LIBRARIES
 ⊙ **250,000 BOOKS** ⊙ **500 STUDY PLACES**
 ⊙ **24-HR ACCESS**
The *arcane-sounding* Sheppard-Worlock Library is open all day, every day and has substantial collections of child education books and, *unsurprisingly enough*, theology. Fans of *soft porn chav-soap* Hollyoaks may find the library eerily familiar – it's used as the set for courtroom scenes.

COMPUTERS
 ⊙ **500 WORKSTATIONS** ⊙ **SPEND PER STUDENT** £££
No workstation is more than four years old as a matter of policy, *although that's still pretty geriatric by today's standards.*

OTHER LEARNING FACILITIES
Drama studio; music rooms; media centre with video recording and editing facilities; radio studio.

ENTERTAINMENT ⊙⊙⊙⊙⊙⊙⊙⊙⊙⊙

THE CITY see University of Liverpool
There are very few pubs in the local area, so students have to venture city-wards to *quench their thirst/get blind stinking trollied.* As far as clubbing goes, Blue Angel (Tues) is the *unofficial Hope night out*, with 95% of the punters being Hope students enjoying the any-drink-for-a-pound-promotion.

UNIVERSITY
 ⊙ **PRICE OF A PINT OF BEER** £1.20
 ⊙ **GLASS OF WINE** £1.60 ⊙ **CAN OF RED BULL** £2
BARS Two small and slightltly tatty boozers at Hope Park. Derwent is *so laid back it's upside down, but buzzes on Friday nights.* Wednesday is sports night and Thursday's open mic night is like *Russian Roulette with talent.* D2 is bigger and gets used for more special events – comedy nights, big screen sports etc. There's a third bar at Everton *but no one gets very excited about it.*
THEATRES The *arty* sorts at Everton put on shows

in the Great Hall each year, but the big event is the Cornerstone drama, music and poetry festival which attracts visiting professionals.
FILM There's a big screen in D2.
MUSIC VENUES Great Hall hosts classical concerts.
CLUBBING Hope is *hardly party central*, but the Derwent Bar has different DJs, themed nights and drinks promos for *low-key light relief*.
FOOD Munchers' paradise: *a big, light and airy* refectory with three food counters dishing up cheap deli-style snacks, hot meals and sandwiches and salads. In the SU, the Derwent Bar does bar snacks and hot dishes at lunch time. There's also a *teeny-tiny* shop for chocs, crisps, and other calorific goodies.
OTHER The Graduation and Christmas Balls are held at the *swanktastic* Adelphi Hotel in town.

SOCIAL ᕮᕮᕮᕮᕮᕮᕮᕮᕮᕮᕮᕮᕮ

LIVERPOOL HOPE STUDENTS' UNION
⊙ **2 SABBATICALS** ⊙ **TURNOUT AT LAST BALLOT** 15%
⊙ **NUS MEMBER**
Although it dresses slightly to the right, a pickled badger is more actively political than LHSU, which concentrates on welfare and providing free ents to its members, though it does get involved in national NUS campaigns and is currently fighting to free up Wednesday afternoons for sporty activities. *The University's religious bent means it disapproves of some of the Union's more raucous activities, eg. a recent plan to chuck condoms into the crowd at the Derwent went down like a lead-filled Durex.*

SU FACILITIES
Derwent House Union Building has: two bars; canteen; four pool/snooker tables; meeting room; Endsleigh Insurance; hairdressers; NatWest bank & ATM; photocopier, fax & printing service; photo booth; payphones; advice centre; TV lounge; juke box; gaming machines; general store; stationery shop; vending machines; bookshop; computer shop; launderette.

CLUBS (NON-SPORTING)
Gospel Choir; Sri Lankan. **See also Clubs tables.**

OTHER ORGANISATIONS
'Liverpool Student' is the free city-wide fortnightly newspaper run jointly with the University of Liverpool and Liverpool John Moores. 'Radio Hope' has just celebrated its first birthday and broadcasts across the city 4pm-12am daily. Rag raises *a quid or two* for good causes and Hope One World sends do-gooders out to Nepal, India, Sri Lanka and Africa to, er, do good.

RELIGIOUS
⊙ **3 CHAPLAINS (COFE; RC; METHODIST)**
LHSU is a *deeply* religious institution so most brands of Christian are well-provided for by the two chapels. There's a muslim prayer room. Religion in Liverpool: see University of Liverpool

PAID WORK
⊙ **JOB BUREAU** ⊙ **PAID WORK:** TERM-TIME: 50 ; HOLS 95
Jobzone at the Career Development Service allows browsing of vacancies. Teacherzone does the same for the more vocationally-minded. The Business Bridge scheme ships 200-300 students into local companies each year.

SPORTS ᕮᕮᕮᕮᕮᕮᕮᕮᕮᕮᕮᕮᕮ

⊙ **RECENT SUCCESSES** MEN'S AND WOMEN'S GAELIC FOOTBALL ⊙ **BUSA RANKING** 82
They may not punch the hardest in the sports ring, but LHSU has an admirable 'have a go' attitude and tries to cater for as many different sports as it feasibly can.

SPORTS FACILITIES
The Sports Hall is independent from the College and self-financing. Students have access to: five pitches (two football, rugby, two all-weather); two tennis courts; sports hall; gym; aerobics studio; dance studio; multigym. £12 a year covers usage costs. Plas Caerdeon is the University's outdoor education centre in North Wales. See University of Liverpool for local facilities.

SPORTING CLUBS
Curling; Gaelic Football; Kick Boxing. **See also Clubs tables.**

ATTRACTIONS see University of Liverpool

ACCOMMODATION ᕮᕮᕮᕮᕮᕮᕮᕮᕮ

IN UNIVERSITY
⊙ **SELF CATERING** 26% ⊙ **COST** £72 (36WKS)
⊙ **1ST YRS LIVING IN** 80% ⊙ **INSURANCE PREMIUM** £
AVAILABILITY Almost all first years have a room if they want one, given the usual deadline and application criteria. Halls are mainly on campus, with one at the Everton site and another at Aigburth (both about four miles away). Facilities are swankier at the top end of the price range. No smoking in communal areas and some halls. Just over half the rooms are en suite. Vending machines, telephones, launderettes and plasma/widescreen/ Sky TV lounges are available on all sites.
CAR PARKING *They'd really rather you didn't, and definitely not permanently.* Student cars being left on local residential streets has caused friction in the past.

EXTERNALLY

⊙ AVE RENT £45

AVAILABILITY see University of Liverpool

HOUSING HELP LHSU provides a list of postcodes that might be worth a glance. See University of Liverpool for services provided by Liverpool Student Homes.

WELFARE ◑◑◑◑◑◑◑◑◑◑◑◑◑◑

SERVICES

⊙ LGBT OFFICER ⊙ MATURE STUDENTS' OFFICER & SOCIETY ⊙ POSTGRAD OFFICER & SOCIETY ⊙ OVERSEAS STUDENTS' OFFICER & SOCIETY ⊙ DISABILITIES OFFICER & SOCIETY ⊙ UNIVERSITY COUNSELLORS 1 FULL/ 2 PART **⊙ CRIME** !!!!

Compass, the Student Services organisation, has a *friendly and competent* welfare arm. The Chaplaincy offers tea and sympathy to all students, regardless of their religion or lack of it, and *the five staff are said to be especially good* at taking international students under their wing.

HEALTH Two visiting doctors look after students in University accommodation every Tues and Wed and there's a full-time College Nurse. Those living out have to register at a recommended GP surgery.

CRÈCHES/NURSERY Hope Park nursery has places for 24 kidlings 3mths-5yrs.

DISABILITIES Access and support for disabled students is very good, with specialised study bedrooms, support workers, note-takers and technological resources for the deaf and blind. An outside agency runs a Study Skills support service.

CRIME *Campus is considered very safe. A copshop on campus helps, as do the links the College fosters with local police.*

FINANCE

⊙ AVE DEBT PER YEAR £3,616

⊙ HOME STUDENT FEES £3,000

FEES International undergrads are charged £6,080.

⊙ ACCESS FUND £450,000 **⊙ SUCCESSFUL APPLICATIONS** 576 **⊙ AVE PAYMENT** £100-3,500

SUPPORT The Uni has £800,000 tucked away to give in scholarships to new UK students from 2006/07. There are busaries of £1,000 plus scholarships of £1,000 and £2,000 for top A level grades and a bunch of smaller awards. From 2009 the top 30 undergrads will be given £5,000 at graduation to fund extra studies.

L

▶ LIVERPOOL HOPE UNIVERSITY COLLEGE
see *Liverpool Hope University*

▶ LIVERPOOL INSTITUTE OF HIGHER EDUCATION (LIHE)
see *Liverpool Hope University*

⊚ **A former Vice-President of Liverpool John Moores Students' Union was hypnotised on 'Richard & Judy' by a dog called Oscar.**

Words in italics are Push's point of view — take it or leave it...

LIVERPOOL JOHN MOORES UNIVERSITY

FORMERLY LIVERPOOL POLYTECHNIC

○ **LIVERPOOL JOHN MOORES UNIVERSITY** Roscoe Court, 4 Rodney Street, Liverpool, Merseyside, L1 2TZ **TEL** (0151) 231 5090 **E-MAIL** recruitment@ljmu.ac.uk **WEBSITE** www.ljmu.ac.uk ○ **THE LIVERPOOL STUDENTS' UNION** The Haigh Building, Maryland Street, Liverpool, Merseyside, L1 9DD **TEL** (0151) 231 4900 **E-MAIL** studentsunion@livjm.ac.uk **WEBSITE** www.l-s-u.com

GENERAL ○○○○○○○○○○○○

A *colossal Merseyside explosion seems to have scattered pieces of LJMU across the city.* Or rather, the merging of four separate colleges (the oldest of which was founded in 1825) in the 60s resulted in a glut of disparate sites and buildings uniting under the name of the bloke who invented the Littlewoods pools. The central site is *smack in the middle of the buzzing* city and has a *beautiful* courtyard plus the SU bars, *which is handy for afternoon slack-offs.* Some University buildings are modern, purpose-built constructions while others, such as the Fine Art Department, are *fine examples* of Georgian and Victorian architecture. Legal eagles study in a converted chapel. The sites are clustered in the city centre, near Liverpool University, and further out around the city's edges. For general information about Liverpool: See University of Liverpool.

🚶🚶🚶🚶🚶🚶🚶🚶🚶🚶🚶🚶🚶🚶🚶🚶🚶🚶🚶🚶

SEX RATIO: ♂46 ♀54	**FOUNDED:** 1970
FULL-TIME U'GRADS: 12,608	**PART-TIME:** 1,704
POSTGRADS: 3,579	**NON-DEGREE:** 3,822
AVE COURSE: 3YRS	**ETHNIC:** 15%
STATE:PRIVATE SCHOOL: 95:5	**FLUNK RATE:** 23%
MATURE: 24%	**INTERNATIONAL:** 8%
DISABLED: 45	**LOCAL:** 43%

ATMOSPHERE

Being distributed across such a lively, fun-stuffed city, LJMU hums with energy. The vibes are more sporty than political since such a huge number of students take sports-related degrees. Academic life can be fairly laidback, but more intense when the pressure's on. Town/gown animosities have been almost entirely resolved thanks to a number of community projects and although students may be on the receiving end of a local's sharp tongue from time to time, there are enough scouser jokes for them to have a comeback at the ready. If they dare.

SITES

Although LJMU can be divided into four main chunks, Mount Pleasant and Byrom Street each have many smaller annexes. There are also associated institutions throughout Merseyside and Cheshire.
MOUNT PLEASANT (4,000 students) The main building sports an *impressive number* of gargoyles outside and a huge, new Learning Resources Centre (aka 'library') inside.

BYROM STREET (8,000 students) A 60s *carbuncle* two mins from the centre.
I M MARSH (1,000 students, Teacher Training, Food & Nutrition, Community & Social Studies, Home Economics) Three miles from the city centre on the *ruralish* outskirts of Aigburth.

LIVERPOOL see University of Liverpool

TRAVEL see University of Liverpool
CAR Permits are required to park on any of the sites.
COLLEGE LJMU operates a shuttle bus between the various sites.

CAREER PROSPECTS

○ **CAREERS SERVICE** ○ **NO. OF STAFF** 8 FULL/5 PART
○ **UNEMPLOYED AFTER 6MTHS** 8%
The Career Development Service provides bulletin boards, interview training, a careers library and arranges job fairs, as well as running skills training programmes for graduate jobseekers.

FAMOUS ALUMNI

Caroline Aherne (The Royle Family); Bill Bryson (writer); Stephen Byers (MP and *truth-deficient* ex-transport secretary); Julian Cope (80s musician); the Dalai Lama; Bill Drummond (KLF); Phil Gayle (TV journalist); Debbie Greenwood (ex-Miss England and TV presenter); Anthony Gormley (artist); Jim King (Cream club runner); John Lennon; Martin 'Chariots' Offiah (rugby league); Phil Selway (Radiohead's drummer); Stu Sutcliffe (fifth Beatle). Liverpool and Everton FCs have honorary degrees.

FURTHER INFO

○ **PROSPECTUSES** UNDERGRAD; POSTGRAD; DEPARTMENTAL; ALTERNATIVE; DVD
○ **OPEN DAYS**
Prospectuses can be requested from the main website. Also guides for mature students and student finance. For info on open days, hit the net, cyberdude.

ACADEMIC ○○○○○○○○○○○○○

Astrophysics and Sports Science both have international reputations for progress in their fields. Varied teaching methods *keep things fresh* in the classroom: lectures, tutorials, seminars, visiting high profile specialists (including Steven Spielberg, and Phil Redmond of Brookside fame). Courses are modular, with students taking a set of modules each year (in theory up to 120 hours of study each). Entry to the second year depends on first year performance. After that, everything counts towards the final grade.

ENTRY POINTS: 120–300	CLEARING: 15%
NO. OF TERMS: 2	LENGTH OF TERMS: 15wks
STAFF TO STUDENT RATIO: 1:22	STUDY ADDICTS: 15%
TEACHING: **	RESEARCH: **
1STS: 8%	2.2S: 42%
2.1S: 40%	3RDS: 10%

ADMISSIONS
○ APPLY VIA UCAS/DIRECT/NMAS FOR NURSING DIPLOMAS/GTTR FOR PGCE
LJMU welcomes applications from mature students and those without formal qualifications but with ability – apply to get special consideration.

SUBJECTS
BUSINESS & LAW 20% **EDUCATION & COMMUNITY & LEISURE** 10% **HEALTH** 16% **MEDIA** 13% **SCIENCE** 20% **TECHNOLOGY** 18%
BEST American Studies; Building, Land & Property Management; Business & Management; Civil Engineering; Communication & Media Studies; Drama, Dance & Cinematics; Economics; Education; Hospitality, Recreation, Leisure & Sport; Land & Property Management; Maths, Statistics & Operational Research; Molecular Biological Science; Nursing; Organismal Biological Science; Pharmocology & Pharmacy; Physics & Astronomy; Politics.; Subjects allied to Medicine;

LIBRARIES
○ 68,500 BOOKS ○ 1,630 STUDY PLACES
○ 24–HR ACCESS
Of the three libraries, the main Aldham Roberts LRC is open 24 hrs, the others *wuss out* at 11pm weekdays. They're called 'Learning Resource Centres' to emphasise services other than books on offer, like the 16,000 e-books and 5,000 e-journals for example. All the LRCs have wireless internet access.

COMPUTERS
○ 1,600 WORKSTATIONS ○ 24–HR ACCESS

OTHER LEARNING FACILITIES
The 'Blackboard' system allows students to access resources and course materials from the comfort of their own modems. Extra-curricular language teaching also available, as well as a drama studio, CAD lab, rehearsal rooms, media centre, sports science labs, practice courtroom and 360-degree ship simulator. The Clinical Practice Suite is a pretend hospital with robotic patients that make realistic groaning noises.

ENTERTAINMENT ○○○○○○○○○

THE CITY see University of Liverpool

UNIVERSITY
○ PRICE OF A PINT OF BEER £1.65
○ GLASS OF WINE £1.80 ○ CAN OF RED BULL £2
BARS The SU building (The Haigh) houses three inter-linked and well-maintained bars, where the atmosphere ranges from swish clubby to traditional pubness. One is non-smoking. Wallet-friendliness makes the SU a popular spot to drink away the night or warm up for a big one on the town. I M Marsh and Byrom Street have watering holes too.
THEATRES *Drama ain't big business here* with only a pocketful of plays performed each year. The theatre's mainly used by drama students.
CLUBBING/MUSIC VENUES The Cooler has club nights most nights, with plenty of takers for dance on a Friday and cheese on a Saturday. Special events include X Factor and poker nights. Gigs have included such *unlikely bedfellows* as Judge Jules, Yousef, Colin Murray, Joe Scully off Neighbours and Chesney *'the one and only, thank God'* Hawkes.
COMEDY/CABARET You guessed it, the Cooler again. Open mic nights and sporadic samplings of up-and-coming but-not-got-there-yet talent.
FOOD There's a refectory at Byrom Street. The Scholar does bar snacks, The Cooler dishes up the likes of beans and chips and The Sanctuary serves paninis. Spendthrifts can bring their own sarnies instead. The campus shop sells all kinds of chompable snack fare.
OTHER Several black tie balls a year: Sportsman's, Graduation and the Snowball (in winter – natch).

SOCIAL ○○○○○○○○○○○○

THE LIVERPOOL STUDENTS' UNION
○ 6 SABBATICALS ○ TURNOUT AT LAST BALLOT 10%
○ NUS MEMBER
LSU claims to be the most popular SU in the country, probably because of its largely free club nights and abolition of joining fees for all societies. For LJMU students, The Haigh is the main social hub and had a recent spruce-up with the likes of student media suites. Interest in politics is *lukewarm at best*, but there are campaigns on local issues and bigger fishes such as fair trade. The University itself enjoys good relations with LSU.

SU FACILITIES
The Haigh contains most of the facilities, which include: three bars; two cafeterias; eight pool tables; Link ATMs; photo booths; payphones; photocopier; fax services; juke boxes; advice centre; late-night minibus; vending machines; post office; and a general store. Other sites contain bars and some smaller shops (including an art supply store).

CLUBS (NON-SPORTING)
Anime; Break Dancing; Cheerleading; Chinese; German; Greek Cypriot; Hellenic; Hindu; Japanese;

L

Mediterranean; Music & Physical Theatre; Pagan; Urban Music. *See also Clubs tables.*

OTHER ORGANISATIONS

'Havoc' is the student magazine. 'Shout FM' hits a few of the SU bars and can be accessed on the web. The Rag committee raises money *and blisters* with fun runs and the like. There's good community action (and karma) through charity projects, conservation and work with the elderly.

RELIGIOUS

○ **3 CHAPLAINS (COFE, RC, METHODIST)**
There are two prayer rooms for use by Muslims and a multi-faith chaplaincy (which includes atheists). City centre locations mean places of worship are *easily accessible to most faiths – everfond of producing guides*, LJMU also do one on faith services in the city.

PAID WORK see University of Liverpool
○ **JOB BUREAU** ○ **PAID WORK** TERM-TIME 68%; HOLS 98%
Two-thirds of students work for their dosh during term. Workbank in the SU is run by an independent company and helps find work during or between terms and 'Business Bridge' helps find work relevant to studies.

SPORTS ◡◡◡◡◡◡◡◡◡◡◡◡◡

○ **RECENT SUCCESSES** FOOTBALL; WOMEN & MEN'S GAELIC FOOTBALL; WOMEN & MEN'S HOCKEY; NETBALL; MEN'S RUGBY UNION ○ **BUSA RANKING** 52
Lycra and studs tend to be donned more for pleasure than for glory, although students at I M Marsh take it all more seriously than those at other sites. Mountaineering is hugely popular, for some reason.

SPORTS FACILITIES

Football pitch; two rugby pitches; four tennis courts; basketball court; sauna/steam room. At the I M Marsh site: two gyms; two dance studios; renovated sports hall; indoor swimming pool; five playing fields; all-weather athletics track. Students at other sites can trek to I M Marsh. Otherwise, it's public facilities (£15 student discount pass) or those at University of Liverpool.

SPORTING CLUBS

Curling; Gaelic Football; Mountaineering. **See also Clubs tables.**

ATTRACTIONS see University of Liverpool

ACCOMMODATION ◡◡◡◡◡◡◡◡◡

IN UNIVERSITY
○ **SELF CATERING** 21% ○ **COST** £67 (36/40/42WKS)
○ **1ST YRS LIVING IN** 80% ○ **INSURANCE PREMIUM** ££
AVAILABILITY Most accommodation is in the city

centre and consists of modern purpose-built halls of residence and flats which are *well laid out and comfortable*. About three-quarters of rooms are en-suite. CCTV, security guards and a student warden system let residents (and anxious parents) sleep easy. First year students are generally posted near their faculty. Cleaning rooms is up to students and *woe betide* anyone caught festering in a pile of pants. Failing the random inspections results in a visit from the cleaners *(actual cleaners, not hitmen)* at your own expense. Most halls have on-site amenities like vending machines and a convenience store, sometimes a bar.
CAR PARKING *Shedloads of space on the city streets* but LMJU *doesn't take kindly* to cars stopping for too long on its land. Some sites and halls require parking permits.

EXTERNALLY
○ **AVE RENT** £50 ○ **LIVING AT HOME** 20%
AVAILABILITY see University of Liverpool
HOUSING HELP LJMU, Liverpool Hope and University of Liverpool jointly run Liverpool Student Homes. It offers advice, legal help, landlord blacklists and vacancy lists *and pledges to find a bed for every wandering urchin who needs one.*

WELFARE ◡◡◡◡◡◡◡◡◡◡◡◡

SERVICES
○ **LGBT OFFICER & SOCIETY** ○ **DISABILITIES OFFICER**
○ **WOMEN'S OFFICER** ○ **MATURE STUDENTS' OFFICER & SOCIETY** ○ **SELF–DEFENCE CLASSES** ○ **UNIVERSITY COUNSELLORS** 4 FULL/9 PART ○ **CRIME RATING** !!!!!
Each student has an academic 'counsellor' and the SU has a 'one stop shop' for welfare needs and financial advice.
WOMEN A women's minibus should start chugging in 2006. Attack alarms are given out.

FINANCE
○ **AVE DEBT PER YEAR** £3,421
○ **HOME STUDENT FEES** £3,000
○ **ACCESS FUND** £970,000
○ **SUCCESSFUL APPLICATIONS (YEAR)** 1,616
○ **AVERAGE PAYMENT** £600
SUPPORT Some local businesses sponsor students through their courses. Various bursaries, scholarships, hardship fund and emergency loans are kicking around, including £2,000 scholarships for local Merseyside students from low-income families, £1,000 a year for *swots* and nominated students from the University's schools network, cash to cover childcare and, *last but definitely not least*, the Vice Chancellor's Award (£10,000 for six of the cleverest students).

L

Words in italics are Push's point of view — take it or leave it...

▶ **LIVERPOOL POLYTECHNIC**
see *Liverpool John Moores University*

▶ **LONDON HOSPITAL MEDICAL COLLEGE**
see *Queen Mary, University of London*

UNIVERSITY OF LONDON

THE INFORMATION, WHICH FOLLOWS, REFERS TO THE UNIVERSITY OF LONDON AS AN AMORPHOUS BLOB. THE SERVICES DESCRIBED ARE THOSE PROVIDED CENTRALLY BY THE UNIVERSITY AND BY ULU, THE STUDENTS' UNION. THE COLLEGES AND INDIVIDUAL UNIONS OF THE UNIVERSITY PROVIDE SERVICES THEMSELVES, AND PUSH COVERS THESE IN INDIVIDUAL ENTRIES. SIMILARLY, THE GENERAL COMMENTS ABOUT LONDON APPLY ON THE WHOLE TO THE CENTRAL AREA, CLOSE TO ULU ITSELF, AND THESE ARE OF EQUAL RELEVANCE TO THE MANY INSTITUTIONS WHICH ARE IN THE CITY BUT NOT PART OF LONDON UNIVERSITY ITSELF. FOR MORE SPECIFIC DISCUSSION OF THE DIFFERENCES BETWEEN NORF 'N' SARF OR HACKNEY 'N' HAMPSTEAD, SEE THE INDIVIDUAL ENTRIES.

○ **UNIVERSITY OF LONDON** Senate House, Malet Street, London, WC1E 7HU **TEL** (020) 7862 8000 **E-MAIL** enquiries@london.ac.uk **WEBSITE** www.lon.ac.uk ○ **UNIVERSITY OF LONDON UNION** Malet Street, London, WC1E 7HY **TEL** (020) 7664 2000 **E-MAIL** general@ulu.lon.ac.uk **WEBSITE** www.ulu.co.uk

GENERAL ◗◗◗◗◗◗◗◗◗◗◗◗◗

London's far too big to be summed up even in one of Push's beautifully succinct epigrams. Something like eight million people live within the boundaries of the M25 *(150 miles of eight-lane car park)*. Since the days of the little Roman village of Londinium on the banks of the Thames, London has come a long way, becoming the country's centre of politics, finance, arts, heritage, tourism, media, pornography, crime, bagel production and so on. Appropriately, the University of London is also big. One in ten of the country's entire higher education population is at one of London University's 20 colleges and 10 institutions. *However, students rarely get a sense of the University as a whole*, especially since some of the larger constituent colleges, such as King's, Imperial and UCL, are big enough to be fairly sizeable universities on their own.

The University's headquarters are in the magnificent art deco Senate House in Bloomsbury about a mile from Trafalgar Square. Students who don't know the place, but are serious about studying here should get hold of one of the less touristy guides. Most years, Time Out magazine does a London Students' Guide (about £3). Push features entries for most of the undergraduate colleges, so read this and then read the separate colleges' entries too because they vary as much as if they were different universities. We don't cover postgraduate-only institutions; we do feature under individual colleges any medical schools or other institutions that are part of particular colleges (eg. King's College Hospital). For the record, these are the London colleges covered by Push:
Birkbeck
Courtauld Institute of Art
Goldsmiths
Heythrop College
Imperial College
King's College London
LSE (London School of Economics)
Queen Mary
Royal Academy of Music
Royal Holloway
Royal Veterinary College
St George's Hospital Medical School
SOAS (School of Oriental & African Studies)
School of Pharmacy
University College London

◉ **Senate House, headquarters of London University, was rumoured to be where Hitler planned to set up his UK headquarters. Supposedly that's why it was never bombed. It's also believed to be the model for Orwell's Ministry of Truth in '1984'.**

Words in italics are Push's point of view — take it or leave it...

....

SEX RATIO: ♀44 ♂56	FOUNDED: 1836
FULL–TIME U'GRADS: 56,040	PART–TIME: 19,665
POSTGRADS: 49,600	NON–DEGREE: 500
AVE COURSE: 3YRS	FLUNK RATE: N/A
STATE:PRIVATE SCHOOL: 43:57	INTERNATIONAL: 24%

LONDON

- **POPULATION** 7,172,091 • **CITY CENTRE** 1 MILE
- **BIRMINGHAM** 106 MILES • **MANCHESTER** 172 MILES
- **EDINBURGH** 423 MILES
- **HIGH TEMP 22** • **LOW TEMP 2** • **RAINFALL** 67

It's easy to feel that you're not making the most of London if you're not spending every waking minute at the theatre, ballet, opera or cinema, in clubs or fashionable markets, in museums and galleries, sports grounds and parks. It's a bit like the salad counter in Pizza Hut – it's up to you to make a selection from the vast selection of goodies and pile them on your plate however you like, but you might end up face-down in a puddle of sweetcorn and Thousand Island dressing while the waiters have a good laugh. In practice most students, and indeed most people who live in London, end up spending most of their time honing in on one particular, um, pizza slice – that being the area in which they live. Even locals often have only a hazy area of what's going on in different areas of town outside the centre and their own immediate hangouts.

The mutual suspicion beneath north and south of the river is well known. Less well known is the new rivalry between west (traditionally cool) and east (new, silly-haircut cool). The good news is that, whereas people in other parts of the country have to be brought up on centuries of distrust to achieve these levels of local rivalry, newcomers to London start to feel that wherever they happen to live is the centre of the universe before they finish unpacking their suitcases. This might be because it's just way too expensive to go anywhere else. There are a number of responses to the high cost of living in London: (1) burst into tears; (2) mug someone; (3) live on credit; (4) ask daddy for lashings of cash. Alternatively, if these don't appeal, you can always use the following methods: (1) limit your spending by only going out when and where you can afford it (ULU fits the bill, offering cheap events for students); (2) buy secondhand – for books, there's ULU, Charing Cross Road and Waterloo and, for clothes, try Camden Market, Greenwich, Brick Lane and Portobello Road; (3) get a job – more London students have part-time jobs than anywhere else.

TRAVEL

TRAINS London is the centre of the network: Birmingham (from £9.90 return); Manchester (£37.70); Leeds (£47.25); Bristol Parkway (£26.50); Glasgow (£62.10).

COACHES London's also the centre of the National Express system and a whole variety of other national bus services (Green Line, Blue Line and so on) letting you ride to Birmingham (£17.60) Manchester (£26.50 and so on. Megabus goes to most cities *for peanuts.*

AIR Served by four airports – Gatwick, Stansted, Luton and Heathrow, the world's busiest. Regular flights to Paris, Belfast, Prague, New York, Timbuktu, anywhere else you care to pluck out of your WH Smith School Atlas *for, often, ridiculously low prices.*

LOCAL TRANSPORT

London's population swells by more than a million every day thanks to commuters, tourists *and those bucket-shaking charity collectors. Unsurprisingly, this can put quite a strain on transport at peak hours. See the excellent* www.tfl.gov.uk *for the lowdown on routes,* timetables and the big spend.

TRAINS Local overground trains are a *speedy and sometimes pleasant way to travel and are moderately efficient. The main problems are ease of use, the high fares (although Travelcards keep costs down a tad) and the early closing* (last trains between 11pm and 1am). *Trains are often the best bet south of the river. The east of the city is covered by the tube/train hybrid, the DLR (Docklands Light Railway) which covers places like Canary Wharf, Mile End and East Ham.*

UNDERGROUND The 'Tube' is the largest underground train system in the world and, generally, *it's okay and takes you just about anywhere you want to go (though not always in east/south-east London). On the down side, it's often crowded, shuts down around midnight during the week, is often disrupted by strikes and breakdowns, and it's expensive. Talking to other tube passengers is tantamount to threatening to slaughter their pets – the only people who do it are tourists, mentalists and people who want to tell you about Jesus.* Nearest tube to Senate House/ULU Building: Goodge Street (Northern Line), Warren Street (Victoria) or Russell Square (Piccadilly) – all Zone 1.

LOCAL BUSES *Buses offer more destinations than tubes and are less crowded and slightly cheaper (just over a quid for anywhere within central London). But the red chuggers are also slow and, until you know your way around, it's difficult to know which ones take you where. After midnight, buses come into their own – night buses are London's only form of all-night public transport and if you don't mind how long it takes, you can go almost anywhere within ten miles of the centre. They congregate at Trafalgar Square, which is a handy central spot to head for post-club/pub/grub.*

TRAVELCARDS The system's split into six zones, with central travel being more expensive than in the outer zones. *Students in full-time education are entitled to a 30% discount on travelcards for bus/local rail/tube travel. Yippee. If you can stump up the readies, it often works out cheaper to pay in advance – a year's Zone 1 & 2 travel card costs from £620. Ouch. But still nearly £200 cheaper than paying for weekly (£15.50) travel cards year-round, which in turn is cheaper than paying for daily tickets or single journeys. Budgeting ahead for travel minimises end-of-loan solitary confinement. Getting about in general is*

Words in italics are Push's point of view – take it or leave it...

cheaper the more you can avoid passing through the central zones, ie. *where the most popular cinemas, museums, shops and Starbucks are located.* A yearly pass for any two consecutive zones other than 1 & 2 costs a *mere* £380. Equivalent fares are also cheaper if you buy them on the Oyster Card, a kind of top-up travelcard, or if you shun the tubes and trains altogether in favour of the buses – a monthly bus pass (£29.60) works out at less than a pound a day. For details of other concessions to students, check with the relevant union.

TAXIS Two types: the classic black cabs, *which are well regulated and enormously expensive; and dodgy merchants in Ford Escorts, which are as regulated as Fallujah on a bad day and are just as expensive as the official ones anyway.* There are now also some run by and for women. *Basically though, forget all taxis, except late at night when all else fails and/or you're in a party of four or more. Far be it from Push to preach, but if you don't know the dangers of using unlicensed cabs when you're on your own, well, you probably haven't evolved opposable thumbs yet either.*

CAR *Parking in Central London is impossible, and although there is only one rush hour every day, it lasts from 6am till midnight (and until club-closing time at the weekend). The introduction of the congestion charge also now means paying to bring a car into central London during office hours, from £8 a day. Disabled drivers get some discounts; students don't.*

BICYCLES *A popular form of student travel given the pros: it's cheap and you zip through traffic jams. But there are the cons: London is big and full of exhaust fumes and bike thieves. The cycle network is making things slightly better all the time, though.*

CAREER PROSPECTS
⊙ CAREERS SERVICE ⊙ NO. OF STAFF 70
See www.careers.lon.ac.uk for vacancies and general information. The main office is at Stewart House in Bloomsbury, but there are also facilities at nine colleges which vary according to subject/professions. The biggest in the country, its goodies include interview advice, CV-checking, mentoring, recruitment fairs and the 'GradClub' and 'C2' to support graduates. Non-London students can also use the service, at a price, naturally.

FURTHER INFO
⊙ PROSPECTUSES UNDERGRAD; POSTGRAD
The University publishes a guide which covers all its colleges, a guide to student life and an *essential* accomodation pamphlet. Contact individual colleges, or see the University's website for general info.

ACADEMIC ⏾⏾⏾⏾⏾⏾⏾⏾⏾⏾⏾⏾⏾

ADMISSIONS
⊙ APPLY VIA UCAS TO INDIVIDUAL COLLEGES

LIBRARIES
⊙ **3,000,000** BOOKS ⊙ **460** STUDY PLACES
The statistics refer to the vast central library at Senate House but individual colleges have their own facilities – see www.ull.ac.uk

COMPUTERS
⊙ **950** WORKSTATIONS
All computers have net access. Colleges also provide their own computers.

ENTERTAINMENT ⏾⏾⏾⏾⏾⏾⏾⏾⏾⏾

THE CITY
⊙ PRICE OF A PINT OF BEER £2.50 ⊙ GLASS OF WINE £2.50
New bars, restaurants, clubs, exhibitions and shows come and go more often than adolescent boy bands. Time Out is compulsory kit for every wannabe London-savvy student. Its weekly listings detail pretty much everything going on around town.

CINEMAS *Many repertory cinemas offer student discounts and the Prince Charles Cinema just off Leicester Square shows a cool mix of Hollywood, cult and independent films, tix from £1.50. By contrast, the Square's also home to red-carpet-and-premier venues where tickets will cost at least ten times as much. Once again, the further from central London, the cheaper. Wood Green's Showcase cinema shows flicks from £3.50. Some fleapits charge a tenner at weekends, but most do student discounts. Pushplugs: Ritzy (Brixton); Everyman (Hampstead); Riverside (Hammersmith); NFT (South Bank, £5.50); the Gate (Notting Hill).*

THEATRES *Student standby tickets are sometimes available for West End shows, but they're still around £12. The National Theatre on the South Bank and the RSC at the Barbican are cheaper and feature some of the country's top talent. Also, don't forget the Fringe (the collective title for all the smaller theatres around town, ranging from back rooms at pubs to full-size auditoria) where you can often see high quality at low cost.*

PUBS *The Jeremy Bentham, Marlborough Arms, University Tavern and Rising Sun are just a few pubs near ULU that are student friendly. Some other London pubs water down their ridiculously expensive beer, but you can often find a decent pint of Young's or Fuller's, or a good selection of guest ales (the Wetherspoon chain is a reliable if characterless starting point). Beyond that, every variety of drinking den, from Irish to Jamaican, from sports bars to wine bars, from plush chrome extravaganzas serving Belgian banana beer with a free half-hour on the net to rough dives that serve phlegmy Carlsberg and a filthy look to outsiders. Many pubs around the City business district, unlike almost anywhere else in the world, close at weekends.*

CLUBBING London has just about *every kind of club imaginable and a lot that aren't.* Fabric, 333 and Heaven have all survived the downturn in dance music's fortunes. There are school discos by the dozen *for those feeling prematurely nostalgic; hip DJ bars like the Embassy in Islington; Soho's*

L

Gossips for heavy metal/*the plain vampiric*; and GAY night at Astoria is *legendary. If you can't find something to move to, you might ask yourself whether you've left your legs on the bus.*

MUSIC VENUES *Somewhere in London there's a band worth checking out every night of the week, it's just a question of finding them.* There are the monster venues like Earl's Court, the hip 'n' happening like Brixton Academy, and the unintimidating, like the Mean Fiddler. But the *best place to see up-and-coming bands for a tenth of the price is the local boozer* – some are occasionally host to impromptu performances by local s'lebs.

COMEDY/CABARET *London's a hot-bed of alternative laugh-mongers. Pushplugs: the Comedy Store near Piccadilly Circus or, more cheaply, Jongleurs (Camden, Battersea, Shepherds Bush); Balham Banana; Hackney Empire. Also, keep a look out for free tickets to TV and radio show recordings* – start with the Beeb's website, www.bbc.co.uk. *Pubs are also great places to catch funny business* – Jimmy Carr used to do a regular spot at the Hen & Chicken in Highbury.

EATING OUT *Nowhere in the country, possibly the world, has a broader choice of eateries. There is every kind of café, restaurant and fast food and then some. Not everywhere is bank-busting either. Head for Soho and Chinatown for affordable food and late night nibbles. For budget fare in the West End, Pushplugs: Pollo's (madhouse Italian); Stockpot (school dinners, but superb value); Gaby's (friendly deli); Poon's (Chinese); Wagamama (Japanese noodles); Pret à Manger (imaginative sarnie chain); Food for Thought (veggie without stodge). If you run out of places to eat, you probably need to go on a diet.*

UNIVERSITY

○ **PRICE OF A PINT OF BEER** £1.70
○ **GLASS OF WINE** £1.80
○ **CAN OF RED BULL** £1.60

Individual College bars are the first port of call for students. At ULU:

BARS The big greenhouse-like Gallery Bar/Diner is *very popular all day* and has TV screens, quiz nights and regular DJ slots. Also Duck 'n' Dive *(typical pub)*; Bar 101 (chrome design, for clubs and big-name gigs), which *confusingly* also goes by the names of Room 101 (for student-only events) and the Venue *(when non-tax shirkers are allowed in)*.

MUSIC VENUES *ULU can hold its own next to any of London's sticky-floored, mid-sized caverns.* Bands like Athlete, Death in Vegas, Coldplay, the Foo Fighters and many others have passed through.

CLUBBING *A smattering of nights go easier on the cheese than most Unions – indie, rock, pop and up-and-coming bands are more their pint of snakebite and black.*

FOOD The Gallery provides *(relatively) healthy* fodder; Duck 'n' Dive *if cholesterol isn't a concern.* The Lunchbox is a *snack-friendly* coffee shop and there's a restaurant in Senate House. Halal, Kosher, veggie, organic and fair-trade options can all be snuffled out.

SOCIAL ○○○○○○○○○○○○○

UNIVERSITY OF LONDON UNION

○ **5 SABBATICALS** ○ **TURNOUT AT LAST BALLOT** 4%

The individual colleges' SUs affiliate separately to NUS and are automatically part of ULU (which isn't a member of NUS) which offers *the most extraordinary level* of facilities at the building in Bloomsbury – open until 11pm or later when hosting an event. ULU (pronounced 'yooloo') is also the students' central representative body and has *effective* officers on most of the University's important committees. They're a *very cosmopolitan crowd* with a large percentage of mature and part-time students. The Union works well with the University but *doesn't shirk on the firebrand front* – recent campaign victories include impartial monitoring of postgrad assessments and more student discounts on transport, plus they back everything from fair trade to Coalition 2010, which opposes removing the £3,000 cap on tuition fees.

SU FACILITIES

At ULU: three bars; coffee shop; cafe/bar, general shop; print shop; photocopying; travel agent; ATMs; Endsleigh Insurance office; opticians; minibus; vending machine; five pool and snooker tables; games and fruit machines; fax service; snack/sandwich shop; 33m swimming pool (the biggest in central London); fitness centre; gymnasium; theatre hall; offices and 20 meeting rooms; *and a partridge in a pear tree.* The University accommodation office and a couple of college careers offices are also in the building. ULU also provides training for staff and student officers of all the member colleges' SUs and handbooks and publications about all aspects of London student life.

CLUBS (NON-SPORTING)

As well as at colleges, there's: AGAPE (Evangelical Christian Society); Art; Ballroom & Latin American Dance (BALADS); Bangladeshi; Breakdance; Buddhist; Capoeira; Chamber Choir; Cyber Geography (works to 'promote a better understanding of the unseen communications that take place within students' geographic boundaries'); ECCO (sustainable development); Gamesoc; Jazz; Koinonia (aims to help students discover the call of God and to give them the support they need to follow the call); LINKS – St John Ambulance; Mountaineering; Overseas Christian Fellowship; People First; Salsa; Sanex: South Asia Nexus; Shaolin Kung Fu; Shorinji Kempo; Singapore Medical; Sub Aqua; Zhuan Shu Kuan. **See also individual Colleges and Clubs tables.**

OTHER ORGANISATIONS

The free fortnightly 'London Student' is Europe's largest student newspaper, and even features a column by Mayor Ken Livingstone *getting down with the yoofs.*

RELIGIOUS
● 6 CHAPLAINS (COFE, BAPTIST, RC, LUTHERAN, METHODIST, ORTHODOX); RABBI

London has religious groups for every denomination from Muslims to Moonies, Jews to Jains. *If you can't find spiritual solace here, please direct your complaint upwards.*

PAID WORK
● JOB BUREAU

Vacancy lists are posted up in the Union and ULU usually has vacancies itself. There are more opportunities in London for part-time work than anywhere else, but there are also more people trying to get those jobs. Students find work *quite easily* in all the usual places like bars and restaurants and also in theatres, offices and shops.

SPORTS ●●●●●●●●●●●●●●

● RECENT SUCCESSES RECENT SUCCESSES: VOLLEYBALL
The basement of ULU has been converted into *one of the best gyms in London*, including an international-sized swimming pool. There is an inter-college league and all the accompanying rivalry.

SPORTS FACILITIES
At the ULU Building, there are all the amenities mentioned above as well as an aerobics studio and sports hall. Students can join the University Health Club for £4 a day, £25 a month or £250 for a whole year. There's also a boathouse at Chiswick on the Thames and sailing facilities at the Welsh Harp reservoir in North London. Not many Colleges have sports fields on site, owing to the sheer urban congestion of the city, *but, like elephants in a mini, it's surprising how much pitch-space can fit it one tightly packed conurbation.*

SPORTING CLUBS
Boat; Canoe Polo; Gymnastics; Ice Hockey; Jitsu; Lacrosse (men's & women's); Lifesaving; Polo; Rifle; Sailing; Ski & Snowboard; Water Polo. **See also individual Colleges and Clubs tables.**

ATTRACTIONS
Depending on promotion and relegation, London generally has about six premiership football

> **One of Coldplay's first concerts was a fundraising gig for London University's Nightline.**

teams, plus all the others scuffling around in the lower divisions. Then there's cricket at Lords and the Oval, rugby at Twickenham, tennis at Wimbledon, athletics at Crystal Palace, plus lots of building sites that *should metamorphose into something miraculous come the 2012 Olympics.*

ACCOMMODATION ●●●●●●●●●

IN COLLEGE
● CATERED 4% **● COST** £123 (40WKS)
● SELF CATERING <1% **● COST** £63 (40/44/52)
● INSURANCE PREMIUM £££££

AVAILABILITY The percentage of London students living in college accommodation varies enormously from college to college, but for those that the colleges don't accommodate, there's a limited number of catered places in the University's eight intercollegiate halls and 500 places in self-catered flats and houses. Halls are mainly mixed.

AMENITIES Conditions in each hall are different but, it's mostly single rooms with showers, a couple of meals provided and minimal cooking facilities. There is also a selection of other amenities including bars, TV rooms, telephones in every room, function, meeting and study rooms, libraries, launderettes, payphones and so on. All have porters and 24-hr security. Depending on the hall, students may be able to enjoy the *delights* of a squash court, darkroom, music room, bike sheds, gardens, videos and in College Hall there's also a hairdressing salon. Prices vary, with flats costing up to £360 a week, but most of the single rooms fall just shy of the £100 a week mark. Not bad for London, especially as meals are included. See www.housing.london.ac.uk for all the gen.

CAR PARKING Don't even go there.

EXTERNALLY
● AVE RENT £93

AVAILABILITY *Contrary to popular belief, it's really not that difficult to find accommodation in London. Thanks to the explosion in buy-to-let in recent years rents have actually been falling by 10-30% in many areas, so it could even be worth haggling with your prospective landlord. Before looking in Loot or the Evening Standard try checking out the excellent www.moveflat.com website or www.findaproperty.com (good for groups in search of houses).*
There's very little housing in Zone 1 even for yuppies, and students come a lot lower in the pecking order. Zone 2 is a bit better, particularly for single rooms in shared flats or houses in places like Wandsworth, Putney and Fulham and wherever the tube system is lacking. Zone 3 is relatively promising, but the catch is that it can take an hour to get to the centre. Zone 4 and beyond are not popular for the same reason, but, as they say, homeless students can't be choosers. Although there are many thousands of people living in

L

cardboard boxes on London's streets, they aren't students. In fact, many students manage to find very comfortable flats for almost reasonable rents.

To be safe, students coming to London should work out where they're going to stay first. Hammersmith, Shoreditch, Islington, Camberwell and Finsbury Park all have student ghettos but it obviously depends where in the city you need to get to every day.

HOUSING HELP The University's *excellent* accommodation office bolsters college facilities and includes a register of 4,500 private landlords, lists of available properties, advice and a series of talks in March-April.

WELFARE ⏾⏾⏾⏾⏾⏾⏾⏾⏾⏾⏾⏾⏾

SERVICES
- LGBT OFFICER ⊙ MATURE STUDENTS' OFFICER
- POSTGRAD STUDENTS' OFFICER & SOCIETY
- INTERNATIONAL STUDENTS' OFFICER ⊙ ETHNIC MINORITIES' OFFICER ⊙ WOMEN'S OFFICER & SOCIETY
- DISABILITIES OFFICER ⊙ NIGHTLINE
- CRIME RATING !!!!!

Currently most welfare services are provided at college-level.

HEALTH Several GP surgeries nearby, plus University College Hospital down the road.

WOMEN ULU's self-defence classes are *well-worth signing up for*. Free attack alarms also available.

LESBIAN, GAY, BISEXUAL & TRANSGENDER *London's gay community is sizeable and proud, and has marked out a large chunk of Soho as pretty much its own. As a result, there are plenty of entertainments which don't conform to heterosexist stereotypes and a few London boroughs make special housing* provisions. *Many of the best clubs have gay nights or even, for a change, straight nights. And don't forget the Pride March & Festival, every summer.*

DISABILITIES Some rooms are inaccessible to wheelchairs but there are ramps and lifts elsewhere (including the library), most lecture theatres have hearing loops and most colleges have a Special Educational Needs Department.

CRIME *London isn't as bad for crime as sensationalists would believe. Bloomsbury is one of the safest areas of central London due to high police presence and CCTV.*

DRUGS *Many Londoners live for years in the capital without ever encountering them. Having said that, every drug you've heard of and a great many beside are readily available on the streets and in the pubs and clubs of London. Cannabis is perpetually prevalent and ecstasy is still around, although not quite as popular as it has been. Cocaine is common currency amongst City and media types. Heroin is more common than in most English cities and the abuse/use of crack is spreading, especially in the South. They're often more expensive than elsewhere, but that shouldn't be regarded as any guarantee of quality – dangerous mixtures are common and the risks are your own. There are a number of help centres (including Narcotics Anonymous (020) 7351 6066) and the authorities usually take a progressive but firm attitude. The University, however, will automatically expel anyone found using illegal drugs. Dealers started to target the campus last year when the local police station temporarily closed, but a police crackdown has been sending crack peddlers away.*

FINANCE
SUPPORT Any cash going is distributed by the colleges.

LONDON METROPOLITAN UNIVERSITY

FORMERLY UNIVERSITY OF NORTH LONDON AND LONDON GUILDHALL UNIVERSITY

⊙ **LONDON METROPOLITAN UNIVERSITY** 166-220 Holloway Road, London, N7 8DB **TEL** (020) 7133 4200
E-MAIL admissions@londonmet.ac.uk **WEBSITE** www.londonmet.ac.uk
⊙ **LONDON METROPOLITAN UNIVERSITY STUDENTS' UNION** MG48, Tower Building, 166-220 Holloway Road, London, N7 8DB
TEL (020) 7133 2769 **E-MAIL** su@londonmet.ac.uk **WEBSITE** www.londonmetsu.org.uk

GENERAL ⏾⏾⏾⏾⏾⏾⏾⏾⏾⏾⏾⏾⏾

2002 saw the *teenage wedding* of London Guildhall University and the University of North London under the new name of London Metropolitan. They're *still in a bit of a honeymoon period*, but all signs *suggest that the merger might give birth to something special*. City campus sits on the outskirts of the financial and business headquarters of the UK and is surrounded by an *enormous wealth* of architectural variety (and money, of course). 16th- and 17th-century buildings give way to Victorian landmarks which give way in turn to the *daunting phalluses* of modern design. Norman Foster's *tremendous todger* of a tower ('The Gherkin') dominates the skyline. To the east *the suits get a bit raggier and the buildings a bit shabbier*: the infamous East End. The area around the London North campus has become *terribly fashionable in recent years, darling, and celeb-infested* Islington and Camden are bustling with bars and shops – *expect to find the 3am Girls plying their scurrilous trade. A wander up the road to Finsbury Park should put things in perspective though.*

SEX RATIO: ♂45 ♀55	FOUNDED: 2002
FULL-TIME U'GRADS: 35,000	PART-TIME: 15,000
POSTGRADS: 2,800	NON-DEGREE: 2,330
AVE COURSE: 3YRS	ETHNIC: 55%
STATE:PRIVATE SCHOOL: 97:3	FLUNK RATE: 25%
MATURE: 50%	INTERNATIONAL: 30%
DISABLED: 425	LOCAL: 44%

ATMOSPHERE
Lots of part-timers, locals and matures make London Met feel more like a community resource centre than a university. There's very little sense of 'young people away from home' and a corresponding lack of silly, drunken tomfoolery but despite this no one takes themselves or their institution too seriously. Many students have no family history of university attendance and set their sights on vocational courses rather than BAs in Post-Feminist Albanian Mythology Studies. Businesslike determination is the order of the day, but the campus becomes the village of the damned at weekends.

SITES
Departments are spread between sites so students *rarely feel the need to cross from one campus to the other. This had led to something of an internal City/North divide and with so little interaction apparent between the two one wonders why they bothered merging in the first place.*
CITY CAMPUS The chunk that used to be London Guildhall.
NORTH CAMPUS The chunk that used to be the University of North London.

LONDON see University of London
⦿ CITY CENTRE 2 MILES

TRAVEL see University of London
TRAINS Liverpool Street, Moorgate and Fenchurch Street for City campus. Holloway Road, Highbury & Islington and Drayton Park for North.
CAR *Both sites are pretty much unparkable and smack in the middle of Congestion Charge Central. Even clamping can work out cheaper and less painful.*
LOCAL *A huge number of bus routes, so both sites are very well serviced.* 15, 25, 40, 253 are just a few numbers for City's SU. 4, 19, 43, 153, 236, 271, 279 for North campus. *Plenty of night-buses too.*
UNDERGROUND City: Moorgate (Northern, Metropolitan, Circle, Hammersmith & City); Aldgate (Metropolitan, Circle); Aldgate East (Hammersmith & City, District); Tower Hill (District, Circle). North: Holloway Road (Piccadilly); Caledonian Road (Piccadilly); Highbury and Islington (Victoria).
BICYCLES *Cheap and green on one hand, difficult and dangerous on the other.*

OTHER Tower Gateway (Docklands Light Railway) is opposite City's Tower Hill site.

CAREER PROSPECTS
⦿ CAREERS SERVICE ⦿ NO. OF STAFF 14 FULL/4 PART
⦿ UNEMPLOYED AFTER 6MTHS 17%
Careers library, newsletters, one-to-one guidance, interview practice, workshop training, bulletin boards and job fairs.

FAMOUS ALUMNI
Celebrities and world-changers are yet to emerge from London Met but from the former institutions: Joy Gardner (*victim of extradition procedures*); Kate Hoey MP (Lab, ex-Spurs physio); Jools Holland (*the prince* of piano); Michael Jackson (TV executive rather than *'troubled' pop monkey*); Nick Leeson (the bloke who broke the bank at Barings); Mike Leigh (film director); Terry Marsh (former boxing champ); Alison Moyet (singer); Vic Reeves; Mark Thatcher (*Maggie's pride and joy*); Jake Chapman (sex and death artist); Garth Crooks (journalist, ex-Spurs star); David Kossof (actor); Martyn Lewis (newsreader); Stephen Platt (editor, New Statesman & Society); Sinead O'Connor (singer); Pete Tatchell (gay activist); Neil Tennant (Pet Shop Boy); Jamie Theakston (TV and radio presenter).

SPECIAL FEATURES
The fresh-faced University's still in a period of gestation with a number of buildings taking shape around its two main sites, including North's Graduate Centre, designed by *top set square user* Daniel Libeskind. There are hopes for a new science centre at North campus in the near future.

FURTHER INFO
⦿ PROSPECTUSES UNDERGRAD; POSTGRAD; SOME DEPART-MENTAL; VIDEO
⦿ OPEN DAYS
Extensive provisions for non-EU students. The University has offices in Bangladesh, Brussels, China, India, Nigeria and Pakistan, among others, and international students get extra-nice treatment, including a special welcome programme and guaranteed accommodation.

ACADEMIC ⦾⦾⦾⦾⦾⦾⦾⦾⦾⦾⦾⦾⦾⦾

Modular courses. Those taking four modules per term can expect to spend 40 hours a week on their studies. If that sounds too daunting, students can switch between full and part-time studying, take a break altogether, or benefit from daytime and evening teaching – handy for those with family or jobs. Many courses involve work placements; there's a *less popular option* to spend time abroad. The many industrial and career-orientated subjects are among the University's *strongest* courses. There are some state-of-the-art learning facilities, but admin and organisation within the University is *a bone of contention among students,* with reports of hours spent waiting in queues.

ENTRY POINTS: 80–240	AVE POINTS: N/A
APPLICATIONS PER PLACE: N/A	CLEARING: 28%
NO. OF TERMS: 2	LENGTH OF TERMS: 15wks
STAFF TO STUDENT RATIO: 1:10	STUDY ADDICTS: N/A
TEACHING: *	RESEARCH: **
YEAR ABROAD: 1%	SANDWICH STUDENTS: 3%
1STS: 5%	2.2s: 42%
2.1s: 29%	3RDS: 24%

ADMISSIONS

○ APPLY VIA UCAS/GTTR FOR TEACHING

London Met attracts a large number of mature students partly because it bases admissions on commitment and experience as much as formal qualifications (unless the particular course requires a basic level of knowledge, eg. biological sciences). International students need an English Language qualification – the minimum for under-grads is IELTS 4.5–5.5.

SUBJECTS

ARCHITECTURE, BUILDING, PLANNING 2%
ART & DESIGN 5%   ARTS/HUMANITIES 1%
BIOLOGICAL SCIENCES 4%   BUSINESS/
MANAGEMENT 29%   COMBINED 17%   COMPUTER
SCIENCE 10%   EDUCATION 6%   LAW 7%
LIBRARIANSHIP & INFORMATION STUDIES 2%
MATHEMATICAL SCIENCES 2%   MEDICAL SCIENCES 2%
SOCIAL SCIENCES 7%
BEST Business & Management.
UNUSUAL Polymer Technology.

LIBRARIES

○ 801,300 BOOKS ○ 2,300 STUDY PLACES

The merger means there are now seven libraries (including a women's library and TUC library) with *an immense volume of volumes* as well as an assortment of multimedia learning resources (DVDs, videos, tapes, online gubbins).

COMPUTERS

○ 2,600 WORKSTATIONS

Four computing centres support course-tailored software programs (including DTP, CAD, statistical analysis and programming languages). North campus boasts an IT technology tower with seven floors of open-access computing facilities and printing.

OTHER LEARNING FACILITIES

City has two new language labs in Moorgate. North's Language Centre is an open-access study area and there's a practice courtroom at the new Goulston Street building. The TV studio and editing suite is set to be complemented by a radio station and a new £27m science centre is in the pipeline for 2006.

ENTERTAINMENT ◖◗◖◗◖◗◖◗◖◗

LONDON see University of London

CAMDEN, ISLINGTON AND EAST END

○ PRICE OF A PINT OF BEER £2
○ GLASS OF WINE £2.80
○ CAN OF RED BULL £1.20

Many local students have their own personal pub preferences peppered across London and don't care for venues near campus. Likewise, few pubs in the area bother with the student market and some are positively unfriendly. North campus has all the *shabby delights of Camden and Islington within reach. City has a lot of trendy wine bars jammed with besuited financiers, but the East End is worth venturing into for Queen Vic style pubbage.*
CINEMAS The Barbican Cinema is a *luxurious* arthouse flickbox and offers 10% NUS discounts. There's an Odeon on Holloway Road.
THEATRES Islington has the Almeida Theatre (new drama, touring opera) and the *wonderful pub theatre, the King's Head (top names, quality drama). The Barbican Arts Centre on the South Bank plays second fiddle to the National but does so at a consistently impressive standard. Good for standbys.*
PUBS Just north of City campus are the *extremely popular* Bricklayer's Arms, the Fox in Paul Street and the *cosy snughole* that is the Griffin. *Pubs in the City tend to go crazy on weekday nights – stuffed with wideboys toasting guzzilion dollar deals.* North campus is better off with the Camden Head (*alcocool*), the Metro (*handy for lecture-avoidance*), the Albion (*beer-gardened and rural*), the York (*bar stool football commentary*), the Duke of Cambridge (*upmarket gastro-pub*) and the *unmistakably Irish* Filthy McNasty's.
MUSIC VENUES *Tons of local bands in Islington and Camden's pubs and on the streets.*
COMEDY/CABARET *The Amused Moose in Camden and Downstairs at the King's Head are top chuckle venues.*
EATING OUT For the City campus, two words suffice: Brick and Lane. *Enough restaurants to give Egon Ronay stress-rashes, most with an Indian flavour.* Pushplugs: Bengal Cuisine, Preem, and Viet Hoa (*great Vietnamese for under a tenner*). Islington Green has the Afghan Kitchen, *which is cheap and quirky.* La Porchetta's pizzas *can get pricey but Italy itself would be hard pressed to top them.*

UNIVERSITY

○ PRICE OF A PINT OF BEER £1.50
○ GLASS OF WINE £1.80 **○ CAN OF RED BULL** £1

There's a feeling that ents could be improved and, partly because of the size of the place, finding out what's going on can be a challenge.
BARS Of seven bars, two are *fighting for supremacy.* City's Sub Bar is two floors and *heaving.* North's The Rocket Complex is *most students' choice for nights of crazy, frolicsome fun.*
THEATRES *Super-keen drama students churn out 15-odd shows a year.*
FILM *Strong culture of film and cinema* but no purpose-built venue. Film showings alternate between the two main bars: two or three a week

L

Words in italics are Push's point of view — take it or leave it...

(£2 admission). The Film Society arranges occasional screenings in the video studies. There's also a deal with Islington's Vue cinema which has a few freebies for Met students.

CLUBBING/MUSIC VENUES The main bars are big enough to accommodate bands and the weekly calendar *is usually jammed with entertainments and club nights*. Wednesdays are the main event at both campuses. Jools Holland has returned to his roots to play here. Other visitors include Artful Dodger, De La Soul, Tim Westwood, Trevor Nelson, and the Prodigy.

COMEDY/CABARET Weekly comic events hit the Rocket Complex and Sub Bar. Norman Lovett has aired his Northern musings here.

FOOD All but one of the food outlets are run by an external catering company so *prices are hiked up at the expense of popularity*. The Diner in Goulston Street *may feel like a greasy spoon full of builders, but at least it's cheap*.

OTHER *Big-assed* May Ball and Winter Ball each year. Formal Sports Awards dinner.

SOCIAL ⏾⏾⏾⏾⏾⏾⏾⏾⏾⏾⏾⏾

LONDON METROPOLITAN UNIVERSITY STUDENTS' UNION
⊙ **5 SABBATICALS** ⊙ **TURNOUT AT LAST BALLOT** 1-2%
⊙ **NUS MEMBER**

The newly-formed SU's still finding its feet. Unlike many other universities, the Union, or 'MetSU', is involved in no commercial operations whatsoever – the University runs the bars – so focuses instead on services and welfare. Guildhall's SU was fairly strong, North London's as limp as lettuce – MetSU looks like settling somewhere in between. Its biggest task at present is to overcome the palpable City/North divide.

SU FACILITIES
Seven bars; four cafeterias; three snack bars; pool tables; Barclays bank; ATMs (Barclays, NatWest, Nationwide); Endsleigh Insurance branch; minibus hire for sporting societies; loads of meeting rooms; photocopiers; fax and printing services; payphones; advice centre; gaming and vending machines; new and secondhand bookshops (Waterstone's, Blackwells); stationery shops; three advice centres.

There's more to student life than poverty and fun... See the clubs & socs tables.

CLUBS (NON-SPORTING)
African Writers; Arab; Aviation; Bangladesh Students; Believers Love World; Hellenic; Hindu; Human Rights Advocacy; Indian; Indonisian; Islamic Sisters; Nigerian; Philosophy; Socan Music; Somali; Salsa; Tamil & Sudanese. **See also Clubs tables.**

OTHER ORGANISATIONS
SU paper 'Student Metro' *hits the litterbins* monthly. The FM-licensed radio station is now ready to roll again – online broadcasts. Rag was born recently, *but has yet to develop motor skills*.

RELIGIOUS
⊙ **3 CHAPLAINS (COFE),** IMAM
A prayer room is available for Muslim men and women.

PAID WORK
⊙ **JOB BUREAU** ⊙ **PAID WORK** TERM-TIME 75%; HOLS 95%
The Careers Development and Employment Service advertises part-time temp/vacation work, work experience and placements. Lots of Met students are employed during term time and the University itself has a large number of clerical positions. Employment Service vacancies are exclusive to Met students. Aspiring attorneys can join LAGREN (Law Graduates Employability Network).

SPORTS ⏾⏾⏾⏾⏾⏾⏾⏾⏾⏾⏾⏾⏾⏾

⊙ **RECENT SUCCESSES** TENNIS, HOCKEY, FOOTBALL, BASKETBALL ⊙ **BUSA RANKING** 21
The University Sports Department takes its responsibilities very seriously. *Eager to establish a sporting rep for themselves they're splashing the cash all over their teams and facilities.*

SPORTS FACILITIES
The facilities shared with Arsenal and Essex Cricket Club include: five football, one rugby and three cricket pitches; two basketball and one netball court; two sports halls; gym; multigym; aerobics studio. Various sports cards allow varying access to facilities (£30-42). There's access to a swimming pool, ice rink, squash and tennis courts and the River Thames from both campuses.

SPORTING CLUBS
See Clubs tables.

ATTRACTIONS see University of London
Arsenal and Tottenham are the local teams for North, *but it's considered bad manners to support them both.*

ACCOMMODATION ⓘⓘⓘⓘⓘⓘⓘⓘⓘ

IN UNIVERSITY
- **CATERED** 1% **COST** £98 (37WKS)
- **SELF CATERING** 3% **COST** £88 (37WKS)
- **INSURANCE PREMIUM** £££££

AVAILABILITY Those hailing from more than 25 miles get priority, and most can be housed as, with so many local students, there's not much call for University accommodation. Many halls are aimed at international students. All North's halls are within walking distance, but City's can be as far as three miles from campus *(a good 40 mins walk)*. *They're not the last word in luxury, but they're comfy enough.* Many have on-site launderettes, Sky TV, common rooms and pool tables and few have on-site bars. Security is tight: entry phones; 24-hr CCTV; 24-hr reception. Single-sex floors available.
CAR PARKING Permits from the council.

EXTERNALLY see University of London
- **AVE RENT** £80

AVAILABILITY Lots of students live at home – many are matures after all. *Standards vary* depending on proximity to the campus. City's expensive because it's the City – *and it's not all that nice in any case. Islington is trendylicious and there are good, roomy student apartments for the taking at the higher prices. But overall, the further away you go, the cheaper it gets.* There are plenty of student hostels around, which can be handy for international students.
HOUSING HELP The Accommodation Service (three full-time staff) lists vacancies and approved landlords and offers legal/contract advice.

WELFARE ⓘⓘⓘⓘⓘⓘⓘⓘⓘⓘⓘⓘ

SERVICES
- **LGBT SOCIETY** **MATURE STUDENTS' OFFICER & SOCIETY** **ETHNIC MINORITIES OFFICER & SOCIETY** **POSTGRAD OFFICER & SOCIETY** **INTERNATIONAL STUDENTS' OFFICER & SOCIETY** **DISABILITIES OFFICER & SOCIETY** **UNIVERSITY COUNSELLORS** 7 FULL
- **CRIME RATING** !!!!!

With no bars to run and half a million squids set aside for welfare this has become the priority. The SU has two sabbatical officers and a squad of volunteers.
HEALTH Health centre at Calcutta House. There's a part-time nurse and doctor.
CRECHES/NURSERY 83 places available in three nurseries for sprogs aged 2-5yrs. Subsidised fees.
DISABILITIES Newer buildings have been built with disabled access in mind so ramps and lifts abound. There's a Dyslexia Resource Centre at City and The Independent Learning Unit at North. The University publishes a handbook for disabled students.
CRIME *City campus is in one of the poorest areas of central London so crime is a very real possibility. North campus's Islington backdrop is safer, although Finsbury Park can get a bit hairy.*

FINANCE
- **AVE DEBT PER YEAR** 4,133 **HOME STUDENT FEES** £3,000
- **ACCESS FUND** £2.5M **SUCCESSFUL APPLICATIONS/YR** 3,000 **AVE PAYMENT** £750

SUPPORT A range of bursaries and scholarships is available.

L

LONDON SOUTH BANK UNIVERSITY

FORMERLY SOUTH BANK UNIVERSITY, SOUTH BANK POLYTECHNIC

1. **LONDON SOUTH BANK UNIVERSITY** 103 Borough Road, London, SE1 0AA **TEL** (020) 7928 8989 **WEBSITE** www.lsbu.ac.uk
 LONDON SOUTH BANK UNIVERSITY STUDENTS' UNION Keyworth Street, London, SE1 6NG **TEL** (020) 7815 6060
E-MAIL su.general.@lsbu.ac.uk **WEBSITE** www.lsbsu.org
2. **EAST LONDON CAMPUS, FACULTY OF HEALTH** Whipps Cross Hospital, Leytonstone, London, E11 1NR **TEL** (020) 7815 4747
3. **ESSEX CAMPUS, FACULTY OF HEALTH AND SOCIAL CARE** Harold Wood Road Hospital, Gubbins Lane, Romford, Essex, RN3 0BE
 STUDENT COUNCIL as above **TEL** (020) 7815 5908

GENERAL ⓘⓘⓘⓘⓘⓘⓘⓘⓘⓘⓘⓘⓘ

The South Bank is *one of London's most vibrant, exciting, beautiful and culturally sophisticated areas.* LSBU's main campus is half a mile away in Elephant & Castle. The immediate surroundings are *drab and depressing.* The worst is the lurid crimson Elephant & Castle Shopping Centre, voted by the London Design Festival as the 5th

Ugliest Landmark In London. *It can feel cheated of the top spot.* A £1.5bn regeneration of the area has been announced – *all very exciting, but unlikely to have any effect beyond builders and roadworks before 2010.* For the time being, LBSU is made up of a number of buildings, *jostling for space and including humungous* new Keyworth Centre, which is *massively impressive.* A new student centre and other sproutings can be expected at the Southwark site sometime soon.

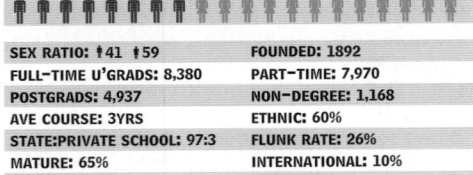

SEX RATIO: ♂41 ♀59	**FOUNDED:** 1892
FULL-TIME U'GRADS: 8,380	**PART-TIME:** 7,970
POSTGRADS: 4,937	**NON-DEGREE:** 1,168
AVE COURSE: 3YRS	**ETHNIC:** 60%
STATE:PRIVATE SCHOOL: 97:3	**FLUNK RATE:** 26%
MATURE: 65%	**INTERNATIONAL:** 10%
DISABLED: 305	**LOCAL:** N/A

ATMOSPHERE

LSBU is a serious university, full of a diverse range of students from all sorts of weird and wonderful backgrounds. They've been out in the real world and, more so than anywhere else, they really are here to study. The flip side of this is that, in the kindest way possible, there's not much atmosphere at all – the university experience isn't much more than a half-way house for those on the way to well-paid graduate jobs. Students are satisfied with their lot and don't pay much attention to the drab surroundings, but they're a cosmopolitan and culturally-rich student body, and friendly with it. When they have time between study sessions, that is.

SITES

Large distances and some navigationally-challenged planning leads to more than a little confusion in getting round – some students don't know whether they're coming or going. Most of the University's Health courses are on the Essex and East London campuses, based at Harold Wood Hospital in Romford and Whipps Cross Hospital in Leytonstone, East London. The Essex campus has its own library and refectory.

LONDON see University of London
○ **CITY CENTRE** 1.5 MILES
ELEPHANT & CASTLE The South Bank is *great*, but the rest of Southwark, while starting to feel some of the knock-on regeneration, is *still pretty grim and grotty. On the other hand, it's cheaper than norf London and not quite so packed with media types with silly haircuts and too much money.*

TRAVEL see University of London
TRAINS Mainline trains from Waterloo or London Bridge, both within ten mins walk or short train hops from Elephant & Castle station.
CAR *There are cars everywhere in the Elephant, most of them hurtling around the notorious gyratory system with the scantest of regard for pedestrians. They tend not to hang around, mainly because there's nowhere to park.* Add the fact that the Elephant borders the Congestion Zone and it should be *pretty clear that it's best to leave the motor at home.*
LOCAL Zone 1 on the Tube: the Bakerloo and Northern Lines pass through Elephant & Castle station (100m from the Southwark Campus) and Thameslink trains serve the train station. Local bus services are frequent and plentiful.
BICYCLES The students union encourages bikes and there's a bike shed, *although convenient railings around campus are apparently more*

popular. London's trademark smog makes two-wheel take-up scarce.

CAREER PROSPECTS
○ **CAREERS SERVICE** ○ **NO. OF STAFF** 7 FULL/3 PART
○ **UNEMPLOYED AFTER 6MTHS** 9%
The Job Shop arranges placements and keeps students posted of vacancies.

FAMOUS ALUMNI
Simone Callender (Commonwealth gold medallist for judo); Jimeoin (comedian); Nick Leslau (property developer); Norma Major (former PM's wife); Bridget Prentice MP (Lab); Greg Searle (Olympic oarsman); Phil Spencer (Location, Location, Location); Jerszy Seymore (Milan-based fashion designer).

FURTHER INFO
○ **PROSPECTUSES** UNDERGRAD; POSTGRAD; INTERNATIONAL; COURSES; VIDEO ○ **OPEN DAYS**
For more admissions info see www.apply.lsbu.ac.uk

ACADEMIC ○○○○○○○○○○○○○

The University has *carved its niche* in teaching vocational and techie courses to mature and local students. That said, it covers a broad base of subjects and is *strongest on education and nursing*. It's also *highly rated as a research university, with a fair amount of one-on-one teaching* across the board.

ENTRY POINTS: 140–240		**AVE POINTS:** 140	
APPLICATIONS PER PLACE: N/A		**CLEARING:** 30%	
NO. OF TERMS: 2		**LENGTH OF TERMS:** 15WKS	
STAFF TO STUDENT RATIO: 1:20		**STUDY ADDICTS:** N/A	
TEACHING: *		**RESEARCH:** ***	
YEAR ABROAD: N/A		**SANDWICH STUDENTS:** 10%	
1STS: 11%		**2.2S:** 39%	
2.1S: 39%		**3RDS:** 9%	

ADMISSIONS
○ **APPLY VIA UCAS/GTTR FOR TEACHING/NMAS FOR NURSING**
A Widening Participation Programme is aimed at mature students without formal qualifications. A summer school gets students up to speed if they need it and a Credit Prior to Learning scheme (APL) turns work or other life experience into academic points.

SUBJECTS
ARTS & HUMAN SCIENCES 17%   **BUSINESS, COMPUTING & INFORMATION MANAGEMENT** 24%   **COMBINED HONOURS** 6 %   **ENGINEERING, SCIENCE & THE BUILT ENVIRONMENT** 22 %   **HEALTH & SOCIAL CARE** 32%
BEST Biological Sciences; Economics; Politics; Psychology; Sociology, Social Policy & Anthropology.

LIBRARIES
◉ **450,000 BOOKS** ◉ **1,500 STUDY PLACES**
◉ **SPEND PER STUDENT** £
The Perry Library in Southwark is open seven days a week; the one on Essex campus is open six days.

COMPUTERS
◉ **2,250 WORKSTATIONS**
The Learning Resource Centre at the main campus runs IT courses available to all students. Almost all students' rooms have internet access, too.

OTHER LEARNING FACILITIES
Language labs, a CAD lab. A new arts and media centre (including recording studios) are pencilled in for the Elephant and Castle re-development.

ENTERTAINMENT ◉◉◉◉◉◉◉◉◉◉

THE CITY see University of London
◉ **PRICE OF A PINT OF BEER** £2
◉ **GLASS OF WINE** £2.60
◉ **CAN OF RED BULL** £1.90
CINEMAS/THEATRES/MUSIC There's the IMAX cinema, the NFT and all the other attractions of the South Bank arts complex, including the National Theatre and Royal Festival Hall. Camberwell up the road has the Blue Elephant Theatre while Peckham, *when it's not sticking a pony in its back pocket*, has the New Varieties theatre. And of course there's the Globe on Southbank itself, with standing tickets from a fiver.
PUBS *There's no real division between students and locals, so there aren't really any studenty or towny pubs. The most popular are the closest (except the Elephant & Castle).* Pushplugs: the Ship and the George on Borough Road; the Duke of York; Bridge House, Zanzibar, and The Flowers of the Forest.
CLUBBING Despite being *well past the peak of its popularity*, the Ministry of Sound is on the doorstep, with the *more happening* the Fridge, the *popular gay club* Heaven, Chunnel Club, The Arches and Cloud 9 *all near enough*.
MUSIC VENUES Brixton Academy is down the road a way, or a couple of stops on the tube. *It may not have the best sound system in the world, but it pulls some big names.* If you like your music sitting down, check out the varied offerings (classical, world, jazz etc) at the Royal Festival Hall.
COMEDY/CABARET The local press is good for finding laughs. Otherwise, try Belushi's
EATING OUT For an *artery-clogging pick-me-up*, students head to Terry's on Suffolk Street, while the *classier* students head to Luperella's on Borough Road or Pizzeria Castello on the other side of the Elephant roundabout. The Nest on London Road is a *popular* caff and Castle Sandwich bar by the station provides *overwhelmingly filled* take-away baps. If you're more braised artichokes than tatties and neeps, a saunter round Borough Food Market on a Sunday is a must. *Foodie heaven*: fresh fast food and not a Pot Noodle in sight.

UNIVERSITY
◉ **PRICE OF A PINT OF BEER** £1.60
◉ **GLASS OF WINE** £2.50
◉ **CAN OF RED BULL** £1.50
BARS The Isobar in the SU is *as studenty as student bars come*, with bar food, music vids on the telly, a stage area and pool tables, but is also – for now – *a smoker's haven and pretty much a no-go for those who like their air oxygenated*. The Tavern on the second floor is a *more traditional* pub, complete with more games machines than you can shake a piggy bank at, as well as big-screen sports and more pool tables. Yet more pool facilities are planned for the Snug next door to the Tavern. *(Why? Are they breeding Steven Hendrys on-site?)*
THEATRES *There's a newish theatre facility but it's more King Kong than King Lear in these parts.*
FILM The Mushroom Film Society puts on *popular flicks as and when they feel like it.*
CLUBBING Isobar is the pre-club Ministry gig; start at 'Let Loose', the *classic Wednesday night cheese-fest*, and entrance to the Ministry is a bargain £2. Raise the Roof is a garage-themed monthly *spectacular*. Recently spotted on the wheels of steel: Lisa Pin-Up, Drez, Renegade, Iron Mike, DJ Neo.
FOOD Grab-a-Bite does everything from sarnies to samosas. Most sites have a refectory, but there are also *lots of local snack huts when Uni food can't be stomached (price- and taste-wise).*
OTHER The Summer Ball and the Athletics Union Ball are the two *posh-frock/penguin-suit blow-outs*. Isobar also hosts end-of-term and Christmas parties.

SOCIAL ◉◉◉◉◉◉◉◉◉◉◉◉

SOUTH BANK UNIVERSITY STUDENTS UNION
◉ **5 SABBATICALS** ◉ **TURNOUT AT LAST BALLOT** 10%
◉ **NUS MEMBER**
Students don't really come to LSBU to party hard so the SU's little more than floor space. The Union does try to pull people together, but events tail off after Freshers' Week once students discover the rest of London. There's not a huge choice of events – and you know what they say about variety – and what does go on isn't much publicised. Students feel a little disconnected from what's happening higher up as a result. The SU building's being put out of its misery shortly in preparation for a face-lift, so don't expect the ents situation to improve for the next couple of years.

SU FACILITIES
Two bars (Isobar doubles as a nightclub); two canteens/coffee bars; five pool tables; meeting room; minibus hire; Endsleigh Insurance; HSBC on site branch and ATM; photocopying/faxing/printing services; crèche; juke boxes; video games; general store; stationery shop; vending machines; new and secondhand bookshop.

L

CLUBS (NON-SPORTING)

Arts & Media; Bible Study; Chinese; Conceptual Wing Chun; Console Gaming; Electronic Workshop; Howard League For Penal Reform; Linux User Group; Model Making; Pan- African; Special Effects (SFX); St John's First Aid; Students Industrial Skills; Stop The War; Tamil. **See also Clubs tables.**

OTHER ORGANISATIONS

Student paper 'Scratch' was itself scratched after one issue, to be swiftly replaced by 'Unity'. *The new paper's been criticised for being 'too political' (unlike the students themselves) but is calming itself down and settling into a monthly affair.* 'ISO FM' broadcasts from the Tavern.

RELIGIOUS

○ **2 CHAPLAINS (RC, COFE)**
Two prayer rooms and a Buddhist temple nearby.

PAID WORK see University of London

○ **JOB BUREAU** ○ **PAID WORK** TERM-TIME 60%; HOLS 75%
Vacancy lists are published in the Union and at the Job Shop.

SPORTS ○○○○○○○○○○○○○○○

○ **RECENT SUCCESSES** RUGBY; TABLE TENNIS; WOMEN'S VOLLEYBALL; MEN'S BADMINTON ○ **BUSA RANKING** 49
Despite a low ranking in the BUSA championship there's been a recent haul of medals and a BUSA award for 'Most Improved University for Sport'. They know there's a fair marathon ahead before they become the 'Loughborough of the south' but have shown willing by investing in the *almost Stalinist-sounding* Academy of Sport, Physical Activity & Well-being to oversee all things sweaty. *Well, most things.*

SPORTS FACILITIES

LSBU boasts: 21 acres of sports fields; four senior football pitches; four junior football pitches; two rugby pitches; three cricket tables (including three artificial wickets in the summer); a fitness suite; free weights room; sports hall (including five-a-side facilities); trampoline; aerobics classes; netball; martial arts; basketball; volleyball; four badminton courts; indoor cricket nets; and on-site physiotherapists. There's a swimming pool in the Elephant & Castle sports centre; *but most students would rather take a plunge in the Thames.*

SPORTING CLUBS

Aikido; Ju-Jitsu; Table Tennis; Wu-Shu-Kwan (Chinese boxing). **See Clubs tables.**

ATTRACTIONS see University of London

The Oval, home of Surrey CCC, is about ten mins walk away.

ACCOMMODATION ○○○○○○○○○○

IN UNIVERSITY

○ **SELF CATERING** 14% ○ **COST** £83 (39/48WKS)
○ **1ST YRS** 45% ○ **INSURANCE PREMIUM** £££££
AVAILABILITY All four halls (1,400 places) are *in walking range* of the campus and are good for making friends. Or losing them, depending on your personal habits. Rooms are arranged in flats with pay-as-you-talk phones, internet access and some en suite facilites. There are *only six* specially adapted rooms for disabled students though. Despite being the oldest, smallest and cheapest, the New Kent Road hall is *prided* for its community feel, pool tables *(surprise)* and BBQ veranda. However, some of the newer ones, such as the favoured McLaren Hall (600 en suite rooms, *conveniently placed*) between the campus and Waterloo) are *quite swish.* Dante Road loves to be hated by residents, David Bomberg is popular with nurses (the building, not the man himself). Most freshers end up at New Kent Road. *Which beats the crap out of being dumped on the Old Kent Road without taxi fare and protective clothing.*
CAR PARKING No spaces, only drop-off points.

EXTERNALLY see University of London

○ **AVE RENT** £103
AVAILABILITY South London is cheaper than north, but the Elephant itself isn't the best place to live, although some *grin and bear it.* Camberwell, Kennington and Oval are the most popular. Brixton is still *a favourite boho haunt,* but students have been increasingly priced-out.
HOUSING HELP Staff at the Accommodation Office dole out leaflets and keep an approved landlord list.

WELFARE ○○○○○○○○○○○○○

SERVICES

○ **LGBT SOCIETY** ○ **WOMEN'S OFFICER** ○ **INTERNATIONAL STUDENTS' OFFICER** ○ **DISABILITIES OFFICER**
○ **SELF-DEFENCE CLASSES** ○ **NIGHTLINE** ○ **TAXI FUND**
○ **UNIVERSITY COUNSELLORS** 4 FULL/2 PART
○ **CRIME RATING** !!!!!
Welfare support from the Personal Development Advice Unit. *Counselling services hang in the balance due to insufficient funding.*
HEALTH A doctor's surgery opposite Southwark campus.
CRECHES/NURSERY 52 places for ankle-biters, 6mths-5yrs, for £135 per week.
DISABILITIES Newer buildings are fully adapted for access, although in the older parts of campus it can be *a bit of a struggle.* Two dyslexia officers are available.

L

FINANCE
- **AVE DEBT PER YEAR** £4,255
- **HOME STUDENT FEES** £3,000
- **ACCESS FUND** £1M **AVE PAYMENT** £250-400

SUPPORT *Top-up fees will be soothed somewhat by a grant available to all home/EU students.* Not means-tested, around £2,250 will be available over three years. LSBU has one of the largest Access funds in the UK, but, with lots of students from backgrounds not exactly typical of more middle-class universities, *it needs it.* There are also lots of sports scholarships (£3,000), the Governers Charitable Fund, the Lawrence Burrow Scholarship (£1,000 grants for ten Asian/West Indian students) and the Minerva Scholarship (£20,000 for Built Environment Students).

⇛ LONDON COLLEGE OF COMMUNICATION
see *University of the Arts, London*

⇛ LONDON COLLEGE OF FASHION
see *University of the Arts, London*

⇛ LONDON COLLEGE OF PRINTING
see *University of the Arts, London*

⇛ LONDON GUILDHALL UNIVERSITY
see *London Metropolitan University*

⇛ LONDON SCHOOL OF ECONOMICS
see *LSE*

⇛ LONDON SCHOOL OF MEDICINE AND DENTISTRY
see *Queen Mary, University of London*

LOUGHBOROUGH UNIVERSITY

 LOUGHBOROUGH UNIVERSITY Loughborough, Leics, LE11 3TU **TEL** (01509) 223 522 **E−MAIL** admissions@lboro.ac.uk **WEBSITE** www.lboro.ac.uk **LOUGHBOROUGH STUDENTS' UNION** Loughborough, Leics, LE11 3TT **TEL** (01509) 635 000 **E−MAIL** president@lborosu.org.uk **WEBSITE** www.lufbra.net

GENERAL ◌◌◌◌◌◌◌◌◌◌◌◌◌

Loughborough, pronounced 'Lufbra' by the locals and 'Loogabarooga' by the crazy and/or drunk, is a *middleweight* market town, set among the wandering countryside and small suburban villages of the East Midlands. Loughborough University sits a mile west of the town centre in *green and pleasant* parkland. The campus buildings are *largely inoffensive*, low-rise blocks on a landscaped, 410-acre site. It's *perfect* for the various playing fields and sporting facilities – sport being *the University's favourite hobby horse – and they sure ride it well.*

SEX RATIO: ♂61 ♀39	FOUNDED: 1908
FULL−TIME U'GRADS: 10,171	PART−TIME: 341
POSTGRADS: 2,060	NON−DEGREE: 435
AVE COURSE: 3/4YRS	ETHNIC: 4%
STATE:PRIVATE SCHOOL: 77:23	FLUNK RATE: 6%
MATURE: 6%	INTERNATIONAL: 17%
DISABLED: 235	LOCAL: 10%

ATMOSPHERE

Someone once said 'It's not the winning, but the taking part that counts.' Push can promise you, they didn't go to Loughborough. Here, it's the winning that matters, along with the training beforehand and the celebration, analysis, recriminations and loud and liver-bothering drinking games afterwards. If you're not particularly interested in sport one way or another, don't be dismayed – there's plenty else to do, plus the influx of new arty types in the wake of the merger with Loughborough College of Art & Design. However, for those who are allergic to track suits and become apoplectic at the hint of exertion, applying here could be construed as a little perverse.

LOUGHBOROUGH
- **POPULATION** 153,600 **LONDON** 100 MILES
- **LEICESTER** 13 MILES **NOTTINGHAM** 17 MILES
- **HIGH TEMP** 20 **LOW TEMP** 1 **RAINFALL** 59

Loughborough's not big enough to fit in more than a few sites of historic interest, but it gives its tuppence worth, including a few old churches and museums (eg. the Bell Foundry, Military and the Ancient Monuments museums). Apart from all the usual shops and public amenities, there's a

twice-weekly street market, some *good independent record stores* and some ethnic jewellery shops. The town is surrounded by the ancient Charnwood Forest – *so ancient that there's not much forest left* – and various waterways flow through the area. Of local note is the Great Central Railway, still steaming its way cross-country.

TRAVEL

TRAINS Loughborough station, 2 miles from the campus has services to London St Pancras and beyond (from £60.05 return).

COACHES Served by local coach company Paul Winson and National Express to Nottingham (£3.50) and London (£20.50) and beyond.

CAR The A6 goes straight through Loughborough and the M1 is less than 2 miles west of the campus.

AIR Nottingham East Midlands Airport (inland and European flights) is 5.5 miles from campus.

HITCHING *The M1's good, but it's a bus ride to the junction.*

LOCAL Local buses run between campus and town.

UNIVERSITY The No. 7 shuttle bus whizzes between campus and the University and the town every 10 mins (£1.10 sgl or £1.80 rtn). The University tuns it's own cab company, ADT.

BICYCLES *Useful for getting into town (and the campus and its sports fields). The theft situation is improving, but it helps not to bring the most expensive, designer mountain bike.*

CAREER PROSPECTS

- **CAREERS SERVICE** - **NO. OF STAFF** 7 FULL/8 PART
- **UNEMPLOYED AFTER 6MTHS** 7%

FAMOUS ALUMNI

Steve Backley (javelin chucker); Sebastian Coe (former runner, ex-MP, now Lord in charge of London's Olympic bid); Michael Fabricant MP (Con); Tanni Grey-Thompson (Para Olympic athlete); Barry Hines (writer, 'Kes'); Jason Lee (England hockey player); David Moorcroft (athlete); Carole Tongue MEP (Lab); Bob Wilson (commentator, ex-Arsenal goalie).

FURTHER INFO

- **PROSPECTUSES** UNDERGRAD; POSTGRAD; ALL DEPTS
- **OPEN DAYS**

ACADEMIC ❍❍❍❍❍❍❍❍❍❍❍❍

Originating as a technical college, which got full university status in 1966, the University continues to evolve and, since the merger with Loughborough College of Art & Design in 1998, has been offering Humanities/Arts courses. Business & Management, Design & Technology, Engineering, Social Sciences & Sports Science *can all hold their own in an academic showdown.* Engineering and Maths recently garnered big cash boosts. Engineering students get help online from the Engineering Student Centre *(with academic stuff, unfortunately, rather than social skills)* and the Maths Learning Support Centre *does its bit for all innumerate students, regardless of their subject area.*

ENTRY POINTS: 260–360	**AVE POINTS:** 310
APPLICATIONS PER PLACE: 7	**CLEARING:** 5%
NO. OF TERMS: 2	**LENGTH OF TERMS:** 15WKS
STAFF TO STUDENT RATIO: 1:17	**STUDY ADDICTS:** 16%
TEACHING: ★★★★★	**RESEARCH:** ★★★★★
YEAR ABROAD: 6%	**SANDWICH STUDENTS:** 38%
1STS: 12%	**2.2S:** 31%
2.1S: 52%	**3RDS:** 5%

ADMISSIONS

- **APPLY VIA UCAS**

SUBJECTS

ENGINEERING 26%   **SCIENCE** 23%
SOCIAL SCIENCES & HUMANITIES 57%

BEST Architecture; Building & Planning; Art & Design; Business; Civil; Chemical & Other Engineering; Communications & Information Studies; Computer Science; Economics; Electronic & Electrical Engineering; English based Studies; Finance & Accounting; Management; Mathematical Sciences; Mechanically-based Engineering; Media Studies; Medical Science & Pharmacy; Physical Geography; Physical Sciences; Politics; Psychology; Sociology; Social Policy & Criminology; Sports Science.

UNUSUAL BSc Ergonomics (Applied Human Sciences).

L

> ◉ **At the 2002 Commonwealth Games, Loughborough University's athletes generated 18 medals for the home nations, including seven Golds. If Loughborough had been a nation, they would have come 9th in the medal table.**

Words in italics are Push's point of view – take it or leave it...

LIBRARIES
⊙ **700,000** BOOKS ⊙ **780** STUDY PLACES

COMPUTERS
⊙ **410** WORKSTATIONS ⊙ **24–**HR ACCESS

All rooms in Halls are connected for phones and t'internet. The 'Learn' server keeps things 21st century with online discussion groups, reading lists, web-based tests, module catalogue, past exam papers.

ENTERTAINMENT ⊙⊙⊙⊙⊙⊙⊙⊙⊙⊙

THE TOWN
⊙ PRICE OF A PINT OF BEER £1.65

CINEMAS The five-screen Curzon is one of the oldest cinemas in the country.

THEATRES Amateur and touring shows in the Town Hall.

PUBS *Local pubs are popular with students who live out or want to get off campus. Pushplugs: the Griffin and the Paget (as studenty as any round here); Barracuda; Lloyds; the Gallery.*

CLUBBING/MUSIC VENUES *Plenty of student nights. Try Wild; Rain; Vice Versa; Echoes on a weekend. The Town Hall puts on classical noisefests; those with other live music tastes will have to head to Leicester or Nottingham.*

EATING OUT *Again, it's necessary to go out of town for serious tastebud tingles but a few establishments are worth a look. Mugals and the Far Pavillion are the most popular curry houses. Moomba is Australian themed. The Loco Lounge and Momentos for Mediteranean, big student discounts at the latter on Mondays and Tuesdays. Also: Cactus Café (Mexican); Mr Chans (cheap Chinese).* There are numerous Indian, Chinese and takeaway places, some open till at least 2am.

UNIVERSITY
⊙ PRICE OF A PINT OF BEER £1.50
⊙ GLASS OF WINE £2.05
⊙ CAN OF RED BULL £1.90

BARS 14 bars: three in residential halls, two on campus and nine in the Union Building, *which are always lively, especially when there's yet another sporting victory to celebrate.* JC's *(old man's pub feel and, surprise surprise, numerous sports screens)* is open until midnight every day. Bar 1 is *classier.* Fusion is a *trendy chill-out bar* with leather sofas and a small stage and the *more intimate* Bocca Bar Café has alternative music, an outdoor balcony and *toasty but environmentally-dubious heaters.*

THEATRES Regular presentations in the Cope Auditorium and a Union-funded troupe in the Sir Robert Martin Theatre.

CINEMAS The film society shows pics and flicks a few times a week (arthouse and blockbuster) in the Union's auditorium.

CLUBBING Several venues with something every night *but students tend to shake their butts on*

the fields more than on the dance floor. For those who need some ents-style exercise, FND (Friday Night Disco) is the most popular club night. Cheese, hiphop and drum & bass all get a chance on the decks, as have Scott Mills and Hard Skool.

MUSIC VENUES The main auditorium tempts up-and-coming acts as well as the likes of Goldie Lookin' Chain, the Bluetones the Foundations.

COMEDY/CABARET Dance/comedy night on Saturdays *(as opposed to comedy dancing every other night of the week).* Sundays are given over to poker.

FOOD In the SU and student village students can find something edible to put in their mouths from 10am to 3am. There's an *imaginative* selection, including the University's own pizza delivery service. Bocca Bar Café does *the cheapest* sarnies and main courses.

OTHER Freshers' week is a blur of ents from surf simulators to bucking broncos. At the other end of a student's stint is the Graduation Ball.

SOCIAL ⊙⊙⊙⊙⊙⊙⊙⊙⊙⊙⊙⊙

LOUGHBOROUGH UNIVERSITY STUDENT UNION
⊙ TURNOUT AT LAST BALLOT 18% ⊙ NUS MEMBER

Politics is a non-issue for most students but the few who take it seriously are very committed indeed. Awareness campaigns go down well. LSU represents students from the University, Loughborough College and the RNIB Vocational College. Although the Union remains part of NUS, *it holds the national body at arm's length.*

SU FACILITIES
A general shop (complete, of course, with sports gear section); nine bars; three catering outlets; travel agency; printing facilities; bookshop (Blackwells); market stalls; three banks (HSBC, Barclays, NatWest) plus other ATMs; Employment Exchange; Endsleigh Insurance office; photocopier; photo booth; games and vending machines; pool tables; juke box; meeting rooms; auditorium; optician; dentist; hairdresser; accommodation letting agency; taxi hire; seven minibuses; recording studio; gallery.

CLUBS (NON-SPORTING)
AIESEC; China Centre; Ballroom & Latin American Dance; Breakdancing; Chinese; CivSoc; Computer; Concert Band; Fever; Hip Hop Dance; Hellenic; Indian; Kenyan LSU Conservative Future; LSU Hindi Students Forum; LSU Saudi; Malaysian; Motor; Motorcycle; MuSoc; RocSoc; Roleplay & Wargaming; Scout & Guide; Singapore; SocSpot; Stage; Transport; Tuxedo Swing. **See also Clubs tables.**

OTHER ORGANISATIONS
The remarkable Rag is about the only thing that distracts anyone from sporting pursuits. It organises fundraisers around the country, netting a commendable £72,888 last year. The Student

L

Community Action group runs other publicly-spirited activities. The student media includes 'Label', the weekly rag financed by the SU but run independently, and the round-the-clock radio station, 'LCR', which is more than 25 years old and gets a month-long FM licence each year. 'LSUTV 'can be seen in the Union Building and on the web.

RELIGIOUS
5 CHAPLAINS (COFE, RC, FC)
There's an ecumenical Christian chaplaincy, a Muslim prayer room and an Islamic library.

PAID WORK
JOB BUREAU ● **PAID WORK** TERM-TIME 50%; HOLS 65-70%
There's a *very successful* employment exchange with a job database for students. It's pretty common for second, third and fourth years to pull in some part-time pennies *(freshers are too busy organising orgies in halls, presumably).*

SPORTS ⊙⊙⊙⊙⊙⊙⊙⊙⊙⊙⊙⊙⊙⊙⊙

● **RECENT SUCCESSES** HOCKEY, RUGBY LEAGUE, LACROSSE
● **BUSA RANKING** 1
Did we mention that Loughborough University is big on sport? Applicants who think that running around a field in shorts, chasing/catching/kicking/throwing a ball is stupid should keep quite quiet about it if they go to Loughborough, unless they want to see grown men and women cry. The University enjoys a vast range of sporting facilities, virtually unmatched by any other, let alone by a university this size. Success in most sports has been phenomenal – they've won the British Universities Sports Association women's championship for the last 26 consecutive years and the men's version for the last 24. A veritable army of students and graduates competed in the 2006 Commonwealth Games. (Perhaps they're all bionic or clones. Has anybody actually checked?)

SPORTS FACILITIES
All sports clubs are fully insured against accidents, *which makes them relatively pricey to join, but the facilities are worth it.* Eight football pitches, five rugby, two hockey, two cricket and three all-weather pitches, five squash, 16 tennis, five basketball and five netball courts, two sports halls, Olympic-sized swimming pool, running track, athletics field, croquet lawn, gym, aerobics studio, multigym, sauna, climbing wall, indoor gymnastics centre. The town doesn't really need to add anything, but the surrounding area does make outdoor sports, such as fell-walking and water-sports, possible. Loughborough is now the regional Centre of Excellence for the English Institute of Sport and to the England and Wales Cricket Board's ECB Academy. The England Rugby Team train at the University.

SPORTING CLUBS
Croquet; Gymnastics; Hiking; Hot Air Ballooning; Mountain Boarding; Lacrosse; LS Flying. **See also Clubs tables.**

ATTRACTIONS
Formula 3 motor racing and motorcycle racing at Donnington.

ACCOMMODATION ⊙⊙⊙⊙⊙⊙⊙⊙⊙⊙

IN UNIVERSITY
● **CATERED** 28% ● **COST** £113 (31WKS
● **SELF-CATERING** 19% ● **COST** £78 (34/38WKS)
● **1ST YRS LIVING IN** 92%
● **INSURANCE PREMIUM** £
AVAILABILITY *Is good, as is quality –it's just a shame the halls look like concrete tower blocks.* There are ten catered and six self-catering halls. They are all mixed (although some blocks or corridors are single sex) and accommodate between 150-650 students. This is enough to house almost all first years who request it and a good number of finalists. 10% of rooms are shared. They are all on or adjacent to campus except one en route to town half a mile away. There are also self-catering flats arranged in courts or in the student village. Between six and eight students share each kitchen.
CAR PARKING Limited permit parking for second and third years (£48).

EXTERNALLY
● **AVE RENT** £60
AVAILABILITY *It's a renter's market and you're unlikely to be left on the pavement. The best places, plucked by the early birds, are around Ashby Road and Storer Road, between the campus and Sainsbury's.* Rents vary from about £40-80, depending on what's included.
HOUSING HELP The Union runs an advice service and the University's student accommodation service holds an accommodation list and offers handy suggestions to new and bemused students. Also see the letting agency in the SU.

WELFARE ⊙⊙⊙⊙⊙⊙⊙⊙⊙⊙⊙⊙⊙

SERVICES
● **LGBT OFFICER & SOCIETY** ● **MATURE STUDENTS' OFFICER & SOCIETY** ● **INTERNATIONAL STUDENTS' OFFICER & SOCIETY** ● **POSTGRAD OFFICER & SOCIETY** ● **DISABILITIES OFFICER & SOCIETY** ● **LATE-NIGHT MINIBUS** ● **UNIVERSITY COUNSELLORS** 4 FULL/4PART ● **CRIME RATING** !!
HEALTH *Comprehensive* medical centre with three doctors, 11 nurses and, naturally, one of the best university physiotherapy and sports injury clinics in the country.

Words in italics are Push's point of view — take it or leave it...

CRECHES/NURSERY 100 places for 6mths-5yrs.
DISABILITIES Modern buildings pose *few* access problems. Support available for students with studying difficulties from the University disabilities and additional needs service.

FINANCE
○ **AVE DEBT PER YEAR** £2,138
○ **HOME STUDENT FEES** £3,000

FEES International students pay £8,850-11,450. Postgrads are charged £3,085-5,670.
○ **ACCESS FUND** £400,000 ○ **SUCCESSFUL APPLICATIONS/YR** 474 ○ **AVE PAYMENT** £1,000
SUPPORT *Sackloads*. International scholarships; music tuition scholarships and bursaries; some dept scholarships; student prizes; some sponsored courses.

LSE

THE SCHOOL IS PART OF THE UNIVERSITY OF LONDON AND STUDENTS ARE ENTITLED TO USE ITS FACILITIES

○ **THE LONDON SCHOOL OF ECONOMICS AND POLITICAL SCIENCE** PO Box 13420, Houghton Street, London, WC2A 2AR **TEL** (020) 7955 7756 **E-MAIL** ug-admissions@lse.ac.uk **WEBSITE** www.lse.ac.uk ○ **LSE STUDENTS' UNION** East Building, LSE, Houghton Street, London, WC2A 2AR **TEL** (020) 7955 7158 **E-MAIL** comms@lse.ac.uk **WEBSITE** www.lsesu.com

GENERAL ❶❶❶❶❶❶❶❶❶❶❶❶❶

London's vim and vigour don't get very much more frantic than where the Strand hits Fleet Street. That's where LSE resides, and *they couldn't have found a much better spot to set up one of the world's leading economics schools*. It's not all E though – *other social sciences are strong too*. The buildings *play sardines* opposite BBC Bush House, a mile or so down the road from Trafalgar Square, *just round the corner* from King's College London and the Courtauld Institute. *It's cramped and busy* with a mixture of *grand old* buildings and modern blocks. For general information about London see University of London.

SEX RATIO: ♂52 ♀48	**FOUNDED:** 1895	
FULL-TIME U'GRADS: 3,808	**PART-TIME:** 51	
POSTGRADS: 4,408	**NON-DEGREE:** N/A	
AVE COURSE: 3YRS	**ETHNIC:** 53%	
STATE:PRIVATE SCHOOL: 62:38	**FLUNK RATE:** 5%	
MATURE: 9%	**INTERNATIONAL:** 47%	
DISABLED: 35	**LOCAL:** N/A	

ATMOSPHERE
LSE's a multicultural intellectual pressure-cooker, which means it's hot with ideas and action, but stay too long and there's a risk of your head exploding. It attracts the most intelligent, the most ambitious and the most jealously competitive from 152 countries, if not flocks of tanked-up party types. There are still *traces of the radical spirit that the college was famed for during the 1960s, but there's more chance of bumping into a young Bill Gates than a young Tony Benn. The lack of fences and boundaries means the main site merges seamlessly into the Capital's heart and the myriad looming buildings all around – it's austere and slightly imposing or safe as houses, depending how you feel about it. The compact site makes getting around between classes is a doddle, but London's also on the doorstep for when the books are finally put away*.

LONDON see University of London

ALDWYCH
Aldwych is *a stone's throw* from the City in the east, the West End in, *er*, the west and the legal fields and *hobos' hang-out* of Lincoln's Inn in the north. *Chuck a stone south, and it'll plop gently into the Thames. Push can't recommend actually hurling stones around the capital, as the Met coppers don't tend to be very sympathetic*.

TRAVEL see University of London
TRAINS Charing Cross is about 500m down the Strand, for trains to London's 'burbs and the South-East. Waterloo and Blackfriars (for Thameslink North London services) are within *sneezing range* too.
CAR *Don't even think about driving around this bit of town*. It's C-Charge central and jam-packed with traffic. Nearest facilities are at Lincoln's Inn Fields, the closest NCP site is at Drury Lane. The Blue Badge disabled drivers scheme operates near LSE and around Camden/Westminster.
LOCAL Buses 16b, 501, 505, RV1, 139, 168 and 243 swing by. Nearest tubes are Temple, Holborn and Charing X.
COLLEGE Free late-night minibus to halls after hours.
BICYCLES *Bikes are predictably popular in this bit of town, but the college could do with more cycle racks on campus*. There are eight racks in the basement area of St Philips north and south buildings.

CAREER PROSPECTS
○ **CAREERS SERVICE** ○ **NO. OF STAFF** 6 FULL/10 INTERNS
○ **UNEMPLOYED AFTER 6MTHS** 5%
Lots of LSE's graduates go on to further training or another degree – *more through naked ambition than addiction to the lie-in lifestyle*. The careers service helps fuel the passion with fairs and forums.

FAMOUS ALUMNI
A Who's Who of the world's movers and shakers: Pat Barker (author); Cherie Booth QC (wife of you-know-who); Eugenia Charles (former PM,

Dominica); Carlos the Jackal (terrorist); Ekow Eshun (journo); Clare Francis (yachtswoman, author); Mick Jagger ('Stone); Judge Jules (DJ); John F Kennedy (US president); Jomo Kenyatta, Mwai Kibaki (first and current president of Kenya); Robert Kilroy-Silk (*permatanned, Arab-baiting* ex-chat-show host); Yu Kuo-Hwa (former PM, Taiwan); Bernard Levin (journalist); Beatriz Merino (Peru's first female PM); Shri KR Narayanan (former Indian president); Mat Osman (Suede); Romano Prodi (Italian PM); Maurice Saatchi (advertising guru); Constantine Simitis (former PM, Greece); George Soros (financier).

FURTHER INFO

⊙ **PROSPECTUSES** UNDERGRAD; POSTGRAD; ALTERNATIVE
⊙ **OPEN DAYS**
See www.lse.ac.uk/collections/undergraduatead-missions or /collections/studentRecruitment for admissions info. The alternative prospectus is at www.lsesu.com.

ACADEMIC ⊙⊙⊙⊙⊙⊙⊙⊙⊙⊙⊙⊙

⊙ **RUSSELL GROUP** ⊙ **1994** GROUP
Deserved reputation for excellence in its fields and a rampant lion in terms of research. Prestigious academic staff and guest speakers, along with great resources. Regular flirtations with the upper echelons of the league tables. Most degrees are comprised for four courses per year, with teaching a mix of lectures, seminars and personal study. There are exams at the end of every year (three-hour unseen papers) but marks are a mix of exam results, coursework and other assignments.

ENTRY POINTS: 300-360	AVE POINTS: 340
APPLICATIONS PER PLACE: 13	CLEARING: 0%
NO. OF TERMS: 3	LENGTH OF TERMS: 10wks
STAFF TO STUDENT RATIO: 1:8	STUDY ADDICTS: 31%
TEACHING: ***	RESEARCH: *****
YEAR ABROAD: 1%	SANDWICH STUDENTS: 0
1STS: 17%	2.2s: 55%
2.1s: 24%	3RDS: 4%

ADMISSIONS

⊙ **APPLY VIA UCAS**
LSE insists on two *proper A Levels (definitely not Business Studies) and the combinations considered are tightly controlled, so thorough research before applying is advisable. There's more chance of fitting a camel in a sexing box than getting in through clearing.*

SUBJECTS

ARTS & DESIGN 12%   **BUSINESS/MANAGEMENT** 19%
SOCIAL SCIENCES 69%
BEST Anthropology; History; Geography; Law; Sociology; Social Policy.
UNUSUAL Anthropology & Law; Economic History; Economic History with Population Studies; International Relations.

LIBRARIES

⊙ **3,684,000** BOOKS ⊙ **1,600** BOOKS
⊙ **SPEND PER STUDENT** ££££
LSE's *huge* main library (the largest social sciences library in the world) goes under the *appropriately grand title* of the British Library of Political & Economic Science and has access to Government publications, bound journals and *all the other top-flight reading matter you'd expect.* Likewise, facilities (assistance, book buddies, collections, security, study rooms, resources for disabled students) are all *excellent*. There are a few hundred laptop points and 480 networked PCs. There are also several small departmental libraries. The Shaw library on the sixth floor of the Old Building has general music & literature collections. The main one has 24-hr access during exam term – *take a sleeping bag.*

COMPUTERS

⊙ **1,000** WORKSTATIONS ⊙ **24-HR** ACCESS
All rooms in halls have internet access and there are network access points across the campus. Many departments have computer rooms designated for postgrads.

OTHER LEARNING FACILITIES

The School's Language Centre for learning other languages, including English for international students.

ENTERTAINMENT ⊙⊙⊙⊙⊙⊙⊙⊙⊙

THE CITY see University of London
⊙ **PRICE OF A PINT OF BEER** £2
⊙ **GLASS OF WINE** £2 ⊙ **CAN OF RED BULL** £2
Aldwych is *convenient* for the bright lights *(and breathtaking prices)* of Leicester Square and Covent Garden. Pubs, theatres, *ritzy* cinemas and *posh* restaurants ago-go. Pubs near the School include the *quafftastic* Bierodrome (Kingsway). The *bright, throbbing lights* of a night out in Islington are a short hop, taxi or bus-ride away. Being at the heart of commuterville means there's a *dazzling array* of eateries around – *some students can afford to eat at, others they'd need to sell their spleen to get in to.* Trusty Wetherspoons 2-4-1 pub dining is close at hand, as well as *high street faves* Benjy's (sarnies) and Pret a Manger (*upmarket* sarnies).

UNIVERSITY
⊙ **PRICE OF A PINT OF BEER** £2.20
⊙ **GLASS OF WINE** £2.30
⊙ **CAN OF RED BULL** £1.75
BARS The Three Tuns Bar (cap 700) is *pretty popular*. The Underground (120) is primarily an events venue and the Beaver's Retreat, *which looks like an old man's pub, gets quite buzzy*. The School's catering services team has acquired the George IV on Portugal Street: *traditional pubbage with a function*

room, open to the public as well but *not so thirsty on the wallet* as other venues around.

THEATRES The drama society won an award in 2004, but *they concentrate on quality over quantity*, putting on around a show a term. Members can also audition for Cambridge University's Edinburgh Fringe productions.

FILM A *mainstream* film a week and a quid for the privilege. *Compared to a tenner a go at the Empire in Leicester Square, that's a snip.*

CLUBBING/MUSIC VENUES The Underground *goes overboard* for its Friday night disco Crush (sets by Jimmy Baker, Rowan Harvey, Judge Jules) and the Quad is used for student bands and the very occasional professional act. *Clubbing's not a passion in these parts, though.* The Underground Bar's the place for a spot of live music.

COMEDY/CABARET Weekly shows at the Three Tuns from pros like Will Smith and *wet-nosed amateurs* like the Cambridge Footlights.

FOOD Brunch Bowl for *cheap* main meals, veggie options and a salad bar. The Garrick is *the best on offer* but the atmosphere and decor don't come cheap. Food's available on both floors – sarnies-to-go on the ground floor, sit down tuck-ins in the basement. Plaza cafe is next to the library – *well-placed for an attack of the study munchies.*

OTHER Global Week held once a year celebrates the School's *impressively diverse* student body.

SOCIAL ◗◗◗◗◗◗◗◗◗◗◗◗◗◗

LSE STUDENTS' UNION

○ **4** SABBATICALS ○ TURNOUT AT LAST BALLOT 26%
○ NUS MEMBER

The Union's dealings are *typically organised and effective*. It hosts Britain's only weekly SU meeting in which all students are able to vote. Being a politically-minded creature elections are a *big deal* and canvassing is a *fine art (after all, this is where future PMs and presidents train-up to be big hitters)*. The *relatively small size* of the School makes for a *good* admin-SU relationship, with the University happy to lend its ear to the student voice, though inter-Union relations are sometimes *a little more strained*.

SU FACILITIES

Three bars; four canteens; snack bar and fast food joint; pool table; meeting rooms; Natwest bank/ATM; printing/fax/photocopying services; payphones; photo booth; crèche; late-night minibus; juke box and games machines; stationery shop; post office; new and secondhand bookshops; travel agent.

CLUBS (NON-SPORTING)

Tent-loads: ABACUS; Africa Forum; AIESEC; Albanian; Alternative Careers; Alternative Entertainments; Alternative Music; American; Anime-Manga; Arabic; Armenian; Arts; Asian Affairs; Asian Careers; Attac; Australia & New Zealand; Austrian; Azerbaijan; Bacchus Friends; Bahai; Bangladeshi; Brazilian; Bridge; Bulgarian; Business; Canadian; Capitalist Worker; Carribean Vibez; Catalan; CEEDS; Chess; Chill Out; China Development Society; Chinese; Chinese Student & Scholar Association (CSSA); Christian Union; Cities; Colombian; Comparative Ideologies; Conservative; Create Commerce; Cypriot; Democrats; Destin; Development; Employment Relations; Entrepreneurs; Eurasia; European; Fight Racism Fight Imperialism; Filipino; Film; French Connection; Friends of Afghanistan; Friends of Palestine; Gaia; Game Theory; German; Globalise Resistance; Go; Grimshaw; Hayek; Health Policy; Hedge Fund; Hellenic; Hindu; Hong Kong Public Affairs; Indian; Indonesian-Bruneian; Information Systems; International; Investment; Israeli; Italian; Japan; Kazakhstan; Kenyan; Kloth Fashion; Knitting; Korean; Krishna Consciousness; Lara (Lager and Real Ale); Latin American; Lebanese Society; Liberty; Literature; Live Music; LLM; London Out; Luxembourg; Malaysia Club; Malaysia Singapore; Mauritian; Mexican; Model United Nations; Modern Dance; Music; Music Business; Naked Punch; OIKOS; Opera; Oriental; Pakistan; People First; Persian; Peruvian; Philosophy; Planning; Poetry; Poker; Polish; Private Equity; Property Investment; Question Time; Real Estate; Regional & Urban Planning; Respect; Risk and Stochastics; Romanian; Russian; Russian Business; SAAR; SHARE; SPICE; Salsa; Scandinavian; Scottish; Secular; Sikh/Punjab; Singapore; SIS Skills; Slavonic; Slovenian; Socialist; Southern African; Spanish; Sri Lankan; Student Action for Refugees (STAR); Stop the War Coalition; Students with Disabilities; Subaltern Soundz; Survival International; Swing Dance; Swiss; Taiwanese; Thai; THC; Turkish; TV; UNICEF; Undergound Dance Music; Vietnamese; Visual Arts; Women in Business. **See also Clubs tables.**

OTHER ORGANISATIONS

SU-published 'the Beaver' is the weekly read (but only 3,500 copies are produced a year, so it's not that highly-read). 'The Script' magazine comes out three times a year on paper and on the net. 'PuLSE' radio broadcasts for 120 hours a week. 'LooSE TV' (not officially part of the Union's media group) broadcasts to the Quad and is shown to prospective students, though its profile and activities *should get a much-needed shot in the arm this year*. Rag *go mad* for a week every year to raise money for charity through bar crawls and other *taxing* stunts.

> ◉ **Mick Jagger, who dropped out of LSE, was later made honorary SU president.**

L

RELIGIOUS
◉ 4 CHAPLAINS (COFE, RC, ORTHODOX, FC)
Also Buddhist & Muslim facilities.
Religion in London: University of London

PAID WORK see University of London
◉ JOB BUREAU ◉ PAID WORK TERM-TIME 50%; HOLS 70%
Work going in the SU services and some opportunities within the University. Part-time jobshop tries to set students up with employers online.

SPORTS ⭕⭕⭕⭕⭕⭕⭕⭕⭕⭕⭕⭕⭕⭕

◉ RECENT SUCCESSES FOOTBALL **◉ BUSA RANKING** 51
Most of LSE's greatest sporting moments are reserved for the Rugby Club Ball. Aldwych's *obviously* not the place for vast playing fields but a *hardy few* make the 40-min train journey to the School's 25 acres of grounds at Berrylands near New Malden way out west. Students can, of course, use ULU's facilities.

SPORTS FACILITIES
20 acres of grounds at Berrylands including playing fields; a croquet lawn, pavilion, bar and restaurant; tennis courts at Lincoln's Inn Fields. On-site there are netball and squash courts; gym (£90/yr – *value for money and good facilities mean places are limited, so be quick*); multigym; aerobics studio; badminton court; snooker table and circuit room.

SPORTING CLUBS
Aerobics; Boxing; Brazilian Jiu jitsu; Capoeira; Japanese Jiu Jitsu; Lacrosse; Muay Thai Boxing; Rock Climbing; Rollerblading; Rowing; Running Club; Shotokan Karate; Table Tennis; Ultimate Frisbee; Yoga. **See Clubs tables.**

ATTRACTIONS see University of London

ACCOMMODATION ⭕⭕⭕⭕⭕⭕⭕⭕⭕

IN COLLEGE
◉ CATERED 18% **◉ COST** £108 (40WKS)
◉ SELF CATERING 19% **◉ COST** £102 (31/40WKS)
◉ 1ST YRS 100% **◉ INSURANCE PREMIUM** £
AVAILABILITY About half of LSE's students live in University of London intercollegiate halls. First years are guaranteed accommodation, and most of them take it. Rooms in halls come with access to common and games rooms and launderettes; some have internet access. Most halls have bars and the communal areas are *kept from rotting by college cleaners.* Those who can't afford to pay £100+ for a *pleasant but poky* college room can pay a little less and share. Passfield Hall's *cheapest, with a good community atmosphere,* whereas Bankside's *pricey and impersonal.*

Commonwealth Hall is *currently in the bad books for general lack.* Roseberry *feels safest. What your money gets you could go further, but the outside world offers less, so all in all it's not too bad a deal.*
CAR PARKING *Horrendously difficult to get a permit, which costs a small fortune.*

EXTERNALLY
◉ AVE RENT £90 **◉ LIVING AT HOME** 10%
AVAILABILITY see University of London
HOUSING HELP LSE has a web-based vacancy system with online waiting lists. There's also the UoL services (see University of London). The Accommodation Office, as well as lots of friendly and sensible advice, produces an A4 book, the London Student Housing Guide, which is a *flat-hunting essential.* Islington is a *student fave but unless you've a knack with the gee-gees or Daddy owns a mansion flat prices and competition don't open many doors.*

WELFARE ⭕⭕⭕⭕⭕⭕⭕⭕⭕⭕⭕

SERVICES
◉ LGBT OFFICER & SOCIETY ◉ WOMEN'S OFFICER ◉ MATURE STUDENTS' SOCIETY ◉ INTERNATIONAL STUDENTS' OFFICER & SOCIETY ◉ POSTGRAD OFFICER & SOCIETY ◉ DISABILITIES OFFICER & SOCIETY ◉ LATE-NIGHT MINIBUS (PRIORITY FOR WOMEN) ◉ NIGHTLINE ◉ COLLEGE COUNSELLORS 3 FULL/2 PART **◉ CRIME RATING** !!!!!
Education and Welfare Officers, and an Advice and Counselling Centre for legal and welfare queries. First years get a student mentor, and have e-mail contact before term starts.
HEALTH St Philips Medical Centre, the on-campus NHS practice, has two GPs, a Gynaecologist, three Practice Nurses, an Osteopath, a Therapeutic Masseuse and a dental service (not free though). There's also 24-hour emergency medical provision for registered students.
WOMEN Free attack alarms and family planning advice. A female staff member is the Advisor to Women Students. The SU's Women's Right to Choose Fund helps out financially both with abortion and baby-raising costs.
CRECHES/NURSERY Places for nine babies and 16 older children, open almost all year-round.
DISABILITIES Adapted accommodation, hearing support systems in all theatres and some classrooms, a support network of note-takers, readers and assistants and a willingness to meet the shortfall. See www.lse.ac.uk/collections/disabilityOffice on what else is available.
CRIME The central London location doesn't help much, and opportunistic crime against students is a particular bugbear.
DRUGS *There's a particular problem in the area around LSE, but the Met Police will come down on offenders like a tonne of breezeblocks.*

L

FINANCE
- **AVE DEBT PER YEAR** £2,763
- **HOME STUDENT FEES** £3,000

FEES International undergrad fees hover around the £10k mark. Postgrads pay £11,196-£12,438 for research degrees. UK postgrads pay £6,162-£6,780.

- **ACCESS FUND** £108,611 **SUCCESSFUL APPLICATIONS/YR** 112 **AVE PAYMENT** £1,200

SUPPORT Around £4.7m in financial assistance awarded every year (undergrads and postgrads), mostly on academic merit or financial hardship. The Union offers assistance on disability and childcare. There's also support for overseas students' who are caught a bit short. Students from Africa, sub-Saharan Africa, Singapore and the Seychelles have specific awards. Advice from current students includes opening an ISA, so clearly there are some who have less need of handouts.

UNIVERSITY OF LUTON

- **UNIVERSITY OF LUTON** Park Street, Luton, Bedfordshire, LU1 3JU **TEL** (01582) 734 111 **E-MAIL** admissions@luton.ac.uk **WEBSITE** www.luton.ac.uk **UNIVERSITY OF LUTON STUDENTS' UNION** Europa House, Vicarage Street, Luton, Bedfordshire, LU1 3HZ **TEL** (01582) 743 286 **WEBSITE** www.ulsu.co.uk

GENERAL ೦೦೦೦೦೦೦೦೦೦೦೦೦

For years Luton's had a hard time living down the image of dropped aitches and having a cheap flight-friendly airport as its most interesting feature. It's an outdated perception – Luton is changing into a lively, growing place with 150 acres of pleasantish greenery and it's not far from the Chiltern Hills. An International Carnival held every May packs more than 140,000 visitors into the town. The University is now one of the kinkiest features and is going hell for leather on the expansion front. It's grown unrecognisably since 1976 when it became a college of higher education. It gained university status in '93 and is getting bigger and more facility-stuffed by the year. A merger with De Montfort University's Bedford campus is planned for the end of 2006, which should see Luton's rebirth under the handle of 'University of Bedfordshire' At time of writing, however, the name had not been finalised. Push is hoping they'll decide to call it 'Dave'.

SEX RATIO: ♂40 ♀60	FOUNDED: 1993
FULL-TIME U'GRADS: 5,956	PART-TIME: 1,896
POSTGRADS: 1,825	NON-DEGREE: 1,056
AVE COURSE: 3YRS	ETHNIC: 53%
STATE:PRIVATE SCHOOL: 99:1	FLUNK RATE: 23%
MATURE: 40%	INTERNATIONAL: 23%
DISABLED: 60	LOCAL: 30%

ATMOSPHERE

Many local students come here because it's on their doorstep, which can give the place the feeling of being an extension of college. Courses are career-focused and the work ethic is dedicated – an attitude the University likes to foster as it keeps up the graduate employability record. Lots of international students add a cosmopolitan feel and with the local element campus is a friendly, happy place – just don't expect life-changing political moments or to achieve nirvana

SITES

PARK SQUARE (Main site) The harsh architecture of Park Square is rather appropriate to the utilitarian philosophy of the courses, although it's balanced by the swish Learning Resources Centre and the new Media Arts Centre.

PUTTERIDGE BURY (500 students – Postgrad Business School) The plush, tranquil country mansion and landscaped gardens are exclusively a postgrad stomping ground four miles from Park Square. Being the prettiest part of the University, it's also hired out for conferences. See www.putteridgebury.com for other details.

LUTON
- **POPULATION** 184,300 **CITY CENTRE** 0 MILES
- **LONDON** 30 MILES **MILTON KEYNES** 21 MILES
- **BEDFORD** 25 MILES **BIRMINGHAM** 80 MILES
- **HIGH TEMP** 21 **LOW TEMP** 1 **RAINFALL** 63

Luton started life as the centre of the hat and lace industry but is now a busy business town with pretty good employment figures. It's the largest town in Bedfordshire, which doesn't say much as Bedford is the only competition. Shops, libraries, banks, markets and the rest exist in plentiful supply but despite the significant ethnic population it's still a bit small town in mentality. At least its residents were cosmopolitan enough to vote it 'Crappest UK Town' in 2004 – narrowly beating Kingston upon Hull to the coveted accolade. Worth a particular mention are the massive modern Arndale Shopping Centre right by the University and the Galaxy Centre, which offers music, TV and multimedia facilities, cinema, art gallery, restaurant and café. Nothing worth changing your trousers for though.

TRAVEL

TRAINS Luton station is five mins walk from the University with trains to London King's Cross (from £13.60 return), Bedford (£25), Milton Keynes (£11.50) and even further afield.

COACHES Green Line and National Express services (London £12, Birmingham £16.60).

L

Words in italics are Push's point of view — take it or leave it...

CAR M1, A6 (straight through town), A1 and A5. Multi-storey parking is available in the Arndale Centre and there's pay & display near Park Street.

AIR Luton Airport is the home of budget airline easyJet and offers inland and international services to Europe, Ireland and the USA.

HITCHING *Despite good connections it's easier to pick up the white lines on the road than pick up a lift in the Home Counties. It's none too safe either and few try it.*

LOCAL 'Hopper' buses scuttle round the town every 30 mins till 11pm, around 60p a trip from the outskirts to Park Square. No local trains around town, but an excellent link into London and good for day-tripping. *However, the last train's too early and all too easy to miss.*

UNIVERSITY Free shuttle bus from Park Square to Putteridge Bury and back again (9am-5pm daily).

TAXIS *Not cheap, but worth using at night when the buses go to bed.*

BICYCLES *Although Luton's flat, few bike it. They're useful for those who live off-site, though, and cycle routes have been cropping up in the town recently.*

CAREER PROSPECTS

○ **CAREERS SERVICE** ○ **NO. OF STAFF** 8 FULL
○ **UNEMPLOYED AFTER 6MTHS** 12%

The Student Centre Careers Service has a careers library with interview training, job fairs, bulletin boards, newsletters and website. Several big businesses in the area offer Graduate Apprenticeship Schemes to Luton students.

FAMOUS ALUMNI

Haji Abi (Mayor of Luton); Ian Drury (Blockhead); Gemma Hunt (CBBC presenter); Julie Pankhurst (founder of Friends Reunited).

FURTHER INFO

○ **PROSPECTUSES** UNDERGRAD; POSTGRAD
○ **OPEN DAYS** ○ **VIDEO**

Prospectuses come with *funky* free lifestyle mag, the Experience *(of the airline seat-pocket type)*. Open days are formally held throughout the year, *but impromptu tours by 'student ambassadors' can be thrown together at a moment's notice.*

ACADEMIC ○○○○○○○○○○○○○○

Since promotion from HE college to university Luton has gained a reputation as a highly-rated new institution. This has been accompanied by a large influx of degree students and an even larger increase in expenditure on buildings and facilities. The focus is decidedly on employment-related skills. *Nice things have been said about its teaching by a lot of people,* including the government, which made it a Centre for Excellence in Teaching and Learning in 2005, *but there's some disgruntlement among students about large seminar groups.*

ENTRY POINTS: 160–200	AVE POINTS: 191
APPLICATIONS PER PLACE: 7	CLEARING: 16%
NO. OF TERMS: 2	LENGTH OF TERMS: 15WKS
STAFF TO STUDENT RATIO: 1:24	STUDY ADDICTS: 18%
TEACHING: *	RESEARCH: *
YEAR ABROAD: <1%	SANDWICH STUDENTS: 5%
1STS: 7%	2.2S: 36%
2.1S: 40%	3RDS: 6%

ADMISSIONS

○ **APPLY VIA UCAS**

Luton takes work and life experience as seriously as academic records, so *it's good news for mature students. A Levels aren't the be all and end all* – Advanced GNVQs, Access courses, foundation degrees and equivalent foreign qualifications all go into the admissions cooking pot. There are international links and regular recruitment from 140 countries worldwide, ranging from China to Estonia. At time of writing, Luton was due to merge with De Montfort University's Bedford site. *Push strongly advises checking with the universities and UCAS for up-to-date information on applications.*

SUBJECTS

CREATIVE ARTS, TECHNOLOGIES & SCIENCES 20%
HEALTH & SOCIAL SCIENCES 46%
LUTON BUSINESS SCHOOL 34%
BEST Business; Computing; Media; Nursing; PR; Psychology; Sport.
UNUSUAL BSc Coaching Science; BSc Computer Games Development.

LIBRARIES

○ **200,000 BOOKS** ○ **979 STUDY PLACES**
○ **SPEND PER STUDENT** ££££

Two Learning Resource Centres and four much smaller hospital libraries spread Luton's collection between them. 24-hr access is available as exams approach at the main Park Square LRC, *which has somehow wound its way on to the Borough Council's must-see tourist itinerary.*

COMPUTERS

○ **1,210 WORKSTATIONS**

If Luton's IT improvement programme continues in the same vein, there'll soon be as many workstations as books. The new Media Arts facility more than doubled the computer provision, adding a legion of high-spec Macs and PCs.

OTHER LEARNING FACILITIES

As well as the drama studio, CAD lab, rehearsal rooms and new psychology lab, the University has splooged £5.5m on a *state-of-the-art* Media Arts facility in Park Square, boasting broadcast TV studio, indoor and outdoor performance spaces, digital radio studios and editing suites – *one of the most impressive (and expensive) facilities of its kind in the country.*

Words in italics are Push's point of view — take it or leave it...

ENTERTAINMENT ◌◌◌◌◌◌◌◌◌

THE TOWN
- **PRICE OF A PINT OF BEER** £1.70
- **GLASS OF WINE** £2.30
- **CAN OF RED BULL** £1.20

CINEMAS Cineworld at the Galaxy Centre has 11 big, mainstream screens with weekday student discount. The smaller Library Theatre shows new and cult releases at NUS discount prices.

THEATRES The Hat Factory is a *lively* council-run arts and media venue in Bute Street just behind the main site, while the Library Theatre produces old favourites, kiddies' theatre and original material.

PUBS *Red Red Red is a sultry chill-out zone with pints and pints of drinks promos. The Park on Park Street may be as dingy as a stoner's kitchen but hefty discounts make it a loud and larking hangout. Pushplugs: Bellini on Chapel Street (recently benefited from an extensive funk-over); Brooks (cheese and pop).*

CLUBBING Edge offers funky, punky, metallic fun for alternative types. Liquid (Gordon Street) and Space (Chapel Street) do a fine line in mainstream dance and charty cheese washed down with cheap booze. Monday is student night (Monkey Madness).

MUSIC VENUES Liquid's *probably Luton's most popular club* and there's also Space in the town centre. Bellini and Brookes are *both smaller but open late* and offer an alternative to the full-on club scene.

EATING OUT *Not great. Brookes on Castle Street does posh all-day brekkie; a cheaper version is to be had at The Caff down the road. The Mona Lisa does Italian eatage and Galaxy does Chinese buffets. Bellini's is the place to take relatives for Italian. Pushplugs: the lunchtime student menu at the Cork & Bull and Balti Nights (curry house).*

OTHER Ten-pin bowling at the Galaxy Centre. *Acne-encrusted 13-year-olds abound. An annual Beer Festival in studenty High Town is the highlight of the calendar for many hopoholics.*

UNIVERSITY
- **PRICE OF A PINT OF BEER** £2
- **GLASS OF WINE** £1.60
- **CAN OF RED BULL** £1.50

BARS *The SU Bar's a modern and cosy daytime stop-off and a busy night-time drink-up with regular quiz nights and society events. The underground Sub Club (open till 2am club nights) is looking less dingy after a bit of a spit and polish and remains popular and bouncy.*

CLUBBING *Getting less popular, with about 275 people turning up for a night. Sporty 'Sin' night in the Sub Club draws the biggest and sweatiest crowd, but there's a wide-ranging weekly calendar. Local DJs get scratchy at Luton more than big name CD spinners and students are*

allowed to step behind the decks. *The Urban club scene's popular with local fly boys 'n gals.*

FOOD The SU toasts paninis and less posh sarnies and plenty of meat gets tossed at summertime bbqs. Local restaurant the Temple has hijacked some counter-space in the SU bar to peddle *cheap and tasty* Afro-Caribbean nibbles.

OTHER There are plans for a summer ball in 2006.

SOCIAL ◌◌◌◌◌◌◌◌◌◌◌

UNIVERSITY OF LUTON STUDENTS' UNION
- **4 SABBATICALS** ● **TURNOUT AT LAST BALLOT** 22%
- **NUS MEMBER**

ULSU is apolitical and takes more care over its societies, ents and advice centre than anything else though the purse ain't overflowing. The sabb team don't have much responsibility, with full-time staff pulling most of strings. There's an Infonet service online: gripes about library hours; books for sale; adverts for swingers parties – whatever really.

SU FACILITIES
The SU building (Europa House, next to Park Square) has: nightclub; bar; coffee bar; pool table; meeting room; club and society area; non-alcoholic area; photocopier; fax and printing service; advice centre; gaming and vending machines; secondhand bookshop; launderette.

CLUBS (NON-SPORTING)
Aylesbury Student Nursing; Believers Love Word; Chocolate Appreciation; Creative Writing; Gaming; Greek & Cypriot; Indian Students; Nigerian; Japanese; Jinx; Law; Nigerian Students; Pakistani; Quran & Sunnah; Sikh; Tolkien. **See also Clubs tables.**

OTHER ORGANISATIONS
SU publications have an *indecent exposure* theme: 'Flasher' is the free paper; 'Streaker' is a free monthly magazine. The University publishes a more official and less risqué newspaper, 'Life'. 'Luton FM' broadcasts for one month each May. Despite the existence of an elected Rag Officer *Luton's charity efforts would make Scrooge blush with shame, although there are seasonal, sponsored events.* The University runs a Student Community Exchange programme which send students off *to be helpful* in the surrounding area.

RELIGIOUS
- **1 CHAPLAIN (COFE)**

The chaplaincy *does its bit for international students* and organises multi-faith events. Prayer rooms for Muslims, meditation-space available upon request. The town has places of worship for most faiths including mosques, synagogue, several Sikh and Buddhist temples and churches for Jehovah's Witnesses, Catholics, Methodists, Anglicans, Baptists and United Reformists.

PAID WORK
◉ JOB BUREAU ◉ PAID WORK TERM-TIME 90%; HOLS 95%
Job shop posts vacancies, gives CV advice and
finds voluntary work for *selfless do-gooders*.
Several companies in Luton (the Airport, the
council, various factories) employ students.

SPORTS ◕◕◕◕◕◕◕◕◕◕◕◕◕

◉ RECENT SUCCESSES FOOTBALL, WOMEN'S BASKETBALL,
WOMEN'S HOCKEY, CRICKET, RUGBY UNION
  ◉ BUSA RANKING 112
*It matters not who wins or loses but whether
there's a bar. The emphasis is on taking part and
pecs are flexed by a good few and admired from
the sidelines by a few more. The University's
own facilities are, in a word, piffling, but deals
have been done with neighbouring sports centres
and Luton is now slowly climbing the student
sports league.*

SPORTS FACILITIES
The Vauxhall Recreation Centre gives students
access to football and hockey pitches, tennis
courts, sports hall, gym, multigym and sauna (£60
a year or on a per session basis). Sports Therapy
students get their hands on Luton's wounded
warriors at the sports massage clinic. The town
has a golf course nearby, plus a swimming pool
and leisure centre. *There are also the hills nearby
for those who enjoy being vertically challenged.*

SPORTING CLUBS
Darts; Martial Arts. **See also Clubs tables.**

ATTRACTIONS
*Luton's biggest sporting non-attraction are 'the
Hatters' (Luton FC).*

ACCOMMODATION ◕◕◕◕◕◕◕◕◕

IN UNIVERSITY
◉ SELF-CATERING 18% **◉ COST** £66 (41WKS)
  ◉ 1ST YRS LIVING IN 100%
  ◉ INSURANCE PREMIUM ££
AVAILABILITY 20 halls, all built in the last 15 years.
All new undergrads and postgrads are

guaranteed a room, priced according to
location/distance. *Cheaper halls are a little basic
but while most tend to be poky, the single study
bedrooms are kitted out with all the necessities
(ie. beds and desks).* The biggest, most central
hall is on Bute Street *and most first years are
drawn to its promise of a pulsing social life.*
Single-sex flats are available. There are wardens
on site. Some halls have gates, which are shut at
11pm. Car owners can buy a key for £30, but
other latecomers are fined £50. *Eeek.*
CAR PARKING Fairly easy, permits cost £120 a year.

EXTERNALLY
◉ AVE RENT £55
AVAILABILITY *There's no real shortage of
appropriate housing, although the beginning of
the year panic is becoming a regular 'mare. The
best areas are High Town, Farley Hill, Park Town,
New Town and the Town Centre, all within
walking distance of the University. Bury Park is
popular with local Asian students, but some
regard it as unsafe. With so many local students,
it's not uncommon for gangs from the same school
to get a house together.*
HOUSING HELP Eight full-time advisors at the
University Accommodation Office provide
vacancy lists and give advice, but are reluctant to
blacklist landlords – the SU does this instead.
*Students reckon they can feel a bit alone in the
house hunt, however, and end up trawling
estate agents.*

WELFARE ◕◕◕◕◕◕◕◕◕◕◕◕

SERVICES
**◉ LGBT SOCIETY ◉ ETHNIC MINORITIES SOCIETY
  ◉ WOMEN'S SOCIETY ◉ MATURE STUDENTS' OFFICER
& SOCIETY ◉ POSTGRAD SOCIETY ◉ INTERNATIONAL
STUDENTS SOCIETY ◉ UNIVERSITY COUNSELLORS** 2
  ◉ SU COUNSELLORS 3 **◉ CRIME RATING** !!!!
The SU advice centre doles out free condoms,
pregnancy tests and attack alarms.
HEALTH No provision on campus, but there's a NHS
practice five mins walk away.
DISABILITIES The new buildings have been
considerately built and all teaching buildings are
wheelchair-friendly. There are adapted study

> ◉ **Seven brothers and sisters from the same
> family have graduated from Southampton
> University – between 1983 and 2002 at least one of
> the siblings was studying for a degree there.**

L

---

bedrooms and induction loops in most lecture theatres. The LRC has a range of software for the use of all disabled students that includes mind-mapping and text-reading programs. Assessment-based provisions for unseen disabilities. Dyslexia screening is available, as is help with libraries and note-taking.

CRIME/DRUGS *Burglaries are not unknown* during the moving-in period in halls. There's a Campus Watch safety scheme to combat this. The SU runs drugs and safe drinking campaigns.

FINANCE
- **AVE DEBT PER YEAR** £1,824
- **HOME STUDENT FEES** £3,000

FEES Part-timers cough up £375 per module. Overseas undergrads pay £7,145. UK postgrads pay £3,850 and overseas postgrads £7,575.
- **ACCESS FUND** £460,646 • **SUCCESSFUL APPLICATIONS**/YR 652 • **AVE PAYMENT** £672

SUPPORT There's a non-assessed bursary scheme giving a minimum of £300 to each student. Some funding from local businesses (£500 handouts). Specific funds are available for members of specific groups: locals, ethnic minorities, matures etc.

▶ LUTON COLLEGE OF HIGHER EDUCATION
see *University of Luton*

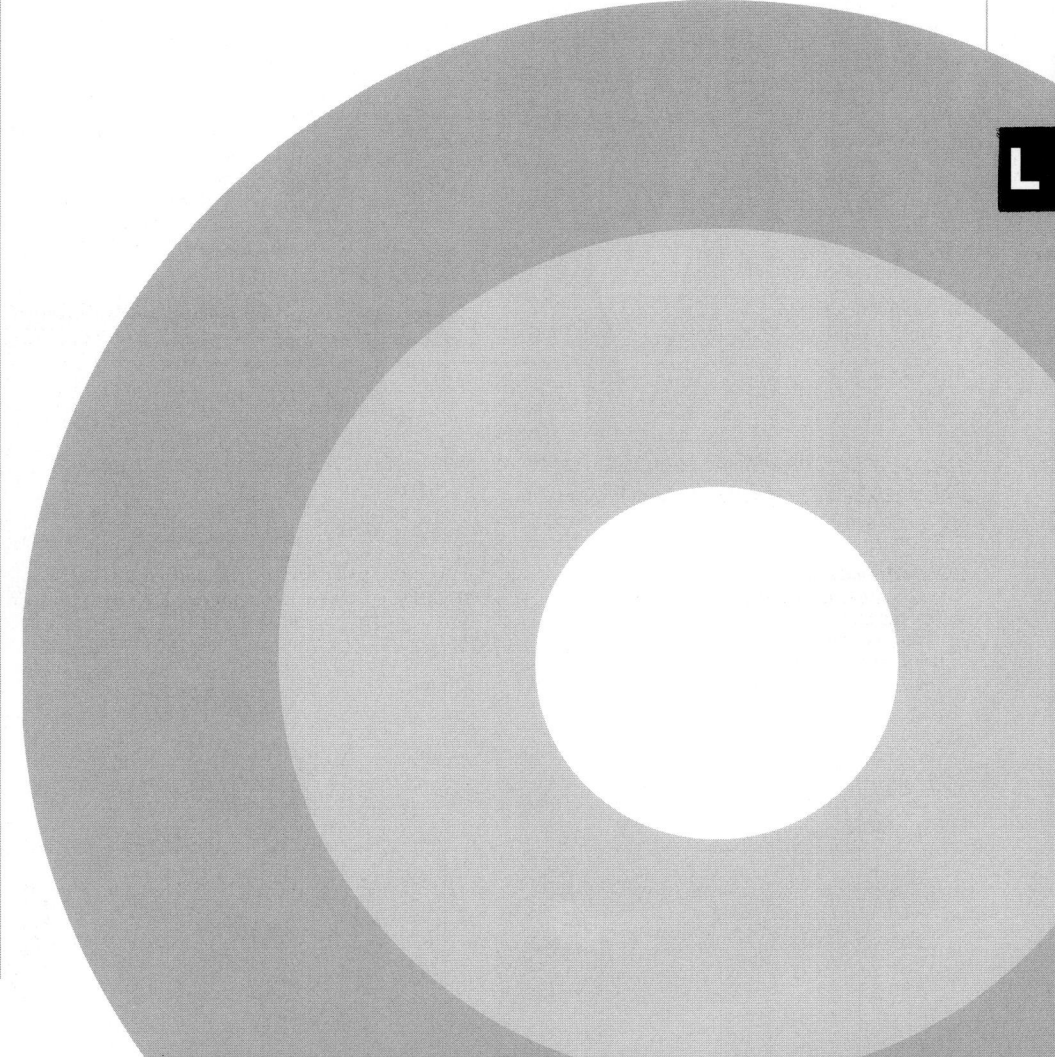

MAGEE
see *University of Ulster*

UNIVERSITY OF MANCHESTER

UNIVERSITY OF MANCHESTER INSITUTE OF SCIENCE & TECHNOLOGY
see *University of Manchester*

MANCHESTER METROPOLITAN UNIVERSITY

MANCHESTER POLYTECHNIC
see *Manchester Metropolitan University*

MIDDLESEX UNIVERSITY

MIDDLESEX POLYTECHNIC
see *Middlesex University*

MOORES, LIVERPOOL JOHN
see *Liverpool John Moores University*

MORAY HOUSE SCHOOL OF EDUCATION
see *University of Edinburgh*

M

UNIVERSITY OF MANCHESTER

⊙ **THE UNIVERSITY OF MANCHESTER** Oxford road, Manchester, M13 9PL **TEL** (0161) 275 2077
E-MAIL ug-admissions@manchester.ac.uk **WEBSITE** www.manchester.ac.uk
⊙ **UNIVERSITY OF MANCHESTER STUDENTS' UNION** Steve Biko Building, Oxford Road, Manchester, M13 9PR **TEL** (0161) 275 2930
WEBSITE www.umsu.manchester.ac.uk

GENERAL ((((((((((((((

Welcome to the 25-hr party town, the battered but mad-for-it sprawl of Britain's second-largest city and the capital of the north-west. The tail-end of the Pennines divides Manchester's Lancashire setting from the posse of Yorkshire counties, and Liverpool's only 30 mins drive away. It's a big place with over a quarter of a million students *loitering* in the Greater Manchester area, including surrounding Salford and Oldham. Most of them – the students, not the towns – belong to the University. The neighbouring UMIST (University of Manchester Institute of Science & Technology) was formally swallowed up in 2004, cementing the University's status as one of the biggest in the country and bolstering both the number of students and the number and quality of learning facilities available. The campus is spread across the city centre. Factor in Manchester Metropolitan University and the other institutions and teaching hospitals and you've got the largest educational complex in Western Europe. *The buildings themselves are a hotchpotch of drab 60s concrete, art nouveau redbrick, Victorian grandeur and stark Thatcherite mingled among more modern offerings. A massive £600m renovation will constitute the biggest, most-botoxed face-lift in Higher Education ever.*

SEX RATIO: ♂46 ♀54	**FOUNDED:** 1824
FULL-TIME U'GRADS: 21,690	**PART-TIME:** 725
POSTGRADS: 10,700	**NON-DEGREE:** 5,990
AVE COURSE: 3-4YRS	**ETHNIC:** 17%
STATE:PRIVATE SCHOOL: 80:20	**FLUNK RATE:** 7%
MATURE: 11%	**INTERNATIONAL:** 13%
DISABLED: 5%	**LOCAL:** 33%

ATMOSPHERE
Although it's always been a big University and has just got even bigger, Manchester's developed a surprisingly close-knit student community. The two halves of the campus are compact and close-by so no one gets isolated. Having said that, the size and constant bustle of the place – particularly the Union building – can put all but the most confident or loudmouthed students into the shade. They're a diverse bunch, with students from about 180 countries. Mancunian businesses are heavily dependent on the student population, meaning lots of cheap bars and student discounts.

MANCHESTER
⊙ **POPULATION** 392,900 ⊙ **CITY CENTRE** 1 MILE ⊙ **LONDON** 167 MILES ⊙ **LIVERPOOL** 28 MILES ⊙ **BIRMINGHAM** 72 MILES ⊙ **HIGH TEMP** 20 ⊙ **LOW TEMP** 1 ⊙ **RAINFALL** 68

Although it's been around since Caesar invented salad, Manchester (as a superpower rather than a settlement) was really built out of cotton during the Industrial Revolution – out of the money from cotton, to be more precise. Industry flooded it and the canals drained it, making the city one of the all-time boomtowns. But it didn't last and Manchester found depression pretty depressing, scarring the city with slums. Some of these, such as Moss Side and Burnage, remain pretty bleak, but many areas have been redeveloped and its chequered history has left Manchester rich in culture. Everything a student could want is here (except perhaps quiet, rural countryside), from shops to galleries to pubs to clubs and back again. It may have lost its 90s title of youth culture capital of the universe, but Manchester can still go a few rounds in the ring with London or any other urban giant. Music still pulses through its veins as the vodka trickles down its throat. Life ain't cheap here, though, and many will need either a job or a trust fund just to get by. Manchester has little of the crowded loneliness or impersonality of London and its sons and daughters are by and large a proud and friendly people – traits which rub off on its students.

TRAVEL
TRAINS Not one but two mainline stations, Manchester Piccadilly for London (from £37.70 return) and the south, and Manchester Victoria for just about everywhere else. Routes go all over, including Birmingham (£18.40), Edinburgh (£35) and more.
COACHES All sorts of coach services to, among most other places, London (£26.50), Birmingham (£12.40), Edinburgh (£24) and beyond.
CAR From the north, M6 (then M61 or M62), A6 or M66; from the east, M62, A58, A62; from the south, M6, A6, A523, A34; and from Wales, the M56. *Parking may well be a problem in central Manchester, but, for the lazy and environmentally feckless, a car doesn't go amiss.*
AIR Manchester Airport's one of the UK's big ones – flights all over the world as well as inland.
HITCHING *Not possible from central Manchester, but quite good on arterial routes out of the city.*
LOCAL Manchester has a major bus network, running all over town, especially up and down Oxford Road. Trains are a *quicker alternative, especially for the outskirts.* The Metrolink tram service trundles around helpfully.
TAXIS *Manchester's centre, being relatively small, means taxi trips are a viable resort.* The black cabs that screech to a halt as you hail them are a lot more expensive than the private traders who are only supposed to pick up phone callers and drop-ins.

Words in italics are Push's point of view – take it or leave it...

BICYCLES *Manchester's quite bike-friendly (flat with a fair few cycle lanes), but theft is rife.*

CAREER PROSPECTS
○ CAREERS SERVICE ○ NO. OF STAFF 12 FULL
○ UNEMPLOYED AFTER 6 MTHS 11%
Manchester has the second biggest careers service in the country. It has over 50 staff in all, *and is accordingly rather brilliant.* Services on offer include the *usual* caboodle of vacancy lists, bulletins, library and *tons of* job fairs, plus interview training (available on video), CV-polishing, psychometric testing, mentoring schemes with professionals and Careers Skills Training courses. They help students find both work placements and life-long careers, arranging around 120 companies-worth of employer presentations. See the dedicated website: www.graduatecareersonline.com.

FAMOUS ALUMNI
Anthony Burgess (writer); Louis de Bernières (author of Captain Corelli's Mandolin); Ben Elton, Rik Mayall, Ade Edmondson, (comedians); Anna Ford (BBC newsreader); Alex Garland (writer, The Beach); Peter Maxwell Davies (composer); Sir Maurice Oldfield (MI6); Christabel Pankhurst (suffragette); Ernest Rutherford (Nobel Prize winner & atom-splitter); Mark Radcliffe, Justin Robertson (DJs); Meera Syal (comedian & actress). **FROM UMIST** Margaret Beckett MP, David Clark MP (Lab cabinet ministers); Sir John Cockcroft (scientist); John Dalton (chemist – *not the condoms and hairspray variety*); Keith Edelman (Chief Executive, Storehouse); Ian Gibson (Chief Executive, Nissan); Sophie Grigson (TV cook); Sir Terry Leahy (Chief Executive, Tesco); Geoff Mulcahy (Chief Executive, Kingfisher Group); Keith Oates (Chief Executive, M&S); Sir Arthur Whitten-Brown (transatlantic pilot).

SPECIAL FEATURES
Manchester degrees are also awarded at the Institute of Advanced Nursing Education in London, Stockport College of Further & Higher Education and University College, Warrington. The newly refurbished and extended Manchester Museum is part of the University.

FURTHER INFO
○ PROSPECTUSES UNDERGRAD; POSTGRAD; SOME DEPTS; ALTERNATIVE; INTERNATIONAL
○ OPEN DAYS
Undergrad and postgrad prospectuses can be ordered via the main website; the alternative prospectus's distributed by the SU. The University runs four open days a year – one of which is exclusively devoted to Medicine. For those who can't make the three annual open days, there are guided campus tours every Wednesday.

ACADEMIC ○○○○○○○○○○○○○

○ RUSSELL GROUP
Manchester's diamond 'ard when it comes to research and academia – both the University and UMIST were fairly solid as separate bodies, so it's no surprise they're good together. Several scholarly folk have changed the world from within its walls: Rutherford did a lot of his work on splitting the atom here and the world's first computer was built here in 1948 – *okay, it was about as sophisticated as an abacus by today's standards but you've got to start somewhere. The University's four faculties are still emitting bright sparks today* and its biomedical research is world-renowned. They're currently leading the way in MRSA research after Sir Jimmy *'now then, now then'* Saville donated 40 grand to pay for it. There's *a huge* variety of joint honours programmes available and *particular undergraduate strengths include: English, Drama, Engineering, Politics, Law and Medicine.*

ENTRY POINTS: 200–340	**AVE POINTS:** 404
APPLICATIONS PER PLACE: 9	**CLEARING:** 8%
NO. OF TERMS: 3	**LENGTH OF TERMS:** 10 WKS
STAFF TO STUDENT RATIO: N/A	**STUDY ADDICTS:** 20
TEACHING: ★★★★	**RESEARCH:** ★★★★★
1STS: 16%	**2.2s:** 22%
2.1s: 49%	**OTHERS:** 7%

ADMISSIONS
○ APPLY VIA UCAS
Manchester considers a wide variety of qualifications when sorting the wheat from the chaff so even though it's heavily subscribed *everyone* gets a look-in.

SUBJECTS
ENGINEERING & PHYSICAL SCIENCES 24%
HUMANITIES 44%   **LIFE SCIENCES** 7%
MEDICAL & HUMAN SCIENCES 25%
BEST Anatomy & Physiology; Anthropology; Archaeology; Business & Management; Chemistry; Civil Engineering; Classics & Ancient History; Computer Science; Dentistry; Drama; Economics; Education; Electrical & Electronic Engineering; Geography; Geology; German; History of Art, Architecture & Design; Iberian Studies; Mannagement & Leisure; Materials Technology; Mathematics, Statistics & Operational Research; Mechanical Engineering; Mechanical, Aeronautical & Manufacturing Engineering; Medicine; Middle Eastern & African Studies; Molecular Biosciences; Music; Nursing; Organismal Biosciences; Other subjects allied to Medicine; Pharmacology & Pharmacy; Philosophy; Physics & Astronomy; Politics; Psychology; Social Policy & Administration; Sociology; Theology & Religious Studies; Town & Country Planning & Landscape.

M

LIBRARIES

○ **4,000,000** BOOKS ○ **3,998** STUDY PLACES
○ **SPEND PER STUDENT:** ££££

The *dullish* brick affair that is John Rylands University Library is much more interesting on the inside. It's second to Oxbridge on size, *but that's still pretty massive.* The range of electronic resources available rivals any other institution and *the sheer number of books can be quite daunting* (and that doesn't include the half million e-books they also stock). It closes at 11.30pm during the week and 9.30pm at weekends.. In addition, there are ten smaller faculty libraries, including the original John Rylands Library at Deansgate which houses the University's special collections and – *sod the books – is probably the most gorgeous example of neo-Gothic architecture the city has to offer.*

COMPUTERS

○ **7,000** WORKSTATIONS ○ **24-HR** ACCESS

The merger with UMIST increased the number and quality of most facilities, but computing benefited in particular. There are four main computer clusters (the main library, Owen's Park, the Arts building and the Manchester Computing Centre) with a range of Pentium PCs, printing facilities and scanners. Other workstations are spread around the faculties. Only in the unlikely event that more than half the students want to use a public computer at the same time would facilities fall short.

OTHER LEARNING FACILITIES

The Language Centre has an extensive library and range of audio-visual material *(loads of arty films)* and allows anyone to learn a foreign tongue. Manchester's science labs are *impressive stuff* and include the famous Jodrell Bank Observatory astronomy research centre. There's also a multi-million pound Interdisciplinary Biocentre. The new music and drama building's *pretty special too,* housing a studio theatre, concert hall, rehearsal rooms, a library and audio-visual facilities.

ENTERTAINMENT ○○○○○○○○○○

THE CITY

○ **PRICE OF A PINT OF BEER** £1.70
○ **GLASS OF WINE** £2.30
○ **CAN OF RED BULL** £2.20

Manchester's a *cultural jamboree,* bringing together the *brightest and the best* in theatre, food, nightlife and, most *recently, music to this* corner of the country. *The Steve Coogan film 24 Hour Party People is essential nostalgic viewing both for a lesson in musical history and for tips for a night on the tiles. Apart from the bit with the hooker.*

CINEMAS A multiplicity of multiplexes and sundry cinemas, everything from the eight-screen Salford Quays multiplex and the cool Cornerhouse (three screens) which shows many an arty flick. With a gallery and café thrown in, *it's a poser's paradise.*

THEATRES *A very thespy city,* with more theatres per head than anywhere else in Europe. The old Cotton Exchange is now the nationally renowned Royal Exchange Theatre – *some of the country's best shows for under a fiver on student standbys.* The Palace and Opera House *do good* pantos while the Green Room is more experimental.

PUBS *Manchester has historic pubs in the truest tradition of the workingman's dive but there's everything from real ales to obscure cocktails to turpentine in a paper bag. If you must be a poseur, pose in Manto and Dry 201 but, for those living somewhere in reality, Pushplugs go to the central Rocket Bar, Revolution on Oxford Road, Jabez Clegg, Baa Baa on Deansgate, the Queen Of Hearts (Fallowfield), Retro Bar and Joshua Brooks.*

CLUBBING *The music is alive but the clubs come and go – The Hacienda, alas, continues only in spirit. Pushplugs: Vodka Island at Tiger Tiger (Mon) Temptation at Home (Weds); the Rock 'n' Roll Bar (indie); Hallelujah at the Paradise Factory; indescribably sticky the Bop at Jabez Clegg; Thursday night is student night at the hysterically tacky Royale. Brutus Gold's Love Train at Ritz (Weds) is a national treasure of tacky 70s retro.* Check for the cheaper NUS-only nights and watch out for flyers for the alighting points of fly-by-night clubs.

MUSIC VENUES The Manchester Evening News Arena lures the hugest names, *for those into binocular-rock. The Apollo, by most towns' standards, would be a best bet; however, all over town there are live venues of every size. Among the many others: The Academy* (run by Manchester University SU); *Boardwalk (indie); Jilly's (rock); Band on the Wall (rootsy); Chorlton Irish Club (folk); P J Bells (jazz); The Bridgewater Hall and the Royal Northern College of Music (classical).* Many of these clubs also stage live bands.

OTHER *A breeding ground for stand-up talent. Live comedy is usually high-octane fun.* Bernard Manning is a local boy – *the world awaits a formal apology. Millionaire students, or at least lucky or stupid ones, will, no doubt, not want to miss Manchester's many casinos.* The more cultured will find many a fond hour to spend in some of the city's *splendid* galleries (The City Gallery, The Cornerhouse and The Whitworth). The Lowry Centre has a theatre and gallery with some of L S Lowry's most famous paintings. As for shopping, head for the Trafford Centre (the mega-mall of the north-west).

EATING OUT Second only to London for number of entries in the Good Food Guide. Chinatown (the oldest in Europe) is stacked with noodleries and Rusholme has half-a-mile of end-to-end Indian restaurants. There's the usual artery-assault of kebab and burger dens but *Pushplugs go to: Generation X; Amigo's (Oxford Road, Mexican); Barca (tapas); Sangam, Shezan (Indian); Green Room (hip veggie with slack service); Dalton Café (greasy spoon and then some).*

Words in italics are Push's point of view — take it or leave it...

THE UNIVERSITY
- **PRICE OF A PINT OF BEER** £1.50
- **GLASS OF WINE** £2.30
- **CAN OF RED BULL** £1.70

The Union's Academy is one of Manchester's main entertainment venues – no mean feat round here.
BARS Since the merger with UMIST there are a number of diverse SU bars spread across town and campus. *Whether you're into sipping Schnapps in silence or swallowing Sambucca by the bucketful, one of them will cater for your needs.*
THEATRES *The University's a honeypot for luvvies and dahlings*, staging close to 30 shows a year as well as some Fringe Festival triumphs. The Contact Theatre has its own resident professional company but also provides a versatile space for student shows. The John Thaw drama studio provides back-up; several black box spaces in the Union building get an airing too. There's an annual month-long student drama festival and competition.
FILM The *huge* film society shows four free films a week to its members, from megabuck thrill-rides to *moodily lit, subtitled ponce-a-thons.*
MUSIC VENUES In addition to the Academy rooms 1, 2 and 3 – which have hosted The Darkness, the *fabulously sullen* Kelly Osbourne, the Arctic Monkeys, Bloc Party, Franz Ferdinand, Space, Keane and Amy Winehouse among many, many others – live bands also play the Hop & Grape and some of the other bars. Academy 1 is due a *wash 'n' brush-up* which will include a massive bar, a viewing gallery properly adapted for disabled access and *bigger, better* dressing rooms so *the Indie bands have more room to iron their ironic, tight-fitting kecks.*
CLUBBING Two or three nights a week, chart and nostalgia efforts such as Tuesdays' Club Tropicana (*80s not orange juice*) and Horny, with occasional guest nights (eg. Talvin Singh, Coldcut, Paul Oakenfold and the *near-legendary* Gatecrasher) for *more serious clubbers.*
FOOD The University Food Court and the SU coffee bar provide an *unimaginative* selection of burgers, sandwiches and chips *but portions are substantial and no one complains about poor value for money.* The refectory's salad bar *does its best to fight the fat.* The Café Express in the Union does light lunches. The bars also do grub. Food's available 24 hrs a day.
OTHER Highlights include the Fresher's Ball and the Graduation Ball but there are departmental shindigs and hall events all year round.

SOCIAL ◖◗◖◗◖◗◖◗◖◗◖◗◖◗◖◗◖◗◖◗◖◗◖◗

UNIVERSITY OF MANCHESTER STUDENTS' UNION
- **6 SABBATICALS** **TURNOUT AT LAST BALLOT** 7%
- **NUS MEMBER**

UMU is as political and inflammatory as a John Prescott sculpture made of turds – and they're damn proud of it, being eager to rouse a rabble or two for all sorts of ethical, equal opportunity and higher education issues. The Fair Trade soc even persuaded the University to adopt the Fair Trade mantle. Right on, sister. Although some students might be deterred by their zealous left-wing energy, most bask in glee at the awesome ents and flabbergasting facilities that the Union provides.

SU FACILITIES
In the *impressively big* Union Building there are: general shop; secondhand bookshop; opticians; travel agency; advice centre; Endsleigh Insurance office; hairdresser; ticket agency; customised nightclubs; photocopiers; coffee and snack bar; two burger bars; four bars and a pub (with satellite TV); Barclays and Halifax ATMs; minibus hire; taxi freephone; video, vending and games machines; TV room; meeting and function rooms; societies resource centre; showers; sauna and solarium; photo booth.

CLUBS (NON-SPORTING)
More than 120, including loads of subject-related socs. Highlights: Arab League; Bangladeshi; Bob Dylan; Brechtian; Buddhist; Chess; Chinese; Choir & Orchestra; Circus Skills; Classics; Cocktail; Cuba Solidarity; Drinking; Egyptian; Extreme (role-play); Fair Trade; First (international student integration); Friends of Palestine; Gilbert & Sullivan; Cypriot; Heavy & Alternative Rock Music; Hindu; Hispanic; History; Indian; Japanimation; Jazz Funk Soul Coalition; Jazz Orchestra; Jeff Forshaw Appreciation; Korean; Laugh Out Loud; Muslim Social Scientists; MUSTV; Malaysian; Manseds Space; Marrow; Mauritian; Mediconcern (Islam & medicine); Megalomaniacs; Middle Eastern; Nigerian; Omani; Pakistani; Panto; Pharmaceutical; Reachout; Respect; Russian-speaking; Samba; Scout & Guide; Seventh Day Adventist; Sikh; Singapore; Spotlights; Stop AIDS; Stop the War Coalition; Syrian; Recordings; Rock; Unisex; Warped (sci-fi); Wilderness Medicine; Wine; Young Jain Students. **See also Clubs tables.**

OTHER ORGANISATIONS
'Student Direct' comes direct once a week, although there's a bundle of other papers and newsletters coming and going. 'Pout', for example, is a monthly women's mag. 'Fuse FM' fills two six-week slots a year and airs all over the city – it's bagged 'Best Student Radio Station' at the National Student Awards. 'MUSTV' gives

Words in italics are Push's point of view — take it or leave it...

wannabe Richards & Judys a place to parade their presenting skills. Manchester charity Rag banked a *whopping* £230,000 recently and a couple of community action groups do nice things with young kiddies and old biddies.

RELIGIOUS
3 CHAPLAINS

There's a multi-faith chaplaincy and Muslim prayer room on campus. *The big Jewish Society is as much social as spiritual and is a strong political force.* The city caters for most creeds' needs: local cathedrals, churches, temples, mosques, synagogues and almost all the usual places of worship.

PAID WORK
JOB BUREAU

The University runs a fully-staffed job shop in the foyer of the Union building, the Careers service posts part-time and vacation vacancies. *Because Manchester's such a big centre for entertainment there are lots of part-time jobs in bars, clubs, shops and restaurants – but, of course, there are lots of people chasing them. Still, the situation's better than in some other parts of the north-west.*

SPORTS ◑◑◑◑◑◑◑◑◑◑◑◑◑

RECENT SUCCESSES RUGBY, FOOTBALL, HOCKEY
BUSA RANKING 14

Both *extensive and plush* facilities and the sheer size of the student body *mean heavy helpings of sporting stardom – one member of the University Squash team represented Kenya at the 2006 Commonwealth Games.* The Athletics Union offers a vast choice of muscle-stretching pastimes *so even the slobbiest slob in slobland should find something sporty to do.* Facilities are *in good nick* on the back of Manchester's own hosting of the Commonwealth Games a couple years back.

SPORTS FACILITIES

There's a variety of sporting spots spread around the University sites. The Wythenshawe Ground is the largest: 60 acres of playing fields (ten acres more are within four miles of campus), totalling 28 pitches for football, rugby and cricket, six tennis courts and a pavilion. Firs Athletic Ground at Fallowfield in South Manchester has 31 acres of playing fields, eight tennis courts, an all-weather pitch and a large pavilion, all near the main student halls of residence. Nearby, the Fallowfield Stadium has amenities for track and field events and a soccer pitch. The Armitage Centre provides a sports hall for indoor ball sports, a climbing room, sauna and solarium, two martial arts dojos, table tennis and a fitness room. The Sugden Sports Centre holds more indoor courts, plus a fitness suite and free weights training area, as well as tennis courts and more outdoor pitches. The Commonwealth pool (the Manchester Aquatics Centre) is in the middle of Oxford Road and is home to the swimming teams. The city offers *everything the discerning* sportsperson could wish for, including the canal for rowing and canoeing, an ice rink, golf course, dry ski slope, a lake, lots of leisure centres and the surrounding hills and caves for those who like to take it outside.

SPORTING CLUBS

Aikido; Capoeira; Dance; Darts; Falun Gong; Free Fall Parachute; Hiking; Hung Kuen Kung Fu; SKUM (Ski-boarding & Ski-ing); Table Football; T'ai Chi Chuan; Wakeboard & Waterski; Wing Tsun Kung Fu. See also Clubs tables.

ATTRACTIONS

Three football teams have swear-words in their names: Arsenal, Scunthorpe and *F***in'* Manchester United. *Real Mancunians (like the brothers Gallagher) tend to back the underdogs and chant for the less successful, but less-despised Man City.* For Test & County Cricket, there's Old Trafford; basketball (The Giants) and ice hockey (The Storm) at the Manchester Evening News Arena; speedway at Broadhurst Park; rugby at Swinton, Salford and Trafford Borough; volleyball at Sale.

ACCOMMODATION ◑◑◑◑◑◑◑◑◑

IN UNIVERSITY
CATERED 10%   **COST** £90 (39WKS)
SELF-CATERING 24%   **COST** £70 (39WKS)
1ST YRS LIVING IN 76%   **INSURANCE PREMIUM** £££££

AVAILABILITY With more than 9,700 accommodation places, Manchester can afford to house just under half its undergraduates and guarantees new arrivals a roof for the first year and international students a bed for the duration. Most accommodation is within two miles of the campuses and is *immensely varied in size, style, catering and cleaning arrangements* – all have internet access though. From traditional and modern halls of residence to smart, modern flats through to small suburban Victorian houses, *there's something to suit all domestic tastes.* Several halls are like little colleges and have their own JCRs *(like mini students' unions), so there's a strong community spirit.* Catered Hulme Hall is the oldest, *sexiest and comfiest* – with larger than average rooms – *so it attracts a lot of attention.* St Anselm's may be all-male but it does formal dinners every night of the week *and is the top choice for returning students. Oak House and Moberly Tower, by contrast, are regarded as lonely.* 243 residences are available for couples and families and the University also leases a fair few private houses for second, third and fourth years, postgrads and families (£40-65 a week).

Words in italics are Push's point of view — take it or leave it...

EXTERNALLY

○ AVE RENT £53

AVAILABILITY *Finding a decent, non-extortionately priced house in Manchester is even easier than a Sunday morning.* There's a huge supply of housing and quality goes up because of the competition. Fallowfield, Victoria Park and Withington are the student ghettos. Didsbury is a bit more suburban but quite accessible. Rusholme can be quite rough but is improving. Levenshulme, Hulme and Moss Side should be treated with caution, although some hardy souls do settle there. There's a whole clutch of decent rooms in private halls of residence – check out www.manchesterstudenthomes.com

HOUSING HELP Manchester Student Housing nudges homemakers in the right direction. They list vacancies, approve landlords and vet properties. The 'Rent Right' campaign gives the skinny on the renting scheme and especially on not falling for the 'this is the last available cardboard box in the city' that *some landlords have been known to try.*

WELFARE ○○○○○○○○○○○○○○

SERVICES

○ LGBT SOCIETY ○ ETHNIC MINORITIES SOCIETY
○ WOMEN'S SOCIETY ○ MATURE STUDENTS'
OFFICER & SOCIETY
○ INTERNATIONAL STUDENTS' OFFICER & SOCIETY
○ POSTGRAD OFFICER & SOCIETY
○ DISABLED STUDENTS' SOCIETY ○ LATE–NIGHT MINIBUS
○ SELF–DEFENCE CLASSES ○ NIGHTLINE
○ UNIVERSITY COUNSELLORS 9 FULL ○ CRIME RATING !!!!!

Half the SU's sabbs have welfare responsibilities and, *overall, the service* – centred on the Union Advice Centre – *is very good.* A night-bus runs students home between 6pm and midnight. *The Union is particularly pro-lesbian, gay and bisexual students, who are a powerfully vocal force amongst the students (and, indeed, in Manchester generally).*

HEALTH A student health centre for broken bones and scabbed knees.

DISABILITIES *Access is improving steadily,* with ramps and lifts for wheelchair users and a study skill room with specialist dyslexia software and support materials.

DRUGS *The hard core of the Manchester scene is ecstasy. This and harder drugs are readily available in the clubs, pubs and on the streets of Manchester. Students' attitudes to drugs vary enormously between individuals and although use of E, acid (LSD), cocaine and cannabis is perhaps more widespread than the norm, the pressure to partake is small. Needless to say, the University comes down hard on anyone it catches.*

FINANCE

○ AVE DEBT PER YEAR £3,690 **○ HOME STUDENT FEES** £3,000

FEES For international students, fees are £8,300 a year for Arts courses, £10,750 for scientists and almost 20 grand for wannabe doctors and dentists. The University website has a handy fees calculator to work out what it'll cost and what bursaries are available/eligible.

SUPPORT Some short-term loans and helpful handouts from both the Union and the University. *A range of supportive bursaries will help take the sting off top-up fees – see their website for the full breakdown.*

M

○ The computer revolution started at Manchester University in June 1948 when a machine built by Tom Kilburn and Sir Freddie Williams, known as 'The Baby' (despite being enormous), ran its first stored programme.

MANCHESTER METROPOLITAN UNIVERSITY

FORMERLY MANCHESTER POLYTECHNIC

⚪ MANCHESTER METROPOLITAN UNIVERSITY All Saints, Oxford Road, Manchester, M15 6BH **TEL** (0161) 247 2000 **E-MAIL** enquiries@mmu.ac.uk **WEBSITE** www.mmu.ac.uk **⚪ MANCHESTER METROPOLITAN STUDENTS' UNION** 99 Oxford Road, Manchester, M1 7EL **TEL** (0161) 247 1162 **E-MAIL** mmsu@mmu.ac.uk **WEBSITE** www.mmunion.co.uk

GENERAL ⚪⚪⚪⚪⚪⚪⚪⚪⚪⚪⚪⚪

The main bit of Manchester Metropolitan at All Saints is part of the biggest educational complex in Western Europe, along with its neighbour the University of Manchester. There are also sites further up the A34 in the Didsbury area and even further away in Cheshire. *This critical mass of students is one reason why Manchester is such a vibrant, artistic place. It's also why so many rock bands from the city have gone in for student favourites like wearing long overcoats and writing songs about topping yourself.* The University's other claim to fame is that they were banned from University Challenge for many years in the 70s after a team answered every question 'Lenin' or 'Marx' as a protest against Oxbridge teams being allowed to enter as individual colleges. Since being allowed back in the 90s they've done very well and, under Paxman's iron rule, no such society-threatening anarchy has occurred. For general info about Manchester see University of Manchester.

🚶🚶🚶🚶🚶🚶🚶🚶🚶🚶🚶🚶🚶🚶🚶🚶🚶🚶🚶🚶🚶🚶🚶

SEX RATIO: ♂41 ♀59	**FOUNDED:** 1970
FULL-TIME U'GRADS: 20,831	**PART-TIME:** 1,822
POSTGRADS: 6,481	**NON-DEGREE:** 3,726
AVE COURSE: 3YRS	**ETHNIC:** 24%
STATE:PRIVATE SCHOOL: 95:5	**FLUNK RATE:** 17%
MATURE: 23%	**INTERNATIONAL:** 6%
DISABLED: 380	**LOCAL:** 53%

ATMOSPHERE

Manchester Met's a bit like Ab Fab's Saffy to Manchester University's Edina: a young upstart that's calmer and more grown-up than it's older relation, probably partly due to a high number of local and mature (and local, mature) students. That's testament to how people feel about the place – they don't want to leave – and there's still yet a large number of students attracted by the party-till-you-puke atmosphere of the 'Madchester' of old, and the sophisticated city of new. Town-gown relations are good – but with the largest student population in Europe students don't really have a choice bar moving somewhere else (or enrolling as students themselves). The Crewe site is currently fattening itself up to lure lots more education-hungry students, matching the recent investment in Crewe itself (cinemas, bars etc), although it's more on the reserve's bench than second fiddle to the Manchester scene. There's no comparison, but the calmer, countryish atmosphere and intimate, friendly feel between students and locals appeal to some.

SITES

ALL SAINTS The main city-centre campus and home to the admin and SU empires. *The buzziest atmosphere, and a magnet for trendies.*
BUSINESS SCHOOL (5,000) half a mile from All Saints and one of the largest business schools in the UK. Close to Piccadilly Station.
JOHN DALTON (5,200) Based in Chester Street, 100 metres from All Saints. Students in the science, engineering and technology departments get to play with petri dishes and capacitors *(whatever they are).*
HOLLINGS (1,700 students – Clothing, Food, Hospitality & Tourism) Three miles (give or take) from All Saints in Fallowfield. Linked with the main campus by *the busiest bus route in Europe.*
DIDSBURY (4,000 – Health, Social Care, Education) About five miles from All Saints. *A leafy site with lively restaurants, bars and good transport links to the centre.*
ELIZABETH GASKELL (3,500) About a mile from the main site. Psychology, Speech Pathology and Health Care students, as well as Law and Community Studies. On the same bus route as the Hollings and Didsbury sites.

The Cheshire 'campus' is made of two sites, at Crewe and Alsager, six miles apart. There's free transport between the two. *Some students feel excluded from the MMU experience and those applying to University for the bright lights should check where they're going to be based. Crewe and Alsager are less than dazzling.*
CREWE (3,300) 28 miles south of Manchester. Home to trainee teachers and research degrees.
ALSAGER (1,592) 34 miles from Manchester in a *leafy* country suburb near Stoke-on-Trent. A variety of arts and sports science courses. *Good sports facilities.*

MANCHESTER see University of Manchester

TRAVEL see University of Manchester

CAREER PROSPECTS

⚪ CAREERS SERVICE ⚪ NO. OF STAFF: 15 FULL-TIME **⚪ UNEMPLOYED AFTER 6MTHS:** 5%

Words in italics are Push's point of view — take it or leave it...

FAMOUS ALUMNI

Terry Christian (ex-Word presenter and Oasis biographer); Steve Coogan, John Thompson (comedians); Bernard Hill, David Threlfall, Julie Walters (actors); Mick Hucknall (Simply Red *soul dwarf*); L S Lowry (painter); Min Patel (cricketer); Bryan Robson (ex-footballer, pundit and *deeply unsuccessful* manager).

FURTHER INFO

- **PROSPECTUSES** UNDERGRAD; POSTGRAD
- **OPEN DAYS**

ACADEMIC ◔◔◔◔◔◔◔◔◔◔◔◔◔

Continued investment means that Manchester Met students benefit from constantly improving academic facilities. Lots of opportunity for work placements and student involvement, such as the Ambassador scheme – *nothing to do with handing out posh chocolates at posh parties* – but paid work at Open Days and the like.

ENTRY POINTS: 80–320	**AVE POINTS:** 180
APPLICATIONS PER PLACE: N/A	**CLEARING:** N/A
NO. OF TERMS: 3	**LENGTH OF TERMS:** 00 WKS
STAFF TO STUDENT RATIO: 1:22	**STUDY ADDICTS:** N/A
TEACHING: ✱✱	**RESEARCH:** ✱✱✱

ADMISSIONS

- **APPLY VIA UCAS**

SUBJECTS

- **ART AND DESIGN** 20% **ENGINEERING & SCIENCE** 25% **FOOD, CLOTHING & HOSPITALITY MANAGEMENT** 15% **HEALTH SOCIAL CARE & EDUCATION** 15% **HUMANITIES, LAW & SOCIAL SCIENCE** 25%
BEST Electronic Engineering; English Studies; Environmental Science; Human & Social Geography; Mechanical Engineering; Physical Geography; Performing Arts; Philosophy; Politics; Social Policy & Anthropology; Sociology; Theology & Religious Studies.

LIBRARIES

- **906,046 BOOKS ◑ 3,356 STUDY PLACES**
- **SPEND PER STUDENT** £££££
Seven libraries spread across the sites.

COMPUTERS

- **3,000 WORKSTATIONS**
There are drop-in 'puters at most University sites, and all bedrooms in halls have internet access.

ENTERTAINMENT ◔◔◔◔◔◔◔◔◔

THE CITY see University of Manchester

THE UNIVERSITY

- **PRICE OF A PINT OF BEER** £1.60
- **GLASS OF WINE** £1.40
- **CAN OF RED BULL** £1.70
BARS The bars in the Union building are large, noisy, *popular* and open from 11.30am till chucking-out/falling-over time. There's a *smaller, quieter* affair at Didsbury, as well as Alsager's Brandies.
THEATRES The acting course has *great* facilities at the Capitol Theatre but the drama society's *not particularly strong*. Performance Art students at Crewe have their own studio.
FILM The University shows three films a week at the Horniman Theatre, free to members.
CLUBBING Three or four club nights a week in the K-Two bar in the Union's main building, including the *popular* 'Flirt'. Revamped to the tune of £500k, charges £3-4 and plays mainly indie, chart and retro. Friday's Double Vision *packs in the biggest crowd and there's more snakebites at Wednesday's sporty back-slap night than a camping trip in the Everglades*. The Cheshire SU thows on transport to Liquid in Stoke *and other local meat markets*.
MUSIC VENUES K-Two's the site for gigs. Eagle Eye Cherrie, Trevor Nelson, Phats and Small, the Chemical Brothers, Dreem Team and Space have appeared in the last few years. MMU students also slope off to the University of Manchester for even bigger names.
FOOD The University Refectory's open 11am-3pm *but the SU coffee bar has a more interesting selection and is open round the clock. Blue, the SU sandwich shop, does exciting things with bread for less than £2. The Uni-owned Brilliant Veggi café is a taste sensation sweeping the nation. OK, it's not, but it's highly-rated across the City.*
OTHER Departmental balls and the annual Athletic Union bash is *popular*.

SOCIAL ◔◔◔◔◔◔◔◔◔◔◔◔◔

MANCHESTER METROPOLITAN STUDENTS' UNION

- **7 SABBATICALS ◑ TURNOUT AT LAST BALLOT** 5%
- **NUS MEMBER**
The Union's main building on Oxford Road is the social hub, and has variously been named after Nelson Mandela, Martin Luther King and Bruce Forsyth, which *gives some idea of the level of political commitment round these parts*. Party political allegiances aren't that strong and *the only thing that gets the students really worked up is money (or lack of it)*.

SU FACILITIES

Main building: two bars; two cafés; travel agency; shop; Barclays and Link ATMs; sandwich shop; vending/games machines; pool tables;

Words in italics are Push's point of view – take it or leave it...

M

photo booth; TV lounge; function rooms; recycling facilities.

CLUBS (NON-SPORTING)

Beer & Real Ale; Brahma Kumaris; Breakdancing; Buddhist & Meditation; Chinese; Cheerleading; Cypriot; Electronic Musicians; Hindu; Poker; Pork Scratching; Respect; Role Play; Russian; Sikh; Student Radio; Yoga. Cheshire campus has: Christian Union; Craft; Cultural Elevation; Drama; Dance; International; LGBT; Music Rock; Pissed up Poets; Urban. **See also Clubs tables.**

OTHER ORGANISATIONS

Free student paper 'Pulp' comes out fortnightly.

RELIGIOUS

MULTI-FAITH CHAPLAINCY
Religion in Manchester see University of Manchester

PAID WORK see University of Manchester
Steam, the University jobshop, has close links with local job networks.

SPORTS ()()()()()()()()()()()

○ **BUSA RANKING** 62
Keeping up with course work and having a quick half in the bar takes precedence over busting a gut on the track, but there are a few brave souls prepared to strain the odd ligament in pursuit of glory.

SPORTS FACILITIES

Sports halls and the Sugden Sports Centre at All Saints. Didsbury has a sports hall too, as well as squash and tennis courts and weight training. There's also a sports hall and Astroturf at Alsager. The best outdoor facilities are at the MMU Cheshire sites, where there are 32 acres of playing fields and an outdoor swimming pool. Manchester Canal comes in handy for rowing, canoeing etc. The All-Saints site is handy for Manchester Aquatics Centre, built for the Commonwealth Games, so *a pretty swish place to make a splash.*

SPORTING CLUBS

Bujinkan; Ching Wu; Gaelic Football; Handball; Kung Fu; Ju Jitsu; Lifesaving; Rowing; Skydiving; Surf; Table Tennis; Trampoline; Ultimate Frisbee. Cheshire campus: Tae kwon do. **See also Clubs tables.**

ATTRACTIONS

A couple of football teams are kicking around, Push forgets their names. See University of Manchester

ACCOMMODATION ()()()()()()()()()

IN UNIVERSITY

○ **CATERED** 2% ○ **COST** £77 (40WKS)
○ **SELF-CATERING** 16% ○ **COST** £62 (40WKS)
○ **1ST YRS LIVING IN** 95% ○ **INSURANCE PREMIUM** £££££
AVAILABILITY All first years are guaranteed accommodation and most make the most of it but virtually everyone moves out again for the remaining years. Rents include insurance. There are halls at all the sites, and all have 24-hour security on-hand *to tuck students in. They're all friendly places with cleaners fighting the good fight against botulism, cholera etc.* The newest housing developments are at Crewe.
CAR PARKING Some halls provide parking although (paid) permits may be necessary.

EXTERNALLY see University of Manchester
○ **AVE RENT** £55
AVAILABILITY *City accommodation is generally of decent quality.* Fallowfield and Withington are *popular choices.*
HOUSING HELP The Accommodation & Welfare Service keep vacancy lists, check properties/contracts and attempts to resolve disputes. A joint housing service is run in conjunction with the University of Manchester. Manchester Student Homes is a private organisation that can find nests for students at either university.

WELFARE ()()()()()()()()()()()

SERVICES

○ **LGBT SOCIETY** ○ **INTERNATIONAL STUDENTS' SOCIETY**
○ **MATURE STUDENTS' SOCIETY** ○ **NIGHTLINE**
○ **UNIVERSITY COUNSELLORS** 3 FULL/6 PART
○ **CRIME RATING** !!!!!
Student advice centres at two of the Manchester sites as well as at Crewe and Alsager.
HEALTH The University has St Augustine's doctors' surgery at All Saints which deals with most minor – and even the odd major – health issues.
DISABILITIES Ramps and lifts are provided in most places.

FINANCE

○ **AVE DEBT PER YEAR** £4,507 ○ **HOME STUDENT FEES** £3,000
fees: International undergraduates pay an average of £7,000/year.
○ **ACCESS FUND** £1767,5351 ○ **SUCCESSFUL APPLICATIONS/YR** 1,974
SUPPORT The SU can give loans of up to £50.

➡ **MANCHESTER POLYTECHNIC**
see *Manchester Metropolitan University*

MIDDLESEX UNIVERSITY

FORMERLY MIDDLESEX POLYTECHNIC

⊙ **MIDDLESEX UNIVERSITY** North London Business Park, Oakleigh Road South, London, N11 1QS **TEL** (020) 8411 5555
E-MAIL admissions@mdx.ac.uk **WEBSITE** www.mdx.ac.uk
⊙ **MIDDLESEX UNIVERSITY STUDENTS' UNION** Bramley Road, London, N14 4YZ **TEL** (020) 8411 6500 **WEBSITE** www.musu.mdx.ac.uk

GENERAL ○○○○○○○○○○○○○

Middlesex used to be a county, *now it only really exists as a postal district, a cricket team and an abstract band down the western side of London. The location of Middlesex University is equally non-specific.* It's based on four major campuses and four hospitals. The London sites range from Trent Park 15 miles from Central London to the Hendon Campus (centre for Business & IT) set in a residential area of North West London. Another campus has just opened in Dubai – *that's how widely dispersed this place is.*

🚹🚹🚹🚹🚹🚹🚹🚹🚹🚶🚶🚶🚶🚶🚶🚶🚶🚶🚶🚶

SEX RATIO: ♂41 ♀59	FOUNDED: 1973
FULL-TIME U'GRADS: 13,625	PART-TIME: 4,490
POSTGRADS: 2,605	NON-DEGREE: 507
AVE COURSE: 3YRS	ETHNIC: 40%
STATE:PRIVATE SCHOOL: 80:20	FLUNK RATE: 27%
MATURE: 45%	INTERNATIONAL: 27%
DISABLED: 309	LOCAL: 57%

ATMOSPHERE
The glut of mature students puts a different emphasis on things and being so spread out means that many students can feel as though they're not exactly cheering for the same team. Students, especially Hendon kids, are loyal to their own campus rather than to the University as a whole. Being so far north of the river means it doesn't really feel like a London university – the bright lights are a long way away – but then, so is the bustle, the smog and the other chaotic hassles of the city centre. With facilities all over the place, it's hard to know what's available and, once discovered, it can be rather an expedition getting there.

SITES
CAT HILL (1,931 students – Textiles, Film Studies, Art && Design, History of Art & Architecture, Electronic Arts) In Barnet, where facilities include a multigym. *Its only bar closed down, leaving students feeling a bit miffed that there's not really anywhere to go.*
ENFIELD (3,084 students – Social Science, Health Studies) Includes ents venue the Forum.
health campus (3,118 students – Nursing) Teaching facilities spread across four North London hospitals.
HENDON (5,708 students – Business, Computing & IT) The largest site in terms of numbers. Now boasts The Sheppard Library – *a pant-moistening* £12m new Learning Resource Centre.

TRENT PARK (3,520 students – Performing Arts, Product Design and Engineering,Teacher Training, Humanities, Languages). A 60-acre country campus set amid woodland and meadows – the main building is an 18th-century style mansion. *Which is nice.*

LONDON see University of London

TRAVEL see University of London
TRAINS Nearest rail/tube stations are Finsbury Park, Seven Sisters and Tottenham Hale (all Victoria line), Oakwood for the Piccadilly line. The University sites are in Zones 3-5.
CAR Free and paid-for parking at or near most sites, *but finding a space can mean a bit of bunfight.* Permits are required to park on campus.
LOCAL The 299, 298 buses run to Cat Hill roundabout. At Enfield, Southbury station or buses 121, 149, 191, 259, 307, 310A, 310B, 313 (to Ponders End bus garage) or 279, 363, 517 to Ponders End High Street. For Hendon campus use Hendon Central stop (Northern line) then bus 183 or walk.
UNIVERSITY The University minibus runs from Oakwood station to Trent Park campus every ten mins in term-time.
BICYCLES Some cycle lanes at most campuses. *Local roads get chocca with motorised smog-sprayers, but there are quieter routes.*

CAREER PROSPECTS
⊙ **CAREERS SERVICE** ⊙ **NO. OF STAFF** 4 FULL/3 PART
⊙ **UNEMPLOYED AFTER 6MTHS** 13%
All the usual gubbins including alumni mentors, computer-based guidance and seminars.

SPECIAL FEATURES
Courses often start in *resolution-breaking* January as well as *tan-fading* September.

FAMOUS ALUMNI
Adam Ant (singer); Tim Campbell (winner of 'The Apprentice'); Ray Davies (Kinks mainman); Nick Harvey MP (LibDem); Allison Goldfrapp (*sultry singer*); James Herbert (novelist); Alison Lloyd (Ally Capellino fashion house); Anish Kapoor (artist); Matthew Marsden (ex-Corrie actor); Helen Mirren (actress); Omar (singer); Stephen Seargeant (sailor); Rianna Scipio (TV presenter); Vivienne Westwood (designer); Johnny Vegas (funny fat man); Arabella Weir (comedian).

M

FURTHER INFO
- **PROSPECTUSES** UNDERGRAD; POSTGRAD; SOME DEPARTMENTS
- **OPEN DAYS**

Two booklets – 'Somewhere To Live' and 'Welcome to Middlesex' – are also available. E-mail openday@mdx.ac.uk for open day information. The University do summer schools for *keen beans.*

ACADEMIC ○○○○○○○○○○○○○○

Academic strengths are training and research in Science, Engineering, Medicine (Middlesex was first to offer a degree in Herbal Medicine), Law, Arts, Languages, Linguistics and Politics. Language teaching and help with study skills are available to any student who fancies dropping in. Some students go for the easy life, but a strong contingent of studious types match the workload of a more traditional university. The work-ethic in the Art & Design Department is particularly hectic. Middlesex was recently decreed a Centre for Excellence in Teaching and Learning in Mental Health and Social Work.

ENTRY POINTS: 180–280	AVE POINTS: 288
APPLICATIONS PER PLACE: 8	CLEARING: 2%
NO. OF TERMS: 2	LENGTH OF TERMS: 15wks
STAFF TO STUDENT RATIO: 1:18	STUDY ADDICTS: 21%
TEACHING: **	RESEARCH: ***
YEAR ABROAD: N/A	SANDWICH STUDENTS: <1%
1STS: 9%	2.2S: 39%
2.1S: 38%	3RDS: 8%

ADMISSIONS
- **APPLY VIA UCAS/GTTR FOR PGCE/NMAS FOR NURSING**

SUBJECTS
- **ARTS** 25% **BUSINESS SCHOOL** 27% **COMPUTING SCIENCES** 21% **HEALTH & SOCIAL SCIENCE** 20%
- **LIFELONG LEARNING & EDUCATION** 5%

BEST Biomedical Sciences; Complementary Health Science; Environment (especially Flood Hazard); Nursing & Midwifery; Psychology.
UNUSUAL Games Design; International Business for China; Psychoanalysis (MA); TV Production.

LIBRARIES
- **750,000 BOOKS** **2,600 STUDY PLACES**

COMPUTERS
- **2,000 WORKSTATIONS**

Courses are supported by online communities, handbooks, presentations and lecture notes on the OASIS virtual learning environment.

OTHER LEARNING FACILITIES
Language labs; drama studio; music rehearsal rooms; CAD lab; media centre; dance studios.

ENTERTAINMENT ○○○○○○○○○○

THE CITY see University of London
- **PRICE OF A PINT OF BEER** £1.70
- **GLASS OF WINE** £2
- **CAN OF RED BULL** £1.85

Etcetera pub theatre, a couple of multiplexes in Finchley, pound-a-pint Tuesdays at the Beef & Barrell in Enfield and *just about everything in Camden.*

THE UNIVERSITY
- **PRICE OF A PINT OF BEER** £1.70
- **GLASS OF WINE** £2
- **CAN OF RED BULL** £1.80

BARS Four are run by the SU on separate campuses, three others by the University. The Enfield set-up is the biggest, but there are others at Trent Park and Hendon.
THEATRES *Not much use is made of* the Simmonds Theatre on the Trent Park campus.
FILM One rabble-rouser a week, courtesy of the Respect Soc – *think radical/political stuff like Outfoxed and Hotel Rwanda. Disney and the Farrelly brothers don't even get a trailer.*
CLUBBING Weekly *Dairylea-infused discos* at Trent Park and the Enfield Forum.
COMEDY/CABARET Monthly, *but no one you'd've heard of.*
FOOD Most catering outlets are now operated by an external contractor. At least two self-service places for snacks, slurps and hot scoff on each campus. No food after 6pm.
OTHER *Middlesex is big on balls.* The Summer extravaganza usually lasts 36 hours and there's a big freshers' do. Lures to lubrication in the often under-used bars include Bar FTSE where the beer prices fluctuate with demand.

SOCIAL ○○○○○○○○○○○○○

MIDDLESEX UNIVERSITY STUDENTS' UNION
- **6 SABBATICALS** **NUS MEMBER**
- **TURNOUT AT LAST BALLOT** 8%

In the past, the SU has been all about services, representation and ents, rather than tearing down barricades and guillotining the University administration. With privatisation creeping across the University facilities, the (largely left-of-centre) students have been getting riled with last year seeing the highest level of student political involvement in a decade. The SU works hard on behalf of a very varied student body, but has its teeth blunted by the University's powers to suspend the president and a lack of cash. Things can seem a bit disorganised and the facilities leave a lot to be desired.

SU FACILITIES

The SU has facilities on all campuses. There are bars, shops, snack bars, a printing service, fax service, photocopier, cashpoints, launderette, games machines, photo booths, meeting rooms, TV lounges and a minibus for hire. *What's there isn't bad, but students would dearly love more events and more places to chill out.*

CLUBS (NON-SPORTING)

African Student; Believers' Loveworld; Chinese Students & Scholars; Cypriot; Elvis Impersonators; Eureka Indian; Herb; Hollywood; International Café; Modern Languages; Public Relations; Stop The War; Traditional Chinese Medicine. **See also Clubs table.**

OTHER ORGANISATIONS

'Mud', the SU mag, is *better than the previous efforts.*

RELIGIOUS

At Hendon there's a Jewish society and a large Jewish community. See University of London for other places of worship around the city.

PAID WORK see University of London
- **PAID WORK** TERM-TIME 10%; HOLS 75%
- **JOB BUREAU**

There's some work to be found at the University and SU, which employ students to marshal car parks, steward at balls, help at Open Days and suchlike.The JobsOnline website has a vacancy service.

SPORTS () () () () () () () () () () () () () ()

- **BUSA RANKING** 67

Various bionic bribes – sorry, sports scholarships – including one hoping to find 2012 Olympic contenders as well as an athlete support team.

SPORTS FACILITIES

The University has five sports halls and three playing fields. There are indoor and outdoor tennis courts, a sauna and steamroom, six multigyms, swimming pools, a hockey and an all-weather pitch. There are real tennis courts at Hendon and, to *kiss it all better,* a rehab clinic at Enfield *(not the Pete Doherty type).* Recent expansion has been helped by Lottery funding.

SPORTING CLUBS

Table Tennis. **See also Clubs tables.**

ATTRACTIONS see University of London

ACCOMMODATION () () () () () () () () () ()

IN UNIVERSITY
- **SELF–CATERING** 17% ● **COST** £83 (40WKS)
- **1ST YRS LIVING IN** 55% ● **INSURANCE PREMIUM** £££

AVAILABILITY There's *not particularly lovable* accommodation for 95% of first years who want it, in one of the seven halls on separate campuses *a hop, skip and a tumble* from most of the teaching sites. *First dibs* go to international and non-local students and those with disabilities get to nose around to see if anything will suit before they commit. Kitchens are shared between 14 or so students. There have been cases where students have had to live at one site when their course is taught at another. *D'oh.* CCTV watches over the entry-phones and night and weekend porters watch over the CCTV.

CAR PARKING First years can't park on site, but later years can get their mitts on the few permits.

EXTERNALLY see University of London
- **AVE RENT** £75

AVAILABILITY *A lot of students live at home. It's not difficult to find somewhere decent since the sites are far enough from the city centre. This is London, mind, so cheap can mean dodgy. Palmers Green is popular and convenient. Wood Green and Turnpike Lane are also handy.*

HOUSING HELP The University runs an accommodation service which helps students find places in shared or self-contained house and flats. It vets properties and keeps an approved landlord list. There's also an online housing service.

WELFARE () () () () () () () () () () () () ()

SERVICES
- **INTERNATIONAL STUDENTS' OFFICER**
- **SELF–DEFENCE CLASSES** ● **CRIME RATING** !!!

The SU's responsible for welfare provision, *but hasn't really got the hang of advertising what's on offer.* University-run website www.mdx.ac.uk/24-7 *is a comprehensive hub of useful student info, welfare-based or otherwise. Poor provision for bewildered international students has left some feeling a bit lost.*

HEALTH Parents' group and first aiders on all campuses.

CRECHES/NURSERY The University's crèche of choice caters for sprogs aged 6wks-5yrs. Nurseries at Enfield, Hendon and Trent Park.

DISABILITIES *Major improvements in access over the last few years, mainly facilitated by the very impressive Able Centre.* Induction loops installed, dyslexia support.

Words in italics are Push's point of view — take it or leave it...

FINANCE
⊙ AVE DEBT PER YEAR £2,676 **⊙ HOME STUDENT FEES** £3,000
FEES International undergrads are charged £9,200, international postgrads from £4,500. UK post-grads pay between £2,100 and £4,800 or, for part-time, £1,700 - £2,200.
SUPPORT Chancellor's scholarships are awarded for academic, sporting, community or cultural achievements. In addition, undergrads with 300 or more UCAS points are entitled to a substantial yearly cash carrot (an Achievement Scholarship) to keep up the donkeywork. Middlesex Scholarships – £10,000 pa for three years – are available to five undergrads who put Middlesex as their first UCAS choice. Short-term loans are available to those in dire straits.

▶ MIDDLESEX POLYTECHNIC
see *Middlesex University*

▶ MOORES, LIVERPOOL JOHN
see *Liverpool John Moores University*

▶ MORAY HOUSE SCHOOL OF EDUCATION
see *University of Edinburgh*

M

⊙ **'If you go straight [to college] from school, unfortunately you turn into a student and you go on pyjama jumps and talk in that student voice' – Jarvis Cocker**

Words in italics are Push's point of view – take it or leave it...

NAPIER UNIVERSITY

▶ NAPIER POLYTECHNIC
see *Napier University*

▶ NENE UNIVERSITY COLLEGE
see *Northampton University*

NEWCASTLE UNIVERSITY

NEWPORT, UNIVERSITY OF WALES

▶ NORTH EAST WALES INSTITUTE (NEWI)

▶ NORTH LONDON UNIVERSITY
see *London Metropolitan University*

NORTHAMPTON UNIVERSITY

▶ UNIVERSITY COLLEGE NORTHAMPTON
see *Northampton University*

NORTHUMBRIA UNIVERSITY

▶ UNIVERSITY OF NORTHUMBRIA AT NEWCASTLE
see *Northumbria University*

▶ NORWICH
see *University of East Anglia*

UNIVERSITY OF NOTTINGHAM

NOTTINGHAM TRENT UNIVERSITY

▶ NOTTINGHAM POLYTECHNIC
see *Nottingham Trent University*

N

NAPIER UNIVERSITY

FORMERLY NAPIER POLYTECHNIC

1. **◉ NAPIER UNIVERSITY** Craiglockhart Campus, Edinburgh, EH14 1DJ **TEL** (08452) 60 60 40 **E-MAIL** info@napier.ac.uk
WEBSITE www.napier.ac.uk **◉ NAPIER STUDENTS' ASSOCIATION (NSA)** 12 Merchiston Place, Edinburgh, EH10 4NR
TEL (0131) 229 8791 **E-MAIL** nsa@napier.ac.uk Website: www.napierstudents.com
2. **◉ MERCHISTON CAMPUS** 10 Colinton Road, Edinburgh, EH10 5DT **TEL** (08452) 60 60 40
3. **◉ CANAAN LANE CAMPUS** 74 Canaan Lane, Edinburgh, EH10 4TB
4. **◉ COMELY BANK CAMPUS** Crewe Road South, Edinburgh, EH14 2LD
5. **◉ CRAIGHOUSE CAMPUS** New Craig, Craighouse Road, Edinburgh, EH10 5LG

GENERAL ◉◉◉◉◉◉◉◉◉◉◉◉◉

Napier is one of the *young upstarts,* growing at a *healthy lick*. There are five sites dotted around a *pleasant, mainly middle-class* area out in the west of the city. The Merchiston campus is home to the majority of students and is built around the 15th-century Tower of Merchiston, where logarithm inventor (and University namesake) John Napier was born in 1550. Science, Engineering and Arts students are based here now and there's a converted house for the Students' Association (NSA). For general info on Edinburgh see University of Edinburgh.

SEX RATIO: ♂47 ♀53	**FOUNDED:** 1992
FULL-TIME U'GRADS: 8,531	**PART-TIME:** 2,549
POSTGRADS: 2,102	**NON-DEGREE:** 150
AVE COURSE: 4YRS	**ETHNIC:** 10%
STATE:PRIVATE SCHOOL: 95:5	**FLUNK RATE:** 22%
MATURE: 67%	**INTERNATIONAL:** 24%
DISABLED: 200	**LOCAL:** 60%

ATMOSPHERE

This is definitely not back-scratching old-boy territory. Students are a practical bunch: they're here to get a job rather than chucking themselves headlong into the social scene. Social bonds are even looser thanks to the disjointed nature of the University – there's a lot of pressure on resources and students spend a lot of their time dashing between the different sites. Relations with the surrounding community are cuddly as custard though, thanks to large proportion of local students and the University's policy of keeping local residents informed of any plans that might affect them and accepting feedback. There's also good support *for the fiddly kind of personal issues which do tend to crop up and get in the way of an education. Not every university is that considerate.*

SITES

MERCHISTON CAMPUS (4,634 students – Faculty of Engineering, Computing and Creative Industries, School of Psychology & Sociology, Life Sciences and Design & Media Art) The largest campus a mile from the city centre. Houses recently refurbished Science and Engineering labs and a 24/7 computer lab with space for 500 bums.
CRAIGHOUSE CAMPUS (1,727 students – Communication Arts, Music) A one-time Victorian loony-bin on top of one of the city's seven hills and a couple of miles from Merchiston in *trendy* Morningside. *Great views over the city.*
CRAIGLOCKHART CAMPUS (4,026 students – Napier University Business School) The 19th-century hospital building (once home to recuperating war poets Siegfried Sassoon and Wilfred 'Gas! Gas!' Owen) houses the main admin centre, a bit of accommodation and a few sports facilities. Following a spot of post-millennial redevelopment, the site acquired what may be a contender for *'Weirdest University Building in Britain'* – a 200-seat lecture theatre inside a giant titanium-clad egg. The Craiglockhart Nature Trail makes getting from here to Craighouse a particularly *pleasant* prospect.
CANAAN LANE CAMPUS (1,651 students – School of Acute & Continuing Care, Nursing and some courses from the School of Community Health, eg. Complementary Therapy, Herbal Medicine) A small campus within the grounds of Astley Ainslie Hospital near Morningside, a couple of miles from Merchiston.
COMELY BANK (1,038 students – Health & Life Sciences, Community Health) It's situated in the north of the city and is an additional base for the Faculty of Health & Life Sciences.

EDINBURGH see University of Edinburgh

TRAVEL see University of Edinburgh
TRAINS The closest stations are Haymarket (Merchiston); Waverley (Marchmont); Slateford (Craiglockhart).
CARS A small number of permits are available to park on University premises, although the spaces available vary from site to site.
BICYCLES Lockable bike racks at all campuses. *Be warned, though, hills are hilly.*

CAREER PROSPECTS
◉ CAREERS SERVICE ◉ NO. OF STAFF 10 FULL
◉ UNEMPLOYED AFTER 6 MTHS 11%
The Careers Advisory Service keeps an *arsenal* of job-hunter's resources, hosts job fairs, offers practice interview sessions and one-on-one guidance, and provides vacancy updates by bulletin board, e-mail and newsletter.

FAMOUS ALUMNI
Colin Baxter (photographer); Jane Franchi, Bill McFarlan, Malcolm Wilson, Cathy McDonald and

Jim White (all Scottish TV presenters); Mark Goodier (radio DJ); Derrick Lee (Scottish rugby player); Lynne Ramsay (film director).

FURTHER INFO
⊙ **PROSPECTUSES** UNDERGRAD; POSTGRAD; INTERNATIONAL; PART-TIME; SOME DEPARTMENTS
⊙ **OPEN DAYS**
Napier produces a range of other publications and pamphlets, including the *straight to the point* 'Show Me the Money' finance guide and a guide to accommodation.

ACADEMIC ◖◖◖◖◖◖◖◖◖◖◖◖◖

The courses are *generally geared* towards the vocational (lots of placements and work experience) and *towards turning students into 9-5ers in the long run. Academic life is more laid back, though – even seminar attendance isn't compulsory. While that leads to a good deal of independence (and lie-ins), it also means those struggling to keep up sometimes aren't recognised until too late.*

ENTRY POINTS: 200-240	AVE POINTS: 200
APPLICATIONS PER PLACE: 4	CLEARING: 11%
NO. OF TERMS: 3	LENGTH OF TERMS: 15WKS
STAFF TO STUDENT RATIO: 1:15	STUDY ADDICTS: 16%
TEACHING: ★★	RESEARCH: ★★★
YEAR ABROAD: <1%	SANDWICH STUDENTS: 25%
1STS: 12%	2.2S: 41%
2.1S: 44%	3RDS: 3%

ADMISSIONS
⊙ **APPLY VIA UCAS/CATCH FOR NURSING**
The University judges each application individually *and isn't a stickler for published requirements.*

SUBJECTS
ARTS & SOCIAL SCIENCES 18% **BUSINESS SCHOOL** 32%
ENGINEERING & COMPUTING 25%
HEALTH & LIFE SCIENCES 25%
BEST Building; Cellular & Molecular Biology; Civil Engineering; Hospitality; Mass Communications; Maths; Organisational Biology; Statistics.

LIBRARIES
⊙ **220,000** BOOKS ⊙ **885** STUDY PLACES
⊙ **SPEND PER STUDENT** £££££
Eight libraries. The *biggest* are at Merchiston (which has an *interesting* war poetry special collection) and Craiglockhart.

COMPUTERS
⊙ **1,034** WORKSTATIONS ⊙ **24-HOUR ACCESS**
⊙ **SPEND PER STUDENT** £££
The Jack Kilby Computing Centre at Merchiston, *which bags architectural accolades by the hatful, has the bulk of 'puters.*

OTHER LEARNING FACILITIES
Digital language learning facilities at Craiglockhart; Sports Science labs, Adaptive Technology Centre and CAD labs at Merchiston; music studio and IT labs at Craighouse. There are several media centres *dotted around too.*

ENTERTAINMENT ◖◖◖◖◖◖◖◖◖◖

THE CITY see University of Edinburgh

UNIVERSITY
⊙ **PRICE OF A PINT OF BEER** £1.75
⊙ **GLASS OF WINE** £1.70
⊙ **CAN OF RED BULL** £1
Ents are *all-but non-existent* at the University, allegedly due to a current cash conundrum. *The SA's kinda thinkin' about maybe kicking the knees-up potential into line but your guess is as good as Push's about when and if it'll all happen.* Higher numbers of local students and those more concerned with degrees than drinks *has probably helped along the demise, as has the unrivalled local scene. Those that are up for it are more than willing to stroll into town for bright lights and boogying, so a lack of on-campus action is no real hardship. The drama and film societies do their bit for student kicks, but facilities aren't great.* Most sites have refectories. Sports and society balls light up the social calendar every so often.

SOCIAL ◖◖◖◖◖◖◖◖◖◖◖◖

NAPIER STUDENTS' ASSOCIATION (NSA)
⊙ **NUS MEMBER**

SU FACILITIES
NSA's converted house park *is pretty much an empty shell* apart from housing the sabbs upstairs. Societies are *as well-advertised and as easy to join as your typical underground, illegal rave.*

CLUBS (NON-SPORTING)
Film; Latin American; United-Left; Whisky.
See also Clubs tables.

OTHER ORGANISATIONS
'Veritas' is the *high-minded (in name at least)* student paper. *Chat show politico Kilroy has nothing to do with it, thankfully.*

RELIGIOUS
⊙ **12** CHAPLAINS (**MULTI-FAITH**)
Two prayer rooms. Religion in Edinburgh see University of Edinburgh

PAID WORK see University of Edinburgh
○ **JOB BUREAU** ○ **PAID WORK** TERM-TIME 96%; HOLS 99%
NSA runs a net-based job bank and the Careers Advisory Service lends a hand by posting temporary or course-related vacancies.

SPORTS ○○○○○○○○○○○○○

○ **BUSA RANKING** 89
Sports facilities *aren't much cop and the University doesn't seem too bothered – it's only a game, innit? – although there's still a ripple of enthusiasm across the campuses.*

SPORTS FACILITIES
Sports Centre at Sighthill (*seven miles from the main campus – getting there and back may be all the exercise you need*) with: two sports halls; multigym; a netball and two basketball courts; aerobics studio; squash courts. Special discount deals at city facilities with an Edinburgh Leisure Card for those who join a sports union club. For Edinburgh's attractions see University of Edinburgh.

SPORTING CLUBS
American Football; Gaelic Football; Jitsu; Kayak; Mountain Bike; Water Polo. **See also Clubs tables.**

ATTRACTIONS see University of Edinburgh

ACCOMMODATION ○○○○○○○○○

IN UNIVERSITY
○ **SELF-CATERING** 11% ○ **COST** £68 (38WKS)
○ **1ST YRS LIVING IN** 60% ○ **INSURANCE PREMIUM** £
AVAILABILITY First years living outside Edinburgh get preference for accommodation – if they apply before the deadline. That means that about 10% of students who want accommodation can't get it. All flats are single-sex and there are six developed for disabled use. No en suite facilities. Everything's *within walking distance* of the city and University or has good public transport links. *It's not the lap of luxury, though – in fact it's more like the arse-end, with some students reporting rat-related activity in kitchens and wall cavities.*
CAR PARKING Parking requires a permit but *that doesn't guarantee a spot.*

EXTERNALLY see University of Edinburgh
○ **AVE RENT** £72
HOUSING HELP *Given university accommodation, most students would prefer to live out, but with local landlords laughing all the way to the bank at students' expense, they're caught between a rock and a big stone.* Three accommodation advisors do their best to match students with pads, warn them about the worst of the local letters, and offer legal advice *for when it all hits the fan.*

WELFARE ○○○○○○○○○○○○

SERVICES
○ **INTERNATIONAL STUDENTS' OFFICER**
○ **UNIVERSITY COUNSELLORS** 4 FULL
○ **CRIME RATING:** !!
NSA, University counsellors and chaplains are available to help with any welfare problems. Counselling service for international and minority ethnic women students.
HEALTH Students are encouraged to register with a local practice when they arrive. The Health & Life Science campus has sessions on aromatherapy, reflexology, alternative medicine and herbal clinics.
DISABILITIES *Although some buildings were built before disabilities were invented, the University keeps an eye on potential access problems and does a bit to overcome them.* Six rooms have been adapted and there are ramps, loops and the Adaptive Technology Centre, which provides specialist equipment, training, software and advice. There's a special needs co-ordinator and a dyslexia support advisor.

FINANCE
○ **AVE DEBT PER YEAR** £2,032 ○ **HOME STUDENT FEES** £1,700
○ **ACCESS FUND** £600,000
○ **SUCCESSFUL APPLICATIONS/YR:** 2,000
○ **AVE PAYMENT** £100-1,200
SUPPORT Scottish students can also apply for the young students' bursary (a grant of £2,100/yr for under-25s from low-income families). Also: a mature students' bursary (means-tested, up to £2,000/yr), hardship loans (up to £500/year) and a childcare fund, which grants up to £200 per child per month towards registered childcare costs.

NAPIER POLYTECHNIC
see *Napier University*

NENE UNIVERSITY COLLEGE
see *Northampton University*

NEWCASTLE UNIVERSITY

○ **UNIVERSITY OF NEWCASTLE UPON TYNE** 6 Kensington Terrace, Newcastle upon Tyne, NE1 7RU **TEL** (0191) 222 5594
E-MAIL enquiries@ncl.ac.uk **WEBSITE** www.ncl.ac.uk ○ **THE UNION SOCIETY** King's Walk, Newcastle upon Tyne, NE1 8QB
TEL (0191) 239 3900 **E-MAIL** union.society@ncl.ac.uk **WEBSITE** www.unionsociety.co.uk

GENERAL ○○○○○○○○○○○○○

No, the Angel of the North isn't Alan Shearer. It's the giant, rusty winged sculpture that gazes over the A1 as it hurtles towards Newcastle upon Tyne, the unofficial capital of the North East and, *as far as many Geordies are concerned, the world*. It's the biggest city on offer between Leeds and Edinburgh and *like most cities (and indeed most coins), it has two sides: fond memories of Sting & The Police on one, ambivalent feelings toward Ant & Dec on the other. It's magnificent, cosmopolitan and happening but, like any city this beefy, it has its poverty-stricken, shabbier areas too*. Its outer areas include the *run-down, like Byker* (of 'Bykah Groahve' fame) and the *luscious and leafy, like Jesmond, known for its nightlife*. The heart of the city is peppered with inspiring Georgian and Victorian architecture amid *nauseating 60s* shopping centres. There are two universities in town: Northumbria University and the University of Newcastle upon Tyne, a classic redbrick campus *just entering its golden years*, with dosh to splosh on new facilities and a rampant desire to expand. The buildings are mostly 19th-century, formed into *attractive* blocks arranged around paved squares, but there are also some drab concrete additions that, *while not quite turning the stomach, certainly give it a bit of a jolt*. The University's keen to cash in on Newcastle's official 'Science City' status, so there are heaps of sci-fi sounding developments currently pushing the boundaries.

🚶🚶🚶🚶🚶🚶🚶🚶🚶🚶🚶🚶🚶🚶🚶🚶🚶🚶🚶🚶🚶🚶🚶

SEX RATIO: ♂49 ♀51	**FOUNDED:** 1834
FULL-TIME U'GRADS: 13,158	**PART-TIME:** 109
POSTGRADS: 4,014	**NON-DEGREE:** N/A
AVE COURSE: 3YRS	**ETHNIC:** 6%
STATE:PRIVATE SCHOOL: 67:33	**FLUNK RATE:** 7%
MATURE: 13%	**INTERNATIONAL:** 15%
DISABLED: 365	**LOCAL:** 15%

ATMOSPHERE

The campus, slap in the city centre, is buzzing and friendly but prone to cliqueiness. Despite the city's rough diamond image, the student body is predominantly middle-class, leading to a bit of a 'posh rich kid' label, especially as far as students at Northumbria University *are concerned, and a traditional rivalry with other posh rich kid* University of Durham *nearby. Mixing between universities and, in turn, with locals isn't uncommon though – partly due to the large number of community action schemes operating from the Union – but the weekend is still largely ruled by locals when it* comes to nightlife. The cost of living is quite low, so students can almost afford to enjoy Newcastle like real people do.

NEWCASTLE UPON TYNE

○ **POPULATION** 259,600 ○ **CITY CENTRE** 0 MILES
○ **LONDON** 255 MILES ○ **EDINBURGH** 94 MILES
○ **MANCHESTER** 112 MILES
○ **HIGH TEMP** 19 ○ **LOW TEMP** 0 ○ **RAINFALL** 54

Newcastle's spirits are far from being moistened by the city's failure to scoop the title 'City of Culture 2008' – not that it means much anyway – and are continuing their thriving cultural renaissance regardless. It's appeared on more than one 'world's best party city' top tens and *its reputation for a kicking nightlife is growing fast*. The past few years of development – bringing with them the *great* glass armadillo that is The Sage musical centre, the iconic Millennium Bridge, a *growing* theatre scene, the *Tate-rivalling* Baltic art gallery and the Dancehouse – *have helped drag the city from the shadows of the black and white stripes.*

The fog on the Tyne no longer belongs to Paul Gascoigne, thank God. It's now trendy, funky, artistic, musical and all the other nice things people usually say when being nice about London. And those who believe that the only way to judge a city is by the strength of its gay scene should stroll across Times Square in the heart of the Centre for Life. This city may be packing the pink, but not everything is rosy. Crime and unemployment still feature on the urban landscape, although they no longer dominate and even in the dodgiest areas the atmosphere is much less Irvine Welsh than it used to be. The Metro Centre at nearby Gateshead is still *pretty humungous, if no longer* Europe's largest shopping centre.

TRAVEL

TRAINS Central Station's about ten mins walk from the city centre campus, two mins by Metro. Direct lines to London (from £60.35 return), Sheffield (£31.90), Edinburgh (£26.55) and all over the country. London (King's Cross) is three and a bit hours away, Edinburgh's a *mere* hour & 20 mins.
COACHES Several coach companies, including Clipper, Blue Line and National Express, offer services to the above destinations and many more. The coach station's ten mins from campus and also accessible by metro.
CAR The A1 hooks round the edge of the city. The A69, A692, A696, A189 and A19 are all useful. There's on-street meter parking around campus. The Union doles out 50 full-time parking permits, and another 25 for out-of-hours (4pm-midnight), £390/yr for either, but spaces tend to be snapped-

N

up by staff in the early morning. There's no shortage of paid parking facilities across the city.
AIR Newcastle Airport, seven miles from the centre, has inland and European flights.
FERRY: North Shields International Ferry Terminal is seven miles away, with daily routes to Norway and Sweden.
HITCHING *Good prospects on routes out of the city, especially the A1.*
LOCAL Bus routes through the city are regular, *reliable and cheap, although travelling the compact city centre can be more of a lurch than a breeze. Walking is the easiest way to get around.*
TAXI *Expect to pay city prices.* The 10-15 min walk between Central Station and campus can be done with feet up for around £6. £15 to the airport, £12 to the ferry terminal.
UNIVERSITY A minibus (priority for women) takes students home from the library, school and Union building, 50p donation, Mon-Fri from 7pm until the Union closes. There's also a public transport discount scheme available to students.
UNDERGROUND *The world's best underground system may be Tokyo's, but Newcastle's Metro is right up there – clean, cheap, reliable and easy to use.* It serves *all the essential* student areas and has now been extended to Sunderland (£4 rtn).
BICYCLES *The city's hilly and trafficky, but that doesn't deter students getting between the University and Heaton, Jesmond and Fenham. Cycle lanes are good, but there aren't many places to leave bikes off-campus without the danger of finding it smaller and with fewer wheels than when you left it. Things are steadily improving though, and there's plenty of parking on campus.*

CAREER PROSPECTS

⊙ CAREERS SERVICE ⊙ NO. OF STAFF 23 FULL/ 3 PART
⊙ UNEMPLOYED AFTER 6 MTHS 4%
Newcastle attracts some *fairly big* employers to *sift through its graduate output.* The careers service has an online database, bulletin boards, newsletters, job fairs, psychometric training, CV clinic and e-mails round vacancies.

FAMOUS ALUMNI

Kate Adie (BBC flak-jacketed *überbabe*); Rowan Atkinson (comedian, who reportedly spent three years in his room); Ed Coode (Olympic rower); Bryan Ferry (Roxy Music); Richard Hamilton (artist); Debbie Horsfield (TV writer); Miriam Stoppard (TV doctor); Paul Tucker (Lighthouse Family).

SPECIAL FEATURES

The Enterprise Centre puts entrepreneurial students in touch with mentoring companies, who help them set up their own business and also provide the odd lecture, seminar or workshop.
The University has *ambitious* blueprints for a 'cultural quarter' – a £40m project with a museum, art gallery and playhouse.
World-renowned architect Sir Terry Farrell has planned the redesign of the University's main entrance.

FURTHER INFO

⊙ PROSPECTUSES UNDERGRAD; POSTGRAD; INTERNATIONAL; DEPARTMENTAL; ALTERNATIVE; VIDEO
⊙ OPEN DAYS
Personalised prospectus can be downloaded from the web. Printed copies can also be ordered from the main e-mail address. Two Visit Days a year and subject area open days after application. Two open days a year: E-mail visit.day@ncl.ac.uk, phone them on (0191) 222 8675 or click on to the website.

ACADEMIC ⊙⊙⊙⊙⊙⊙⊙⊙⊙⊙⊙⊙⊙

⊙ RUSSELL GROUP
Newcastle acquits itself admirably in the majority of its 200+ degree programmes, although things go particularly swimmingly in English, Maths and Sciences. Employability is the buzzword, and practical teaching extends to facilities like practice courtrooms and the Enterprise Centre. Medicine and Dentistry are *for the long haul*, at five years apiece. Students need around 120 credits/yr to progress.

ENTRY POINTS: 260-360	**AVE POINTS: 200**
APPLICATIONS PER PLACE: 6	**CLEARING: 11%**
NO. OF TERMS: 2	**LENGTH OF TERMS: 15WKS**
STAFF TO STUDENT RATIO: 1:14	**STUDY ADDICTS: 16%**
TEACHING: ★★★	**RESEARCH: ★★★**
YEAR ABROAD: 2%	**SANDWICH STUDENTS: 25%**
1STS AND 2.1S: 69%	**2.2S AND 3RDS: 31%**

ADMISSIONS

⊙ APPLY VIA UCAS/GTTR FOR TEACHING
Applications for Medicine or Dentistry should be sent off early, usually by the preceding October. Mature students without recognised qualifications are assessed on an individual basis.

SUBJECTS

ARTS, HUMANITIES & SOCIAL SCIENCES 46%
MEDICAL SCIENCE 22%   **SCIENCE & ENGINEERING** 32%
BEST Agriculture; Biology; Computer Science; English; European Languages; History & Archaeology; Law; Mathematical Sciences; Medicine & Dentistry; Medical Sciences & Pharmacy; Other Medical Sciences; Performing Arts; Philosophy; Physical Geography & Environmental Sciences; Physical Sciences; Politics.
UNUSUAL Geomatics; Folk & Traditional Music; Marine Environmental Engineering.

LIBRARIES

⊙ 1,000,000+ BOOKS ⊙ 2,000 STUDY PLACES
⊙ SPEND PER STUDENT ££££
The *comfy, well-stocked* Robinson Library has a Relative Humidity of around 50%, *which may be part of the reason* Newcastle's library services have four charter marks for excellence. *Who knows?* Anyhow, it's the only UK university library that does. There's also the Walton Library

and the Law library. *We can't tell you the humidity there. Sorry.* All have *brief* windows of opening during weekends, but the Law Library shuts up shop completely on a Sunday.

COMPUTERS
⊙ **1,445** WORKSTATIONS ⊙ **24-HOUR ACCESS**
⊙ **SPEND PER STUDENT** £££££
45 computer clusters around the University, not all 24-hr. 200 of them live in the library. Some halls have IT clusters too, and they're working on hooking 90% of student rooms up to the net by the end of 2006. A wireless network is on the technocards and laptops have started appearing on the grass.

OTHER LEARNING FACILITIES
Aside from the 55 – yes, 55 – language labs (40 languages available for anyone and their dog to learn), rehearsal rooms, photo studio and darkroom, TV centre, art gallery and drama studio, Newcastle has several subject-specific facilities, including a marine laboratory, a biology field station, its own farms and 'Bernicia', a research boat on the Tyne. Most recently landed are the £11m cancer research centre and an eco-licious £19m environment & e-science institute. There's also a lab for computer science students known as the Virtual Cave, which offers the *full Lawnmower Man experience.* Geography students get a soil-inspecting lab. *Whoop de do.*

ENTERTAINMENT ⊙⊙⊙⊙⊙⊙⊙⊙⊙

NEWCASTLE
⊙ **PRICE OF A PINT OF BEER** £2
⊙ **GLASS OF WINE** £2
⊙ **CAN OF RED BULL** £1.90
Newcastle is as stuff-stuffed a city as the next and rivals Leeds, Manchester and almost London when it comes to music, clubs, pubs and restaurants. Any bar worth its salt will have a free listings mag or six on the counter. Those on a low-sodium diet might be interested in the many free perks around: the Millennium Bridge, the Laing Art Gallery and a couple of nature reserves. Castle Keep (local history) and the Life Sciences Centre for those who don't get enough learning during the day, do discounted student entry. Multicultural festivals light-up the streets every now and then.
CINEMAS There's a ten-screener in the Gate Complex (NUS discounts), five mins from the city centre, the excellent Tyneside Arts Cinema (four screens) and the *diddy wee* Side Cinema on the Quayside – *all within walking distance of the University.* There's also a multiplex at the Metro Centre, *though this isn't used much by students as it's further out.*
THEATRES Newcastle has plenty of theatres ranging from *great stages to smaller poncing-boards.* Pushplugs: The Theatre Royal *(touring RSC and West End shows)*; The Playhouse *(RSC seasons, local prods)*; and The Live Theatre, *which*

has been pumped full of cash to produce innovative new writing. The People's Theatre is home to am-dram while the Journal Tyne Theatre is mainly for musical events and panto.
PUBS Many, many pubs, some *rougher than students might like,* but plenty serve a welcome brew, not least a pint of the ubiquitous Newcastle Brown (aka 'Newky Brown' or 'Dog'). *The Hancock opposite campus gets points for convenience but medics prefer their traditional haunt, North Terrace. Diverse and atmospheric, Trent House is the coolest pub in Newcastle – it's official. Revolution's range of flavoured vodkas is a big draw, and the Cluny in Byker provides live music and a welcoming atmosphere. Bar 55 and the Attic are the places to go to feel important after lottery wins. Quayside has plenty of sexy quaff-houses. Bar Ha Ha and Goose are highlights while Jazz is popular for jazz, funnily enough.*
CLUBBING *A huge part of Geordie life and there's always some kind of boogy to be found within stumbling distance of campus.* Pushplugs *(among others)*: Tiger Tiger; Foundation; Blue Bambu; Mood; World HQ; Sea; Baja Beach Club; Digital *has three floors of mostly R'n'B. Sports club members get discounts at Attic.*
MUSIC VENUES *The Metro Radio Arena has big names on its posters, but spoils it with the X Factor Tours. The Cluny gets a few cult heroes.* The new Carling Academy's *trying to get one over though with big sounds from the likes of the Coral and Athlete.* The Norman Foster-designed Sage Gateshead Music Centre on the South Bank houses the Northern Sinfonia and the Folkworks programme (involved with the University's BA Folk & Traditional Music course). *For a mixed playlist of blues, Irish and open mic, local pubs like the Cumberland Arms are worth a peek. Sneaking into Northumbria University's Union isn't unheard of, either.*
EATING OUT *Newcastle's got everything from classy bistros to bacterial blubber in a bun. Somewhere in between,* Pushplugs: Rumpolis; Marco Polo's & Don Vito's *(Italian)*; Cradlewell *(all-day breakfasts)*; King Lau *(Chinese)*; Est, Est, Est *(Italian). The Playhouse and the Tyneside Coffee Rooms are the places to pose and Stowell Street (in Newcastle's own mini-Chinatown) is the place to go for Chinese food.*
OTHER Comedy is common in various bars and pubs. *Try the Hyena Café for starters.*

UNIVERSITY
⊙ **PRICE OF A PINT OF BEER** £1.70
⊙ **GLASS OF WINE** £2.25
⊙ **CAN OF RED BULL** £1.50
BARS The Union Building houses six bars, all open six days a week. The Mens Bar is not for men only, but named after the University motto, 'Mens agitat molem' *('subterranean rodents create havoc in the gents'). However, it does retain a pretty laddish, sporty atmosphere.* The Cochrane Lounge is *quieter, comfy* and smoke-free. The Global has a continental café style and doubles as a small

N

Words in italics are Push's point of view — take it or leave it...

gig venue. The Green Room, Beats and the Bassment are mainly for weekend clubs and gigs. *They're all dark.*

THEATRES The drama group, NUTS, is highly active, putting on around two plays a semester, and is frequently to be found at the Edinburgh Fringe or in the campus Playhouse theatre.

FILM The film society (£4 membership) shows two weekly flicks, *generally recent arthouse hits (if that's not an oxymoron), but with so many mainstream cinemas in town offering a glimpse of Will Smith's bottom, loyalties are torn. The film production society is more into making films than watching them.*

MUSIC VENUES The Global and the Bassment have brought in some *huge hitsters*: the Darkness, Keane, Damien Rice, the Zutons and Snow Patrol have all paid a visit. Friday nights in both venues showcase chart, indie, techno and jazz (Bassment) and hip hop, R'n'B and local bands (the smaller Global).

CLUBBING The Bassment's big enough to bring in the big guns, including Groove Armada, Groove Rider and DJ Yoda. Friday's Solution is *the cream of Union club nights.* Top national nights also get monthly outings, including: Brighton Beach (indie, non-cheesy retro, £5); Turbulence (drum'n'bass, £10); and Universal (*straight-friendly* monthly gay night, £3). There's nothing mid-week, though.

COMEDY/CABARET The Global has fortnightly comedy on a Monday. Highlights have been Perrier-darling Daniel Kitson, Andre Vincent and Eddie Brimson.

FOOD The Chilli OU and Hot Stuff do, *um*, hot stuff as well as salads and sandwiches. The Martin Luther King is *small, bright,* smokeless and veggie. The Global does international café fare, with exotic hot paninis gracing its menu. The Cochrane Lounge boasts the cheapest coffee going alongside its *pubby* menu. Campus Coffee *pulls no surprises* and is open 8-8 Mon-Sat.

OTHER At least four balls a year plus a five-day Freshers' binge and a Christmas Ball for each department. The Cochrane Lounge's regular quiz night gets *busy*. Arcane, the termly charity extravaganza, burns the midnight oil well beyond midnight.

SOCIAL ◑◑◑◑◑◑◑◑◑◑◑◑◑◑

THE UNION SOCIETY

◉ **6 SABBATICALS** ◉ **TURNOUT AT LAST BALLOT** 20%
◉ **NUS MEMBER**

Newcastle's SU is as active and frantic as its bar staff on a Friday night. The colossal Union building is buzzing with entertainments and facilities and the ever-growing society lists offer something for everyone, no matter how twisted a fun fetish they may have. Relations with the University are good, but that doesn't matter one jot really since the SU is completely independent in every way and stands firmly on its own two feet, jumping up and down on its substantial piles

of cash. Members sit on many a University committee, and have persuaded them to embrace Fair Trade, which is the hot potato at the moment.

SU FACILITIES

An entire floor of the Union building's devoted to franchise outlets, including bookshops and a ticket agency. In addition: shop; post office; hairdresser; six bars; café bar; eight pool tables; four meeting rooms; minibus hire; van hire; Endsleigh Insurance office; ATMs; photocopiers; fax & printing services; photo booth; payphones; advice centre; TV lounge; juke boxes; gaming & vending machines; dry cleaning.

CLUBS (NON-SPORTING)

Acoustic Music; Agent (Anglo German); Breakfast Club (break dancing); Change Ringers (bell ringing); Cheerleading; Chess; Chinese students; Chinese students and scholars; Fell walking; Fine Art; Gilbert and Sullivan; ICCHS Gallery and Culture Club; Indonesian; Iranian; Latin and Ballroom; Libyan; Link society (St John's Ambulance); Malaysian; Mauritian; Music; Newcastle Racing & Motor Sport; Norwegian; NUTS (Theatre); Omani; Planning; Politics; Questland (role play); Saudi; Singapore; Shorts (film); South Asian; STAR (Student Action for Refugees); Stop Aids; Swing Dance; Syrian; Thai; Wind band. **See also Clubs tables.**

OTHER ORGANISATIONS

The weekly paper, 'the Courier', has the free 'Pulp' entertainment and listings magazine tucked into it. Newcastle Student Radio's run jointly with Northumbria University and echoes around the city on FM twice a year for a month at a time. The charity Rag *regularly endangers lives for cash*, netting £17,000 in 2005 (double what they raised the year before) but SCAN (Student Community Action Newcastle) has around 5,000 members, its own fundraising shop and about 90 do-gooding projects on the go, some of which qualify for the Millennium Volunteers Award, and others which even count as course credits. Additionally, there's the university 'Students into Schools' programme, *where student tutors help local schoolkids become as clever as them.*

RELIGIOUS

◉ **5 CHAPLAINS (COFE, RC, BAPTIST, METHODIST, URC);
2 RABBIS**

The chaplaincy maintains links with various Christian churches in the city, as well as appointing visiting Orthodox and Reform Jewish, Muslim and Buddhist worship-leaders. The building has a common room, quiet room and a kitchen. There's a mosque on campus. Most faiths will find a *godshop* in Newcastle. If not, the Tyne & Wear conurbation will have something.

PAID WORK

◉ **JOB BUREAU** ◉ **PAID WORK** TERM-TIME 52%; HOLS 75%

The Union runs a jobshop which also monitors conditions and pay. It has links with 500 employers and posts around over 1,000 vacation and term-time vacancies. Registering students receive an induction on job-related issues. The Union has two recruitment fairs a year, with opportunities to stock the coffers in local bars, shops, the theatres and *no end of soul-destroying* work at the Metro Centre.

SPORTS ❍❍❍❍❍❍❍❍❍❍❍❍❍❍

❍ **RECENT SUCCESSES** SKIING, SNOWBOARDING, BADMINTON, FENCING, GOLF, VOLLEYBALL, RUGBY
❍ **BUSA RANKING** 19

Fittingly for such a sporting city, Newcastle's also pretty stoked up about sport. They're no stranger to the BUSA league tables and the Athletics Union (which has its own sabbatical officer) pumps hundreds of thousands into University sport each year. There's also a selection of sporting bursaries to encourage the future greats. *The downside is that, while the ethos is supposedly 'sports for all', there can be a bit of an elitist streak in the more popular sports which discourages wide participation. A £5.5m indoor sports and dance facility is now up and running /sweating, and is part of the cunning plan to* make Newcastle one of the country's best universities for sports, but *pocket-sorry* prices (£150/yr all-in) *lend more appeal to a culinary threesome with both Ben and Jerry.*

SPORTS FACILITIES
On campus, there are facilities in the Claremont Sports Hall (sports hall, four squash courts). There are outdoor amenities on five sites: Heaton (medics' playing fields); Close House (ten miles out, 18-hole golf course, hockey pitches); Cochrane Park (playing fields); Longbenton (more playing fields); and Newburn Boat House on the Tyne for rowers. Also 18 football, one hockey, one all-weather, six rugby and two cricket pitches, 11 tennis and eight netball courts, aerobics studio, four squash and two basketball courts, multi-gym, lacrosse pitch. There are 50 acres of playing fields in total, *covering everything it's possible to do on grass except croquet.* The city has many other leisure facilities, including an ice rink, dry ski slope and a lake, plus student discounts at Close House Golf Club ten miles west of Newcastle. The Northumbrian countryside has enough caves and hills to keep outdoor-types exhausted.

SPORTING CLUBS
Aikido; American Football; Athletics and Cross Country; Boat; Canoe Polo; Caving; Freestyle Karate and Kickboxing; Hapkido; Ice Hockey; Jitsu; Lacrosse; Lifesaving; Mountain Bike; Mountaineering; Parachute; Rifle; Yachting; Snowboarding; Surf; Water Polo; Table Tennis; Thai Boxing; Ultimate Frisbee; Windsurf. **See also Clubs tables.**

ATTRACTIONS
Newcastle United's Toon Army of fans aren't the most self-effacing in the country and chances are even the most unsporty will recognise the stripy soldiers. The Falcons Rugby Club were much more low-profile – until people became aware that HRH Jonny Wilkinson, lord of the drop-kick, plays for them. The Newcastle Eagles basketball squad and the Vipers ice hockey team have dedicated followers too. Rugby League and Horse-Racing's knocking about, with sadists plumping for surfing off freezing Tynemouth beach (not that the weather deterred the National Championships, mind). The regions pouring a whole load more cash down the sporting gullet, so expect a slew of major sporting events over the coming decade.

ACCOMMODATION ❍❍❍❍❍❍❍❍❍

IN UNIVERSITY
❍ **CATERED** 11% ❍ **COST** £82 (38WKS)
❍ **SELF-CATERING** 19% ❍ **COST** £71 (38WKS)
❍ **1ST YRS LIVING IN** 73% ❍ **INSURANCE PREMIUM** ££
AVAILABILITY Housing's guaranteed to all first years who meet the various criteria, but sharing may be a necessity early-on. Limited space for other years, but it's self-catering all the way. 1,500 catered rooms, the majority at the traditional Castle Leazes. Henderson Hall does some en suite – though it's three miles away and pretty quiet with it, plus *some have described the food as 'minging'. Not Push, natch.* Catered halls come with a small kitchen, common room, laundrettes, computer clusters, TV, games & music rooms. There are another 2,000 self-catered halls littering the city, mostly a 15-min walk away, with shared flats at Bowsden Court. St Mary's is way out in Fenham (30-min walk away), *which is a bit of a bummer if your flatmates turn out to be knobheads.* All students get regular visits from *a cleaning hit squad, but only for the communal areas, not for personal pants squalor.* Night porters, entry phones and security patrolling *are all appreciated.* Some couples and families can be housed, and there are some mixed/single sites. Students at Freeman's Hall pay less – *not out of University generosity* – but because they're *turfed out* during vacations.
CAR PARKING Limited and, at £195/yr, it's *all but cheaper to get clamped.*

EXTERNALLY
❍ **AVE RENT** £62 ❍ **LIVING AT HOME** 22%
AVAILABILITY *Tricky and expensive in the city centre, but there's not much problem elsewhere. Plenty of rip-off merchants are all too happy to take advantage of virgin house-hunters. Stick to accredited channels. Jesmond has the advantage of proximity to bars, the Metro and fun, but its prices are inflating faster than Jordan's boobs. Heaton's cheaper but doesn't have much going on*

except for takeaway fans. *Gosforth's slightly further out but inoffensive, if a little staid. Sandyford's small, but somewhere between the two when it comes to balancing the rent/nightlife ratio. Fenham isn't too bad, though its houses aren't as safe as the proverb says and Benwell and Scotswood shimmer in the twilight with the light from burning cars, so students try to keep clear. Parking's restricted around the city centre and many find it too much effort keeping a car.*

HOUSING HELP The University Accommodation Service lists approved houses and flats, runs a landlord accreditation scheme and provides help, advice and contract guidance.

WELFARE

❤ 👎

SERVICES

- LGBT OFFICER & SOCIETY
- ETHNIC MINORITIES OFFICER & SOCIETY
- MATURE STUDENTS' OFFICER & SOCIETY
- INTERNATIONAL STUDENTS' OFFICER & SOCIETY
- POSTGRAD OFFICER & SOCIETY
- DISABILITIES OFFICER & SOCIETY
- LATE-NIGHT/WOMEN'S MINIBUS ● NIGHTLINE
- SELF-DEFENCE CLASSES
- UNIVERSITY COUNSELLORS 1 FULL/5 PART
- CRIME RATING !!!

The Union has two welfare sabbaticals and *numerous* officers with specific responsibilities. All advice comes from trained personnel.

HEALTH On campus the NHS practice has 17 GPs, 12 nurses, four dentists and an optician. Medical and dental practices abound throughout Newcastle, in particular in student suburbs like Jesmond and Heaton.

CHILDCARE No nursery. Equipment (ie. harnesses, car seats) can be loaned from the university.

WOMEN: Free alarms, condoms and sanitary products.

DISABILITIES Many Victorian buildings limit access, but there have been a number of useful adaptations, especially in the Union Building, which is now accessible on every level. Wheelchair-friendly routes have been designated, but they generally involve going the long way round. Adapted housing's available for mobility- and hearing-impaired students. The University's disabilities unit has a trained dyslexia advisor who provides study skills support. Loop system in some lecture theatres; hardware loans scheme.

FINANCE

- AVE DEBT PER YEAR £3,144 ● HOME STUDENT FEES £3,000

FEES International (including EU) students pay between £8,500 (classroom-based) and an *eye-watering* 20 grand for lab or fieldwork-based courses. UK p/t undergrads pay £100 for 10 credits, with a maximum of 60 credits a year.

- ACCESS FUND £598,166

SUPPORT Around £500,000 available through 200 scholarships, plus £1,000 for 29 best A-Level results (if Newcastle's first choice). Also financial rewards for best-performing students in each year. The South African Scholarship provides funds for a South African student to study at Newcastle. The Abbeydale mathematicians and sportsmen & women; the Charles Letts Memorial for Marine Science and Technology.

NEWPORT, UNIVERSITY OF WALES

FORMERLY UNIVERSITY OF WALES COLLEGE, NEWPORT; PART OF THE UNIVERSITY OF WALES

● **UNIVERSITY OF WALES** Newport, Caerleon Campus, PO Box 101, Newport, NP18 3YG **TEL** (01633) 432 432
E-MAIL uic@newport.ac.uk **WEBSITE** www.newport.ac.uk ● **STUDENTS' UNION, CAERLEON CAMPUS** College Crescent, Caerleon, NP18 3YG **TEL** (01633) 432 076 **E-MAIL** students.union@newport.ac.uk **WEBSITE** www.newportunion.com

GENERAL

In the south-east of Wales, a *hop and skip* from Cardiff, is the *industrial* city of Newport, home to the University's two sites. The main site's near the pre-Roman village of Caerleon, which many historians and mythologists believe to have been the site of Camelot *(where King Arthur kept his Round Table before IKEA even thought of selling them)*. Nowadays, it's more notable for the University, which began its life as a Mechanics Institute, became a University College in 1996 and finally succeeded in its quest for the grail of full University status in 2003. The main building's dominated by an *impressive* clock tower and fronted by lawns where students play football when the sun shines – *much to the annoyance of the Vice-Chancellor, whose windows overlook them. Campus is a quiet, attractive place in the summer, filled with barbecuing and picnicking in the halls' courtyard and sunbathers on the grass.*

> ● **One of Newcastle University's halls of residence is on the site of a former morgue.**

Words in italics are Push's point of view – take it or leave it...

SEX RATIO: ♂47 ♀53	FOUNDED: 1841
FULL-TIME U'GRADS: 2,941	PART-TIME: 6,123
POSTGRADS: 365	NON-DEGREE: N/A
AVE COURSE: 3YRS	ETHNIC: 2%
STATE:PRIVATE SCHOOL: 99:1	FLUNK RATE: 23%
MATURE: 60%	INTERNATIONAL: 5%
DISABLED: 145	LOCAL: 45%

ATMOSPHERE

Caerleon campus is intimate and friendly, and feels more a like a college than a full-blown university – in part due to lots of local students who go home at the end of the day. It's home to the Art, Media & Design School, so there are lots of funky students wandering around (that's funky as in looks, not smell). The atmosphere is relaxed and laid-back, with students preferring to party hard than hit the books, but they know how to knuckle-down when it counts. Bands (idolising them and being in them) are the bee's knees in this part of the world, so everything comes with a side order of music appreciation. Doings with the locals are hunky-dory, with lots of community support for students. The Allt-yr-Yn campus is (for now) set in an posh area a mile and a half from Newport. There's less local interaction in that neck of the woods, and students are more likely to commute from other 'burbs, or from halls on the Caerleon campus. The whole circus is up and moving to Newport City Centre in the next couple of years. The University is the biggest recruiter of state school students in Britain, which is an interesting pub quiz fact. Or not. As well as being a working class bastion, there's a down-to-earth pragmatism – most students are here ultimately to get a good job, or improve the one they've already got.

OTHER SITES

ALLT-YR-YN CAMPUS (830 students – Business & Management, Computing & Engineering, Social Studies & Art Foundation) The smaller campus is ten mins walk from the city centre in one of Newport's affluent, leafy suburbs and much better placed for travel links and city nightlife. It houses specialist learning facilities for computing and engineering; two refectories; an art supply shop; LRC; Student Services office; careers service and the Enterprise Research Centre – Newport university's commercial arm.

NEWPORT

⊙ **POPULATION** 145,000 ⊙ **CITY CENTRE** 4 MILES
⊙ **LONDON** 140 MILES ⊙ **CARDIFF** 17 MILES
⊙ **HIGH TEMP** 21 ⊙ **LOW TEMP** 2 ⊙ **RAINFALL** 87
Many people could be forgiven for thinking that Newport is an industrial wasteland with occasional bouts of remission. It's certainly not a pretty place, but despite losing core industries in past decades, re-investment and redevelopment is smoothing over the cracks and making the city less depressing to look at. The current bout of regeneration should get the city geared up with everything a growing girl needs: cinema, bars and restaurants, and generally for fewer pence than in many other parts of the UK. The centre is compact and navigable with a Norman castle floundering on the banks of the Usk. High street and trendy label shops sit amongst ex-catalogue discount stores, and the enormous Transporter Bridge dominates the skyline. Postcards for parents tend to come from Caerleon village, which is pretty, quaint and unspoilt – which makes it sound more like a model village than a real place – and sports a fine example of a Roman amphitheatre, if that's your bag. The Spar's the only supermarket in the village, but a trip to Newport lays the world of cut-price own-brands at the starving student's feet. Newport's notable neighbouring attractions include the Big Pit mining museum, the Brecon Beacons and Cardiff.

TRAVEL

TRAINS Newport station is on the Cardiff–Birmingham line and is directly linked to London. Cardiff (from £5 return, 20 mins); London (£27.70); Manchester (£30.65).
COACHES The station's right in the city centre and has local and National Express services, including coaches to Gatwick and Heathrow. Direct services to London (£26) and Birmingham (£18.40), amongst others. Megabus services can be picked up in Cardiff, see University of Cardiff.
CAR The M4's handiest.
AIR Cardiff International Airport is 30 miles away and has cheap flights (RyanAir and BMIBaby).
HITCHING A bad idea from the city centre. The M4 offers glimmers of hope.
LOCAL Regular and cheap. Buses 2 and 7 wind their way up to Caerleon from stand 25 at the bus station, 95p (sgl) until 11pm.
UNIVERSITY An hourly shuttle bus between the Caerleon Campus and Allt-yr-Yn campus 20 mins away (9am-6pm).
TAXIS £5–6 from Newport centre to Caerleon Campus – handy after a night out; sharing brings costs down.
BICYCLES A hilly area and narrow roads, so cycling can be tiring and dangerous. Cycle bays and areas to lock bikes are provided on campus.

CAREER PROSPECTS

⊙ **CAREERS SERVICE** ⊙ **NO. OF STAFF** 4 FULL/ 3 PART
⊙ **UNEMPLOYED AFTER 6 MTHS** 7%
Part of the admirable Student Services department, with support available even after graduation: vacancy updates; newsletters; interview practice; job fairs; career counselling; workshops; placements and employer links.

FAMOUS ALUMNI

Asif Kapadia (film director with a BAFTA or two); Justin Kerrigan (writer and director of cult clubber movie Human Traffic); Terry Matthews (industrialist and Wales's richest man); Ian Watkins (Lost Prophet).

N

FURTHER INFO

❂ PROSPECTUSES UNDERGRAD; POSTGRAD; PART-TIME
❂ OPEN DAYS

International students should contact the International Office (international@newport.ac.uk) for admissions enquiries.

ACADEMIC ❶❶❶❶❶❶❶❶❶❶❶❶❶

The four schools have a range of highly innovative course options, many vocational. The highly-subscribed Newport School of Art, Media & Design has *proved its mettle* on many occasions, particularly when it comes to animation, photography, film and graphics. Its high academic and research rep *tends to overshadow other departments a bit, which puts a few noses out of joint.* The University *still intends to treat its little darling, though* – it's to move to a new, £60m development at Newport River Bank next year.

Newport Business School's *pretty hot* too and the University's been voted best in Wales for Entrepreneurship Action – but then, it did produce the country's *most minted* industrialist, so *not really a surprise.* The International Film School of Wales, which is based at Newport, is one of Britain's two *top-flight* film schools. Social Sciences, Computing and Teaching Training are also on offer. Teaching's a mix of seminars and lectures. Assessment is by exam and coursework – extensions are hard won and late work is heavily penalised. *You have been warned.*

ENTRY POINTS: 200–300	AVE POINTS: 230
APPLICATIONS PER PLACE: 3	CLEARING: 20%
NO. OF TERMS: 3	LENGTH OF TERMS: 12WKS
STAFF TO STUDENT RATIO: 1:10	STUDY ADDICTS: 6%
TEACHING: **	RESEARCH: ***
YEAR ABROAD: N/A	SANDWICH STUDENTS: 0%
1STS: 7%	2.2S: 38%
2.1S: 46%	3RDS: 13%

ADMISSIONS

❂ APPLY VIA UCAS/GTTR FOR TEACHING

SUBJECTS

ARTS, MEDIA & DESIGN 37%   **BUSINESS & MANAGEMENT** 7%
COMPUTING & ENGINEERING 9%   **EDUCATION** 16%
HUMANITIES & SCIENCE 15%   **SOCIAL STUDIES** 11%
BEST Business & Administrative Studies; Education Studies; Engineering & Technology; Historical & Philosophical Studies; Social Studies. Students at the Film School and Photography department regularly win national awards.
UNUSUAL Computer Games Design; Digital Special Effects & Animatronics; Games Development & Artificial Intelligence Photography for Advertising & Fashion.

LIBRARIES

❂ 156,641 BOOKS ❂ 370 STUDY PLACES
Two libraries, one for Business & Computing, t'other for the Humanities and Art & Design. Both open seven days a week. Specialist collections include documentary photography and local teaching practice. Also on offer: self-service photo copying, a limited number of 'puters, inter-library loans and dissertation-binding facilities. The availability of books has *rattled a few cages and the five-volume loan limit prompts the occasional four-letter outburst at the issue desk. A tendency to leave deadlines as long as possible* can end up with everyone fighting over the same five books at the same time. *It's not pretty.*

COMPUTERS

❂ 850 WORKSTATIONS ❂ 24-HOUR ACCESS
Caerleon site's computer rooms hum through the wee hours; Allt-yr-Yn's close at 9pm most evenings. 100 Macs are spread between campuses in addition to the PCs, and video conferencing equipment is available. Labs come with printers, scanners and photocopiers. Internet sockets in all on-campus bedrooms. The University also has its own text-messaging system.

OTHER LEARNING FACILITIES

There are language labs on the Allt-yr-Yn campus (which any student can use for free) and music rehearsal rooms on both. Study Zone is a learning skills initiative that helps with things like revision planning and essay writing. A Distance Learning Centre provides IT support and general assistance for those off-campus.

ENTERTAINMENT ❶❶❶❶❶❶❶❶❶

THE CITY

❂ PRICE OF A PINT OF BEER £2
❂ GLASS OF WINE £2
❂ CAN OF RED BULL £1.80
CINEMAS The new-release City Cinema in Newport has the largest screen in Wales and offers £3 student tickets. The *fancy* retail park UGC has *four million screens (or many, at least) and a complicated concessions arrangement.*
THEATRES The Riverfront Theatre is invaded by touring productions, pantos and youth theatre, as well as the University's drama department (see below). Otherwise, Cardiff offers more boards for the treading.
PUBS The old town of Caerleon has about ten pubs, all of which are student-friendly. *The Drover's Arms, Minstrels and the Olde Bull have the advantage of being closest to campus.* Tennyson is said to have written his Arthurean epics from the window seat of the Hanbury Arms. *Jocks head to Walkabout in Newport. A drinking outing in some of Newport's shabbier areas has a 30% chance of resulting in minor injury or hurt pride.*
CLUBBING *Several ever-changing student nights in the city but Wednesday is 'the big night out'.* The Union has discount deals with Walkabout and Vodka bar – *both good weekday venues. Breeze*

N

and Shout! are good studenty bets too. Club Night and Basement (for moshers) also run the gauntlet until 4am. A bus runs from campus to dancers' paradise Cardiff Creation every Monday (£4).

MUSIC VENUES *The near-legendary TJ's is the premier live music venue, having had the likes of Oasis and the Stone Roses passing out in its dressing rooms.* Newport City Live Arena does some large-scale touring events. There's also foot-tapping to be done at Newport Leisure Centre and The Riverfront Centre.

EATING OUT *Caerleon can be a bit pricey when it comes to wining and dining, but the Priory is just about worth it, the Olde Bull does good pub grub and Curo's is a top Spanish restaurant.* There are takeaways open till 12.30am, but there's always food to be had for those who know where to look.

UNIVERSITY

- ○ **PRICE OF A PINT OF BEER** £1.80
- ○ **GLASS OF WINE** £1.50
- ○ **CAN OF RED BULL** £1.80

A large number of students living out and a good many matures mean the Union has a tricky job of arranging an events schedule to keep everyone happy – some feel campus entertainment's a little lame. Everyone and his wife and their dog head into Newport of a Wednesday evening in any case.

BARS Clarence Bar is the only place *to drown your studies* on campus and is very busy as a result – probably only because it's very small – with plasma screens, sports screenings, pool table, juke box, plenty of quizzes (Tuesdays, good prizes), and live bands (Thursdays). Opens until midnight at the moment, but may get a permanent later licence in 2007.

MUSIC VENUES The Main Hall regularly showcases local talent and – *often enough* – the Lost Prophets. Indie/rock is the big thing. *Just like in Twin Town.*

CLUBBING Occasional clubbing collaborations with Cardiff University on Fridays, or in the Main Hall whenever the mood takes 'em.

FOOD *Apparently there's no feeding students after dark – they turn into gremlins, or something.* In any case, *opening hours are pants*. The refectory at Caerleon ladles out main meals and munchies 9am-2pm Mon-Fri & 10am-3pm at weekends. Clarence Fast Food Outlet isn't as junkie as the name suggests: baguettes and main meals, as well as curry and chilli nights during the week, 10am-8pm Mon-Thurs & 10am-2pm Fri. Allt-yr-Yn's got the Take Five snack bar, with similar hours and supplies. Upper refectory opens lunchtimes for... lunches, *d'uh.*

OTHER Halloween Freak Fest, Snow Ball (Christmas) and Valentines Dance in the Main Hall. *All are massive, but the May Ball is the annual sell-out must-do:* a third of the Union's budget gets blown on this mother every year, and tix still cost from £30.

STUDENTS' UNION

- ○ **4 SABBATICALS** ○ **NUS MEMBER**

Politics is beaten out of the two Union offices with a big stick of neutrality – even though the Socialist Worker Society is the most active on campus. The student body quibbles with the Union's entertainment schedule and level of representation, but is generally too indifferent to get actively involved. They threw in their two cents' worth at the anti top-up rally in London, but generally SU concerns are much closer to home: parking restrictions and keeping Wednesday afternoons free for sport are top of the list. *What they want, they get, though –* the SU overturned the University's attempts to stop students parking at residences by appealing to the council. *For now, they use their powers for only good, not evil.* The sabbs have a drop-in centre, but they generally refer to Student Services who are in a much better position to offer help.

SU FACILITIES

Bar; shop; Main Hall; ATM; payphone.

CLUBS (NON-SPORTING)

Circus Skills; Literate Soup; Socialist Workers; Students Against Anti-Social Behaviour. **See also Clubs tables.**

OTHER ORGANISATIONS

'Report' is the bi-termly magazine. Keep your eyes 'n' ears peeled for the likely prospect of an SU TV/Radio station in the near future. Rag week's *pulled its socks up* and shook buckets to the tune of £1,200 last year. There's a Newport Student Volunteering Group which does work in the local community but is independent of the University/Union. There's lots of work to be had empowering disadvantaged local women.

RELIGIOUS
- ○ **1 CHAPLAIN (METHODIST)**

A prayer room's open to all denominations and Newport has a wide range of places of worship. *Cardiff's is wider still.* Visiting chaplains bring prayer to the people on campus. A prayer room/mosque is currently in the offing.

PAID WORK
- ○ **JOB BUREAU**

Many work part-time both in term and out. The University job bureau is essentially the Careers Service in a different hat. Acorn Recruitment visits the Fresher's Fayre each year to *hunt down fresh temping meat*. Some SU work's to be had – bar, library, shop, IT suites, marketing – and in the local area, mainly in shops, pubs, clubs and call centres.

N

SPORTS

⊙ RECENT SUCCESSES BASKETBALL **⊙ BUSA RANKING** 122
The state-of-the-art sports centre's shared by University and locals – it does beauty treatments, personal training and kiddy parties. Sport is open to all, and there are also some *impressive* victories from dedicated athletes. The University's *keen to attract* the sporty to its hallowed halls and offers six £1,000 scholarships to prospective students of professional standard. In addition, £500 bursaries can be awarded to cover training and competition costs for national- or international-level jocks.

SPORTS FACILITIES
The University use football and all-weather pitches at a local school, and make use of Newport city's athletics field. Facilities at the Sports Centre include: gym/fitness suite; a range of classes; outdoor pitches & courts; floodlit tennis & netball courts; modern fitness suite with resistance and cardiovascular machines. The Velodrome is two miles away for *when the need to cycle round in a great big circle takes hold*, and there are a dry ski slope, swimming pool, lake and other facilities in the immediate area.

SPORTING CLUBS
Extreme Sports; Mountain Sports; Snowboarding. **See also Clubs tables.**

ATTRACTIONS
The Newport Gwent Dragons rugby team play nearby. The Millennium Stadium is 20 mins by train. The Celtic Manor Golf Course – owned by Terry Matthews – will be hosting the 2010 Ryder Cup.

ACCOMMODATION

IN UNIVERSITY
⊙ SELF–CATERING 22% **⊙ COST** £53 (39WKS)
⊙ 1ST YRS LIVING IN 70% **⊙ INSURANCE PREMIUM** £
AVAILABILITY The rise in students wanting accommodation has outstripped what the University can provide – some international students even had to be housed in Cardiff last year. Prices, *presumably to put some people off even asking*, are set to rise over the next few years. First years are guaranteed a place in the self-catered campus halls, which are divided between en suite and 'traditional' accommodation – *the tradition presumably being some ancient toilet-sharing custom*. En suite rooms are arranged in clusters with shared kitchen and lounge. Cleaning materials are also provided, *though whether they're actually used is another matter*. Cleaners muck in to muck out communal areas. Halls are grouped close to the main

campus building, forming a cosy student village but there's an 11pm curfew. A 24-hr reception close to the student village co-ordinates security. Single and mixed-couple accommodation is available in special cases, although the University keeps this fact to itself where possible.
CAR PARKING Not many spaces and the University's *dead against*. The SU's *pooh-poohed* their objections, but the toss is still being argued. Cars parked in the nearby village are open to vandalism if left too long. There's a pay & display on campus and a permit-only car park (£40/yr or £10 if car-sharing).

EXTERNALLY
⊙ AVE RENT £50 **⊙ LIVING AT HOME** 31%
AVAILABILITY Caerleon's not big enough to house everyone so many end up living in Newport itself or the smaller towns surrounding it. With such varying proximity, a car – *or an obliging friend with one* – are almost prerequisites. *Some areas of Newport are not the most habitable. Cwmbran, Cardiff and Caldicott are other locations of choice.*
HOUSING HELP Accommodation Services provide regularly updated housing lists and various leaflets. They will help with looking over contracts, *but they reserve the right to have no responsibility if everything goes tits up.*

WELFARE

SERVICES
⊙ LGBT OFFICER & SOCIETY
⊙ WOMEN'S OFFICER & SOCIETY
⊙ ETHNIC MINORITIES OFFICER
⊙ MATURE STUDENTS' OFFICER & SOCIETY
⊙ POSTGRAD OFFICER ⊙ DISABILITIES OFFICER
⊙ NIGHTLINE ⊙ SELF–DEFENCE CLASSES
⊙ UNIVERSITY COUNSELLORS 2 PART
⊙ CRIME RATING !!!!
The award-winning Student Services are the first point of contact for anyone in difficulty.
HEALTH The University Medical Centre has a doctor and two nurses to plaster scraped knees. There's a *legion* of trained first aiders on campus.
CRECHES/NURSERY The Tiny Tots Day-Care Nursery on the Caerleon site can take kids between 18mths-5yrs. Holiday clubs for older children kick in during vacations and are held at both campuses.
DISABILITIES Once the steep hill that leads to the campus is out of the way, access is rather good with lifts, ramps and electronic doors throughout the main building. There are some problems with narrow doorways and cramped teaching rooms. Once you're actually in, compensation includes provision of note-takers, IT equipment and help with applications for the Disabled Students' Allowance. One-to-one tuition's available for dyslexics, plus extended loans and specialist software programs. Hearing loops are in many lecture theatres.

N

Words in italics are Push's point of view — take it or leave it...

CRIME The University itself is a secure place to be. The city's *a different story* and although Newport's *climbing down from the No. 1 spot for violent crime thanks to more police beating the streets, pick-pocketing and other social disturbances are fairly common.*
DRUGS Smoking's only permitted in Clarence Bar and designated areas outside. Harder drugs aren't a problem on campus but *Newport itself has a bit of a rep.*

FINANCE
❍ AVE DEBT PER YEAR £3,458 ❍ HOME STUDENT FEES £1,200
FEES International students pay between £7,050 and £8,250. Welsh students studying in Wales are entitled to £1,800 fees grants (not means tested), and can then top-up with a loan. Non-Welsh folk, however, will be £3K worse off a year.
❍ ACCESS FUND £461,442 ❍ SUCCESSFUL APPLICATIONS/YR 625
❍ AVE PAYMENT £200-2,000
SUPPORT An emergency loan scheme slips skint students a few notes in sticky situations. The National Bursary Scheme and the Assembly Learning Grant (see www.learning.wales.gov.uk) both help Welsh students studying in Wales. The Reginald Salisbury Photography Awards is for aspiring photographers *(not paparazzi wannabes, Push presumes).* Professional advice is also available on budgeting, loans, funding and benefits.

NORTH EAST WALES INSTITUTE

PART OF THE UNIVERSITY OF WALES

1. ❍ NORTH EAST WALES INSTITUTE OF HIGHER EDUCATION Mold Road, Wrexham, LL11 2AW TEL (01978) 290 666
E-MAIL sid@newi.ac.uk Website: www.newi.ac.uk ❍ STUDENTS' UNION TEL (01978) 293 225
2. NORTH WALES SCHOOL OF ART AND DESIGN Regent Street, Wrexham

GENERAL ◖◖◖◖◖◖◖◖◖◖◖◖◖

Wrexham's often described as the capital of North Wales, *which probably says more about the wilds of North Wales than it does about the metropolis of Wrexham.* Just over the border from England, this small-but-perfectly-formed market town is home to the North East Wales Institute of Higher Education, one of the country's newest universities. NEWI's been kicking around in one form or another since 1887, however, when the first post-compulsory education was established in Wrexham. Originally a School of Science and Art, it's best known for the latter, with renowned 1950s architecture and Grade II listed tiles in the main foyer (designed by Peggy Angus to represent a flow of learning with a Welsh background, apparently). It became a university college in 1975 and was made a full member of the University of Wales in 2004. The buildings are clean and modern, apart from the *grotty* Union which gets busy nonetheless. Most of the action takes place on the Plas Coch (Red Hall) campus while the Regent Street campus is the home of NEWI's North Wales School of Art & Design.

ATMOSPHERE
Not the liveliest of campuses, but a happy one. Students usually have a smile on their faces and get on well with staff. More than two thirds come from the local area and so, predictably, town/gown relations are pretty pally. A similar number are mature and part-time undergrads outnumber their full-time countreparts.

OTHER SITES
NORTH WALES SCHOOL OF ART & DESIGN (693 students, er, Art & Design) Just five minutes walk from Plas Coch, students have their own snack bar and art shop but otherwise are handy for all the fun of main campus.

WREXHAM
❍ POPULATION 128,477 ❍ CITY CENTRE 0.5 MILES
❍ CHESTER 14 MILES
❍ HIGH TEMP 17 ❍ LOW TEMP 5 ❍ RAINFALL 42
The historic town has seen new investment lately with industrial and business parks springing up. The centre is a flurry of high street shops plus specialist stores. Locally there are castles, Erddig National Trust property and the great outdoors, *to occupy those that can drag themselves away from the TV.*

TRAVEL
TRAINS Trains to Cardiff (from £9.85 return) and London (£33.65).
COACHES Bus depot is in the town centre. Services to London (£30), Cardiff (£7.50), Manchester (£30).
CAR M6, A451, A483 and A55 aren't far away. *Plenty of car parks in Wrexham, or it's free to pull up a motor on campus (permit required). Many local students have cars, though wheels aren't essential as the town centre is compact and nearby.*

SEX RATIO: ♂48 ♀52	FOUNDED: 1887
FULL-TIME U'GRADS: 2,179	PART-TIME: 2,882
POSTGRADS: 480	NON-DEGREE: 460
AVE COURSE: 3YRS	ETHNIC: 1%
STATE:PRIVATE SCHOOL: 99:1	FLUNK RATE: 27%
MATURE: 60%	INTERNATIONAL: 6%
DISABLED: 185	LOCAL: 68%

Words in italics are Push's point of view — take it or leave it...

AIR Liverpool or Manchester are the nearest airports.
LOCAL Buses and trains zip around the vicinity.
UNIVERSITY NEWI lays on an *eclectic transport* selection, collecting international students from the airport and shipping student teachers to work placements in local schools.
TAXIS *Reliable cabs for those with cash to spare.*
BICYCLES Lanes throughout the town and bike stands on campus *give budding Lance Armstrongs all the encouragement they need.*

CAREER PROSPECTS
○ **CAREERS SERVICE** ○ **NO. OF STAFF** 10 FULL
○ **UNEMPLOYED AFTER 6 MTHS** 7%
Super-keen careers service with bulletin boards all over the place. Also interview training, careers library, job placements and, *for Alan Sugar types*, advice on starting a business.

FAMOUS ALUMNI
Brian Fleet MBE (Airbus); Joey Jones (footballer); Karen Sinclair AM.

FURTHER INFO
○ **PROSPECTUSES** UNDERGRAD; POSTGRAD; ALL DEPARTMENTS
○ **OPEN DAYS**

ACADEMIC ○○○○○○○○○○○○○

Cosy links with industry, with work placements common and many degrees leading to exemptions from relevant professional bodies. *Art & Design, Health, Engineering and Education are all strong points.*

ENTRY POINTS: 60–180	AVE POINTS: 160
APPLICATIONS PER PLACE: 2	CLEARING: 10%
NO. OF TERMS: 2	LENGTH OF TERMS: 15WKS
STAFF TO STUDENT RATIO: 1:13	STUDY ADDICTS: 26%
TEACHING: *	RESEARCH: N/A
YEAR ABROAD: 0%	SANDWICH STUDENTS: 0%
1STS: 11%	2.2s: 31%
2.1s: 45%	3RDS: 7%

ADMISSIONS
○ **APPLY VIA UCAS/DIRECT**
NEWI welcomes applications from anyone committed to their subject, whether or not they have the qualifications to prove it, and may accept outside-the-box applicants after an interview.

SUBJECTS
ART & DESIGN 10% **BUSINESS/MANAGEMENT** 11%
COMPUTING 6% **EDUCATION** 11%
HEALTH, SOCIAL CARE, SPORT & EXERCISE 23%
HUMANITIES 7% **SCIENCE & TECHNOLOGY** 32%
UNUSUAL Criminal Justice; Estate Agency; Illustration for Children's Publishing; Performance Car Technology; Substance Use; Traditional Chinese Medicine.

LIBRARIES
○ **150,000 BOOKS** ○ **314 STUDY PLACES**
○ **SPEND PER STUDENT** £
The Edward Llwyd Centre houses the library and the computer suites (plus the international and student support centres, *if a reason to skive off study were needed*). It's open until 9pm during the week, and from 10am-5pm on term-time Saturdays.

COMPUTERS
○ **320 WORKSTATIONS** ○ **SPEND PER STUDENT** £
13 computer suites, most of which welcome all-comers, but there are a few specialist labs for the likes of Computing, Engineering and Art & Design bods. Opening hours are the same as the library. All student rooms have internet access and wireless hotspots are popping up on campus *like spots on a teenager*. Blackboard is the virtual learning environment of choice.

OTHER LEARNING FACILITIES
Art gallery; CAD lab; media centre; drama studio; radio/recording studio; performance car lab.

ENTERTAINMENT ○○○○○○○○○

THE TOWN
Wrexham has more nightspots than nearby Chester, but Liverpool and Manchester scratch the places North Wales can't reach.
PUBS Independent bars *jostle for space* with the big chains – Lloyds; Yates; Wetherspoons...*you know the score*. Late licences are common.
CLUBBING/MUSIC VENUES Plenty of pub strummers. Central Station gets big(ger) names and doubles as a nightclub. Funeral for a Friend, Girls Aloud, Wet Wet Wet and the Coral have all performed, as have DJs Boy George and Justin Robertson. Clubbers are well catered for, *by small town standards at least.*
EATING OUT A decent range of restaurants and more takeaways that you could shake a tree at.
OTHER Wrexham Arts Centre and Museum do their bit for culture vultures.

UNIVERSITY
○ **PRICE OF A PINT OF BEER** £1.50
○ **GLASS OF WINE** £1.70
○ **CAN OF RED BULL** £1.40
BARS Degrees Bar (Plas Coch campus) has events throughout the year, including balls, live bands, discos and, just for a minute when the SU thought it was in the Balearics rather than North Wales, a foam party. Fellows Bar (cap 150) opens its doors when there's something kicking off in the concert hall. It's also a coffee shop and snackspot during the day.
THEATRES Student and proper productions in the campus theatre, NEWI William Aston Hall.

N

CLUBBING/MUSIC VENUES As well as the shenanigans in Degrees Bar, there's a weekly student night at the Century Club, which is near the campus. William Aston Hall gets touring bands.

FOOD The main chomp palace is Scholar's Rest, which does snacks, 'home cooking', baguettes and jacket potatoes. Fellows has baguettes, paninis and more spuds plus fairtrade caffeine juice and Caffi Darganfod has snacks and sarnies.

SOCIAL ◔◔◔◔◔◔◔◔◔◔

NEWI STUDENTS' UNION
❷ 2 SABBATICALS ❷ NUS MEMBER
The apolitical SU concentrates on keeping its members safe and happy and gets on swimmingly with the University as a result, with students represented on various boards and committees.

SU FACILITIES
Degrees is the SU building. The SU or University provides: a bar; music venue; canteen/cafeteria; snack/coffee bar; fast food outlet; pool/snooker table; meeting room; photocopier; printing service; payphone; advice centre; crèche/nursery; jukebox; video/gaming machine; vending machine; new/second-hand bookshop; launderette.

CLUBS (NON-SPORTING)
International. **See also Clubs tables.**

OTHER ORGANISATIONS
Rag *pimps its ass* in the name of charidee. 'The Wal', NEWI's radio studio, is used by students and locals alike.

PAID WORK
❷ JOB BUREAU
The careers service advertises part-time and holiday jobs and the University runs a paid ambassador scheme for student recruitment activities.

SPORTS ◔◔◔◔◔◔◔◔◔◔◔

❷ BUSA RANKING 122
The sports centre is run as a separate company and welcomes locals alongside students. Academic use gets priority from 9am-5pm and the SU runs a sports programme *to get students out of the bar.* NEWI's hosted the National Badminton Championship and European Hockey Championship, *which suggests its facilities are up to scratch.*

SPORTS FACILITIES
Three football pitches; hockey pitch; netball court; basketball court; sports hall; gym; aerobics studio; multigym. The University can also use six more

footy pitches; two rugby pitches; six tennis courts and an athletics track. An astro-turf pitch shuld also be in place by September 2006. Various levels of sports membership, with student rates available. Lots of golf courses nearby.

SPORTING CLUBS
Aikido; Ju-Jitsu; Table Tennis; Thai kickboxing; Thai Chi. **See also Clubs tables.**

ATTRACTIONS
Walking, diving, white-water rafting, climbing, horse-riding, mountaineering *and hide and seek* in nearby Snowdonia.

ACCOMMODATION ◔◔◔◔◔◔◔◔◔

IN COLLEGE
❷ SELF-CATERING 13% **❷ COST** £58 (37WKS)
❷ INSURANCE PREMIUM £
AVAILABILITY Many students already live locally anyway, but there's housing available for most first years that want it (8% are disappointed). Most of the accommodation is on campus in the student village and Plas Coch Hostel, with the rest a ten minute walk away. Kitchens are shared and most rooms are en suite – *perfect for those that prefer to pee in private.* There are some rooms for couples and disabled students and a 24-hr porter *makes sure the bed bugs don't bite.*
CAR PARKING Free and easy.

EXTERNALLY
❷ AVE RENT £55
AVAILABILITY 156 rooms in a privately-run hostel in town, plus the usual roster of shared flats and houses to rent.
HOUSING HELP NEWI keeps a list of good and bad landlords, plus an online vacancy list and fire/gas certificate checks.

WELFARE ◔◔◔◔◔◔◔◔◔◔◔

SERVICES
❷ LGBT OFFICER & SOCIETY
❷ WOMEN'S OFFICER & SOCIETY
❷ INTERNATIONAL STUDENTS' SOCIETY
❷ MATURE STUDENTS' OFFICER & SOCIETY
❷ COLLEGE COUNSELLORS 1 FULL/2 PART
❷ CRIME RATING: !
The student support centre in the Edward Llywd building is the first port of call for advice and welfare needs.
HEALTH Two nurses on campus.
CRECHES/NURSERY 41 places for kiddywinks aged 3mths-7yrs and a school holiday club.
DISABILITIES *Access in NEWI is good on the whole,* but the North Wales School of Art is a listed

N

building and doesn't have a lift. Dyslexia help includes an assessment centre, visiting educational psychologists, a one-to-one student support suite and IT support suite.

FINANCE
○ **AVE DEBT PER YEAR** £3,886 ○ **HOME STUDENT FEES** £1,200 **FEES** Fees will be topped up to £3,000 from 2007,

although Welsh students will get extra handouts to cover the difference. International students pay £6,150 (undergrad) or £8,000 (postgrad).
○ **ACCESS FUND** £250,000 ○ **SUCCESSFUL APPLICATIONS**/YR 400
○ **AVE PAYMENT** £250-1,000
SUPPORT Around 40% of new students should get some kind of bursary from 2006.

NORTH LONDON UNIVERSITY
see _London Metropolitan University_

NORTHAMPTON UNIVERSITY

FORMERLY NENE COLLEGE, UNIVERSITY COLLEGE NORTHAMPTON

○ **UNIVERSITY OF NORTHAMPTON** Park Campus, Boughton Green Road, Northampton, NN2 7AL **TEL** (0800) 358 2232
E-MAIL study@northampton.ac.uk **WEBSITE** www.northampton.ac.uk ○ **UNIVERSITY OF NORTHAMPTON STUDENTS' UNION**
Park Campus, Bougton Green Road, Northampton, NN2 7AL **TEL** (01604) 892 818 **WEBSITE** www.ucnu.org

GENERAL ○○○○○○○○○○○○○

800-year-old Northampton's a _large, pleasant and unassuming_ market town, smack between Brum and London, _a bit too far east to be properly in the Midlands and too far north to be in the Home Counties_. Its nearest neighbour is the _much maligned_ Milton Keynes, but there's some lovely countryside nearby to get lost in. Historically, _there's no business like shoe business_ and Northampton has been British footwear capital in past decades – the leather industry still has a strong _foothold_. Northampton is about 2.5 miles away on two landscaped campuses – Park and Avenue _(the Manhattan-based pun isn't entirely coincidental)_ – with modern developments _tastefully arranged around lovely rolling lawns where little bunny rabbits scamper_. One of the country's newest 'universities proper', it got 'University College' status in 1999 and after a few years of _trying, waiting and hoping_, recently bloomed into the fully-feathered University of Northampton.

in. _The University's small enough not to get lost in, but large enough to dissuade exclusive cliques from forming. The academic atmosphere at Park Campus errs on the sensible and serious side, while the number of arts students based at Avenue gives that campus a more trendy and flamboyant air._

OTHER SITES
PARK CAMPUS The main campus, just outside the town centre, housing Science and Humanities students, as well as the Business School and School of Healthcare (complete with on-site 'ward'). The newest kid on the block is 2005's Student Centre, giving space to, among other things, Student Services, more student housing and a GP surgery.
AVENUE CAMPUS (3,000 students; Art, Design, Fashion, Performing Arts & Technology) A mile from Park Campus, the _pleasant_ Avenue has all the facilities to function independently: specialist library, drama and dance studios, a CAD lab, 24-hr computer suite, a new accommodation block (housing 500) and bar and catering facilities. It's linked with Park via a free shuttle service (every 15 mins).

NORTHAMPTON
○ **POPULATION** 194,458 ○ **CITY CENTRE** 2 MILES
○ **LONDON** 63 MILES ○ **BIRMINGHAM** 52 MILES
○ **MANCHESTER** 137 MILES
○ **HIGH TEMP** 21 ○ **LOW TEMP** 0 ○ **RAINFALL** 49
As big as a town can get without becoming a city, Northampton has managed to maintain its ancient market square (the largest in Britain) in _something approaching good nick_ and there are some admirable examples of Georgian and Victorian architecture around the centre. _Some of the outer reaches are closer to prefab hell, however._ In among the urban planning exercise

SEX RATIO: ♂37 ♀63	FOUNDED: 1999
FULL-TIME U'GRADS: 7,230	PART-TIME: 2,625
POSTGRADS: 275	NON-DEGREE: N/A
AVE COURSE: 3YRS	ETHNIC: 18%
STATE:PRIVATE SCHOOL: 98:2	FLUNK RATE: 19%
MATURE: 29%	INTERNATIONAL: 7%
DISABLED: 220	LOCAL: 25%

ATMOSPHERE
Northampton is home to a broadly blended bunch of all ages and accents. They're friendly, far from pretentious and there's a strong sense of community, particularly amongst those who live

Words in italics are Push's point of view — take it or leave it...

there's the Sol Central entertainment complex and the usual array of banks, malls, supermarkets, bookshops, galleries and museums, *although the Leather Museum isn't as much fun as it could be.* Other attractions include regular hot-air balloon festivals and one of the *best-preserved* Norman round churches in the country.

TRAVEL
TRAINS Northampton station is four miles from the Park campus and offers mainline services to London (from £15.10 return), Birmingham (£8.65), Edinburgh (£55.70) and others.
COACHES The coach station about four miles from Park runs National Express, Midland Fox and local services to various towns and cities, including London (£13.20) and Birmingham (£6.20).
CAR The M1 zooms past the town – although there's at least three wiggly miles between it and the University. The A45, A50 and A43 also come in handy. *On campus, permits are needed and overnight stays are charged.*
AIR Luton Airport is closest, *though if it's of use is another matter.* Some of the budget airlines (like easyjet) use it though. Rail links to Birmingham Airport.
HITCHING *M1 junctions are good pick-up spots and there are enough major roads to make hitching possible.*
LOCAL The bus station is *utterly horrid, but services are reliable enough.* Trips between town and University cost 90p each way.
UNIVERSITY There's a free bus service for students and staff between the main campus and the town's bus and train stations.
TAXIS *Not too expensive and not too hard to get hold of.*
BICYCLES There are some cycle lanes but the constantly busy roads make traffic dodging *something of a bloodsport.*

CAREER PROSPECTS
○ **CAREERS SERVICE** ○ **UNEMPLOYED AFTER 6 MTHS** 6%
Students are treated to interview assistance, CV-writing lessons, psychometric and aptitude tests, bulletin boards and one-on-one advice sessions. Facilities are available until three years after graduation.

FAMOUS ALUMNI
Andrew Collins (BBC 6 DJ); David J (Bauhaus/Love & Rockets); Lord Hesketh (Formula 1 team manager); Des O'Connor (*the poor man's Michael Parkinson*); Derek Redmond (athlete); Jonathon Waller (artist).

SPECIAL FEATURES
The School of Leather Technology has on display a *fine* specimen of a blue whale's foreskin.

FURTHER INFO
○ **PROSPECTUSES** UNDERGRAD; POSTGRAD; INTERNATIONAL; PART-TIME
○ **OPEN DAYS**
All prospectuses except international can be downloaded or ordered from the main website.

The University runs open days in spring and autumn (tel. (0800) 3582232 or e-mail study@northampton.ac.uk for info). Tours can be booked online.

ACADEMIC ○○○○○○○○○○○○

Gold stars for Healthcare, Education, business-related courses and the Art & Design department. The Park Campus is a 9-5 affair; things are a little looser at Avenue. Tutors are approachable rather than ivory tower-ensconced types.

ENTRY POINTS: 180–240		AVE POINTS: 180	
APPLICATIONS PER PLACE: N/A		CLEARING: 10%	
NO. OF TERMS: 3		LENGTH OF TERMS: 12WKS	
STAFF TO STUDENT RATIO: 1:17		STUDY ADDICTS: 6%	
TEACHING: **		RESEARCH: *	
YEAR ABROAD: 5%		SANDWICH STUDENTS: 5%	

ADMISSIONS
○ **APPLY VIA UCAS/NMAS FOR NURSING AND MIDWIFERY/GTTR FOR TEACHING**

SUBJECTS
APPLIED SCIENCE 9%   **ARTS** 18%   **EDUCATION** 12%
HEALTH 21%   **NORTHAMPTON BUSINESS SCHOOL** 23%
SOCIAL SCIENCES 17%
UNUSUAL LEATHER TECHNOLOGY, LIFT TECHNOLOGY

LIBRARIES
○ **250,000 BOOKS**

COMPUTERS
○ **24-HOUR ACCESS**
Each campus has an IT centre offering Broadband net access, available 24-hrs all week long. Free IT courses are available for the technologically backward and there's a plug-in area for student laptops.

OTHER LEARNING FACILITIES
Drama studio, media centre, digital video editing suite in the Park Campus library. The Centre for Academic Practice on the Avenue Campus *(unmanageably acronymed CfAP)* offers courses in study skills.

ENTERTAINMENT ○○○○○○○○○

THE TOWN
○ **PRICE OF A PINT OF BEER** £2.50
○ **GLASS OF WINE** £2.80
○ **CAN OF RED BULL** £1.80
It's a ten minute drive or bus hop to town, where all the delights of the not-quite-a-city await.
CINEMAS The Sol Central development has a Vue multiplex in the town centre. Also a UGC just outside town.
THEATRES The Royal puts on traditional stuff,

mainly rep. The Derngate is a flexible, multi-purpose venue with lots of touring productions and the Roadmender puts on experimental material.

PUBS Northampton now has three Wetherspoons *and, for some reason, they're proud of it. Big cheap chains have been colonising, although small independent places still get their share of student custom. Pushplugs: the White Elephant and Picturedrome near the Avenue Campus; the Charles Bradlaugh (massive mixing pot for students and staff). In the summer, the various country pubs around campus are a good bet for wiling away the hours with a local cider.*

CLUBBING *Northampton's nightspots are on the up, but slowly. Monday night at Time & Envy is the big student dance hole* – sponsored by the Union. *Chicago Rock is also okay for aboozin' and a-boogyin'.*

MUSIC VENUES The Roadmender is a *fair-to-middling* indie stop-off and sells tickets via the Union. The Soundhouse also houses, er, sounds.

EATING OUT Northampton has the usual range of eateries, including burgers and pizzas till 4am. *Wellingborough Road is the best bet for value and variety. Pushplugs: Buddies (American diner, legend has it no one has managed to finish a meal because they're so big); Sorrebtino's.*

UNIVERSITY

- **PRICE OF A PINT OF BEER** £1.50
- **GLASS OF WINE** £1.80
- **CAN OF RED BULL** £1.50

A recent makeover with a new stage and sound system has been reeling more students into the Union, both during the day and at night.

BARS Laidback is the only place to escape the campus's *stringent* anti-smoking policy and even then only in the evenings, *when it lives up to its name a bit more. Just because it's got 'sophisticated European-style café bar' written all over its décor doesn't stop it being a class A piss-up venue,* and it's also got big screen sport, pool, open mic nights and karaoke to offer. George's at Avenue has a theme night or two, including the *legendary Friday 13th night (£13 entry, drink the bar dry). The Pavilion's more chilled out,* and the NN2 club spot has theme nights.

FILM/MUSIC VENUES/COMEDY NN2 is used to pamper local (and not so local) bands, show films and fill the air with laughter. Editors, Bodyrockers and Biffy Clyro have *popped up. Or down.*

CLUBBING Weekend nights keep NN2 open till 2am. *Unlike every other Union in the country, Northampton students have protested against cheesy pop and the ents people are providing more diverse music.* Trevor Nelson and local girl Jo Whiley have DJ'd, as have Cut Up Boys.

FOOD Big Al's Diner does the *cheapest nosebag. Grubby grub at Laidback.* The University refectory *is more expensive, though the food's far from great.*

OTHER The Xmas Ball is popular but the Freshers' Ball hasn't been drawing in the punters – *most of them are too busy and bleary-eyed to attend.*

SOCIAL 🙂🙂🙂🙂🙂🙂🙂🙂🙂🙂🙂

UNIVERSITY OF NORTHAMPTON STUDENTS' UNION

- **4 SABBATICALS** ● **TURNOUT AT LAST BALLOT** 14%

Lucky UNSU has not one but three buildings, two at Park and one on Avenue, but the facilities at Avenue have a cloud over their heads and risk closure unless there's enough money down the back of the sofa to keep them afloat. Meanwhile, the Union doesn't attract much attention from the student body except as an ents and services provider. As suggested by their disaffiliation from NUS, when it comes to politics, the Union doesn't give a flying monkey's, really, though because the place is so small the sabbs have a good track record is seeing pet projects through. It gets on all right with the University itself now that they've started talking to each other.

SU FACILITIES

Three bars; café; three pool tables; minibus hire; advice centre; payphones; photocopiers; fax and printing service; photo booth; Endsleigh Insurance office; NatWest and Co-op ATMs.

CLUBS (NON-SPORTING)

Internaional Hat (made it on tour to Barcelona, apparently). **See also Clubs tables.**

OTHER ORGANISATIONS

'Wave' is the Union newsletter. Rag rakes in some cash relief for a different charity each month. Volunteers is an organisation that visits people in need of visiting and smoothes things over with the locals.

RELIGION

- **2 CHAPLAINS (ECUMENICAL, MULTI-FAITH)**

The chaplaincy centre on campus is open to all faiths on the Avenue campus, *mainly for chatting and coffee.* There's a Muslim prayer room on each site. Northampton is big enough to support all but the most esoteric spiritual requirements.

PAID WORK

- **JOB BUREAU** ● **PAID WORK** TERM-TIME 20%; HOLS 50%

Between them, the SU and University's Student Services unit run Jobs Junction which links up with local employers and posts a vacancy notice board. The Union and local bars and shops often have jobs going. Students can make extra pennies acting as student ambassadors, *or, in English, tour guides.*

SPORTS 😐😐😐😐😐😐😐😐😐😐😐😐

- **BUSA RANKING** 92

Enthusiasm outstrips the facilities and trophy collection. Outside sponsorship has perked things up, though successes are mostly down to the women. Still, the banter between sports clubs keeps things lively in the Union.

SPORTS FACILITIES

The Park Campus has: sports hall with fitness suite; 25 acres of fields; pavilion. Nothing exclusively for the University at Avenue but it's close to the town's rugby/football pitches and has access to the swimming pool in the school next door and to the River Nene (not for swimming though). Use of the facilities costs £20 per year. There are leisure centres in Northampton, there's a lake nearby and Milton Keynes Snowdome is 20 mins away.

SPORTING CLUBS

American Football; Gaelic Football; Lacrosse. **See also Clubs tables.**

ATTRACTIONS

Northampton Rugby Club (aka the Saints) are local heroes. There's also Northampton Town FC (known, not entirely inaccurately, as the Cobblers) and not far away, the Silverstone Formula 1 circuit, home of the British Grand Prix. The Nene Whitewater Centre is within splashing distance. The County Cricket Club is a ball's throw from Avenue.

ACCOMMODATION ◖◖◖◖◖◖◖◖◖

IN UNIVERSITY

○ **SELF-CATERING** 22% ○ **COST** £63 (40WKS)
○ **1ST YRS LIVING IN** 78% ○ **INSURANCE PREMIUM** £
AVAILABILITY Northampton has around 1,400 places in seven halls of residence, all but 250 of which are reserved for first years, meaning everyone can have a room on arrival. A handful have to share. Very few in successive years live in. Halls are on campus, so lie-ins are a regular feature of life here. Kitchens facilities are basic but the atmosphere makes up for the lack of Agas and espresso machines. The en suite facilities at West Hall and Spencer Perceval put them in demand. Bassett Lowke – the only hall at the Avenue Campus – is a popular en suite complex of generally single-sex flats. Charles Bradlaugh Hall has been kicking around a good many years and is beginning to look like it. Accommodation for couples is available on application. Security and lighting have been souped up recently. CCTV, scan keys and night porters conquer the forces of evil and there's a warden to watch over every ten students.
CAR PARKING Not exactly a piece of Battenburg. Permits are around £120 yearly (not needed for day-parking).

EXTERNALLY

○ **AVE RENT** £45
AVAILABILITY Local housing is pretty good and reasonable, although the hike between town and campus can get a little wearisome. Nearby Kingsthorpe and Abington are the best bets. Semilong can be a bit rough, though a clean-up operation's in progress.
HOUSING HELP Student Services keep vacancy lists, approve landlords and offer a placement service. All first years are guaranteed a local home address at the beginning of the year.

WELFARE ◖◖◖◖◖◖◖◖◖◖◖◖◖

SERVICES

○ **LGBT OFFICER & SOCIETY**
○ **MATURE STUDENTS' OFFICER** ○ **POSTGRAD OFFICER**
○ **INTERNATIONAL STUDENTS' OFFICER & SOCIETY**
○ **NIGHTLINE** ○ **LATE-NIGHT BUS**
○ **UNIVERSITY COUNSELLORS** 10 FULL/7 PART
○ **CRIME RATING:** !!!!
The Union runs a drop-in Welfare & Advice Service that lends an ear. A PAL (Partners in Academic Life) scheme has been set up, whereby eight students act as points of contact for academic concerns. Nightline is open four nights a week – so don't get suicidal on a Wednesday. First Aid and other courses are available for free.
HEALTH There's a GP surgery on the Park Campus and plenty of doctors and dentists available in the town.
DISABILITIES Renovation has made most buildings very accessible. Both campuses have relief pens for guide dogs and induction loops have been installed in several lecture theatres. Good level of support and equipment for unseen disabilities.
CRIME Some mild vandalism comes a cropper of CCTV.

FINANCE

○ **AVE DEBT PER YEAR** £3,686 ○ **HOME STUDENT FEES** £2,500
FEES Northampton is one of the few Universities resisting the temptation to squeeze every penny out of home students, fees-wise. Part-timers pay £200-400 a module, international undergrads are charged between £5,000 and £8,400 and UK postgrads pay £3,010 a year (£1,000 part-time). HNDs and Foundation Courses cost £1,200.
○ **ACCESS FUND** £17,479 ○ **SUCCESSFUL APPLICATIONS/YR** 20%
SUPPORT There's an emergency loan of £150 available when things get tight. Also bridging loans of £200 and opportunity bursaries for undergrads with low-income families of up to £2,000.

NORTHAMPTON UNIVERSITY COLLEGE

see _Northampton University_

NORTHUMBRIA UNIVERSITY

FORMERLY NEWCASTLE POLYTECHNIC

1. ○ **NORTHUMBRIA UNIVERSITY** Newcastle City Campus, Ellison Place, Newcastle upon Tyne, NE1 8ST **TEL** (0191) 227 4604
E-MAIL er.admissions@northumbria.co.uk **WEBSITE** www.northumbria.ac.uk ○ **NORTHUMBRIA UNIVERSITY STUDENTS' UNION**
Newcastle City Campus, 2 Sandyford Road, Newcastle upon Tyne, NE1 8SB **TEL** (0191) 227 4757 **WEBSITE** www.mynsu.co.uk
2. ○ **NORTHUMBRIA UNIVERSITY** Coach Lane Campus, Coach Lane, Benton, Newcastle upon Tyne, NE7 7XA **TEL** (0191) 215 6000
E-MAIL su.president@northampton.ac.uk **WEBSITE** www.mynsu.co.uk

GENERAL ◖◖◖◖◖◖◖◖◖◖◖◖◖◖

Newcastle's newer university started from humble beginnings as the city's little poly, *but there's no denying it's now a hefty player.* The main campus, plop in the middle of the city and stuck next to a busy motorway, is the study centre for most courses, with around 15,700 students knocking around at any given time. It's a *distressing muddle* of 1880s municipal buildings, such as the original redbrick Sutherland Building, and 60s concrete architecture, *made easier on the eye by some charming* 19th-century buildings in Ellison Place. *Being just a continuation of buildings and no greenery, it's difficult to tell exactly where the town stops and campus starts.* New development 'City Campus East' continues the academic sprawl: work has started, and the new buildings should be ready for September 2007. *If the name suggests a laboured commute to a site tucked away in the far eastern edges of Newcastle, don't be misled* – it's 100m away from the main campus, on the other side of the motorway...

SEX RATIO: ♂45 ♀55	
FULL-TIME U'GRADS: 13,715	**PART-TIME:** 3,873
POSTGRADS: 4,804	**NON-DEGREE:** 2,616
AVE COURSE: 3YRS	**ETHNIC:** 16%
STATE:PRIVATE SCHOOL: 91:9	**FLUNK RATE:** 15%
MATURE: 33%	**INTERNATIONAL:** 13%
DISABLED: 230	**LOCAL:** 36%

ATMOSPHERE
Local relations are good since more than half the students come from the local area. With two universities in town, one in six of the city's population during term is a student, *so there's plenty of likeminded folk around. Things can still get a bit hairy on a Friday or Saturday night – but then they'd still be hairy and lairy with or without students. Like many universities in a thriving city, the campus itself can empty pretty quickly after lectures as everybody scarpers off to the city's heaving fleshpots. The Union building remains a little more lively than its surroundings – busy if not buzzy. The same can't be said of the Coach Lane campus which is dogged by a feeling of isolation.*

THE CITY see <u>Newcastle University</u>

TRAVEL see <u>Newcastle University</u>
UNIVERSITY The University operates its own *infrequent* bus service between the campuses with a last bus after midnight. Bike sheds are *finally starting to sprout* around campus.

OTHER SITES
COACH LANE (3,653 students – Health, Community & Education Studies) Three miles from the main site in Benton *(quite a rough suburb)* is the Coach Lane site, a modern and recently expanded campus, clean and green, with enough pubs and shops around *not to feel too unloved.*

CAREER PROSPECTS
○ **CAREERS SERVICE** ○ **NO. OF STAFF** 7 FULL
○ **UNEMPLOYED AFTER 6 MTHS** 5%
The careers service has limited outposts at both campuses and *tries to plug gaps with its website.*

FAMOUS ALUMNI
Emmanuel Bajyewv (Lighthouse Family); Jeff Banks (fashion designer/former Clothes Show presenter); Steve Bell (cartoonist); Sarah Blackwood (Dubstar); Steve Cram (athlete); Robson Green (actor/singer of '& Jerome' fame); Scott Henshall (fashion designer); Jonathan Ives (inventor of iMac); Vaughan Oliver (artist/designer); Sting (*pompous* pop star & tantra king); Kevin Whateley (actor – Inspector Morse).

FURTHER INFO
○ **PROSPECTUSES** UNDERGRAD; POSTGRAD; INTERNATIONAL; PART-TIME; ALL DEPARTMENTS
○ **OPEN DAYS**

ACADEMIC ◖◖◖◖◖◖◖◖◖◖◖◖◖

Northumbria prides itself on being a practical, get-stuck-in kind of university and they have links with industries in the area. Many courses offer work placements and students can nab academic credit by acting as ambassadors to local schools. Several courses have been nationally recognised as *top-banana* – the University's in the UK top 20 for subjects including: Nursing; Librarianship & Information; Management; Drama; Dance; Cinematics; Social Work; and Art & Design. Despite the academic plaudits, time-tabling's *a bit of a shambles*, with several students repeatedly misinformed about days and times of lectures and seminars – which takes the biscuit when trying to fit in a part- or even full-time job around studies. *A lack of classroom space is to blame, but the main site's expansion should alleviate the worst of it.*

ENTRY POINTS: 200-320	AVE POINTS: 200
APPLICATIONS PER PLACE: 2	CLEARING: 33%
NO. OF TERMS: 2	LENGTH OF TERMS: 12WKS
STAFF TO STUDENT RATIO: 1:20	STUDY ADDICTS: 11%
TEACHING: **	RESEARCH: *
1STS: 10%	2.2S: 35%
2.1S: 42%	3RDS: 6%

ADMISSIONS
○ APPLY VIA UCAS/NMAS FOR NURSING
Fair range of Access schemes for those from non-traditional routes. Disabled applicants and mature students with qualifications from the University of Life are *warmly* welcomed.

SUBJECTS
ARTS & SOCIAL SCIENCES 18%   **BUILT ENVIRONMENT** 7%
COMPUTING, ENGINEERING & INFORMATION SCIENCES 13%
HEALTH, COMMUNITY AND EDUCATION STUDIES 20%
DESIGN 6%   **LAW** 7%   **NEWCASTLE BUSINESS SCHOOL** 18%
PSYCHOLOGY & SPORTS SCIENCE 5%   **SCIENCES** 7%
BEST Art & Design; Building; Business & Management; Dance & Cinematics; Design & Film; Drama; Economics; Education Studies; Electrical & Electronic Engineering; History of Art; Housing Studies; Information & Library Management; Land & Property Management; Maths & Statistics; Modern Languages; Molecular Biosciences; Nursing; Physics; Politics; Psychology; Sociology; Sport Sciences; Subjects allied to Medicine.
UNUSUAL Computer Forensics; Computer Game Studies.

LIBRARIES
○ 500,000 BOOKS ○ 1,600 STUDY PLACES
○ 24-HOUR ACCESS
The main library has been given an overhaul and is now a *nice, airy place* to while away bouts of essay mania. There's even a basement lounge, with newspapers, armchairs, email facilities and – *crucially* – a doughnut vending machine, which turns out also to be *popular with drunks who stumble in in the early hours* (there's 24-hour access with a swipe card). The shiny, *crazy lifts have minds of their own and should be avoided wherever possible.*

COMPUTERS
○ 5,500 WORKSTATIONS ○ 24-HOUR ACCESS
IT facilities at both campuses and a new 24-hour lab. All students gets their own hard-disk space to store important files. A wireless network covers most of both campuses and some course resources are available with the e-learning portal. Some departments also loan laptops.

OTHER LEARNING FACILITIES
The Study Skills Centre assists students with all the basic but crucial aspects of student life such as literacy, numeracy, essay writing and IT.

ENTERTAINMENT ○○○○○○○○○

THE CITY see <u>Newcastle University</u>
The *worryingly-named* Mr Lynch in Jesmond and Tynemouth's Cumberland Arms are *student faves whilst not being overly studenty pubs themselves. Those less fond of their teeth* head for the city's Bigg Market. There's *almost infinite choice* around the city centre and Quayside.

UNIVERSITY
○ PRICE OF A PINT OF BEER £1.70
○ BOTTLE OF WINE 2.50
○ CAN OF RED BULL £2
BARS The Union runs four bars: Reds (pool, darts, games machines and the *hideously sinful temptation* of Pro-Evolution Soccer on the big-screen), the *clubbier* Venue (gig nights), the *pub-style* Bar One and Coach Lane (pool tables and club nights). Stage 2 (cap 600) is host to a variety of musical and big, big-screen sporting events.
MUSIC The Venue is *humongernormous* and *perfect for visiting bands:* Feeder, Girls Aloud, Moby and The Coral have warbled their way through it.
THEATRE Open-air productions take place when weather and interest permit, otherwise there's *token* board-treading in the Venue.
CLUBBING Red's Bar (500) is host to the self-explanatory 'Wiggle' – *cheesy, charty pop thrills* – and, for punk/ska/hiphop fans, there's 'Get Y'Skates On'. Wednesday's are Vodka Sensation; Pimp My Uncle *(as it were)* on a Thursday is R'n'B central and Friday's TFI kicks off the weekend with DJs and games from 3pm.
CINEMA Sporadic film soc screenings. The International Students' Society is *more celluloid-focused*, with regular foreign language films on Stage 2's screen.
COMEDY Stage 2 on a Monday night (£3 NUS members) features acts from the London comedy circuit.
FOOD The Venue has a small food court *but it's nowt to write home about.* Bar One is usually rammed, on the other hand, and sells burgers, wraps, sarnies and Costa Coffees. The Union

Northampton's School of Leather Technology has a fine specimen of a blue whale's foreskin.

building also houses a small deli/sandwich shop.
OTHER Weekly quiz night, *disturbingly* regular karaoke and Christmas, Graduation and departmental balls.

SOCIAL ()()()()()()()()()()()()()

NORTHUMBRIA UNIVERSITY STUDENTS' UNION
○ **4 SABBATICALS** ○ **TURNOUT AT LAST BALLOT** 10%
○ **NUS MEMBER**

Bawdy seaside postcards have more politics in them than Northumbria's students, but the Union organises a *frantic* diary of social events during Freshers' Week. Its building, situated on the main campus opposite the library, is *enormous and facility-stuffed. It doesn't stop the exec pushing for a new one once City Campus East is completed, though.* Coach Lane campus has little more than an office and bar on site. As well as clubs and societies, there's a *packed* schedule of free/ cheap taster events, such as Learn to DJ, Tibetan Head Massage, Jewellery Design and, *like a kind of good-will Esperanto, there's, er,* 'Laarn y'salf Geordie'.

SU FACILITIES
Four bars; a café; two coffee bars; two pool tables; eight meeting rooms; Lloyds TSB/Barclays ATM; photocopier; photo booth; general store; stationery shop; vending and gaming machines; travel agency; late night minibus; bookshop; TV lounge; advice centre.

CLUBS (NON-SPORTING)
Anime; Card Game; Chinese; Darts 501; Fair Trade; Fine Arts; Gaming & Roleplay; GLOBE (LGBT); Green; Hellenic; Homelessness; Humanist; Indonesian; I (International); Libyan; Links (St Johns' Ambulance); Make Poverty History; Malaysian; Motorsports; Mountain Biking; Music; Newcastle Indian; Northern Ireland Supporters' Club; Paganism; Pub Crawl; Red Cross; Salsa; Snowsports; Sri Lankan; Student action for Refugees STAR; Student Newspaper; Student Scouts & Guides Organisation (SSAGO); Taiwanese; Thai; Vegetarian; Vietnam. **See also Clubs tables.**

OTHER ORGANISATIONS
'Northumbria Student' is the monthly SU *bog-reading matter*. Runs a 'best in lecture doodle' comp. A radio station is run jointly with Newcastle University and has an FM licence for a couple of weeks each term. *Rag has its sights set on complete and utter global domination.* Last year they raised £26,000 – 160% up on the year before, and they plan to outstrip that again this year, mostly through pyjama pub crawls, bucket-shaking and a Rag Ball at St James' Park. A voluntary group co-ordinates community work.

RELIGION
○ **7 CHAPLAINS (COFE, RC, URC, METHODIST, QUAKER, SALVATION ARMY)**
The main Christian godshops have chaplains and there are links with most religions, including the Catholic Student Society, Chinese Christian Fellowship, Christian Student Action, Islamic Society, Jewish Society and Methodist Student Society. Religion in Newcastle: see Newcastle University.

PAID WORK
○ **JOB BUREAU**
20% of the students are registered with Job Shop, which employs two full-time staff and some casual student assistants during term. They pass on CVs to employers looking for *cheap, exploitable – sorry, flexible, enthusiastic* – labour. See Newcastle University for details of the city's *manifold* opportunities.

SPORTS ()()()()()()()()()()()()()

○ **RECENT SUCCESSES** MEN'S FOOTBALL, FENCING, RUGBY UNION ○ **BUSA RANKING** 10

SPORTS FACILITIES
Most outdoor facilities are based at the Bullocksteads Sports Ground. These include 13 football and rugby pitches and an all-weather pitch. The *freshly kitted* fitness suite at City Campus includes three squash courts and a fitness conditioning centre. The University's in talks with Newcastle City Council to build an eight-lane 50m swimming pool as well, but until then there's a public pool right next to the main campus, which has Turkish baths, saunas, sunbeds and fitness suites as well as just water. Student facility membership costs £70 for one year, £190 for three. See Newcastle University for the city's facilities.

SPORTING CLUBS
Gaelic Football; Hapkido; Ice Hockey; Jitsu; Kendo; Lacrosse; Mountain Biking; Outdoor Activities (OUTAC); Rugby League; Rugby Sevens; Table Tennis. **See also Clubs tables.**

ATTRACTIONS see Newcastle University

ACCOMMODATION ()()()()()()()()()

IN UNIVERSITY
○ **CATERED** 2% ○ **COST** £88 (38WKS)
○ **SELF-CATERING** 20% ○ **COST** £75 (43WKS)
○ **1ST YRS LIVING IN** 50% ○ **INSURANCE PREMIUM** ££
AVAILABILITY Anyone who applies before August is guaranteed a place in halls if they want one. They might want one in *popular* Camden Court – the newest halls and the nearest to the city

N

centre. The older ones further out used to have a bad reputation (poorly maintained with dodgy showers) but things are improving. They all have a residents' manager to *whinge at* anyway. Some rooms are adapted for disabled students. Internet access is mostly limited to common rooms.
CAR PARKING Parking *isn't too difficult* with a (free) permit.

EXTERNALLY see Newcastle University
○ **AVE RENT** £60
AVAILABILITY There are a couple of privately-run halls all close to the University, which are newer but pricier (£80-100/week). *Jesmond's a popular student enclave* (clean, tidy, with a glut of *good* bars and restaurants). Sandyford's cheaper (around £60-65 a week) and Heaton's even more cut-price (£45/week). Fenham's dirt cheap and *cultishly cool – but that could just be posturing by those who choose to live so far from the University for the sake of a £30/week rent.*
HOUSING HELP The University runs an accommodation office with an *extremely thorough and detailed* flat-finding guide online. The accreditation scheme recommends landlords who come up to scratch.

WELFARE ◗◗◗◗◗◗◗◗◗◗◗◗◗

SERVICES
○ **LGBT SOCIETY** ○ **INTERNATIONAL STUDENTS' SOCIETY**
○ **SELF-DEFENCE CLASSES** ○ **NIGHTLINE**
○ **UNIVERSITY COUNSELLORS** 4 FULL ○ **CRIME RATING:** !!!
The part-time 'Chair of Equal Opportunities' – *that's a person, not an item in the IKEA catalogue* – covers all minority groups in one go.
HEALTH The City and Coach Lane Campus health centres are staffed by nurses, who ship anyone they can't fix off to local doctors.
CHILDCARE Although there's no crèche, *generous*, means-tested funding is available towards childcare for full-time students with sprogs up to 5yrs.
DISABILITIES Wheelchair-adapted housing at Claude Gibb Hall, Lovine Flats, Stephenson and Rothbury. Some rooms designed for students with hearing impairments. Also *comprehensive* facilities and support for sight- and hearing-impaired and dyslexic students.

FINANCE
○ **AVE DEBT PER YEAR** £2,397 ○ **HOME STUDENT FEES** £3,000
FEES International undergrads pay £7,700-8,150. International postgrads pay up to £14,150.
○ **ACCESS FUND** £1.1M ○ **SUCCESSFUL APPLICATIONS/YR** 457
○ **AVE PAYMENT** £500-3,000
SUPPORT Apart from the access fund (which runs out quickly) several awards to the lucky few and some scarce loans for those in urgent need, there's *not really enough* support to go around.

N

UNIVERSITY OF NORTHUMBRIA AT NEWCASTLE
see *Northumbria University*

NORWICH
see *University of East Anglia*

UNIVERSITY OF NOTTINGHAM

1. ○ **THE UNIVERSITY OF NOTTINGHAM** University Park Nottingham, NG7 2RD **TEL** (0115) 951 5151
E-MAIL undergraduate-enquiries@nottingham.ac.uk **WEBSITE** www.nottingham.ac.uk
○ **UNIVERSITY OF NOTTINGHAM UNION** Portland Building, University Park, Nottingham, NG7 2RD **TEL** (0115) 846 8800
E-MAIL studentsunion@nottingham.ac.uk **WEBSITE** www.su.nottingham.ac.uk
2. **UNIVERSITY OF NOTTINGHAM SUTTON BONINGTON** nr Loughborough, Leicestershire, LE12 5RD **TEL** (0115) 951 5151

GENERAL ◗◗◗◗◗◗◗◗◗◗◗◗◗

Famous in days of yore as the haunt of a robbing do-gooder and his band of merry men, Nottingham has come a long way since the days of the evil sheriff. The largest city in the East Midlands is about half an hour by horse from the Peak District. A handful of high-profile gun crimes have earned Nottingham the nickname of

'assassination city', but for the vast majority of the students that call the place home, it's just as safe as any big city. About three miles from the city centre is the University Park Campus, which manages to retain a distinct whiff of the countryside with 330 hugely spacious acres of charming views, parkland, lake and a mixture of majestic old buildings (such as the main admin centre and the Union) and newer blocks (such as the white concrete flying saucer which disguises

itself as the Hallward Library). Two miles away, the brand new Jubilee Campus is built around a man-made lake. Ten miles south, at Sutton Bonington near Loughborough (see Loughborough University for general details), the University has another self-contained campus, a *huge* 400 acres, which will have the UK's first new school of Veterinary Science for half a century. *Nottingham's expansion ambitions don't stop there,* with an on-campus hotel and student TV station plus a £200million extension of the Jubilee Campus in the pipeline. *Robin would have been proud.*

SEX RATIO: ♂51 ♀49	FOUNDED: 1881
FULL-TIME U'GRADS: 19,656	PART-TIME: 4,161
POSTGRADS: 7,654	NON-DEGREE: 6,549
AVE COURSE: 3-4YRS	ETHNIC: 10%
STATE:PRIVATE SCHOOL: 73:20	FLUNK RATE: 4%
MATURE: 6%	INTERNATIONAL: 22%
DISABLED: 365	LOCAL: 10%

ATMOSPHERE

The buzz and hum on the campus is like a vibrator powered by bees. The social life flows with honey and the clubs milk the efforts of almost all students, yet, a staggering number of students still get involved in the successful Rag and Community Action group. *Undiluted essence of life is bottled and served in large quantities at centres around the campus and it would take considerable effort to be bored.* Relations with locals would be rosy were it not for a few over-exuberant party animals keeping the town's uglier residents from their beauty sleep.

OTHER SITES

JUBILEE (Business, Computing, Education) This new, ethically built (and soon to be expanded) site is on the western edge of the city. Built as a crescent around the lake, it has accommodation and other facilities including a library, a shop, a café and a canteen.
SUTTON BONINGTON AND NURSING SITES AT LINCOLN, DERBY, MANSFIELD, GRANTHAM, BOSTON AND NOTTINGHAM CITY CENTRE (900 students – Agricultural, Nursing) This site has its own Student Guild (funded by the Union) which runs a shop and some social events. There's a bar and some sporty stuff at Sutton Bonington, but nothing formal at the nursing sites. *Sutton Bonington is self-contained and has all the basic necessities for life, but, if it all gets too claustrophobic, escape into Loughborough or Nottingham is easy.*
THE UNIVERSITY OF NOTTINGHAM MALAYSIA CAMPUS On the outskirts of Kuala Lumpur, *it's out of the reach of most undergrads – unless you're reading this in Malaysia – a bit like...*
THE UNIVERSITY OF NOTTINGHAM CHINA CAMPUS which is in China, *if you hadn't guessed. The site in Ningbo is a recent notch on the University's bedpost.* See www.unnc.edu.cn.

NOTTINGHAM
- **POPULATION** 267,000 - **CITY CENTRE** 3 MILES
- **LONDON** 117 MILES - **BIRMINGHAM** 47 MILES
- **LOUGHBOROUGH** 13 MILES
- **HIGH TEMP** 20 - **LOW TEMP** 1 - **RAINFALL** 59

The city's had to cope with a big influx of students over the past few years (see Nottingham Trent University), *which hasn't exactly been welcomed by all locals. However, town/gown relations have stayed surprisingly sweet, with any bad feeling directed at the universities (which do what they can to smooth things over) rather than individual students (except the noisy ones). Nottingham's big enough to have all the amenities a social animal could desire, but small and cosy enough to avoid urban angst. It has its dank and squalid corners,* but the main areas with *shops galore* and developments like the Victoria Centre are *clean and spacious. The city centre has been rejuvenated with huge cosmopolitan bars.* Areas such as Hockley, among others, offer *trendy* little bars, *trendy* little designer shops and *trendy* big secondhand markets. Some of the *daintiest* features include the Goose Fair every October (the largest temporary fun fair in Europe), the famous old lace market (an old quarter of the city where lace is still sold wholesale), Nottingham Castle (*more of a mansion really*), Slab Square for sitting amidst pigeons, and 'Ye Olde Trip to Jerusalem' (built into caves) and 'Salutation Inn', two of the country's oldest pubs. *Students particularly enjoy* 'The Tales of Robin Hood', a heritage centre aimed at kids of all ages.

TRAVEL

TRAINS Nottingham Midland and Beeston stations both offer services all round the country (north and south are simpler than east and west), including London (from £26.25 return), Birmingham (£10.85), Manchester (£19.60) and Edinburgh (£58.55).
COACHES National Express services to, among other places, London (£22), Birmingham (£8.10) and Glasgow (£43.50).
CAR Nottingham is five mins off the M1 and is also easily reached by the A6, A47, A52 and the A1 (20 miles away). The M1 and A52 are best for the University. Parking permit required on campus.
AIR Nottingham East Midlands Airport, 12 miles outside town, has regular and budget flights inland and to Europe.
HITCHING *The M1 is good for wild rovers.*
UNIVERSITY Free shuttle bus service between the three campuses. Free Hopper bus services also available.
TAXIS *Pretty reasonable rates in the city centre.*
BICYCLES Flat with a major network of cycle lanes connecting the city centre, University Park and Jubilee campuses. *Laxity with locks can leave legs with little to lever.*

CAREER PROSPECTS
- **CAREERS SERVICE** - **UNEMPLOYED AFTER 6 MTHS** 6%

FAMOUS ALUMNI

Matthew Bannister (ex-controller, Radio 1); D H Lawrence (writer); Mary March (Director of NSPCC and Childline); Brian Moore (former England rugby player); Sir Robert Phillis (chairman of Guardian Media Group); Tim Robinson (cricketer); Sultan Raja Azlan Shah (King of Malaysia); David Ross (co-founder of Carphone Warehouse).

SPECIAL FEATURES

The University makes a big deal out of the fact that D H Lawrence was a student here and it's the foremost centre for research into his works, *although Lawrence's attitude to the University was, to say the least, ambivalent.*
Two recent Nobel Prizes (Medicine, Economic Science) *have got the research scientists all giddy.*

FURTHER INFO

○ **PROSPECTUSES** UNDERGRAD; POSTGRAD; VIDEO
○ **OPEN DAYS**

ACADEMIC ○○○○○○○○○○○○○

○ **RUSSELL GROUP**
35 schools and six departments are grouped into six faculties. All courses (bar Medicine, *thankfully*) are modular, meaning students can pick what they want to study. *Within reason.*

ENTRY POINTS: 240-360	AVE POINTS: 411
APPLICATIONS PER PLACE: 10	CLEARING: 7%
NO. OF TERMS: 2	LENGTH OF TERMS: 14/6WKS
STAFF TO STUDENT RATIO: 1:12	STUDY ADDICTS: 20%
TEACHING: ★★★★	RESEARCH: ★★★★★
YEAR ABROAD: 6%	SANDWICH STUDENTS: 4%
1STS: 15%	2.2S: 19%
2.1S: 61%	3RDS: 3%

ADMISSIONS

○ **APPLY VIA UCAS/NMAS FOR NURSING**

SUBJECTS

ARTS 17%   **BUSINESS, LAW & SOCIAL SCIENCES** 24%
EDUCATION 19% **ENGINEERING** 9%
MEDICINE & HEALTH SCIENCES 12%
BEST Agriculture; Biology; Civil, Chemical & Other Engineering; English-based Studies; European Languages & Area Studies; Finance & Accounting; History & Archaeology; Human & Social Geography; Law; Maths; Mechanically-based Engineering; Medicine & Dentistry; Other Languages & Area Studies; Philosophy; Physical Science; Psychology; Theology & Religious Studies.

LIBRARIES

○ **1,500,000** BOOKS ○ **4,150** STUDY PLACES
There's the main Hallward library, a medical library and a library on the Jubilee and Sutton sites. *Very good facilities, although nocturnally-inclined students aren't happy* about the 9.45pm closing time – they go 24-hr in exam time though.

COMPUTERS

○ **1,600** WORKSTATIONS ○ **24-HOUR ACCESS**
The Cripps Computing Centre is the base of the excellent University network, which is steadily moving into pastures wireless. All departments are being encouraged to jump on the e-learning bandwagon.

OTHER LEARNING FACILITIES

Language lab; media centre. Autumn 2006 sees the first 100 students walk through the doors of the *gleaming* new School of Veterinary Science – the first in the country for 50 years.

ENTERTAINMENT ○○○○○○○○○○

THE TOWN

○ **PRICE OF A PINT OF BEER** £2
○ **GLASS OF WINE** £2.50
○ **CAN OF RED BULL** £1.80
CINEMAS Nottingham has two multiplexes, one a mile from University Park and the other in the Cornerhouse complex in the city centre. There are three independent cinemas: the Nottingham Film Theatre shows arty pics and the Broadway offers student discounts. The Savoy is a rare instance of a cinema you can smoke in and also has double seats and an ice cream lady.
THEATRES The Royal Theatre is Nottingham's largest theatre and shows mainstream stuff, as well as opera and ballet. The Playhouse offers top rep and the Lace Market and Co-op Theatres host local amdram and fringe shows.
PUBS The local brew is Hardy & Hansons. The Lace Market/Hockley area of the city centre is the *buzziest. Pushplugs: Bluu; Geisha; the Market Bar (all in the centre); the Bag O' Nails; the Old Peacock; the Grove and the Ropewalk (all well-placed and have friendly atmospheres); Ye Olde Trip to Jerusalem (the country's oldest pub). Most local pubs are student friendly, though a few boozers in Beeston might be better avoided.*
CLUBBING *For the discerning clubber, Nottingham has many sweaty cattle markets where students can bop their socks off. Pushplugs: student nights at the Isis (sports night, Weds); Revolver at Obsessions (indie rock); Firefly at Lenton (drum & bass); Monday nights at Oceana; Monday Club at Snug; Climax at Faces.*
MUSIC VENUES Rock City is Nottingham's main indie/rock venue. The Social, Stealth and the Rescue Rooms are more intimate; The Strokes appeared recently. The Royal Concert Hall has classical concerts and more mainstream ents. The Nottingham Ice Arena melts down for big gigs. *Girls Aloud did Nottingham recently. Yes, they were rather tired afterwards.*
EATING OUT *Plenty to satisfy the most jaded palate, including the usual run of franchises and dodgy kebabberies. Pushplugs: Severez; Sapnars (Indian); Mayflower (Chinese); San Rimo's, Capocci (Italian & Mexican); Antibo's; Topo Gigio (Italian); Fat Cats (gorgeous cheesy garlic bread); Hogs Head*

Words in italics are Push's point of view — take it or leave it...

N

(very tasty burgers); Punchinellos (for that parental visit); Wok-u-like (bad name, good food).

UNIVERSITY
- **PRICE OF A PINT OF BEER** £1.65
- **GLASS OF WINE** £1.80
- **CAN OF RED BULL** £1.50

BARS There are well-patronised bars in the halls of residence and the sports centre, but the focal point is The Ark bar, which is *surprisingly dinky* (*plans are afoot to beef it up*) but stays open late at weekends. Campus 14 is a tried and tested bar crawl around halls, which still goes on *despite being outlawed by the sheriffs of Nottingham University.*

THEATRES The New Theatre and D H Lawrence Pavilion are used for 12 productions a year (student and professional). The University Arts Centre, Lakeside, hosts a year-round programme of theatre, comedy, dance and exhibitions (www.lakesidearts.co.uk).

FILM The cinema, Unifilms, screens three films a week – a nice balance of independent and mainstream offerings, from Starsky & Hutch to El Crimen del Padre Amaro.

CLUBBING The Ark puts on two club nights a week with cheesy 'classics' and recent hits.

COMEDY/CABARET A fortnightly session in The Ark *bags top chucklemonsters on tour.*

MUSIC VENUES *The Ark does a decent line in rock/indie student strummers, but has its sights set on bigger bands post-redevelopment.* The Summer Party is the *biggun*, though, bringing several thousand punters to the outdoor venue and big names including Trevor Nelson, Basement Jaxx and, er, Dr Karl Kennedy off 'Neighbours'.

FOOD The bars do *reasonable* sarnies to soak up the booze. The University-run Lakeside Diner and Food Court have a wider range *but they're a bit pricey.* The Ballroom is a *rather swanky continental-style* café and the Portland Dining Room has a *good* veggie variety. The Ark serves up nosh until midnight at weekends.

OTHER A *whopping* 80 balls a year including the Graduation extravaganza and the Snowflake Ball for Rag. The Hugh Stewart Hall has a 'formal' every fortnight – *think tuxes, gowns and three-course grub.* The University has its own art galleries, art bookshop, museum and a cafeteria (Café Lautrec).

SOCIAL ◗◗◗◗◗◗◗◗◗◗◗◗◗◗

UNIVERSITY OF NOTTINGHAM UNION
- **8 SABBATICALS** ● **TURNOUT AT LAST BALLOT** 22%
- **NUS MEMBER**

It's a very moderate union, concentrating on slickly-run services rather than identifiable political commitment, though demos have been more successful here than elsewhere. Relations between the Union and the University authorities are very good.

SU FACILITIES
The Portland Building is the centre of operations: bar; travel agent; three shops; advice centre; jobshop; theatre; rehearsal room; print shop and photocopying; record/CD/video library; car and minibus hire; NatWest and HSBC Banks (with cashpoints); games and vending machines; Endsleigh Insurance office; record & CD library; photo booth; pool table; juke box; TV lounge; eight meeting rooms; car parking.

CLUBS (NON-SPORTING)
Action For Earth; AIESEC; American; Arab; Archaeology; Baha'i; Bands; Bassic; Bell Ringing; Bike; Blade; Blow (flute and things, not Johnny Depp high as a kite); Bouncy Castle; Breakdance; Brunotts; Buddist; Chess & Backgammon; Capoeira; CCMP; Chinese; Chocolate; Christian Focus; Christians in Sport; Classical; Cocktail; CSSA; Culture; Cymsoc (Welsh); Cyprus; Duke of Edinburgh; Dark Celluloid; Darts; Drum and Bass; Exchange; Fashion; Feast; Flair; Football Supporters; Forest Supporters'; Frontside (skateboarding); Funk; Gaba (Going Abroad, Being Abroad); Gilbert & Sullivan; Guinness; Graduate Christian Fellowship, Gym, Hedonizm; Hellenic; High; Hindu; Hispanic; House, Humanist, Indian; Investment; Iranian; ISS (Pro Evolution Soccer gaming); Jazz; Juggling; Jumpers for Goalposts (kickabout footie); Kebab; Korean; Latin & Ballroom Dancing; Law; Living History; Magic; Mexican; Malaysian & Singapore; Model United Nations; Music; Mutant; Neuroscience; Nordic; New Lit; NSPM (peace); Orchestra; Omani; Pakistan; Politics; Role Play; Russian; Scout & Guide; Scribble; Seventies; Sikh; Slavonic; Soul; Star; Taiwan; Thai; Turkish; Wine. **See also Clubs tables.**

OTHER ORGANISATIONS
'Impact' (monthly magazine) and 'Grapevine' (weekly paper) are the press, but it's 'University Radio Nottingham' that wins the awards. A new Union mag and TV station are also brewing. Also 'Karnival', the charity Rag, is the country's biggest, raising more than £565,000 last year. The University's *tremendously successful* Community Action group – the biggest in the country – involves nearly 3,000 students in 75 projects and *can claim some responsibility for the excellent student/community relations.*

RELIGION
- **2 CHAPLAINS, OTHER MULTI-FAITH LEADERS**

Chapel and two Muslim prayer rooms in the Portland Building. Local places of worship for most Christian denominations, Muslims, Jews, Sikhs, Hindus and Buddhists.

PAID WORK
- **JOB BUREAU** ● **PAID WORK** TERM-TIME 45%; HOLS 85%

The Centre for Career Development runs job agency 'Nucleus'. Apart from the usual money scrambles, students have been known to sell themselves as guinea pigs at the medical school.

SPORTS ⏾⏾⏾⏾⏾⏾⏾⏾⏾⏾⏾⏾⏾

⊙ RECENT SUCCESSES RUGBY, HOCKEY, VOLLEYBALL, ROWING **⊙ BUSA RANKING** 7
Outstanding facilities. *Top-level sport is strong and there's a concerted effort to spread the exercise bug* with inter-hall competitions and taster sessions.

SPORTS FACILITIES
Most outdoor facilities are at Grove Farm, a mile from the campus, but some are also on campus. In all, there are 120 acres of playing fields including a floodlit artificial hockey pitch and a croquet lawn/bowling green. There's also the University lake, a 2,000m rowing course near the campus and the University Boathouse on the Trent. The sports centre on University Park campus has the biggest and *most efficient* sports hall in the country, a 25m eight-lane pool, two tennis courts, 12 indoor sports courts, a smaller hall, seven squash courts, a climbing wall, fitness room, table tennis, snooker room, bar and coffee shop. There's a state-of-the-art sports centre on the Jubilee Campus and another proposed for the Sutton Bonington site. There are bursaries for the best.

SPORTING CLUBS
10-Pin Bowling; Aikido; American Football; Bat Polo; Boat; Boxing; Canoe; Canoe Polo; Caving; Darts; Exploring; Gliding; Hand Ball; Ice Hockey; Inline Hockey; Ju-Jitsu; Korfball; Kung Fu; Lacrosse; Lifesaving; Mountaineering; Motorsport; Munro; Nin Jutsu; Parachuting; Paragliding; Polo; Rambling; Rifle & Clay; Rugby League; Snooker; Snowsports; Softball; Surfing; Table Tennis; Thai Boxing; Triathlon; Ultimate Frisbee; Water Polo; Water Skiing; Weight Training; Wing Chun. See also Clubs tables. **See also Clubs tables.**

ATTRACTIONS
In addition to Nottingham Forest and Notts County FCs, the Rugby Club and the County Cricket, there are geegees and woof-woofs racing at Colwick, the ice rink (where Torvill and Dean learned their craft), the National Watersports Centre and one of Europe's largest Lawn Tennis Association Centres.

ACCOMMODATION ⏾⏾⏾⏾⏾⏾⏾⏾⏾

IN UNIVERSITY
⊙ CATERED 20% **⊙ COST** £112 (31WKS)
⊙ SELF-CATERING 15% **⊙ COST** £76 (44WKS)
⊙ 1ST YRS LIVING IN 92% **⊙ 2ND YRS LIVING IN** 12%
⊙ FINALISTS LIVING IN 5% **⊙ POSTGRADS LIVING IN** 26%
⊙ INSURANCE PREMIUM ££££
AVAILABILITY Every first year is offered the chance to live in one of the catered halls or self-catering flats. Accommodation is available at Broadgate Park, Jubilee Campus, Raleigh Park, St. Peter's Court and *the most popular*, University Park. *The community atmosphere's very strong and there's a friendly rivalry with inter-hall competitions and so on.* There are 3,000 self-catering places in flats of five, six or seven students within Broadgate Park, Raleigh Park and St Peter's Court, within 5-25 mins walking radius of the University Park and Jubilee sites. New self-catered flats have been springing up *with glee abandon* in recent years. The privately-rented St Peters Court and Raleigh Park are *more expensive and less popular, though they have good bars.* There's some accommodation for married students and disabled students. There are also 200 university-owned houses for returning students.
CAR PARKING *No chance on campus except for students with special circumstances, which doesn't include not wanting to walk too far in heels.*

EXTERNALLY
⊙ AVE RENT £60 **⊙ LIVING AT HOME** 3%
AVAILABILITY *A decent supply of private housing. Lenton and Dunkirk (not that Dunkirk) are good places to look, lying as they do between the campus and the city. Burglaries are all too common in Lenton, so house contents insurance is an essential. The Park is popular and Beeston is also a student spot, but slightly further out. Stapleford and Ilkeston are a bit far and students tend to avoid Radford (none too safe) and The Meadows. Wollaton is an option for the more sedate scholars.*
HOUSING HELP The Accommodation Office has plenty of advisors to help with property vetting and contract approval. There's a vacancy list, approved landlord list and a bulletin board. The Union offers a few hints and tips too.

N

Words in italics are Push's point of view — take it or leave it...

WELFARE ⓾⓾⓾⓾⓾⓾⓾⓾⓾⓾⓾⓾⓾

SERVICES
- ⊙ LGBT OFFICER & SOCIETY
- ⊙ WOMEN'S OFFICER & SOCIETY
- ⊙ MATURE STUDENTS' OFFICER ⊙ POSTGRAD SOCIETY
- ⊙ INTERNATIONAL STUDENTS' OFFICER & SOCIETY
- ⊙ DISABILITIES OFFICER & SOCIETY
- ⊙ ETHNIC MINORITIES OFFICER & SOCIETY
- ⊙ LATE-NIGHT MINIBUS ⊙ WELFARE OFFICER
- ⊙ SELF-DEFENCE CLASSES ⊙ NIGHTLINE
- ⊙ UNIVERSITY COUNSELLORS 4 FULL
- ⊙ SU COUNSELLORS 4 FULL/6 PART ⊙ CRIME RATING !!!!!

The Students' Union Student Advice Centre is *its pride and joy*, co-ordinating all its welfare work from advice and help for all to the International Students' Bureau. It also offers Union solicitors for consultation (free for the first session).

HEALTH Cripps Health Centre has four doctors, an occupational health specialist and nurses, and offers extra care for a £12 annual subscription. Physios at the Sports Centre.

WOMEN Free attack alarms available from the Union, which also provides occasional self-defence classes. The late-night minibus runs every night.

CRECHES/NURSERY Some childcare facilities are available.

DISABILITIES Nottingham's been making *steady* efforts in improving access. There are adapted facilities, rooms for personal assistants, an alternative formats service and a disabled students' minibus.

FINANCE
- ⊙ AVE DEBT PER YEAR £4,008 ⊙ HOME STUDENT FEES £3,000

FEES No fees for a handful of courses in Physiotherapy, Nutrition or Nursing. Postgrad fees are around £2,840-£17,000. International undergrads have to pay between £9,210 and £21,950; international postgrads £5,400-£18,290.
- ⊙ ACCESS FUND £613,000 ⊙ SUCCESSFUL APPLICATIONS/YR 695
- ⊙ AVE PAYMENT £100-3,500

SUPPORT £3,000 grants each year for students from the poorest backgrounds. Cash bursaries for those with household incomes below £41,500 – about half the students, the University reckon.

NOTTINGHAM TRENT UNIVERSITY

FORMERLY NOTTINGHAM POLYTECHNIC, TRENT POLYTECHNIC

1. ⊙ **THE NOTTINGHAM TRENT UNIVERSITY** Burton Street, Nottingham, NG1 4BU **TEL** (0115) 941 8418
E-MAIL marketing@ntu.ac.uk **WEBSITE** www.ntu.ac.uk ⊙ **THE NOTTINGHAM TRENT UNIVERSITY UNION OF STUDENTS**
Byron House, Shakespeare Street, NG1 4GH **TEL** (0115) 848 6200 **E-MAIL** generaloffice@su.ntu.ac.uk
WEBSITE www.trentstudents.org
2. ⊙ **CLIFTON CAMPUS** Clifton, Nottingham. Contact details as city campus above.
3. ⊙ **BRACKENHURST CAMPUS** Brackenhurst, Southwell, Notts, NG25 0QF **TEL** (01636) 817 000

GENERAL ⓾⓾⓾⓾⓾⓾⓾⓾⓾⓾⓾⓾⓾

Once upon a time there was Trent Poly, then it became Nottingham Poly, and now it's in its third incarnation as a university. There are three campuses, the largest and *if the truth be known*, the main one is the *bustling City site* in the city centre. Life is more laid back at the more modern Clifton site, four miles away, and the third site at Brackenhurst 14 miles from the city centre. Over the last few years money has been thrown at Nottingham Trent *like it was a stripper at a rugby bash*, so it's got a bundle of modern facilities.

SEX RATIO: ♀50 ♂50	**FOUNDED:** 1992
FULL-TIME U'GRADS: 15,926	**PART-TIME:** 3,531
POSTGRADS: 5,317	**NON-DEGREE:** 8,722
AVE COURSE: 3YRS	**ETHNIC:** 18%
STATE:PRIVATE SCHOOL: 92:8	**FLUNK RATE:** 15%
MATURE: 13%	**INTERNATIONAL:** 5%
DISABLED: 320	**LOCAL:** 28%

ATMOSPHERE
It's a right ol' mix of ages and backgrounds. Students are scattered geographically, because most live out and they're spread across three sites. Despite that, they like nothing more than getting together and solemnly discussing the state of the world and the price of chips. Perhaps with a drink or two thrown in, for social lubrication purposes only.

SITES
CITY SITE (Art & Design, Business, Architecture, Design and the Built Environment, Law & Economics, Social Sciences) On the edge of the city centre, the University's main campus is a *jumble* of Victorian three- and four-storey houses, slabs of clean concrete and tower blocks (such as the main Newton Building) with *sparse* green areas in between. The Union's main centre is in a block designed as a swimming-pool complex. *It's an ugly building but with a lively atmosphere that endears it to the regulars.*
CLIFTON CAMPUS (5,950 students – Arts, Communication & Culture, Education, Biomedical & Natural Sciences, Computing & Informatics) Set

on a hill overlooking the River Trent and its valley, near where D H Lawrence set 'Sons and Lovers', Clifton is a *small, friendly and modern site with so much to offer that students can get isolated from city life*. It also boasts one of the only Environmental Chambers in the UK – *so eco-boffins can control a little bit of the weather. It feels more laid-back than the City Campus, as does Brackenhurst*.

BRACKENHURST (1,345 – Animal, Rural & Environmental Sciences) Full of *eager beavers* enjoying catering and sports facilities, library, SU and bar. It's all set in *tranquil* farmland and woods and has a commercial farm alongside its educational facilities.

NOTTINGHAM see University of Nottingham

TRAVEL
LOCAL Nottingham station is a mile from the City site, buses cost between 50-80p (or a quid return) from the City Centre to Clifton with several companies running regular services. There's also an inter-campus bus service every 15 mins (£1.20 single) which covers late-night antics and a tram service running through the city campus into town. Parking is free at Brackenhurst and cars are more common than on the other sites.

CAREER PROSPECTS
○ **CAREERS SERVICE** ○ **NO. OF STAFF** 6 FULL/11 PART
○ **UNEMPLOYED AFTER 6 MTHS** 6%
The careers service employs a shedload of people itself and has bulletin boards, library and advice.

FAMOUS ALUMNI
Steve Dixon (Sky News); Jonathen Glazner (director); Paul Kaye (comedian); Reynold Pearce & Andrew Fionda (fashion designers); Paul Ratcliffe (Olympic silver medallist, canoeing); Alan Simpson MP (Lab); Simon Starling (Turner prize winner); Steve Trapmore (Olympic gold rower).

FURTHER INFO
○ **PROSPECTUSES** UNDERGRAD; POSTGRAD; DEPARTMENTAL
○ **OPEN DAYS**

ACADEMIC ○○○○○○○○○○○○○○○

Along with a *chunky* amount of investment in new facilities the University is *vocationally very aware*. Strong industry links mean extensive opportunities for student placements and a high rate of graduate employment. The Law and Business schools have *good reps*. Nottingham Trent also has a *good* research rep and plenty of their *bizarre* discoveries find their way into the papers, from findings about female Russian suicide bombers to the psychological perils of watching TV news.

ENTRY POINTS: 160-360	AVE POINTS: 220
APPLICATIONS PER PLACE: 5	CLEARING: 12%
NO. OF TERMS: 3	LENGTH OF TERMS: 10WKS
STAFF TO STUDENT RATIO: 1:15	STUDY ADDICTS: 23%
TEACHING: **	RESEARCH: ****
YEAR ABROAD: N/A	SANDWICH STUDENTS: 34%
1STS: 7%	2.2S: 39%
2.1S: 45%	3RDS: 6%

ADMISSIONS
○ **APPLY VIA UCAS**

SUBJECTS
ARCHITECTURE, DESIGN & BUILT ENVIRONMENT 12%
ART & DESIGN 10%   **ARTS, COMMUNICATION & CULTURE** 10%
BUSINESS 20%   **BIOMEDICAL & NATURAL SCIENCES** 6%
COMPUTING & INFORMATION 4%   **EDUCATION** 7%   **LAW** 10%
SOCIAL SCIENCES 17%
BEST Biology; Civil, Chemical & Other Engineering; Communications & Information Studies; Economics; Education Studies; English; European Languages & Area Studies; History & Archaeology; Human & Social Geography; Law; Media Studies;Other subjects Allied to Medicine; Physical Science; Politics.
UNUSUAL Fashion, Knitwear Design & Knitted Textiles; Landscape & Heritage; Equine Sports Science.

LIBRARIES
○ **531,000 BOOKS** ○ **1,300 STUDY PLACES**
○ **24-HOUR ACCESS** ○ **SPEND PER STUDENT** £
There are three libraries shared between the campuses, most open 12 hrs a day, spiced up with 24-hr access at the Boots library. *Rather short on books, though.*

COMPUTERS
○ **7,000 WORKSTATIONS** ○ **24-HOUR ACCESS**
○ **SPEND PER STUDENT** ££££
Each site has its own IT centre, Clifton's is open round the clock. Most terminals have internet access and all halls are wired so students can dial-up to IT facilities.

OTHER LEARNING FACILITIES
Silly amounts of recent investment: £3m teaching and lab facility at Brackenhurst; £1.2m biomedical science building at Clifton campus; a new glass-fronted Art & Design building; currently developing a bioscience and healthcare innovation centre; a joint Toyota/University-built £3m training centre at Clifton – the only one of its kind in Europe (*which doesn't necessarily make it special, only rare*).

N

ENTERTAINMENT ()()()()()()()()()

THE CITY see University of Nottingham
- **PRICE OF A PINT OF BEER** £2
- **GLASS OF WINE** £2.50
- **CAN OF RED BULL** £1.80

UNIVERSITY
- **PRICE OF A PINT OF BEER** £1.75
- **GLASS OF WINE** £1.90
- **CAN OF RED BULL** £1.60

BARS Glo Bar at the City site is designed to be like a modern loft, *or an attic or something. It's popular anyway.* The Sub Bar's downstairs opens out into a night spot, *but closes unexpectedly from time to time.* Clifton has the Point, and *is quite happy about that.* The Museum bar at Brackenhurst is *less civilised than its name suggests, with karaoke and fancy dress nights going down a storm.*

THEATRES *One customised theatre and two lecture rooms with stages and drama soc shows at all of them.*

CLUBBING/MUSIC Byron House pulses with live tunes every Saturday and Climax (disco/soul/chart/R'n'B) every Friday. Editors, Vernon Kay and Roy Walker from 'Catchphrase' have all appeared recently and JK & Joel and Bodger & Badger have shown up at the weekly Flirt night at the Point. There's a weekly open mic night and a monthly amateur/stand-up night in Glo Bar and also a weekly Athletic Union event and monthly Union club night at Ocean in town.

FOOD The Sports Diner, Sandwich City and Chaucer Late deal with all fast food requirements. *The school dinners at the University's Legoland-like refectory pale by comparison.* Café Eliot feeds the Clifton site.

OTHER Balls are mostly handled by the societies but the SU does the *big* summer bash.

SOCIAL ()()()()()()()()()()

NOTTINGHAM TRENT STUDENTS' UNION
- **8 SABBATICALS** ● **TURNOUT AT LAST BALLOT** 21%
- **NUS MEMBER**

NTSU shuns politics, *preferring to stress its position as a commercial organisation.* The prez sits on the board of governors and student reps have a say at faculty board meetings.

SU FACILITIES
NTSU has facilities at all three sites, in Byron House on the City site and in the Benenson Building at Clifton. Byron's got: two bars; café; minibuses; travel agents; photocopying; shop; games and vending machines; pool tables; juke box; HSBC bank; recycling; meeting rooms;

insurance office. Clifton has: a bar; coffee shop; shop; bookshop; printing; pool tables; recycling; games machines. Both sites have employment stores and ticket agencies.

CLUBS (NON-SPORTING)
Chinese; Bangladeshi; Chinese Christian Fellowship; Current & Social Affairs; Dance; International Students; Malaysian; Mystro Singers; Nottingham Forest Supporters; Pro Evolution (computer game); Sikh; Skateboarding. **See also Clubs tables.**

OTHER ORGANISATIONS
'Platform', the free Union newspaper, is distributed free fortnightly during term. 'Fly FM' transmits for a month, twice a year. Do-gooders *do well* – there's an active RAG, the Student Festival Week raises cash for charity and Junction does *noble things in the wider world.* Stride offers courses on motivational and business skills, stress management and the like.

RELIGION
- **6 CHAPLAINS (COFE, RC, FC)**

The Christian Union is extremely forthright and influential. Muslim prayer space also available.

PAID WORK see University of Nottingham
- **JOB BUREAU** ● **PAID WORK** TERM-TIME 70%; HOLS 80%

The Students in Classrooms scheme lets undergrads earn money while studying. Students are recruited to work in local schools and further education colleges.

SPORTS ()()()()()()()()()()()()()

- **BUSA RANKING** 27

NTSU sorts out anything that may be considered sporty, but they don't call it sport, they call it *recreation, which reveals the University's attitude to all things healthy. It's not the winning that's important, it's the having a laugh, not being obese and, if possible, developing a six-pack.* The Athletic Union holds its own in the BUSA leagues and, *perhaps more importantly,* against their rivals at the University of Nottingham. The annual fee for facilities is a fiver and then there are *smaller additional* charges after that. The Coach4Sport scheme gets students teaching local kids and earning coaching qualifications in the process.

SPORTS FACILITIES
Sports facilities and 32 acres of playing fields are spread between three sites.

CITY Sports hall; indoor cricket nets; climbing wall; badminton; netball; volleyball court; fitness suites; aerobics studio; two squash courts; gym. *Enthusiasm gets a bit of a slap as access to the pitches is tricky.*

CLIFTON Sports hall; two gyms; multigym; two squash courts; playing fields; all-weather pitches; athletics track; cricket pitch.

BRACKENHURST Facilities for cricket, football and netball. Also home to the University's riding club.

SPORTING CLUBS
10-pin bowling; Airsoft (Japanese version of paintball); American Football; Capoeira; Cheerleading; Ice hockey; Ju-Jitsu; Korfball; Rowing; Surf; Table Tennis; Thai boxing; Trampolining; Ultimate Frisbee; Waterskiing. **See also Clubs tables.**

ATTRACTIONS see University of Nottingham

ACCOMMODATION 000000000

IN UNIVERSITY
- **SELF-CATERING** 21% ○ **COST** £73 (40WKS)
- **1ST YRS LIVING IN** 80% ○ **INSURANCE PREMIUM** ££££

AVAILABILITY Students *would be wise to apply early,* but those with unconditional offers or international students *need not worry.* 18 halls are spread out across the city – some within *spitting distance* of campus and others a 30min bus trek away. *The box-fresh Gill Street hall is a popular choice because it's so close to the campus and city centre.* All halls have secure entry systems, *which is handy as some, eg. Norton Court, aren't in the nicest of areas.* Clifton and Brackenhurst both have places and the University runs a head tenancy scheme *for students who can't be bothered to look for their own flat.*

CAR PARKING Parking permits allow a handful of deserving students to get at the *gold dust* spaces.

EXTERNALLY see University of Nottingham
- **AVE RENT** £55 ○ **LIVING AT HOME** 28%

HOUSING HELP The University's Accommodation Service keeps an office on each site has a register of the *least-offensive* housing. They help with contracts, run a landlord accreditation scheme and produce a helpful booklet. NTSU runs an introduction to house-hunting course for first years and does its own booklet.

WELFARE 0000000000000

SERVICES
- **MATURE STUDENTS' OFFICER & SOCIETY**
- **INTERNATIONAL STUDENTS' OFFICER & SOCIETY**
- **DISABILITIES OFFICER & SOCIETY**
- **LATE-NIGHT/WOMEN'S MINIBUS**
- **SELF-DEFENCE CLASSES**
- **UNIVERSITY COUNSELLORS** 3 FULL/5 PART
- **CRIME RATING:** !!!!!

The Union has an advice service, but the University has the *strongest helping hand,* offering counselling and student support services.
HEALTH Medical centres at the City and Clifton sites have doctors and nurses.
WOMEN Free attack alarms available.
CRECHES/NURSERY Both sites have daily nurseries for 1-5yrs and a holiday play scheme for 5-14yrs.
DISABILITIES The self-catering hall in Peel Street has wheelchair-friendly accommodation. Students are advised to contact the University's Disability Support Service to sort out any issues before they happen. *Having said that, access to lots of buildings is pretty dire.*

FINANCE
- **AVE DEBT PER YEAR** £3,609 ○ **HOME STUDENT FEES** £3,000
- **ACCESS FUND** £1,028,314
- **SUCCESSFUL APPLICATIONS/YR** 1,374
- **AVE PAYMENT** £100-£3,500

SUPPORT A spread of bursaries to *soothe* the top-up fees sting, with up to £3,700 for students from the poorest families.

NOTTINGHAM POLYTECHNIC
see *Nottingham Trent University*

◉ **The Northumberland building at Northumbria University was going to be powered by the biggest solar panels in Europe, until a passing student pointed out they were facing the wrong way.**

THE OPEN UNIVERSITY

➤ ORIENTAL STUDIES
see *SOAS*

UNIVERSITY OF OXFORD

Balliol college, Oxford
Brasenose College, Oxford
Christ Church, Oxford
Corpus Christi College, Oxford
Exeter College, Oxford
Greyfriars Hall, Oxford
Harris Manchester College, Oxford
Hertford College, Oxford
Jesus College, Oxford
Keble College, Oxford
Lady Margaret Hall, Oxford
Lincoln College, Oxford
Magdalen College, Oxford
Mansfield College, Oxford
Merton College, Oxford
New College, Oxford
Oriel College, Oxford
Pembroke College, Oxford
The Queen's College, Oxford
Regent's Park College, Oxford
Somerville College, Oxford
St Anne's College, Oxford
St Catherine's College, Oxford
St Edmund Hall, Oxford
St Hilda's College, Oxford
St Hugh's College, Oxford
St John's College, Oxford
St Peter's College, Oxford
Trinity College, Oxford
University College, Oxford
Wadham College, Oxford
Worcester College, Oxford

OXFORD BROOKES UNIVERSITY

➤ OXFORD POLYTECHNIC
see *Oxford Brookes University*

O

THE OPEN UNIVERSITY

○ **THE OPEN UNIVERSITY**, Walton Hall, Milton Keynes, MK7 6AA **TEL**: (01908) 274 066 **E-MAIL**: general-enquiries@open.ac.uk
WEBSITE: www.open.ac.uk ○ **OPEN UNIVERSITY STUDENTS' ASSOCIATION**, PO Box 397, Walton Hall, Milton Keynes, MK7 6BE
TEL: (01908) 652 026 **E-MAIL**: ousa@open.ac.uk **WEBSITE**: www.open.ac.uk/ousa/

GENERAL ◑◑◑◑◑◑◑◑◑◑◑◑◑◑

There was a time when most people's idea of the Open University was a mysterious realm of late-night BBC2 populated by tweedy, shock-headed academics. But the times are a-changing, and younger students who want to avoid major debt, or feel they're *not quite cut out for a conventional university experience, are attracted in growing numbers*. It's *especially well-suited* to disabled students, who might have access difficulties elsewhere. Courses are run by 'supported distance-learning', so there are TV and radio programmes (an increasing number produced with the BBC and aired during primetime), DVDS, CD-Roms and a host of swanky internet tools to *bolster the books*. Technological leaps and bounds are throwing up new teaching methods at a rate of gigabytes. All degrees are part-time, *and require particular powers of dedication, especially to resist the dubious temptations of Channel 5 in the middle of a lecture*. Some courses require attendance at one of the 297 regional centres or day schools as well as the substantial amount of self-study students need to undertake. No qualifications are necessary to enrol – hence their name.

SEX RATIO: ♂37 ♀63	**FOUNDED:** 1969
POSTGRADS: 19,239	**PART-TIME:** 149.744
AVE COURSE: 6YRS	**NON-DEGREE:** 643
MATURE: 88%	**ETHNIC:** 10%
DISABLED: 10,348	**FLUNK RATE:** N/A
INTERNATIONAL: 11%	

ATMOSPHERE

Open University students hit the books wherever they might be. *For some that means living rooms, local libraries or cafés. For others it has meant while 20,000 leagues beneath the sea in a Navy submarine, living homeless on the streets of London, on board a yacht, in the Bosnian war zone, while on kidney dialysis or while banged up at Her Majesty's pleasure. The closest real place the OU could find to reflect the essentially virtual location is lego-inspired Milton Keynes. Of course, most students are lucky enough never to visit.* They make use of official study centres attached to other universities and colleges around the country (most recently the Tremough campus in Cornwall, part of the Combined Universities Initiative and run in conjunction with Exeter and Plymouth – see Exeter University for more details). Most OU students are mature *(in attitude, as well as age) and tend to juggle study with other commitments (kids, jobs, mortgages,*

prison, etc.). One student even perfpormed as a circus contortionist. But, like the man says, 'OU students do it on their own', which means the atmosphere is a totally individual thing.

CAREER PROSPECTS
○ **CAREERS SERVICE** ○ **NO. OF STAFF** 2 FULL
Most OU students already have jobs – often their employers are shelling out for them in the first place. But the University lays on workshops, newsletters and bulletin boards to *keep job-hunters' options open*.

FAMOUS ALUMNI
Joan Armatrading (singer); Connie Booth (actress/writer); Craig Brown CBE (former Scotland football manager); Brian Burrige (Air Chief Marshal); Julie Christie (actress); Micky Dolenz (ex-Monkee); Jerry Hall (actress, model); Sheila Hancock (actress); Matthew Kelly (TV presenter); Lord Gardiner (former Lord Chancellor); Dave Sexton (football manager); Vikram Solanki (cricketer); Susan Tully (actress); Meles Zenawi (Prime Minister of Ethiopia). Honorary degrees given to Bill Bryson (author), Alan Ayckbourn (playwright) and Heather Mills-McCartney (former model and wife of Sir Paul).

SPECIAL FEATURES
In March 2000 the OU held the world's first Virtual Degree ceremony. *It sounds like something from The Matrix*, but was actually to award MAs to students in eight different countries who had taken their entire degrees online.
The BBC's 'Child In Our Time' programme is produced along with the OU.

FURTHER INFO
○ **PROSPECTUSES** UNDERGRAD; POSTGRAD; DEPARTMENTAL
○ **OPEN DAYS**
There are student advisors at regional campuses. For further info on courses – many of which are introductory, non-degree or tied in with the BBC – see www.open.ac.uk/courses.

ACADEMIC ◑◑◑◑◑◑◑◑◑◑◑◑◑◑

Unlike most universities, there are no academic qualifications required to study. The OU has a *well-earned* reputation for teaching excellence, *which it shows off by regularly trouncing the Oxbridge upstarts on University Challenge*. Assessment varies from course to course, with a mix of written assignments, oral or practical assessments, exams and dissertations. Tutors are available via phone or e-mail if support is needed. The days of kipper-tied

BBC2 professors warbling about particle physics are long gone and these days you're more likely to encounnter glossier OU-made programmes like Child of Our Time or Coast. *As always, the emphasis is on the individual* – so it's up to students how, when and where they work. *Sounds like a slacker's paradise, but it takes Herculean commitment and motivation.*

LENGTH OF TERMS Traditionally the OU academic year has run from February to October, but many courses now offer multiple start dates.

STAFF TO STUDENT RATIO: 1:81	STUDY ADDICTS: N/A
TEACHING: ★★★★★	RESEARCH: ★★★
1STS: 18 %	2.2s: 31%
2.1s: 41%	3RDS: 10%

ADMISSIONS
◉ **APPLY DIRECT**
No formal qualifications are necessary, though the OU will advise students on what level of course is best suited. Younger students are being actively recruited (around 20% of newbies are under 25); even prisoners can apply.

LIBRARIES
◉ **200,000+ BOOKS** ◉ **150 STUDY PLACES**
There's a 200,000 volume central library in Milton Keynes, although most students are more likely to use OU regional study centres. Students can also use several thousand e-books, as well as many local and other institution libraries.

COMPUTERS
More and more courses are conducted on the net, and in many cases the courses actually demand computer access. Electronic resources are excellent. An online library contains core text books and more than 4,000 others as well as a conference system that allows students in 150 courses to join in discussion forums. NA dthese days, students are as likely to slide in a DVD as they are to open weighty tomes. It's up to students to make the practical arrangements, though, either privately or through local colleges and libraries.

SUBJECTS
ART & DESIGN 9%   **BUSINESS** 14%   **COMPUTER SCIENCE** 5%   **EDUCATION** 9%   **ENGINEERING** 8%   **HEALTH & SOCIAL WELFARE** 8%   **HUMANITIES** 12%   **(MODERN) LANGUAGES** 7%   **MATHS** 5%   **MEDICAL SCIENCES** 9%   **SCIENCES** 16%   **SOCIAL SCIENCES** 14%   **BEST** All

SOCIAL �

OPEN UNIVERSITY STUDENTS' ASSOCIATION (OUSA)
OUSA isn't a political organisation, and it concentrates fairly exclusively on academic and welfare issues. 19 part-time officers run OUSA (not affiliated to the NUS) and the minority of students apply for membership.

SU FACILITIES
No central facilities, although OUSA do sell stationery and products by mail order, co-ordinate some societies and organise occasional ents at summer schools.

CLUBS (NON-SPORTING)
Astronomy & Planetary Science; Change Ringers; Chemistry; Christian Fellowship; Computing; Correspondence Chess; Development & Environment; Geological; History; Law; London; London Arts; M500; Mountaineering; Music; Physics; Poetry; Postgraduate Students; Psychological; Science; Technology and Space; Shakespeare; Students for Ethical Science; Tadpoles; Travel & Study. **See also Clubs tables.**

OTHER ORGANISATIONS
'OU Student' is published bi-monthly, although this is designed and published alongside 'Sesame', the official University newspaper. 'Open Eye' is published for graduates. OUSET is the charity fund-raising body, which also provides funds for students. This occupies the gap *usually filled by Rag.*

PAID WORK
All students *pull in the pennies* and around four in five OU students already work full-time while studying.

WELFARE illillillillillillillill

SERVICES
Student advisors at regional campuses are on hand to provide academic advice and personal support. Childcare's available on campus. There is also an online peer support network, run via OUSA.

FINANCE
FEES The estimated cost of a BA/BSc degree is £5,000, which students pay for module-by-module. This was once regarded as expensive, but in contrast to the cost of a degree in a conventional university, *it's starting to look like pretty good value*, especially if an employer is forking out. Also, since most students are earning while learning, there's no spectre of debt looming over them on graduation. UK postgrads pay £300-£2,795 per course.
◉ **ACCESS FUND** £1,005,000
◉ **SUCCESSFUL APPLICATIONS/YR** 27,909
SUPPORT The average access payment covers the cost of almost 1.5 60-point modules (an honours degree requires 360 points). The student fundraising body OUSET is responsible for handing out assistance, and looks at cases on individual merit. There are £500/year loans available for students on benefits or low incomes, and a hardship fund and grants for help with course and living costs – last year 1,800 students benefited.

Words in italics are Push's point of view — take it or leave it...

➡ **ORIENTAL STUDIES**
see *SOAS*

UNIVERSITY OF OXFORD

⊙ **UNIVERSITY OF OXFORD**, University Offices, Wellington Square, Oxford, OX1 2JD **TEL** (01865) 288 000
E-MAIL undergraduate.admissions@admin.ox.ac.uk **WEBSITE** www.ox.ac.uk ⊙ **OXFORD UNIVERSITY STUDENT UNION**
Thomas Hull House, New Inn Hall Street, Oxford, OX1 2DH **TEL** (01865) 288 450 **E-MAIL** enquiries@ousu.org **WEBSITE** www.ousu.org

GENERAL ◖◖◖◖◖◖◖◖◖◖◖◖◖◖

Oxford is the oldest university in the country and, along with its great rival Cambridge, *probably the most famous in the world.* Like Cambridge, the university itself is a *shadowy hard-to-pindown sort of thing* – students only really see it in the shape of the 39 colleges and seven private halls. *They've all got their own quirks and characteristics.* The town's *elegantly lovely,* surrounded by *quaint* little villages in *gently rolling* countryside. The 'dreaming spires' of the older colleges' chapels *really are impressive,* but they're set apart from the *otherwise unassuming* centre of town. *Students and townies generally keep out of each other's way, although everyone curses and trips over the tourists. There are loads of hearty picture postcard moments, of ruddy-faced bright young things sailing around on bicycles, in boats on the rivers (Cherwell and Isis) and in states of essay-induced panic.*

SEX RATIO: ♂53 ♀47	**FOUNDED:** c.1150
FULL-TIME U'GRADS: 11,225	**PART-TIME:** 0
POSTGRADS: 6,491	**NON-DEGREE:** 0
AVE COURSE: 3-4YRS	**ETHNIC:** 15%
STATE:PRIVATE SCHOOL: 52:48	**FLUNK RATE:** 2%
MATURE: 6%	**INTERNATIONAL:** 12%
DISABLED: 170	**LOCAL:** 2%

ATMOSPHERE

Everyone's stereotypes of Oxford – elitism, snobbery, Pimm's, punts, death-defying cyclists, gowns and mortar-boards, dreaming spires and Inspector Morse – are at least partly true. But like most stereotypes, there are an awful lot of exceptions. Oxford's awash with tradition, pomposity and circumstance. Life, both at work and out of it, is *intense* and lots of students exist in a *flurry of hyperactivity. It can look intimidating, but there's something for everyone,* whether it's sport, music, drama, debating, fly-fishing or just propping up the college bar. Student life's *centred* around the colleges, where everyone lives, sleeps, eats, drinks, works, plays and socialises. *Each has its own freaks and foibles, and it would be a fool indeed who tried to generalise.* They vary in size from the *miniscule* (Greyfriars, Campion Hall) to the *massive* (Christ Church, Keble), and in personality from the stuffy

(Magdalen) to the street (Wadham fancies itself as a bit edgy). *It's no mean feat to pick one, but a bit of careful selection pays off.*

OXFORD
⊙ **POPULATION** 134,428 ⊙ **CITY CENTRE** 0 MILES
⊙ **LONDON** 55 MILES ⊙ **BRISTOL** 55 MILES
⊙ **BIRMINGHAM** 55 MILES
⊙ **HIGH TEMP** 21 ⊙ **LOW TEMP** 0 ⊙ **RAINFALL** 54
Oxford's not exactly the party centre of the universe. Forget the glamour – it's a small city that can get a bit parochial and dull after just a few weeks. It has a *functional* civic bit (Cornmarket Street) with *regular* high-street shops and a couple of *fairly underwhelming* arcades. *But the intensity of life, provided by the University, makes it more than the sum of the parts.*

TRAVEL

TRAINS Trains draw up at Oxford Station, close enough to the steps of the city's most central colleges. Mainline services to London (£11.20), Bristol (£17.80), etc.
COACHES As well as National Express serving London (£7), Bristol (£12) and all points beyond, there are other coach companies (Oxford Express) serving London all through the night, with Oxford Airline also going to and from Heathrow and Gatwick.
CAR Ten mins off the M40. Also on the A40, A34, A423, A43 and A420. However, there's very restricted access to the city centre and parking is either *limited or expensive.*
HITCHING *Pretty good on the M40 or the larger local A roads, but get out of the city by bus.*
LOCAL Several local bus companies with *frequent and cheap* services (40p to get as far as digs in Jericho), but they're not really worth it for shorter trips.
UNIVERSITY OUSU runs a nightbus.
TAXIS *Black cabs and minicabs aplenty, but they're happy to charge a small fortune for a smaller journey.*
BICYCLES Oxford's flat, some roads are closed to cars and most colleges have sheds. *A few words of warning: (i) a good lock and a cheap bike is the safest defence against theft; (ii) Pedestrians – watch out for two-wheeled lunatics.*

CAREER PROSPECTS
⊙ **CAREERS SERVICE** ⊙ **NO. OF STAFF** 16 FULL
⊙ **UNEMPLOYED AFTER 6 MTHS** 5%
Forget any romantic notions of being headhunted straight out of Oxford into the City, the BBC or the

Foreign Office. Oxford grads have to scrap it out with *the rabble nowadays. So it's a good job* the careers service has vacancy lists, careers library, talks and counselling.

FAMOUS ALUMNI
See individual colleges.

SPECIAL FEATURES
Oxford's *full of ritual*, especially when it comes to exams. Students have to dress in subfusc (formal clothes) and *look like Batman on the way to the Oscars.* It's a well-known myth that once a student turned up for his final exams and demanded a glass of sherry in accordance with an ancient rite. After the exam, he was fined a shilling by his college authorities for not wearing his sword during his exam – another forgotten statute. *Rites like these seem positively sane compared with some of the continuing traditions.* Speaking of which, it's worth pointing out that while the official HESA figures show a high number of part-time students, it includes those on continuing education and graduate courses – you can't actually apply to do a part-time undergrad degree at Oxford. *What do you think this is, the Open University?*

FURTHER INFO
○ **PROSPECTUSES** UNDERGRAD; POSTGRAD; DEPARTMENTAL; VIDEO ○ **OPEN DAYS**
Most colleges produce their own prospectuses and some JCRs also have alternative guides.

ACADEMIC ○○○○○○○○○○○○○

○ **RUSSELL GROUP**
Workloads are *tough* compared to the *mere mortal* unis, but facilities are *a world apart.* Terms are *short* (eight weeks), although most students stay longer, boning up for exams with *weird* and *wonderful* titles like 'mods', 'collections', 'prelims' and, er, 'finals'. The newer parts of the Uni include the Begbroke Business and Science Park and the *impressive* glass-fronted Said Business School.

ENTRY POINTS: 340–360	AVE POINTS: N/A
APPLICATIONS PER PLACE: 4	CLEARING: 0%
NO. OF TERMS: 3	LENGTH OF TERMS: 8WKS
STAFF TO STUDENT RATIO: 1:8	STUDY ADDICTS: 36%
TEACHING: ★★★★★	RESEARCH: ★★★★★
YEAR ABROAD: 5%	SANDWICH STUDENTS: 0
1STS: 24%	2.2S: 9%
2.1S: 65%	3RDS: 1%

ADMISSIONS
○ **APPLY VIA UCAS**

LIBRARIES
○ **6,000,000** BOOKS ○ **2,500** STUDY PLACES
○ **24**-HR ACCESS
The famous Bodleian Library is the collective title given to the University's main research libraries (including the Radcliffe Science Library, Bodleian Law Library and Indian Institute Library, mainly housed in the Old and the New Library Buildings, and all the *marvellous* others). It is one of the country's five copyright libraries which means that it can demand a copy of any book published in the UK and, as a consequence, it has over six million books (*including The Push Guides*). 948,000 of these – yup, a mere 948,000 – are on open shelves and most of them can't be borrowed, though students can view them *if they ask nicely.* In fact, Oxford students don't have the right to use the Bodleian until they've undergone one of the University's many *bizarre* initiation rituals. This one involves swearing *oddly practical* oaths such as agreeing not to set fire to the buildings. *Nude dancing and sacrificing virgin goats is not usually an essential part of this ceremony.* Each college and most University departments also have their own libraries, most of which lend books.

COMPUTERS
○ **2,500** workstations ○ **24**-hr access
Most colleges have *woken up to the idea of an IT revolution* and upgraded from their clapped-out Amstrads. The Computer Teaching Centre has 100 networked terminals and the Computer Service which provides support for students' research when their departments fall short. 24-hr access during term-time.

SUBJECTS
ARTS/HUMANITIES 35.5% **MEDICAL SCIENCES** 6.9% **SCIENCES** 37.4% **SOCIAL SCIENCES** 20.2%
BEST Archaeology; Biochemistry; Biological Sciences/Forestry; Classics/Ancient History; Economics; Engineering; Fine Art; Materials; Maths; Medicine/Physiology; Modern Languages; Oriental Studies; Philosophy; Physics; Politics; Psychology.

ENTERTAINMENT ○○○○○○○○○

THE CITY
○ **PRICE OF A PINT OF BEER** £2.50
○ **GLASS OF WINE** £2.60 ○ **CAN OF RED BULL** £2.50
CINEMAS For standard blockbusters there are two ABC Cinemas (three screens at one, one at the other) *and for the slightly higher brow*, The Phoenix (two screens) in Jericho and the Ultimate Picture Palace in Cowley.
THEATRES The New Theatre has *standard* family fare with pantos at Xmas and summer specials after the end of term. It also hosts the occasional concert. The Playhouse tends towards *brainier* offerings, including a few big student productions and a decent comedy lineup. The Pegasus Theatre's *on the fringe in every sense* with experimental productions and a bit of a trek to get there and also shows student productions. The *recently tarted-up* Old Fire Station also hosts student stuff.

PUBS The old-school charm of many of Oxford's pubs comes at *premium price*. As a result, they aren't too popular with *pocket-conscious* students. *Pushplugs: The King's Arms ('The KA' as it's affectionately known); The Turf; The Bullingdon Arms; The Lamb & Flag (now owned by St John's); The Eagle and Child (C S Lewis and Tolkien used to quaff there). The Jolly Farmers is the main gay haunt.*

CLUBBING *Ungracious dogholes in the main. The Bridge is the best of the bunch. Other slightly more dubious, but still popular options are Po Na Na, the Purple Turtle and the Coven.*

MUSIC VENUES The music scene's *booming*, with *loads* of local bands dreaming of *doing a Coldplay. Pushplugs: The New Theatre (big, mainstream); The Pub Oxford; The Zodiac (indie).*

EATING OUT Various kebab vans open *till they run out of domestic animals or 3am – whichever is sooner.* Cowley Road in general is good for cheap eats. *Pushplugs: Browns (perfect parent parlour); Jamal's (Indian); Queen's Lane Coffee House; George and Davis (ice cream); Radcliffe Arms (pub grub); La Cappanina (Italian, Supergrass ate here).*

THE UNIVERSITY

BARS Each college has a bar, some of which only serve their own students. The Union (debating society) has a bar, *but it's closed to the riff-raff*: Members Only.

THEATRES The Old Fire Station, the Burton-Taylor Theatre (above The Playhouse) and the larger Newman Rooms host student stuff. In summer there are outdoor productions in many College gardens.

MUSIC VENUES Student bands play in any room large enough – bars usually – and the Sheldonian Theatre and Holywell Music rooms host classical concerts. However, because the University has no single big venue, *it doesn't often attract big names*, except at ball-time.

CLUBBING The SU runs club nights througout the week at various clubs, under the brandname Zoo. Most colleges have weekly, fortnightly or termly 'bops' – *sweaty and intensive pissups that often serve as hotbeds for college scandal.*

COMEDY/CABARET The Oxford Revue (student comedy group which pursues a healthy rivalry with Cambridge's Footlights) performs stand-up and improv at the Comedy Cellar at the Union and does other special shows.

FOOD Oxford tends to go for formal meals in a big way, although the frequency, quality and number of gongs and Latin grace-readings *differs* from college to college. There are cafeterias, often known *(predictably obscurely)* as butteries. There are few University facilities – no central refectory, although some faculties have caffs.

BALLS Most colleges have an annual ball where everyone *dons their dapperest and thrills* to the strains of live bands, discos, cabarets, casinos, hypnotists, karaoke, in fact *anything that becomes a lot more fun when completely wrecked. Some love them; others resent shelling*

out £80 for a spruced-up night out in college. Either way, balls are an Oxbridge institution. Some colleges have a cheaper alternative called an event, which usually doesn't involve the get-up or the grub and costs nearer £20.

OXFORD UNIVERSITY STUDENTS' UNION
◎ 6 SABBATICALS

OUSU doesn't have a union building, as there are 39 other common rooms for students to *hang around shooting pool and dodging lectures* in. The main role of OUSU is to *make a lot of noise* campaigning and representing students at University level. Each college has a Junior Common Room (JCR), which is usually a committee as well as a building. They're all affiliated to OUSU, and although OUSU isn't affiliated to the NUS, some JCRs are. *Keeping up? Anyway, OUSU co-ordinates a swamp of societies and prints alternative prospectuses, freshers' guides and so forth. It's generally leftier than the average and run by cracks and hacks on their way up the greasy pole.*

CLUBS

Aegisiety (genocide prevention); Air Squadron; Alternotives; Arcadian Singers (acapella); Asia Pacific; Australia New Zealand; B-Boy Breaks; Beaufort; Belly Dancing; Buddhist; Caribbean; Carrom Club; Chamber Music; Chess; Chinese; Comedy; C S Lewis; Donut Kings; Dutch; Gamelon (Javanese percussion); Finest-Jazz; Flamenco; Food; Free Tibet; Future Flyers; Greek; Hertford College Music; Hindu; Hispanic; The Hive (debate); Indian; Korean; Jacari (home teaching); Jain; The Jazz Band; Latin Reading & Conversation; Learning Together; LGBT; Malaysian; Malaysia-Singapore; Mexican; Officer Training Corps; Out of the Blue (acapella); Oxford Belles; Oxford Development Abroad; Oxford Entrepreneurs; Oxford Fund for Victims of the War; Oxford Guild; Oxford Imps (comedy); Oxford Link Africa Student; Oxford Reform; Palestine; Persianiety; Polish; Progress Eritrea; Quiz; Red Soul Brigade (soul band); Reformed Church; Rock Gospel Choir; Scandanavian; Science; Scottish; Scottish Dance; Stop Aids; Student Action for Refugees; Students Supporting Street kids; Student Pugwash (armed conflict/nuclear disarmament); Tabs are for Flying (Theatre technicians and design); Taiwanese; Tarvithorn (Tolkien); Thai; Tory Reform; Trance and House; Travelaid; Tiddlywinks; Ukrainian; United Nations Association; United World Colleges. **See also Clubs tables.**

OTHER ORGANISATIONS

Students who spend their days at Oxford doing nothing but their degrees are *made to feel like David Beckham at a Mensa meeting*. There are plenty of fields of endeavour to choose from including various sports, OUSU and college JCRs as well as the following:

THE OXFORD UNION SOCIETY Not to be confused with OUSU (the Students' Union), the Union is Oxford's *world famous* debating society. Ted Heath, Edwina Currie and Benazir Bhutto are among its ex-presidents. Its *high profile* has attracted some of the world's most famous speakers to take part in debates and discussions, from Yasser Arafat to Vinny Jones, JFK to Kermit the Frog. The Union is also the name of the HQ building which offers a social scene, a bar, restaurant, the Comedy Cellar, a library and all the paraphernalia of traditional gentlemen's clubs, but women can join too. *That's the good news. The bad news is that it costs £100 and the Union is a nest for some of the University's most arrogant and obnoxious knob-ends.*

OXFORD UNIVERSITY DRAMATIC SOCIETY (OUDS) Almost every day of every term, the population of Oxford is faced with a choice of several student theatrical performances. Thesps visit each other's productions and thus the shows go on. The standard often reaches a *thoroughly professional* level, but sometimes, *well, it doesn't,* and the selection is as diverse as any *legal* experience in a theatre can get. Whether the star of Spielberg's last pic or the third sheep in the primary school nativity effort, new talent is welcomed to auditions with *open arms, kisses on both cheeks and the words 'lovely, daaahling'.* The post-audition reception is *more discriminating and bitter cries of 'Clique!' have echoes of truth,* although drama at Oxford is so *widespread* that even the *most wooden pretenders* get a chance to try their board-treading technique. Meanwhile, there are *just as many* opportunities to play the non-singing part of unsung hero backstage. OUDS is the organisational body which co-ordinates and supports this plague of plays and runs the Cuppers drama competition.

MEDIA Magazines come and go *as fast as the tourists* in Oxford but there are several long-standing publications with *excellent* reputations. Primarily, there's 'Cherwell', Oxford's award-winning weekly student newspaper. *Last of the newspapers and least,* is OUSU's 'Oxford Student'. For magazines, there's 'Isis', the students' answer to Vogue and *verbosity,* and various others such as 'International Review', 'Amazon' (women's), 'Phoenix' (termly magazine of student writing, both poetry and prose) and a *recycling binful* of college gossip/scandal rags and societies' newsletters. 'Oxide', the radio station, rides above the usual amateur airwave-hogging with sophistications like recording its DJs live from a club once a week.

RAG With its own sabbatical co-ordinator, Rag raises more than £50,000 a year with all the standard pranks, stunts and events, including Jailbreak, where students have to travel as far as they can in 24hrs without shelling out a penny – so far Japan and Canada are the distances to beat.

STUDENT VOLUNTEER ACTION The relationship between students and locals *can't be described as nasty – they just tend to misunderstand or ignore each other.* Volunteer Action links students up with nearly 40 help groups both in the University and the local community, *going some way to improve matters in the process.* All sorts of other activities incude KEEN which works with kids and young adults with special needs.

RELIGIOUS

Put any group of self-consciously intellectual people together – such as Oxford students – and within minutes they'll have established as many different religious groups as they can invent and then some. Many of the colleges owe their existence to funding from Christian sinners in fear of hell. *There's not so much quaking at impending damnation any more, but the fervour for activity amongst Oxford students extends to religion as much as anything else.*

CHRISTIANITY Students at Christ Church who say they're popping down to the college chapel are talking about Oxford's Anglican cathedral. The other colleges have less high-church chapels and most have at least one chaplain. Other Christian denominations are also catered for around town: Catholics, Baptists, Evangelicals, Methodists, URC, Seventh-Day Adventists, Christian Scientists, Pentecostals, Unitarians, Quakers, Orthodox, *Cliff Richard Fan Club* and so on. The Inter-Collegiate Christian Union (OICCU) brings these Christian groups together.

ISLAM Mosque and prayer room at the Islamic Studies centre.

JEWS Local synagogue and large Jewish student population.

OTHERS Three Buddhist centres locally and a Sikh Gurdwara in Headington.

PAID WORK
○ JOB BUREAU

Students are banned from working during term-time (*not that most of them would be able to find time*). That's not to say that no one does and Oxford has *plenty* of shops and bars around to take students on. The Careers Service has a vacation employment service, and a wide range of jobs and internships are available.

SPORTS ○○○○○○○○○○○○○

○ RECENT SUCCESSES ROWING **○ BUSA RANKING** 8

One of the highest accolades in University sport (apart from being able to drink a pint of beer in under three seconds) is an Oxbridge blue. To earn one, you've got to be selected for one of the University's major sports teams. These teams often compete on a first class level, which doesn't necessarily mean that they're better than all the other University teams, just that they're highly respected and they expect great things. The biggest grudge is the Oxbridge rivalry, Oxford generally having the edge over Cambridge in football and rugby in recent years. A more cynical observer than Push might say the University admissions procedure becomes a whole lot more flexible if you have an international sporting reputation. Push would (for legal reasons) like to distance itself from any suggestion of the sort. Suffice it to say that the University places emphasis and funding on its *impressive* record in sports, both minor and major. Sport at a college level is more *geared to fun and fitness* and is *very welcoming*, even to students who aren't quite Olympians.

SPORTS FACILITIES

All colleges have their own facilities to *varying degrees* and the University has an *excellent* range of central amenities: floodlit all-weather hockey pitch; playing fields; sports halls; swimming pool; squash courts; athletics field; bowls and croquet in the quads; tennis courts; gym (with multi-gym); and, of course, the Rivers Isis and Cherwell. The town also has a golf course, ice rink and two swimming pools.

SPORTING CLUBS

Aikido; American Football; Australian Rules Football; Boat Club; Bowling; Boxing; Caving; Cheerleading; Croquet; Dancesport; Eton Fives; Floorball; Gaelic Football; Gliding; Gymnastics; Handball; Hurling; Ice Hockey; Jitsu; Kendo; Kickboxing; Korfball; Kung Fu; Lacrosse; Lifesaving; Pentathlon; Pistol; Polo; Pool; Power lifting; Punting; Rowing; Rackets; Real Tennis; Rifles; Surfing; Table Tennis; Tai Chi; Triathlon; Ultimate Frisbee; Underwater Exploration; Windsurfing; Wrestling; Yachting. **See also Clubs tables.**

ATTRACTIONS

The Combined Oxford Universities Cricket team is a joint effort with Oxford Brookes. Oxford United FC are the *lowly* local team and the city also has its own ice hockey side.

ACCOMMODATION ◗◗◗◗◗◗◗◗◗◗

IN COLLEGE
- **CATERED** 87% ○ **1ST YRS LIVING IN** 100%
- **INSURANCE PREMIUM** ££

AVAILABILITY *One of the best* features of the Oxford colleges is that accommodation is guaranteed in college rooms *(often of an excellent standard)* for all first years. Most colleges also provide for finalists and so, if they want, students can usually stay in college for all but one of their years – though some can even stay in for their whole University career. What's more, rooms are cleaned, beds are made and sleeping partners are embarrassed by 'scouts' in most colleges. Each college has its own quirks and quiddities – details can be found in the entries following. The SU reckon rents can vary to the tune of £30 a week in different colleges. Centrally, the University has no accommodation other than a

few flats – about 390 places – for families, couples and single graduates, *but you can offer to snog the Chancellor to get them and it still won't help.*

CAR PARKING Oxford city council have done their very best to make it *nigh-on impossible* to park in the city centre and most colleges won't let students bring cars without a very, very good reason.

EXTERNALLY
○ Ave rent £83

AVAILABILITY Housing in Oxford *rivals London* for costliness, *although there's more to be had for the money.* Cowley Road and Jericho are the most *popular* locations.

HOUSING HELP The *best* way of finding a house is to get friendly with someone who's got one the year before you need it. You can also turn to agencies who'll charge a supplement, or to ads on notice boards around the colleges. The University-run Accommodation Office with four full-time staff, a vacancies list and bulletin board *usually points students in the right direction.* The local Housing Rights Centre is much frequented by students, but, like OUSU, they can only offer free advice and don't have any vacancies to dish out.

WELFARE ◗◗◗◗◗◗◗◗◗◗◗◗◗◗

SERVICES
- ○ **LGBT OFFICER** ○ **POSTGRAD OFFICER**
- ○ **MATURE STUDENTS' OFFICER** ○ **DISABILITIES OFFICER**
- ○ **ETHNIC MINORITIES OFFICER** ○ **INTERNATIONAL STUDENTS OFFICER** ○ **WOMEN'S OFFICER**
- ○ **LATE-NIGHT MINIBUS** ○ **NIGHTLINE** ○ **CRIME RATING** !!

The OUSU Welfare Officer can advise and refer students with most problems. Law students give free advice at OUSU two days a week.

WOMEN St Hilda's is the last all-female college. *Life in the male-dominated colleges can have a testosterone-y aftertaste.* A nightwalk service accompanies women walking alone at night and there's a women-only bus.

CRECHES/NURSERY Two nurseries with 94 places for 5mths-5yrs.

DISABILITIES Access is *gradually improving* and efforts include OUSU's disabled access guide, a disability co-ordinator and Taylor House, an accommodation block with special facilities. Some colleges have Braille machines, etc.

FINANCE
- ○ **AVE DEBT PER YEAR** £2,774
- ○ **HOME STUDENT FEES** £3,000

FEES International student fees: £8,880 (Arts), £10,360 (Social Sciences & Humanities), £11,840 (Sciences), £21,700 (Medicine).

SUPPORT Bursaries for anyone with a household income of less than £37,425 and sackloads more from individual colleges.

BALLIOL COLLEGE, OXFORD

THIS COLLEGE IS PART OF THE UNIVERSITY OF OXFORD AND STUDENTS ARE ENTITLED TO USE ITS FACILITIES

- **BALLIOL COLLEGE**, Oxford, OX1 3BJ **TEL** (01865) 277 748 **E-MAIL** admissions@balliol.ox.ac.uk **WEBSITE** www.balliol.ox.ac.uk
- **BALLIOL COLLEGE JCR**, Oxford, OX1 3BJ **TEL** (01865) 277 744 **E-MAIL** jcr.admissions@balliol.ox.ac.uk **WEBSITE** www.ballioljcr.org/jcr

GENERAL

Balliol's one of the oldest, largest, *famous-est and central-est* colleges, just 350 metres from the Carfax chippy. *Academic standards are high, yet the atmosphere remains relatively relaxed, with a cosmopolitan flavour lent by the proportion of international students. Looks-wise, buildings range from idiosyncratically Gothic through silly Disney to unpleasant and stripey.*

SEX RATIO: ♂59 ♀41	**FOUNDED: 1263**
FULL-TIME U'GRADS: 405	**PART-TIME: 0**
POSTGRADS: 253	**MATURE: 1%**
STATE:PRIVATE SCHOOL: 35:65	**INTERNATIONAL: 25%**
ACADEMIC RANKING: 3	**DISABLED: 16**

Two bars; a handful of sweaty bops per term in The Lindsay Bar (cap 250); May Event (not Ball) has a big-name band, but no penguin suits. Music Soc recitals in dining hall (cap 450); choral groups. JCR Arts festival with drama, poetry, film and photography; theatre (Michael Pilch Studio); weekly news-sheet ('John de Balliol') in loos. TV room; secondhand book sale service. Art loans for room decoration. Anglican chapel. Library (100,000 modern books, 10,000 pre-1800); 35 computers with 24-hr access; *decent* sports facilities and *does okay in a variety of sports*; sports fields 5 mins away. All students live in except 55% of second years; pay-as-you-eat self-service; *legendary* JCR pantry. Hardship funds, living-out grants; doctor, nurse. Welfare reps for postgrads, international students, ethnic minorities, disabled students, LGBT support group; taxi fund; free condoms, rape alarms and tampons; crèche with 16 places for 3mths-5yrs; morning nursery for 18mths-4yrs, £10 a day.

FAMOUS ALUMNI

Rabbi Lionel Blue (writer, broadcaster); Richard Dawkins (scientist and God-basher); Graham Greene (writer); King Harald of Norway; the late Sir Edward Heath (former Con PM); Aldous Huxley (author); Gerard Manley Hopkins (poet); Lord Jenkins (Oxford University Chancellor); Boris Johnson MP (*straw-headed* Tory *buffoon*); Howard Marks (dope evangelist); King Olaf V of Norway; Chris Patten (last governor of Hong Kong); Adam Smith (economist); Algernon Swinburne (*perverse* poet); Stephen Twigg (ex-Labour MP); the late Hugo Young (The Guardian).

BRASENOSE COLLEGE, OXFORD

THIS COLLEGE IS PART OF THE UNIVERSITY OF OXFORD AND STUDENTS ARE ENTITLED TO USE ITS FACILITIES

- **BRASENOSE COLLEGE**, Radcliffe Square, Oxford, OX1 4AJ **TEL** (01865) 277 510 **E-MAIL** admissions@bnc.ox.ac.uk **WEBSITE** www.bnc.ox.ac.uk ● **BRASENOSE JCR**, Radcliffe Square, Oxford, OX1 4AJ **E-MAIL** jcr.president@bnc.ox.ac.uk **WEBSITE** www.bnc-jcr.co.uk

GENERAL

Brasenose College is named after its brass door knocker (made in 1279 and now hanging over the high table) which is shaped like an animal's face with a pronounced snout (brazen nose, *geddit?*). *The College is ideally situated at the heart of the University in Radcliffe Square and 300 metres from Carfax. Brasenose was the first Oxford college to accept women and there's an emerging arty side (Law, PPE, History and English)* which provides the University with a steady stream of journalists for Cherwell and *other hackery.*

SEX RATIO: ♂55 ♀45	**FOUNDED: 1509**
FULL-TIME U'GRADS: 365	**PART-TIME: 0**
POSTGRADS: 180	**MATURE: 1%**
STATE:PRIVATE SCHOOL: 55:45	**INTERNATIONAL: 25%**
ACADEMIC RANKING: 18	**DISABLED: 4**

Fabulous split-room bar (cap. 120) with darts, table football, games machines, jukebox, quiz nights and karaoke. Student bands in the dining hall (200); 'cabaret and cocktails' jazz nights; *sexy* JCR (100) and digital TV room with film nights, Sky, Playstation, vending & quiz machines; cosy basement room (100); three bops a term; annual drama and arts mini-festival; annual panto; biennial ball. Termly newspaper 'Sanesober'. CofE chapel with regular concerts. Two libraries

Words in italics are Push's point of view — take it or leave it...

(60,000 books), one law with Ethernet points; 10 computers (6 online), 24hrs. *Bit nifty in law and medicine.* Tennis and squash courts; playing fields *a ball's throw* from College; pavilion with bar (drinks on a tab) and table tennis; boathouse (shared with Exeter College). *Good record in rugby, football and hockey.* Nearly all undergrads live in, majority en suite; wide variety of accommodation; few cooking facilities but *microwaves ago-go.* Gertie's Tea Bar serves up snacks. CCTV, locked gates with entry-phones; doctor, nurse; attack alarms issued. Disabled access to JCR. LGBT, Women's, Men's, Disabilities, Ethnic Minorities and International Welfare Officers. Assorted funds, travel grants (£150-£200) and bursaries available. Alternative prospectus.

FAMOUS ALUMNI

Lord Jeffrey Archer (briefly, so he claims, but it wasn't a degree course); David Cameron (Tories' leader *and last chance*), Colin Cowdrey (cricketer); Stephen Dorrell MP (Con); William Golding (Nobel Prize writer); Field Marshall Earl Haig (WW1); Michael Palin (Monty Python, global traveller); Lord Runcie (late Archbishop of Canterbury); Lord Saville (Law Lord); Andrew Linsay (Olympic gold medallist).

CHRIST CHURCH, OXFORD

THIS COLLEGE IS PART OF THE UNIVERSITY OF OXFORD AND STUDENTS ARE ENTITLED TO USE ITS FACILITIES

○ **CHRIST CHURCH**, St Aldgate's, Oxford, OX1 1DP **TEL** (01865) 276 181 **E–MAIL** admissions@chch.ox.ac.uk **WEBSITE** www.chch.ox.ac.uk ○ **CHRIST CHURCH JCR**, St Aldgate's, Oxford, OX1 1DP **TEL** (01865) 276 166 **E–MAIL** president@chchjcr.org **WEBSITE** www.chchjcr.org

GENERAL

*Wh*oever *first linked the words 'dreaming spires' with Oxford was looking at Christ Church's pointy bits when they did.* 'The House', as it's known, is 200 metres from Carfax and is the closest college to the river. It's also home to the city's *sumptuous* Anglican cathedral. *It's a stunning place, with idyllic gardens and gorgeous, almost intimidating architecture – the living embodiment of romantic dreams of Oxford (something the Harry Potter filmmakers realised when they chose it as the setting for Hogwarts). The College – largest in the University – is burdened with champagne-quaffing toff stereotypes but, while it's still possible to see tuxedoed undergrads downing bottles of bubbly in Tom Quad, most students prefer the relaxed and more down-to-earth environs of the bar.* Known for serious academia, the natives still find time for high levels of involvement in University-wide arty, sporty and musical activities – *especially the latter: the College's very own cathedral resonates with choral song on a daily basis.*

SEX RATIO: ♂56 ♀44	**FOUNDED:** 1525
FULL–TIME U'GRADS: 420	**PART–TIME:** 0
POSTGRADS: 261	**MATURE:** 2%
STATE:PRIVATE SCHOOL: 55:45	**INTERNATIONAL:** 6%
ACADEMIC RANKING: 9	**DISABLED:** 8

Lovely stone-floored Undercroft bar ('the Undie'), with pool, table football and jukebox; *active* drama society, garden shows; own picture gallery with works by Michelangelo and Raphael; *internationally renowned* choir and long musical tradition; frequent recitals, jazz evenings, gigs and bops; annual ball. Two libraries (one 16th-century, one for law – 24hrs), main library open till midnight – *among the finest college facilities in Oxford*; reading rooms; 16 24-hr computers in two rooms; art room; 'Chit Chat' newsletter; *apolitical JCR good on charity work. A whopping five Rag reps – hot on fundraising.* Anglican chaplain (*comes free with breathtaking cathedral*). *Almighty* Boat Club, *also good in tennis and football; excellent* sports facilities (and bar) five mins away. Everyone can live in (£84/28wks); *decent rooms (with fridges), poor kitchen facilities*; keypad entry; *very formal dinner every night in what many will recognise as the Hogwarts dining hall; nightmare parking.* LGBT, Postgrad, Women's and International Officers; Cake Rep (for emergency cake delivery – there's even a cake song); nurse, doctor and counsellor; attack alarms; *old building poor for access* but being improved; specialised accommodation available. *Generous* financial help: entrance bursaries (£1,000), hardship funds, interest-free 5-yr loans (£1,000), travel and book grants, academic prizes.

FAMOUS ALUMNI

W H Auden (poet); Lewis Carroll (author and don); Alan Clark (late *raunchy* MP and diarist); David Dimbleby (broadcaster); 13 prime ministers (including Gladstone); John Mortimer (barrister, author and playwright); Richard Curtis (screenwriter, *reason Hugh Grant has a career*); Einstein (*briefly*); Lord Hailsham (late Lord Chancellor); Lord Nigel Lawson (*slimming guru* and ex-Chancellor); Anna Pasternak ('Di & Hewitt' *hack*); Auberon Waugh (controversialist).

CORPUS CHRISTI COLLEGE, OXFORD

THIS COLLEGE IS PART OF THE UNIVERSITY OF OXFORD AND STUDENTS ARE ENTITLED TO USE ITS FACILITIES

CORPUS CHRISTI COLLEGE, Merton Street, Oxford, OX1 4JF **TEL** (01865) 276 700 **E-MAIL** admissions@ccc.ox.ac.uk **WEBSITE** www.ccc.ox.ac.uk **CORPUS CHRISTI COLLEGE JCR**, Merton Street, Oxford, OX1 4JF **TEL** (01865) 276 700 **E-MAIL** jcr.president@ccc.ox.ac.uk **WEBSITE** www.corpusjcr.org

GENERAL

Tucked away down Merton Street, overlooking Dead Man's Walk, Corpus is one of Oxford's *diddiest* colleges. *It's an unstuffy sort of place (despite a strong academic rep* and a 2005 University Challenge triumph), with the *famous* Pelican sundial at the front of the College. Originally intended for training monks, the College got sidetracked into churning out well-rounded Renaissance men *and still does five centuries on* (nowadays producing Renaissance ladies in equal quantities). An *elegant* Tudor building borders the main quad.

SEX RATIO: ♂59 ♀41	FOUNDED: 1517
FULL-TIME U'GRADS: 246	PART-TIME: 0
POSTGRADS: 115	MATURE: 0%
STATE:PRIVATE SCHOOL: 43:42	INTERNATIONAL: 11%
ACADEMIC RANKING: 16	DISABLED: 2

The Beer Cellar Bar (cap. 120, closed Sat nights); bops fortnightly; theme nights, quizzes and gigs in the bar, concerts in New Music room; biennial Summer Ball; Burns night with haggis and pipes. *Involved* 'Owlets' drama soc; annual Arts Week and panto. 16th-century library (80,000 books, 24hrs); reading rooms; 15 computers in private 'pods', 24hrs. JCR with two TV rooms, Playstation, DVD/video and snack machines.

'Smallprint' mag and weekly newsletter; annual tortoise race with Balliol for charity. Playing fields (five acres) 15 mins walk; shares a boathouse; *emphasis on participation and fun rather than sporting honours but rugby, basketball and, um, tiddlywinks are on top form.* Annual sports tournament with Corpus Christi, Cambridge, *who tend to lose.* Everyone can live in College in *pretty good* rooms (£600-£750 a term, 35 en suite), either on site or in one of many College-owned houses dotted around Oxford; phone/internet points in all rooms; some accommodation for couples. *Excellent* food, veggie options – though nearby Ahmed's Kebab Van proves *irresistable* to many; weekly formal dinners. Female 'Corpuscles' can enjoy Women's Tea every Sunday. Male Welfare, Female Welfare, LGBT, Cultural Relations and Equal Opps Officers (also Tortoise Keeper and Poet Laureate posts). Doctors and nurse; dentist; wheelchair access ramps; *excellent* welfare. *Comprehensive* alternative prospectus online.

FAMOUS ALUMNI

Dr Arnold (of Rugby fame); Al Alvarez (writer and poker buff); Sir Isaiah Berlin (writer and philosopher); Robert Bridges (Poet Laureate); Erasmus (humanist, declared Corpus library to be 'the eighth wonder of the world'); Lord Fisher (Archbishop of Canterbury, 1906); Richard Hooker (theologian); General Oglethorpe (founded Georgia); David & Ed Miliband (MPs, Lab); Brough Scott (racing commentator); Vikram Seth (novelist).

O

EXETER COLLEGE, OXFORD

THIS COLLEGE IS PART OF THE UNIVERSITY OF OXFORD AND STUDENTS ARE ENTITLED TO USE ITS FACILITIES

EXETER COLLEGE, Oxford, OX1 3DP **TEL** (01865) 279 600 **E-MAIL** admissions@exeter.ox.ac.uk **WEBSITE** www.exeter.ox.ac.uk
EXETER JCR, Exeter College, Oxford, OX1 3DP **TEL** (01865) 279 635 **WEBSITE** jcr.exeter.ox.ac.uk

GENERAL

Oxford's fourth oldest college, Exeter is slap bang in the middle of the academic heart of Oxford on

semi-pedestrianised Turl Street, right next door to the Bodleian Library and 250 metres from Carfax. *It's a small, close-knit and friendly place with buildings spanning five centuries and magnificent views from the garden – no wonder Inspector Morse chose to die in the front quad.* Access to

 The last Inspector Morse episode was filmed on the front quad of Exeter College, Oxford.

Words in italics are Push's point of view – take it or leave it...

the walls makes it possible to snipe from on-high at tourists below. *The location and compact layout make it ideal for students allergic to walking.*

SEX RATIO: ♂58 ♀42	**FOUNDED:** 1314
FULL-TIME U'GRADS: 328	**PART-TIME:** 0
POSTGRADS: 165	**MATURE:** 1%
STATE:PRIVATE SCHOOL: 52:48	**INTERNATIONAL:** 13%
ACADEMIC RANKING: 7	**DISABLED:** 3

The Undercroft Bar (cap. 200) open 11-11 seven days a week with College bops every two weeks (*be warned*: students are fined for drunken vomiting); a black-tie ball once a year. Library (70,000 books, 62 study places with Ethernet) with 24-hr access; 14 computer workstations with internet access; music rehearsal rooms; CofE chapel;

boathouse and playing fields (1.5 miles away). All first years live in *old-fashioned but spacious rooms*, £80-£100 a week, most rooms have ether-net points and swipecard entry, 11% share; most other years live out. All eat in hall, fortnightly 'theme nights' (*quirky* menus, guest speakers, etc). College doctor and nurse. Women's advisor, subsidised attack alarms; hearing loops in lecture theatres; disabled access rooms in College and in main hostels. Variety of bursaries and hardship funds.

FAMOUS ALUMNI
Martin Amis, Alan Bennett, Will Self, J R R Tolkien (writers); Sir Roger Bannister (first to run the 4-minute mile); Wllliam Morris (designer and social pioneer); Phillip Pullman (*Christian-baiting* children's author); Ned Sherrin (broadcaster); Imogen Stubbs (actress).

GREYFRIARS HALL, OXFORD

THIS COLLEGE IS PART OF THE UNIVERSITY OF OXFORD AND STUDENTS ARE ENTITLED TO USE ITS FACILITIES

○ **GREYFRIARS HALL,** Iffley Road, Oxford, OX4 1SB **TEL** (01865) 243 694 **WEBSITE** www.greyfriars.ox.ac.uk
○ **GREYFRIARS HALL JCR,** Greyfriars Hall, Iffley Road, Oxford, OX4 1SB **TEL** (01865) 246 665 **WEBSITE** www.greyfriars.ox.ac.uk/jcr

GENERAL
The *beautiful and serene* Greyfriars Hall is one of Oxford's smallest colleges. *Very small – the entire population could take a double-decker together.* In fact, technically it's not even a college but a 'Permanent Private Hall', *although not many people know that and fewer still notice the difference.* It's home to 50 undergrads (including women since 1992) and seven Franciscan Friars and maintains a strong tradition of Catholicism and the teachings of St Francis of Assisi in particular (hence the Friars). *However, students' own spiritual preferences reflect a bigger smorgasbord of world religions. A hefty chunk of its under-graduates ended up here through the pooling system – after all, a working friary isn't the most obvious destination for the student experience – but a bulky slice of them end up being pleased they found themselves in such a uniquely cosy place.* The hall is some way from the centre of town, on Iffley Road.

SEX RATIO: ♂50 ♀50	**FOUNDED:** 1224
FULL-TIME U'GRADS: 50	**PART-TIME:** 0
POSTGRADS: 5	**MATURE:** 2%
STATE:PRIVATE SCHOOL: 50:50	**INTERNATIONAL:** 20%
ACADEMIC RANKING: N/A	**DISABLED:** 0

No bar, just a drinks shelf in the kitchen and free Pimm's at *renowned* summer garden parties; one bop per year; regular parties in the basement. *Strongly involved in drama and politics; good* on student media and *journalism.* Pool table, Sky TV, weights room. Catholic church. *Well-equipped* specialist library (10,000 volumes, 25 study spaces); 3 PCs, 24hrs; JCR IT officer; all rooms have Ethernet access. JCR with kitchen, living/Sky TV room, weights/pool room. Recent sporting successes in rugby, karate and rowing, for which students join the Balliol banner *(where they dominate the women's first boat),* own boat arriving as a result. Just over half the students live in, including all first years. Food is included in catered cost (£80/wk), but rebates are provided for uneaten meals. Eight self-catered bedrooms (£60). Smart formal dinner every evening – students take turns to serve, black toe guest dinners every term. Bike lock-ups, limited car parking. LGBT and women's officer and free attack alarms; self-defence classes. Scholarships for academic excellence, drama, sport, journalism, charity, first and third years. Most arts/humanities subjects can be accommodated; no sciences or medicine.

FAMOUS ALUMNI
Roger Bacon (scholar and polymath); Robert Grosseteste (13th-century Bishop of Lincoln); William of Ockham (of 'Ockham's Razor' philosophy fame); John Duns Scotus (theologian).

HARRIS MANCHESTER COLLEGE, OXFORD

THIS COLLEGE IS PART OF THE UNIVERSITY OF OXFORD AND STUDENTS ARE ENTITLED TO USE ITS FACILITIES

○ HARRIS MANCHESTER COLLEGE, Mansfield Road, Oxford, OX1 3TD **TEL** (01865) 271 006 **E-MAIL** enquiries@hmc.ox.ac.uk **WEBSITE** www.hmc.ox.ac.uk **○ HARRIS MANCHESTER COLLEGE JCR**, Mansfield Road, Oxford, OX1 3TD **TEL** (01865) 271 006 **E-MAIL** jcr.president@hmc.ox.ac.uk

GENERAL

Harris Manchester only admits mature students. *As a result the atmosphere can be more cardigans and slippers than quaffing contests and meat-market bops.* The buildings are late Victorian Gothic (there are some *lovely* Pre-Raphaelite stained glass windows in the chapel) as the College has only been in them since its move from Manchester (via London) in 1889. *Push was disappointed to learn that the College takes its name not from Rolf, Chopper or even Bomber, but from Lord Harris of Peckham.*

SEX RATIO: ♂50 ♀50	**FOUNDED:** 1786
FULL-TIME U'GRADS: 89	**PART-TIME:** 0
POSTGRADS: 54	**MATURE:** 100%
STATE:PRIVATE SCHOOL: N/A	**INTERNATIONAL:** 20%
ACADEMIC RANKING: 30	**DISABLED:** 3

Small bar; film club; ball every three yrs. Three libraries (70,000 books); ten computers, 24hrs; internet in all rooms. *Cordial* staff/student relations. Chapel; Unitarian chaplain, weekly choral recitals. *No real sports facilities 'cept the Royal Yacht (the College punt) and a croquet lawn; free membership to city gym and pool softens the blow. Recent emergence* in University football and cricket. Most first years and finalists can live in on site (at a steep £140 a week); non-smoking; no married accommodation (*a bit rich since everyone's mature); excellent* food, *decent veggie* option; two formal dinners a week; no self-catering. *Poor* wheelchair access *(being jazzed up)*; induction loops; one adapted bedroom. CCTV; doctor; Women's and LGBT Officers; academic prizes (£50-£100), hardship and travel funds, book grants (£30/year).

FAMOUS ALUMNI

Gareth Morgan (youngest MP in South African parliament).

HERTFORD COLLEGE, OXFORD

0

THIS COLLEGE IS PART OF THE UNIVERSITY OF OXFORD AND STUDENTS ARE ENTITLED TO USE ITS FACILITIES

○ HERTFORD COLLEGE, Catte Road, Oxford, OX1 3BW **TEL** (01865) 279 400 **E-MAIL** admissions@ hertford.ox.ac.uk **WEBSITE** www.hertford.ox.ac.uk/main **○ HERTFORD COLLEGE JCR**, Catte Road, Oxford, OX1 3BW **WEBSITE** jcrweb.hertford.ox.ac.uk/main

GENERAL

Hertford has a *long and slightly dodgy history*, having gone by turns bankrupt and by the names of Hart Hall and Magdelen Hall before now. *It's large and diverse, whacked* straight into the middle of Oxford right next to the Bodleian library. Its bridge *(which looks a bit like the Rialto in Venice if you squint) is a tourist magnet. The College is pretty inclusive and has traditionally been one of the more liberal — one of the first to unbar its gates to the girlies— and is attractive if not pant-ruiningly gorgeous.*

SEX RATIO: ♂48 ♀52	**FOUNDED:** 1282
FULL-TIME U'GRADS: 370	**PART-TIME:** 0
POSTGRADS: 170	**MATURE:** <1%
STATE:PRIVATE SCHOOL: 65:35	**INTERNATIONAL:** 20%
ACADEMIC RANKING: 6	**DISABLED:** 0

Student-run bar; *strong* drama and music; Baring Room (cap. 250) *is one of the best venues in any Oxford college*; themed bop cellar Saturday nights. JCR with pool table. games machines and Sky TV, DVD library. new Moroccan chill-out room. Twice weekly JCR bulletins; College magazine 'Simpkins' (after the College cat). Catholic church, CofE chapel. Library (47,000 books); 27 computers, 24hrs, JCR IT Officer. Sporty, *excelling* in rowing and rugby; four tennis courts, squash courts, boathouse 10 mins by bike, multigym and weights room in College. All accommodated (first years in College, later years in annexes), but quality, size and location are a *mixed* bag; all rooms have broadband access; self-catering available; twice weekly formal dinners, (charged retrospectively) termly black tie dos, cafeteria, new coffee bar. Bike lock-ups, *limited* car parking CCTV; doctor and nurse; Women's, Men's, LGBT and two Welfare Officers; *good* security. Scholarships for academic whizzkids.

FAMOUS ALUMNI
John Donne (poet); David Elleray (football ref); Charles James Fox (18th-century politician); Thomas Hobbes (philosopher); Henry Pelham (ex-PM); Jonathan Swift (satirist); William Tyndale (translator of international best-seller the Bible); Evelyn Waugh (writer).

JESUS COLLEGE, OXFORD

THIS COLLEGE IS PART OF THE UNIVERSITY OF OXFORD AND STUDENTS ARE ENTITLED TO USE ITS FACILITIES

⊙ JESUS COLLEGE, Turl Street, Oxford, OX1 3DW **TEL** (01865) 279 700 **E—MAIL** schools.liaison@jesus.ox.ac.uk **WEBSITE** www.jesus.ox.ac.uk **⊙ JESUS COLLEGE JCR**, Jesus College, Turl Street, Oxford, OX1 3DW **TEL** (01865) 287 261 **E—MAIL** jcr.admissions@jesus.ox.ac.uk **WEBSITE** jcr.jesus.ox.ac.uk

GENERAL
The *eye-grabbing* Tudor turrets of Jesus are just 250 metres from both Carfax and the Bodleian. It was founded by Queen Elizabeth (the first one) and traditionally it was rumoured to be full of Welsh students *(still a little true)* and rahs *(not really true)*. Nowadays, *students from all social backgrounds and levels of fondness for daffodils sunbathe and revise (allegedly)* in the *dinky* second quad.

SEX RATIO: ♂56 ♀44	FOUNDED: 1571
FULL—TIME U'GRADS: 330	PART—TIME: 0
POSTGRADS: 130	MATURE: 0%
STATE:PRIVATE SCHOOL: 65:35	INTERNATIONAL: 4%
ACADEMIC RANKING: 13	DISABLED: 3

Bar (cap. 150), *usually packed*; happy hours, quizzes, occasional bands; bops every Friday; termly black tie shindig; annual events – College has a hand in the Turl Street Arts Festival; graduate common room with Sky TV, VCR & DVD, pool table and snack kiosk; holds dinners, cocktail nights and DVD nights on Sundays; lots of one-off events and trips. Evensong choir every Sunday; interdenominational chapel. Library (36,000 volumes); 45 computers, 48 power-points for laptop use (24hrs), internet in all student rooms. 'Sheepshagger' newspaper. *Excellent* sports facilities 1.5 miles from college, pavilion with multigym, conference rooms and bar; tennis courts; *good reputation* in tennis and football, new mixed lacrosse team. All can live in, but majority of non-first years live in College-owned flats, shared between three or four(Herbert's Close complex is *the most popular*); Flats for couples and some adapted rooms for disabled students. food on a credit system; No parking permits for those living in College, but those in the two outside complexes allocated one permit per flat. CCTV, free attack alarms; Men's, Women's and Diversity Officers; doctor, nurse; hardship grants; scholarships.

FAMOUS ALUMNI
William Boyd (author); Paul Jones (singer); T E Lawrence (of Arabia); Sian Lloyd, Kirsty McCabe (weatherpeople); Magnus Magnusson (former 'Mastermind' inquisitor); Norman Manley (first president of Jamaica); Edward 'Beau' Nash *(dandy)*; Henry Vaughn (poet); Lord Wilson (former PM).

KEBLE COLLEGE, OXFORD

THIS COLLEGE IS PART OF THE UNIVERSITY OF OXFORD AND STUDENTS ARE ENTITLED TO USE ITS FACILITIES

⊙ KEBLE COLLEGE, Parks Road, Oxford, OX1 3PG **TEL** (01865) 272 727 **E—MAIL** enquiries@keble.oxford.ac.uk **WEBSITE** www.keble.ox.ac.uk **⊙ JUNIOR COMMON ROOM**, Keble College, Parks Sreet, Oxford, OX1 3PG **TEL** (01865) 272 755 **WEBSITE** jcr.keble.ox.ac.uk

GENERAL
Keble is just under 800 metres north of Carfax, right next to the University Science Area. Well placed for OUSU, the Lamb & Flag pub and the *excellent* Maison Blanc patisserie. It's a big and relatively modern college – a mere *spring chicken* at 134 years old. The main buildings are Victorian redbrick, *some of them resembling vast* *Battenburg cakes. These buildings – and the unforgettable* chapel – *contrast almost violently with the spaceship which landed one night in the rear quad and claimed it was the bar. Keble students like to get out and about and are often involved in high profile University activities, especially sports, despite a fairly casual crew.*

0

SEX RATIO: ♂60 ♀40	FOUNDED: 1870
FULL-TIME U'GRADS: 440	PART-TIME: 0
POSTGRADS: 190	MATURE: 2%
STATE:PRIVATE SCHOOL: 60:40	INTERNATIONAL: 10%
ACADEMIC RANKING: 10	DISABLED: 0

Large, *popular, recently extended* bar; two or three themed bops a term, big ball every other year. *Feisty* Rag and *strong* drama at the O'Reilly Theatre; music rehearsal rooms at the Sloane Robinson Building with several pianos and a harpsichord. Library (40,000 books), 25 computers, 24hrs. Anglican chapel with *successful* recording choir. 'The Brick' termly for college news. *Very sporty* (loads of 'Blues') and *excellent* facilities including gym, weights room and rowing boat about a mile away. *Especially strong at rugby and hockey*. Keble can house most of its many undergrads and postgrads due to new *conference-type* rooms (most en suite); catered pay-as-you-eat credit system (you have to buy 30 meals in advance) and *limited* self-catering; six formals a week; network points in all rooms. Nurse, doctor, Women's, Welfare, Charities and Equal Opps Officers and rep for ethnic minorities and international students; ramp for wheelchair access; scholarships, bursaries, hardship fund.

FAMOUS ALUMNI

Michael Croft (founder, National Youth Theatre); Imran Khan (cricketer); Timmy Mallett (*children's TV legend/hammer-wielding maniac*); Rev Chad Varah (founder, the Samaritans); Andreas Whittam Smith (founder, The Independent) – *yes, Keble's your college if you're planning to found something*.

LADY MARGARET HALL, OXFORD

THIS COLLEGE IS PART OF THE UNIVERSITY OF OXFORD AND STUDENTS ARE ENTITLED TO USE ITS FACILITIES

◉ **LADY MARGARET HALL**, Oxford, Lady Margaret Hall, Oxford, OX2 6QA **TEL:** (01865) 274 310
E-MAIL academic.officer@lmh.ox.ac.uk **WEBSITE** www.lmh.ox.ac.uk
◉ **LADY MARGARET HALL JCR**, Lady Margaret Hall, Oxford, OX3 6QA **TEL** (01865) 274 277 **WEBSITE** www.lmh-jcr.ox.ac.uk

GENERAL

Lady Margaret Hall is a late 19th-century redbrick college set in *extensive* riverside gardens. It began as strictly girls-only, but in 1979 – 100 years after its foundation – LMH *invited the blokes in to play*. *Two iffy* purpose-built five-floor residential blocks *poo on the idyllic setting and handsome architecture, but they're really popular with those inside*. Being 1,200 metres from the city centre *doesn't put a dampener on University-level involvement. As Oxford goes, LMH-ers are among the most down-to earth*.

SEX RATIO: ♂50 ♀50	FOUNDED: 1878
FULL-TIME U'GRADS: 440	PART-TIME: 0
POSTGRADS: 182	MATURE: 4%
STATE:PRIVATE SCHOOL: 50:50	INTERNATIONAL: 5%
ACADEMIC RANKING: 29	DISABLED: 4

Bar (cap. 200). Two libraries (one for Law, 70,000 books, 60 study bays); 35 computers, 24-hr access. Ecumenical chapel. *Strong* drama at the Beaufort Literary Society founded by actor Sam West. Sports facilities a mile away (multigym and squash on site); *strong on netball, hockey and rowing*. First years, finalists and most second years live in; dining hall with fixed payments for meals (whether eaten or not) or pay-as-you-eat. *Better disabled access than most colleges*. Doctor; nurse; First year, Welfare and Women's Officers; free tampons and condoms.

FAMOUS ALUMNI

Benazir Bhutto (ex-President, Pakistan); Caryl Churchill (writer); Lady Antonia Fraser (historian); Eglantyne Jebb (founder, Save the Children); Nigella Lawson (domestic goddess); Barbara Mills (Director of Public Prosecutions); Diana Quick (actress); Matthew Taylor MP (Lib Dem); Lady Warnock (educationalist); Sam West (actor); Anne Widdecombe MP (Con).

0

> ◉ Oxford's Bodleian Library is the second largest in the country after the British Library and has six million books and more than 100 miles of shelving.

LINCOLN COLLEGE, OXFORD

THIS COLLEGE IS PART OF THE UNIVERSITY OF OXFORD AND STUDENTS ARE ENTITLED TO USE ITS FACILITIES

○ **LINCOLN COLLEGE**, Oxford, OX1 3DR **TEL** (01865) 279 800 **E-MAIL** admissions@lincoln.ox.ac.uk **WEBSITE** www.lincoln.ox.ac.uk
○ **LINCOLN COLLEGE JCR**, Lincoln College, Oxford, OX1 3DR **WEBSITE** www.lincolnjcr.com

GENERAL

200 metres from Carfax is Lincoln, *a miniature version of a picture-book Oxford college, though it considers itself to be forward-looking and progressive. If Ikea decided to make a range of dreaming spires, they might look a bit like the sand-blasted stone quad. Students tend to stick to College affairs rather than roam too far, contributing to the fun, familial atmosphere.*

SEX RATIO: ♂50 ♀50	FOUNDED: 1427
FULL-TIME U'GRADS: 303	PART-TIME: 0
POSTGRADS: 240	MATURE: 0%
STATE:PRIVATE SCHOOL: 55:45	INTERNATIONAL: 7%
ACADEMIC RANKING: 16	DISABLED: 13

Attractive Deep Hall Bar (cap. 200); quizzes, bops, karaoke, pool, cabaret; biennial ball. 'Imperative' newsletter twice a term. Music society recitals, opera. Converted 17th-Century church library (40,000 books); 20 computers in two rooms, 24hrs.

CofE chapel, chaplain. *Rowing, rugby, football, netball and croquet are popular,* sucesses in hockey and football; sports fields 10 mins bike ride away. Everyone lives in and eats at formal and/or informal dinners every night; *best food in Oxford; self-catering available to second and third years.* Nurse, doctor, NNHS dentist. Women's tutor; harassment support; access fund and College bursaries; Oxford Bursaries up to £1,000; scholarships and College prizes. *Good college welfare includes Men's and Women's,* International and Rag Officers plus the *essential* wine committee, food reps and steak fairy. *No, really. Glamourpuss* Lucy Pinder is an honorary member of the JCR, along with the *somewhat less photogenic* Boris Johnson.

FAMOUS ALUMNI

John le Carré (writer); Steph Cook (pentathlete); Sir Rod Eddington (British Airways CEO); Howard Florey (found penicillin); Tom Paulin (poet); Theodore 'Dr Seuss' Geisel (*crazy-rhyming* 'Cat in the Hat' author); JA. Hobson (political thorist); Manfred von Richtofen (the Red Baron); Edward Thomas (poet); John Wesley (founder of Methodism).

MAGDALEN COLLEGE, OXFORD

THIS COLLEGE IS PART OF THE UNIVERSITY OF OXFORD AND STUDENTS ARE ENTITLED TO USE ITS FACILITIES

○ **MAGDALEN COLLEGE**, Oxford, OX1 4AU **TEL** (01865) 276 063 **E-MAIL** admissions@magd.ox.ac.uk **WEBSITE** www.magd.ox.ac.uk
○ **MAGDALEN COLLEGE JCR**, Magdalen College, Oxford, OX1 4AU **TEL** (01865) 276 001 **E-MAIL** president@jcr.magd.ox.ac.uk **WEBSITE** www.magdjcr.co.uk

GENERAL

Magdalen (pronounced 'Maudlin') is one of Oxford's biggest, *richest* colleges. Its *superb* buildings, 800 metres from Carfax, are set in 100 acres of grounds, which include over a mile of riverside walks and a deer park. The surroundings attract a *plague* of tourists and plenty of film crews. The *old-fashioned* bar (crossed oars, etc.) overlooks the river. The Magdalen May Morning celebration *is especially enchanting,* coming to a climax when the choir welcomes summer from the top of Magdalen Tower. *The students are a tolerant and friendly bunch, hard-working but not freakish human beavers.*

SEX RATIO: ♂54 ♀46	FOUNDED: 1458
FULL-TIME U'GRADS: 390	PART-TIME: 0
POSTGRADS: 219	MATURE: 1%
STATE:PRIVATE SCHOOL: 50:50	INTERNATIONAL: 5%
ACADEMIC RANKING: 4	DISABLED: 12

Bar used for student bands, pool, quizzes, bops and snacks; *monster* events each term; tea-parties; punting trips; classical concerts in the chapel; fortnightly bops and cocktail parties; music auditorium; Commemoration Ball every three years, *one of the biggies.* Five libraries including a special Law Library and a rare books library (120,000 books in total, 100 study places, 24hrs); 28 computers, open 24hrs. CofE chapel. Grammy-nominated choir. Auditorium for film screenings; darkroom run by JCR photography rep. *Active (and minted)* JCR; weekly student 'Bogsheet'. Two common rooms (one known as

'Father Dominic of Bulgaria', one known *less romantically* as 'Dave'); Sky, DVD players, free pool table, cornershop with *trashy* novels to loan, wine shop (unique to Magdalen) with largest free DVD lending library in Oxford. *Great* sports fields 10 mins walk; three squash courts in College; *excellent* gym; boathouse and punts; *women's squash strong, as are rounders and cricket.* Almost everyone lives in; *very spacious, modern* rooms, and *some olde worlde woody beam affairs*, all with network points; all room rents are equal; 27 kitchens for undergrads, *lousy food – better in the bar but bring your Hobnobs, anyway.* International Students', Women's and Ethnic Minorities Officers. *College is responsive to students' problems.* Free attack alarms provided.

Wheelchairs *hampered* by cobbles. Hardship funds, scholarships, book and travel grants.

FAMOUS ALUMNI
John Betjeman (poet, sent down); Lord Alfred 'Bosie' Douglas (lover of Oscar Wilde); Edward Gibbon (historian); Darius Guppy (*fraudster*); William Hague MP (ex-Con Leader); Seamus Heaney (poet); Ian Hislop (editor, Private Eye); C S Lewis (writer); Dudley Moore (comedian/ actor/pianist); Desmond Morris (socioanthropologist); John Redwood MP (Con); David Rendel MP (LibDem); Dr Edwin Shrodinger (physicist who had a cat – or did he?); A J P Taylor (historian); Oscar Wilde (writer); Cardinal Wolsey.

MANSFIELD COLLEGE, OXFORD

THIS COLLEGE IS PART OF THE UNIVERSITY OF OXFORD AND STUDENTS ARE ENTITLED TO USE ITS FACILITIES

⊙ **MANSFIELD COLLEGE**, Mansfield Road, Oxford, OX1 3TF **TEL** (01865) 282 920 **E-MAIL** admissions@mansfield.ox.ac.uk **WEBSITE** www.mansfield.ox.ac.uk ⊙ **JUNIOR COMMON ROOM**, Mansfield College, Mansfield Road, Oxford, OX1 3TF **TEL** (01865) 270 889 **WEBSITE** www.mansfieldjcr.org.uk

GENERAL
Mansfield sprung into being in Birmingham in 1835, *but packed its satchel* for Oxford half a century later. The main Victorian buildings are set around the *huge* circular lawn. *Outside it looks inspiring and spacious. Rowing's popular* and the College has its own boathouse – Mansfield was the home of Donald McDonald, the rower made *famous(ish)* by the film 'True Blue'. *It used to be a Free Church centre and prides itself on a tradition of being the source of many a minister. The atmosphere's friendly and less 'keep out, mortal' than some colleges and there's a strong tradition of supplying hacks to the SU and journos to Cherwell. Mansfield's turning more of an admiring eye to applicants from FE colleges.*

Black Bottle bar, *packed* at the weekend; *thespy*, with annual Arts Fesival; *eclectic* film soc; handful of bops termly and bands in the JCR (cap. 225); Winter Ball every three years; cabaret; Sky; pool tables; games machines. Weekly 'Bogsheet'. Two libraries (35,000 volumes, 72 study places including specialist law and theology library); 21 PCs (14 networked), 24hrs; internet access in all rooms on campus and 30 sockets in the library; specialist science software packages. *Greenish JCR with a charitable streak.* URC chapel. Tennis courts, basketball court; most sports amenities are run jointly with Merton College. Varied accommodation for all first and third years/ finalists. Students eat in College dining halls except Sundays. CCTV, night wardens, computerised entry. Ramps available; one room for a wheelchair user; College nurse; counselling team; Women's and LGBT Officers; free attack alarms. *Limited* maintenance awards for those on the wrong side of the breadline.

FAMOUS ALUMNI
Paul Crossley (concert pianist); C H Dodd, Albert Schweitzer (theologians); Philip Franks (actor); Guy Hands (*übercapitalist*); Donald McDonald (*mutinous rower*); Adam von Trott (tried to kill Hitler).

SEX RATIO: ♀53 ♂47		**FOUNDED:** 1886	
FULL-TIME U'GRADS: 207		**PART-TIME:** 0	
POSTGRADS: 48		**MATURE:** 1%	
STATE:PRIVATE SCHOOL: 60:30		**INTERNATIONAL:** 10%	
ACADEMIC RANKING: 19		**DISABLED:** 4	

O

> **New College, Oxford constructed a cess pit that was so large it didn't have to be drained for the first 300 years. It's since been cleaned out and is now a student common room. Lucky students.**

MERTON COLLEGE, OXFORD

THIS COLLEGE IS PART OF THE UNIVERSITY OF OXFORD AND STUDENTS ARE ENTITLED TO USE ITS FACILITIES

○ **MERTON COLLEGE**, Merton Street, Oxford, OX1 4JD **TEL** (01865) 276 310 **E–MAIL** undergraduates@admin.merton.ox.ac.uk
WEBSITE www.merton.ox.ac.uk **MERTON COLLEGE JCR**, Merton College, Merton Street, Oxford, OX1 JD
E–MAIL president@mertonjcr.org **WEBSITE** www.mertonjcr.org

GENERAL

Merton is *one of Oxford's oldest and prettiest colleges*, 600 metres from Carfax, with *magical* gardens (where Tolkien wrote Lord of the Rings), a *beautiful* chapel and *bizarre* gargoyles. The Mob Quad is the oldest quad in Oxford and home of the library (the oldest in England), which is supposedly haunted and contains Chaucer's Astrolabe. *Merton's not only big and clever, but darn loaded too*, counting Corpus Christi College, the Turf Tavern and a *hefty chunk* of Coventry among its assets. *The atmosphere's laid-back but academically stellar students have made their mark in University journalism, drama and music. Token archaic* traditions include walking backwards around the quad drinking port for an hour when the clocks go back. *Like you do.*

SEX RATIO: ♂58 ♀42	FOUNDED: 1264
FULL–TIME U'GRADS: 321	PART–TIME: 0
POSTGRADS: 150	MATURE: 0%
STATE:PRIVATE SCHOOL: 50:42	INTERNATIONAL: 7%
ACADEMIC RANKING: 1	DISABLED: 3

Large bar with fortnightly bops — *bonzer 90p* toasties; weekly quizzes, karaoke, casino and open-mic comedy nights. Drama in the gardens in May Week; Xmas Ball; *mighty* Choral soc; weekly Merton Newspaper. Library (70,000 books) with a *cramped* 88 study places; 15 computers, 24hrs.

Ethernet connections in all on-site rooms and at intervals in library. JCR with Sky, kitchen, free pool and table football; DVD rental service; *charity-happy Exec.* Chapel. Two tennis courts and sports grounds 10 mins away shared with Mansfield College; annual Sports Day – *there's more of an emphasis on having a go than on thinking you're hard enough, although badminton, pool and women's rugby are top notch.* Everyone can live in *high-quality* catered accommodation for 25 weeks of the year (£86/wk); *some very elegant rooms; not many* kitchens; daily formals ('cept Sat) with *tasty chow; termly black tie meal.* Entry phones and night porters; doctor and shared nurse; Men's and Women's Welfare Officers; Equal Opps and two LGBT reps; free attack alarms, condoms, pregnancy tests; welfare tea and movie nights. *Narrow doorways and paths make wheelchair access tricky.* Access bursaries (£4,000 in the first year, £3,000 in successive years, dependent on household income); scholarships, grants towards books and overseas work and travel. Alternative prospectus.

FAMOUS ALUMNI

Roger Bannister (athlete); Max Beerbohm (caricaturist & writer); Frank Bough (broadcaster); Howard Davies (deputy Governor, Bank of England); T S Eliot (poet); Mark Haddon (author, 'The Curious Incident of the Dog...'); William Harvey (discoverer of circulatory system); Kris Kristofferson (singer/songwriter); Robert Morley (actor); Crown Prince Naruhito (Japanese heir apparent); Sir Andrew Wiles (mathematician); John Wycliffe (religious reformer).

NEW COLLEGE, OXFORD

THIS COLLEGE IS PART OF THE UNIVERSITY OF OXFORD AND STUDENTS ARE ENTITLED TO USE ITS FACILITIES

○ **NEW COLLEGE**, Holywell Street, Oxford, OX1 3BN **TEL** (01865) 279 555 **E–MAIL** admissions@new.ox.ac.uk
WEBSITE www.new.ox.ac.uk ○ **NEW COLLEGE JCR**, Holywell Street, Oxford, OX1 3BN **TEL** (01865) 279 577
WEBSITE www.newcollegejcr.org.uk

GENERAL

New College, *ironically* one of the oldest colleges *(those crazy jokers)*, is *so prettily Gothic that it wouldn't look out of place in Disneyland*, with the city wall running through its *pleasant* grounds. It was founded originally to replace members of the clergy wiped out by the Black Death, but *these days things are much less gloomy* and bubonic. The College is only 600 metres from Carfax, but it's hidden to a certain extent from the *swarms* of tourists. The social scene rotates around the Beer Cellar, a refurbished medieval cave attracting students from all over Oxford.

SEX RATIO: ♂50 ♀50	FOUNDED: 1379
FULL-TIME U'GRADS: 430	PART-TIME: 0
POSTGRADS: 172	MATURE: 1%
STATE:PRIVATE SCHOOL: 48:52	INTERNATIONAL: 4%
ACADEMIC RANKING: 15	DISABLED: 10

Bar (cap. 200); classical music in Anglican chapel. Biggest ents budget in the University; themed bops ('100 Greatest Musicals', etc.), jazz and student bands in the Long Room (200); student DJ nights *popular*, open to non-college members. *Strong music and theatre; famous choir.* Music rehearsal rooms. Library (100,000 books, including 30,000 antiquarian) with enormous DVD collection; 45 computers, 24hrs. Eight acres of playing fields nearby. Most years ('cept a few thirds) can be housed in College; art gallery – students can borrow paintings for their rooms. All students eat in hall; daily formal dinner; self-catering in new buildings. Doctor; nurse; Men's, Women's and Welfare Officers, LGBT rep – *good welfare*. Various bursaries, prizes and study grants available.

FAMOUS ALUMNI
Tony Benn (former Lab MP); Kate Beckinsale (Brit movie celeb); Angus Deayton (*disgraced, resurgent* TV presenter); John Fowles, John Galsworthy (writers); Hugh Grant (*er*, actor); Bryan Johnston (late *effusive* cricket commentator, after whom the pavilion is named); Revd W A Spooner (*jerbal vuggler*); Naomi Woolf (feminist writer).

ORIEL COLLEGE, OXFORD

THIS COLLEGE IS PART OF THE UNIVERSITY OF OXFORD AND STUDENTS ARE ENTITLED TO USE ITS FACILITIES

○ **ORIEL COLLEGE**, Oxford, OX1 4EW **TEL** (01865) 276 522 **E-MAIL** admissions@oriel.ox.ac.uk **WEBSITE** www.oriel.ox.ac.uk
○ **JCR, ORIEL COLLEGE**, Oxford, OX1 4EW **TEL** (01865) 276 587 **E-MAIL** jcr.president@oriel.ox.ac.uk **WEBSITE** www.orieljcr.org

GENERAL
One of the oldest and smallest colleges, the *beautiful* College of Oriel is 300 metres from Carfax, *cunningly hidden* down a side-street. *It remains fairly conservative and was the last Oxford college to go co-educational (in 1985). Its quiet, closed quads and tight, communal spirit can be either inspiring or suffocating. The sporting reputation it prides itself on has been dwindling in recent years – although the celebratory drinking sessions persist with aplomb (and considerable rowdiness).*

SEX RATIO: ♂56 ♀44	FOUNDED: 1326
FULL-TIME U'GRADS: 296	PART-TIME: 0
POSTGRADS: 147	MATURE: 1%
STATE:PRIVATE SCHOOL: 50:50	INTERNATIONAL: 9%
ACADEMIC RANKING: 26	DISABLED: 17

Humming bar with pool table, dartboard, table football and games machines, *unsettlingly popular karaoke;* varied weekly recitals and film screenings; *respected* chapel choir; regular cabaret; ball every three years. *Well-funded* library (100,000 books, 74 study places) split into Junior and Senior sections, Junior Library open 24hrs; 21 networked computers in two suites; all rooms have Ethernet. Anglican chapel with termly RC masses; TV room *(sorry, 'Noam Chomsky Entertainment Wing')* with video and Sky, arcade and pinball machines. *Left-wing* JCR, currently withholding subscription from OUSU (students are still technically members though). Squash courts, multigym, 6.5 acres of playing fields a mile away; *ideally positioned for the river; rowers by tradition, darts and rugby also doing well;* annual KPMG-sponsored regatta. All students can live in (£82-112/25wks), either on-site or at James Mellon Hall a mile away; about half en suite; *quality mixed but improving;* some entry phones; students eat in hall; formals six days a week; *moderate* food but *carbolicious* all-you-can-eat breakfasts. LGBT, Postgrad, International, Male and Female Welfare Officers, welfare-organised self-defence classes; nurse available five mornings a week, free condoms, cheap attack alarms. *Older bits bad for access,* adapted rooms at JMH. Range of scholarships, prizes and bursaries (£500-1,200) including JCR hardship fund. Oxford Opportunity bursaries for u'grads. Alternative prospectus.

FAMOUS ALUMNI
Matthew Arnold (poet); Beau Brummel (dandy); Sir Thomas More (executed by Henry VIII); Cardinal Newman (Oxford Movement); Sir Walter Raleigh (potatoes and general swash buckling); Cecil Rhodes (*dodgy imperialist*); A J P Taylor (historian).

 The Queen's College, Oxford, is allowed to shut down the High Street for archery practice.

Words in italics are Push's point of view – take it or leave it...

PEMBROKE COLLEGE, OXFORD

THIS COLLEGE IS PART OF THE UNIVERSITY OF OXFORD AND STUDENTS ARE ENTITLED TO USE ITS FACILITIES

◉ **PEMBROKE COLLEGE**, Oxford, OX1 1DW **TEL** (01865) 276 444 **E-MAIL** admissions@pmb.ox.ac.uk **WEBSITE** www.pmb.ox.ac.uk
◉ **PEMBROKE COLLEGE JCR**, Oxford, OX1 1DW **WEBSITE** www.pembrokejcr.com

GENERAL

Pembroke's quads, 300 metres from Carfax, *range from medieval marvels to modern misdemeanours, but even Alan Titchmarsh could get some tips from their gardens. They're known for sporting prowess – despite their wussy pink colours – but academic achievement hovers around the adequate mark (by Oxford standards). One of their more deranged* traditions is the 'burning of the boats' after rowing victories – with the crew still on board – *leaving a 60 metre scorch mark on the North Quad for most of the year. The College has been the butt of some jokes about its financial wellbeing (or lack of it) in recent years – not helped by the word 'broke' in its name. A recent staff turnaround is restocking the treasury, however.*

SEX RATIO: ♂59 ♀41	FOUNDED: 1624
FULL-TIME U'GRADS: 406	PART-TIME: 0
POSTGRADS: 90	MATURE: 1%
STATE:PRIVATE SCHOOL: 50:50	INTERNATIONAL: 7%
ACADEMIC RANKING: 17	DISABLED: 60

College bar (bops, quizzes, theme nights, pool table and video games) and private bar for postgrads; ball every other year; regular *muck-raking* 'Bogsheet'; *raucous* Yearbook. Modern library (40,000 books, 64 study places, 24 with network sockets), open 24 hours during term. 24 computers for undergrads; MCR computer room (four PCs); web access in all rooms (£25 a year). Interdenominational chapel with CofE chaplain. Claims to have best attended JCR meetings in Oxford – *not big on out-of-college issues though;* common room with pool, arcade games; TV room with DVD player. *Hugely sporty:* won Sporting College of the Year Award 2006 and made Oxford rowing history in 2004 when both men's and women's 1st VIIIs won the Headship in the annual Summer Eights competition. All first years and most others live in; *relatively high quality* rooms (£98-£163 for 24wks), priced according to size; *modern* Geoffrey Arthur Building *most sought after* – mainly finalists; Macmillan Building *is the obligatory 60s carbuncle, but buzzing inside;* no one shares; three formal dinners a week – *pretty much compulsory for first years; decent* food (£207 a term) complemented by JCR pantry (8am-5pm); *limited parking* – only available at GAB. Postgrad Officer and soc; LGBT Officer and soc; Women's Officer and soc; free attack alarms, condoms, sanitary towels, pregnancy tests; doctor; nurse on site 2hrs a day. *Limited* hardship fund; Oxford Opportunity Bursaries; £200 scholarships for First-nabbers, £100 to those who come close; assortment of prizes.

FAMOUS ALUMNI

William Blackstone (lawyer); Denzil Davies MP (Lab); Michael Heseltine (former MP, Con); Samuel Johnson (wrote the first dictionary); John Pym (socialist, historian, revolutionary); James Smithson (founded Washington DC's Smithsonian Institute). Roger Bannister (4-min mile runner) is a former Master of the College. J R R Tolkien was a fellow for 19 years.

THE QUEEN'S COLLEGE, OXFORD

THIS COLLEGE IS PART OF THE UNIVERSITY OF OXFORD AND STUDENTS ARE ENTITLED TO USE ITS FACILITIES

◉ **THE QUEEN'S COLLEGE**, High Street, Oxford, OX1 4AW **TEL** (01865) 279 120 **E-MAIL** admission@queens.ox.ac.uk **WEBSITE**: www.queens.ox.ac.uk ◉ **JCR, THE QUEENS COLLEGE**, High Street, Oxford, OX1 4AW **TEL** (01865) 279 120 **WEBSITE** www.queens.ox.ac.uk/jcr

GENERAL

Queen's may be dribbling with history and tradition, but it maintains a surprisingly laid-back attitude. Technically, students can still order servants into the cellar to fetch them beer, but now prefer to go themselves – because the cellar's a pub. The *superb* buildings, 600 metres from Carfax, *dominate* the High Street, and Queen's quad and cupola (designed by *celeb-architect* Hawksmoor) leave quite an impression. More northern students are attracted to Queen's than most colleges *and the atmosphere is refreshingly unpretentious.*

SEX RATIO: ♂55 ♀45	FOUNDED: 1341
FULL-TIME U'GRADS: 300	PART-TIME: 0
POSTGRADS: 100	MATURE: 0%
STATE:PRIVATE SCHOOL: 54:46	INTERNATIONAL: 12%
ACADEMIC RANKING: 20	DISABLED: 6

Bar – the Beer Cellar (cap. 150) – with *friendly staff* and *slap-up dinners* preceded by fanfare and afternoon teas; Queen's Hall (cap. 350) and JCR (75) used for ents and bands; ball every three years; Library (200,000 books); 12 computers, 24hrs; JCR with pool, TV and snackage. Anglican chapel with *talented* mixed recording choir. Drama and medical socs; *strong musical streak. Queen's students' sport of choice is darts*; tennis/netball courts and football/hockey pitches (a mile away), gym, track, multigym, squash courts, bowling green, pavilion. Annual sports day with bouncy castle and tug-of-war with *gentleman* rivals, St Edmund Hall. Everyone lives in College halls or flats, some self-catering, dining hall. LGBT group; LGBT, Minorities, Welfare, Men's and Women's Officers; academic and food reps, doctor and nurse. Bursaries, scholarships and hardship funds, *oh my.* Open days May-June.

FAMOUS ALUMNI
Rowan Atkinson (comedian); Jeremy Bentham (philosopher); Tim Berners-Lee (invented the www); Edmund Halley *(named some comet)*; Henry V (king); Gerald Kaufman MP (Lab); Oliver Sacks (writer, psychiatrist); Brian Walden (journalist).

REGENT'S PARK COLLEGE, OXFORD

THIS COLLEGE IS PART OF THE UNIVERSITY OF OXFORD AND STUDENTS ARE ENTITLED TO USE ITS FACILITIES

○ **REGENT'S PARK COLLEGE**, Pusey Street, Oxford, OX1 2LB **TEL** (01865) 288 120 **E-MAIL** admissions@ rpc.ox.ac.uk **WEBSITE** www.rpc.ox.ac.uk ○ **JCR, REGENT'S PARK COLLEGE**, Pusey Street, Oxford, OX1 2LB **TEL** (01865) 288 120 **E-MAIL** info@regentsjcr.org.uk **WEBSITE** www.regentsjcr.org.uk

GENERAL
Through an *unassuming* little door off the *beautiful* boulevard of St Giles' is the *unassuming* little college of Regent's Park, one of Oxford's smallest. It began its life as a London training institution for Baptist ministers and missionaries and although it's long since been absorbed into Oxford University and opened its door to different denominations (becoming thoroughly ecumenical), it's still got a heavy theological slant – it's the national Centre for Baptist History and Heritage. *It remains relatively unknown in the Oxbridge scheme of things, although involvement in the University SU is improving. While many other colleges struggle with the pressures of celebrity, snobbery and the old boys' network, the small number of Arts & Humanities students based here (technoboffins beware) are happy simply to get on with things, while maintaining a high level of involvement with University-wide activities.* The College doesn't require faith commitments from students, welcomes families and has a *quietly homely atmosphere that warms the cockles other colleges can't reach.*

SEX RATIO: ♂45 ♀55	FOUNDED: 1810
FULL-TIME U'GRADS: 85	PART-TIME: 20
POSTGRADS: 40	MATURE: 30%
STATE:PRIVATE SCHOOL: 60:40	INTERNATIONAL: 10%
ACADEMIC RANKING: N/A	DISABLED: 4

Very cheap, tiny bar, but drinking space in the JCR; karaoke, gameshow nights; *fairly strong dramatic activity*, usually at least one major production a year; two bops a term; annual 'Final Fling' mini ball; ad hoc ents; strawberries and Pimm's summer outings, punting trips; London theatre trips. *Very involved JCR, keen on charity work*; common room with newspapers, VCR/DVD/Sky. Two libraries (40,000 books, 50 study places), including Angus Library of early Baptist Documents – *good for theology, philosophy and English.* Six 24-hr computers; free intranet in all rooms. Ecumenical chapel. *Football, netball and rowing doing well*; snooker, table football and table tennis table; no playing fields. Nearly all live in; flats for couples/single sex; no en suite. *High-quality*, waiter service meals provided weekdays but *kitchen facilities are good*; laundry facilities; no parking. College gates close at 10pm, swipecard access; overnight guests must be registered – *rather kills the mood, don't you think?* CCTV; free attack alarms; Postgrad, Women's, Men's, LGBT, Harassment and Welfare Officers; doctor; *disabled access needs improvement.* Various bursaries.

FAMOUS ALUMNI
Paul Fiddes, Henry Wheeler Robinson (theologians); the bloke who directed Spiceworld – *his name can't be given to protect his own safety*; Maltus Wells (explorer).

ST ANNE'S COLLEGE, OXFORD

THIS COLLEGE IS PART OF THE UNIVERSITY OF OXFORD AND STUDENTS ARE ENTITLED TO USE ITS FACILITIES

ST ANNE'S COLLEGE, Woodstock Road, Oxford, OX2 6HS **TEL** (01865) 274 800 **E-MAIL** enquiries@st-annes.ox.ac.uk **WEBSITE** www.st-annes.ox.ac.uk **JCR, ST ANNE'S COLLEGE**, Woodstock Road, Oxford, OX2 6HS **TEL** (01865) 274 870 **WEBSITE** www.stannesjcr.org

GENERAL

St Anne's is ten mins walk from the city centre and gets *a fair bit of stick* for being 'miles' away as a result. It was initially a women-only affair, linked to the rise of education for Oxford women in 1878. It became an affiliated college in 1952 and let the boys in to play in 1979. Because of its past it maintains a strict halfway balance of men and women both in the student body and the teaching staff. The 1930s main building is made of *warm* Cotswold stone with a battlement top; most of the others were constructed *with more slapdash aesthetics* in the 50s and 60s and the newest building appeared in 2005. *The modern style doesn't sit well with the prestige of some other colleges and architectural snobs occasionally turn up noses. The students are a no-nonsense bunch – not much petty student politicking. They prefer to put their energies into charity Rag events, the wealth of drama and music societies or a sociable bevy now and then. St Anne's trumpets equality from the rooftops, has recently appointed its first male principal, claims to be particularly open to applications from minorities and its students are reputed to be 'normal'. Which is comforting.*

 *(sex ratio figure)*

SEX RATIO: ♂50 ♀50	**FOUNDED:** 1952
FULL-TIME U'GRADS: 445	**PART-TIME:** 0
POSTGRADS: 140	**MATURE:** 0%
STATE:PRIVATE SCHOOL: 50:50	**INTERNATIONAL:** 10%
ACADEMIC RANKING: 8	**DISABLED:** 0

Bar with pub quizzes, darts and bar Olympics on offer; *active* drama society (the St Anne's Players), comedy soc; large lecture theatre with screen and collapsible stage; bands in JCR and *whopping bops*; yearly arts festival with drama, comedy, music, photos and *all things arty*. A *spacious* library, (110,000 books, growing by 2,000 every year); 16 networked computers and Ethernet access in most rooms. There's a scheme for students to buy computers off the College, paying in instalments. 'Double Standards' and 'Agent Orange' are the JCR mags – 'Bogsheet' is for gossip-mongers. *Strong on women's football*; sports facilities are shared with St John's, 800m away. Everyone except some postgrads lives in but *there are grumbles a-rumblin' over the rent – the JCR is struggling for reductions. Rooms fairly standard, though sexy new pads are being built. Catering arrangements a bit restrictive; plenty of formal dinners; small kitchens on each staircase.* Some parking. LGBT, Ethnic Minorities and Women's Officers; doctor, nurse, student counsellor; *reasonable wheelchair access.* Travel grants, book allowances; scholarships to study in Japan available.

FAMOUS ALUMNI

Maria Aitken (actress); Edwina Currie (ex-MP, romance novelist and *John Major's bit of stuff*); Penelope Lively, Iris Murdoch, Zoe Heller, Jenny Uglow (writers); Libby Purves (journalist); Sir Simon Rattle (conductor); Baroness Young (politician).

ST CATHERINE'S COLLEGE, OXFORD

THIS COLLEGE IS PART OF THE UNIVERSITY OF OXFORD AND STUDENTS ARE ENTITLED TO USE ITS FACILITIES

ST CATHERINE'S COLLEGE, Manor Road, Oxford, OX1 3UJ **TEL** (01865) 271 703 **E-MAIL** admissions@stcatz.ox.ac.uk **WEBSITE**: www.stcatz.ox.ac.uk **THE JCR**, St Catherine's College, Manor Road, Oxford, OX1 3UJ **WEBSITE** jcr.stcatz.ox.ac.uk

GENERAL

Catz, as St Catherine's is *affectionately* known, *far from the typical sandy-stoned Oxford college*, is a modernist concoction of glass and concrete a mile from Carfax. *The relatively progressive architecture reflects the forward-looking, unstuffy atmosphere inside.* It's a large college and what it

lacks in architectural sex appeal it makes up for with mod cons: warm rooms, showers, kitchens, purpose-built bar, even a grassy amphitheatre and water gardens. *There are plenty of ents and they are keen on maintaining their up-for-it ambience, so for students who want to go to Oxford for the academic kudos, but want to steer clear of the Ivory Tower mentality of the more traditional settings, Catz's a good bet. Students are proud to be here, but even concrete can't quite* stave off that inimitable Oxford smugness. It still has that one big happy family feel, mainly because of its comparatively detached setting.

SEX RATIO: ♂60 ♀40	**FOUNDED:** 1962
FULL-TIME U'GRADS: 447	**PART-TIME:** 0
POSTGRADS: 187	**MATURE:** 1%
STATE:PRIVATE SCHOOL: 44:56	**INTERNATIONAL:** 14%
ACADEMIC RANKING: 22	**DISABLED:** 4

Lively all-day bar is the largest in Oxford – but the famous Turf Tavern is five mins away. Mightily theatrical: JCR and Bernard Sunley Theatres; Music House used for bands; May Ball; very popular weekly bops in JCR and MCR; library (57,000 books); 40 networked PCs, 24hrs. All rooms have internet access. No chapel. JCR with 18 e-mail stations, shop, snack bar, photocopier. Not half bad at rowing; football &

cricket pitches, squash court, gym; the rest 15 mins away. All first, third and most second years live in; new accommodation block with seminar rooms; large car park behind College, around £8.50 for three meals/day; formal dining hall in the evenings; Pete's Caff for snack meals; buttery. LGBT, Postgrad and Women's Officers and socs; College doctor, nurse; good disabled access.

FAMOUS ALUMNI
John Birt (former Director General, BBC); Phil De Glanville (former England rugby captain); Joseph Heller (writer, Catch-22); Richard Herring (tubby comedian of Lee & Herring fame); Sir Cameron Mackintosh (honorary fellow, musical magnate, producer of, you guessed it, Cats); Peter Mandelson (EU Commissioner, New Labour svengali); A A Milne (writer, Winnie the Pooh); Matthew Pinsent (four-time Olympic gold rower); Sara Ramsden (controller of Sky One); Simon Winchester (author); Jeanette Winterson (writer).

ST EDMUND HALL, OXFORD

THIS COLLEGE IS PART OF THE UNIVERSITY OF OXFORD AND STUDENTS ARE ENTITLED TO USE ITS FACILITIES

⊙ **ST EDMUND HALL**, Queens Lane, Oxford, OX1 4AR **TEL** (01865) 279 011 **E-MAIL** admissions@seh.ox.ac.uk **WEBSITE** www.seh.ox.ac.uk ⊙ **JCR**, St Edmund Hall, Queens Lane, Oxford, OX1 4AR **WEBSITE** jcr.seh.ox.ac.uk

GENERAL
Small, cute and cuddly, Teddy Hall, as its undergrads know it, is a mixture of ancient and modern buildings set 650 metres from Carfax. Although St Edmund's has only been a college in the strictest sense since 1957, its academic and architectural roots stretch back to the 13th-Century and it has a legitimate claim to being the first institution ever to educate undergrads anywhere. The buildings include a Norman church (now the library) and its attached graveyard (de-consecrated) and crypt. The students are a friendly, confident lot radiating freedom of spirit and intimacy and they definitely know how to party - after all, no other college plays 'The Teddy Bear's Picnic' during matriculation. They're strong in journalism, drama and, especially, sport – indeed, there was a time when it seemed like the College only accepted talented athletes, but now even those who are rubbish at sport are in with a chance – provided they can at least down a pint with the chaps after the big games.

SEX RATIO: ♂53 ♀47	**FOUNDED:** 1263
FULL-TIME U'GRADS: 403	**PART-TIME:** 0
POSTGRADS: 129	**MATURE:** 1%
STATE:PRIVATE SCHOOL: 30:52	**INTERNATIONAL:** 14%
ACADEMIC RANKING: 24	**DISABLED:** 20

Dinky buttery bar with legendary fortnightly bops in Wolfson Hall; ancient dining hall; two JCR party rooms. Keenly dramatic – John Oldham Society puts on three plays per year; plenty of theatre trips arranged; annual black tie Summer Event; two sumptuous black tie dinners a term; choral concerts and recitals. Library open till 1am, some parts 24hrs; over 50,000 books, 85 study places, 24 computers, 24hrs; most rooms have Ethernet, College helps fund net access for rooms that don't; photography darkroom. Excellent College magazine, 'The Insider', two JCR news 'Bogsheets' a term. CofE chapel and chaplain. Small JCR with games and pool machines, Sky and free condoms. Dedicated JCR committee. Sports facilities five mins from site, multigym. All can live in, wide variety of rooms available, most spacious and well-fitted (£100/25wks); students eat in ancient dining hall – pricey food (£50/wk); optional Sunday formal dinner. Unique JCR butler serves 'Chaps Tea' of toasted teacakes and other goodies every weekday in the coffee bar; self-catering facilities vary. LGBT Officer; JCR Welfare Officer; doctor, nurse; one adapted bedroom for wheelchair-users; access not brilliant; £800 a year bursary scheme for low income students, more financial help in the offing. Alternative prospectus from alt.seh.ox.ac.uk

FAMOUS ALUMNI
Sir Robin Day (broadcaster); Nicholas Evans (author of 'The Horse Whisperer'); Terry Jones (Monty Python); Graham Kentfield (former chief cashier, Bank of England); Stewart Lee (comedian, 'Jerry Springer: The Opera'); Al Murray (pub landlord); John Oldham (17th-century poet).

Words in italics are Push's point of view — take it or leave it...

ST HILDA'S COLLEGE, OXFORD

THIS COLLEGE IS PART OF THE UNIVERSITY OF OXFORD AND STUDENTS ARE ENTITLED TO USE ITS FACILITIES

○ **ST HILDA'S COLLEGE**, Oxford, OX4 1DY **TEL** (01865) 276 884 **E–MAIL** college.office@st-hildas.oxford.ac.uk **WEBSITE** www.st-hildas.ox.ac.uk ○ **JCR**, St Hilda's College, Oxford, OX4 1DY **TEL** (01865) 276 846

GENERAL

St Hilda's College, almost a mile from Carfax, is the last all-female college in Oxford and they plan to keep it that way. In 2004 men did try to *crowbar* their way in, but the motion was *swiftly overturned by the JCR. Despite the strong sense of sisterhood, this is no nunnery – most students are drawn to an environment where macho attitudes don't impinge on academic life, but they don't object to associating with blokes after hours – after all, the only ones around have been hand-picked. The large population of international students lends a cosmopolitan tinge to College social life. The 'Hildabeasts' enjoy a strong sense of communal identity but still manage a high level of involvement with University-wide shenanigans.*

SEX RATIO: ♂0 ♀100	**FOUNDED:** 1893
FULL–TIME U'GRADS: 418	**PART–TIME:** 0
POSTGRADS: 114	**MATURE:** <1%
STATE:PRIVATE SCHOOL: 56:44	**INTERNATIONAL:** 25%
ACADEMIC RANKING: 23	**DISABLED:** 0

Student-run buttery bar with snacks and juke box, pool, table football, quizzes and karaoke, open all-night May Eve; JCR for student bands and jazz nights; *cheapest* May Ball in town; annual arts festival week. Termly 'Hilda Guardian' mag and weekly 'Loo News'. Two libraries, (60,000 books, 120 study places) one for law, 24hrs; 24 computers, free printing and Ethernet in all rooms. Music rehearsal rooms in the Jacqueline du Pré building – *one of Oxford's best concert venues. Competent JCR with high level of student involvement.* Non-denominational chapel. Near Iffley Road Sports Centre; punts, boathouse and tennis court on-site and swimming pool next door. *Very strong on rowing.* A third of students live out – Accommodation Office lists vacancies; all first years and most thirds live in (170 catered places, 287 self-catered with meal tickets). *Spacious modern rooms* and new *(if pricey)* accommodation block. Formal dinners at weekends – *damn good food.* CCTV; night porter; doctor; nurse; JCR reps for Equal Opportunities, Disabilities, Overseas Students, Lesbians and Bisexuals; no JCR access for wheelchair users; two adapted bedrooms; ramps; disability adviser; adaptations as required; hardship fund; travel grants; £50 book grant for first years, £200 music bursary. Alternative prospectus available on web.

FAMOUS ALUMNI

Zeinab Badawi (newscaster); Wendy Cope (poet); Helen Jackson MP (Lab); Susan Kramer (London mayoral candidate, Lib Dem); Hermione Lee (writer); Val McDermid (crime novelist); Rosalind Miles (writer); Kate Millett (writer); Barbara Pym (writer); Baroness Gillian Shephard (former Con MP). Jacqueline du Pré (cellist) was an Honorary Fellow.

ST HUGH'S COLLEGE, OXFORD

THIS COLLEGE IS PART OF THE UNIVERSITY OF OXFORD AND STUDENTS ARE ENTITLED TO USE ITS FACILITIES

○ **ST HUGH'S COLLEGE**, St Margaret's Road, Oxford, OX2 6LE **TEL** (01865) 274 900 **E–MAIL** admissions@st-hughs.ox.ac.uk **WEBSITE** www.st-hughs.ox.ac.uk ○ **JCR**, St Hugh's College, St Margaret's Road, Oxford, OX2 6LE **TEL:** (01865) 274 425 **WEBSITE**: www.hughsjcr.com

GENERAL

St Hugh's *spacious but unglamorous juxtaposition* of redbrick, Edwardian, art deco and *brutal* 60s buildings are a mile from Carfax, protecting it from the tourist hordes. The College was founded *almost by accident* by Elizabeth Wordsworth for women's education. *It's known for its unstuffy, creative vibe.* Having survived for a century without them, St Hugh's started enrolling men in 1986. *This apparently resulted in an increase of rugby songs and associated lewdness in the bar –* *though as often as not, it's the women's football team to blame – and the College is welcoming with a tight-knit community atmosphere. Hugh's students plague almost every activity at a University level.*

SEX RATIO: ♂48 ♀52	**FOUNDED:** 1886
FULL–TIME U'GRADS: 404	**PART–TIME:** 0
POSTGRADS: 237	**MATURE:** 8%
STATE:PRIVATE SCHOOL: 57:43	**INTERNATIONAL:** 15%
ACADEMIC RANKING: 28	**DISABLED:** 3

Words in italics are Push's point of view – take it or leave it...

Bar: Wordsworth Room and Lee House (for functions); Morden Hall theatre, *lots of musicals*; frequent *popular* bops in JCR; opera and jazz trips. Two libraries (88,503 books – *good on suffragette movement*); four computer rooms (20 workstations), 24-hr access. *Sporadic* 'Hugh's News' and *excellent* College newsletter; *charitable* JCR with *strong environmental concerns*; interdenominational chapel. *Fairly sporty*; two basketball courts, lawns for croquet, tennis and frisbee; other facilities shared with Wadham 800m away. All can live in, 40% en suite rooms; cafe for snacks and surfing (the net variety); weekly formal meal in dining hall. Two Welfare, International, Ethnic, Women's and Disability Officers; visiting doctor, nurse. Access fund varies between £100-500 a pop. Alternative prospectus online.

FAMOUS ALUMNI
Baroness Barbara Castle (late Lab MP); Emily Davison (suffragette martyr); Ruth Lawrence (mathematical prodigy); Mary Renault (historical novelist); Aung San Suu Kyi (Burmese Nobel Peace Prize winner); Joanna Trollope (Aga saga writer).

ST JOHN'S COLLEGE, OXFORD

THIS COLLEGE IS PART OF THE UNIVERSITY OF OXFORD AND STUDENTS ARE ENTITLED TO USE ITS FACILITIES

○ **ST JOHN'S COLLEGE**, Oxford, OX1 3JP **TEL** (01865) 277 318 **E-MAIL** admissions@sjc.ox.ac.uk **WEBSITE** www.sjc.ox.ac.uk
○ **JCR**, St John's College, Oxford, OX1 3JP **TEL** (01865) 277 422 **E-MAIL** jcr-president@sjc.ox.ac.uk **WEBSITE** jcr.sjc.ox.ac.uk

GENERAL
St John's, one of the oldest and *minted-est* colleges in Oxford, is 800 metres from Carfax. Its *awesome* 15th-, 17th- and 18th-century buildings are arranged around six quads for the public gaze and the largest garden in Oxford. *Meanwhile – like poor relations or pornographic tattoos – the modern additions are kept wisely out of sight. The only sounds during the day are the pen-jotting, page-flicking or pencil-chewing of diligent students. At night, though, students remove their thinking caps, let their hair down and get down to the bar, already full of the women rowers (the Sirens). Its reputation as an academically snooty workhouse isn't entirely justified* – Tony Blair's rock career began (and ended) here, after all.

Largest bar is the Sirens' bop venue; others in the Larkin Room, the Prestwich Room and the *post-modern* Basement band venue; auditorium used by St John's Mummers drama group; four bops a term; ball every three years; two libraries (one for law) with 75,000 books, *massive* manuscripts selection; 40 computers, 24hrs; internet in most rooms. Fortnightly College mag 'TW'; Anglican chapel with Sunday choir service. *Active* JCR with *strong* anti-fees sentiments; reading room; TV and games room; juke box; vending machine and photocopier. *Motivated Rag.* 10 acres of sports fields a mile away; two tennis courts and netball court. *Women's rowing doing well – as usual; tiddlywinks also popular, but there you go.* All live in catered halls (£67-76/24wks); 10% en suite; 5-8 share kitchens with oven; *very respectable quality rooms* ranging from 16th-century to 90s style; daily formal halls. LGBT, Ethnic Minorities, Women's and Disabilities Officers. Doctor, nurse, counsellor. Free condoms, cheap attack alarms for women; *better disabled access than most*; £30,000 access fund; *fat wads* of grants, scholarships, bursaries and hardship funds available.

SEX RATIO: ♂56 ♀44	FOUNDED: 1555
FULL-TIME U'GRADS: 398	PART-TIME: 0
POSTGRADS: 200	MATURE: 1%
STATE:PRIVATE SCHOOL: 69:31	INTERNATIONAL: 6%
ACADEMIC RANKING: 2	DISABLED: 4

FAMOUS ALUMNI
Sir Kingsley Amis, Robert Graves, A E Houseman, Philip Larkin, John Wain (all writers/poets); Tony Blair MP (PM).

○ **University College, Oxford celebrated its 1,000th anniversary in 1872 despite knowing that claims it was founded by King Alfred were faked by 13th-century scholars to win a land argument.**

Words in italics are Push's point of view — take it or leave it...

ST PETER'S COLLEGE, OXFORD

THIS COLLEGE IS PART OF THE UNIVERSITY OF OXFORD AND STUDENTS ARE ENTITLED TO USE ITS FACILITIES

○ **ST PETER'S COLLEGE**, New Inn Hall Street, Oxford, OX1 2DL **TEL** (01865) 278 863 **E-MAIL** Admissions@spc.ox.ac.uk **WEBSITE** www.spc.ox.ac.uk ○ **ST PETER'S COLLEGE JCR**, New Inn Hall Street, Oxford, OX1 2DL **TEL** (01865) 278 900 **WEBSITE** www.spcjcr.co.uk

GENERAL

The *small and cosy* St Peter's College is 250 metres from Carfax, just off Oxford's main High Street and round the corner from the newly developed Castle site. Originally founded by a *disgruntled Liverpudlian Bishop* in the hope of offering a university education to those who might not be otherwise able to afford it, it became an Oxford college in 1961 *and the worthy Bishop's plans went out the window (although it still maintains a strong open access policy)*. Its buildings are a *low-key* collection of Georgian, Victorian and *nasty 70s affairs* arranged around four grass quads. *St Peter's is a friendly and relaxed college, noted for its strengths in sport, art, music and drama, as well as its spectrum of joint honours courses.*

SEX RATIO: ♂55 ♀45	**FOUNDED:** 1929	
FULL-TIME U'GRADS: 390	**PART-TIME:** 0	
POSTGRADS: 125	**MATURE:** 5%	
STATE:PRIVATE SCHOOL: 50:50	**INTERNATIONAL:** 17%	
ACADEMIC RANKING: 27	**DISABLED:** 26	

Bar with adjacent games room – *more students drink in town; strong and diverse drama;* student bands and four bops a term in the JCR; choral concerts and recitals; occasional club events in town; black tie dinner each term, ball every other year; two libraries – one law, (40,000 books in total) open 24hrs; 15 PCs and more for student hire; Ethernet in all rooms. Anglican chapel. Fortnightly mag, 'Peterphile'. Piazza for *snackish delights. Sporty – football, cricket and tennis doing well on the bloke front, netball and hockey women-wise;* darts club; shares sports fields with Exeter and Hertford Colleges (football, rugby, squash, hockey, cricket, tennis, gym). All first and third years live in, most second years scavenge their own beds; accommodation split between main site (£95/25wks), College annexes (£92-£98/38wks) and self-catered College houses in town (£85/38wks); St Peter's has planned to accommodate more of its undergrads by building some *fancy new annexes five mins away; rooms small but pleasant* (35% en suite); *better kitchen facilities off main site;* optional formal dinners; termly fixed meal charge (£133-£306 depending on housing); *parking next to impossible. Welfare-heavy* JCR; LGBT Officer and soc, Postgrad Officer and soc, Women's Officer, *disabled access okay except in library.* Access fund: £500-1,500 a time; means-tested bursary scheme; travel funds and exam-tested scholarships. DVD prospectus available.

FAMOUS ALUMNI

Edward Akufo Addo (ex-President of Ghana); Carl Albert (former speaker, US House of representatives); Revd W Awdry (creator of Thomas the Tank Engine); Simon Beaufoy (screenwriter, 'The Full Monty'); Lord Condon (former Met Police Commissioner); Ken Loach (film director); Sir Paul Reeves (former Governor General of New Zealand); Peter Wright (author, 'Spycatcher').

SOMERVILLE COLLEGE, OXFORD

THIS COLLEGE IS PART OF THE UNIVERSITY OF OXFORD AND STUDENTS ARE ENTITLED TO USE ITS FACILITIES

○ **SOMERVILLE COLLEGE**, Woodstock Road, Oxford, OX2 6HD **TEL** (01865) 270 600 **E-MAIL** admissions@some.ox.ac.uk **WEBSITE** www.some.ox.ac.uk ○ **JCR**, Somerville College, Woodstock Road, Oxford, OX2 6HD **TEL** (01865) 270 593 **E-MAIL** jcr.president@some.ox.ac.uk **WEBSITE**: student.some.ox.ac.uk/jcr

GENERAL

Somerville's 800 metres from the town centre, near the *trendy* area of Jericho. It's a *relaxed, peaceful* college of mixed, rather institutional architecture and *gorgeous gardens. The small bar, with its merry happy hours, is a vital social lubricant.* Men are a *controversial* recent addition (1994) *but the atmosphere hasn't become as blokey as some hoped/feared. Informality and tolerance is the rule and Somervillians opt out of some of Oxford's dafter traditions (students can walk on the grass, for example), although its political folk are ubiquitous in positions of authority across OUSU and the Union (debating).*

Words in italics are Push's point of view – take it or leave it...

SEX RATIO: ♂49 ♀51	**FOUNDED:** 1879	
FULL-TIME U'GRADS: 392	**PART-TIME:** 0	
POSTGRADS: 100	**MATURE:** 1%	
STATE:PRIVATE SCHOOL: 63:37	**INTERNATIONAL:** 15%	
ACADEMIC RANKING: 12	**DISABLED:** 4	

Bar next to digital TV room – also near the *legendary* Duke of Cambridge pub (happy hour) and Brown's restaurant *(not near much else; students need a bike)*; Flora Anderson Hall for bands; *active* drama, JCR drama rep; *busy* music soc; summer Event; ball every three years. *Good* library (100,000+ books); 20 computers, most rooms have Ethernet; music rehearsal rooms. Non-denominational chapel, Catholic church next door. *Lots* of charity projects; *gallant JCR valiantly fighting against* increasing rents. *Some sporting talent, especially in football, netball, rugby and rowing;* gym; shared fields with Wadham. All first years live in, all finalists can if they wish; *varied but generally spacious rooms*;

JCR Equalisation scheme (£80/term) helps second years with costs of living out. Pay-as-you-eat meal system; weekly formal hall. *Parking impossible.* LGBT, Postgrad, Women's, International Students' and LGB reps and Ethnic Minorities Officer; doctor, nurse; crèche with 16 places; *not bad wheelchair access*; adapted rooms for disabled students; means-tested awards (£5-500), travel and sports grants from JCR, scholarships, book prizes, well-endowed hardship fund. Alternative prospectus online.

FAMOUS ALUMNI
Sunethra Bandaranaike (Sri Lanka's former PM); Indira Ghandi (India's former PM); Dorothy Hodgkin (Nobel Prize winner); Iris Murdoch (writer); Baroness Park (spymaster); Esther Rantzen (*toothy* TV celeb); Dorothy L Sayers (crime writer – wrote about the College in Gaudy Night); Baroness Margaret Thatcher (former PM); Baroness Shirley Williams (Lib Dem) – *clearly the college of choice for would-be baronesses and PMs*.

TRINITY COLLEGE, OXFORD

THIS COLLEGE IS PART OF THE UNIVERSITY OF OXFORD AND STUDENTS ARE ENTITLED TO USE ITS FACILITIES

○ **TRINITY COLLEGE**, Broad Street, Oxford, OX1 3BH **TEL** (01865) 279 900 **E-MAIL** admissions@trinity.ox.ac.uk
WEBSITE www.trinity.ox.ac.uk ○ **JCR**, Trinity College, Broad Street, OX1 3BH **TEL** (01865) 279 900 **E-MAIL** jcr@trinity.ox.ac.uk
WEBSITE www.trinity.ox.ac.uk/jcr

GENERAL
Originally Trinity students had to take holy orders, lead monastic lifestyles of study and contemplation and never marry. *Entry requirements have relaxed – now students just have to be clever.* Trinity College *sits very prettily* in extensive gardens, 400 metres from Carfax and within walking distance of the University's main facilities. *The College is generally moderate – in size, sporting/political activity and cost – and though it maintains a keenly academic tilt, has plenty of journos, politicos and thespos too.*

SEX RATIO: ♂52 ♀48	**FOUNDED:** 1555	
FULL-TIME U'GRADS: 295	**PART-TIME:** 0	
POSTGRADS: 124	**MATURE:** 5%	
STATE:PRIVATE SCHOOL: 50:50	**INTERNATIONAL:** 17%	
ACADEMIC RANKING: 14	**DISABLED:** 26	

Bar; student bands; three clubbing nights a term in Beer Cellar (cap. 150); small weekly ents events; ball every three years. Arts week. Library (86,000 books, 86 study spaces), 24hrs; 21 computers. Internet access in all rooms. Soundproof practice room. *Involved* JCR. 'Broadsheet' College newspaper, Rag, debating, drama, music and wine societies. *Eye-smacking* Anglican chapel and *ear-stroking* choir. Five acres of shared sports fields 1.5 miles away *(a bit discouraging for students); strong in fencing, football and athletics.* Almost all students live in College accommodation and eat in the dining hall or Beer Cellar; *good veggie options*; one kitchen for self-catering; night porter; CCTV; doctor; nurse; counsellor; Ethnic Minorities, Men's and Women's Officers; bursaries; travel funds; scholarships; hardship fund.

FAMOUS ALUMNI
Richard Burton (explorer and Arabian Nights translator); Sir Kenneth Clark (art historian); Cardinal Newman (theologian); William Pitt, Lord North (ex-PMs); Terrance Rattigan (playwright).

 Gangly funny man Hugh Laurie was a rower in the Cambridge v Oxford Boat Race in 1980.

Words in italics are Push's point of view – take it or leave it...

UNIVERSITY COLLEGE, OXFORD

THIS COLLEGE IS PART OF THE UNIVERSITY OF OXFORD AND STUDENTS ARE ENTITLED TO USE ITS FACILITIES

○ **UNIVERSITY COLLEGE**, Oxford, OX1 4BH **TEL** (01865) 276 602 **E—MAIL** admissions@univ.ox.ac.uk **WEBSITE** www.univ.ox.ac.uk
○ **JCR**, University College, Oxford, OX1 4BH **TEL** (01865) 276 606 **E—MAIL** jcr.president@univ.ox.ac.uk

GENERAL

Though they freely admit claims that King Alfred established it in the 9th-Century are hokum, University College is still the oldest in Oxford. It presents an *imposing facade* to the High Street but is *cosily habitable inside*, with a massive marble memorial to Shelley (who actually got expelled) lurking down one of its quieter corridors. *The College has been a bit insular in the past but now the environment's relaxed and friendly enough, so students aren't easily tempted to stray too far in search of fun. There's a healthy fondness for sporty and dramatic knockabouts and a proud tradition of hardcore academia.*

SEX RATIO: ♂63 ♀37	**FOUNDED:** 1249
FULL-TIME U'GRADS: 430	**PART-TIME:** 0
POSTGRADS: 112	**MATURE:** 1%
STATE:PRIVATE SCHOOL: 22:53	**INTERNATIONAL:** 11%
ACADEMIC RANKING: 5	**DISABLED:** 22

Bar (cap. 150) with pool, darts, jukebox, games machines and regular karaoke; three bops a term; jazz evenings; regular dramatic and musical offerings; weekly recitals. Formal ball every three years. Two libraries (50,000 books, growing by a 1,000 a year), 24hrs; 35 computers; internet access in all student rooms. One reverend; inter-denominational chapel. JCR with coffee and snacks, TV and video room. Termly politico-cultural mag 'Cognito'; 'MouthSpeech' creative writing mag. Univ students have access to an Alpine chalet (joint with Balliol and New College). *Strong in sports, especially rowing and women's teams*; 7.5 acres of sports pitches, boathouse 1.5 miles away, tennis, gym, darts, badminton. All years can live in. Cafeteria-style food, formal meal six nights a week. Night porter; CCTV. LGBT, Minorities' and Women's Officers; nurse; *keen to adapt things for disabled students*. Book fund, travel fund, vacation study grants, bursaries, graduate scholarships.

FAMOUS ALUMNI

Clement Atlee (ex-PM); William Beveridge (founded the welfare state); Bill Clinton (ex-US Prez); Chelsea Clinton (his offspring); Paul Gambaccini (broadcaster); Bob Hawke (ex-Australian PM); Stephen Hawking (cosmologist); Richard Ingrams (founder, Private Eye); Armando Ianucci (satarist, writer); C S Lewis (author); Warren Mitchell, Michael York (actors); Andrew Motion (Poet Laureate); Festus Mogae (Botswana's Prez); V S Naipaul (writer); Willie Rushton (late broadcaster and satirist); P B Shelley (poet); Peter Sissons (newsreader); Peter Snow (BBC presenter); Harold Wilson (ex-PM); Prince Youssoupov (killed Rasputin).

WADHAM COLLEGE, OXFORD

THIS COLLEGE IS PART OF THE UNIVERSITY OF OXFORD AND STUDENTS ARE ENTITLED TO USE ITS FACILITIES

○ **WADHAM COLLEGE**, Parks Road, Oxford, OX1 3PN **TEL** (01865) 277 900 **E—MAIL** admissions@wadh.oxford.ac.uk **WEBSITE** www.wadham.ox.ac.uk **WADHAM COLLEGE SU**, Parks Road, Oxford, OX1 3PN **TEL** (01865) 277 969 **E—MAIL** su.president@wadh.oxford.ac.uk **WEBSITE** su.wadham.ox.ac.uk

GENERAL

Opposite the Bod (Bodleian Library), 300 metres from Carfax, are the golden-grey Jacobean stones of Wadham. Founded by a woman (Dorothy Wadham) and one of the first to admit women, *Wadham's a progressive, tolerant and diverse college*. The *picturesque* main buildings centre around a grassy quad and, along with the newer library, SU and halls, are set amongst neat lawns and gardens. *The SU plays an important part of Wadham life – it's the only Oxford college that has one instead of a JCR. Wadham is liberal, politically* active (but not party political) and its ents are revered and feared throughout the University.*

SEX RATIO: ♂48 ♀52	**FOUNDED:** 1610
FULL-TIME U'GRADS: 450	**PART-TIME:** 0
POSTGRADS: 150	**MATURE:** 5%
STATE:PRIVATE SCHOOL: 67:33	**INTERNATIONAL:** 20%
ACADEMIC RANKING: 11	**DISABLED:** 20

Comfy bar; Moser theatre with eight shows a term; classical concerts in Holywell Music Room (cap. 150); fortnightly bops, cabaret in JCR, including 'Queer Bop' and 'Wadstock' music festival. Library (40,000 books), 24hrs; 25 computers. Chapel. JCR with pool, table football, video games and Sky; women's room, U shop. Six acres of playing fields 1.5 miles away; tennis and squash courts; weights room; *strong in rowing and cricket*. All 1st years and finalists live in on site, a handful of second years live 1.5 miles away near the sports fields – most live out; *good self-catering facilities; food available in Refectory (self-service) and Hall (table service)*; *rare* formal dinners. LGBT, Minorities' and Women's groups and Officers; nurse; free tampons, rape alarms and condoms; lots of spiral staircases – disabled ramps available. Adapted rooms for wheelchair users and deaf students. Warden's exhibition fund; hardship fund; travel grants; bursaries.

FAMOUS ALUMNI

Melvyn Bragg (broadcaster); Alan Coren (columnist); Cecil Day-Lewis (poet); Michael Foot (Labour leader 1980-83); C B Fry (cricketer); Rosamund Pike (actress and Bond girl); Rowan Williams (Archbishop of Canterbury); John Wilkins (scientist); John Wilmott (*saucy poet and Earl of Rochester*); Sir Christopher Wren (architect).

WORCESTER COLLEGE, OXFORD

THIS COLLEGE IS PART OF THE UNIVERSITY OF OXFORD AND STUDENTS ARE ENTITLED TO USE ITS FACILITIES

⊙ WORCESTER COLLEGE, Walton Street, Oxford, OX1 2HB **TEL** (01865) 278 300 **E-MAIL** admissions@worc.ox.ac.uk
WEBSITE www.worc.ox.ac.uk **JCR**, Worcestor College, Walton Street, Oxford, OX1 2HB **TEL** (01865) 278 380

GENERAL

Worcester's a *beautiful* college with both medieval and modern buildings and surrounded by 26 acres of *stunning* gardens, complete with a lake and a family of ducks *for when the students get peckish (don't worry, not really)*. Although some of its buildings date way back to the 13th-Century, *in Oxford college terms it's a spring chicken at 300 years old. Worcester students are a warm, welcoming bunch and politics is forgotten in the College's enthusiasm for sport* (it's one of the few colleges to have all its facilities on site) *and dedication to music and having a good time. While working like dam-busting beavers, obviously.*

👤👤👤👤👤👤👤👤👤👤👤👤👤👤👤👤👤👤👤👤

SEX RATIO: ♂50 ♀50	**FOUNDED:** 1714
FULL-TIME U'GRADS: 408	**PART-TIME:** 0
POSTGRADS: 188	**MATURE:** 2%
STATE:PRIVATE SCHOOL: 47:53	**INTERNATIONAL:** 4%
ACADEMIC RANKING: 20	**DISABLED:** 12

Cellar Bar (cap. 100) *for boozing* and Buttery bar *for a cup of tea and a bit of a sit down*. For bops: hall (150); JCR (100); Morley Fletcher Room (100). Soundproof room; ball every three years; *tons of live music*; choir; weekly recitals; *hefty thespian leanings*; termly boat club cocktail party; annual Arts Week festival. Newsletter 'the Worcester Source'. Three libraries (100,000 books); 22 computers. *Involved* JCR. Chapel. 12 acres of sports fields on site; boathouse; gym; tennis courts; *renowned women's football*. All first and second years live in, plus a handful of finalists (they're aiming to have everyone living in within a year) for £680-£820 a term; rooms range from *gorgeous* 15th-Century affairs to *functional* 60s blocks. Phone and Ethernet in all rooms; most eat in hall; optional formal dinners – *mighty fine food; limited* self-catering; CCTV. Nurse, dentist; LGBT and Women's Officers; *limited but improving disabled access*; book allowance, travel and vacation study grants, bursaries, scholarships, hardship funds.

FAMOUS ALUMNI

Richard Adams (author, 'Watership Down'); Sir Alistair Burnett (newscaster); Toby Litt (writer); Rupert Murdoch (media mogul); John Sainsbury (founder, Sainsbury's).

◉ In the mid-70s smarty pants at University College, Oxford were banned from competing in 'University Challenge' for winning too many times.

OXFORD BROOKES UNIVERSITY

FORMERLY OXFORD POLYTECHNIC

1. ○ **OXFORD BROOKES UNIVERSITY**, Headington Campus, Gipsy Lane, Oxford, OX3 0BP **TEL** (01865) 741 111
E−MAIL query@brookes.ac.uk **WEBSITE** www.brookes.ac.uk **OXFORD BROOKES UNIVERSITY STUDENTS' UNION**, Helena Kennedy Student Centre, Headington Hill Campus, Oxford, OX3 0BP **TEL** (01865) 484750 **E−MAIL** obsu@brookes.ac.uk **WEBSITE** www.thesu.com
2. ○ **OXFORD BROOKES UNIVERSITY**, Harcourt Hill Campus, Oxford, OX2 9AT
3. ○ **OXFORD BROOKES UNIVERSITY**, Wheatley Campus, Wheatley, Oxford, OX33 1HX

GENERAL ○○○○○○○○○○○○○

Oxford Brookes is unlike its famous neighbour in many ways. Despite being in the same city of ivory towers and dreaming spires, Oxford Brookes dodges any of the dusty stuffiness of the University of Oxford. The students, however, are just as partial to punting, falling in the river and strolling through Christchurch meadows. It has four campuses as well as a site based at the John Radcliffe Hospital. Two of the campuses (Gipsy Lane and Headington Hill) are basically the same site (even the University is inconsistent about the distinctions), consisting of 25 acres of modern, pretty functional, if slightly schooly, buildings (not as bad as it sounds), spread along either side of Headington Road, a mile outside Oxford's centre in the suburbs, away from that hazy churn of academic ritual. Headington's leafy and green, but it doesn't have much to offer the discerning shopper, diner or party-goer. There are a couple of smaller sites at Harcourt Hill (five miles west) and Wheatley (five miles east).

👤👤👤👤👤👤👤👤👤👤👤👤👤👤👤👤	
SEX RATIO: ♂40 ♀60	**FOUNDED:** 1865
FULL−TIME U'GRADS: 8,840	**PART−TIME:** 4,160
POSTGRADS: 5,040	**NON−DEGREE:** 399
AVE COURSE: 3YRS	**ETHNIC:** 15%
STATE:PRIVATE SCHOOL: 75:25	**FLUNK RATE:** 15%
MATURE: 64%	**INTERNATIONAL:** 18%
DISABLED: 405	**LOCAL:** 21%

ATMOSPHERE
Brookes attracts a higher proportion of Home Counties trendies than most of the former polys, probably drawn by the Oxford name-tag (without such demanding entrance requirements). That said, there are plenty of mature students and others who don't necessarily fit the mould and everyone is included in the sporty, boozy lifestyle.

SITES
HEADINGTON CAMPUS The main campus is divided into two: Headington Hill, 15 acres that used to belong to the Captain Dodgy himself, Robert Maxwell, on the north side of Headington Road; and Gipsy Lane, 11 more cramped acres on the south side.
HARCOURT HILL The newest site is a spacious and green 95 acres, on the outskirts of the other side of Oxford, about two miles from the city centre, housing the Institute of Education and some halls.

WHEATLEY The Wheatley site houses the business courses and a hall of residence on its 65 acres, five miles further out east into the countryside.

OXFORD see University of Oxford
○ **CITY CENTRE** 1 MILE

TRAVEL see University of Oxford
UNIVERSITY OBSU's late night minibus runs from 9pm-3am anywhere within the ringroad for a £1 donation. Also a University bus runs around the various sites. A pass costs £150 and is automatically included in halls fees. Some students are less than overjoyed at this, particularly those in the halls right next to the campus.

CAREER PROSPECTS
○ **CAREERS SERVICE** ○ **NO. OF STAFF** 3 FULL/5 PART
○ **UNEMPLOYED AFTER 6 MTHS** 7%
The careers service provides bulletin boards, job fairs, careers library and interview training.

FAMOUS ALUMNI
Jonathan Djangoly MP (Con); Andy Gomersall (World Cup-winning England rugby player); Oliver Heath (designer); John Pilkington (BBC); Adrian Reynard (motorsport entrepeneur); Tim Rodber (rugby player); Richard Younger-Ross MP (Lib Dem).

SPECIAL FEATURES
There's a no-smoking rule in all areas of the University, except the SU Bars.
The University's Chancellor is Jon Snow (Channel 4 News Presenter).

FURTHER INFO
○ **PROSPECTUSES** UNDERGRAD; POSTGRAD ○ **OPEN DAYS**

ACADEMIC ○○○○○○○○○○○○○

In terms of traditional academic pursuits, Brookes isn't a patch on its famous neighbour, but it offers something different and its reputation is far from tatty, especially in business and traditional techie subjects. The University has recently changed from a three term to a two semester system, much to the chagrin of students who don't like having to focus for 12 weeks at a stretch.

ENTRY POINTS: 80-340	AVE POINTS: 168
APPLICATIONS PER PLACE: N/A	CLEARING: 13%
NO. OF TERMS: 2	LENGTH OF TERMS: 15WKS
STAFF TO STUDENT RATIO: 1:12	STUDY ADDICTS: 18%
TEACHING: ****	RESEARCH: *
1STS: 9%	2.2S: 37%
2.1S: 48%	3RDS: 2%

ADMISSIONS
○ APPLY VIA UCAS

SUBJECTS
ARTS/HUMANITIES 13%
BIOLOGICAL & MOLECULAR SCIENCES 6%
BUILT ENVIRONMENT (ARCHITECTURE, PLANNING) 10%
HEALTH AND SOCIAL CARE 14%
SCHOOL OF MATHEMATICAL SCIENCES 5%
SCHOOL OF TECHNOLOGY 5%   SOCIAL SCIENCES & LAW 10%
WESTMINSTER INSTITUTE OF EDUCATION 16%
BEST Anthropology; Built Environment; English; French; German; History; Law; Sociology; Town & Country Planning.
UNUSUAL Brewing Science; Midwifery; Motorsport Technology & Engineering; Publishing.

LIBRARIES
○ 500,000 BOOKS ○ 1,100 STUDY PLACES
The main library at the Gipsy Hill campus in Headington is the biggest and there are smaller, specialised collections at Wheatley and Harcourt Hill. The University's lengthened opening hours and splashed out on more copies of in-demand books recently.

COMPUTERS
○ 750 WORKSTATIONS ○ 24-HR ACCESS
All halls have internet points and college intranet access, *but even with 24-hr access, it's not enough computers.* There's a *swish* system for spotting which computers are free on a big monitor, but the machines themselves are *pretty archaic.*

ENTERTAINMENT ○○○○○○○○○

THE CITY see University of Oxford

UNIVERSITY
○ PRICE OF A PINT OF BEER £1.85
○ GLASS OF WINE £1.90 ○ CAN OF RED BULL £1.80
BARS Four to choose from. Morals bar at Morrell Hall is the biggest (cap. 550) and it doubles as a club venue. Hart's Bar (350) – so-called because it was opened by Tony Hart – does karaoke and quiz nights, as does the Harcourt Hill Bar. The Mezzanine Bar at Headington Hill opens less often but is still *very popular.*
THEATRES The two drama societies are *pretty popular* and there's a theatre at the Harcourt Hill campus.
MUSIC VENUES Brookes pulls in the *biggest names in Oxford.* Recent visits from Coldplay, Ash, and The Coral.

CLUBBING *Distractions of the dancing variety six nights a week.* FUBAR (Weds) and Pleasuredome (Fri) are the biggies at the Venue. Morals Bar puts on a trio of tuneage and the Sunday Session at Harts Bar makes sure the week kicks off with a hangover. Paul Oakenfold, Pete Tong and David Holmes have DJ'd.
FOOD *Heaps* of eateries to cater *for all tastes,* though they're not particularly cheap.

SOCIAL ○○○○○○○○○○○○

OXFORD BROOKES STUDENTS' UNION
○ 6 SABBATICALS ○ TURNOUT AT LAST BALLOT 11%
○ NUS MEMBER
OBSU is a *busy, enthusiastic, high-profile* organisation, which does a *rather good job* of looking after its students and railing against the University suits *whenever the opportunity presents itself.* Most facilities are in the Helena Kennedy Student Centre at Headington.

SU FACILITIES
Ents venue; three bars; canteen; coffee bar; minibus hire; shops; juke boxes; pool table; vending and games machines; pool tables; photocopying; minibus; TV room; insurance agent; dentist; travel agents; Natwest bank; cash machines.

CLUBS (NON-SPORTING)
8 Dragons (martial arts); Alternative Frisbee; Alternative Rock; Arab Culture; Asian; Bass Associates (drum & bass); Black Box (backstage production); Board Games; Brookes Entrepreneurs; Business and Retail; CHAOS (choral and orchestra); Contemporary Ideology Forum; Concentio (chamber choir); East African; Extreme (sports); Football Appreciation; Formula Brookes (racecar); Fortune Players (musical theatre); French; Friends of Aang Serian; Friends of Falun Gong; Fusion; German; Harlequin; Hockey Appreciation; Hollow Way (halls society); Indonesian; Japanese; Jazz; Musical Appreciation; Oxucation (charity); Polish; Postgraduate; Real Ale; RAG; Shotgun-Not; Skating; Spanish; Talksign (sign language); T-shirts and Tie; Turkish. **See also Clubs tables.**

OTHER ORGANISATIONS
Monthly newspaper 'OBScene' is the main SU vehicle for rants against the University authorities. There are usually *lots of strange and wonderful charity events* – one recent stunt was a 72-hr bus tour of Britain's other student unions. Community action group STAX arranges about 300 do-gooding opportunities.

RELIGIOUS
○ 9 CHAPLAINS (ECUMENICAL, COFE, RC, METHODIST, BAPTIST, RUSSIAN ORTHODOX, URC, OXFORD COMMUNITY)
Prayer provisions in the University for Christians, Sikhs and Muslims. Religion in Oxford see University of Oxford.

Words in italics are Push's point of view – take it or leave it...

PAID WORK
◉ JOB BUREAU ◉ PAID WORK TERM-TIME 30%; **HOLS** 40%
The SU runs a jobshop with specialist staff filling over 1,500 vacancies a year. Unlike their University of Oxford counterparts, Brookes students are allowed to take part-time jobs and lots of them do.

SPORTS ◖◗◖◗◖◗◖◗◖◗◖◗◖◗◖◗

◉ RECENT SUCCESSES FOOTBALL **◉ BUSA RANKING** 54
Sport is one of the few things that can drag Brookes students out of the bar. *They live to put one over on the Oxford University teams* and recently toasted a glorious victory on the football field. *Rowing is a perennial strong point.* *Unusually*, the SU isn't involved in running sports – the University sports centre manages it all.

SPORTS FACILITIES
Most are in Headington: five football pitches; rugby, hockey, cricket and all-weather pitches; fitness suite; weights room; five badminton courts; basketball court; three squash courts; climbing wall; eight tennis courts; two astroturf pitches; golf course; fitness trail; indoor swimming pool; river. See also University of Oxford

SPORTING CLUBS
American Football; Chinese Martial Arts; Karting; Korfball; Lacrosse; Polo; Outdoor Pursuits; Rowing; Waterpolo. **See also Clubs tables.**

ATTRACTIONS see University of Oxford

ACCOMMODATION ◖◗◖◗◖◗◖◗◖◗

IN UNIVERSITY
◉ CATERED 7% **◉ COST** £108 (38WKS)
◉ SELF-CATERING 32% **◉ COST** £83 (38WKS)
◉ 1ST YRS LIVING IN 90% **◉ INSURANCE PREMIUM** ££
AVAILABILITY A recent spate of refurbs has *smartened the halls up a bit,* but it can be hard to get a place, as the Oxford catchment area for denying applications includes most of London. In total there are nine halls open to first years and one for *oldies,* housing 3,700 students in total. Six are close to Headington, two are a bus ride away and there's one apiece at Harcourt Hill and Wheatley. *Cheney and Clive Booth (great Saturday night club ents) are the most popular. Wheatley is really grim, although those unlucky enough to get stuck there often develop an obstinate devotion to the place.* There's some single-sex and disabled accommodation.
CAR PARKING The University clamps cars anywhere near halls. Students have to agree not to bring a car to Oxford.

EXTERNALLY see University of Oxford
◉ AVE RENT £75
HOUSING HELP The SU Advice Centre will check contracts.

WELFARE ◖◗◖◗◖◗◖◗◖◗◖◗◖◗

SERVICES
◉ LGBT OFFICER & SOCIETY ◉ POSTGRAD SOCIETY
◉ ETHNIC MINORITIES OFFICER ◉ WOMEN'S OFFICER
◉ INTERNATIONAL STUDENTS' OFFICER
◉ DISABILITIES OFFICER
◉ LATE-NIGHT MINIBUS (9PM–3AM)
◉ UNIVERSITY COUNSELLORS: 6 FULL/8 PART
◉ UNION COUNSELLORS 3 PART **◉ CRIME RATING** !!
HEALTH On-campus health centre (four GPs and nurses) for students at Headington and a dentist causing *scary drilling sounds.*
WOMEN Attack alarms provided and lasses get priority on the safety bus.
CRECHES/NURSERY A crèche looks after young children.
DISABILITIES *Better in the new buildings than the old. Access isn't great,* although there's a system of improvement underway to try and sort it out.

FINANCE
◉ AVE DEBT PER YEAR £2,409 **◉ HOME STUDENT FEES** £3,000 **◉ ACCESS FUND** £588,000 **◉ SUCCESSFUL APPLICATIONS/YR** 973 **◉ AVERAGE PAYMENT** £864
SUPPORT John Henry Brookes bursary scheme is a limited fund to provide bursaries for hardship cases.

➡ **OXFORD POLYTECHNIC**
see *Oxford Brookes University*

◉ In 1881, the entire student body of University College, Oxford was sent down after the Dean's Room was screwed shut (with the Dean inside).

Words in italics are Push's point of view – take it or leave it...

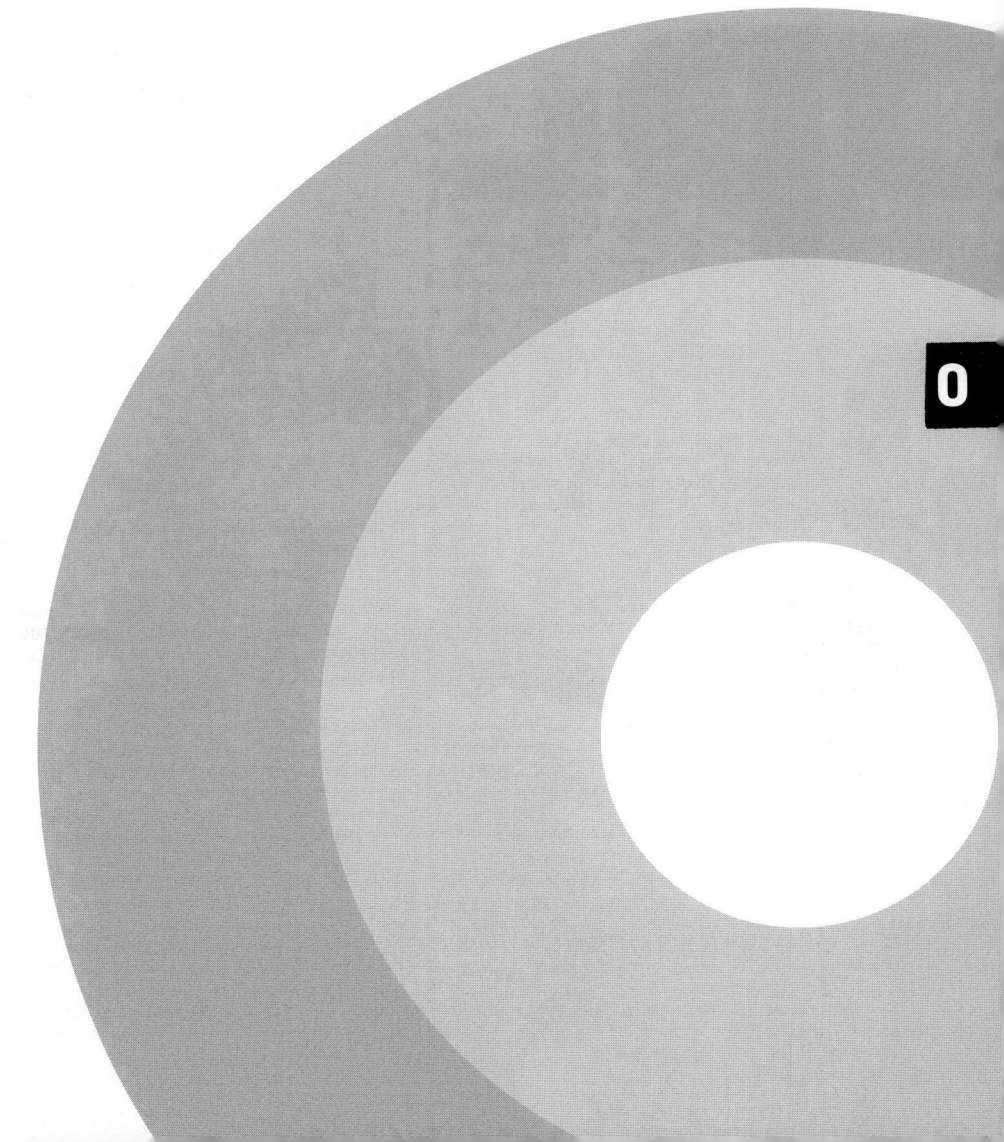

O

PAISLEY UNIVERSITY

▶ **PCL (POLYTECHNIC OF CENTRAL LONDON)**
see *University of Westminster*

▶ **PENINSULA MEDICAL SCHOOL**
see *University of Plymouth*

▶ **POLYTECHNIC SOUTH WEST**
see *University of Plymouth*

▶ **PHARMACY, SCHOOL**
see *The School of Pharmacy, University of London*

UNIVERSITY OF PLYMOUTH

UNIVERSITY OF PORTSMOUTH

▶ **PORTSMOUTH POLYTECHNIC**
see *University of Portsmouth*

▶ **PRINTING**
see *University of the Arts, London*

PAISLEY UNIVERSITY

FORMERLY PAISLEY COLLEGE

⊙ **UNIVERSITY OF PAISLEY** High Street, Paisley, PA1 2BE **TEL** (0141) 848 3000 **E—MAIL** uni-direct@paisley.ac.uk
WEBSITE www.paisley.ac.uk ⊙ **PAISLEY UNIVERSITY STUDENTS' ASSOCIATION** Paisley Campus Union, Storie Street, Paisley, PA1 2HB
TEL (0141) 849 4157 **E—MAIL** president@upsa@org.uk **WEBSITE** www.upsa.org.uk. See below for details of other sites

GENERAL ⊙⊙⊙⊙⊙⊙⊙⊙⊙⊙⊙⊙

Paisley made its name flogging the eponymous patterned cloth to proto-golfer types in the 19th-Century. These days it's not quite so well-off, but despite its proximity to Glasgow, it could be described as a smaller, more run-down version of Edinburgh. There are the same leg-testing hills and the Edwardian and Victorian architecture balanced by some of its rougher elements. To the south there's beautiful countryside in the shape of Glennifer Braes County Park and to the north there's the somewhat less beautiful Glasgow International Airport. With the inexplicably cheap prices offered by budget airlines, you could probably fly here for less than the price of a hamburger. The fact that most students don't (80% are from the local area) does mean that the University has a relatively insular feel, but with Scotland's biggest beer festival here every April there's no reason why that shouldn't change. There are also sites in Dumfries and Ayr. See below for details of each site.

SEX RATIO: ♂35 ♀65	FOUNDED: 1897
FULL—TIME U'GRADS: 5,988	PART—TIME: 5,621
POSTGRADS: 1,685	NON—DEGREE: 98
AVE COURSE: 3–4YRS	ETHNIC: 7%
STATE:PRIVATE SCHOOL: 98:2	FLUNK RATE: 22%
MATURE: 46%	INTERNATIONAL: 4%
DISABLED: 120	LOCAL: 80%

ATMOSPHERE

Students don't go to Paisley for the party scene. In fact you could hardly say most of them 'go' here at all – they grew up here, their parents grew up here and, very probably, their great-great-grandparents grew up here too. On the plus side, this does mean that the University's far more integrated with the town than many institutions and the lack of anything approaching a social whirl (more of a gentle social waltz, really) means you might actually get some work done. There is, however, a bit of a townie (or as they say in these part, 'neddy') culture which gets a bit inyerface sometimes.

OTHER SITES

See below for details of University Campus Ayr (in Ayr) and Crichton University Campus (in Dumfries).

PAISLEY
⊙ **POPULATION** 176,970 ⊙ **TOWN CENTRE** 0 MILES
⊙ **LONDON** 412 MILES ⊙ **EDINBURGH** 56 MILES
⊙ **GLASGOW** 10 MILES
⊙ **HIGH TEMP** 19 ⊙ **LOW TEMP** 1 ⊙ **RAINFALL** 96
You can't spend centuries making psychedelic swirling shapes without a fair amount of artiness rubbing off on you. Right opposite the University is the town's museum and art gallery. Along with shops and the like, there's Paisley Abbey (parts of which date back to the 12th century), the Coats Observatory and the Weaver's Cottage, but Paisley isn't one of Scotland's bigger tourist destinations, despite it being voted the '29th Most Romantic Place in Scotland' apparently.

TRAVEL
TRAINS The nearest mainline station is 5 mins walk from Gilmour Street. Regular direct services to Glasgow (£3 return) with the last train at night at 11.54pm, and London (£62.20).
COACHES Served nationally by Scottish Citylink, via Glasgow.
CAR M8's a mile from the town, also the A737 and A726. The large car park beside the Union has been voted 'Scotland's Best Car Park' – presumably by the same people behind the romantic poll (see above) – but parking on campus is still very difficult, nevertheless.
TAXIS Relatively cheap. There's a huge rank by the station.
HITCHING Generally not recommended due to the local, heroin-fuelled crime problem.
LOCAL Buses allow easy, short hops: the 85p single fare to Glasgow's cheaper than the train and runs till 3am.
BICYCLES The hills and the fact that there's nowhere to store bikes on campus doesn't stop some students giving it a go. Bikes shouldn't be left in the town without landmines and electric fencing, however.

CAREER PROSPECTS
⊙ **CAREERS SERVICE** ⊙ **NO. OF STAFF** 4 FULL/2 PART
⊙ **UNEMPLOYED AFTER 6 MTHS** 6%
As well as student/grad job facilities there's help with writing CVs and coping with psychometric testing (those personality tests popular with firms not confident of spotting lunatics at interviews). They've also had guest lectures from the likes of John McCormick (former BBC controller), former Scotland football manager Craig Brown and Travis star Fran Healy.

FAMOUS ALUMNI
Gavin Hastings (ex-Scottish rugby union captain); Graeme Obree (cyclist).

Words in italics are Push's point of view – take it or leave it...

FURTHER INFO
- **PROSPECTUSES** UNDERGRAD; POSTGRAD; ALL DEPARTMENTS; INTERNATIONAL
- **OPEN DAYS**

ACADEMIC ◖◖◖◖◖◖◖◖◖◖◖◖◖

People come to Paisley, not for wishy-washy ideas about bettering themselves, but because they want to get a good, solid job when they finish, and the courses reflect this. All degrees provide work experience and the University has links with VW, Shell and Scottish Power. The Media Studies courses also emphasise practical skills – students have been placed with the BBC and Channel Four among others.

ENTRY POINTS: 140–240	AVE POINTS: 168
APPLICATIONS PER PLACE: N/A	CLEARING: 14%
NO. OF TERMS: 2	LENGTH OF TERMS: 15WKS
STAFF TO STUDENT RATIO: 1:20	STUDY ADDICTS: N/A
TEACHING: **	RESEARCH: ****

ADMISSIONS
- **APPLY VIA** UCAS/CATCH (NURSING)/DIRECT (POSTGRAD, PART-TIME)

A *flexible* admissions policy. A wide range of qualifications, including GCSEs and the Scottish Wider Access Programme, are accepted for certain courses.

SUBJECTS
BUSINESS 13%   **ENGINEERING** 11%   **HEALTH** 29%
ICT 10%   **SOCIAL SCIENCES** 7%
BEST Accountancy & Economics.
UNUSUAL Commercial Music; Complementary Therapies; Events Management; Forensic Sciences; Music Technology; Performance for Stage & Screen; Sports Injury Rehabilitation; MA Scottish Creative & Cultural Industries.

LIBRARIES
- **340,000** BOOKS ● **1,145** STUDY PLACES

There are three library sites – Paisley, Ayr and Alexandra Hospital. The main one is the (deep breath) Robertson Trust Library and Learning Resource Centre. *Despite the severe sounding name this is a great place to work. The desks are big enough so that you can spread your books out without them falling on the floor and it's bright, airy and dotted with pot-plants (that's plants in pots, not... oh never mind). Students at Ayr and Dumfries can suffer from IBS (Inadequate Books Syndrome) but they have the option of ordering books from Paisley. It's quicker on the train, however.*

COMPUTERS
- **305** WORKSTATIONS ● **24-HOUR** ACCESS

The Paisley campus has a new internet café with 30 computers as well as facilities planned for students to connect wirelessly via their laptops. *Again, Ayr and Dumfries are a tad under-facilitied and await a computer boost.*

ENTERTAINMENT ◖◖◖◖◖◖◖◖◖

THE TOWN
- **PRICE OF A PINT OF BEER** £2.30
- **GLASS OF WINE** £2.50
- **CAN OF RED BULL** £2

CINEMAS The CAC has two screens (£3.50), the Arts Centre also has regular screenings (£2).
THEATRES Paisley Arts Centre hosts popular touring companies.
PUBS *Pushplugs: Café Borgia; Cellar Bar (very close to University); Fiddlers Green; O'Neill's and Paddy Malarkey's (Irish); Vodka Wodka (Scotland's first vodka bar).*
CLUBBING The subtly titled *Shag at Furry Murry's, Toledo and Utopia are all popular.*
MUSIC VENUES *The Arts Centre is the only hot-spot. Well, more of a luke-warm spot, really.*
EATING OUT *Pub lunches are a reliable source of sustenance. Other Pushplugs: Café Borgia in the Arts Centre; A Taste of Europe (bargain lunches); Kaldi's Coffee House; Vodka Wodka (excellent value at £2 for two colossal courses).*

UNIVERSITY
- **PRICE OF A PINT OF BEER** £1.80
- **GLASS OF WINE** £2.50
- **CAN OF RED BULL** £2

BARS *The Big Bar isn't ironically named. With its space-age seats and vast windows it puts you in mind of an airport. That spaciousness can be detrimental to the atmosphere, except on the major party nights. It's not the sort of place where you find yourself chatting to the person next to you purely because their elbow's in your beer.*
FILMS A film a week on art house and world cinema lines. The cinema at Ayr campus is used for teaching media students as well as screening their work.
CLUBBING Friday night is the Big Cheese chart-dance night in the Big Bar, which keeps at it till 3am. Radio 1 DJs have been known to spin the musical wheels.
MUSIC Speedway played here recently. *Who? Exactly. For anything beyond local and tribute bands Paisleyites go to Glasgow.*
FOOD *The refectory fare is so-so. Nosh from the SU is cheap and cheerful.* There's also a Starbucks. *Woohoo.*
COMEDY There are comedy nights every couple of months at the Big Bar and the likes of Phil Kay, Jerry Sadowitz and Lee Evans have appeared.
OTHERS One formal ball a year and a big bash at a nightclub in Glasgow once a term. Major sports events every week in the SA.

P

SOCIAL ⓤⓤⓤⓤⓤⓤⓤⓤⓤⓤⓤ

PAISLEY UNIVERSITY STUDENTS' ASSOCIATION
- **3 SABBATICALS** - **TURNOUT AT LAST BALLOT** 6%
- **NUS MEMBER**

The Student Association, based in a run-down building, is hardly rabidly political. The last big campaign was for Wednesdays off for people playing sport but this is contested by lecturers who don't see kicking a ball around as important. The SA has also joined the campaign against tuition fees. *The low turnout for elections reflects the fact that so many of the students are part-time and don't really care.*

SA FACILITIES
Two bars; café; shop; Bank of Scotland ATM; eight pool tables; photocopiers; games and vending machines; juke box; TV lounge; two meeting rooms; advice centre; general store; stationery shop; new & secondhand bookshops; customised night club; launderette.

CLUBS (NON-SPORTING)
Buddhism; Juggling; Sci-fi Role Play; Scottish Socialism. **See also Clubs tables.**

OTHER ORGANISATIONS
Weekly paper, 'the Banter', *is hardly broadsheet journalism, but is worth its weight in giggles.* 'UCA Radio' broadcasts locally.

RELIGION
- **4 CHAPLAINS (RC, COFS, BAPTIST, EPISCOPAL)**

The multi-faith chaplaincy at the Thomas Coats Memorial Church has provisions for the above plus a Muslim prayer room, Episcopalian and lay preachers and links with the local Rabbi and Muslim leaders.

PAID WORK
- **JOB BUREAU**

The Student Advisory Service lists vacation vacancies and potential term-time jobs in local pubs and restaurants. The SA also recruits staff early on each year.

SPORTS ⓤⓤⓤⓤⓤⓤⓤⓤⓤⓤⓤⓤ

- **BUSA RANKING** 122

Sport isn't a major obsession, but the Robertson Trust Sports Centre gets a few people dragging their Kappa Slappa Lycra out of the closet.

SPORTS FACILITIES
The Sports Centre, two miles from campus, includes rugby and football pitches, a sports hall and a fitness room. *Extensive* local facilities and reciprocal agreements with other educational establishments nearby mean students have access to a lake, swimming pool, golf course, squash and tennis courts, croquet lawn, sauna/solarium and ice rink.

SPORTING CLUBS
Aikido; American Football; Cheerleading; Gaelic Football; Mountaineering; Pool; Snowsport; Wrestling. **See also Clubs tables.**

ATTRACTIONS
The local football heroes are St Mirren.

ACCOMMODATION ⓤⓤⓤⓤⓤⓤⓤⓤⓤ

IN UNIVERSITY
- **SELF-CATERING** 13% - **COST** £48 (31WKS)
- **1ST YRS LIVING IN** 35% - **INSURANCE PREMIUM** £££

AVAILABILITY The University has nearly 800 places for self-catering students – priority goes to first years hailing from more than 25 miles away. Most places are within ten mins of the campus, such as Underwood Residence, which has 168 places (single rooms, some adapted for disabled students' needs). *Thornly Park, about two miles from the Paisley campus, is sociable and desirable, as is the modern hall at Christie Street. Underwood's less popular.* There are rooms for singles and sharers at Ayr campus.

CAR PARKING Some accommodation sites have on-site parking.

EXTERNALLY
- **AVE RENT** £55

AVAILABILITY 94% of students live outside University accommodation but *it's reasonably easy to find places in Paisley and the standard's okay. West End Park should be avoided on safety grounds and Ladylane and Storie Street are best left alone too, not because they're rough, but because houses have a propensity for growing mould. Many students live in the East End of Glasgow.*

HOUSING HELP The Residential Accommodation Unit employs three full-time staff, offering residential places when available, a register of local private accommodation and gas safety checks.

WELFARE ⓤⓤⓤⓤⓤⓤⓤⓤⓤⓤⓤⓤ

SERVICES
- **LGBT OFFICER & SOCIETY**
- **INTERNATIONAL STUDENTS' SOCIETY & OFFICER**
- **ETHNIC MINORITIES SOCIETY** - **WOMEN'S OFFICER**
- **MATURE STUDENTS' OFFICER & SOCIETY**
- **POSTGRAD SOCIETY** - **DISABILITIES OFFICER**
- **LATE-NIGHT MINIBUS** - **NIGHTLINE**
- **UNIVERSITY COUNSELLORS** 4 FULL - **CRIME RATING** !!

P

VARIOUS HELP ORGANISATIONS the Student Advisory Service employs four counsellors; Student Welfare Association; the Student Health Service with nurse; another counsellor and a full-time welfare advisor in the SA. They also provide Copeline on (0800) 056 8181 – a freephone service to help with issues like anxiety, depression and relationship problems. A free party bus takes students home to Thornly Park and Underwood every night.
CRECHES/NURSERY Ten places for 2-year-olds and 24 places for 2-5 year-olds at the Paisley Campus.
DISABILITIES Ramps are in place for wheelchair users. A Special Needs service to help students with specific problems with exams.
DRUGS/CRIME Paisley is one of the hard drug blackspots of the UK *but problems haven't really filtered into the University*.

FINANCE
◯ **AVE DEBT PER YEAR** £3,546 ◯ **HOME STUDENT FEES** £1,700
FEES *Scottish students have it easy compared to other UK-ers (the whole £3,000 caboodle) and international undergrads*, who pay £7,900/yr for the privilege of a British education.
◯ **ACCESS FUND** ◯ **SUCCESSFUL APPLICATIONS/YR** 627
◯ **AVE PAYMENT** £100-2,500
SUPPORT Bursary system and hardship fund (£10,000) from Student Welfare for those who can't get other help. Loans from the access fund available in as little as 48hrs, with mature students able to apply for parts of the pot as well as help with childcare and housing. The Welfare Service can refer students to external trusts and scholarships such as Renfrewshire Educational Trust, Carnegie Trust, Elizabeth Nuffield Educational Fund and so on.

UNIVERSITY CAMPUS AYR

◯ **UNIVERSITY OF PAISLEY** University Campus Ayr, Beech Grove, Ayr, KA8 0SR **TEL** (01292) 886 000
◯ **UNIVERSITY OF PAISLEY STUDENTS' ASSOCIATION** Ayr, KA8 0SR **TEL** (0141) 849 4169

GENERAL
In marked contrast to the *earnest* business and techie types at Paisley, Ayr's 2,500 students are a *creative bunch*. The half studying Media or Music add an *arty sparkle to the close-knit atmosphere and mix well with the (predominantly female) Education and Nursing students*. It's set in 20 acres of parkland bordering the River Ayr, but the building itself *looks and feels rather like a high school*.

AYR
◯ **POPULATION** 69,378 ◯ **CITY CENTRE** 1.2 MILES
◯ **LONDON** 409 MILES ◯ **EDINBURGH** 83 MILES
◯ **GLASGOW** 38 MILES
◯ **HIGH TEMP** 12 ◯ **LOW TEMP** 6 ◯ **RAINFALL** 82
At the heart of South Ayrshire, the land of Robert Burns, Ayr is an 800-yr-old *pedestrian* town by the coast. The 18th-century Culzean Castle is reckoned to be the National Trust of Scotland's top visitor attraction.

TRAVEL
Trains and regular express coaches to Glasgow, an hour's drive away. The M77 links Ayr to the UK's motorway network. There's an international airport at Prestwick, two miles away. Students at Ayr have no academic reason to travel to the University's other sites, other than hunting obscure books at Paisley's library.

ACADEMIC
The campus holds the departments of Education, Cultural & Creative Industries and Health and there are some Business School students (mainly third years). The recently refurbished library has all the requisite facilities, *but on a smaller scale than at Paisley*. There are just 30 computers and study space is in *short supply*. Ayr's strong point is its *excellent specialist media facilities*: two TV studios; four radio suites; editing suite; two art studios; two computer studios; three recording studios; one of the UK's largest facilities for Pro-Tools, the industry standard digital-recording studio equipment. The *under-used* Careers Service is geared towards the subjects offered on-site and the Paisley-based Careers Advisor visits weekly.

ADMISSIONS
◯ **APPLY VIA UCAS/CATCH (NURSING)/DIRECT (POSTGRAD, PART-TIME)**
A *flexible* admissions policy. A wide range of qualifications, including GCSEs and the Scottish Wider Access Programme, are accepted for certain courses.

ENTERTAINMENT
AYR *Pushplugs: The Meridian Pub (pricey wine bar); Treehouse; Harley's; Powerhouse, Madisons (clubs); Cecchini's (Italian).*
SITE The social centre is Fresh Ayr, the SU building, *which is small, cosy and frequently mobbed*. Events throughout the week keep things moving until 12.30 or 1am: karaoke (Mon); quiz night (Tue); live music (Wed); alternate music eg. hiphop, rock (Thurs); TFI and Playstation competitions (Fri). Commercial music students also *treat their peers to regular live events*. The SU bar dishes up *cheap* snacks and lunches, or peckish peeps can eat *school-dinneresque fare* or *slightly more palatable sandwiches* and coffee at the University refectory.

SOCIAL
The SU building has a bar/diner, events area, games room and a student shop. There's also a *tiny* bookshop. Ayr has its own SU sabbatical officer, Christian Union, LGBT Society, radio

P

station (UCA Radio), student handbook (Ayrmail), bar and Rag, which does good deeds fundraising and working with underprivileged children.

SPORTS

There's a gym for teaching purposes. Ayr has its own football and hockey teams.

ACCOMMODATION

ON SITE ◯ **SELF-CATERED COST** £45

Self-catering halls on campus have space for 112 in single or shared study bedrooms with communal facilities. *Standards are pretty basic, but demand for places is increasing.*

WELFARE

The Student Advisory Service has a welfare advisor, two chaplains (Epicostal, CofS) and a special needs counsellor. A health and safety service has various leaflets on breast cancer, meningitis, flu and Copeline numbers. *Disabled access is easy as the campus is on one level.*

FINANCE

Lots of tourists mean part-time work is *easy to come by* in the hotels of Ayr. The Careers Service works with the JobCentre to help students find ways to pull in the pennies.

CRICHTON UNIVERSITY CAMPUS

◯ **UNIVERSITY OF PAISLEY** Crichton University Campus, Maxwell House, Dumfries, DG1 4UQ **TEL** (01387) 702 075
E-MAIL crichton@paisley.ac.uk **WEBSITE** www.crichton.ac.uk

GENERAL

Set in Dumfries, this *resolutely local campus* works with local colleges to act as a learning hub for the people of Dumfries and Galloway. Close to the town centre, it's set in 80 acres of parkland and woods in the former Crichton Royal Hospital and overlooks the River Nith and the Galloway Hills.

DUMFRIES

◯ **POPULATION** 8,000 ◯ **CITY CENTRE** 1.5 MILES
◯ **LONDON** 336 MILES ◯ **EDINBURGH** 81 MILES
◯ **GLASGOW** 78 MILES
◯ **HIGH TEMP** 11 ◯ **LOW TEMP** 4 ◯ **RAINFALL** 136
Dumfries has city-like facilities – high street and independent shops, pubs, clubs, restaurants, cinemas, health clubs – but it's a small place. For culture vultures there are stunning castles and arty towns in the local area. The nearby countryside has Britain's largest forest park and mountain-biking opportunities aplenty.

TRAVEL

The campus is a quick stroll, drive or bus ride away from the town centre. Public transport runs to the other University sites.

ACADEMIC

Business and ICT courses are the main areas of study at Crichton. Childhood Studies and Health

Studies are also on campus. To encourage local learners, programmes tend to be flexible with opportunities for part-time, evening or daytime study. A lot of students come from Dumfries and Galloway College to top up HNCs and HNDs into a full- or part-time degree. The library is in the Rutherford McCowan Building and has a *peaceful* study area and IT resources.

ENTERTAINMENT

DUMFRIES *What the nightlife lacks in scale is made up for by the cheap prices.*
SITE Students rub shoulders with locals *(who, after all, are usually one and the same)* at Ay-Jay's, a non-Union pub on campus. It has a café/bar and restaurant.

SOCIAL

As well as Ay-Jay's, there's an advisory service, student association office, bookshop and games room.

SPORTS

Football pitch and nine-hole golf course.

ACCOMMODATION

Not a bed on-site. Lists of private accommodation are available from the residential accommodation unit.

▶ **PCL (POLYTECHNIC OF CENTRAL LONDON)**
see *University of Westminster*

▶ **PENINSULA MEDICAL SCHOOL**
see *University of Plymouth*

▶ **POLYTECHNIC SOUTH WEST**
see *University of Plymouth*

▶ **PHARMACY, SCHOOL**
see *The School of Pharmacy, University of London*

Words in italics are Push's point of view — take it or leave it...

UNIVERSITY OF PLYMOUTH

FORMERLY POLYTECHNIC SOUTH WEST

1) ○ **UNIVERSITY OF PLYMOUTH** Drake Circus, Plymouth, PL4 8AA **TEL** (01752) 232 137 **E-MAIL** admissions@plymouth.ac.uk
WEBSITE www.plymouth.ac.uk ○ **UNIVERSITY OF PLYMOUTH STUDENTS' UNION** University of Plymouth, Drake Circus,
Plymouth, PL4 8AA **TEL** (01752) 238 500 **E-MAIL** suenquiries@su.plymouth.ac.uk **WEBSITE** www.upsu.com
2) ○ **UNIVERSITY OF PLYMOUTH** Faculty of Arts & Education (Exeter Campus), Earl Richards Road North, Exeter, EX2 6AS
TEL (01392) 475 010
3) ○ **UNIVERSITY OF PLYMOUTH** Faculty of Arts & Education (Exmouth Campus), Douglas Avenue, Exmouth, EX8 2AT
TEL (01395) 355 522

GENERAL ○○○○○○○○○○○○○

If Plymouth were any further south-west, it would be Cornwall. If it were any further south it'd be in the English Channel. As it is, it's a port around the Plymouth Sound (the bay) on the south coast of Devon near *wild and windy* Dartmoor. Plymouth has a claim to founding the USA – the Pilgrim Fathers set off in the Mayflower from Plymouth Harbour (arriving Stateside in Plymouth Harbour – *what are the chances?*). It was also from here that Sir Francis Drake sailed to whip the Spanish Armada's arse. According to the myth, Frankie psyched himself up by playing bowls on the Hoe, a patch of greenery by the sea – *not a giant Elizabethan prostitute*. The University's got a number of sites, but centralisation is the buzz word at the mo', which means there's going to be an *almighty upheaval over the next few years* as Plymouth gathers all its darlings together in one place in stead of *littering* students across the South West. Applications for courses formerly held at Seale have doubled since moving back to Plymouth, so *it's clearly a good idea – but students on the Exeter and Exmouth campuses a couple of years from now should be prepared to pack up and relocate to a completely different city miles from where they started.*

SEX RATIO: ♂39 ♀61	FOUNDED: 1970
FULL-TIME U'GRADS: 24,537	PART-TIME: 6,535
POSTGRADS: 955	NON-DEGREE: 3,723
AVE COURSE: 3YRS	ETHNIC: 2%
STATE:PRIVATE SCHOOL: 92:8	FLUNK RATE: 14%
MATURE: 43%	INTERNATIONAL: 8%
DISABLED: 910	LOCAL: N/A

ATMOSPHERE
The south-west as a whole is a pretty mellow place and although Plymouth students are largely laidback, they are capable of perking up when it comes to work (there's lots of careerist zeal) and drinking unfeasible quantities of beer. *The smaller sites have their own quirks, but the Plymouth campus is a haven for surfer dudes and dudettes – why else would anyone wear Bermuda shorts in March? Loads of* voluntary projects help bridge town/gown divides. *The University's won some Centre of Excellence Awards, which meant a total*

£18m prize – it sure beats a scratchcard. The money's going to prettify the place up a bit and make it taller. That and the 'big move' means the main campus resounds to the tune of hammers and buzzsaws rather than larks and nightingales. A bit like in town really – the whole place is having a Changing Rooms moment. Carole Smilie is thankfully absent.

OTHER SITES
EXETER (Art) 44 miles from Plymouth. A redbrick campus two miles from the city centre, next to the hilly countryside that surrounds Exeter. It was purpose-built as Exeter Art College. For a more detailed low-down on the ups and downs of Exeter, see <u>Exeter University</u>, which, *for students who are willing to mix with the Sloanes, is a social life-saver*. The Branch of the Plymouth SU based here has its own cosy bar with sofas and pool tables, as well as a refectory. Being art-based, the campus houses a *fairly artsy crowd* of under 1,000 students – *a good many with imaginatively coloured hair. Skateboards are the de rigeur mode de transport.*
EXMOUTH (Education) 50 miles from Plymouth, the town of Exmouth is, unsurprisingly, at the mouth of the River Exe on the east bank of the wide estuary. *This is a small town (but the largest seaside resort in Devon), a bit of a baby brother to Exeter eight miles upstream.* Exmouth *thumps above its weight* for live music scene and has a theatre and the Pavilion on the seafront, which stage a variety of entertainments. *Samantha's, Matrix and Q club are preferred night-time destinations. Two miles of golden sands make it a cute little place but Exeter is a vital standby for students who want more from life than pretty sea views.* The campus is a *tasteful* combination of old, new and recently refurbished, giving an academic home to around 3,000 English, Geoography and Education students, *who are generally more than averagely good-looking – it must be the surfer thing.* The Exmouth branch of the Union is a *warm and bustling place that maintains a 1am bar licence on Saturdays and holds regular events and theme nights.* 'Rolle-up' is the *little but busy* site magazine. A new accommodation block provides rooms for over 200 students.

P

PLYMOUTH

- **○ POPULATION** 241,000 **○ CITY CENTRE** 0 MILES
- **○ LONDON** 200 MILES **○ EXETER** 37 MILES **○ BRISTOL** 106 MILES
- **○ HIGH TEMP** 19 **○ LOW TEMP** 4 **○ RAINFALL** 76

Apart from a few buildings dating back to the days of Drake, most of Plymouth was *hastily thrown back together* after WWII bombing raids. *After a few years as a pug ugly duckling next to other West Country tourist traps it's being re-designed by David Mackie, who re-designed Barcelona. It's in its in-between stage at the moment, though, which is a nice way of saying the worst bits are hidden behind scaffolding and sheets. A new cultural quarter should be one of the highlights, and for those more Prada than Picasso, a £2m shopping centre will be ringing to the sound of myriad cash registers later this year. Unlike Bournemouth and Eastbourne, it's not a waiting room for the afterlife – there's a healthy mix of young and old and all social classes are represented in the population.* Articles of interest include the *quaint* red and white lighthouse, Smeaton's Tower, the City Museum & Art Gallery and the National Aquarium with its shark theatre and deep reef tank.

TRAVEL

TRAINS Plymouth's the nearest station to the main site, about five mins away. Services to London (from £37.60 return), Bristol (£25.75), etc. Most stop at Exeter (on the same line).
COACHES National Express and Western National services from Plymouth's Bretonside Bus Station (ten mins from campus) to London (£35) and beyond.
CAR The A38 links Plymouth with Exeter. The M5, M4 and A303 are also useful. *There's no student parking, however, and the city centre multi-storeys can only hold so many.*
AIR Flights inland and to Ireland from Plymouth Airport, roughly six miles away.
HITCHING *Okay along the A38 for he (and she) that waits, except up the Cornwall end.*
LOCAL No. 7 is the *most useful* route, going from the popular student area of Mutley to the city centre (£1.10).
UNIVERSITY Subsidised bus services between sites.
TAXIS Plymouth has its fair share of black cabs and minicabs, *but students only really use them for the ride home after a night out (about £3.20 from town to Mutley).*
BICYCLES *Plymouth's a bit hilly for the lazier cyclist, but the more energetic can find wheeled exploration pleasant on a summer's day.* The University has secure bike stores, and there's bike parking in town.

CAREER PROSPECTS

- **○ CAREERS SERVICE ○ NO. OF STAFF** 12 FULL/6 PART
- **○ UNEMPLOYED AFTER 6 MTHS** 10%

Plymouth Careers Service does the usual rounds of job fairs, vacancy bulletins and interview training, plus some *sexy* cyber-resources like career databases and aptitude tests. The Uni's Gradsouthwest website also helps students find voluntary and graduate jobs.

FAMOUS ALUMNI

David Braine (BBC weather); Jules Leaver (founded Fat Face clothing company); Clare Nasir (GMTV weather); Pam St Clement (Eastenders' Pat); Michael Underwood (BBC children's TV presenter); Peter Winterbottom (rugby player).

FURTHER INFO

- **○ PROSPECTUSES** UNDERGRAD; POSTGRAD; DEPARTMENTAL
- **○ OPEN DAYS**

Prospectuses can be ordered from the *rather labyrinthine* website, or there's an edited version online.

ACADEMIC ○○○○○○○○○○○○○

Plymouth's interested in what they call student-centric learning – which probably explains some of the crazier courses on offer. The academic structure's undergone some hefty rejiggery recently as they attempt to integrate the six dispersed faculties into some kind of spiritual whole. This means a *tonne* of new facilities including computer labs, a Faculty of Arts building with exhibition and gallery space and beefed-up library provision. Plymouth has a *highly successful* network of partner colleges around the Southeast (including the Peninsula Medical School, run together with Exeter University). The academic year is split into two semesters and one assessment month.

ENTRY POINTS: 80–370	AVE POINTS: N/A
APPLICATIONS PER PLACE: N/A	CLEARING: 18%
NO. OF TERMS: 3	LENGTH OF TERMS: 12WKS
STAFF TO STUDENT RATIO: N/A	STUDY ADDICTS: N/A
TEACHING: ★★	RESEARCH: ★★★

ADMISSIONS

○ APPLY VIA UCAS/NURSING FOR NURSING/ GTTR FOR TEACHING

'Proper' qualifications are the norm, but enthusiasm and commitment also get applicants a look-in. Deferred entry is possible, *if not quite encouraged.*

SUBJECTS

BEST Aeronautical & Manufacturing Engineering; Computer Science; Civil Engineering; Electrical & Electronic Engineering; Environmental Studies; Geography; History of Art; Architecture & Design; Local Government & Election Studies; Mechanical; Psychology; Social Policy & Administration; Sociology.
UNUSUAL Brewing & Licensed Trade Management; Cruise Operations Management; Equine Studies; Media Make-up; Merchant Shipping; Cruise Administration; Plant Discovery & Exploitation; Popular Music; Robotics; Surf Science & Technology (which has been franchised to Australia).

Words in italics are Push's point of view – take it or leave it...

LIBRARIES
○ **518,212 BOOKS** ○ **982 STUDY PLACES**
Figures above are for all three campuses, although the *recently extended* main library at Plymouth has around half the total resources. *The Marine Biology section is one of the best in the country.*

OTHER LEARNING FACILITIES
In addition to the drama studio, open-access language labs, IT training, rehearsal rooms and audio/TV centre Plymouth is also *the only university in the UK* to have a *state-of-the-art* diving centre, mainly used by Marine Biologists and, *um,* Civil Engineers. *The planetarium is to be turned into a digi-dome, a kind of gigantic virtual reality headset – they're calling it an 'immersive learning centre'. Users will get a chance to feel what it's like to be on the inside of the human body, just like in Fantastic Voyage. Lets hope killing Donald Pleasence off with a giant lymphocyte doesn't prove too upsetting.* The Pilgrims' Café at the Business School is a working model which *allows wannabe Basil Fawltys to practice on unsuspecting members of the public.*

ENTERTAINMENT ◖◖◖◖◖◖◖◖◖◖

PLYMOUTH
○ **PRICE OF A PINT OF BEER** £2
○ **GLASS OF WINE** £3
○ **CAN OF RED BULL** £3
CINEMAS The 15-screen Vue cinema *comes straight out of the generic multiplex box. The three-screen ABC is similar, but on a smaller scale. The Plymouth Arts Centre may only have one screen but it's got a proper bohemian ethos, with a veggie restaurant to prove it.* All have student discounts.
THEATRES *It may be a seaside town, but theatre is far from limited to Blackpool trademark end-of-the-pier musical rubbish. The Barbican shows a more unusual blend of drama, comedy and dance. The Drum Theatre is for cutting-edge contemporary and classics, while the Plymouth Athenaeum shows quirky amateur efforts.*
PUBS *Flagonfuls of pubs along the Barbican, in Mutley and on the North Hill in the town centre and in and around the major student areas. Pushplugs: the Skiving Scholar (a very literal title); the Fresher and Professor (ditto, with a VW Beetle on its roof); BacBar; Varsity.*
CLUBBING *Most of the nightspots the city has to offer are on Union Street with some smaller clubs on the Barbican. Pushplugs: Boogie Nights at C103 (indie, hiphop, old skool; R'n'B – SU venue of choice). Walkabout, Pilgrimage and C103 have deals with University/Union.*
MUSIC VENUES Classical at the Theatre Royal and the Guildhall; pop and comedy at the Plymouth Pavilions, and a mix of orchestral and big name events at Powderham Castle. Try The Cooperage for local bands. Peninsula Arts *often throws something together* in conjunction with the SU.

OTHER The Plymouth Festival in July is a city-wide funkathon of all kinds of music and fun from international and regional artists. *There's not many laughs to be had either on or off campus. Occasional wandering minstrels and court jesters have been known to put in a visit at Plymouth campus.*
EATING OUT Apart from the usual chain restaurants, *Pushplugs: the milkshakes at the Joint Internet Café; the Fresher and Professor pub; Jake's (fast food); Veggie Perrins (veggie Indian).*

UNIVERSITY
○ **PRICE OF A PINT OF BEER** £1.75
○ **GLASS OF WINE** £2
○ **CAN OF RED BULL** £1.80
BARS The SU has Illusion, Ignition and Fishbowl, plus four bottle bars. The new 4-storey building will be called the Hive and will have coffee rooms, computer suites and a non-alcoholic area, and *should be buzzing by 2007.*
FILM Films nights in Illusion. The Faculty of Arts is planning to open a cinema a couple of years down the line.
THEATRE *Occasional boardwalking* by the School of Art & Performance. The Musical Theatre Group stages something once a year.
MUSIC VENUES Ignition gets a few DJs in – Scott Mills has dropped by with the Radio 1 Roadshow crew and Electric Six have played. The University choir and orchestra puts on a *diverse* show, with global links to draw on for *back-up.*
CLUBBING SU events held Thu, Fri and Sat – *it's the town clubs on other nights.* Ignition does party tunes and guitar-thwanging at Illusion (Fridays). Thursday is Stock Exchange night, when the bars get turned into mini stock markets – *the more you buy of a certain drink, the more expensive it gets and vice versa – anyone for Special Brew, then?*
FOOD Seven eateries in all. The Union Café's *simple, cheap and edible. Loafers Two's queues stretch out the door for lunchtime sarnies.* The Babbage Refectory *has lovely food and lovely views.* There's also the Cookworthy, Hoe Centre, Portland and Pilgrim's Cafés. The SU shop gets Fair Trade and local produce in.
OTHER *Big fat daddy of a Summer Ball.*

SOCIAL ◖◖◖◖◖◖◖◖◖◖◖◖

UNIVERSITY OF PLYMOUTH STUDENTS' UNION
○ **7 SABBATICALS** ○ **TURNOUT AT LAST BALLOT** 19%
○ **NUS MEMBER**
The SU has facilities on all sites, usually in buildings shared with the University. *Students aren't out to change the world – they're not even out to give it a bit of a refurb.* The SU's trying to get students behind causes rather than just courses, and *so far they've succeeded in*

P

encouraging, er, *a Conservative club*. The SHAG campaign (sexual health), drink-spiking awareness and a *nice 'n' fluffy* 'be ethical' campaign have all run over the past year. *Union and University get on like houses at the moment, though who knows how things will fare once students start getting shunted about.*

SU FACILITIES
Nightclub; four bars at Plymouth; one each at Exeter and Exmouth; canteen; cafés; fast food outlet; advice centre at all sites; six pool tables; meeting room; six minibuses for hire; car/van hire; Endsleigh Insurance office; HSBC bank and ATMs; photocopying; fax and printing service; photo booth; payphones; juke boxes; gaming and vending machines; general store.

CLUBS (NON-SPORTING)
Computer Games; Musical Theatre. **See also Clubs tables.**

OTHER ORGANISATIONS
Plymouth campus produces 'Fly' magazine, free, Mondays. Exmouth has 'Rolle-up' and Exeter has 'Slack'. 'Juice' is a collaboration between all of them. 'UP's the radio station. Rag week focuses charitable donations with parades and other events. VIP – Volunteering in Plymouth – works everything from local projects cleaning beaches/feeding the primates at Cornwall Monkey Sanctuary to international affairs.

RELIGION
❍ **7 CHAPLAINS (ECUMENICAL, COFE, RC, ORTHODOX, URC, BAPTIST, METHODIST, NEW FRONTIERS)**
There are chaplaincies at all campuses. Plymouth's has a chapel, lounge and quiet room. Locally there are worship centres for most spiritual needs.

PAID WORK
❍ **JOB BUREAU**
Apart from the usual bar work and all that, there are a few tourist and maritime-based jobs in Plymouth. *The SU's employment register can be fruitful, as can hopping over the Tamar to Cornwall in the summer.*

SPORTS ⭕⭕⭕⭕⭕⭕⭕⭕⭕⭕⭕⭕⭕

❍ **RECENT SUCCESSES** FOOTBALL, TRAMPOLINING, SAILING, DANCE ❍ **BUSA RANKING** 57
Okay, they may have an unfair advantage, but Plymouth has the best surf team in the country. Things were looking bleak for a while, with the closure of the Exmouth playing fields (the sports facilities at the smaller campuses are still fairly cruddy) but the University threw over £70,000 at new sailing boats and has a number of sports scholarships for national and international athletes. On the whole: pretty good, but only for those based at the Plymouth campus.

SPORTS FACILITIES
PLYMOUTH Fitness room; squash courts; sports hall; aerobics studio; playing fields; all-weather pitch; seven-hole golf course; swimming pool; sailing boats; watersports centre. The city provides facilities for watersports, a bowling green, a baseball diamond, swimming pools and ski slope and ice skating.
EXMOUTH Rolle Fitness Suite.
EXETER Facilities are mainly hired playing fields.

SPORTING CLUBS
Aerobics; Argentinean Tango; Body Combat; Fitness Circuit; Gymnastics; Mountain biking; Yachting; Yoga. **See also Clubs tables.**

ATTRACTIONS
Plymouth Argyle for footie. Plymouth is one of the UK's big surf spots and ain't a bad choice for regattas and sailing events either.

ACCOMMODATION ⭕⭕⭕⭕⭕⭕⭕⭕⭕⭕

IN UNIVERSITY
❍ **SELF-CATERING** 8% ❍ **COST** £88 (52WKS)
❍ **1ST YRS LIVING IN** 35% ❍ **INSURANCE PREMIUM** £
AVAILABILITY Only special needs and non-EU students are guaranteed places in halls, for the rest it's the luck of the draw. No one lives in after the first year. At Plymouth halls are within two miles of the campus and are integrated into a *lively student village with cute little streets running through it. The buildings are all well maintained and attractive, but Robbins with its kitchen balconies is a top choice, as are cheap, sociable Gilwall and modern Pilgrim.* 60% of rooms are en suite, most kitchens have internal telephones, most halls have laundry rooms. Exeter runs a head tenancy scheme and Exmouth has benefited from some new rooms – more housing developments are planned in Plymouth. *CCTV records prowlers and streakers.*
CAR PARKING FOR PLYMOUTH *No, no, and once again, no.*

EXTERNALLY
❍ **AVE RENT** £65
AVAILABILITY IN PLYMOUTH *There's just about enough for those who are quick off the mark, but students who bend down to tie their laces or check the mirror for zits may look round to find they've missed the boat. Recommended areas include: Mutley, Greenbank, Stoke, Peverell and St Judes. All are reasonably nearby. Accommodation for families can be harder to come by.*
HOUSING HELP The University runs a *well-staffed* accommodation service on each campus offering vacancy lists, property vetting, contract approval and annual property inspections.

WELFARE ⓤⓤⓤⓤⓤⓤⓤⓤⓤⓤⓤⓤⓤⓤ

SERVICES
- **LGBT OFFICER & SOCIETY**
- **POSTGRAD STUDENTS' OFFICER & SOCIETY**
- **ETHNIC MINORITIES OFFICER & SOCIETY**
- **WOMEN'S OFFICER & SOCIETY**
- **MATURE STUDENTS' OFFICER & SOCIETY**
- **INTERNATIONAL STUDENTS' SOCIETY & OFFICER**
- **DISABILITIES OFFICER & SOCIETY**
- **SELF–DEFENCE CLASSES**
- **UNIVERSITY COUNSELLORS** 2 FULL/10 PART
- **SU COUNSELLORS** 2 PART ⊙ **CRIME RATING** !!!

The Union's advice centre *lends an ear to student woes* and runs both one-to-one counselling and workshops, eg. on dealing with exam stress. The SU don't run a nightline, but instead donate money to the Samaritans. The international student team does orientation *(no, not running around the countryside with a map and a compass)*, social events and provides free language support to students and their partners.
HEALTH A nurse is available at most sites and there are regular surgeries at Exmouth and Plymouth. Exeter's students are advised to register with local practices.
CRIME On-campus security centres.
CRECHES/NURSERY The Plymouth Freshling's nursery has 50 places for 0-5yrs and a play centre. Prices are reasonable and competition fierce.

DRUGS There's zero-tolerance on campus, but counselling's available for those who get into trouble.
DISABILITIES The ASSIST service helps prospectives co-ordinate their applications. *Access could be better at Plymouth but they're trying their best.* There are disabled toilets and ramps, portable hearing loops in the libraries, induction loops in some lecture theatres, tape/Braille transcription facilities and text/ minicom phones. Students with unseen disabilities are offered study skills support, a taping service in exams and specialist equipment.

FINANCE
- ⊙ **AVE DEBT PER YEAR** £2,960 ⊙ **HOME STUDENT FEES** £3,000
- ⊙ **ACCESS FUND** £1.2M ⊙ **SUCCESSFUL APPLICATIONS/YR** 1,300
- ⊙ **AVE PAYMENT** £300-700

SUPPORT The SU has some say in where Access money goes. Mature students *can scoop up to* £1,500 for relocation costs plus £500 for financial hardships. There are handouts towards the cost of compulsory field trips (UK/EU students). The Drake Marine Scholarship offers a grand for national competition in sailing, canoeing, etc. The Babbage Scholarship dishes out a generous £3,000 for academic excellence. The Reynold's Scholarship does something similar with a *meagre* £500 for Chemists, Modern Languagers and others. There's a good choice of bursaries too.

UNIVERSITY OF PORTSMOUTH

P

FORMERLY PORTSMOUTH POLYTECHNIC

1) ⊙ **UNIVERSITY OF PORTSMOUTH** University House, Winston Churchill Avenue, Portsmouth, PO1 2UP **TEL** (02392) 848484
E-MAIL admissions@port.ac.uk **WEBSITE** www.port.ac.uk ⊙ **UNIVERSITY OF PORTSMOUTH STUDENTS' UNION**
The Student Centre, Cambridge Road, Portsmouth, PO1 2EF **TEL** (02392) 843640 **WEBSITE** www.upsu.net

GENERAL ⓤⓤⓤⓤⓤⓤⓤⓤⓤⓤⓤⓤⓤ

Flanked by the ocean and speared by the Solent, Portsmouth sits within rowing distance of the Isle of Wight. For 400 years it was one of Britain's foremost naval ports *and the nautical influence is still inescapable*. The city, built on Portsea Island (a peninsular rather than a real island), is one of Europe's most densely populated – *it's a small place that can't grow without getting wet*. The University's main site in the city centre has benefited from a £6.2m Union building – *with very swanky glass wall and reception desk* – that now forms the social centre of student life. A £300,000 Virtual Reality Centre and the new Creative Arts Faculty are the latest toys. The satellite campus at Langstone is the sporting and residential centre.

SEX RATIO: ♂55 ♀45	**FOUNDED:** 1992
FULL-TIME U'GRADS: 13,429	**PART-TIME:** 1,485
POSTGRADS: 4,020	**NON–DEGREE:** 500
AVE COURSE: 3YRS	**ETHNIC:** 26%
STATE:PRIVATE SCHOOL: 93:7	**FLUNK RATE:** 19%
MATURE: 35%	**INTERNATIONAL:** 11%
DISABLED: 495	**LOCAL:** N/A

ATMOSPHERE
Portsmouth has enjoyed a relatively smooth and hassle-free growth recently and is now consolidating its powers on the main Guildhall site, which provides a busy working environment for the relaxed and down-to-earth student crowd. They really do like to be beside the seaside here – summertime brings books to the beaches and students lounge around the University gardens topping up tans. Relations with locals are mild

and unthreatening, helped by the fact that so many students are locals and halls aren't in residential areas.

SITES

The Guildhall campus in the city centre is decidedly the focus of university life. The Langstone campus just outside the city is now mainly halls of residence and sports facilities with very little academia or party action going down.

PORTSMOUTH

○ **POPULATION** 186,900 ○ **CITY CENTRE** 0 MILES
○ **LONDON** 70 MILES ○ **SOUTHAMPTON** 20 MILES
○ **HIGH TEMP** 22 ○ **LOW TEMP** 4 ○ **RAINFALL** 66

Portsmouth is a *compact if not pocket-sized place*, easily explored on foot. The *lovely, leafy seafront makes for pleasant strolling and there are shiploads of maritime marvels on display.* HMS Victory, the Mary Rose, the Warrior and the Royal Marines are all *intriguing and impressive titbits of Britain's military history* while Southsea House – pied á terre of Henry VIII – and Charles Dickens's birthplace provide tickboxes on the tourist's checklist. The millennium project, Spinnaker Tower, is also proving a popular amusement, partly due to the lift breaking down the day it launched. The beach, pier and funfair provide their quota of laughs too. Gunwharf Quays boasts over 70 factory outlets from Ralph Lauren to Levi's. Those who prefer leeks to labels will want to try the daily fruit and veg market. *Although there's little eyebrow-raising architecture or stunning scenery in the city centre, the stepped and columned Guildhall – with its rideable stone lions – provides an attractive and inspiring graduation venue. Portsmouth's worked hard at building up the impression of an affluent, harbour community, but irrepressible Vicky Pollards don't stay hidden for too long. Sha' aap!*

TRAVEL

TRAINS Portsmouth and Southsea station runs connections to London Waterloo (from £15.20), Brighton (£12.95) and Southampton (£9.40).
COACHES National Express services travel around the country from the coach station – a mile from Guildhall.
CAR The A27, which runs along the south coast, becomes the M27 between Portsmouth and Southampton. The A3 connects the city with London. *Plentiful Portsmouth parking provision*, but use of University spaces (around 850 at each site) costs £25 a year.
AIR Southampton International Airport is 15 miles away with *cheap* flights from Skybus, flyBe and ScotAirways.
FERRIES Regular ferries (and even quicker hovercrafts) to the Isle of Wight, Spain and France (St Malo, Cherbourg, Caen, Le Havre).
HITCHING *Langstone is too far out of town to be any good for thumbing it. Guildhall is a slightly better idea, but not many are prepared to stop on the busy roads.*
LOCAL Buses and local trains are reliable – around £2 for either – *but, since most distances are*

walkable, students tend to get by on foot.
UNIVERSITY A free shuttle bus service runs between Langstone halls and the city centre between 7.30am and 11pm.
TAXIS *Cabs are cheap enough for most students to use semi-regularly, particularly those in the studentish area of Southsea (£2). Those going from the campus to Langstone are less lucky.*
BICYCLES *Plenty of cycle routes and obliging topography make pedalling a pleasure. Despite this, most students don't bother with bikes as walking is as good a means as getting around as any.* The University provides lockable sheds (£20 a year) and stacks of racks.

CAREER PROSPECTS

○ **CAREERS SERVICE** ○ **NO. OF STAFF** 10 FULL/3 PART
○ **UNEMPLOYED AFTER 6** MTHS 9%

The careers service offers loads of online resources like vacancy bulletins, personality and career guidance and downloadable info leaflets. *Luddites might be more comfy* with the one-on-one discussion sessions, CV surgeries, job fairs and the careers library.

FAMOUS ALUMNI

David Chidgey MP (Lib Dem); Shirley Conran (writer); Ron Davies MP (Lab); Ben Fogle (Castaway chap and TV presenter); Rachel Lowe (Dragon's Den *victim who had the last laugh* when Hamley's snapped up her taxi-based board game); Grayson Perry (2003 Turner Prize winning transvestite); Nicky Wire (Manic Street Preachers) dropped out because he was 'having a thoroughly miserable time'.

FURTHER INFO

○ **PROSPECTUSES** UNDERGRAD; POSTGRAD; SOME DEPARTMENTAL; INTERNATIONAL
○ **OPEN DAYS**

The University runs regular Preview Days for anyone interested in applying and there are also invitation-only departmental open days for more specific academic info. Prospectuses can be ordered online.

ACADEMIC ⚇⚇⚇⚇⚇⚇⚇⚇⚇⚇⚇⚇

Portsmouth reckons that unique, specialised and vocational courses are what hooks new students. *They must be on the nose*, as applications are up by 67% – more than any other university in England, and *even more impressive in light of top-up trauma which has seen numbers falling off* elsewhere. Developments include an expanded Business School, a new Sports Science centre, a Marine Biology lab and a school for dental sciences – a *canny move considering the nation's shortage of teeth-cleaners.* Currently it's offering courses in the dental hygiene line, but an upgrade to full dentistry school status could be on the cards. It's a high-tech subject taught in a replica hospital with a mixture of *freaky* VR/ plastic heads and *local guinea pigs*.

As treatments are cheap/free and students on the course are eligible for certain bursaries, *it's proving rampantly popular.* Teaching is a mix of conventional methods and e-learning. Arts students can expect a *mere* hour of timetabled study a week (with a lot of self-study); Science boffins can expect around 20 hours. 30 credits are taken over three years, and allow a flexible approach to subject choice (many are plumping for languages). Final degree class is based on the 'best of three' idea: whatever's best out of the second year marks, third year marks or the overall grade is what the student walks out with.

ENTRY POINTS: 160–300	AVE POINTS: N/A
APPLICATIONS PER PLACE: 6	CLEARING: 1%
NO. OF TERMS: 2	LENGTH OF TERMS: 15WKS
STAFF TO STUDENT RATIO: 1:20	STUDY ADDICTS: 24%
TEACHING: **	RESEARCH: ***
YEAR ABROAD: <1%	SANDWICH STUDENTS: 9%
1STS: 7%	2.2s: 37%
2.1s: 34%	3RDS: 7%

ADMISSIONS
⊙ APPLY VIA UCAS/DIRECT FOR POSTGRAD
Direct application forms for postgrad study and courses not covered by UCAS. Forms can be downloaded from the website.

SUBJECTS
ENVIRONMENT 16%   **HUMANITIES & SOCIAL SCIENCES** 26%
PORTSMOUTH BUSINESS SCHOOL 20%   **SCIENCE** 21%
TECHNOLOGY 18%
BEST Biology; Chemical Engineering; Economics; Education Studies; English Studies; European Languages; Finance & Accounting; Media Studies; Medical Science; Physical Science; Politics; Psychology; Sports Science.
UNUSUAL Criminology & Criminal Justice; E-Business; Real Estate Management. Palaeontology is what all the cool kids are up to these days, and the Isle of Wight, with its Jurassic Park-style history is the place to do it, courtesy of the University's course.

LIBRARIES
⊙ 380,000 BOOKS ⊙ 680 STUDY PLACES
  ⊙ SPEND PER STUDENT £££
The main Frewen Library is *mostly* open till midnight and is getting an £11m, three-storey extension this year. It will contain more teaching rooms, 200 computers and an extra 200m of shelving *to take the pressure off the bulging stacks.* There are a host of smaller departmental libraries, including the Faculty of Environment's Portland LRC which has books, audio-visual materials, IT suites, reprographics facilities *(ie. photocopiers)* and an art shop.

COMPUTERS
⊙ 4,200 WORKSTATIONS ⊙ SPEND PER STUDENT ££
The campus is getting more and more wireless as time goes on. Broadband is available in all rooms in halls. The Anglesea Building has drop-in internet facilities (as well as a Dr. Who Tardis and a Dalek, *but that's beside the point*).

OTHER LEARNING FACILITIES
Drama studio; music rooms; open-access language labs; design lab; media centre.

ENTERTAINMENT ◡◡◡◡◡◡◡◡◡

THE CITY
⊙ PRICE OF A PINT OF BEER £1.75
⊙ GLASS OF WINE £2
⊙ CAN OF RED BULL £2
CINEMAS *More blockbusters than you could point your remote control at:* UCI and Odeon in the city, Carlton Cinema and No.6 in the dockyard *for adventures in artier celluloid.* Gunwharf also has a Vue nestled in among the trendy boutiques and boats. The Third Floor Arts Centre holds film festivals from time to time.
THEATRES The King's Theatre is *beloved but doomed* – a last-minute cash injection may save it, but it's on the critical list. The historic Theatre Royal does *a good line* in student discounts, and has the Othello Café.
PUBS *The waterholes around the University have cottoned on to the profit possibilities of the student market* and have a parade of discounts and promos, particularly earlier in the week. Old Portsmouth and *increasingly trendy* Southsea *are sure bets for a good night out.* Wetherspoons *may be evil,* but the one in Guildhall Walk lures in *plenty of students for cheap food and beer (along with the billions of other bars on the same street). Pushplugs: Registry (pre-drinks, fab discounts – get a yellow card to get the best deals); Yates's; V Bar; Bar Me; Fuzzy Duck.* Albert Road is the other pub hub: try *One-Eyed Dog; Wonky Donkey (99p drinks); the Wedgewood Rooms.*
CLUBBING *Portsmouth has as many clubs as a Canadian seal-culling expedition, especially around Southsea and the Guildhall area. Pushplugs: Tiger Tiger, Time, Envy, Route 66.*
MUSIC VENUES The Guildhall is Portsmouth's premier venue, mixing pop, rock, classical and comedy. There are a handful of other places, including, *bizarrely,* the Pyramids – a swimming pool more famed for its wave and slide action – which also hosts live bands. The Wedgewood Rooms *is a good place to unearth local talent.*
COMEDY Jongleurs at Gunwharf. Lee Evans, Eddie *'action transvestite'* Izzard and Jack Dee have all made wry and witty observations from the Wedgewood Rooms.
OTHER Portsmouth is on the coast so there's piers, candyfloss, whelks, the beach and all the fun of the fair. Gunwharf has a bit of everything, from bowling to casino antics.
EATING OUT *Loads of cheap deals* in the pubs around Guildhall and Southsea, as well as some swankier restaurants, curry houses and pizza parlours. *Fish-lovers will be happy (that's if they love to eat fish – nothing to do with indulging bizarre eel fetishes) thanks to the ocean harvest.* Gunwharf *satisfies global appetites,* and Albert Road's there for *booze-induced* munchies.

P

UNIVERSITY
- **PRICE OF A PINT OF BEER** £1.70
- **GLASS OF WINE** £2
- **CAN OF RED BULL** £1.50

BARS *The Waterhole is the big daddy bar – always busy thanks to its late licence (2am), pool tables, games machines and big screen sport. CO2 next to Lux is for chilling out. There's also the small Embassy Bar for quieter, less frenetic drinking.*
FILM Screenings every Tuesday.
CLUBBING The second largest venue in Portsmouth. Three rooms cater for *varied musical, if not aesthetical, styles.*
COMEDY/CABARET A *packed* schedule at Union every Thursday keeps students *giggling.*
FOOD *Waterhole Kitchen for hot stuff (temperature-wise rather than culinary flair). The Pit Stop does 99p pies.* Via Lattea is a veggie coffee shop.
OTHER Christmas and Freshers' balls.

SOCIAL ◑◑◑◑◑◑◑◑◑◑◑◑

UNIVERSITY OF PORTSMOUTH STUDENTS' UNION
- **7 SABBATICALS** • **NUS MEMBER**

UPSU's strongest strengths are sporty and social – although Portsmouth's boys and girls haven't been afraid to throw in their lot with the futile fight against fees. Some of the sabbs have been up to London to lobby Parliament about the quality of student housing. Relations with the University continue to be cosier than cocoa and candy, with students represented on most committees and having a say in most decisions.

SU FACILITIES
The Student Centre contains the three bars, the Lux club, café, canteen, the Pitstop, Endsleigh Insurance office, stationery shop, pool tables, juke boxes, gaming and vending machines, ATMs advice centre and a 24-hr Blockbuster video and DVD rental machine. Also: fax and printing service; payphones; photocopiers; new bookshop; general store.

CLUBS (NON-SPORTING)
Big Band; Break Dance; Computer Games; Drum & Bass; Duke Of Edinburgh; Fantasy Role Play; Hindu; Hong Kong; Music; New Music; Metal; Mixing; Mature; Malaysian; Juggling. **See also Clubs tables.**

OTHER ORGANISATIONS
'Pugwash' (Portsmouth University Guild of Writers) is the monthly UPSU paper. The Union's sports and societies newsletter, 'Purple Wednesdays', comes out weekly. Radio station 'Pure' broadcasts daily on the net, and tries but mostly fails to get an FM licence. *The Portsmouth Rag is like a hyperactive kid but shares out the*

madness by giving everyone a chance to make tits out of themselves for charity with pub-crawls, slave auctions and the rest. Volunteering in Portsmouth (VIP) arranges voluntary projects for *do-gooders* that come with certificates for *CV-embellishers* as well.

RELIGION
- **5 CHAPLAINS (COFE, RC, BAPTIST, FC)**

On campus there's a chaplaincy meeting room and Muslim prayer room. Most religions are served in the city, which has synagogues, mosques, Hindu and Sikh temples, a Buddhist Monastery *and enough churches of various colours to guarantee a place in heaven.*

PAID WORK
- **JOB BUREAU** • **PAID WORK** TERM TIME 33%

The job shop in the Union does its bit to help cash-hunters and with all the bars, ferries, shops and tourists in and around Southsea, chances of finding work are above average.

SPORTS ◑◑◑◑◑◑◑◑◑◑◑◑

- **RECENT SUCCESSES** FOOTBALL, NETBALL, GOLF, SQUASH
- **BUSA RANKING** 41

The Athletics Union does a jolly good job of organising sporting events and keeping the jocks happy. Portsmouth's teams have made quite a name for themselves in the leagues of late and and there's a strong 'sports for all' ethos: couch potatoes are encouraged through the social side, with the Hockey Soc leading the way with Wednesday night dress-ups (everything from wetsuits to pirate gear, we hear). Sporting socs can join an annual booze-up in Spain.

SPORTS FACILITIES
On the main site, there's the Nuffield Sports Centre with cricket bays, a gym, two weights rooms with multigym, two squash courts, two dance studios and four multi-purpose courts. It hosts 42 fitness classes every week, ranging from boxercise to pilates. St Paul's has a sports hall and four floors of free weights, resistance and cardiovascular gym gear. Near the halls, the four acres of sports fields by Langstone Harbour include four soccer pitches, two mini-football fields, two rugby fields, lacrosse pitch and a full-size artificial pitch. The University also has a host of facilities to be used on the Solent, *a flood of fun for those who get wet for water sports.* Annual membership of the sports centres costs £97 a year and the gym costs £3 a time. An Olympic-sized swimming pool is planned for the Mountbatten Centre, though Push can't say when. Locally there are sports centres, tennis courts, golf courses, a swimming complex, and sailing and windsurfing in the Solent.

SPORTING CLUBS
10 Pin Bowling; Off Shore Sailing; Paintball; Polo;

P

Roller Hockey; Table Tennis; Rowing; Softball; Sky Diving; Ultimate Frisbee; Waterpolo. **See also Clubs tables.**

ATTRACTIONS

This is decidedly Portsmouth FC's territory, but there's also the greyhound racing track and Hampshire Cricket Club's second ground.

ACCOMMODATION ◖◖◖◖◖◖◖◖◖

IN UNIVERSITY

● **CATERED** 5% ● **COST** £91 (36WKS)
● **SELF-CATERING** 16% ● **COST** £85 (36WKS)
● **1ST YRS LIVING IN** 20% ● **INSURANCE PREMIUM** £
AVAILABILITY Although international students are guaranteed places and a large proportion of rooms are reserved for first years, 10% of each year's intake gets left out in the cold. Most first years are locals who live at home the first year. James Watson is the newest hall, housing 726 students in *relative* en suite *luxury* in three tower blocks, D, N and A *(geddit?)*. Most of the halls are within ten mins of Guildhall or Langstone campus, but *Langstone can be a drag because of its distance from the city centre and the main student scene. Rooms tend to be of decent quality and neutral décor* – 84% are en suite *– although some of the older halls, like Bateson at Langstone, are a bit poky and ugly lookin'. The most popular are Trafalgar Hall and the studio flats opposite the Guildhall buildings – these are the most modern and comfortable. Rees Hall may be the furthest away of the city centre halls but its spectacular sea views and Edwardian appearance make it a favourite for the wealthier students.* Those living catered get between five and 14 meals a week (depends how much they pay) and a microwave for packaged snacks. Self-catered students share kitchens with three to eight people. All halls have laundry rooms, satellite TV lounges and games rooms. Hall reps are there to keep an eye on residents, arrange midnight feasts and other social activities and act as go-between to the University. Events for international students answer housing questions and needs. *Single-sex flats are available if you ask the Housing Office nicely. Night security patrols shoot bogeymen on sight.*
CAR PARKING Only available at the halls around Langstone – with permit.

EXTERNALLY

● **AVE RENT** £55
AVAILABILITY *No shortage of nesting places. The most appropriate places are in the large Victorian houses which have been split into tenement flats and bedsits, usually shared by two to four people. The best places are Southsea, Fratton and North End. Eastney, Somerstown and Paulsgrove are too rough to be worth it. Albert Road, with its generous mix of amenities and lottery of bars and restaurants is particularly worth a peek.*
HOUSING HELP The Student Housing Office publishes regular bulletins and keeps a list of respectable digs. 'Find a Home' days at the beginning of each year help match students with potential housemates, ie. *non-kleptomaniacs who don't bottle their own urine.*

WELFARE ◖◖◖◖◖◖◖◖◖◖◖◖◖

SERVICES

● **LATE-NIGHT MINIBUS** ● **SELF-DEFENCE CLASSES**
● **UNIVERSITY COUNSELLORS** 2 PART
● **CRIME RATING** !!!!
There's a woeful lack of individual welfare officers, though the University has counselling provisions for students who demonstrate a need. *ie. not for trauma caused by bad hair days.* The late-night bus service deposits *boozy* folk on their doorstep for 50p.
HEALTH NHS practices on both Langstone and Guildhall campuses with three GPs and nurses.
CRECHES/NURSERY 38 places for precious things aged 6mths-5yrs.
DISABILITIES *Access is good in the newer bits and improving in the older ones.* There are wheelchair ramps and lifts in most buildings and specialised rooms available in almost all halls. Induction loops are fitted in lecture theatres and dyslexia screening and support is available from the Disability Advice Centre.

FINANCE

● **AVE DEBT PER YEAR** £4,083 ● **HOME STUDENT FEES** £3,000
FEES International students can pay between £7,250 and £8,350 depending on their course. UK Postgrads pay £3,010.
● **ACCESS FUND** £1,215,945
● **SUCCESSFUL APPLICATIONS/YR** 1,806
● **AVE PAYMENT** £600-800
SUPPORT As well as the Hardship Fund (£750,000), there's a bursary scheme for low-income families.

P

⇒ **PORTSMOUTH POLYTECHNIC**
see *University of Portsmouth*

⇒ **PRINTING**
see *University of the Arts, London*

QUEEN MARGARET UNIVERSITY COLLEGE, EDINBURGH

QUEEN MARY, UNIVERSITY OF LONDON

➡ **QUEEN MARY & WESTFIELD COLLEGE**
see *Queen Mary, University of London*

➡ **QUEEN'S COLLEGE, GLASGOW**
see *Glasgow Caledonian University*

QUEEN'S UNIVERSITY BELFAST

Q

QUEEN MARGARET UNIVERSITY COLLEGE, EDINBURGH

1) ● **QUEEN MARGARET UNIVERSITY COLLEGE**, Clerwood Terrace, Edinburgh, EH12 8TS **TEL** (0131) 317 3000
E-MAIL admissions@qmuc.ac.uk **WEBSITE** www.qmuc.ac.uk ● **QUEEN MARGARET UNIVERSITY COLLEGE STUDENTS' UNION**,
Clerwood Terrace, Edinburgh, EH12 8TS **TEL** (0131) 317 3400 **E-MAIL** su-staff@qmuc.ac.uk **WEBSITE** www.qmucsu.org.uk
2) ● **LEITH CAMPUS**, Duke Street, Leith, Edinburgh, EH6 8HF **TEL** (0131) 317 3353
3) ● **THE GATEWAY**, Gateway Theatre, Leith Walk, Edinburgh, EH7 4AH **TEL** (0131) 317 3900

GENERAL ◗◗◗◗◗◗◗◗◗◗◗◗◗◗

Made of three campuses dotted around the *beautiful and culturally vibrant* city of Edinburgh (see University of Edinburgh for more info), QMUC is a *pleasantly mixed bag.* The main site is in the Corstorphine area, four miles from the city centre, in a residential area, neighbouring a nature reserve, and itself surrounded by mature gardens on a 24-acre greenfield site. *Unfortunately half the buildings look like 60s comprehensive schools with maze-like corridors to confuse everybody.* The next is seven miles away in Leith, a mile from the Edinburgh's East End. The other is The Gateway on Leith Walk, five minutes from town, with its own theatre. Come 2007, these are set to close their doors and pass on the baton to the new campus right on the other side of town in Craighall, near Musselburgh, opens with, we're promised, fab facilities including an 'academic village', a new Students' Union, shops and cafes, sports paraphernalia, accommodation and *a luxury cruise liner. Well, Push can dream. Although the move to the other side of the city could take a bit of getting used to, the promised wonders of the new campus should be a vast improvement on QMUC's current buildings. Let's just hope the building work gets completed on schedule.*

SEX RATIO: ♀23 ♂77	FOUNDED: 1875
FULL-TIME U'GRADS: 2,950	PART-TIME: 239
POSTGRADS: 445	NON-DEGREE: 875
AVE COURSE: 4YRS	ETHNIC: N/A
STATE:PRIVATE SCHOOL: 93:7	FLUNK RATE: 13%
MATURE: 39%	INTERNATIONAL: 11%
DISABLED: 95	LOCAL: 68%

ATMOSPHERE
Friendly and intimate with perky and enthusiastic students. There's a bit of a hefty female ratio, which can be terrific or torture for either sex depending on their mood and how horny they're likely to get.

SITES
CORSTORPHINE (3,000 students) The main campus and the heart of admin, academic and SU services.
LEITH CAMPUS (600 students) The Health Studies site, where students study Podiatry, Radiography, Physiotherapy, Occupational Therapy and Art Therapy. *Leith's a nice area by the water* with a shopping centre and the Royal Yacht Britannia.

While the *facilities don't rock,* there are pubs, restaurants and clubs enough to satisfy most entertainment urges. The *ethos is more work-orientated though.*
THE GATEWAY (200 students – Drama) The Gateway is located in the New Town area of Edinburgh. Despite its name, New Town has some beautiful old buildings and is very close to the city centre. Houses excellent facilities for students of production, drama and performance.

EDINBURGH see University of Edinburgh
● **CITY CENTRE** 4 MILES

TRAVEL see University of Edinburgh
A shuttle bus nips between the three campuses a couple of times a day and there are local buses too. *About as much chance of finding a parking space as there is of running into a Westlife fan in a heavy metal club.*

CAREER PROSPECTS
● **CAREERS SERVICE** ● **UNEMPLOYED AFTER 6 MTHS** 6%
QMUC job shop offers interview training, bulletin boards and help with applications and CVs.

FAMOUS ALUMNI
Dougie Anderson (TV presenter); Matt Baker (Blue Peter); Edith Bowman (Radio One); Jimmy Chisholm (actor); Angel Coulby (actress); David Crystal (linguistics guru); Andy Gray (actor); Sally Gray (TV presenter); Ashley Jensen ('Extras'); Simone Lahbib (actress); Brian Marjoribanks (ex-footballer and presenter); Kevin McKidd (actor); Lloyd Quinan (Scottish weatherman).

FURTHER INFO
● **PROSPECTUSES** UNDERGRAD; POSTGRAD ● **OPEN DAYS**

ACADEMIC ◗◗◗◗◗◗◗◗◗◗◗◗

QMUC isn't afraid of getting down with the kids and trying new things, academically speaking. The College specialises in Business, Theatre and Healthcare subjects and quite a few students end up in work placements of one sort or another. *Its small size makes for cosy class sizes, which is good because it means lecturers will always know your name, and bad ... for precisely the same reason.* At the moment, QMUC is building a 'virtual' campus, *an online excuse for students to study in bed.*

ENTRY POINTS: 160–340	AVE POINTS: 289
APPLICATIONS PER PLACE: 6	CLEARING: 14%
NO. OF TERMS: 2	LENGTH OF TERMS: 15wks
STAFF TO STUDENT RATIO: 1:18	STUDY ADDICTS: N/A
TEACHING: *	RESEARCH: *
1STS: 4%	2.2S: 17%
2.1S: 24%	3RDS: 1%

ADMISSIONS
- **APPLY VIA UCAS**

SUBJECTS
BUSINESS & ENTERPRISE 14%
DRAMA & CREATIVE INDUSTRIES 8%
HEALTH SCIENCES 56%   **INTERNATIONAL HEALTH** 1%
INTERNATIONAL STUDY CENTRE 2%   **JOINT DEGREES** 2%
SOCIAL SCIENCES, MEDIA & COMMUNICATION 17%
UNUSUAL logopaedics (that's studying speech defects to the rest of us).

LIBRARIES
- **121,000 BOOKS** ● **350 STUDY PLACES**
- **SPEND PER STUDENT** ££

The library *is well-equipped, except that it doesn't actually have all that many books. It also doesn't open very late.*

COMPUTERS
- **390 WORKSTATIONS** ● **SPEND PER STUDENT** ££

Often housed in *small, stuffy rooms, computers are scattered around the campuses, fewest in Gateway. There aren't enough to go round, which stings at peak times, as does the lack of 24-hr access.* Hall bedrooms come with internet points though.

OTHER LEARNING FACILITIES
Movement studios; voice studios; rehearsal rooms; TV and radio studios; wardrobe and design facility; theatre; training restaurant; photographic studio; dark room; video conferencing; CAD lab.

ENTERTAINMENT ◑◑◑◑◑◑◑◑◑

THE CITY see University of Edinburgh

IN COLLEGE
- **PRICE OF A PINT OF BEER** £1.80
- **GLASS OF WINE** £1.60

Anything involving the stage is mighty, everything else sucks slightly, but with the variety of Edinburgh just outside, someone must have thought 'why bother?'. Students go off-campus to find most entertainment.

BARS/MUSIC/CLUBBING The Union Bar (cap. 350) is popular on a Wednesday and *the comfy sofas are in demand during the day.* Open late with a *tiny* DJ/stage area. Sporadic club nights, usually with one themed or sponsored shindig a week.

THEATRES Teeming with drama and stage management students, the Gateway Theatre houses various productions and QMUC doubles

as a Fringe venue during the Festival in the summer. All students are encouraged to get stuck into the theatre.

FILM The film soc is involved in screening independent flicks from the arty to the *ones only the director has heard of.* Occasional theme nights.

COMEDY/CABARET Rarely anything on site but Edinburgh's comedy and stand-up clubs *keep faces smiling.*

FOOD A *stodgy* canteen, a *student-wallet-unfriendly* Café Ritazza and *average pub grub* in the Union Bar. If none of that appeals, the shop does sarnies.

OTHER Christmas, Summer and Sports & Societies balls.

SOCIAL ◑◑◑◑◑◑◑◑◑◑◑◑◑

QUEEN MARGARET UNIVERSITY COLLEGE STUDENTS' UNION
- **2 SABBATICALS** ● **NUS MEMBER**

Picking up political pace since the tuition fees brouhaha, students are willing to demonstrate and walk out of lectures for a worthy cause. Internally, the SU enjoys a productive relationship with College and students, and has recently established a student parliament – the first student representation system of its kind in the UK.

SU FACILITIES
Nothing fancy: bar; canteen; photocopier; stationers; pool table; meeting room; payphone; juke box; TV lounge; games machines; advice centre; ATM (£1.50 to withdraw cash); *tiny* Waterstones. Common rooms at the other campuses.

CLUBS (NON SPORTING)
Bike; Poker. **See also Clubs tables.**

OTHER ORGANISATIONS
The monthly paper is 'the Echo'. Community relations are discussed with local representatives twice a year. Links with local charities – Barnardos, First Hand (single parents), Shelter and the Edinburgh Volunteer Centre – for do-gooders. *Rag is small but effective.*

RELIGIOUS
A meeting room is supplied for anyone feeling all spiritual.

PAID WORK see University of Edinburgh
- **JOB BUREAU**

Crust-earners usually have to head to the city centre for work. JobShop helps students find part-time and vacation work as well as vocational employment related to their degree. There's a good amount of these jobs around Festival time, but that's during the summer break.

SPORTS

❍ RECENT SUCCESSES FOOTBALL **❍ BUSA RANKING** 122
If treading the boards counted as sport, QMUC would have its eye on the Olympics but, alas, sports provisions are limited and, in the eyes of the students, under-funded. Even so, QMUC passes muster at football.

SPORTS FACILITIES
QMUC has an all-weather playing field, tennis, netball and basketball courts, swimming pool, sauna and an *under-equipped* fitness suite. Students are charged a small fee to use them.

SPORTING CLUBS
Cheerleading. **See also Clubs tables.**

ATTRACTIONS see University of Edinburgh

ACCOMMODATION

IN COLLEGE
❍ CATERED 5% **❍ COST** £80 (38WKS)
❍ SELF-CATERING 14% **❍ COST** £64 (38WKS)
❍ INSURANCE PREMIUM £
AVAILABILITY Corstorphine Campus has three *old, tired* halls: Guthrie Wright Hall (151 catered single rooms), Stevenson Hall (153 self-catered singles) and Grainger Stewart Hall (139 self-contained flats). Leith and Gateway have Halmyre Street flats as off-site accommodation. Catered halls comes in both full-board and B&B flavours, prices reflects this. Self-caterers can buy 'season tickets' for canteen food *if the uphill trek back from the shops to share cooking space with 10-15 others seems like too much hard work.* About 25-30% of students in halls of residence are international students. Others opt to stay at home or get private flats in the city centre. The head tenancy scheme finds beds for 92 students.

EXTERNALLY see University of Edinburgh
❍ AVE RENT £65
AVAILABILITY *Students tend to prefer living in Haymarket, Leith, Dalry and Corstorphine. Leith is the most popular, being cheaper, more plentiful, modern and down by the water. Prices have been creeping up in the New Town. Finding housing isn't a problem; finding affordable and non-skanky housing requires a bit more effort. Many lettings agents are keen to take student pounds.*
HOUSING HELP The Accommodation Office is *helpful,* having an approved list of landlords and some directly leased properties owned by the College.

WELFARE

SERVICES
❍ EQUAL OPPORTUNITIES OFFICER
❍ UNIVERSITY COUNSELLORS 1 FULL **❍ CRIME RATING** !!
The Union advice centre is at Corstophine and the medical centre offers family planning, emergency contraception, general health checks and vaccinations. Also a registered nurse, GP and a full-time counsellor. CCTV on campus keeps things safe (*or maybe just provides amusing video of late night student japes*).
CRECHES/NURSERY The Corstorphine campus has a nursery with some free, part-time places available.
DISABILITIES *Access isn't helped by the split sites, which are based in the city or in areas with lots of stairs.* The College has started to provide special disabled accommodation and improved disabled sports facilities, particularly for visually impaired people.

FINANCE
❍ AVE DEBT PER YEAR £2,873
❍ HOME STUDENT FEES £1,700
FEES International undergrads pay around £7,600-8,400. UK postgrads are charged £3,085-7,000. Part-time students pay by the module.
❍ ACCESS FUND £235,953 **❍ SUCCESSFUL APPLICATIONS/YR** 319 **❍ AVE PAYMENT** £100-4,000 (HIGH PAYMENTS ARE USUALLY TO HELP WITH CHILDCARE COSTS)
SUPPORT The College has £16,000 to hand out each year in hardship loans as well as £86,372 for hardship grants and £71,873 worth of mature students' bursaries.

 Queen Mary University of London's campus has a cemetery slapbang in the middle of it.

Words in italics are Push's point of view — take it or leave it...

QUEEN MARY, UNIVERSITY OF LONDON

FORMERLY QUEEN MARY & WESTFIELD COLLEGE, LONDON
THE COLLEGE IS PART OF THE UNIVERSITY OF LONDON AND STUDENTS ARE ENTITLED TO USE ITS FACILITIES

1) ⊙ **QUEEN MARY, UNIVERSITY OF LONDON**, Mile End Road, London, E1 4NS **TEL** (020) 7882 5555 **E−MAIL** admissions@qmul.ac.uk **WEBSITE** www.qmul.ac.uk ⊙ **QUEEN MARY STUDENTS' UNION**, Mile End Site, 432 Bancroft Road, London, E1 4DH **TEL** (020) 7882 5390 **E−MAIL** su-genoff@qmul.ac.uk **WEBSITE** www.qmsu.org
2) ⊙ **BARTS & THE LONDON SCHOOL OF MEDICINE & DENTISTY**, Turner Street, London E1 2AD **TEL** (020) 7377 7611 **E−MAIL** medicaladmissions@qmul.ac.uk. ⊙ **BARTS & THE LONDON STUDENTS' ASSOCIATION**, Stepney Way, London, E1 2JJ **TEL** (020) 7377 7640 **E−MAIL** su-vpassociation@qmul.ac.uk

GENERAL ◖◗◖◗◖◗◖◗◖◗◖◗◖◗

Situated in East London, close to Canary Wharf and the Docklands and a hair's breadth away from the City, Queen Mary is the only campus college in the University of London. A mish-mash of different buildings, from the *fine old* Queen's building (complete with clock tower) to some 50s art deco and 60s *eyesores,* and strangely, a Jewish cemetery. With 19th-century origins, it was set up to educate East-Enders, while Westfield (now dropped from the name) was a pioneering college for women. Near Regent's Canal and East London's greenbelt as well as having a variety of bustling markets and boozers nearby, Queen Mary *shows the best the East End has to offer* and is only 15 mins tube journey from Trafalgar Square. For general information on London: see University of London.

SEX RATIO: ♂51 ♀49	**FOUNDED:** 1887
FULL−TIME U'GRADS: 8,532	**PART−TIME:** 526
POSTGRADS: 2,454	**NON−DEGREE:** 494
AVE COURSE: 3YRS	**ETHNIC:** 31%
STATE:PRIVATE SCHOOL: 86:14	**FLUNK RATE:** 10%
MATURE: 22%	**INTERNATIONAL:** 23%
DISABLED: 45	**LOCAL:** 48%

ATMOSPHERE

Multi-racial, multi-national, the cultural gumbo that is QM mirrors the vibrant diversity of the local community, making for a learning experience in itself. It rubs off on the students who mix with each other and the locals with relish. The University spirit loves serious study as much as a proper social life. Early on Friday afternoon the bars fill up, but the study areas also get rammed. Commitment to local volunteering and a general enthusiasm about the area suggest an easy relationship with surrounding East London.

SITES

THE MEDICAL SCHOOL Barts and The London School of Medicine and Dentistry is located on two sites in Whitechapel and the City. Students are allowed to use all the main site's facilities, if they have the time.

WHITECHAPEL (170 students) *Friendly and approachable (at least in comparison with some other medical schools)*, the Royal London Hospital is right opposite Whitechapel tube in an impressive brick edifice, 800 metres from the main QM site.
WEST SMITHFIELD (730 students) Bart's Hospital is housed in a *lovely* Georgian-fronted building near Smithfield Meat Market *(don't bother, they've heard all the jokes about where the corpses end up).* It's located a mile from QM's main campus. There are also sites in Charthouse Square, Chislehurst and Mile End.

LONDON see University of London

TRAVEL see University of London
TRAINS Liverpool Street and Stratford are five minutes by tube or a 20min walk.
BUSES Numbers 339, 25, 106 and night buses N25, N8 and N15.
CAR City and Tower Hamlets councils have quite stringent restrictions and there are the usual traffic/parking concerns.
UNDERGROUND Mile End (Central, District, Hammersmith & City lines) and Stepney Green (District, Hammersmith & City lines, peak times only). Whitechapel (District, East London Line, Hammersmith & City) for the London Hospital, St Paul's or Barbican for Bart's.
BICYCLES There's a bicycle users' group (BUG) run by the SU and plenty of cycle racks in the student village and on campus.

CAREER PROSPECTS
⊙ **CAREERS SERVICE** ⊙ **NO. OF STAFF** 5 FULL
⊙ **UNEMPLOYED AFTER 6MTHS** 5%
Library, interview training, bulletin boards, job fairs.

FAMOUS ALUMNI
Dr Barnardo (liked kids); Malcolm Bradury, Eva Figes, Ruth Prawer Jhabvala, Andrea Newman (writers); Bernard Butler (Suede guitarist); Graham Chapman (Monty Python); Bruce Dickinson (ex-Iron Maiden); Peter Hain MP (Lab); Sir Roy Strong (former director, V&A museum); David Sullivan (ex-footballer, porn baron); Frederick Treves (treated the Elephant Man).

Words in italics are Push's point of view — take it or leave it...

FURTHER INFO
- **PROSPECTUSES** UNDERGRAD; POSTGRAD; DEPARTMENTAL
- **OPEN DAYS**

ACADEMIC ○○○○○○○○○○○○

Not just a great big medical love-in but also training and research in Science, Engineering, Medicine, Law, Arts, Linguistics and Politics. Students can also learn a language and computing skills if they fancy it.

ENTRY POINTS: 180–340	AVE POINTS: 328
APPLICATIONS PER PLACE: N/A	CLEARING: 8%
NO. OF TERMS: 3	LENGTH OF TERMS: 12WKS
STAFF TO STUDENT RATIO: 1:8	STUDY ADDICTS: 3%
TEACHING: ★★★	RESEARCH: ★★★★
1STS: 13%	2.2S: 24%
2.1S: 41%	3RDS: 6%

ADMISSIONS
- **APPLY VIA UCAS**

SUBJECTS
ARTS 18% **ASSOCIATES/FOUNDATION** 5%
ENGINEERING & MATHEMATICAL SCIENCES 24%
LAW & SOCIAL SCIENCES 20%
MEDICINE & DENTISTRY 22% **NATURAL SCIENCES** 11%
BEST Biology & Related Science; Computer Science; English-based Studies; European Languages; History; Human & Social Geography; Physical Geography & Environmental Science; Law; Mathematical Sciences; Mechanically-based Engineering; Physical Science; Politics; Subjects allied to medicine; Technology.
UNUSUAL Astronomy; Avionics & Space Systems; Cities; Journalism & Contemporary History; Materials with Forensic Science; Physics & Finance.

LIBRARIES
- **650,000 BOOKS** ○ **1,400+ STUDY PLACES**

The Law and Medical libraries are quietly impressive, the general one is okay too, having won awards in the past, though they certainly weren't for opening hours.

COMPUTERS
- **1,000 WORKSTATIONS** ○ **24-HR ACCESS**

Extra computers in most departments as well.

OTHER LEARNING FACILITIES
Language lab; drama studio; media centre.

ENTERTAINMENT ○○○○○○○○○○

THE CITY see University of London
- **PRICE OF A PINT OF BEER** £2.40
- **GLASS OF WINE** £2.60
- **CAN OF RED BULL** £1.60

The New Globe, Hayfield and Coborn pubs are popular as they do special student promos – the Hayfield gets a special student thumbs up. The six-screen Odean cinema does student prices (£3) and there's a local comedy club for when practising autopsies on dead bodies just isn't funny any more.

UNIVERSITY
- **PRICE OF A PINT OF BEER** £1.70
- **GLASS OF WINE** £2
- **CAN OF RED BULL** £1.60

Hard-working students need to blow off steam and take some of the weight off their wallets so they can get to lectures quickly in the morning. College ents lose some of their novelty after the first year and students start pounding the wider stomping ground of the Big Smoke.
BARS The SU runs four bars. The e1 Venue Bar, remarkably, is at it's best when it's being a venue for QM's *wide range* of ents. The Drapers Arms (cap. 350) is the bop shop, Whitechapel has its Association Bar and Smithfield has Bart's Bar. Others are the Forest Bar (popular with staff and postgrads) and the non-smoking Balcony Bar.
THEATRES *Like a drama ninja.* 25 productions were put on last year and shows are regularly taken to the Fringe. *Hai-ya!*
CLUBBING/MUSIC Fizz (themed, Sat) goes down well, as do hiphop, R'n'B and Bhangra nights. The e1 in its nightclub guise hosts the likes of Dreem Team, DJ Luck and Morcheeba.
COMEDY/CABARET Top mirth merchants peddle their donkeys once a month at e1.
FOOD The refectory spreads over three floors, *quality and value are pretty good.* Bar Med and Global Village have lunch menus. Infusion in the SU does coffees and pastries. For general groceries there's the village shop in the Student Village.
OTHER Beer festivals, annual Valentine's Ball and a gallery in the College with local artists' work.

SOCIAL ○○○○○○○○○○○○

QUEEN MARY STUDENTS' UNION
- **5 SABBATICALS** ○ **TURNOUT AT LAST BALLOT** 10%
- **NUS MEMBER**

The SU does well on the ents front with more time channelled into these than political causes. Big picture campaigns don't do so well as ones with immediate relevance to QM students. The SU has been working more closely with the University bigwigs of late, but that's not to say that they see eye to eye.

SU FACILITIES
Five bars; two eateries; two retail outlets; pool tables; meeting room; minibus; car hire; insurance; bank; ATMs; photocopier; fax; printing; photobooth; payphone; advice; TV lounge; juke box; vending machines; bookshops.

CLUBS (NON SPORTING)

Bengali; Business; Chinese; Cocktail; Creative Arts Film; Cypriot; Muslim Women's Cultural; Economics; Engineering; Every Nation Christian; Faldo Sociey (clubbing); Friends of Palestine; Hellenic; Hindu; Hispanic; Krishna Consciousness; Law; Malaysian; Music; Now! Music (live music); Oriental; Persian; PSI Star (Physics & Science); Queer Mary (LGBT); Salsa; Sikh; Singapore; Somali; SPUE (Society for the Promotion of Universal Ethics); Sri Lankan; Technical (Engineering & Electronics); Theatre Company; Wine Appreciation; World Revival (debate). **See also Clubs tables.**

OTHER ORGANISATIONS

'CUB' and 'MaD' are the monthly student papers. The community action group is the biggest in London and Rag is huge at Bart's.

RELIGIOUS

○ 3 CHAPLAINS
Muslim prayer rooms available.

PAID WORK see University of London

○ JOB BUREAU ○ PAID WORK TERM-TIME 35% **HOLS** 50%
QMSU and the College run job shops advertising opportunities for students. There's a part-time work website, notice boards and workshops. Lots of opportunity to make cash within the SU.

SPORTS ○○○○○○○○○○○○○○

○ BUSA RANKING 79
Sport, like entertainment, acts as a uniting force for QM's disparate colleges and someone's generally being successful at something (for an inner-city institution at any rate), though exactly what varies from year to year.

SPORTS FACILITIES

Football, rugby, (two) cricket, all-weather and hockey pitches; four tennis, two squash, two basketball and two netball courts; gym; climbing wall; sports hall; multigym; sauna; river.

SPORTING CLUBS

Aikido; Boat; Boxing; Croquet; Ju-Jitsu; Mary Angels (cheerleading); Women's Football; Women's Rugby; Wu Shu Kwan. **See also Clubs tables.**

ATTRACTIONS see University of London

West Ham and Leyton Orient are the local football sides and there's a dog track, an indoor climbing wall and an ice rink.

ACCOMMODATION ○○○○○○○○○

IN UNIVERSITY

○ SELF-CATERING 27% **○ COST** £92 (38WKS)
○ 1ST YRS LIVING IN 35% **○ FINALISTS LIVING IN** 25%

○ POSTGRADS LIVING IN 33%
○ INSURANCE PREMIUM £££
AVAILABILITY The College's own accommodation has around 2,115 self-catered places. Another 220 find a roof in the University's inter-collegiate halls. That covers most of the first years that want housing, but one in ten have to look elsewhere. The new student village at Mile End *scrubs up well with a view of Regent's Canal. It's expensive, even for London (some rents can be as much as £107 a week).*
CAR PARKING Students can't park on campus before 4pm.

EXTERNALLY see University of London
○ AVERAGE RENT £90 **○ LIVING AT HOME** 56%
AVAILABILITY It's fairly easy to get hold of accommodation in the local area (Mile End), and affordable stuff is out there. *The East End is fun but quality can be variable and not all parts are safe.*
HOUSING HELP The College accommodation office has approved landlord and vacancy lists, property vetting and local papers for perusal.

WELFARE ○○○○○○○○○○○○○

SERVICES

○ LGBT OFFICER ○ WOMEN'S OFFICER
○ MATURE STUDENTS' OFFICER ○ INTERNATIONAL STUDENTS' OFFICER ○ ETHNIC MINORITIES OFFICER
○ POSTGRAD OFFICER ○ LATE-NIGHT/WOMEN'S MINIBUS
○ NIGHTLINE ○ UNIVERSITY COUNSELLORS 1 FULL/5 PART
○ CRIME RATING !!!!!
The SU runs the Matthew Spencer Support Centre, but when Matthew Spencer doesn't need support it looks after students. There is a welfare suite, counsellors, welfare officers, a health centre with two doctors, a senior nurse and a visiting psychiatrist. All of the different groups, LGBT, women's and so on, regularly meet and arrange support groups and advice within their remits.
DISABILITIES *Access in College accommodation is okay but is variable in other buildings.* There's a part-time dyslexia support worker and induction loops in all lecture halls.

FINANCE

○ AVE DEBT PER YEAR £1,715
○ HOME STUDENT FEES £3,000
○ ACCESS FUND £354,000 **○ SUCCESSFUL APPLICATIONS/YR** 519 **○ AVERAGE PAYMENT** £795
SUPPORT Undergraduate bursaries of £1,500 per annum for a lucky few. Plans for more handouts are in the pipeline.

Words in italics are Push's point of view — take it or leave it...

⟐ **QUEEN MARY & WESTFIELD COLLEGE**
see *Queen Mary, University of London*

⟐ **QUEEN'S COLLEGE, GLASGOW**
see *Glasgow Caledonian University*

QUEEN'S UNIVERSITY BELFAST

1) ❍ **QUEEN'S UNIVERSITY BELFAST**, University Road, Belfast, BT7 1NN **TEL** (028) 9024 5133 **E–MAIL** admissions@qub.ac.uk
WEBSITE www.qub.ac.uk ❍ **QUEEN'S UNIVERSITY BELFAST STUDENTS' UNION**, University Road, Belfast, BT7 1NF
TEL (028) 9097 3106 **WEBSITE** www.qubsu.org

GENERAL ◗◗◗◗◗◗◗◗◗◗◗◗◗◗

On the River Lagan, where the Lough (the bay) opens out into the Irish Sea, lies the largest city in Northern Ireland. The Queen of Queen's University was the *unamused* Victoria – the *tasteful* University buildings date mostly from her time. The University has taken over much of the prosperous surrounding Belfast suburb, so that the houses of the nearby Victorian terraces are more likely to contain one of the University's facilities (or schools) than any Victorians. Given the surrounding greenery – many parks and the nearby botanical gardens – it can be hard to believe that Belfast City Centre is only 800 metres away and the Shankill and Falls Roads 800 metres beyond that. The University's currently on a shopping spree *that would put Coleen McLoughlin to shame* – altogether £200m is being splurged on re-developing accommodation, the SU, sports facilities and the Health Sciences and Physical Sciences buildings, plus *whacking* up a brand new library.

🚶🚶🚶🚶🚶🚶🚶🚶🚶🚶🚶🚶🚶🚶🚶🚶🚶🚶🚶🚶

SEX RATIO: ♂42 ♀58	**FOUNDED:** 1845
FULL–TIME U'GRADS: 12,756	**PART–TIME:** 1,387
POSTGRADS: 4,174	**NON–DEGREE:** 5,855
AVE COURSE: 3YRS	**ETHNIC:** 2%
STATE:PRIVATE SCHOOL: 99:1	**FLUNK RATE:** 13%
MATURE: 9%	**INTERNATIONAL:** 6%
DISABLED: 314	**LOCAL:** 88%

ATMOSPHERE
Most students are down to earth with a broad range of social backgrounds (though lots are local and some Northern Ireland state schools are a bit public-like). Belfast is a politically and socially active university, with plenty of entertainment and close to town centre so there's no oppressive small campus feeling. Relations with locals are very good, especially with local businesses, and the University has just taken on a Community Relations Officer to make sure things stay sweet. The University is largely untouched by the ever-changing Northern Ireland situation, apart from vigorous debate. The worst of the troubles has passed it by, especially since it's in a

prosperous suburb of South Belfast, away from the profoundly sectarian parts, so most of the tension on campus is reserved for essays and exams. The rest is reserved for being rude about University of Ulster, and hardcore drinking.

BELFAST
❍ **POPULATION** 350,000 ❍ **CITY CENTRE** 1,200 METRES
❍ **LONDON** 364 MILES ❍ **DUBLIN** 105 MILES
❍ **DERRY** 75 MILES
❍ **HIGH TEMP** 18 ❍ **LOW TEMP** 2 ❍ **RAINFALL** 71
The first impression of Belfast is of a collection of *earthy* Victorian civic buildings and a *monstrously* modern shopping centre. The city is *blossoming* under recent investment, making it quite a happening place, with more tourists than ever. Lying in an *attractive* bay ringed by mountains, when the rain clears *(once or twice a year)* it's possible to enjoy the city's gifts of shopping malls, supermarkets, bookshops, museums, all served up with a *ruthless, tourist-trapping portion of blarney. The debris of the troubles, like murals and protection rackets, lingers on but the locals are a friendly bunch and Belfast is fun-on-a-stick with pubs and clubs doing a roaring trade.*

TRAVEL
TRAINS All of Ireland's main cities and towns, north and south, are just a train journey away, including Derry (from £14 return) and Coleraine (£13.50). A *nippy* train service, the Enterprise (boldly going where it went yesterday), does Dublin from £25.
COACHES Translink serves most destinations in Northern Ireland and the Republic, but a direct coach from Britain is difficult to catch (what with the Irish Sea and all). National Express runs a service to London (£56).
CAR *The centre of Belfast's a pain for driving in, though parking's easy enough.*
AIR Regular flights from all over Britain and Europe go to Belfast. Competition between budget airlines have reduced the costs of flights to Belfast and prices vary.
FERRIES Services to Stranraer, Holyhead and Liverpool, and a fast Sea Cat service.
HITCHING *Better than most places in the UK, especially heading south or west, but not to the ports or airport.*
LOCAL Frequent buses provide a ten minute

journey into the city centre for around 50p. Translink discount cards (£7) get cheaper train and bus travel and season tickets are available. **TAXIS** Loads of the buggers, minimum fare £2.50. **BICYCLES** *Theft's not a problem, the rain is.*

CAREER PROSPECTS
- **CAREERS SERVICE** ● **NO. OF STAFF** 12 FULL
- **UNEMPLOYED AFTER 6MTHS** 5%

A mixture of full-time staff and student assistants offer advice, services and work placements.

FAMOUS ALUMNI
John Alderdice (former Alliance Party leader); Simon Callow, Liam Neeson, Stephen Rea (actors); Seamus Heaney (Nobel prize-winning poet); Lord Hutton; Patrick Kielty (comedian); Mary McAleese (President of Rep. of Ireland); Ian Paisley Jnr, David Trimble (politicians); Nick Ross (TV presenter); Dawson Stelfox (mountaineer).

FURTHER INFO
- **PROSPECTUSES** UNDERGRAD; POSTGRAD; DEPARTMENTAL
- **OPEN DAYS**

ACADEMIC ◑◑◑◑◑◑◑◑◑◑◑◑◑

Excellent research record especially in science and humanities with several international research centres and great opportunities to stay on and get involved. Good links to industry means help in getting a placement especially in science subjects. Learning is structured with an emphasis on teaching, especially tutorials, lectures and seminars, with some aided application and laboratory work. Students normally have to pass six modules to make it onto the next year of the course and assessment is usually a combination continuous assessment and final exams. No rest for the wicked, eh?

ENTRY POINTS: 200–420	**AVE POINTS: 355**
APPLICATIONS PER PLACE: 7	**CLEARING: 3%**
NO. OF TERMS: 2	**LENGTH OF TERMS: 15 WKS**
STAFF TO STUDENT RATIO: 1:16	**STUDY ADDICTS: 27**
TEACHING: ****	**RESEARCH:** ****
1STS: 16 %	**2.2S: 27 %**
2.1S: 53%	**3RDS: 4 %**

ADMISSIONS
- **APPLY VIA UCAS**

SUBJECTS
BIOLOGICAL SCIENCES 5%   **BIOMEDICAL SCIENCE** 2% **CHEMISTRY & CHEMICAL ENGINEERING** 2% **ELECTRONICS, ELECTRICAL ENGINEERING & COMPUTER SCIENCE** 8%   **ENGLISH** 5% **GEOGRAPHY, ARCHAEOLOGY & PALAEOECOLOGY** 5%   **HISTORY & ANTHROPOLOGY** 5% **LANGUAGES, LITERATURES & ARTS** 5%   **LAW** 6% **MANAGEMENT & ECONOMICS** 7% **MATHEMATICS & PHYSICS** 4%   **MECHANICAL & AEROSPACE ENGINEERING** 4%   **MEDICINE & DENTISTRY** 7%   **MUSIC & SONIC ARTS** 2%   **NURSING &**

MIDWIFERY 11% **PHARMACY** 3%   **PLANNING, ARCHITECTURE & CIVIL ENGINEERING** 6%   **POLITICS & PHILOSOPHY** 3% **PSYCHOLOGY** 4%   **SOCIOLOGY, SOCIAL POLICY & SOCIAL WORK** 5%   **THEOLOGY** 1%

LIBRARIES
- **1,200,000** BOOKS ● **2,530** STUDY PLACES
- **24-HR ACCESS** ● **SPEND PER STUDENT** ££££

Despite five libraries and vast quantities of books, students get a little narky about limited book availability. 24-hr access during exam time. A £44m library is slated for 2009.

COMPUTERS
- **1,003** WORKSTATIONS ● **24-HR ACCESS**
- **SPEND PER STUDENT** £££

Lots of computers. *Printing's a bit of a lottery and 24-hr access is again just during exam time,* otherwise it's 9-11. *A toe is being dabbled into shiny new waters of e-learning.*

ENTERTAINMENT ◑◑◑◑◑◑◑◑◑◑

THE CITY
- **PRICE OF A PINT OF BEER** £2.30
- **GLASS OF WINE** £1.80 ● **CAN OF RED BULL** £1

Most Belfast nightlife happens in the Golden Mile that stretches from Queen's to the city centre. *What with the students, the tourist industry and the, frankly silly, amounts of money pumped into Belfast nightlife since the 90s, it's pretty good.* **CINEMAS** *The UGC and the Movie House show the Hollywood fodder where Tom Cruise simply never dies, while the Queen's Film Theatre shows those films where everyone dies, in Czech with subtitles.* **THEATRES** *You can't throw a stone without it hitting a theatre, and bouncing off another one. There's* seven in all, including the Waterfront, the Lyric Theatre and the *legendary* Belfast Grand Opera House, and visits from touring companies like the Royal Shakespeare or An Culturlann, an innovative Irish language company. **PUBS** *Stout strong enough to stand pencils in, drunken blarney-merchants called Jon arguing with strangers about military tactics, chrome-plated trend pits with a lifespan of three days, Belfast has a pub for all tastes (and some with no taste). Pushplugs: Botanic; Pott House (glass floors) Kelly Cellars (traditional). The main gay venue is the Crow's Nest.* **CLUBBING** *Belfast's developing quite a reputation as a clubber's paradise. Stiff Kitten and the Coach in Banbridge get big(ish) names. Pushplugs: Limelight (indie, retro, jazz nights); The Brunswick (soul and hardcore, four separate floors); Network Club (dance/hiphop); M Club (student nights); Thompson's Garage (house); the New Storm.* **MUSIC/COMEDY** Ulster Hall for big names, Empire Music Hall for medium-sized and comedy nights, Waterfront Hall for pretty much anything and *innumerable small-scale gigs anywhere they can find space – most pubs and bars lay on tunes of some description.* **EATING OUT** *A strong café culture and top notch*

Chinese. Lisburn Road, close to the campus, has a lot of decent cafés, patisseries and Chinese and Indian takeaways. An Culturlann (Falls Road) is *the place for traditional Irish fare. Pushplugs: Bishops (chippie); Speranza's (pizzas, a student institution); the Other Place (bring your own booze); Oasis (cheap); the Mad Hatter; Which Sandwich; many of the pubs do nice nosh too.*

UNIVERSITY
- **PRICE OF A PINT OF BEER** £2.20
- **GLASS OF WINE** £2.30
- **CAN OF RED BULL** £1.80

Wine, women and song are the name of the day along with men and lashings of beer.
BARS Four SU drinking holes, including the *clubtastic* Mandela Hall and smaller venues with pub quizzes and DJs. The Bunatee Bar (cap. 300) and the Speakeasy (550) are packed by 7pm.
FILM/THEATRE There's a Drama & Film Centre. The University has its own cinema, which hosts regular film festivals and the annual Belfast Film Festival Season. The weekly movie club shows just what it says on the tin.
MUSIC VENUES Deftones, Ordinary Boys, Editors and Graham Coxon have all recently performed in Belfast's 1,400 capacity music venue, Mandela Hall.
CLUBBING Mandela Hall, *with a sound system to go deaf for,* stomps to a bunch of different beats on most nights of the week, one of the best being Shine (Saturday) which attracts guest DJs and big acts like moths.
COMEDY/CABARET National Comedy Network shows, fortnightly.
FOOD Nine cafés and restaurants on campus do daytime grub. *Chapters café is the cheapest. There's a new(ish) food court and the Speakeasy is as cheap as chips but has about as much range as a dead archer. The Beech Room and the Cloisters also whore their culinary abilities.*
OTHER *Queen's students like their balls and there are up to seven a year, including Freshers', Rag and St Paddy's. Most facilities have some kind of formal too. The Annual Belfast Festival held at Queen's is up there with Edinburgh, with ballet, theatre, comedy and pretty much anything that might conceivably be entertaining chucked on stage.*

If you have any comments about Push, or fancy being involved in the next edition, drop us a line: editor@push.co.uk

QUEEN'S UNIVERSITY BELFAST STUDENTS' UNION
- **5 SABBATICALS** **TURNOUT AT LAST BALLOT** 7%
- **NUS MEMBER**

Most strands of political thought are tangled up in the machinations of the SU. The majority, of course, just regard the SU as a convenient source of booze and opportunities to get laid. The Union is housed in a 60s monstrosity, which is in the process of getting a £9m facelift, luckily.

SU FACILITIES
Bars; canteens; advice centre; Bank of Ireland bank/ATM; launderette; showers; supermarket; writing room; secondhand bookshops; sports shop; insurance office; travel centre; computer shop; hairdresser; snooker room; games room; vending and games machines; photocopier; function rooms; photo booth; crèche; women's room; shop; payphones; jukebox; printing.

CLUBS (NON SPORTING)
Anthropology; Archaeology; Chemical Engineering; English; Ethnommusicology; History; Queens Radio; Dragonslayers (gaming); Student Community Action; South Asisan Students; Singapore students. **See also Clubs tables.**

OTHER ORGANISATIONS
'Gown' and 'the Craic' are the student newspapers. Rag is *particularly effective* and the Community Workshop does its things for local relations.

RELIGIOUS
- **4 CHAPLAINS**

Four assigned chaplaincy centres covering 14 different flavours of faith with even a church for deaf people. Belfast fills in the blanks.

PAID WORK
- **JOB BUREAU**

250 bar jobs provided by the University every year. Plenty of part-time work available in town. 12 week work placements are a part of many courses and the careers service can also set students up with companies for part-time work, work experience, a year out, etc.

- **BUSA RANKING** 71

Rugby, soccer and hockey are all pretty strong in both men and women's varieties and *sport in general is a popular pastime.* Facilities are *extensive* and students who make the University look good at anything are awarded Blues (which is like being capped), like at Oxbridge colleges.

Words in italics are Push's point of view — take it or leave it...

SPORTS FACILITIES

100 acres of sports fields, 13 football/rugby, two hockey, one cricket and two all-weather pitches; ten squash, two handball, one tennis and four basketball courts; two sports halls; two netball courts; athletics track; 25m swimming pool; martial arts area. There's a £7m plan to improve the facilities with two studios, a gym, a climbing wall and specialist coaching stuff on the way.

SPORTING CLUBS

Aikido; Camogie (traditional Irish); Caving; Cricket; Ladies' Gaelic Football; Harriers; Hurling (Irish sport); Ju-Jitsu; Men's Boat; Motor; Mountaineering; Parachute; Riding; Seiokan Karate; Ladies' Soccer; Squash; Surf; Tae Kwon Do. **See also Clubs tables**.

ATTRACTIONS

The local ice hockey team is the Belfast Giants. Rugby team Ulster play in local Ravenhill. Northern Ireland play in Windsor Park which is also local, not to mention various Gaelic teams and football teams, like Glentoran and Linfield.

ACCOMMODATION ◡◡◡◡◡◡◡◡◡

IN UNIVERSITY
- **SELF-CATERING** 15% ○ **COST** £65 (39/50WKS)
- **INSURANCE PREMIUM** £

AVAILABILITY The University are in the process of replacing their accommodation – old-school ten-storey halls about 800m from campus – with a £45m student village (1,727 en suite places). *Swanky, eh?*

CAR PARKING Plentiful but costly.

EXTERNALLY
- **AVE RENT** £45 ○ **LIVING AT HOME** 45%

AVAILABILITY Many students are locals. Those who start searching in early summer shouldn't have problems, last-minuters might have difficulties. The Holyland area (Jerusalem Street, Palestine Street, etc.) is the *most popular as it's cheap* and close to the University, the Union, the Golden Mile and the gym. *Also popular are Stranmillis, Malone Road and Lisburn Road. Ormeau Road used to be dodgy but is improving – and is dirt cheap.*

HOUSING HELP Several housing associations look after the students, as do the Union welfare office and the University accommodation office.

WELFARE ◡◡◡◡◡◡◡◡◡◡◡◡

SERVICES
- **WOMEN'S OFFICER** ○ **MATURE STUDENTS' SOCIETY**
- **INTERNATIONAL STUDENTS' SOCIETY**
- **POSTGRAD SOCIETY** ○ **LATE-NIGHT/WOMEN'S MINIBUS**
- **SELF-DEFENCE CLASSES** ○ **NIGHTLINE** ○ **TAXI FUND**
- **UNIVERSITY COUNSELLORS** 1 FULL/1 PART
- **CRIME RATING** !!!

The Union's small counselling service meets most needs for troubled souls, while troubled bodies are mended by the Health Centre. The legally troubled can see a solicitor who visits four times a week.

HEALTH Free NHS treatment in the clinics including regular check-ups. There's a sports injury clinic for those needing the deep heat treatment.

WOMEN Rape alarms from the SU welfare service. Also a free-phone taxi service, self-defence classes and 'Shrewd' magazine.

CRECHES/NURSERY 48-wk crèche with 84 places.

DISABILITIES Lots of large, old 60s-style buildings but all with lifts. The University is spread throughout 250 buildings in the Belfast area so it can take a while to get around. All have ramps, lifts, specialist books, accommodation and audio equipment. Deaf students are particularly well cared for by Joint Universities Deaf Education (JUDE).

DRUGS *Apart from the standard dangers, the drugs trade has paramilitary connections, so tread carefully.*

FINANCE
- **AVE DEBT PER YEAR** £3,523 ○ **HOME STUDENT FEES** £3,000
- **ACCESS FUND** £900,000
- **SUCCESSFUL APPLICATIONS/YR** 900
- **AVE PAYMENT** £500-3,500

SUPPORT Various scholarships including the Guinness sports bursaries and bursaries for students from poorer families.

Words in italics are Push's point of view – take it or leave it...

UNIVERSITY OF READING

▶ **RICHMOND**
see _Roehampton University_

ROBERT GORDON UNIVERSITY

▶ **ROBERT GORDON INSTITUTE OF TECHNOLOGY**
see _Robert Gordon University_

▶ **ROEHAMPTON INSTITUTE OF HIGHER EDUCATION**
see _Roehampton University_

ROEHAMPTON UNIVERSITY

ROYAL ACADEMY OF MUSIC

ROYAL AGRICULTURAL COLLEGE

ROYAL COLLEGE OF MUSIC

▶ **ROYAL HOLLOWAY AND BEDFORD COLLEGE**
see _Royal Holloway, University of London_

ROYAL HOLLOWAY, LONDON

▶ **ROYAL POSTGRAD MEDICAL SCHOOL**
see _Imperial College, London_

ROYAL SCOTTISH ACADEMY OF MUSIC AND DRAMA

ROYAL VETERINARY COLLEGE, LONDON

R

UNIVERSITY OF READING

1. ○ **UNIVERSITY OF READING** Whiteknights, PO Box 217, Reading, RG6 6AH **TEL** (0118) 378 6586
E-MAIL student.recruitment@reading.ac.uk **WEBSITE** www.reading.ac.uk ○ **READING UNIVERSITY STUDENTS' UNION** Whiteknights, University of Reading, PO Box 230, Reading, RG6 6AZ **TEL** (0118) 986 0222 **E-MAIL** president@rusu.co.uk
WEBSITE www.rusu.co.uk
2. . ○ **BULMERSHE CAMPUS** Bulmershe Court, Early, Reading, RG6 1HY **TEL** (0118) 987 5123 ○ **READING UNIVERSITY STUDENTS'**
UNION address as campus **TEL** (0118) 378 8693

GENERAL ○○○○○○○○○○○○○

Reading is commuter-belt country and *suspiciously close to Staines. It's not the most inspiring part of Britain*, although some of the *ultra-wealthy* Thames-side commuter villages in the area are *gently pretty*. The University is based on the large Whiteknights campus, under two miles from the town centre and set in 320 acres of parkland, lake and wood. The buildings vary from Victorian to very modern, *all managing to be ugly in their own little way*. The second campus about two miles away at Bulmershe, where about 2,000 other students are holed up, *feels a million miles away*. There are plans to unite both sites on the main campus, *but they're far off yet. A bit like Bulmershe itself.*

SEX RATIO: ♂46 ♀54	**FOUNDED:** 1892
FULL-TIME U'GRADS: 11,198	**PART-TIME:** 2,911
POSTGRADS: 6,320	**NON-DEGREE:** 5,000
AVE COURSE: 3-4YRS	**ETHNIC:** 10%
STATE:PRIVATE SCHOOL: 83:17	**FLUNK RATE:** 10%
MATURE: 19%	**INTERNATIONAL:** 16%
DISABLED: 285	**LOCAL:** 20%

ATMOSPHERE

Whiteknights is a cosy campus given a sense of *friendly community* by the *large* number who live there. The atmosphere is *middle-class and middle-England*, although there are *more than enough exceptions to test the rule, especially from visiting Erasmus students*. Sport's *high on the agenda, possibly because most students are in training to high-tail it at the weekend* – the student body's predominantly southern and Reading's well-placed for popping home for Sunday lunch. Campus life is a little isolated from town but students don't seem too bothered. The University is pumping several squillions into new developments, but the real cost has seen several departments (*Music, Sociology) going the way of the Dodo.*

SITES

BULMERSHE CAMPUS 2,000 students – Institute of Education, School of Health & Social Care, Film Theatre & TV

READING

○ **POPULATION** 143,200 ○ **HIGH TEMP** 22 ○ **LOW TEMP** 1
○ **CITY CENTRE** 1.5 MILES ○ **LONDON** 40 MILES ○ **OXFORD** 25 MILES ○ **BRISTOL** 74 MILES ○ **RAINFALL** 48

Supposedly the statue of Queen Victoria on the edge of the city centre points away from the town because her highness disliked the place that much. Still, although it's dominated by office blocks and *doesn't have beauty on its side*, Reading has a *good* shopping centre and a *vast array* of supermarkets, bookshops, restaurants, bars and a cinema. The modernised city centre has quaint touches, the river and smaller arcades, but the outer edges are increasingly *neglected mostly 'cause the mammoth Oracle shopping mall in the centre acts like a great big money sucker.*

TRAVEL

TRAINS The station is about 1.5 miles from the main campus. Trains go direct to London Paddington (£12.60 rtn), Oxford (£11.55) and *pretty much anywhere* to the west.
COACHES National Express lead their magical mystery (*guess how late the bus will arrive*) tours all over the UK.
CAR M4/A4 for London and M1 via the M25/M40. *Parking in town can be tricky.*
AIR Heathrow is 45 mins by coach.
LOCAL Buses connect town to campus, £1.30 each way.
UNIVERSITY The SU runs a free night bus service to the halls every day during term time (except Sundays) until 15 mins after the last bar on campus closes. There's also a (free) shuttle bus that connects the Bulmershe campus to the central hub.
TAXIS Campus to town costs £5-6.
BICYCLES *Reading is as flat as a starched and ironed pancake – perfect for pedal power.*

CAREER PROSPECTS

○ **CAREERS SERVICE** ○ **NO. OF STAFF** 18 FULL/2 PART ○ **UNEMPLOYED AFTER 6 MTHS** 5%

FAMOUS ALUMNI

James Cracknell (Olympic rower); Jamie Cullum (*warbling* jazz pixie); Nigel de Gruchy (general secretary, ASUWT); Glynn Ford MEP (Lab); Richard Sambrook (Director of the BBC World Service); Gustav Holst (composer) lectured here; Sir Steve Redgrave (rower) holds an honorary degree.

FURTHER INFO

○ **PROSPECTUSES** UNDERGRAD; POSTGRAD; DEPARTMENTAL
○ **OPEN DAYS**
A handbook for students with special needs is available. This and more from www.rdg.ac.uk

Words in italics are Push's point of view — take it or leave it...

ACADEMIC ◯◯◯◯◯◯◯◯◯◯◯◯◯

● 1994 GROUP

A flexible first-year course with the option to take modules from other faculties, but it's *demanding* and capped by *tough* exams. After that *bitter pill* there's the *honey-sweet knowledge* that there's no crossing swords with another exam paper until finals. A *strong coursework* element should keep you busy in the meantime.

ENTRY POINTS: 160–340	AVE POINTS: 362
APPLICATIONS PER PLACE: 11	CLEARING: 1%
NO. OF TERMS: 3	LENGTH OF TERMS: 10WKS
STAFF TO STUDENT RATIO: 1:6	STUDY ADDICTS: 16%
TEACHING: ★★★★	RESEARCH: ★★★

ADMISSIONS
● APPLY VIA UCAS

SUBJECTS
ARTS/HUMANITIES 41%   LIFE SCIENCES 12%
ECONOMIC & SOCIAL SCIENCES 19%   SCIENCES 28%
BEST Archaeology; Art & Design; Biology; English; Environmental Sciences; Geography; History; Languages; Law; Management; Philosophy; Psychology.
UNUSUAL Cybernetics; International Securities; Investment & Banking.

LIBRARIES
● 1,000,000 BOOKS ● 400 STUDY PLACES
● 24-HR ACCESS
Main library is at Whiteknights. Bulmershe and other faculties have their own smaller libraries.

COMPUTERS
● 600 WORKSTATIONS

OTHER LEARNING FACILITIES
Three museums attached to the University – zoology, archaeology and the Museum of English Rural Life. All students can dabble in foreign tongues if they wish. The International Capital Market Association, unique in Europe, *lets budding brokers indulge their stocks and shares fantasies*.

ENTERTAINMENT ◯◯◯◯◯◯◯◯◯

THE TOWN
● PRICE OF A PINT OF BEER £2.20
● GLASS OF WINE £2.50
● CAN OF RED BULL £2.20
CINEMAS *More screens than a film buff could poke an overpriced hot dog at*, courtesy of two multiplexes.
THEATRES The Hexagon stages *high-profile mainstream stuff*, including snooker and ballet. Alternative drama at the Progress Theatre.

PUBS Commuters have brought London prices with them. Boozing costs and not all of the town's pubs are happy to rub shoulders with students. Pushplugs: Upin Arms; Wetherspoons; the Hope Tap; Pavlov's Dog; the Lyndhurst (not as studenty but homey and good ale selection); the College Arms; the Purple Turtle.
CLUBBING *Provincial clubs mean bad sound rigs and sticky carpets.* 'After Dark' *is a well-kept secret (...not anymore)*, off the beaten track and playing everything from 70s and 80s to underground dance.
MUSIC VENUES *Reading's August festival has long been (after Glasto) the highlight of the summer. Fez club host good but not-quite-there yet artists.* The Hexagon theatre is home to bigger names (Craig David, Goldfrapp, Morrissey). Rivermead Centre also has some noteworthy gigs (Sugababes). South Street's also worth a mention with a heady mix of folk and world music on the agenda.
COMEDY Jongleurs and South Street *are both worth a chuckle.*
EATING OUT Chain restaurants *by the stack*, with a few grub-pubs to make up numbers. *Escape the Oracle shopping mecca to find those of more interest.* Pushplugs: Blue Ginger (Indian – *check out the Sunday £6 buffet*); Café Iguana (veggie); Global Café (hippy); Art of Siam (Thai).

UNIVERSITY
● PRICE OF A PINT OF BEER £1.80
● GLASS OF WINE £1.50
● CAN OF RED BULL £2
BARS Mojo's is the *main* joint, sports themed with a late licence and a double-life as a small band venue. Shows Neighbours on a lunchtime. The *centre of social gravity* at Bulmershe is Legends Bar.
THEATRES The thesp scene churns out an array of plays, mainly Shakespeare and musicals – *they're not too keen on anything too heavy*. Wolfgang Van Emden Theatre is home to the drama soc.
FILM A private film company shows three or four films a week *to all and sundry* in one of the lecture theatres, *usually on the indie side of mainstream* (eg. Corpse Bride, A History of Violence, Broken Flowers).

R

The original site of Reading University was the backyard of the Huntley and Palmer biscuit factory.

Words in italics are Push's point of view – take it or leave it...

MUSIC VENUES 3Sixty's the main University club and pulls some *big* names. Recent visitors include Goldie Lookin' Chain, Athlete and the *lesser-spotted* Minogue (Dannii). Mojo's also does free live music and drinks offers on Mondays – the highlights are repeated on radio on Sundays.

CLUBBING NUS has rated 3Sixty one of the best student clubs in the land for its *sleek modern design and lively atmosphere*. It crams in almost 2,000 punters at a time for three *big* club nights a week.

COMEDY/CABARET Comedy/open mic night on alternative Tuesdays at Mojo's, too.

FOOD There are six tucker huts on campus, including those serving food hot (Mojo's Munchies) on the hop (Mondial coffee and pastries), and destined for the hips (Mojo's *reasonably-priced, all-day pub grub*). University-owned Cedar Food Court, next to the Union, does *all kinds, cheaply.*

OTHER Three balls a year: Freshers, Grand Summer (last year featuring Rolf '*digeridoo*' Harris) and the Sport Federation's.

SOCIAL ⦿⦿⦿⦿⦿⦿⦿⦿⦿⦿⦿⦿

READING UNIVERSITY STUDENTS' UNION (RUSU)
⦿ **6 SABBATICALS** ⦿ **TURNOUT AT LAST BALLOT** 10%
⦿ **NUS MEMBER**
Top-notch facilities provide the centre of daily life. RUSU is very active, running loads of clubs and societies. The SU particularly snubs the weekend deserters with a bustling social calendar. There's a growing campaigning ethic with volunteer groups pushing lots of worthy causes. SU:Uni relations are generally toastier than thick-sliced.

SU FACILITIES
Travel shop; welfare office; three bars; purpose built club/music/comedy venue; stationery shop; bookshop; general/wholefood shop; Endsleigh Insurance office; Lloyds TSB bank and ATM; other services such as photocopying and vending machines; launderette.

CLUBS (NON-SPORTING)
Afro-Caribbean; Aiesec (Business); Anime; Armed Forces; Art; Asian; Believer's Love World; Brazilian & Portuguese; Blessed Melody Gospel Choir; Catholic; Chinese Students & Scholars Association; Circus Skills; Drama; Duke of Edinburgh; Electronic Music; Entrepreneur; ERASMUS; Fair trade; Fantasy & Horror; Games & Role-playing; Go Green campaign; Guides and Scouts; Hellenic; Indie; Literature & Journalism; Millennium Volunteers; Motorbike; Photographic; Poker; Reading LAN (online community); Rock; Sci-Fi; Spanish & Latin American; SPEAK (Christian focus); St John's Ambulance; Student Bands & Live Music; Student Stop AIDs Society; Thai; Vegetarian & Vegan; Writers; Young Greens. *See also Clubs tables.*

OTHER ORGANISATIONS
Weekly student paper 'Spark' is *trumped* by the award-winning radio station 'Junction 11'. Rag is *very busy* and holds an annual fundraising week. Push *is loving* the MASIV (Modular Accreditation for Students Involved in Volunteering), which lets students count community volunteering as degree credits.

RELIGIOUS
Chaplaincy centres and prayer rooms for Christians and Muslims. Prayer places in town for Muslims, Hindus, Sikhs, Jews.

PAID WORK
⦿ **JOB BUREAU**
Jobshop advertises vacancies of no more than 16 hours a week – *study comes first, children*. Local work in bars, restaurants and shops is easy to come by during term, *nigh-on impossible outside it*.

SPORTS ⦿⦿⦿⦿⦿⦿⦿⦿⦿⦿⦿⦿⦿

⦿ **RECENT SUCCESSES** JITSU, ROWING AND CHEERLEADING, RAH, RAH, RAH ⦿ **BUSA RANKING** 31
There are *plenty* of places to work up a sweat and this patch of the Thames is excellent for canoeing and rowing, but *many find the University's priority to elite sports and Sir Redgrave's honorary degree more irritating than a sweaty jock-strap*. £2m is being channelled into a *ginormous* sports centre on the Wolfenden site, which should meet the needs of a *highly sporty* student body. Bulmershe residents make use of discounted local facilities.

SPORTS FACILITIES
Wolfenden Sports Centre currently has badminton, archery, basketball, cricket, fencing, five-a-side football, hockey, martial arts, netball, table tennis, trampolines, tennis courts, gym and a brand new Astroturf pitch. There's also a squash centre, gym and weights room at Bulmershe. Outdoors: athletics pavilion; playing fields for cricket, football and rugby; an all-weather surface and running track. The town adds numerous swimming pools and rowing and sailing on the river.

SPORTING CLUBS
Aikido; American Football; Boat Club; Break Dance; Caving; Cheerleaders; Clay Pigeon; Dance; Floorball; Inline Hockey; Ju-Jitsu; Kick Boxing; Kung Fu; Polo; Surf; Ultimate Frisbee. **See also Clubs tables.**

ATTRACTIONS
Reading's *not a football-loopy town*, but the FC's doing better than okay. If you're feeling flush, the local racing (in boats at Henley Regatta and on nags at Ascot, Windsor and Newbury) is *first rate*. Madjeski stadium is accessible to students, *when London Irish aren't throwing their premiership balls around, and not too intimidating either.*

Words in italics are Push's point of view — take it or leave it...

ACCOMMODATION ()()()()()()()()()

IN UNIVERSITY
- **CATERED** 17% - **COST** £116 (30/31WKS)
- **SELF-CATERING** 23% - **COST** £95 (30/51WKS)
- **1ST YRS LIVING IN** 95%
- **INSURANCE PREMIUM** £

AVAILABILITY First years applying by June (ie. not via clearing) are guaranteed University accommodation, most will be offered catered housing. Those with Reading as their first choice can take their pick of halls, most of which are within a mile of Whiteknights. Rooms are single with shared kitchens (although there are 45 flats for married couples with or without children), but many have en suite bathrooms. Standard is high but prices rival London. Around a third of finalists return to halls.

CAR PARKING A limited number of halls parking permits are available for second and third years and postgrads (£10).

EXTERNALLY
- **AVE RENT** £65

AVAILABILITY *It's no big deal to find a place to call home in town, although quality varies from luxurious to last-turkey-in-the-shop.* Wokingham Road, Addlington Road, Erleigh Road, Basingstoke Road and Southampton Road *are all kings of the castle*; Mandela Court, Prospect Park and Oxford Road *are all dirty rascals, and pretty far to boot. Given the choice, most would prefer to live-in.*

HOUSING HELP The Accommodation Office (five staff) provides online vacancy lists. Landlords are vetted by the local council. RUSU run presentations on house-hunting, and *many of the best digs are found on the RUSU notice board, handed down from previous tenants.*

WELFARE ()()()()()()()()()()()

SERVICES
- **LGBT OFFICER** - **ETHNIC MINORITIES OFFICER**
- **WOMEN'S SOCIETY** - **MATURE STUDENTS' SOCIETY**
- **INTERNATIONAL STUDENTS' SOCIETY**
- **POSTGRAD SOCIETY** - **ETHNIC STUDENTS' SOCIETY**
- **DISABILITIES SUPPORT GROUP** - **LATE-NIGHT MINIBUS**
- **NIGHTLINE** - **UNIVERSITY COUNSELLORS** 6 FULL/5 PART
- **SU COUNSELLORS** 3 FULL/1 PART - **CRIME RATING** !!!!

Advice and help from tutors or the Welfare Office. There's a full-time equal ops and ethics sabbatical officer. A £6.5m one-stop welfare shop opened on campus in 2006.

HEALTH The Health Centre has five doctors, two dentists, a physiotherapist and various nurses. Annual registration charge, but students are entitled to reduced rates for vaccinations and medical examinations.

WOMEN Women have priority on the nightbus. RUSU provide attack alarms, £3.

CRECHES/NURSERY 40 places (3mths-5yrs).

DISABILITIES: A special needs co-ordinator looks after particular requirements including notetaking, sign language, English language support and personal care. The University makes an effort to adapt buildings for access and there are dedicated rooms with disabled facilities in halls.

FINANCE
- **AVE DEBT PER YEAR** £3,100
- **HOME STUDENT FEES** £3,000

FEES International students pay between £8,500 and £10,800 a year, postgrads between £3,000-£15,000. Top-up fees have shunted down the number of applicants per place.

- **ACCESS FUND** £340,000 - **SUCCESSFUL APPLICATIONS/YR** 600 - **AVE PAYMENT** £600

SUPPORT The University doesn't actually splash its own cash, but points students in the right direction in applying for bursaries. The music department's been razed to the ground, but in its place are bursaries to allow gifted musicians to continue playing alongside their studies. Entrance bursaries in: Agriculture; Biology; Chemistry; Food Sciences; Maths; Modern Languages; Natural Sciences; Pharmacy; and Physics. Other small academic bursaries for freshers include an English book award for A Level work and three full scholarships for International Baccalaureate holders.

R

▶ RICHMOND
see *Roehampton University*

ROBERT GORDON UNIVERSITY

FORMERLY ROBERT GORDON INSTITUTE OF TECHNOLOGY

◉ ROBERT GORDON UNIVERSITY Schoolhill, Aberdeen, AB10 1FR **TEL** (01224) 262 728 **E-MAIL** admissions@rgu.ac.uk **WEBSITE** www.rgu.ac.uk **◉ ROBERT GORDON UNIVERSITY STUDENTS' UNION** 60 Schoolhill, Aberdeen, AB10 1JQ **TEL** (01224) 262 263

GENERAL ◉◉◉◉◉◉◉◉◉◉◉◉

Bonny Bobbie Gordon's been around for over 200 years, but 1992's cull of polytechnics saw it awarding university degrees for the first time. Aberdeen is dribbling with students (see University of Aberdeen) and *those from RGU mix well with all the others – just as well, perhaps, since RGU's own Students' Union building doesn't exactly deliver fun in a box. Perhaps the integration comes from the fact that RGU is based on two sites covering quite a bit of ground* across the city. The city centre campus (where few students, but the SU and University admin are based) huddles around an original 1729 site at Schoolhill. *The larger* Garthdee campus is two miles away, to the south-west of the city.

👤👤👤👤👤👤👤👤👤👤👤👤👤👤👤👤👤👤👤👤

SEX RATIO: ♂42 ♀58	**FOUNDED:** 1750
FULL-TIME U'GRADS: 6,729	**PART-TIME:** 1,742
POSTGRADS: 3,411	**NON-DEGREE:** 2,233
AVE COURSE: 4YRS	**ETHNIC:** 11%
STATE:PRIVATE SCHOOL: 94:6	**FLUNK RATE:** 17%
MATURE: 28%	**INTERNATIONAL:** 20%
DISABLED: 105	**LOCAL:** 52%

ATMOSPHERE
RGU students are a friendly, practical bunch who are clearly cut out for careers in helpful and/or useful industries like nursing, engineering and science. Many are from the area, which means that they tend to hang out in the city itself rather than the SU a lot of the time.

SITES
GARTHDEE CAMPUS (Aberdeen Business School, Gray's School of Art, the Scott Sutherland School, Faculty of Health and Social Care) *More attractive than its city centre sibling,* Garthdee's large modern buildings overlook the River Dee, surrounded by rolling parkland. *The site is less convenient, but peaceful and conducive to contemplative study.*
SCHOOLHILL CAMPUS (Schools of Engineering, Pharmacy, Life Sciences and Computing) Around a quarter of RGU's students are based here.

ABERDEEN see University of Aberdeen

TRAVEL see University of Aberdeen
UNIVERSITY A shuttle bus, well, shuttles between the Garthdee and City Centre sites every 15 mins – *if it's on time.* £3 weekly pass.

CAREER PROSPECTS
◉ CAREERS SERVICE ◉ NO. OF STAFF 6 FULL-TIME

◉ UNEMPLOYED AFTER 6 MTHS 2%
The *highly-rated* Careers Service *does a good job* of shifting students into industry (as well as part-time work in term), offers CV workshops, interview preparation, career fairs and a library.

FAMOUS ALUMNI
Ena Baxter (of the soups); Calum Innes (artist, Turner Prize nominee); Donnie Munro (Runrig singer).

FURTHER INFO
◉ PROSPECTUSES UNDEGRAD; POSTGRAD; INTERNATIONAL
◉ OPEN DAYS
Individual course brochures and an Access prospectus are also available from the admissions office.

ACADEMIC ◉◉◉◉◉◉◉◉◉◉◉◉

The University's strong in Health Sciences, Art & Design, Architecture & Engineering – especially renewable and sustainable energy (*which must go down well in a city built on oil profits*). Applied learning is the order of the day *and students enjoy knowing they're learning something useful for post-study life.*

ENTRY POINTS: 96-252	**AVE POINTS:** N/A
APPLICATIONS PER PLACE: 3	**CLEARING:** 15%
NO. OF TERMS: 3	**LENGTH OF TERMS:** 18WKS
STAFF TO STUDENT RATIO: 1:10	**STUDY ADDICTS:** N/A
TEACHING: ★★★★	**RESEARCH:** ★
YEAR ABROAD: <1%	**SANDWICH STUDENTS:** 50%
1STS: 10%	**2.2S:** 40%
2.1S: 42%	**3RDS:** 8%

ADMISSIONS
◉ APPLY VIA UCAS/CATCH FOR NURSING
Alternative qualifications include Access courses run by the University, equivalent overseas qualifications and SQA, NVQs and BTEC.

SUBJECTS
ART & DESIGN 17%   **BUSINESS/MANAGEMENT** 26%
COMPUTING 6%   **ENGINEERING** 8%
MEDICAL SCIENCES 30%   **SCIENCES** 6%
SOCIAL SCIENCES 5%

LIBRARIES
◉ 255,877 BOOKS ◉ 902 STUDY PLACES
◉ 24-HR ACCESS ◉ SPEND PER STUDENT ££
Reasonable hours and weekend opening, although *not the best friend to night-owls and early birds.*

COMPUTERS
◉ 1,600 WORKSTATIONS ◉ SPEND PER STUDENT ££

R

OTHER LEARNING FACILITIES

3-D sports motion analysis system; CAD lab; language labs; practice courtroom; X-ray suite.

ENTERTAINMENT

THE CITY see University of Aberdeen

UNIVERSITY

- **PRICE OF A PINT OF BEER** £1.70
- **GLASS OF WINE** £1.70

Students prefer the increasingly bright lights in town, although there's some cross pollination of RGU students in Aberdeen's Union, and vice versa. A £3m-refurb is on the cards, but the SU's got its poker face on about when the new facilities/bistro will open.
BARS Two bars, one a pool-playing *DJ-hut*, the other a *chilled-out, food-serving, DJ-loving, Wednesday sports fest. Both bars give away prizes like cinema tickets and travel vouchers to keep the punters coming in.*
EATING OUT The café on the first floor of the Union building does *an uninspiring* selection of cafeteria food.

SOCIAL

ROBERT GORDON UNIVERSITY STUDENTS' UNION

- **TURNOUT AT LAST BALLOT** 15% **NUS MEMBER**

SU FACILITIES

The four-floor Union building at Schoolhill has: two meeting rooms; Information Centre; ATM (Clydesdale); general store; stationery shop; vending and games machines.

CLUBS

Charities; European Exchange; GAP (Gray's Art in Places); International; Malaysian/Indian; Rogues (drama); Tunnels (entertainment). **See also Clubs tables.**

OTHER ORGANISATIONS

'Cogno' ('knowledge' in Latin) is the monthly Union tabloid. The Volunteering Co-ordinator can arrange Millennium Volunteering projects (which come with a CV-boosting certificate).

RELIGIOUS

- **2 CHAPLAINS (COFS, SCOTTISH EPISCOPAL)**

No places of worship on campus but Aberdeen has something for most religious palates – churches, chapels, mosques, synagogue and a Hindu cultural centre. See University of Aberdeen for more.
PAID WORK see University of Aberdeen
- **JOB BUREAU**

SPORTS

- **BUSA RANKING** 101

The Robert Gordon Sports Centre has *impressive* facilities, including: gym; climbing wall; swimming pool; indoor hockey/basketball/football/tennis hall; sports injury clinic; sports shop. Garthdee's also got a dry ski-slope. Beyond that, we're talking city facilities – see University of Aberdeen

SPORTS FACILITIES

Gaelic Football; Ju-Jitsu; Mountaineering; Rifle; Rowing. **See also Clubs tables.**

ATTRACTIONS see University of Aberdeen

ACCOMMODATION

IN UNIVERSITY

- **CATERED** 18% **COST** £75 (31WKS)
- **INSURANCE PREMIUM** £
- **1ST YRS LIVING IN** 28%

AVAILABILITY All first years who live 15 or more miles away are guaranteed a place in halls. *Most prefer to live in the city centre rather than at the mercy of the Garthdee shuttle bus. Most are happy with their lot.* Rooms in halls come with communal areas, internet access and contents insurance. Cleaners *keep bubonic plague at bay*, while CCTV, night porters and entry phones keep PlayStation-pilferers out. Some rooms have en suite facilities and even fewer are available for families and long leasers (50 wks).
CAR PARKING *Limited, and not free, but two-wheeled, motorless car equivalents (as the kids are calling bikes nowadays) can be locked up securely.*

EXTERNALLY

- **AVE RENT** £65

HOUSING HELP The RGU accommodation service keeps lists of vacancies and approved landlords.

R

In a poll at Robert Gordon University, 70% of students said the communal fridge is the biggest cause of student flat disputes.

Words in italics are Push's point of view – take it or leave it...

WELFARE ⓤⓤⓤⓤⓤⓤⓤⓤⓤⓤⓤⓤⓤ

SERVICES
- ⦿ INTERNATIONAL STUDENTS' OFFICER & SOCIETY
- ⦿ POSTGRAD OFFICER ⦿ DISABILITIES OFFICER & SOCIETY
- ⦿ SELF-DEFENCE CLASSES ⦿ UNIVERSITY COUNSELLORS
3 FULL-TIME ⦿ CRIME RATING !!!

HEALTH Health practice with two GPs and a nurse.
CRECHES/NURSERY 90 places for precious ones aged 0-5yrs.
DISABILITIES The Centre for Student Access (CenSA) provides advice and support for mobility-impaired, dyslexic and other disabled students.

FINANCE
- ⦿ AVE DEBT PER YEAR £1,747
- ⦿ HOME STUDENT FEES £1,700

FEES International students pay around £8/9k (undergrad) up to around £12k for postgrads. It's £3,085 for UK postgrads, the full £3,000 whack for UK undergrads.
- ⦿ ACCESS FUND £212,910
- ⦿ SUCCESSFUL APPLICATIONS/YR 424
- ⦿ AVE PAYMENT £600

SUPPORT As well as the hardship fund there's also a mature students' bursary with over £200,000 in the kitty, which splashes out an average of £1,700 each for around 100 successful applicants.

▶ ROBERT GORDON INSTITUTE OF TECHNOLOGY
see _Robert Gordon University_

▶ ROEHAMPTON INSTITUTE OF HIGHER EDUCATION
see _Roehampton University_

ROEHAMPTON UNIVERSITY

FORMERLY ROEHAMPTON INSTITUTE

1) ⦿ **ROEHAMPTON UNIVERSITY** Froebel College, Roehampton Lane, London, SW15 5PJ **TEL** (020) 8392 3470
E-MAIL enquiries@roehampton.ac.uk **WEBSITE** www.roehampton.ac.uk
⦿ **ROEHAMPTON STUDENTS' UNION** Froebel College, Roehampton Lane, London, SW15 5PJ **TEL** (020) 8392 3221
E-MAIL info@roehamptonstudent.com **WEBSITE** www.roehamptonstudent.com
2) **DIGBY STUART COLLEGE** Roehampton Lane, London, SW15 5PH **TEL** (020) 8392 3213
3) **SOUTHLANDS COLLEGE** 80 Roehampton Lane, London, SW15 5SL **TEL** (020) 8392 3400
4) **WHITELANDS COLLEGE** Holybourne Avenue, London, SW15 4JD **TEL** (020) 8392 3500

R

GENERAL ⓤⓤⓤⓤⓤⓤⓤⓤⓤⓤⓤⓤ

An Anglican, a Catholic, a Methodist and an agnostic walked into a bar... well, it wasn't a bar it was a London borough, and the upshot of it was they decided to join their respective colleges together and form a fully-fledged university. Roehampton University officially came into the world in late 2004 and represents the _holy communion_ of four neighbouring Victorian teacher training institutes. _The campus itself is located in one of the few pockets of London that isn't crowded by bricky, urban mess but by attractive parkland._ Within reach of the West End and only a brief stroll from Richmond Park, _Roehampton is well-placed to enjoy both suburban serenity and the bright lights of the big city._ For general information on London see _University of London._

SEX RATIO: ♀23 ♂77	FOUNDED: 1841
FULL-TIME U'GRADS: 5,784	PART-TIME: 270
POSTGRADS: 1,566	NON-DEGREE: 427
AVE COURSE: 3YRS	ETHNIC: 37%
STATE:PRIVATE SCHOOL: 95:5	FLUNK RATE: 17%
MATURE: 26%	INTERNATIONAL: 7%
DISABLED: 265	LOCAL: 57%

ATMOSPHERE
Roehampton's four colleges are pleasant, picturesque places and those qualities seem to be reflected by the students that inhabit them. Like Londoners in general, they're a diverse, metropolitan crowd, and though there are differences in atmosphere from one college to another, everyone's on the same wavelength and the University-wide sense of community is strong. Nevertheless, a little intercollegiate sporting/drinking rivalry never hurt anyone, did it?

Words in italics are Push's point of view — take it or leave it...

COLLEGES

Roehampton is a collegiate institution, meaning that its student body is divided into four roughly equal chunks – each living, socialising and loitering at a different college. Though the colleges are self-contained in those respects, teaching is done at a university-wide level, thus students can find themselves travelling between college sites to utilise different facilities. Applicants can specify a particular college upon application, but there's *no enormous distinction to be made between them*, except in terms of architecture, facilities and religious background. All colleges have their own bar, halls and canteen.

FROEBEL (Early Childhood Research Centre, the Education Studies Centre, the Roehampton Education Development Centre) Named after the inventor of the kindergarten and surrounded by four acres of *jaw-dropping* landscaped gardens, the College centres on the Grade II listed Grove House, *which looks a lot like the stately home of some minor royal*. It was founded in 1892 as a centre for educational reform and is the only College without a historical religious bias.

DIGBY STUART (Arts) Founded in 1872 as a teacher training college for women by a nun from the Society of the Sacred Heart, 'Digby' is a *friendly and relaxed* place with strong Catholic roots. Roehampton's main library facility is based here, but *more importantly*, the Belfry Bar has an off-licence.

SOUTHLANDS (Business, Social Sciences) *Like some sort of wandering Methodist minstrel*, Southlands was a latecomer to Roehampton, entering the world in 1872 and passing through Westminster, Battersea and Wimbledon in various incarnations before joining the other three Colleges in 1975. It too began as training ground for women teachers but has been offering non-educational degree programmes since 1905. Southlands has only been wearing its present buildings since 1997 and so has the most contemporary look and feel of the four. *It's a sleek and attractive place, but given architectural shelf life, will probably be called hideous in 20 years.*

WHITELANDS (School of Human & Life Sciences) Founded in 1841, it's the oldest of the colleges and has just relocated closer to its three brethren (though it's still 15mins walk away). The new campus centres around an 18th-century Palladian villa that was once home to poet Gerard *'not very'* Manly Hopkins. Whitelands was also a women's teacher training college, this time with Anglican leanings. It boasts a stained glass window by Pre-Raphaelite painter, Edward Burne-Jones, as well as William Morris-designed altar screens.

LONDON see University of London
○ **CITY CENTRE** 6 MILES

TRAVEL see University of London
CARS The A3 and A205 swing *handily by but, as everywhere in London, prospective students should think twice, weigh up the pros and cons and consult a palmist before bringing a car to the city.*
UNIVERSITY An hourly bus service shuttles between the colleges.

LOCAL Buses 72, 265, 493, 33 and 337 are useful for getting around – fares hover around £1.20. For those who prefer rail, Barnes is the local overland service and there's a tram service from Wimbledon.
UNDERGROUND Hammersmith (Hammersmith & City line) and Putney (District line) stations are the most accessible Tube stops.
BICYCLES Bikes are *generally safe* on campus, where 100 shed spaces are provided, and there are cycle lanes and paths throughout the borough.

CAREER PROSPECTS
○ **CAREERS SERVICE** ○ **NO. OF STAFF** 6 FULL/4 PART
○ **UNEMPLOYED AFTER 6** MTHS 5%

FAMOUS ALUMNI
Toby Anstis (Heart 106.2); Alice Beer (TV presenter); Enid Blyton (children's author, *of lashings of golliwogs infamy*); Naomi Rowe (radio presenter); Darren Shan (children's author).

SPECIAL FEATURES
Whitelands College holds an annual May Day beauty pageant. It's the legacy of art critic, *latent paedophile and pubic-hair-phobe*, John Ruskin, who in 1881 decided that students should elect 'the nicest and likeablest' girl to be the May Queen, who would then be inaugurated by a visiting bishop. It still goes on, but in these less rampantly misogynous times, students elect a 'May Monarch' of either sex. *Ruskin must be writhing in his grave.*

FURTHER INFO
○ **PROSPECTUSES** UNDERGRAD; POSTGRAD; SOME DEPARTMENTAL; INTERNATIONAL
○ **OPEN DAYS**

ACADEMIC ○○○○○○○○○○○○○

Roehampton's reputation rests on its teaching and education-orientated courses, but it does offer a range of other subjects and, now it's got a proper university hat on, is likely to expand its empire in the coming years. It has a good research record for a new University and has just been awarded £4.5million for a touchy-feely Centre of Excellence in Social Justice, Human Rights & Citizenship. Degree structures are flexible, with more than 1,500 module combinations possible and students are encouraged to take 12-week foreign language evening classes, which contribute academic credits to their degrees. The Roehampton Education Development (RED) centre sorts out study skills training, *which is nice.*

ENTRY POINTS: 120–260	AVE POINTS: 236
APPLICATIONS PER PLACE: 5	CLEARING: 10%
NO. OF TERMS: 2	LENGTH OF TERMS: 16/8WKS
STAFF TO STUDENT RATIO: 1:21	STUDY ADDICTS: 7%
TEACHING: ✱✱	RESEARCH: ✱✱
YEAR ABROAD: 3%	SANDWICH STUDENTS: 0%
1STS: 7%	2.2S: 45%
2.1S: 46%	3RDS: 3%

R

Words in italics are Push's point of view – take it or leave it...

ADMISSIONS
○ **APPLY VIA UCAS**
Roehampton also deals with the CAT (Credit Accumulation and Transfer) scheme.

SUBJECTS
ARTS 37%   **BUSINESS & SOCIAL SCIENCES** 17%
EDUCATION 23%   **HUMAN & LIFE SCIENCES** 23%
BEST Education Studies; English-based Studies; History & Archaeology; Philosophy; Sports Science; Theology & Religious Studies.
UNUSUAL Integrative counselling

LIBRARIES
○ **400,000 BOOKS** ○ **600 STUDY PLACES**
○ **SPEND PER STUDENT** £
The Digby Learning Resource Centre is six floors of *hot library action, although its opening hours aren't quite so spicy* (till 9pm/7pm Fridays). Weekend opening *makes up for it.*

COMPUTERS
○ **490 WORKSTATIONS** ○ **24-HOUR ACCESS**
New suites at Whitelands have *put a smile on students' faces* and software training is available to anyone. IT suites in the halls of residence.

OTHER LEARNING FACILITIES
The University has an Educational Development Centre (RED) which provides study skill, literacy and numeracy and English language support. Also: language labs; drama studio; rehearsal rooms; CAD lab; TV Roehampton video recording and editing suite.

ENTERTAINMENT ○○○○○○○○○○

THE CITY see University of London
Putney and the other areas near the University have a flavour of night life *all their own.* For everything from stadium bands to cutting-edge rock chic, there's the Shepherd's Bush Empire, the Hammersmith Apollo and the Half Moon. There are cinemas nearby, plus the Putney Arts Centre and the Richmond Theatre, and *plenty* of pubs to sup, quaff or chug in.

UNIVERSITY
○ **PRICE OF A PINT OF BEER** £1.60
○ **CAN OF RED BULL** £1.65
A veritable ice cream parlour of different ents flavours during the week, nothing but a soggy wafer at weekends.
BARS Each college has its own bar, all with pool tables and occasional late licences. Digby's Belfry Bar is the main venue and has bands nights on Thursdays.
THEATRES A *wide* array of regular productions are put on in the dance and theatre studios, as well as Montfiore Hall.

FILM The film society arranges double bills every Sunday evening (£2 for two *mainstream* films) and the Union takes students, *school trip-like,* to a local cinema once a month.
MUSIC VENUES Montfiore Hall and the bar at Digby get some *small* bands – *we're not talking musical midgets –* and Jason Donovan-sized acts.
CLUBBING Froebel College has a weekly Friday bop that attempts to cater for all music tastes – *barring silly ones, like Country & Western.*
COMEDY/CABARET Monthly gagmeisters in Belfry Bar.
FOOD *Reasonably healthy, reasonably priced and yummy enough to tempt even the likes of Gillian McKeith to put away a proper meal once in a while.* Each college has a canteen serving food until 8pm, as well as a café and hot & cold food vending machines. Food at Whitelands' Dining Room is cooked in full view of diners – *no need to check sarnies for bogies.*
OTHER Annual ball.

SOCIAL ○○○○○○○○○○○○○

ROEHAMPTON STUDENT UNION
○ **4 SABBATICALS** ○ **NUS MEMBER**
RSU has over 40 elected officers – *which looks a lot like overkill, given the mid-size student body and lack of political activism beyond a stringent recycling policy –* but in fact reflects the diverse needs of students. *Good on welfare and services.*

SU FACILITIES
In the Hirst Union Building at Froebel: meeting rooms; Endsleigh Insurance; photo booth; advice centre; launderette.

CLUBS (NON-SPORTING)
Anthropology; Alpha; Broken Bass Jazz; Cheerleaders (reminding boys of the reason for their mindless competitiveness); Creative Writing; Deviant; Education; Entrepreneur; Horse Riding; Human Rights; International Students; Japanese Cultural; Junglist Mashup (drum & bass nutters); Krishna Consciousness Vedic; Philosophy; Mature Students; 'Neighbours'; Psychology; Self-defence; UNICEF; Volunteering & Fundraising; The Wednesday Activity Club (mid-week limber-up). **See also Clubs tables.**

OTHER ORGANISATIONS
Tabloid-style 'Fresh' comes out on the first Monday of every month, followed hot on the heels by 'Funsize Fresh', its diminutive e-mail equivalent. A radio station should assault the airwaves from September 2006. *The Rag committee isn't going to make a million any time soon but it's good to know they're around and working their charitable socks off.*

RELIGIOUS
○ **8 CHAPLAINS (COFE, RC, METHODIST), RABBI**
Roehampton's strong religious heritage is reflected in Digby Stuart, Whitelands and Southlands own

chaplaincies, each reflecting the College's denominational background. There's also a Jewish Resource Centre and two Muslim prayer rooms. For religion in London: see University of London

PAID WORK see University of London
◉ **JOB BUREAU** ◉ **PAID WORK** TERM-TIME 65%; HOLS 80%
The Employment and Careers Service posts part-time local vacancies and helps students find jobs relevant to their field of study.

SPORTS ◖◗◖◗◖◗◖◗◖◗◖◗◖◗

◉ **RECENT SUCCESSES** FOOTBALL ◉ **BUSA RANKING** 106
At Roehampton it's less 'sports for all' than 'sports for none' – campus facilities are sparser than rainforests in the desert. Although there's an admirably low-key attitude to the recreational end of the sports pitch, those involved in the competitive side are mainly in it for the drinking. Both Union and University are hankering after more cash, so extra goodies should be on the horizon.

SPORTS FACILITIES
Football pitch, two tennis courts and a netball court. Students are obliged to use local facilities, which include: seven leisure centres; boating and fishing lakes (at Battersea Park); athletics track; a sports hall; swimming pool; golf course; more tennis courts.

SPORTING CLUBS
Rowing. **See also Clubs tables.**

ATTRACTIONS
The Lawn Tennis Association's national centre is in Roehampton. Fulham FC and Rosslyn Park RFC are the local teams. Putney Bridge is the starting point for the *irresistible anachronism that is the* Oxbridge Boat Race. See also University of London

ACCOMMODATION ◖◗◖◗◖◗◖◗◖

IN UNIVERSITY
◉ **CATERED** 7% ◉ **COST** £90 (38-48WKS)
◉ **SELF–CATERING** 20% ◉ **COST** £70 (38-48WKS)
◉ **INSURANCE PREMIUM** £
AVAILABILITY Priority is given to those who pick Roehampton as *their absolute favourite university ever* and get their forms in before the July 31 deadline. Livers-in are spread between the four colleges (Froebel holds the most). There's a wide variation in facilities and standards – reflected in rents – but *there's nothing to be scared of*. The newer halls are *particularly well-kitted out* and are mainly en suite. Security is tight and there are laundry facilities. Only pillows are provided, so students should bring their own bedding. Women-only accommodation available in

Montfiore at Froebel.
CAR PARKING *Pigs will be soaring through the frozen underworld eating their own headwear before a student parks on campus without a very good excuse.*

EXTERNALLY
◉ **AVE RENT** £80
HOUSING HELP An off-campus accommodation service publishes vacancies and offers a mediation service.

WELFARE ◖◗◖◗◖◗◖◗◖◗◖◗◖◗

SERVICES
◉ **LGBT OFFICER & SOCIETY** ◉ **MATURE STUDENTS' OFFICER & SOCIETY** ◉ **POSTGRAD OFFICER** ◉ **WOMEN'S OFFICER** ◉ **INTERNATIONAL STUDENTS' OFFICER & SOCIETY** ◉ **ETHNIC MINORITIES OFFICER** ◉ **DISABILITIES OFFICER & SOCIETY** ◉ **SELF–DEFENCE CLASSES** ◉ **UNIVERSITY COUNSELLORS** 1 FULL/2 PART ◉ **CRIME RATING** !!
HEALTH There's an NHS medical practice unit on site, but *if you're really broken*, Queen Mary's Hospital is just over the road.
CRECHES/NURSERY Limited places for kidlets aged 5mths-5yrs at the Froebel College nursery. The University runs a crèche service at special events.
DISABILITIES *Buildings are old and access limited.* The fact Roehampton's on a slope doesn't help either. *They do make an effort, however*, and hearing loops, ramps, adapted accommodation and a special education support unit make things *a little easier*.

FINANCE
◉ **AVE DEBT PER YEAR** £4,525 ◉ **HOME STUDENT FEES** £3,000
FEES International students hand over £7,160 for an undergraduate course or £600 for each ten credit module. UK part-timers can take modules for £250 each. UK postgrads pay £3,204-9,000.

◉ **ACCESS FUND** £519,254 ◉ **AVE PAYMENT** £100-3,500
SUPPORT *Surprisingly straightforward:* students that qualify for the government maintenance grant get an annual £500 bursary and those getting more than 320 points at A level are given an annual £1,000 scholarship. *Not bad.*

R

There's more to student life than poverty and fun... See the clubs & socs tables.

ROYAL ACADEMY OF MUSIC

THE COLLEGE IS PART OF THE UNIVERSITY OF LONDON AND STUDENTS ARE ENTITLED TO USE ITS FACILITIES

○ **ROYAL ACADEMY OF MUSIC** Marylebone Road, London, NW1 5HT **TEL** (020) 7873 7393 **E−MAIL** admissions@ram.ac.uk
WEBSITE www.ram.ac.uk ○ **ROYAL ACADEMY OF MUSIC STUDENTS UNION** Marylebone Road, London, NW1 5HT
TEL (020) 7837 7337 **E−MAIL** su@ram.ac.uk

GENERAL ◑◑◑◑◑◑◑◑◑◑◑◑◑

South of Regent's Park, along Marylebone Road from Madame Tussaud's, stands the *striking Edwardian edifice* that houses the Royal Academy of Music (or RAM, *if slightly confusing acronyms are your gig*). It's one of the *pre-eminent music schools in the country, possibly the world, with the notes of budding geniuses harmonising with the echoes of past greats.* The place is steeped in history and music tradition. RAM is *too posh* to be small, but *too hardworking and vocational (with students as poor as the next) to be petite, so Push would call it cosy.* For general information about London: see University of London.

†††††††††††††††††††††††††

SEX RATIO: ♂43 ♀57	**FOUNDED:** 1822
FULL-TIME U³GRADS: 305	**PART-TIME:** 0
POSTGRADS: 328	**NON-DEGREE:** 14
AVE COURSE: 4YRS	**ETHNIC:** 25%
STATE:PRIVATE SCHOOL: 75:25	**FLUNK RATE:** 6%
MATURE: 10%	**INTERNATIONAL:** 40%
DISABLED: 0	**LOCAL:** N/A

ATMOSPHERE

Like a classically educated kung fu midget, it's small and frenetic with a well-spoken student body. People are friendly with it too, but make no mistake, this isn't an artsy institution but a training ground for the cut-throat classical music biz. Okay, it's a bit artsy. But in a cut-throat sort of way. There's a leaning towards cliqueyness, despite well-meaning attempts at integrating the 50 nationalities represented, partly because students are so work-focussed. But, while you'd expect a classical institution in the heart of Marylebone to be dominated by Hooray Henrys, there is actually a good spread of social backgrounds and little evidence of snobbery.

LONDON see University of London

TRAVEL see University of London

CAREER PROSPECTS
○ **CAREERS SERVICE** ○ **NO. OF STAFF** 1 FULL
○ **UNEMPLOYED AFTER 6 MTHS** 6%
RAM has the Career Surgery, tutor advice, newsletters and support for graduates, including fellowships for the promising. Many go on to be freelance musicians, which *means work levels varying from none to world-famous concert stardom.*

FAMOUS ALUMNI
Sir John Barbirolli (conductor); Harrison Birtwhistle (composer); Johnny Dankworth (jazz musician); Lesley Garrett (opera singer); Evelyn Glennie (percussionist); Dame Myra Hess (pianist); Sir Elton John (*wig-wearer extraordinaire*); Graham Johnson (pianist); Aled Jones (former chorister, *grans loved him*); Annie Lennox (pop diva); Joanna MacGregor (pianist); Michael Nyman (composer); Simon Rattle (conductor); Sir Arthur Sullivan (Gilbert's other half); Mark Wigglesworth (conductor).

FURTHER INFO
○ **PROSPECTUSES** UNDERGRAD; POSTGRAD; ALTERNATIVE
○ **OPEN DAYS**

ACADEMIC ◑◑◑◑◑◑◑◑◑◑◑◑◑

Weekly lessons and tutorials, and not just in classical music - there's also music for TV, jazz etc. The *world-class* teaching veers more towards *practical* and is *highly rated* by students, as well as everyone else - the Academy houses many famous musicians' personal collections. There's *strong emphasis* on the business side of the Music Biz, and students are equally driven – *and we don't just mean in Range Rovers.* Staff/ student relations are *comfy-cosy.* Expect to spend most of every day practising; orchestras and bands *help take the edge off the loneliness.* Entrance is by audition.

ENTRY POINTS: N/A		**AVE POINTS:** N/A	
APPLICATIONS PER PLACE: 4		**CLEARING:** 0%	
NO. OF TERMS: 3		**LENGTH OF TERMS:** 10WKS	
STAFF TO STUDENT RATIO: 1:1		**STUDY ADDICTS:** 20%	
TEACHING: *****		**RESEARCH:** ****	
YEAR ABROAD: 0%		**SANDWICH STUDENTS:** 0%	
1STS: 41%		**2.2S:** 8%	
2.1S: 37%		**3RDS:** 2%	

ADMISSIONS
○ **APPLY DIRECT**

SUBJECTS
MUSIC 100%

LIBRARIES
○ **125,000 BOOKS** ○ **26 STUDY PLACES**
○ **SPEND PER STUDENT** £££
There are scores of scores, of course, as well as other music-related manuscripts. 100 practice rooms on campus.

COMPUTERS
◉ **58** WORKSTATIONS   ◉ **SPEND PER STUDENT** ££££
RAM's got two IT centres and facilities in
the library.

ENTERTAINMENT ⦿⦿⦿⦿⦿⦿⦿⦿⦿

THE CITY see University of London

ACADEMY
◉ **PRICE OF A PINT OF BEER** £2
◉ **GLASS OF WINE** £2.20
◉ **CAN OF RED BULL** £1.80
The work:fun balance *has its chakras out of joint
– students are a hard-working lot, and the Union's
attempts to jolly things up a bit tend to fall on
Beethoven's ears.* Off-campus, the Prince Regent
on Marylebone High Street is a *home away from
home – and does better food, too.* Having
Regent's Park on the doorstep is a *source of
smugness in the summer while the rest of
London disappears up its own exhaust pipe.* The
Academy has only the one bar, see University of
London for other entertainment needs.
BARS The RAM bar (250 cap.) is open 5-11pm
during the week, hosts a variety of music nights
and has a pool table and arcade games.
THEATRES The Sir Jack Lyon Theatre hosts a few
student productions.
MUSIC VENUES Students do their own music
(recitals etc.).
CLUBBING Around once a month, ie. School
Disco, Brazilian.
FOOD The canteen, open 8.30am-6pm Mon-Fri
is the social hub, with *tasty food* and a *fun
atmosphere.*

SOCIAL ⦿⦿⦿⦿⦿⦿⦿⦿⦿⦿⦿

RAMSU (THE ROYAL ACADEMY OF MUSIC STUDENTS' UNION)
◉ **1** SABBATICAL   ◉ **TURNOUT AT LAST BALLOT** 35%
◉ **NUS** MEMBER
*RAM students are apolitical, preferring to
wave batons rather than banners.* Having said
that, there are close links between the SU and
admin, with the President getting a vote on all
major issues.

SU FACILITIES
A *comfy* lounge with a pool table, Sky TV; bar;
cafeteria; meeting room; photocopier, printing
and fax services; vending machines; ATM.

RELIGIOUS
◉ **1** CHAPLAIN (COFE)
Religion in London: see University of London

PAID WORK
◉ **JOB BUREAU**   ◉ **PAID WORK** term-time 75%; hols 90%
Most students pick up paid gigs or get involved
in teaching. There's also regular opera and
concert stewarding and occasional admin work to
be fought over.

SPORTS ⦿⦿⦿⦿⦿⦿⦿⦿⦿⦿⦿⦿⦿

◉ **RECENT SUCCESSES** 5-A-SIDE FOOTBALL
No RAM-specific facilities – but those who can be
lured away from the harpsichord head for the
University of London, and there's Regents Park just
behind the Academy for the odd game of footie.

SPORTING CLUBS
Massage; Tai Chi; Yoga. **See also Clubs tables.**

ATTRACTIONS see University of London

ACCOMMODATION ⦿⦿⦿⦿⦿⦿⦿⦿⦿

IN COLLEGE
◉ **CATERED** 3%   ◉ **COST** £142 (43WKS)
◉ **1ST YRS LIVING IN** 49%
◉ **INSURANCE PREMIUM** ££££
AVAILABILITY *Tricky.* Many first years are not able to
be housed by the college, though for what's available
they and international students get priority (halls five
mins walk away). No second or third years live in
and only a tiny percentage of postgrads do. Housing
is a mixture of flats and halls. The flats are closer to
college and recently refurbished; halls are *less
popular* as they involve sharing.
CAR PARKING Central London – *say no more.*

EXTERNALLY see University of London
◉ **AVE RENT** £110   ◉ **LIVING AT HOME** 2%
AVAILABILITY Willesden, Kilburn and Cricklewood
are grotty round the edges but cheap and *popular*
choices: they're close enough to the Academy, but
far enough away to avoid the worst of the *merry
band of cut-throats that are London landlords.*

WELFARE ⦿⦿⦿⦿⦿⦿⦿⦿⦿⦿⦿⦿

SERVICES
◉ **INTERNATIONAL STUDENTS' SOCIETY** ◉ **POSTGRAD
OFFICER** ◉ **DISABILITIES OFFICER** ◉ **WOMEN'S OFFICER**
◉ **COLLEGE COUNSELLORS** 1   ◉ **CRIME RATING** !!!!!
Those in need of help or advice can see the
Welfare Officer, the full-time counsellor or their
tutors, but with so many specialist teachers in on
a part-time basis, the *pastoral side can be
strained.* The health centre is 15 mins away and

R

for self-defence students can learn tai chi – *presumably the nasty variety or they're in trouble.* Some parts of the library and other areas still aren't wheelchair-friendly.

FINANCE
⊙ **AVE DEBT PER YEAR** £2,246
⊙ **HOME STUDENT FEES** £3,000
FEES *RAM has championed top-up fees, but*

bursaries should help soak up any resentment. International students have more to sop up though, with fees of £13,650. Postgrads pay around six grand.
⊙ **ACCESS FUND** £35,000 ⊙ **SUCCESSFUL APPLICATIONS/YR** 25% ⊙ **AVE PAYMENT** £1,000
SUPPORT A *whopping* 250 different bursaries to be seized, ranging from £20 to £10,000 especially rewarding merit.

ROYAL AGRICULTURAL COLLEGE

⊙ **ROYAL AGRICULTURAL COLLEGE** Stroud Road, Cirencester, Gloucestershire, GL7 6JS **TEL** (01285) 652531
E-MAIL admissions@rac.ac.uk **WEBSITE** www.rac.ac.uk
⊙ **RAC STUDENTS' UNION** Stroud Road, Cirencester, Gloucestershire, GL7 6JS **TEL** (01285) 652 531

GENERAL ◡◡◡◡◡◡◡◡◡◡◡◡◡

When, in 1868, Charles Dickens visited the UK's oldest agricultural college, about a mile outside the Cotswold town of Cirencester, he wrote: 'That part of the holding of a farmer or landowner that pays best for cultivation is the small estate within the ring fence of his skull' or in less roundabout English, 'Farmers need brains'. This is where they go to get them. Just outside the Roman town of Cirencester, the RAC – *great at farming, useless when your car breaks down* – occupies some *truly treasurable Oxbridge-esque* buildings – the ancient farmhouse and 16th-century tithe barn are *complemented* by the surrounding Victorian Gothic architecture. In Dickens's day, and until 2001, the College was a private institution. In 1995 it became the first agricultural college to award its own degrees and now receives public funding too. Nonetheless, the College's alumni are said to own, manage or administer over 80% of the UK between them. *Conspiracy-theorist heaven or what?*

CIRENCESTER
⊙ **POPULATION** 8,400 ⊙ **TOWN CENTRE** 1 MILE
⊙ **LONDON** 95 MILES ⊙ **CHELTENHAM** 16 MILES
⊙ **BRISTOL** 40 MILES
⊙ **HIGH TEMP** 22 ⊙ **LOW TEMP** 1 ⊙ **RAINFALL** 60
Cirencester, 'capital of the Cotswolds', is a *quintessentially English town*. Not much of the original Roman remains, er, remain, but the *genteel* 16th- and 17th-Century architecture and the gleaming Cotswold stone *do brighten things up a bit – which helps considering the weather often doesn't*. It's far from cosmopolitan, but there's a good selection of banks and cafés. For the weekly shop there's Tesco, Somerfield and a large Waitrose, *which tells you a bit about the locals*. Cheltenham (see University of Gloucestershire) *is relatively more sophisticated and fashionable, but the many tourists stopping off here on their way through the beautiful Cotswolds haven't come for fashion.* Students who want that will probably end up heading for Bristol, but in its own way Cirencester's a *quiet, charming place*.

TRAVEL
TRAINS Kemble Train Station is three miles away. Great Western rail services from London Paddington to Kemble (from £22.45 return). From Kemble trains also go to Cheltenham (£9.25) and Bristol (£9.55).
COACHES National Express coach services run from Cirencester to London (£20), an express service to Heathrow also operates.
CARS The M4 from the south, the M5 from the north, leading to the A433 which gets you to Cirencester. Parking's easy and costs are included in rents. Most students have cars - but if you don't, lifts are *easily found and freely given*.
HITCHING *Can be a useful means of getting about for the carless and out of pocket.* The best pick-ups are on Stroud Road, usually from sixth form college students – *which is a bit demeaning, really*.
AIR Approximately 11–2-hr drive from Heathrow, Birmingham and Bristol airports, all of which have international and budget airlines.
COLLEGE There's talk of a local bus service to be

SEX RATIO: ♀61 ♂39	
FULL-TIME U'GRADS: 670	PART-TIME: 15
POSTGRADS: 140	NON-DEGREE: 65
AVE COURSE: 3YRS	ETHNIC: 2%
STATE:PRIVATE SCHOOL: 40:60	FLUNK RATE: 5%
MATURE: 25%	INTERNATIONAL: 22%
DISABLED: 45	LOCAL: 20%

ATMOSPHERE
Living-in in such a small, cut-off community has been likened by some students to being at board-ing school, so if Mallory Towers ain't your thing, you might want to consider living in town. Despite the perils of claustrophobia, most enjoy the close, friendly feel of campus life, and there are few complaints about the rolling, unspoilt countryside all around. Staff-student fraternisation is the norm, which keeps things relaxed and infor-mal (which you might not expect in a cord-wear-ing, pashmina-draped student body).

R

Words in italics are Push's point of view — take it or leave it...

run jointly with the FE College down the road, in an attempt to reduce the number of student cars clogging up the place, but Cirencester's a mere 15-min walk from College.

LOCAL Buses from Cirencester marketplace stop close to the College, but friendly bus drivers have been known to drop a fortunate few at the front door. The service runs every 60-90mins, 80p (sgl) until 5.30pm. Buses from Kemble train station are patchy (around every two hours) and only one stops outside the College during the week.

BICYCLES Great cycle path between College and town.

TAXIS The trip from Kemble Station to the College (three miles) costs £9.

CAREER PROSPECTS
⊙ **CAREERS SERVICE** ⊙ **NO. OF STAFF** 1 FULL/1 PART ⊙ **UNEMPLOYED AFTER 6MTHS** 16%

The Careers Service do all the usual stuff in terms of advice, but an extra advantage for RAC students is that they can put you in touch with the old boy (*and occasional girl*) network scattered around the globe. A networking organisation called 'The 100 Club' also puts students in touch with the big names in agribusiness.

FAMOUS ALUMNI
Plenty of useful name-dropping for agri-careers: Marcus Armitage (Grand National rider & winner); Euan Cameron (former President of the Country Landowners' Association); Henry Cecil (racehorse trainer); Geoffrey Clifton-Brown (MP); Jonathan Dimbleby (broadcaster); Sir David Naish (former president of the National Farmers Union).

FURTHER INFO
⊙ **PROSPECTUSES** UNDERGRAD; POSTGRAD; ALL DEPARTMENTS
⊙ **OPEN DAYS**

Two open days a year, which should be booked in advance. Also two-day taster courses.

ACADEMIC ⓤⓤⓤⓤⓤⓤⓤⓤⓤⓤⓤⓤⓤ

As well as agriculture, the College runs industry-specific courses in land management, property and a *horse course* (or 'equine degree' as they call it). All Agriculture and Business students take on a six-month work placement in the second year. Learning is hands-on throughout, there's a strong business element and things are generally geared up to getting students into related employment – *but then, you wouldn't spend three years messing around with cows udders if you weren't already serious, would you?* Courses are modular – around eight a year for a three-year degree. There's talk of doings with the local FE college, which could mean more combined courses on offer in future.

ENTRY POINTS: 40–220	AVE POINTS: 210
APPLICATIONS PER PLACE: 3	CLEARING: 1%
NO. OF TERMS: 3	LENGTH OF TERMS: 12WKS
STAFF TO STUDENT RATIO: 1:13	STUDY ADDICTS: 2%
TEACHING: ★★★★	RESEARCH: ★★★
YEAR ABROAD: 2%	SANDWICH STUDENTS: 65%
1STS: 2%	2.2s: 33%
2.1s: 54%	3RDS: 11%

ADMISSIONS
⊙ **APPLY VIA UCAS**

All applicants are interviewed – international students are encouraged to visit before making a decision. Disabled applicants are welcomed, but should declare their disability upon application. Students with fewer than 160 UCAS points can do a four-year course at the College that includes a foundation year.

SUBJECTS
AGRICULTURE 47%   **BUSINESS** 10%   **RURAL ECONOMY & LAND MANAGEMENT** 43%

LIBRARIES
⊙ **32,000** BOOKS ⊙ **160** STUDY PLACES

The *spacious* Garner Building library is open till 12.30am during term and contains a dedicated IT wing. There's *reasonable* stockage of academic journals, too.

COMPUTERS
⊙ **56** WORKSTATIONS ⊙ **24-HR ACCESS**

OTHER LEARNING FACILITIES
The RAC farm (2,200 arable acres) has a 300-cow dairy herd and 1,500 breeding ewes. There are also language and media labs, and a practical training centre where you can *indulge your love of boys toys* learning tractor-driving, welding and the *slightly sinister-sounding* embryo transfer.

ENTERTAINMENT ⓤⓤⓤⓤⓤⓤⓤⓤⓤ

CHELTENHAM see University of Gloucestershire

CIRENCESTER
⊙ **PRICE OF A PINT OF BEER** £2.60
⊙ **GLASS OF WINE** £2.60
⊙ **CAN OF RED BULL** £1.40

CINEMAS There are UGCs in Bristol, Swindon and Gloucester and an Odeon in Cheltenham, all of which are good for *popcorn fodder flicks*.

PUBS *Enough* for a decent crawl. *Pushplugs: Somewhere Else (tapas and atmosphere); the Crown (good for large groups). Push doesn't plug: the Bear.*

CLUBBING The Rock and Havana *are your lot.* Havana has been known to open just for RAC students on a Friday.

EATING OUT Local pubs, an Indian and a Thai takeaway and a Pizza Express: *midnight feasts take a bit of a battering.*

R

Words in italics are Push's point of view — take it or leave it...

COLLEGE
- **PRICE OF A PINT OF BEER** £2.20
- **GLASS OF WINE** £2.40
- **CAN OF RED BULL** £1.40

Given it's a small college, this is reflected in types of ents. Links with students in Oxford mean occasional trips up and down.
BARS The Tithe Bar is run jointly by the SU and College and opens lunchtimes and evenings. There's a regular smattering of themed/fancy-dress events and live local bands/DJs. *It's no God's Kitchen, though,* and there are equally regular pub-crawls through town.
FILM Occasional screenings in the Tithe Barn on Saturday nights.
CLUBBING Occasional rock nights and a disco till 2am on Fridays.
FOOD The College diner ladles out three meals a day – free for those living in, others can buy meal tickets from the porter's lodge (around £6 in total for breakfast and lunch, including a drink). The College shop does snacks 'n' sandwiches.
OTHER Five black-tie balls a year, including the Hunt Ball. Recent highlights have included: dancing to the Blueshounds, a horn-blowing competition, a fundraising raffle and fairground rides. There's also the Freshers' Ball, Christmas Ball, Rag Ball and the Beagle Ball in May.

SOCIAL ⓊⓊⓊⓊⓊⓊⓊⓊⓊⓊⓊⓊⓊ

ROYAL AGRICULTURAL COLLEGE STUDENTS UNION
- **TURNOUT AT LAST BALLOT** 61%

The Union isn't affiliated to NUS – it's run by the College, but students are involved in managing its facilities. *'Compact and bijou'* about sums it up – there's not masses on offer, but the student body is fairly small. Students pay £100 each up-front at the start of the year to cover SU running costs. Facilities include a small bar and a common room with a real fire and a *cosy, Emmerdale farm-feel to it*. Postgrads will soon be able to hibernate in a new common room.

SU FACILITIES
The Tithe Barn Union facilities include: bar; canteen; coffee bar; TV lounge; pool table; meeting rooms. Plus, run by the College: photocopier; general store; printing service; launderette; advice centre; secondhand bookshop.

CLUBS (NON-SPORTING)
See Clubs tables.

OTHER ORGANISATIONS
A new student paper *could be winging its way from the ashes sometime soon. Ish.*

RELIGIOUS
- **4 CHAPLAINS (COFE, METHODIST, RC, BAPTIST)**
Chapel on campus.

PAID WORK
- **JOB BUREAU** • **PAID WORK** TERM-TIME 20%; HOLS 30%
Vacancy boards keep the students updated. Opportunities vary, but in-season there's well-paid but heavy-duty work harvesting and lambing.

SPORTS ⓊⓊⓊⓊⓊⓊⓊⓊⓊⓊⓊⓊⓊⓊ

- **RECENT SUCCESSES** HOCKEY • **BUSA RANKING** 104

The College clay pigeon shooting club is the largest in the country; they stock their own guns for students to borrow. There's also a gym (£20/month) and a steadfast hunt supporters' club, complete with a Master of Beagles. Sporting rivalry with Harper Adams is *legendary – RAC's still mourning the loss of its pantomime horse's head.*

SPORTS FACILITIES
Football pitch; two hockey pitches; a cricket pitch; four tennis courts; one netball court; three rugby pitches; an all-weather pitch; three squash courts; and a clay pigeon shooting range. All clubs have subscription fees. Cirencester has a sports hall, swimming pool, ice rink, bowling green, golf courses *galore* and lakes nearby. See University of Gloucestershire for facilities in Cheltenham.

SPORTING CLUBS
Beagles; Clay Pigeon Shooting; Lacrosse; Polo. See also Clubs tables.

ATTRACTIONS see University of Gloucestershire

ACCOMMODATION ⓊⓊⓊⓊⓊⓊⓊⓊⓊⓊ

IN COLLEGE
- **CATERED** 46% • **COST** £135 (30WKS)
- **1ST YRS LIVING IN** 95%
- **INSURANCE PREMIUM** £

AVAILABILITY Nearly all first years can live in , but if there's unexpected demand those living locally already may not get a place. Normally, though, around half of the undergrad population lives in, and about a quarter share. The rooms are *fine* and those in Coad Court or Woodland Lodge have *calming* country views. West Lodge *isn't awful* but it's old, without en suite, and the views are a bit *uninspiring*. Some halls have en suite rooms, net access, phone points and TV aerial sockets, the newest is reserved for postgrads and is set back a little from the main campus and have kitchen facilities. Women are not housed on the ground floor wherever possible – *just to give them more exercise*. Rents are reduced for students living in during holidays. A £500 deposit

R

(£300 for sharers) is required before moving into halls *in case students trash the place*.
CAR PARKING *Bountiful*. The Stroud Road car park has room for 500 cars.

EXTERNALLY
O AVE RENT £60 **O LIVING AT HOME** 10%
AVAILABILITY Cheaper housing on offer in Cirencester (but won't include parking costs).
HOUSING HELP Most 2nd and 3rd years find pads in town through the accommodation service, which approves landlords, posts vacancies and offers property vetting and contract approval services.

WELFARE ◖◖◖◖◖◖◖◖◖◖◖◖

SERVICES
O DISABILITIES OFFICER O WELFARE OFFICER O COLLEGE COUNSELLORS 1 FULL **O CRIME RATING** !
The College motto may be 'Avorum Cultus Percorumque' (or 'Caring for the fields and the beasts'), but they do give some thought to their students in the old welfare department too. Counselling is paid for by the College but takes place off-campus and is available 24/7.
HEALTH Nurse; GP surgery four days a week.
DISABILITIES Around 17% of the students have some form of dyslexia and receive extra tuition as well as access to a dyslexia officer. *All courses claim to be accessible with ramps etc., but some buildings are just too damn old to be practical.*

FINANCE
O AVE DEBT PER YEAR £1,840
O HOME STUDENT FEES £3,000
FEES International undergrads pay £6,800/year, as do part-timers (per eight modules). Everyone pays for an *alarming number* of extras: study visits and field trips, gun storage and beagle fee (optional), compulsory campus fee, compulsory caution money, *optional breathing tax*.
O ACCESS FUND £90,000
O SUCCESSFUL APPLICATIONS/YR 40
SUPPORT The bursary scheme takes the load off top-up fees for the eligible. Scholarships include sports, outstanding achievement, Dick Harris (students born in Scotland, Cumbria or Northumbria), the Sir Emrys Bursary, similar but for students with a Welsh connection.

ROYAL COLLEGE OF MUSIC

O ROYAL COLLEGE OF MUSIC Prince Consort Road, London, SW7 2BS **TEL** (020) 7589 3643 **E−MAIL** info@rcm.ac.uk
WEBSITE www.rcm.ac.uk **O THE STUDENTS' ASSOCIATION ROYAL COLLEGE OF MUSIC** Prince Consort Road, London, SW7 2BS
TEL (020) 7591 4350

GENERAL ◖◖◖◖◖◖◖◖◖◖◖◖◖

Right next to the Albert Hall, over the road from Kensington Gardens (where Peter Pan lives, honest) is the *imposing* Victorian edifice of the Royal College of Music. It was founded by the Prince of Wales who went on to become the chubby, popular Timothy West lookalike Edward VII. He also had it off with numerous actresses, *but we're drifting from the point*. We're talking music, not drama here. *The RCM has a worldwide reputation, especially for chamber music and opera. Things are quite laid-back (although the workload isn't) and the college all-but shuts down at weekends.* For general information about London see University of London

ATMOSPHERE
Small with a friendly and supportive atmosphere. Students here are approachable, bright and united by an enthusiasm for music. They can sometimes be found practising with their vocal chords in and around campus. A very high work ethic and competitive environment. It's like the 'X Factor' in chinos.

LONDON see University of London

SEX RATIO: ♂47 ♀53	FOUNDED: 1882
FULL−TIME U'GRADS: 610	PART−TIME: 5
POSTGRADS: 200	NON−DEGREE: 230
AVE COURSE: 4YRS	ETHNIC: 14%
STATE:PRIVATE SCHOOL: 50:50	FLUNK RATE: 3%
MATURE: 5%	INTERNATIONAL: 35%
DISABLED: 5	LOCAL: N/A

> **Royal College of Music students have been banned from practising in the disabled toilets.**

Words in italics are Push's point of view − take it or leave it...

KENSINGTON

Posh Kensington is home to millionaires and museums, perhaps not the first place you'd choose to plonk a load of cash-strapped students. Shopping is designer and pricey but close tube and transport links means the rest of London's easily accessible.

TRAVEL see University of London

Number 52, 9 and 10 buses all serve the site. The nearest tubes are South Kensington, (a five minute *amble* from College), Gloucester Road and Knightsbridge and the nearest rail station is Paddington.

CAREER PROSPECTS

⊙ UNEMPLOYED AFTER **6** MTHS 2%

The Woodhouse Centre does the advice/work-experience/bulletin board thing.

FAMOUS ALUMNI

Janet Baker, Peter Pears, Joan Sutherland, Jonathan Lemalu (singers); Julian Bream (guitarist); Benjamin Britten, Gustav Holst, Michael Tippet, Mark Anthony Turnage, Julian Anderson, Ralph Vaughan Williams (composers), Andrew Lloyd Webber (also a, *ahem*, composer); Colin Davis, Neville Marriner (conductors); Barry Douglas (pianist); James Galway (flautist); Belcea Quartet (string quartet).

FURTHER INFO

⊙ PROSPECTUS ⊙ OPEN DAYS

ACADEMIC ◯◯◯◯◯◯◯◯◯◯◯◯◯

RCM does music, *and does it very intensely and very well*. Exchange schemes are in place with the Universities of California and Western Ontario. There are Alexander Technique classes and visits from leading musicians (*it's never time for Chico then?*).

ENTRY POINTS: N/A	AVE POINTS: N/A
APPLICATIONS PER PLACE: N/A	CLEARING: N/A
NO. OF TERMS: 3	LENGTH OF TERMS: 10WKS
STAFF TO STUDENT RATIO: 1:3	STUDY ADDICTS: 2%
TEACHING: ★★★★	RESEARCH: ★★★
YEAR ABROAD: 2%	SANDWICH STUDENTS: N/A
1STS: 16%	2.2S: 27%
2.1S: 54%	3RDS: 2%

ADMISSIONS

⊙ APPLY VIA CUKAS

All applicants are auditioned. *Spoon players need not apply.* You can apply to CUKAS (the Conservatoires UK Admissions Service) online – see www.cukas.ac.uk.

SUBJECTS

MUSIC 100%.

UNUSUAL Physics and Music (run jointly with Imperial College).

LIBRARIES

⊙ **300,000** BOOKS ⊙ **29** STUDY PLACES

Students can also use Imperial College library and public music libraries in Kensington and Westminster. *Unsurprisingly, there's a world-class music collection.*

COMPUTERS

⊙ **50** WORKSTATIONS ⊙ **24**-HR ACCESS

Includes internet café, stations in the library and 20 access terminals in halls.

OTHER LEARNING FACILITIES

Custom-built opera house; rehearsal rooms; recording studio. The Centre for Performing History has instruments dating back from the 15th-Century.

ENTERTAINMENT ◯◯◯◯◯◯◯◯◯

THE CITY see University of London

KENSINGTON

Kensington's *not a clubber's paradise* but with London on your doorstep, you won't miss out. A-list acts and events are the lifeblood of the Albert Hall, and London Fashion Week also operates from the area.

COLLEGE

⊙ PRICE OF A PINT OF BEER £1.80
⊙ GLASS OF WINE £1.50
⊙ CAN OF RED BULL £1

The students, being entertainers themselves, sometimes spontaneously erupt into music. Disconcerting for other Tube travellers.

BARS SA bar, most often used after concerts and for parties and *sporadic but packed* events on a Friday evening. It closes at 8pm otherwise, and many students head over to the Union at Imperial College.

THEATRES The theatre is mostly used for musical, rather than dramatic, offerings.

MUSIC VENUES *The whole College is essentially built out of potential music venues, but the Concert Hall and the Britten Theatre are the biggest.*

CLUBBING Themed parties and live jazz on campus roughly fortnightly.

FOOD The bar does snacks and the canteen provides *cheap, heavenly, made-to-order* sandwiches, *but Kensington's got more variety, if you've got the money.*

OTHER Summer Ball in June and a *pretty epic Freshers' Week.*

SOCIAL ()()()()()()()()()()()()

ROYAL COLLEGE OF MUSIC STUDENTS' ASSOCIATION
O 1 SABBATICAL O TURNOUT AT LAST BALLOT 40%
If more politicians announced their policies in the style of a Gilbert & Sullivan musical, RCM students might take more interest. They did manage a canteen boycott that lowered food prices, though. The small SA has games machines; pool tables; TV lounge; bar and meeting rooms. There's also a College photocopier; 'Upbeat' termly mag; Rag association and Rag week (raising money for the Brain Research Trust through 'chav & pikey' parties); Catholic chaplain and Christian Union.

PAID WORK
O JOB BUREAU O PAID WORK TERM-TIME 90%; HOLS 90%
The Woodhouse Centre finds paid performances, stewarding and admin work and teaching spotty school-kids and adults *(we don't know if they're spotty too).*

SPORTS ()()()()()()()()()()()()()

All sports facilities are shared with Imperial College, London. Football, salsa, netball and yoga are the main physical activities.

ACCOMMODATION ()()()()()()()()()

IN COLLEGE
O SELF CATERING 28% **O COST** £90 (30WKS)
O 1ST YRS LIVING IN 95%
O INSURANCE PREMIUM £
AVAILABILITY First years are housed in College Hall (a converted bank) in Hammersmith (nearest tube Ravenscourt Park), where there are common rooms, shared kitchens, gardens, practice rooms and a resident cat and dog. *Some students don't appreciate how far away from College it is.* Rents are *reasonable*, for London, with twin rooms starting at £63/week per person.
CAR PARKING *Difficult, although there are some of the world's most expensive parking meters right outside the College.*

EXTERNALLY see University of London
O AVE RENT £100 **O LIVING AT HOME** 10%
AVAILABILITY Houses and flats to be had all over London – most RCM students live in the west. Also hostels and inter-collegiate lodgings.
HOUSING HELP Advice and a list of suitable housing *(landlords who don't mind a bit of noise).* RCM students can also use Imperial College's services.

WELFARE ()()()()()()()()()()()()()

SERVICES
O COLLEGE COUNSELLORS 1 **O CRIME RATING** !!!
The Welfare team offers advice and support and refers students elsewhere if in need of further help. *The welfare's good, largely because students can also use Imperial College's facilities,* which include counselling and psychotherapeutic services. *Disabled access is variable – a case of old-building syndrome –* but lifts and ramps have been installed.

FINANCE
O AVE DEBT PER YEAR £2,780 **O ACCESS FUND** £3,000
O SUCCESSFUL APPLICATIONS/YR 48
O AVE PAYMENT £150-2,000
SUPPORT Scholarships, study support grants, instrument loan fund, hardship money available ranging from £150 to £1,500. The Junion Scholarship Bursary coughs up to the tune of £8,000 to enable skill development. *On the whole, quite a soft cushion relatively.*

R

➡ ROYAL HOLLOWAY AND BEDFORD COLLEGE
see *Royal Holloway, London*

ROYAL HOLLOWAY, LONDON

THE COLLEGE IS PART OF THE UNIVERSITY OF LONDON AND STUDENTS ARE ENTITLED TO USE ITS FACILITIES

1) **◉ ROYAL HOLLOWAY** Egham Hill, Egham, Surrey, TW20 8BL **TEL** (01784) 434 455 **E−MAIL** liaison-office@rhul.ac.uk
WEBSITE www.rhul.ac.uk **◉ ROYAL HOLLOWAY STUDENTS' UNION** Egham Hill, Egham, Surrey, TW20 0EX **TEL** (01784) 486 300
E−MAIL reception@su.rhul.ac.uk **WEBSITE** www.su.rhbnc.ac.uk
2) **◉ BEDFORD SQUARE** 2 Gower Street, London **TEL** (020) 7307 8600

GENERAL ◖◗◖◗◖◗◖◗◖◗◖◗◖◗

R oyal Holloway's part of the University of
London, despite being 20 miles away from
the capital, and a mile from Egham in Surrey,
near Thorpe Park and Windsor. It is sometimes
called London's country campus – *it's certainly as
green as the University gets, even if it is all mani-
cured and tamed splendour.* The *extensive* park
grounds on a *steep* hill on the fringe of Windsor
Park set off the College's *astoundingly beautiful*
Founder's Building, an ornate red brick and stone
structure, based on the Château Chambord in the
Loire Valley in France. It's arranged as a square
around grass courtyards with turrets, domes and
ornamental carvings all over. *Fancy, eh?* For general information about London see University of
London

🚶🚶🚶🚶🚶🚶🚶🚶🚶🚶🚶🚶🚶🚶🚶🚶🚶🚶🚶🚶

SEX RATIO: ♂40 ♀60	**FOUNDED:** 1886
FULL−TIME U'GRADS: 5,494	**PART−TIME:** 640
POSTGRADS: 1,010	**NON−DEGREE:** 250
AVE COURSE: 3YRS	**ETHNIC:** 20%
STATE:PRIVATE SCHOOL: N/A	**FLUNK RATE:** 6%
MATURE: 7%	**INTERNATIONAL:** 26%
DISABLED: 80	**LOCAL:** N/A

ATMOSPHERE

*Royal Holloway's starting to shrug off its right-
wing past and become much more open and
multi-cultural, with a high proportion of mature
students. It's just the right size and location
(small but not claustrophobic, close to London
but still green) for fun and friendship and most of
the students seem glad to be here. It's a campus
university rather than part of the metropolis –
those after a central London experience may feel
isolated.*

SITES

BEDFORD SQUARE (History, Health & Social Care,
Media, Arts, Music) A *small* building (four floors)
45 mins from the main site in the relative bustle
near Tottenham Court Road. *Facilities are sparse
– a communal kitchen and common room – but
it's a good place for students to meet and
socialise in central London.* There's just one student flat, usually filled with postgrads.

LONDON see University of London

EGHAM

The closest town to the campus is Egham, about

a mile away. *It's a typically small, suburban, com-
mutery-type place which can't truthfully be
described as either groovy or student-oriented.
Staines, where Ali G's posse hangs, is nearby.*

TRAVEL see University of London

TRAINS Trains to Waterloo from Egham every 15
mins.
COACHES *Infrequent and expensive* but there's a
College service every 15 mins or so and an SU
bus late at night.
CAR Egham's just outside the M25 London ring
road, north of where the M3 crosses it on the way
south-west. The A30 goes right through the
town. *A car is obviously handier than at other
London sites but parking's tricky on campus.*
BICYCLES *If cycling up the slight hill doesn't put
students off, bikes are useful.*

CAREER PROSPECTS

◉ CAREERS SERVICE ◉ NO. OF STAFF 3 FULL/2 PART **◉
UNEMPLOYED AFTER 6MTHS** 5%
Services are open to students and recent gradu-
ates and are run by the University of London.

FAMOUS ALUMNI

David Bellamy (naturalist); Richmal Crompton
(writer, Just William); Emma Freud (broadcaster
and Mrs Richard Curtis); Felicity Lott, Susan
Bullock (opera singers); Francis Wheen (journalist).

FURTHER INFO

◉ PROSPECTUSES UNDERGRAD; POSTGRAD; DEPARTMENTAL;
VIDEO
◉ OPEN DAYS
The SU produces a handbook and a guide for
mature students.

ACADEMIC ◖◗◖◗◖◗◖◗◖◗◖◗◖◗

◉ 1994 GROUP
Arts & Humanities, Geography, Music, French,
German and Drama *are fairly muscular.* Science is
highly-rated for research and the outreach programme includes master classes and workshops.
Compulsory lectures in all subjects; some degrees
may include workshops (drama), seminars, computer sessions (maths) and video conferencing
(classics).
      Most degrees have one-to-one or small
group tutorial sessions with a personal tutor once
or twice a week. Shared teaching with the Royal

R

College of Music is available for the best music students. The language centre has online access to self-study resources including satellite TV. Foundation or core courses in the first year give way to more options in later years. Assessment's usually through exams and essays, though different subjects vary (especially drama). First year marks don't count towards final degree; second and third year marks usually count for 30% and 70% respectively.

ENTRY POINTS: 240-340	AVE POINTS: N/A
APPLICATIONS PER PLACE: N/A	CLEARING: 14%
NO. OF TERMS: 3	LENGTH OF TERMS: 12wks
STAFF TO STUDENT RATIO: 1:15	STUDY ADDICTS: N/A
TEACHING: ✶✶✶✶✶	RESEARCH: ✶✶✶✶
YEAR ABROAD: N/A	SANDWICH STUDENTS: <1%
1STS: 12%	2.2S: 27%
2.1S: 54%	3RDS: 6%

ADMISSIONS
❂ APPLY VIA UCAS/DIRECT FOR POSTGRADS
Most departments invite potential undergrads to visit, meet current students and staff and generally *have a bit of a nose around*. The college has a high proportion of mature students and some postgraduate courses can be undertaken part-time by distance learning.

SUBJECTS
BIOLOGY 8%   **CLASSICS** 3%   **COMPUTER SCIENCE** 5%   **DRAMA** 6%   **ECONOMICS** 8%   **ENGLISH** 8%   **EUROPEAN STUDIES** 2%   **FRENCH** 4%   **GEOGRAPHY** 5%   **GEOLOGY** 3%   **GERMAN** 1%   **HISTORY** 8%   **ITALIAN** 2%   **MANAGEMENT** 15%   **MATHS** 4%   **MEDIA ARTS** 5%   **MUSIC** 3%   **PHYSICS** 2%   **PSYCHOLOGY** 6%   **SPANISH** 2%   **SPS** 4%
BEST Biochemistry; Biology; Classics; Drama; Economics; French; Geography; Italian; Management; Maths; Media Arts; Physics; Psychology; Social & Political Sciences; Sociology.

LIBRARIES
❂ 548,815 BOOKS ❂ 634 STUDY PLACES
Three libraries: Bedford, Founders and Music. *Facilities are pretty good but there's still room for improvement.*

COMPUTERS
❂ 580 WORKSTATIONS ❂ 24-HR ACCESS (WITH A SWIPE CARD)

OTHER LEARNING FACILITIES
Language lab; Electron Microscopy centre; drama studio/theatre; computer-aided design lab; music rehearsal rooms.

ENTERTAINMENT ◖◖◖◖◖◖◖◖◖◖

THE CITY see University of London
❂ PRICE OF A PINT OF BEER £1.80
❂ GLASS OF WINE £2.30
❂ CAN OF RED BULL £1.55

Egham's about as lively as a flattened hedgehog, although there's no shortage of places to get a drink. Students looking for the high life go into London instead.
CINEMAS The ten-screen Vue in Staines is five mins away from the College. Cineworld in Eltham is slightly further afield.
THEATRES The Orange Tree Theatre in Richmond (20 mins by train) does discounted tickets. A few seats every Tuesday are available on a pay-as-much-as-you-like basis, *which sounds pretty good to Push*. The National Theatre lays on free events for students.
PUBS No shortage of watering holes. The Monkey's Forehead, opposite the college, is *popular.*
MUSIC VENUES The Exchange.
EATING OUT There are student deals to be munched at local pizza, Indian, Italian, Chinese, seafood and fish 'n' chip places. *Pushplugs: Perfect Pizza (buy one, get one free); Red Rose for Indian (10% discount); Jack's for fishy pleasures.*

UNIVERSITY
❂ PRICE OF A PINT OF BEER £1.70
❂ GLASS OF WINE £1.20
❂ CAN OF RED BULL £1
BARS There are six bars in all *(it's rumoured that the Queen Mum once had a sneaky dram in one of them)*. The busiest drink-spot is Tommy's *(perhaps because it's on the ground floor of the SU and not such an effort to reach)*; there's also Stumble Inn and the Union Bar. Holloway's is *popular with the sporty set.*
THEATRES Two (including one Japanese) are used for student and professional productions. The drama and musical theatre socs put on regular plays and productions in London.
FILM The SU shows a film Sat and Sun, *usually mainstream.*
MUSIC VENUES Raghav played recently.
CLUBBING *Something for everyone. Cheap and cheerful cheese and R'n'B nights are popular. For the more discerning clubber,* the Union attracts names like Trevor Nelson, Shorty Blitz and Tim Westwood, and arranges group nights to the *über* London clubs.
COMEDY/CABARET The Stumble Inn draws the likes of Tony Hall and John Maloney every three weeks.
FOOD The SU-run TWZO's offers *the best range (including a decent vegetarian selection)* but *some find it a bit pricey. Students who live on campus tend to prefer the University dining halls.* Café Jules provides chic and sophisticated dishes.
OTHER *More balls than a snooker table:* society, sports, Christmas and summer black tie events. The fashion show in March is a *massive* three-day event.

R

SOCIAL

ROYAL HOLLOWAY STUDENTS' UNION
○ **4** SABBATICALS ○ TURNOUT AT LAST BALLOT 12% ○ NUS MEMBER

The SU has good reason to smile. It's finally lost the right-wing tag that dogged it for so many years and is now considered a very fair and democratic union by many. Socially, it excels, with a rapidly-expanding roster of clubs and societies to cater for every taste. It even enjoys massive student support, something that most SU's would sell their kidneys for.

SU FACILITIES
Nightclub; music venue; bars; coffee bar; cafeteria; fast food outlet; 15 pool/snooker tables; photo booth; photocopier; fax service; printing service; payphones; advice centre; TV lounge; three minibuses; games machines; vending machines; NatWest bank on campus; shop; ticket agency; launderette; Waterstones.

CLUBS (NON-SPORTING)
Absolute Harmony; BALADS (dance); Chinese; Cinema; Comedy; Historical re-enactment; Lebanese; Manga & Anime; Poker; Wine & Cheese Appreciation. **See also Clubs tables.**

OTHER ORGANISATIONS
'The Orbital' mag is published by the SU three times a year. The Radio-One-award-winning student radio station '1287 AM Insanity' broadcasts full-time in the Union. There's a Community Action Group and Rag's *on the increase*, with all the societies and sports clubs getting in on the charity act.

RELIGIOUS
Chapels and a Muslim prayer room can be found in College or nearby.

PAID WORK see University of London
○ JOB BUREAU

Plenty of job opportunities on campus or locally *for those in need of an extra bob or two.* The College and the SU provide vacancy boards, and there's a job file and two members of staff to *make job-hunting that bit easier.*

SPORTS

○ BUSA RANKING 70

The Royal Holloway's been declared London's best sporting college by the University of London Union (ULU) and there's a good smattering of facilities on campus and locally, including a new sports hall and renovated fitness 'suite' *(nothing to do with lounging in an armchair watching Jade Goody's danceaerobics though).*

SPORTS FACILITIES
Tennis, basketball, squash and netball courts; five football pitches; rugby and cricket fields; multigym; aerobics studio; sports hall. The nearby Thames and Datchet Reservoirs provide sailing and watersport opportunities.

SPORTING CLUBS
American Football; Boots; Cheerleading; Dragonfly (karate); Lacrosse; Ninjitsu; Polo; Scuba; Tukkong Moosul; Thai kick-boxing; MACS (climbing). **See also Clubs tables.**

ATTRACTIONS see University of London
Wentworth Golf Course is nearby.

ACCOMMODATION

IN COLLEGE
○ CATERED 21% ○ COST £83 (30-38WKS)
○ SELF CATERING 18% ○ COST £88 (30-50WKS)
○ **1**ST YRS LIVING IN 20%
○ INSURANCE PREMIUM £

AVAILABILITY First years are guaranteed accommodation (deadlines apply and the numbers suggest most miss it, or prefer to live elsewhere). Big and modern halls or, for spacious rooms *and kudos*, there are rooms in the Founder's Building. 3% have to share. Some accommodation is single-sex. First years bed down in Founders and Kingswood, although the latter's *less popular* because of distance from the main campus. Gowar and Wedderburn are slightly newer blocks.

CAR PARKING Parking is by permit only and *very limited.*

EXTERNALLY see University of London
○ AVE RENT £68

AVAILABILITY Privately rented houses are easy enough to find and without the London price-tags. Englefield Green is the most convenient area but many prefer Staines (one train stop away) for the better social life it offers – *better than Egham, that is.*

HOUSING HELP The College Accommodation Service provides vacancy sheets and standard contracts.

WELFARE

SERVICES
○ LGBT SOCIETY ○ MATURE STUDENTS' OFFICER ○ POST-GRAD STUDENTS' OFFICER ○ INTERNATIONAL STUDENTS' SOCIETY ○ DISABILITIES STUDENTS' SOCIETY ○ ETHNIC MINORITIES SOCIETY ○ LATE-NIGHT/WOMEN'S MINIBUS ○ SELF-DEFENCE CLASSES ○ NIGHTLINE ○ COLLEGE COUNSELLORS 5 FULL/5 PART ○ CRIME RATING !

The SU has a Welfare Officer. Other services

R

include an alcohol awareness programme.

HEALTH There's an on-campus health centre with two GPs and a part-time dentist.

WOMEN The SU lays on self-defence classes and a late-night minibus.

DISABILITIES Access is *pretty bad* in the older parts of the campus. Receipt of a major grant has improved things a bit with, for example, more ramps being installed. Potential applicants should contact the Educational Support Officer. There's accommodation for disabled students and facilities for the hearing-impaired.

FINANCE
- **AVE DEBT PER YEAR** £2,780
- **HOME STUDENT FEES** £3,000

FEES International undergrads have to stump up between £7,975 and £11,750 a year.

- **ACCESS FUND** £217,344 **SUCCESSFUL APPLICATIONS/YR** 335 **AVE PAYMENT** £630

SUPPORT There are a few extra bursaries on offer *for the crème de la crème*. Bedford Entrance Scholarships give £1,000 and guaranteed accommodation to *the cleverest undergrads*. Bioscience Entrance Scholarships dish up the *same goodies* to students of that subject. Choral, Organ and Instrumental Scholarships give guaranteed accommodation and between £100-300 to the musically gifted. Sporty students who compete at national or international level may get up to £750, guaranteed accommodation, discounted physio and free access to local sports centres under the Student Talented Athlete Recognition Scheme (STARS). Separate scholarships are available for international students, particularly those from India.

⮞ **ROYAL POSTGRAD MEDICAL SCHOOL**
see *Imperial College London*

ROYAL SCOTTISH ACADEMY OF MUSIC AND DRAMA

 ROYAL SCOTTISH ACADEMY OF MUSIC AND DRAMA 100 Renfrew Street, Glasgow, G2 3DB **TEL** (0141) 332 4101 **E–MAIL** registry@rsamd.ac.uk **WEBSITE** www.rsamd.ac.uk **RSAMD STUDENTS UNION** 100 Renfrew Street, Glasgow, G2 3DB **TEL** (0141) 270 8296 **E–MAIL** supresident@rsamd.ac.uk **WEBSITE** www.forums.rsamd-su.org.uk

GENERAL ͰͰͰͰͰͰͰͰͰͰͰͰ

The heart of a Scottish city renowned for its *industrial past may not appear to be the ideal spot to establish a community of artists and performers*, but for the past 150 years RSAMD has been churning out *some of the best musicians in the world and some of the UK's most respected actors*. Right in the middle of the busiest part of Glasgow, near the Glasgow Film Theatre, the Theatre Royal and the Scottish TV Centre, the Academy has now enjoyed more than a decade in its new, *attractively modern*, purpose-built home. The campus – *or rather, the building* – is more of a cluster of performance spaces than a conventional college. Its state-of-the-art concert halls, auditoria and theatre spaces offer a continuous and *wide-ranging* programme of music, drama and opera to paying punters – performed by both students and visiting professionals. *As an arts venue, even the most thesp-hating cynic would be reduced to tears and flower-throwing.* As a university college, it's a totally unique place to study – *its prestigious atmosphere is generated and justified by the portraits of famous alumni and celeb glitterati that line the walls.*

SEX RATIO: ♀33 ♂67	FOUNDED: 1847
FULL–TIME U'GRADS: 560	PART–TIME: 0
POSTGRADS: 115	NON–DEGREE: N/A
AVE COURSE: 4YRS	ETHNIC: N/A
STATE:PRIVATE SCHOOL: N/A	FLUNK RATE: 11%
MATURE: 16%	INTERNATIONAL: 14%
DISABLED: 35	LOCAL: N/A

ATMOSPHERE
Constant public performances and continuous assessment creates a vibrant, humming atmosphere. The Academy never stands still and the students are as busy and on the go as rabbits at an orgy – leaving them with little time to pursue extra-curricular activities. It goes without saying that they're an artsy bunch, determined to take their first steps into professional arts careers. No prima donnas though – many are mature in outlook as well as age and the small size of the College makes for a tight-knit and welcoming family atmosphere and the students enjoy close relationships with, and undivided attention from, their tutors.

GLASGOW see University of Glasgow

TRAVEL see University of Glasgow
CAR The M8 is the best road for getting to RSAMD and there's a car park around the corner. *Parking elsewhere in Glasgow is a major bitch*, however, and not many students keep cars.
LOCAL Bus routes 40, 41 and 61 are handy for halls. Fares average out at £1.15.
BICYCLES *Navigating the busy roads can get a bit lairy at times but cycling is generally an easy way to travel to and from the Academy, thanks to the subways*. There are spaces to chain up bikes with cameras overlooking the area.

CAREER PROSPECTS
○ **UNEMPLOYED AFTER 6 MTHS** 1%
There's no specific careers service like in most institutions – *but then, RSAMD isn't like most institutions, is it?* Students have the option of using the University of Glasgow's careers resources *but most don't need to*. RSAMD receives regular visits from professionals (BBCScottish Symphony Orchestra etc.), who offer advice on performance, business planning and self-promotion. Successful alumni – *of which there are many* – come back to offer advice to *their eager former selves*. Students get practical help with career management, including assistance with CVs, headshot photos and auditions and a yearly job fair and careers day. *Students have every chance to learn the tricks of the trade, rub shoulders with the pros and butter up any potential employers.* Actors, for example, receive guidance from casting directors in their final year and an Acting Showcase invites agents and directors to check out the talent, *browsing over student profiles like hawks in a hamster farm.* Final year students in the School of Drama are assigned a graduate mentor who offers personal advice on career choices and auditions, as well as introducing them to professional contacts.

FAMOUS ALUMNI
Billy Boyd (hobbit); Robert Carlyle (Trainspotting, The Full Monty); Tom Conti (actor); Alan Cumming (The High Life, Goldeneye); Sheena Easton (For Your Eyes Only); Hannah Gordon (Watercolour Challenge); John Hannah (Four Weddings and a Funeral, Sliding Doors); James McAvoy (Mr Tumnus, Band of Brothers); James Macpherson (Taggart); Lisa Milne (soprano); Marina Nadiradze (pianist); Daniela Nardini (This Life); David Tennant (Doctor Who); Ruby Wax (mouthy presenter). *More or less any orchestra worth its strings will have a graduate of RSAMD's music school sat in its ranks.*

SPECIAL FEATURES
The Academy has close relationships with similar conservatoires across the globe, often sending students to Norway, Warsaw, California and Paris among other places. Contemporary Theatre Practice students do professional placements with companies in Glasgow and Edinburgh and often do secondments in other cities and countries.

FURTHER INFO
○ **PROSPECTUSES** UNDERGRAD; POSTGRAD; DEPARTMENTAL; AUDIO ○ **OPEN DAYS**
All prospectuses, including the audio version, are available from the general office. Book in advance for open days.

ACADEMIC ○○○○○○○○○○○○○

RSAMD is a conservatoire – *not a French sun lounge*, but rather an institution dedicated to training musicians, actors and production technicians to professional levels of ability. As such, studying here is a vocational affair *(or rather a matter of personal 'calling')* and Academy students benefit from *highly specialised* facilities, *tight* links with relevant industries and an intensely focused environment. Most degree courses are largely practical (recitals, workshops, rehearsals etc.) with theoretical elements thrown into the mix in the form of essays and written exams. *Studying here is a 9-to-5 job and then some – there's time to relax, but the pressure of regular public performance can make life both exciting and stressful.*

ENTRY POINTS: N/A		**AVE POINTS:** N/A	
APPLICATIONS PER PLACE: N/A		**CLEARING:** 0%	
NO. OF TERMS: 3		**LENGTH OF TERMS:** 12wks	
STAFF TO STUDENT RATIO: 1:1		**STUDY ADDICTS:** 25%	
TEACHING: N/A		**RESEARCH:** *	
YEAR ABROAD: <1%		**SANDWICH STUDENTS:** 0%	

ADMISSIONS
○ **APPLY VIA CUKAS/DIRECT FOR DRAMA**
Applications should be made at www.cukas.ac.uk, except for BEd Music, for which students should apply via UCAS to the University of Glasgow. All applicants are interviewed and/or auditioned – if not in person, then by video submission – and *it's performing ability that cuts mustard more than academic qualifications.* Wannabe actors are required to perform two speeches. RSAMD will accept anyone they think is talented enough, regardless of background, although anyone over 30 is normally considered past it for most departments – however younger mature students with professional musical experience still stand a chance. The Academy is part of the GOALS scheme, which pulls in pupils from schools in West Scotland that don't send many on to higher education.

SUBJECTS
DRAMA 36%   **MUSIC** 64%
UNUSUAL All courses are unique among universities, particularly Scottish Music, Digital Film & Theatre, Musical Theatre and Technical & Production courses.

LIBRARIES
○ **90,000 BOOKS** ○ **32 STUDY PLACES**
The Whittaker Library is home to one of the UK's most extensive collections of musical and

dramatic performance materials, *including enough CDs, vids and DVDs to keep a dodgy market stall in business for millennia. The place is a tiny thespian Tardis and although there aren't that many study places or books in total, with such a large component of the courses being practical, there doesn't need to be.*

COMPUTERS
○ **30 WORKSTATIONS**
The IT provision in the Ainslie Millar Room is a *bit limp compared to most universities*, but, again, the facilities are entirely tailored to music and drama students. Computer training available. Fifteen IT stations are dotted around campus so students can check e-mail on the go. Wi-fi is on the way.

OTHER LEARNING FACILITIES
Countless rehearsal rooms for music and other performances, as well as *the indescribably fancy Groves Studio* offering digital film and TV-making facilities and editing suites. And, of course, loads of performance spaces.

ENTERTAINMENT ()()()()()()()()()

THE CITY see University of Glasgow

ACADEMY
○ **PRICE OF A PINT OF BEER** £1.80
○ **GLASS OF WINE** £2
○ **CAN OF RED BULL** £1.50
BARS *The Café Bar is not a bar in the usual lager-soaked sense, but more of a back-slapping social centre for after performances. It's relaxed and friendly*, lined with pictures of the celebs that studied and drank here, *but the booze stops flowing at 9pm*. There's also a bar in the common room, but with no permanent bar staff, opening is *sporadic at best*.
THEATRES Over a third of the students study drama, so the Academy wouldn't get far without its two theatres – the Athenaeum and the Chandler, both constantly in use. *There are too many plays to count* and acting students also tread a large number of local boards, including the Edinburgh Fringe. Performances are directed by professionals so *there's little risk of school nativity-style dramatic catastrophes*. Several students have been up for Olivier awards in recent years.
MUSIC VENUES Four concert venues showcase a variety of student and visiting musicians. Academy musicians are frequently booked to perform at other venues in Glasgow and further afield. Vladimir Ashkenazy, Idlewild, Jane Eaglen have all played recently.
FOOD Snacks are available in the Café Bar and after extensive student campaigning, a new catering team has been shipped in *to drag the sub-standard* Aramark Canteen *out of the doldrums. The current*

favourite is the Granden Yoghurt Bar – there've been fights over the last pot.
OTHER *Special events tend to be highbrow and high profile including art exhibitions and special concerts. The Summer Ball is the biggest annual event and there's a spattering of comedy nights.*

SOCIAL ()()()()()()()()()()()()

ROYAL SCOTTISH ACADEMY OF MUSIC AND DRAMA STUDENTS' UNION
○ **1 SABBATICAL** ○ **NUS MEMBER**
It's such a tiny place, with such cosy ties between students and staff, that the Union has very little to do. The SU is consulted on most issues relating to the College and receives strong support from the authorities. *There's little time for political rallying or armchair revolutions, but they give a nod to national campaigns for performers' rights.*

SU FACILITIES
Minimal but adequate. The College runs the canteen, meeting rooms, photocopying, payphones, printing and fax service, vending machines and advice centre. The SU takes charge of the bar, common rooms, jukebox and pool table.

CLUBS (NON-SPORTING)
Many students join societies at neighbouring universities. **See also Clubs tables.**

OTHER ORGANISATIONS
Rag raises an *admirable* £5,000 through buskathons and *other less arty wheezes*.

RELIGIOUS
The Christian Union runs a Bible study group, morning prayer sesh and the odd lecture. Religion in Glasgow: see University of Glasgow

PAID WORK see University of Glasgow
○ **JOB BUREAU**
Despite hectic schedules, most students work during and out of term. The Union keeps noticeboards of vacancies, mainly relating to the arts, but with the odd wallet-top-up job in sales or call centres. Ushering work is available in the Academy, there's also an informal musicians agency, *for more enterprising students*.

SPORTS ()()()()()()()()()()()()()

Maybe it's nature, maybe it's nurture, but the fact is that artistic people have never been much into sport. RSAMD has no sweat-generating facilities, although students can use Glasgow Caledonian's Arc Centre and the SU sports officer arranges football tournaments.

R

SPORTING CLUBS

Occasional dance and massage sessions. That's it at RSAMD, and other University's sports clubs are a no-go because of insurance issues. *Oh well.*

ATTRACTIONS see University of Glasgow

ACCOMMODATION ()()()()()()()()()()

IN COLLEGE
- **SELF CATERING** 20% **COST** £80 (35-50WKS)
- **1ST YRS LIVING IN** 90%
- **INSURANCE PREMIUM** £££

AVAILABILITY Although guarantees given to first years coming from outside Glasgow, 10% of locals don't get a place to crash. Academy accommodation is grouped with the independent Glasgow Student Village on Queen Street. Rooms are either in self-catering hostels or self-contained flats – first years and internationals tend to get the former. There's also en suite rooms, fitted kitchens with dining areas, TV aerial points and internet access – subject to a fee. 24-hr security. *Students aren't exactly satisfied, however.*
CAR PARKING *None at residences.*

EXTERNALLY see University of Glasgow
- **AVE RENT** £50-70 **LIVING AT HOME** 25%

WELFARE ()()()()()()()()()()()()

SERVICES
- **COLLEGE COUNSELLORS** 1 FULL **CRIME RATING** !!!

An *active* student-advisor system is overseen by the Academy Counsellor. Most teaching staff are keen to offer help and support. The SU's Equal Opportunities Officer is responsible for women, international students, students with disabilities and LGBTs.
HEALTH The Woodside Health Centre is nearest. The Dental Hospital is five minutes away. There's an on-site Alexander Technique specialist.
DISABILITIES *Access is good*, with lifts, ramps and toilets in the Academy building. The Fife lecture theatre and all auditoria are fitted with hearing loops and have wheelchair spaces. Note-takers and scribes are available. Many RSAMD students are dyslexic, *so support is particularly good.*
CRIME *The area around Sauchiehall Street is known as a bit dodgy, so students should take care. But then, they should take care everywhere really.*

FINANCE
- **AVE DEBT PER YEAR** £1,644
- **HOME STUDENT FEES** £1,175

FEES Costs vary widely, depending on the size of the course's practical element, but international undergrad fees start at £10,323. UK undergrads have to fork out a fistful more than Scottish types.
SUPPORT Some bursaries are available for new students and married students over 25 can be eligible for a Mature Student's Bursary, mainly for childcare. Entrance scholarships ranging from £100-1,000 are awarded on the basis of admittance auditions. Plus loads of other awards and scholarships, most of them aimed at promoting exceptional talent.

R

ROYAL VETERINARY COLLEGE, LONDON

THE COLLEGE IS PART OF THE UNIVERSITY OF LONDON AND STUDENTS ARE ENTITLED TO USE ITS FACILITIES

1) **THE ROYAL VETERINARY COLLEGE** Royal College Street, London, NW1 0TU **TEL** (020) 7468 5000 **E–MAIL** registry@rvc.ac.uk **WEBSITE** www.rvc.ac.uk
2) **HAWKSHEAD** Hawkshead Lane, North Mymms, Hatfield, Herts, AL9 7TA **TEL** (01707) 666 333 **THE ROYAL VETERINARY COLLEGE STUDENTS' UNION SOCIETY** Hawkshead Campus, Hawkshead Lane, North Mymms, Hatfield, Herts, AL9 7TA **TEL** (01707) 666 310 **E–MAIL** sucommunications@rvc.ac.uk

GENERAL ()()()()()()()()()()()()()

You *won't be surprised to learn that* RVC (as its chums call it) mostly teaches students how to be vets. The College's main site is one and a quarter miles from Trafalgar Square, in Camden,

which has a reputation *as one of the trendiest, buzziest areas of London, but is getting a bit saggy and complacent nowadays.* Students spend two years at the redbrick Camden site, *falling over minor indie bands and over-eyelinered types every time they go down the pub*, and then move out to the *almost tediously tranquil* countryside of Hawkshead to do their clinical study. The Hawkshead campus, a couple of miles from Hatfield, is an extensive, *s elf-contained and green arrangement, set in relaxed, commuter belt* countryside (see University of Hertfordshire). For general information about London see University of London.

SEX RATIO: ♂80 ♀20	FOUNDED: 1791
FULL-TIME U³GRADS: 1,153	PART-TIME: 11
POSTGRADS: 338	NON-DEGREE: 0
AVE COURSE: 5YRS	ETHNIC: 10%
STATE:PRIVATE SCHOOL: 40:60	FLUNK RATE: 0%
MATURE: 13%	INTERNATIONAL: 8%
DISABLED: 10	LOCAL: 6%

ATMOSPHERE
Despite the fact they're ludicrously busy learning how to tell if an elephant's got cystitis or a budgerigar's got scrofula, students still find time to have fun. There's a closer relationship between students and staff than in many universities, with tutor-tutee socials taking place on a regular basis. *Bonds are bound to form in an atmosphere this fast-paced and close-knit, and graduating students often take a post-finals holiday together.*

SITES
HAWKSHEAD (500 students) The flagship campus. *There's even more of an atmosphere of frantic work than there is at Camden,* because by the time students move here they're well on the way to becoming vets. The College keeps its own farm here and *there are few nicer places to finish off a degree (or stick your hand up a cow's rectum, if you must).* For those wanting to get back to the capital, the site is just about walkable from Potters Bar station (15mins), *but it's not the easiest of hikes.*

LONDON see University of London

TRAVEL see University of London
LONDON see University of London
HAWKSHEAD see University of Hertfordshire

CAREER PROSPECTS
Students (in London, at least) can use the University of London facilities.

SPECIAL FEATURES
The College is the only place in England to be accredited by the American Veterinary Medicine Association, *which suggests its facilities are top-notch, especially for a limey institution.*

FURTHER INFO
O PROSPECTUSES UNDERGRAD; POSTGRAD
O OPEN DAYS
The college has been trying to widen access and the lower grades needed by some of the newer courses are helping to mix things up slightly.

ACADEMIC ❍❍❍❍❍❍❍❍❍❍❍❍❍

The teaching's mostly based in small groups and on practical experience *(bring the longest, thickest pair of rubber gloves imaginable). Not the place for an easy ride* – there are year-round assessments and failing end-of-year exams more than once means the red card. *The final year may be lecture-free, but it's also more intense than David Tennant in a staring competition.*

ENTRY POINTS: 20–340	AVE POINTS: N/A
APPLICATIONS PER PLACE: 4	CLEARING: 8%
NO. OF TERMS: 3	LENGTH OF TERMS: 11WKS
STAFF TO STUDENT RATIO: 1:2	STUDY ADDICTS: N/A
TEACHING: ★★★	RESEARCH: ★★★★
YEAR ABROAD: 0%	SANDWICH STUDENTS: 0%

ADMISSIONS
O APPLY VIA UCAS
The College runs a summer school for Year 11 pupils interested in veterinary degrees.

SUBJECTS
SCIENCES 12% **VETERINARY MEDICINE** 75%
VETERINARY NURSING 13%

LIBRARIES
O 28,000 BOOKS O 178 STUDY PLACES
There are libraries at both Camden and Hawkshead. *Early closing* (8pm) *raises a few hackles.*

COMPUTERS
O 250+ WORKSTATIONS
Plenty of computers. The College intranet service has a number of *useful* resources online (lecture notes, databases and the ilk). Wireless networks on both campuses.

OTHER LEARNING FACILITIES
Farm; language labs; drama studio; media centre. The Museum of Veterinary History is stuated on the Camden campus.

R

O **If you have any comments about Push, or fancy being involved in the next edition, drop us a line: editor@push.co.uk**

Words in italics are Push's point of view — take it or leave it...

ENTERTAINMENT ()()()()()()()()()()

LONDON see University of London
*Obviously there's a lot more going on near
Camden than Hawkshead, but prices are higher.
The famous Camden weekend market's still pretty
cool, especially for young, slightly alternative
Japanese tourists. If you're not one, it can get a
bit samey.* Pushplugged pubs at Hawkshead: the
Bridge; the Maypole; *avoid* Williots. In Camden:
*plenty of pintworthy places around Camden Lock.
Castle's is a popular Pie & Mash shop near the
College.*

UNIVERSITY
● PRICE OF A PINT OF BEER £1.30
BARS The bars on each campus are as popular
with staff as with students and *the two groups
mix well.*
THEATRE Hawkshead has a *small* theatre
production company which gears itself towards a
successful annual production.
CLUBBING A boogie bus runs from the Hawkshead
site stopping at several pubs and a club in Enfield
or Hatfield. *Serious* clubbers at the Camden site
head into town or the West End. ULU facilities
are open to RVC students.
FOOD Both Camden and Hawkshead have
refectories – the former's is open all day and the
latter's serves at evenings and weekends too –
good quality and choice, but not that cheap.
There's also a café and a buttery bar, *which isn't
actually smeared with margarine, luckily.*
OTHER An *infamous* 12-hr ball every year.

SOCIAL ()()()()()()()()()()()()

THE ROYAL VETERINARY COLLEGE STUDENTS' UNION SOCIETY
● NUS MEMBER
*Blink and you'd miss it. There are plans to
relocate and improve the SU's Camden facilities
but at the moment these stretch to a couple of
under-used common rooms.*

SU FACILITIES
Welfare services; shop; vending machine; travel
agency; pool table; minibus.

CLUBS (NON-SPORTING)
Clinical; Countryside Sports & Rural Affairs;
Officer Training Corps; Overseas Development;
Project Africa (yearly research project); Royal
Naval Unit; University Air Squadron; Zoological.
See also Clubs tables.

OTHER ORGANISATIONS
RAG pops into existence for one *enthusiastic*
charity-stuffed week a year.

RELIGIOUS
● 1 CHAPLAIN (COFE)
*For religious advice the sole reverend is willing to
help worshippers of any persuasion with matters
ecumenical or snooker-related (apparently he's
quite good).*
Religion in London see University of London
Religion in Hatfield see University of
Hertfordshire

PAID WORK see University of London
● JOB BUREAU ● PAID WORK HOLS 60%
There's a jobs board but holidays are few and
students are expected to spend time on animal
placements (eg. lambing) so there isn't much time
for other work.

SPORTS ()()()()()()()()()()()()()

● RECENT SUCCESSES ROWING, RUGBY, WOMEN'S RUGBY,
RIDING **● BUSA RANKING** 75
*Certainly sporty, verging on the bionic. RVC has
taken home the Small College's Cup for the past
two years running. Being a vet keeps you fit and
a liking for the great outdoors is second nature.
However, grimy Camden isn't very conducive to
exercise, so all of the sports facilities bar the
gym are based in Hawkshead.* There are also the
facilities at ULU.

SPORTS FACILITIES
Football, rugby, hockey and cricket pitches; tennis
and netball courts; swimming pool; gym; squash
courts. See University of London and University of
Herfordshire for local facilities.

SPORTING CLUBS
Lacrosse; Mountaineering; Pool; Rowing;
Shooting. **See also Clubs table.**

ATTRACTIONS see University of London

ACCOMMODATION ()()()()()()()()()

IN COLLEGE
● CATERED 5%   **● COST** £90 (46/50WKS)
● SELF CATERING 55%   **● COST** £83 (46/50WKS)
● 1ST YRS LIVING IN 95%
● 2ND YRS LIVING IN 15%
● 3RD YRS/FINALISTS LIVING IN 30%
● POSTGRADS LIVING IN 10%
● INSURANCE PREMIUM ££££
AVAILABILITY The privately-run halls are a *popular
choice, if not particularly cheap,* and standards
are *pleasantly habitable.* Almost all first years can
be housed. Camden has self-catering rooms for

R

£95-112 a week, all are en suite. Students can also apply to inter-collegiate halls. Accommodation at Hawkshead costs £64-75 a week: there are 30 places in Odiham Hall (which can be catered for £105 a week) and 17 new-ish houses two mins from college with six bedrooms apiece. All accommodation is in single rooms. There are some rooms suitable for wheelchair users at both campuses.

CAR PARKING *A real problem in Camden.* In Hawkshead it's free *and there's plenty of it.*

EXTERNALLY see University of London
○ AVE RENT £100 **○ LIVING AT HOME** 3%
CAMDEN *Most Camden students live in Kentish Town which is a bit cheaper than Camden.* The College and SU keep details of housing and run lectures on the pitfalls of renting. The University of London accommodation office is there to be consulted.
HAWKSHEAD *Potter's Bar is the best place to look but there's competition from University of Hertfordshire students.*

SERVICES
○ LGBT SOCIETY ○ INTERNATIONAL STUDENTS' OFFICER ○ POSTGRAD OFFICER & SOCIETY ○ CRIME RATING !!!!!
Not many welfare provisions but students can use the extensive University of London facilities.
DISABILITIES *The physically demanding nature of the course could make it difficult for some students. Both sites have accessible toilets, lifts and induction loops in the main lecture theatre. There's a residential unit adapted for wheelchair users at both campuses.* See www.rcvs.org.uk for disability guidelines for vets.
HEALTH Occupational health service available.

FINANCE
○ AVE DEBT PER YEAR £3,807
○ HOME STUDENT FEES £3,000
FEES Postgrads pay a steep £4,370-7,264. International students pay from £7,284 to £17,526 for courses.
○ ACCESS FUND £67,000 **○ SUCCESSFUL APPLICATIONS/YR** 70 **○ AVERAGE PAYMENT** £650
SUPPORT Bursaries for students from poorer families range from £1,000 to a *Bill Gates-style generous* £5,700.

R

S

SALFORD UNIVERSITY

◉ THE UNIVERSITY OF SALFORD The Crescent, Salford, M5 4WT **TEL** (0161) 295 5000 **E–MAIL** course-enquiries@salford.ac.uk
WEBSITE www.salford.ac.uk **◉ UNIVERSITY OF SALFORD STUDENTS' UNION** University House, The Crescent, Salford, M5 4WT
TEL (0161) 736 7811 **E–MAIL** students-union@salford.ac.uk **WEBSITE** www.salfordstudents.com

GENERAL ◖◖◖◖◖◖◖◖◖◖◖◖◖◖

At the western end of Manchester (just two miles from the centre) is the city of Salford, but screw up your eyes and you can't see the join. Salford isn't magically different, nor is it sufficiently far away to make it properly distinct and so everything we say about Manchester (see University of Manchester) applies equally to Salford. It's kind of like Canada's relationship with America, though, in that a lot of famous Mancs are actually Salfordians in disguise. Even uber-Mancunians The Smiths were famously pictured in front of Salford Lads Club on the cover of their The Queen Is Dead album. Salford's certainly not the posh end of Manchester, but the 34-acre site of the University is quite green and less hideous than many modern campuses. With a few red-brick exceptions, the buildings have all been built in the last few decades and it'll be a good ten years more before they're officially declared ugly.

👤👤👤👤👤👤👤👤👤👤👤👤👤👤👤👤👤👤👤👤

SEX RATIO: ♂45 ♀55	**FOUNDED:** 1896
FULL–TIME U'GRADS: 15,369	**PART–TIME:** 2,800
POSTGRADS: 2,928	**NON–DEGREE:** 68
AVE COURSE: 3–4YRS	**ETHNIC:** 18%
STATE:PRIVATE SCHOOL: 97:3	**FLUNK RATE:** 17%
MATURE: 33%	**INTERNATIONAL:** 16%
DISABLED: 310	**LOCAL:** 50%

ATMOSPHERE

Many of the students are local – part of the community rather than apart from it – and they'd laugh off the suggestion that Salford is a dangerous place to be. Try Moss Side for that sort of thing. But Salford is a more down-to-earth area than Manchester proper (which isn't exactly an airy-fairy place itself). So it's wise to avoid activity that screams 'student' or 'Southern pansy'. The campus is fairly quiet because many students either go home or head for the bright lights outside hours. It's the best of both worlds: a campus university in a small neighbourhood town with the metropolitan high life of Manchester just around the corner, although the latter tends to overshadow any specifically Salfordian local colour.

SITES

PEEL PARK, FREDERICK ROAD AND ADELPHI The majority of students are based at these three campuses, all within ten mins walk of each other. There's also Irwell Valley, a further ten mins from Frederick Road, near the Castle Irwell Student Village.

MANCHESTER

see University of Manchester

SALFORD

◉ POPULATION 392,900
◉ HIGH TEMP 20 **◉ LOW TEMP** 1 **◉ RAINFALL** 68
Salford has its own small and friendly community. Occasionally, it looks somewhat like a Lowry painting, full of matchstick men and matchstick cats and dogs, factory gates and the rest of it. Not surprising really, since this is Lowry's home town. There's a spectacular gallery to show off his work. Occasionally, Salford also looks like a scene from Coronation Street. Again, no surprise, chuck, as this is where it's set. But far more often, it is the rebuilt Salford that shows its face. The docklands have been developed and right in the heart of the North are all sorts of new constructions: high rise blocks, shopping malls and supermarkets, libraries, bookshops, banks and everything else a growing boy needs, including three museums, an 'urban heritage park' and its own nightlife.

TRAVEL see University of Manchester
LOCAL Salford is covered by Manchester's bus and train networks which are reliable, comprehensive and generally cheap. Salford Crescent station is actually on the campus, although for national services it may be necessary to change at one of Manchester's stations (trains every 15 mins). Buses go to Manchester city centre every three mins.

CAREER PROSPECTS

◉ CAREERS SERVICE ◉ NO. OF STAFF 15 FULL
◉ UNEMPLOYED AFTER 6 MTHS 10%
As well as the usual rigmarole of finding a job, the careers service provides graduates with help starting their own business as well as placements in local industry.

FAMOUS ALUMNI

Bill Beaumont (ex-England rugby captain); John Cooper Clarke (poet); Christopher Eccleston (former Dr Who); Ieaun Evans (rugby); Peter Kay (Phoenix Nights creator); L S Lowry (artist); Jonathan Morris (actor); Norman Whiteside (ex-Man Utd footballer).

FURTHER INFO

◉ PROSPECTUSES UNDERGRAD; POSTGRAD; ALTERNATIVE SOME DEPARTMENTAL; INTERNATIONAL
◉ OPEN DAYS
Campus tours are conducted every Wednesday – call (0161) 295 5762 to book. Individual depart-ments arrange open days throughout the year.

Words in italics are Push's point of view – take it or leave it...

ACADEMIC ⭘⭘⭘⭘⭘⭘⭘⭘⭘⭘⭘⭘

The media courses are all heavily over-subscribed, especially the likes of Performance, TV and Radio Technology. *Salford is big on making sure degrees count in the job market and they're very chummy with local industry, organising placements,* some of which count towards final degree marks. A new law course for wannabe legal eagles should be in place by September 2007, along with an £8m law school.

ENTRY POINTS: 180–300	**AVE POINTS:** 200
APPLICATIONS PER PLACE: N/A	**CLEARING:** 10%
NO. OF TERMS: 2	**LENGTH OF TERMS:** 19wks
STAFF TO STUDENT RATIO: 1:6	**STUDY ADDICTS:** N/A
YEAR ABROAD: N/A	**SANDWICH STUDENTS:** N/A
TEACHING: **	**RESEARCH:** ***
1STS: 9%	**2.2S:** 35%
2.1S: 41%	**3RDS:** 15%

ADMISSIONS
◉ APPLY VIA UCAS/NMAS FOR NURSING
The Admissions Office takes work and experience into account for applicants with no formal qualifications.

SUBJECTS
ARTS MEDIA & SOCIAL SCIENCE 24%
BUSINESS & INFORMATICS 26%
HEALTH & SOCIAL CARE 35%
SCIENCE, ENGINEERING & ENVIRONMENT 15%
BEST Biological Sciences; Sports Science; Business; Finance & Accounting; Management; Engineering & Technology; English Studies; Languages; Politics.
UNUSUAL Aircraft Engineering with Pilot Studies; Aviation Technology with Pilot Studies; Physics with Space Technology.

LIBRARIES
◉ 629,000 BOOKS ◉ 1,557 STUDY PLACES
◉ 24–HR ACCESS
Seven libraries dotted about. *The weekend opening hours are pretty weak though* – three hours on Saturday, six on Sunday.

COMPUTERS
◉ 768 WORKSTATIONS ◉ 24–HR ACCESS

OTHER LEARNING FACILITIES
Language labs; drama studio; rehearsal rooms; media centre; TV & radio studio.

ENTERTAINMENT ⭘⭘⭘⭘⭘⭘⭘⭘⭘

MANCHESTER see University of Manchester
SALFORD
◉ PRICE OF A PINT OF BEER £2.20
◉ GLASS OF WINE £2.40
Manchester's the daddy when it comes to nightlife round here, but Salford isn't without larks of its own.
CINEMAS Even Mancunians leave their more local cinemas to come to the eight-screen multiplex at Salfod Quays.
THEATRES *High-brow hijinks and the obligatory* panto at the plush Lowry at Salford Quays, home to local and national touring productions.
PUBS The real Coronation Street has been demolished long since, *but the spirit of the Rover's Return continues in many a local, although many are quite rough and you don't get Betty's hotpots. Pushplugs: the Old Pint Pot; the Crescent; the Black Horse; Wallness Tavern.*
FOOD *Pushplugs: Pizza Express; Frankie & Benny's at Salford Quays; Punter's Bistro.*

UNIVERSITY
◉ PRICE OF A PINT OF BEER £1.75
◉ GLASS OF WINE £2
◉ CAN OF RED BULL £1.50
BARS *The main bars are Lowery's, which is packed at lunchtimes and which the great man would undoubtedly have turned into a heartwarming picture of matchstick men playing the fruities, or* home-from-home the Pavilion ('Pav'), *which has value grub,* free Playstation, pool tables, big screen sport and a 2am licence. Also the Sub Club on Frederick Road for lunch.
THEATRES Most dramatic posturing happens in and around the Robert Powell Theatre on campus.
FILM Four films a week, usually of the 'modern classic' variety (Withnail & I, Donnie Darko etc).
FOOD What with a restaurant, six cafeterias, two sandwich bars and various bar snacks, the campus has 24-hr munchability. Try the Adelphi Cafeteria or Milliways.
CLUBBING/MUSIC VENUES The Pav is the Union's customised club venue with regular club nights, live bands, comedy and open mic nights. Live music tends to be local and/or cover bands, but Atomic Kitten and Chesney Hawkes have passed through.
OTHERS Regular quiz nights, talent spots and live football in the Pav. Also there's a gallery, sometimes exhibiting student work and a campus pottery. Five balls a year.

S

SOCIAL

UNIVERSITY OF SALFORD STUDENTS' UNION
- **4 SABBATICALS** - **TURNOUT AT LAST BALLOT** 7%
- **NUS MEMBER**

We're talking more beer than barricades here. The Union's main thrust is its professionally handled services and entertainments. It even has its own company, SUPER Services, which runs the student pub among other things.

SU FACILITIES
At University House: three bars; eight cafés; four pool tables; eight meeting rooms; Endsleigh Insurance; various ATMs; fax & printing service; advice centre; late-night minibus; TV lounge; women's room; gaming machines; stationery shop; post office; new and secondhand bookshops; ticket agency.

CLUBS (NON-SPORTING)
Almost Famous; CAMRA; High Rollers; Linux; Literary; Man Utd; War games. **See also Clubs tables.**

OTHER ORGANISATIONS
The weekly newspaper, 'Student Direct', is part of University of Manchester's paper (with an added Salford section) and is Europe's widest circulating student publication. 'Channel M' is the University's television station and there's also a radio station (www.shockradio.co.uk) that broadcasts on FM for 12 weeks a year throughout the city. The Community Services Group involves a *healthy* 200 or so students in a range of local projects.

RELIGION
- **4 CHAPLAINS (COFE, RC, METHODIST, URC)**

The various Christian denominations have a prayer room and there's an on-site mosque and a visiting local rabbi. Religion in Manchester see University of Manchester.

PAID WORK see University of Manchester
The careers service also runs the jobshop in the Union building.

SPORTS

- **BUSA RANKING** 102

While Salford may not be nationally toasted for its sporting record, enthusiasm and facilities are at least worth an admiring nod.

SPORTS FACILITIES
The University has got over 50 acres for students to run, jump, kick balls and throw things across. There are 18 floodlit football pitches, four cricket pitches, a running track, a croquet and bowling lawn and six rugby pitches as well as facilities for hockey, tennis, netball, squash and basketball. There's also a leisure centre right next to the Union building with a multigym, swimming pool sauna and climbing wall. Gym/Swim membership, giving year-long access to the pool, spa, sauna and fitness rooms, costs £95. A discount card is available for other facilities. See University of Manchester for facilities in the local area.

SPORTING CLUBS
Breakdancing; Cheerleading; Circus & Juggling; Diving; Ninjutsu; Roller Hockey; Snooker. **See also Clubs tables.**

ATTRACTIONS see University of Manchester

ACCOMMODATION

IN UNIVERSITY
- **SELF-CATERING** 21% - **COST** £44 (40WKS)
- **INSURANCE PREMIUM** £££££

AVAILABILITY First years are guaranteed a place in halls if they apply before 1st September. On campus there are the Horlock and Constantine Halls. Then, about ten mins away, there's Castle Irewell. Near the Adelphi site is Eddie Colman and John Lester. All have phone and internet facilities of some description. On average there's 6-12 students *fighting over the toaster* in the self-catering blocks, with kitchens on all floors. Some rooms available for couples.

CAR PARKING Parking's *not a problem* so long as students have applied for a (free) permit.

EXTERNALLY see University of Manchester
- **AVE RENT** £50

WELFARE

SERVICES
- **LGBT OFFICER & SOCIETY**
- **MATURE STUDENTS' OFFICER & SOCIETY**
- **POSTGRAD OFFICER & SOCIETY**
- **INTERNATIONAL STUDENTS' SOCIETY**
- **ETHNIC MINORITIES OFFICER & SOCIETY**
- **WOMEN'S OFFICER & SOCIETY**
- **DISABILITIES OFFICER & SOCIETY**
- **SELF-DEFENCE CLASSES** - **MINIBUS**
- **UNIVERSITY COUNSELLORS** 3 FULL - **SU COUNSELLORS** 1
- **CRIME RATING:** !!!!

The Union runs its own advice centre with a visiting solicitor every Thursday. International students can turn to the Overseas Student Secretary or the University's Overseas Students Counsellor.

HEALTH Nurses at the campus health centre on the third floor of the Maxwell building will see students without an appointment.
CRECHES/NURSERY 104 places for children aged 6mths-4yrs.
DISABILITIES All the newer buildings have ramps and *wheelchair access is generally good and the Equality & Diversity Office is particularly helpful.*

FINANCE
○ **AVE DEBT PER YEAR** £4,256 ○ **HOME STUDENT FEES** £3,000
FEES HND students stump up around £7,500 a year for undergrad and postgrad courses. International students pay that for courses like English and Languages and up to a *whopping* ten grand for Media, Computing and the like.

⏩ **SCHOOL OF ORIENTAL & AFRICAN STUDIES**
see *SOAS*

THE SCHOOL OF PHARMACY, UNIVERSITY OF LONDON

THE COLLEGE IS PART OF THE UNIVERSITY OF LONDON AND STUDENTS ARE ENTITLED TO USE ITS FACILITIES

○ **THE SCHOOL OF PHARMACY, UNIVERSITY OF LONDON** 29-39 Brunswick Square, London, WC1N 1AX **TEL** (020) 7753 5831
E-MAIL registry@ulsop.ac.uk **WEBSITE** www.ulsop.ac.uk ○ **THE SCHOOL OF PHARMACY STUDENTS' UNION**
29-39 Brunswick Square, London, WC1N 1AX **TEL** (020) 7753 5809

GENERAL ○○○○○○○○○○○○○

Don't be fooled by the location. Russell Square may be crash-bang in central London, *but there's not a lot else crash-bang about it.* The Bloomsbury locale is a *quiet, leafy island* between King's Cross and Holborn, home to a *few* plush hotels and a *lot of very rich people.* The School of Pharmacy's *easy on the eye,* with *huge windows and an art deco entrance.*

SEX RATIO: ♂35 ♀65	**FOUNDED:** 1842
FULL-TIME U'GRADS: 720	**PART-TIME:** N/A
POSTGRADS: 200	**NON-DEGREE:** N/A
AVE COURSE: YRS	**ETHNIC:** 85%
STATE:PRIVATE SCHOOL: 70:30	**FLUNK RATE:** 4%
MATURE: 20%	**INTERNATIONAL:** 25%
DISABLED: 5	**LOCAL:** N/A

ATMOSPHERE

The School of Pharmacy only runs one course *(no prizes for guessing what),* so it attracts the *career-headed and studious. It feels very much like a school, rather than a university, and is full of class swots who at the age of 18 thought 'I'm going to be a pharmacist – yes! I can make my own drugs!'. Any rogue party fiends have to make their way to UCL or ULU for the action. There's a high proportion of Asian students and many of the budding pharmacists are generously subsidised by their parents – debts and part-time jobs are rare.*

LONDON see University of London
○ **CITY CENTRE** 1,200M
Bloomsbury's *quiet and refined,* but nearby King's Cross is *squalid, noisy and until the redevelopers move them on, swarming with ≠hookers and junkies. On the other side, Covent Garden and Leicester Square are by turns exhilaratingly busy and intolerably rammed.*

TRAVEL see University of London
TRAINS King's Cross and Euston both *within walking distance,* connections to the Midlands, East Anglia and the North.
BUSES 17, 45, 46, 68, 168 swing past.
CAR *Cataclysmically costly* to park, even if there's a space to be snapped up. Right in the middle of the congestion zone.
UNDERGROUND Russell Square (Piccadilly line); King's Cross (Northern line, Victoria, Circle, Hammersmith & City and Metropolitan lines); Euston (Northern & Victoria).
BICYCLES Bikes can be secured on railings across the road from the school.

CAREER PROSPECTS
○ **CAREERS SERVICE** ○ **UNEMPLOYED AFTER 6 MTHS** 0%

FURTHER INFO
○ **PROSPECTUSES** UNDERGRAD; POSTGRAD

S

Words in italics are Push's point of view – take it or leave it...

ACADEMIC

Everything's geared towards the MPharm and students are expected to put in about 40 hours a week of study. Students spend at least 12wks on placement *honing their skills in the real world.*

ENTRY POINTS: 300	AVE POINTS: N/A
APPLICATIONS PER PLACE: 6	CLEARING: 1%
NO. OF TERMS: 2	LENGTH OF TERMS: 15wks
STAFF TO STUDENT RATIO: 1:14	STUDY ADDICTS: 5%
TEACHING: ★★★	RESEARCH: ★★★★★
YEAR ABROAD: 5%	SANDWICH STUDENTS: N/A
1STS: 8%	2.2s: 36%
2.1s: 54%	3RDS: 2%

ADMISSIONS
- APPLY VIA UCAS

SUBJECTS
MEDICAL SCIENCES 100%
BEST Medical Science & Pharmacy.

LIBRARIES
- **50,000** BOOKS - **75** STUDY PLACES

Narkingly closed at weekends, though students have full borrowing rights at the UCL library to carry them through Sat-Sun.

COMPUTERS
- **52** WORKSTATIONS - **24**-HOUR ACCESS

OTHER LEARNING FACILITIES
The practice pharmacy is *a trainee chemist's playroom.*

ENTERTAINMENT

THE CITY see University of London
- PRICE OF A PINT OF BEER £2.30
- GLASS OF WINE £2.50
- CAN OF RED BULL £2.30

CINEMAS Leicester Square for the *biggest, priciest* screens around.
THEATRES The West End *is as good as theatre gets.*
PUBS The Goose is a *popular* joint, as are the Lord Russell, Aunt Mabel's and the Rocket (yellow card).
CLUBBING La Scala in King's Cross is *one of the best in London. Just don't hang around outside unless you're looking for crack.*
EATING OUT The Hare and Tortoise noodle bar *fulfils the cravings* for Chinese, Deepak Tandoori for Indian and The Piazza and Valtores *also get the thumbs up.*

UNIVERSITY
- PRICE OF A PINT OF BEER £1.50
- GLASS OF WINE £2
- CAN OF RED BULL £1.60

BARS The bar is only open one night a week, on Fridays. *Wouldn't want to go too crazy on a school night now, would we?*
FILM The Renoir, an arthouse screen next door to the school, shows arty and foreign films.
FOOD The JCR is open from 8.30am-4.30pm and serves cheap, *school-dinner* fare. A new place is in the offing for September.

SOCIAL

SCHOOL OF PHARMACY STUDENTS' UNION
The gnat-sized SU has no full-time officers.

SU FACILITIES
Bar; cafeteria; juke box; meeting rooms; photocopier; pool table; vending machine.

CLUBS (NON-SPORTING)
Chinese; Hindu; Krishna Consciousness; Sikh. **See also Clubs tables.**

OTHER ORGANISATIONS
An unusually active Rag raises stacks of cash for good causes.

PAID WORK see University of London
Students are expected to take work placements during vacations.

SPORTS

Sport's virtually dropped off the bottom of the agenda. This is bookworm country.

SPORTING CLUBS
See Clubs tables.

ATTRACTIONS see University of London
The local footie teams are Arsenal, Spurs and, er, Barnet.

ACCOMMODATION

IN COLLEGE
- CATERED 12% - COST £107 (38WKS)
- INSURANCE PREMIUM £££££

AVAILABILITY Accommodation is in UoL intercollegiate halls. Places only available to non-Londoners. All halls have wheelchair access.

S

Words in italics are Push's point of view — take it or leave it...

CAR PARKING The few spaces that exist are mostly reserved for staff.

EXTERNALLY see University of London
○ **AVE RENT** £105 ○ **LIVING AT HOME** 50%
AVAILABILITY Housing *isn't too hard to come by, but will blow a hole in the budget.* Angel, Camden and Holloway are all *popular* choices.
HOUSING HELP Run through the UoL accommodation office.

WELFARE ○○○○○○○○○○○○○

SERVICES
○ **INTERNATIONAL STUDENTS' OFFICER**
○ **POSTGRAD OFFICER & SOCIETY** ○ **DISABILITIES OFFICER**
○ **COLLEGE COUNSELLORS** 1
○ **CRIME RATING:** !!!!!
The college *leans* on UoL and ULU welfare facilities.
DISABILITIES *Wheelchair access is difficult – the college building is stair crazy.*

FINANCE
○ **AVE DEBT PER YEAR** £1,603 ○ **HOME STUDENT FEES** £3,000
○ **ACCESS FUND** £45,000

▶ SCHOOL OF SLAVONIC & EAST EUROPEAN STUDIES
see University College London

▶ SCOTTISH COLLEGE OF TEXTILES
see Heriot Watt University

UNIVERSITY OF SHEFFIELD

○ **UNIVERSITY OF SHEFFIELD** Western Bank, Sheffield, S10 2TE **TEL** (0114) 222 1255 **E-MAIL** study@sheffield.ac.uk **WEBSITE** www.shef.ac.uk/asksheffield ○ **THE UNIVERSITY OF SHEFFIELD UNION OF STUDENTS** Western Bank, Sheffield, S10 2TG **TEL** (0114) 222 8500 **E-MAIL** union@sheffield.ac.uk **WEBSITE** www.sheffieldunion.com

GENERAL ○○○○○○○○○○○○○

Sheffield, England's fourth largest city, just north-east of the Derbyshire Peak District and equidistant from Leeds and Manchester, is also one of the furthest places from the coast in the whole of Britain. *Most people immediately connect it with the steel industry, which is what made the place famous* and, to the east, there's still a *stark* reminder of industrial demise. Now the city is a *busy, bustling but friendly place* with a modern centre and compact Victorian suburbs. The University's 15 mins walk west from the city centre on a campus extending over a mile, with buildings *smeared* into the surrounding urban setting. Almost all of them are less than a century old and *have been carefully constructed rather than thrown up as required.* Mostly they're *attractive* redbrick buildings, although there are a few more modern structures – the arts tower and library, which are Grade II listed, are *functional rather than appealing* glass high-rises.

SEX RATIO: ♂45 ♀55	FOUNDED: 1905
FULL-TIME U'GRADS: 16,216	PART-TIME: 2,826
POSTGRADS: 4,801	NON-DEGREE: 515
AVE COURSE: 4YRS	ETHNIC: N/A
STATE:PRIVATE SCHOOL: 83:17	FLUNK RATE: 8%
MATURE: 9%	INTERNATIONAL: 17%
DISABLED: 330	LOCAL: 20%

ATMOSPHERE
The University buzzes with activity especially around the Union, which is the social and political centrepiece. That's not to say it's a student bubble – they're well integrated into the community (after the first year most live out), and a campus

S

Researchers at Sheffield University developed a contraceptive pill for squirrels.

Words in italics are Push's point of view — take it or leave it...

spread across the city centre means there's a relaxed and fun town/gown atmosphere, especially in local pubs. The University's closely involved with community issues and representatives from it and the SU sit on community forums. Sport, politics and insane party action all have prominent places in student life – though the libraries and study areas can get as crowded as the bars when they need to. Many students stay in the city after graduation – which can't be a bad thing.

SHEFFIELD
- **POPULATION** 513,100 **CITY CENTRE** 1 MILE
- **LONDON** 169 MILES **LEEDS** 35 MILES
- **MANCHESTER** 37 MILES
- **HIGH TEMP** 21 **LOW TEMP** 1 **RAINFALL** 48

A sign on the city outskirts reads 'Welcome to Sheffield, the home of British cutlery' *but honestly, it's got platefuls of stuff going for it. The popular image of Sheffield as a gritty northern town populated by ex-steelworkers stripping for cash isn't complete gibberish, but it's a fairly narrow view nowadays.* The old industrial area has been redeveloped *(the outskirts are still rather grim)* and Sheffield is *well set for leisure and sports facilities.* The suburbs in the south-west, where the University accommodation is based, are *greenish and pretty. Amenities: local luxuries* like late-night shops; 52 parks; street markets; museums; galleries (the City Museum, the Mappin Art Gallery and now the Winter Garden and Millennium Galleries). *The vast Meadowhall Shopping Centre is one of Europe's largest. It's known as Meadow-hell to some, but its sheer range and size is both crude and astonishing.*

TRAVEL
TRAINS Sheffield Station, less than a mile from the University, offers services to London (£35), Birmingham (£19.45), Edinburgh (£51.50) and more.
COACHES The Sheffield Interchange, also less than a mile, runs National Express and Stagecoach Express services. A trip to London costs £19.60.
CAR Ten mins off the M1, also A57, A61, A616 and A631. 20 mins off the end of the M18. Parking's *fairly easy in the city centre* and there are plenty of park & ride spots in the outskirts. University *parking is a different story* – permits needed (£78.60) are not generally available to undergrads.
AIR Doncaster/Sheffield Robin Hood and Leeds/Bradford for short haul budget flights, Manchester also does longer trips.
HITCHING *A bus trip to the M1 is the first step. An imploring look and an outstretched thumb is the second.*
LOCAL Local buses run all day and all night and are *frequent, reliable and quite cheap. Local minibuses are even better because they go everywhere. The Supertram is best of all, though, 'cause it's fun and cheap* (£80p from the train station to the University, on the Yellow line).
UNIVERSITY The SU provides the Union Safety Bus for women (runs at night till 2.15am, SU to halls, £1).

TAXIS *Taxi ranks are common as muck* and are indicated on University maps. Taxi companies are informed of Union events so there's enough on hand at fall-out time. *Black cabs circle like vultures around Glossop Road and Western Bank, but private companies offer a cheaper deal.*
BICYCLES The University is keen on bikes and positively bribes its students to use them – free soup and rolls for cyclists are dished out on certain days. *Bumpy geography puts some off but there are comprehensive cycle lanes and routes in the city centre.* The police stamp postcodes on students' bikes in Freshers' week – *as if that makes a difference.*

CAREER PROSPECTS
- **CAREERS SERVICE** **NO. OF STAFF** 20 FULL/7 PART
- **UNEMPLOYED AFTER 6 MTHS** 9%

The *extensive* service includes a careers library, interview training, job fairs, employer presentations and graduate workshops, some aimed specifically at mature and disabled students. The Student Directions website is *stuffed with helpful advice and job-hunting aids.* OpUS is a subdivision that focuses on finding work experience opportunities and promotes work-based learning in academic departments.

FAMOUS ALUMNI
Carol Barnes (newsreader); David Blunkett MP (Lab); Sir Sze-yuen Chung (Hong Kong politician); Stephen Daldry (theatre and film director); David Davies (Football Association); Joanne Harris (writer); Eddie Izzard (*action transvestite/* comedian); Amy Johnson (pioneer airwoman); Harry Kroto (Nobel prize-winning scientist); Sir Peter Middleton (Chairman, Barclays Bank); Jack Rosenthal (late writer); Richard Roberts (another Nobel prize-winning scientist); Helen Sharman (Britain's first astronaut); Linda Smith (late comedian); Ann Taylor (Lab peer); Dave Weatherall (footballer); Phil Wheatley (Director General of the Prison Service).

FURTHER INFO
- **PROSPECTUSES** UNDERGRAD; POSTGRAD; DEPARTMENTAL; INTERNATIONAL; DVD
- **OPEN DAYS**

ACADEMIC))))))))))))

- **RUSSELL GROUP**

Sheffield *is strong across the academic board.* There's a big law department and a medical school. All courses (with the exception of Medicine and Dentistry, *luckily*) are modular, meaning students get some choice in the subjects they study. Most courses have the option to study abroad and there's a self-access centre for *anyone that fancies picking up a foreign lingo.* The SU stays open round-the-clock in exam time, offering sofas and tables to last-minute revisers.

Words in italics are Push's point of view — take it or leave it...

ENTRY POINTS: 260–360	AVE POINTS: N/A
APPLICATIONS PER PLACE: 7	CLEARING: 9%
NO. OF TERMS: 2	LENGTH OF TERMS: 15WKS
STAFF TO STUDENT RATIO: 1:14	STUDY ADDICTS: 20%
TEACHING: ★★★★	RESEARCH: ★★★
YEAR ABROAD: 5%	SANDWICH STUDENTS: 0%
1STS: 14%	2.2S: 22%
2.1S: 54%	3RDS: 4%

ADMISSIONS
⊙ APPLY VIA UCAS/NMAS FOR NURSING & MIDWIFERY
'Academic suitability' is Sheffield's only *vague
criterion* for admissions. They don't always demand
the standard three A Levels and are happy to
consider other qualifications or experience,
particularly in the case of mature students.

SUBJECTS
ARCHITECTURE 4%   ARTS 16%   ENGINEERING 10%
MEDICINE & BIOMEDICAL SCIENCES 24%   SCIENCES 17%
SOCIAL SCIENCES 21%
BEST Architecture; Biology; Building & Planning;
Medicine; Dentistry; Civil, Chemical & Other
Engineering; Communication & Information
Studies; Computer Science; Electronic & Electrical
Engineering; English; European Languages &
Area Studies; Finance & Accounting; History &
Archaeology; Human & Social Geography; Law;
Mechanically-based Engineering; Medical Science
& Pharmacy; Performing Arts; Physical
Geography & Environmental Science; Physical
Science; Philosophy; Politics; Psychology; Social
Policy & Antropology; Sociology; Theology.
UNUSUAL Aerospace Engineering with Private Pilot
Instruction; Motor Sports Engineering Management.

LIBRARIES
**⊙ 1,400,000 BOOKS ⊙ 2,233 STUDY PLACES
⊙ SPEND PER STUDENT ££££**
The main library and the St Georges Library both
open till 9.30pm Mon-Thu, closing earlier at the
weekend. There are also nine or ten smaller,
departmental libraries. A new LRC is due for
October 2006, with 100,000 books and 900 study
places, most with computer provision.

COMPUTERS
**⊙ 1,385 WORKSTATIONS ⊙ 24-HOUR ACCESS
⊙ SPEND PER STUDENT £**
Wireless access across campus.

OTHER LEARNING FACILITIES
The academic arsenal includes language labs, drama
studio, rehearsal rooms, CAD lab and media centre.

ENTERTAINMENT ◗◗◗◗◗◗◗◗◗◗

THE CITY
**⊙ PRICE OF A PINT OF BEER £1.80
⊙ GLASS OF WINE £2
⊙ CAN OF RED BULL £1.50**
CINEMAS Three mainstream multiplexes (Odeon
and Cineworld in the centre, Vue at Meadowhall)

and the Showroom in the centre for *wobbly
cameras and subtitles* – student tickets £2.50
on Mon/Thur.
THEATRES The Union box office flogs tickets for
shows at the Crucible Theatre (of World Snooker
Championships fame) and its alternative-leaning
studio, plus the Lyceum next door – student
discounts often available *if you ask nicely*.
Everything from West End tours to local stuff.
PUBS *Drinkers would have to be pretty darn picky
not to find a suitable watering hole in Sheffield –
hundreds of pubs ranging from nasty chain bars
with no atmosphere to crumbling locals. West
Street (a five minute stumble from the University)
has as good a selection as anywhere. Pushplugs:
West Street Live (oodles of different music nights);
the Lounge (foreign beers); Halcyon (cheapish
cocktails). Students are welcome pretty much
everywhere in the city centre. Further out the
unpleasantness and accusations of
sheep-tampering start.*
CLUBBING *The legendary Gatecrasher breaks into
Republic once a month and is one of the North's
best nights. The Leadmill holds indie/alternative
nights and Hot Pants at City Hall on Saturdays is
another biggie (two rooms of retro tat). Kingdom
holds what may be the best-named gay night
around (Fairy Liquid) and R'n'B on Sundays. If
there really is nothing on the Sheffield groovy
train to take you up where you belong then
Leeds and Manchester are a six-pack and train
ride away.*
MUSIC VENUES Sheffield Arena and Don Valley
Stadium deal with the sort of acts *punters are
happy to watch through binoculars*, ranging from
top touring bands to wrestling and show
jumping. *City Hall copes with the smaller-scale
mainstream.* The Leadmill and the Plug are the
major indie venues (Mogwai, Futureheads).
COMEDY Touring comedians drop in at the City
Hall, biggies like Little Britain crash the Arena
and Takapuna does a weekly comedy club.
EATING OUT If animal grease and BSE aren't up
your street – *they're up most of Sheffield's* – then
there's plenty of tastier options, mainly focused
around Division Street and Devonshire Green. *Lots
of choice but tapas is the current student
favourite. Pushplugs: BB's Wokmania (all-you-can-
eat Chinese); Nibbles (pizza); Valente (Italian).*

UNIVERSITY
**⊙ PRICE OF A PINT OF BEER £1.60
⊙ GLASS OF WINE £1.70**
*Sheffield SU has its many fingers in many pies –
most of them lavishly flavoured with student
entertainment. The extent of its involvement in
music, club nights, pubbing and food is both
staggering and profitable.*
BARS *Bar One is one of the liveliest and longest-
running, and crammed with promos, competitions,
big-screen sport, DJs and an eight-table pool
room. The swish Interval has international beers
plus fairtrade coffee and food. The dinky Raynor
Lounge can be booked for free three nights a*

week. The SU also has the keys to a pub, the beer-gardened Fox & Duck in Broomhill.

THEATRES The Drama Studio is an old converted church *and its inhabitants are a busy bunch*, putting on stageloads of plays.

FILM The Film Unit is a cinema-space and shows several films a week (new release, classics, arthouse) and is kitted out with hearing loops, Dolby surround sound and wheelchair access.

MUSIC VENUES The Octagon (cap 1,400) hosts quality crooners including the Zutons, Maximo Park and the Charlatans. The Foundary (cap 1,200) host gigs, while acoustic sets can be heard in Interval and Coffee Revolution.

CLUBBING Five nights a week including the *brazenly naff, astonishingly popular* Pop Tarts retro night, the *renowned* Tuesday Club, which has featured Coldcut and High Contrast, Frouk (cheesy chart), plus *cutting edge indie* at the Fuzz Club. There's also a gang of monthly nights, including gay-friendly Climax and dancey Urban Gorilla, which attracts the likes of James Lavelle and Layo & Bushwacka. Tickets go on sale the morning of the event and *invariably sell out*.

COMEDY/CABARET The Last Laugh Comedy Club hits Bar One every Sunday, *but doesn't bring household names*.

FOOD *Many* outlets. One to Go, for scrumptious junk. Interval offers classier snackable fare. Loxley's Food Court has a *magnificent* breakfast bar and Coffee Revolution (organic coffee, fair trade paninis) is one of the Union's major money-spinners. Legions of other snack kiosks and coffee stops too.

OTHER End of Year Carnival, Freshers, Sports and departmental balls. The Octagon hosts an international cultural evening.

SOCIAL ʊʊʊʊʊʊʊʊʊʊʊʊ

THE UNIVERSITY OF SHEFFIELD UNION OF STUDENTS

○ **8 SABBATICALS** ○ **TURNOUT AT LAST BALLOT** 20%
○ **NUS MEMBER**

Sheffield's Union is nearly one of the most powerful forces in the universe. Well, in Sheffield at least. Communication between the Union and the University is a particular plus point – the SU pays students to represent Union issues to University departments and acts as a first point of contact for fellow students, exactly like trade union representatives. The 'Union Links' scheme keeps things sweet between the SU and the authorities. Politics is a scorching leftie potato – campaigns are plentiful and the Union, which has fair trade status, puts its money where its mouth is, pushing ethical and environmentally-friendly products whenever it can.

SU FACILITIES

Two purpose-built nightclubs; two bars; two pubs; four snack bars; three cafeterias; fast food joint; ten pool tables; seven meeting rooms; Endsleigh Insurance office; Oxfam and Natwest banks, five major bank ATMs; general store; stationery shop; bookshop; quiet room; mature students' lounge; nursery; women's room; photocopier; fax and printing services; payphones; photo booth; advice centre; gaming and vending machines; travel agency; ticket box office; launderette; music practice room.

CLUBS (NON-SPORTING)

Alternative Ironing; Animal Rights; Arab; Army Officer Training; Bangaladesh; Basque; Bollywood; Bolshevik Debating; Brasov Orphanage (raises funds for Romanian orphans); Broad Left (left-wing pressure group); Business Stimulation; Celidh; Cheerleaders; Computer Gaming; Cornish Language; East Asian Cinema; Flying Teapots (circus skills); Gospel Choir; Hellenic; Hindu Students; Hong Kong; Indonesean; Iranian; Kenyan; Knitting; Krishna Counsiousness; Malaysian; Medieval Re-enactment; Mexican & Latin American; 'Neighbours' Appreciation; Oxfam; Pakistani; Palestine; Poetry; Poker; Pro-life (anti-abortion campaigners); Quidditch; Real Ale; Samba; Scandinavian; Sheffield Assassins Guild (game-playing, not real killing); Shopping; Sikh; Slavonic; Speak (evangelical campaigning); Sri Lankan; Star Trek; Stings (scouts and guides); Student Action for Refugees; Student CND; Stop the War; Tea Drinking; Thai; Turkish; Vegetarian & Vegan; Welsh. **See also Clubs tables.**

OTHER ORGANISATIONS

Top class student newspaper 'Sheffield Steel' is published fortnightly, accompanied by a weekly 'What's On?' event listings, the Union magazine, 'Stainless', a Nursing & Midwifery newsletter and SheffieldBase.com. Radio station 'Sure' broadcasts on the web but is angling for an AM licence. Sheffield Rag is *alive and kicking*, arranging a *clustered calendar of cash-creating capers*. SheffieldVolunteering is *highly active* working with schools, refugees, special needs kids, the homeless and the elderly.

RELIGION

○ **9 CHAPLAINS** (**COFE, URC, PENTECOSTAL, UNITARIAN, JEWISH, MUSLIM, HINDU, SIKH, BUDDHIST, BAHA'I**)

As well as the multi-faith chaplaincy centre there are several Muslim prayer rooms and halal food available on campus. The chaplaincy produces a guide to religious provision around the town (churches, mosques, synagogues, temples and two cathedrals – RC and CofE).

PAID WORK

○ **JOB BUREAU**

Potential in bars and shops on campus and in town. Also some departmental envelope-stuffing-type daywork. There's a University and Union-run Jobshop in the Union to help with finding work, although students aren't supposed to graft for more than 15 hours a week.

S

SPORTS ΟΟΟΟΟΟΟΟΟΟΟΟ

○ **RECENT SUCCESSES** MEN'S BADMINTON; MEN'S SQUASH; WOMEN'S RUGBY ○ **BUSA RANKING** 30

The sporting amenities are among the best in the country. It's not all about winning though: beginners and casual participants are encouraged to give it a go and even the most dedicated, crisp-encrusted couch potato will find something to do. Varsity is the annual competition against Sheffield Hallam.

SPORTS FACILITIES

45 acres of sports grounds, including: four football, four rugby, three synthetic (hockey) and two cricket pitches; four squash, four tennis and two netball/basketball/volleyball courts; sports hall; swimming pool; gym; aerobics studio; multigym; sauna and climbing wall. Membership *ain't cheap* – £160 a year (off-peak) or £308 (peak) – but everything except the gym can be used on a pay & play basis, with discounts at off-peak hours. Sheffield caters for everything its University doesn't. Ponds Forge, Sheffield Arena and The Don Valley Stadium are all world-class sports centres, the city has two ice rinks, and the River Don and the Ogston reservoir are there for watersports. The *glorious* Peak District provides nature's own sports centre for ramblers, cavers, mountaineers, hang gliders and other outdoor types. Sheffield's also home to Europe's largest artificial ski resort.

SPORTING CLUBS

Pretty much all of them. Here's a few: 10 Pin Bowling; Akido; American Football; Caving; Ju-Jitsu; Korfball; Lacrosse; Rowing; Snowboarding; Table Tennis; Ultimate Frisbee. **See also Clubs tables.**

ATTRACTIONS

Sheffield Wednesday and United FCs; Sheffield Eagles (rugby); Steelers (ice hockey); Sharks (basketball); speedway at Owlerton Stadium.

ACCOMMODATION ΟΟΟΟΟΟΟΟΟ

IN UNIVERSITY

○ **CATERED** 17% ○ **COST** £99 (30/38WKS)
○ **SELF-CATERING** 14% ○ **COST** £74 (42WKS)
○ **1ST YRS LIVING IN** 94% ○ **POSTGRADS LIVING IN** 12%
○ **INSURANCE PREMIUM** £££

AVAILABILITY Most first years guaranteed University accommodation – most in large, brick-heavy halls catered halls 20 mins away from campus or self-catering flats. A handful (3%) have to share. There are plans for a spruce up by 2007-8 – watch this space. *Ranmoor is the largest hall and Sorby is avoided like an ugly 60s tower block. Because it is one. Facilities and furnishings are*

generally decent, but it's a bit like booking a hotel – if you want a minibar and trouser press, you have to shell out a bit more. Note: minibars and trouser presses are not available in University accommodation. There are also brickloads of university-owned houses, ranging from *cutesy* terrace cottages to Victorian town houses.

CAR PARKING *Problematic.* Broad Lane Court has 27 spaces *and that's about it.* Permits are only given to the most needy *(or argumentative).*

EXTERNALLY

○ **AVE RENT** £53

AVAILABILITY Those living externally find it fairly easy to get hold of reasonable homes in proximity of the campus. Broomhill and Crookes are popular areas because they're nearby, have plenty of pubs and a large student population. Private provider UNITE are opening *swankier* pads.

HOUSING HELP The University accommodation office runs a website with house-finding database. The advice centre provides a recommended contract for tenants. *Most students use word of mouth, notice boards in the Union and ads in shops.*

WELFARE ΟΟΟΟΟΟΟΟΟΟΟΟ

SERVICES

○ **LGBT SOCIETY** ○ **ETHNIC MINORITIES SOCIETY**
○ **WOMEN'S OFFICER & SOCIETY**
○ **MATURE STUDENTS' SOCIETY** ○ **TAXI FUND**
○ **INTERNATIONAL STUDENTS' OFFICER & SOCIETY**
○ **POSTGRAD SOCIETY** ○ **SELF-DEFENCE CLASSES**
○ **LATE-NIGHT WOMEN'S MINIBUS** ○ **NIGHTLINE**
○ **UNIVERSITY COUNSELLORS** 6 FULL/3 PART
○ **CRIME RATING:** !!!

The sabbatical welfare officer operates an open door policy. One officer sits on postgrad and mature students meetings but has no special responsibility for either. Halls have resident tutors and each student is assigned a personal tutor, *so there are always plenty of people to turn to – the biggest problem is deciding which one.*

HEALTH The University Health Service has nine doctors, five nurses, in-patient facilities and a website.

WOMEN Late-night minibus (till 2.15am) between SU-halls/houses, £1, Woman's pack (from Women's Officer) contains magazine, alarm, welfare handbook and contacts list.

CRECHES/NURSERY SU nursery has 64 places, to 5yrs. Holiday playscheme for 4-12yrs.

DISABILITIES Town's awkward for wheelchairs. University is trying to improve access, but a couple of buildings are effectively out-of-bounds. There's *pretty good* support to seen/unseen disabilities in general. Some specially adapted accommodation is available for those with limited mobility or hearing. The SU has good access and there are provisions for the dyslexic and visually/hearing-impaired.

S

CRIME Sheffield's remarkably safe for a city of its size.

FINANCE
- **AVE DEBT PER YEAR** £3,621 - **HOME STUDENT FEES** £3,000
FEES Cheaper fees for students on years abroad, *thank God*. Postgrads cost £3,085-£15,085. International fees also vary enormously: £8,100-19,900. Part-timers pay pro-rata.
- **ACCESS FUND** £915,016 - **SUCCESSFUL APPLICATION/YR** 617

SUPPORT About 20 sports scholarships for *bionic people*. Bursaries of £400-£650 for those with household incomes below £33,000 and up to £800 for those on Outreach schemes. Academic scholarships of up to £1,550 in certain subjects, depending on income.

▶ **SHEFFIELD CITY POLYTECHNIC**
see *Sheffield Hallam University*

SHEFFIELD HALLAM UNIVERSITY

FORMERLY SHEFFIELD CITY POLYTECHNIC

- **SHEFFIELD HALLAM UNIVERSITY** City Campus, Howard Street, Sheffield, S1 1WB **TEL** (0114) 225 5555
E-MAIL enquiries@shu.ac.uk **WEBSITE** www.shu.ac.uk - **SHEFFIELD HALLAM UNIVERSITY UNION OF STUDENTS**

GENERAL ()()()()()()()()()()()()

Sheffield Hallam's spread across three campuses in town, with the main site (the imaginatively-named City campus) built around a big, glass atrium. Psalter Lane and Collegiate Crescent campuses are *living the high life in posh Hallam*, which is lined with boutique shops, gourmet restaurants and, remarkably, student houses. There's not a lot of site-hopping to be done, but even if there were, it's not too difficult. Nonetheless, applicants should check on which site their course would be based. The Peak District is on the doorstep, *which makes a change from the regular semi-skimmed.*

SEX RATIO: ♂47 ♀53	**FOUNDED:** 1969
FULL-TIME U'GRADS: 15,246	**PART-TIME:** 1,930
POSTGRADS: 7,261	**NON-DEGREE:** 3,484
AVE COURSE: 3YRS	**ETHNIC:** 12%
STATE:PRIVATE SCHOOL: 95:5	**FLUNK RATE:** 12%
MATURE: 63%	**INTERNATIONAL:** 2%
DISABLED: 605	**LOCAL:** 48%

ATMOSPHERE
Hallam's high on postgrads and part-timers. Chuck in the fact that lots of students are local, and the spread-out location, and it's no surprise the University gets on well with the town. The whole place feels like home – mainly because, for most people, it is. Self-contained sites have their benefits for those based there, but on the other hand are fragmented and insular. Posh-boy Psalter Lane is particularly bereft, with little passing trade with other campuses and few student essentials like cash machines and budget supermarkets. Plans are chalked-up to integrate it

into City campus towards the end of the decade. Collegiate Crescent will eventually also only contain the Health & Wellbeing and Sports Science departments.

SHEFFIELD see University of Sheffield
- **CITY CENTRE** 0 MILE

SITES
CITY CAMPUS (most subjects and SU) Main city centre site, at Pond Street.
COLLEGIATE CRESCENT (Health, Education – 3,500 students) *Lots* of green space and a *mix* of buildings. A *few* sports facilities, halls and student houses.
PSALTER LANE (Cultural Studies, Art, Design, Film) *Eclectic, arty* territory three miles from the City campus. It's got a Union-run shop and *a few other facilities to call its own.*

TRAVEL see University of Sheffield
CAR A lot of local students drive to University, although the time saved on the journey is *usually eaten up going round in circles looking for somewhere to park.*
LOCAL Buses *can be a bit of a gamble*, and prices are ever on the up. The Supertram's *not all that super* for Hallam students as it manages to avoid both campus and residences. It's good for Meadowhall shopping and Hallam Arena, though. £2.70 day ticket.

CAREER PROSPECTS
- **CAREERS SERVICE** - **NO. OF STAFF** 13 FULL
- **UNEMPLOYED AFTER 6 MTHS** 7%

Words in italics are Push's point of view – take it or leave it...

FAMOUS ALUMNI

Richard Caborn (Minister for Sport); David Kohler (footballer); Bruce Oldfield (fashion designer); Nick Park (animator, Wallace & Gromit big cheese); Howard Wilkinson (football manager with *whatever the opposite of the Midas touch is*). *Honorary celebs are being snapped up like the last loo roll on the shelf.* Sean Bean, Michael Palin and Derek Jacobi are all on the rollcall.

FURTHER INFO

- **PROSPECTUSES** UNDERGRAD; POSTGRAD; DEPARTMENTAL; VIDEO
- **OPEN DAYS**

ACADEMIC ◖◖◖◖◖◖◖◖◖◖◖◖◖

There's a *hands-on, pragmatic* approach to learning with the emphasis on *getting out there and doing something*. There are more sandwich courses *than a student could poke a Sub at* (more than anywhere else in the UK, in fact) and a lot of courses include a year abroad. The degrees offered are *mostly vocational and a bit techie*. Teaching and support over a wide range of courses are highly rated by students.

ENTRY POINTS: 140–300	AVE POINTS: 264
APPLICATIONS PER PLACE: 6	CLEARING: 15%
NO. OF TERMS: 2	LENGTH OF TERMS: 13wks
STAFF TO STUDENT RATIO: 1:23	STUDY ADDICTS: 12%
TEACHING: **	RESEARCH: ***
YEAR ABROAD: <1%	SANDWICH STUDENTS: 39%
1STS: 8%	2.2S: 38%
2.1S: 48%	3RDS: 7%

ADMISSIONS

- **APPLY VIA UCAS**

The University's *hot* for local, part-time and mature students, and there are a number of bursaries to entice them in. Mature students can be assessed on work experience rather than qualification.

SUBJECTS

ARCHITECTURE, BUILDING & PLANNING 5%
ART & DESIGN 7%   **ARTS & HUMANITIES** 2%
BUSINESS/MANAGEMENT 22%   **COMBINED** <1%
COMPUTING 9%   **EDUCATION** 5%   **ENGINEERING** 7%
MATHS 1%   **MEDIA:** 3%   **MODERN LANGUAGES** 3%
MEDICAL SCIENCES: 8%   **SCIENCES** 13%
SOCIAL SCIENCES 13%
BEST Accounting; Agriculture & Other Veterinary Sciences; Anatomy; Physiology; Pathology; Architecture; Biology/Biological Sciences; Building; Business & Administrative Studies; Education; English Studies; European Languages & Related Studies; Finance; Food & Beverage Studies; Historical & Philosophical Studies; History & Archaeology; Human & Social Geography; Languages; Law; Management Studies; Materials & Minerals Technology; Mathematics & Statistics; Medical Science &

Pharmacy; Physical Science; Sociology; Social Policy & Anthropology; Sport Science; Technology.
UNUSUAL Interactive product design; bespoke courses run in association with Network Rail and the Army.

LIBRARIES

- **513,943 BOOKS** ◗ **4,011 STUDY PLACES**
- **24-HOUR ACCESS** ◗ **SPEND PER STUDENT ££££**

There's a library on each campus and a 'learning centre' apiece at the City and Collegiate Crescent campuses. As well as winning design awards *(apparently it looks like a seagull, go figure)* it includes mobile phone tolerant zones and chillout rooms. The ALL (Access to all Libraries for Learning) scheme means students have reading rights in all the town libraries, including those at University of Sheffield.

COMPUTERS

- **2,091 WORKSTATIONS** ◗ **24-HOUR ACCESS**
- **SPEND PER STUDENT ££££**

An online learning system suits the nocturnal or the just plain shy.

OTHER LEARNING FACILITIES

Students can all-but gain a degree from under their duvets, as the University's channelled a lot of, um, 'creative vision' into their e-learning strategy. Students can access a virtual learning portal, including the Blackboard system.

ENTERTAINMENT ◖◖◖◖◖◖◖◖◖

THE CITY see University of Sheffield
The Showroom cinema is opposite Hallam Union, *and is the largest arthouse cinema in the universe. Well, outside London, anyway.* Regular talks, festivals and live music, plus bar and a wide range of flicks make it a top, *rocking joint*. The Devonshire Cat on the city fringes is *popular* with Hallamites for its unusual range of beers. The city-centre Globe is good for *inter-lecture refreshment*; the Porter Cottage on Ecclesall Road is a *non-studenty student fave*. Kingdom nightclub is as vast as the name suggests and runs co-ordinated nights with the Union (chart, cheese, RnB, friendly vibe). The Lescar Hotel off Ecclesall Road is home to the Last Laugh Comedy Club. Jumbo (Chinese buffet) in the city centre is an obvious choice *for students with bottomless stomachs and a limited budget.*

UNIVERSITY

- **PRICE OF A PINT OF BEER** £1.70
- **GLASS OF WINE** £1.80
- **CAN OF RED BULL** £1.90

City campus is getting a wash 'n' brush-up, which extends to a new Union building (the former site of the National Centre for Popular Music) – all

S

part of the future centralisation, y'see. Goodies including a public bar serving hot food and snacks, an SU-managed shop, a student bar, areas for live bands and meeting rooms for clubs and societies.

BARS The Phoenix is the main bar, *aided and abetted by* The Furnace (comedy nights and small ents). The Phoenix's 'Boozie 100' *operates like the FTSE minus the knobs in pin-stripe jackets*: drinks prices go up and down depending on what is and isn't selling. Worthies can come down to 70p a pint – spirits slurpers are advised to stand well away from the bar for safety's sake.

THEATRES Not a *buzzing* drama scene, but definitely a *burgeoning* one. The drama society has *plenty of enthusiastic members*. There are occasional theatre facilities in the Union building.

FILM Sunday night screenings in the SU – *everything from the cult* (Back To The Future) *to the crap* (Harry Potter).

MUSIC VENUES The Works (cap 1,000) has recently entertained the crowds with the Bluetones, Big Brovas, Malibu Stacey, The Nolans and *pert-buttocked Romanian novelty* act the Cheeky Girls. New Music Backlash is a monthly showcase for local talent. The SU has DJ facilities/space *but they're yet to pop the cherry, as it were*.

CLUBBING Mid-week knees-ups in indie, metal, cheese and retro. The old National Centre for *Pap Muzak* is a *perfect* clubbing den – its four 'pods', three dancefloors and atrium have even enticed Psalter Lane out to play.

FOOD Sandwiches from the Union shop for grub on the go. Phoenix bar does food until 7pm daily – the *usual pubby concoctions*. Psalter Lane has Steeley's Restaurant, City Campus has Cutting Edge and Collegiate Crescent has Miller's *for ruining appetites between lectures*.

OTHER Regular black tie bashes.

SOCIAL 🅤🅤🅤🅤🅤🅤🅤🅤🅤🅤🅤🅤

SHEFFIELD HALLAM UNIVERSITY UNION OF STUDENTS
○ 5 SABBATICALS ○ TURNOUT AT LAST BALLOT 12%
○ NUS MEMBER

The SU *knows its place* and busies itself supporting *whatever kind of activity* students want to get involved with, so setting up new societies is *dead easy. Not much* politicking goes on, except when a big issue like fees rears its head. University and Union are *tight as a nut*, with the University even opening up its wallet to see the SU through the move to the new facilities.

SU FACILITIES
In the SU building: One bar (plus another four in the nightclub rooms upstairs); Union shop; pool tables; video game arcade; photo booth; ATM; computer points; vending machines; advice centre; plus a giant resource centre with PCs/printers/meeting rooms.

CLUBS (NON-SPORTING)
Breakdancing; Chinese; DJ; E-soc (Entrepreneurs); Hindu; Juggling; Live Music; Malaysian; Pro-evolution; Salsa & Merengue; Volleyball Supporters. **See also Clubs tables.**

OTHER ORGANISATIONS
Stage Service is a hands-on techie training group that works the rigs at SU ents. 'Shu-Print' is the *re-vamped* SU newsrag. 'Rush' radio gets occasional two-week FM licences. The Volunteering Office has six full-time staff members co-ordinating more than 40 annual local projects. Hallam runs the Devonshire Jam music festival, which *pulls in the crowds* every summer.

RELIGION
○ 1 CHAPLAIN (MULTI-FAITH)
A multi-faith chaplaincy caters for most religious persuasions.

PAID WORK see University of Sheffield
○ JOB BUREAU ○ PAID WORK TERM TIME 62%
Network job fairs help circulate CVs to prospective employers. Finding term-time pocket money is easy enough, *with a seemingly endless supply of bars and shops to trawl*.

SPORTS 🅤🅤🅤🅤🅤🅤🅤🅤🅤🅤🅤

○ RECENT SUCCESSES WOMEN'S BASKETBALL, MEN'S VOLLEYBALL **○ BUSA RANKING** 17
Sport Hallam oversees *decent* facilities and supports budding athletes.

SPORTS FACILITIES
The University hires a lot of local amenities (see Sheffield University) but it also has a fair few facilities of its own: Club Hallam (*state-of-the-art* gym); three fitness suites; two fitness studios; swimming pool; squash courts; tennis; Astroturf pitch; 23 acres of playing fields; three sports halls; sports injury clinic. Costs range from £40-110 a year, non-members can pay-as-they-go. Coaching badges and qualifications can also be studied.

SPORTING CLUBS
10 Pin Bowling; American Football; Boxing; Clay Pigeon Shooting; Gaelic Football; Gymnastics; Hurling; Korfball; Lacrosse; Modern Biathlon/Pentathlon; Rifle; Rowing; Rugby League; Snooker; Snowboard; Surfing; Table Tennis; Triathlon. **See also Clubs tables.**

ATTRACTIONS see University of Sheffield

ACCOMMODATION ⦿⦿⦿⦿⦿⦿⦿⦿⦿⦿

IN UNIVERSITY
◉ **CATERED** 3% ◉ **COST** £102 (39WKS)
◉ **SELF-CATERING** 9% ◉ **COST** £65 (39/42/44WKS)
◉ **1ST YRS LIVING IN** 80% ◉ **INSURANCE PREMIUM** £££
AVAILABILITY Most first years can be housed.
Rooms are *pretty well furnished* and well within
hiking range of the campuses. Self-catered
accommodation has shared kitchens and there
are some single-sex flats. Security is *nice and
tight*, with CCTV, swipe cards and night patrols.
CAR PARKING Permit-parking is available at
some halls.

EXTERNALLY see University of Sheffield
◉ **AVE RENT** £55
AVAILABILITY The house-hunting season before
term is a good time to find the right place to hole
up in, but even with another university on the
scene there's no *'this town ain't big enough for
the both of us'* – there's enough to go around.
Manor Park and Manor Top *aren't as grand as the
names imply* and students tend to steer clear.
Bramall Lane's good for those on a tight budget,
while Ecclesall Road is *'where it's at'* – *whatever
'it' is*. There are several private halls in town,
including Unite's, but quality's an *unfixed variable*
– the Forge site gets a particular thumbs down
from residents for noise, cost, poor ventilation
and over-priced internet hook-ups.
HOUSING HELP The Housing and Accommodation
Centre provides lists of registered
accommodation and a database called Online
House Search, which allows students to trawl
through options according to area, amenities,
street name, number of rooms and so on.

WELFARE ⦿⦿⦿⦿⦿⦿⦿⦿⦿⦿⦿⦿

SERVICES
◉ **SELF-DEFENCE CLASSES**
◉ **UNIVERISTY COUNSELLORS** 2 FULL/7 PART
◉ **CRIME RATING** !!!
There are no individual issues officers, but the f/t
Equal Opportunities and p/t Multicultural &
International and Welfare Executives wear many
hats. The Union Advice Centre has drop-in
sessions every afternoon.
HEALTH Independent practice on City Campus
(GPs, nurses) and a purpose-built surgery near
the Collegiate Crescent campus. 24-hr GP service
for emergencies.
WOMEN Hallam Union Women's Unit offers free
attack alarms.
CRECHES/NURSERY 74 places (6mths-5yrs).
DISABILITIES Access varies between campuses. It's
best at City campus and there's disabled parking
at all sites. Dyslexia support is *excellent*.

FINANCE
◉ **AVE DEBT PER YEAR** £2,609 ◉ **HOME STUDENT FEES** £3,000
FEES UK postgrads are charged around a grand a
year; international undergrads pay £7,175-£10,245;
international postgrads pay £5,400-£10,495.
◉ **ACCESS FUND** £1,257,038
◉ **SUCCESSFUL APPLICATION/YR** 1,577 ◉ **AVE PAYMENT** £549
SUPPORT Bursaries have multiplied in reaction to
top-up fees trauma. The Hallam Access Bursary
doles out £300/yr to undergrads paying top up
fees and who've come from partner schools. High
achievers can aim for a £1,000 scholarship. Those
not entitled to a Higher Education Grant can
apply for £500 through the Access to Learning
Fund, but there are various rules and regs. As the
University's got *a bit of a soft spot* for widening
access, others who are struggling and who are
long-term unemployed, single parents, local
students etc. can apply for various handouts.
There are various prize funds for enterprising
students who start their own business.
Hillsborough Trust memorial bursaries, an
international prize, scholarships and hardship
funds. A loan of £50 cash or food vouchers is
available in extreme emergencies.

S

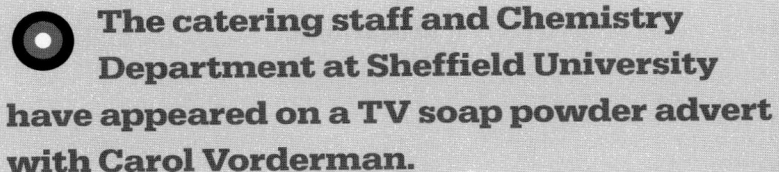

**The catering staff and Chemistry
Department at Sheffield University
have appeared on a TV soap powder advert
with Carol Vorderman.**

SOAS

THE COLLEGE IS PART OF THE UNIVERSITY OF LONDON AND STUDENTS ARE ENTITLED TO USE ITS FACILITIES

1. ○ **SCHOOL OF ORIENTAL & AFRICAN STUDIES (SOAS)** Thornhaugh Street, Russell Square, London, WC1H 0XG **TEL** (020) 7637 2388 **E-MAIL** study@soas.ac.uk **WEBSITE** www.soas.ac.uk ○ **SOAS STUDENTS' UNION** Thornhaugh Street, Russell Square, London, WC1H 0XG **TEL** (020) 7898 4996 **E-MAIL**: fin.com@soas.ac.uk **WEBSITE** www.soasunion.org
2. ○ **VERNON SQUARE CAMPUS** Vernon Square, Penton Rise, London, WC1X 9EL **TEL** (020) 7074 5100

GENERAL ○○○○○○○○○○○○○

With students from over 100 nations and the occasional foreign royalty, SOAS is a *diverse and highly respected institution*. It's part of the central complex of the University of London in Bloomsbury, *which makes it convenient for students wanting to wallow in the luxury of University of London Union's (ULU's) services*. Directly over the road is the University's Senate House and Birkbeck College is just round the corner. The whole caboodle is on the streets parallel to Tottenham Court Road, bang in the middle of London and less than a mile north of Trafalgar Square. SOAS itself is a 30s brick building, *depressingly uniform* and overshadowed by the vast Brunei Gallery (a gift from the Sultan) opposite. Originally a training ground for people about to go off and look after the empire, *the tone is now decidedly post-imperial and right on*. For general information on London see University of London

SEX RATIO: ♂41 ♀59	**FOUNDED:** 1916
FULL-TIME U'GRADS: 1,925	**PART-TIME:** 2
POSTGRADS: 1,694	**NON-DEGREE:** 170
AVE COURSE: 3-4YRS	**ETHNIC:** 46%
STATE:PRIVATE SCHOOL: 69:31	**FLUNK RATE:** 13%
MATURE: 26%	**INTERNATIONAL:** 37%
DISABLED: 35	**LOCAL:** N/A

ATMOSPHERE
SOAS is small enough for everyone to know everyone else, by sight at least. There's a wide mix of religious and ethnic backgrounds, a fascinating example of multi-culturalism. Most dive headfirst into the melting pot and are chuffed to bits to be here. ULU offers an escape from the potential pressure cooker of academic life, as well as being the main source of extra-curricular activity.

SITES
VERNON SQUARE CAMPUS Between Kings Cross and Islington, 15 mins from the main site, Vernon Square is *more a few extra square metres for the School to play with rather than a true campus*. It's right next door to some of the School's accommodation and has some administrative departments (including the Registry) and an internet café. Many undergrads have classes in the new teaching rooms here.

LONDON see University of London

TRAVEL see University of London

CAREER PROSPECTS
○ **CAREERS SERVICE** ○ **NO. OF STAFF** 1 FULL/2 PART ○ **UNEMPLOYED AFTER 6 MTHS** 8%
SOAS's 'Grad Club' is run by the University of London's Careers Service. It has a careers library, bulletin boards, interview training and weekly seminars.

FAMOUS ALUMNI
Zeinab Badawi (newsreader); Dom Joly (Trigger Happy comedian); Jomo Kenyatta (ex-president of Kenya); Enoch Powell (*unmourned* MP); Paul Robeson (singer); Princess Sirindhorn of Thailand.

FURTHER INFO
○ **PROSPECTUSES** UNDERGRAD; POSTGRAD; DEPARTMENTAL ○ **OPEN DAYS**

ACADEMIC ○○○○○○○○○○○○○

As the name suggests, SOAS specialises in any course even remotely related to Asia or Africa and, perhaps less obviously, the Middle East. Provision for its specialist subjects is *excellent*, with *skyscraper high* staff: student ratios and visiting speakers, though *things can be a bit more hit-and-miss in other areas*. In recent years, there's been a bit of a shift from final exams to coursework.

ENTRY POINTS: 240-360	**AVE POINTS:** N/A
APPLICATIONS PER PLACE: 8	**CLEARING:** 5%
NO. OF TERMS: 3	**LENGTH OF TERMS:** 11WKS
STAFF TO STUDENT RATIO: 1:11	**STUDY ADDICTS:** 28%
TEACHING: ★★★	**RESEARCH:** ★★★★
YEAR ABROAD: 24%	**SANDWICH STUDENTS:** 46%
1STS: 15%	**2.2S:** 22%
2.1S: 62%	**3RDS:** 21%

ADMISSIONS
○ **APPLY VIA UCAS**
'Academic suitability' is SOAS's only vague criterion for admissions. They don't always demand the standard three A Levels and are happy to consider other qualifications or experience, particularly in the case of mature students.

Words in italics are Push's point of view — take it or leave it...

SUBJECTS
ARTS/HUMANITIES 26%   **LANGUAGES & CULTURE** 34%
LAW & SOCIAL SCIENCES 40%
BEST Economics; History & Archaeology; Other Languages & Area Studies; Politics; Social Policy & Anthropology; Sociology.

LIBRARIES
◉ 1,200,000+ BOOKS ◉ 650 STUDY PLACES
The main library is *impressive* with *a shelf-busting* selection on African and Oriental music and around 4,000 languages represented overall. *Undergrads have complained about the lack of books for them (but they haven't got a strong case) and about the general organisation and opening hours, but a recent expansion should shut them up a bit.* Many departments have their own little libraries.

COMPUTERS
◉ 300 WORKSTATIONS
Not as many computers as the students need, but what's there is all sufficiently 21st-century. There's internet access on all lab computers, all computers are multilingual, they all have statistics and economic software and there are network points for laptop users. SOAS was one of the pioneer VLE (Virtual Learning Environment) institutions, meaning students have access to online resources, assessment and academic forums.

OTHER LEARNING FACILITIES
Five language labs; music rehearsal rooms; recording studio for audio/video tapes; and the Brunei Gallery. The new research centre provides four floors of, um... research for postgrads and profs.

ENTERTAINMENT ◖◗◖◗◖◗◖◗◖◗◖◗

THE CITY see University of London
Situated in Central London, *local entertainments range from chopsticks in Chinatown to mummy-mooning in the British Library. Not for the faint of wallet however.*

UNIVERSITY
◉ PRICE OF A PINT OF BEER £1.80
Multi-cultural entertainment is at the heart of SOAS's supply of fun, with visiting acts and troupes from many different nations and traditions. *Drinking and clubbing play a half-hearted second-fiddle.*
BARS *The bar is relaxed and informal and provides a good melting pot for the School's cultural combo, often playing opera during the day. Wednesdays are quiz nights and Fridays get live bands, but the doors stay shut at weekends.*
FILM A weekly film night on each campus.
MUSIC VENUES Many bands perform – the majority of them are Asian and African, though other nationalities get a look in. Scala, the Palestinian

Society, hosts Arabic parties, but *hardcore clubbers go elsewhere for a fix (often Cheapskates for 70p drinks).*
FOOD *The JCR Snack Bar is the best value* but there's also a refectory. Another snack bar and *posh* café are to be found in the Brunei Gallery. The Vernon Square Campus has an internet café. Hari Krishnas give out free vegetarian food *and chanty orangeness.*
OTHER Many of the international clubs provide ents that attract many people from outside the School. There have been Indonesian Gamelan recitals, Laotian dancing, African groups, Capoeira demonstrations, Ghanian drumming, food and music evenings and a traditional Thai concert featuring former student the Princess of Thailand. SOAS also has two balls a year.

SOCIAL ◖◗◖◗◖◗◖◗◖◗◖◗◖◗◖◗◖◗◖◗◖◗

SOAS STUDENTS' UNION
◉ 2 SABBATICALS ◉ TURNOUT AT LAST BALLOT 33%
◉ NUS MEMBER
The SU champs at the revolutionary bit and has students assigned to watch every aspect of School life. Campaigns, when they happen, stir the masses, and come election time, there's a stampede to the ballot box. It's had its bust-ups with the authorities, including a bout of wrist-slapping which ended in the SU having its bar taken away, and recently the SU and students kicked up enough fuss about two specialist librarians being made unceremoniously redundant to get the pair reinstated.

SU FACILITIES
A shop; snack bar; newsagents; crèche; jukebox; pool tables; games machines.

CLUBS (NON-SPORTING)
Abacus (network of Chinese students); Africa; Angels of Harlem (Gospel Choir; awesome name); Anime; Anti-Colonial Resistance; Asian Music; Capoeira; Chinese; Cultural; Culture of Myanmar/Burma; Fight Racism!; Fight Imperialism!; Food Appreciation; Friends of Africa; Giant BLT (LGB); Go Soc; Hong Kong Film; International Campaigns; Investment Banking; Israel; Jammu and Kashmir (Jaks); Japanese; Know the Ledge; Korea; Krishna Consciousness; Latin American; Mature Students Soc; MUN (Model United Nations); Music soc; Natural Remedies; Nordic; Openair Radio; Palestine; People First (finds jobs in the UK for Japanese speakers); Persian Soc; Respect; Spirit magazine; Sri Chaitanta Saraswata Soc (Hinduism); Student Action For Refugees; Taiwanese; Thai; Tibet Soc; UNYSA (UN Youth and Student Association); Volunteering; War on Want; Women's. **See also Clubs tables.**

OTHER ORGANISATIONS
'The New Spirit' is published independently and monthly.

Words in italics are Push's point of view — take it or leave it...

RELIGION
⦿ 3 CHAPLAINS (RC, COFE, FG)
Muslim prayer room on campus and pretty much everything else around the city. Religion in London see <u>University of London.</u>

PAID WORK see <u>University of London</u>
⦿ JOB BUREAU ⦿ PAID WORK TERM TIME 25%; HOLS 50%
Students use the University's of London's facilities. *In any case, London's a fiesta of part-time work opportunities.*

SPORTS ⦿⦿⦿⦿⦿⦿⦿⦿⦿⦿⦿⦿⦿

⦿ BUSA RANKING 122
The budget goes elsewhere and the School's facilities don't stretch past squash courts and a gym. Students do have access to the ULU's fancy facilities when the sporting bug grabs them. For most SOAS students, *sports are for relaxation rather than rivalry.*

SPORTING CLUBS
Dentokan (martial art); Penkat Silat (another martial art); Shorinji Kempo (and again); Thai Boxing. **See also Clubs tables.**

ATTRACTIONS see <u>University of London</u>

ACCOMMODATION ⦿⦿⦿⦿⦿⦿⦿⦿⦿

IN UNIVERSITY
⦿ SELF-CATERING 40% **⦿ COST** £113 (38/51WKS)
⦿ 1ST YRS LIVING IN 44% **⦿ 2ND YRS LIVING IN** 23%
⦿ POSTGRADS LIVING IN 30%
⦿ INSURANCE PREMIUM £££££
AVAILABILITY SOAS uses 11 different residences of varying quality for students to rest their heads. It sounds a lot but only two, right next to the Vernon Square Campus (20 mins walk from the main site), actually belong to the School. Two others are run by a private outfit and the rest are the University of London's intercollegiate halls, which are shared by colleges all over London (and which include an all-female hall). New students get priority, *but there are no guarantees.*

Halls *bristle* with security guards and are mostly the standard study-bedrooms-around-a-shared-kitchen set-up. *Accommodation can seem prison-like sometimes, but not as cheap* (and there's a £200 deposit for the School's halls).
CAR PARKING *Hahaha, that's a good one.*

EXTERNALLY see <u>University of London</u>
⦿ AVE RENT £113
HOUSING HELP The Student Accommodation Advisor and ULU provide a *respectable* amount of help getting those hard-to-find places to hang one's hat.

WELFARE ⦿⦿⦿⦿⦿⦿⦿⦿⦿⦿⦿

SERVICES
⦿ LGBT OFFICER ⦿ MATURE STUDENTS' OFFICER
⦿ INTERNATIONAL STUDENTS' OFFICER
⦿ POSTGRAD OFFICER ⦿ DISABILITIES OFFICER
⦿ WOMEN'S OFFICER ⦿ ETHNIC MINORITIES OFFICER
⦿ UNIVERSITY COUNSELLORS 3 PART
⦿ CRIME RATING: !!!!!
Students solve health quandaries via the University of London Hospital. There's a crèche on campus and advice to be had from tutors. For mobility-impaired students, *access is okay, but there are still many annoying little oversights.* CCTV and undercover police have been attempting to do something about soft drugs *(stopping them, that is, not procuring them).*

FINANCE
⦿ AVE DEBT PER YEAR £2,598 **⦿ HOME STUDENT FEES** £3,000
FEES Most postgrads pay £3,510, but fees vary more than Madonna's hairstyle. Full-time fees for international students are £10,450.
⦿ ACCESS FUND £141,000 **⦿ SUCCESSFUL APPLICATION/YR** 181
⦿ AVE PAYMENT £6,000
SUPPORT There are a number of funds, such as the hardship fund for EU/overseas students, and bursaries, such as those from the Zoroastrian Studies Fund and Opportunity Bursaries for disadvantaged UK undergrads. Access funds are available *if students' pennies are feeling the pinch.*

▶ **SOUTH BANK POLYTECHNIC**
see *<u>London South Bank University</u>*

▶ **SOUTH BANK UNIVERSITY**
see *<u>London South Bank University</u>*

▶ **SOUTHAMPTON INSTITUTE**
see *<u>Southampton Solent University</u>*

S

Words in italics are Push's point of view — take it or leave it...

UNIVERSITY OF SOUTHAMPTON

1. ☉ **UNIVERSITY OF SOUTHAMPTON** Highfield, Southampton, SO17 1BJ **TEL** (02380) 595 000 **E–MAIL** prospenq@soton.ac.uk **WEBSITE** www.soton.ac.uk ☉ **SOUTHAMPTON UNIVERSITY STUDENTS' UNION** Highfield, Southampton, SO17 1BJ **TEL** (02380) 595 233 **E–MAIL** susu@soton.ac.uk **WEBSITE** www.susu.org
2. ☉ **UNIVERSITY OF SOUTHAMPTON BOLDREWOOD CAMPUS** Biomedical Sciences Building, Bassett Crescent East, Southampton, SO16 7PX
3. ☉ **UNIVERSITY OF SOUTHAMPTON AVENUE CAMPUS** Highfield Road, as Highfield Campus
4. ☉ **NATIONAL OCEANOGRAPHY CENTRE, SOUTHAMPTON** University of Southampton, Waterfront Campus, European Way, Southampton, SO14 3ZH **TEL** (02380) 596 666
5. ☉ **SOUTHAMPTON GENERAL HOSPITAL** Tremona Road, Southampton, SO16 6YD **TEL** (02380) 777 222
6. ☉ **WINCHESTER SCHOOL OF ART** Park Avenue, Winchester, SO23 8DL **TEL** (02380) 596 900
   ☉ **WINCHESTER SCHOOL OF ART STUDENTS' UNION** Park Avenue, Winchester, SO23 8DL **TEL** (01962) 840 772

GENERAL ◖◖◖◖◖◖◖◖◖◖◖◖◖

Southampton's the wizened old sea dog of the south coast. It's salty, not particularly pretty and it's even got the scars to prove it tangled with the Luftwaffe during World War II. There's lots to see in the surrounding countryside – the Isle of Wight to the south; to the west lies the ancient, 145 sq-mile New Forest; beyond the forest is Bournemouth, *which is the closest to Miami that England does (not very close at all, but there's a beach and a few bars);* to the north lie the cathedral cities of Salisbury and Winchester, and to the east lies Southampton's *fearsome* rival, Portsmouth. The University – *typical of the rest of the city* – has redbrick buildings that survived the war, along with post-war geometric blocks that won awards in the 60s and look *pretty hideous* now, mostly on a landscaped campus, two miles from the city centre. The main site is dotted with sculptures including some by Barbara Hepworth.

SEX RATIO: ♂39 ♀61	**FOUNDED:** 1952
FULL–TIME U'GRADS: 13,045	**PART–TIME:** 3,305
POSTGRADS: 2,900	**NON–DEGREE:** N/A
AVE COURSE: 3–4YRS	**ETHNIC:** 8%
STATE:PRIVATE SCHOOL: 81:19	**FLUNK RATE:** 7%
MATURE: 16%	**INTERNATIONAL:** 16%
DISABLED: 535	**LOCAL:** 16%

ATMOSPHERE
On arrival at Southampton, students tend to turn into unpretentious, vaguely scruffy types no matter what their background. Most of them were white and middle class to begin with, but there's not much attitude about the place.

SITES
BOLDREWOOD CAMPUS (1,000 students – Biomedical Sciences) Less than a mile from the main campus is this *large, squat Lego-box* building. Even though it's within *easy* walking distance it's a separate community where the student medics make their own entertainment.
AVENUE CAMPUS (3,000 students – English, Film, History, Philosophy, School of Modern Languages, Archaeology) A short walk from the main campus, served by the University's bus service,

housing most arts students, except musicians and artists.
NATIONAL OCEANOGRAPHY CENTRE, SOUTHAMPTON (600 students – School of Ocean & Earth Science) A purpose-built site taking advantage of Southampton's natural environment. It's three miles from the main campus but there's a *regular* shuttle bus service.
WINCHESTER SCHOOL OF ART (1,000 students – Art, Design & Textiles) This member of the Southampton family merged with the University in 1996. It's in the *historic* city of Winchester (12 miles from Southampton), maintains a separate identity and is creative and predominantly female.

SOUTHAMPTON
☉ **POPULATION** 217,600 ☉ **CITY CENTRE** 2 MILES
☉ **LONDON** 74 MILES ☉ **PORTSMOUTH** 16 MILES
☉ **WINCHESTER** 12 MILES
☉ **HIGH TEMP** 22 ☉ **LOW TEMP** 3 ☉ **RAINFALL** 66
Southampton's a gentle, pleasant enough place to live, but the fun doesn't come neatly packaged and left by the front door. Fortunately, for students who go looking for it, there's the best part of 30,000 student partners in crime (including the Southampton Solent population). The locals have learned to put up with the droves of students.

TRAVEL
TRAINS Southampton Central offers services to London (£20.40), Bristol (£17.75), Manchester (£50.55) and others.
COACHES National Express services all over the country, including London (£16.40), Manchester (£28.50) and all points beyond.
CAR The A27 splits for a brief spell into the M27 and the continuing A27 around Southampton. There's also the A31, A33, A36 and A336 and the M3. Parking's *tough* in town and a University permit (£126) *hard to come by.*
AIR Flights inland, to Europe, Ireland and the Channel Islands from Southampton Airport.
LOCAL Buses are *cheap and reliable.* Local trains are *regular* with connections all over Hampshire and there are seven stations around the city, but *it's not the cheapest or most practical way of getting around.*
UNIVERSITY Uni-link links the city and the campuses (£1 single/£2 all-day pass). The Union runs a safety bus every evening.

S

Words in italics are Push's point of view — take it or leave it...

TAXIS *Not a bad way to get around, if you can afford it.* Typical journey, city centre to the 'burbs – £5-7.

BICYCLES *Good* bike facilities on campus and bike sheds at halls. Cycle routes through city and parks. The city centre around the University is *generally fairly flat.*

CAREER PROSPECTS
- **CAREERS SERVICE** - **NO. OF STAFF** 14
- **UNEMPLOYED AFTER 6 MTHS** 6%

Careers fairs, vacancy lists, psychometric tests and various others.

FAMOUS ALUMNI
Laura Bailey (model); Miriam and Guin Batten (Olympic rowers); Roger Black (athlete turned BBC athletics commentator); John Denham MP (Lab, ex-SU President); Jeremy Hardy (comic); John Inverdale (BBC sports presenter); Dominic Mohan (the Sun); Chris Packham (Really Wild Show); John Sopel (BBC correspondent); Lord Tonypandy (former speaker of House of Commons).

FURTHER INFO
- **PROSPECTUSES** UNDERGRAD; POSTGRAD; MOST DEPTS
- **OPEN DAYS**

ACADEMIC ((((((((((((((

- **RUSSELL GROUP**

Good academic credentials, even with the *young upstart* Southampton Solent hot on the University's heels. *Lots of support* for budding young entrepreneurs.

ENTRY POINTS: 160-370	**AVE POINTS:** 389
APPLICATIONS PER PLACE: 7	**CLEARING:** 9%
NO. OF TERMS: 2	**LENGTH OF TERMS: 16**WKS
STAFF TO STUDENT RATIO: 1:14	**STUDY ADDICTS:** 25%
TEACHING: ****	**RESEARCH:** ****
YEAR ABROAD: N/A	**SANDWICH STUDENTS:** N/A
1STS: 17%	**2.2s:** 24%
2.1s: 50%	**3RDS:** 5%

ADMISSIONS
- **APPLY VIA UCAS/NMAS FOR NURSING/GTTR FOR TEACHING**

SUBJECTS
ART & DESIGN 4%   **BIOLOGICAL SCIENCES** 6%
BUSINESS/MANAGEMENT 3%   **CHEMISTRY** 2%
CIVIL ENGINEERING & THE ENVIRONMENT 3%
EDUCATION 1%   **ENGINEERING** 5%
ELECTRONICS & COMPUTER SCIENCE 6%   **GEOGRAPHY** 3%
LAW 3%   **MATHEMATICS** 2%   **MEDICINE** 6%
NURSING & MIDWIFERY 20%   **OCEAN & EARTH SCIENCE** 4%
PHYSICS & ASTRONOMY 1%   **SOCIAL SCIENCES** 9%
BEST Computer Science; Engineering; Medicine; Physical Geography & Environmental Science.
UNUSUAL Electrical Engineering; Sport Management & Leadership.

LIBRARIES
- **2,649,300 BOOKS** - **1,932 STUDY PLACES**
- **SPEND PER STUDENT** £££££

Seven libraries – the main one is the Hartley Library in the centre of the campus. Facilities are *fair to middling,* with *helpful* opening hours.

COMPUTERS
- **1,635 WORKSTATIONS** - **24-HOUR ACCESS**

There are wireless areas on campus and most hall bedrooms have network points and internet.

ENTERTAINMENT (((((((((

THE CITY
- **PRICE OF A PINT OF BEER** £2.20
- **GLASS OF WINE** £2.10
- **CAN OF RED BULL** £2.40

CINEMAS A seven-screen multiplex at Ocean Village. 14-screen multiplex at Leisure World. Harbour Lights is an arthouse/mainstream cinema also in the Ocean Village area. Also has a fortnightly film quiz in the bar.

THEATRES The Nuffield specialises in modern drama, the Mayflower in the touring blockbusters.

PUBS *A wide* selection, many with extended opening. *Pushplugs: Goblets; the Crown; Gordon Arms; Talking Heads; the Hogshead; the Lizard Lounge; Varsity; the Giddy Bridge. The Crown & Sceptre and the Gate are best avoided.*

CLUBBING *Plenty of sweat-pits, including a few student faves. Pushplugs: Rhino Club (disco/ indie nights); Lennons (rock/indie); Nexus (hip hop, drum 'n bass, alternative nights); Kaos (pop/chart); Frog and Frigate (cheesy classics); Bambuubar. The Hobbit is legendary for its massive beer garden and relaxed atmosphere.*

MUSIC VENUES The Joiners for *middling* indie, the Mayflower and the Guildhall for bigger names (Supergrass, The Vines, Jamelia, Motorhead).

EATING OUT *Cheap meal deals at pubs, but loads of other snack-shacks to choose from, particularly around Oxford Street. Pushplugs: Poppadom Express; Goodies Diner (film-themed); Cook House (sarnies, coffee bar); Chutneys (Indian).*

UNIVERSITY
- **PRICE OF A PINT OF BEER** £1.80
- **GLASS OF WINE** £1.20
- **CAN OF RED BULL** £1.50

BARS The Stag's Head (main Union Bar, cap 400) is fairly pubby. There's also a sports bar with board games and Twister *for those who need to flex their competitive instincts.* The bar at the School of Art at Winchester has recently been refurbished.

THEATRES A couple of societies put on musicals and mainstream theatre. There's a *once-a-year glitzy extravaganza* at the Nuffield, a professional theatre on the Highfield Campus, and regular trips to Edinburgh.

Words in italics are Push's point of view – take it or leave it...

FILM The film society puts on three flicks every week, *from mainstream favourites to strange leftfield arthouse numbers.* Membership's £12 a year.

MUSIC VENUES The West Refectory receives touring bands with 800 *sets of open arms.* Recent shows from Razorlight and Athlete and Electric Six.

CLUBBING *Big* nights at the Cube (cap 1,800) with rock, urban and the *ubiquitous cheesefests* during the week. Occasional DJ sets from national names (eg. Dave Pearce, Judge Jules and, *er,* Dr Karl Kennedy).

COMEDY/CABARET Weekly comedy nights at the Bridge with *ribs tickled* by John Ryan, Sarah Kendall, Craig Campbell and more.

FOOD Hot/cold fodder and *the best hot chocolate for miles* at the SUSU café. Bar snacks at the Bridge and school dinners at Piazza. *More choice around the campuses than a gastronome could shake Michael Winner at.*

OTHER Graduation ball and faculty balls throughout the year.

SOCIAL ◖◖◖◖◖◖◖◖◖◖◖◖

SOUTHAMPTON UNIVERSITY STUDENTS' UNION
◉ 5 SABBATICALS ◉ TURNOUT AT LAST BALLOT 19%
The left-leaning, NUS-shunning Union Council tries to rouse some political interest and *stretches the net a little wider* than moping about top-up fees. *They've been working on playing nicely with the University lately.*

SU FACILITIES
Dry cleaners; hairdressers; guarded cloakroom; lockers; photo booth; pottery studio; minibus; two bars; café; cheap driving school; showers and baths; launderette; market stalls each Monday; sports equipment and hire service; Barclays, HSBC, Lloyds TSB and NatWest banks/ATMs; TV rooms; Interflora; darkroom; meeting rooms; customised disco; ballroom; retail centre with a shop; travel agency; sports shop.

CLUBS (NON-SPORTING)
145 including: AIESEC; Airsoft; Ballet; Ballroom & Latin Dance; Bel Canto (two choirs); Breakdance; Circus; Comedy; Concert Band; Contemporary Dance; Jazz Dance; Jazz Manics; Live Music; Lopsoc (light opera); Medics Revue; Showstoppers (performing arts); Sinfonietta; Stagsoc (backstage craft); SU Singers; SOJO (jazz); SUSO (symphony orchestra); Symphonic Wind Orchestra; Tap Dance; Theatre Group; Wessex Films. **See also Clubs tables.**

OTHER ORGANISATIONS
The SU mag 'Wessex Scene' comes out every three weeks. 'Surge' radio broadcasts on AM and the web. SUSU Rag does the fundraising number and SCA (community action) make an effort in the local community.

RELIGION
◉ 3 CHAPLAINS (COFE, FC, RC)
There are many faiths represented in Southampton, with a mosque, Hindu temple, Gurdwara and Christian places of worship for most denominations.

PAID WORK
◉ JOB BUREAU ◉ PAID WORK TERM TIME 60%; HOLS 70%
As well as *the usual gamut* of bar and shop slog, students can *rake in the cash* at the boat show in the summer. The job shop, Openings, matches students to taskmasters.

SPORTS ◖◖◖◖◖◖◖◖◖◖◖◖◖

◉ RECENT SUCCESSES WINDSURFING, SAILING, RIFLE, FENCING, EQUESTRIANISM **◉ BUSA RANKING** 13
The Athletic Union funds 74 flavours of sporting society, making use of decent facilities in the area. A SportRec card (£45) gives year-long sporting access.

SPORTS FACILITIES
On campus there's a large sports hall, six squash courts, climbing wall (outdoors), judo room, table tennis, aerobics room, tennis courts, snooker room and, after all that, an injuries clinic. New indoor sports centre with swimming pool, badminton court and gym. Off campus there are 90 acres of playing fields, a rifle range and a boatyard. The city adds a golf course, dry ski slope, bowling green and a cycle track.

SPORTING CLUBS
10-pin Bowling; Aikido; American Football; Badminton; Baseball; Boat; Boxing Chess; Bujincan BudoTiajutsu; Canoe; Canoe Polo; Darts; Fencing; Gojo Ryu; Golf; Handball; Hang Gliding; Hillwalking; Ju-Jitsu; Judo; Karate-do Shotokai; Kickboxing; Kite Surfing; Ko-do Ryu; Kung Fu Wu Shu; Lacrosse; Lifesaving; Motor; Mountain Bike; Mountaineering; Okinawan Shorin Ryu Karate; Paragliding; Riding; Rifle; Roller Hockey; Shaolin Kung Fu; Shorinji Kempo; Ski & Snowboarding; Skydive; Snooker; Surf; Table Tennis; Tae Kwon Do; Trampolining; Triathlon; Trident Paintball; Ultimate Frisbee; Vixens Cheerleading; Volleyball; Water Polo; Water Ski & Wakeboard & Windsurf. **See also Clubs tables.**

ATTRACTIONS
The Scummers (as rivals Portsmouth know them – fans know them as Saints, neutrals as plain old Southampton) play Championship football and occasionally hold vicious fights with arch-rival Portsmouth fans. Hampshire CCC play at the Rose Bowl, and Cowes Week sees *rich folk swan around* the Solent *in boats.*

S

ACCOMMODATION ◡◡◡◡◡◡◡◡◡

IN UNIVERSITY
- **CATERED** 5% ○ **COST** £108 (34/38WKS)
- **SELF-CATERING** 35% ○ **COST** £78 (38/51WKS)
- **1ST YRS LIVING IN** 90% ○ **POSTGRADS LIVING IN** 30%
- **INSURANCE PREMIUM** ££

AVAILABILITY *Most of the halls are liveable-in,
although some more so than others.* Connaught
Halls *get the biggest thumbs up.* Glen Eyre student
village is close to the campuses and *good craic.*
CAR PARKING Permit needed, 1st years aren't
allowed cars.

EXTERNALLY
- **AVE RENT** £55 ○ **LIVING AT HOME** 7%

AVAILABILITY It's *very easy* to find accommodation
– *two days' search max to find somewhere
(though if it takes longer, don't come crying to
Push).* There's *some good housing* about,
particularly around Portswood, Highfield and
Bevois Valley, *within staggering distance of the
best* student pubs. *Avoid some parts of
Swaythling, Bassett Green and Bitterne which are
about as welcoming as a Strangeways reception
committee. Students should also avoid letting
anyone convince them to sort it out too long in
advance.* Landlords shove up prices and charge
for renting over the summer. *It takes guts, but this
is the time to wait and hold on till the landlords
are a little more anxious to fill their places.*
HOUSING HELP The University accommodation

office in Winchester is developing a full private
rented sector property service. In Southampton
all landlords are asked to produce safety
certificates before they can have their property
advertised. The Union has a vacancies board.

WELFARE ◡◡◡◡◡◡◡◡◡◡◡◡◡

SERVICES
- **LGBT SOCIETY** ○ **WOMEN'S OFFICER**
- **MATURE STUDENTS' SOCIETY**
- **INTERNATIONAL STUDENTS' SOCIETY**
- **POSTGRAD SOCIETY** ○ **SELF-DEFENCE CLASSES**
- **LATE-NIGHT MINIBUS** ○ **NIGHTLINE**
- **UNIVERSITY COUNSELLORS** 8 FULL/10-12 PART
- **CRIME RATING:** !!!!

HEALTH Two health centres. The University health
service at Highfield has five GPs and three nurses.
CRECHES/NURSERY 108 places for ages 2-5yrs.
DISABILITIES *Reasonable* access and residences for
students who need care assistance. The Learning
Differences Clinic looks out for dyslexics,
dyspraxics and anyone else who needs extra help.

FINANCE
- **AVE DEBT PER YEAR** £2,767 ○ **HOME STUDENT FEES** £3,000

FEES Part-timers pay £750 and postgrads £3,085.
International students cough up between £8,300
and £11,300 a year.
- **ACCESS FUND** £672,000 ○ **SUCCESSFUL APPLICATION/YR** 1,458

SUPPORT In addition to the access fund, the
University runs a hardship fund for people whose
circumstances change mid-course. SUSU also
gives short-term emergency loans.

▶ **SOUTH WEST POLYTECHNIC**
see *University of Plymouth*

S SOUTHAMPTON SOLENT UNIVERSITY

FORMERLY SOUTHAMPTON INSTITUTE

○ **SOUTHAMPTON SOLENT UNIVERSITY** East Park Terrace, Southampton, SO14 0YN **TEL** (023) 8031 9039
E-MAIL enquiries@solent.ac.uk **WEBSITE** www.solent.ac.uk ○ **SOLENT STUDENTS' UNION** Students Union Building, East Park
Terrace, Southampton, SO14 0YN **TEL** (023) 8023 2154 **E-MAIL** suadmin@solent.ac.uk **WEBSITE** www.solentsu.co.uk

GENERAL ◡◡◡◡◡◡◡◡◡◡◡◡

Solent, which became a university in 2005, is
located at a modern campus in the middle of
Southampton, set apart from the very centre of
town by *big* gardens – *perfect for chilling out in
the summer.* The second site, which does
merchant navy training, is nine miles up the
coast at Warsash.

SEX RATIO: ♂56 ♀44	**FOUNDED:** 1984
FULL-TIME U'GRADS: 8,684	**PART-TIME:** 1,740
POSTGRADS: 260	**NON-DEGREE:** 2,066
AVE COURSE: 3YRS	**ETHNIC:** 12%
STATE:PRIVATE SCHOOL: 96:4	**FLUNK RATE:** 17%
MATURE: 24%	**INTERNATIONAL:** 11%
DISABLED: 285	**LOCAL:** 30%

Words in italics are Push's point of view — take it or leave it...

ATMOSPHERE

The Solent campus is *busy, although not necessarily with academic work* – watersporters are particularly noticeable, *taking full advantage of the river with which the University shares its name*. There's a *tight* community feel and *everyone knows everyone else's business*.

SITES

WARSASH MARITIME CENTRE A merchant navy training centre with practical and watersports facilities. *It's self-contained and has its own SU bar, but some students can feel a bit isolated from action at the main site.*

SOUTHAMPTON see University of Southampton
⊙ **CITY CENTRE** 400M

TRAVEL see University of Southampton
Being closer to the city centre than Southampton University, Solent is handy for local bus and train stations.
UNIVERSITY A University coach service connects the main campus with Warsash.
TAXIS Several ranks close to Solent. Typical journey, city centre to the 'burbs, costs £5-7.
BICYCLES *Good bike* facilities on campus and bike sheds at halls. Cycle routes through city and parks. The city centre around the University is *generally fairly flat.*

CAREER PROSPECTS

⊙ **CAREERS SERVICE** ⊙ **NO. OF STAFF** 3 FULL/6 PART
⊙ **UNEMPLOYED AFTER 6 MTHS** 9%

FAMOUS ALUMNI

Ed Dubois (yacht designer); Peter Long (CEO, First Choice holidays); Jenny Packham (fashion designer); David Quayle (the Q in B&Q).

FURTHER INFO

⊙ **PROSPECTUSES** UNDERGRAD; POSTGRAD
⊙ **OPEN DAYS**
The University website has some *rather snazzy* student-produced videos that show off the facilities.

ACADEMIC ⊙⊙⊙⊙⊙⊙⊙⊙⊙⊙⊙⊙⊙⊙

Solent specialises in vocational courses and *dabbles in* sponsorship and work with local businesses *in order to give its graduates as sparkly a CV as possible*. Its specialities include business, technology, media arts and maritime courses. Last year the University took an outside broadcast truck to Glastonbury *to give budding MTV presenters a chance to practice in the (muddy) field. Beats sitting in a classroom, Push reckons.*

ENTRY POINTS: 100-260	AVE POINTS: N/A
APPLICATIONS PER PLACE: 3	CLEARING: 13%
NO. OF TERMS: 3	LENGTH OF TERMS: 13wks
STAFF TO STUDENT RATIO: 1:22	STUDY ADDICTS: 8%
TEACHING: *	RESEARCH: *
YEAR ABROAD: 1%	SANDWICH STUDENTS: 9%
1STS: 4%	2.2s: 35%
2.1s: 50%	3RDS: 8%

ADMISSIONS

⊙ **APPLY VIA UCAS**
A widening participation programme is in place.

SUBJECTS

MEDIA, ARTS & SOCIETY 31%
SOUTHAMPTON BUSINESS SCHOOL 33%
TECHNOLOGY 25%   **WARSASH MARITIME CENTRE** 11%
UNUSUAL Computer & Video Games; Fine Arts Valuation; Football Studies; Watersports Studies & Management; Yacht & Powercraft Design.

LIBRARIES

⊙ **230,000+ BOOKS** ⊙ **836 STUDY PLACES**
The Mountbatten libraries are on the city campus. *Students' demand is a touch higher than the libraries' ability to supply.*

COMPUTERS

⊙ **750 WORKSTATIONS**
Data network and internet points in student rooms.

OTHER LEARNING FACILITIES

Language lab with multimedia facilities, towing tank for testing hull designs and, at Warsash, navigational and bridge simulation equipment.

ENTERTAINMENT ⊙⊙⊙⊙⊙⊙⊙⊙⊙

THE CITY see University of Southampton

UNIVERSITY

⊙ **PRICE OF A PINT OF BEER** £1.80
⊙ **GLASS OF WINE** £1.80
BARS *Inventive naming ahoy*. There's the Top Bar (*pubby* and *busy* most days, especially for happy hour), the Bottom Bar (café-style bar/*sociable loitering centre* with hot and cold meals and trendy seating) and, *guess what*, the Middle Bar (*chilled-out space for chatting or study*).
THEATRES Central Hall just down the road is also used by Performing Arts students. There's no student drama society, though.
MUSIC VENUES Top Bar has acoustic music on Mondays – student bands and DJs welcome.
CLUBBING All three bars have dance space but things tend to wind up around 11pm, leaving clubbers to hit Southampton's *many* student nights.
FOOD Lots of options, from snacky, greasy burgery treats at the Bottom Bar, pizza/pasta/panini from the Works food court and sandwiches from Delice Express. Other cafés too. No nosh after 7pm.

Words in italics are Push's point of view — take it or leave it...

OTHER Three balls every year (freshers, grad and summer, which is often held in conjunction with Winchester). 11 tonnes of sand was scattered around for last year's freshers Hawaiian Beach Bash – *Southampton's answer to 'the OC'?*

SOCIAL ⭕⭕⭕⭕⭕⭕⭕⭕⭕⭕⭕⭕

SOLENT STUDENTS' UNION
- **2 SABBATICALS** - **TURNOUT AT LAST BALLOT** 16%
- **NUS MEMBER**

About as political as a box of biscuits, the Union is primarily there to keep students safe and entertained. To this end it runs three bars, a shop and a welfare office as well as giving several other private outlets a roof over their heads. *The Union and University are united in the desire to make students happy and as a result their working relationship is group hug rather than daggers drawn.* The Union is looking into ways to improve links with the *slightly neglected* Warsash site.

SU FACILITIES
City: three bars; four minibuses for hire; advice centre; two shops (books, stationery, sweets); ATMs (Barclays, NatWest); photo booth; games and vending machines; pool tables; juke boxes; two meeting rooms; satellite TV; dry cleaning. Warsash: shop; bar; refectory.

CLUBS (NON-SPORTING)
Breakin' Ground (breakdancing); Circus; Darts; Gaming (roleplay, board & computer); Maritime; Poker; Officer Training Corps; St. Johns Ambulance; Welsh. **See also Clubs tables.**

OTHER ORGANISATIONS
'Re:Sus' is the *light-hearted* magazine (seven issues a year); 'SIN' radio broadcasts across in bars and halls and there are plans for a TV station. SSU student volunteers *muck in* with a load of charitable schemes and causes. The Union has a full-time volunteer co-ordinator. RAG *is growing slowly with money-spinners including a Vegas night, dodgeball tournament and skydive.*

RELIGION
- **3 CHAPLAINS (RC, COFE, INTERNATIONAL)**
There's also a multi-faith quiet room.

PAID WORK see University of Southampton
- **JOB BUREAU** - **PAID WORK** TERM TIME 65%; HOLS 75%
The SU street team employs students to do promos for the Union. The Jobshop e-mails and advertises vacancies to students after a job.

SPORTS ⭕⭕⭕⭕⭕⭕⭕⭕⭕⭕⭕⭕⭕

- **RECENT SUCCESSES** YACHTING - **BUSA RANKING** 43
Sport falls into the in-tray of Team Solent, a

partnership between University and Union: the University owns and runs the sports centre, playing fields and watersports centre and provides facilities, the SU runs the clubs and teams. There's a sports scholarship scheme and all sorts of coaching and instructing courses. Sailing is the *big thing* at Solent, *which regularly trounces* all comers, whether national or international.

SPORTS FACILITIES
Could do with a revamp – some wheels are in motion, apparently. Main site: sports hall; health suite; sailing facilities; two fitness centres (including teaching lab); multigym; circuit training; 12 acres of playing fields three miles away; use of squash and tennis courts. Warsash: small sports hall; multigym; sailing/water sports on the Hamble and Itchen. The University has links with local sports centres who provide concessionary deals at golf courses, climbing wall, athletics facilities, riding stables, artificial ski-slope and boxing ring.

SPORTING CLUBS
American Football; Cheerleaders; Ju-Jitsu; Kickboxing; Kung Fu; Mountain Sports; Roller Hockey; Rowing; Snowboarding; Surf; Triathlon; Ultimate Frisbee; Wakeboarding & Waterskiing. **See also Clubs tables.**

ATTRACTIONS see University of Southampton

ACCOMMODATION ⭕⭕⭕⭕⭕⭕⭕⭕⭕

IN UNIVERSITY
- **SELF-CATERING** 24% - **COST** £84 (40/48WKS)
- **1ST YRS LIVING IN** 60% - **INSURANCE PREMIUM** £
AVAILABILITY The *modern* accommodation is dished out to those *who stick their hands up first*, but there's enough to cope with first year demand. Most students reckon it's *a bit pricey*, but they appreciate *tight* security, *cushy* facilities and the proximity to the University (all halls are within walking distance). Nearly half the rooms are en suite and there are specially adapted disabled flats. Emily Davies is the *slightly cheaper* postgrad hall (from £40 a week) but the undergrad accommodation costs £68 or more.
CAR PARKING A few parking spaces at each hall (£350 a year), far more bike-sheds for pedal pushers.

EXTERNALLY see University of Southampton
- **AVE RENT** £68
HOUSING HELP The Accommodation Office supplies an accredited housing list, shared with the University.

WELFARE ⭕⭕⭕⭕⭕⭕⭕⭕⭕⭕⭕⭕⭕

SERVICES
- ⭕ LGBT SOCIETY ⭕ EQUAL OPPORTUNITIES OFFICER
- ⭕ POSTGRAD SOCIETY ⭕ MATURE STUDENTS' SOCIETY
- ⭕ INTERNATIONAL STUDENTS' SOCIETY
- ⭕ DISABILITIES SOCIETY ⭕ LATE-NIGHT MINIBUS
- ⭕ SELF-DEFENCE CLASSES
- ⭕ UNIVERSITY COUNSELLORS 2 FULL/3 PART
- ⭕ CRIME RATING: !!!!

The Student Support Network co-ordinates helpdesks throughout the University, SU, finance and accommodation offices. It brands them all 'Students First' centres, *although whether that's a good excuse to queue-jump is uncertain*. The Student Advice Centre is now known as the Source to *funky up welfare awareness*. Angels and Guardian Angels (*that's the SU-run version rather than the celestial*) show freshers the best and safest places to go out. Newsletter for disabled students, work placements and mentoring scheme for ethnic minorities.

HEALTH Close links with St Mary's Surgery nearby, which runs regular surgeries at halls.
WOMEN Free personal attack alarms from the Union advice centre.
DISABILITIES Wheelchair access to most teaching areas, but some remain inaccessible. The campus is quite compact, which a lot of disabled students find helps. Specialist help with dyslexia and other impairments.
CRIME The Police Liaison Officer helps keep an eye on campus wrongdoing.

FINANCE
- ⭕ AVE DEBT PER YEAR £3,547 ⭕ HOME STUDENT FEES £3,000
- ⭕ ACCESS FUND £566,763 ⭕ SUCCESSFUL APPLICATION/YR 850
- ⭕ AVE PAYMENT £100-3,500

SUPPORT A wide range of financial safety nets. Bursaries for poorer students on a sliding scale of up to £1,000 to students eligible for a full government maintenance grant. £250 for local students or those living in halls. Four Lisa Wilson awards (£1,000) for the hardest-up. Sports scholarships help with equipment, training etc.

UNIVERSITY OF ST ANDREWS

⭕ **UNIVERSITY OF ST ANDREWS** Education Liaison Office, Admissions Reception, St Katharine's West, The Scores, St Andrews, KY16 9AJ **TEL** (01334) 462 245 **E-MAIL** ed-liaison@st-andrews.ac.uk **WEBSITE** www.st-andrews.ac.uk
⭕ **THE UNIVERSITY OF ST ANDREWS STUDENTS' ASSOCIATION** St Mary's Place, St Andrews, Fife, KY16 9UZ **TEL** (01334) 462 700 **E-MAIL** union@st-andrews.ac.uk **WEBSITE** www.yourunion.net

GENERAL ⭕⭕⭕⭕⭕⭕⭕⭕⭕⭕⭕⭕

The *postcard-perfect vista* of the Scottish east coast is home to St Andrews, oldest university in Scotland and beaten only to the same title in England by Oxford and Cambridge. The University buildings – which occupy a large amount of town-space – reflect the heritage, spreading from the 15th century to the modern day to some *classic* 16th and 17th-century architecture. Just as a large part of the town is university, a large number of inhabitants are students, accounting for a third of the population. *The town is so small that it's more like one big campus. St Andrews has been unfairly classed as a dumping ground for Oxbridge rejects – both the town and the University may be pint-size, but they're certainly not featherweight.*

ATMOSPHERE
Tradition oozes from every crack in the stonework. Student life is peppered with ritual, ceremony and a healthy drizzle of custom dating back to the darkest recesses of history. The town itself is a small, quiet place, and the University follows suit. It's easygoing, laid back, with none of the frenetic urban pace of Glasgow or Edinburgh. There's little hostility between locals and students, mainly because the University is the major local employer. Many students work alongside locals in the town, which is difficult to cross without bumping into a familiar face. All in all, it's as cosy as cocoa.

ST ANDREWS
- ⭕ POPULATION 18,000 ⭕ CITY CENTRE 1 MILE
- ⭕ LONDON 371 MILES ⭕ DUNDEE 13 MILES
- ⭕ EDINBURGH 55 MILES
- ⭕ HIGH TEMP 19 ⭕ LOW TEMP 0 ⭕ RAINFALL 55

Mix golf and history and you've either got the most boring lesson ever, or something like St Andrews. With six courses, including the oldest in the world, the town attracts Rupert Bear look-alikes like students to a traffic cone. The history part is what brings the tourists in, flocking over to soak up the tradition that drenches the place, and to enjoy the magnificent scenery and architecture. The cathedral and the castle are the most photogenic chunks and although shops and

SEX RATIO: ♂59 ♀41	FOUNDED: 1413
FULL-TIME U'GRADS: 5,788	PART-TIME: 157
POSTGRADS: 1,053	NON-DEGREE: 1,000
AVE COURSE: 4YRS	ETHNIC: 14%
STATE:PRIVATE SCHOOL: 67:33	FLUNK RATE: 2%
MATURE: 23%	INTERNATIONAL: 29%
DISABLED: 160	LOCAL: N/A

S

Words in italics are Push's point of view — take it or leave it...

tea rooms are geared toward the tourist trade decent clothing stores and internet caffs are beginning to crop up too. It's a three-street urban oasis flanked by sandy beaches, rocky coast and countryside. Oh, and golf courses.

TRAVEL

Public transport is thin on the ground *so it can feel cut off from the outside world.*
TRAINS Leuchars station is five miles from the main University buildings with direct lines to London (£63.75), Dundee (£4,60) and Edinburgh (£9.95). For other services, passengers *(sorry, customers)* must change at Edinburgh or Dundee.
COACHES National Express coaches run from Dundee, 13 miles away, to London (£41), Glasgow (£12) and beyond.
CAR A915 south, A91 west to M90 (to Edinburgh).
HITCHING *Difficult to get from St Andrews to anywhere. Better from Edinburgh (A1) or Dundee if thumbsters can get there.*
LOCAL Buses every half hour but rarer at night, although they're quite cheap (£1.40). *St Andrews is generally small enough to walk everywhere.*
UNIVERSITY Late night minibus (Friday till 1.40am).
TAXIS *A taxi ride into Leuchars is expensive at £8.50;* some firms offer student discounts.
BICYCLES *The best way to get around short of a chauffeur-driven limo. St Andrews is small and quite flat with limited traffic.*

CAREER PROSPECTS

○ **CAREERS SERVICE** ○ **NO. OF STAFF** 8 FULL
○ **UNEMPLOYED AFTER 6 MTHS** 8%
Careers library, bulletin boards and interview practice programme. Also a regular newsletter and a bundle of online resources.

FAMOUS ALUMNI

Sir James Black (Nobel Prize scientist); Crispin Bonham-Carter (*drippy* BBC period drama actor); Hazel Irvine (sports presenter); Edward Jenner (discovered smallpox vaccination); John McAllion (Scottish Socialist Party member); Madsen Pirie (Adam Smith Institute); Siobhan Redmond (actress); Alex Salmond MP (SNP); Fay Weldon (writer and feminist); HRH William (pin-up prince and heir to the throne). Former Rectors (elected by students) include Rudyard Kipling and John Cleese, who advised students not to let their degrees get in the way of their education.

SPECIAL FEATURES

Donning an undergrad gown gets students free entry to the castle. *Surely some kind of ID card would be easier?*

ACADEMIC ○○○○○○○○○○○○○○

○ **1994 GROUP**
Four faculties, between them containing 18 schools. An £8m Faculty of Art building should be ready for 2006 entry, and will house the School

of International Relations. Like other Scottish universities, first years study more than one subject (usually three), and streamline their study in the second or, for arts students, third year.

ENTRY POINTS: 228–336	AVE POINTS: 320
APPLICATIONS PER PLACE: 8	CLEARING: 0%
NO. OF TERMS: 2	LENGTH OF TERMS: 15WKS
STAFF TO STUDENT RATIO: 1:10	STUDY ADDICTS: 34%
TEACHING: ★★★★	RESEARCH: ★★★★
YEAR ABROAD: N/A	SANDWICH STUDENTS: 1%
1STS: 12%	2.2S: 16%
2.1S: 60%	3RDS: 1%

ADMISSIONS

○ **APPLY VIA UCAS**
Andy's is trying to pull in more locals and international students.

SUBJECTS

ARTS 65% **DIVINITY** 1% **MEDICAL SCIENCE** 7% **SCIENCES** 27%
BEST Cellular & Molecular Biology; Chemistry; Economics; European Languages; Geography; History; Maths & Statistics; Organismal Biology; Physics; Psychology.
UNUSUAL Astrophysics; International Terrorism; Social Anthropology.

LIBRARIES

○ **1,000,000 BOOKS** ○ **1,046 STUDY PLACES**
○ **SPEND PER STUDENT** ££££
Five libraries (two departmental) ensure there's always a place to go to learn stuff. Not at night, mind you – they close around 10pm weekdays. *The sheer quantity of books is very impressive for a relative tiddler of a university.*

COMPUTERS

○ **500 WORKSTATIONS** ○ **24-HOUR ACCESS**
○ **SPEND PER STUDENT** ££
Rooms have network points and phone lines as standard (requires a small annual surcharge).

OTHER LEARNING FACILITIES

Language labs, rehearsal rooms, a computer design lab and a debating chamber are all present and correct for student use.

ENTERTAINMENT ○○○○○○○○○○

THE CITY

○ **PRICE OF A PINT OF BEER** £2.40
○ **GLASS OF WINE** £3.40
○ **CAN OF RED BULL** £2.40
Even though it's a teeny town, there are a fair few pens to play in.
CINEMAS The New Picture House's three screens juggle mainstream releases and culty, studenty classics (no discounts).
THEATRES Two tiny stages: the Byre Theatre and the Crawford Arts Centre, with occasional back up from the castle itself.

PUBS *More pubs drain tourists' wallets than students', but Raisin is cheap and sporty, with the more upmarket Lizard also a popular haunt.*
CLUBBING *The only swinging clubs here are on the golf course.* There's a bus service to Dundee's nightclubs, *for those who prefer their socialising without a Pringle knit.*
MUSIC VENUES Jazzy goings-on at Younger Hall and the Vic Café, which also hosts blues and folk music. The Gin House has live bands every Thursday. Aikman's (bar & bistro) does live rock, blues and folk, accompanied by *pubby* fare (fajitas, chilli, lasagne).
EATING OUT *A wide selection of ethnic eateries (Indian, Mexican, Thai et al). Pubs are often a good bet.* Pushplugs: Balaka (Bangladeshi); Vine Leaf (for romantic liaisons à deux); Ziggys (decent burgers and pizza); North Point (tea shop); Coffee House (15 blends and hotly tipped bacon sarnies); Le Rustique (good value, tasty lunches). Broons does a bizarre blend of Scottish-French cuisine. The indefatigable Starbucks (must be all that coffee) finally has a presence, but the locals still won't stomach McDonalds.*

UNIVERSITY
○ **PRICE OF A PINT OF BEER** £1.60
○ **GLASS OF WINE** £2.50
○ **CAN OF RED BULL** £1.80
BARS The Union Bar is *the biggie* with the latest licence in town. Those who prefer to do their quaffing in the comfort of their own front room can get the bevies in from the Union's late-licensed offie.
THEATRES *Thesparama.* Dramatoids tread the boards at the local theatres as well as the campus's Venue 1. Scores of shows make the short trip to the Edinburgh fringe each year and every student is automatically a member of the Mermaids drama soc.
FILM Three film clubs show a range of flicks from arty to mainstream and Manga. Free to members.
MUSIC VENUES The Union Theatre doubles as a gig venue, and has hosted the likes of Toploader, Mull Historical Society and Snow Patrol.
CLUBBING Three weekly club nights compose the night scene of the whole city, with *popular cheesy Fridays* and other events pulling in the locals. Judge Jules, Toby Anstis and the ever-ready Pat Sharpe have itched and scratched here.
COMEDY/CABARET Fortnightly comedy gigs have drawn Al Pitcher, Andy Zaltzman and John Oliver to perform. *It's a textbook touring talent stop.*
FOOD The Main Bar includes a restaurant which *doles out everything from snacks to full feasts that can only be described as canteen style.* The Old Union coffee bar also deals in nibbles.
OTHER Raisin Week sees freshers initiated into university life by their student 'parents': the whole shebang culminates in a massive foam fight. *Black tie events are as common as wombles.* The May Ball event starts with a dip in the sea at sunrise and carries on from there. Between them, socs, halls and faculties hold about one a week.

UNIVERSITY OF ST ANDREWS STUDENTS' ASSOCIATION
○ **4 SABBATICALS** ○ **TURNOUT AT LAST BALLOT** 20%
SASA is made of two parts: the Student Representative Council (SRC), which does all the shouting, and the Students' Services Council (the Union), which dishes out services. *The SRC ditched the NUS in 1979 and has been going solo ever since.*

SA FACILITIES
The Union building has three floors of facilities and more dotted across campus: three bars; cafeteria; fast food joint; snack bar; travel agency; general shop; Royal Bank of Scotland ATM; TV lounge; Blackwell's bookshop; launderette; photocopying; photo booth; payphones; fax service; printing service; two minibuses for hire; sexual health clinic; games & vending machines; six pool tables; snooker table; juke box; five meeting rooms; two conference halls; parking.

CLUBS (NON-SPORTING)
Applied Eastern Philosophy; Art; Canadian; DocSoc (Doctor Who); Fine Wine & Cheese; Fly-fishing; Flying; Gilbert & Sullivan; Global Investment Group; Hispanic; Italian; Jazz; Juggling; Middle East; Music; Officer Training Corp; Photosoc; Polish; Scottish National Party; St Andrews in Europe. **See also Clubs tables.**

OTHER ORGANISATIONS
The award-laden 'Saint' is the 50p bi-weekly independent paper competing for attention with union-run 'the Vine', which is churned out once a month. St Andrew's Radio can – sometimes – be heard online, see www.standrewsradio.com. There's the *very active* Student Voluntary Service (SVS) and the Rag, Scotland's *most successful,* raises at least £35,000 every year. There's also the Kate Kennedy Club (named after the niece of the University's founder), a *strangely* all-male charitable group.

RELIGION
○ **8 CHAPLAINS (COFS, COFE, EPISCOPALIAN, EDEN FELLOWSHIP, RC, BAPTIST)**
The University chaplaincy, city churches, meetinghouses, and cathedral cater for most types of Christianity. An Orthodox rabbi is also available and there's a Muslim prayer room.

PAID WORK
○ **JOB BUREAU** ○ **PAID WORK** TERM TIME 48%; HOLS 93%
Advertises local vacancies – *mainly involving gimping for golfers (caddying) and other tourist-related hotel and bar work.* The SA publicises part-time jobs on its website.

S

Words in italics are Push's point of view — take it or leave it...

SPORTS ⭕⭕⭕⭕⭕⭕⭕⭕⭕⭕⭕⭕⭕

⊙ RECENT SUCCESSES GOLF, LACROSSE, RUGBY, SQUASH, HOCKEY **⊙ BUSA RANKING** 36
Excellent facilities (especially for golf). Participation and enthusiasm are strong (especially for golf). There's an impressive number of sporting societies for a university this size, but noteworthy success remains elusive.

SPORTS FACILITIES
60 acres of sports fields with eight football pitches; three rugby pitches; three all-weather pitches; three squash courts; hockey pitch; cricket wicket; three tennis courts; basketball court; two sports halls; four jogging trails; shinty pitch; ultimate frisbee pitch; multigymn; climbing wall; aerobics studio; running track and golf course, *natch.* Facilities have small charges per usage. Watersports, climbing, skiing and riding are all catered for in the nearby area.

SPORTING CLUBS
Aikido; Boxing; Clay Pigeon; Dance; Jujitsu; Korfball; Lacrosse; Life Saving; Polo; Rifle; Rowing; Shinty; Sky-Diving; Table Tennis; Ultimate Frisbee; Waterpolo. **See also Clubs tables.**

ATTRACTIONS
What part of 'six golf courses' don't you understand? Students and locals pay the same rates.

ACCOMMODATION ⭕⭕⭕⭕⭕⭕⭕⭕⭕

IN UNIVERSITY
⊙ CATERED 24% **⊙ COST** £110 (31/50WKS)
⊙ SELF-CATERING 19% **⊙ COST** £67 (31/51WKS)
⊙ 1ST YRS LIVING IN 98% **⊙ INSURANCE PREMIUM** £
AVAILABILITY The gaggle of 13 halls at St Andrews is dispersed across the *weeny town* so all are within walking distance of everything else. All first years are guaranteed walls, floors and ceilings if they meet the housing deadline. Most hang around for a year and then do their own thing for the next two, though the trend reverses for postgrads, who can also live in for almost the whole year if they wish. Undergrads clear out during vacations. Around 20% of the rooms are shared, *so better leave the X-Factor tribute album and The Great Mould Experiment at home.* Kitchens in self-catering apartments come with dishwashers, *so hands that do dishes really do feel as soft as your face.* Students in catered halls don't have to wash up (three meals a day, two at weekends included in rents) and have cleaners and bed linen – *so just like being at home, then.* The gender divide is made literal in a few places, with male/female-only wings and floors. *The gorgeous St Salvator's halls are highly in demand*

because of their lurvely old architecture and central location. CCTV is everywhere, so put your pants back on. David Russell (self-catered hall) has en suite apartments as well as bar, bistro and shop. Rents are on a gradual rise but the University has promised no private sector sell-outs for at least 20 years.
CAR PARKING *Lousy in town.* Permits are dished out only to staff, and the campus area *is usually too damned busy to park.*

EXTERNALLY
⊙ AVE RENT £80 **⊙ LIVING AT HOME** 7%
AVAILABILITY Rentable housing is fairly easy to come by in the town although the lack of parking pushes some nests further afield in nearby villages. Prices can get *unpleasant* but there are bargains to be had too.
HOUSING HELP Student Accommodation Service with five full-timers provides vacancy lists, bulletin board, and legal help. The SA and local estate agents are also happy to give a nudge in the right direction.

WELFARE ⭕⭕⭕⭕⭕⭕⭕⭕⭕⭕⭕⭕

SERVICES
⊙ LGBT SOCIETY ⊙ ETHNIC MINORITIES OFFICER & SOCIETY
⊙ WOMEN'S OFFICER ⊙ MATURE STUDENTS' OFFICER
⊙ INTERNATIONAL STUDENTS' OFFICER
⊙ POSTGRAD OFFICER ⊙ DISABILITIES OFFICER
⊙ SELF-DEFENCE CLASSES ⊙ LATE-NIGHT MINIBUS
⊙ NIGHTLINE ⊙ UNIVERSITY COUNSELLORS 5 PART
⊙ CRIME RATING: !!
The Director of Representation is the sabbatical officer to turn to in times of personal or academic cataclysm whereas legal worries can be addressed at a free weekly solicitor's clinic. Student Support Services and the SA Welfare Advisor are also available to tackle students' concerns. Upon arrival, undergraduates aquire 'student families' who offer academic guidance. *And alcohol, if you're lucky.*
HEALTH Local health centre with dedicated student practice.
WOMEN Free attack alarms are available as necessary. *Women are in the majority, but Girl Power hasn't landed yet.*
CRECHES/NURSERY There is a crèche facility with 60 places for kids aged 3mths-12yrs.
DISABILITIES *Access is good in the more modern buildings but pretty hopeless in the listed ones. Residences are better.* Dyslexia sufferers can get extra exam time, one-to-one proof reading, scribes and special computers. There are 52 adapted rooms with wheelchair computer desks and other specialised furniture available.

Words in italics are Push's point of view – take it or leave it...

FINANCE
- **AVE DEBT PER YEAR** £2,136 ⊙ **HOME STUDENT FEES** £1,700 **FEES** International undergrads are looking at upwards of £10,000 in fees. UK or EU postgrads need to cough up £3,085 (£1,542 part-time).
- ⊙ **ACCESS FUND** £200,000 ⊙ **SUCCESSFUL APPLICATION/YR** 450
- ⊙ **AVE PAYMENT** £400

SUPPORT In addition to the access fund, bursaries and scholarships, the University can provide interest-free loans in extreme cases through the Director of Student Support Services. Mature students have a stab at special bursaries and there's an emergency grant or two for internationals.

ST DAVID'S UNIVERSITY COLLEGE
see *Lampeter, University of Wales*

ST GEORGE'S HOSPITAL MEDICAL SCHOOL, LONDON
see *St George's, University of London*

ST GEORGE'S, UNIVERSITY OF LONDON

THE COLLEGE IS PART OF THE UNIVERSITY OF LONDON AND STUDENTS ARE ENTITLED TO USE ITS FACILITIES; FORMERLY ST GEORGE'S HOSPITAL MEDICAL SCHOOL

⊙ **ST GEORGE'S HOSPITAL** University of London, Cranmer Terrace, Tooting, London, SW17 0RE **TEL** (020) 8672 9944 **E-MAIL** medicine@sgul.ac.uk **WEBSITE** www.sgul.ac.uk **THE SCHOOL CLUB** St George's, University of London, Cranmer Terrace, Tooting, London, SW17 0RE **TEL** (020) 8725 5201 **E-MAIL** stuuni@sgul.ac.uk **WEBSITE** www.students.sghms.ac.uk

GENERAL ◗◗◗◗◗◗◗◗◗◗◗◗◗◗

Six miles from Nelson's Column sits one of the few self-contained teaching hospital campuses in London. St George's Hospital Medical School is the only independent medical school in the UK, although it's part of the University of London. Tooting (odds-on favourite for the silliest London district name) hasn't much to distinguish it from anywhere else in the capital other than its Victorian streetlights and the 70s redbrick campus which houses the working hospital and all attendant teaching facilities.

This is partly due to the student support structure: first years are assigned a 'mum' or 'dad' in the year above, who in turn have a 'mum' or 'dad' in the year above them, which means a great, family-like network of step-siblings and second cousins twice removed. The small student body and campus also means fraternising and friendly faces are easily come by. The informal atmosphere (rare in other med schools) and inter-year mixing are missed when students are carted off to other teaching hospitals. As far as town/gown relations go – no one likes students but everyone likes doctors. So Tooting residents don't know what to think.

SEX RATIO: ♂45 ♀55	**FOUNDED:** 1752
FULL-TIME U'GRADS: 1,340	**PART-TIME:** 0
POSTGRADS: 64	**NON-DEGREE:** 16
AVE COURSE: 5YRS	**ETHNIC:** 50%
STATE:PRIVATE SCHOOL: 45:55	**FLUNK RATE:** 10%
MATURE: 40%	**INTERNATIONAL:** 10%
DISABLED: 0	**LOCAL:** 70%

ATMOSPHERE
Being at St George's can feel more like being in a hospital than a university, mainly because it is one. The corridors bustle with healthcare professionals, patients, visitors and students and the unique eau de hospital aroma fills the air. But for all the bustle, students are relaxed and approachable with a bar-side manner seemingly at odds with the hectic and debt-crippled lifestyle they're compelled to lead for five or more years.

SITES
Some degrees (Pharmacy, Nursing) are offered jointly with Kingston University, so require moving between sites: Kingston's around ten miles from central London and on the overground train network. See the Kingston profile for the low-down.

LONDON see *University of London*

TRAVEL see *University of London*
TRAINS Tooting is the closest station, though it's not hugely useful.
BUSES 44, 57, 77, 155, 264, 270, 280, 355 & G1 for campus sites and surrounding areas.
UNDERGROUND Tooting Broadway (Northern line).
CAR Outside the Congestion Charging Zone, but very limited parking on or around campus.
BICYCLES Most students live within ten mins of the hospital, so pushbikes are *particularly popular.*

Words in italics are Push's point of view – take it or leave it...

CAREER PROSPECTS
◑ **UNEMPLOYED AFTER 6 MTHS** <1%
It's a vocational institution, so a careers service is largely unnecessary, although facilities are accessible at the University of London. A med school employee is on hand for vocational advice.

FAMOUS ALUMNI
Henry Gray (of Gray's Anatomy fame); Harry Hill (*neckless* comic); Edward Jenner (smallpox vaccine inventor); Mike Stroud (Antarctic explorer); Edward Wilson (accompanied Scott to death in the Antarctic).

SPECIAL FEATURES
First years are welcomed in with a mammoth 'Fresher's Fortnight' as opposed to the standard week. *If they can survive such extended alcohol intake, they'll presumably do well as medics.*

FURTHER INFO
◑ **PROSPECTUSES** UNDERGRAD; POSTGRAD
◑ **OPEN DAYS**
The SU website has admissions info, as does the University site.

ACADEMIC ◑◑◑◑◑◑◑◑◑◑◑◑◑

George's is the only med school in London that offers a full range of healthcare education on a single site. Teaching is a combination of classroom and clinic and assessment is based both on written exam and clinical performance. Unlike many other medical schools, exams are also taken on-site, which works out less stressful, and means *there's no danger of leaving the lucky pig's trotter at home.* The first year starts with general medical studies before becoming more specialised. Teacher-student relations are good and staff are approachable. Problem-based and Case-based Learning are an academic focus – students frequently have to 'treat' hypothetical patients, usually other students – *anyone fancy a sponge bath?* Communication skills modules (bedside manner) are popular. Equally beloved are the course handbooks which contain all the lecture notes and other thoughtful bits of info *(not the exam answers though).* Assignments to other teaching hospitals are common. Terms are 10-11 weeks in length, but some can stretch to 15.

ENTRY POINTS: 210–300	AVE POINTS: 380
APPLICATIONS PER PLACE: 15	CLEARING: 1%
NO. OF TERMS: 3	LENGTH OF TERMS: 10/11wks
STAFF TO STUDENT RATIO: 1:7	STUDY ADDICTS: 5%
TEACHING: ✶✶✶✶✶	RESEARCH: ✶✶✶✶
YEAR ABROAD: 0%	SANDWICH STUDENTS: 0%

ADMISSIONS
◑ **APPLY VIA UCAS**

SUBJECTS
MEDICAL SCIENCES 100%
BEST Medicine; Dentistry.
UNUSUAL Diagnostic and Therapeutic Radiography. The forthcoming Bioinformatics course will train the NHS's future IT specialists.

LIBRARIES
◑ **45,000 BOOKS** ◑ **382 STUDY PLACES**
◑ **SPEND PER STUDENT** £££££
The Med school library is open till 10pm most nights but closed on Sundays. Stocks videos (*teaching-related, not Buffy, Push assumes*) and other multimedia materials.

COMPUTERS
◑ **110 WORKSTATIONS** ◑ **24-HOUR ACCESS**
George's halls of residence have computer rooms with web access. Wireless access *all over the shop*, with free loan of wireless cards to laptop owners.

OTHER LEARNING FACILITIES
There's an audio/TV centre for media buffs and Clinical Skills Labs to *practice saying 'ooh matron'* as well as more practical things like resuscitation techniques.

ENTERTAINMENT ◑◑◑◑◑◑◑◑◑

LONDON see University of London
St George's social life gravitates around the Bar *(both its name and function).* Those who venture beyond the SU like Spirit Bar, the Tramshed and Hoochi Mama's. JJ Moon's (Wetherspoon) should be avoided like Ken Livingston should avoid journalists. Tooting is close to being the curry house capital of London, *which makes a meal for a fiver a real and tasty possibility.* The Trafalgar Arms is there for *students craving stodgy hangover fare,* with a medics discount to boot. *On-screen antics can be had at Wandsworth Cineworld and Wimbledon Odeon. There are hi-jinks a-plenty of all kinds in Central London.*

UNIVERSITY
◑ **PRICE OF A PINT OF BEER** £1.60
◑ **GLASS OF WINE** £1.65
◑ **CAN OF RED BULL** £1.20
BARS The Bar can quench 600 thirsts in one sitting and is open 9am-11pm weekdays, later on weekend club nights. There's a non-alcoholic lounge, and the whole venue is no-smoking. Also does table tennis (*well, if you're not smoking and not drinking, you'll need to do something with your hands*).
THEATRES *Medics love to dress-up, cross-dress and fancy dress.* The Monkton Theatre puts on scriptloads of shows each year and hosts the Revue.

FILM Flicks with faint medical undertones tend to be shown in the bar every so often. Admission: £1.

CLUBBING/MUSIC VENUES The bar gives stage-room to local and student bands and hosts a bundle of late-licence club nights with the usual cheesy themes, the fortnightly Friday disco *(fancy dress – not 'Doctors & Nurses' Push is guessing)* always goes down a storm.

COMEDY/CABARET The Georges Medics – *a very popular student review and Edinburgh favourite –* steal the stage at Monkton on a monthly basis.

FOOD Peabodies café has recently opened beside the bar *offering a good gossip spot for latte addicts.* Sandwiches are nicer and pricier, *but the looks are posh enough to make it worth it.* The NHS canteen is a cut-price favourite, and the School Shop also does cheap sarnies and snacks.

OTHER Four balls a year normally held off-campus: Fresher's, RAG, Grad and Summer.

SOCIAL 🍵🍵🍵🍵🍵🍵🍵🍵🍵🍵🍵🍵

THE SCHOOL CLUB
- **3 SABBATICALS** - **TURNOUT AT LAST BALLOT** 30%
- **NUS MEMBER**

The SU is as political as a pencil sharpener – it's primarily concerned with welfare, courses and facilities. Where there are issues, they're solved with debate rather than demonstration.

SU FACILITIES
Bar; four pool/snooker tables; café; three meeting rooms; two minibuses; gaming machines; juke box; new and secondhand bookshops are run by the Union. The hospital offers: a canteen; photocopier; fax service; printing service; payphones; advice centre; general store; stationery shop and vending machines. There's a NatWest on campus.

CLUBS (NON-SPORTING)
Appreciation Of Persian Culture; Book Club; Diwali; International Students; Links (First Aid); Modern Languages; Salsa; Sexpression (teaching sex education in schools); Student Action For Refugees; Wilderness. **See also Clubs tables.**

OTHER ORGANISATIONS
The *aptly named* 'Sharp' is the independent twice-termly Union paper. Rag is a big money spinner. Rag Week last year raised £100,000 just by being daft *(including, naturally, cross-dressing stunts where bucket-rattlers take to the tubes and scare the bejesus out of commuters for charity). It's all very competitive and creative.* Eight community action groups are managed by a sabbatical officer, *who ensures students do their bit for the good of humanity as well as healing the sick.* Student Action for Refugees also take refugee children on days out.

RELIGION
No chaplain yet. There's a multi-faith prayer room in the hospital and a mosque nearby.

PAID WORK see University of London
- **JOB BUREAU** - **PAID WORK** TERM TIME 33%; HOLS 50%

Advice, suggestions and vacancies are posted on the School Club notice board, but trainee doctors and nurses rarely have time for work beyond the first and second years.

SPORTS 🍵🍵🍵🍵🍵🍵🍵🍵🍵🍵🍵🍵🍵

- **RECENT SUCCESSES** TENNIS, RUGBY, NETBALL
- **BUSA RANKING** 107

Sports involving balls are doing particularly well in inter-collegiate leagues at the moment. Sporting societies are easily set up.

SPORTS FACILITIES
Five football pitches; rugby pitch; two cricket wickets; three squash courts; four tennis courts; basketball court; sports hall; gym; aerobics studio; multigym; climbing wall. The fields are found in Cobham. The Rob Lowe Sports Centre *(no, not that Rob Lowe)* has a weight room, cardio room, exercise machines, squash courts and sports hall, and classes at lunchtimes and evenings. Tooting has Kinetika at Tooting Leisure Centre, with a gym and swimming pool. Water babies can take advantage of a deal the School's made with the pool for discounted prices. Oarsmen can wield their blades on the Thames at Chiswick. Sailors can hornpipe their way to Burnham-on-Crouch.

SPORTING CLUBS
Martial Arts; Open-Water Swimming; Rowing; Snowboarding. **See also Clubs tables.**

ATTRACTIONS see University of London

ACCOMMODATION 🍵🍵🍵🍵🍵🍵🍵🍵🍵

IN COLLEGE
- **SELF-CATERING** 19% - **COST** £71 (42WKS)
- **1ST YRS LIVING IN** 50% - **INSURANCE PREMIUM** ££

AVAILABILITY First year students are guaranteed rooms, either catered in Friendship House or in one of the 13 self-catering University houses on the self-contained St George's Grove Estate (15 mins walk). *There's a lick of paint and smear of elbow grease planned for 2007, which may affect quantity as well as quality. Currently things are loveably shabby and very friendly.* Common/TV rooms at the centre of each block *encourage get-togethers.* Also central computing and cheap laundry facilities. *The housing estate next door isn't the nicest of views.* Kitchens are usually shared with 6-8 other people *so plenty of sticky labels wouldn't go amiss.* 24-hr security; three rooms for international students; all other years live out.

CAR PARKING Free permits for those mad enough to want to bring a car. No parking at the hospital. Locked garages are available for bikes.

Words in italics are Push's point of view — take it or leave it...

EXTERNALLY see University of London
- **AVE RENT** £83
AVAILABILITY Rents around the hospital are reasonable. For London. Tooting, the student's friend, is 10-20 mins walk from the main site.
HOUSING HELP see University of London

WELFARE ◖◖◖◖◖◖◖◖◖◖◖◖◖◖

SERVICES
- **LGBT SOCIETY** ⊙ **MATURE STUDENTS' OFFICER**
- **INTERNATIONAL STUDENTS' OFFICER & SOCIETY**
- **POSTGRAD STUDENTS' OFFICER AND SOCIETY**
- **DISABILITIES OFFICER** ⊙ **SELF-DEFENCE CLASSES**
- **NIGHTLINE** ⊙ **TAXI FUND**
- **COLLEGE COUNSELLORS** 3 PART
- **CRIME RATING:** !!!

First years in halls can claim a free personal attack alarm. *Presumably those not in halls have to learn Ninjitsu and cross their fingers.* All sites are non-smoking (part of the NHS ban) so smokers currently have to leave campus to have a fag. Many of the welfare facilities are run in conjunction with those at ULU – see University of London.

HEALTH *It's a hospital. Go figure.* There's a staff-student health centre with one doc and a few senior nurses for occupational health problems (i.e. needle stick injuries) – not a confidential service.

WOMEN Women-only minibus for large Union events.

DISABILITIES Facilities are a strong point. *Vocationally speaking, it's advisable to check with the assistant registrar to see if some disabilities are compatible with certain specialities.*

FINANCE
- **AVE DEBT PER YEAR** £5,217 ⊙ **HOME STUDENT FEES** £3,000
FEES International students can expect £10,825 in fees. Foundation For Medicine students will be exempt the top-up fee in 2006-7. Radiography and Physiotherapy courses are supported by the NHS. International undergrads *need a trustfund* to pay charges of around £20,000/year.
- **ACCESS FUND** £113,000 ⊙ **SUCCESSFUL APPLICATION/YR** 102
- **AVE PAYMENT** £20-3,500
SUPPORT Bursaries and scholarships available, some from the NHS, plus a fistful of prizes and awards.

▶ **ST MARTIN'S COLLEGE, LANCASTER**
see Lancaster University

▶ **ST THOMAS'S HOSPITAL**
see King's College London

STAFFORDSHIRE UNIVERSITY

FORMERLY STAFFORDSHIRE POLYTECHNIC

1. ⊙ **STAFFORDSHIRE UNIVERSITY** College Road, Stoke-on-Trent, ST4 2DE **TEL** (01782) 294 000 **E-MAIL** admissions@staffs.ac.uk **WEBSITE** www.staffs.ac.uk ⊙ **STAFFORDSHIRE UNIVERSITY STUDENTS' UNION** Staffordshire University, College Road, Stoke-on-Trent, ST4 2DE **TEL** (01782) 294 629 **E-MAIL** theunion@staffs.ac.uk **WEBSITE** www.staffsunion.com
2. ⊙ **STAFFORDSHIRE UNIVERSITY BEACONSIDE** Stafford, ST18 0AD **TEL** (01785) 353 253
⊙ **STAFFORDSHIRE UNIVERSITY SU** Beaconside Campus, Stafford, ST18 0AD tel (01785) 353 311

GENERAL ◖◖◖◖◖◖◖◖◖◖◖◖◖◖

Staffordshire is a *fairly gentle* part of the north-west Midlands. One site is on the outskirts of Stafford, a *small and pretty* country town. It's a greenfield campus with a mix of buildings, some of which got a good dose of 60s technical-college architecture. *They're trying to hide those bits behind the new stuff,* including a 100-seater broadcast studio for film students. The Stoke bit of the University is split over two sites at College Road and Leek Road in the city centre of Stoke-on-Trent. Leek Road has more of the feeling of a self-contained campus with playing fields and accommodation on site, and is

Staffordshire University pioneered the use of sewage for making bricks and floor tiles.

Words in italics are Push's point of view — take it or leave it...

due a £2m refurb project which has been designed with students' input. *Which is chancey as there's always a risk the University could end up commissioning a giant Boohbah statue.* Current plans, though, are for a new social arena, with space for live music, cultural activities, big screens, water features and a tower.

SEX RATIO: ♂51 ♀49	FOUNDED: 1970
FULL-TIME U'GRADS: 8,914	PART-TIME: 3,880
POSTGRADS: 2,557	NON-DEGREE: 2,900
AVE COURSE: 3YRS	ETHNIC: 13%
STATE:PRIVATE SCHOOL: 97:3	FLUNK RATE: 21%
MATURE: 55%	INTERNATIONAL: 14%
DISABLED: 235	LOCAL: 35%

ATMOSPHERE
The Stoke campus is friendly, artsy and has a warm community feel about it, even in relations with the locals. A lot of students are on part-time or professional courses.

SITES
BEACONSIDE CAMPUS (5,000 students – Engineering, Business, Computing, School of Health) The Stafford site might unkindly be descibed as rather geeky, although the techies who make up the student population would probably point to a lively drinking culture to dispute that.

STOKE-ON-TRENT
○ **POPULATION** 240,000 ○ **CITY CENTRE** 1.5 MILES
○ **LONDON** 165 MILES ○ **BIRMINGHAM** 44 MILES
○ **MANCHESTER** 38 MILES
○ **HIGH TEMP** 20 ○ **LOW TEMP** 0 ○ **RAINFALL** 56
STOKE Stoke *didn't come out well* from a couple of decades of urban decline. Robbie Williams may have lived here once, *but he's a lot better off in his mansion in LA.* In Hanley there's a shopping centre and Festival Park, once the site of the National Garden Festival, an excellent swimming pool and various other attractions. *Like many more run-down places, it breeds a defiant sort of love among the students who live there, but then love is blind. Stoke is the original 'good personality, shame about the legs' town.* Those who tire of the Alton Towers scream park can instead go say hello to 140 free-roaming Barbary Macaque monkeys at Trentham's Monkey Forest, which is also *just* down the road.
STAFFORD *Inside every twisted nightmare of urban planning there's a pleasant market town wishing they'd left it alone.* Stafford's no different. There's a market, *obviously* (although the days of herding livestock are long gone) and a modest shopping centre. *Little to set the heart aflutter, though.*

TRAVEL
TRAINS Stafford and Stoke both connect to London (£28.50 and £31 rtn respectively) on the Merseyside and Manchester services. The main Stoke site is about 500 metres from the station.
COACHES National Express, including Manchester (£31), Liverpool (£8.90), Birmingham (£8.90)

and London (£21).
CAR The M6 and A34 connect the two towns. Stafford is also served by the A518 and A513. The A50 provides handy links to Derby and Nottingham. A parking permit is a tenner a term.
AIR MyTravel and BMI fly out of Manchester International.
HITCHING *There's the nearby ringroad at Stoke. The M6 is good for both towns.*
LOCAL The X1 (also known as the Bakerbus – it's run by Baker's) shuttles between the two campuses, £2 sgl or £3.50 rtn. Buses leave Hanley bus station hourly (7am-6pm), with the return leaving Beaconsfield hourly between 8am-7pm Mon-Fri. Two-hourly services on Saturdays. Special staff and student season tickets can be got for Baker's Buses and Central Trains.
TAXIS *Loads on offer in both towns.* Grab a cab from the station in Stoke.
BICYCLES This is a *flat* part of the world, so bikes are *popular*, but there's no secure cycle parking at University residences.

CAREER PROSPECTS
○ **CAREERS SERVICE** ○ **NO. OF STAFF** 4 FULL/10 PART
○ **UNEMPLOYED AFTER 6 MTHS** 11%

FAMOUS ALUMNI
Jim Davies (aka a Chemical Brother); Editors (the band).

SPECIAL FEATURES
Applicants under 21 and resident in Staffordshire, Shropshire or Cheshire are guaranteed an offer depending on the usual entry requirements. Staffordshire recently became the UK's first university to open an art gallery in New York. The University has its own nature reserve *hibernating round the back of the Leek Road.*

FURTHER INFO
○ **PROSPECTUSES** UNDERGRAD, POSTGRAD, PART-TIME,DEPARTMENTAL, VIDEO, DVD
○ **OPEN DAYS**

ACADEMIC ○○○○○○○○○○○○○○

Staffordshire has *flung itself into the millennium with real vigour.* There are all sorts of modern learning facilities, and the teaching is *decent* across a range of *unusual* subjects: Geography's particularly accolated. Learning spreads across two semesters of 12 weeks each, with assessments and exams scheduled around May. The University embraces technology, especially where it supports students – the Forensic Science department even sends feedback to students on mp3 files via email, so they can be downloaded and listened to later. *Anything that keeps Kelly Osbourne out of iPod playlists can only be a good thing.*

Words in italics are Push's point of view — take it or leave it...

ENTRY POINTS: 200–300	AVE POINTS: 211
APPLICATIONS PER PLACE: 5	CLEARING: 22%
NO. OF TERMS: 2	LENGTH OF TERMS: 12WKS
STAFF TO STUDENT RATIO: 1:20	STUDY ADDICTS: N/A
TEACHING: **	RESEARCH: *
YEAR ABROAD: N/A	SANDWICH STUDENTS: N/A
1STS: 8%	2.2s: 42%
2.1s: 39%	3RDS: 11%

ADMISSIONS
○ APPLY VIA UCAS
Mature students can apply direct – in the first instance, pay a visit to the HE shop on College Road. There's some flexibility in entrance requirements to suit individual circumstances.

SUBJECTS
ARTS, MEDIA & DESIGN 20%   **BUSINESS & LAW** 26%
COMPUTING, ENGINEERING & TECHNOLOGY 24%
HEALTH & SCIENCES 30%
BEST Geography.
UNUSUAL Football Technology; Forensic Science.

LIBRARIES
○ 314,811 BOOKS ○ 1,331 STUDY PLACES
○ SPEND PER STUDENT £
The libraries on both sites are open until 3am throughout the week, although *there aren't quite enough books to keep students occupied until the wee hours.* Online journals take up the slack.

COMPUTERS
○ 2,600 WORKSTATIONS ○ SPEND PER STUDENT £££
IT facilities are excellent and up-to-date. Laptops can be rented from the IT department.

OTHER LEARNING FACILITIES
The forensic science department has its own crime house, *nicknamed the House of Horror.* There's also an *incredible* virtual reality room. Distance and online learning are also options.

ENTERTAINMENT ○○○○○○○○○

THE TOWNS
○ PRICE OF A PINT OF BEER £1.60
○ GLASS OF WINE £1.65
○ CAN OF RED BULL £1.20
CINEMAS The Apollo in Stafford only has three screens but Stoke's got two flicks (Odeon and Warner). All do student discounts. Stoke on Trent Film Theatre is situated on the College Road campus, but is a public affair. Two films a week, blockbuster and world cinema.
THEATRES Stoke Repertory Theatre, the New Vic in Newcastle under Lyme near Stoke and the Gatehouse in Stafford.
PUBS Most pubs are *student-friendly*, especially those closest to college. *Stoke Pushplugs: the Terrace; the Fawn; the Roebuck. Stafford: Bird in Hand; HogsHead; Telegraph; Wagon & Horses; Potterhouse.*
CLUBBING Stoke has *more clubs than you could*

shake a rhythm stick at, including Sugarmill; New York, New York (buy a drink at the Lounge for free entry on Tuesday's student night); Reynold's.
MUSIC VENUES The Darkness have played Sugarmill. Stafford's got the Surgery (live bands as well as comedy, drag, DJs and performance artists) and the Grapes (live music bar opposite the Apollo).
EATING OUT *Typical* chain pub offerings. Two meals for a fiver deals are *predictably popular.* Hanley and Newcastle are good for global gourmets (Thai, Italian, Indian and the rest).
OTHER Alton Towers is *just down* the road.

UNIVERSITY

○ PRICE OF A PINT OF BEER £1.55
○ GLASS OF WINE £2.50
○ CAN OF RED BULL £1.60
BARS The Ember Lounge at College Road campus has a *post-refurb glow about it,* with DJ facilities to boot. Leek Road has LRV, *recently botoxed to the tune of £500,000 and money well spent. It's a stylish but relaxed place for daytime lounging and eating, with a dance floor for burning the calories off later on.* In Stafford there's Legends (nightclub bar), which has a day guise as the Lounge *(compact and bijou coffee bar with good atmos).*
THEATRES The drama and theatre students *entertain the masses* with a couple of productions per semester.
MUSIC VENUES The Leek Road Venue holds the most gigs. Recent visitors include Electric 6, Shed 7 and Kosheen *(8?).*
CLUBBING Heaps of clubnights, including Revolver (alternative) on Monday's in LRV, Gobble (cheese) on Wed, Super Friday on Fri, natch, and Smooch (R'n'B) on Sat. Flirt at Legends (Fri) is the new charty addition to the ents calendar.
COMEDY/CABARET A *hugely popular* Thursday comedy night at the Leek Road. It features the likes of Brendon Burns, Mitch Benn and Toby Foster.
FOOD Ember Lounge for a full, global menu (English brekkies, Tortilla wraps), available until 1am. LRV does *good veggie* options. Stoke has the Courtyard Café at College Road (8am-3.30pm) and Bush House (cafeteria food) at Leek Road. Stafford's got Dol.cHe Vita which is a smart coffee bar with *pretentious punctuation.* The Terrace Café, *as the name implies,* has good views of the campus.
OTHER A summer ball *finishes each year off drunken-stylee.*

SOCIAL ○○○○○○○○○○○

STAFFORDSHIRE UNIVERSITY STUDENTS' UNION
○ 5 SABBATICALS ○ TURNOUT AT LAST BALLOT 15%
○ NUS MEMBER
The SU's responsible for representing, entertaining and looking out for the student body at large. It

S

gets on *very well* with the University and students seem to be *pretty happy* with the job it does. Sabbs are on hand for student queries, quibbles and quandaries weekdays between 12-2pm.

SU FACILITIES
Three bars/clubs/venues; three cafés/snack bars; eight pool tables; meeting rooms; three shops (two at Stoke, one at Stafford); two advice centres; Endsleigh Insurance; Lloyds TSB, NatWest and Co-op banks/ATMs (not NatWest).

CLUBS (NON-SPORTING)
Alternative Music; International Students; Chinese; Heartical Sounds (music); Law; Ministry of Justice; Myth & Role-play; South Asian; Stop Down (photography). **See also Clubs tables.**

OTHER ORGANISATIONS
'GK News' is the monthly SU rag. 'GK radio' broadcasts every day over the intranet. Sponte is the University's community volunteer scheme, with opportunities in conservation, outreach, mentoring, working with animals, etc. 'Plastic Tree Records' is an independent record company set up by enterprising students *(or Simon Cowell wannabes, perhaps)*. As well as recording opportunities, there's promotion and performance prospects.

RELIGION
The College Road campus has the Faith House (meeting rooms for groups, prayers and the like) and Chaplains for all denominations. Both towns have churches for all the main denominations. A Muslim prayer room is available at Stafford and there are places of worship in Stoke for Jews, Muslims, Hindus and Sikhs.

PAID WORK
◉ JOB BUREAU
Bar and shop work is available in both towns and a University workbank to help around 200 students a year find it.

SPORTS ◖◖◖◖◖◖◖◖◖◖◖◖◖

◉ RECENT SUCCESSES CRICKET, AMERICAN FOOTBALL
◉ BUSA RANKING 122
There's a wide participation in sports; *some clubs have a higher standard than others, though.* With a football technology degee, sport's on the syllabus as well as off it.

SPORTS FACILITIES
STOKE 40 acres of fields; three floodlit synthetic pitches; sports hall; activities studio; fitness suite. The Riverside recreation centre slap in the centre of town has swimming facilities.
STAFFORD 30 acres of fields; two synthetic pitches; sports hall; dance studio; fitness suite.

SPORTING CLUBS
American Football; Boxing; Cheerleading; Dodgeball; Dance; Hula-Hoop (the sport not the snack); Lacrosse; Snowsports; Surf; Ultimate Frisbee. **See also Clubs tables.**

ACCOMMODATION ◖◖◖◖◖◖◖◖◖

IN UNIVERSITY
◉ SELF-CATERING 21% **◉ COST** £66 (38WKS)
◉ 1ST YRS LIVING IN 60% **◉ INSURANCE PREMIUM** £
AVAILABILITY Rooms in halls are *fairly plush.* Most are en suite and *decent* sizes. Broadband's available free at all sites. All are *relatively close* to campus and much accommodation in both towns has been rebuilt in the last three years. Residents get a welcome pack which contains *scores of fab freebies,* including: bedding (plus duvet and pillow), mug, microwaveable/oven-proof dish, saucepan, washing-up liquid, a tin-opener and a corkscrew. TV licensing and insurance are also included. 72 rooms are disabled-adapted (physical and sensory impairments). International students are guaranteed accommodation upon meeting relevant deadlines. There's 24-hr security, some communal cleaning and a launderette service too.
CAR PARKING *Ample* and free.

EXTERNALLY
◉ AVE RENT £43 **◉ LIVING AT HOME** 40%
AVAILABILITY *Lots* of housing, some of it through the University's private landlord scheme. There's a *student infestation* in virtually all the streets between Stoke's Leek and College Roads (the Shelton area). Highfields is a good bet at Stafford.
HOUSING HELP The accommodation office keeps a website and register of landlords. Any of three advisors can help with things like contract approval.

WELFARE ◖◖◖◖◖◖◖◖◖◖◖◖

SERVICES
**◉ LGBT SOCIETY ◉ ETHNIC MINORITIES SOCIETY
◉ INTERNATIONAL STUDENTS' OFFICER & SOCIETY
◉ POSTGRAD SOCIETY ◉ DISABILITIES OFFICER
◉ TAXI FUND
◉ UNIVERSITY COUNSELLORS** 5 FULL
◉ SU COUNSELLORS 3 FULL/1 PART
◉ CRIME RATING: !!!!
Students are *very impressed* with the welfare provisions. The SU, university tutors and counsellors and a legal clinic help out with all sorts of problems. On-site cop shop (community copper). The taxi fund means students aren't ever stranded – the University covers the cost of a cab, which is repaid later on. There's also an 'official' cab company which handles all uni business.

S

Words in italics are Push's point of view — take it or leave it...

HEALTH Medical centres on both campuses with trained health staff.
WOMEN Subsidised attack alarms from SU shops.
CRECHES/NURSERY Nursery places are available for children up to 5yrs.
DISABILITIES *No real problems with access as most of the college buildings are modern or newly renovated.*

FINANCE
- **AVE DEBT PER YEAR** £3,334 ● **HOME STUDENT FEES** £3,000
- **ACCESS FUND** £75,000 ● **SUCCESSFUL APPLICATION/YR** 1,385
- **AVE PAYMENT** £100-3,500

SUPPORT Up to 30 Ashley scholarships are awarded to local applicants who face particular difficult circumstances in going to university (financial/social/physical). The Union has around £85,000 in reserve for hardship loans.

▶ **STAFFORDSHIRE POLYTECHNIC**
see *Staffordshire University*

STIRLING UNIVERSITY

1. ● **UNIVERSITY OF STIRLING** Stirling, FK9 4LA **TEL** (01786) 467046 **E-MAIL** recruitment@stir.ac.uk **WEBSITE** www.stir.ac.uk
● **STIRLING UNIVERSITY STUDENTS' ASSOCIATION** SUSA Office, The Robbins Centre, University of Stirling, Stirling, FK9 4LA **TEL** (01786) 467 166 **E-MAIL** susa@stir.ac.uk **WEBSITE** www.susaonline.org.uk
2. ● **HIGHLAND CAMPUS** University of Stirling, Department of Nursing and Midwifery, Raigmore Hospital, Old Perth Road, Inverness, IV2 3SG **TEL** (01463) 704 315
3. ● **WESTERN ISLES CAMPUS** University of Stirling, Department of Nursing and Midwifery, Western Isles Hospital, Macaulay Road, Stornaway, Isle of Lewis, HS1 2AF **TEL** (01851) 704 704

GENERAL ◑◑◑◑◑◑◑◑◑◑◑◑

Stirling is tucked away in the heart of Scotland, surrounded by the *picturesque* scenery of the Southern Highlands and Trossachs. The castle, on a cliff face, *dominates* the landscape and was the royal home in Scotland until 1600. Much of the historic architecture survives in the Old Town. The University is two miles out of the city just before you get to the small town of Bridge of Allan and, *like Stirling itself, it's small.* The students, who account for one in five of the local population, have a campus reputed for its beauty and set in 310 acres of landscaped grounds, complete with the 18th-century Airthrey Castle, a golf course and a loch with a bridge, separating the residences from the academic buildings and providing a home for wild fowl *and a fun feature for wild students. Apart from the castle,* which houses departments and offices, *the University's other buildings are less impressive than the setting.* Most (for now) are grey or white flat-topped oblongs, usually three or four floors high, but, shaded with trees, they blend in somehow. Meanwhile, the towering Wallace Monument (dedicated to William 'Braveheart' Wallace) presides over the goings on.

ATMOSPHERE
There's a lively feel to Stirling, as if everyone knows exactly where they're going, although they're always prepared to take a detour for a coffee and a chat. Many of the students are sporty – and dress the part in hoodies, jogging bottoms, trainers and baseball caps. The international students (from over 80 countries at any one time) add to the general feeling of laidback, but energetic and cosmopolitan campus life. There's plenty of space to study and relax, especially after the dark Scottish winter passes and students make the most of the natural setting through the summer months. The campus is self-sufficient (right down to post office, travel agency and pharmacy) and many students rarely feel the need to leave – though those that do move out after the first year get on just dandily with the local residents. More than two-thirds of them are Scottish themselves.

SITES
There are two other sites which are both part of the Department of Nursing and Midwifery.
HIGHLAND CAMPUS (370 students) On the outskirts of Inverness (which can be reached on the regular bus) in the grounds of Raigmore Hospital is the medical school.
WESTERN ISLES CAMPUS (60 students) Accessible only by boat, this part of Lewis Hospital in Stornoway on the island of Lewis is *probably the UK's most remote university site.* Almost all the students are drawn from the local population.

SEX RATIO: ♀42 ♂58	**FOUNDED:** 1967
FULL-TIME U'GRADS: 6,030	**PART-TIME:** 1,160
POSTGRADS: 2,020	**NON-DEGREE:** 285
AVE COURSE: 4YRS	**ETHNIC:** 3%
STATE:PRIVATE SCHOOL: 91:9	**FLUNK RATE:** 13%
MATURE: 15%	**INTERNATIONAL:** 14%
DISABLED: 125	**LOCAL:** 14%

Words in italics are Push's point of view — take it or leave it...

STIRLING
- ○ **POPULATION** 85,220 ○ **CITY CENTRE** 2 MILES
- ○ **LONDON** 378 MILES ○ **GLASGOW** 27 MILES
- ○ **EDINBURGH** 33 MILES
- ○ **HIGH TEMP** 19 ○ **LOW TEMP** 0 ○ **RAINFALL** 79

Up 246 steps, from the top of the Wallace Monument, *the surrounding natural beauty provides some of Scotland's finest views.* But Stirling itself is one of the UK's newest cities, having been upgraded from a town as part of Her Maj's jubilee bash in 2002 – *but it's still a small town by most standards.* Also the newness doesn't apply to the mostly 17th- and 18th-Century architecture or *the quaint and traditional* shops selling antiques and crafts. Meanwhile, the Thistle Centre, the city's major shopping area, does the normal high street brands with a few independent outlets too – especially around the Arcade and King Street where there are specialist music shops, bookstores and toy shops.

TRAVEL
TRAINS Stirling Station, two miles from campus, has half-hourly services to London (£63.75) and the main cities in Scotland, including Glasgow (£7.40) and Edinburgh (£7.80) in under an hour.
COACHES National Express services to major cities in Scotland and England, such as Glasgow (£6.50) and London (£36) car: A9 and M9.
AIR It's 1hr 20mins to Glasgow Airport and 45mins to Edinburgh Airport, both with flights all over the place, including budget operators such as easyJet and Britannia Direct.
HITCHING *Fairly easy to Edinburgh if you start from the outskirts of town.*
LOCAL First Buses (Nos 52, 53, 54, 58, 62, 63) operate between campus and the town centre and cost 75p to £1.20. Ferguson Coaches scoot along to the train station and students can hire them for a 20% discount.
TAXIS Taxis are *easy to find* and cost £2.50 to £3 from town to campus. A late night trip in the other direction costs up to a fiver.
BICYCLES *Despite the winter wind and rain, the cheap, green option is increasingly popular on campus.*

CAREER PROSPECTS
- ○ **CAREERS SERVICE** ○ **NO. OF STAFF** 13 FULL/2 PART
- ○ **UNEMPLOYED AFTER 6** MTHS 6%

The *busy* Career Development Centre does the business from pre-university, through student life on into graduate careers. Services range from long-range advice to a jobshop for part-time and vacation work. Apart from the usual newsletters and bulletin boards, they do CV clinics, aptitude tests and even a four-day course about what a career in management is all about. *All this entices quite a few employers to visit and sniff out the talent as graduation approaches.*

FAMOUS ALUMNI
Iain Banks (writer); Mark Cousins (film-maker and former director of the Edinburgh Festival); Mark Daly (journalist); Neil Davidson, QC (Scotland's Solicitor-General 2001-2); Bruce Flockhart (Badminton champ); Mhairi Love (Paralympic swimmer & silver medallist); Catriona Matthew (golfer); Jack McConnell MSP (Scottish First Minister); Vicky Nash (director of Ofcom Scotland); Nick Neckles (Olympic swimmer); John Reid MP (Health Secretary); Gordon Sherry (golfer); Gordon Smith, CBE (Chairman IBM Scotland). The current Chancellor is ex-Avenger Dame Diana Rigg (aka Emma Peel).

FURTHER INFO
- ○ **PROSPECTUSES** UNDERGRAD; POSTGRAD; INTERNATIONAL; SOME DEPARTMENTS; CD-ROM
- ○ **OPEN DAYS**

Open evenings, adult learners evenings and applicants' days can be booked on (01786) 467 046.

ACADEMIC ○○○○○○○○○○○○○

Over the years Stirling has been quite cutting edge in its approach to courses. The Film and Media Studies course, for example, just turned 25, making it one of the oldest in Britain. It was the first University in the UK to have two 15-week semesters a year rather than three terms and most courses are modular which means students get to try different things before committing to their main subject. They also use lots of continuous assessment – *good for those who hate exams, bad for those who prefer their efforts to be seasonal.* Some of the latest innovations include the option of starting a degree in February or studying in the evenings. *It also has a good track record for widening access.*

ENTRY POINTS: 220-280	AVE POINTS: 280
APPLICATIONS PER PLACE: 11	CLEARING: 6%
NO. OF TERMS: 2	LENGTH OF TERMS: 15WKS
STAFF TO STUDENT RATIO: 1:15	STUDY ADDICTS: 17%
TEACHING: ★★★	RESEARCH: ★★★★
YEAR ABROAD: 5%	SANDWICH STUDENTS: N/A
1STS: 10%	2.2s: 41%
2.1s: 20%	3RDS: 4%

ADMISSIONS
○ **APPLY VIA UCAS/CATCH FOR NURSING**
The University deals with Highers rather than UCAS points in terms of entry qualifications. DAICE (Division of Academic Innovation and Continuing Education) helps students who've just missed the required grades to bring them up to par and for part-timers and adult learners. *There's also strong links with local schools and colleges.*

SUBJECTS
ARTS/HUMANITIES 31% **BUSINESS/MANAGEMENT** 36% **HUMAN SCIENCES** 23% **NATURAL SCIENCES** 8%
BEST Administration & Social Work; Earth & Environmental Studies; Economics; European Languages; History; Politics & International Relations; Social Policy.
UNUSUAL Criminology; European Film & Media; Freshwater Science.

S

LIBRARIES
- **505,000 BOOKS** ● **900 STUDY PLACES**
- **SPEND PER STUDENT** £

The main University Library, which houses four computing libraries, *has decent opening hours and subscribes to a whopping 9,000 journals.* There are other little libraries for student teachers and language students and at the Highland and Western Isles sites. The main library's been due a refurb for several years, with one promised always just around the corner. *The wait goes on.*

COMPUTERS
- **950 WORKSTATIONS** ● **24–HOUR ACCESS**

Students can plug into the net from their bedrooms in Murray Hall and Geddes Court (more network points in rooms are planned) or surf from their own laptop in the library. There are four IT labs accessible to students (most 24-hr), and the library information centre provides guidance on using University systems.

OTHER LEARNING FACILITIES
Language lab; state-of-the-art Film & Media Studies newsroom with design and audio-visual editing software and equipment.

ENTERTAINMENT ❍❍❍❍❍❍❍❍❍❍

THE CITY
- **PRICE OF A PINT OF BEER** £1.50
- **GLASS OF WINE** £1.80
- **CAN OF RED BULL** £1.20

Before you judge too harshly, remember Edinburgh and Glasgow are less than an hour away. An hour's an hour, though.

CINEMAS The Carlton (Allan Park) has two screens, *but it's not up to much.*

THEATRES The Tollbooth and the Cowane Centre offer stuff from panto to Pinter. Student discounts available at both.

PUBS *Quite a few are tolerant of, even friendly to, students, but some, such as the Rob Roy and the Caperceilidh, deserve a wide berth. Pushplugs: the Meadow Park Hotel, aka 'the Med', situated at the bottom of the campus; Hog's Head (for good pub grub); Courtyard; Hydes; the Westerton Arms (in Bridge of Allan). The Whistlebinkies pub is a snug place for a winter warmer.*

CLUBBING A couple of *tacky* clubs in town. *The FU Bar and Enigma have student nights on Thursdays.* Beat is Stirling's latest club, offering 3 for 2 drinks and 2 for 1 meals.

MUSIC VENUES *Stirling Council have finally realised that castles can be fun.* Stirling Castle now hosts open air concerts. Several pubs have folk nights and the Albert Bar hosts jazz.

EATING OUT *The best food in town is probably to be found in the pubs* but there's the standard range of Indian, Italian and fast food feeders as well. *Pushplugs: Pacos; Smilin' Jack's (both Mexican); Littlejohns (American); Riverhouse (classy joint owned by Carol Smiley's husband); the Bistro.* The

Clive Ramsay delicatessen in Bridge of Allan has a café attached. *For fish and chips, the Allan Water Café cannot be beaten.*

OTHER Ten-pin bowling in Stirling at AMF Bowling (Riverside). Hillbillies and Frames provide pool and snooker tables respectively.

UNIVERSITY
- **PRICE OF A PINT OF BEER** £1.60
- **GLASS OF WINE** £1.10
- **CAN OF RED BULL** £1.50

The SU's ents scene *has won national accolades by the fistful.* The MacRobert *attracts a fair slew of famous faces* for lectures including Anthony Minghella and Iain Banks.

BARS As well as the Robbins Student Centre (the Union building), Stirling's got five other bars. Studio is the newest and largest with a full menu available till 8pm. During the day, its deck is *packed with chompers, chatterers and those just taking in the great view. Inside, the plasma screens, sofas and movie memorabilia, make it popular after dark too.* Tuesdays are 'Karaoke Idol' night and Sunday brings the pub quiz. The club venue Glow has three bars: the Long Bar *(packed at night),* the Cocktail Bar (with, er, cocktails) and the Glow Bar itself. The Gannochy Sports Bar next to the Sports Centre shows big screen sports fixtures and hosts regular film and rock nights to boot.

THEATRES The Drama Society (SUDS) struts the boards of the local Tollbooth Theatre or, occasionally, the MacRobert Arts Centre (equipped with both a 466-seat theatre and 140-seat studio), which also feature touring thesps.

FILM The MacRobert Arts Centre is also *film central* with 20-30 movies a week and a late bar with *top snacks.* It's just £3 a movie for anything from blockbusters to *arty farty* fare.

MUSIC VENUES In recent times, Shola Ama, Sophie Ellis Bextor, Wheatus, Idlewild and Shed 7 have performed at the SU's Robbins Student Centre, which has also played host to *less illustrious* local and student bands. Head down to the MacRobert for jazz, funk and classical.

CLUBBING *Glow is the place on campus for dancing, prancing and falling over.* Most nights have a different theme: hip hop, cheese and rock'n'pop from the 60s to 90s. Also, big club names such as Ministry of Sound and Artful Dodger turn up from time to time.

COMEDY/CABARET Every few weeks, the MacRobert hosts comic stylings.

FOOD Haldanes and the Pathfoot Dining Room are the two main scoff stops, *both good value.* Oscar's Snack bar sells *simple* snacks and main meals. Meanwhile, in the Andrew Miller Building, Roberto's serves fast food (pizzas, chips and baked potatoes at £2.50 for a meal deal) and Stir C@fé does *posh but pricey* coffees and sandwiches. The MacRobert Bar sells paninis, snacks and sandwiches, with specials on lunch and pre-theatre menus. Similar snack fare is available from the Long Bar in the Union *(good*

S

smoothies) and Studio *(busy throughout the day)*. Students can buy their grub in bulk at the beginning of each semester by topping up their smart card which also gives them serious discounts.
OTHER Three balls a year and the *anarchic* 'Final Fling'.

SOCIAL ○○○○○○○○○○○○○○

STIRLING UNIVERSITY STUDENTS' ASSOCIATION
○ **4** SABBATICALS ○ **TURNOUT AT LAST BALLOT** 15%
○ **NUS MEMBER**
Nothing too political – they prefer to concentrate on winning awards for ents. Relations with the University remain just fine.

SA FACILITIES
As well as the top notch bars, clubs and catering facilities (see above), SUSA provides a general shop, print room, photo booth, two meeting rooms, five pool/snooker tables and a bunch of web-based stuff. Royal Bank of Scotland is on campus (with cash machine).

CLUBS (NON-SPORTING)
Air TV; Air3 1350 (radio station); Book Club; Celtic Music; Chess Club; Chinese; Comic; Creative Writing ; DANCE@SU; Dyslexia; Gesture (deaf awareness); International; Law Society; Live Music; Mature Students; Poker; Psychology Society; Rock; Scottish Nationalist Association; Sci-Fi & Fantasy (SHAZAM!); Socialist; Spanish; Strategy Gaming & Role Playing; Wildwatchers. **See also Clubs tables.**

OTHER ORGANISATIONS
'Brig' is Stirling's long-running and award-winning free monthly student paper. 'Air3 1350' sends out sounds across campus from 11am to 11pm daily. Meanwhile 'Air TV' does pictures too, but only a few times a week in the campus cinema. Stirling RAG's recent readies-raising events have included a bean-eating competition. Sounds like a gas.

RELIGION
○ **6** CHAPLAINS (BAPTIST, RC, COFE, METHODIST, CONGREGATIONALIST, COFS)
The campus chaplaincy is basically Christian, but tries to put others in touch with other faith groups and there's a Muslim prayer room.

PAID WORK
○ **JOB BUREAU** ○ **PAID WORK** TERM TIME 40%; HOLS 90%
The jobshop is part of the Career Development Centre and it finds jobs for quite a few students on campus or in the pubs and restaurants in Bridge of Allan and Stirling. *But local employment is a bit scarce on the ground and so time and money may be needed to heigh-ho it off to Glasgow or Edinburgh.*

SPORTS ○○○○○○○○○○○○○

○ **RECENT SUCCESSES** GOLF, SWIMMING, TENNIS
○ **BUSA RANKING** 16
Stirling gives Loughborough University a run (and a swim and a putt) for its money. The successful sports bursary scheme has done the University proud. Apart from notable triumphs in international sports competitions for students, in recent years Stirling has spawned five Olympians, a Paralympian swimming medallist and 12 Commonwealth Games athletes. The sports scholarship has helped two amateur golfers turn pro; three students have gone on to compete in the Walker Cup. It's also home to the HQ of the Scottish Institute of Sport.

SPORTS FACILITIES
23 acres of playing fields including artificial pitches, football pitch, rugby pitch, hockey pitch and all-weather pitch; sports hall; squash courts; two basketball courts; athletics field and running track; loch (for angling, sailing, canoeing *and the occasional skinny dip)*; croquet lawn/bowling green; the expanding Scottish National Tennis Centre; all-weather pitch; multigym; running track; sauna and solarium. In addition to a nine-hole golf course, there's a Golf Centre with a short game practice area and three target greens. Jogging routes are situated around the campus. The Olympic swimming pool has been highly commended for disabled access: Mhairi Love trained here for the 2006 Games *(the Commonwealth, not the TV series)*. The town adds a curling and skating rink, ten-pin bowling and the River Forth. Skiing facilities are close by.

SPORTING CLUBS
American Football; Canoe Polo; Capoiera; Cheerleading; Kayak; Lacrosse; Ladies Gaelic; Octopush; Rowing; Sen-no-Kai Karate; Snow Sports; Tenshinkan Karate; Ultimate Frisbee; Water Polo. **See also Clubs tables.**

S

ACCOMMODATION ○○○○○○○○○

IN UNIVERSITY
○ **SELF-CATERING** 56% ○ **COST** £63 (37WKS)
○ **1ST YRS LIVING IN** 100% ○ **INSURANCE PREMIUM** £
AVAILABILITY First years get the pick of accommodation on campus (self-catering study bedrooms with shared kitchens and bathrooms): Andrew Stuart Hall and Geddes Court are the *most lively and popular*. En suite rooms are available, *but it costs extra to spend a penny in private. Rooms are basic and in desperate need of the Llewellyn-Bowen treatment.* There's also space for some third years, finalists and postgrads, both on campus and in the off-site flats. Most second years prefer to make their own

arrangements closer to the centre of town. International students can live in for their whole course. 2% of students have to share. A small number of married couples can be housed, mainly in the 130 *sought-after* off-campus flats maintained by the University. There's a women-only flat, specially adapted facilities for disabled students and 24-hr campus security from what are known as the 'Green Meanies'. After 11pm on campus, students must show their student ID and first-year guests have signing in times.

CAR PARKING No spaces for first years, but for others *a permit costs a whopping £65 a year.*

EXTERNALLY

○ **AVE RENT** £59+ ○ **LIVING AT HOME** 30%

AVAILABILITY *Finding a comfy rented pad isn't always easy. Quality varies dramatically. Bridge of Allan, the local friendly town, is most popular. Raploch and Cornton less so.*

HOUSING HELP The Union website has an accommodation search facility and the University has seven full- and three part-time home-hunt helpers. Services include an approved landlord list, property vetting, legal advice and a bulletin board.

WELFARE ○○○○○○○○○○○○○

SERVICES

○ **LGBT SOCIETY** ○ **WOMEN'S OFFICER & SOCIETY**
○ **MATURE STUDENTS' OFFICER**
○ **INTERNATIONAL STUDENTS' OFFICER**
○ **POSTGRAD OFFICER** ○ **DISABILITIES OFFICER & SOCIETY**
○ **NIGHTLINE** ○ **UNIVERSITY COUNSELLORS** 1 FULL/2 PART
○ **SU COUNSELLORS** 3
○ **CRIME RATING:** !

SUSA provides an Advice & Support Centre which doles out advice as well as condoms and attack alarms. Welfare volunteers help with academic, accommodation and mental health concerns.

HEALTH The on-campus NHS and dental practice has four full-time GPs and one other doctor one day a week and offers sexual health surgeries.

CRECHES/NURSERY The Bright Beginnings Nursery is next-door to the University and looks after kids from 6wks-5yrs, where, with help from the Council, some spaces are subsidised. The Psychology Department also runs a playgroup for children from just under 3-5yrs.

DISABILITIES *The campus designers have really given access some serious thought.* Rooms and facilities have been adapted, lifts have been installed and doorways have been widened. Lecture theatres have induction loops and help is available for students with dyslexia. The Disabilities Officer is there to iron out other creases. Stirling has been nationally recognised for spot-on IT provisions to assist disabled students.

CRIME *Almost none – safe as houses.*

FINANCE

○ **AVE DEBT PER YEAR** £3,060 ○ **HOME STUDENT FEES** £1,700

FEES *Here's a blast from New Labour's past:* First-time Scottish students don't pay fees, top-up or not. That may well change in the future, and it doesn't mean other UK students don't still have to pay (currently it's a *bargainacious* £1,150/yr). Scottish students will still need to contribute a couple of grand when they graduate. International full-timers pay £7,965-£9,880 (under-grad courses) and £7,965-£10,500 (postgrad). UK postgrads pay £3,080/yr or £220 per module.

○ **ACCESS FUND** £243,903 ○ **SUCCESSFUL APPLICATION/YR** 370
○ **AVE PAYMENT** £200-500

SUPPORT The University distributes hardship loans or non-repayable bursaries to students who have received their full loan but are still finding it difficult to make ends meet. These are administered by SISS (the Student Information and Support Service) which also provides financial advice. Among other scholarships for international, local and UK/EU students, the Stirling Minds Fund bails out students with the brains but not the bucks. There's also a Mature Students' Bursary which doles out around £100,000 a year.

S

➡ **STOCKTON**
see *Durham University*

○ The **Dissertation Dash (15th May)** is where staff and students congregate on the hills at **Sussex University** to cheer on those rushing to hand in tightly bound scripts and quaff ale. Nice.

Words in italics are Push's point of view — take it or leave it...

UNIVERSITY OF STRATHCLYDE

1. ○ **UNIVERSITY OF STRATHCLYDE** 16 Richmond Street, Glasgow, G1 1XQ **TEL** (0141) 552 4400 **E-MAIL** scls@mis.strath.ac.uk
WEBSITE www.strath.ac.uk ○ **UNIVERSITY OF STRATHCLYDE STUDENTS' ASSOCIATION** 90 John Street, Glasgow, G1 1JH
TEL (0141) 567 5000 **E-MAIL** admin@theunion.strath.ac.uk **WEBSITE** www.strathstudents.com
2. ○ **JORDANHILL CAMPUS** University of Strathclyde, 76 Southbrae Drive, Glasgow, G13 1PP
○ **UNIVERSITY OF STRATHCLYDE STUDENTS' ASSOCIATION** Jordanhill Campus, 76 Southbrae Drive, Glasgow, G13 1PP
TEL (0141) 950 3256

GENERAL ○○○○○○○○○○○○

Strathclyde University is situated on a number of hills slap in the middle of Glasgow and right in the city's central business district. The campus is *modern and fairly brutal, having hit a few branches of the ugly tree on the way out of the architect's office, but it blends inconspicuously with the rest of this part of the city.* The original University building, *an out-of-place redbrick construction, is quite lost* among more modern post-60s structures. The compact campus consists of large department buildings and tower blocks and is being rapidly developed and re-developed. The 'merger' with Jordanhill College created a second site housing the Faculty of Education.

🚹🚹🚹🚹🚹🚹🚹🚹🚹🚹🚹🚹🚹🚹🚹🚹🚹🚹🚹🚹🚹

SEX RATIO: ♂44 ♀56	**FOUNDED:** 1796
FULL-TIME U'GRADS: 11,530	**PART-TIME:** 2,510
POSTGRADS: 2,875	**NON-DEGREE:** 0
AVE COURSE: 4YRS	**ETHNIC:** 10%
STATE:PRIVATE SCHOOL: 90:10	**FLUNK RATE:** 17%
MATURE: 16%	**INTERNATIONAL:** 17%
DISABLED: 180	**LOCAL:** 70%

ATMOSPHERE

For every student of Glasgow University taking an artsy non-vocational course, there are about ten at Strathclyde intent on gathering CV points and winding up richer than their parents. The vast majority are from the West of Scotland, *blend seamlessly into the Glaswegian backdrop and don't look at university life in the same way as international or English students might – for them it's a case of turn up, tune in, get out.* Many get here and are reunited with school friends, so there's a ready-made social life to drop into. The Union fosters new friendships with many *screamingly drunken nights on the schedule, and an emphasis on getting involved in extra-curricular activity. Music and club nights are relentlessly arranged, although the lactose-intolerant would do well to be wary of all that cheese.*

SITES

JORDANHILL CAMPUS (2,000 students – Applied Arts, Education, Social Work, Speech & Language Therapy) Formerly Jordanhill College, the *green and leafy* site is five miles from the main John Anderson campus in Glasgow's largely residential West End. It has *good* sports facilities mainly used for teaching, a bar, library, computer rooms and the Crawford Auditorium, which doubles as a

multimedia performance space. There's a high proportion of mature and female students. *In theory Jordanhill is completely integrated with the main campus, but in practice it functions almost autonomously.* There's not much need for students to travel between campuses, but there's a free bus for those who want to – *presumably more out of curiosity than anything else.*

GLASGOW see University of Glasgow

TRAVEL see University of Glasgow
TRAINS Queen's Street and Central Stations are the mainline stations and run regular services to London, Edinburgh, Birmingham and other major cities.
UNIVERSITY The shuttle bus links John Anderson Campus and Jordanhill eight times a day till 5pm.
BICYCLES Steep hills and good local transport links make bikes unnecessary at John Andersen campus, though the University is keen to encourage cycling. *Jordanhill isn't half as mountainous as both bits of its name sound.*

CAREER PROSPECTS
○ **CAREERS SERVICE** ○ **NO. OF STAFF** 5 FULL/3 PART
○ **UNEMPLOYED AFTER 6 MTHS** 7%
Careers service open Tue-Fri 1-5pm: 24-hr online help; website; special needs services, especially for international, disabled and mature students. Several job fairs offer permanent/summer positions, plus the *enormous* annual Work Fair.

FAMOUS ALUMNI
Belle & Sebastian (posterchildren of lo-fi pop); Craig Brown (former Scotland football coach); Malcom Bruce MP (Lib Dem); Michael Connarty; Ian Davidson; Dougie Donnelly (sports commentator); Maria Fyfe; Tom Hunter (founder of Sports Connection); James Kelman (Booker-winning author); Helena Kennedy QC; Paul Laverty (Cannes-winning screenwriter); John Logie Baird (inventor of TV and *picnic-stealing friend of Boo-Boo*); John McFall, Jim Murphy (Labour MPs); Yvonne Murray (Olympic runner); Andrew O'Hagan (author); Lord Reith (BBC founder); Elaine Smith (actress); Tartan Amaebas (band); Teenage Fanclub.

SPECIAL FEATURES
The Hunter Centre for Enrepreneurship unique to Strathclyde allows students to combine entrepreneurial studies with any degree.

FURTHER INFO
○ **PROSPECTUSES** UNDERGRAD; POSTGRAD; INTERNATIONAL; ALTERNATIVE; VIDEO

S

Words in italics are Push's point of view — take it or leave it...

OPEN DAYS

See online for prospectuses, e-mail scls@mis.strath.ac.uk for open day info. The Arts and Social Sciences departments run faculty afternoons (baby open days). The alternative prospectus is available in cassette form, call (0141) 548 2814.

ACADEMIC ◖◖◖◖◖◖◖◖◖◖◖◖◖

Strathclyde employs every teaching method you could shake a stick at, and then some. The University has embraced the potential of cyberspace as a learning environment alongside more traditional classroom teaching. Courses are directed towards employability – *hence the small number of graduates who don't find careers quickly. The Hunter Centre, founded on the premise that having ideas generates money, has kick-started many a student business.* Departmental mergers mean fewer profs to go around, though.

ENTRY POINTS: 120-360	AVE POINTS: N/A
APPLICATIONS PER PLACE: N/A	CLEARING: 10%
NO. OF TERMS: 3	LENGTH OF TERMS: 12wks
STAFF TO STUDENT RATIO: 1:17	STUDY ADDICTS: 20%
TEACHING: ★★★	RESEARCH: ★★★★
YEAR ABROAD: N/A	SANDWICH STUDENTS: N/A

ADMISSIONS
APPLY VIA UCAS

Strathclyde is big on widening access to those who might not consider university. Representatives also go off to exhibitions around the world to net more international students. Entry requirements are *highly flexible* for mature students – there's a Mature Student Guide with details.

SUBJECTS

ARTS & SOCIAL SCIENCES 19%   **BIOLOGY** 19% **BUSINESS/MANAGEMENT** 25% **CHEMISTRY** 26% **COMPUTING** 15%   **EDUCATION** 15%   **ENGINEERING** 20% **PHYSICS** 20%
BEST Politics.
UNUSUAL Elective classes in Entrepreneurship; Highly specialised Education courses; Forensic Biology; Prosthetics; Orthotics.

LIBRARIES
761,900 BOOKS ## 2,260 STUDY PLACES

In addition to the main Andersonian library, there are some smaller departmental ones, a Law library and the one at Jordanhill (the biggest education library in Scotland). *The main library is starting to look a bit raggy* but the large number of laptop plug-in points, extended opening hours in exam periods and the *psychedelically decorated* Orbit Café *more than make up for any aesthetic issues.* The Royal Scottish Geographical Society keeps a collection of rare books and manuscripts here.

COMPUTERS
1,000+ WORKSTATIONS

All rooms in halls come with data points; off-campus there's access to the Virtual Private Network. There are 16 PC labs on John Anderson campus, plus Sunray terminals in two labs. The Jordanhill campus has two labs. The Education faculty provides Mac facilities. Business School students are eligible for free laptop loans *to help them look the part* when sat on the train.

OTHER LEARNING FACILITIES

Language labs are open to all. There's also a design lab, rehearsal rooms and a film and TV studio. Drama students get the *magnificent* Ramshorn Theatre to frolic in. Strathclyde's not afraid of technology when it comes to learning methods, pioneering the Personal Response System (PRS), where as many as 350 students in one lecture can express their views through personal handsets – *just like on Who Wants to be a Millionaire?* The Centre for Academic Practice offers study skill seminars and workshops.

ENTERTAINMENT ◖◖◖◖◖◖◖◖◖

THE CITY see University of Glasgow

UNIVERSITY
PRICE OF A PINT OF BEER £1.95
GLASS OF WINE £1.95
CAN OF RED BULL £1.80

When they're not out and about in fun-crammed Glasgow (especially in the nearby Ark pub), Strathclyders have so much going on in the Union it's amazing they don't die of liver failure.
BARS *Thank the heavens for Scottish licensing laws. The vast Union's six bars keep the pumps pumping till 3am most nights. Sunday closing in many gives students a chance to calm down and dry out. The Barony is pubby and popular – not least on account of DJ Phil's infamous TFI Friday.* The newly refurbished Gameszone is really a pool hall with beer but the 26 tables draw in a *huge* daytime crowd. There's also: Darkroom *(baguettes by day, bops by night);* Miller's *(baguettes by day, chill-out zone by night);* the Priory *(beer by day, more beer by night,* non-smoking) and the University-run Lord Todd. Toby's Bar at Jordanhill has theme nights almost every evening and *serves a wicked breakfast.*
THEATRES The Ramshorn Theatre hosts productions from the award-winning Strathclyde Theatre Group as well as well as a range of touring, professional and student productions. Trips to the Edinburgh Fringe are regular events.
FILM The *passionate* Film Society shows *a huge variety of films from blockbusters to art house* as well as films made by its members. Classic movies are also shown in the debating chamber.
MUSIC VENUES The Union has a *good reputation,*

especially for giving a kick-start to local bands and it's also hosted the likes of E-17, the Bluetones, Travis, Wheatus and the Cheeky Girls. Every bar in the Union building is equipped for big sounds from big names, and Vertigo in particular is a conference suite moonlighting as a mosh-pit.

CLUBBING At least three club nights a week, spread between the Barony, the Darkroom and Vertigo. *'12 Hour Tuesday', where all drinks are 99p, is a particular favourite.*

COMEDY/CABARET Fortnightly comedy in Miller's has included visits from Phil Kaye, the Reverend Obediah Steppenwolf and Hugh Lennon and his Hypnodog.

FOOD The food courts in the Darkroom and Miller's offer traditional stodge and curries, while Delice de France does *healthy* baguettes. *Burgery junk* is to be had in the Gameszone, while the Lord Todd serves a range of traditional, veggie and international cuisine till 2pm.

OTHER The Sports Ball is the biggest and most regular; many departments have their own dos. Freshers week is also pretty social. Christmas all-nighters (8pm-8am) aren't unknown. Jordanhill has its own May Ball on campus.

SOCIAL ⊍⊍⊍⊍⊍⊍⊍⊍⊍⊍⊍⊍⊍⊍⊍

UNIVERSITY OF STRATHCLYDE STUDENTS' ASSOCIATION

❍ **6 SABBATICALS** ❍ **TURNOUT AT LAST BALLOT** 13%
❍ **NUS MEMBER**

The SA's *tightly organised and intimately involved with the concerns of the student body. It offers a phenomenal number of commercial services and is good in student development (like the National Student Learning Programme). It's in no way party political, but that's not to say it isn't strongly concerned with ethical and democratic issues –* there's been a recent ban on smoking in the Priory Bar and an embargo on Nestlé products in the SA building. The Deputy President spearheads a committee responsible for issues at Jordanhill.

SA FACILITIES

The Association's ten-floor building houses: six bars; nightclub/music venue; café; fast food outlet; pool tables; four meeting rooms; minibus and car hire service; Endsleigh Insurance office; NatWest bank with three ATMs; payphones; photocopier; photo booth; fax and printing service; advice centre; gaming and vending machines; jukeboxes; travel agency; general and stationery shops; secondhand bookshop; conference suite. Jordanhill has: bar; coffee shop; tea bar; welfare office; USSA office and campus shop.

CLUBS (NON-SPORTING)

Armchair Sports; Chorus; GameSoc; GeekSoc; Hellenic Cultural; Jousting; SAIN (Student Anti Imperialist Network); Scottish National Party; Spanish; Stop the War; Student Scouting &

Guiding Organisation; SURGe (Strathclyde University Role-play Gaming etc.); SURGS (Strathclyde University Retro Gaming Society). **See also Clubs tables.**

OTHER ORGANISATIONS

The SA's 'Strathclyde Telegraph' comes out every three weeks and has a circulation of around 5,000. It's an *impressive* publication and was awarded the Herald Student Newspaper of the Year award a few years ago. 'Fusion' radio station survives on an intermittent FM licence and broadcasts on the internet. The sabbatical-run charity Rag is *very active*, generating £56,850 of philanthropic cash last year. They organise a range of events, from urban abseiling to battle of the bands. Cactus is a Community Action Group that specialises in working with single parent kids.

RELIGION

❍ **8 CHAPLAINS (SCOTTISH EPISCOPAL, COFE, URC, RC, FC, METHODIST, BAPTIST); RABBI**

The chaplaincy service (St Paul's building) has a chapel, library, common room and ARK café and caters for most flavours of biblical faith, plus Muslim and Jewish students. A number of International Student Chaplains work at the centre also. *It's a pro-active service* with a busy calendar of speakers, art exhibitions, ceilidhs and films. Religion in Glasgow see University of Glasgow.

PAID WORK see University of Glasgow

❍ **JOB BUREAU**

The careers service has a database of part-time and vacation opportunities. There are several jobs going in the University doing bar work and the like. The Union keeps its own vacancy board.

SPORTS ⊍⊍⊍⊍⊍⊍⊍⊍⊍⊍⊍⊍⊍⊍

❍ **RECENT SUCCESSES** WOMEN'S ATHLETICS, CROSS COUNTRY, BADMINTON, MEN'S RUGBY, SAILING, CURLING
❍ **BUSA RANKING** 32

Sport at Strathclyde is as much a social activity as a competitive one but they still have their fair share of almighty victories. A University member took home an Olympic gold medal in curling in 2002 and in 2003 Strathclyde scooped all the trophies for sailing they had going at the Student Yachting World Championships. There are 42 sporting clubs and counting.

SPORTS FACILITIES

45 acres of playing fields; sports centre with gym and multigym; six squash courts; swimming pool; aerobics studio. Jordanhill's facilities include: astroturf and grass pitches; six badminton courts; swimming pool; fitness suite and weights room. Membership of the USSA is a one-off £20 fork-out that includes accident insurance. Nature's gifts to the University include a lake and the River Clyde for watersports.

S

Words in italics are Push's point of view – take it or leave it...

SPORTING CLUBS

Aikido; Basketball; Boxing; Handball; Kickboxing; Mountaineering; Parachuting; Rowing; Shinty; Snowsports; Surfing; Tukido; Xtreme Street Sports; Ultimate Frisbee. **See also Clubs tables.**

ATTRACTIONS see University of Glasgow

ACCOMMODATION ◖◖◖◖◖◖◖◖◖◖

IN UNIVERSITY
- **CATERED** 1% - **COST** £75 (35WKS)
- **SELF-CATERING** 12% - **COST** £66 (37/50WKS)
- **1ST YRS LIVING IN** 15% - **INSURANCE PREMIUM** £££

AVAILABILITY Accommodation is limited to full-time students coming from over 25 miles away. First years who meet these criteria are guaranteed a room *but not necessarily a nice one.* Self-catered flats (housing four to six) are dotted about but catered accommodation is only to be found at Jordanhill campus and includes two meals a day during the week only (*so Sunday lunch could mean a Pot Noodle and a cheese bap*). Residences generally come with wash basins and internet access in rooms plus shared showers, baths and kitchens on each floor. Also provided are common rooms, coin-op launderettes and cleaning services in some halls (*bring a duster for James Blyth or Thomas Campbell Court*). The majority of students in all years live out – which in Strathclyde's case means with mum. The University has two flats in the city for married couples – families aren't so lucky and have a lengthy wait on their hands before any of the few three-bed flats 14 miles away become available.
CAR PARKING Patrick Thomas Court has 12 spaces, allocated on a first come, first parked basis. 45 spaces are available at Andrew Ure. Permits not required.

EXTERNALLY see University of Glasgow
- **AVE RENT** £55

HOUSING HELP The University helps find private housing and there is a Glasgow-wide student housing website.

WELFARE ◖◖◖◖◖◖◖◖◖◖◖◖

SERVICES
- **LGBT SOCIETY** - **WOMEN'S OFFICER**
- **MATURE STUDENTS' OFFICER**
- **INTERNATIONAL STUDENTS' SOCIETY**
- **POSTGRAD STUDENTS' SOCIETY**
- **UNIVERSITY COUNSELLORS** 3 FULL/2 PART
- **SU COUNSELLORS** 2 FULL/5 PART
- **CRIME RATING:** !!

The ASK4 service in the Union has two student advisors to help with personal, academic, housing and financial problems.
HEALTH The Student and Occupational Health Service runs a daily clinic and weekly family planning clinic. Glasgow Royal Infirmary is a block away and the Dental Hospital 15 mins walk.
WOMEN: Attack alarms sold for £1.
CRECHES/NURSERY The SA crèche on the John Anderson campus is free of charge for students' children aged 3-5yrs. Kidcare Ltd runs a custom-built nursery facility for pre-school children on a paying basis.
DISABILITIES The hills around John Anderson make access tricky and those with mobility problems *should visit before applying.* Disabled students are guaranteed University accommodation and rooms can be specially adapted according to individual needs. Six of the Union building's ten floors have wheelchair access, though there are some rooms in various buildings which still present problems. For the partially sighted/dyslexics the Special Needs Service's Technology Support Officer assists in getting and using specialist software and equipment. There are speaking lifts with Braille buttons.
CRIME The arrival of CCTV has *heavily reduced* crime in the campus village but there are still regular incidents of theft from student rooms, mainly because of open windows.

FINANCE
- **AVE DEBT PER YEAR** £1,887 - **HOME STUDENT FEES** £1,700

FEES Scottish students have £1,700 to pay, but not till they graduate, thanks to the Scottish Graduate Endowment Fund. Other UK folk fork out £3,000. International and postgraduate fees vary from school to school.
- **ACCESS FUND** £8,000 - **SUCCESSFUL APPLICATION/YR** 1,000
- **AVE PAYMENT** £400

SUPPORT Sports bursaries of up to £1,000 are available from the University (with Glasgow City Council). The Royal and Ancient Golf Club awards £1,500 bursaries to the rising stars of golf. The Mature Student's Bursary fund helps with childcare costs. Also other hardship funds and short-term loans available.

Led Zeppelin played their first gig at Surrey University

Words in italics are Push's point of view — take it or leave it...

SUNDERLAND UNIVERSITY

FORMERLY SUNDERLAND POLYTECHNIC

1. ○ **THE UNIVERSITY OF SUNDERLAND** Edinburgh Building, Chester Road, Sunderland, SR1 3SD **TEL** (0191) 515 3000
E-MAIL student-helpline@sunderland.ac.uk **WEBSITE** www.sunderland.ac.uk ○ **UNIVERSITY OF SUNDERLAND STUDENTS' UNION**
Wearmouth Hall, Chester Road, Sunderland, SR1 3SD **TEL** (0191) 514 5512 **E-MAIL** sac@sunderland.ac.uk
WEBSITE www.sunderlandsu.ac.uk
2. ○ **ST PETER'S CAMPUS** Chester Road, Sunderland **TEL** (0191) 515 3000

GENERAL ○○○○○○○○○○○○○

Way up on the map, just south of Newcastle, on the north-east coast of Blighty sits the city of Sunderland, a *sprawling* industrial port that forms part of the Tyne & Wear conurbation. *Or so it was.* It's still a port and hasn't moved, but it has had a *face-lift, getting the botox treatment* from such attractions as the Stadium of Light, the National Glass Centre, Sunderland Marina, Riverside Regeneration, Winter Gardens, the Metro and Crowtree Leisure Centre. Most of the rest of the city centre was shoved up in the 60s *and looks like it.* It is, however, close to the Northumbrian coast, the moors and two of Europe's biggest shopping complexes, Gateshead's Metro Centre and Newcastle's Eldon Square (see Newcastle University). Sunderland University itself is scattered across the city like someone just dropped it. City Campus in the city centre is composed of early 60s tower blocks which match most of the city's architecture in style *and complete lack of aesthetic appeal.* An on-going £8.5m refurb may help, but for now is focussing on providing a one-stop shop for students' issues, and a sports injuries clinic. The St Peter's campus, by the river, *is easier on the eyes though.*

SEX RATIO: ♂55 ♀45	**FOUNDED:** 1901
FULL-TIME U'GRADS: 17,355	**PART-TIME:** 8,620
POSTGRADS: 2,102	**NON-DEGREE:** 5,227
AVE COURSE: 3YRS	**ETHNIC:** 38%
STATE:PRIVATE SCHOOL: 97:3	**FLUNK RATE:** 27%
MATURE: 47%	**INTERNATIONAL:** 20%
DISABLED: 150	**LOCAL:** 61%

ATMOSPHERE

The University makes a specific point of attracting local students and for many in this once deprived corner of the country, it can be a life-changing experience. Neither the city nor the Uni will win any beauty contests (they've won architecture awards, but that's something different altogether) but they make up for it in friendliness, enthusiasm and perky hedonism.

SITES

ST PETER'S CAMPUS (7,000 students – Business, IT and Media) St Peter's is *Naomi Campbell to City Campus' Kathy Burke.* All curves and exposed woodwork, it's an *attractive* site composed of a cluster of five buildings, some of which actually won a Sunday Times Buildings of the Year award a while back.

SUNDERLAND

○ **POPULATION** 280,800 ○ **CITY CENTRE** 200M
○ **LONDON** 257 MILES ○ **NEWCASTLE** 10 MILES
○ **DURHAM** 13 MILES
○ **HIGH TEMP** 19 ○ **LOW TEMP** 0 ○ **RAINFALL** 54

No one would claim this is an architecturally appealing city – unless they were an architect – but as we've said, it's on the up. There are two museums, some interesting bridges and, a little way inland, the Penshaw Monument, a big folly that looks like a Greek temple and can be seen for miles around. As can the Angel of the North a bit further away outside Gateshead.

TRAVEL

TRAINS Sunderland station is ten mins walk from the City campus. There are direct trains to Newcastle (£2.40) and Middlesbrough (£9.80) and connections to the rest of the country.
COACHES Blueline and National Express services to many destinations including London (£34) and Manchester (£21.50).
CAR Eight miles off the A1(M) on the A123, A19 and A690.
AIR Newcastle International and Teesside Airports are both under an hour's drive away.
FERRIES From Newcastle and Hull, serving Europe and Scandinavia.
HITCHING *Good prospects once out of Sunderland, particularly on the A1 heading north or south.*
LOCAL The Newcastle Metro Link now runs to Sunderland (and back again) taking in Gateshead on the way. *It's punctual, clean and has proved a godsend for easing traffic,* and touches several University sites, including halls of residence. A yearly student pass costs £20. *Local buses are cheap and reliable.*
UNIVERSITY A free campus bus service runs between all key University buildings, halls of residence and Manor Quay nightclub until the early hours.
TAXIS *Sunderland is small, so taxi fares are pretty cheap.* The Union has struck a deal with Station Taxis where if you hand over your Union card to the driver, the Union is billed the next day. Pay back your fare and get your Union card back.
BICYCLES There are bike lanes between Consett and the coast and between Sunderland and Whitehaven in Cumbria, *but biking's not popular. Problems with theft are decreasing, but there aren't many secure places to leave bikes in town.*

S

Words in italics are Push's point of view — take it or leave it...

CAREER PROSPECTS
- **CAREERS SERVICE** - **NO. OF STAFF** 4 FULL/2 PART
- **UNEMPLOYED AFTER 6 MTHS** 6%

FAMOUS ALUMNI
Alan Ahlberg (children's writer); Terry Deary (author of the Horrible Histories); Tony Scott (movie mogul).

SPECIAL FEATURES
(Lord) David Puttnam is the University Chancellor, which means he shakes hands and doles out degrees once a year.
The Hatchery incubates enterprise ideas and helps students who think they're Sir Alan Sugar – *with business advice, not psychological help, we mean.*

FURTHER INFO
- **PROSPECTUSES** UNDERGRAD; POSTGRAD
- **OPEN DAYS**

ACADEMIC ((((((((((((((

The University's *strong* on widening participation, and as a result there are lots of students who are the first in their family to attend university. Having so many locals, Sunderland also has strong links with local industry, particularly Nissan who churn out Micras nearby. So the Automotive Engineering course is *strong*, as are Pharmacy/Pharmacology and, partly thanks to £20m spent recently on the new media arts centre at St Peter's Campus, so is Media Studies. The University has attracted some *high-calibre names* in recent years (former Ed Sec Estelle Morris and England's Chief Pharmaceutical Officer Dr Jim Smith) but it remains a students' university *rather than one for posturing academics waiting for a spot on Newsnight Review. It's a radical idea, but Push likes it.*

ENTRY POINTS: 80–240	AVE POINTS: 159
APPLICATIONS PER PLACE: N/A	CLEARING: 19%
NO. OF TERMS: 3	LENGTH OF TERMS: 10WKS
STAFF TO STUDENT RATIO: 1:18	STUDY ADDICTS: N/A
TEACHING: **	RESEARCH: **
YEAR ABROAD: 0%	SANDWICH STUDENTS: 8%
1STS: 9%	2.2s: 39%
2.1s: 42%	3RDS: 6%

ADMISSIONS
- **APPLY VIA UCAS**

At interview, personality and suitability count for just as much as official points and there's clearly a fondness for locals.

SUBJECTS
ART & DESIGN 7%   **ARTS/HUMANITIES** 3%
BUSINESS/MANAGEMENT 15%
COMPUTING/DIGITAL MEDIA 11%   **EDUCATION** 12%
HEALTH & ENVIRONMENT 5%   **MEDIA** 13%

LAW 2%   **LIFE-LONG LEARNING** 10%   **PSYCHOLOGY** 3%
SPORTS & LESIURE 4%
BEST Anatomy & Physiology; Art & Design; Media Studies; Molecular Bio-sciences; Nursing; Pharmacology/Pharmacy.

LIBRARIES
- **500,000 BOOKS** - **1,900 STUDY PLACES**
- **24-HR ACCESS**

There are main libraries on both campuses, both have 24-hour access by swipe card (but there's no access to information staff outside normal hours). The libraries also act as collection and drop-off points for academic work, which *partly explains why you'll find so few students actually inside them. The rest of the explanation involves a trip round the SU's bars.* There are further departmental libraries as well as the Ashburne Library.

COMPUTERS
- **1,250+ WORKSTATIONS** - **24-HR ACCESS**

OTHER LEARNING FACILITIES
The 'media centre' concentrates on TV and radio, with facilities provided by Sony. It was opened by Estelle Morris in September 2003. *Cutting edge and very impressive. The centre, not Estelle Morris.*

ENTERTAINMENT ((((((((((

THE TOWN
- **PRICE OF A PINT OF BEER** £2.10
- **GLASS OF WINE** £2
- **CAN OF RED BULL** £1.80

Newcastle is like Sunderland's flashier big brother, but don't under-estimate the little guy, he's got some moves.
CINEMAS A three-screen mainstream house and a 12-screen Virgin cinema ten miles out of town.
THEATRES The Empire shows mainstream plays, pantos and concerts and the Royalty has local offerings. The Seaburn Centre also hosts visits from the RSC.
PUBS *Cheap, cheerful and mostly friendly. Pushplugs: Fitzgerald's; Baroque (a huge Gothic style pub); Royalty Museum Vaults; Ivy House (very student friendly); the Windsor Castle is a cool gay hang-out; Varsity is popular; Lampton Worm is a cheap Weatherspoons.* Most do student discounts in some form. *Posh bars include Ttonic, Berlins, Lunar and Chase.*
CLUBBING The Beach is a *two-floor boogie wonderland.* Annabel's is a Sunderland institution (chart). Quayside Exchange has resident DJs.
COMEDY The Point is home to chucklemeisters on Tuesdays. Otherwise there's the Comedy Club.
MUSIC VENUES *Sunderland is mainly a local bands town* with the Ropery, Royalty, Greens and Bar 36 all hosting live music. The Town Hall hosts *mum-friendly* tunes. Once a month, the Blue Velvet Caberet at the Mowbray Park Hotel oozes live music, comedy, poetry and art.

S

EATING OUT The Panda (all-you-can-eat Chinese) *is very, very popular. Naz does the same thing but with Asian flavours. The Amalfi's good for early bites: any pizza or pasta for £3.20 before 7pm. Otherwise, pick from the normal array of kebab and burger joints.*

UNIVERSITY
- **PRICE OF A PINT OF BEER** £1.70
- **GLASS OF WINE** £1.90
- **CAN OF RED BULL** £1.50

BARS By day, students frequent The Roker Bar, waiting for somewhere else to open or wishing they'd gone to the *chirpier* Wearmouth Bar on Chester Road. By night, they go to a converted warehouse called the Bonded Warehouse or cram themselves into the SU's major nightspot, Manor Quay.

THEATRES Enthusiastic, *but outside of academia, facilities are limited.* There are occasional stints at the Sunderland Empire.

FILM Recent films are shown in the Sony Media Centre's cinema at the St Peter's Campus.

MUSIC VENUES *Manor Quay's got an eye for up-and-coming talent – they showcased the Artic Monkeys before they were famous.*

CLUBBING Manor Quay offers a variety of nights out, from cheesy to serious funk, plus drinks promotions. Let's not forget the Bonded Warehouse which flaunts its late licence on a Friday and Saturday and is a venue for local live bands.

COMEDY/CABARET One-off events during Freshers' Week. Wearmouth's Sunday night quiz is the regular big draw.

FOOD Manor Quay has a pizza shack (food till 11pm). GJs does food until 6pm.

OTHER May Ball and the April Sports Ball, a black tie event usually held at the Stadium of Light.

SOCIAL ⓊⓊⓊⓊⓊⓊⓊⓊⓊⓊⓊⓊ

UNIVERSITY OF SUNDERLAND STUDENTS' UNION
- **5 SABBATICALS**

The students are almost aggressively uninterested in all things political. The SU isn't even affiliated to NUS. Instead, *they try to snuggle up to local businesses for cheap prices and special deals for students.* There are two SU discount cards: the *glitzy* Gold Card (a fiver) is good for a wider radius, including trips to Liverpool and free entry to museums. Like the rest of the University, SU facilities and buildings are spattered over both campuses.

SU FACILITIES
Only the bare essentials: three bars which serve food, two small shops, print shop, gaming lounge and a photocopier.

CLUBS (NON-SPORTING)
Hong Kong; Games; Self-Protection. **See also Clubs tables.**

OTHER ORGANISATIONS
'Degrees North' (DN) is a *pretty pukka* monthly mag and has a sabbatical editor. Meanwhile, 'Utopia FM' won three gongs at the BBC-backed Student Radio Awards. The Community Bridge campaign puts students to work coaching local kids or painting buildings. Rag is *piss poor,* though not for lack of intention. It's recently re-started and, despite raising a *miserable* grand last year, *the committee still has fire in the loins for even bigger and better sponsored karaoke.*

RELIGION
- **1 CHAPLAIN (COFE)**

On-campus mosque and an ecumenical team.

PAID WORK
- **JOB BUREAU**

The Union employs around 100 students but the local area *isn't exactly a job hotbed.* The well-staffed jobshop (combined with the careers service) will help find what there is. Students aren't supposed to work for more than 16 hours a week – *hedonism doesn't come cheap, though, and there are more than a handful who work longer hours.*

SPORTS ⓊⓊⓊⓊⓊⓊⓊⓊⓊⓊⓊⓊ

- **BUSA RANKING** 89

Sport's *neither popular nor well-catered for,* but talk of an Olympic swimming pool *may get couch potatoes out of jim-jams and into training. Those with a passion for getting hot, sweaty and out-of breath would do better to get a willing partner, or look to discounted local facilities instead.*

SPORTS FACILITIES
The sports centre on Chester Road has a 25m pool, sports hall and two gyms. St George's House has a dance studio and training room. At Seaburn and Hendon, there are ten acres of playing fields and the University is finalising a deal with Sunderland FC so students can have a crack at their facilities. Sunderland has squash, badminton and basketball courts, a dry ski-slope, football, rugby and cricket pitches. The local Crowtree Centre also has a pool, ice skating and hockey and boxing facilities. Silksworth outdoor complex has a tennis centre, dry ski-slope, running track, lake and orienteering courses. Sunderland Marina for water sports, the coast for surfing and rock-climbing.

SPORTING CLUBS
Aikido; American Football; Boxing; Dance; Duk Moo; Gaelic Football; Parachute; Salsa; Snow Sports; Surf. **See also Clubs tables.**

S

Words in italics are Push's point of view – take it or leave it...

ATTRACTIONS
Sunderland FC play football and grumble about Newcastle not far off.

ACCOMMODATION ○○○○○○○○○○

IN UNIVERSITY
○ **SELF-CATERING** 23% ○ **COST** £78 (50WKS)
○ **1ST YRS LIVING IN** 35% ○ **INSURANCE PREMIUM** £££££
AVAILABILITY First years who want to live in can do so, but only a third want to (most are local, anyway). Nearly a third of other undergrads *should also be in luck*. No one has to share. The facilities range from purpose-built halls to *ageing* tower blocks, from *swish* self-catering flats with en suite facilities to 450 places under a head tenancy scheme. Security is *good* with 24-hr watch on all sites, CCTV, swipe card entry systems and mobile and foot patrols.
CAR PARKING *Mostly easy* although not at St Peter's.

EXTERNALLY
○ **AVE RENT** £48 ○ **LIVING AT HOME** 51%
AVAILABILITY *Wise students bide their time and don't jump at the first pad that comes along. It's not hard to find good, cheap, safe, but, well, studenty housing near the University or University-linked Metro station. Students who can't aren't looking hard enough. Avoid Hendon and Pennywell. Students only ever go there in heavily-armed groups of 30 or more and are still never seen again.*
HOUSING HELP The University-run accommodation service *is small and doesn't need to do much.*

WELFARE ○○○○○○○○○○○○

SERVICES
○ LGBT OFFICER & SOCIETY
○ INTERNATIONAL STUDENTS' OFFICER
○ WOMEN'S OFFICER & SOCIETY ○ CRIME RATING: !!
CRECHES/NURSERY In conjunction with Ofsted, the University has two nurseries on the go, offering places to children as old as 12.
CRIME Two bobbies on the beat are *probably more Randall & Hopkirk than Starsky & Hutch* but have reduced on-campus crime by, *ooh, loads*.
DISABILITIES Most buildings, particularly at St Peter's, which is purpose-built, have good access. The major problems come with old Langham Tower, which is so *bad* that its services are slowly being relocated and, we guess, the Tower will eventually be melted down and made into disability ramps. A *small* disabled support team and help for dyslexics.

FINANCE
○ **AVE DEBT PER YEAR** £3,426 ○ **HOME STUDENT FEES** £3,000
FEES Scottish students have £1,700 to pay, but not till they graduate, thanks to the Scottish Graduate Endowment Fund. Other UK folk fork out £3,000. International and postgraduate fees vary from school to school.
○ **ACCESS FUND** £8,000 ○ **SUCCESSFUL APPLICATION/YR** 1,000
○ **AVE PAYMENT** £400
SUPPORT Sports bursaries of up to £1,000 are available from the University (with Glasgow City Council). The Royal and Ancient Golf Club awards £1,500 bursaries to the rising stars of golf. The Mature Student's Bursary fund helps with child-care costs. Also other hardship funds and short-term loans available.

▶ **SUNDERLAND POLYTECHNIC**
see *Sunderland University*

S

SURREY UNIVERSITY

○ **UNIVERSITY OF SURREY** Guildford, Surrey, GU2 7XH **TEL** 0800 9803 200 **E-MAIL** information@surrey.ac.uk **WEBSITE** www.surrey.ac.uk ○ **UNIVERSITY OF SURREY STUDENTS' UNION** Union House, University of Surrey, Guildford, Surrey, GU2 7XH **TEL** (01483) 689 223 **E-MAIL** info@ussu.co.uk **WEBSITE** www.ussu.co.uk

GENERAL ○○○○○○○○○○○○○○

Think of Surrey and *the first (and probably only) thing that comes to mind is serious, stockbroker money tucked into the big houses* of the commuter belt around London. *Some of this cash seems to have fallen into the pockets of the University, too.* In the last few years they've garnished the centre of their home town of Guildford with several *swanky modern buildings – a vast improvement* on the older parts of the campus, *some of which look like Lego dipped in porridge. The University stands on a hill at the western end of town, near the glum, postwar cathedral where Gregory Peck famously came to a sticky end in 'The Omen'. Bored Civil Engineering students have put it about that the* whole campus is slowly sliding down hill (probably something to do with Damien) but the newer buildings and the air of prosperous industriousness suggests a University very much on the up.

SEX RATIO: ↑41 ↑59	FOUNDED: 1966
FULL-TIME U'GRADS: 6,633	PART-TIME: 495
POSTGRADS: 4,579	NON-DEGREE: 743
AVE COURSE: 4YRS	ETHNIC: 10%
STATE:PRIVATE SCHOOL: 88:12	FLUNK RATE: 11%
MATURE: 29%	INTERNATIONAL: 16%
DISABLED: 80	LOCAL: 10%

ATMOSPHERE

Students come to Surrey University because they want to do well and doing well, in this context, means getting a good job and making lots of money. Not that this means they spend all day swotting. There's plenty of creative, extra-curricular activity going on, it's just that you get the feeling that if there's not a prize, an award or some other kind of CV-boosting kudos attached to it, they don't want to know. The atmosphere is 'posh and proud of it' but for career-minded students there are few better places to go and, in the evenings, it livens up considerably. Town goes with gown like pipe and slippers in these parts. There's wasn't even any knee-jerk panic about 24-hour drink licensing as the students are such a trustworthy lot. Things remain on an even keel through vacations as well, which either means the students have integrated really well into city life, or that they haven't really made an impression. Everybody's all goose-pimply about the impending changes to city and campus, including the new Manor Park accommodation.

GUILDFORD

⊙ **POPULATION** 129,701 ⊙ **TOWN CENTRE** 800M
⊙ **LONDON** 35 MILES
⊙ **HIGH TEMP** 24 ⊙ **LOW TEMP** -3 ⊙ **RAINFALL** 60

Guildford's done well so far to maintain its own character in the face of the relentless pressure to be nothing more than a dormitory for London. That's all about to change, though, as 2007 will see the start of a major refurbishment to update the city centre and bus and train stations. Whether the quaint, cobbled streets and rustic atmosphere withstand the posh housing and gyms planned is yet to be seen – some time around 2014. There's also the ruined Norman castle built by William the Conqueror (although it wasn't a ruin when he built it), and a museum dedicated to Lewis Carroll of 'Alice In Wonderland' fame. Despite the historical attractions the centre's got all the obligatory chain stores and chain pubs.

TRAVEL

TRAINS Guildford's on the main London (Waterloo) to Portsmouth line, with a good service. Fast trains to Waterloo (£11.90) take 40 mins. There's an alternative line with a slower service, via Cobham which takes around an hour.

COACHES National Express coach No. 030 runs between Victoria Coach Station and Guildford Park Barn every two hours from 6.40am to 9.15pm (70 mins, £10.90 rtn).

CAR If approaching from London (A3) or the M25 (Junction 10), remain on A3 until the exit signed to Cathedral and University – don't take the exit signed to Guildford.

AIR Via Heathrow: coaches from Terminal 4 for Woking Station 7.20am-11.10pm, picking up from Terminals 2, 3 and 1 (£8 sgl). Via Gatwick: hourly trains for Guildford between 5.10am and 12.20am (38 mins).

LOCAL Arriva bus numbers 17 (hourly), 27 (every 20 mins/30 mins Sunday) and 37 run from the Friary Bus Station to the campus.

UNIVERSITY A free bus back to Hazel Farm, the off-campus hall of residence.

CAREER PROSPECTS

⊙ **CAREERS SERVICE** ⊙ **NO. OF STAFF** 5 FULL/2 PART
⊙ **UNEMPLOYED AFTER 6 MTHS** 3%

Tops for jobs for grads, so they say, and they do it with a mixture of career counselling, job fairs, careers library and jobshop. DAVE - Development, Accreditation, Volunteering, Employability – is run by students and offers skills for CV-polishers.

FAMOUS ALUMNI

Robert Earl (Planet Hollywood founder); Kirsten Lawton (world No. 1 trampolinist); Alan Parker (MD, Whitbread plc); Professor Sir Martin Sweening (founded Surrey Satellite Technology – see below); Sir David Varney (Executive Chairman, HM Revenue & Customs).

FURTHER INFO

⊙ **PROSPECTUSES** UNDERGRAD; POSTGRAD; DEPARTMENTAL
⊙ **OPEN DAYS**

There's a virtual campus tour on the main website. Guided and self-guided tours of the real thing are also possible. The University organises school visits and fairs. Personalised prospectuses tailored online make recruits feel all warm and fuzzy.

ACADEMIC ◖◖◖◖◖◖◖◖◖◖◖◖◖

⊙ **1994 GROUP**

Although it's rigorously academic Surrey courses are also very practical. The University's home to one of the most successful Research Parks in Europe and to Surrey Satellite Technology Ltd – the only company in the country designing, building and launching satellites into space. They're not just highly rated for research, though: teaching of Business, Economics, Education and Music, among others, has been commended by official bods. The brand-spanking new Medical School (a £14m development) and Management building knock the aesthetic socks off some of the fugly older blocks. Around 80% of students

S

plump for the University's placement year, with a high chance of landing experience in their dream jobs. Assessments come after Christmas and Easter, *when students have been lulled into a false sense of security by too much chocolate.* Some testing also occurs through group work or practical/lab sessions. Core and non-core modules mean degrees are varied and personalised.

ENTRY POINTS: 240–340	AVE POINTS: 327
APPLICATIONS PER PLACE: 5	CLEARING: 4%
NO. OF TERMS: 2	LENGTH OF TERMS: 15wks
STAFF TO STUDENT RATIO: 1:3	STUDY ADDICTS: 16%
TEACHING: **	RESEARCH: *****
YEAR ABROAD: 20%	SANDWICH STUDENTS: 69%
1STS: 12%	2.2s: 33%
2.1s: 47%	3RDS: 6%

ADMISSIONS
◐ APPLY VIA UCAS/NMAS FOR NURSING
Mature applications are *encouraged*, even where standard qualifications aren't in hand, the same goes for international mature students. There are links with local colleges and those on access courses also get a look-in.

SUBJECTS
ARTS, COMMUNICATION & HUMANITIES 13%
BIOMEDICAL & MOLECULAR SCIENCES 9%
ELECTRONICS & PHYSICAL ENGINEERING 15%
ENGINEERING 10% **EUROPEAN INSTITUTION OF HEALTH AND MEDICAL SCIENCES** 21%   **HUMAN SCIENCES** 14%
MANAGEMENT 18%
BEST Biological Sciences; Psychology; Computer Science; Civil, Chemical & Other Engineering; Politics; Social Policy & Anthropology; Sociology.
UNUSUAL Dietetics, International Hospitality Management, International Hospitality & Tourism Management; Retail Management; Space Technology & Planetary Exploration.

LIBRARIES
◐ 500,000 BOOKS ◐ 743 STUDY PLACES
◐ SPEND PER STUDENT ££
There's a European documentation centre with everything you need to know about the EU.

COMPUTERS
◐ 725 WORKSTATIONS ◐ 24-HR ACCESS
The campus' network is available both on and off it. Additional learning support; print shop; laptop corner; broadband's being installed in halls. The assisted technology centre has *loads of goodies* for disabled students.

OTHER LEARNING FACILITIES
The Language Centre gives foreign students a hand with essay writing, technical writing and grammar revision, *as well as introducing them to the delicate delights of British humour* and other aspects of British culture. There are 12 music practice rooms, mostly with pianos and a well-stocked audio room with scores, CDs etc.

ENTERTAINMENT ◖◖◖◖◖◖◖◖◖

THE TOWN
◐ PRICE OF A PINT OF BEER £2.39
◐ GLASS OF WINE £2.40
◐ CAN OF RED BULL £1.20
CINEMAS The nine-screen Odeon does a 10% student discount.
THEATRES The Electric Theatre hosts arty screenings, student productions and local amateurs. The Yvonne Arnaud Theatre is *one of the UK's top regional theatres* and is home to pre-West End plays, opera, ballet and more. The New Victoria in nearby Woking is the South East's largest auditorium with West End shows (after London, *natch*).
PUBS Guildford's home to many a chain pub but locals tend to drink in more traditional places, students stick to JD Wetherspoon and other bars on Bridge Street such as Bar Med and Edward's. The Star on the High Street is popular for its traditional vibe and live music.
CLUBBING Pulse, the Loft and Time are popular – the SU puts on a free bus to the latter.
MUSIC VENUES The Powerhouse holds open mic nights. The *cherished* Guildford Civic is still undergoing a nip 'n' tuck. Guilfest, held in Stoke Park, *turns more heads every year.*
EATING OUT *The well-heeled* might like to pop along to one of the many French restaurants in the town. Or there's Ken Hom's Chinese. Or, *for those who can bear to eat food cooked by someone who hasn't been on TV,* there're loads of Italians and Café Rouge, Café de Paris, Café Nero, Café Uno – *you get the idea* – try up Chapel Street. Joe Schmoe (US-style eatery) is still pretty new.

UNIVERSITY
◐ PRICE OF A PINT OF BEER £1.80
◐ GLASS OF WINE £1.80
◐ CAN OF RED BULL £1.50
BARS The main bar and restaurant Chancellors ('Channies') is so popular that students want signs giving the queuing time so they don't keep missing lectures. Other bars are the Varsity, which is popular with sports clubs; Helyn Rose, which competes with 'Channies' for *fine* breakfasts; the SU bar (actually five bars, cap 1,600); Roots café (*relaxed*); and Hari's, which is open in the afternoons.
FILM SU screenings on alternate Sunday nights. Outdoor screenings could be on the cards.
MUSIC VENUES A *nice* mix of up-and-coming acts like Reuben and Martin Grech have been through the SU Bar, as well as *old-stagers* like Boney M. Roots has Thank Funk it's Friday (*d'you see what they did there?*).
CLUBBING *Surrey's a major point on the superstar DJ circuit:* Carl Cox, Paul Oakenfold, Judge Jules and Seb Fontaine have all *scratched their way*

through. *Loads* of themed nights – everything from school disco to drag. Rubix has top notch sound 'n' light. Friday's Flirt! Has ex-Radio 1 DJ Dan Bailey at the wheel of steel. Tease is the gay night which happens roughly once a month. **COMEDY/CABARET** Comedy evenings fortnightly in Channies, £3/4. Open mic nights at both Rubix and Roots.
FOOD As well as Channies and the other Union bars the University has Pizzaman (free delivery), Rushes (for quick snacks), Seasons (for *serious* lunches), the Ivy Room (does private bookings) and Wates House which is a bar, function room and self-service restaurant. *With their never-ending yen for innovation and modernity* the University have even provided an online baguette ordering service from Rushes and Seasons – no delivery though. Young's Oriental Café serves up Chinese through the day, *but then does a Clark Kent in a nearby phonebooth,* emerging as UniK, a kebab hatch which stays open until 5am. Local fruit and veg is sold in the SU every Thurs *for those who actually know how to use a gas ring.* **OTHER** Three formal balls a year.

SOCIAL ○○○○○○○○○○○○

UNIVERSITY OF SURREY STUDENTS' UNION
○ **4 SABBATICALS** ○ **TURNOUT AT LAST BALLOT** 9%
○ **NUS MEMBER**

The *huge* 30-strong Union executive have won awards for campaigns against fees and for greater safety measures on the fringes of campus, but they don't intend to sit on their laurels, and there are plans for turning the SU into a *honed and sexy uber-machine. Or something.* There's a good rapport with the *bigwigs,* and the Union's say-so is listened to and has amended Uni strategy in the past.

SU FACILITIES
Bar/nightclub; music venue; two bars; canteen; snack bar; fast food place; two pool tables; meeting room; five minibuses and van for hire; Endsleigh Insurance office; NatWest Bank; NatWest and Barclays ATMs; fax and printing service; payphones; advice centre; games machines; general store; stationery shop; new and secondhand bookshops.

CLUBS (NON-SPORTING)
Alt Music; Arabic; Asian; Ballroom Dancing; Big Band; Breakdance; Change Ringing (Bellringing); Chinese Asian; Cyprus; Chinese Student & Scholar Association; Electronics & Amateur Radio Society (EARS); European; Game; GU2 (Radio Station); Hellenic; Iranian; Korean; La Latina; Love Music Society; Madsoc; Magick & Pagan; Malaysian Students; Mauritian; Meditation; Orthodox; Oscar Film Unit; Paintball; Pakistan; Poker; Presha (Music); Photography; Sikh; Singapore; St.John LINKS; Stage Crew; Surrey Gurners; Switchgear; Taiwanese; Tamil; Thai; Turkish; University Of Surrey Society Of Russia (USSR); 'V' Scheme (Volunteer Scheme); Wind Band; West Country Society. **See also Clubs tables.**

OTHER ORGANISATIONS
Free fortnightly, award-winning newspaper, 'Barefacts', has a 4,000 print-run and can be downloaded too. The Student Radio station 'GU2 1350AM' runs 24-hrs during the academic year and has also picked up a couple of Student Radio Station awards. Engineering students can get involved in reassembling Concorde (or one of 'em); it'll eventually be displayed at the Brooklands Museum in Weybridge. 'V' volunteering projects get staff and students involved in community projects. Give It a Go organises community events but not necessarily for charity. There's a Rag society, but activities are on the sparse side.

RELIGION
○ **3 CHAPLAINS (COFE, RC, FC)**
Lots of inter-faith mingling, senior advisors for most faiths and plans for a multi-faith prayer space. The Cathedral in town holds Greek Orthodox masses.

PAID WORK
○ **JOB BUREAU**
The University has links with various local stores (Tesco, Debenham's, House of Fraser) and there's *plenty* of bar work in the area. The campus recruitment agency gets students into jobs within the Uni.

SPORTS ○○○○○○○○○○○○

○ **RECENT SUCCESSES** TRAMPOLINING, GYMNASTICS, ROWING, GOLF, NETBALL, VOLLEYBALL, BASKETBALL, AMERICAN FOOTBALL ○ **BUSA RANKING** 60

In sport, *as in everything else they do,* SurreySport play to win and usually score well in the BUSA league.

SPORTS FACILITIES
Sports Centre: two squash courts; 180ft climbing wall; fitness centre; main hall for ball sports; smaller rooms for martial arts; dance & aerobic classes. Varsity Centre: five squash courts; nine tennis courts & netball courts; floodlit artificial turf pitch; pitches for football, rugby & cricket; archery field. It's also home to the England Squash Centre of Excellence and the National League Squash. Locally there's a leisure centre, swimming pool and athletics track. The Spectrum has an Olympic-sized ice-rink, gym, bowling, arena, pool and diving boards.

SPORTING CLUBS
Aikido; American Football; Boat; Cheerleading; Rifle; Gliding; Ju-Jitsu; Kendo; Kite Sports (Extreme Sport); Mountain Biking;

S

Words in italics are Push's point of view – take it or leave it...

Mountaineering; Ski & Snowboarding; Table tennis; Tai Jitsu; Ultimate Frisbee; Water Polo. **See also Clubs tables.**

ATTRACTIONS

The nearby Spectrum Leisure Centre's home to local ice-hockey team the Guildford Flames.

ACCOMMODATION ◡◡◡◡◡◡◡◡◡◡

IN UNIVERSITY

◉ **SELF-CATERING** 61% ◉ **COST** £75 (32/52WKS) ◉ **1ST YRS LIVING IN** 85% ◉ **INSURANCE PREMIUM** £

AVAILABILITY All first years and finalists who want to can usually live in. International students without families and partners are guaranteed places. Most rooms are *well furnished*: desk, reading-lamp, wardrobe, bookshelves. The *most popular* are at the *expensive* Twyford and University Courts. *More reasonable* rents are at Battersea and Surrey Courts right in the middle of campus. *Less desirable* is Bellerby Court, about 500m from campus or Hazel Court, about three miles away. Guildford Court is *old, small, and may be knocked down if it doesn't fall down first.* Split-level rooms are available for sharers. Some shared flat and modern en suites are available. The 'Courts' share reception buildings, where there are also TV lounge and games. Manor Park's the *new kid on the block*, and has 700 en suite, fully furnished rooms arranged in flats for 5-8 people, as well as some family accommodation. University Court, Millennium House and Manor Park are managed by Pavilion Housing Association. CCTV, security guards and panic phones around campus *keep everything as safe as the proverbial.*

CAR PARKING *Not easy.* Pay and display parking near campus. Disabled students with the right colour badges can get free permits for campus spaces.

EXTERNALLY

◉ **AVE RENT** £75

AVAILABILITY The University manages around 450 rooms off-campus. Listings are published every February. Guildford's a commuter town so *cheap housing's in short supply.* Most students live near the train station at Guildford Park or north of the University in *quieter* Bellfields. Park Barn to the west is a *bit rough but less painful on the pocket.*

HOUSING HELP Bulletin boards, landlord vetting, lots of useful leaflets and help with contracts from the Accommodation Office.

WELFARE ◡◡◡◡◡◡◡◡◡◡◡◡◡

SERVICES

◉ **LGBT OFFICER & SOCIETY** ◉ **WOMEN'S OFFICER** ◉ **ETHNIC MINORITIES OFFICER** ◉ **MATURE STUDENTS' OFFICER** ◉ **DISABILITIES OFFICER** ◉ **INTERNATIONAL STUDENTS' SOCIETY** ◉ **POSTGRAD OFFICER & SOCIETY** ◉ **NIGHTLINE** ◉ **SELF-DEFENCE CLASSES** ◉ **UNIVERSITY COUNSELLORS** 10 FULL ◉ **CRIME RATING** !

Personal tutors, counsellors and the Student Advice and Information Service *all battle it out* to lend an ear. Nightline takes up the slack 8-8 Mon, Wed, Fri and Sat.

HEALTH 24-hr sick bay and health centre staffed by a doctor and nurses.

CRECHES/NURSERY New nursery for 52 kids 3mths-5yrs for staff and students first, plus some external parents. Open all year.

CRIME Guildford's one of the safest towns in Surrey, *for what it's worth.* Drug offences off-campus have risen but there's on-campus advice for students.

DISABILITIES The University's on a hill but most areas can be accessed in a wheelchair. The Assistive Technology Centre has workstations with software for dyslexic students. Learning support sessions/tutors; technology & software (including a Braille maker and text readers); adapted accommodation; note-taking and induction loop system for deaf students; library access and special loans.

FINANCE

◉ **AVE DEBT PER YEAR** £1,620 ◉ **HOME STUDENT FEES** £3,000

FEES International undergrads pay £8-10k a year. A foundation year costs £1,200. The Professional Placement Year costs £450.

◉ **ACCESS FUND** £233,850 ◉ **SUCCESSFUL APPLICATION/YR** 715 ◉ **AVE PAYMENT** £1,000

SUPPORT Scholarships of up to £1000 for academic performance, sports, various departmental, choral and organ, as well as a whole bag of funding-related and widening participation bursaries of up to £2000.

⯈ **SURREY INSTITUTE OF ART & DESIGN**
see *Creative Arts University College*

⯈ **UNIVERSITY OF SURREY, ROEHAMPTON**
see *Roehampton University*

Words in italics are Push's point of view — take it or leave it...

SUSSEX UNIVERSITY

UNIVERSITY OF SUSSEX Sussex House, Falmer, BN1 9RH **TEL** (01273) 678 416 **E-MAIL** ug.admissions@sussex.ac.uk
WEBSITE www.sussex.ac.uk **UNIVERSITY OF SUSSEX STUDENTS' UNION** Falmer House, Falmer, BN1 9RH **TEL** (01273) 678 152
E-MAIL ussu-coms@sussex.ac.uk **WEBSITE** www.ussu.info

GENERAL ◐◐◐◐◐◐◐◐◐◐◐◐◐

Three and a half miles inland from Brighton, just before the *stunning* South Downs roll into the landscape, sprawls the 200-acre campus of Sussex University, just beside the *quiet* village of Falmer. *Swathes of gentle greenery* provide the foundation for the *thoroughly modern* Basil Spence University buildings – all arches, courtyards, concrete pillars and redbrick. *It's not ugly, although some might use the word 'interesting' through gritted teeth.* Some of the buildings were designed to look like certain objects from the air, Falmer House is a camera, the arts building is an insect – *all very well, but passing pilots probably feel like they're tripping.* The Medical School – a joint venture with the University of Brighton, which has a site nearby – is a *more attractive construction, inside and out. It's certainly close to nature, occasionally too close, as drunken students have fallen foul of (or rather 'over') the many badgers with whom they share their environment.*

SEX RATIO: ♂42 ♀58	**FOUNDED:** 1961
FULL-TIME U'GRADS: 6,976	**PART-TIME:** 451
POSTGRADS: 3,136	**NON-DEGREE:** 1,640
AVE COURSE: 3YRS	**ETHNIC:** 12%
STATE:PRIVATE SCHOOL: 85:15	**FLUNK RATE:** 11%
MATURE: 26%	**INTERNATIONAL:** 24%
DISABLED: 330	**LOCAL:** 30%

ATMOSPHERE
Sussex students are a friendly bunch with a tendency to lie back and let education and fun wash over them, but are far more proactive on politics. The bars and cafés fill up at lunchtimes and evenings – chatting is a major pastime here, along with getting riled about the ills of society. The campus quietens down at the weekend as many students go off to nearby Brighton, playground of the funky.

BRIGHTON see University of Brighton
 CITY CENTRE 3.5 MILES

TRAVEL see University of Brighton
TRAINS Falmer station is 200m away from the campus, from where frequent connections to Brighton (£2) – and therefore the rest of the country (£lots) – are possible.
CAR The A27 links Sussex with the A23. There are car parks around campus, *but not enough space for everyone.* Permits cost £300 a year or £1 a day. *The University's trying to get car-sharing going.*

LOCAL *Buses are reliable both when it comes to turning up on time and in taking convoluted routes.* Weekly passes cost £10.
TAXIS There are no cabs around campus. Catching one in Brighton to campus costs about a tenner.
BICYCLES *The University's attempts to coax people into cycling pale somewhat in comparison with the mind-numbing terror of weaving in and out of busy main roads filled with manic drivers, and the exhausting prospect of uphill pedalling.*

CAREER PROSPECTS
 CAREERS SERVICE **NO. OF STAFF** 7 FULL/16 PART
 UNEMPLOYED AFTER 6 MTHS 6%
The Careers Development & Employment Centre hosts career workshops, interview training, job fairs and employer presentations.

FAMOUS ALUMNI
Alun Anderson (editor, New Scientist); Rob Bonnet (BBC news reporter); Simon Fanshawe (broadcaster/writer); Brendan Foster (athletic commentator); Peter Hain MP (Lab); Hattie Hayridge (female Holly on 'Red Dwarf'); Billy Idol (*bleached 80s rocker*); Simon Jenkins (journalist); Thabo Mbeki (President of South Africa); Ian McEwan (writer); Bob Mortimer (Vic Reeves's *gaunt* friend); Andrew Morton (biographer/Diana interviewer); Dermot Murnaghan (BBC newsreader); Nigel Planer (Neil from 'The Young Ones'); Gail Rebuck (chief exec of Random House); Alexandra Shulman (editor, Vogue UK); Julia Somerville (journalist); Virginia Wade (last female Briton to win a Wimbledon singles title). Honorary awards: Paul McCartney (Beatle); Henry Moore (*curve-happy* sculptor); Anita Roddick (founder of Body Shop); Tom Stoppard (playwright).

FURTHER INFO
 PROSPECTUSES UNDERGRAD; POSTGRAD; SOME DEPARTMENTS; INTERNATIONAL; VIDEO
 OPEN DAYS
Open days in autumn and summer, campus tours for schools run every week.

ACADEMIC ◐◐◐◐◐◐◐◐◐◐◐◐◐

 1994 GROUP
Sussex has a range of vocational and non-vocational courses and a strong research basis. The Sussex Institute, which handles professional stuff like Law, Education and Social Care has recently expanded. *The latest stripe on its shoulder is* the new Medical School, opened in

S

partnership with the University of Brighton. The Psychology course is a *national favourite*. *Never ones to miss a chance to start the revolution*, up to 100 students organised an unofficial sit-in at the library last year over claims that the University had cut courses and teaching time.

ENTRY POINTS: 290-360	AVE POINTS: 345
APPLICATIONS PER PLACE: 7	CLEARING: 2%
NO. OF TERMS: 3	LENGTH OF TERMS: 10wks
STAFF TO STUDENT RATIO: 1:13	STUDY ADDICTS: 22%
TEACHING: **	RESEARCH: *****
YEAR ABROAD: 12%	SANDWICH STUDENTS: 1%
1STS: 13%	2.2S: 23%
2.1S: 56%	3RDS: 5%

ADMISSIONS
○ APPLY VIA UCAS
Part-timers and postgrads can apply direct.

SUBJECTS
ARTS/HUMANITIES 28%   DEVELOPMENT STUDIES 1%
SCIENCES 16%   SCIENCE & TECHNOLOGY 16%
SOCIAL SCIENCES 20%   SUSSEX INSTITUTE 17%
BEST American Studies; Economics; Education; Electrical & Electronic Engineering; French; History of Art; Linguistics; Maths & Statistics; Media Studies; Molecular Biosciences; Organismal Biosciences; Philosophy; Physics & Astronomy; Politics & International Relations; Sociology.
UNUSUAL Artificial Intelligence; Landscape Studies.

LIBRARIES
○ 786,000 BOOKS ○ 1,000 STUDY PLACES
In addition to the two libraries, there's the Geography Resource Centre, which holds over 80,000 maps. The electronic library gives access to a number of databases and online publications.

COMPUTERS
○ 550 WORKSTATIONS ○ 24-HR ACCESS
There are a few Macs and Unix systems as well as the PCs kept in all-night computer clusters around campus/in the libraries. The wireless service lets laptops connect to the network in most academic buildings.

OTHER LEARNING FACILITIES
The language labs are open to students who fancy speaking in tongues. The Media Centre's equipped with a TV studio, sound studio and digital editing suite – it isn't exclusively the domain of media students; anyone can have a go. There's also a design lab, rehearsal rooms and a drama studio.

ENTERTAINMENT ○○○○○○○○○○

BRIGHTON see University of Brighton

UNIVERSITY
○ PRICE OF A PINT OF BEER £1.90
○ GLASS OF WINE £2
○ CAN OF RED BULL £1.50
BARS The *dingy but cosy* East Slope (big screens inside, wooden patio outside) is the *most popular* of the four bars, although the Falmer bar fills up at mealtimes. The Park Village Lounge is a *good spot to cosy-up with a cocktail*, whereas the University-operated Grapevine is open daily all year, *or as good as*.
THEATRES The Gardner Arts Centre hosts student productions and touring shows, and displays art exhibitions. Sussex's drama and musical theatre societies are *far from inert*.
FILM Three films of the *mildly artsy* breed are shown every week (£2).
MUSIC VENUES Mandela Hall is the largest. Smaller bands and student musos twang away regularly in the bars. Occasional open mic stuff in Park Village bar.
CLUBBING The Hothouse (*dinky* 300 cap) churns the tunes and hosts regular nights run by various clubs and socs, or by Brighton promoters. Friday (R'n'B) and Saturday (retro cheese) are the *biggest and bestest*.
FOOD Laines Restaurant leads the way with large-scale refectory fodder. There's an assortment of café-style snack stops, including the fair trade Dhaba and the new Doctor's Orders café at the Medical School.
OTHER The Summer and Fresher's Balls are *massive* but not formal annual events. There's the Sports Federation Ball and the Clubs & Societies Oscars, where awards are dished out – *American High School Prom style*, plus smaller events like the Halloween Ball and Valentine's Party.

SOCIAL ○○○○○○○○○○○○

UNIVERSITY OF SUSSEX STUDENTS' UNION
○ 6 SABBATICALS ○ TURNOUT AT LAST BALLOT 25%
○ NUS MEMBER
USSU has a stubborn streak and some very pointy teeth when it comes to politics. Relentlessly left-wing, they're committed to greening up the University and have passed a number of eco-friendly policies. Imperialist American politics stick in SU teeth and anti-war organisations spit a lot of bile. The Vice-Chancellor has his work cut out trying to get along with them – SU passed a vote of no confidence in him for failing to retract his pro

S

top-up stance in the face of massive student opposition. But then, relations with the University have never been peachy – the Union reckons it's being charged over the odds for rent on Falmer House and isn't afraid to say so.

SU FACILITIES
Across campus: four bars; nightclub; cafeteria; four coffee bars; pool tables; meeting rooms; three minibuses for hire; Endsleigh Insurance office; Barclays and HSBC banks with ATMs; photocopiers; fax and printing services; payphones; photo booth; advice centre; general and stationery stores; post office; travel agency; bookshop; gaming and vending machines; launderette.

CLUBS (NON-SPORTING)
Baha'i; Ballet; Breaking & Streetdance; Buddhist Meditation; Chamber Choir; Chess; Chinese; Circus; Cuban Arts Aid; Dirty Weekenders (conservation); Fair Trade; Friends of Palestine; Japanese; Model United Nations; Open Mic; Poker; Shisha Pipe; War & Roleplay; Wine; Writers. **See also Clubs tables.**

OTHER ORGANISATIONS
'The Badger' is the weekly SU newspaper, backed up by the termly mag 'Pulse'. The *super-active* 'URF' (University Radio Falmer) broadcasts daily around campus plus online with an intermittent FM licence. The charity Rag gets up to the usual *silly things* for money: pubcrawls; slave auctions; blind dates. Project V aims to get the locals and the students working together on community projects.

RELIGION
6 CHAPLAINS (COFE, RC, METHODIST, BAPTIST, EVANGELICAL), RABBI
An Interdenominational Meeting House holds the Chaplaincy and quiet rooms. There's a Muslim Student Centre and Baha'i faith group operating on campus. Religion in Brighton see University of Brighton.

PAID WORK see University of Brighton
JOB BUREAU ● PAID WORK TERM-TIME 40%; HOLS 70%
The Careers Service dredges through the local employment scene and points students in the direction of part-time or vacation work.

SPORTS ○○○○○○○○○○○○○○

BUSA RANKING 48
Despite the top-notch facilities and the range of classes on offer (yoga, dance, martial arts and so on), sport doesn't change lives at Sussex. There are some bursaries available for talented sports people but the focus is on the social rather than the competitive. The victory table pepped up when the University slung the Union an extra £30,000 towards coaching, but Sussex is used to losing out to local (and sports student-infused) rivals Brighton.

SPORTS FACILITIES
The University owns two sports centres. The Falmer Sports Complex contains: two-floor fitness suite with Sky TV; three squash and six tennis courts; floodlit artificial pitch; cricket nets; playing fields; café bar. Sportcentre has: two sports halls; four squash courts; dance and martial arts studio; Lifestyles studio; solarium; sports shop. £18.50 gets annual membership but then there are some *sneaky* sessional charges on top of that (eg. £1.40 for a squash court).

SPORTING CLUBS
Aikido; Cheerleaders; Surfing; Kickboxing; Shaolin Kung Fu; Ultimate Frisbee. **See also Clubs tables.**

ATTRACTIONS see University of Brighton

ACCOMMODATION ○○○○○○○○○○

IN UNIVERSITY
SELF-CATERING 38% ● **COST** £64 (39/48WKS)
INSURANCE PREMIUM £
AVAILABILITY A recent surge in student numbers meant that about 200 first years were housed with host families last year, but there should be accommodation for all newbies by 2007, thanks in part to some new privately-owned, university-run and *non-too-cheap* halls springing up. Sussex's no issues about giving local students rooms – *no one should be forced to live with parents any longer than they have to.* Accommodation comprises self-catering halls and self-contained flats, mostly on campus with about one in ten in Brighton, with a scattering of students in head tenancy schemes nearby. *Quality kitchens are divided between 5-12 students and there are a few en suite rooms.* Some rooms are shared. Several flats are available to families and married couples (both must be studying at Sussex). Single sex housing comes in female and female Muslim-only. *Most halls are of decent-ish standards, the glaring exception East Slope attempting gradual structural suicide.*
CAR PARKING Students resident on campus aren't allowed cars except for some disabled students and residential advisors (the guys who live on site and look after new students).

EXTERNALLY see University of Brighton
AVE RENT £70
AVAILABILITY *The house hunt is as easy as shooting fish in a barrel. From a great distance. With a bent peashooter.* Most students find something a mile or two away.
HOUSING HELP The University Housing Office – *more a man with a pile of classifieds* – runs workshops in how to find a house, produces vacancy lists and manages an online database. The Union gives advice and produces a booklet.

S

WELFARE ()()()()()()()()()()()()()()

SERVICES

- ○ LGBT OFFICER & SOCIETY
- ○ WOMEN'S OFFICER & SOCIETY
- ○ ETHNIC MINORITIES OFFICER & SOCIETY
- ○ MATURE STUDENTS' OFFICER & SOCIETY
- ○ DISABILITIES OFFICER & SOCIETY
- ○ INTERNATIONAL STUDENTS' OFFICER & SOCIETY
- ○ POSTGRAD OFFICER & SOCIETY
- ○ UNIVERSITY COUNSELLORS 9 PART
- ○ SU COUNSELLORS 3 FULL
- ○ CRIME RATING: !!!

There's a welfare sabbatical and a *huge* number of part-time support group exec officers. USSU runs a daily drop-in centre at Falmer House where students can unload their troubles. Unisex is a *heavily-staffed* office (in conjunction with the University of Brighton) doling out *nookie-related* advice, cheap pregnancy tests and condoms and screening for *itchy downstairs diseases.*

HEALTH The NHS runs the University Health Service with four GPs, nurses, dentist and chemist.
CRECHES/NURSERY 44 places available for children from 4mths and up.
DISABILITIES *Wheelchair access is okay, though there are lots of slopes on campus and some difficult buildings.* There are specialist units for dyslexia and mental health, and adapted accommodation is reserved for students with mobility difficulties. Ramps and hearing loops are abundant.

FINANCE

- ○ AVE DEBT PER YEAR £3,914 ○ HOME STUDENT FEES £3,000

FEES *Not even the SU's wrath could stop* fees from being topped up to the max. International students pay £8,850-£11,800.
SUPPORT *Plenty to chew on.* An annual £1,000 to students with family incomes of less than £17,500, plus a further 200 payments for those with family incomes of less than £24,000. Several £1,000 scholarships for those with top exam results, plus sports bursaries.

SWANSEA UNIVERSITY

PART OF THE UNIVERSITY OF WALES

○ **SWANSEA UNIVERSITY** Swansea, Singleton Park, Swansea, SA2 8PP **TEL** (01792) 205 678 **E-MAIL** admissions@swansea.ac.uk
WEBSITE www.swansea.ac.uk ○ **SWANSEA STUDENTS' UNION** Singleton Park, Swansea, SA2 8PP **TEL** (01792) 295 466
E-MAIL generaloffice@swansea-union.co.uk **WEBSITE** www.swansea-union.co.uk

GENERAL ()()()()()()()()()()()()()()

Swansea sits on the arm of the Gower Peninsula, *a landscape artist's wet dream,* covered in beaches, forests and general green bits on the south coast of Wales. The peninsula was the first place in Britain to be officially designated an Area of Outstanding Natural Beauty. About two miles out of town, past the cricket ground, following the coast road, is the campus of Swansea University. Made of rolling mini-hills, red-brick and concrete, the University has the beach on its doorstep and parkland around it. The *little* city of Swansea itself is in turn *modern, attractive, run-down and comedically nondescript,* depending on where wandering feet lead. Applications increased by 10% last year, *something of which most universities (particularly those wading into top-up fee territory) could only dream.*

SEX RATIO

SEX RATIO: ♂42 ♀58	**FOUNDED:** 1920
FULL-TIME U'GRADS: 8,074	**PART-TIME:** 515
POSTGRADS: 1,601	**NON-DEGREE:** 851
AVE COURSE: 3YRS	**ETHNIC:** 8%
STATE:PRIVATE SCHOOL: 93:7	**FLUNK RATE:** 10%
MATURE: 17%	**INTERNATIONAL:** 8%
DISABLED: 220	**LOCAL:** 26%

ATMOSPHERE

Laid-back and pleasant, Swansea students enjoy taking in the view – the effects of the vast stretch of beach just outside eventually rub off on them. With the Gower having some of the best surf in Britain, the University has its fair share of board-loving types swanning around too. Students have a good life and get on well with local residents. The work ethic is quietly studious.

SWANSEA

- ○ **POPULATION** 223,200 ○ **CITY CENTRE** 2.5 MILES
- ○ **LONDON** 160 MILES ○ **CARDIFF** 40 MILES
- ○ **BRISTOL** 60 MILES
- ○ **HIGH TEMP** 20 ○ **LOW TEMP** 2 ○ **RAINFALL** 105

Dylan Thomas described Swansea as 'the graveyard of ambition' because once discovered, no one wants to leave (Dylan, of course, left). *Perhaps more accurately,* he also called it his 'ugly, lovely town'. It's a *strange mix of beauty and grime,* gleaming pubs and streets half boarded up. In the summer, the surrounding countryside and beaches are *extraordinarily* scenic and the town becomes a pit stop for tourists. *Most locals are cheerful and always willing to have a chat (or, more likely, an epic conversation); one or two aren't.* While small, Swansea has most amenities, high street shops and banks, as well as the opportunity to try lavabread (*like fishy spinach made from seaweed*).

TRAVEL

TRAINS Direct trains from Swansea station, three miles from campus, to Cardiff (£9.85) and London (£38.95); book at least a week early to avoid the price doubling.

COACHES Services to London (£30), Cardiff (£7.50), Manchester (£30). Again, book early.

CAR A465, A48 and five miles off the M4. Parking is limited in residential areas around the campus, but there are a couple of car parks five mins amble from Singleton.

AIR Nearest *useful* airport is Cardiff.

LOCAL Frequent public services pootle between University sites and the city centre.

TAXIS Free phone on campus for students with flammable cash. *Not as expensive as in some towns.*

BICYCLES Bikes are *perfect* between campus and town and the *ecologically-minded University is a real pedal pusher.* The local hills and scenery are *gorgeous* in the right weather and *full of bikeable* trails.

CAREER PROSPECTS

⊙ **CAREERS SERVICE** ⊙ **NO. OF STAFF** 25 FULL/6 PART
⊙ **UNEMPLOYED AFTER 6** MTHS 6%

A well-organised and friendly job shop. They do interview training, jobs fairs, workshops, lectures and job placements and have an extensive range of online services.

FAMOUS ALUMNI

Lord Anderson (Labour peer); Ian Bone (founder of Class War); Daniel Caines (Olympic runner); Andrew Davies AM (Welsh Assembly Government Minister); Richey Edwards, Nicky Wire (Manic Street Preachers); Nigel Evans MP (Con); Dr Hwyel Francis MP (Lab); Steve James, Adrian Dale (England cricketers); Jason Mohammed, Mavis Nicolson (TV presenters); Prof. Colin Pillinger (space *boffin*); Paul Thorburn, Robert Howley, Adedayo Adebayo, Dafydd James, Dwayne Peel, Richie Pugh (rugby players); Two Hats (Goldie Lookin' Chain); Julia Wheeler (BBC Gulf correspondent); Alan Williams MP (Lab).

SPECIAL FEATURES

Campus includes the Egypt Centre, containing a *considerable* collection of artefacts and curios. The University is already home to the Multidisciplinary Nanotechnology Centre *(a big name for the study of very little things)* and is currently developing the £50m Institute of Life Science, which will include a 'visualisation centre' that could be good news for healthcare and medical innovations.

FURTHER INFO

⊙ **PROSPECTUSES** UNDERGRAD; POSTGRAD; ALL DEPARTMENTS; INTERNATIONAL; VIDEO
⊙ **OPEN DAYS**

ACADEMIC ⦿⦿⦿⦿⦿⦿⦿⦿⦿⦿⦿⦿⦿

All subjects are modular and some modules are more optional than others. Students can submit exams or projects in Welsh. *Engineering, the Clinical School, Sports Science and Arts & Humanities are considered pretty perky.* Vocational courses (eg. Nursing and Social Work) involve plenty of practicals. Most undergrads are expected to do a dissertation in their final year and continuous assessments and presentations are increasingly common. The virtual campus (Blackboard) is making its presence felt, particularly in the Department of Adult Continuing Education, where it is often the main method of teaching. Swansea's big on skill development and English language teaching and study skill support are there *for those that want 'em.*

ENTRY POINTS: 240-360	AVE POINTS: 304
APPLICATIONS PER PLACE: 5	CLEARING: 12%
NO. OF TERMS: 3	LENGTH OF TERMS: 7/10/12wks
STAFF TO STUDENT RATIO: 1:13	STUDY ADDICTS: N/A
TEACHING: ★★★★★	RESEARCH: ★★★
YEAR ABROAD: 1%	SANDWICH STUDENTS: 1%
1STS: 9%	2.2s: 39%
2.1s: 44%	3RDS: 8%

ADMISSIONS

⊙ **APPLY VIA UCAS/DIRECT FOR POSTGRADS AND INTERNATIONAL APPLICANTS**

Mature applications are encouraged, even where standard qualifications aren't in hand, the same goes for international mature students. There are links with local colleges and those on access courses also get a look-in.

SUBJECTS

ARTS, LANGUAGES & SOCIAL STUDIES 36%
BUSINESS STUDIES, ECONOMICS & LAW 16%
ENGINEERING 9%   **MEDICAL SCIENCES** 18%   **SCIENCES** 21%
BEST Biology & Related Sciences; Business; Civil, Chemical & Other Engineering; Computer Science; Economics; English-based Studies; European Languages & Area Studies; History & Archaeology; Human & Social Geography; Law; Management; Mechanically-based Engineering; Media Studies; Physical Geography & Environmental Science; Physical Science; Politics; Psychology; Sociology, Social Studies & Anthropology; Sports Science.
UNUSUAL Egyptology.

LIBRARIES

⊙ **820,000** BOOKS ⊙ **1,298** STUDY PLACES
⊙ **SPEND PER STUDENT** £££

Swansea did have four different libraries, but from 2006 they're being condensed into one.

COMPUTERS

⊙ **1,855** WORKSTATIONS ⊙ **SPEND PER STUDENT** £££

There are five students to every computer, *which is good as long as they don't all use it at once. A*

S

Words in italics are Push's point of view — take it or leave it...

cross-campus wireless network reaches its cyber tentacles as far as student bedrooms, giving broadband net access to anyone with a clever enough laptop.

OTHER LEARNING FACILITIES

Language laboratory; rehearsal rooms; CAD lab; media centre; drama studio; practice court room.

ENTERTAINMENT ◑◑◑◑◑◑◑◑◑

THE CITY
- **PRICE OF A PINT OF BEER** £1.95
- **GLASS OF WINE** £1.20
- **CAN OF RED BULL** £1.80

Swansea's *best* for liquid entertainment, being *full* of pubs and clubs. The Kingsway, where most of the clubs hide, teems with revellers at the weekend. The Mumbles Mile, a pub crawl along the seafront, is known as far away as America *(perhaps where someone woke up after trying it)*.

CINEMAS Ten-screen multiplex for mainstream films and the Dylan Thomas arts centre for *films in need of York Notes.*

THEATRES The Grand theatre is *popular and successful, but tends to excel more at panto than Pinter.*

PUBS Mumbles, the Uplands and Wine Street are *popular* for sheer variety and quality of pub. Some pubs on the outskirts should be approached with caution. *Pushplugs: Ice Bar; Rhydding's; Walkabout.*

CLUBBING Swansea boasts some *fine* clubs; people come from miles around to visit *(because there's very little elsewhere). Pushplugs: Escape (top DJs and indie hangout at weekends); Time (broke the largest student night record when 3,000 freshers turned up); Jumpin' Jacks.*

MUSIC VENUES Dozens of pubs are hosts to live music, especially in the Uplands area.

EATING OUT *The range, quality and price of Indian restaurants, especially on St Helen's Road, beggars rational belief.* Night nibbles are available till at least 2am and deliveries till midnight, but only till 10pm in the Mumbles. *Pushplugs: Café Mambo (Mexican); Mozart's (Austrian); Viceroy (Indian); Slow Boat (Chinese); Angellettos (Italian).*

UNIVERSITY
- **PRICE OF A PINT OF BEER** £1.40
- **GLASS OF WINE** £1.20

The Taliesin Arts Centre is the crown of the campus with a host of entertainment facilities (from exhibitions to film and music) and *makes up for the city's musical and arty limitations.* In October it's the focus of the Swansea Fringe Festival (the second biggest in Britain after Edinburgh).

BARS JC's (cap 400) *is the new toy.* Diva's (cap 450) and Idols (400) are the main bars, putting on a bunch of different nights throughout the year. The Taliesin also has a bar.

THEATRES Swansea students love their drama and like to put on a production or twelve in the Taliesin's theatre (cap 350) when the major touring companies aren't using it.

FILM The film society shows two or three a week, usually arthouse or foreign. There's also a gay film season. The Taliesin shows a bit of everything.

MUSIC VENUES When a big band's in Swansea, *it's probably lost, but if it's meant to be there,* it'll be in The Refectory (cap 800). Recently it's seen the likes of Snow Patrol and 22-20s. Brangwyn Hall sometimes gets a look-in too.

CLUBBING Swansea student craziness revolves around Diva's, more stuff's in town and the SU have been known to hire out popular clubs for the night.

FOOD *The Refectory is cheap and has a nice selection, including fodder for the veggie trough. Diva's looks like a chippie with delusions of grandeur.* There's also the free internet café Impressions, Le Café, Café West and Coffee Culture *(they're keen on coffee, y'see). Raging carnivores enjoy the bloody pleasures of the Bayview Carvery at lunchtimes.*

OTHER Lots of balls. The grand finale is the summer ball *with thumping bass that keeps grannies awake for miles around.* Goldie Lookin' Chain and Kosheen featured at the '05 bash.

SOCIAL ◑◑◑◑◑◑◑◑◑◑◑◑

SWANSEA STUDENTS' UNION
- **6 SABBATICALS** **TURNOUT AT LAST BALLOT** 12%
- **NUS MEMBER**

As a rule, the student body doesn't let politics interfere with their lack of politics, but they do care about the issues that influence them (fees, racism etc.). The college administration are regularly accosted by the SU for various discussions in the name of Swansea students, but facilities are *adequate enough to discourage the laidback learners from kicking up much of a fuss.*

SU FACILITIES

Three bars; canteen; two fast food outlets; advice centre; crèche; printing; stationers; travel agent; media centre; insurance shop; pool tables; laundry; video and vending machines; phones; ATMs; photo booth. Hendrefoilan Student Village has: a general shop; bar; licensed diner; vending machines; laundry; payphones.

CLUBS (NON-SPORTING)

Alternative Music; Amnesty International; Art; Asian Society; Baha'I; Buddhist Meditation; Catholic; Capoeira; Cheerleaders; Chinese; Chemistry; Choral; Club 52% (women); Club Kontiki; Computing; Conservative; Conservation; Crazy Society; Dance; Drama; Drinking Wine; Duke of Edinburgh; Economics; Engineering;

EWB-Swansea; Film; French; Friends of CU; Geography; German; Go Swansea; Gym-Gym (Welsh); HEAL; History; Hong Kong; Indian; International Development; Irish; Islamic; Italian; Labour; LAN Cymru; Law; Live Music; Malaysian; Mature; Media; Medsin-Swansea; Multi-Cultural Society; Musicians; No Cuts, No Closures; Off Campus; Pagan; Physics; Plaid Cymru; Psychology; Real Ale; Refugees; Respect; Royal Naval Unit; St John Ambulance LINKS; Scouts and Guides; Socialist Workers; Spanish; Students Agains War; SUMA (anime); Tactical Airsofting; Undercurrents; Visual Art; White Wolf; Xtreme; Yoga. **See also Clubs tables.**

OTHER ORGANISATIONS

'Waterfront' is the rather *good* newspaper, 'Xtreme 963' is the rather *loud* radio station and Discovery is the rather *large* community dooda that's been running projects for the needy for more than 40 years. RAG pulls in the pennies for good causes.

RELIGION

○ **3 CHAPLAINS (COFE, RC, URC); RABBI**
Campus has a chapel and a mosque and Swansea is well stocked for places of worship.

PAID WORK

○ **JOB BUREAU** ○ **PAID WORK** TERM-TIME 60%; HOLS 85%
Worklink's services include: duty careers advice sessions; specialist follow-up sessions; CV and application workshops; skills workshops; psychometric testing workshops; employer talks programme; careers fair; six dedicated jobs and placements advisors. Swansea is part of the GO Wales programme so summer jobs in tourism *are not hard to come by. In addition to SU and University opportunities on campus, several employers in the vicinity are sensitive to student situations and offer flexible hours.*

SPORTS ◡◡◡◡◡◡◡◡◡◡◡◡◡◡

○ **BUSA RANKING** 45
No shortage of facilities, and the healthy sea air has furnished students with success on a national level in the past and given them something to do when not studying.

SPORTS FACILITIES

Swansea's *impressive* collection of facilities include: the Swansea Sports Village, consisting of an athletics track, two all-weather pitches and an indoor training centre. There's: 32 acres of playing fields for football, rugby, cricket and hockey; six tennis, one netball, six squash and two basketball courts; swimming pool; indoor and outdoor running tracks; climbing wall; martial arts dojos; golf course; sports hall; river; lake; gym; multigym; athletics field; and, *when all that sport gets too strenuous,* a physiotherapy room. Gym visits cost £2 a time; everything else is £1.

Students can also purchase passes (term's gym use: £50, Annual: £140, Annual Activity Pass: £65 plus 50p court booking fee).

SPORTING CLUBS

Aikido; Bodyboarding; Caving; Go-karting; Harriers; Ju-Jitsu; Lacrosse; Lifesaving; Mountaineering; Mountain Biking; Rowing; Running; Surfing; Ultimate Frisbee; Windsurfing. **See also Clubs tables.**

ATTRACTIONS

Swansea's got the sea, with all its sailing, surfing and other such soggy stuff, a dry-ski slope, a swanky new footy stadium to watch the Swans' *latest defeat* and St Helens to watch the rugby. Wales National Pool is a *bit snazzy* – a 50m pool in an £11m complex, and they're tacking on bits to the outside like the floodlit athletics track. It's a joint University and City/County councils initiative.

ACCOMMODATION ◡◡◡◡◡◡◡◡◡

IN UNIVERSITY

○ **CATERED** 7% ○ **COST** £79 (32WKS)
○ **SELF-CATERING** 25% ○ **COST** £57 (40/41/51WKS)
○ **1ST YRS LIVING IN** 98% ○ **INSURANCE PREMIUM** £
AVAILABILITY Almost all first years get accommodation, as do a handful of others; *only local clearing students are unlucky.* The 600 catered students get a *measly* seven meals (brekkies) a week. The self-contained student village in Hendrefoilan is a *little gem,* quite far from campus but featuring a cute cluster of purpose-built housing (with shop). 1,600 students pay £55 a week to call it home. En suite self-catering rooms (in a different hall) are £19 a week dearer. A handful of rooms are shared and some rooms and flats are available to couples and families. There are also about 150 spaces in University-managed houses. Phones in all rooms.
CAR PARKING There's no student parking on campus but permits are issued free to those wishing to stow the motor at Hendrefoilan.

EXTERNALLY

○ **AVE RENT** £48
AVAILABILITY *Swansea is student-friendly and there's little difficulty finding a relatively nice house in a relatively good area. Good places include Brynmill, Uplands and Sketty. Bad places include Townhill and Bonymaen.*
HOUSING HELP Accommodation Office offers sharing lists, advice leaflets, general advice and a bulletin board. The SU provides its own handbook to help avoid unscrupulous landlords and a local accreditation scheme allows trustworthy landlords to advertise at slightly higher rates.

S

WELFARE ⦾⦾⦾⦾⦾⦾⦾⦾⦾⦾⦾⦾⦾

SERVICES
- ◎ LGBT OFFICER & SOCIETY
- ◎ ETHNIC MINORITIES OFFICER & SOCIETY
- ◎ WOMEN'S OFFICER & SOCIETY
- ◎ INTERNATIONAL STUDENTS' OFFICER & SOCIETY
- ◎ MATURE STUDENTS' OFFICER & SOCIETY
- ◎ POSTGRAD OFFICER & SOCIETY
- ◎ DISABILITIES OFFICER & SOCIETY ◎ NIGHTLINE
- ◎ UNIVERSITY COUNSELLORS 2 FULL/5 PART
- ◎ CRIME RATING: !!

There's a central Student Support Services Department and an on-campus police officer. Extra counsellors are called in *at times of high trauma.*

HEALTH The University runs a health centre with Mental Health Co-ordinator and counselling services. The NHS practice on campus has four GPs, two nurses and a dentist.

WOMEN Free attack alarms and advice are offered to women – *who should avoid Singleton Park behind the University at night if they don't like being flashed at.*

CRECHES/NURSERY 32 places for munchkins aged 3mths-7yrs.

DISABILITIES *The Welsh hills make for difficult times for wheelchair users, though most buildings have access.* There are tactile pathways and a centre for blind students as well as weekly classes by a dyslexia tutor. The Disability Office provides note-takers and co-ordinates a Voluntary Support Worker Scheme that offers non-medical human support. Its Assessment and Training Centre offers academic support, including alternative examination provisions, IT training and equipment loan. Several adapted rooms are available.

FINANCE
- ◎ AVE DEBT PER YEAR £3,715 ◎ HOME STUDENT FEES £1,200

FEES Fees will be topped up to £3,000 from 2007, though Welsh students will get extra handouts to cover the difference. International students pay £8,420-£10,700.
- ◎ ACCESS FUND £550,000 ◎ SUCCESSFUL APPLICATION/YR 1,280
- ◎ AVE PAYMENT £100-3,500

SUPPORT Department scholarships are worth £400-£1,100 to *cleverclogs and paupers.* Ten sports scholarships of £1,000 a year. There's also an EU and overseas hardship fund and a cashpot for international students with disabilities.

SWANSEA INSTITUTE OF HIGHER EDUCATION (SIHE)

PART OF THE UNIVERSITY OF WALES

1. ◎ **SWANSEA INSTITUTE OF HIGHER EDUCATION** Mount Pleasant, Swansea, SA1 6ED **TEL** (01792) 481 000
E-MAIL enquiry@sihe.ac.uk **WEBSITE** www.sihe.ac.uk
2. ◎ **TOWNHILL CAMPUS** Townhill Road, Townhill, Swansea, SA2 0UT

GENERAL ⦾⦾⦾⦾⦾⦾⦾⦾⦾⦾⦾⦾⦾

Swansea Institute was welcomed into the University of Wales's fold in 2004, *which makes it sound as deceptively young as a freshly face-lifted Joan Collins.* The *newly-crowned* University College has actually been *knocking around* for 150 years in various forms, rising from a melting pot of technology, art and teacher training colleges to receive independent HE status in 1992. It's split over several sites, the biggest being the main Mount Pleasant campus in the city centre.

SEX RATIO: ♂56 ♀44	FOUNDED: 1976
FULL-TIME U'GRADS: 2,812	PART-TIME: 1,591
POSTGRADS: 665	NON-DEGREE: N/A
AVE COURSE: 3YRS	ETHNIC: N/A
STATE:PRIVATE SCHOOL: N/A	FLUNK RATE: 20%
MATURE: N/A	INTERNATIONAL: 7%
DISABLED: 55	LOCAL: 66%

> ◉ **Swansea University's degree in surfing was axed because people couldn't stop taking the mickey out of it.**

ATMOSPHERE
Not unlike a conker, a beautiful interior awaits those who dare venture within the less appealing shell of the Institute's buildings. Students tend to stick to their own haunts rather than getting down and dirty with the locals. The drabness of the campus means the atmosphere could be accused of bordering on the bleak, although the lively little city of Swansea and the kind of natural beauty that sends poets into delirium is never far away.

SITES
TOWNHILL (Humanities, Education) Two miles away from the main site, the campus has a canteen, sports hall, multigym and the Institute's only bar, as well as *academic bricks and mortar.* It's currently undergoing a £3m facelift.
DYNEVOR (Art & Design) The newest campus opened its doors in 2005.

SWANSEA see University of Swansea
○ CITY CENTRE 0.25 MILES

TRAVEL see University of Swansea
Good news for the walk-shy – the Institute is much closer to the city centre than Swansea University and the train station is a five minute stroll away.
BUS *Lots*, including the no. 81 First Cymru service, which *shoots* between the campuses and costs £1.35 from the furthest campus to the city centre.
CAR The A483 and M4 are the nearest arteries. There's a reasonable amount of parking locally, but nowt on the main campus and *not enough* on the Townhill campus.
TAXIS £4-5 to get into town from the furthest campus.
BICYCLES Bike racks and showers for sweaty cyclists, *but the hills put off all but the keenest of trouser-clippers.*

CAREER PROSPECTS
○ CAREERS SERVICE ○ UNEMPLOYED AFTER 6 MTHS N/A
The Careers Advisory Service offers *the standard CV-building services* – careers library; job fairs; interview training; newsletters; bulletin boards.

FAMOUS ALUMNI
Robert Croft (Cricketer); David Pickering (Chairman of the WRU and former rugby international); Richard Webster (Cardiff Blues coach and former rugby international).

FURTHER INFO
○ PROSPECTUSES UNDERGRAD; POSTGRAD; SOME DEPTS
○ OPEN DAYS

ACADEMIC ○○○○○○○○○○○○○

There are three faculties – Applied Design & Engineering, Humanities and Art & Design – divided into ten schools. Each faculty *keeps on its toes* with strong links with industry, giving students opportunities for work experience and career prospect *healthiness.* Students take six modules a year, choosing from more than 40 in the first year and an increasingly specialised pool in further years. The year is divided into three 11-week terms.

ENTRY POINTS: 120–240	**AVE POINTS:** N/A
APPLICATIONS PER PLACE: N/A	**CLEARING:** N/A
NO. OF TERMS: 3	**LENGTH OF TERMS:** 11WKS
STAFF TO STUDENT RATIO: 1:3	**STUDY ADDICTS:** N/A
TEACHING: **✶✶	**RESEARCH:** N/A
YEAR ABROAD: N/A	**SANDWICH STUDENTS:** N/A

ADMISSIONS
○ APPLY VIA UCAS/DIRECT/GTTR FOR TEACHER TRAINING
Mature applications are encouraged, even where standard qualifications aren't in hand, the same goes for international mature students. There are links with local colleges and those on access courses also get a look-in.

SUBJECTS
BEST Art & Design; Business.

LIBRARIES
○ 180,000 BOOKS
A trio of libraries. Owen Library (Mount Pleasant campus) is the main bookstash. The library at Dyvenor is open from 9am-7.30pm while those at Mount Pleasant and Townhill let learners linger until 9pm.

COMPUTERS
Open access computers *hum* on each campus and student accommodation has internet points.

OTHER LEARNING FACILITIES
Drama studio/theatre; music rehearsal rooms; CAD lab; media centre.

ENTERTAINMENT ○○○○○○○○○

THE CITY see University of Swansea

UNIVERSITY
○ PRICE OF A PINT OF BEER £1.60
○ GLASS OF WINE £1.20
○ CAN OF RED BULL £1.30
BARS The Islwyn Bar (Townhill) is open evenings and weekday lunchtimes. There's a quiz on Sundays and the *vocal drunken humiliation* of karaoke on Tuesdays.

THEATRES Townhill Theatre provides a stage for student and professional thesps. Drama's *popular*, although there's no official society.

FOOD Two refectories, one at Townhill, churn out hot meals, sandwiches and jacket potatoes during the daytime. The student centre does fast, *fattening* food including a burger meal for £3.50 and there's a patisserie area (sarnies, chocs and pastries).

OTHER There's an active ball in March and a summer ball, plus other bits and bobs including a visiting comedy-hypnotist *(apparently there is such a thing).*

SOCIAL ◖◖◖◖◖◖◖◖◖◖◖◖◖◖

SWANSEA INSTITUTE STUDENTS' UNION
○ **3** SABBATICALS ○ **TURNOUT AT LAST BALLOT** 7%
○ **NUS MEMBER**

Sharing a building and a toasty working relationship, the Union and University get on like Dick & Dom, though (hopefully) without the sexual tension. There's some student representation at all levels and the Union lobbies for better facilities.

SU FACILITIES
Bar; three canteens/cafés; minibus for hire; four pool/snooker tables; meeting room; ATM (Moneybox); photocopier; fax; printing service; payphones; advice centre; jukebox; video/gaming machines; general store; stationery shop; vending machines; launderette.

CLUBS (NON-SPORTING)
See Clubs tables.

OTHER ORGANISATIONS
There's an *embryonic* RAG. That's about it.

RELIGION see University of Swansea

PAID WORK
○ **JOB BUREAU**
There's a GO Wales jobshop. For work prospects in Swansea see University of Swansea

SPORTS ◖◖◖◖◖◖◖◖◖◖◖◖◖◖

○ **BUSA RANKING** 119

SPORTS FACILITIES
There's a sports hall and a multigym at the University. *The rest is left to the town and the great outdoors.* For facilities in the local area see University of Swansea

SPORTING CLUBS
See Clubs tables.

ATTRACTIONS see University of Swansea

ACCOMMODATION ◖◖◖◖◖◖◖◖◖

IN UNIVERSITY
○ **SELF-CATERING** 11% ○ **COST** £44
○ **INSURANCE PREMIUM** £
AVAILABILITY There are 302 self-catering places, which leaves 18% of *room-hungry* first years to fend for themselves. All accommodation is mixed and there's some for couples. Other students shouldn't have to share. There's a launderette and a 24-hr porter to *keep things clean and safe.*
CAR PARKING A *small* car park, *too small.* A permit costs a *winceable* £200 a year.

EXTERNALLY see University of Swansea
○ **AVE RENT** £40
HOUSING HELP The Residential Services Officer gives accommodation advice and has a bulletin board, approved landlord list and vacancy list *for those that ask nicely.*

WELFARE ◖◖◖◖◖◖◖◖◖◖◖◖◖◖

SERVICES
○ **LGBT SOCIETY** ○ **WOMEN'S OFFICER & SOCIETY**
○ **MATURE STUDENTS' OFFICER**
○ **INTERNATIONAL STUDENTS' OFFICER**
○ **DISABILITIES OFFICER & SOCIETY**
○ **UNIVERSITY COUNSELLORS** 2 FULL
○ **CRIME RATING:** !!

There's a University welfare service and the SU is on hand to wipe those teary eyes.
DISABILITIES Access can be *tricky*, with split sites, old buildings and, *perhaps worst of all, the ruddy great hills everywhere.* Still, the University has some special accommodation, ramps, lifts and hearing loops, plus support workers and dyslexia help.
DRUGS *There's a small problem with the use of cannabis on site, apparently, though whether the potheads themselves would call it a problem is another matter.*

FINANCE
○ **AVE DEBT PER YEAR** £3,097 ○ **HOME STUDENT FEES** £1,200

UNIVERSITY OF TEESSIDE

▶ TEESSIDE POLYTECHNIC
see *University of Teesside*

▶ THAMES COLLEGE OF HEALTHCARE STUDIES
see *Greenwich University*

▶ THAMES POLYTECHNIC
see *Greenwich University*

THAMES VALLEY UNIVERSITY

▶ TRENT UNIVERSITY
see *Nottingham Trent University*

TRINITY COLLEGE, CARMARTHEN

T

UNIVERSITY OF TEESSIDE

FORMERLY TEESSIDE POLYTECHNIC

○ **UNIVERSITY OF TEESSIDE** Middlesbrough, Tees Valley, TS1 3BA **TEL** (01642) 218 121 **E-MAIL** recruit@tees.ac.uk
WEBSITE www.tees.ac.uk ○ **UNIVERSITY OF TEESSIDE STUDENTS' UNION** Middlesbrough, TS1 3BA **TEL** (01642) 342 234
E-MAIL enquiry@utsu.org.uk **WEBSITE** www.utsu.org.uk

GENERAL ○○○○○○○○○○○○○

Middlesbrough is a *crouton in the sprawling industrialised urban soup* that used to go by the name of Cleveland. More than a million Teessiders (that's local folk, not students) are squeezed into Middlesbrough, Stockton, Redcar and Hartlepool. There's been *broad* regeneration in recent years and the University *is part and educational parcel* of it all. There's also a *mammoth* new shopping centre and a leisure complex and a brand new modern art gallery. *And should the urban existence start to jar, the Swampy centre (more properly known as Nature's World) is on hand to provide mud, grass and all other things rural. Except Foot and Mouth disease.*

SEX RATIO: ♀41 ♂59	**FOUNDED:** 1992
FULL-TIME U'GRADS: 6,702	**PART-TIME:** 1,256
POSTGRADS: 2,341	**NON-DEGREE:** 10,386
AVE COURSE: 3YRS	**ETHNIC:** 9%
STATE:PRIVATE SCHOOL: 98:2	**FLUNK RATE:** 9%
MATURE: 35%	**INTERNATIONAL:** 19%
DISABLED: 190	**LOCAL:** 47%

ATMOSPHERE
Like one of Big Daddy's skimpier leotards, the Teesside campus is straining at the seams, with loads of modern facilities and a welcoming, friendly body of students that draws heavily from the local population. It's a clean, green kind of campus and the most recent buildings really are impressive. Let's hope the forthcoming £11m Institute of digital Media and the £7m Centre for Creative Technologies add to the architectural eye-candy.

MIDDLESBROUGH
○ **POPULATION** 134,800 ○ **CITY CENTRE** 500M
○ **LONDON** 256 MILES ○ **YORK** 49 MILES
○ **NEWCASTLE** 39 MILES
○ **HIGH TEMP** 19 ○ **LOW TEMP** 0 ○ **RAINFALL** 51
Middlesbrough's not a *million miles away from the Corrie end credits – military lines of Victorian terraces and plenty of hills (although the days of bluff northern chaps doffing their flat caps are long past).* Many of the older manufacturing industries are just shadows of former glories. There's a *rich seam of shops to be mined,* including bookshops and four massive shopping centres. *In the fine tradition of the trendification of northern cities (see also: Newcastle, Liverpool),*

Middlesbrough's docks are set for a good spit and polish with £500m of investment in the pipeline. The Tees Valley runs alongside the North York Moors so those who like to go out and about can, um... go out and about.

TRAVEL
TRAINS Middlesbrough Station offers direct links to Newcastle (from £11 return), Manchester (£25.50) and other major interchanges. For London (£58.75) change at Darlington.
COACHES Coach services courtesy of Blue Line, City Link, Swiftline and National Express to London (£34), Manchester (£18.80) and all over.
CAR The A19 south to York and north to Newcastle runs straight past Middlesbrough. There's the A66 cross country to the Lakes, and the A1 runs past Darlington, 15 miles to the west.
AIR Durham Tees Valley Airport's 12 miles away: domestic flights and to Europe and Scandinavia.
LOCAL Buses are *cheap and fairly regular* (until 11pm). Trains run all over the Teesside conurbation.
TAXIS *Reasonably* priced (£2 across town) and *readily* available.
BICYCLES The town is flat, *but small enough to render pedalling purely recreational.*

CAREER PROSPECTS
○ **CAREERS SERVICE** ○ **NO. OF STAFF** 6 FULL-TIME
○ **UNEMPLOYED AFTER 6MTHS** 8%
The careers service ticks all the right boxes, providing students with bulletin boards, a careers library, job fairs, individual guidance, employer presentations and psychometric testing. There are good links with national companies and graduates' careers are kick-started through Knowledge Transfer Partnerships – *the modern equivalent of having an uncle on the board of directors.*

FAMOUS ALUMNI
David Bowe (MEP); Chris Newton (Olympic bronze medallist, Sydney 2000); Skin (singer, once of Skunk Anansie).

SPECIAL FEATURES
Technotronic Teesside hosts Animex each year – a major international animation and computer games festival that attracts designers, animators and general *geeks* from around the world. The Animex Student Animation Awards are held and judged here.

FURTHER INFO
○ **PROSPECTUSES** UNDERGRADS; POSTGRADS; DEPARTMENTAL; VIDEO; CD-ROM ○ **OPEN DAYS**

ACADEMIC

Toasty hot on media-related subjects, particularly where computers are involved. Also strong for Health and Sport Studies.

ENTRY POINTS: 120–300	AVE POINTS: 217
APPLICATIONS PER PLACE: 4	CLEARING: 8%
NO. OF TERMS: 3	LENGTH OF TERMS: 12wks
STAFF TO STUDENT RATIO: 1:17	STUDY ADDICTS: 17%
TEACHING: ***	RESEARCH: *
YEAR ABROAD: <1%	SANDWICH STUDENTS: 30%
1sts: 8%	2.2s: 40%
2.1s: 34%	3rds: 7%

ADMISSIONS
○ APPLY VIA UCAS/NMAS FOR NURSING

SUBJECTS
ARTS & MEDIA 14%   **BUSINESS SCHOOL** 11%
COMPUTING 21%   **HEALTH & SOCIAL CARE** 18%
LIFELONG LEARNING 1%   **SCIENCE & TECHNOLOGY** 12%
SOCIAL SCIENCES & LAW 22%
BEST Biology & Related Sciences; Education Studies; English-based Studies; Law; Nursing; Psychology; Social Policy & Anthropology; Sociology.
UNUSUAL Animation & Visual Effects Programming; Computer Games Design; Digital Visual Effects; Forensic Chemistry; Fraud Science; Policing; Sport & Exercise Psychology; Sports Management.

LIBRARIES
○ **378,397 BOOKS** ○ **1,307 STUDY PLACES**
○ **SPEND PER STUDENT** £££
The new Learning Resource Centre is visually and technologically *impressive, but students complain that there just aren't enough books to go round. The Union wants 24-hr opening but, as mums irritatingly tell small children, "I want never gets". Sadly, in this case mother seems to know best.*

COMPUTERS
○ **1,813 WORKSTATIONS**
Internet access in all hall bedrooms.

OTHER LEARNING FACILITIES
Plenty of added bonuses, including: language labs open to all; the *elaborate* Crime Scene House Laboratory; the nanotechnology centre; a Vehicle Examination Centre *(for rozzers in training* and Forensics students*)*; sports testing labs and a drop-in study skills centre. The Institute of Digital Innovation and the Centre for Creative Technologies will land in 2007, *much to the delight of* Computing, Media and Design students.

ENTERTAINMENT

THE TOWN
○ **PRICE OF A PINT OF BEER** £2.05 ○ **GLASS OF WINE** £2
○ **CAN OF RED BULL** £1.60
CINEMAS Two new multiplexes. The UGC does a discount for students.
THEATRES The Middlesbrough Theatre and Little Theatre show *mainstream* performances with the Arc doing the *diversity* bit.
PUBS *Plenty of competition keeps things cheap and cheerful. Popular pubs* on Southfield Road (at the centre of the campus). Linthorpe Road is a *spanking new stretch of boozers and bars. Pushplugs: Dickens Inn (events and a beer garden); the Cornerhouse; the Star & Garter.*
CLUBBING *Pushplugs: Empire (dance, indie and live music); the Cornerhouse. Best of a borderline bunch.*
MUSIC VENUES/COMEDY The Town Hall hosts *big-to-middling* rock and pop acts plus funnymen like Dara O'Briain and Jimmy Carr *(okay, so maybe we lied about the funny).*
EATING OUT Curry houses *galore can't overshadow the student institution that is* Roy's Café. *Roy's an honorary lifetime SU member. Pushplugs: Jo Rigatonies (Italian); the Purple Onion; Royal Palace; Khans (Indian).*

THE UNIVERSITY
○ **PRICE OF A PINT OF BEER** £1.50 ○ **GLASS OF WINE** £1.40
○ **CAN OF RED BULL** £0.85
BARS The cosy Terrace Bar (cap 650) is right in the middle of the campus and serves hot meals. More to the point, it's open for *boozing* seven days a week.
FILM The film society shows four a week, from *classics (Brighton Rock)* to *mainstream favourites* (Pirates of the Caribbean) and latest releases.
MUSIC VENUES *The Terrace Bar and Club One have thrown in the touring band towel and focus on acoustic nights and student bands rather than anyone you'd've heard of.*
CLUBBING Nothing during the week. On non-school nights the *tatty* Club One (cap 1,000) is the *favourite,* with rock, R'n'B, cheesy pop and retro nights plus DJ sets from circuit names like John Digweed, the Freestylers and Tim Delux.
COMEDY/CABARET The Joke Joint (fortnightly at Club One) features *minor* names. The Phoenix Nights cast pitch up *now and again.*
FOOD *Digestible fayre at* the Terrace Bar and the Gallery. The Studio does snacks and, *if all else fails, there are various pre-packed things at the shop.*
OTHER Black tie and ballgowns at the ready for the Annual Awards Dinner and Graduation ball.

Words in italics are Push's point of view — take it or leave it...

SOCIAL ◖◗◖◗◖◗◖◗◖◗◖◗◖◗

UNIVERSITY OF TEESSIDE STUDENTS' UNION
○ **4 SABBATICALS** ○ **TURNOUT AT LAST BALLOT** 12%
○ **NUS MEMBER**
The award-winning SU is *known for putting extra effort into ents.*

SU FACILITIES
Two bars; general shop; cash machine (HSBC); Endsleigh Insurance; advice centre; new activities and skills centre; pool tables; vending machines; market stalls and other general services such as phones, photocopiers and photo booths.

CLUBS (NON-SPORTING)
See Clubs tables.

OTHER ORGANISATIONS
'PTO' is the monthly student newspaper. *Rag's place in heaven is secure – it amasses a few grand every year for charity.* Student action organises good work in the community. The Give It A Go campaign helps people make friends by trying new things – *think salsa and trips to the moors rather than Class A drugs.*

RELIGIOUS
○ **2 CHAPLAINS (COFE, RC)**
No Islamic prayer room on campus as yet, but they're working on it. Churches, mosques and synagogues are all available in Middlesbrough.

PAID WORK
○ **JOB BUREAU**
The Student Job Centre helps students find part-time work and the SU employs more than 150 students every year.

SPORTS ◖◗◖◗◖◗◖◗◖◗◖◗◖◗

○ **RECENT SUCCESSES** VOLLEYBALL ○ **BUSA RANKING** 95
The SU did win a Sport England VIP recognition award, but sporting successes are *thin on the ground* – shocking, given the mighty state of the ground (*a frankly awesome* £6.5m two-storey building, which houses *every sporting facility imaginable*). *The University is aware of all this wasted potential and has a 'try it, you might like it' attitude.* Wednesday afternoons are left free for mucking about on the pitch.

SPORTS FACILITIES
Saltersgill Sports Ground has 65 acres of playing fields for football, rugby and hockey – including one all-weather; netball court; two squash courts; basketball court; two sports halls; gym; climbing wall; watersports centre; *bizarre and extravagant* temperature-controlled environment centre which can simulate any climate in the world. *No, really.* Disabled access is good and there's a wellbeing centre which does fitness evaluations along with aromatherapy *and other hippy-dippy claptrap.* With a sports card (£40), almost everything is free. Locally: leisure centre; golf course; watersports lake; ski slope; swimming pool.

SPORTING CLUBS
10-Pin Bowling; American Football; Cheerleading; Freestyle Dance; Handball; Hapkido (Korean self-defence); Iaido (traditional Japanese swordmanship); Jeet Kune Do Adaptive Combat Systems (martial arts); Kickboxing; Kung Fu; Mountaineering; Paintballing; Pool; Rollerhockey; Rowing; Snow Sports; Surfing; Table Tennis; Tae Kwondo. **See also Clubs tables.**

ATTRACTIONS
Middlesbrough FC recently won their first trophy for 127 years; West Hartlepool rugby union; horse racing at Redcar; speedway at Stockton. Tees Barrage is an 11-mile stretch of world-class white water for rafting and canoeing.

ACCOMMODATION ◖◗◖◗◖◗◖◗◖◗◖◗

IN UNIVERSITY
○ **SELF-CATERING** 19% ○ **COST** £47 (37/38WKS)
○ **1ST YRS LIVING IN** 30% ○ **INSURANCE PREMIUM** £££££
AVAILABILITY All first years firmly accepting a place are now being guaranteed a bed. Accommodation ranges from *positively plush to pretty poor* but is all *close* to college – *so close that it can get a bit inyerface.* King Edward's Square and Parkside Flats *get the thumbs up.* Parkside Hall (shared study bedrooms) and Woodlands (*pricey* rooms) *get a thumbs down. But, on the other hand, it's as cheap as David Dickinson's fake tan.*
CAR PARKING £65 (£20 of which is refundable) buys a year-long parking pass for college and halls.

EXTERNALLY
○ **AVE RENT** £40
AVAILABILITY *Good value at twice the price* and all the student neighbourhoods are in *spitting distance* of campus. Accommodation is *ridiculously easy* to find, and, since the North York Moors and the North Sea Coast are on the doostep, *the view's always pretty.* A new private hall in town is also on the way.
HOUSING HELP Five full-time staff are on hand at the University Accommodation Service.

WELFARE ◑◑◑◑◑◑◑◑◑◑◑◑◑

SERVICES
- **LGBT OFFICER & SOCIETY** **ETHNIC MINORITIES OFFICER & SOCIETY** **WOMEN'S OFFICER & SOCIETY**
- **MATURE STUDENTS' OFFICER & SOCIETY**
- **INTERNATIONAL STUDENTS' OFFICER & SOCIETY**
- **DISABILITIES OFFICER & SOCIETY**
- **POSTGRAD OFFICER** **TAXI FUND**
- **SELF-DEFENCE CLASSES**
- **UNIVERSITY COUNSELLORS** 3 FULL/2 PART
- **CRIME RATING** !!!!!

Welfare provision at the University Advice Centre is *top dollar,* and the SU/University collaborate *to keep things that way.*
HEALTH *Loads* of medical practices in the town centre.
CRECHES/NURSERY 66 places for children aged 6wks-5yrs.

DISABILITIES The low-level, ramped-up campus is *big* on access. The Learning Resource Centre has a reading edge scanner, large-screen PC, braille machine and tactile diagram facility. Hearing loops are installed around the campus. The University provides specialist dyslexia support and a mental health co-ordinator.

FINANCE
- **AVE DEBT PER YEAR** £2,440
- **HOME STUDENT FEES** £3,000

FEES Placement years cost £750 and postgrads have to cough up £3,700 or £8,250 for an MBA. International students pay £7,250-8,250 (or £10,000 for an MBA).
- **ACCESS FUND** £800,000 **SUCCESSFUL APPLICATIONS/YR** 1,972 **AVE PAYMENT** £100-£3,500

SUPPORT Bursaries of up to £1,300 a year for the poorest students and scholarships of £1,000 a year. *Incredibly,* all UK and EU students receive a £500 welcome grant, just for showing up.

➡ TEESSIDE POLYTECHNIC
see *University of Teesside*

➡ THAMES COLLEGE OF HEALTHCARE STUDIES
see *Greenwich University*

THAMES VALLEY UNIVERSITY

FORMERLY POLYTECHNIC OF WEST LONDON

1. **THAMES VALLEY UNIVERSITY** St Mary's Road, Ealing, London, W5 5RF **TEL** (0800) 036 8888 **E-MAIL** learning.advice@tvu.ac.uk **WEBSITE** www.tvu.ac.uk **THAMES VALLEY STUDENTS' UNION** Thames Valley University, St Mary's Road, Ealing, London, W5 5RF **TEL** (020) 8231 2573 **E-MAIL** student.services@tvu.ac.uk **WEBSITE** www.tvu.ac.uk/student-services
2. **THAMES VALLEY UNIVERSITY** Wellington Street, Slough, Berkshire, SL1 1YG **TEL** (01753) 534585
3. **THAMES VALLEY UNIVERSITY** King's Road, Reading, Berkshire, RG1 4HJ **TEL** (0118) 967 5000

GENERAL ◑◑◑◑◑◑◑◑◑◑◑◑◑

Thames Valley University is made up of three sites, following the winding path of the Thames through Reading, Slough and Ealing. In 1991, Thames Valley College Slough merged with London College of Music which merged with Queen Charlotte's College of Healthcare Study to form the Polytechnic of West London. A year later it became Thames Valley University. In January 2004, Reading College was sucked into the mix. *It also tried to merge with a passing milkman, but he was having none of it.* The University has a strong commitment to the local area and encouraging entry through non-traditional routes. Most students are at the main Ealing site, in the suburban west of London, ten miles from Trafalgar Square. For general information about London see University of London.

SEX RATIO: ♂ 35 ♀ 65	**FOUNDED:** 1992
FULL-TIME U'GRADS: 4,463	**PART-TIME:** 1,016
POSTGRADS: 2,113	**NON-DEGREE:** 16,028
AVE COURSE: 3YRS	**ETHNIC:** 67%
STATE:PRIVATE SCHOOL: 98:2	**FLUNK RATE:** 25%
MATURE: 75%	**INTERNATIONAL:** 16%
DISABLED: 50	**LOCAL:** 57%

ATMOSPHERE
Diverse and then some, TVU takes in large numbers of students who are mature, international or from the ethnically diverse local community. There are also many students on part-time, day-release and evening courses and those studying for degrees are in the minority. *There's also quite a chunk who've rolled in off the roulette wheel of clearing. This all means TVU is about as far as you can get from the stereotypical university (20-year-old white males with posh*

voices, reading poetry in college scarves). The main campus at Ealing is quiet and away from the main, gritty urban splat of London. Students are always in a hurry – as if they're worried that if they stand still the University will try to merge with them.

SITES

SLOUGH CAMPUS (Hotel & Catering, Science, Computing, Accounting, Business & Finance, Nursing & Healthcare) More space and free facilities than Ealing, it's got a gym and an expanded range of courses but, *of course,* it's in Slough, 13 miles from Ealing. *A heroically unimpressive commuter satellite town, with a name like a groinal infection in sheep, Slough is perhaps best known as the fictional setting for the Office and best described by John Betjeman 'Come friendly bombs and fall on Slough. It's not fit for humans now'.* So it's just as well £4m has been slated for rejuvenating the town centre. The train station's right opposite, *which is dead handy for a fast getaway.*

READING COLLEGE (Fine Art, Fashion, Chemical Science, Building Studies) Still further west out of London (Ealing, 25 miles; Slough, 21 miles). *There's fierce rivalry with Slough in the dullness stakes, but Oxford* (20 miles) *is easy to get to from Reading for more aesthetic pleasures. Trains to Paddington are fairly regular and speedy* (30 mins), *so a night out in the West End is doable (though you don't want to stay out too late).*

LONDON see <u>University of London</u>

EALING

Ealing is an *easily accessible* part of West London and *mostly affluent* with *posh* shops flogging stuff alongside the budget. *South Ealing has things a bit harder.* The main campus is halfway between the two. The area is known as a haunt for would-be celebs – Ealing Studios is opposite the University. Situated by a private estate, local noise-related friction has caused sparks in the past, ably sorted out by the University wading in and threatening to ban ents and bars.

TRAVEL see <u>University of London</u>
TRAINS Nearest station is Ealing Broadway, 800m away.
BUSES Buses serving Ealing are 65, 207, 83 E1, E2, E7, E8, E9, E10, E11, PR1, 297, 607 and night buses too. *Enough, already.*
COACHES Nearest stop is Hammersmith, ten mins by Tube.
UNDERGROUND Ealing Broadway, Ealing Common and South Ealing (all zone 3) are all less than a mile away.
CAR *The four-wheeled monsters are common among students.* There are short-term parking meters throughout central Ealing. The University has limited parking for students at £5 per day. Also a number of council-run car parks in the area.
TAXIS Cab ranks at Ealing Broadway and South Ealing station *for those that can't face the walk.*

UNIVERSITY A free bus service connects the Ealing and Slough campuses and the Paragon halls, running hourly in term time between 7am and 7pm.
BICYCLES Bikes are a *popular option,* with sheds at all buildings and sites. Although Ealing has no cycle lanes, there a large number of parks, *which makes for peaceful cycling.*

CAREER PROSPECTS
○ **CAREERS SERVICE** ○ **NO. OF STAFF** 8 FULL/2 PART
○ **UNEMPLOYED AFTER 6MTHS** 9%
A well-stocked careers service, with career planning and management, appointments, workshops, student-employer meetings and employer presentations.

FAMOUS ALUMNI
Emma Anderson (musician); John Bird (Big Issue founder); Tim Campbell (winner of 'The Apprentice'); Sergey Ivanov (Russian defence minister); James Larlett (ex British hockey captain); Alan Lee (illustrator); Freddie Mercury (Queen, *RIP*); Robert Rankin (writer); Pete Townshend (the Who); Ron Wood (Rolling Stones). Honorary Awards have gone to David Frost, Neil Kinnock and Alexi Sayle and recently Gary Rhodes and Brian Turner.

FURTHER INFO
○ **PROSPECTUSES** UNDERGRAD; POSTGRAD; DEPARTMENTAL; VIDEO ○ **OPEN DAYS**

ACADEMIC ◡◡◡◡◡◡◡◡◡◡◡◡

The big idea is to provide education from FE (A Levels etc.) right the way through to postgrad, and *it shows TVU is always willing to make the most of what they've got and give new things a bash (especially if they're cheap).* For starters, 'Blackboard', a virtual campus, is in place, designed to help distance learning. There's also a 'credit accumulation scheme', where students can take a break from study, change the structure of their course or obtain a certificate for the work they've done if they quit. Employers get on board in designing courses and the University is proud of its work-related facilities, like a kitchen showroom where *spiky* chef Gary Rhodes has shown off his slicing and dicing. Workshops, group work, case studies, lectures and seminars are the norm with assessment concentrated on the third year. *Many students think it's all a bit disorganised, partly due to the recent Reading merger.*

T

ENTRY POINTS: 40–280	AVE POINTS: 205
APPLICATIONS PER PLACE: N/A	CLEARING: 15%
NO. OF TERMS: 4	LENGTH OF TERMS: 10wks
STAFF TO STUDENT RATIO: N/A	STUDY ADDICTS: 20%
TEACHING: *	RESEARCH: *
YEAR ABROAD: 10%	SANDWICH STUDENTS: 10%
1STS: 11%	2.2s: 34%
2.1s: 39%	3RDS: 7%

ADMISSIONS
◉ APPLY VIA UCAS
Courses start in February as well as Autumn.

SUBJECTS
ARTS 52% **HEALTH & HUMAN SCIENCES** 13%
PROFESSIONAL STUDIES 35%
There's also a fair amount of Technology, but this is mainly at FE rather than University level.
BEST Nursing; Psychology; Tourism, Hospitality & Leisure.
UNUSUAL Acupuncture; Credit Management.

LIBRARIES
◉ 326,951 BOOKS ◉ 900 STUDY PLACES
◉ SPEND PER STUDENT ££
TVU has five libraries, the two main ones being at Ealing and at Slough in the *fancy* Paul Hamlyn Resource Centre *(which looks like a train station). The opening hours are uninspiring, the latest being 10pm.*

COMPUTERS
◉ 800 WORKSTATIONS ◉ 24-HR ACCESS
Three different labs, with both Macs and PCs and special provision for disabled students. All the new University bedrooms have broadband, *for all your all-night porn needs.*

OTHER LEARNING FACILITIES
Audio, TV and video studio, CAD lab, language laboratory; photography studio; Pillers kitchen and restaurant; Asian kitchen.

ENTERTAINMENT ◯◯◯◯◯◯◯◯◯◯

THE CITY see University of London
◉ PRICE OF A PINT OF BEER £2.50 **◉ GLASS OF WINE** £3 **◉ CAN OF RED BULL** £2.50
With a better than average selection of bars and restaurants, Ealing has enough to mean treks into central London can be kept for occasions worth the extra hassle and expense.

THEATRE & CINEMA The three-screen Cineworld is the flick-pit of choice. There are more further out. Ealing has the small Questors with fringe performances, but the *top-notch* Lyric Hammersmith and Riverside ain't far away and *usually have an innovative programme.* Watermans Arts Centre is ten mins by bus and does arthouse cinema, exhibitions etc.
PUBS *Most local pubs have the feel of a middle-class family day out, but are still fun with the right crowd. There are a couple of chain pubs about too.* Pushplugs: O'Neill's (live music at weekends); Edward's (student night on Tuesdays); Finnegans Wake (student comedy night).
CLUBBING/MUSIC/COMEDY A range of music at the Priory, which is dinky enough to bump into other students. Oceana in Kingston is also *popular.* Live music is mainly pub-based but the Labatts Apollo (Hammersmith) and the Shepherds Bush Empire are within easy reach. Ha Bloody Ha on Ealing Green gets comedians, *but half of the fun is trying to find the place.*
EATING OUT All sorts of multi-cultural scoff shops. *Pushplugs: New Leaf (Chinese); the Lantern Tavern (Greek). Monty's does cult Indian eating.*

THE UNIVERSITY
◉ PRICE OF A PINT OF BEER £1.70 **◉ GLASS OF WINE** £1.80
◉ CAN OF RED BULL £1.50
Plenty of space club-wise, but this isn't exactly TVU's forte. Variety lacks, so students have adventures off-campus in search of the missing fun.
BARS A *small but cosy* bar in Ealing with pool tables, table football and telly, plus two bars in Slough.
THEATRE/FILM Not technically, but the drama society put on the odd show in Lawrence Hall and there's a film society.
MUSIC/CLUBBING Lawrence Hall (cap 500) hosts a bunch of events including a weekly live music and comedy night. Tribute bands turn up a lot and *inexplicably* aren't chased away. The monthly *sports club-dominated* Night Fever is the *big shindig.*
FOOD Snacks and sandwiches from the SU coffee shop (daytimes only) are *about as good as it gets. Still, at least it's cheap.*
OTHER Societies stage cultural events at the SU throughout the year. Each site has its own annual ball: welcome balls, the black tie sports awards and the ten-hour extravaganza that is the Annual May Ball.

T

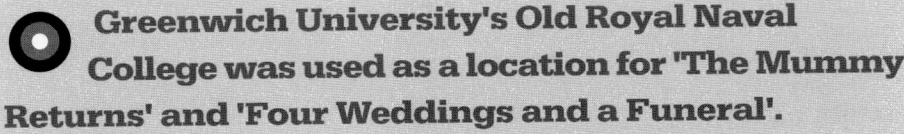

◉ **Greenwich University's Old Royal Naval College was used as a location for 'The Mummy Returns' and 'Four Weddings and a Funeral'.**

Words in italics are Push's point of view — take it or leave it...

SOCIAL ◐◐◐◐◐◐◐◐◐◐◐◐

THAMES VALLEY STUDENTS' UNION
○ **4 SABBATICALS** ○ **TURNOUT AT LAST BALLOT** 11%
○ **NUS MEMBER**
All campuses are united in not giving a flying fig about politics. Good relations exist between the University and the SU. Students sit on the governing and academic boards and *get to hear and have a say in most things that go on.*

SU FACILITIES
The main SU is a converted Victorian Grammar School with a bar, minibuses, coffee shop, photocopying, printing, snack shop, vending and games machines.

CLUBS (NON-SPORTING)
Chess; Chinese; Gaming; 3D Knowledge Group; Mooting; Malaysian Students; TUBE Radio. **See also Clubs tables.**

OTHER ORGANISATIONS
Monthly student newsletter, 'the Valley'; on-air and online radio station 'the Tube' plus online rival 'Blast' at the Reading campus. *TVU students are charitable souls,* with a RAG week on each campus.

RELIGIOUS
○ **2 CHAPLAINS** (COFE, RC), **RABBI**
World Faith Room in the North Building.

PAID WORK see University of London
○ **JOB BUREAU** ○ **PAID WORK TERM-TIME** 90%; **HOLS** 95%
The Careers & Employment Service has various opportunities including bar work, marketing, IT support, office admin, retail, translation, marketing and charity work. TVU Temps is the place for part-time vacancies.

SPORTS ◐◐◐◐◐◐◐◐◐◐◐◐◐

○ **RECENT SUCCESSES** RUGBY, NETBALL, BASKETBALL, FOOTBALL ○ **BUSA RANKING** N/A
The students have been developing a keen interest in sports, despite the lack of facilities (marginally less bad at the Slough campus), for which they pay £20 a year. They signed up to play with other unis in BUSA last year.

SPORTS FACILITIES
Football, hockey, cricket and rugby pitches; basketball and squash courts, sports hall; gym; multigym. Locally, Grasshoppers Sportsclubs give students a cheaper deal. See also University of London

SPORTING CLUBS
Aerobics; Capoiera; Ju-Jitsu; Thai Boxing; Yoga. **See also Clubs tables.**

ATTRACTIONS see University of London

ACCOMMODATION ◐◐◐◐◐◐◐◐◐◐

IN UNIVERSITY
○ **CATERED** 2% ○ **COST** £90 (42/44WKS)
○ **SELF-CATERED** 19% ○ **COST** £122 (42/44WKS)
○ **INSURANCE PREMIUM** ££
AVAILABILITY TVU's first proper accommodation block will open its 868 doors in 2006 – priority will go to those with disabilities or long commutes *but there's likely to be a stampede.* The University reckons the block, at the Paragon site in a residential area a mile and a half from the main campus, will attract more 'traditional' and international students – *Push suggests free beer tokens might swing it.* Rooms are certainly very swanky, arranged in eight-bedroom flats with en suite, 24-hour security plus a small number of studio flats. There's also a hall on the Reading campus. Otherwise, the University *does its best to locate living spaces for its students in the local area.*
CAR PARKING Various campus car parks cost an *off-putting* £5 a day.

EXTERNALLY
○ **AVE RENT** £87 see University of London
AVAILABILITY *As well as Ealing itself, Northfields; Hanwell; Greenford; Northolt; Brentford; Acton; Perivale and Alperton are popular and cheapish, though Acton is a bit dull. The rest of Ealing is avoided because it's costly. Slough: the last thoughts of many a victim of horrible deaths are probably 'Oh well, at least I don't live in Slough'. Those with worse luck close their eyes and plump for a pad in central Slough, Langley, Burnham or Datchet. Windsor is near, but very expensive.*
HOUSING HELP The Administration Department runs an *excellent* housing help service, *probably because they have to.* They have approved housing lists, vetted properties, advice and so on.

WELFARE ◐◐◐◐◐◐◐◐◐◐◐◐

SERVICES
○ **WOMEN'S OFFICER** ○ **INTERNATIONAL STUDENTS' OFFICER** ○ **DISABILITIES SOCIETY** ○ **SELF-DEFENCE CLASSES** ○ **LATE NIGHT MINIBUS**
○ **UNIVERSITY COUNSELLORS** 2 FULL/3 PART
○ **CRIME RATING** !!!!
TVU's student advice team, personal tutors and counsellors supply general help and wisdom, alongside the SU's case workers (available by appointment only). There's help available at Reading too.
HEALTH Nursing staff are available at Ealing and Slough and a GP visits the Ealing campus four

times a week. A GP surgery at Reading and other bits and bobs like acupuncture and massage.
CRECHES/NURSERIES A *double whammy* at Reading, one for 0-5yrs and t'other for 2-5yrs.
WOMEN Self-defence classes are run through the sports department.
DISABILITIES *Wheelchair access is excellent* and there are induction loops, dyslexia support, talking lifts and an assistive technology suite with computers that have Jaws, Kurswell 3000 and Texthelp. There's some disabled accommodation available.

FINANCE

AVE DEBT PER YEAR £4,449 **HOME STUDENT FEES** £2,700 **ACCESS FUND** £1,000,000 **SUCCESSFUL APPLICATIONS/YR** 596 **AVE PAYMENT** £100-3,500 **SUPPORT** £500-1,000 is the standard student bursary, depending on *neediness*. Also various trusts and charitable donations can be had and scholarships are available through the faculties (aka academic departments).

▶ TRENT UNIVERSITY
see *Nottingham Trent University*

TRINITY COLLEGE, CARMARTHEN

PART OF THE UNIVERSITY OF WALES

 TRINITY COLLEGE CARMARTHEN College Road, Carmarthen, South Wales, SA31 3EP **TEL** (01267) 676 767
E-MAIL registry@trinity-cm.ac.uk **WEBSITE** www.trinity-cm.ac.uk

GENERAL ◗◗◗◗◗◗◗◗◗◗◗◗◗

Towards the westernmost tip of south-west Wales, set in *eye-poppingly beautiful* coastal countryside, is the small town of Camarthen. On its outskirts is Trinity College, a *small but (almost) perfectly-formed* institution offering degrees in Education and the Arts. Founded in 1848 as a church college (there's even still an old church building on site to prove it), it now falls into the broad parish of the University of Wales. *They're Welsh and proud here*, with everything written in two languages and *the one that looks like elvish usually in pride of place*.

SEX RATIO: ♂24 ♀76	FOUNDED: 1848
FULL-TIME U'GRADS: 1,242	PART-TIME: 514
POSTGRADS: 254	NON-DEGREE: 82
AVE COURSE: 3YRS	ETHNIC: 6%
STATE:PRIVATE SCHOOL: 60:1	FLUNK RATE: 26%
MATURE: 75%	INTERNATIONAL: 5%
DISABLED: 35	LOCAL: N/A

ATMOSPHERE
Like Camarthen, the College is quiet, but pleasant. The site is nearly as pretty as the surrounding countryside, though its aesthetic copybook is blotted by a handful of shabby-ish accommodation. The student body is a friendly bunch and can almost feel like a family, albeit one with more than 1,000 members. Mature students are in the majority. A car is a handy accessory for days when the isolation (and time-consuming transport links) start to grind.

CARMARTHEN
 POPULATION 173,635 **CITY CENTRE** 1 MILE
 SWANSEA 27 MILES
 HIGH TEMP 18 **LOW TEMP** 6 **RAINFALL** 42
Supposedly the birthplace of Arthurian wizard Merlin, Camarthen stokes students up with entertainment, shopping and part-time work rather than magic potions. The learners like the town and the locals like them. Aw. Green joys like the National Botanic Garden of Wales and Aberglasney Gardens aren't far away.

TRAVEL
Can be tricky to get around both the town and the wider wilds of Wales.
TRAINS Direct trains from the town station, a 15-20 minute walk from campus. Services to London (from £35.65 return) and beyond.
COACHES Services from the train station, including London (£30) and Birmingham (£27).
CAR A48 and M4 are the nearest fast roads. *Ridiculously cheap to stash a motor* and there's a *decent-sized* car park at the College.
AIR Nearest airport is Swansea, nearest *useful* airport is Cardiff.
BICYCLES A *deservedly popular* way to get around, with covered bike-sheds at the College.

CAREER PROSPECTS
 CAREERS SERVICE **NO. OF STAFF** 3 FULL/1 PART
 UNEMPLOYED AFTER 6MTHS 5%
A *good* range of guidance. Paid graduate-level ten week work placements can be arranged and one advisor also works for GO Wales, which organises taster sessions that get a *big thumbs-up* from students.

T

Words in italics are Push's point of view — take it or leave it...

FAMOUS ALUMNI

Dt Stuart Burrows (operatic tenor); Carwyn James (former British Lions coach); Barry John (Wales and British Lions outside half); *loads* of S4C presenters.

FURTHER INFO

○ **PROSPECTUSES** UNDERGRAD; POSTGRAD (LEAFLETS); OVERSEAS POSTGRAD ○ **OPEN DAYS**

ACADEMIC ○○○○○○○○○○○○○

Teacher training is biggest area in terms of student numbers, Theatre & Performance is biggest in terms of buzz. Sports are also strong. Students get a *fairly average* 10-20 hours of lectures a week, plus self-directed study, tutorials and seminars *to keep them busy*. There are two semesters lasting 15 weeks each. The College is keen on language planning and bilingual development. All students get a personal tutor.

ENTRY POINTS: 80-360	AVE POINTS: N/A
APPLICATIONS PER PLACE: N/A	CLEARING: N/A
NO. OF TERMS: 3	LENGTH OF TERMS: 8/11/14wks
STAFF TO STUDENT RATIO: N/A	STUDY ADDICTS: N/A
TEACHING: ✦✦✦	RESEARCH: ✦✦✦

ADMISSIONS

○ **APPLY VIA UCAS/GTTR FOR TEACHER TRAINING**
There's a widening access co-ordinator.

SUBJECTS

ARTS & SOCIAL SCIENCES 46% **EDUCATION & TRAINING** 54%
UNUSUAL Bilingual (MA).

LIBRARIES

○ **120,000** BOOKS ○ **144** STUDY PLACES
○ **24-**HR ACCESS
There's a main library/llyfrgell and teacher resource centre (TRC/CAA), depending on your language of choice. Access is round the clock during term, *patchier* at other times.

COMPUTERS

○ **150** WORKSTATIONS
Computers are available 18 hours a day *(maybe more if you sweet-talk the porter)*. Wireless access is popping up all over the campus.

OTHER LEARNING FACILITIES

Drama studios and theatre; rehearsal rooms; CAD lab.

ENTERTAINMENT ○○○○○○○○○

THE TOWN

Camarthen's no seething entastic metropolis, but by the standards of the West Wales pond, it's a trout rather than a tadpole. Just. Swansea isn't

inaccessibly far away for those that crave occasional city pleasures – befriend a (non-drinking) driver. Otherwise it's down to the Union to distract students from swotting too late into the night.

THE UNIVERSITY

○ **PRICE OF A PINT OF BEER** £1.80 ○ **GLASS OF WINE** £2.00
○ **CAN OF RED BULL** £1.50
BARS Unity bar (cap 500) *is the fat cat*, with a stage and big dancefloor. It only opens its doors three nights a week, but doesn't shut 'em until 1am. Attic (cap 100), which has satellite TV, pool, darts and other drink-related distractions, is open until midnight Mon-Fri and a few hours on Sunday. There are also a couple of bars in the University conference suites.
THEATRES The 375-seater Halliwell Theatre *is well-used by the supremely keen* luvvie contingent. It's set for when the Theatr Genedlaethol Cymru (Welsh National Theatre Company) is set to move to college.
CLUBBING/MUSIC VENUES Unity's one of the best entertainment venues in West Wales, *not that there's much competition. Republica and Wheatus have performed recently, suggesting to Push that the music scene in these parts lags somewhat behind the rest of the galaxy.*
FOOD Merlin Restaurant for sandwiches and *wallet-friendly* canteen fare, plus a few snack stops.
OTHER Four balls a year. The summer ball wipes the floor with the others, with a funfair, marquee and live music to keep students dancing until dawn.

SOCIAL ○○○○○○○○○○○○

TRINITY STUDENTS' UNION

○ **2** SABBATICALS ○ **NUS** MEMBER
Unity/Undod is the SU's nest, a jolly place where the staff are friendly and the politics doesn't get in the way of ents and welfare. Relations with the University are glowing.

SU FACILITIES

Nightclub & music venue; two bars; canteen; snack bar; pool tables; meeting rooms; minibus hire; photocopier; fax; printing; payphone; advice centre; nursery; jukebox; video and vending machines; general store; stationery shop; travel agent.

CLUBS (NON-SPORTING)

American; Archaeology; Tower; Erasmus; Welsh.
See also Clubs tables.

OTHER ORGANISATIONS

RAG *sells its soul* for charidee.

RELIGIOUS
- **COFW CHAPLAIN**

PAID WORK
- **JOB BUREAU** - **PAID WORK TERM-TIME** 71%

Staff-hunting employers often come directly to the college with vacancies of the bar/shop/childcare varieties. Casual work, work experience and *proper jobs* throughout Wales are advertised through the GO Wales programme.

SPORTS ()()()()()()()()()()()()()

- **RECENT SUCCESSES** RUGBY, ATHLETICS
- **BUSA RANKING** 122

The University owns most of the facilities and the Union rallies the students into clubs and teams to make use of them. The *mighty* rugby team *shows the rest of the UK that Wales is where egg-chasing's at.* £120 buys a *well-intentioned* annual membership of the new health suite.

SPORTS FACILITIES
Two football pitches; hockey pitch; cricket pitch; rugby pitch; all-weather pitch; four tennis courts; three netball courts; swimming pool; sauna/steam room; gym; aerobics studio; climbing wall; basketball court; two sports halls. *This is great outdoors country*, with a river and the Millennium and Pembrokeshire National Coastal Paths within reach.

SPORTING CLUBS
Canoe; Dance; Gym; Lifesaving; Outdoor Pursuits; Surf. **See also Clubs tables.**

ACCOMMODATION ()()()()()()()()()()

IN COLLEGE
- **CATERED** 25% - **COST** £83 (41WKS)
- **SELF-CATERING** 23% - **COST** £65 (41WKS)
- **1ST YRS LIVING IN** 52% - **INSURANCE PREMIUM** £
AVAILABILITY The College tries to squeeze in all first years but makes no promises. International

and special needs students get priority; after that it's first come, first housed. All halls are together on one campus and the self-catering accommodation has en suite facilities. There are three catered halls, Myrddin, Tower (ten floors, *reputed to be the tallest building in West Wales*) and Non (in the centre of campus). Nosh is dished up in Merlins restaurant and the coffee shop and students can choose between a seven-day package or five-day package if they scoot off home for the weekend. There's a launderette and 24-hour porter and self-catering halls have a communal lounge.
CAR PARKING Parking's easy to come by but costs £150 a year.

EXTERNALLY
- **AVE RENT** £45

HOUSING HELP There's one full-time advisor. The College gives out a vacancy list but leaves students to suss out the landlords for themselves.

WELFARE ()()()()()()()()()()()()()

SERVICES
- **LGBT OFFICER & SOCIETY**
- **INTERNATIONAL STUDENTS' OFFICER & SOCIETY**
- **CRIME RATING** !

The University's Student Services Centre tries to keep students on an even keel with academic, welfare and career advice. It calls on other staff, including a specialist counsellor, when necessary.
CRECHES/NURSERY The bilingual nursery takes 48 dinky people from fresh out of the womb to 7yrs.

FINANCE
- **AVE DEBT PER YEAR** £4,704 - **HOME STUDENT FEES** £1,200
FEES Fees will soon rise to £3,000, although Welsh students will get extra payments to cover the difference. International students are charged a low £6,000 and postgrads an *even lower* £2,700. Part-timers get charged by the module.
- **ACCESS FUND** £82,720

T

In March 2006, Sussex University held a Vagina Week, including among other things a Vagina Painting Workshop and chocolate vaginas.

⇒ UCE
see *UCE Birmingham*

UCE BIRMINGHAM

UCL

⇒ UEA
see *University of East Anglia*

⇒ UEL
see *University of East London*

⇒ UMIST
see *University of Manchester*

⇒ THE UNITED MEDICAL AND DENTAL SCHOOLS (UMDS)
see *King's College, London*

⇒ UNIVERSITY COLLEGE LONDON
see *UCL*

⇒ UNIVERSITY COLLEGE STOCKTON
see *Durham University*

⇒ UNIVERSITY OF CENTRAL ENGLAND
see *UCE Birmingham*

UNIVERSITY OF ULSTER

⇒ UNIVERSITY OF WALES INSTITUTE, CARDIFF
see *UWIC*

⇒ UNIVERSITY OF THE WEST OF ENGLAND
see *UWE, Bristol*

UWE, BRISTOL

UWIC

⇒ UXBRIDGE
see *Brunel University*

U

▶ UCE
see *UCE Birmingham*

UCE BIRMINGHAM

FORMERLY BIRMINGHAM POLYTECHNIC

○ **UNIVERSITY OF CENTRAL ENGLAND** UCE Birmingham, Perry Barr, Birmingham, B42 2SU **TEL** (0121) 331 5000
EMAIL info@ucechoices.com **WEBSITE** www.ucechoices.com ○ **UCE UNION OF STUDENTS** Perry Barr, Birmingham, B42 2SU
TEL (0121) 331 6802 **EMAIL** union.president@uce.ac.uk **WEBSITE** www.uceunion.com

GENERAL ◑◑◑◑◑◑◑◑◑◑◑◑

Birmingham, the pug-ugly duckling that got silicone implants and a facelift, is home to the ten very different campuses of UCE. Most of the sites are close to the city centre, except Bournville which is away on its own, *being arty and mysterious, but secretly just eating chocolate.* Perry Barr is the main site, catering for at least half of the students and it's only three miles from the centre. *Today's Birmingham is a culturally varied, exciting and modern city despite its mass of council housing and factories.* See also University of Birmingham

SEX RATIO: ♂40 ♀60	**FOUNDED:** 1968
FULL-TIME U'GRADS: 12,757	**PART-TIME:** 4,010
POSTGRADS: 1,159	**NON-DEGREE:** 397
AVE COURSE: 3YRS	**ETHNIC:** 46%
STATE:PRIVATE SCHOOL: 99:1	**FLUNK RATE:** 16%
MATURE: 21%	**INTERNATIONAL:** 16%
DISABLED: 200	**LOCAL:** N/A

ATMOSPHERE
Students have picked up on the determined, easy-going cheerfulness common to people in less than perfect surroundings and have a business-like attitude to work. UCE Brum offers many FE courses and free courses for the unemployed, so the social mix isn't just the usual bunch of undergrads. *The University's been splashing out recently on refurbishment and new buildings, but there's little reason for students to hang around once their lectures are out. Still, the city's got plenty to do so boredom's rarely an issue.*

SITES
PERRY BARR Despite being the main site, Perry Barr's not too big. Students stride *around purposefully, getting an education. Perry Barr is a fairly grubby part of the city (although the campus itself is a large and pleasant enough island). Its best features are a good number of local shops, a greyhound stadium opposite the campus and a station to get the hell out of there.*
WESTBOURNE ROAD/EDGBASTON (Education and Nursing) Six miles from Perry Barr, the site is

about to remove the bandages to reveal the fruits of a £24m makeover. Its other main advantage is the social scene offered at Broad St, five mins away. It attracts students from all around – the nurses have nothing to do with it, honest.
BOURNVILLE (Art & Design) Four miles from the city centre, near the choccy factory, Bournville is one of four sites housing art and design courses. *Unsurprisingly, students are arty, and like a good, boozy laugh.*
OTHERS Gosta Green (Art & Design); Margaret Street (Art & Design); the Birmingham Conservatoire (Music); the Jewellery School (Maths?) in the city's Jewellery Quarter, *which is turning touristy.* Recent addition the Birmingham School of Acting brought luvvies into the fold in 2005. There's also the Technology Innovation Centre at Millennium Point.

BIRMINGHAM see University of Birmingham

TRAVEL see University of Birmingham
With no inter-site transport laid on by the University, cars are handy. There are buses and two trains an hour between Perry Bar and the city centre.

CAREER PROSPECTS
○ **CAREERS SERVICE** ○ **NO. OF STAFF** 11 FULL/1PART
○ **UNEMPLOYED AFTER 6 MTHS** 7%
Careers advice; interview training; jobs fairs and the *ever-useful* bulletin board are on hand for job needs.

FAMOUS ALUMNI
Alfred Bestall (creator, Rupert the Bear); Jim Crace (novelist); Betty Jackson (fashion designer); Larry (cartoonist); Nigel Mansell (ex-F1 driver); Jas Mann (Babylon Zoo); Frank Skinner (comedian).

FURTHER INFO
○ **PROSPECTUSES** UNDERGRAD; POSTGRAD ○ **OPEN DAYS** .

ACADEMIC ◑◑◑◑◑◑◑◑◑◑◑◑

UCE's got a stonking range of courses, grouped into several faculties: the Birmingham

Conservatoire; the Birmingham Insititute of Art & Design; Business School; Innovation Centre; Health & Community Care; Law, Humanities & Social Sciences. Many of the courses are career-related (nurses especially tend to go straight into work) and *zillions* of part-time and sandwich courses are up for grabs. *Good news for public sector hopefuls* – the University is part of a Centre for Excellence in Teaching and Learning along with two local hospitals and the education department is highly-rated.

ENTRY POINTS: 180–260	AVE POINTS: 256
APPLICATIONS PER PLACE: 6	CLEARING: 10%
NO. OF TERMS: 3	LENGTH OF TERMS: 12WKS
STAFF TO STUDENT RATIO: 1:18	STUDY ADDICTS: 20%
TEACHING: ∗	RESEARCH: ∗∗∗
YEAR ABROAD: 22%	SANDWICH STUDENTS: 47%
1STS: 9%	2.2s: 34%
2.1s: 54%	3RDS: 3%

ADMISSIONS
◉ APPLY VIA UCAS FOR MOST F/T COURSES

SUBJECTS
BIRMINGHAM INSTITUTE OF ART & DESIGN 15%
BUSINESS SCHOOL 14%   COMPUTING 9%
EDUCATION 7%   HEALTH 27%   LAW, HUMANITIES & SOCIAL SCIENCES 6%   MUSIC 2%   PROPERTY & CONSTRUCTION AND PLANNING & HOUSING 6%
BEST Finance & Accounting; Law; Media Studies; Performing Arts.
UNUSUAL Gemmology; Horology.

LIBRARIES
◉ 691,316 BOOKS ◉ 897 STUDY PLACES
A good variety of books, but competition can be fierce. Perry Barr has the main Kenrick Library and there are seven more specialist libraries on the different sites for the courses based there. *New kid on the shelf* the Mary Seacole library (Westbourne site) is one of the biggest health education libraries in the UK.

COMPUTERS
◉ 900 WORKSTATIONS
Each site has its own computer rooms, not all have internet access. There's wireless access and loanable laptops. All University bedrooms have phone lines and a connection to the University network.

OTHER LEARNING FACILITIES
Lecture notes, discussion forums and course updates are online on Moodle, the virtual learning environment, *which is handy for anti-social types that want to stay in bed all day.*

ENTERTAINMENT ◌◌◌◌◌◌◌◌◌◌

CITY see University of Birmingham
There's a shopping centre with a couple of fast food outlets opposite the campus.

UNIVERSITY
◉ PRICE OF A PINT OF BEER £1.75
◉ GLASS OF WINE £1.90
◉ CAN OF RED BULL £1.40
BARS The main ones are the Bar 42 (Perry Barr – cap 600, leather sofas and weekly karaoke); thepavilion (Moor Lane Sports Centre); Village Inn (Hampstead) and iBar (Millennium Point, city centre). There's also a bar at the Conservatoire.
THEATRES/FILM *A drama group has been relentlessly doing stuff like Grease for the past few years, but people love it.* The film club shows blockbusters, world cinema and old favourites twice a week.
MUSIC VENUES/CLUBBING Big name bands are a rare sight, but Birmingham itself is always on the route of famous musicians passing through. Friday's Toons night (£2.50) at the Union Bar is *charty and cheesy*. Monday's Bounce is for R&B freaks (£2), Saturday's Summit 4 (free) is house and trance.
COMEDY/CABARET Funsters pop into thepavilion every fortnight.
FOOD Every site has an eatery; kosher and vegan meals are now on the menu. Café Quad does *pricey but bog-standard* canteen fare.
OTHER Two sports balls a year and various faculties and societies like to put on a bit of a do.

SOCIAL ◡◡◡◡◡◡◡◡◡◡◡

UCE BIRMINGHAM STUDENTS' UNION
◉ TURNOUT AT LAST BALLOT N/A ◉ NUS MEMBER
This was the first SU to become a limited company. *The local MP has an office on site, but that doesn't mean this is a hotbed of politicos. Split sites, limited facilities and downright disorganisation don't inspire confidence. They're good with awareness campaigns though.*

SU FACILITIES
The Union has facilities on five sites. At the SU's main centre at Perry Barr, there's a cheap bar, shop, advice centre, Endsleigh Insurance office, games machines, photo booth and photocopier.

CLUBS (NON-SPORTING)
ACS; Asian; BIAD; Breakdancing; Cheerleading; Chinese; Clubbing & DJing; Drum & Bass; Global; Hindu; Law; LINKS; Mooting; Nigerian; R 'n' B; Rock Soc; Scout & Guide; Sikh; SWSS; SocieTIC; Transform; Urban. **See also Clubs tables.**

OTHER ORGANISATIONS
Spaghetti Junction is the *picture-laden* student newspaper; SCRatch radio; charity Rag; community action group (involved in projects to help homeless amongst others).

RELIGIOUS
○ 5 CHAPLAINS (COFE, RC, METHODIST, URC)
In addition to the chaplaincy, there's a Muslim prayer room.

PAID WORK
○ JOB BUREAU
The University job bureau (part of the careers service) helps find work on campus, locally, during holidays and after graduation.

SPORTS ○○○○○○○○○○○○○○

○ RECENT SUCCESSES HOCKEY, FOOTBALL
○ BUSA RANKING 112
UCE Birmingham's set its sights on becoming a sporting champion. Investment in stonking new facilities like the pavilion is a hurdle in the right direction and there's plenty more development already in progress.

SPORTS FACILITIES
Sports-for-all policy tries to get as many as possible off their bottoms or out of the pubs. Charges for facilities are kept low, between 30p and £2 a pop. Facilities include: six football and rugby pitches; hockey and all-weather pitches; squash courts; basketball and netball courts; running track; croquet/bowling green; gym/multi-gym. Investment is going into three new sports developments, the biggest to be near the Perry Barr campus.

SPORTING CLUBS
Athletics; Boardriders; Boxing; Frisbee; Ice Hockey; Ju-Jitsu; Kick Boxing; Sky Diving; Table Tennis. **See also Clubs tables.**

ATTRACTIONS see University of Birmingham

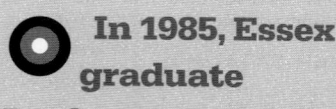

In 1985, Essex graduate Professor Rodolfo Neri Vela became Mexico's first astronaut, aboard the US Atlantis space shuttle.

ACCOMMODATION ○○○○○○○○○○

IN UNIVERSITY
○ CATERED 8% **○ COST** £69 (40WKS)
○ SELF-CATERING 11% **○ COST** £67 (40WKS)
○ INSURANCE PREMIUM ££
AVAILABILITY Five halls, mostly self-catering, two at the Perry Barr, one in the city centre and one each at the Wesbourne Road and Hampstead campuses. A student village in Perry Barr has 650 study bedrooms and University-leased houses and flats for 850 bodies. 3% share, some first years can't get a place. *Most halls are reputable and the en suite rooms at Oscott Gardens in Perry Barr inspire a spot of jealousy. There are a few self-contained studio flats (£65-85/wk) for post-grads and couples.*

EXTERNALLY see University of Birmingham
○ AVE RENT £65
AVAILABILITY *Houses aren't hard to get, quality varies significantly with price; £35 a week pays for a hovel in a ghetto, £55 a week will get something almost posh, by comparison.*
HOUSING HELP The accommodation service runs the head tenancy scheme and there's a register of approved housing.

WELFARE ○○○○○○○○○○○○

SERVICES
○ LGBT SOCIETY ○ LATE-NIGHT/WOMEN'S MINIBUS
○ UNIVERSITY COUNSELLORS 1 FULL/3 PART
○ CRIME RATING !!!!
Three campuses have drop-in advice centres and there's CCTV on every site.
HEALTH Nurses are based on three of the sites and local NHS practices are recommended.
Out-of-hours appointments are available as are Well Women Clinics and blood donor sessions.
CRECHES/NURSERY Perry Barr and Westbourne Road have nurseries for children aged 12mths-5yrs.
DISABLED A Disability Action Officer potters around the various campuses, making improvements; a Student Services Co-ordinator helps students with special needs, and the library has facilities for sight- and hearing-impaired people.

FINANCE
○ AVE DEBT PER YEAR £4,393
○ HOME STUDENT FEES £3,000
FEES International students pay £8,270. Foundation degrees cost £1,200.
○ ACCESS FUND £778,045
○ SUCCESSFUL APPLICATIONS/YR 2,174
SUPPORT Bursaries for students from low-income backgrounds.

Words in italics are Push's point of view — take it or leave it...

UCL

THE COLLEGE IS PART OF THE UNIVERSITY OF LONDON AND STUDENTS ARE ENTITLED TO USE ITS FACILTIES

⊙ **UNIVERSITY COLLEGE LONDON** Gower Street, London, WC1E 6BT **TEL** (020) 7679 2000 **E-MAIL** degree-info@ucl.ac.uk
WEBSITE www.ucl.ac.uk ⊙ **UNIVERSITY COLLEGE LONDON UNION** 25 Gordon Street, London, WC1H 0AY **TEL** (020) 7387 3611
E-MAIL ucl.union@ucl.ac.uk **WEBSITE** www.uclunion.org

GENERAL ◌◌◌◌◌◌◌◌◌◌◌◌◌

University College London (UCL) is the largest college in the University of London and *big enough to be a whopper university on its own*. Faculties and accommodation are concentrated in Bloomsbury, *so UCL's the nearest thing the University of London has to a campus in the city*. It was founded by a group of worthies influenced by the ideas of Jeremy Bentham, the famous Utilitarian philosopher, to promote equality and the crossing of class barriers. It had no religious leanings – which was unique in those days – and was also the first university college to admit women. The main building is *beautiful* with steps leading to an *impressive* portico at the main entrance. The library dome can be seen behind it. Three stone cloisters edge a big grass lawn. It's all a bit like an inner city stately home. *Unfortunately, the other buildings, humdrum brick, aren't all like that.* For general information on London see University of London.

SEX RATIO: ♂47 ♀53	FOUNDED: 1826
FULL-TIME U'GRADS: 11,894	PART-TIME: 190
POSTGRADS: 7,005	NON-DEGREE: 581
AVE COURSE: 3YRS	ETHNIC: 35%
STATE:PRIVATE SCHOOL: 59:41	FLUNK RATE: 7%
MATURE: 26%	INTERNATIONAL: 27%
DISABLED: 165	LOCAL: 34%

ATMOSPHERE

Most applicants think they're going to like being a student at UCL, and the University rarely disappoints. The increasingly middle-class student body are a fairly laid-back bunch – the atmosphere is one of drinking beer, contemplating navels and putting off that library stint for another hour. The size of the college and its proximity to all the temptations of the West End combine to dilute any specific college spirit, but it's not an unfriendly place.

SITES

ROYAL FREE AND UNIVERSITY COLLEGE MEDICAL SCHOOL The Royal Free Hospital site (about four miles away in Hampstead), and the Whittington Hospital site (at Archway). The Royal Free Hospital, an early 70s concrete building, is based in the *very upmarket and trendily wealthy London district of Hampstead. It's a relaxed environment and students demonstrate a team spirit which is usually put into practice on the sports field*. The School of Slavonic and East European Studies

(SSEES) merged with UCL in 1999 and is based in Bloomsbury. Space science and astronomy students have access to sites in Mill Hill (London) and Dorking (Surrey) with specialist observatories and equipment.

LONDON see University of London

TRAVEL see University of London
TRAINS Nearest tube to Senate House/ULU Building is Goodge Street (Northern Line).
CAR The University's slapbang in the middle of London, which means the congestion charge applies to vehicles on the roads around it. On-campus parking is *non-existent*.

CAREER PROSPECTS
⊙ **CAREERS SERVICE** ⊙ **NO. OF STAFF** 11 FULL
⊙ **UNEMPLOYED AFTER 6 MTHS** 5%
UCL has its own careers service, complete with job fairs, careers library and interview training.

FAMOUS ALUMNI
Britpoppers Brett Anderson (Suede) and Justine Frischmann (Elastica); Rabbi Lionel Blue (writer/broadcaster); Raymond Briggs (writer/illustrator); A S Byatt (novelist); Tom Courtney (actor); Jonathan Dimbleby (broadcaster); Ken Follet (writer); Sir Norman Foster (architect); Hugh Gaitskell (late former Labour leader); Mahatma Gandhi; David Gower (cricketer); Margaret Hodge MP (Lab); Derek Jarman (film director); Dr Hilary Jones (TV doctor); Jonathan Miller (writer/director); Sir Eduardo Paolozzi (artist/sculptor); Raj Persaud (celebrity shrink); Dr Mark Porter (another TV doctor); Stanley Spencer (artist); Marie Stopes (birth control pioneer); all of Coldplay.

SPECIAL FEATURES
UCL includes the Slade School of Fine Art – *dead prestigious and nothing to do with an 'It's Chriiiiiiistmas'-hollering yob-rock quartet from Wolverhampton.*

FURTHER INFO
⊙ **PROSPECTUSES** UNDERGRAD; POSTGRAD; SOME DEPARTMENTS ⊙ **OPEN DAYS** .

ACADEMIC ◌◌◌◌◌◌◌◌◌◌◌◌◌

⊙ **RUSSELL GROUP**
64 academic departments are grouped into eight faculties.

U

ENTRY POINTS: 240–360	AVE POINTS: 275
APPLICATIONS PER PLACE: N/A	CLEARING: 9%
NO. OF TERMS: 3	LENGTH OF TERMS: 10–11wks
STAFF TO STUDENT RATIO: N/A	STUDY ADDICTS: N/A
TEACHING: ★★★★★	RESEARCH: ★★★★★
1STS: 19%	2.2s: 21%
2.1s: 54%	3RDS: 6%

ADMISSIONS
○ APPLY VIA UCAS

SUBJECTS
ART & DESIGN 16%   **BUILT ENVIRONMENT** 5%
CLINICAL SCIENCES 11%   **ENGINEERING SCIENCES** 10%
LAW 5%   **LIFE SCIENCES** 20%
MATHEMATICAL & PHYSICAL SCIENCES 14%
SOCIAL & HISTORICAL SCIENCES 19%
BEST *for pretty much everything*: Art & Design;
Biology & Related Sciences; Building & Planning;
Business; Civil, Chemical & Other Engineering;
Communications & Information Studies;
Economics; Electronic & Electrical Engineering;
English-based Studies; European Architecture;
Finance & Accounting; History & Archaeology;
Human & Social Geography; Languages & Area
Studies; Law; Management; Mathematical
Studies; Mechanically-Based Engineering;
Medical Science & Pharmacy; Medicine &
Dentistry; Philosophy; Physical Science; Theology
& Religious Studies; Politics; Psychology;
Sociology, Social Policy & Anthropology; Subjects
allied to Medicine.

LIBRARIES
○ **1,500,000** BOOKS ○ **1,514** STUDY PLACES
Apart from the Main library there are 15
specialist book barns and another at the Royal
Free. The British Library's nearby to *plug
any gaps.*

COMPUTERS
○ **781** WORKSTATIONS
Advance booking for computers available and
some 24-hr access.

OTHER LEARNING FACILITIES
Language lab; drama facilities and music
rehearsal rooms at Bloomsbury Theatre; limited
media centre at the Slade.

ENTERTAINMENT ◖◗◖◗◖◗◖◗◖◗

THE CITY see University of London
○ PRICE OF A PINT OF BEER £2.40
○ GLASS OF WINE £2.80
○ CAN OF RED BULL £2

UNIVERSITY
○ PRICE OF A PINT OF BEER £1.50
○ GLASS OF WINE £1.75
○ CAN OF RED BULL £1.50

*Students gripe that UCL's ents, particularly in the
clubbing department, are limp as old celery.
Something of which the bright lights and
wallet-draining delights of London town could
never be accused, luckily.*
BARS There are eight bars around the campus and
in its halls of residence, the central one being the
pub-like Phineas. Others include the sporty
second floor Bar, the vast Windeyer and Gordon's
Café Bar. Another three bars are at the Royal Free
site – the Doctors', Students' and Hospital Bars.
THEATRES The Bloomsbury Theatre hosts student
and professional productions. There's also a
smaller theatre, the Garage, *where fringe stuff
gets to see the light of day.*
FILM There's a cinema in the Union and a
film society.
MUSIC VENUES Occasional theme nights (eg. salsa)
with live bands. Royal Free has the New JCR
(cap 200) for live bands and the Peter Samuel
Hall for classical music. Easy J's has live music on
a Tuesday.
CLUBBING *A mouldy low-fat sarnie rather than a
deep-fill triple pack with extra cheese. Some
events on offer, but they don't satisfy many.*
COMEDY/CABARET Ross Noble, Ricky Gervais and
other *examples of laughing gas in human form*
have appeared at the fortnightly Ministry of
Comedy nights .
FOOD Food in the Union *ain't cheap or particulary
tasty, but there is plenty of it* – snack and
sandwich bars and food served in six of the bars
as well as cafés in some departments. There are
also three University refectories, the hospital
canteen, bars and a servery at the Royal Free.
OTHER Three black tie balls a year *for those who
can't resist the lure of the penguin suit.*

SOCIAL ◖◗◖◗◖◗◖◗◖◗◖◗

UNIVERSITY COLLEGE LONDON UNION
○ **6** SABBATICALS ○ TURNOUT AT LAST BALLOT 11%
○ NUS MEMBER
*UCLU as a whole isn't renowned for political
activity, although individual student parties are
strong and top MPs often drop by to debate the
issues of the day. It's very close to ULU, so those
desperate for a soap box or frantic for fantastic
facilities don't have far to go.*

SU FACILITIES
In UCLU's main building: four bars; fast food and
sandwich bars; two shops including a general
shop; print shop; travel agency; advice centre;
HSBC ATM; hairdresser; games machines and
pool tables. There's a shop; various games; pool
table; Lloyds TSB ATM and satellite TV at the
Royal Free site.

CLUBS (NON-SPORTING)
Anime; Balls (juggling); Bongos; BTV (TV-makers);
Cheese Grater Magazine; Human Pals; Jazz; Live
Music; MD's Comedy Revue; Modo (Fashion);

Music; Musical; Muslim Media Forum; Pi Magazine; Prawn Magazine; Rare FM; Salsa; Stage Crew; Urban Music; VOCE (gospel choir); Abacus (helps Chinese students integrate); Ahmadiyya Muslim; Arab; Bangla; Card Gaming; Chess; Chinese; Christian Medics RUMS; Cypriot; Duke Of Edinburgh; European; Friends Of Palestine; German; Hellenic; Hindu; Human Powered Flight; Indian; Investment; Japan; Malaysian; Masaryk (Eastern Europe); Medical Ethics; Medieval; Model United Nations; Pagan; Pakistan; Persian; Rag; Russian; Sikh; Singapore; Social Forum; Sri Lankan; Stop the War; Student Industrial (extra skills training); Taiwanese; Thai; Turkish; Volunteering; Welsh. **See also Clubs tables.**

OTHER ORGANISATIONS

'PI' is the official monthly rag. The award-winning television station 'BTV' can be seen occasionally at Union venues. 'Rare FM' (www.rarefm.co.uk) has been the most-listened-to online student radio station and does an *old-style* FM broadcast one month a year. Union Volunteers organises voluntary placements in the local community. At the Royal Free there's Spectrum community action group and a Rag week.

RELIGIOUS

Despite UCL's *godless foundations*, the Christian Union is one of London's largest. In the Union there's a multi-purpose meditation room and the University's church (the Church of Christ the King) is in Byng Place.

PAID WORK see University of London

● **JOB BUREAU**

This being London, many students need to earn a bit of extra cash. Luckily, the capital has no shortage of opportunities for bar and shop work and the Union-run Workstation is invaluable in finding flexible, part-time work. A bunch of student entrepreneurs make money from their IT skills, running website companies and the like.

SPORTS ()()()()()()()()()()()()()

● **BUSA RANKING** 48

All faculties keep Wednesday afternoons free for sports, although facilities are not so free – there's an annual charge for the Bloomsbury Fitness Centre. *Royal Free has a strong sporting reputation among the London medical schools.*

SPORTS FACILITIES

In the Bloomsbury Fitness Centre (also open to the public) there are: squash courts; aerobics, fencing and dance halls; weights gym. The sports centre at Somers Town is ten mins walk from campus. The UCLU sports grounds at Shenley in Hertfordshire provide good facilities and is also Watford FC's training ground.

SPORTING CLUBS

5-a-side football; Boat RUMS; Darts; Fives Handball; Gliding; Ju-Jitsu; Kendo; Lacrosse; Shaolin Gong Fu; Shorinji Kempo; Skate; Skydive; Snooker & Pool; Table Tennis; Thai Martial Arts; Ultimate Frisbee; Waterpolo; Wing Chun Kung Fu. **See also Clubs tables**.

ATTRACTIONS see University of London

There is no end to London's sporting attractions: from tennis and strawberries at Wimbledon to football and fighting at Millwall; from cricket at Lords to croquet at Hurlingham; from athletics at Crystal Palace to rugby at Twickers; from... *well, as we said, there's no end.*

ACCOMMODATION ()()()()()()()()()()()

IN COLLEGE

● **CATERED** 6%   ● **COST** £103 (37 WKS)
● **SELF-CATERING** 22%   ● **COST** £106 (37WKS)
● **INSURANCE PREMIUM** £££££

AVAILABILITY All first years who apply in time get college accommodation. Second years are almost certainly on their own, but a few finalists come back. In addition to UCL's accommodation there are places in the University's intercollegiate halls. There's also accommodation at the Royal Free. Catered halls provide breakfast and evening meals every day, except Ifor Evans which doesn't at weekends and has cooking facilities instead. Self-catering flats and houses have *good, big* kitchens with a couple of cookers and fridges between ten people. Facilities include launderettes, TV lounges, games rooms and computer rooms and bars, depending on the place. *Halls tend to be in better nick than flats and are a pretty cheap way to live in England's extortionate capital.*

CAR PARKING Only available at Max Rayne, Ifor Evans and Langton Close. *Parking is by permit only and permits are like gold dust. This is London, after all.*

EXTERNALLY see University of London

● **AVE RENT** £110

AVAILABILITY Many UCL students live in Stoke Newington (the number 73 bus runs to UCL) and the Finsbury Park/Manor House ghetto or Camden *if they're feeling flush. The areas around the Royal Free are more expensive.*

HOUSING HELP UCL keeps information on private and College accommodation and publishes a regular bulletin.

WELFARE ⊙⊙⊙⊙⊙⊙⊙⊙⊙⊙⊙⊙⊙⊙

SERVICES
- ⊙ LGBT OFFICER ⊙ MATURE STUDENTS' OFFICER
- ⊙ POSTGRAD OFFICER ⊙ DISABILITIES OFFICER
- ⊙ INTERNATIONAL STUDENTS' OFFICER
- ⊙ SELF-DEFENCE CLASSES ⊙ NIGHTLINE
- ⊙ COLLEGE COUNSELLORS 3 FULL/5 PART
- ⊙ CRIME RATING !!!!!

Students' welfare needs are *well-tended*. The University provides counsellors and personal tutors, while the SU lays *on a host of advisors*.
HEALTH The Gower Street Health Centre has three GPs, dentists and a practice nurse.
WOMEN The SU has two advisors for female students. Subsidised attack alarms *can be picked up* from the Union shop.
CRECHES/NURSERY 38 places are available for kiddies aged between 3mths-5yrs.

FINANCE
- ⊙ AVE DEBT PER YEAR £3,118
- ⊙ HOME STUDENT FEES £3,000
- **FEES** International students pay £8,270. Foundation degrees cost £1,200.
- ⊙ ACCESS FUND £778,045
- ⊙ SUCCESSFUL APPLICATIONS/YR 2,174
- **SUPPORT** There's an access fund and cash from others eg. the Friend's Trust, is occasionally available – notices are posted by the Registry department.

▶ **UEA**
see *University of East Anglia*

▶ **UEL**
see *University of East London*

▶ **UMIST**
see *University of Manchester*

▶ **THE UNITED MEDICAL AND DENTAL SCHOOLS (UMDS)**
see *King's College, London*

▶ **UNIVERSITY COLLEGE LONDON**
see *UCL*

▶ **UNIVERSITY COLLEGE STOCKTON**
see *Durham University*

▶ **UNIVERSITY OF CENTRAL ENGLAND**
see *UCE Birmingham*

⊙ **UCL removed the preserved head of philosopher Jeremy Bentham from its display case after a group of King's College students 'borrowed' it for a game of football.**

ULSTER UNIVERSITY

1) **● UNIVERSITY OF ULSTER** Cromore Road, Coleraine, Co. Londonderry, BT52 1SA **TEL** (08700) 400 700 **E-MAIL** online@ulster.ac.uk **WEBSITE** www.ulster.ac.uk **● UUSU** University of Ulster, Cromore Road, Coleraine, Co. Londonderry, BT52 1SA **TEL** (028) 7032 4323 **E-MAIL** info@uusu.org **WEBSITE** www.uusu.org
2) **● THE UNIVERSITY OF ULSTER** Jordanstown, Shore Road, Newtonabbey, Co. Antrim, BT37 0QB
3) **● THE UNIVERSITY OF ULSTER** York Street, Belfast, BT15 1ED
4) **● THE UNIVERSITY OF ULSTER** Magee Campus, Northland Road, Londonderry, BT48 7JL

GENERAL ◖◖◖◖◖◖◖◖◖◖◖◖◖◖◖

Once upon a time, there was a university and a polytechnic in Northern Ireland. Then, in 1984, they merged and became one large university with four distinct sites, *thinly* spread across three of the six counties. The largest is Jordanstown, the former poly site on the hills above Belfast overlooking the Lough (bay), and the smallest (housing Art & Design) is in Belfast city centre. The University HQ is on the outskirts of Coleraine, nearly 60 miles north of Belfast on the *beautiful* Antrim coast. 30 miles to the west of that is the fourth site, Magee College in (London)Derry. Each site may be part of the same institution, but *geography will be geography and no grand integration plan is going to prevent them from maintaining their own separate and unique atmospheres. Indeed, all that Jordanstown and Coleraine have in common are a beautiful, isolated setting and unlovable modern concrete buildings.*

👤👤👤👤👤👤👤👤👤👤👤👤👤👤👤👤👤👤👤👤

SEX RATIO: ♂40 ♀60	**FOUNDED:** 1968
FULL-TIME U'GRADS: 15,192	**PART-TIME:** 3,027
POSTGRADS: 4,816	**NON-DEGREE:** 6,791
AVE COURSE: 3YRS	**ETHNIC:** N/A
STATE:PRIVATE SCHOOL: 100:0	**FLUNK RATE:** 17%
MATURE: 21%	**INTERNATIONAL:** 12%
DISABLED: 375	**LOCAL:** N/A

ATMOSPHERE
We're talking about four different sites here which, despite the University's best efforts towards integration and certain similarities in the make-up of the student body (a strong sense of community thanks to so many being local), still stubbornly remain up to 80 miles apart. Failing divine intervention, they'll remain geographically separate, so that's how we'll treat them.

SITES
JORDANSTOWN (14,075 students) The largest site swallows the vast majority of the student population and is still *greedily* expanding. Belfast, seven miles away, is the nearest town of any size. *There is a slight degree of isolation though the campus is well-connected and the attractive grounds and views over the bay provide some compensation. Designed around a central mall, some buildings hail from the 70s and some are younger, altogether it's a bit of a maze-like hotchpotch. Most of the students go home every weekend, so there's no room for claustrophobia. Relaxed and occasionally a bit vacant.*

COLERAINE (5,524 students) The original site of the University and its current administrative HQ. The campus is on the edge of the *small, quiet and nearly-but-not-quite-happening* market town of Coleraine, and less than five miles from the coastal resorts of Portrush and Portstewart, where most students live. The neighbouring towns make up 'the Triangle' – not an apocalyptic cult, but an *amiable threesome* of seaside tourist spots. The campus is surrounded by green countryside and nearby the Giant's Causeway reaches out across the Irish sea towards Scotland. *It's a studious, peaceful place – sometimes a tad too peaceful. Every night at 6pm the campus sputters to a halt. This is true for weekends too (so if you're after a blinding Saturday night, better be inventive). There is grooving to be had, though, in the pubs and clubs in Portrush and Portstewart.*

MAGEE (2,980 full-time students) An *attractive* campus on the River Foyle, just north of the old city of (London)Derry. The £3m centre for Dramatic Arts has *increased the pulse somewhat.*

BELFAST (1,213 students) Art & Design students are housed on York Street, just a mile away from Queen's University Belfast, *whose facilities they share and which is the focus of their social life. A £30m redevelopment programme is underway, which should make it something to stop and gawp at while in Belfast.*

BELFAST see Queen's University Belfast

COLERAINE/PORTRUSH/PORTSTEWART
The three towns form a triangle with the two ports to the north providing accommodation, jobs and *sporadic* nightlife, and Coleraine at the south tip providing what could only be called amenities. A town of 25,000 give or take a few, Coleraine has a *fair sprinkling of cheapy* supermarkets, Irish and UK banks and bookshops. *It's an isolated, parochial, coastal and touristy outpost.*

(LONDON)DERRY
An ancient and *scenic* city and Northern Ireland's second biggest. The huge stone walls betray the city's turbulent history. *People's lives aren't ruled by terrorism though, but by the normal, mundane concerns like getting down the pub. (Okay, the London prefix thing: saying 'Londonderry' marks a person as pro-Unionist, saying Derry ruffles the feathers the other way. Either way, students are stuffed. No wonder most come from Northern Ireland – at least they understand the questions, even if they don't know the answers.)*

TRAVEL see Queen's University Belfast
TRAINS Direct lines from Coleraine to Belfast and (London)Derry only on Northern Ireland Railways. Trains are frequent and *frequently dirty*. Trains for Dublin can also be picked up from Belfast.
COACHES Goldline Express and Ulsterbus link Belfast, (London)Derry and Coleraine.
CAR The M2 and the A26 provide *a fast route between Jordanstown and Coleraine.*
AIR Flights to the UK and mainland Europe from Belfast International. Other flights go to the UK from Belfast City Airport and Derry airport in the north-west.
HITCHING *Good between Coleraine and the ports, otherwise only with the greatest care.*
LOCAL *Comprehensive and expensive local bus routes*, but half-price for students around Coleraine. Ulsterbus does various student discounts.
TAXIS *Readily available and cheap if shared.*
BICYCLES *With the hills and inclement weather, cycling's only for the hardy, but bike theft's not too much of a worry.*

CAREER PROSPECTS
○ CAREERS SERVICE ○ NO. OF STAFF 4 FULL
○ UNEMPLOYED AFTER 6 MTHS 5%
The main office is, predictably, at Jordanstown but each site puts on some kind of effort. Coleraine's looks after students up to three years after graduation.

FAMOUS ALUMNI
Gerry Anderson (radio personality); Brian Friel (playwright); Kate Hoey MP (Lab); Brian Keenan (ex-hostage); Brian Robinson (Irish rugby). Honorary graduates include: Amanda Burton (TV actress); James Nesbitt (Cold Feet); Ewan McGregor (actor).

SPECIAL FEATURES
It's rare to have to travel between the sites, rarer still because of a video conferencing facility. It's not for chats about the weather, though. The Jordanstown site has a pet cemetery. *Don't all cry at once.*

FURTHER INFO
○ PROSPECTUSES UNDERGRAD; POSTGRAD; DEPARTMENTAL
○ OPEN DAYS

ACADEMIC ◖◖◖◖◖◖◖◖◖◖◖◖

Ulster's a busy and rampantly progressive institution. Public speaking and debating are encouraged because they're seen as being useful in the workplace. *Students have a good deal of independence in their own learning, something the University encourages.*

ENTRY POINTS: 160–360	AVE POINTS: 228
APPLICATIONS PER PLACE: 6	CLEARING: 1%
NO. OF TERMS: 3	LENGTH OF TERMS: 12WKS
STAFF TO STUDENT RATIO: 1:18	STUDY ADDICTS: 15%
TEACHING: ✱✱✱	RESEARCH: ✱✱✱
YEAR ABROAD: <1%	SANDWICH STUDENTS: 46%
1STS: 12%	2.2S: 34%
2.1S: 51%	3RDS: 3%

ADMISSIONS
○ APPLY VIA UCAS
Admissions are taken on academic ability only. If the points are met, the student's in.

SUBJECTS
ARTS 14%   **BUSINESS/MANAGEMENT** 22%
ENGINEERING 25%   **LAW** 5%
LIFE & HEALTH SCIENCES 25%
SOCIAL SCIENCES 25%
BEST Business & Management; Celtic Studies; Economics; Education; Hospitality, Leisure, Sport & Tourism; Maths, Statistics & Operational Research; Nursing; Other Subjects Allied to Medicine; Philosophy; Politics; Psychology.
UNUSUAL Dance; Postgrad diplomas in: Belfast: The Social & Cultural History of a Changing City; Coastal Zone Management; Dementia Studies; Disaster Relief; Peace & Conflict Studies.

LIBRARIES
○ 750,000 BOOKS ○ 2,831 STUDY PLACES
○ SPEND PER STUDENT £
University libraries are sprinkled across the campuses. Jordanstown's has just been vamped up, in Coleraine it's considered *adequate*, Belfast has the arts books, Magee the Irish ones *(so Push wonders where students of Irish Art go)*. *It's tricky to travel to some of the other campuses to work, but the ambitious* virtual campus (www.campusione.ulster.ac.uk) attempts to link everyone cybernetically, at least.

COMPUTERS
○ 6,000 WORKSTATIONS ○ 24 HR ACCESS
Each facility has its own computers and there are up to four IT centres on each campus. There are ports for laptops, including net access but with extra charges for printing.

OTHER LEARNING FACILITIES
Graphics centre; TV studio; language lab.

ENTERTAINMENT ◖◖◖◖◖◖◖◖◖

THE CITY see Queen's University Belfast

COLERAINE
○ PRICE OF A PINT OF BEER £1.80
○ GLASS OF WINE £2.20
○ CAN OF RED BULL £1.20
Coleraine's *far from the beating heart of the fun monster and what there is can be jealously guarded by a hulking, tattooed section of the local*

U

population. *Any nightlife is found in Portrush and Portstewart.*

CINEMAS Coleraine has the Jet Centre, *a little more dynamic-sounding than it really is.* Portrush has the Playhouse, a student fave that shows all sorts of *quality flicks.*

PUBS *Burberry's is the only pub of note in Coleraine itself, but the Derry and Harbour Inn at Portrush and the Anchor and O'Hara's in Portstewart are pretty pro-student money.* The Bushmill's distillery is nearby and does guided tours.

CLUBBING Trax (Portrush) is the *student meat market* on a Monday.

MUSIC VENUES *Loads of the bars and clubs host bands, some are less impressive than others such as Snappers in Portstewart.* Pushplugs: O'Hara's in Portstewart (traditional music).

EATING OUT *The ports have all the chips and candyfloss a fat kid could ever want, but only during the summer season.* Pushplugs: Morelli's in Portstewart (for ice cream).

UNIVERSITY

○ **PRICE OF A PINT OF BEER** £2.20
○ **GLASS OF WINE** £2.20
○ **CAN OF RED BULL** £1.80

Not entertainmentsville by a long shot; students actually prefer to seek out the local hotspots.

BARS Jordanstown and Magee have two bars apiece; *nothing at Coleraine but plans to open a boozer at Belfast.*

THEATRES The *jewel in the crown* is the Riverside Theatre at Coleraine, the third-largest professional theatre in Northern Ireland. The Riverside programme incorporates drama, music recitals, rock bands, contemporary dance, ballet, opera, variety, children's shows, pantomimes and recordings for TV and radio. There's a smaller effort at Jordanstown.

MUSIC VENUES Local bands call in at all the sites. *Jordanstown comes out best with its Assembly Hall, though Coleraine's Biko Hall ain't bad either and the Riverside occasionally pulls something out of the hat.*

CLUBBING *The most popular night out is Kelly's in Portrush. The Saturday night raves at Conor Hall in Belfast are popular too and can attract big DJs. Most campuses will have something quietly rocking along most nights.*

COMEDY/CABARET Something to watch or laugh at – *and Push doesn't mean your flatmates* – at each site.

FOOD All sites except Belfast have *cheap but basic* canteens run by the SU. Belfast has no catering facilities. Banside canteen at Coleraine may *be best avoided.*

OTHER Freshers ball every year and various others. The Hallowe'en festival in Derry is like a mini Mardi Gras.

THE UNIVERSITY OF ULSTER STUDENTS' UNION (UUSU)

○ **10** SABBATICALS ○ **TURNOUT AT LAST BALLOT** 5%
○ **NUS MEMBER**

Coherent political identity is a tall order at the best of times, but when everything's so spread out it's almost impossible. Technically speaking, the SU co-ordinates ents and facilities across all sites but is distant and unapproachable and has difficulty achieving any kind of global view. Most students think the SU is just a bar.

SU FACILITIES

All sites have bars and snack bars or cafeteria facilities as well as music venues. In the South Building at Coleraine: general shop; ATM; pool tables; crèche; travel agents; hairdresser; launderette; printing facilities; vending machines; jukebox. At Jordanstown: shop; travel agents; ATM; insurance office; secondhand bookshop; car and van hire; photocopying. At Belfast: art shop; games room; free shuttle after SU ents. Magee: general shop; photocopier; photo booth.

CLUBS (NON-SPORTING)

Applied Arts; Arts & Crafts; Civil Engineering; International; Irish Language; Law; Political; Silversmith, plus a handful more on the other sites. **See also Clubs tables**.

OTHER ORGANISATIONS

Each site has its own publication and there's an all-site publication called – *wait for it* – 'Foursite', as well as the Coleraine-based publication 'Euphoria'. The combined Rag raises a trickle of money every year with *wacky stunts and zany antics and student groups do good work – sorry about this* – 'fourging' links with their respective local communities.

RELIGIOUS

Non-denominational prayer rooms are available. *Non-Christians will be a bit pushed to find a handy worship stop.*

PAID WORK see University of London

○ **JOB BUREAU**

The University employs around 300 people throughout the year. There's plenty of part-time/vacation work to be had in local bars, cafés and other tourist traps.

○ **RECENT SUCCESSES** KARATE, ATHLETICS
○ **BUSA RANKING** 48

Sport's an enthusiasm on a campus-wide rather than a University-wide basis. *The best facilities*

are inevitably centred on Jordanstown and Coleraine, but the nearby coast offers a host of opportunities for hydrophiliacs.

SPORTS FACILITIES

Coleraine and Jordanstown have over 40 acres of playing fields (collectively); sports centres; athletics tracks; steam rooms; squash and tennis courts. Coleraine has floodlit hockey and soccer pitches; fitness suite; netball; multigym and gym. Centre at Somers Town is ten mins walk from campus. The UCLU sports grounds at Shenley in Hertfordshire provide good facilities and is also Watford FC's training ground.

SPORTING CLUBS

8-ball Pool; Aikido; Camogie; Gaelic Football (Men's & Women's); Hurling; Ju-Jitsu; Mountaineering; Surf; Table Tennis. **See also Clubs tables**.

ATTRACTIONS see Queen's University Belfast
The Antrim coast provides *some of the best* surfing, wind surfing and swimming conditions in the British Isles, *though it can be ferocious at times*. Fishing is popular too, as is rock climbing, mountaineering, parachuting and rowing. Irish games such as hurling, camogie and Gaelic football should be experienced, and the rugby teams are in the highest Irish leagues.

ACCOMMODATION ◖◖◖◖◖◖◖◖◖◖

IN UNIVERSITY
- **SELF-CATERING** 17% - **COST** £48 (37WKS)
- **1ST YRS LIVING IN** 65%
- **INSURANCE PREMIUM** £

AVAILABILITY All first years can be housed, as can international students if they meet the 1st August deadline. Jordanstown has six-bedroom houses and flats, Coleraine offers four lots of halls and flats and Magee has three blocks and a student village. Belfast art students need to find their own pads, though there's a head tenancy scheme to help them.
CAR PARKING Car parking is easy and without the hassle of needing a permit.

EXTERNALLY see Queen's University Belfast
- **AVE RENT** £55 - **LIVING AT HOME** 35%
AVAILABILITY *Pretty easy to find*. Many of those at the main campus live in Belfast. Most students at Coleraine live in the port towns, *where housing is*

exceptionally cheap and more affluent students fork out a bit more for a single flat. The University's renting scheme shares houses at the ports that are given up to tourists during the summer. *Most are more than happy with a comfortable room in a shared house. Cars make life simpler at Coleraine and parking is not problem.*
HOUSING HELP Both the SU and the accommodation office dispense advice.

WELFARE ◖◖◖◖◖◖◖◖◖◖◖◖

SERVICES
- **LGBT OFFICER** - **POSTGRAD SOCIETY**
- **WOMEN'S OFFICER & SOCIETY**
- **INTERNATIONAL STUDENTS' OFFICER & SOCIETY**
- **MATURE STUDENTS' OFFICER & SOCIETY**
- **SELF-DEFENCE CLASSES**
- **UNIVERSITY COUNSELLORS** 3 FULL/3 PART
- **CRIME RATING** !

There's a parent support group and the University is proud of its childcare provision with *well-run* crèches at all sites. There are counsellors on every site and a full-time mental health advisor. The SU adds three welfare officers. The SU solicitor's on hand once a week with legal advice. The chaplaincy runs a non-alcoholic bar at Jordanstown.
HEALTH The University of Ulster has a health clinic on each site.
DISABILITIES Sites have ramps, parking, special accommodation, automatic doors, talking lifts, Braille signs, toilet facilities and dropped kerbs. Also there's the Coalition for Disability Awareness and the Joint Universities Deaf Education. *A significant effort is being made to improve things.*

FINANCE
- **AVE DEBT PER YEAR** £3,251
- **HOME STUDENT FEES** £3,000
FEES International students pay £8,270. Foundation degrees cost £1,200.
- **ACCESS FUND** nearly £1m
- **AVE PAYMENT** £500-£3,500
- **SUCCESSFUL APPLICATIONS**/YR 200
SUPPORT Several kinds of financial aid are available, including endowments for home students, the *amusingly named* Visa Card Royalty Fund, the Royal & Ancient Golf Bursary Scheme of £1,500 a year for outstanding golfers plus other sports bursaries. Fee waivers are available for *impoverished but capable* students. Most of these involve an interview with the Student Funding Advisor.

➡ **UNIVERSITY OF WALES INSTITUTE, CARDIFF**
see *UWIC*

➡ **UNIVERSITY OF THE WEST OF ENGLAND**
see *UWE, Bristol*

UWE, BRISTOL

1) **◉ UWE, BRISTOL, FRENCHAY CAMPUS** Coldharbour Lane, Bristol, BS16 1QY **TEL** (0117) 328 3333 **E-MAIL** admissions@uwe.ac.uk **WEBSITE** www.uwe.ac.uk **◉ UWE STUDENTS' UNION, FRENCHAY CAMPUS** Coldharbour Lane, Bristol, BS16 1QY **TEL** (0117) 328 2577 **E-MAIL** union@uwe.ac.uk **WEBSITE** www.uwesu.net
2) **◉ GLENSIDE CAMPUS** Blackberry Hill, Bristol, BS16 1DD **TEL** (0117) 328 8534 **◉ SU TEL** (0117) 328 8514
3) **◉ ST MATTHIAS CAMPUS** Oldbury Court Road, Fishponds, Bristol, BS16 2JP **TEL** (0117) 328 4458 **◉ SU TEL** (0117) 328 4435
4) **◉ BOWER ASHTON CAMPUS** Kennel Lodge Road, Bristol, BS3 2JT **TEL** (0117) 328 4716 **◉ SU TEL** (0117) 328 4725

GENERAL ◑◑◑◑◑◑◑◑◑◑◑◑◑

UWE is divided into four campuses with a main campus five miles north of the city centre at Frenchay. *It's been facelift central since the late 90s* with new lecture theatres, a five-floor library, a new Education facility, new Architecture studios, a £1m Genomics lab, a £1m Revolutionary Machining lab and, newest of all, a new student village and sports facilities in 2006. *Phew.* The other campuses, described below, are spread out around Bristol. They have their own courses and are *roughly* self-contained, although all students are allowed to use facilities at the main campus. For general information about Bristol see University of Bristol.

🚶🚶🚶🚶🚶🚶🚶🚶🚶🚶🚶🚶🚶🚶🚶🚶🚶🚶🚶🚶

SEX RATIO: ♂41 ♀59	**FOUNDED:** 1992
FULL-TIME U'GRADS: 15,229	**PART-TIME:** 931
POSTGRADS: 7,388	**NON-DEGREE:** 3,275
AVE COURSE: 3YRS	**ETHNIC:** 10%
STATE:PRIVATE SCHOOL: 87:13	**FLUNK RATE:** 16%
MATURE: 22%	**INTERNATIONAL:** 8%
DISABLED: 285	**LOCAL:** 35%

ATMOSPHERE
The University's a bit fragmented, with the subsidiary sites feeling a bit lonely. The city, though, lends itself to student shenanigans. There's a safe, middle-class feel about, although the SU has been known to raise up some political agitation in the past. There's occasional tension with locals, though no more than at other student cities.

SITES
GLENSIDE CAMPUS (3,375 full-time students – Faculty of Health & Social Care) A Victorian edifice, 1.5 miles from Frenchay, with refectory, bar and so on.

ST MATTHIAS CAMPUS (3,000 – Schools of Cultural Studies, English & Drama, History) Two and a half miles from Frenchay with a Graduate School and two halls of residence. *By far the best-looking site* with a Gothic-style listed building and sunken lawn. *It feels more like Hogwarts than a University.* A tight-knit community and *almost a college in its own right.*
BOWER ASHTON CAMPUS (1,600 – Bristol School of Art, Media & Design) Two miles from the city centre near the Clifton Suspension Bridge, but *with the advantage of being in a studenty area.* 7.5 miles from Frenchay, this is *an overwhelmingly white concrete and glass oblong, not built to appeal to the aesthetic nature of students based here, but hopefully the forthcoming recevelopment will sexy things up a bit.* Surrounded by *pleasant* fields, and again almost entirely separate from the main campus.

BRISTOL see University of Bristol

TRAVEL see University of Bristol
LOCAL *Not enough of it and too pricey, according to the Union,* who've been lobbying a local bus company for improvements.
UNIVERSITY There's a free inter-campus bus every 30 mins. Hourly student shuttle bus to/from city centre student accommodation to Frenchay campus for £1 (sgl).

CAREER PROSPECTS
◉ CAREERS SERVICE ◉ NO. OF STAFF 8 FULL/4 PART **◉ UNEMPLOYED AFTER 6MTHS** 7%

FAMOUS ALUMNI
Kyran Bracken, Simon Shaw (England World Cup rugby players); David Hempleman-Adams (adventurer); Dawn Primarolo MP (Lab); Geoff Twentyman (ex-footballer now BBC sports presenter).

> **◉ When 'Mastermind' was filmed at Ulster University, students kidnapped the Black Chair. When the BBC refused to pay a ransom, the chair was pushed into the River Bann.**

Words in italics are Push's point of view – take it or leave it...

FURTHER INFO
- **PROSPECTUSES** UNDERGRAD; POSTGRAD; SOME DEPARTMENTAL; CD-ROM
- **OPEN DAYS**

ACADEMIC

UWE has a *slight techie bias*, although it's *pretty competent* for arts and humanities.

ENTRY POINTS: 160–360	AVE POINTS: 260
APPLICATIONS PER PLACE: 6	CLEARING: 6%
NO. OF TERMS: 3	LENGTH OF TERMS: 11WKS
STAFF TO STUDENT RATIO: 1:20	STUDY ADDICTS: 19%
TEACHING: **	RESEARCH: **
YEAR ABROAD: 3%	SANDWICH STUDENTS: 15%
1STS: 12%	2.2S: 35%
2.1S: 46%	3RDS: 5%

ADMISSIONS
- **APPLY VIA UCAS/NMAS FOR NURSING/GTTR (TEACHING)**

SUBJECTS
APPLIED SCIENCES 9%   ART, MEDIA & DESIGN 8%
BRISTOL BUSINESS SCHOOL 15%   BUILT ENVIRONMENT 10%   COMPUTING, ENGINEERING & MATHEMATICAL SCIENCES 11%   EDUCATION 3%
HARTPURY COLLEGE 5%   HEALTH & SOCIAL CARE 10%
HUMANITIES, LANGUAGES & SOCIAL SCIENCES 24%
LAW 6%

BEST Art, Media & Design; Biological & Biomedical Sciences; Building & Quantity Surveying; Business & Management; Cultural & Media Studies; Economics; Education; Electronic Engineering; English; French, German, Spanish & Linguistics; Land & Property Management; Law; Maths, Statistics & Operational Research; Nursing & Midwifery; Physiotherapy, Occupational Therapy, Radiography; Politics; Psychology; Sociology; Town & Country Planning & Housing.
UNUSUAL Forensic Sciences.

LIBRARIES
- **567,962 BOOKS** ● **2,118 STUDY PLACES** ● **24-HR ACCESS** ● **SPEND PER STUDENT** £
There are libraries on all campuses relating to the studies based there.

COMPUTERS
- **1,820 WORKSTATIONS** ● **24-HR ACCESS**
60 computer rooms, one open round the clock. *Still not enough machines.* Internet access all over the University, with cyber kiosks in two bars on Frenchay campus. Wi-fi zones in the main library.

OTHER LEARNING FACILITIES
Movable walls in the Architecture building; mock courtroom; mock crime room and outdoor crime scene area; language lab (non-linguists welcome); studio space at Spike Island Studios and the Arnofini (for Bower Ashton arty types).

ENTERTAINMENT

THE CITY see University of Bristol

UNIVERSITY
- **PRICE OF A PINT OF BEER** £1.65
- **GLASS OF WINE** £1.60
- **CAN OF RED BULL** £1.50
BARS The Escape bar's the *social hub* but the Venue stays open late and hosts events. Core 24 is run by the University. All do food of some description.
FILM/THEATRE Musicals and *proper plays* at the theatre run by the Centre for Performing Arts. Occasional film screenings in the Union.
MUSIC VENUES Battle of the Bands and local strummers often sell out at Venue and Core 24 (cap 1,000). Babyshambles, Athlete and Lemar have taken to the stage.
CLUBBING Crunchie (cheese/R'n'B) is the Friday night spectacular. Saturday night's Escapism (hip hop, funk, soul, metal) at the Escape bar is a *refuge against cheese*. Scott Mills and DJ Spoony have played.
COMEDY/CABARET Glenside campus gets regular touring comedians for a fiver a night.
FOOD The University Refectory is the main scoff stop. The Escape bar does all-day brekkies and pub grub and the other bars serve up snacks. Coffee bars in each department and a shop plug the gaps.
OTHER Four black tie balls a year.

SOCIAL

UNIVERSITY OF THE WEST OF ENGLAND STUDENTS' UNION
- **4 SABBATICALS** ● **TURNOUT AT LAST BALLOT** 10%
- **NUS MEMBER**
UWESU has at least an office on each campus and usually a bar and common room as well, but the *main centre's* at the Frenchay campus. The Union stays politically neutral. Relations with the University are *generally lovely*.

SU FACILITIES
Bars and shops on each campus; meeting and training rooms; computing facilities; photocopying/printing/fax services; games and vending machines; pool table; juke box; nursery; launderette.

CLUBS (NON-SPORTING)
Archaos History; Baha'i; Ballroom Dancing & Other Forms of Dance; Capoeira; Chess; Comets; Duke of Edinburgh; Hellenic; Howard League Penal Reform; LINKS (St Johns Ambulance); Literature; Malaysian Students; Pagan; Paintball;

Pole Dancing; Scandinavian; People & Planet; Postgrad; Real Deal Poker; Respect; Self-defence; Sign; St Matts Drama; Students & Scholars; Urban; Vietnamese; Welsh; X Indie. **See also Clubs tables.**

OTHER ORGANISATIONS

'Western Eye' is the fortnightly union paper. 'Westworld' is the monthly mag and 'Hub AM' broadcasts over the internet and in student bars. There are two drama groups (one for musicals and performing arts, one *pure thesp*) and the University runs a Community Volunteering project.

RELIGIOUS

○ 16 RELIGIOUS ADVISORS (COFE, RC, METHODIST, URC, EASTERN ORTHODOX, QUAKER), RABBI
The Octagon houses the University's multi-faith chaplaincy centre. There's also a separate Islamic prayer room.

PAID WORK also see University of Bristol
○ JOB BUREAU ○ PAID WORK TERM-TIME 60%
Two staff and weekly emails to get students lining their own pockets. Around 7,000 jobs a year get advertised in teh SU Jobshop.

SPORTS ○○○○○○○○○○○○○

○ RECENT SUCCESSES FOOTBALL, RUGBY, HOCKEY, NETBALL, ROWING **○ BUSA RANKING** 65
UWE has a *fearsome urge* to put one over on its *notoriously sporty* neighbour (Bristol). They've even hired three sporting development officers.

SPORTS FACILITIES

Nine acres of *shabby* pitches include: two football, one all-weather and one cricket pitch. *Sports facilities aren't great at the mo'* but a new Sports Hall (badminton, basketball, footie and aerobics facilities) is due to be open 2006, with two squash courts; aerobics studio; fitness room; eight badminton court hall and climbing wall *to make up for past ills.* UWE hires out some of the city's facilities √ see University of Bristol.

SPORTING CLUBS

Aikido; American Football; Boxing; Canoe';Climbing; Fencing; Gliding; Ju-Jitsu; Kickboxing; Mountain & Hillwalking; Mountain Bike; Polo; Power Kite; Riding; Rowing; Shotokan Karate; Skater Hockey; Skydive; Snowsports;; Surf and Skate; Table Tennis; Tae Kwon Do; Ultimate Frisbee; Waterpolo; Waterski & Wakeboard; Windsurf. **See also Clubs tables.**

ATTRACTIONS see University of Bristol

ACCOMMODATION ○○○○○○○○○○

IN UNIVERSITY
○ SELF-CATERING 29% **○ COST** £77 (42/46WKS)
○ 1ST YEARS LIVING IN 72%
○ INSURANCE PREMIUM £
AVAILABILITY First years get priority, but some *come away keyless.* There are halls at Glenside and St Matthias, a student village at Frenchay and some new developments in the city centre *(better for all the fun of Bristol, worse for making that 9am lecture).* The 17 older halls charge £60-76 while en suite rooms in Frenchay's just-built student village (housing 1,932) cost £90 a week. Insurance is included in fees.
CAR PARKING By permit only. *It's easier to find a space than climb a mountain, but not much.*

EXTERNALLY see University of Bristol
○ AVE RENT £60 **○ LIVING AT HOME** 10%
AVAILABILITY *Clifton, Gloucester Road, the City Centre and Fishponds are all popular roosts.*
HOUSING HELP Advisors in the accommodation office keep a register of properties and lists of vacancies and dodgy landlords.

WELFARE ○○○○○○○○○○○○○

SERVICES
○ INTERNATIONAL STUDENTS' SOCIETY ○ POSTGRAD SOCIETY ○ DISABILITIES OFFICER ○ LATE-NIGHT MINIBUS ○ SELF-DEFENCE CLASSES ○ NIGHTLINE (8PM-8AM) ○ UNIVERSITY COUNSELLORS 4 FULL/4 PART **○ CRIME RATING** !!!!!
Drop-in advice centre (10am-4pm)
HEALTH Local doctor holds a surgery at Frenchay every lunchtime.
CRECHES/NURSERY Halley Nursery at St Matthias campus takes more than 20 children (6mths-5yrs), but there's a waiting list.
DISABILITIES *Good* access at Frenchay, but at the older buildings, especially St Matthias, it's *not the best.* There's a Disability Resource Centre for advice. Special accommodation is available, full details on the website.
CRIME/DRUGS See University of Bristol

FINANCE
○ AVE DEBT PER YEAR £3,509 **○ HOME STUDENT FEES** £3,000
FEES International students pay £7,830-£8,280.
○ ACCESS FUND £1,075,000 **○ SUCCESSFUL APPLICATIONS/YR** 1,552 **○ AVE PAYMENT** £100-3,500
SUPPORT *Lakes of cash for those in need.* Bursaries of £750-£1,250 for around half the student body and £1,250 for students liable for the full £3,000 fee who've done an Access course.

UWIC

PART OF THE UNIVERSITY OF WALES

◉ UNIVERSITY OF WALES INSTITUTE CARDIFF Western Avenue, PO Box 377, Llandaff, Cardiff, CF5 2SG **TEL** (029) 2041 6070 **E−MAIL** uwicinfo@uwic.ac.uk **WEBSITE** www.uwic.ac.uk **◉ UWIC STUDENTS' UNION** Central Union Offices, UWIC, Cyncoed Road, Cardiff, CF23 6XD **TEL** (029) 2041 6138 **E−MAIL** studentunion@uwic.ac.uk **WEBSITE** www.uwicsu.co.uk

GENERAL ◖◗◖◗◖◗◖◗◖◗◖◗◖◗◖◗◖◗◖◗

Splattered over one residential and four academic sites – all within four miles of the centre of Cardiff – sits UWIC, an institution with the power vested in it to award degrees in a mixedpalette of courses though it chooses to award those from the University of Wales. It's attracted attention in recent years: undergrads are reaching record numbers and its access policy embraces all those 'non-traditional' students *that the Government seems so concerned about.*

SEX RATIO: ♂47 ♀53	**FOUNDED:** 1976
FULL-TIME U'GRADS: 6,000	**PART-TIME:** 1,500
POSTGRADS: 2,000	**NON−DEGREE:** 1,900
AVE COURSE: 3YRS	**ETHNIC:** 10%
STATE:PRIVATE SCHOOL: 95:5	**FLUNK RATE:** 16%
MATURE: 45%	**INTERNATIONAL:** 5%
DISABLED: 360	**LOCAL:** 60%

ATMOSPHERE

UWIC's babies are sporty, unpretentious vocational types who are here to get a useful qualification, maybe have a bit of a laugh, but not do anything too crazy on the way. Many of them are from Wales, and nearly half are mature students for whom UWIC is primarily a means to an end rather than a three-year bonanza marking the death of youth. The campus has a busy, upcoming vibe, not unlike the city in which it's set.

SITES

LLANDAFF CAMPUS (Science, Art & Design, Health & Social Sciences, Product & Engineering Design) The administrative heart of the University.
CYNCOED CAMPUS (Education & Sport) Also houses the Union's Head Office and most of the sports facilities.
COLCHESTER AVENUE CAMPUS (Business, Hospitality, Tourism & Leisure) Hospitality students have access to the Celtic Suite – a practice restaurant for would-be gourmet chefs.
HOWARD GARDENS CAMPUS (Art & Design) Has a *useful* general store specialising in artists' materials.

CARDIFF

see Cardiff University

TRAVEL see Cardiff University
COLLEGE The various sites are linked by UWIC Rider, the hourly college bus service.

CAREER PROSPECTS

◉ CAREERS SERVICE ◉ NO. OF STAFF 10 FULL
◉ UNEMPLOYED AFTER 6MTHS 6%
There's a drop-in service on each site once a week during term. As well as giving advice on gripping the various rungs of the career ladder, they provide bulletin boards, interview training, job fairs, career planning computer software, careers library and career workshops.

FURTHER INFO

◉ PROSPECTUSES UNDERGRAD; POSTGRAD; PART-TIME
◉ OPEN DAYS
Prospectuses can be requested online via the main website, by e-mailing uwicinfo@uwic.ac.uk, or by calling (029) 2041 6044. Open days come in two hues: general and career-focused. Contact the Open Day Officer on (029) 2041 6042 for more info and booking.

ACADEMIC ◖◗◖◗◖◗◖◗◖◗◖◗◖◗◖◗◖◗◖◗

The UWIC *mantra* is 'vocation, vocation, vocation'. Almost all courses are career-orientated *and getting a job in a field that doesn't make them want to bang their heads into desks is the main motivation of UWIC students, rather than buying into that 'student experience' malarkey.* Sports, Art & Design, Health and Teacher Training programmes are on the specials board here.

ENTRY POINTS: 100–240		**AVE POINTS:** 177
APPLICATIONS PER PLACE: 4		**CLEARING:** 10%
NO. OF TERMS: 3		**LENGTH OF TERMS:** 10WKS
STAFF TO STUDENT RATIO: 1:15		**STUDY ADDICTS:** 20%
TEACHING: ✶✶		**RESEARCH:** ✶✶
YEAR ABROAD: N/A		**SANDWICH STUDENTS:** 20%
1STS: 12%		**2.2S:** 40%
2.1S: 38%		**3RDS:** 10%

ADMISSIONS

◉ APPLY VIA UCAS
UWIC *loves to get down and dirty* with mature students, international students and part-timers. The First Campus project, of which UWIC is a flagship institution (with Glamorgan University), is designed to get school drop-outs and those dissatisfied with education into Higher Education courses.

U

SUBJECTS
ART & DESIGN 17%   **BUSINESS/MANAGEMENT** 27%
EDUCATION 14%   **HEALTH SCIENCE** 25%   **SPORT** 17%
BEST Psychology; Subjects Allied to Medicine;
Teacher Training.
UNUSUAL Complementary Therapies; Trading
Standards.

LIBRARIES
○ **250,000** BOOKS ○ **660** STUDY PLACES
○ **SPEND PER STUDENT** £
Four libraries, one on each of the main sites, and
open till around 9pm Mon-Thu during term (earlier
closing at weekends and completely on a Sunday).
There's a slide library at Howard Gardens but this
is a one-man-show *and its hours and facilities are as
predictable as a monkey with a chainsaw.*

COMPUTERS
○ **1,000** WORKSTATIONS ○ **24-HR ACCESS**
Computer facilities at Llandaff and Colchester Avenue
are available through the small hours. The libraries all
have networked workstations for students.

OTHER LEARNING FACILITIES
Language labs; drama studio; CAD lab; media centre.

ENTERTAINMENT ○○○○○○○○○

CARDIFF see Cardiff University

UNIVERSITY
○ **PRICE OF A PINT OF BEER** £1.20
○ **GLASS OF WINE** £1.30
○ **CAN OF RED BULL** £1.50
BARS The Union runs five: one's a nightclub bar in
Cardiff city centre; there are others on each site.
Cyncoed's is the *fattest* of these and is
particularly sexy to sporty types. Howard Gardens
is a testing-ground for student bands, Llandaff's
is a pre-club DJ promo spot, and *Colchester
Avenue isn't much use to anyone since it closes
at 3pm.*
THEATRES Drama's *almost unheard of* outside the
teaching course.
MUSIC VENUES A few student bands gig in Howard
Gardens, *but only if the Union can convince them
to put their dignity at stake.*
CLUBBING The Union club in the centre of Cardiff
hosts a few club nights a week (often with free
bus from halls), the most remarkable being
Saturday's the Amp – a rocky, indie night mar-
keted as 'the alternative to shit music' – *simple
and to the point. We like it.*
COMEDY/CABARET Fortnightly comedy network.
FOOD *Nowt to shout about.* There's a cafeteria
on each campus, plus a snack bar on the
Cyncoed site.
OTHER The Christmas Ball at the Cardiff
International Arena induces all-night queuing
when tickets go on sale and sell out in hours.

SOCIAL ○○○○○○○○○○○○○

UNIVERSITY OF WALES INSTITUTE, CARDIFF STUDENTS' UNION
○ **3** SABBATICALS ○ **TURNOUT AT LAST BALLOT** 5%
○ **NUS MEMBER**
Aside from running bars and shops, *UWICSU
doesn't really have all that much to do politically.*
Sports and welfare are its *biggest* hitters, with
rather lacklustre efforts at keeping the kids in the
halls entertained and at arranging the epic
Freshers' Fortnight.

SU FACILITIES
Spread over the four sites and managed by either
University or Union: five bars; four cafeterias; two
snack bars; three minibuses; ATMs; nursery;
advice centre; three general/stationery/clothes
shops; vending machines; launderette.

CLUBS (NON-SPORTING)
Humanities. **See also Clubs tables.**

OTHER ORGANISATIONS
'Retro' is the free monthly *'newspaper'*, backed up
by a weekly 'What's On?' e-zine which students
can subscribe to.

RELIGIOUS
○ **1** CHAPLAIN (COFE) see Cardiff University
UWIC has a chapel and Cardiff is well stocked
with mosques and churches.

PAID WORK see Cardiff University
○ **JOB BUREAU**
Many UWIC students work during term and the
Careers Service runs a job shop to help. The SU
employs bar staff and shop assistants.

SPORTS ○○○○○○○○○○○○○

○ **RECENT SUCCESSES** RUGBY UNION, SQUASH, ATHLETICS,
WOMEN'S HOCKEY ○ **BUSA RANKING** 4
UWIC's Athletics Union copes superhumanly
with limited funding – *students may need to fork
out the cash to participate in national events* –
and the facilities it uses are modern and
*impressive for such a relatively new, small and
disparate institution.*

SPORTS FACILITIES
Football, rugby and Astroturf pitches; tennis
centre; squash courts; indoor athletics centre;
basketball court; gym; swimming pool. There's
also the river for those who like their sport moist.
Membership costs £15/yr, on top of which it's £1
per use. Cardiff's ice rink, dry ski slope and
assorted leisure centres are accessible too.

Words in italics are Push's point of view – take it or leave it...

SPORTING CLUBS
Aquatics; Canoe; Ju-Jitsu; Lacrosse; Triathlon.
See Clubs tables.

ATTRACTIONS see <u>Cardiff University</u>

ACCOMMODATION ◑◑◑◑◑◑◑◑◑

IN COLLEGE
◉ **CATERED** 9% ◉ **COST** £93 (39WKS)
◉ **SELF-CATERING** 11% ◉ **COST** £80 (39WKS)
◉ **1ST YEARS LIVING IN** 90%
◉ **INSURANCE PREMIUM** £
AVAILABILITY Halls are available at the Cyncoed
Campus, the Plas Gwyn Residential Campus
(within walking distance of Llandaff) and at
Evelian Court (a mile from Llandaff). All
campuses, the city centre and popular areas for
private student accommodation are served by the
UWIC Rider. Most students loiter in the halls
closest to the campus in which they're based.
CCTV and 24-hr security patrols keep the peace.
CAR PARKING Permits aren't required, *but camels
and eyes of needles spring to mind.*

EXTERNALLY see <u>Cardiff University</u>
◉ **AVE RENT** £50 ◉ **LIVING AT HOME** 20%
AVAILABILITY Most students manage to wrangle a
shared house within reach of campus. *Quality of
accommodation, however, is like a box of chocolates
– some are lovely, others are just stinky brown goo.*
HOUSING HELP The Accommodation Office
publishes a vacancy list and organises
'meet-the-landlord-of-your-dreams' fairs for
students that didn't make it into halls.

WELFARE ◑◑◑◑◑◑◑◑◑◑◑◑◑

SERVICES
◉ **LGBT OFFICER** & **SOCIETY** ◉ **NIGHTLINE**
◉ **UNIVERSITY COUNSELLORS** 2FULL/2PART
◉ **CRIME RATING** !!!!
HEALTH There are nurses on each campus and a
drop-in doctor's surgery on the Cyncoed campus,
weekdays.
CRECHES/NURSERY Places for 40 kids aged up to 5.
DISABILITIES Some adapted bedrooms and a
dyslexia support centre. Contact the Disability
Department before applying.

FINANCE
◉ **AVE DEBT PER YEAR** £4,056 ◔ **HOME STUDENT FEES**
£1,200
FEES Fees are going up to £3,000 from 2007, but
Welsh students should be eligible for the
standard Assembly grant to cover the difference.
SUPPORT The University throws a few quid at
students with dependants, disabilities, or just
whopping big overdrafts. Hardship funds and
sports scholarships have a wee *bit o' cash in
them.*

▶ UXBRIDGE
see *Brunel University*

**The World's first mock mass grave was
constructed at Bournemouth University as
part of a unique training programme ran by
Inforce, the International Forensic Centre of
Excellence for the Investigation of Genocide.**

Words in italics are Push's point of view — take it or leave it...

▶ POLYTECHNIC OF WALES
see *Glamorgan University*

UNIVERSITY OF WALES

▶ UNIVERSITY OF WALES, CARDIFF
see *Cardiff University*

▶ UNIVERSITY OF WALES CARDIFF INSTITUTE
see *UWIC*

▶ WALES COLLEGE OF MEDICINE
see *Cardiff University*

▶ WALES UNIVERSITY, ABERYSTWYTH
see *Aberystwyth, University of Wales*

UNIVERSITY OF WARWICK

▶ UNIVERSITY OF THE WEST OF ENGLAND
see *UWE, Bristol*

▶ WEST SURREY COLLEGE OF ART AND DESIGN
see *Creative Arts University College*

UNIVERSITY OF WESTMINSTER

▶ WINCHESTER ART SCHOOL
see *University of Southampton*

▶ UNIVERSITY COLLEGE WINCHESTER
see *University of Winchester*

▶ UNIVERSITY COLLEGE WORCESTER
see *University of Worcester*

UNIVERSITY OF WINCHESTER

UNIVERSITY OF WOLVERHAMPTON

UNIVERSITY OF WORCESTER

▶ WRITTLE COLLEGE
see *University of Essex*

▶ WYE COLLEGE
see *Imperial College London*

W

▶ POLYTECHNIC OF WALES
see *Glamorgan University*

UNIVERSITY OF WALES

◉ UNIVERSITY OF WALES King Edward VII Avenue, Cathays Park, Cardiff, CF10 3NS **TEL** (02920) 382 656 **E-MAIL** uniwales@wales.ac.uk **WEBSITE** www.wales.ac.uk

GENERAL ⏾⏾⏾⏾⏾⏾⏾⏾⏾⏾⏾⏾⏾

The University of Wales is the third largest in the country after Open University and University of London, and like these, it's rather unusual. It's a federal university, a collection of colleges which operate almost entirely independently of each other. *Many students in Wales don't even realise that their colleges aren't, technically, fully feathered universities.* Interested students shouldn't start writing off to the University of Wales for its prospectus or wondering why they can't find the campus on the map. Try investigating instead the individual colleges, which are, of course, included elsewhere in *Push*, as follows:

Aberystwyth, University of Wales
Bangor, University of Wales
University of Wales Insititute, Cardiff
Lampeter, University of Wales
Newport, University of Wales
North-East Wales Institute
Swansea, University of Wales
Swansea Institute of Higher Education
Trinity College, Carmarthen

UCAS applications are made to the individual colleges.

▶ UNIVERSITY OF WALES, CARDIFF
see *Cardiff University*

▶ UNIVERSITY OF WALES CARDIFF INSTITUTE
see *UWIC*

▶ WALES COLLEGE OF MEDICINE
see *Cardiff University*

▶ WALES UNIVERSITY, ABERYSTWYTH
see *Aberystwyth, University of Wales*

UNIVERSITY OF WARWICK

◉ UNIVERSITY OF WARWICK Coventry, Warwickshire, CV4 7AL **TEL** (02476) 523 648 **E-MAIL** student.recruitment@warwick.ac.uk **WEBSITE** www.warwick.ac.uk **◉ STUDENTS' UNION UNIVERSITY OF WARWICK** Coventry, Warwickshire, CV4 7AL **TEL** (02476) 572 777 **E-MAIL** sunion@sunion.warwick.ac.uk **WEBSITE** www.sunion.warwick.ac.uk

GENERAL ⏾⏾⏾⏾⏾⏾⏾⏾⏾⏾⏾⏾⏾

Warwick Castle is in Warwick. Warwick University isn't. This 500-acre piece of civic lost property has been left somewhere in the hinterland between Coventry and Leamington Spa. Coventry already has a university and Leamington Spa *is too weedy to deserve one, so, short of calling it the University of Somewhere-In-The-South-East-Midlands, 'Warwick University' is* probably the best option. *The hilly surroundings can make it seem deceptively remote*, although it's only three miles to the centre of Coventry and 25 to Birmingham's. The campus is *a crazed and colourful creation: smeared with sculptures, kid's play-block buildings* and three artificial lakes. Built in the 60s, *when 'bland' was the standard architectural blueprint, Warwick stands out as being not as depressingly dull as some universities' token monoliths. But there sure is a lot of white around.*

Words in italics are Push's point of view — take it or leave it...

SEX RATIO: ♂49 ♀51	**FOUNDED:** 1964
FULL-TIME U'GRADS: 10,266	**PART-TIME:** 1,257
POSTGRADS: 7,485	**NON-DEGREE:** N/A
AVE COURSE: 3–4YRS	**ETHNIC:** 34%
STATE:PRIVATE SCHOOL: 77:23	**FLUNK RATE:** 5%
MATURE: 36%	**INTERNATIONAL:** 33%
DISABLED: 115	**LOCAL:** 5%

ATMOSPHERE

Although it attracts a sizeable middle-class contingent and a fair few Oxbridge rejects, the campus is buzzing, cosmopolitan and enormous. Situated far from the city centre, it's almost entirely self-sufficient. Indeed, most first year students who live there never actually need to leave. It's been called a 'bubble' or a 'holiday camp' in the past and it can all get a bit 'Prisoner' from time to time. Campus fever can be relieved by jaunts into Leamington or Coventry, where students are tolerated fairly well.

COVENTRY see Coventry University

LEAMINGTON SPA

More Warwick students live in Leamington Spa than in Coventry, and it's a pretty, park-filled place that still pulls in quite a few tourists. As far as shops and night activities go, *they're limited but respectable,* with two student-angled clubs, plenty of posh eateries (tourists) and coffee shops. *The town is basically divided into the good and the ugly. Past the railway bridge into South Leamington, the picturesque stops and the cheap, rough area begins. This means many takeaways and no pretty houses. Overall, a quaintly cheerful little town with an unprecedented number of skater kids and good music stores. Birmingham and Coventry are better bets for bigger fun, though.*

TRAVEL see Coventry University

TRAINS The main station is two miles away in Coventry but there's a line running through Leamington Spa and Warwick.
CAR *It's in the middle of nowhere and the University likes to keep it that way.* There's room for 1,000 cars on campus but permits are the order of the day. The M6 is handy for drivers.
AIR Ten miles to Birmingham International.
LOCAL From the bus stops on campus, the numbers 12, 12A and 112 run into Coventry centre via the train station every ten mins until 11pm (80p-£1). There are similar services to

Leamington and Kenilworth. Late-night services during term-time.
TAXIS It's almost inevitable that students will get trapped on campus in the witching hour at some point. That's where the on-site taxi rank comes in handy. Fares to Coventry vary around £6, while Leamington can cost over a tenner.
BICYCLES *Helpful for getting around campus, but no one fancies seven miles to Leamington twice a day unless they want really big calves.* Bike racks and cycle lanes dotted around the site.

CAREER PROSPECTS

○ **CAREERS SERVICE** ○ **NO. OF STAFF** 11 FULL/8 PART
○ **UNEMPLOYED AFTER 6MTHS** 6%
Newsletters, bulletin boards, a full careers library, job fairs and interview prep.

FAMOUS ALUMNI

Baroness Amos (Leader of the House of Lords); Jenny Bond (former BBC correspondent); David Davis MP (senior Tory); A L Kennedy, Hari Kunzru (authors); Timmy Mallett (hammer-wielding TV prat); Simon Mayo (DJ); Sheila McKechnie (late campaigner); Stephen Merchant ('The Office' and 'Extras' co-creator); Dave Nellist (Militant ex-MP); Stephen Pile (writer); Frank Skinner (comedian); Gary Sinyor and Vadim Jean (film makers); Sting (for a term).

SPECIAL FEATURES

The campus has the biggest *and most active* university Arts Centre outside London. There's a roaring trade in conferences, which means there are some *excellent* facilities and accommodation is better whilst *being relatively cheap. It also means students can feel like they're an inconvenience stuck between the real business of travelling salesmen's piss-ups and dandruff-dripping, navel-gazing academics reading logarithms to each other.*

FURTHER INFO

○ **PROSPECTUSES** UNDERGRAD; POSTGRAD; ALTERNATIVE; SOME DEPARTMENTAL; ALTERNATIVE; VIDEO
○ **OPEN DAYS**

ACADEMIC ○○○○○○○○○○○○○

○ **RUSSELL GROUP** ○ **1994 GROUP**
A hard-hitter right across the academic board. Highly-rated for teaching and research plus cosy industry links to boot. There's an *upcoming* medical school. Grades for some courses are dependent on

> **Supposedly, the corridors in the University of Warwick's halls of residence are all exactly one riot shield wide.**

second and third year performance, *making the first year a test merely to determine whether students stay on*. Meanwhile, some science courses count first year grades as up to 20% of the final degree mark. Optional/compulsory modules for each course are detailed on the University website.

ENTRY POINTS: 300–420	AVE POINTS: 425
APPLICATIONS PER PLACE: 9	CLEARING: 3%
NO. OF TERMS: 3	LENGTH OF TERMS: 10/11wks
STAFF TO STUDENT RATIO: 1:12	STUDY ADDICTS: 28%
TEACHING: ✭✭✭✭✭	RESEARCH: ✭✭✭✭✭
YEAR ABROAD: 6%	SANDWICH STUDENTS: N/A
1STS: 22%	2.2S: 16%
2.1S: 58%	3RDS: 4%

ADMISSIONS
❂ APPLY VIA UCAS/GTTR FOR PGCE
Warwick is *weak at the knees* for widening participation (access schemes and so on) and accepts postgrad applications directly through its online system.

SUBJECTS
ARTS 20%   **MEDICINE** 6%   **SCIENCE** 42%
SOCIAL STUDIES 32%
UNUSUAL Women & Gender. MORSE (Maths, Operational Research, Statistics & Economics) and Film & Italian are unique to Warwick.

LIBRARIES
❂ 1,000,000 BOOKS ❂ 1,600 STUDY PLACES
❂ 24–HR ACCESS ❂ SPEND PER STUDENT: £££
In addition to the *book-stuffed* main library (open till midnight), there are various smaller departmental libraries. The Resource Centre has 10,000 'core texts' stuffed onto its shelves. The new Learning Grid group study facility is proving *popular – not a place for peaceful, reflective learning.*

COMPUTERS
❂ 1,000 WORKSTATIONS ❂ 24–HR ACCESS
Internal correspondence is becoming increasingly dependent on e-mail. All campus bedrooms come complete with broadband portal – *no need for brown paper bags for porn, then.*

OTHER LEARNING FACILITIES
Language labs, drama studio, rehearsal rooms and media centre.

ENTERTAINMENT ◡◡◡◡◡◡◡◡◡

COVENTRY see Coventry University

LEAMINGTON
❂ PRICE OF A PINT OF BEER £1.70
❂ GLASS OF WINE £1.40
❂ CAN OF RED BULL £1.50
Excellent facilities on campus compensate for Leamington's deficiencies.
PUBS Pushplugs: Moo Bar *(retro)*; Jug & Jester *(old school)*; Robin's Well. *Don't win on the bandit in the Guardsman – it upsets the locals.*

CINEMAS Two with seven screens between them. *The Rubin Cinema is a bit artier than the Apollo.*
THEATRE The Royal Spa is a *standard* regional rep house but Leamington is on a direct rail route to the *bard-licious* Stratford-upon-Avon.
CLUBBING/MUSIC VENUES Mirage (*zillions of student nights*) and Colosseum are top bop spots. Evolve (commercial dance, £6) heaves on Thursdays and Sugar puts on a 'hip' night of student carnage (£4). Birmingham refreshes the gig-going parts Coventry can't reach.
EATING OUT *Again, not a huge deal, although, this being the Midlands, there's a number of excellent value Balti houses. Pushplugs: Mongolian Wok Bar in Coventry (buffet lunch); Ali Baba (Balti).* Spun End Balti does deliveries to campus.

UNIVERSITY
❂ PRICE OF A PINT OF BEER £1.50
❂ GLASS OF WINE £2 **❂ CAN OF RED BULL** £1.80
BARS The principal bars are Cholo and the Cooler *(actually rather warm)* which doubles as a club. Others include: Graduate *(pubby)*; two Bottles & Shots bars; *blingtastic* Rococos *(champagne cocktails, cigars and a VIP area)*; Xananas; the Bar (University-run). There are also supping stops at the Arts Centre and in the Sports Pavilion.
ARTS CENTRE *The Arts Centre on campus is fantastic in every respect – it looks as though it's sprung from some futuristic fantasy and has facilities to dream about:* two theatres; conference hall; film theatre; art gallery; sculpture court; concert hall; music centre and bookshop. *250,000 people a year flock to bathe in its glory.*
THEATRES In the Arts Centre, the main theatre attracts touring companies (drama, dance, opera etc.), as well as big student shows. The studio theatre lends itself to smaller scale productions. *Students enter into the dramatic fray with thespian gusto.*
CINEMAS The Cinema Society shows classics and blockbusters for around £2, while the Arts Centre provides *a less commercial counterbalance* at higher prices, *ironically enough.*
CLUBBING The Cooler (cap. 1,400) is the main venue. Six events a week: everything from world music (Heat) to R'n'B (Pure) and cheese (Top Banana) to hiphop/drum & bass (Coalition). Crash (rock/indie) includes a live band. DJs have included Tim Westwood, Hanif (MTV's The Lick) and Grandmaster Flash.
MUSIC VENUES The Union's Market Place (1,200 capacity) is the biggest. Reel Big Fish, London Electricity and Dizzee Rascal have all played recently. Graduate (cap. 400) hosts jazz, DJs and open mic nights. Massive Butterworth Hall in the Arts Centre features a variety of music, mostly classical, and attracts top international performers. The University Chorus and orchestra perform here *between Wembley Stadium gigs.*
COMEDY/CABARET Fortnightly comedy spurts from various venues. *Past masters* include Andy Zaltzman, Paul Chowdhury and Rob Dearing.
FOOD *More grub than the bottom of a gardener's wellies.* Cholo Food (*filling luches*); South Central

W

Words in italics are Push's point of view — take it or leave it...

(Subway-esque sarnies); Xananas (posh nosh); Eat (expensive); Fat Tony's (pizza delivery); Battered (fish'n'chips); Bar Food (junk) and Café Library (grab and go). If all else fails there's always the Costcutter supermarket.

OTHER Several varyingly sized balls a year as well as the February Real Ale and One World Week Festivals. Scissor Sisters, Ash and Goldie Lookin' Chain have played at the SU's Final Fling.

SOCIAL ◡◡◡◡◡◡◡◡◡◡◡◡

UNIVERSITY OF WARWICK STUDENTS' UNION (UWSU)

○ **7 SABBATICALS** ○ **TURNOUT AT LAST BALLOT** 15%
○ **NUS MEMBER**

The Union building is the biggest in Europe. The SU juggles *a varied and unfaltering social calendar* with serious representation: they managed to kill off the threat of compulsory student laptops a while back. *The Club & Socs list at Warwick is longer than a supermarket sweep receipt – even the most eccentric student should find enough like-minded weirdos to feel cosy.*

SU FACILITIES

In and around the Union building: nightclub; nine bars; cafeteria; two coffee bars; fast food joint; five meeting rooms; four banks with ATMs; Endsleigh Insurance branch; Costcutter; stationery shop; computers for sale; fax and printing services; photo booth; photocopiers; payphones; travel agency; launderette; opticians; hairdressers; pool and snooker tables; juke boxes; gaming and vending machines; late-night campus bus; advice centre; DTP suite; darkroom; three minibuses and a car for hire; TV lounges.

CLUBS (NON-SPORTING)

More than any other Union in the country: Amazonia (campaigning); Animal Rights & Vegetarian; Anime & Manga (Japanese animation); Arabic; Art of Living (health); Backgammon; Baha'i; Band; Bangladeshi; Baobab – Your Window to Africa (cultural); Beatdown; Bell Ringing; Belly Dance; Bhangra; Big Band; Biker; BJS (Blues Jazz Soul); Boar (newspaper); Bollywood; Brass; Break Dancing; Bridge; Buddhist; Bulgarian; Capoeira; Catalan & Basque; Caribbean Heat (cultural); Caribbean Riddims (cultural); Ceilidh; Celtic; Centre for Alternative Culture (C4aC); Chamber Music; Cheemu (DJing); Cheese & Chocolate; Chill Out; Chinese; Chinese Chess & Cards; Chorus; Classical & Modern Dance; Cloakroom (charity); Clublands; Codpiece (drama); Comedy; Comic Book; Conceptual Art Performance; Curry; Cypriot; Dancasianal (dance); Dance Mat (virtual gaming); Darts; Deck Masters (sci-fi collectable card games); Decriminalise Cannabis; Diversity (students with disabilities); Duke of Edinburgh; Dutch; Dynamics of Alcoholic Fluids Team; Eastern European Central Asian; Eastern Food; European; European School; Exotic Dance; Expedition; Fresh Blood Theatre;

Football Fans; Francophone; Free Spirits; Free Tibet (campaigning); Friends of Palestine; Get Decked (DJing); G-Force (DJing); Globalise Resistance (campaigning); Go; Goffbeat; Greens (campaigning); Hack (charity); Hellenic; Hindu; Horror; Human Rights Debating; Indian; Indonesian; Jailbreak (fundraising); Japanese; Jubilee (children with Autistic Spectrum Disorder ASD); Juggling; Kernow (Cornwall appreciation); Knitting & Craft; Korean; Krishna Consciousness; LARPS (Live Action Role Play); Laser Quest; Latin American; Light Aircraft (flying enthusiasts); Link Africa (campaigning); Love; Mah Jong; Malaysian Students Association; Mauritian; Medsin (campaigning); Melange (Warwick students united); Music Festival; Music Theatre Warwick; New Writing; Nightline; Noise; Nordic; North American; Northern Ireland; Offbeat; One (DJing); Pagan; Paintball; Parkour; Persian; Photographic; Poker; Portuguese Speaking; Pottery; Power & Traction Kite; Psyche (DJing); Punk Soc; Quiz; RaW (radio); Real Ale; Respect; Revelation Rock-Gospel Choir; RIP Soc (Research in Production); ROAR; Russian Speaking; Salsa Dancing; SANZA (South Africa/New Zealand/Australia); Scavenger Hunt; Scottish; SIFE (Students In Free Enterprise); Sikh; Sikh Urban Music; Singapore; Spanish; Socialist Street Vibe; Students; Spanish; Speak (campaigning); Sri Lankan; St. John Ambulance LINKS; Stop The War Coalition; Student Scout & Guide (SSAGO); Stunt; Table Football; Taiji Quan (exercise); Taiwan; Tap Dancing; Taste; Tech Crew; Thai; The Hooka (smokers); The Really Wild (Mature Students); Tibet Support (campaigning); Touring Band; Travel; Turkish; Woodcraft Folk (campaigning); Ultimate Jenga; UNICEF Warwick; United Nations; Underground (DJing); United World Colleges (cultural); Video Game Design; Vietsoc; Warwick Anti-Sexism; Warwick Fashion; Warwick Hong Kong; Warwick Off-Broadway; Warwick Piano; Warwick Polonia (Polish); Warwick STAR (campaigning); Warwick Student Opera; Warwick TV; Warwick Volunteers; Welsh; WERL Records (music/band promotion); Wine & Whisky Appreciation; Women's Group; WUDS (drama); Young Jains Students Warwick. **See also Clubs tables.**

OTHER ORGANISATIONS

'Boar' newspaper is *in no way as dull as it sounds*. Union mag 'the Word' comes out every couple of weeks. Radio station 'RaW' *pulses relentlessly* through local radio waves. Newly created WTV broadcasts around the Union and campus halls. Rag *rakes it in* – recently staging the world's largest pillow fight with over 300 combatants beating each other with soft feathery clubs – and *is so cocky* it has its own website (www.warwickrag.co.uk). Warwick Volunteers gets students involved in local help projects.

RELIGIOUS

○ **3 CHAPLAINS (COFE, RC, FC), RABBI**

Multi-faith chaplaincy and a Muslim prayer room. Coventry and around is *intensely multi-cultural with according religious provision.*

Words in italics are Push's point of view — take it or leave it...

PAID WORK
see Coventry University
○ JOB BUREAU
Unitemps on campus gives advice and posts vacancies. With such a conference-heavy vacation agenda, there's always plenty of work to be had looking after visitors. The SU itself employs 300 students.

SPORTS ○○○○○○○○○○○○○

○ RECENT SUCCESSES SQUASH, GOLF, WOMEN'S RUGBY
○ BUSA RANKING 24
Sport plays as much a part of life as academia, with a £3m shell-out on a gleaming new facility. *The ethos is not only 'sport for all', but 'all sport for all' with a baffling range on offer, although Warwick's jocks take great pride in trashing the* Coventry University *whenever they can.* Most facilities are based on campus.

SPORTS FACILITIES
Bucketloads: sports pavilion; 25m swimming pool; 16m learner/training pool; six squash courts; three multi-purpose sports halls; eight lane mondo running track; fitness suite; activities room; aerobics studio; conditioning room/performance weights room; dance studio; sauna; 12 tennis courts (three artificial); seven football and three rugby pitches; two cricket squares (one artificial); seven outdoor netball courts; three all-weather pitches; American football pitch; lacrosse pitch; ultimate frisbee pitch; climbing centre with bouldering walls.

SPORTING CLUBS
10 Pin Bowling; Aerobics; Aikido; American Football; Canoe Polo; Cheerleaders; Croquet; Eskrima (martial art); Five-a-side Football; Gliding; Ice Hockey; Kempo Ju-Jitsu; Lacrosse; Latin & Ballroom; Lifesaving; Motorsport; Mountaineering; Polo; Pool; Rifle; Roller Hockey; Rowing; Samarai Jiu Jitsu; Shotokan Karate; Skydive; Snooker; Submission Wrestling; Surf; Table Tennis; Thai Boxing; Triathlon; Ultimate Frisbee; Water Skiing; Weight Training; Windsurf; Wing Tsun (self-defence); Yoga; Zhuan Shu Kuan (Chinese kung fu). **See also Clubs tables.**

ATTRACTIONS see Coventry University
Birmingham NEC and any Midland team are within chanting distance.

ACCOMMODATION ○○○○○○○○○

IN UNIVERSITY
○ SELF-CATERING 50%   **○ COST** £77 (30-39/43-50WKS)
○ 1ST YEARS LIVING IN 90%   **○ 2ND YEARS LIVING IN** 5%
○ 3RD YEARS LIVING IN 25%   **○ POSTGRADS LIVING IN** 80%
○ INSURANCE PREMIUM ££
AVAILABILITY *Although some of the rooms are small*

hobbit dwellings, others are fairly plush (around a third en suite) *and some border on luxurious – primarily to attract conference-goers, which means as well as paying more, those in better rooms are at risk of temporary eviction when the vacations begin.* First years are guaranteed a room if they get their form in on time. Broadband access is a *bonus* as are the *beefy* security measures: dog patrol, CCTV, entry phones and 24-hr porters. The head tenancy scheme plonks 1,650 students in shared houses off-campus. *The cleaners are a thorough bunch*, laundering linen, hoovering rooms and swabbing the kitchen.
CAR PARKING *Permits* (£250) *are required, but first years aren't allowed cars on campus anyhow.* Some pay & display available.

EXTERNALLY see Coventry University
○ AVE RENT £53
AVAILABILITY *Coventry is getting to be more and more at the cheaper end, but Leamington is still the most popular. Earlsdon ain't a bad bag either. Union Court does student accommodation near the centre of Leamington.*
HOUSING HELP The Accommodation Office has 14 staff who post and approve vacancies, help negotiate contracts and offer legal help. The Union do their bit to help and there's no shortage of cash-hungry lettings agents.

WELFARE ○○○○○○○○○○○○○

SERVICES
○ LGBT OFFICER & SOCIETY ○ ETHNIC MINORITIES OFFICER & SOCIETY ○ WOMEN'S OFFICER & SOCIETY ○ MATURE STUDENTS' OFFICER & SOCIETY ○ INTERNATIONAL STUDENTS' OFFICER & SOCIETY ○ POSTGRAD OFFICER & SOCIETY ○ DISABILITIES OFFICER & SOCIETY ○ LATE-NIGHT MINIBUS ○ NIGHTLINE ○ UNIVERSITY COUNSELLORS 6 FULL/3 PART
○ SU COUNSELLORS 2 PART **○ CRIME RATING** !
The SU runs an Advice & Welfare Centre with four staff and a sabbatical officer. Each hall has a resident tutor *who doesn't 'tute' anything but* will help with personal problems if Nightline seems too impersonal.
HEALTH A fully staffed health centre with several GPs *helps clear your nose and soothes your throat.*
WOMEN Free personal alarms and late-night minibus around campus (not just for women).
CRECHES/NURSERY Facilities for children aged 3mths-4yrs.
DISABILITIES *Wheelchair access is among the best in the country* with ramps, lifts and specialised rooms. Hearing loops, specialist learning facilities and Braille signs on some buildings.
CRIME Campus is largely safe and security heavy. Coventry's no ghetto either.
DRUGS *Bongfuls of middle-class arts students have given Warwick a bit of a rep for cannabis culture,* but the University claims to come down hard on users.

W

FINANCE
- **AVE DEBT PER YEAR** £4,817
- **HOME STUDENT FEES** £3,000
FEES Non-EU students pay £8,700-£11,300. UK postgrads are charged £4,750.

- **ACCESS FUND** £441,194 ○ **SUCCESSFUL APPLICATIONS/YR** 420 ○ **AVE PAYMENT** £100-£3,500
SUPPORT Bursaries for students with a family income of less than £35,000, plus music scholarships, sports bursaries and a hardship fund.

▶ UNIVERSITY OF THE WEST OF ENGLAND
see *UWE, Bristol*

▶ WEST SURREY COLLEGE OF ART AND DESIGN
see *Creative Arts University College*

UNIVERSITY OF WESTMINSTER

FORMERLY POLYTECHNIC OF CENTRAL LONDON

○ **UNIVERSITY OF WESTMINSTER** 309 Regent Street, London, W1B 2UW **TEL** (020) 7911 5000 **E-MAIL** admissions@wmin.ac.uk **WEBSITE** www.wmin.ac.uk ○ **UNIVERSITY OF WESTMINSTER STUDENTS' UNION** 35 Marylebone Road, NW1 5LS **TEL** (020) 7915 5454 **E-MAIL** supresi@wmin.ac.uk www.uwsu.com

GENERAL ◑◑◑◑◑◑◑◑◑◑◑◑◑

Originally founded as the Royal Polytechnic Institute in order to educate the public on engineering and all matters scientific, Westminster has gone through all manner of changes and expansions since Victorian times. This has resulted in a tapestry of different architectural styles, from the *handsome* pre-war headquarters building on Regent Street to the more modern constructions at Harrow. *Three sites are close enough to Trafalgar Square to offer students the West End on a big, glitzy over-priced plate, while the Harrow site nudges the suburbs and is lovingly smudged* with greenery. For general information about London see University of London.

SEX RATIO: ♂46 ♀54	**FOUNDED:** 1838
FULL-TIME U'GRADS: 10,900	**PART-TIME:** 6,450
POSTGRADS: 5,900	**NON-DEGREE:** 4,211
AVE COURSE: 3YRS	**ETHNIC:** 62%
STATE:PRIVATE SCHOOL: 94:6	**FLUNK RATE:** 23%
MATURE: 32%	**INTERNATIONAL:** 28%
DISABLED: 180	**LOCAL:** N/A

ATMOSPHERE
Undergrads are a diverse bunch with a big ethnic mix and a high proportion of mature and international students. Although most campuses are relatively close together inhabitants tend to stick like glue to their own site's bars and facilities so there's little sense of one big cohesive family. Still, with all the fun of the West End on their doorsteps there's no excuse to be bored. Jimmy 'The Solo' Hendrix played here, and Cherie 'The Lips' Blair taught at the law school.

SITES
REGENT (School of Law, School of Social Sciences, Humanities & Languages, Diplomatic Academy of London, Health & Fitness Centre) The admin centre for both University and SU. *For fans of fancy stonework*, the historic Headquarters building holds an *elegant* 1911 marble foyer.
CAVENDISH (Biosciences, Integrated Health, Computer Science) Still *glowing* from a recent £35m campus facelift.
HARROW (Formerly Harrow College of Higher Education, 5,000 students – Arts & Design, Business School, Computer Science, Media) 12 miles – or *20 mins on a good Tube day* – from the Central London campuses, Harrow houses the *prestigious* Media School (which has garnered top BBC awards), as well as some *swanky* computer labs, photography and music studios thanks to open purse strings in recent years.
MARYLEBONE Home to the *fabtastic* careers service (CaSE), plus the Counselling and Housing services, the Educational Initiative Centre, Architecture & the Built Environment courses and Westminster Business School. Not forgetting Marylebone Books and Intermission, the SU's new social space.

LONDON see University of London

TRAVEL see University of London
TRAINS Euston is closest at 20 mins stroll away.
CAR *Driving in London is naturally a dumb idea*, but there are pay & displays at the Harrow campus – which, together with the Marylebone site, is outside the Congestion Charge Zone.
UNDERGROUND For Cavendish: Warren Street (Northern, Victoria); for Marylebone: Baker Street (Bakerloo, Circle, Jubilee, Metropolitan, Hammersmith & City); for Regent: Oxford Circus (Bakerloo, Central, Victoria); for Harrow: Northwick Park (Metropolitan) and Kenton (Bakerloo).

Words in italics are Push's point of view – take it or leave it...

CAREER PROSPECTS

○ **CAREERS SERVICE** ○ **NO. OF STAFF** 9 FULL/11 PART
○ **UNEMPLOYED AFTER 6MTHS** 10%

CaSE covers all aspects of employment during and after study, from job fairs to CV advice – *the whole nine yards*. See www.wmin.ac.uk/careers for online resources.

FAMOUS ALUMNI

Christopher Bailey (Burberry creative director); Sir Anthony Caro (sculptor); Baroness Chalker (Tory peer); Baroness Cox (lobbyist); Trisha Goddard (TV presenter); Annie Nightingale, Lisa I'Anson (current and former Radio 1 DJs); Michael Jackson (former C4 chief exec, not Wacko); Nico Ladenis (restaurateur); Markus Lupfer (fashion designer); Nick Mason and Roger Waters (Pink Floyd); Julian Metcalfe and Sinclair Beecham (creators of Pret à Manger); Anand Tucker (director); Ian Ritchie (architect); Jon Ronson (journo); Philip Sycamore (ex-Law Society president); Timothy West (actor); Vivienne Westwood (fashion designer).

SPECIAL FEATURES

Marylebone campus building hosted the first International Business & Development Conference.

FURTHER INFO

○ **PROSPECTUSES** UNDERGRAD; POSTGRAD; DEPARTMENTAL; INTERNATIONAL ○ **OPEN DAYS**

Several campus open days and course presentations throughout the year.

ACADEMIC ○○○○○○○○○○○○○

Many courses are of a vocational nature, with relevant industries closely involved in the development of course programmes, *ensuring that teaching is up to date as well as up to scratch. There has been a ripple of discontent in the student body, however, who feel that some courses are heavy on the academic side with not enough on the practical.*

ENTRY POINTS: 40-340	AVE POINTS: 108
APPLICATIONS PER PLACE: 4	CLEARING: 30%
NO. OF TERMS: 2	LENGTH OF TERMS: 13/18WKS
STAFF TO STUDENT RATIO: 1:15	STUDY ADDICTS: 18%
TEACHING: **	RESEARCH: ***
YEAR ABROAD: <1%	SANDWICH STUDENTS: 9%
1STS: 11%	2.2S: 33%
2.1S: 53%	3RDS: 2%

ADMISSIONS

○ **APPLY VIA UCAS**

Contact the Enquiries and Student Finance Office directly for part-time courses and postgrad degrees.

SUBJECTS

ARCHITECTURE & BUILT ENVIRONMENT 8%
BIOSCIENCES 5%   **BUSINESS SCHOOL (HARROW)** 4%
BUSINESS SCHOOL (WESTMINSTER) 18%
MEDIA, ARTS & DESIGN 11%   **COMPUTER SCIENCE** 9%
EDUCATIONAL INITIATIVE CENTRE 0.2%

INTEGRATED HEALTH 3%   **LAW** 7%
SOCIAL SCIENCES, HUMANITIES & LANGUAGES 23%
BEST Arabic; Building; Chinese; French; Housing & Surveying; Media & Communications; Psychology; Subjects allied to Medicine; Tourism.
UNUSUAL Complementary Therapies; Urban Redevelopment.

LIBRARIES

○ **420,000 BOOKS** ○ **1,900 STUDY PLACES**

Four libraries are distributed around the campuses, including a Learning Resource Centre (*which is the same thing really*) at Harrow. Its second floor is devoted to special needs learning resources, including books software and AV material.

COMPUTERS

○ **3,500+ WORKSTATIONS**

Each site has a number of computer labs, most open till 9pm. Many courses employ the Blackboard system, an online learning facility with e-journals, past papers etc.

OTHER LEARNING FACILITIES

Regent has a Learning Advice Centre, open to all. Harrow has music rehearsal rooms and broadcast-quality TV and radio studios. Marylebone boasts a CAD lab.

ENTERTAINMENT ○○○○○○○○○

LONDON see University of London
○ **PRICE OF A PINT OF BEER** £2.30
○ **GLASS OF WINE** £2.40
○ **CAN OF RED BULL** £1.60

UNIVERSITY
○ **PRICE OF A PINT OF BEER** £1.80
○ **GLASS OF WINE** £2 ○ **CAN OF RED BULL** £1.35

When they're not rampaging through the West End, swanning through Bloomsbury pubs or drinking neighbouring Imperial College's bar dry, Westminster students enjoy a limited but lavish range of domestic entertainments.
BARS Marylebone has the brand new Intermission, which has alcohol-free areas and a tabletop ordering system *that make it feel more like a private members' club than a typical student dive.* The Undercroft at Harrow *attracts an arty crowd* and has a wide range of *cheapish* beers. Regular events and happy hours – DJs every Monday and live music at the weekend.
THEATRES The Drama Soc *rally round* for a couple of shows a year at Harrow.
FILM There's a big screen at Harrow. Student-made films are shown occasionally *and Manga flicks are pretty popular.* The Animation Soc shows something every month.
CLUBBING/MUSIC VENUES Area 51 at Harrow hosts a weekly mix of club nights and gigs, with frequent acoustic sets from music students and the odd big

name. Raghav and Pendulum have played recently.
FOOD There are University-run outlets at each site *but despite recent efforts to improve things, students aren't happy about the cost or the taste.* SU outlets are *cheaper.* Bars dish out snackage as well.
OTHER Annual May Ball and some large-scale Freshers' events, plus Valentines and Halloween Balls. *Boat parties (an excuse to get drunk on the river) are the New Big Thing for societies.*

SOCIAL ⓊⓊⓊⓊⓊⓊⓊⓊⓊⓊⓊⓊⓊ

UNIVERSITY OF WESTMINSTER STUDENTS' UNION
- **4 SABBATICALS** - **TURNOUT AT LAST BALLOT** 8%
- **NUS MEMBER**

The hardworking exec is prepared to stand up to the administration but the students don't seem to know or care what's going on. They have been trying to organise political protests and whip up a revolutionary fervour, but enthusiasm and interest among students remain rather reserved. The offices at Marylebone are cramped but functional.

SU FACILITIES
Two bars; purpose-built nightclub; four cafeterias; two snack/coffee bars; fast food outlet; four pool tables; table football; jukeboxes; minibus for hire; Barclays ATMs; photocopiers; fax and printing services; photo booth; payphones; advice centre; TV lounge; gaming and vending machines; general store and stationery shop; art supply store at Harrow; new and secondhand bookshops.

CLUBS (NON-SPORTING)
Amsterdam (organises trips to Amsterdam); Animation; Bhangra; Book; Campaigning; Cedar (recognising the interests of the Lebanese and Arab population in the university); Comedy; Computing; Dialogue & Debate (aims to engage in dialogue between Muslims and non-Muslims); Drama; Electronic Dance Music; Fashion; Freshers' Angels Cheerleading Squad; Fun (pool, Playstation, sumo wrestling, bungee jumping); Greek; Hindu; Indie Culture (music events); International Human Rights; Law; Live Music; Literature & Culture; Medical; Model United Nation; Persian; Psychology; Shisha; Sikh; Socialist Worker; Soul Train; Uzbekistan Awareness; Wu Style Qi Gong & Tai Ji (martial art). **See also Clubs tables.**

OTHER ORGANISATIONS
Monthly 'the Smoke' is the *well-worth thumbing* student paper. 'Smoke radio' wafts across the Harrow campus via the internet. Community volunteering is on the up, but *after a bit of a kerfuffle,* there's still no Rag. WISPA is Westminster's International Student Programme of Activities, *rather than an extinct chocolate bar.*

RELIGIOUS
- **3 CHAPLAINS (COFE, RC, METHODIST)**

Muslim and multi-faith prayer rooms available on each campus. One associate chaplain volunteers at Harrow and another helps run worship and discussion groups. See University of London for wider religious provisions.

PAID WORK
See University of London
- **JOB BUREAU**

Along with CaSE, the SU runs a job shop (external jobs and employment within the SU).

SPORTS ⓊⓊⓊⓊⓊⓊⓊⓊⓊⓊⓊⓊ

- **RECENT SUCCESSES** RUGBY, NETBALL
- **BUSA RANKING** 98

Bearing in mind the urban location and the lack of cohesion between sites, sporting success is nowhere near as lame as might be expected. The campuses try to whoop each other's asses in regular matches but it's hands on deck against local Varsity rivals TVU. The men's rugby team have a good record in the SESSA league, and though there are relatively few sporting teams, those that exist are buff enough to kick ass when they have to.

SPORTS FACILITIES
The Regent Street site has badminton and snooker facilities, a gym, a sauna, solarium and multigym – these are being redeveloped for the 2006–07 academic year. At Harrow there's a fitness centre and a sports hall. There's a sports ground at Chiswick, complete with running track, boathouse, bar and 55 acres of pitches. There's also a gym and all-weather pitches. *A ridiculously complicated swimming payback scheme lets students pay £20 and then claim back the admission cost of up to 15 swims at Cally Pool and Harrow Leisure Centre.*

SPORTING CLUBS
Ju-Jitsu; Rowing; Women's Basketball; Women's Football; Women's Hockey. **See also Clubs tables.**

ATTRACTIONS see University of London

ACCOMMODATION ⓊⓊⓊⓊⓊⓊⓊⓊⓊ

IN UNIVERSITY
- **SELF–CATERING** 11% - **COST** £93 (37WKS)
- **1ST YEARS LIVING IN** 26%
- **INSURANCE PREMIUM** £

AVAILABILITY Limited: a quarter of first years looking for a room aren't going to find one, with priority going to those coming from the 'wrong' side of the M25. In most of the five halls, kitchens and bathrooms are shared by 6-12 people. In Harrow's *pricey* on-site flats, however, some rooms have en suite facilities and no more than six share kitchen facilities. Students from the Central London campuses have half an hour on public transport to get from bed to study – *Harrovians are luckier*. Most halls have TV common rooms and launderettes. Single sex accommodation is available upon request and mixed sex couples can share. Marylebone Hall is closing in 2006 with a view to opening *bigger and better* doors in 2007.

CAR PARKING *No sir.*

EXTERNALLY see University of London
○ **AVE RENT** £99
HOUSING HELP The University-run Student Housing Service at the Marylebone and Harrow sites provides a notice board, approval scheme and advice. Temporary accommodation available in September during house-hunting season.

WELFARE ○○○○○○○○○○○○

SERVICES
○ LGBT OFFICER & SOCIETY ○ WOMEN'S OFFICER & MUSLIM WOMEN'S SOCIETY ○ MATURE STUDENTS' OFFICER & SOCIETY ○ INTERNATIONAL STUDENTS' OFFICER ○ DISABILITIES OFFICER ○ ETHNIC MINORITIES

OFFICER ○ LATE-NIGHT/WOMEN'S MINIBUS ○ NIGHTLINE ○ UNIVERSITY COUNSELLORS 9 FULL/11 PART ○ CRIME RATING !!!!!
HEALTH Clinics at Harrow and Marylebone. A University nurse deals with most complaints and administrates a GP referral service. There are a number of advice clinics on travel vaccines and contraception etc., and several trained first-aiders to hand. The University pays for psychiatric referrals when necessary.
CRECHES/NURSERY There's a 20-place nursery at Marylebone and a 12-place playgroup at Harrow. Both take 2-5-yr-olds.
DISABILITIES The Central London campuses and location aren't wheelchair-friendly. Harrow is a lot better, with full access and converted accommodation on-site. Two disability advisors are there to help.

FINANCE
○ **AVE DEBT PER YEAR** £2,215
○ **HOME STUDENT FEES** £3,000
FEES Part-timers pay £380 per module. International undergraduates pay £8,750 depending on course. Postgrad fees range from £3,500-14,000.
○ **AVE PAYMENT** £100-£3,000
SUPPORT 1,800 bursaries of £300 are doled out according to household income. Scholarships of up to £4,000 based on pre-university achievement. Emergency loans of up to £100 are available.

▶ WINCHESTER ART SCHOOL
see University of Southampton

▶ UNIVERSITY COLLEGE WINCHESTER
see University of Winchester

▶ UNIVERSITY COLLEGE WORCESTER
see University of Worcester

W

◎ According to legend, a student at the University of York tried to hand in a copy of a published paper for an essay – in which the paper was one of the references in the question. After failing his degree the student turned up at graduation anyway, complete with gown, cap and parents.

UNIVERSITY OF WINCHESTER

○ UNIVERSITY OF WINCHESTER West Hill, Winchester, Hampshire, SO22 4NR **TEL** (01962) 841515
E−MAIL course.enquiries@winchester.ac.uk **WEBSITE** www.winchester.ac.uk
○ UNIVERSITY OF WINCHESTER STUDENTS' UNION Sparkford Road, Winchester, Hampshire, SO22 4NR
TEL (01962) 827418 **E−MAIL** su_admin@winchester.ac.uk **WEBSITE** www.winchesterstudents.co.uk

GENERAL ○○○○○○○○○○○○○

When King Alfred wasn't out burning the cakes, he was hanging out in Winchester pondering how to get the Danes out of the country. The city was then the capital of Wessex, the now non-existent southern county that Thomas Hardy was so keen on. *These days, Winchester is about as urban as Hampshire gets.* On a *pleasant* wooded hillside overlooking the quaint cathedral city, sits the University of Winchester, once a training ground for Anglican priests, now a rapidly evolving university (only just – they gained university status in 2005). The main campus is a small, self-contained combination of olde worlde churchy buildings and some *moderately attractive* redbrick affairs, *which blend into each other almost seamlessly.* There's another campus in Basingstoke, exclusively for postgrads and part-time students.

England, it's gone the way of similar cities like Norwich, York and Canterbury and now exists as a small, but busy snapshot of the days when kings were kings and architecture wasn't rubbish. You've only to look at the *magnificent* cathedral (in which Winchester's students have *the honour* of graduating), the West Gate or the Great Hall (now home to King Arthur's round table) to feel the medieval legacy breathing down your neck. Jane Austen is buried here *and it's understandable why – the city's not so different in spirit from her home town of Bath.* It's more than just a museum piece though, nowadays Winchester is home to the *usual* collection of high street chains and franchises (many in the Brooks Shopping Centre), as well as blink-and-you'll-miss-them boutiques and quirky ickle shops and art galleries. There's street theatre at the annual Hat Fair and Folk Festival, *but those who like their social calendar a bit more frantic head to nearby Southampton.* Those who like it sparser can head off into the beautiful Hampshire countryside, with its *picturesque* villages and market towns and of course, the South Downs.

SEX RATIO: ♂35 ♀65	**FOUNDED:** 1840
FULL−TIME U'GRADS: 2,953	**PART−TIME:** 189
POSTGRADS: 1,351	**NON−DEGREE:** 1,148
AVE COURSE: 3YRS	**ETHNIC:** 4%
STATE:PRIVATE SCHOOL: 96:4	**FLUNK RATE:** 11%
MATURE: 21%	**INTERNATIONAL:** 4%
DISABLED: 140	**LOCAL:** 15%

ATMOSPHERE

The small and leafy campus may seem dull in winter, but when the summer sun cracks through the clouds, students breathe a contented sigh and admire the fantastic views. It's a dinky place, with a strong sense of community, but those wanting non-stop party thrills will probably sulk a bit here. Those that want a friendly, safe and welcoming atmosphere will be laughing, though. It's luvvie-heaven with a sizeable thesp contingent to liven the campus up a bit – or rather, to do a bit of air-kissing and shriek 'Dahling, you were maaarvellous!' at every possible opportunity. Since students make up around 10% of Winchester's population, they play a big part in the city's economy, so the townsfolk are happy to have them. *It can get a tad desolate during the holidays, though.*

WINCHESTER
○ POPULATION 40,000 **○ CITY CENTRE** 1 MILE
○ LONDON 64 MILES **○ SOUTHAMPTON** 14 MILES
○ HIGH TEMP 22 **○ LOW TEMP** 3 **○ AVE RAINFALL** 66
Winchester is only really a city in the 'having a cathedral' sense of the word, and even though it was once the capital of Alfred the Great's

TRAVEL

TRAINS Winchester mainline station runs direct services to Southampton (£5 rtn) and London (£20 travelcard), where connections across the country are available.
CAR The M3 and the A34 are useful for getting to the city, but the compact centre and tricky parking makes cars both redundant and awkward. Only students living more than five miles away can park on campus, and they have to fork out £20/yr for the privilege.
AIR Southampton airport is just 15 minutes away by car, and Gatwick and Heathrow are just about reachable for journeys further afield.
LOCAL Most of the city is navigable on foot, but the No.5 bus from campus to halls and the city centre (45p) can be a leg-saver when the big hill becomes a turn-off.
TAXIS *Plentiful, reasonably priced and rarely used.*
BICYCLES Once again, the fact that the Uni is plonked on a hilltop can strain a few hamstrings, but theft is almost non-existent and most places around town are easily bikeable. UoW has bike lockers and operates a cycle loan scheme.

CAREER PROSPECTS
○ CAREERS SERVICE ○ NO OF STAFF 1 FULL/3 PART
○ UNEMPLOYED AFTER 6 MONTHS 4%
The *dinky* Careers Service runs the *usual gamut* of job fairs, newsletters and bulletin boards, plus luring visiting speakers, workshops and careers skill sessions.

FAMOUS ALUMNI

Martin Bashir (journalist and Michael Jackson/Princess Di interviewer); Mike Bushell (TV sports reporter); Sara Coburn (TV business reporter); Steven Furst (comedian); Dirk Maggs (radio producer); John McIntyre (reporter); Michael Rose (producer of *child-catching* West End musical 'Chitty Chitty Bang Bang'); Angus Scott (sports broadcaster).

FURTHER INFO

- **PROSPECTUSES** UNDERGRAD; POSTGRAD; INTERNATIONAL; VIDEO
- **OPEN DAYS**

ACADEMIC ◐◐◐◐◐◐◐◐◐◐◐◐◐

Teaching is the *traditional raison d'être*, but humanities and arts subjects such as drama, performing arts and archaeology are now among the University's star-hitters. Drama, in particular, *lives near the top of the tree* with rehearsal and performance spots – including an outdoor space and a *scary-sounding but very high-tech* Performance Gym – littered around the campus and, *as if that wasn't enough show-off space,* *strong* links with local venues. The courses available are generally academic (English, say) but vocational courses (like journalism) are now getting a look-in too. Assessment is increasingly project-based to emphasise skills and employability rather than bookishness. *Courses are as flexible* as a rubber band with various joint honours or subsidiary subject combos available.

ENTRY POINTS: 160–260	**AVE POINTS: 220**
APPLICATIONS PER PLACE: 5	**CLEARING: 10%**
NO. OF TERMS: 2	**LENGTH OF TERMS: 20**wks
STAFF TO STUDENT RATIO: 1:22	**STUDY ADDICTS: 1%**
TEACHING: ★★★	**RESEARCH: N/A**
YEAR ABROAD: 2%	**SANDWICH STUDENTS: N/A**
1STS: 6%	**2.2S: 37%**
2.1S: 52%	**3RDS: 2%**

ADMISSIONS

- **APPLY VIA UCAS/DIRECT FOR PART-TIME**

'Widening' and 'participation' are buzzwords, meaning those with non-traditional backgrounds are welcomed with open arms.

SUBJECTS

ARTS 45% **EDUCATION** 30% **SOCIAL SCIENCES** 30%
BEST Archaeology; Business & Management; Drama/Performing Arts; Education; Psychology; Religious Studies & Theology; Sports studies.

LIBRARIES

- **225,000 BOOKS** ● **450 STUDY SPACES**
- **SPEND PER STUDENT** ££££

COMPUTERS

- **500 WORKSTATIONS** ● **24-HR ACCESS**
- **SPEND PER STUDENT** £££££

Computers are spread between the library and assorted IT clusters. Students are offered techno-training and those that need it can attend one-to-one 'IT surgeries'. Internet access in halls.

OTHER LEARNING FACILITIES

Dance and drama studios, CAD lab and a media centre.

ENTERTAINMENT ◐◐◐◐◐◐◐◐◐

THE CITY

- **PRICE OF A PINT OF BEER** £2
- **GLASS OF WINE** £2.20
- **CAN OF RED BULL** £2.20

CINEMAS The Screen in the city centre has two screens and offers 10% student discounts (and, more importantly, a bar).
THEATRES The Theatre Royal *does the stuff that all small town theatres called 'Theatre Royal' usually do: touring shows, pantos, comedy, crap for the oldies, etc.* More offbeat stuff at the Chesil Theatre and the Cultural Centre Gallery.
PUBS Winchester has a claim to having more pubs per square mile than any other city in the country. There aren't that many square miles though. Boozers range from local joints to swanky bars. Wetherspoon and Muswells are favourites – for cheapness, if not atmosphere.
CLUBBING Beyond dancefloors and late licences in certain bars, the only party action that goes on is in the Union, or in Southampton.
MUSIC VENUES The Railway pub is a haven for alt/indie guitar twangers.
EATING OUT The standard range of cosmopolitan eats – Italian, Mexican, Venusian and so on. Okay, maybe not the last one. Main courses range from £4 to £8.

UNIVERSITY

- **PRICE OF A PINT OF BEER** £1.70
- **GLASS OF WINE** £1.80
- **CAN OF RED BULL** £1.50

BARS Bar 22 stays open till 12 or 1am twice a week and multi-tasks theme nights, comedy, live music and club nights. The Lounge lives up to its name with a plasma screen and bar snacks and C2H at Westdowns Student Village provides a more chilled vibe.
THEATRES Drama is a major player on the University club scene, so the newly expanded Stripe theatre is never short of board-treaders.
MUSIC VENUES Bar 22 juggles local and student bands once a month.
CLUBBING BOP, every Wednesday, throws open both bars for cheap drinks, cheese, R'n'B and proper rock. The Radio One crew have sunk a pint or two.
COMEDY/CABARET Weekly stand-up shows *get 'em rolling in the aisles.*
FOOD Destination ladles out chomps to suit all tastes (*except, perhaps, for cannibalism – that*

W

would just be weird. And illegal) and D2Go sells basic shop fodder.

OTHER Three balls a year: Freshers', Christmas and the Summer Fair.

SOCIAL

UNIVERSITY OF WINCHESTER STUDENTS' UNION
⊙ **2 SABBATICALS** • **TURNOUT AT LAST BALLOT** 20%
⊙ **NUS MEMBER**

The University does its best to listen to the students and enjoys an open relationship with the SU (not that they sleep with other people or anything). The new four storey Student Centre (due for 2007) will hopefully improve the social side and give the Union some real clout.

SU FACILITIES
Three bars; cafeteria; two snack bars; four pool tables; ten meeting rooms; Alliance & Leicester ATM; photocopier; photobooth; payphones; games and vending machines; general store; stationery shop; new and secondhand bookshops; launderette.

CLUBS (NON-SPORTING)
Akido; Alternative Music; Archaeology; International Students; Magazine; Jung Shin Hapkido; LGB; Performing Arts Winchester; Ski & Snowboard; The Voice (radio); Winchester Association of Roleplayers and Gamers. **See also Clubs tables.**

OTHER ORGANISATIONS
The 'Big Fish, Little Pond' paper is distributed every term. 'The Voice' radio broadcasts in the Union and 'Rubber Duck' TV also rides the airwaves. A charity Rag raises small but perfectly formed sums each year.

RELIGIOUS
⊙ **1 CHAPLAIN (COFE)**

In addition to the University's chapel and Muslim prayer room, Winchester provides 30 churches, ensuring all brands of Christian are catered for. Other faiths might have to find other trees to bark up, though.

PAID WORK
⊙ **JOB BUREAU** ⊙ **PAID WORK** TERM-TIME 70%; HOLS 80%
Plenty of cash-catching opportunities in and around the city, advertised by Student Services.

SPORTS

⊙ **RECENT SUCCESSES** HOCKEY, FOOTBALL, BASKETBALL ⊙ **BUSA RANKING** 122
Dominance in the local leagues is one thing. BUSA is a different kettle of fish.

SPORTS FACILITIES
On or near campus: two football, one rugby, one hockey and one cricket pitch; squash, tennis, basketball and netball courts; sports hall; sports pavilion; gym; multigym; aerobics studio. Use of the facilities costs £10 a year. Winchester offers a leisure centre, tennis and squash courts, swimming pool and golf course. The hills nearby offer outdoor-pursuers outdoor pursuits.

SPORTING CLUBS
Leisure classes include Yoga and Street Dance. **See also Clubs tables.**

ACCOMMODATION

IN UNIVERSITY
⊙ **CATERED** 7% ⊙ **COST** £98 (30WKS)
⊙ **SELF–CATERING** 24% ⊙ **COST** £90 (40WKS)
⊙ **1ST YEARS LIVING IN** 95%
⊙ **INSURANCE PREMIUM** £

AVAILABILITY Students are advised to get their forms in on time, but there's room at the inn for most first years anyway. Winchester's halls are almost oozing with sexiness and have awards to prove it. The Centre Parcs-like Westdown Student Village in particular has a 'that was the best year of my life' type reputation. Nearly all first years can get rooms if they want them and about a third are en suite. Most other years live out. All halls are either on or within five minutes walk of campus. Loud music has to be off by 11pm, though, otherwise it's a visit from the boys, got that?
CAR PARKING If you must – and only if you must – it's £40/yr.

EXTERNALLY
⊙ **AVE RENT** £73

AVAILABILITY On the pricey side, but the quality of the area tends to be worth it – especially if students go for houses garlanded with the Winchester Housing Accreditation Award. Nearly everyone ends up with something nearby campus.
HOUSING HELP The Accommodation Office runs a housing fair each year and provides a vacancy list, bulletin board, legal help and blacklists naughty landlords.

WELFARE

SERVICES
⊙ **LGBT OFFICER & SOCIETY** ⊙ **ETHNIC MINORITIES OFFICER** ⊙ **WOMEN'S OFFICER & SOCIETY** ⊙ **MATURE STUDENTS' OFFICER** ⊙ **INTERNATIONAL STUDENTS' OFFICER** ⊙ **DISABLED STUDENTS' OFFICER** ⊙ **POSTGRAD OFFICER** ⊙ **UNIVERSITY COUNSELLORS** 4 FULL/3 PART
⊙ **CRIME RATING** !

The SU are able to arrange a free solicitor's

Words in italics are Push's point of view — take it or leave it...

consultation for students with legal queries.

HEALTH The uni's medical officer works from the nearby health centre. The university's nurse also on hand.

WOMEN Free attack alarms available (for men too).

CRECHES/NURSERY The University crèche has 20 places for students' studentlings, aged 6mths-4yrs.

DISABLED The hill, the stairs and the old buildings don't make for great wheelchair access but there is some specialised accommodation available in halls, and automatic doors, lifts, ramps and induction loops have been installed and the dyslexia support on offer is top notch.

DRUGS Not permitted on campus.

FINANCE

- **AVE DEBT PER YEAR** £4,100
- **HOME STUDENT FEES** £3,000 ● **ACCESS FUND** £187,000
- **SUCCESSFUL APPLICATIONS** 568
- **AVE PAYMENT** £200-£600

SUPPORT A range of bursaries and scholarships, including the £1,300 Winchester Scholarship for UK undergrads.

UNIVERSITY OF WOLVERHAMPTON

FORMERLY WOLVERHAMPTON POLYTECHNIC

1) ● **UNIVERSITY OF WOLVERHAMPTON** Wulfruna Street, Wolverhampton, WV1 1SB **TEL** (01902) 322 222
E-MAIL enquiries@wlv.ac.uk **WEBSITE** www.wlv.ac.uk ● **UNIVERSITY OF WOLVERHAMPTON STUDENTS'**
UNION Wulfruna Street, Wolverhampton, WV1 1LY **TEL** (01902) 322 021 **E-MAIL** uwsu@wlv.ac.uk **WEBSITE** www.wolvesunion.org
2) ● **COMPTON PARK CAMPUS** Compton Road West, Wolverhampton, WV3 9DX **TEL** (01902) 323 604
3) ● **WALSALL CAMPUS** Gorway Road, Walsall, WS1 3BD **TEL** (01902) 323 200
4) ● **TELFORD CAMPUS** Shifnal Road, Priorslee, Telford, TF2 9NT **TEL** (01902) 323 900

GENERAL ○○○○○○○○○○○○○

Wolverhampton may be part of the Birmingham *urban spill* but it has an *identity of its own – woe betide anyone who mixes the two up*. The 13 miles to the centre of Brum are taken up with Dudley, West Bromwich and Walsall and each has its *own distinctive feel*. Wolves is *far more residential* than Brum and moves at a *much slower pace*. But the differences shouldn't disguise the fact that all the towns in the conurbation are part of the same family, *which is just as well*, as Wolves Uni *squats* across all of them *without a definitive centre of gravity*. Education is taught at Walsall, while *right out in the sticks* and split between the *almost rural towns* of Telford and Compton, is the Business School.

SEX RATIO: ♂42 ♀58	
FULL-TIME U'GRADS: 12,461	PART-TIME: 7,135
POSTGRADS: 4,026	NON-DEGREE: N/A
AVE COURSE: 3YRS	ETHNIC: N/A
STATE:PRIVATE SCHOOL: 96:4	FLUNK RATE: 24%
MATURE: 67%	INTERNATIONAL: 16%
DISABLED: 210	LOCAL: 72%

ATMOSPHERE

This part of the Midlands is still struggling to convince the rest of the UK that it's not just smoggy, clogged up and thoroughly short on glam. *After years of jibes and bad Black Country impressions, it's a thankless task, but locals know the truth. As a result, there's a large body of local students, which smoothes town/gown relations and gives airs, graces and pretensions short shrift.*

SITES

CITY CAMPUS The modern main campus is about one and a half miles from the city centre. The main building is *scrubbed to a clinical gleam*, although it's actually a bit *disconcertingly institutional – like going to college in a hospital*. It's *slap* in the centre of Wolves, *handy for the hub of social life* that is the 24-hr Asda.

COMPTON PARK CAMPUS (Business Studies) A *smart* campus about one and a half miles from the centre of town. Students get *the best of both worlds*: a close community with a fair bit of greenery and easy links to the concrete jungle on the University shuttle bus.

WALSALL CAMPUS (Education, Sport, Performing Arts, Health) Walsall can feel a bit *isolated*, but the social life is *more than enough to make up for that*. It's a *sporty* sort of place with *recently refurbished* halls and facilities, and is *very popular* with residents.

TELFORD (Business, Engineering, Social Work) Telford's *very definitely a campus unto itself*. It's 16 miles from Wolves, almost into the Shropshire countryside and attracts a healthy contingent of international students. Like Compton, it's a *pleasant enough* place to be, *but the intensity of community spirit borders on cabin fever*.

W

BIRMINGHAM see University of Birmingham

TRAVEL see University of Birmingham
TRAINS Wolverhampton station's ten mins from the City campus. It's a piece of cake to get to London (from £24.75 return), Edinburgh (£54.20), Manchester (£16.05), Reading (24.15) and all over.
COACHES National Express does London (£17.60), Manchester (£12.40), Edinburgh (£38.50) etc.
CAR M5, M54, M6 for Wolves and Walsall, A41, M54 for Telford.
LOCAL Regular buses to the 'burbs. The supertram Metro links Wolves to Brum. £2.30 to Brum on the train, or the ever-popular night special, £1.40 rtn (last train 3am). There's also a 50p night bus from Brum to Walsall.
UNIVERSITY Shuttle buses (free with NUS ID) ferry between lectures on different sites. They're *reliable*, but some take *the closest thing that Wolves has to a scenic route*. There's a late-night safety bus that does doorstep drop-offs within a three mile radius of university events. Women get first dibs.
BICYCLES *Not the best idea, unless heavy sweating and crippling thigh pain is the goal.*

CAREER PROSPECTS
○ **CAREERS SERVICE** ○ **NO. OF STAFF** 22 FULL
○ **UNEMPLOYED AFTER 6MTHS** 10%
Comprehensive service with newsletters, bulletin boards, library, job fairs, interview coaching, psychometric testing and vacancy database.

FAMOUS ALUMNI
Trevor Beattie (advertising guru); Sir Terence Beckett (deputy chairman, CEGB); Jenny Jones, Michael Foster (MPs); Mark O'Shea (TV snake expert); Suzi Perry (TV presenter); Vernie (Eternal).

FURTHER INFO
○ **PROSPECTUSES** UNDERGRAD; POSTGRAD; SOME DEPTS; ALTERNATIVE
○ **OPEN DAYS**
Get online for more info, including the SU website for alternative bumf.

ACADEMIC ○○○○○○○○○○○○○○

Wolves is a *typical* 'new' university with lots of vocational courses, *a healthy dose* of mature and local students and some *off-the-wall* degree

subjects: Complementary Therapies, Virtual Reality, E-commerce and a totally online degree (Business Administration). New building projects are improving teaching facilities and study support is taken seriously, with *staff available for hand-holding as much as possible. How touchy-feely.*

ENTRY POINTS: 140–300	**AVE POINTS:** 288
APPLICATIONS PER PLACE: 5	**CLEARING:** 2%
NO. OF TERMS: 2	**LENGTH OF TERMS:** 15WKS
STAFF TO STUDENT RATIO: 1:17	**STUDY ADDICTS:** 21%
TEACHING: ★★★★	**RESEARCH:** ★★★
YEAR ABROAD: <1%	**SANDWICH STUDENTS:** <1%
1STS: 12%	**2.2S:** 40%
2.1S: 38%	**3RDS:** 10%

ADMISSIONS
○ **APPLY VIA UCAS**

SUBJECTS
APPLIED SCIENCES 8%   **ART & DESIGN** 9 %
BUSINESS/MANAGEMENT 12%   **COMPUTING & INFORMATION TECHNOLOGY** 8%   **ENGINEERING & BUILT ENVIRONMENT** 7%   **HUMANITIES, LANGUAGES & SOCIAL SCIENCES** 11%   **LEGAL STUDIES** 12%
SCHOOL OF EDUCATION 12%   **SCHOOL OF HEALTH** 17%
SPORT, PERFORMING ARTS & LEISURE 5%
BEST Art & Design; Business & Management; Economics; Education; Hospitality, Leisure & Sport Tourism; Maths, Statistics & Operational Research; Molecular & Organismal Bio-sciences; Nursing; Other subjects allied to Medicine; Philosophy; Politics; Psychology; Theology.
UNUSUAL Deaf Studies; Glass; Popular Music.

LIBRARIES
○ **300,000 BOOKS** ○ **900,000 STUDY PLACES**
○ **24-HR ACCESS**
There's a library on each site and a modern Learning Centre, *which has everything except enough books to go around.* The Social Learning Environment is a combined coffee bar and study area. The most popular ones are now on four-hour loan, *which means that everyone can get them, but no one has time to read them.*

COMPUTERS
○ **2,000 WORKSTATIONS** ○ **24-HR ACCESS**
Many departments have their own computer rooms with specialist software available. Lecture notes and discussion forums (*for subject-related chit-chat, not 'Big Brother' gossip*) are on the *swanky* intranet – WOLF (Wolverhampton Online Learning Framework). Most student halls have wi-fi access.

◉ **Some real clubs and societies: Tennent's Lager Appreciation (Strathclyde); Human Powered Flight Club (UCL); Extreme Ironing (Aston); Queueing (Wolverhampton).**

Words in italics are Push's point of view — take it or leave it...

ENTERTAINMENT ()()()()()()()()()

THE CITYsee University of Birmingham
- **PRICE OF A PINT OF BEER** £2.20
- **GLASS OF WINE** £2.50
- **CAN OF RED BULL** £1.60

CINEMAS The 12-screen Cineworld's a *short* bus or taxi-ride from the City campus.

THEATRES The Grand Theatre takes *pride of place* in Wolves and there's a lefty sort of arts place on campus.

PUBS *Perfect student territory: lots of cheap beer deals in student-happy chain pubs. Pushplugs: Scream; Varsity (cheap); Crooked House (tilted building with a big beer garden). There are also some hard, tattooed and aggressively towny venues (the Feathers, for instance).*

CLUBBING *A reasonable selection of places to shake a tailfeather, but perhaps serious clubbers' alarm bells should be ringing when the Civic Centre (most popular nights – soul & pop on Fridays, indie on Saturdays) is the best of the bunch.*

MUSIC VENUES *Best make a break for Brum to catch big-league live acts, but the Civic (next to the University) gets the likes of the Arctic Monkeys. Goldie Lookin' Chain and Julian Cope have played at Wulfrun Hall and the teensy Little Civic gets as-yet-unknown strummers.*

COMEDY *Occasional laughs (of the Jimmy Carr and Jerry Sadowitz variety, not just at fellow gig-goers' outfits) to be had at the music venues.*

OTHER The zoo and castle in Dudley are *worth a peek*, as is the West Midlands Safari Park and the Black Country Living Museum. Wolverhampton and Walsall have art galleries; Walsall even has a leather museum. Contemporary exhibitions and local archive paintings at the *popular* art gallery.

EATING OUT Lots of choices, most of them the *typical Midlands ethnic jumble. Pushplugs: Bilash Tandoori; Imperial (Chinese); Dilshad Tandoori; Gepetto's (Italian).*

UNIVERSITY
- **PRICE OF A PINT OF BEER** £1.50
- **GLASS OF WINE** £2 **CAN OF RED BULL** £1.40

All campuses have their own SU buildings and bars.

BARS *A trio of well-attended watering holes. Fat Mick's (City campus) is the main hang-out, Poly Bar is loungey and Zone 34, clubby.*

THEATRES The Arena puts on student drama, small companies and experimental gubbins (about 70 productions a year).

CLUBBING Zone 34 can pack in *an impressive* 1,360 people *but faces fierce competition from the city nightspots.* DJ-wise, Fingerthing and Easy Rollers have stopped by recently.

COMEDY/CABARET The odd special event, such as a recent Bar Idol competition with heats at each campus.

FOOD A *big* University refectory, a couple of Costas and pre-packed sarnies in the Union.

OTHER Graduation balls are organised by departments. There's a *huge* end of year ball for all and sundry.

SOCIAL ()()()()()()()()()()()()

UNIVERSITY OF WOLVERHAMPTON STUDENTS' UNION
- **6 SABBATICALS** **TURNOUT AT LAST BALLOT** 10%
- **NUS MEMBER**

Woefully apolitical but the SU's *central* to student life in *more practical ways* (social ents and welfare).

SU FACILITIES
SU building on each campus; nightclub/music venue; five bars; four canteens; seven pool tables; meeting rooms; seven minibuses; people carrier; Endsleigh Insurance; ATMs; photocopying, fax, printing services; photo booth; payphones; crèche; late-night minibus; juke boxes; video games; general store; stationery shop; vending machines; new and secondhand bookshop; launderette; printing and graphics shop; hairdressers; optician.

CLUBS (NON-SPORTING)
Afro-Caribbean; Anime; Bring It On (fresher mentoring); Chinese; Computer Games; Greek & Cypriot; Links (1st Aid); Malaysian; Nigerian; Sikh; Single Parents. **See also Clubs tables.**

OTHER ORGANISATIONS
'Cry Wolf' is the *well-read* student mag. Each campus has a Rag, which raise a *respectable* £20,000 altogether.

RELIGIOUS
- **4 CHAPLAINS (COFE, RC, FC)**

There's a multi-faith chaplaincy and a Muslim prayer room.

PAID WORK see University of Birmingham
- **JOB BUREAU** **PAID WORK** TERM-TIME 75%; HOLS 80%

Wolves work is *easy to come by*, with loads of pubs, bars and restaurants in town. The University Job Shop can also help.

SPORTS ()()()()()()()()()()()()

- **BUSA RANKING** 91

Walsall's the site for sports courses and the new national judo centre. It's part of a new sports centre development with 12 indoor courts, a full-size all-weather pitch and an athletics track.

SPORTS FACILITIES
Five football pitches; three rugby pitches; two hockey pitches; two all-weather pitches; two squash courts; nine tennis courts; nine multi-purpose courts; 12 netball courts; four sports halls;

Words in italics are Push's point of view – take it or leave it...

swimming pool; running track; athletics field; gym; aerobics studio. The local area has a leisure centre; running track; squash courts; swimming pool; ice rink; croquet lawn; golf course. Of course, *then there are the delights* of Brum.

SPORTING CLUBS
Aikido; Frisbee; Ju-Jitsu; Kung Fu. **See also Clubs tables.**

ATTRACTIONS see University of Birmingham Wolves *hover* between Premiership and Championship status. The University's practically on top of the Molineux stadium and there's also Birmingham City, Aston Villa, West Brom and Walsall.

ACCOMMODATION ◗◗◗◗◗◗◗◗◗◗

IN UNIVERSITY
◉ **SELF-CATERING** 19% ◉ **COST** £61 (37WKS)
◉ **INSURANCE PREMIUM** ££
AVAILABILITY Students need to live more than 15 miles from town to qualify for halls. *Even then, they're dished out to the first takers*; only disabled students are guaranteed accommodation. There's housing at each of the four sites and 40% of rooms are en suite. Halls are *generally pretty habitable* – prices vary according to *poshness. Despite their ghastly appearance*, Randall Lines are *popular, sociable and cheap*. Walsall used to be the pits, but new buildings have changed that.
CAR PARKING Telford is the easiest campus for parking. Finding a spot at City or Walsall *is no joke*.

EXTERNALLY see University of Birmingham
◉ **AVE RENT** £43
AVAILABILITY *Easy to find and even easier on the pocket.* Whitmore Reans and Penfield are student strongholds. Heath Town's so grotty that the housing service won't even advertise properties there.

HOUSING HELP The accommodation office has online vacancy lists, property vetting, landlord blacklists and housing checks.

WELFARE ◗◗◗◗◗◗◗◗◗◗◗◗◗◗

SERVICES
◉ **LGBT OFFICER** ◉ **ETHNIC MINORITIES SOCIETY**
◉ **MATURE STUDENTS' OFFICER** ◉ **INTERNATIONAL STUDENTS' OFFICER** ◉ **DISABILITIES OFFICER**
◉ **WOMEN'S OFFICER** ◉ **LATE-NIGHT MINIBUS**
◉ **SELF-DEFENCE CLASSES**
◉ **UNIVERSITY COUNSELLORS** 3 FULL/3 PART
◉ **CRIME RATING** !!!
The SU Advisory team is at City campus, with a once-weekly service at Telford and Walsall. They deal with everything from health and housing to debt.
HEALTH The SU deals with sexual health and there's an opticians on site. *But if it's not eyes or genitals causing the problem, look to town.*
WOMEN Attack alarms are available from the Union.
CRECHES/NURSERY Limited places for 2-5-yr-olds.
DISABILITIES Best in Telford (hearing loops, ramps, adapted rooms) and *okay* in City, particularly for wheelchair access. Building work at Walsall means *access is pretty poor*. There's a dyslexia unit and advisor.
CRIME *There've been thefts on campus but security is tight.*

FINANCE
◉ **AVE DEBT PER YEAR** £3,671
◉ **HOME STUDENT FEES** £3,000
FEES Students from local colleges may get £1,000 off their fees.
◉ **ACCESS FUND** £3M ◉ **AVE PAYMENT** £50-1,000
SUPPORT The University's Start Right Bursary Scheme soothes the fee sting by topping up government grants awarded to poorer students to £3,000. University hardship loans and bursaries and there's a fund for black South African students.

UNIVERSITY OF WORCESTER

◉ **UNIVERSITY OF WORCESTER** Henwick Grove, Worcester, WR2 6AJ **TEL** (01905) 855 000 **E-MAIL** study@worc.ac.uk **WEBSITE** www.worc.ac.uk ◉ **WORCESTER STUDENTS' UNION** University of Worcester, Henwick Grove, Worcester, WR2 6AJ **TEL** (01905) 740 800 **WEBSITE** www.worcsu.com

GENERAL ◗◗◗◗◗◗◗◗◗◗◗◗◗◗

Just south of Birmingham, the historic city of Worcester is, *predictably enough*, the county town of Worcestershire – the River Severn's last stop on its way into Wales. Just south of its banks, in a *greenish* suburb of this pretty city, the compact campus *quietly* and *leafily minds its own business*. Built on the site of an old RAF base, the buildings are a collection of nice modern buildings, *slightly marred* by the *stubborn vestiges* of 70s architecture and *what are essentially a few run-down shacks*. Overall, however, the effect is one of *unassuming charm*.

Words in italics are Push's point of view — take it or leave it...

SEX RATIO: ♂24 ♀76	**FOUNDED:** 1947
FULL-TIME U'GRADS: 3,462	**PART-TIME:** 533
POSTGRADS: 1,501	**NON-DEGREE:** 3,081
AVE COURSE: 3YRS	**ETHNIC:** 5%
STATE:PRIVATE SCHOOL: 96:4	**FLUNK RATE:** 18%
MATURE: 33%	**INTERNATIONAL:** 4%
DISABLED: 110	**LOCAL:** 24%

ATMOSPHERE

You could scarcely call it an academic powerhouse, but while Worcester's students are as keen for a drink and a knees-up (in the bar or on the sports field) as much as anyone else, they're by no means slackers – timetables for their predominantly vocational courses can get pretty packed. *They're a relaxed lot, with a pleasant, welcoming and strongly communal attitude –* since everything's effectively on the doorstep, the campus functions as a small village within the city. Many courses, like teaching and nursing, rely heavily on work placements in the wider community, *which is quite fond of its students in return. Finally, male students might like to note the gender ratio – three girls to every bloke should appeal to anyone who fancies a touch of Worcester sauce...*

WORCESTER

- **POPULATION** 93,000 ● **CITY CENTRE** 1,200M
- **LONDON** 115 MILES ● **BIRMINGHAM** 52 MILES
- **LEEDS** 190 MILES
- **HIGH TEMP** 22 ● **LOW TEMP** 1 ● **RAINFALL** 60

People have been living in and around Worcester for thousands of years. The Romans came and went. Those great gifts to English spelling, the Saxons, knew it affectionately and unpronounceably as 'Weagornoceaster', and the Middle Ages saw it grow into a prosperous town heavily involved with the cloth industry and its famous porcelain. Its rich history is reflected in its current appearance – contemporary buildings share space with Tudor houses and medieval churches. The skyline is pierced with spires – *not quite dreaming like Oxford, but at least twitching in their sleep.* Reasons to visit include the ancient and impressive cathedral with its 200-metre tower and medieval cloisters, the birthplace of composer Edward Elgar and the reputed tomb of the *villified* King John. Reasons to stay include an *adequate* variety of pubs, shops and restaurants, a *surprisingly lively* nightlife, and the *beautiful* surrounding countryside. *Okay, so it's not a throbbing metropolis, but that's what Birmingham – less than an hour away – is for.*

TRAVEL

TRAINS Both Worcester's mainline stations – Forgate Street and Shrub Hill – are within a mile of the University and have frequent connections all over the country (Birmingham, from £7.05 rtn).
COACHES National Express services stop in the city centre.
CAR The M5, A443, A44 and A38 are some of Worcester's *favourite roads. Parking isn't much of*

an issue as there are plenty of pay & displays around and 500 spaces on campus (£1.20/day, 60p after 6pm). Permits cost £25 a term – but conditions apply.
AIR Birmingham International 45 mins away serves both national and international destinations.
LOCAL *Handy* bus 31 goes in and out of town for £1.20.
UNIVERSITY Free minibuses are laid on for certain nursing and education classes.
TAXIS *Reliable* but *unhailable* services. Several firms have an understanding with the University and are always around at peak times.
BICYCLES *Cycle fever hasn't really hit Worcester the town or Worcester the University, but* campus storage facilities are *more than adequate* in any case.

CAREER PROSPECTS

- **CAREERS SERVICE** ● **NO. OF STAFF** 2 FULL
- **UNEMPLOYED AFTER 6MTHS** 8%

Newsletters, bulletin boards, interview training, job fairs and a careers library. The Careers Service itself used to be an RAF morgue and still has the sloping floors. *No jokes about 'dead-end jobs' please* – that'd be tasteless.

FAMOUS ALUMNI

Matt Beechey (rower); Jacqui Smith MP (Education Minister); Andy Train (Olympic canoeist); Jo Yapp (England Women's Rugby captain).

FURTHER INFO

- **PROSPECTUSES** UNDERGRAD; POSTGRAD; INTERNATIONAL
- **OPEN DAYS**

ACADEMIC ◡◡◡◡◡◡◡◡◡◡◡◡

Traditionally a training ground for nurses and teachers, Worcester's *rapidly becoming a rising star* in the fields of digital arts and sports science. All undergrad courses are modular, allowing students to tackle various subjects in varying depth over their course of study.

ENTRY POINTS: 120–200	**AVE POINTS:** 217
APPLICATIONS PER PLACE: 2	**CLEARING:** 9%
NO. OF TERMS: 2	**LENGTH OF TERMS:** 19WKS
STAFF TO STUDENT RATIO: N/A	**STUDY ADDICTS:** 17%
TEACHING: ✦✦✦	**RESEARCH:** ✦
YEAR ABROAD: 0%	**SANDWICH STUDENTS:** 1%
1STS: 6%	**2.2s:** 38%
2.1s: 39%	**3RDS:** 15%

ADMISSIONS

- **APPLY VIA UCAS/NMAS FOR NURSING/GTTR FOR PGCE**

Mature students without formal qualifications can be admitted via interview and essay assessment.

SUBJECTS

APPLIED SCIENCES, GEOGRAPHY & ARCHAEOLOGY 9%
ARTS, HUMANITIES & SOCIAL SCIENCES 24%   **BUSINESS SCHOOL** 13%

BEST Art & Design; Biology; Business; Education; Nursing; Psychology; Sociology; Sport.

LIBRARIES
⊙ **150,000 BOOKS** ⊙ **408 STUDY PLACES**
⊙ **SPEND PER STUDENT** ££££
Perks include the collection housed on behalf of the Worcestershire Archaelogical Society and a *treasure trove* of kids' lit.

COMPUTERS
⊙ **444 WORKSTATIONS**
Computer provision isn't Worcester's strongest point and students must pay extra to jack into the net in halls. There's wireless access across campus, though.

OTHER LEARNING FACILITIES
In addition to the drama studio-cum-theatre, dance studio, language labs and recording studio, there's a *particularly sexy* digital arts centre containing a video production studio. *Even fancier*, however, is MARRC – the Motion Analysis Research and Rehabilitation Centre which uses cameras, sensors and animation to create 3D computer models. The English polo and cricket teams have been using it recently. *Sports Science has never tasted so good.* The nursing department has two simulation hospital wards.

ENTERTAINMENT ⓊⓊⓊⓊⓊⓊⓊⓊⓊⓊ

THE CITY
⊙ **PRICE OF A PINT OF BEER** £2.30
⊙ **GLASS OF WINE** £3.10 ⊙ **CAN OF RED BULL** £2
CINEMAS The six-screen Odeon and ten-screen Vue (free popcorn deal on Tuesdays) do NUS discounts.
THEATRES The Swan Theatre and Huntingdon Hall are *small* venues nearby, but *if all the world's a stage, Worcester ain't included.* Stratford-Upon-Avon and the Royal Shakespeare Company is 30 mins away by car if you fancy a bit of thesp-action.
PUBS *Worcester has plenty to offer the discerning student beer fiend, from traditional pubs to wine bars to alternative joints and all the winding, staggering way back again.* Local establishments have embraced the University with open arms and the sports team-sponsoring Crown & Anchor begins each term by hoisting its *notorious* 'Drinking Term commences soon. Enrol today' banner. The Garibaldi and the Bedwardine have their share of live-outers as regulars. *The only bar Push wouldn't prop up is the Brewers Arms, since it seems peculiarly keen on elderly men.*
CLUBBING *Nothing particularly diverse or alternative, but if good, wholesome chart dance gets your party started,* Tramps (four clubs, R&B, cheese, dance) should do the trick. *Other Pushplugs: Bamboo; Bushwalkers; Jill.*
MUSIC VENUES *Birmingham gets the stars of the stadium. Worcester makes do with* live pub sessions at places like the Marrs Bar, Keystones and Drummonds.
EATING OUT *A fair range of reasonable eateries.*

Most Worcesterites are happy with the kebabulous Shakeey's after a night out, but since Push is way too classy for that, a plug goes to the cheap and sizeable portions at Keystones.

UNIVERSITY
⊙ **PRICE OF A PINT OF BEER** £1.60
⊙ **GLASS OF WINE** £2 ⊙ **CAN OF RED BULL** £1.50
BARS The *unashamedly named* Dive is the only bar on campus and probably the only student bar to be made out of an old RAF aircraft hangar. *Apparently, the spirits of long dead pilots still turn up for a pint.* It's busy *most of the time, luring* students in with pool tables, Sky TV and *enough promo deals to floor a bull elephant.*
THEATRES Two societies perform *irregularly* in the drama studio, *which masquerades as a theatre.*
FILM Occasional screenings in the Dive.
MUSIC VENUES The Dive has a small stage for bands: mostly tributes and Chesney.
CLUBBING The SU is *willing* but the venue is *weak,* at least until they get their licensing sorted. The Dive has a DJ booth and dance floor, *and the atmosphere often buzzes in a clubby way,* but there are no bona fide club nights. Trevor Nelson and Chappers and Dave have taken time out from the Radio One airwaves to pop down.
COMEDY/CABARET An open mic comedy night is planned.
FOOD Snak Attack *can't spell but they can cook – usually artery-clogging fare,* but a pasta option exists for health-freaks. The Food Court canteen is the lunch venue of choice, with an extensive selection and vegetarian options. Café Connections and Ritazza make the kind of food you eat with coffee. Berry's *(like Subway, but on a budget)* fills many a tummy.
OTHER The Colours Ball is an awards night/*piss-up* for sportsfolk.

SOCIAL ⓊⓊⓊⓊⓊⓊⓊⓊⓊⓊⓊⓊⓊ

WORCESTER STUDENTS' UNION
⊙ **3 SABBATICALS** ⊙ **TURNOUT AT LAST BALLOT** 10%
⊙ **NUS MEMBER**
'Politically ferocious lobbying machine' is not a phrase you'll ever see used in conjunction with Worcester's Union (except here) because representation and service matters are their main hobby horse, although to be fair, they knocked together some banners and dusted off some surly expressions for the anti top-up demos. Relations with the University itself are comfily co-operative.

SU FACILITIES
Bar; music venue; two cafés; canteen; five pool/snooker tables; meeting room; Alliance & Leicester ATM; photo booth; fax & printing service; payphones; women's room; games & vending machines; juke box; general store; Waterstone's books; stationery shop.

Words in italics are Push's point of view — take it or leave it...

CLUBS (NON-SPORTING)

Archaeology; History; Psychology; W.I.N. (Worcester Innovators Network – wannabe entrepeneurs); Yu Gi Oh (Japanese Anime). **See also Clubs tables.**

OTHER ORGANISATIONS

SU newspaper, 'the Voice', is hot off the press twice termly or so. *Small but warm-hearted* Rag releases its own yearly magazine and arranges a Rag Week and various events throughout the year.

RELIGIOUS

◑ ❶ 1 CHAPLAIN (COFE)

There's a multi-faith chaplaincy and prayer room on campus but, *for those who like their places of worship a touch more bespoke*, the city offers a variety of Christian churches and a mosque.

PAID WORK

• **PAID WORK** TERM-TIME 65%; HOLS 90%

Worcester is the UK's first University to introduce a Job Pod scheme, where students can search for part-time or temporary work via a touch-screen databank, all without having to leave the SU. A free phone connects straight through to local and national Job Centres. Worcester has a few bar and shop jobs kicking around and the campus employs tour guides, note-takers for disabled students and other SU workers.

SPORTS ◖◗◖◗◖◗◖◗◖◗◖◗◖◗

◑ RECENT SUCCESSES BASKETBALL **◑ BUSA RANKING** 38
Worcester seems to be more successful at dealing with injuries than opposing teams, thanks to its Sports Performance Labs and BUPA clinic on campus, but they're by no means afraid to roll around in the mud with the best of them. Seven (count 'em) different football clubs cater for all standards from *the not bad at all to the completely deluded.*

> Worcester's careers service is built in a former RAF morgue. No jokes about 'dead-end jobs', please – that'd be tasteless.

SPORTS FACILITIES

There are a couple of *scrappy* pitches and some Astroturf on campus, but most of the sporting larks happen off-site on the three competition pitches. There's also: a floodlit *but tatty* tennis court; two training and one full-size basketball court; two netball courts; Sports hall; gym; multigym; aerobics studio, and the river nearby. Students pay £25 a term for access to the fitness suite; eveything else is free. Members of the public can use the Sports Hall and gym at *the extortionate prices that members of the public deserve.* The city adds various other leisure facilities, including a golf course, a running track and, fairly nearby, outdoor adventure activities areas. The county cricket ground is in pebble-hurling distance of campus.

SPORTING CLUBS

American Football; Mountain Boarding. **See also Clubs tables.**

ATTRACTIONS

If it weren't for the fact they knocked Liverpool out of the FA Cup in 1959, *footie pub bores would never have heard of* Worcester City FC. Worcester's Zurich Premiership Rugby Union team dangle over relegation, while the *not-quite-brilliant* Worcester Wolves basketball boys bounce about in Division One.

ACCOMMODATION ◖◗◖◗◖◗◖◗◖◗◖◗◖◗◖◗

IN UNIVERSITY

◑ SELF–CATERING 24%   **◑ COST** £55 (37+WKS)
◑ INSURANCE PREMIUM £
AVAILABILITY University accommodation – *and there isn't much of it* – is allocated on a first-come, first-housed basis and only students from Worcestershire are exempt from applying. *Miraculously,* only 1% of first years go away disappointed. Halls are composed of flats for four or six people, sharing large kitchens and communal areas which *add to the homey feel (in both the domestic and gangsta senses of the word).* All halls are either on or within a mile of campus and most are new, *attractive* blocks – *Worcester Halls being the newest and attractivest. Chandler halls are the oldest and most basic, but their practically-giving-it-away rent keeps students happy.* Security patrols, CCTV and entry phones *keep the outside out whilst, on the inside, third year hall wardens keep their power-crazed eyes on the inmates within.* All halls are non-smoking.
CAR PARKING £25-permits are only available to teaching students or those on work placements.

EXTERNALLY

◑ AVE RENT £56
AVAILABILITY The St John's area is *easily meanderable* from campus and has a wide range of *affordable* options. *Corner Gardens, Corner Road and Laughere Road are all popular, shame the*

W

same can't be said about Happylands. *No, really.*
HOUSING HELP The SU and Student Services jointly pen the anuual Housing List each March. Landlords are approved or blacklisted *according to their relative moral status*, vacancy lists and bulletin boards are maintained and legal help is offered.

WELFARE ◗◗◗◗◗◗◗◗◗◗◗◗◗◗

SERVICES
- ◉ LGBT SOCIETY ◉ INTERNATIONAL STUDENTS' OFFICER
- ◉ POSTGRAD OFFICER ◉ DISABILITIES OFFICER
- ◉ EQUAL OPPORTUNITIES OFFICER ◉ NIGHTLINE
- ◉ UNIVERSITY COUNSELLORS 2 PART
- ◉ SU COUNSELLORS 1 FULL ◉ CRIME RATING !!

The advice centre scratches welfare and finance itches.
HEALTH The Health Centre on campus is staffed by a medical attendant and several trained staff. An NHS practice is available locally.
CRÈCHES/NURSERY The University nursery has 36 places for students' spawn 3mths-5yrs, though there are plans to expand in order to keep up with the waiting list.
WOMEN Attack alarms are doled out to the *fragrant sex.*

DISABILITIES A University-wide overhaul has added ramps, sliding and automatic doors and a disabled lift *(no, that doesn't mean it's been turned off)*. Some of the older areas *present obstacles to access* – especially on the door front. Four rooms have been adapted for wheelchair users and adjacent rooms for carers are also available. Assistant Disability Co-ordinators have responsibility for visually- and hearing-impaired students and there are several adapted rooms, support tutors, hearing loops, vibrating pagers, a Braille embosser and specialised computer software available. Dyslexics benefit from sensitive marking and software support.
DRUGS *All sorts of unpleasent things are done to campus drug users.*

FINANCE
- ◉ AVE DEBT PER YEAR £3,527
- ◉ HOME STUDENT FEES £3,000

FEES Part-timers pay £375 a module and postgrads cough up £3,100 or £6,025 (for Management Studies). The international contingent are charged £7,600.
- ◉ ACCESS FUND £399,461
- ◉ SUCCESSFUL APPLICATIONS 470

SUPPORT Some sports scholarships are available to athletic *supermen and women*, and there's an emergency hardship fund. As far as fees go there are £700 bursaries for those on the maintenance grant – £500 for everyone else.

▶ **WRITTLE COLLEGE**
see *University of Essex*

▶ **WYE COLLEGE**
see *Imperial College London*

W

UNIVERSITY OF YORK

UNIVERSITY OF YORK

○ **UNIVERSITY OF YORK** Heslington, York, North Yorkshire, YO10 5DD **TEL** (01904) 430 000/433 533
E-MAIL admissions@york.ac.uk **WEBSITE** www.york.ac.uk ○ **YORK UNIVERSITY STUDENTS' UNION**
The Daw Suu Centre, Goodricke College, Heslington, York, North Yorkshire, YO10 5DD **TEL** (01904) 433 724
E-MAIL su-enquiries@york.ac.uk **WEBSITE** www.yusu.org

GENERAL ○○○○○○○○○○○○○○

For some reason, all civil wars seem to occur between North and South. York (or 'Jorvik', for the more Viking-minded) didn't come out of the War of the Roses too well, by all accounts, but a few centuries and several judicious beheadings later, *York is now a scenic, peaceful city, pulsing with an intense cultural and historical atmosphere*. Half the hike from London to Edinburgh, a *seagull's throw* from the coast and *within puking distance* of Leeds – major transport node of the north-east – it's *thoroughly accessible* by land, sea or air. The University itself is a *relative spring-chicken* at just over 40 years old. Rather than sharing the *glorious architecture* of the Minster, the off-city campus was *designed in the days when meaning something was more important than looking sexy, so the landscaped concrete 'concept' campus may not be to all tastes*, although the 200 acres of surrounding parkland and the central lake are *undeniably pretty*. The concept itself is 'discovery around every corner' – *that's not to say you're likely to stumble over copulating couples behind every department, but that the architects were trying to imbue the very buildings with the essence of learning. They didn't do a bad job* – York has *one of the best* academic reputations of any concrete university.

🚶🚶🚶🚶🚶🚶🚶🚶🚶🚶🚶🚶🚶🚶🚶🚶🚶🚶🚶🚶🚶

SEX RATIO: ♂46 ♀54	**FOUNDED:** 1963
FULL-TIME U'GRADS: 7,631	**PART-TIME:** 1,117
POSTGRADS: 2,778	**NON-DEGREE:** 1,656
AVE COURSE: 3YRS	**ETHNIC:** 6%
STATE:PRIVATE SCHOOL: 80:20	**FLUNK RATE:** 5%
MATURE: 12%	**INTERNATIONAL:** 19%
DISABLED: 140	**LOCAL:** 10%

ATMOSPHERE

York, like Oxbridge, is a collegiate university, *although the resemblance ends there*. There are eight colleges with roughly 1,000-odd students *stashed away* in each. The system is *more a convenient means of breaking the student body into manageable chunks than brewing up true collegiate spirit*. You can ask for a specific college though requests aren't guaranteed. The *large* and still expanding Heslington campus (in a *wee* village one and a half miles south-east of the *famous* city walls) *isn't exactly a frenetic hub of activity (especially at the weekend, when the silence of death pervades), but there is a quiet sense of community all around – even if it's just among the ubiquitous waterfowl. Relations between students and locals are largely amicable.*

YORK

○ **POPULATION** 181,300 ○ **CITY CENTRE** 1 MILE
○ **LONDON** 205 MILES ○ **LEEDS** 23 MILES
○ **HIGH TEMP** 21 ○ **LOW TEMP** 2 ○ **RAINFALL** 53
From the moment the striking city walls come into view, it's clear that York has a lot to offer the cultural historian or flash-happy tourist (that's photography, not indecent exposure). It's the top British *tourist lure* after London, what with the Minster, the castle, the oldest street in the country and the *intentionally musty* Jorvik Viking Centre. *York is a melting pot of intriguing architecture*: Viking huts, Roman affairs and a host of *elegant* Georgian buildings. *Abounding in pubs and all the high-street trimmings, the city's full of diversions for the dedicated party player as well as those more interested in tinkly-dangly crafty shops.*

TRAVEL

TRAINS York Station is right next to the city centre, about two miles from the campus. Direct trains to Edinburgh (from £43.90 return), London (£47.50) and Manchester (£12.70). Most other destinations involve travelling via Leeds.
COACHES National Express runs coaches to most destinations from the rail station.
CAR The A64, A1, A19, M1 and M62 are all accessible from York. Parking in the city *can be tricky*, however, as the city council's green transport policy has resulted in parking restrictions. The University will only issue parking permits in exceptional circumstances (free to disabled students, £18 to others). There are four pay & display car parks on campus, which *aren't too evilly priced. Most students opt for bikes instead of cars, which are generally only used for out-of-city travel.*
AIR Leeds Bradford Airport is 24 miles away (40 mins by car) and has a few budget airlines on offer (Ryanair, BMI, Jet2, British European). Direct train link to Manchester Airport.
HITCHING *Prospects are uncertain, but the M1 and A1 are busy enough to ensure a trip somewhere.*
LOCAL *Good on the legs, less so on the pocket*: bus No. 4 goes from campus to the city centre in about 10 mins and costs £1.50 one way or £2.50 for a day ticket.
UNIVERSITY The SU runs a free minibus service from the city centre to the campus, and from there to student homes off-campus, *so everyone can get home unscathed*. Donations appreciated, but aren't obligatory.
TAXIS Local services are *reasonably* priced and *popular* with students. A journey from the large rank outside the station to the Heslington campus costs around a fiver.
BICYCLES *Flat York is best navigated by bicycle,*

Y

making the campus seem like the aftermath of an explosion in a bike shop. It's often quicker and more efficient than a car, and the campus is well provisioned for the two-wheeled wonders with numerous bike sheds dotted around the campus for storage or playground canoodling purposes. The city itself is blessed with extensive cycle routes. Be warned: thieves also get far too many pieces of the pedal action.

CAREER PROSPECTS
○ **CAREERS SERVICE** ○ **NO. OF STAFF** 8 FULL/4 PART
○ **UNEMPLOYED AFTER 6** MTHS 6%
The Careers Service boasts bulletin boards, interview practice, a careers library and a programme of employer presentations to start students off in the big bad world of work.

FAMOUS ALUMNI
Tony Banks, Robin Cook (late Labour MPs); Jung Chang (writer); Greg Dyke (the ex-Director-General of the BBC and the University's Chancellor); Harry Enfield (comedian); Harriet Harman MP, Oona King MP; Peter Lord (of Aardman Animations, the cartoon boffins behind Wallace & Gromit); Victor Lewis-Smith (comedian/journalist); Denise O'Donohue (HatTrick TV); Genista McIntosh (theatre director); Dominic Muldowney (composer); John Witherow (editor, Sunday Times).

FURTHER INFO
○ **PROSPECTUSES** UNDERGRAD; POSTGRAD; ALTERNATIVE; VIDEO
○ **OPEN DAYS**
All info from the Admissions and Schools Liaison by phone on (01904) 433 196 or online at www.york.ac.uk/admissions. The SU flogs an alternative prospectus at £1 a pop.

ACADEMIC ○○○○○○○○○○○○○

○ **1994 GROUP**
York is heavy on research, with glowing teaching standards across the board. All courses are credit-based, with students taking 120 credits a year, divided across an assortment of compulsory and optional modules. Assessment is very much course dependent, with some departments shunning end of year exams altogether. Wannabe doctors apply to the Hull York Medical School, which involves 65 places each at Hull and York.

ENTRY POINTS: 260–340	AVE POINTS: 418
APPLICATIONS PER PLACE: 9	CLEARING: 5%
NO. OF TERMS: 4	LENGTH OF TERMS: 10WKS
STAFF TO STUDENT RATIO: 1:12	STUDY ADDICTS: 28%
TEACHING: *****	RESEARCH: *****
YEAR ABROAD: 7%	SANDWICH STUDENTS: 4%

ADMISSIONS
○ **APPLY VIA UCAS/NMAS FOR NURSING/GTTR FOR PGCE**
York's trying to bump up its mature and international student numbers.

SUBJECTS
ARCHAEOLOGY 3% **BIOCHEMISTRY** 2% **BIOLOGY** 5% **CHEMISTRY** 5% **COMPUTER SCIENCE** 4% **EDUCATIONAL STUDIES** 1% **ELECTRONICS** 4% **ENGLISH** 7% **ENVIRONMENT** 3% **HISTORY** 9% **HISTORY OF ART** 2% **LANGUAGE & LINGUISTIC SCIENCE** 4% **MANAGEMENT** 3% **MATHS** 5% **MEDICINE** 6% **MUSIC** 2% **NURSING & MIDWIFERY** 11% **PHILOSOPHY** 2% **PHYSICS** 4% **POLITICS, PHILOSOPHY & ECONOMICS** 10% **PSYCHOLOGY** 5% **SOCIAL SCIENCES** 4%
BEST Archaeology; Biology; Computer Science; Education; English; History; Management; Maths; Psychology.

LIBRARIES
○ **800,000** BOOKS ○ **750** STUDY PLACES
○ **SPEND PER STUDENT** ££££
The Raymond Burton library for humanities has freed up shelf space in the main J B Morrell library, which is lovely and modern inside, but ugly concrete externally. It stays open till 10pm on weekdays in term and you can issue books yourself so you don't always have to deal with unnecessary librarians.

COMPUTERS
○ **1,387** WORKSTATIONS
Open access computer rooms in seven of the colleges as well as the libraries, all with networked, internet-enabled PCs. High-speed connection points are available in all on-campus student rooms, which they can hook up to for £20 a term.

OTHER LEARNING FACILITIES
York's Language For All (LFA) programme has 14 languages to pick from, at all levels of competence. Students can learn a foreign language in addition to their course, night-school style. In-coming students can also take a basic research and IT course named Information Literacy in all Departments (or ILIAD – someone worked hard for that acronym) which introduces useful skills for studying. There's even a certificate. Wow. Other facilities include: language labs, music rehearsal rooms (for music students and the Music Society), a drama studio (for drama students) and media centre (the University's TV station's base).

ENTERTAINMENT ○○○○○○○○○

THE CITY
○ **PRICE OF A PINT OF BEER** £2.20
○ **GLASS OF WINE** £2
○ **CAN OF RED BULL** £1.50
CINEMAS Three to choose from, including the usual Odeon and Warner Village (Vue) multiplexes and City Screen – a baby three-screener, with a classic/cult bias and regular stand-up comedy nights. And, most importantly, a bar. All offer student discounts.
THEATRES The Theatre Royal is the largest venue for mainstream plays and comedy, and the Grand

Opera House supplies *fat women singing and dying.*

PUBS *York is dribbling with traditional olde worlde British pubs like the Old White Swan, Punch Bowl and the Royal Oak, which boast proper northern ales. There are a few more lively and swanky establishments, including Harker's, Fiesta Mehicana, Ha!Ha! Bar and the Gallery. For retro boozage: Flares (dedicated to 1970s) and Reflex (where the 80s never ends. The horror, the horror).*

CLUBBING *Although a bit naff and meat-markety, there's fun to be had in the York club scene.* Monday through to Wednesday there's at least one student night on at Ikon, Diva, Toffs or the Gallery, which fills three rooms with mainstream, pop and dance, indie and acid, jazz and chill out *vibes. And students, of course. The more reliable hardcore club scene lingers alluringly in Leeds.*

MUSIC VENUES York has a *middleweight* music scene, with many pubs presenting regular live n' local music nights. Fibbers (200 cap) *reels in the bigger fish,* like Badly Drawn Boy and Franz Ferdinand. *Around a fiver to get in and it's friendly and sweaty. Yum.*

EATING OUT *Nothing too special, but a good range of cheap eats,* including some *quality* curry houses. *Pushplugs: Oscar's wine bar; Caesar's and Fellini's for Italian; the Cello for coffee and edible coffee accessories; the Willow – a Chinese that, much like Cinderella, becomes a cheesy disco at midnight.* There's a new Wetherspoon's in town with *very cheap food and criminally inexpensive drink. Oh, and any visit to York is incomplete without a stop in Betty's Tea Rooms, where cake looks, tastes and is priced like a work of art.*

UNIVERSITY

- **PRICE OF A PINT OF BEER** £1.60
- **GLASS OF WINE** £1.70
- **CAN OF RED BULL** £1.25

Without a big daddy SU to take charge of their evenings, the individual colleges make their own amusement like a bunch of raucous siblings. Rather like the Waltons, but with rather more beer.

BARS Seven college-run bars ensure a *wide variety* of surroundings *to lose bodily control in.* Henry's (at Alcuin College) is a *trendy* city-style café bar; Café Sol (Derwent) has a Mediterranean theme. Hoggies (Langwith) is *more central and traditional,* while Vanbrugh bar is the show house of the York Brewery and, along with Goodricke bar, is *pretty popular.* Edge (Wentworth) is a *popular postgrad haunt with a sophisticated continental style* and JJ's (Halifax) is *the place to be* for big screen premiership matches and cocktail pitchers. Hours are *pretty standard, although weekend drinking doesn't usually start until the evening.*

THEATRES Drama is *strong* with several drama societies and three theatres on the go. The Drama Barn, Jack Lyons Concert Hall and Central Hall stage numerous student productions.

FILM The University-built cinema shows four current mainstream titles per week and the odd bit of arthouse for £2.50 admission. By contrast, the Word Cinema Society picks out independent celluloid to screen each week.

MUSIC VENUES There are no purpose-built music venues on campus, but the SU sets up the four large dining halls as *gig-holes when the need arises.* Visitors have included Mark Owen, Electric Six and Editors. The SU runs a yearly Battle of the Bands and a 'Woodstock' festival competition to showcase local and student talent. *Or lack of it.*

CLUBBING Various ents are held regularly at various colleges, such as 'Langwith Large', 'GSpot' and 'Club D'. 'Planet V' at Vanbrugh is the latest *pop fest.* 'Breakz' is an alternative dance night, spotlighting techno, house, D&B and breakbeat. On top of these Platinum Society runs hip hop nights. The Indie soc does, er, Indie nights.

COMEDY/CABARET Wentworth College hosts three comedy nights a term.

FOOD Most of the college bars offer snacks or more substantial edibles, as well as dining halls. JJ's, for example, offers free pizza delivery to all houses in Halifax College and all porters' lodges. Royston's at Langwith is a *giant* (300+) Fish'n'Chip emporium. Roger Kirk's Galleria restaurant serves all kinds of *quick food.* Several departments and a library have their own cafeteria or snack bar too, *so students are never far from a meal. Until after 7pm, that is. Then it's Costcutter or starvation.*

OTHER Different colleges and societies run a number of black tie balls, totalling around 15 every year. The biggest is the £60 Graduation Ball, sometimes held at York Race Course, which includes a three-course meal and *top* acts headlining.

SOCIAL ◖◗◖◗◖◗◖◗◖◗◖◗◖◗

YORK UNIVERSITY STUDENTS' UNION (YUSU)

- **6 SABBATICALS** ◉ **TURNOUT AT LAST BALLOT** 11%
- **NUS MEMBER**

YUSU has survived many years without a centralised union building and still lacks its own bar/music venue. *It's only real problem with the University authorities has been the repeated rejection of proposals to get one. The collegiate system can work against Union-awareness on campus, so YUSU has had to work particularly hard to combat this,* implementing an electronic voting system so that students can have their say on union issues online, without having to leave their room. It takes just three members to set up a society, *so weird and wonderful groups abound.*

SU FACILITIES

Student facilities, not all in the SU: seven bars; seven canteens, two snack bars; 11 pool tables; meeting room; six minibuses for hire; Endsleigh Insurance; ATMs: Link and NatWest; photocopier;

fax service; printing service; photo booth; payphones; advice centre; crèche; late night minibus; TV lounge; juke box; video machines; general store; stationery shop; vending machine; secondhand bookshop; video gaming machines.

CLUBS (NON-SPORTING)

Aid for Chinese; Amnesty International; Anime & Manga; Astronomy; Ballet; Birdwatching; Book Group; Bridge; City (posh job-hunting); Comedy; Folk; Fragsoc (computer games); Friends of Antara (helping provide healthcare in India); Gilbert & Sullivan; Hellenic; Hitch to Morocco; It's a Ducks Life (mental health); Japanese; Juggling; Karen Hilltribe Volunteers; Legalisation of Cannabis; LINKS; Love; Loud (against discrimination of loud people); Medieval; Meditation; Mexican; Namaskar; 'Neighbours'; Oriental; Outdoor; Pagan; Pantomime; People & Planet; Photo; Poker; ProEvo; Quiet; RESPECT; Singapore; STAR (action for refugees); Stop AIDS; Tea; Tentelini; Theatre; United Nations; Veggie; Wine; World Cinema. **See also Clubs tables.**

OTHER ORGANISATIONS

Vision (tabloid) and Nouse (*arm-aching* broadsheet) are the two free titles published by independent bodies regularly each term. There's also a free SU magazine containing articles on student life and union events. University Radio was one of the first student stations in the country and *stays at the top of the tree*, hitting the campus airwaves 24 hrs a day. YSTV (the student-run TV station) is shown in campus bars and JCRs for five hours or so each day. Plans are afoot to feed the signal into all student bedrooms. The York Rag is a *busy little bee*, arranging campus events, *sponsored life-endangerment* and students escape into Europe with a bucket to jangle. The Community Action Group *is equally active*, with a large number of local and international welfare projects, including drama in prisons, AIDS awareness campaigns in Africa and conservation and education work.

RELIGION

⊙ 3 CHAPLAINS (COFE, METHODIST, RC) VISITING CHAPLAINS OF OTHER DENOMINATIONS

For Anglicans, the Minster, home to one of England's two archbishops, *has an inspiring influence, which has rubbed off on other Christian denominations. Following an incident involving a Jewish massacre nearly 1,000 years ago,* there's no synagogue in York, but there are meetings, prayers and accommodation for four people at the Jewish Centre on campus. The nearest synagogue is *awkwardly* 20 mins away in Leeds. There are churches of most denominations in York and a mosque *very close* to campus.

PAID WORK

⊙ JOB BUREAU

The *thriving* tourist industry ensures job opportunities for students in the high seasons. Museum, tearoom, restaurant and pub work is easy to get *to fill the piggy bank*. The University operates a job centre and Unijobs, a *helpful* agency that links students up with local businesses. Target assists first and second years in finding vacation or gap-year work in *all corners* of the globe.

⊙ RECENT SUCCESSES CRICKET, MEN'S BASKETBALL, WOMEN'S FOOTBALL, WOMEN'S BADMINTON
⊙ BUSA RANKING 33

York has something of a communist attitude to sporting activity: a firmly held 'sports for all' credo, whether at college or university level. The Athletics Union co-ordinates all sporting events on the *well-equipped* campus. Membership includes personal accident insurance, discounts in sports stores and the chance to join any one of York's many athletics clubs. The pole exercise (*writhing up and down a pole in the name of fitness*) club is *titillatingly popular*. *The bitter taste of history returns* at the annual Roses Tournament with Lancaster University, the largest intervarsity event in the country. *Beheadings are blessedly rare.*

SPORTS FACILITIES

40-acre sports area; eight football/rugby pitches; hockey pitch; all-weather pitch; two cricket pitches; squash courts; six tennis courts; one basketball/netball court; two sports halls; running track; athletics field; croquet/bowling green; aerobics studio; climbing wall; seven badminton courts; sports hall. Locally: a swimming pool, golf course and opportunities for mountaineering, potholing or *mucking about* on the river.

SPORTING CLUBS

Aerobics; Aikido; Boat; Boxing; Caving & Potholing; Croquet; Cycling; Dance Sport; Frisbee; Gliding; Ju-Jitsu; Karting; Lacrosse; Paintball; Pole Dancing; Pool; Squash; Street Hockey; Surf; Waterpolo; Yoga. **See also Clubs tables.**

ATTRACTIONS

York Race Course is nearby, for *big-hatted gambling types*.

IN UNIVERSITY

⊙ SELF-CATERING 40% **⊙ COST** £67 (34/38WKS)
⊙ 1ST YRS LIVING IN 100% **⊙ 2ND YRS LIVING IN** 45%
⊙ 3RD YRS LIVING IN 45% **⊙ POSTGRADS LIVING IN** 50%
⊙ INSURANCE PREMIUM £

AVAILABILITY Barring exceptional circumstances (*eg. getting the form in late*), all first year students are guaranteed a room and many others can be *safely tucked up* in college accommodation.

Students who are *very deeply in lurve* have a stab at obtaining one of the five double rooms in Holgates Hall, while students with families *on their backs* have some limited accommodation available to them. Fairfax House (off-campus) attracts mature students *like bees to a honeypot*. The halls of residence themselves are *fairly similar* (being no more than 40 years old), although some of the newer accommodation blocks *can seem a smidge antisocial*, since tight security limits mixing between corridors. Rooms are divided into four price bands (or 'luxury bands' technically), ranging from economy to superior en suite. The price range differs by just over a tenner a week. Some halls have *decent* kitchen facilities, others are near pay-as-you-eat canteens. *There are a few rooms that are ready to be taken out to the barn and shot, but overall, York accommodation is good value for money.*
CAR PARKING Parking is restricted to those with disabilities or exceptional requirements (a permit costs £18), *so unless the car can be easily disguised as modern sculpture, forget it.* Lockable bike sheds are available at most colleges, though.

EXTERNALLY
○ AVE RENT £53 **○ LIVING AT HOME** 4%
AVAILABILITY Just over half of undergraduates live out and *no one has so far been unable to find a spot to crash in.* Recently, however, the house hunt *has been getting trickier and more competitive. Nearby Heslington Road is the first choice for living out, but Bishopthorpe Road and South Bank are also getting quite popular. Fulford prices tend to be prohibitive. Luckily, no real dodgy areas since York is relatively free from crime. Relatively.*
HOUSING HELP The Accommodation Office holds a list of properties that comply with guidelines. It also posts vacancies on its bulletin board and blacklists *iffy* landlords.

WELFARE ○○○○○○○○○○○○○

SERVICES
○ LGBT OFFICER & SOCIETY ○ RACIAL EQUALITY OFFICER
○ WOMEN'S OFFICER & SOCIETY
○ MATURE STUDENTS' ASSOCIATION
○ OVERSEAS STUDENTS' ASSOCIATION
○ GRADUATE STUDENTS' ASSOCIATION
○ DISABILITIES OFFICER & SOCIETY
○ LATE-NIGHT/WOMEN'S MINIBUS ○ NIGHTLINE
○ TAXI FUND ○ UNIVERSITY COUNSELLORS 7 FULL
○ CRIME RATING !!
The University provides trained counsellors, a legal support service and personal tutors responsible for pastoral care (*no sheep involved*).
HEALTH Students have the option of registering with the University Health Centre on campus or any York GP.
WOMEN There are weekly women's committee meetings and a frequently updated notice board. The Well Women service on campus can provide breast examination and cervical smear testing. There's a women's bookshop and women have priority on the late-night minibus. YUSU provides free attack alarms and pregnancy tests.
CRECHES/NURSERY University facilities for 30 children aged 2-5yrs and nine children aged 3mths-2yrs.
DISABILITIES The equal opps policy should mean full access to all facilities and activities. There's a *good* record of admitting and supporting disabled students and there are lifts in almost every building, *plenty* of ramps, adapted accommodation and hearing induction loops. The dyslexia support centre offers diagnosis and advice and those with unseen disabilities receive support from the Disability Services Office.

FINANCE
○ AVE DEBT PER YEAR £4,800 ○ HOME STUDENT FEES £3,000
FEES Fees for non-EU nationals vary between £8,430 and £11,130 depending on the course. For postgrads, we're talking between £3,085 (UK) and £11,130 (non-EU) a year.
○ ACCESS FUND £500,000 ○ AVE PAYMENT £600-1,400
SUPPORT The SU can provide a hardship loan of £100 on the spot. There are some bursaries and sponsorships available, particularly for international or mature students.

○ According to York University regulations students can be chucked out if they eat the ducks that live on the campus lake.

Words in italics are Push's point of view — take it or leave it...

PUSH, OF COURSE

HOW TO USE 'PUSH, OF COURSE'.

On the next few pages are listed the courses available at each of the universities in the UK. If you know what you want to study, find it in the list (or the closest thing to it) and below you'll find the names of the universities where you can study it. But not so fast, speedy. There's a few things it may be handy to know.

First off, the **course names**. Because there are around 20,000 individual courses, we've simplified the names and grouped them together. So, 'English Literature' and 'Literature in English' have been bundled in under 'English' (along with 'English Studies', 'Studies in English', 'Twentieth Century English Fiction' and, quite probably, 'Nursery Rhyme Studies'). And English is grouped together with 'Literature, Linguistics, Classics, etc'. Some of these groups may seem a little odd at first, but blame UCAS (where we got our information from) and they can blame the universities (where they got it). We've added cross-references which should make it pretty straightforward.

That means if you want to study Guatemalan History, try thinking a bit wider: in this instance, 'History, specialising in a specific country or area'. But be warned, the universities listed there may not offer Guatemalan History per se, but they will offer the closest thing possible. **Check with the university in question for the exact range of courses on offer.**

Next up: the order that the universities are listed indicates the **entrance requirements** needed to get in. The first ones only accept students with the highest grades and the last listed may not expect you to have much more than a bronze swimming certificate. (Those requiring the same grades are listed alphabetically.)

Bear in mind that some courses are harder to get into than others: they don't let people with half an A Level and a scout's badge study Medicine, for instance. **Again, check with the university itself for the exact grades they'd want from you.**

The courses listed are often available in **combinations** – just occasionally, they're only available jointly with other subjects. Yet again, the university itself will have the latest details.

This list – with loads more detail and search and sort facilities – is also available in the members' area of **Push Online (www.push.co.uk)** and UCAS's own website (www.ucas.com) has its own version. Once you've found which universities offer your chosen course, check out their profiles to see whether you like the place and what else they have to offer.

CHOOSING A COURSE

For every different student, there's probably a different way to choose a course. Many take one look at the list of courses available and run screaming into the night. Others stick to their 'best' subject at A Level, without giving a thought to the fact that maths at A Level and maths as a degree can be about as similar as watching a Formula 1 car racing and standing in front of one.

Others pick a degree based on the career they want to follow. This is usually sound but don't forget that you can get a career in the media without a media studies degree and not all accountants studied accountancy at university.

The safest bet is always to pick a course you'll enjoy. If you enjoy it, it'll be worthwhile and you'll do better. You'll also be qualified for jobs you might enjoy.

Check out a university you like the sound of. Visit or phone the relevant departments of the subjects you're considering. Then talk to the students who're studying it and the tutors who teach it to find out what it's all about.

Choose carefully – you can sometimes change your course once you've started it, but at some universities it's about as difficult, exhausting and painful as listening to Britney Spears mincing a badger.

JOINT HONOURS COURSES

Forget any notion of lazy, hazy Sunday afternoons – these are degrees where you study two subjects instead of just the one, usually in two separate departments of the university.
Most universities offer combinations of courses. Obvious ones are language courses (eg. French and German), but more adventurous bods may want to tackle something less likely – physics and music, anyone?

Don't presume, however, that just because two separate subjects are available at one institution that you can do both together. Check with the prospectus and/or in the UCAS listings.
How the courses are combined also varies. Some are 'interdisciplinary' (meaning you do a course which combines stuff from both subjects) and some are independent of each other – in effect you're doing two separate half-courses.

Just to confuse you even more, some mix 50% of each course and others offer the option of picking one subject as a 'major' (though you usually don't have to decide which until after your first year). Some students find the workload on joint courses is heavier than on single honours equivalents and that communication levels between departments seem to predate the telephone. As a result, the students' organisational skills need to be as watertight as a lilo in a shark-infested paddling pool. But at the end of it all you should have a wider range of skills, be less likely to be fed up with your subjects and have had the chance to make loads more friends.

For those who really like to live on the edge (or who can't make up their minds and pick just one course), there are combined honours courses where you study not one, not two, but three or more subjects.

MODULAR COURSES

Most universities now offer modular courses. This means you can pick and choose a range of options across the academic spectrum. You go through university life successfully completing (hopefully) individual 'modules' in different subject areas and collecting credits. When you've got enough credits, you can trade them in for a degree – like collecting tokens off the back of cereal packets.

This system is particularly good for students with outside commitments, since you can often accumulate credits, go back to full-time work for a year and then pick up again where you left off.
It's also great for people who don't know at the time of application what sort of subjects will interest them.

LENGTH OF COURSE

Most full-time degrees are three years in length while some – eg. Engineering, most languages – tend to take a wee while longer, being four years. That's not to say that all Engineering and language courses take four years nor that all other courses are only three. Push probes where others fear to smell, but we all have limits, so contact the college or university in question to find out the exact length of the course you're interested in. The difference often depends on the letters at the beginning of the course name – BA/BSc will usually be three years of hard and fruitful graft and make you a 'bachelor' of your subject. Meanwhile MA/MSc/MEng/etc. will be a four-year course (if not five) and mean you're a 'master' ('...but only a master of evil, Darth').

Most undergraduate courses in England and Wales are bachelor courses, but in Scotland, they usually head to masters degrees and so take an extra year.

For added relish, 'sandwich' courses are four years in length, but get you a bachelor degree. A sandwich course contains some time (usually a year, but often in more than one bit) doing a work placement (and getting paid for it) or studying abroad, usually betwen your second and final year, in a country, industry or bed, as appropriate to your degree.

Medicine, Dentistry and Veterinary Science are just far too long for all but the mad, dedicated, perverted or rich, being a whacking five or six years of studenthood. But don't let Push stop you. We want dentists to have all the training they can get before anyone starts drilling our teeth, thank you.

AGRICULTURAL, VETERINARY SCIENCES ETC.

PRE-CLINICAL VETERINARY MEDICINE Liverpool, Bristol, Cambridge, Nottingham, Royal Veterinary, Edinburgh, UWE, Middlesex

CLINICAL VETERINARY MEDICINE & DENTISTRY Royal Veterinary, Glasgow, Bristol

ANIMAL SCIENCE Sheffield, Gloucestershire, Newcastle, Reading, Chester, Aberystwyth, Glamorgan, Plymouth, Nottingham Trent, Bristol, UWE, Canterbury Christ Church, Central Lancashire, Greenwich

AGRICULTURE Harper Adams, Nottingham, Newcastle, Bangor, Reading, Royal Agricultural, Aberystwyth, Glamorgan, Plymouth, Aberdeen, Bristol, UWE, Brighton

FORESTRY Bangor, Aberdeen, Central Lancashire, Brighton

FOOD & BEVERAGES Harper Adams, Leeds Metropolitan, Reading, Huddersfield, Manchester Metropolitan, Abertay Dundee, London Metropolitan, Nottingham, Heriot-Watt, Surrey, Wolverhampton, Bath Spa, Sheffield Hallam, Abertay Dundee, Teesside, UWIC

OTHER SIMILAR & RELATED Liverpool, Newcastle

AMERICAN STUDIES see Languages & Literature, Eastern, Asian, African, etc.

ANCIENT HISTORY see History, Philosophy, etc. & Literature, Linguistics, Classics, etc.

ANCIENT LANGUAGES see Literature, Linguistics, Classics, etc.

ANTHROPOLOGY see Social Studies

ARCHAEOLOGY see History, Philosophy, etc

ARCHITECTURE, BUILDING & PLANNING

ARCHITECTURE Liverpool, London Metropolitan, London South Bank, Manchester Metropolitan, Manchester, Westminster, Nottingham, Sheffield, Bath, Liverpool, Newcastle, Edinburgh, Plymouth, Queens Belfast, UCL, UWIC, UCE, Leeds, Nottingham Trent, Sheffield Hallam, Strathclyde, Bristol, UWE, East London, Anglia Ruskin, De Montfort, Huddersfield, Leeds, Lincoln, Portsmouth, Robert Gordon, Greenwich, Brighton, Glamorgan, Leeds Metropolitan, Southampton Solent

BUILDING Heriot-Watt, Wolverhampton, Central Lancashire, Nottingham Trent, UCE, Brighton, Bristol, UWE, UWIC, Newport, Leeds Metropolitan, Southampton Solent, Westminster

LANDSCAPE DESIGN Nottingham Trent,

Gloucestershire, Glamorgan, Buckinghamshire Chilterns, Bournemouth

PLANNING (URBAN, RURAL & REGIONAL): Birmingham, Heriot-Watt, Newcastle, Queen's Belfast, Aberdeen, Sheffield Hallam, Bristol, UWE, Manchester, Brighton, Central Lancashire, UCE, London South Bank, Cardiff, Leeds, Aston, Glamorgan, Bolton

OTHER SIMILAR & RELATED Heriot-Watt, NEWI, Sheffield Hallam, UCE, Glamorgan, Greenwich, Anglia Ruskin, Middlesex, UWIC, Bristol, UWE, Manchester, Nottingham Trent, Bolton, London South Bank

ART & DESIGN

FINE ART Goldsmiths, Leeds Metropolitan, London Metropolitan, Luton, Middlesex, NEWI, Westminster, Oxford, Reading, Southampton, Edinburgh, Leeds, St Andrews, Kent, Lancaster, Chester, Brighton, UCE, De Montfort, Dundee, Huddersfield, Lincoln, Newcastle, Nottingham Trent, Aberystwyth, Chichester, Bath Spa, Glamorgan, Newport, Plymouth, Sheffield Hallam, Anglia Ruskin, Coventry, Dundee, Canterbury Christ Church, UWIC, Central Lancashire, East London, Hertfordshire, Manchester Metropolitan, Portsmouth, Staffordshire, Derby, Wolverhampton, Bolton, Sunderland, Trinity Carmarthen, Buckinghamshire Chilterns, Southampton Solent, Salford, UCL, Bristol, UWE, Chichester, Gloucestershire, Loughborough, SIHE

DESIGN Goldsmiths, Luton, Middlesex, Loughborough, Liverpool, Wolverhampton, Hull, Queen Mary, Sheffield Hallam, Greenwich, Glamorgan, Napier, Plymouth, Strathclyde, Central Lancashire, East London, Edinburgh, Leeds Metropolitan, Manchester Metropolitan, Salford, Staffordshire, Teesside, Worcester, Sunderland, Thames Valley, De Montfort, Southampton Solent, Anglia Ruskin, Bath Spa, London South Bank, Leeds, Sussex, Brighton, Nottingham Trent, Brunel, Nottingham, Queen's Belfast, Swansea, Aston, UCE, Lincoln, Middlesex, Nottingham Trent, Bristol, UWE, Heriot-Watt, Huddersfield, Bristol, Coventry, Portsmouth, Bradford, UWIC, Dundee, Bournemouth, Hertfordshire, Manchester, NEWI, Bolton, Derby, Buckinghamshire Chilterns, Paisley, Robert Gordon, SIHE

MUSIC Goldsmiths, Royal Holloway, Cambridge, Durham, King's, Manchester, Nottingham, Oxford, Surrey, Bristol, Durham, Liverpool, Newcastle, Sheffield, York, City, Edinburgh, Glasgow, Huddersfield, Sheffield, Southampton, Sussex, Aberdeen, Birmingham, Brunel, Cardiff, East Anglia, Hull, Lancaster, Leeds, Sheffield, Staffordshire, Surrey, Bangor, Keele, Queen's Belfast, Salford, SOAS, Winchester, York, Central Lancashire, Southampton Solent, Aberdeen, Chester, Wolverhampton, UWE, UCE, Glamorgan,

Hertfordshire, Manchester Metropolitan, Bath Spa, Coventry, Gloucestershire, Middlesex, Napier, Sunderland, Chichester, Leeds Metropolitan, Plymouth, Teesside, Thames Valley, Anglia Ruskin, Canterbury Christ Church, Strathclyde, UWIC, Roehampton, Buckinghamshire Chilterns, Royal Academy of Music, Brighton, Chichester, RSAMD, Westminster

DRAMA London South Bank, Manchester, Royal Holloway, East Anglia, Essex, Goldsmiths, Hull, Loughborough, Queen Mary, Sussex, Aberystwyth, Birmingham, Bristol, Bristol, Brunel, Exeter, Hull, Queen Margaret, Aberystwyth, Queen's Belfast, Chester, Winchester, Wolverhampton, UWE, Huddersfield, Kent, Salford, Chester, Bath Spa, Lincoln, Manchester Metropolitan, Southampton Solent, Winchester, Glamorgan, Middlesex, Newport, Roehampton, Staffordshire, Anglia Ruskin, Canterbury Christ Church, UWIC, Central Lancashire, East London, Thames Valley, Wolverhampton, Worcester, De Montfort, Sunderland, Buckinghamshire Chilterns

DANCE Leeds, Surrey, Chester, Wolverhampton, Bath Spa, Chichester, UWIC, Coventry, Manchester Metropolitan, Middlesex, Roehampton, Sunderland, Central Lancashire, Roehampton, De Montfort, Brighton

FILM STUDIES & PHOTOGRAPHY Luton, Falmouth, Westminster, Kent, Leeds, Nottingham, Kent, Bolton, Manchester Metropolitan, Bath Spa, UCE, Newport, Bath Spa, Bolton, Buckinghamshire Chilterns, SIHE, Nottingham Trent, Gloucestershire, Central Lancashire, De Montfort, East London, Derby, Middlesex, Portsmouth, NEWI, Southampton Solent, Buckinghamshire Chilterns, RSAMD, Newport, Paisley, Leeds Metropolitan, London South Bank, Chester, Napier, Plymouth, Staffordshire, Sunderland, Anglia Ruskin, Central Lancashire, Roehampton, Thames Valley, Wolverhampton, Sunderland, Robert Gordon, Brighton

CRAFTS Manchester Metropolitan, Coventry, Anglia Ruskin, Brighton, London Metropolitan, Dundee, Sheffield Hallam, Buckinghamshire Chilterns, UCE, Wolverhampton, Huddersfield, SIHE, Middlesex, NEWI, Lincoln

CREATIVE WRITING London Metropolitan, London South Bank, Luton, Manchester Metropolitan, NEWI, Essex, Bolton, Portsmouth, Chester, Glamorgan, Middlesex, Winchester, Newport, Staffordshire, Anglia Ruskin, Bolton, Bradford, Central Lancashire, East London, Greenwich, Roehampton, Wolverhampton, Trinity Carmarthen, Buckinghamshire Chilterns, De Montfort, Derby, Chichester

OTHER SIMILAR & RELATED London Metropolitan, London South Bank, Luton, Middlesex, Kent, Leeds, Lancaster, Bangor, De Montfort,

Manchester Metropolitan, Bolton, Manchester Metropolitan, Newport, Greenwich, Paisley, Derby

ASIAN LANGUAGES see <u>Languages & Literature, Easter, Asian, African, etc.</u>

BIOLOGY, ETC

BIOLOGY Hull, Keele, Durham, Imperial, East Anglia, Nottingham, Royal Holloway, Bath, UCL, York, Cardiff, Edinburgh, Lancaster, Leeds, Loughborough, Reading, Southampton, Birmingham, Bristol, Aston, Liverpool, Manchester, Newcastle, Queen Mary, Sheffield, Strathclyde, Sussex, Swansea, Aberystwyth, Bristol, Exeter, Gloucestershire, Lancaster, Plymouth, St Andrews, Surrey, Chester, Wolverhampton, Bangor, Bolton, Dundee, Essex, Glasgow, Hull, Keele, Kent, Staffordshire, Brighton, Coventry, Sheffield Hallam, Stirling, Anglia Ruskin, Bath Spa, Central Lancashire, Glamorgan, Gloucestershire, Huddersfield, Manchester Metropolitan, Nottingham Trent, Plymouth, Portsmouth, Aberdeen, Wolverhampton, UWE, Salford, East London, Manchester Metropolitan, Queen Margaret, Robert Gordon, Roehampton, Paisley, Worcester, Derby

BOTANY Durham, Sheffield, Edinburgh, Nottingham, Bristol, East Anglia, Manchester, Aberystwyth, Reading, Glasgow, Aberdeen, Wolverhampton, Worcester, Glamorgan

ZOOLOGY Imperial, Durham, Royal Holloway, Sheffield, UCL, Edinburgh, Leeds, Newcastle, Nottingham, Reading, Southampton, Bristol, Cardiff, Liverpool, Manchester, Queen Mary, Swansea, Aberystwyth, Queen's Belfast, Bangor, De Montfort, Dundee, Glasgow, Staffordshire, Stirling, Anglia Ruskin, Roehampton, Wolverhampton, Worcester, Brighton, Derby, Bangor

GENETICS Sheffield, UCL, York, Edinburgh, Leeds, Newcastle, Nottingham, Liverpool, Manchester, Queen Mary, Swansea, Aberystwyth, Surrey, Glasgow, Queen's Belfast, Anglia Ruskin, Aberdeen, Bristol, UWE, Wolverhampton, Cardiff

MICROBIOLOGY London Metropolitan, Westminster, Glasgow, Imperial, Bristol, Leeds, Newcastle, Nottingham, Reading, Cardiff, Liverpool, Manchester, Queen Mary, Aberystwyth, Surrey, Bradford, Queen's Belfast, Glamorgan, Hertfordshire, Napier, Nottingham Trent, Portsmouth, Aberdeen, UWE Bristol, Heriot-Watt, Nottingham Trent, Leeds Metropolitan, Wolverhampton, Salford, Warwick

SPORTS SCIENCE London Metropolitan, London South Bank, Luton, Paisley, Bath, Durham, Sheffield, Bath, Heriot-Watt, Hertfordshire, Leeds, Salford, Birmingham, Bolton, Gloucestershire, Sheffield Hallam, Staffordshire, Swansea, Bangor, Brighton, Chichester, De Montfort, Edinburgh,

`Huddersfield, Leeds Metropolitan, Portsmouth, Queen Mary, Aberystwyth, Chester, Brunel, Central Lancashire, Chichester, Essex, Glasgow, Kent, Nottingham Trent, Robert Gordon, Aberdeen, Abertay Dundee, Chester, Hull, Manchester Metropolitan, Napier, Anglia Ruskin, UWE Bristol, UWIC, Coventry, Glamorgan, Huddersfield, Lincoln, Plymouth, Greenwich, Teesside, Portsmouth, Southampton Solent, Wolverhampton, Trinity Carmarthen, Buckinghamshire Chilterns, Anglia Ruskin, Derby

MOLECULAR BIOLOGY, BIOPHYSICS & BIOCHEMISTRY
Keele, London Metropolitan, Plymouth, Westminster, Imperial, Oxford, Leeds, Nottingham, Sheffield, UCL, York, King's, Newcastle, Nottingham, Reading, Lancaster, Liverpool, Manchester, Queen Mary, Swansea, Hull, Kent, Greenwich, Hertfordshire, Huddersfield, Portsmouth, Aberdeen, Heriot-Watt

PSYCHOLOGY Liverpool, London Metropolitan, London South Bank, Luton, Open, Westminster, Royal Holloway, Cardiff, Reading, Bath, City, Durham, Exeter, Leeds, Loughborough, Oxford, Reading, Sheffield, Southampton, St Andrews, UCL, Bristol, Leicester, Liverpool, Manchester, Newcastle, Nottingham, St Andrews, Stirling, Surrey, Sussex, Bristol, York, Aston, Brighton, Edinburgh, Essex, Kent, Lancaster, Manchester Metropolitan, Portsmouth, Queen's Belfast, Sheffield Hallam, Birmingham, Coventry, Goldsmiths, Hertfordshire, Hull, Lancaster, Nottingham Trent, Swansea, Wolverhampton, Bangor, Brunel, Central Lancashire, Huddersfield, Lincoln, Strathclyde, Chester, Anglia Ruskin, Bolton, UWE, Buckingham, De Montfort, Dundee, Glasgow, Gloucestershire, Leeds Metropolitan, Manchester Metropolitan, Queen Margaret, Salford, Sheffield Hallam, Staffordshire, Thames Valley, Aberdeen, Bradford, Glamorgan, Hertfordshire, Plymouth, Southampton Solent, Sunderland, Winchester, Bath Spa, UWIC, UCE, Chichester, Glamorgan, Gloucestershire, Greenwich, Leeds Metropolitan, Manchester Metropolitan, Napier, Newport, Nottingham Trent, Aberdeen, Abertay Dundee, Bournemouth, Roehampton, Teesside, Canterbury Christ Church, East London, Middlesex, Worcester, Paisley, Buckinghamshire Chilterns, De Montfort, Paisley, Bolton, Derby, SIHE, Warwick, Westminster

OTHER SIMILAR & RELATED COURSES London Metropolitan, London South Bank, Anglia Ruskin, Huddersfield, Manchester Metropolitan, Derby, Manchester, Newcastle, UCL, Leeds, Bangor, Bolton, Lincoln, Greenwich, Leeds Metropolitan

BUSINESS, MANAGEMENT & ADMINISTRATION

BUSINESS Leeds Metropolitan, London Metropolitan, London South Bank, Luton, Newport, Open, Durham, City, Bath, Aston, Lancaster, Queen Mary, Sheffield, Cardiff, Edinburgh, Exeter, Glasgow, Liverpool, Reading,

Stirling, Strathclyde, Birmingham, Wolverhampton, Aston, De Montfort, Durham, East Anglia, Heriot-Watt, Liverpool, Queen Mary, Surrey, Sheffield Hallam, Brunel, Coventry, Queen's Belfast, Salford, Swansea, Aberystwyth, Chester, Bolton, UWE Bristol, Buckingham, Gloucestershire, Hertfordshire, Huddersfield, Manchester Metropolitan, Middlesex, Nottingham Trent, Staffordshire, Aberdeen, Abertay Dundee, Bradford, Wolverhampton, Anglia Ruskin, Bournemouth, Brighton, Chichester, Abertay Dundee, Winchester, UCE, Bolton, De Montfort, Glamorgan, Kent, Lincoln, Napier, Nottingham Trent, Plymouth, Portsmouth, Staffordshire, Sunderland, Teesside, UWIC, Central Lancashire, Queen Margaret, Bournemouth, Canterbury Christ Church, East London, Glasgow Caledonian, Greenwich, NEWI, Paisley, Roehampton, Southampton Solent, Thames Valley, Trinity Carmarthen, Worcester, Buckinghamshire Chilterns, Derby, Chichester, SIHE, Thames Valley, Westminster

MANAGEMENT Harper Adams, Keele, Lampeter, Leeds, London Metropolitan, London South Bank, Manchester Metropolitan, Sussex, Warwick, City, Durham, Lancaster, Sheffield, Southampton, St Andrews, Bath, King's, Lancaster, Manchester, Newcastle, Nottingham, Reading, Royal Holloway, York, Cardiff, Essex, Hull, Loughborough, Strathclyde, Essex, Leicester, SOAS, Exeter, Heriot-Watt, Keele, Kent, Manchester, Queen's Belfast, Stirling, Swansea, Chester, Bangor, De Montfort, Gloucestershire, Hertfordshire, Huddersfield, Middlesex, Plymouth, Robert Gordon, Salford, Warwick, Sheffield Hallam, Wolverhampton, Nottingham Trent, Bangor, UWE Bristol, UCE, Coventry, Glamorgan, Gloucestershire, Lincoln, Napier, Plymouth, Sunderland, Central Lancashire, Leeds Metropolitan, Queen Margaret, Teesside, Thames Valley, Anglia Ruskin, Central Lancashire, East London, Glasgow Caledonian, Middlesex, Paisley, Robert Gordon, Buckinghamshire Chilterns, De Montfort, Southampton Solent, Bolton, Derby, Bath Spa, Royal Holloway, SIHE, Aberdeen, Abertay Dundee

FINANCE Keele, London Metropolitan, Manchester Metropolitan, Westminster, LSE, Lancaster, Manchester, Nottingham, East Anglia, Essex, Queen's Belfast, Strathclyde, Brunel, Heriot-Watt, Keele, Aberystwyth, Bournemouth, Buckingham, Dundee, Hertfordshire, Manchester Metropolitan, Portsmouth, Robert Gordon, Salford, Staffordshire, Stirling, Aberdeen, Bath Spa, Abertay Dundee, UCE, Lincoln, Napier, Portsmouth, Hertfordshire, Anglia Ruskin, East London, Greenwich, Middlesex, De Montfort

ACCOUNTING Leeds, London Metropolitan, London South Bank, Luton, Lancaster, Manchester, Newcastle, Southampton, Bath, Aston, Leeds, Loughborough, Newcastle, Queen's Belfast, Reading, Sheffield, Surrey, Exeter, Hull, Liverpool, Manchester, Birmingham, Wolverhampton,

Durham, Essex, Cardiff, Coventry, East Anglia, Heriot-Watt, Kent, Bangor, Bournemouth, Buckingham, De Montfort, Essex, Gloucestershire, Hertfordshire, Huddersfield, Manchester Metropolitan, Nottingham Trent, Portsmouth, Sheffield Hallam, Staffordshire, Strathclyde, Abertay Dundee, Bradford, Bristol, Chester, Brighton, Glamorgan, Leeds Metropolitan, Aberystwyth, UWE, Lincoln, Napier, Newport, Plymouth, Sunderland, UWIC, Central Lancashire, Derby, Anglia Ruskin, East London, Greenwich, Middlesex, Paisley, Teesside, Thames Valley, Wolverhampton, Southampton Solent, Derby, SIHE, Warwick, Westminster

MARKETING Keele, Leeds Metropolitan, London Metropolitan, London South Bank, Luton, Westminster, Aston, Lancaster, Newcastle, Hull, Liverpool, Stirling, Strathclyde, Aberystwyth, Wolverhampton, Coventry, Essex, Keele, Chester, Bangor, Bolton, Brighton, Buckingham, De Montfort, Gloucestershire, Hertfordshire, Huddersfield, Manchester Metropolitan, Plymouth, Portsmouth, Sheffield Hallam, Staffordshire, Bradford, Winchester, Bath Spa, UCE, UWE Bristol, Glamorgan, Lincoln, Napier, Newport, Sunderland, Bournemouth, Central Lancashire, Queen Margaret, Derby, Anglia Ruskin, Canterbury Christ Church, Glasgow Caledonian, Greenwich, Middlesex, NEWI, Paisley, Roehampton, Southampton Solent, Teesside, Buckinghamshire Chilterns, De Montfort, Southampton Solent, UWIC, SIHE

HUMAN RESOURCES MANAGEMENT Keele, London Metropolitan, London South Bank, Luton, Westminster, Leeds, LSE, Liverpool, Stirling, Strathclyde, Wolverhampton, Keele, Bolton, Hertfordshire, Portsmouth, Staffordshire, Bradford, Bolton, Huddersfield, Manchester Metropolitan, Coventry, Glamorgan, Gloucestershire, Sunderland, Derby, Anglia Ruskin, Central Lancashire, Greenwich, Middlesex, Paisley, Roehampton, Teesside, Wolverhampton, Buckinghamshire Chilterns, Southampton Solent

OFFICE SKILLS Huddersfield, London Metropolitan, London South Bank, Heriot-Watt, Middlesex

TOURISM, TRANSPORT & TRAVEL Harper Adams, London Metropolitan, London South Bank, Luton, Westminster, Glasgow, De Montfort, Hertfordshire, Manchester Metropolitan, Stirling, Chester, Hull, Bath Spa, UWE Bristol, UWIC, Glamorgan, Glasgow Caledonian, Kent, Leeds Metropolitan, Lincoln, Napier, Plymouth, Aberystwyth, Hertfordshire, Huddersfield, Queen Margaret, Bolton, Canterbury Christ Church, Greenwich, Middlesex, Paisley, Trinity Carmarthen, Bournemouth, Derby, SIHE

OTHER SIMILAR & RELATED Abertay Dundee, Chichester, Anglia Ruskin, Central Lancashire, Glasgow Caledonian, Trinity Carmarthen, Derby

CELTIC see Literature, Linguistics, Classics, etc.

CHEMISTRY see Physical Sciences

CHINESE see Languages & Literature, Eastern, Asian, African, etc.

CLASSICS see Literature, Linguistics, Classics, etc.

COMMUNICATIONS & MEDIA

INFORMATION & LIBRARY SERVICES Manchester Metropolitan, Loughborough, Sheffield, Aberystwyth, Paisley, Brighton

PUBLICITY, PR, ETC.: London Metropolitan, Luton, Wolverhampton, Swansea, Huddersfield, Leeds Metropolitan, Queen Margaret, UCE, Gloucestershire, Lincoln, Southampton Solent, Sunderland, Central Lancashire, Teesside, Thames Valley, Buckinghamshire Chilterns, SIHE, Westminster

MEDIA STUDIES Lampeter, London Metropolitan, London South Bank, NEWI, Royal Holloway, Westminster, Goldsmiths, Birmingham, York, Glasgow, Manchester, Sussex, UCE, Newcastle, Sheffield Hallam, Swansea, Aberystwyth, Glamorgan, Huddersfield, Bradford, Chester, Wolverhampton, Bolton, Plymouth, Portsmouth, Salford, Bradford, De Montfort, Leeds Metropolitan, Nottingham Trent, Queen Margaret, Southampton Solent, Sunderland, Winchester, Napier, Staffordshire, Sunderland, Teesside, UWE Bristol, Chichester, Derby, Anglia Ruskin, UWIC, Central Lancashire, Middlesex, Paisley, Thames Valley, Worcester, Trinity Carmarthen, Buckinghamshire Chilterns, SIHE, Westminster

PUBLISHING Loughborough, Robert Gordon, Gloucestershire, Anglia Ruskin, Middlesex

JOURNALISM London Metropolitan, London South Bank, Luton, Cardiff, Bournemouth, Brighton, City, Nottingham Trent, Queen Mary, Sheffield, Salford, Staffordshire, Stirling, Strathclyde, Chester, Glasgow Caledonian, Lincoln, Southampton Solent, Wolverhampton, Bangor, Central Lancashire, Glamorgan, Napier, Portsmouth, Sheffield Hallam, Middlesex, Roehampton, Sunderland, Falmouth, Coventry, Anglia Ruskin, East London, Middlesex, Thames Valley, Buckinghamshire Chilterns, De Montfort, Westminster

OTHER SIMILAR & RELATED Keele, London Metropolitan, Leeds, Leicester, Keele, Liverpool, Swansea, Leeds Metropolitan, Lincoln, Bath Spa, Hertfordshire, Anglia Ruskin, Greenwich, Manchester Metropolitan, Middlesex

EASTERN EUROPEAN LANGUAGES see Languages & Literature, European

ECONOMICS see Social Studies

EDUCATION

TRAINING TEACHERS Newport, Chester, Gloucestershire, Canterbury Christ Church, Sheffield Hallam, Leeds Metropolitan, Hertfordshire, Nottingham Trent, Hull, Manchester Metropolitan, Bath Spa, Paisley, Bangor, Worcester, Plymouth, Wolverhampton, Trinity Carmarthen, Derby, Roehampton, Gloucestershire, UWE Bristol, East London

RESEARCH AND STUDY SKILLS IN EDUCATION Bolton

ACADEMIC STUDIES IN EDUCATION Hull, Keele, London Metropolitan, Luton, Newport, Durham, York, Aberystwyth, Edinburgh, Cardiff, Exeter, Keele, Bolton, Brighton, Brunel, UWIC, Chichester, Dundee, Staffordshire, Anglia Ruskin, Manchester Metropolitan, Stirling, Winchester, Bath Spa, UWE Bristol, Sunderland, Glamorgan, Leeds Metropolitan, Roehampton, Sheffield Hallam, UWIC, Central Lancashire, East London, Glasgow, Greenwich, Middlesex, Roehampton, Strathclyde, Wolverhampton, Trinity Carmarthen, Derby, De Montfort, Worcester, Queen's Belfast, SIHE

OTHER SIMILAR & RELATED Huddersfield, Liverpool, Goldsmiths, Leeds Metropolitan, Glamorgan, Trinity Carmarthen, Buckinghamshire Chilterns, Derby, Manchester Metropolitan, NEWI, Nottingham Trent, Plymouth, Bath Spa, Bolton

ENGINEERING

GENERAL ENGINEERING Leicester, London South Bank, Manchester, Southampton, Durham, Oxford, Swansea, Edinburgh, Exeter, Newcastle, UCL, Birmingham, Lancaster, Newcastle, Brunel, Strathclyde, Aberdeen, Brighton, City, Manchester Metropolitan, Bradford, Chester, Aston, UWE Bristol, UCE, Heriot-Watt, Central Lancashire, Greenwich, Portsmouth, UWIC, Portsmouth, Greenwich, Bolton, Coventry, Anglia Ruskin, Abertay Dundee

CIVIL ENGINEERING London South Bank, Imperial, Liverpool, Warwick, Durham, Manchester, Newcastle, East London, Edinburgh, Exeter, Loughborough, Plymouth, Queen's Belfast, Salford, Sheffield, Surrey, Birmingham, Bradford, Bristol, Cardiff, Leeds, Nottingham Trent, Nottingham, Coventry, Heriot-Watt, Aberdeen, Wolverhampton, Brighton, City, Dundee, Glasgow, Greenwich, Portsmouth, Bradford, Napier, Glamorgan, Abertay Dundee, Anglia Ruskin, UWE Bristol, Leeds Metropolitan, Teesside, Central Lancashire, Newport, Bolton, Paisley, SIHE, Bath

MECHANICAL ENGINEERING Hull, Leicester, London South Bank, Bristol, Imperial, Liverpool, Sheffield, Southampton, Bath, Warwick, Durham, Manchester, Newcastle, Swansea, UCL, Aston, Edinburgh, Exeter, King's, Loughborough,

Nottingham, Queen Mary, Robert Gordon, Salford, Sheffield Hallam, Strathclyde, Surrey, Sussex, Birmingham, Bradford, Cardiff, Lancaster, Leeds, Newcastle, Staffordshire, Aston, Brunel, Coventry, Glasgow, Huddersfield, Queen Mary, Queen's Belfast, Swansea, Aberdeen, Brighton, City, Glamorgan, Greenwich, Hertfordshire, Manchester Metropolitan, Plymouth, UWE Bristol, UCE, Heriot-Watt, Napier, Aberdeen, Sunderland, Teesside, Central Lancashire, De Montfort, Plymouth, Portsmouth, Wolverhampton, Bolton, UWIC, Paisley, Southampton Solent, SIHE

AEROSPACE ENGINEERING Liverpool, Sheffield, Southampton, Bath, Imperial, Manchester, Swansea, Hertfordshire, Queen Mary, Surrey, Liverpool, Strathclyde, Brunel, Coventry, Salford, UWE Bristol, Glamorgan, Salford

NAVAL ARCHITECTURE UCL, Newcastle, Strathclyde, Southampton Solent

ELECTRONIC & ELECTRICAL ENGINEERING Hull, Imperial, Leeds Metropolitan, Leicester, London South Bank, Durham, Liverpool, Manchester, Newcastle, Bath, UCL, Bangor, Edinburgh, Exeter, Newcastle, Portsmouth, Queen Mary, Queen's Belfast, Robert Gordon, Strathclyde, Sussex, Swansea, Birmingham, Bristol, Brighton, Cardiff, Essex, Glasgow, Bath, Brunel, Glamorgan, Nottingham, Aberdeen, Bangor, City, Dundee, Greenwich, Hertfordshire, Hull, Manchester Metropolitan, Plymouth, Portsmouth, Sheffield Hallam, Aston, UWE, UCE, East London, Heriot-Watt, Anglia Ruskin, Bolton, Central Lancashire, Glamorgan, Heriot-Watt, Huddersfield, Liverpool, Robert Gordon, Teesside, Coventry, Derby, NEWI, Southampton Solent, Sunderland, Abertay Dundee

PRODUCTION & MANUFACTURING ENGINEERING Leeds Metropolitan, Cambridge, Bath, Warwick, Loughborough, Queen's Belfast, Strathclyde, Coventry, Liverpool, Bradford, Glamorgan, Sunderland, Teesside, SIHE, Durham, Cardiff, Nottingham, Greenwich, Hertfordshire, UWIC, East London, SIHE

CHEMICAL, PROCESS & ENERGY ENGINEERING Newcastle, Heriot-Watt, Strathclyde, Teesside, Paisley, Imperial, Cambridge, Sheffield, Manchester, Bath, Edinburgh, Leeds, Nottingham, Queen's Belfast, Surrey, Swansea, UCL, Birmingham, Aston, Strathclyde, Paisley

OTHER SIMILAR & RELATED London South Bank, Newcastle, Leeds, Loughborough, Nottingham, Lancaster, Queen Mary, Bristol, Napier, NEWI, Bradford

ENGLISH see Literature, Linguistics, Classics etc.

FOOD & BEVERAGES see Agriculture

GEOLOGY see Physical Sciences

GEOGRAPHY, PHYSICAL & ENVIRONMENTAL see Physical Sciences

GEOGRAPHY, HUMAN & SOCIAL see Social Studies

GERMAN see Linguistics & Literature, European

GREEK, CLASSICAL see Literature, Linguistics, Classics etc.

HISTORY, PHILOSOPHY, ETC

HISTORY, GENERAL OR SPECIALISING IN A SPECIFIC PERIOD Keele, Lampeter, London Metropolitan, NEWI, Open, Westminster, Durham, Cambridge, Exeter, King's, Liverpool, Manchester, Nottingham, Sheffield, St Andrews, Bristol, Leeds, Cardiff, East Anglia, Edinburgh, Glasgow, Kent, Lancaster, Leicester, Reading, Sheffield, Sussex, Aberystwyth, Birmingham, Bristol, Brunel, Cardiff, Essex, Goldsmiths, Huddersfield, Kent, Liverpool, Hull, Kent, Bangor, Bolton, UWE, UCE, Dundee, Nottingham Trent, Aberdeen, Bradford, Chester, Wolverhampton, Anglia Ruskin, Brighton, Central Lancashire, De Montfort, Gloucestershire, Hertfordshire, Lincoln, Manchester Metropolitan, Newcastle, Nottingham Trent, Bath Spa, Coventry, Glamorgan, Newport, Chichester, Leeds Metropolitan, Derby, UWIC, East London, Greenwich, Middlesex, Wolverhampton, Worcester, Worcester

HISTORY, SPECIALISING IN A SPECIFIC COUNTRY OR AREA Portsmouth, Aberystwyth, Plymouth, Aberdeen, St Andrews, Edinburgh, Glasgow, Stirling, Dundee, Bangor, East Anglia, Kent, UCL, Swansea, Bradford, Anglia Ruskin, Essex, Canterbury Christ Church

HISTORY, SPECIALISING IN A SPECIFIC TOPIC Portsmouth, UCL, Warwick, York, Queen Mary, SOAS, Southampton, UCL, Stirling, Strathclyde, SOAS, Swansea, Sheffield Hallam, De Montfort, Winchester, Staffordshire, Sunderland, Roehampton, Canterbury Christ Church, Worcester, Teesside, De Montfort, Derby, Royal Holloway

ARCHAEOLOGY Lampeter, Durham, Oxford, Manchester, Nottingham, Sheffield, York, East Anglia, Edinburgh, Southampton, UCL, Birmingham, Cardiff, King's, Leicester, Liverpool, SOAS, Exeter, Kent, Newcastle, Queen's Belfast, Reading, Bradford, Chester, Winchester,, Bournemouth, Central Lancashire, Trinity Carmarthen, Worcester, Royal Holloway

PHILOSOPHY Lampeter, London Metropolitan, Durham, UCL, Cambridge, Durham, King's, LSE, Oxford, Sheffield, St Andrews, Sussex, Bristol, Warwick, York, Essex, Lancaster, Liverpool, Manchester, Cardiff, East Anglia, Edinburgh, Exeter, Glasgow, Leeds, Newcastle, Nottingham, Reading, Southampton, Birmingham, Hull, Kent, Lancaster, Essex, Queen's Belfast, Bolton, Dundee, Stirling, Aberdeen, Hertfordshire, Manchester Metropolitan, UWE Bristol, Glamorgan, Newport, Staffordshire, Roehampton, Bradford, Anglia Ruskin, Central Lancashire, Greenwich, Middlesex, Wolverhampton

THEOLOGY & RELIGIOUS STUDIES Lampeter, SOAS, Oxford, Edinburgh, Glasgow, Manchester, Kent, King's, Lancaster, Cardiff, Bangor, Stirling, Aberdeen, Gloucestershire, Winchester, Bath Spa, Canterbury Christ Church, Huddersfield, Roehampton, Wolverhampton, Chester, Durham, St Andrews, Leeds, Nottingham, Birmingham, Chichester, Exeter, Hull, Queen's Belfast, Bristol, Bangor, De Montfort, Aberdeen, Greenwich, Roehampton

OTHER SIMILAR & RELATED Cambridge, Bangor, Lampeter, Luton, Glasgow, Birmingham, Exeter, Leeds, Central Lancashire, Oxford, UCL, Manchester, Trinity Carmarthen, Manchester, Cardiff

ITALIAN see Languages & Literature, European

JAPANESE see Languages & Literature, Eastern, Asian, African, etc.

JOURNALISM see Communications & Media

LANGUAGES & LITERATURE EASTERN, ASIAN, AFRICAN, ETC.

CHINESE Westminster, Cambridge, Oxford, Edinburgh, Nottingham, Sheffield, Leeds, SOAS, Central Lancashire

JAPANESE Cambridge, Oxford, SOAS, Edinburgh, Leeds, Sheffield, Central Lancashire

SOUTH ASIAN STUDIES SOAS, Cambridge, Sheffield, Leeds

OTHER ASIAN STUDIES SOAS, Newcastle, Sheffield, Central Lancashire

AFRICAN STUDIES Birmingham, SOAS

MODERN MIDDLE EASTERN STUDIES Oxford, St Andrews, SOAS, Edinburgh, UCL, Leeds, Manchester

AMERICAN STUDIES Keele, Lampeter, London Metropolitan, Manchester Metropolitan, Manchester, Kent, King's, Nottingham, Warwick, Hull, Leicester, Nottingham, Sussex, Birmingham, Essex, Swansea, East Anglia, Keele, Lancaster, Dundee, Portsmouth, Aberystwyth, Wolverhampton, UWE Bristol, Central Lancashire, Lincoln, Winchester,, UWE Bristol, Derby, Canterbury Christ Church, Middlesex, Plymouth, Sunderland, Wolverhampton, De Montfort, Derby

OTHER SIMILAR & RELATED Cambridge, Oxford, Newcastle, Nottingham, Hull, King's, SOAS, Leicester, SOAS, Manchester Metropolitan, Nottingham Trent

LANGUAGES & LITERATURE EUROPEAN

FRENCH Keele, Leeds, Liverpool, London Metropolitan, Open, Westminster, Durham, Manchester, St Andrews, UCL, King's, Lancaster, Royal Holloway, Southampton, Bath, Warwick, York, Edinburgh, Exeter, Glasgow, Lancaster, Liverpool, Manchester, Newcastle, Queen Mary, Stirling, Aberystwyth, Birmingham, Aston, Coventry, Heriot-Watt, King's, Nottingham, Sheffield, Aberystwyth, Bristol, Cardiff, Essex, Hull, Kent, Leicester, Queen's Belfast, Reading, Southampton, Aberystwyth, Bristol, Wolverhampton, Bangor, Brighton, Salford, Swansea, Aberdeen, Chester, Anglia Ruskin, Leeds Metropolitan, Nottingham Trent, UWE Bristol, Coventry, Portsmouth, Sheffield Hallam, Manchester Metropolitan, Anglia Ruskin, Canterbury Christ Church, Central Lancashire, Middlesex, Paisley, Roehampton

GERMAN Open, Durham, King's, Manchester, Nottingham, St Andrews, Lancaster, Royal Holloway, Southampton, St Andrews, Bath, Warwick, York, Edinburgh, Glasgow, Newcastle, Sheffield, St Andrews, Aberystwyth, Birmingham, Aston, Heriot-Watt, Liverpool, Nottingham, Reading, UCL, Cardiff, Exeter, Hull, Kent, Leeds, Queen's Belfast, Bristol, Bangor, Brighton, Salford, Stirling, Swansea, Aberdeen, Wolverhampton, Nottingham Trent, UWE, Portsmouth, Sheffield Hallam, Anglia Ruskin, Central Lancashire, Leeds Metropolitan, Manchester Metropolitan, Paisley, Queen Mary, Royal Holloway

ITALIAN Durham, Manchester, St Andrews, Lancaster, Royal Holloway, St Andrews, Bath, Edinburgh, Glasgow, Lancaster, Manchester, Birmingham, Hull, Leeds, Reading, UCL, Cardiff, Exeter, Kent, Leicester, Warwick, Bristol, Bangor, Salford, Swansea, Nottingham Trent, Sheffield Hallam, Manchester Metropolitan, Aberystwyth

SPANISH London Metropolitan, Durham, St Andrews, Lancaster, Southampton, St Andrews, Bath, Edinburgh, Glasgow, Leeds, Manchester, Newcastle, St Andrews, Stirling, Aberystwyth, Birmingham, Aston, Heriot-Watt, Hull, Liverpool, Bristol, Cardiff, Essex, Exeter, Hull, Kent, Leicester, Queen's Belfast, Wolverhampton, Bangor, Salford, Sheffield Hallam, Swansea, Aberdeen, Chester, Bangor, Leeds Metropolitan, Nottingham Trent, UWE, Coventry, Portsmouth, Anglia Ruskin, Central Lancashire, Metropolitan, Middlesex, Paisley, Roehampton, Queen Mary, Royal Holloway

PORTUGUESE King's, Manchester, Birmingham, Nottingham, Bristol, Salford

SCANDINAVIAN Edinburgh, UCL

RUSSIAN & EAST EUROPEAN Nottingham, Durham, Manchester, SOAS, St Andrews, Edinburgh, Glasgow, Sheffield, St Andrews, Bath, UCL, Birmingham, UCL, Exeter, Leeds, Queen Mary, Bristol, Royal Holloway, Bristol

OTHER SIMILAR & RELATED London Metropolitan, Open, Cambridge, Oxford, King's, Manchester, Lancaster, Newcastle, Aberystwyth, Liverpool, UCL, Goldsmiths, Hull, Leicester, Aberdeen, Manchester Metropolitan, Nottingham Trent, Lincoln, Nottingham, East Anglia, Bangor, Dundee, UWE Bristol, Leeds Metropolitan

LATIN see Literature, Linguistics, Classics, etc.

LAW

LAW, GENERAL OR SPECIALISING IN A SPECIFIC COUNTRY OR AREA Keele, Leeds, Leicester, London Metropolitan, London South Bank, Manchester Metropolitan, Open, Plymouth, Cambridge, Durham, East Anglia, Manchester, Newcastle, Sheffield, SOAS, Southampton, UCL, Birmingham, City, East Anglia, Exeter, King's, Lancaster, Liverpool, Oxford, Queen's Belfast, Reading, Bristol, Brunel, Essex, Queen Mary, Strathclyde, Surrey, Sussex, Aberystwyth, Wolverhampton, Cardiff, Edinburgh, Glasgow, Hull, Keele, Staffordshire, Aberdeen, Bradford, Anglia Ruskin, Bangor, UCE, Coventry, Glamorgan, Nottingham Trent, Plymouth, Derby, Bournemouth, UWE, Sheffield Hallam, Bolton, Buckingham, Dundee, Gloucestershire, Hertfordshire, Huddersfield, Napier, Portsmouth, Robert Gordon, Stirling, Swansea, Thames Valley, UWE, Central Lancashire, Sunderland, UWE, East London, Glamorgan, Gloucestershire, Middlesex, Derby, Central Lancashire, Paisley, Teesside, Wolverhampton, Buckinghamshire Chilterns, De Montfort, Southampton Solent, Warwick, Westminster

LAW, SPECIALISING IN A SPECIFIC TOPIC De Montfort, Glasgow Caledonian, Aberystwyth, Leeds Metropolitan, Chester, Bangor, Bolton, Plymouth, Anglia Ruskin, UCE, Bradford, Greenwich, Westminster, London Metropolitan, Westminster, Aberystwyth, Glamorgan, De Montfort, Huddersfield, Middlesex, Buckinghamshire Chilterns, Southampton Solent, Westminster, Brunel, London Metropolitan, Manchester Metropolitan

OTHER SIMILAR & RELATED Leeds, Manchester Metropolitan, Middlesex

LITERATURE, LINGUISTICS, CLASSICS, ETC.

LANGUAGE/LINGUISTICS Westminster, SOAS, York, Sheffield, Cardiff, Edinburgh, Essex, Lancaster, Manchester, Newcastle, St Andrews, Sussex, Bath, UCL, Birmingham, York, Leeds, Queen's Belfast, Aberystwyth, Chester, Wolverhampton, Bangor, Salford, Aberdeen, Bristol, Glamorgan, Nottingham Trent, UWE Bristol, Anglia Ruskin, Central Lancashire, Greenwich, Wolverhampton

COMPARATIVE LITERATURE Glasgow, King's,

Liverpool, Kent, Manchester, Essex, Sunderland, Manchester Metropolitan, Queen Mary

ENGLISH Hull, Keele, Lampeter, London South Bank, NEWI, Open, Bristol, Cambridge, Durham, Exeter, Manchester, Oxford, Sheffield, Southampton, St Andrews, UCL, York, King's, Liverpool, Loughborough, Manchester, Nottingham, Reading, Royal Holloway, Southampton, Sussex, Warwick, York, East Anglia, Goldsmiths, Huddersfield, Leicester, Manchester, Queen Mary, Stirling, Swansea, Birmingham, Brighton, UWE, Brunel, Coventry, East Anglia, Kent, Reading, Sheffield Hallam, Bristol, Coventry, Exeter, Huddersfield, Lincoln, Queen's Belfast, Strathclyde, Chester, Wolverhampton, Bangor, Bolton, Brighton, Buckingham, Coventry, Dundee, Glamorgan, Keele, Nottingham Trent, Plymouth, Portsmouth, Sheffield Hallam, Aberdeen, Winchester, Chichester, De Montfort, Manchester Metropolitan, Salford, UWE, Newport, Sunderland, Anglia Ruskin, Bolton, Leeds Metropolitan, Manchester Metropolitan, Bradford, Derby, Canterbury Christ Church, UWIC, UCE, Central Lancashire, Greenwich, Wolverhampton, Worcester, Teesside, Trinity Carmarthen, Worcester, Buckinghamshire Chilterns, Bournemouth, Derby, Chichester, SIHE

ANCIENT LANGUAGES Oxford, Westminster, SOAS, Edinburgh, St Andrews

CELTIC STUDIES Edinburgh, Glasgow, Aberystwyth, Aberdeen

LATIN Lampeter, Durham, Edinburgh, Glasgow, King's, Manchester, Nottingham, UCL, Exeter, Leeds, Swansea, Royal Holloway

CLASSICAL GREEK Durham, St Andrews, Edinburgh, Glasgow, King's, Manchester, Leeds

CLASSICS Lampeter, Cambridge, Oxford, Durham, Newcastle, Nottingham, St Andrews, Bristol, Warwick, Edinburgh, Exeter, Glasgow, King's, Manchester, Newcastle, UCL, Birmingham, Liverpool, Kent, Leeds, Reading, Swansea, Bristol, Roehampton, Royal Holloway

OTHER SIMILAR & RELATED Exeter, Nottingham, Leeds, Manchester, Aberystwyth, London Metropolitan, Aston, East Anglia, Swansea, Middlesex, Roehampton, Birmingham

MARKETING see Business, Management & Administration

MATHS & COMPUTING

MATHEMATICS Keele, Liverpool, London Metropolitan, Newport, Open, Royal Holloway, Durham, Imperial, Sheffield, Bath, Bristol, Cambridge, Durham, East Anglia, Leeds, Nottingham, Oxford, Southampton, St Andrews, Surrey, Aberystwyth, UCL, Warwick, York, East Anglia, Kent, King's, Lancaster, Leicester,

Manchester, Newcastle, Queen's Belfast, Reading, Royal Holloway, Southampton, Strathclyde, Sussex, Bristol, Cardiff, De Montfort, Edinburgh, Exeter, Loughborough, Stirling, Surrey, Aberystwyth, Birmingham, Essex, Queen Mary, Aston, Brunel, Heriot-Watt, Kent, Chester, Bolton, Brighton, UWE, City, Coventry, Dundee, Glasgow, Nottingham Trent, Swansea, Aberdeen, Glamorgan, Manchester Metropolitan, Plymouth, Portsmouth, Sheffield Hallam, Bournemouth, Chichester, Glasgow Caledonian, Hertfordshire, Canterbury Christ Church, Central Lancashire, Greenwich, Wolverhampton, Derby, East Anglia, Royal Holloway, Sunderland

OPERATIONAL RESEARCH Greenwich, Warwick, Lancaster

STATISTICS Leeds, Bath, Newcastle, St Andrews, UCL, Reading, Aberystwyth, Lancaster, Queen Mary, Heriot-Watt, Glasgow, UWE Bristol, Glamorgan, Hertfordshire, Greenwich, Middlesex, Wolverhampton

COMPUTER SCIENCE Hertfordshire, Huddersfield, Hull, Keele, Liverpool, London Metropolitan, London South Bank, Luton, Napier, Newcastle, Open, Westminster, Cambridge, Durham, Strathclyde, City, Imperial, Oxford, Southampton, Bath, Warwick, East Anglia, Kent, King's, Leeds, Manchester, Nottingham, Sheffield, St Andrews, UCL, Bristol, York, Cardiff, Edinburgh, Lancaster, Leicester, Loughborough, Queen Mary, Queen's Belfast, Reading, Surrey, Sussex, Swansea, Aberystwyth, Birmingham, Coventry, Lincoln, Staffordshire, Bath, Brunel, Essex, Exeter, Goldsmiths, Chester, Wolverhampton, Bangor, Brighton, UWE, Buckingham, De Montfort, Dundee, Glasgow, Greenwich, Manchester Metropolitan, Nottingham Trent, Plymouth, Portsmouth, Salford, Sunderland, Aberdeen, Bradford, Aston, UCE, Glamorgan, Gloucestershire, Heriot-Watt, Anglia Ruskin, Central Lancashire, Middlesex, Napier, Nottingham Trent, Sheffield Hallam, Stirling, Aberdeen, Abertay Dundee, Bradford, Bournemouth, UWIC, Chichester, Leeds Metropolitan, Newport, Teesside, Derby, Canterbury Christ Church, Central Lancashire, De Montfort, East London, Greenwich, NEWI, Paisley, Robert Gordon, Thames Valley, Roehampton, Trinity Carmarthen, Wolverhampton, Worcester, Buckinghamshire Chilterns, Leeds Metropolitan, Southampton Solent, Paisley, Royal Holloway

INFORMATION SYSTEMS Keele, Liverpool, London Metropolitan, London South Bank, Luton, Napier, Westminster, Imperial, City, Strathclyde, Bath, Leeds, King's, Newcastle, Cardiff, Lincoln, Brunel, Bangor, Bolton, UWE Bristol, Hertfordshire, Manchester Metropolitan, Nottingham Trent, Aberdeen, Bradford, UCE, Glamorgan, Gloucestershire, Heriot-Watt, Sheffield Hallam, Staffordshire, Stirling, Anglia Ruskin, Bournemouth, Hertfordshire, Napier, Portsmouth,

Teesside, Abertay Dundee, Leeds Metropolitan,
Thames Valley, Derby, Greenwich, Paisley, UWIC,
Trinity Carmarthen, Southampton Solent, SIHE

SOFTWARE ENGINEERING Hull, Luton, Napier,
Westminster, Imperial, Manchester, City,
Southampton, Strathclyde, Aberystwyth,
Sheffield, Coventry, Durham, Edinburgh,
Greenwich, Loughborough, Newcastle,
Wolverhampton, Essex, Heriot-Watt, Salford,
Aston, Brighton, UWE Bristol, Glasgow, Lincoln,
Nottingham Trent, Portsmouth, Abertay Dundee,
Bradford, UCE, Manchester Metropolitan,
Staffordshire, Stirling, Anglia Ruskin, Glamorgan,
Hertfordshire, Huddersfield, Sheffield Hallam,
Sunderland, Teesside, Bournemouth, Leeds
Metropolitan, Central Lancashire, De Montfort,
East London, Paisley, Wolverhampton,
Southampton Solent, SIHE

ARTIFICIAL INTELLIGENCE Luton, Manchester,
Imperial, Sheffield, Edinburgh, Liverpool,
Birmingham, Robert Gordon, Aberystwyth,
Portsmouth, Salford, UWE Bristol, Heriot-Watt,
Manchester Metropolitan, Staffordshire, UWE,
Hertfordshire, Sunderland, De Montfort,
Westminster

MEDIA see Communications & Media

MEDICINE & HEALTH

MEDICINE Hull, King's, Leicester, Manchester,
Nottingham, Oxford, Cambridge, Queen's Belfast,
Dundee, East Anglia, Imperial, Leeds, Open,
Sheffield, Birmingham, Sussex, Edinburgh,
Thames Valley, Exeter, Cardiff, Southampton,
Aberdeen, Bristol, York, UCL, Swansea, Essex,
Queen Mary

DENTISTRY Dundee, Glasgow, Leeds, Manchester,
Newcastle, Birmingham, Bristol, Manchester,
King's, Queen Mary, Queen's Belfast, Cardiff,
Sheffield, Portsmouth

ANATOMY, PHYSIOLOGY & PATHOLOGY Oxford,
Newcastle, Staffordshire, Liverpool, Bristol, St
Andrews, Queen's Belfast, Dundee, Glasgow,
Sheffield Hallam, Sheffield, Edinburgh, King's,
Leeds, Leicester, UCL, Bristol, Manchester,
Wolverhampton, Dundee, Essex, Swansea,
Hertfordshire, Manchester Metropolitan,
Nottingham Trent, Aberdeen, UWE, Leeds
Metropolitan, Sunderland, Cardiff, Westminster

PHARMACOLOGY, TOXICOLOGY & PHARMACY London
Metropolitan, Edinburgh, King's, Leeds,
Newcastle, Southampton, Bath, UCL, Bristol,
Manchester, Bradford, Wolverhampton, Dundee,
Glasgow, Sheffield Hallam, Brighton,
Hertfordshire, Nottingham Trent, Portsmouth,
Aberdeen, Sunderland, Portsmouth, Sunderland,
Greenwich, Huddersfield, Napier, East London

COMPLEMENTARY MEDICINE Central Lancashire,
Glamorgan, Salford, Anglia Ruskin, Bournemouth,

UWIC, Central Lancashire, East London,
Greenwich, Middlesex, Derby, Wolverhampton,
Brighton, Westminster

NUTRITION London Metropolitan, London South
Bank, Luton, King's, Nottingham, Newcastle,
Surrey, Wolverhampton, Glamorgan, Huddersfield,
Sheffield Hallam, Abertay Dundee, Greenwich,
Thames Valley, Leeds Metropolitan, Queen
Margaret, Robert Gordon, UWIC, Westminster

NURSING Luton, Middlesex, NEWI, Coventry, City,
Edinburgh, Birmingham, Coventry, Liverpool,
Nottingham, Cardiff, Glamorgan, Glasgow, Leeds,
Manchester, Brighton, Bangor, UCE, Lincoln,
Queen Margaret, Anglia Ruskin, UWE Bristol,
Anglia Ruskin, Canterbury Christ Church, Central
Lancashire, Abertay Dundee, Wolverhampton,
Buckinghamshire Chilterns, St George's Medical
School, Staffordshire, Stirling, Sunderland

MEDICAL TECHNOLOGY Imperial, Southampton, Bath,
Queen Mary, Surrey, Cardiff, Wolverhampton,
Bradford, Canterbury Christ Church, Portsmouth

OTHER SIMILAR & RELATED Hull, London
Metropolitan, Luton, Open, Imperial, Manchester,
King's, Manchester, Lancaster, Bradford,
Nottingham Trent, Chester, Central Lancashire,
Manchester Metropolitan, Leeds Metropolitan,
Portsmouth, Greenwich, Exeter, Cardiff,
Huddersfield, Durham, Kent, UWE Bristol,
Hertfordshire, Lincoln, Abertay Dundee,
Bournemouth, Paisley

MIDDLE EASTERN STUDIES AND LANGUAGES see
Languages & Literature, Eastern, Asian, African,
etc.

NURSING see Medicine & Health

PHILOSOPHY see History, Philosophy, etc.

PHYSICAL SCIENCES

CHEMISTRY Hull, Keele, London Metropolitan,
Newcastle, Nottingham Trent, Durham,
Southampton, Warwick, Cambridge, Imperial,
Oxford, East Anglia, Imperial, Manchester,
Sheffield, Southampton, Edinburgh, Leicester,
Liverpool, Manchester, Nottingham, St Andrews,
Sussex, Bath, Birmingham, Reading, Cardiff, De
Montfort, Leeds, Loughborough, Nottingham,
UCL, York, Kent, Surrey, Bradford, Glasgow,
Surrey, Aberdeen, Aston, Bangor, Heriot-Watt,
Glamorgan, Huddersfield, Queen's Belfast,
Sunderland, Aberdeen, Greenwich, UWE Bristol,
Central Lancashire, Manchester Metropolitan,
Paisley

MATERIALS SCIENCE Oxford, Imperial, Manchester,
Sheffield, Loughborough, Queen Mary, Swansea,
Birmingham, St Andrews, Imperial, Leeds,
Swansea, Manchester Metropolitan, Liverpool

PHYSICS Hull, Imperial, Kent, Durham, Cambridge,

Nottingham, Oxford, Bath, King's, Lancaster, Leeds, Leicester, Liverpool, Manchester, Queen's Belfast, Sheffield, Southampton, St Andrews, Sussex, York, Cardiff, Edinburgh, Loughborough, Royal Holloway, Surrey, Swansea, Aberystwyth, UCL, Birmingham, Bristol, Kent, Queen Mary, Reading, Strathclyde, Cardiff, Exeter, Royal Holloway, Dundee, Glasgow, Nottingham Trent, Salford, Aberdeen, Nottingham Trent, Heriot-Watt, Hertfordshire, Central Lancashire, Paisley, Royal College of Music, Warwick

FORENSIC & ARCHAEOLOGICAL SCIENCE Bournemouth, Greenwich, Keele, London Metropolitan, London South Bank, NEWI, Strathclyde, Anglia Ruskin, Bournemouth, Queen Mary, Central Lancashire, Kent, Bradford, UWE Bristol, Glamorgan, Lincoln, Nottingham Trent, Abertay Dundee, Coventry, Nottingham Trent, Sheffield Hallam, Napier, Portsmouth, Sheffield Hallam, Teesside, UWE, De Montfort, Teesside, Canterbury Christ Church, East London, Robert Gordon, Wolverhampton, Paisley, Derby, Staffordshire, Westminster

ASTRONOMY Sheffield, UCL, Queen Mary, Central Lancashire, Glasgow, Nottingham Trent, Glamorgan, Hertfordshire

GEOLOGY Keele, Cambridge, Southampton, Imperial, Liverpool, Royal Holloway, UCL, Birmingham, Durham, Edinburgh, Lancaster, Leeds, Leicester, Manchester, Aberystwyth, UCL, Bristol, Cardiff, Leeds, Southampton, Exeter, Brighton, Keele, Plymouth, Glamorgan, Aberdeen, Greenwich, Derby, Portsmouth

OCEAN SCIENCES Southampton, Liverpool, Bangor, Plymouth, Southampton Solent

PHYSICAL GEOGRAPHY & ENVIRONMENT Aberystwyth, Aberdeen, Bath Spa, East Anglia, Coventry, Central Lancashire, Chester, Sheffield Hallam, Bradford, Bolton, UWE Bristol

OTHER SIMILAR & RELATED Bath Spa, Liverpool, Open, Leeds, York, Aberdeen, Canterbury Christ Church, Aston

POLITICS see Social Studies

PORTUGUESE see Language & Literature, European

PSYCHOLOGY see Biology, etc.

RELIGIOUS STUDIES see History, Philosophy, etc.

RUSSIAN see Languages & Literature, European

SCANDINAVIAN LANGUAGES see Languages & Literature, European

SOCIAL STUDIES

ECONOMICS Keele, London Metropolitan, Open, Plymouth, Cambridge, Durham, LSE, Nottingham, UCL, City, Durham, Oxford, St Andrews, Bath, Warwick, York, Aston, Lancaster, Leicester, Loughborough, Manchester, Newcastle, Sheffield, SOAS, Southampton, Birmingham, Cardiff, East Anglia, Edinburgh, Essex, Exeter, Glasgow, Hull, Leeds, Leicester, Liverpool, Queen Mary, Reading, Stirling, Strathclyde, Sussex, Aberystwyth, Brunel, Kent, Surrey, Bristol, Coventry, Goldsmiths, Heriot-Watt, Queen's Belfast, Bangor, Buckingham, Dundee, Hertfordshire, Manchester Metropolitan, Nottingham Trent, Salford, Staffordshire, Swansea, Aberdeen, Bradford, Wolverhampton, UWE, UCE, Glamorgan, Napier, Newport, Portsmouth, Central Lancashire, East London, Greenwich, Middlesex, Paisley, Royal Holloway, Abertay Dundee

POLITICS London Metropolitan, SOAS, Durham, Manchester, Royal Holloway, Warwick, Durham, Essex, Hull, Nottingham, Sheffield, Southampton, Stirling, Sussex, Bath, Birmingham, Bristol, York, Aston, Edinburgh, Exeter, Glasgow, Leeds, Newcastle, Queen Mary, Strathclyde, Aberystwyth, UCL, East Anglia, Essex, Kent, Lancaster, Leicester, Liverpool, Reading, Surrey, Bradford, Cardiff, Goldsmiths, Queen's Belfast, Strathclyde, Bristol, Brunel, Buckingham, Dundee, Loughborough, Portsmouth, Salford, Swansea, Aberdeen, Glamorgan, Manchester Metropolitan, Nottingham Trent, UWE, Coventry, Huddersfield, Leeds Metropolitan, Lincoln, Sunderland, Anglia Ruskin, Canterbury Christ Church, UWIC, Central Lancashire, East London, Greenwich, Middlesex, Wolverhampton, Paisley, De Montfort, Westminster

SOCIOLOGY London Metropolitan, London South Bank, Plymouth, Bristol, City, Royal Holloway, Durham, Bath, Birmingham, Aston, East Anglia, Edinburgh, Glasgow, Leeds, Manchester, Newcastle, Nottingham, Sheffield, Stirling, Sussex, Warwick, Essex, Goldsmiths, Lancaster, Liverpool, Southampton, York, Brighton, Cardiff, Coventry, Exeter, Hull, Kent, Leicester, Loughborough, Queen's Belfast, Strathclyde, Surrey, Brunel, De Montfort, Nottingham Trent, Portsmouth, Salford, Sheffield Hallam, Aberdeen, Chester, Wolverhampton, Bangor, Manchester Metropolitan, Queen Margaret, Bath Spa, UWE, UCE, Glamorgan, Gloucestershire, Huddersfield, Leeds Metropolitan, Plymouth, Staffordshire, Sunderland, Worcester, Bradford, Anglia Ruskin, UWIC, Central Lancashire, East London, Greenwich, Middlesex, Teesside, Thames Valley, Abertay Dundee, Worcester, Paisley, Buckinghamshire Chilterns, Roehampton, Derby, Bath, Westminster

SOCIAL POLICY London Metropolitan, London South Bank, Durham, Royal Holloway, LSE, Birmingham, Cardiff, Edinburgh, Nottingham, Sheffield, Stirling, Brighton, Leeds, Sheffield, Southampton, York, Kent, Queen's Belfast, Bristol, Bangor, Portsmouth, Sheffield Hallam, Swansea, Wolverhampton, Anglia Ruskin, Hull, Gloucestershire, Lincoln, Salford, Bradford, Anglia Ruskin, Central Lancashire, East London,

Middlesex, Newport, Wolverhampton, Paisley, Roehampton, Bath

SOCIAL WORK London Metropolitan, London South Bank, Luton, Manchester Metropolitan, Middlesex, Open, Birmingham, Edinburgh, Queen's Belfast, Sussex, Wolverhampton, Goldsmiths, Lancaster, Leeds, Reading, Sheffield, York, Hull, Manchester, Stirling, Bath, Bradford, Chester, Brunel, Chichester, Dundee, Greenwich, Nottingham Trent, Robert Gordon, Southampton, Swansea, Huddersfield, Lincoln, NEWI, Strathclyde, Anglia Ruskin, Coventry, Glamorgan, Huddersfield, Kent, Leeds Metropolitan, Plymouth, Staffordshire, Teesside, De Montfort, Bournemouth, UWE Bristol, Canterbury Christ Church, UCE, Central Lancashire, East London, Hertfordshire, Newport, Portsmouth, Sheffield Hallam, Sunderland, Paisley, Buckinghamshire Chilterns, UWIC, Gloucestershire, Salford, Teesside, Derby, Brighton, Southampton Solent, St George's Medical School

ANTHROPOLOGY Lampeter, Durham, LSE, Glasgow, Goldsmiths, Sussex, UCL, Birmingham, Southampton, Kent, Aberdeen, Glamorgan, East London, Roehampton

HUMAN & SOCIAL GEOGRAPHY Keele, King's, Nottingham, Oxford, Leeds, Manchester, Newcastle, Birmingham, Edinburgh, Lancaster, Liverpool, LSE, London, Reading, Southampton, UCL, Queen Mary, Sheffield Hallam, Gloucestershire, Leicester, Queen's Belfast, Brighton, Dundee, Hull, Portsmouth, Staffordshire, UWE Bristol, Central Lancashire, Manchester Metropolitan, Nottingham Trent, Glamorgan, Gloucestershire, Hertfordshire, Leeds Metropolitan, Wolverhampton, Worcester, Royal Holloway, Westminster

OTHERS SIMILAR & RELATED London Metropolitan, Open, Aberystwyth, Hull, Leeds, Liverpool, Manchester, Lancaster, Glasgow, Chester, Bangor, Leeds Metropolitan, Nottingham Trent, Bath Spa, Newport, Anglia Ruskin, Greenwich, Middlesex, Edinburgh, Swansea, Aberdeen, Manchester Metropolitan, Goldsmiths, Leeds, Aston, Lincoln, Glamorgan, Napier, Greenwich, Bolton

SPANISH see Language & Literature, European

SPORTS see Biology, etc.

TECHNOLOGIES

MINERALS TECHNOLOGY Leeds, Exeter

METALLURGY Sheffield, Birmingham

CERAMICS & GLASSES Wolverhampton, SIHE, Sheffield, Canterbury Christ Church, UWIC, Buckinghamshire Chilterns, Bath Spa, Westminster

POLYMERS & TEXTILES Sheffield, Queen Mary,

Manchester Metropolitan, Napier, Manchester, Bolton, UCE, UWIC

Technology relating to other materials Loughborough, Plymouth, Buckinghamshire Chilterns, UCE

MARITIME TECHNOLOGY Southampton Solent, Newcastle, Southampton, Plymouth, Gloucestershire, Greenwich

INDUSTRIAL BIOTECHNOLOGY Aberdeen, Nottingham

OTHER SIMILAR & RELATED London South Bank, Leeds, Birmingham, Aston, Glasgow, Huddersfield, Manchester Metropolitan, Bournemouth, Loughborough, Bath Spa, SIHE, Loughborough, Coventry, Aston, Portsmouth, Wolverhampton, De Montfort

THEOLOGY see History, Philosophy, etc.

TOURISM see Business, Management & Administration

VETERINARY SCIENCES see Agriculture

ZOOLOGY see Biology, etc.

ENTRANCE REQUIREMENTS

However much you might like to choose from every university in this book, not every one will have you. The best way of knowing in advance which ones would welcome you with open arms and which would give you the finger is to check out the entrance requirements.

Who they'll accept is usually based largely on points that students collect by passing exams and qualifications. A Levels, obviously, but also Highers, AS Levels, NVQs and any one of the new bits of paper that pass for proof of intelligence.

Each grade in each qualification is worth a different number of points and, in theory, once you've got enough points for a particular course, you should stand a good chance of being accepted. **See the table below for the 'UCAS points tariff'.**

However, it's not that simple. (Is it ever?) All points are supposed to be equal, but some are a lot more equal than others.

First off, it matters what qualifications you've got. Whatever the points score says, some universities don't take AS Levels or vocational A Levels quite as seriously as an equal number of points at A Level.

Then there's the subject you've studied. In practice, points gained in a relevant subject count for more than points in something completely unrelated. For example, if you want to do a science degree, but all you've got is arts A Levels, only universities desperate for students aren't going to look at your application and snigger.

The whole system of points is more than a bit dubious at the edges, not least because many mature students will be accepted without traditional qualifications and the set-up of

modular courses throws a spanner in the works. Besides, come Clearing, universities with vacancies to fill will throw their list of requirements out the window and take what they can get.

Heed that huge health warning and the additional advice that it's best to check with the actual department you're applying to for what grades they'd be likely to want from you, given the subjects and qualifications you're taking.

Having said that, here's Push's exclusive guide to grades.

Have a look at the points table on the following pages, which is a quick reference to help you narrow down where to study, depending entirely on what points you already have or expect to get. It's a good tool for seeing the range of points required to get in where you want.

In the past, UK students took an average of three or four A Levels. Now you're more likely to sit four AS exams in the first year and three A2 exams in the second year of A Level studies, giving you up a maximum of 420 UCAS points. But, as Push likes to keep it simple, for now we've shown the maximum points as 360, which is what most universities are still dealing with.

Some universities offer a narrow range of points. For example, Oxford expects you to have a minimum of 340 points (AAB) for most courses, and Cambridge a minimum of 360 points (AAA). With anything from 240 to 340 (CCC to AAB), Aston's courses span a wider range of abilities and at Central Lancashire, the spread is even wider – from just 40 up to 300 (from a D to BBB).

Of course, remember that these are the minimum requirements for their various courses. Whether you've a penchant for Portuguese at Paisley or a hankering for Higher Maths at Heriot-Watt, when Push comes to shove you'll need to check with the department involved exactly what they want from you before you apply.

A LEVELS		HIGHERS		ADVANCED HIGHERS		VOCATIONAL A LEVELS		AS LEVELS		KEY SKILLS		BTEC DIPLOMA	
GRADE	PTS	GRADE	PTS	GRADE	PTS	GRADE	PTS	GRADE	PTS	GRADE	PTS	GRADE	PTS
A	120	A	72	A	120	A	240	A	60	4	30	DDD	360
B	100	B	60	B	100	B	200	B	50	3	20	MMM	240
C	80	C	48	C	80	C	160	C	40	2	10	PPP	120
D	60	D	42	D	72	D	120	D	30				
E	40					E	80	E	20				

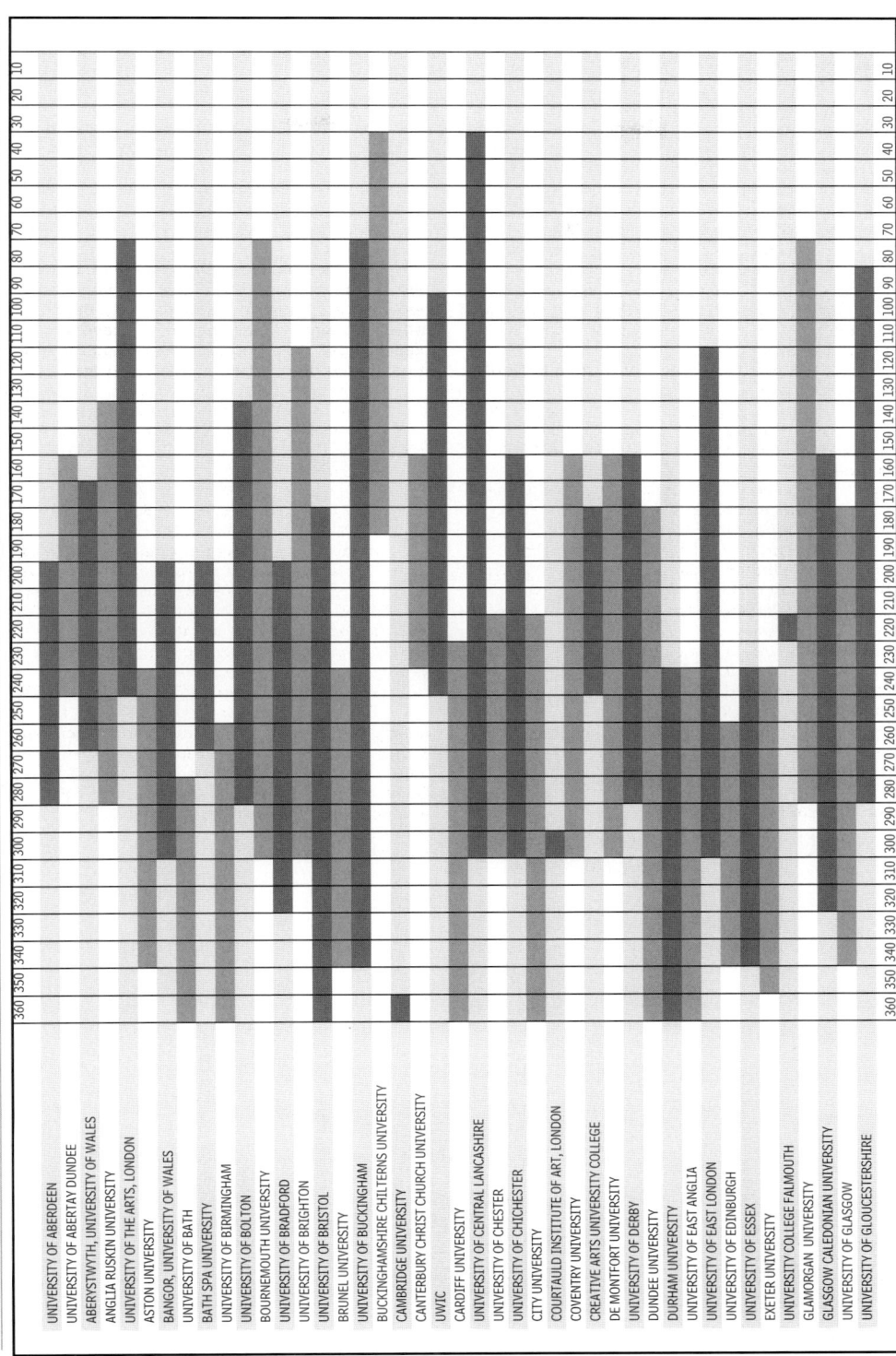

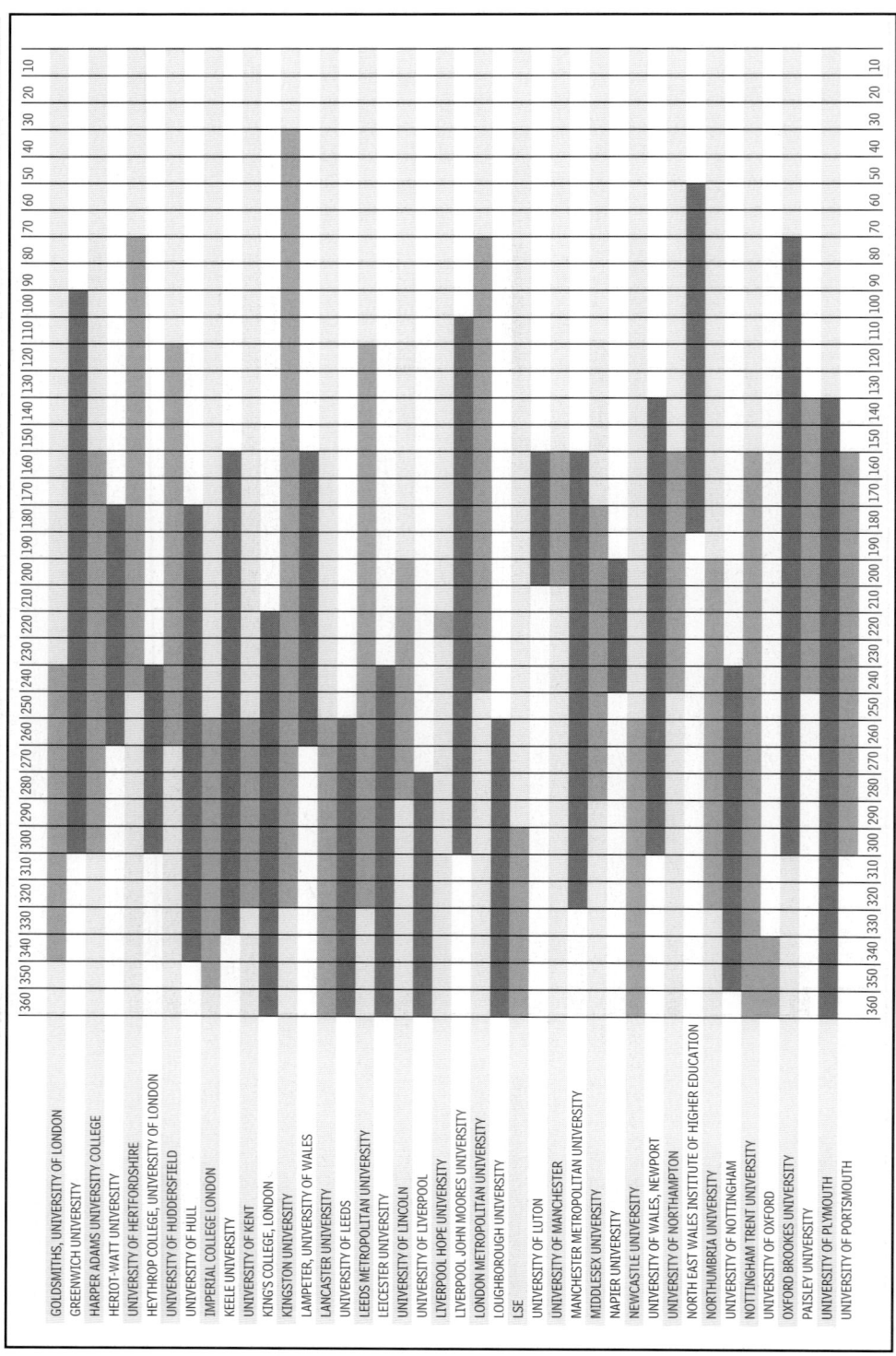

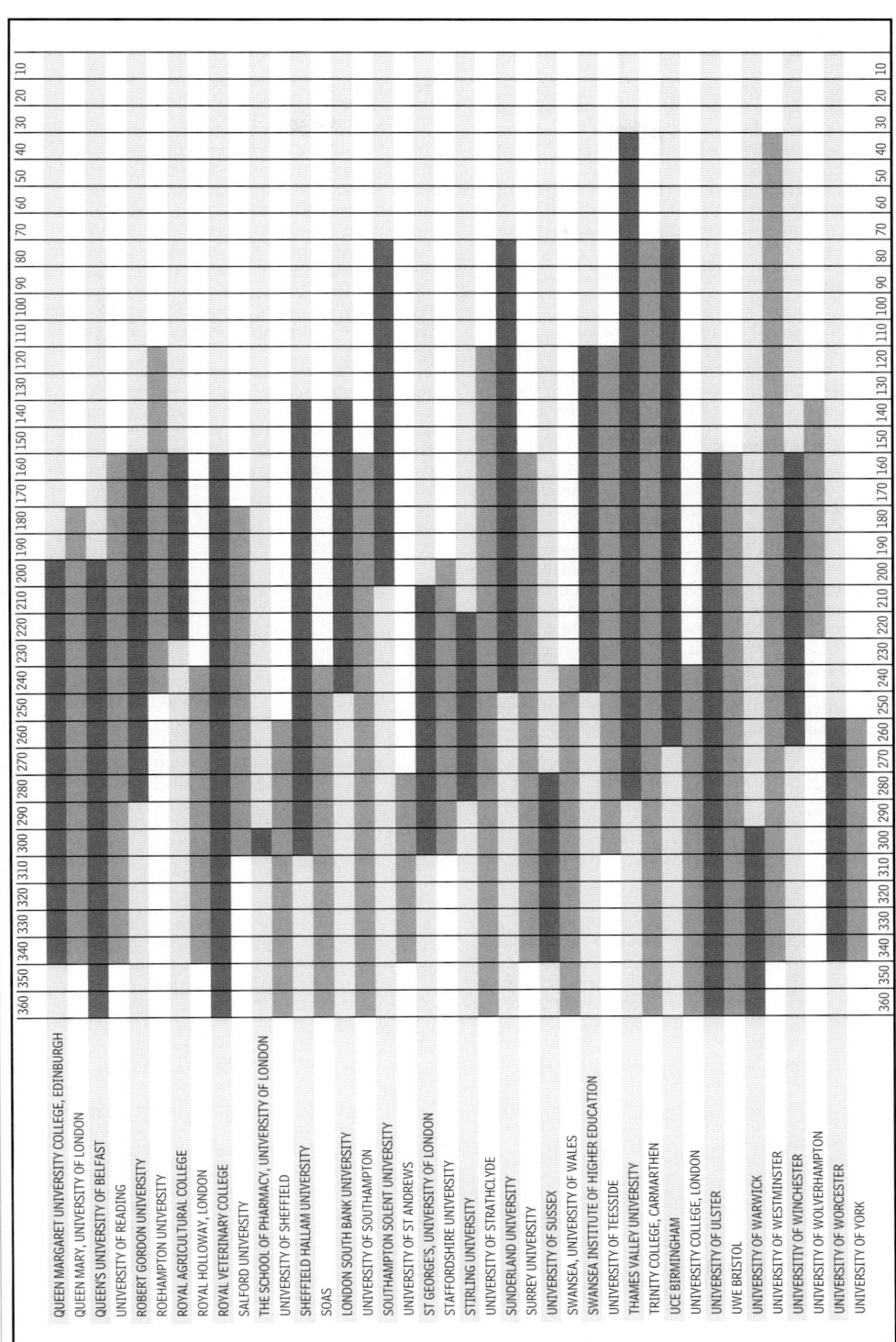

PUSH TABLES

Where would education be without tables? There's a great tradition from the Periodic Table, times tables and timetables to the Government's own league tables. And of course school desks, which are tables. Sort of.

Never one to buck a trend, Push introduces the tables to end all tables – the crucial guides to clubs and sports and the controversial reality of hard facts.

CLUBS

Some clubs and societies are available at most institutions. So, rather than bore you rigid listing them in every university profile, Push has detailed them in the following pages so you can see if there's rock at Reading or karate at Keele.

VITAL STATISTICS

What you want to do is get those universities up against the wall and see how they look side by side. So on the following pages Push has distilled the finest facts and charted them: the sex ratio; founding year; student numbers; the level of care; the numbers of those who enter through clearing; the numbers who flunk; cost and availability of housing; the cost of booze (average of a pint of beer, glass of wine and a Red Bull); employment prospects; and the average yearly student debt (including student loans).

For a fuller explanation of Push's statistical data, please see 'How to use Push' (page ???).

TOP 10S

Top 10s are eye candy – found everywhere from Top of the Pops to Viz, recording everything from the biggest-selling records to the world's fastest slugs. They're also an easy way to decode information without having to do much at all apart from raise the occasional eyebrow.

Push's Top 10s shouldn't be taken too seriously. Anyone choosing a university solely on the basis that it tops the charts for cheap beer has maybe not made a full and rounded decision. But all else being equal, it's as good a clincher as any.

Furthermore, taken together our Top 10s tell you quite a bit. Every university has its good and bad points and we help you pinpoint the strongest strengths and weakest weaknesses. (It also provides a quick guide to cheap rent, top totty and bargain beer.)

Universities (columns across the chart):

UNIVERSITY OF SOUTHAMPTON, SOAS, SHEFFIELD HALLAM UNIVERSITY, UNIVERSITY OF SHEFFIELD, SCHOOL OF PHARMACY, LONDON, SALFORD, ROYAL VETERINARY COLLEGE, ROYAL SCOT ACADEMY MUSIC/DRAMA, ROYAL HOLLOWAY, LONDON, ROYAL COLLEGE OF MUSIC, ROYAL AGRICULTURAL COLLEGE, ROYAL ACADEMY OF MUSIC, ROEHAMPTON, ROBERT GORDON, READING, QUEEN'S BELFAST, QUEEN MARY, LONDON, QUEEN MARGARET, EDINBURGH, PORTSMOUTH, PLYMOUTH, PAISLEY, OXFORD BROOKES, OXFORD, NOTTINGHAM TRENT, NOTTINGHAM, NORTHUMBRIA, NORTHAMPTON, NEWI, NEWPORT, NEWCASTLE, NAPIER, MIDDLESEX, MANCHESTER METROPOLITAN, MANCHESTER, LUTON, LSE, LOUGHBOROUGH, LONDON SOUTH BANK, LONDON METROPOLITAN, LIVERPOOL JOHN MOORES, LIVERPOOL HOPE, LIVERPOOL, LINCOLN, LEICESTER, LEEDS METROPOLITAN, LEEDS, LANCASTER, LAMPETER, KINGSTON, KING'S, KENT, KEELE, IMPERIAL, HULL, HUDDERSFIELD, HERTHROP, HERTFORDSHIRE, HERIOT-WATT, HARPER ADAMS, GREENWICH, GOLDSMITHS, GLOUCESTERSHIRE, GLASGOW CALEDONIAN, GLASGOW, GLAMORGAN, FALMOUTH, EXETER, ESSEX, EDINBURGH, EAST LONDON, EAST ANGLIA, DURHAM, DUNDEE, DERBY, DE MONTFORT, COVENTRY, COURTAULD INSTITUTE, CITY, CHICHESTER, CHESTER, CENTRAL LANCASHIRE, UCE, UWIC, CARDIFF, CANTERBURY CHRIST CHURCH, CAMBRIDGE, BUCKINGHAMSHIRE CHILTERNS, BUCKINGHAM, BRUNEL, UWE BRISTOL, BRISTOL, BRIGHTON, BRADFORD, BOURNEMOUTH, BOLTON, BIRMINGHAM, BIRKBECK, BATH SPA, BATH, BANGOR, ASTON, THE ARTS LONDON, ANGLIA RUSKIN, ABERYSTWYTH, ABERTAY DUNDEE, ABERDEEN

Societies (rows along the bottom):

NON-SPORTING: AFRICAN-CARIBBEAN, AMNESTY, ANIMAL RIGHTS, ANTI-RACIST/ANTI-NAZI, ASIAN, BUNAC, CATHOLIC, CHRISTIAN UNION, CINEMA CLUB, CONSERVATION, CONSERVATIVE, DANCE, DEBATING, DRAMA, FILM MAKING, GREEN/ENVIRONMENT, INDUSTRIAL SOCIETY, IRISH, ISLAMIC, JEWISH, LABOUR, LGBT, LIB DEM, (ORCHESTRAS), PEOPLE & PLANET, PHOTOGRAPHY, ROCK/INDIE MUSIC, SF & FANTASY, SOCIALIST WORKER

SPORTING: ARCHERY, ATHLETICS, BADMINTON, BASKETBALL, CANOEING, CHESS, CLIMBING, CRICKET, CROSS COUNTRY, CYCLING, FENCING, FOOTBALL, GOLF, HILL WALKING, HOCKEY, HORSE RIDING, JUDO, KARATE, NETBALL, ORIENTEERING, RUGBY, SAILING, SKIING, SQUASH, SUB-AQUA, SWIMMING, TAE KWON DO, TENNIS, TRAMPOLINING, VOLLEYBALL

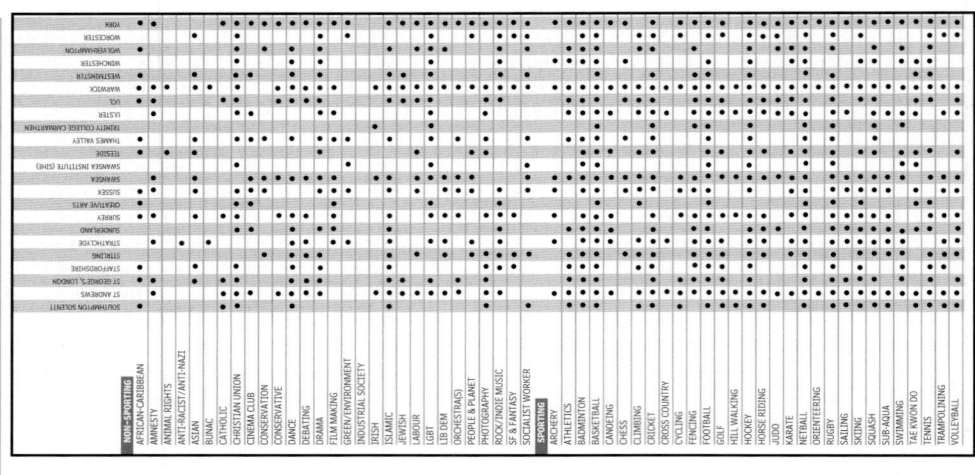

Universities (rows): YORK, WORCESTER, WOLVERHAMPTON, WINCHESTER, WESTMINSTER, WARWICK, UCL, ULSTER, TRINITY COLLEGE CARMARTHEN, THAMES VALLEY, TEESIDE, SWANSEA INSTITUTE (SIHE), SWANSEA, SUSSEX, CREATIVE ARTS, SURREY, SUNDERLAND, STRATHCLYDE, STIRLING, STAFFORDSHIRE, ST GEORGE'S, LONDON, ST ANDREWS, SOUTHAMPTON SOLENT

NON-SPORTING: AFRICAN-CARIBBEAN, AMNESTY, ANIMAL RIGHTS, ANTI-RACIST/ANTI-NAZI, ASIAN, BUNAC, CATHOLIC, CHRISTIAN UNION, CINEMA CLUB, CONSERVATIVE, DANCE, DEBATING, DRAMA, FILM MAKING, GREEN/ENVIRONMENT, INDUSTRIAL SOCIETY, IRISH, ISLAMIC, JEWISH, LABOUR, LGBT, LIB DEM, ORCHESTRA(S), PEOPLE & PLANET, PHOTOGRAPHY, ROCK/INDIE MUSIC, SF & FANTASY, SOCIALIST WORKER

SPORTING: ARCHERY, ATHLETICS, BADMINTON, BASKETBALL, CANOEING, CHESS, CLIMBING, CRICKET, CROSS COUNTRY, CYCLING, FENCING, FOOTBALL, GOLF, HILL WALKING, HOCKEY, HORSE RIDING, JUDO, KARATE, NETBALL, ORIENTEERING, RUGBY, SAILING, SKIING, SQUASH, SUB-AQUA, SWIMMING, TAE KWON DO, TENNIS, TRAMPOLINING, VOLLEYBALL

	SEX RATIO M:F	STAFF-STUDENT RATIO	FOUNDED	NUMBER OF UNDER-GRADUATES	NUMBER OF PART-TIME STUDENTS	NUMBER OF POSTGRADS	% IN THROUGH CLEARING	% OF MATURE STUDENTS	% OF OVERSEAS STUDENTS	NUMBER OF DISABLED STUDENTS	STATE: PRIVATE STUDENTS	AVERAGE ENTRY POINTS	AVERAGE HOUSING PER WEEK	% IN COLLEGE HOUSING	BOOZE INDEX	% OF GRADS UNEMPLOYED AFTER 6 MONTHS	NUMBER OF STUDENTS PER COUNSELLOR	FLUNK RATE (%)	AVERAGE DEBT PER YEAR
UNIVERSITY OF ABERDEEN	46:54	N/A	1495	10,300	1,060	3,159	6	19	19	165	84:16	300	£67.90	27	2.10	5	3,158	17	£1,509
UNIVERSITY OF ABERTAY DUNDEE	51:49	1:17	1888	4,009	506	450	10	32	19	90	97:3	N/A	£51.16	19	2.05	5	979	15	£1,897
ABERYSTWYTH, UNIVERSITY OF WALES	51:49	1:15	1872	6,163	1,493	757	7	12	8	290	94:6	303	£63.22	58	1.81	7	1,917	11	£2,860
ANGLIA RUSKIN UNIVERSITY	34:66	1:30	1989	11406	11307	4310	15	71	20	180	97:3	207	£75.22	11	1.70	5	3562	17	£4,097
UNIVERSITY OF THE ARTS, LONDON	40:60	1:17	1989	9,022	600	1,607	4	30	30	415	97:3	330	£97.11	19	2.34	9	3,123	13	£3,586
ASTON UNIVERSITY	49:51	1:15	1895	6,300	259	1,200	8	8	15	75	90:10	342	£59.67	38	1.75	6	935	8	£3,747
BANGOR, UNIVERSITY OF WALES	37:63	1:17	1884	6,221	2,210	1,933	2	29	9	295	94:6	288	£51.01	31	2.51	6	6,173	17	£4,004
UNIVERSITY OF BATH	54:46	1:14	1966	8,285	1,222	2,977	2	21	19	215	73:27	324	£67.04	31	2.15	6	3,118	4	£2,683
BATH SPA UNIVERSITY	30:70	1:22	1983	3,360	117	1,302	5	40	7	190	80:20	180	£76.75	42	1.47	6	1,349	12	£3,173
BIRKBECK, UNIVERSITY OF LONDON	48:52	1:18	1823	6	4,030	3,436	N/A	99	5	0	N/A	N/A	£92.50	0	2.50	N/A	1,868	N/A	£776
UNIVERSITY OF BIRMINGHAM	43:57	1:14	1900	19,548	4,180	7,500	4	12	25	375	80:20	320	£60.28	30	1.76	4	4,856	12	£3,546
UNIVERSITY OF BOLTON	51:49	1:15	1982	2,641	1,588	1,388	25	86	25	35	97:3	174	£43.08	21	2.10	7	9,646	32	£3,356
BOURNEMOUTH UNIVERSITY	45:55	1:12	1976	10,106	3,569	1,526	7	21	8	410	93:7	259	£86.69	15	2.07	21	3,354	13	£3,162
UNIVERSITY OF BRADFORD	49:51	1:22	1966	6,900	1,645	1,220	18	32	22	140	93:7	268	£46.80	23	1.78	7	3,350	19	£3,001
BRIGHTON UNIVERSITY	63:37	1:22	1853	15,937	4,440	4,080	10	51	13	365	92:8	240	£60.53	58	2.31	8	4,448	15	£1,895
UNIVERSITY OF BRISTOL	47:53	1:10	1876	10,600	3,900	2,663	0	10	20	180	69:31	280	£73.80	36	2.05	6	3,803	4	£2,224
BRUNEL UNIVERSITY	55:45	1:19	1966	8,933	848	2,515	23	25	18	215	79:8	276	£72.90	36	2.31	11	2,968	12	£3,403
UNIVERSITY OF BUCKINGHAM	45:55	1:9	1974	486	40	137	0	61	75	N/A	N/A	220	£78.87	72	1.91	11	428	4	£6,311
BUCKINGHAMSHIRE CHILTERNS UNIVERSITY	43:57	1:10	1893	5,830	2,940	320	19	30	13	185	N/A	140	£52.60	19	2.33	10	1,425	12	£2,983
CAMBRIDGE UNIVERSITY	52:48	1:12	1284	11,982	0	5,499	0	7	13	50	57:43	520	£66.67	N/A	1.59	3	1,665	1	£1,488
CANTERBURY CHRIST CHURCH UNIVERSITY	28:72	N/A	1962	6,438	5,097	3,089	21	50	7	170	97:3	160	£63.65	37	1.85	4	12,075	16	£3,611
CARDIFF UNIVERSITY	44:56	1:6	1883	15,548	292	3,882	3	15	17	250	85:15	375	£57.44	33	1.87	5	3,263	5	£3,457
UNIVERSITY OF CENTRAL LANCASHIRE	47:53	1:18	1828	11,894	2,951	7,005	21	26	27	360	59:41	220	£58.61	10	1.84	6	5,006	19	£3,937
CHESTER UNIVERSITY	38:62	1:19	1839	5,321	510	1,579	3	19	3	75	97:3	282	£69.17	21	2.06	3	4,770	13	£3,137
UNIVERSITY OF CHICHESTER	32:68	1:17	1839	2,620	315	1,133	5	40	4	145	95:5	236	£65.46	13	2.11	9	411	9	£3,115
CITY UNIVERSITY	43:57	1:14	1894	6,506	1,730	4,568	N/A	42	29	5	30:70	320	£88.57	11	2.41	5	2,170	15	£2,825
COURTAULD INSTITUTE OF ART	40:60	1:8	1932	150	0	200	0	10	15	5	40:60	478	£90.00	27	2.18	5	350	1	£1,575
COVENTRY UNIVERSITY	53:47	1:15	1843	9,635	1,508	2,384	14	30	15	290	96:4	230	£58.77	23	2.57	8	1,965	18	£3,831
CREATIVE ARTS UNIVERSITY COLLEGE	N/A	N/A	2005	N/A	N/A	N/A	16	26	5	N/A	N/A	N/A	N/A	N/A	N/A	N/A	493	8	£4,713
DE MONTFORT UNIVERSITY	41:59	1:19	1969	12,570	1,519	3,751	16	26	5	365	96:4	229	£56.34	22	1.88	9	3,416	16	£2,495
UNIVERSITY OF DERBY	59:41	1:22	1851	8,592	2,951	2,476	N/A	33	3	170	95:5	210	£48.03	24	1.88	6	1,195	27	£2,960
DUNDEE UNIVERSITY	37:63	1:10	1967	9,454	1,417	4,993	7	29	9	140	N/A	240	£67.50	14	2.21	4	3,789	16	£1,461
DURHAM UNIVERSITY	47:53	1:19	1832	11,410	97	1,047	3	7	15	80	61:33	426	£85.78	56	1.74	16	1,563	4	£1,975
UNIVERSITY OF EAST ANGLIA	39:61	1:17	1963	8,508	2,461	2,127	7	53	15	125	88:12	276	£56.39	40	1.86	7	1,318	13	£2,601
UNIVERSITY OF EAST LONDON	45:55	1:29	1970	8,980	3,052	5,186	46	75	25	475	96:2	210	£80.10	10	2.04	8	3,138	26	£2,313
UNIVERSITY OF EDINBURGH	44:56	1:19	1582	15,870	840	5,200	5	13	18	420	N/A	240	£72.21	31	1.94	8	2,223	6	£2,884
UNIVERSITY OF ESSEX	51:49	1:14	1964	5,610	234	2,211	11	17	38	475	96:4	311	£60.65	53	1.82	9	713	14	£2,683
EXETER UNIVERSITY	48:52	1:14	1955	8,460	1,509	3,589	5	10	13	345	76:24	360	£87.13	73	1.67	5	3,201	6	£3,199
UNIVERSITY COLLEGE FALMOUTH	42:58	1:3	1902	1,706	58	193	3	30	9	225	93:7	220	£70.90	18	2.04	N/A	482	17	£3,617
GLAMORGAN UNIVERSITY	49:51	1:17	1913	9,833	8,521	2,972	20	40	13	180	97:3	210	£47.00	11	1.93	6	3,103	25	£2,170
UNIVERSITY OF GLASGOW	42:58	1:17	1451	15,890	4,565	3,780	2	15	13	215	86:14	380	£63.45	22	1.97	4	5,620	14	£2,419
GLASGOW CALEDONIAN UNIVERSITY	39:61	1:10	1875	10,662	2,836	2,362	3	44	3	145	97:3	285	£65.62	6	2.03	7	2,407	18	£3,496
UNIVERSITY OF GLOUCESTERSHIRE	45:55	1:20	2001	6,446	3,204	1,573	6	30	7	185	96:4	200	£61.04	21	1.94	5	4,810	14	£2,861

	SEX RATIO M:F	STAFF:STUDENT RATIO	FOUNDED	NUMBER OF UNDER-GRADUATES	NUMBER OF PART-TIME STUDENTS	NUMBER OF POSTGRADS	% IN THROUGH CLEARING	% OF MATURE STUDENTS	% OF OVERSEAS STUDENTS	NUMBER OF DISABLED STUDENTS	STATE:PRIVATE STUDENTS	AVERAGE ENTRY POINTS	AVERAGE HOUSING PER WEEK	% IN COLLEGE HOUSING	BOOZE INDEX	% OF GRADS UNEMPLOYED AFTER 6 MONTHS	NUMBER OF STUDENTS PER COUNSELLOR	FLUNK RATE (%)	AVERAGE DEBT PER YEAR
GOLDSMITHS, UNIVERSITY OF LONDON	33:67	1:10	1891	3,406	1,255	2,612	19	34	15	75	91:9	285	£74.83	28	2.23	3	2,658	18	£1,923
GREENWICH UNIVERSITY	47:53	1:20	1890	9,121	1,781	5,203	21	46	19	190	95:5	200	£95.67	11	2.20	14	5,072	25	£3,343
HARPER ADAMS UNIVERSITY COLLEGE	62:38	1:7	1901	929	11	83	3	16	4	75	78:22	220	£75.54	60	1.70	3	2,034	13	£2,459
HERIOT-WATT UNIVERSITY	60:40	1:14	1821	5,100	250	1,600	7	39	28	100	91:9	N/A	£70.53	32	2.12	10	6,825	17	£1,655
UNIVERSITY OF HERTFORDSHIRE	45:55	1:30	1952	20,300	3,800	3,330	15	23	11	250	97:3	230	£69.59	17	1.95	12	4,255	18	£2,869
HEYTHROP COLLEGE, UNIVERSITY OF LONDON	53:47	1:8	1614	277	4	359	12	26	8	N/A	80:20	240	£104.47	13	2.24	8	638	17	£2,738
UNIVERSITY OF HUDDERSFIELD	44:56	1:8	1992	8,242	1,219	3,404	13	55	8	235	97:3	189	£54.09	21	1.83	5	3,064	20	£3,815
UNIVERSITY OF HULL	47:53	1:15	1927	9,769	7,575	2,387	10	30	10	380	93:7	253	£54.01	26	1.85	6	3,596	12	£4,113
IMPERIAL COLLEGE, LONDON	63:37	1:9	1907	7,850	0	3,827	3	13	33	25	59:41	341	£113.02	39	1.74	4	4,757	4	£4,542
KEELE UNIVERSITY	40:60	1:11	1962	5,500	12	3,000	6	15	8	70	83:9	240	£61.28	58	1.79	4	1,547	10	£2,335
UNIVERSITY OF KENT	49:51	1:16	1965	9,442	2,970	1,504	8	18	10	185	88:12	321	£74.39	42	2.04	3	2,072	13	£3,446
KING'S COLLEGE, LONDON	40:60	1:9	1829	12,101	1,743	5,693	7	29	15	115	71:21	389	£78.36	27	2.49	4	2,667	7	£3,099
KINGSTON UNIVERSITY	48:52	1:11	1971	12,192	1,691	2,552	N/A	32	14	240	92:8	200	£82.96	20	1.84	4	3,897	17	£3,092
LAMPETER, UNIVERSITY OF WALES	39:61	1:8	1822	829	118	503	8	37	11	105	60:40	200	£47.84	61	1.82	9	464	23	£2,448
LANCASTER UNIVERSITY	47:53	1:15	1964	8,216	42	2,834	9	8	24	185	91:9	293	£60.68	57	2.10	6	1,582	5	£2,803
UNIVERSITY OF LEEDS	45:55	1:15	1904	22,175	1,519	6,210	4	10	9	525	74:26	387	£65.73	32	1.94	10	2,649	8	£2,883
LEEDS METROPOLITAN UNIVERSITY	49:51	1:18	1970	14,151	1,871	3,241	10	21	10	320	97:3	236	£58.29	22	1.94	4	2,618	15	£3,458
LEICESTER UNIVERSITY	47:53	1:13	1921	7,853	170	8,448	5	10	8	175	88:12	370	£66.45	52	1.80	5	660	4	£3,556
UNIVERSITY OF LINCOLN	45:55	1:18	1861	8,292	662	692	12	49	3	365	97:3	247	£79.81	16	2.19	18	3,105	18	£3,112
UNIVERSITY OF LIVERPOOL	50:50	1:13	1881	13,623	622	927	5	21	11	215	93:7	340	£62.72	25	1.84	4	4,954	6	£4,730
LIVERPOOL HOPE UNIVERSITY	34:66	1:23	1844	4,176	991	1,180	N/A	30	6	200	N/A	220	£51.82	26	1.67	6	2,926	24	£3,616
LIVERPOOL JOHN MOORES UNIVERSITY	46:54	1:22	1970	12,608	1,704	3,579	15	24	8	45	95:5	220	£53.45	21	1.72	8	2,005	23	£3,421
LONDON METROPOLITAN UNIVERSITY	45:55	1:10	2002	35,000	15,000	2,800	28	50	30	425	97:3	180	£80.34	3	2.25	17	6,471	26	£4,133
LONDON SOUTH BANK UNIVERSITY	41:59	1:20	1892	8,380	7,970	4,937	30	65	10	305	97:3	140	£99.61	14	2.42	9	0	26	£4,255
LOUGHBOROUGH UNIVERSITY	61:39	1:17	1908	10,171	341	2,060	5	6	17	235	77:23	310	£78.07	47	2.34	7	2,067	6	£2,138
LSE	52:48	1:8	1895	3,808	51	4,408	0	9	47	35	62:38	340	£95.40	36	1.93	5	2,060	5	£510
UNIVERSITY OF LUTON	40:60	1:24	1993	5,956	1,896	1,825	16	40	23	60	99:1	191	£57.03	18	1.73	12	2,910	23	£1,824
UNIVERSITY OF MANCHESTER	46:54	N/A	1824	21,690	725	10,700	8	11	13	520	80:20	404	£60.58	35	2.04	11	2,848	8	£4,507
MANCHESTER METROPOLITAN UNIVERSITY	41:59	1:22	1970	20,831	1,822	6,481	N/A	23	6	360	95:5	180	£56.58	18	2.02	5	4,704	20	£3,690
MIDDLESEX UNIVERSITY	43:57	1:18	1973	11,144	1,375	3,884	30	47	31	330	80:20	220	£76.29	17	2.12	13	3,929	25	£2,676
NAPIER UNIVERSITY	47:53	1:15	1992	8,531	2,549	2,102	11	67	24	200	95:5	200	£71.60	11	1.85	11	2,977	22	£2,032
NEWCASTLE UNIVERSITY	49:51	1:14	1834	13,158	109	4,014	6	13	15	365	67:33	338	£64.56	31	1.90	4	4,922	7	£3,144
NEWPORT, UNIVERSITY OF WALES	47:53	1:10	1841	2,941	6,123	1,100	20	60	5	145	99:1	230	£50.75	22	1.84	7	4,002	23	£3,458
NORTHAMPTON UNIVERSITY	37:63	N/A	1999	7,230	2,625	275	10	29	7	220	73:20	180	£48.78	22	1.88	19	645	19	£3,686
NORTH EAST WALES INSTITUTE (NEWI)	48:52	1:13	1975	2,179	2,882	480	10	60	6	185	99:1	160	£55.42	13	1.95	N/A	2,050	27	£3,886
NORTHUMBRIA UNIVERSITY	45:55	1:20	1969	13,715	3,873	4,804	33	33	13	230	91:9	200	£63.51	13	2.20	5	5,696	15	£2,397
UNIVERSITY OF NOTTINGHAM	51:49	1:12	1881	19,656	4,161	5,909	7	6	22	365	73:20	411	£73.02	36	1.94	4	2,513	4	£4,008
NOTTINGHAM TRENT UNIVERSITY	50:50	1:15	1992	15,926	3,531	5,317	12	13	5	320	92:8	220	£58.79	21	2.09	3	4,183	15	£3,609
THE OPEN UNIVERSITY	41:59	1:81	1969	0	149,744	19,239	N/A	88	5	10348	N/A	N/A	N/A	N/A	N/A	N/A	N/A	N/A	N/A
UNIVERSITY OF OXFORD	53:47	1:8	1150	11,225	0	6,491	0	6	12	170	52:48	480	N/A	N/A	1.58	5	2,531	2	£2,774
OXFORD BROOKES UNIVERSITY	40:60	1:12	1865	8,840	4,160	5,040	13	64	18	405	75:25	168	£80.70	42	1.76	7	1,388	15	£2,409
PAISLEY UNIVERSITY	35:65	1:20	1897	5,988	5,621	1,685	14	46	4	120	98:2	168	£54.05	13	2.25	6	2,621	22	£3,546
UNIVERSITY OF PLYMOUTH	39:61	N/A	1970	16,715	6,895	1,505	18	43	8	910	92:8	260	£75.60	8	2.31	9	6,384	14	£2,960
UNIVERSITY OF PORTSMOUTH	55:45	1:20	1992	13,429	1,485	4,020	1	35	11	495	93:7	240	£61.75	21	2.49	9	3,638	19	£4,083

Institution	SEX RATIO M:F	STAFF STUDENT RATIO	FOUNDED	NUMBER OF UNDER-GRADUATES	NUMBER OF PART-TIME STUDENTS	NUMBER OF POSTGRADS	% IN THROUGH CLEARING	% OF MATURE STUDENTS	% OF OVERSEAS STUDENTS	NUMBER OF DISABLED STUDENTS	STATE: PRIVATE STUDENTS	AVERAGE ENTRY POINTS	AVERAGE HOUSING PER WEEK	% IN COLLEGE HOUSING	BIQUE INDEX	% OF GRADS UNEMPLOYED AFTER 6 MONTHS	NUMBER OF STUDENTS PER COUNSELLOR	FLUNK RATE (%)	AVERAGE DEBT PER YEAR
QUEEN MARGARET UNIVERSITY COLLEGE, EDINBURGH	23:77	1:18	1875	2,950	239	445	14	39	11	95	93:7	289	£65.70	19	1.90	6	3,515	13	£2,873
QUEEN MARY, UNIVERSITY OF LONDON	51:49	1:8	1887	8,532	526	2,454	8	22	23	45	86:14	328	£91.44	27	2.28	5	3,214	10	£1,715
QUEEN'S UNIVERSITY BELFAST	42:58	1:16	1845	12,756	1,387	4,174	5	9	6	314	99:1	355	£47.94	12	1.56	3	11,990	13	£3,523
UNIVERSITY OF READING	46:54	1:6	1892	11,198	2,911	6,320	1	19	16	285	83:17	362	£80.53	40	2.09	5	1,581	10	£3,100
ROBERT GORDON UNIVERSITY	42:58	1:10	1992	6,729	1,742	3,411	15	28	20	105	94:6	240	£66.08	18	2.08	2	5,506	17	£1,747
ROEHAMPTON UNIVERSITY	23:77	1:21	1841	5,784	270	1,566	10	26	7	285	95:5	236	£78.68	26	1.90	6	3,743	17	£4,555
ROYAL ACADEMY OF MUSIC	43:57	1:1	1822	305	0	328	0	10	40	0	75:25	320	£111.13	3	2.19	6	633	6	£2,246
ROYAL AGRICULTURAL COLLEGE	61:39	1:13	1845	670	5	175	1	25	22	45	40:60	210	£95.00	46	2.00	16	0	5	£1,840
ROYAL COLLEGE OF MUSIC	47:53	N/A	1882	360	0	230	N/A	5	35	5	50:50	N/A	£97.21	28	2.32	2	605	3	£2,780
ROYAL HOLLOWAY	40:60	1:15	1886	5,494	480	1,602	14	7	26	80	N/A	340	£74.55	39	1.65	6	988	6	£2,780
ROYAL SCOTTISH ACADEMY OF MUSIC AND DRAMA	33:67	1:1	1847	560	0	115	0	16	14	35	N/A	N/A	N/A	78	1.83	1	675	11	£1,644
ROYAL VETERINARY COLLEGE	80:20	1:2	1791	1,153	11	338	8	13	8	10	40:60	450	£90.10	60	2.12	2	272	0	£3,807
SALFORD UNIVERSITY	45:55	1:16	1896	15,369	2,800	2,928	10	33	16	310	97:3	200	£50.74	21	2.07	10	0	17	£4,256
THE SCHOOL OF PHARMACY, UNIVERSITY OF LONDON	37:63	1:13	1842	720	0	200	1	20	25	5	70:30	300	N/A	75	1.45	0	920	4	£1,603
UNIVERSITY OF SHEFFIELD	45:55	1:14	1905	16,216	2,826	6,902	9	9	17	330	83:17	400	£63.93	31	1.73	9	3,057	8	£3,621
SHEFFIELD HALLAM UNIVERSITY	47:53	1:23	1969	15,246	1,930	7,261	15	63	2	605	95:5	264	£57.19	11	1.86	7	2,235	12	£2,609
SOAS	41:59	1:11	1916	1,925	2	1,694	5	26	37	35	69:31	330	£112.35	40	2.15	8	2,413	13	£2,598
UNIVERSITY OF SOUTHAMPTON	39:61	1:14	1952	13,810	2,375	5,370	9	16	16	535	81:19	389	£60.11	40	1.94	6	1,594	7	£2,767
SOUTHAMPTON SOLENT UNIVERSITY	56:44	1:22	1984	8,684	1,730	540	13	24	11	285	96:4	230	£71.32	24	2.13	9	2,967	17	£3,547
UNIVERSITY OF ST ANDREWS	59:41	1:10	1413	5,788	157	1,053	0	23	29	160	67:33	320	£84.60	43	2.41	8	2,768	2	£2,136
ST GEORGE'S HOSPITAL MEDICAL SCHOOL, LONDON	45:55	1:7	1752	1,340	1,085	64	9	40	10	0	45:55	305	£80.32	19	2.31	1	936	10	£5,217
STAFFORDSHIRE UNIVERSITY	51:49	1:20	1970	8,914	3,880	2,557	22	55	14	235	97:3	211	£47.70	21	1.92	10	1,578	21	£3,334
STIRLING UNIVERSITY	42:58	1:15	1967	6,030	1,160	2,020	6	15	14	125	91:9	320	£61.03	56	1.43	6	4,315	13	£3,060
UNIVERSITY OF STRATHCLYDE	44:56	1:17	1796	11,530	2,510	2,875	10	16	17	180	90:10	320	£56.61	14	2.04	10	1,842	17	£1,887
SUNDERLAND UNIVERSITY	55:45	1:18	1901	7,355	8,620	2,102	19	47	20	150	97:3	159	£54.65	23	1.83	6	3,581	27	£3,426
SURREY UNIVERSITY	41:59	1:15	1966	6,633	495	4,579	4	29	16	80	88:12	328	£74.82	61	1.81	3	1,146	11	£1,620
SUSSEX UNIVERSITY	42:58	1:13	1961	6,976	451	3,136	2	26	24	330	85:15	345	£67.79	38	2.01	6	2,297	11	£3,914
SWANSEA UNIVERSITY	42:58	1:13	1920	8,074	515	1,601	12	17	8	220	93:7	304	£52.47	32	2.11	6	2,804	10	£3,715
SWANSEA INSTITUTE OF HIGHER EDUCATION (SIHE)	56:44	N/A	1992	2,812	1,591	665	N/A	N/A	7	55	N/A	230	£40.38	11	N/A	N/A	2,136	20	£3,097
UNIVERSITY OF TEESSIDE	41:59	1:17	1992	6,702	1,256	2,341	8	35	9	190	98:2	217	£39.92	19	1.59	8	2,418	19	£2,440
THAMES VALLEY UNIVERSITY	35:65	N/A	1992	4,463	1,016	2,113	15	75	16	50	98:2	205	£115.91	21	2.65	9	2,024	25	£4,449
TRINITY COLLEGE CARMARTHEN	24:76	N/A	1848	1,242	514	254	N/A	57	5	35	N/A	N/A	£59.25	48	1.87	5	1,753	26	£4,704
UCE BIRMINGHAM	40:60	1:15	1971	12,757	6,341	3,680	10	54	5	200	97:3	240	£52.85	16	1.84	7	7,843	16	£4,393
UNIVERSITY COLLEGE, LONDON	47:53	1:3	1826	11,894	190	7,005	9	26	27	165	59:41	410	£108.59	29	2.17	5	3,453	7	£3,118
UNIVERSITY OF ULSTER	40:60	1:18	1968	15,192	3,027	4,816	1	21	12	375	100:0	228	£53.77	17	2.08	5	4,782	17	£3,251
UWE, BRISTOL	41:59	1:20	1992	15,229	931	7,388	6	22	8	285	87:13	260	£64.93	27	2.26	7	3,847	16	£3,509
UWIC	47:53	1:15	1976	6,000	1,500	2,000	10	45	5	360	95:5	177	N/A	6	1.62	6	1,675	16	£4,056
UNIVERSITY OF WARWICK	49:51	1:12	1964	10,266	1,257	7,485	3	36	33	115	77:23	435	£64.75	50	2.27	6	2,205	5	£4,817
UNIVERSITY OF WESTMINSTER	46:54	1:15	1838	10,900	6,450	5,750	30	32	28	180	94:6	108	£97.91	11	2.06	10	1,381	23	£2,215
UNIVERSITY OF WINCHESTER	35:65	1:22	1840	2,953	189	1,351	10	21	4	140	96:4	220	£78.57	30	1.99	N/A	800	11	£4,100
UNIVERSITY OF WOLVERHAMPTON	42:58	1:28	1983	12,461	7,135	4,026	N/A	67	16	210	96:4	200	£45.96	19	2.01	8	4,456	24	£3,671
UNIVERSITY OF WORCESTER	24:76	N/A	1947	3,462	533	1,501	9	33	4	110	96:4	220	£55.65	24	2.26	10	2,809	18	£3,527
UNIVERSITY OF YORK	46:54	1:16	1963	7,631	1,117	2,778	5	12	19	140	80:20	418	£58.25	40	1.75	6	1,567	5	£4,800

TOP TEN: CHEAPEST CAMPUS PINT

- EXETER
- SCHOOL OF PHARMACY
- DURHAM
- UWIC
- LIVERPOOL
- LIVERPOOL HOPE
- LINCOLN
- GLASGOW
- BRISTOL
- ROYAL VETERINARY COLLEGE

TOP TEN: HIGHEST MALE SEX RATIO

- SIHE
- ST ANDREWS
- ROYAL VETERINARY COLLEGE
- ROYAL AGRICULTURAL COLLEGE
- LOUGHBOROUGH
- IMPERIAL
- HERIOT-WATT
- HARPER ADAMS
- DERBY
- BRIGHTON

TOP TEN: CHEAPEST COLLEGE ACCOMMODATION

- TEESSIDE
- CANTERBURY CHRIST CHURCH
- SIHE
- PAISLEY
- ULSTER
- LAMPETER
- NEWPORT
- SALFORD
- WORCESTER
- BOLTON

TOP TEN: LOWEST EXTERNAL RENT

- BOLTON
- BRADFORD
- SIHE
- TEESSIDE
- WOLVERHAMPTON
- STAFFORDSHIRE
- BANGOR
- QUEEN'S BELFAST
- DERBY
- GLAMORGAN

TOP TEN: HIGHEST FEMALE SEX RATIO

- BATH SPA
- CANTERBURY CHRIST CHURCH
- CHICHESTER
- GOLDSMITHS
- LIVERPOOL HOPE
- QUEEN MARGARET, EDINBURGH
- ROEHAMPTON
- RSAMD
- TRINITY CARMARTHEN
- WORCESTER

TOP TEN: LOWEST UNEMPLOYMENT AFTER 6 MONTHS

- SCHOOL OF PHARMACY
- RSAMD
- ST GEORGE'S HOSPITAL MED SCHOOL
- ROBERT GORDON
- ROYAL COLLEGE OF MUSIC
- ROYAL VETERINARY COLLEGE
- ABERDEEN
- CHESTER
- GOLDSMITHS
- HARPER ADAMS

TOP TEN: HIGHEST PROPORTION LIVING IN

- RSAMD
- SCHOOL OF PHARMACY
- EXETER
- BUCKINGHAM
- SURREY
- LAMPETER
- ROYAL VETERINARY COLLEGE
- HARPER ADAMS
- KEELE
- BRIGHTON

TOP TEN: BEST AT STUDENT SPORT

- LOUGHBOROUGH
- BATH
- BIRMINGHAM
- UWIC
- DURHAM
- CAMBRIDGE
- NOTTINGHAM
- OXFORD
- EDINBURGH
- NORTHUMBRIA

TOP TEN: HIGHEST PRIVATE:STATE SCHOOL RATIO

- CITY
- COURTAULD INSTITUTE
- ROYAL AGRICULTURAL COLLEGE
- ROYAL VETERINARY COLLEGE
- ST GEORGE'S HOSPITAL MED SCHOOL
- ROYAL COLLEGE OF MUSIC
- OXFORD
- CAMBRIDGE
- CENTRAL LANCASHIRE
- IMPERIAL COLLEGE, LONDON

TOP TEN: HIGHEST PROPORTION LIVING OUT

- BIRKBECK
- ROYAL ACADEMY OF MUSIC
- LONDON MET
- GLASGOW CALEDONIAN
- UWIC
- PLYMOUTH
- EAST LONDON
- CENTRAL LANCASHIRE
- WESTMINSTER
- SIHE

TOP TEN: HIGHEST PERCENTAGE OF MATURE STUDENTS

- BIRKBECK
- OPEN UNIVERSITY
- BOLTON
- THAMES VALLEY
- EAST LONDON
- ANGLIA RUSKIN
- WOLVERHAMPTON
- NAPIER
- SOUTH BANK
- OXFORD BROOKS

TOP TEN: HIGHEST FLUNK RATE

- BOLTON
- ABERTAY DUNDEE
- NEWI
- SUNDERLAND
- DERBY
- EAST LONDON
- SOUTH BANK
- TRINITY COLLEGE, CARMARTHEN
- THAMES VALLEY
- LONDON METROPOLITAN

WHEN PUSH COMES TO SHOVE

In the world of higher education, there's a whole language of weird words and interminable terminology. Ever true to our no-nonsense, cut-the-brown-smelly-stuff approach, The Push Guide takes you on a ramble through the jargon jungle, explaining all the terms to help anyone pass themselves off as a student.

THE 1994 GROUP A band of about 20 universities that likes to think of themselves as fairies on the top of the Christmas tree of higher education. Like the better-known Russell Group, there's some truth to their claims because they attract a lot of moolah for research and have high teaching standards. Although a couple of universities have joined both groups (more party invitations, we suppose), the 1994 Group universities tend to be slightly smaller, which one could argue, makes them less prestigious.

A LEVELS Strictly speaking A Levels are split in two: AS levels in Year 12 (lower sixth) and A2s in Year 13, but however you slice it, A Levels are the exams most students take at the end of school or college (further education) in England and Wales. Usually students heading for university take three or four A Levels and, unless there are other factors, finding a place will be tough with fewer than at least two. Those other factors might well include having other qualifications, such as Highers in Scotland or an International Baccalaureate earned abroad or other qualifications such as vocational A Levels and AS Levels.

ACCOUNTANCY/ACCOUNTING Not a professional qualification, just a background course giving prospective accountants the necessary insight into finance, investment, tax, management and business.

ADMISSIONS The admissions office of any university or college handles the applications and enrolments. That's the department to ask for when you phone up to talk about getting in.

ALUMNI 'Old boys' and 'old girls', ie. former students. Singular: alumnus. Feminine singular: alumna. Feminine plural: alumnae. Neuter ablative plural: go ask a Latin student.

AMERICAN STUDIES Often dismissed as a doss subject (eg. 'you just watch films and listen to old jazz records') this is a multi-disciplinary subject, covering the culture (what culture?), history and current affairs of the US. Usually includes a period spent in the States – a big draw for people who like Oreo cookies, country music and drive-by shootings.

ARCHAEOLOGY You might think three years risking the wrath of disturbed Egyptian mummies is a cool way to spend a degree course, but archaeology courses are more 'Time Team' than 'Indiana Jones', using a combination of history, science, languages and other disciplines, as well as practical fieldwork.

ARCHITECTURE Architecture requires a combination of technical knowledge of forms and structures (sciencey) with creative and aesthetic talents (arty), as well as history, economics and environmental studies.

ART(S) Arts subjects include pretty much anything creative. You know, painting, drama, music and all that. It often overlaps with humanities.

ATHLETICS UNION/SPORTS UNION The student organisation that runs student sports clubs and sometimes sports facilities. They're usually hot-beds of sexism, alcohol abuse and hairy chests... and that's just the women.

BACHELOR of... Arts, Science, Education, Engineering, etc. At English and Welsh universities, this is the degree that most undergraduate students are heading for. When you get it, you can put BA, BSc, BEd, BEng or whatever else is appropriate at the end of your name, but if you feel you have to boast about it like that, anyone else who's got one will think you're a bit of a nob – and so will people who haven't.

BALLS Big black-tie and posh frock parties, of course. Why? What did you think it meant? Many student balls include not only a slap-up dinner and much drinking, but also bands (often including quite big has-been names), a club night, casinos, fun-fairs, cabaret acts, fortune-tellers, snogging and vomiting. Hardy ball-goers often party all night and occasionally the event is rounded off with a champagne breakfast and 'survivors' photo' (not a pretty sight).

BOPS A dance night more in the school disco style than a hardcore club night.

BOTANY The plant bit of Biology.

BUSINESS STUDIES The study of business, obviously, but it also includes maths and economics and, less predictably, bits of psychology and sociology. And what with Europe and all that stuff, languages are becoming increasingly unavoidable.

CAMPUS The area of land on which a collection of college buildings are built. So, a campus university is one built entirely or mainly on a single campus. A civic campus is a campus in a town. And a greenfield campus is not. Just to confuse things, some universities use 'campus' as a synonym for 'site' and vice versa, so it could mean anything from a single building to an almost entirely separate college.

CHAPLAIN Chaplains hang around universities offering religious guidance and support to those who want it. They usually come in a variety of religious flavours.

CLEARING Each year after the A Level results are published, many students find they haven't got the place they wanted and many universities find they haven't filled their courses. Having participated in a sophisticated applications and admissions process up to then, the universities and students throw caution to the wind and often try to shove square pegs into round holes. Clearing tends not to result in the best possible matches. There's more about making the most of clearing without making a meal of it at Push Online (www.push.co.uk).

COLLEGE A vague word that could mean (a) a sixth form college where students do A Levels, (b) a semi-self-contained unit in a collegiate university, (c) an institution of higher education that isn't allowed to call itself a university or (d) any university, college of higher education, its buildings and/or its administrative authorities.

COMBINED HONOURS An undergraduate degree course that involves several subject areas – usually three – in approximately equal parts (to start with at any rate).

CONVOCATION A fancypants term for graduation – the formal ceremony when you receive your degree.

COURT A square surrounded by buildings, usually covered in grass and commonly found in Oxbridge colleges. Only at Oxford they call them quads, just to be difficult.

DEGREE A higher education qualification of a certain level. They're split into undergraduate degrees or first degrees which are usually Bachelorships and various postgraduate degrees (masters, doctorates, PGCEs and so on). A university isn't a university if it doesn't teach degrees although some do other higher education qualifications too like Higher National Diplomas (HNDs).

DEPARTMENT Most universities break down different subject areas into departments and students 'belong' to whichever department teaches their course. It gets more complicated if they study more than one subject, because they may end up in several departments. Some universities don't have departments, they have schools or faculties instead (or even as well), but they're basically the same thing.

DESMOND Slang for a lower-second class honours degree, ie. a Desmond Tutu (two-two. Geddit?). For the record, a first is known as 'a Geoff' (Hurst), a 2.i is 'an Attila' (the Hun) and a third is a 'Douglas' (Hurd).

DONS Dons are Mafia bosses, but in the context of universities, particularly Oxbridge, they're more likely to be lecturers, tutors or other academics who teach.

ECONOMICS Economists will tell you that their subject is 'the study of the allocation of scarce resources'. In fact, they mean it's about the way money changes hands, affecting society (and managing never to reach you and me).

EDUCATION A Bachelor of Education degree teaches teachers to teach, within a specialised field at any rate (usually determined by age group, academic subject, or both). Some take a 'normal' first degree (BA, BSc, etc.) instead and study for a further year to get a Postgraduate Certificate of Education (PGCE). Either way, after four years of being a student, they know how to work for low pay and look moth-eaten.

ENGINEERING Engineering is the study of how to create things that make people's lives easier/healthier/safer/better. There are sub-divisions such as: chemical engineering (studying how materials change); civil engineering (transport, sewage, etc.); electrical engineering and so on. Engineers usually work phenomenally hard, play X-Box for hours and tell you their subject is 'really interesting, actually'.

ENTS Short for entertainments, which are usually run by the students' union and include such larks as gigs, hypnotists and, if you're unlucky, karaoke.

ENVIRONMENTAL STUDIES A relatively new discipline that takes bits of biology, chemistry, geology and social sciences and investigates how environmental problems occur, how to prevent them and how to chain yourself to a bulldozer.

EUROPEAN STUDIES French, Spanish and Italian aren't just languages, nowadays there are courses which combine learning how to talk with learning something to talk about. A French course might include bits about French culture, business, law, history and Thierry Henry's tackling techniques.

FACULTY Old lecturers never die, they just lose their faculties. Universities are usually divided into departments (see above). Just in case these departments feel lonely, they're allowed to club together into faculties. So, the physicists join their chemistry and biology chums in a Science Faculty and the musicians get together with the drama luvvies in an Arts Faculty and everybody's happy. Except the lawyers, who usually have a faculty on their own. Maybe they smell.

FINALS/FINALISTS Finals are the exams in the final year of study that decide whether or not the last three or four years have been worth living in abject poverty for. Hence, finalists are students in their final year with their heads on the exam block.

FIRST Not what you get when you don't drink enough, but the top-scoring honours degree.

FLUNKING To flunk is to drop out of university or fail. Hence the proportion of students who do it is the flunk rate.

FORMALS Posh universities and colleges (the Oxbridge ones, for a start) sometimes have formal dinners where students are supposed to dress up sometimes in black tie, sometimes in suits or sometimes in gowns over their combats and T-shirts. Such formals may be compulsory or voluntary or they may be so popular that students have to sign up to attend (especially if the formals are followed by ents of some sort). Some places have formals every night, some have them only once a term.

FOUNDATION DEGREE A relative newbie – they've been on offer since 2001 – these are employment-related courses studied over two years (if taken full-time, but part of the lure is the flexible approach). While a university might offer a foundation degree, its content could be planned and even taught by employers.

FRESHERS Freshers are first year students in their first few weeks – when the pace is faster than curry through a dog with diarrhoea and the main topics of conversation are home towns, A Level grades and UCAS codes. During students' time as freshers, they are likely to spend 99% of their student loan, join student clubs whose events they will never attend and get staggeringly drunk most nights. After three weeks of this, they are hungover, broke and wiser – ie. fully-fledged students.

FRESHERS' WEEK Also known as Week One, Orientation Week, Intro Week and 'Cyril' for all we know, this is the first week of the first term of the first year of a student's university career. It's packed with events and ents designed to help students settle in, make friends and to tell them everything they need to know about how the university and students' union work. In the process, they tend to both drink and spend too much, but have a damn good time. See Freshers, above.

FURTHER EDUCATION (FE) Further education is what comes after primary and secondary education. In other words it's usually what 16- to 18-year-olds do. In yet other words, it's A Levels, Highers and the like. And in other, other, other words, it's what you have to do to be qualified to go on to higher education (universities and the like).

GAP YEAR Many students decide to take a year off – or a year out or a gap year – after school or college and before going to university. This is best not spent in front of the TV, but getting work experience, earning money, travelling or doing something exciting or mind-expanding. Or a mixture of all of the above. See 'Pushing the Boat Out' at the front of the book.

GEOLOGY Geologists study the structure of the earth and the rocks, fossils, minerals and all the general gunk that's in it.

GRADUAND A student in the few months between finishing their course and being awarded their degree.

GRADUATE Someone who's successfully completed a degree. A graduate student is a glutton for punishment who's embarking on another degree, usually a postgraduate degree.

GRADUATION Also known as convocation. When you're officially awarded your degree.

GRANTS Once upon a time, students used to get grants which paid for everything from beer to Biros. The magical money gifts went to ground for a few years, before coming back a paler imitation of their former selves. From 2006, the hardest-up students get a higher Education Maintenance Grant, worth up to £2,700 a year. Although not as generous as in ye olde days, it's still free money that doesn't have to be paid back. Ever. Yippee.

GUILD OF STUDENTS/STUDENTS' GUILD Another name for a students' union.

HACK Not the sound of a bad cough or a lozenge to cure it, but a person who is utterly committed to their extra-curricular activities. Usually refers to those involved in SUs or student journalism. You can tell a hack because they're the ones claiming everyone else is apathetic.

HALLS At most colleges, when students talk about halls, they mean 'halls of residence', the accommodation blocks, which traditionally provide catered meals (but increasingly are becoming self-catered), cleaners, heat, light and electricity and a variety of amenities such as launderettes, common rooms and TV lounges. Oxbridge, of course, has to be different. At Oxford or Cambridge, halls are the formal dining rooms.

HEAD TENANCY SCHEME Rather than handing out cardboard boxes or have students cluttering up the gym floor, some universities do the house-hunting themselves. They get a group of landlords together, rent all their brick boxes that pretend to be homes and then sublet them to students, often at cheaper rates or on better terms.

HIGHER EDUCATION (HE) After primary school, there's secondary school, then further education and, finally, higher education which takes place at universities, colleges of higher education and so on. HE includes undergraduate and postgraduate degrees, higher national diplomas (HNDs) and a few other things like certain vocational qualifications (such as LPCs for lawyers, for instance).

HIGHERS In Scotland, instead of A Levels, students take Highers.

HND The Higher National Diploma is based on vocational studies and is generally aimed at prepping students for a particular career or industry. It can lead to or count towards a degree course.

HONOURS DEGREE When people boast about having an honours degree, don't be too impressed. Most degrees are honours degrees and, depending on how you do in your exams or coursework, are split into: first class honours (or firsts), upper second class or 2.i (pronounced 'two-one'), lower-second class or 2.ii (a 'two-two', more commonly called a Desmond) and third class honours, or a third. If a student does badly, but not quite badly enough to fail, that's when they might not get an honours degree, but an ordinary degree instead.

HUMANITIES The study of human creative endeavour, whether it's literature, art, music or whatever. 'Richard & Judy' probably doesn't count. Humanities aren't quite the same as actually doing the creative bit, ie. the Arts (which includes almost anything likely to get Lottery funding).

INTRO WEEK Another name for Freshers' Week.

JOBSHOP A student employment agency usually run by the students' union. Apart from advertising vacancies, jobshops are sometimes more proactive and actually look for appropriate paid work for students. They also sometimes impose minimum pay and conditions and check that the employer's not a crooked slave-driver. Unlike most job agencies, they usually don't take a cut and often students get work in the jobshop or students' union itself.

JOINT HONOURS Not an honours degree in cooking big roasts or rolling spliffs, but, like a combined honours degree, a course involving more than one subject. In this case, two subjects.

JUNIOR COMMON ROOM (JCR) Another name for a students' union, but usually quite a modest affair such as in an Oxbridge college or a hall of residence. It's also usually a real common room too for undergrad students.

LAW An LLB course will not qualify a student to don a silly wig and act like Judge John Deed. In theory, it teaches the workings of the legal system (usually the English one) and how laws are applied. It also includes the skills and methods that the legal profession requires, such as learning to shout 'you can't handle the truth!'. Not all degrees are qualifying law degrees – meaning you'll still need to sit the Common Professional Examination (CPE). Even with an undergrad law degree under your belt you'll need to do further vocational training to become a barrister or solicitor.

LEA Your friendly, neighbourhood Local Education Authority. They're the nice people you hope will give you money towards fees and living expenses. Slowly being superseded by Students' Parents.

LEARNING RESOURCES CENTRE (LRC) In the old days (when there were knights and vikings and people thought Tony Blair was great) universities used to have libraries (with books in them) and computer rooms (with computers). Now they're just as likely to have LRCs which are vast buildings that contain books, computers, videos and machines that beep when you put a book near them.

LECTURE Someone once defined a lecture as the process of transferring words from the notes of the lecturer to the student without passing through the brain of either. Lectures are one of the main teaching method of universities. They tend to be larger than regular school classes and less interactive. (Seminars are more like school.) Usually attendance is not compulsory, but missing them isn't likely to help your studies.

LECTURER Apart from the obvious – ie. someone who gives a lecture – lecturers are academics at a certain level in the hierarchy well above postgraduates but below professors and deans.

MATURE STUDENTS It is not necessarily true that mature students behave any more maturely than conventional ones. Nor are they necessarily old fogeys – some are as young as 21 – but, generally, they are older than most other students and are probably returning to education rather than being fresh out of school. (Having a year out counts as being fresh, having 10 years out living in a brothel counts as matured.)

MEANS TESTING Local Education Authorities (LEAs) assess how much money students have at their disposal before handing out any money for their tuition fees. Similarly student loans are based on a means test. However it may seem, they're not called that because they're trying to see how mean they can be.

MEDIA STUDIES A heavily over-subscribed course, often by students who think (i) it'll get them straight into the BBC or Hollywood or (ii) it's a doss course. Both are wrong. Media courses usually cover practical and theoretical training in all areas of mass communication and while the experience and contacts might give students an edge in pursuit of a glittering career full of men with pony-tails, unfortunately, life-membership of the Groucho Club is not automatic and there are many other routes to media infamy.

MIDDLE COMMON ROOM (MCR) Like a Junior Common Room, but for postgrads only.

MODULAR COURSES A sort of pick'n'mix course comprising a number of components (modules), either within just one department or across a range of subjects.

NIGHTLINE All students have times when the skin on the cocoa of life is just a bit too thick and Nightline services, available in most colleges worth their salt, are there for those times. They are telephone counselling services, a bit like the Samaritans, run (usually) by students for students.

NON-COMPLETION/NON-PROGRESSION RATE A politer term for what we at Push call the flunk rate (see flunking).

NUS The National Union of Students, run by students who never got tired of it, provides research, welfare information and services to SUs which are affiliated. NUS is also the national body which represents and campaigns on behalf of students. At a day-to-day level students deal with their own university's students' union.

NUS CARD You'll get your NUS card from your students' union. Guard it with your life: it can get you into nightclubs and museums for free or money off very useful things like undies, train tickets, books or even (most importantly) booze.

NVQ The National Vocational Qualification is usually taken when you've already got a job (or work experience) and, basically, it's a bit like your boss sending you off to study, but only the bits she really wants you to know about. They're taught at an industry-agreed standard, so employers in those industries can be keen if you've got one on your CV.

OPEN DAYS An opportunity for prospective students to be shown around the university. Beware only being shown the good parts and take the opportunity to talk to the inmates, er, students.

ORDINARY DEGREE An 'ordinary degree' is somewhat less than ordinary, because most students get an honours degree. You only get an ordinary degree if either you decide to aim lower for some reasons or you fail an honours degree, but don't fail so badly you get nothing.

OXBRIDGE The collective name for the two oldest universities in the country, Oxford and Cambridge, both collegiate, both traditional, both highly respected (not least by themselves). It's strange that Camford never caught on.

PERSONAL TUTORS/MORAL TUTORS At many, if not most, universities, students are assigned to a personal tutor who is charged with responsibilities beyond the purely academic. The extent of their remit and of their usefulness varies enormously. Some have regular meetings to discuss everything from exams to sex, others introduce themselves to their tutees at the beginning of their college career with some Ernst & Julio and limp cheese and don't see them again till graduation day. Sometimes they're called moral tutors, but expecting academics to give moral guidance is like asking a fish to run a marathon.

PGCE A Postgraduate Certificate in Education is a one-year postgraduate course that graduates can take and which qualifies them to become teachers. At the moment, most students get six grand just for doing the course and might get their student loan paid off too if they go on to become a teacher in a subject where there's a shortage. A PGCE's not the only way to become a teacher – you can also do a four-year Bachelor of Education undergrad degree, or just do a regular degree and then pimp your knowledge to the private sector.

PHILOSOPHY 'What is philosophy?' is a philosophical question, but, ever ready to ponder even the deepest mysteries, Push's definition is that it's about asking the complex questions behind other subjects. Without necessarily expecting an answer. So, when philosophers ask 'Does God exist?', they're more interested in the ideas and arguments involved, than His mobile number (for that you want theology).

POLITICS Of course, nobody with the intelligence and decency to read The Push Guide would want to become anything as vile as a politician, but you might wish to study how these creatures operate. Politics (aka Political Studies, Government, etc.) uses elements of history, economics, statistics and more to investigate how people govern themselves and each other and whether Gordon Brown will ever smile.

POLYTECHNIC Once upon a time there was something called 'the binary divide' which distinguished between universities and polytechnics. It never meant much anyway and now it means nothing at all. Polytechnics tended to have a slant towards vocational courses and an often unfair reputation for lower academic standards than universities. Now they've all become universities themselves, but the old poly prejudices seem to linger about like last week's dirty socks, again somewhat unfairly.

POSTGRADUATE/POSTGRAD A student doing a postgraduate degree, ie. they've already got one degree and now they're doing another higher one such as a masters degree, a doctorate (PhD) or a postgraduate certificate in education (PGCE).

PRACTICAL A form of teaching, or probably more accurately, of learning, usually used in sciencey type subjects. It involves doing experiments and the like.

PROFESSOR A big cheese in an academic department – often the head – but, at any rate, someone who has climbed the brain hierarchy.

PSYCHOLOGY If, at university, you ever get pestered by students wielding clipboards and asking intimate questions about sexuality and your favourite colour, chances are they're either chatting you up or they're psychologists (or both). Psychology is the study of the way people think and behave, using elements of biology, sociology, maths and other disciplines. And sometimes they make cute little mazes for rats to run around in. Aw.

QUAD A square surrounded by buildings, usually covered in grass and commonly found in Oxbridge colleges. Only at Cambridge they call them courts, just to be difficult.

RAG Rag (from 'Raise and Give') is an excuse to dress up in stupid clothing and get up to wacky, irresponsible and sometimes illegal antics – and all in the name of charity. Collectively, student charity Rags raise millions of pounds with stunts like parachute jumps, sponsored hitch-hikes and so-called 'Rag raids' where students (usually dressed as rabbits, nuns, characters from Little Britain, etc.) accost strangers in the street and try to milk their human kindness.

RAH (OR RA) aka Yah or Sloane. Certain universities – Oxbridge, Durham, Bristol and Exeter spring to mind – tend to attract a certain sort of posh student, ex-public school, dressed in country casuals (and probably able to say what exactly 'country casuals' means) and, when gathered in herds, from a distance their braying makes a 'ra, ra, ra' sound. Hence the name. They're harmless enough, but if you're not one of them, you may find them almost inexplicably irritating.

REDBRICK A redbrick building or campus does not necessarily have to have a single red brick. Instead, it refers to a style of building, or a period from around the turn of the century through to the Second World War. What redbrick means is not very precise, but what it doesn't mean is easier to explain. A campus is described as redbrick if it isn't an Oxbridge rip-off or a modern concrete monstrosity.

THE RUSSELL GROUP A band of 20 universities, including Oxbridge, that like to think of themselves as the whipped cream on the top of the frappucino of lesser universities. It's true that they have cornered a big share of the research funding and they do tend to have excellent teaching. It would be fair to label them 'elite' (or even 'elitist'), but the word 'best' shouldn't be bandied about without extreme care. See also The 1994 Group.

SABBATICAL Every year at most colleges, a few students either take a year off their studies or hang around after them because they've got nothing better to do. In the meantime they are employed (sub-peanut wages) by various student bodies in official roles, such as in SUs, Rags, newspapers, athletics unions and so on. Not just anyone can do this though – they almost always have to be elected by the other students, who then spend the rest of the sabbatical's year of office wondering why they ever voted for them. Just like real politics.

SANDWICH COURSE Not a catering course (although, come to think of it, you could do a sandwich course in catering), but a course that involves vocational experience. So, the bread in a sandwich course is academic study and the filling is a work placement usually in business or industry. Usually it takes a year to fill a sandwich (as a result, most last four years), but there are thin and thick versions that involve different amounts of filling dispersed between different thicknesses of bread. Push eagerly awaits the introduction of toasted and club sandwich courses.

SEMESTER A semester is the American word for a term and is used in Britain to describe American-style college terms that are longer (usually about 15 weeks) than British ones (between 8–11 weeks). Generally speaking, universities have either two semesters or three terms.

SEMINAR A teaching class, overseen by a lecturer, in which anything from half a dozen to about 35 students discuss and maybe even do exercises. Sound familiar? Basically, we're talking about what any normal person would call 'a lesson'.

SENIOR COMMON ROOM (SCR) Like a Junior or Middle Common Room, but this is for the fully qualified academics and the emphasis is exclusively on the room itself and a few clubby activities, rather than on any kind of students' union or representative role.

SINGLE HONOURS An undergraduate degree involving one main subject.

SOCIAL SCIENCE A social science is any subject which uses scientific methods to study human society, rather than the natural world. Originally regarded as a soft option, some social scientists can now earn big wads by going on the telly and talking lots.

SOCIOLOGY The study of how people operate within social groups (eg. families, tribes, football crowds). Sociologists have to use a variety of skills, such as dealing with data and statistics. Sociology still has an undeserved reputation as a dumping ground for left-wing under-achievers, but it's as intellectually rigorous (and attractive to employers) as any other social science subject.

SOCS Short for 'societies', these are the student clubs which range from serious political battlegrounds to sporting teams, from cultural groups to seriously silly socs, such as the Rolf Harris Appreciation Club and Up Shit Creek Without A Paddle Soc – both genuine.

STUDENTS' ASSOCIATION (SA) Just another name for a students' union really. Common in Scotland.

STUDENTS' REPRESENTATIVE COUNCIL/COMMITTEE (SRC) Yet another name for a students' union or part of one, especially the part that focuses on representation. Sometimes, an SRC may be the group of students within a department elected to represent other students' views.

STUDENTS' UNION (SU) Almost all colleges have a students' union and students are usually automatically members. As a rule, an SU is usually a services and representative organisation run by students for students or the building in which such services are housed.

SUBSIDIARY COURSE A course that acts as a side dish to the main course, usually in a single honours course.

TARIFF The list of points you score for each of your further education qualifications. Collect enough points and you might have enough to get into a particular degree at a particular university. As it happens, the tariff is at least partly fiction because most universities tend to rely on the student's whole application, not just their grades.

THEOLOGY The study of God, gods and religion.

THESP An arty-farty acting type.

TOP-UP FEES The unofficial name for the tuition fees that universities are now allowed to directly charge students in most parts of the UK. What you have to pay varies at each university, though most charge the maximum allowed – currently three grand. See 'Hard Pushed' at the front of the book for details on the whole fees shebang.

TOWN/GOWN An expression which describes the relationship between locals and the student and academic staff community. People say 'town/gown' even though students these days are more at home in a Gap T-shirt and a pair of scuffed Vans than a gown and mortar board. Come Graduation Day, though, students are geared up in 'subfusc', as the outfit is called, and photos are taken of them. Embarrassment guaranteed.

TUTEE A student whose work (and/or well-being) is overseen by a particular tutor. It's pronounced more like 'chew tea' than like 'tutty'.

TUTOR An academic who oversees or supervises the work of individual students (tutees).

TUTORIAL A small group of students – definitely no more then five otherwise it's a seminar whatever they claim – who meet up with a tutor and discuss their studies. If they're lucky, students get one-to-one tutorials which are a great opportunity to discuss individual ideas, thoughts and problems with work.

UCAS The Universities & Colleges Admissions Service is the organisation that handles most university applications. Prospective students register online and fill out a UCAS Form, which UCAS sends to the universities the student wants to apply to. After the decision process and interviews the student either gets accepted or not, and UCAS oversees the process to check no one finds themselves with more than one place and to try to match students with spaces as efficiently as possible.

UNDERGRADUATE A student doing their first degree.

UNION Usually this is just another name for a students' union or the building in which the students' union and/or its facilities and services are based. As such, it's often the students' main hang-out on campus. However, at Oxbridge (and various other universities that just have to be awkward), the Union might also be the Union Society, a debating club with some highly exclusive (even elitist) facilities attached.

UNIVERSITY Not nearly as easy to define as you might have thought, although officially a UK university has to be founded by Parliamentary Statute. There are plenty of places like certain university colleges and, for instance, the colleges of London University that deserve the name as much as many of the places that have it. The long and the short of it is that a university is a place to get a higher education.

UNIVERSITY COLLEGE Officially, a college that has the power to award its own degrees, but isn't a fully-fledged university, or a college run by a fully-fledged university. HE colleges which are independent, but whose degrees are rubber-stamped by a university, aren't allowed to use the 'University' bit, but to the student on the ground they're pretty much the same thing.

VICE-CHANCELLOR Aka principals, wardens, masters etc. These are the big cheeses – the Stilton amongst the Dairyleas of academia. Students rarely get to meet them, but basically they run the place. Where there are vice-chancellors, there are also chancellors, who are the token heads of the institutions (often minor royals or B-list celebs), but they usually don't do much more than shake students' hands at the graduation ceremony. The allegations that vice-chancellors have anything to do with vice are entirely unfounded.

VOCATIONAL COURSE Any course that is intended at least to train students for a particular profession, career or job. They often involve practical experience in a work environment, such as placements, or doing projects similar to what goes on in real world jobs.

WOMEN'S STUDIES (AKA GENDER STUDIES) A multi-disciplinary subject that studies how women (and men) are treated in fields as diverse as law, history and health and the reasons or gender differences in behaviour, communication, pay and more. Oh, and men are allowed to apply.

ZOOLOGY The animal bit of biology.

SHORT, SHARP PUSH

The abbreviations used in Push:

AU	Athletics Union
BUNAC	British Universities North American Club
BUSA	British Universities Sports Association
CAP	capacity
CATS	Credit Accumulation and Transfer Scheme
CDL	Career Development Loan
COFE	Church of England
COFS	Church of Scotland
COFW	Church of Wales
CUKAS	Conservatoires UK Admissions Service
DFES	Department for Education and Skills
ENTS	entertainments
FC	Free Church
GTTR	Graduate Teacher Training Registry
HND	Higher National Diploma
HE	higher education (ie. degree/HND-level or above)
HEFCE	Higher Education Funding Council for England
HESA	Higher Education Statistics Agency
JCR	Junior Common/Combination Room (usually Oxbridge)
LEA	Local Education Authority
LGBT	Lesbian, Gay, Bisexual, Transgender
LRC	Learning Resources Centre
NHS	National Health Service
NMAS	Nursing and Midwifery Admissions Service
NSS	National Student Survey
NUS	National Union of Students
POLY	polytechnic
POSTGRADS	postgraduates
RC	Roman Catholic
SA	Students' Association (usually Scotland)
SABB	sabbatical officer
SCR	Senior Common Room
SLC	Student Loans Company
SNP	Scottish National Party
SOC	society or club
SRC	Student Representative Council
SU	Students' Union
SWSS	Socialist Workers' Student Society
UCAS	The Universities and Colleges admissions service
U'GRADS	undergraduates
ULU	University of London Union
URC	United Reform Church

PUSHING ON

Where to go from here. A guide to useful
publications, websites and other resources:

GENERAL

BOOKS

The Push Guide to Which University 2007/08, Alice
Tarleton, Anthony Leyton & Ruth Bushi, ed. Johnny
Rich (Hodder Arnold, 2006)
ISBN 0340 929588, £15.99
E: editor@push.co.uk

*Everything You Need to Know About Going to
University*, Sally Longson (Kogan Page, 2003)
ISBN 07494339858, £9.99

Choosing Your Degree Course & University, Brian
Heap (Trotman, 2006)
ISBN 1844550710, £21.99

*The Big Guide 2006 (University & College Entrance:
The Official Guide)*, UCAS
ISBN 1843610361, £32.50
Includes an entry requirements CD-Rom

*The Sixthformer's Guide to Visiting Universities and
Colleges 2006*, Carol Coe (ISCO, 2006)
ISBN 1905057032, £10.95

Student Life – A Survival Guide, Natasha Roe
(Lifetime Careers, 2002)
ISBN 1904979017, £10.99

WEBSITES

www.push.co.uk
Push Online
Loads of information for anyone even thinking of
university, links to hundreds of students and university
websites and, well, it's just generally fab (though we
probably would say that). Particularly magnificent is
the unique interactive University Chooser feature.

www.ucas.com
The UCAS website
Register and apply to university online. Details of the
application procedure, order forms for books, forms
and resources and a course search facility for finding
which universities do the course you're after. Also the
Stamford Test to help choose a suitable subject to
study.

www.aimhigher.ac.uk
A Government-funded site plugging higher education,
but with lots of handy stuff on it.

ACADEMIC GUIDES &
APPLICATIONS PROCEDURE

CONTACTS
Prospectuses
Individual colleges publish prospectuses for
admissions and many students' unions produce
alternative prospectuses. To get hold of a copy, use
the contact details in the profiles in The Push Guide
to Which University or Push Online (www.push.co.uk)
or see your careers adviser/library.

UCAS
www.ucas.com
Rosehill, New Barn Lane, Cheltenham, Gloucs, GL52 3LZ.
T: 01242 222444 E: enquiries@ucas.ac.uk. Apply online.
Details of the application procedure, an order forms for
books, forms and resources and a course search facility
for finding which universities do the course you're after.

Scottish students: SAAS
Student Awards Agency for Scotland
www.saas.gov.uk
Gyleview House, 3 Redheughs Rigg, Edinburgh EH12
9HH. T: 0845 1111711. E: saas.geu@scotland.gsi.gov.uk
Student Support in Scotland. Publishes a booklet each
year called *A Guide for Undergraduate Students*.

Northern Irish students: DELNI
The Department of Employment and Learning
Northern Ireland
www.delni.gov.uk
Adelaide House, 39–49 Adelaide Street, Belfast BT2
8FD. T: 02890 257 777 E: info.tea@delni.gov.uk
Publishes its own version of *Financial Support for
Students in Higher Education*.

Welsh-speaking students: NWA National Assembly
for Wales
www.hefcw.ac.uk
Higher Education Funding Council for Wales, Linden
Court, Ilex Close, Llanishen, Cardiff CF14 5DZ. T: 029
2076 1861. Different arrangements for hardship funds
and bursaries exist in Wales. Contact the Further and
Higher Education Division of the National Assembly
for Wales on 029 2082 6318.

BOOKS
*The Big Guide 2006 (University & College Entrance:
The Official Guide)*, UCAS
ISBN 1843610361, £32.50
Includes an entry requirements CD-Rom

Scottish Guide 2006, UCAS
ISBN 1843610388, £14.95

*How to Complete Your UCAS Application: For 2007
Entry to University and College*, Tony Higgins
(Trotman, 2006)
ISBN 1844550761, £11.99

Choosing Your Degree Course & University, Brian
Heap (Trotman, 2006)
ISBN 1844550710, £21.99

Degree Course Offers 2007 Entry, Brian Heap (Trotman, 2006)
ISBN 1844550702, £28.99

You want to study what? Vol. 1, Dianah Ellis (Trotman, 2003)
ISBN 0856608939, £14.99

You want to study what? Vol. 2, Dianah Ellis, Trotman, 2003)
ISBN 0856608947, £14.99
A guide to some of the more unusual degree courses.

Trotman's Green Guides, £9.99 each (Trotman)
Individual guides for various subject areas from engineering to performing arts, (Business Courses, Engineering Courses, Healthcare Courses, Physical Science Courses, Art, Design & Performing Arts Courses)

Directory of University and College Entry 2007/8 (Trotman, 2006)
ISBN 1844550729, £39.99

British Vocational Qualifications (Kogan Page, 2005)
ISBN 079444851, £40

NVQs and How to Get Them, Hazel Dakers (Kogan Page, 2002)
ISBN 07949437111, £9.99

Getting into Business & Management Courses, Kate Smith (Trotman, 2005)
ISBN 1844550192, £11.99

Getting Into Dental School, James Burnett & Andrew Long (Trotman, 2005)
ISBN 1844550214, £11.99

Getting Into Law, Carl Lygo (Trotman, 2006)
ISBN 1844550672 £11.99

Getting Into Medical School, Joe Ruston and James Burnett (Trotman, 2006)
ISBN 1844550745, £11.99

Getting Into Psychology, James Burnett & Maya Waterstone (Trotman, 2006)
ISBN 1844550699, £11.99

Getting into Veterinary School, Mario Di Clemente (Trotman, 2005)
ISBN 1844550206, £11.99

Getting into Oxford & Cambridge, Sarah Alakjia (Trotman, 2005)
ISBN 1844550222, £11.99

Q & A Studying Art & Design (Trotman, 2000)
ISBN 0856605700, £4.99

Q & A Studying Business & Management (Trotman, 2000)
ISBN 0856605719, £4.99

Q & A Studying Chemical Engineering (Trotman, 2000)
ISBN 0856605778, £4.99

Q & A Studying Computer Science (Trotman, 2000)
ISBN 0856605727, £4.99

Q & A Studying Drama (Trotman, 2000)
ISBN 0856605735, £4.99

Q & A Studying English (Trotman, 2000)
ISBN 0856605743, £4.99

Q & A Studying Law (Trotman, 2000)
ISBN 0856605751, £4.99

Q & A Studying Media (Trotman, 2000)
ISBN 085660576X, £4.99

Q & A Studying Psychology (Trotman, 2000)
ISBN 056605786, £4.99

Q & A Studying Sports Science (Trotman, 2000)
ISBN 0856605794, £4.99

WEBSITES
www.ecctis.co.uk
UK Course Discover, ECCTIS+, subscription CD and website
Covers 100,000 courses at universities and colleges in the UK. Available at schools, colleges, careers offices and training access points (TAP).

www.student.co.uk
Helpful site for information on completing a UCAS form.

GAP YEARS AND TRAVELLING

BOOKS
Taking a Year Off, Val Butcher (Trotman, 2002)
ISBN 0856608505, £11.99

The Gap Year Guidebook 2006 (John Catt Educational)
ISBN 1904724213, £11.95

Taking a Gap Year, Susan Griffith (Trotman, 2005)
ISBN 188458328X, £12.95

The Virgin Travellers' Handbook, Tom Griffiths (Virgin, 2002)
ISBN 0753506335, £14.99

Planning your Gap Year, Nick Vandome, (How To Books, 2005)
ISBN 1845280105, £9.99

Work your Way around the World, Susan Griffith (Vacation-Work. 2005)
ISBN 1854583298, £12.95

Opportunities in the Gap Year (ISCO, 2003)
ISBN 0901936995, £7.95

A Year Off... A Year On? Tessa Doe et al (Lifetime Careers, 2005)
ISBN 1902876865, £10.95
Ideas on what to do, where to go and how to use your time constructively.

The Rough Guides
Many of their guide books are reproduced on their website at www.roughguides.co.uk

WEBSITES

www.gap-year.com
Provides good information on taking a year out.

www.gapwork.com
A guide to working holidays and current vacancies.

www.yearoutgroup.org/organisations.htm

www.raleigh.org.uk
Raleigh International
A charity-run scheme giving young people the opportunity to go on 3-month expeditions all over the world for varied project work. Over 20,000 young people (including Prince William) have taken part in a total of 168 expeditions in 35 countries since 1984. T: 020 7371 8585.

www.gap.org.uk
Gap Activity Projects (GAP)
An independent educational charity founded in 1972, which organises voluntary work overseas in 30 different countries. T: 0118 959 4914.
E: volunteer@gap.org.uk

www.yini.org.uk
The Year in Industry Scheme
Contact National Director, University of Southampton, Southampton SO17 1BJ.
T: 023 8059 7061. E: enquiries@yini.org.uk, or visit their website for an online application form.

www.vso.org.uk
The Voluntary Service Organisation (VSO)
Runs special overseas youth programmes for under 25s. T: 020 8780 7500
E: enquiry@vso.org.uk

www.csv.org.uk
Community Service Volunteers (CSV)
Full-time voluntary placements throughout the UK for people between 16 and 35. Allowance, accommodation and food provided. T: 0800 374 991.

www.volunteerafrica.org
Voluntary opportunities in Africa.
E: support@volunteerafrica.org

www.spw.org
Students Partnership Worldwide
Challenging and rewarding 4–9 month projects in developing countries. T: 020 7222 0138.

www.gapadvice.org
Does what it says on the web address.

www.teaching-abroad.co.uk
Teaching & Projects Abroad
Foreign travel and experience in teaching English, conservation work, medicine, journalism, etc. Countries include China, Ghana, India, Thailand, Mexico and South Africa. T: 01903 859911.

www.aventure.co.uk
Africa and Asia Venture
4 and 5 month schemes offering great scope for cultural and interpersonal development in Kenya, Tanzania, Uganda, Malawi, Zimbabwe, India and Nepal. Mainly unpaid teaching work, with extensive travel and safari opportunities. 10 Market Place, Devizes, Wiltshire SN10 1HT. T: 01380 729009.
E: av@aventure.co.uk.

www.kiliproject.org
Village Education Project
Mint Cottage, Prospect Road, Sevenoaks, Kent TN13 3UA. T: 01732 743000
E: project@kiliproject.org
8-month teaching projects in Tanzanian, no teaching qualification required.

www.bunac.org
BUNAC (British Universities North America Club)
Offers a range of work/travel programmes worldwide, from a few months to a whole year, depending on destination and programme. T: 020 7251 3472.

www.kibbutzvolunteer.com
www.kibbutz.org.il/eng
If you fancy working on a kibbutz, contact: Kibbutz Representatives, 1a Accommodation Road, London NW11 8ED.

www.uk-sail.org.uk
UKSA
'The perfect marriage of gap year, radical watersports and awesome experience.' Windsurfing, kayaking, sailing, professional crew and skipper training. T: 01983 294941.

www.world-challenge.co.uk
Gap Challenge/World Challenge Expeditions
Varied schemes for students 18–25, from voluntary conservation projects to paid hotel work in many different countries. T: 020 8728 7200.
E: welcome@world-challenge. co.uk

www.madventurer.com
Madventure
The Old Casino, 1–4 Forth Lane, Newcastle NE1 5HX.
T: 0808 168 1996
E: team@madventurer.com
Africa, South America, Asia and South Pacific, take part in combined community project and adventure.

www.lonelyplanet.com
Lonely Planet Guides
They also do guidebooks

www.letsgo.com
Let's Go Guides
They do guidebooks too

STUDYING ABROAD

CONTACTS
ERASMUS
UK Socrates–Erasmus Council, Rothford, Giles Lane,
Canterbury CT2 7LR. T: 01227 762712
E: info@erasmus.ac.uk   www.erasmus.ac.uk
Comenius action 2.2,
Leonardo da Vinci, Central Bureau for International
Educational Education and Training
The British Council, 10 Spring Gardens, London SW1A
2BN. T: 020 7389 4004
E: leonardo@centralbureau.org.uk

UK NARIC
ECCTIS Ltd
Oriel House, Oriel Road, Cheltenham, Gloucestershire
GL50 1XP. T: 0870 990 4088. E: info@naric.org.uk
www.naric.org.uk

British Council
10 Spring Gardens, London SW1A 2BN. T: 0161 957
7755. E: general.enquiries@british council.org
www.britcouncil.org

Commission of the European Communities (London
Office)
8 Storey's Gate, London SW1P 3AT. T: 020 7973 1992
www.cec.org.uk

BOOKS
GET 2006 Careers in Europe (Hobsons/Trotman)
ISBN 190463852X, £9.99

Experience Erasmus 2006 (Trotman, 2005)
ISBN 000380278, £16.95
Lists degree and diploma courses which incorporate
study in Europe

Getting Into American Universities, Margaret Kroto
(Trotman, 2006)
ISBN 0856609781, £11.99.

WEBSITES
www.educationuk.org.uk
Info about UK courses and qualifications available and
also those in the home countries of international
students.

www.eua.be/eua
European University Association
For European Universities.

www.australian-universities.com
For Australian universities.

www.student.com
About college life in the USA.

FINANCE, GRANTS AND SPONSORSHIP

CONTACTS
The Student Loans Company
100 Bothwell Street, Glasgow G2 7JD.
T: 0800 40 50 10. For information about student loans.
www.slc.co.uk

Department for Education and Skills
Publications Centre, PO Box 2193, London, E15 2EU.
T: 0870 000 2288. The riveting Government missives
on student funding are also available on their website
at www.dfes.gov. uk/studentsupport

Form HC1
Can be used to claim help with prescriptions, dental
and eye care charges. See www.ppa.org. uk/ppa/low_
income.htm for more details.

The National Union of Students
NUS produces a series of info sheets on student
finance. Send an A4 stamped self-addressed envelope
with details of the subject you need info about, to: The
Welfare Unit, NUS, 461 Holloway Road, London N7
6LJ. T: 020 7272 8900 www.nusonline.co.uk

Education Grants Advisory Service (EGAS)
501–505 Kingsland Road, Dalston, London E8 4AU.
(Enclose a stamped addressed envelope with enquiry
letters) T: 020 7254 6251
www.egas-online.org

The Windsor Fellowship
Runs undergraduate personal and professional
development programmes (such as sponsorships,
community work and summer placements). Primarily
for gifted black and Asian students. The Stables,
138 Kingsland Road, London E2 8DY. T: 020 7613 0373
www.windsor-fellowship.org E: office@windsor-
fellowship.org

Association for Sandwich Education and Training
Professional body for work-based learning
practitioners. 3 Westbrook Court, Sharrow Vale Road,
Sheffield S11 8YZ. T: 0114 2212902
E: aset@aset.demon.co.uk

BOOKS
The Push Guide to Student Money 2007/08, Alice
Tarleton & Johnny Rich (Hodder Arnold, 2006)
ISBN 034092960X, £9.99.
Push's guide to what funds you're entitled to, where it
all goes, how to make it stretch and what to do if it
doesn't. Full of handy tips and the only guide to give a
breakdown of key costs at every UK university. Money
advice is also available at www.push.co.uk

University Scholarships and Awards, Brian Heap
(Trotman, 2004)
ISBN 0856609773, £14.99.

The Educational Grants Directory 2004/05, Alan French et al (Directory of Social Change, 2004)
ISBN 190399151X, £34.95
Lists all sources of non-statutory help for students in financial need.

Students' Money Matters, Gwenda Thomas (Trotman, 2005)
ISBN 1844550281, £14.99
A reference book about student finance, with student case studies and 'thrift tips' throughout.

Balancing your Books, Josephine Warrior (ECCTIS/CRAC, 2004)
ISBN 0954756517, £6.99

Find it – Keep it: The Guardian/ NUS Guide to Student Finance, Jimmy Leach, (Guardian Books, 2004)
ISBN 1843543184, £6.99

WEBSITES
www.push.co.uk
Push Online
Helpful advice and information on all aspects of student money.

www.scholarship-search.org.uk
Has a free funding search facility for all undergraduate and postgraduate students. You can search by subject, type of award or region. Student Money, Hotcourses Ltd, 150–152 King Street, London W6 9JG.

www.hefce.ac.uk
Higher Education Funding Council for England.

www.studentuk.com
A general student guide including a good money section.

www.studentmoneynet.co.uk
Offers some sound advice and general financing info.

www.work-experience.org
Part-time work opportunities and student placements.

www.loot.com
Has a student section listing work placements and part-time vacancies.

www.hotrecruit.co.uk
Student-specific jobs nationwide.

www.jobpilot.co.uk/content/ channel/student
Student jobs.

www.guardian.co.uk
Job vacancies section.

www.dti.gov.uk/er/pay.htm
Tells you about the national minimum wage and hours of employment and also has a 'young worker' section.

www.student.co.uk
Guide to dealing with debt.

www.uniservity.net
Academic, social and financial web resources.

www.interstudent.co.uk
Sound advice, with a great money section.

www.uni4me.com
Government-funded site promoting going to university

www.student123.com
Student deals

OVERSEAS STUDENTS

CONTACTS
The British Council
10 Spring Gardens, London SW1A 2BN. T: 0161 957 7755. E: general.enquiries@british council.org www.britcouncil.org has information on coming to university in Britain and a 'virtual campus' to introduce you to life at UK universities.

EU students (non-UK): Department for Education and Skills
The European Team, DfES, Podium Room 38, Mowden Hall, Staindrop Road, Darlington, County Durham DL3 9BG. T: 01325 391199 www.dfes.gov.uk/student support/eustudents

BOOKS
A Guide to Studying and Living in Britain, Kris Rao (CRAC/Hobsons, 2005)
ISBN 1845280458, £10.99.

WEBSITES
www.ukcosa.org.uk
The Council for International Education
Support organisation for international students.

www.prospects.ac.uk
Advice for international postgrad students. See the 'International Students in the UK' section.

MATURE STUDENTS

BOOKS
The Mature Students' Directory, 2005 (Trotman, 2004)
ISBN 0856609854, £19.99.

Coming Back to Learning: A Handbook For Adults, Tessa Doe et al (Lifetime Careers, 2004)
ISBN 1902876881, £11.99

POSTGRADUATE STUDY

CONTACTS

Biotechnology and Biological Sciences Research Council (BBSRC)
Polaris House, North Star Avenue, Swindon SN2 1UH. T: 01793 413200 Source of Government funding for relevant scientific research. www.bbsrc.ac.uk

Economic and Social Research Council (ESRC)
Address as above, (Postcode SN2 1UJ). T: 01793 413000 Source of Government funding for social sciences research work. www.esrc.ac.uk

Engineering and Physical Sciences Research (EPSRC)
Address as above (Postcode SN2 1ET). T: 01793 444000 Source of Government funding for relevant scientific research. www.epsrc.ac.uk

Natural Environment Research Council (NERC)
Address as above (Postcode SN2 1EU). T: 01793 411500 Source of Government funding for relevant scientific research. www.nerc.ac.uk

Particle Physics and Astronomy Research (PPARC)
Address as above (Postcode SN2 1SZ). T: 01793 442000 Source of Government funding for relevant scientific research. www.pparc.ac.uk

Medical Research Council (MRC)
20 Park Crescent, London W1B 1AL. T: 020 7636 5422 Source of Government funding for medical research work. www.mrc.ac.uk

The Arts and Humanities Research Board (AHRB)
Whitefriars, Lewins Mead, Bristol BS1 2AE. T: 0117 987 6500 (Postgrad Awards Division) Source of Government funding for arts research work. www.ahrb.ac.uk

Council for the Central Laboratory of the Research Councils (CCLRC)
Rutherford Appleton Laboratory, Chilton, Didcot, Oxon OX11 0QX. T: 01235 445000 www.cclrc.ac.uk

The Association of Graduate Careers Advisory Service (AGCAS)
AGCAS Administration Office, Millennium House, 30 Junction Road, Sheffield S11 8XB. T: 0114 251 5750 www.agcas.org.uk

Royal Society Research Fellowships
Research Appointments Department, 6-9 Carlton House Terrace, London SW1Y 5AG. T: 020 7451 2500. www.royalsoc.ac.uk

BOOKS

How to Get a PhD, Estelle Phillips & Derek Pugh (Open University Press, 2005)
ISBN 03335216846, £18.99

How to Manage your Postgraduate Course, Lucinda Beacker (Palgrave Macmillan, 2004)
ISBN 140391656X, £12.99

Directory of Postgraduate Studies, Hobsons, £109.99
At this price, don't buy it, try the library.

WEBSITES
www.prospects.ac.uk
Posgraduate section.

STUDENTS WITH DISABILITIES

BOOKS
Applying to Higher Education: Guidance for Disabled People, Skill, £2.50
Available from Skill, Chapter House, 18–20 Crucifix Lane, London SE1 3JW or download from www.skill.org.uk T: 020 7450 0620

Funding for Disabled Students in Higher Education, Skill, £2.50
Booklet containing info about social security entitlements, available to buy or download from Skill (details as above).

The Disabled Students' Guide to University, Emma Caprez (Trotman, 2004)
ISBN 0856609463, £21.99.
Provides information on the financial, practical (eg housing, transport), social and academic provisions each university has for disabled students.

Disabled Students 2005 (Hobsons, 2004)
ISBN 1904638198, £9.99)

WEBSITES
www.skill.org.uk
Skill
Offers information for students and careers and details of how to get hold of Skill publications. Also has loads of student jobs.

www.afbp.org
Action for Blind People
Grants Officer, 14–16 Verney Road, London SE16 3DZ. T: 020 7635 4800.

www.asbah.org.uk
Association for Spina Bifida and Hydrocephalus
ASBAH House, 42 Park Road, Peterborough PE1 2UQ. T: 01733 555988.

www.dyslexia-inst.org.uk
The Dyslexia Institute
Park House, Wick Road, Egham, Surrey TW20 0HH. T: 01784 222300 Has a bursary fund offering extra financial support for students with dyslexia.

www.snowdonawardscheme. org.uk
Snowdon Award Scheme
22 City Business Centre, 6 Brighton Road, Horsham, West Sussex RH13 5BB. Helps disabled students aged 17-25 in further, higher or adult education. T: 01403 211252.

STUDENT WELFARE

CONTACTS

NHS Direct 0845 4647 www.nhsdirect.nhs.uk
24-hour health advice from nurses.

Samaritans 0345 909090 E: jo@samaritans.org
www.samaritans.org.uk
Confidential helpline for emotional problems of all
kinds.

National Aids Helpline 0800 567123
24-hour support and advice.

National Drugs Helpline 0800 776600.
24-hour support and advice.

See below for other helplines.

BOOKS

The Push Guide to Student Money 2007/08, Alice
Tarleton & Johnny Rich (Hodder Arnold, 2006)
ISBN 034092960X, £9.99
Advice on avoiding and coping with student debt.

Coping with Stress at University: A Survival Guide,
Stephen Palmer & Angela Puri (Sage, 2006)
ISBN 1412907330, £12.99

*What every parent should know before their child
goes to university*, Jane Bidder (White Ladder, 2005)
ISBN 0954821912, £9.99

WEBSITES

www.push.co.uk
Push Online
Plenty of advice about all aspects of student welfare
and handy links.

www.nusonline.co.uk
National Union of Students
Information on student related issues including
welfare and offers links to Students' Unions
throughout the country.

www.netdoctor.co.uk
Advice on depression, smoking, hangovers, stress,
medicines, sexual health and any other health
concerns. E-mail your questions to doctors.

www.who.int
World Health Organisation.

www.edauk.com
Eating Disorder Association T: 0845 634 1414

www.meningitis-trust.org.uk
Explains what meningitis is, symptoms and support.
T: 0845 6000 800.

www.depressionalliance.org
Depression helpline.

www.cre.gov.uk
Commission for Racial Equality
T: 020 7828 7022

www.somebodycares.org.uk
Comprises 4 charities: Addaction, National AIDS Trust
(NAT), Homeless Link and Prisoner Abroad.

www.sexualhealth.org.uk
Advice on contraception and family planning.

www.llgs.org.uk
London Lesbian and Gay Switchboard
T: 020 7837 7324

www.tht.org.uk
Terrence Higgins Trust
HIV and AIDS charity.

www.survive.org.uk
Rape advice.

www.alcoholics-anonymous. org.uk
Alcoholics Anonymous
Helpline 0845 7697555

www.alcoholconcern.org.uk
National agency on alcohol misuse

www.ukna.org
Narcotics Anonymous
T: 020 7730 0090

www.drugscope.org.uk
Drug charity.

www.hit.org.uk
UK charity providing drug information.

www.talktofrank.com
Non-directive, non-judgemental drugs advice from a
Government-funded scheme. Helpline: 0800 776600
E: frank@talktofrank.com

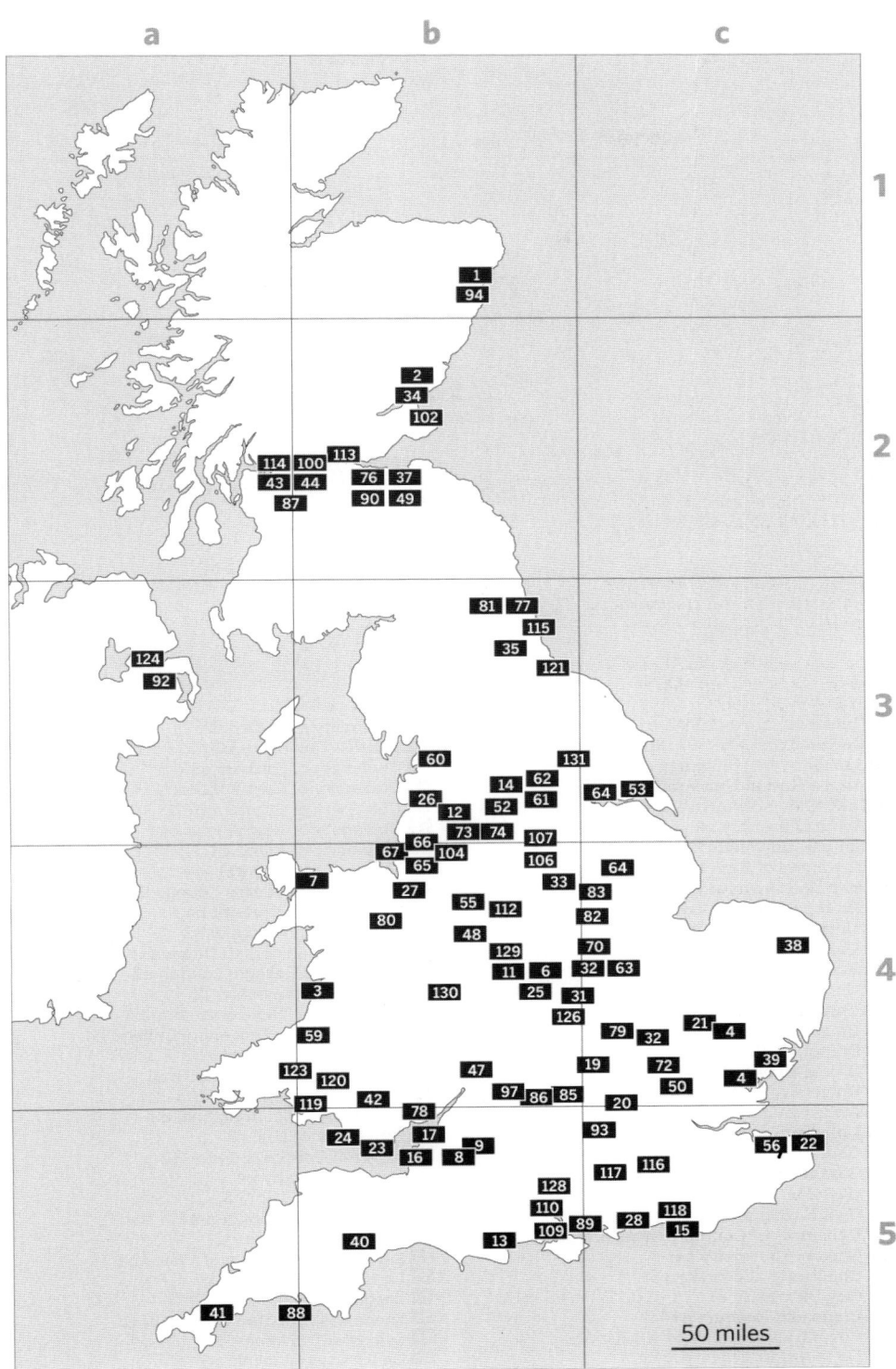

a

b

c

1

2

3

4

5

1
94

2
34
102

114 100 113
43 44 76 37
87 90 49

81 77
115
35
121

124
92

60
131
26 14 62
12 52 61
66 73 74
67 104 107
65 106
7
27 33 83
80 82
55 112
48 70
129 32 63
11 6
3 130 25 31
126
59 79 21 4
32
47 19 72
123 120 97 86 85 50 4
119 42 20 39
78 93
24 23 17 56 22
16 8 9 117 116
128 118
110 28 15
40 109 89
13

64 53
64

38

50 miles

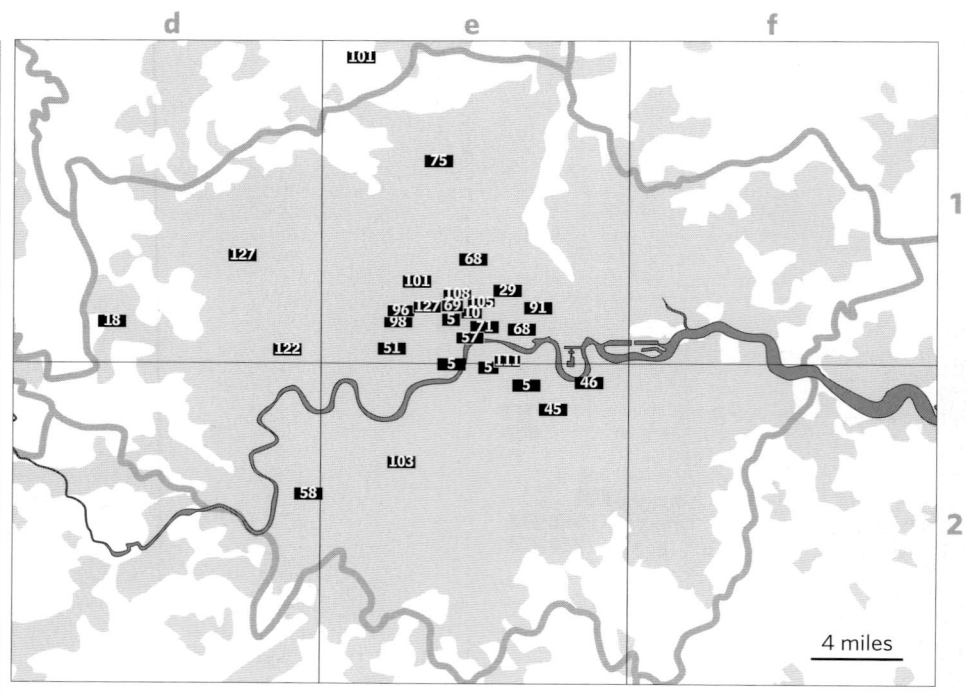

4 miles

1. University of Aberdeen b1
2. University of Abertay Dundee b2
3. Aberystwyth, Unversity of Wales b4
4. Anglia Ruskin University c4
5. University of the Arts, London e1, e2
6. Aston University c4
7. Bangor, University of Wales b4
8. University of Bath b5
9. Bath Spa Univeristy b5
10. Birkbeck College, London e1
11. University of Birmingham c4
12. University of Bolton b3
13. Bournemouth University b5
14. University of Bradford b3
15. University of Brighton c5
16. University of Bristol b5
17. Bristol, UWE b5
18. Brunel University d1
19. University of Buckingham c4
20. Buckinghamshire Chilterns University c4
21. University of Cambridge c4
22. Canterbury Christ Church University c5
23. Cardiff University b5
24. UWIC b5
25. UCE Birmingham c4
26. University of Central Lancashire b3
27. Chester University b4
28. Chichester University c5
29. City University e1
30. Courtauld Institute e1
31. Coventry University c4
32. De Montfort University c4
33. University of Derby c4
34. Dundee University b2
35. University of Durham c3
36. University of East London f1
37. University of Edinburgh b2
38. University of East Anglia c4
39. University of Essex c4
40. Exeter University b5
41. Falmouth University College a5
42. Glamorgan University b4
43. University of Glasgow b2
44. Glasgow Caledonian University b2
45. Goldsmiths College, London e2
46. Greenwich University f2
47. University of Gloucestershire b4
48. Harper Adams University College b4
49. Heriot-Watt University b2
50. University of Hertfordshire c4
51. Heythrop College, London e2
52. University of Huddersfield c3
53. University of Hull c3
54. Imperial College, London e2
55. Keele University b4
56. University of Kent c5
57. King's College, London e1
58. Kingston University d2
59. Lampeter, University of Wales b4
60. Lancaster University b3
61. Leeds University c3
62. Leeds Metropolitan University c3
63. Leicester University c4
64. University of Lincoln c3

● The quad at Brasenose, Oxford, is known as the Deer Park, even though there are no deer in it. Legend has it that Brasenose undergrads stole a deer from Magdalen College, who weren't very happy and ordered its return – at which point the students cooked and ate it.

INDEX

WHY DO FLUNK RATES MATTER?

WHY SHOULD I CARE WHETHER A UNIVERSITY'S BIG OR SMALL, ANCIENT OR MODERN?

WHAT'S THE POINT OF A ROLF HARRIS APPRECIATION SOCIETY?

The Push Guide to Choosing University has all the answers and more, showing you the ins and outs of applications and the ups and downs of student life.

This is a decision that will stay with you for the rest of your life and cost you a bundle—so you might as well make the right choice, eh?

THE PUSH GUIDE TO CHOOSING A UNIVERSITY
The like-it-is guide to making the best choice of university for you.

£4.99. ISBN 0340 929596

EDUCATION & CAREERS

ONLY IN

THE INDEPENDENT

EVERY THURSDAY